DATE DUE

WITNESS TO HOPE

ALSO BY GEORGE WEIGEL

Tranquillitas Ordinis: *The Present Failure and Future Promise of American Catholic Thought on War and Peace*

Catholicism and the Renewal of American Democracy

American Interests, American Purpose: Moral Reasoning and U.S. Foreign Policy

Freedom and Its Discontents: Catholicism Confronts Modernity

Just War and the Gulf War [with James Turner Johnson]

The Final Revolution: The Resistance Church and the Collapse of Communism

Idealism Without Illusions: U.S. Foreign Policy in the 1990s

Soul of the World: Notes on the Future of Public Catholicism

WITNESS TO HOPE

The Biography of Pope John Paul II

GEORGE WEIGEL

Cliff Street Books

An Imprint of HarperCollins*Publishers*

HarperCollins books may be purchased for educational, business,
or sales promotional use. For information please write: Special Markets Department,
HarperCollins Publishers, Inc., 10 East 53rd Street, New York, NY 10022.

FIRST EDITION

Designed by Pagesetters, Inc.

Library of Congress Cataloging-in-Publication Data
Weigel, George.
    Witness to hope: the biography of Pope John Paul II/George
Weigel.—1st ed.
        p.   cm.
    Includes bibliographical references and index.
    ISBN 0-06-018793-X
    1. John Paul II, Pope, 1920–   . 2. Popes—Biography.   I. Title.
BX1378.5.W45   1999
282'.092—dc211   99-26340
    [B]

99 00 01 02 03 ❖/ RRD 10 9 8 7 6 5 4 3 2 1

For Joan,

Gwyneth, Monica, and Stephen

Contents

Contents

A Brief Note
on Pronunciation

Polish pronunciation can seem daunting, but it is, in fact, more regular than English. As one introduction to Polish puts it, the English speaker learning to pronounce Bydgoszcz, Szczecin, and Śląsk, having learned the invariable rules of Polish pronunciation, will have an easier time of it than the native Polish speaker—or even the native "American" speaker!—trying to figure out Gloucester, Leicester, and Slough.

There is no need for a comprehensive treatise on Polish pronunciation here. The following rules and examples should be helpful.

The letters *ą* and *ę* are pronounced as a nasal *aw* and *en* in English.
C is pronounced as *ts* in English.
Ch is pronounced as a hard *h* in the Scottish "loch."
Cz is pronounced as *ch* in "church."
Dz is pronounced as *j* in "jeans."
I is pronounced as *ee* in English.
J is always pronounced as *y* in English.
Ł and *ł* are pronounced as *w* in English.
Ó is pronounced as *oo* as in the English "cool."
Ś is pronounced as *s* in "sure."
Sz is pronounced as the English *sh*.
W is pronounced as *v* in English.
Y is pronounced as a *y* in the English "myth."
The accent in Polish is almost always on the second-to-last syllable.

Thus . . .
Częstochowa is pronounced *Chens-toe-HOE-vah*.
Dziwisz is pronounced *JEE-vish*.
Kraków is pronounced *KRA-koov*.
Malecki is pronounced *Mah-LETS-kee*.
Rybicki is pronounced *Rih-BEETS-kee*.
Stanisław is pronounced *STAN-is-wahv* (an exception to the accent rule).
Środowisko is pronounced *Shroe-doe-VEES-koe*.
Wałęsa is pronounced *Vah-WHEN-sah*.

Wawel is pronounced *VAH-vel.*
Wojtyła is pronounced *Voy-TEE-wah.*
Wujek is pronounced *VOO-yek.*
Wyszyński is pronounced *Vih-SHIN-skee.*

The surnames of married men and women are masculine and feminine, thus "Stanisław Rybicki" and "Danuta Rybicka." These have been retained, but for the sake of simplicity, the masculine plural form is used when referring to couples together rather than the Polish plural, which in this instance would be "the Rybyccy."

PROLOGUE

The Disciple

Stealing quietly through Kraków's blacked-out streets, the audience and the actors who would perform for them arrived at an apartment in the city's Dębniki district, across the frozen Vistula River from ancient Wawel Castle. It was the 1,181st evening in the long, dark night of the Polish soul, and they took great care to avoid the armed patrols that enforced the Nazi Occupation's curfew. For what they were doing was an act of defiance that, detected, would have sent everyone involved to the death camps. This particular night, November 28, 1942, the Rhapsodic Theater, an avant-garde troupe committed to a "theater of the living word" without props or elaborate costumes, was performing an adaptation of Adam Mickiewicz's epic poem *Pan Tadeusz*, a classic of the Polish Romantic tradition.

The apartment blinds were drawn; the lights were lowered; a clandestine act of cultural resistance began. It did not go unchallenged. During the performance, Nazi megaphones outside began blaring the news of another victory by the invincible Wehrmacht. To some in the audience, that rasping, intrusive propaganda, interrupting a brief respite from the terrors of life in occupied Poland, seemed an apt metaphor for the hopelessness of their situation.

The twenty-two-year-old actor then speaking, an underground seminary student named Karol Wojtyła, paid no attention whatsoever to the racket outside. Unfazed, he continued his recitation as if the harsh static of the principalities and powers of the age simply did not exist . . .

Almost thirty-seven years later, on June 2, 1979, Karol Wojtyła addressed another audience: the largest gathering to that point in the history of Poland. The former actor no longer spoke in a darkened apartment. Rather, he said what he had to say before 1 million of his countrymen gathered in and around Warsaw's massive Victory Square. In some respects, though, things were curiously similar. Once again, Karol Wojtyła, now Pope John Paul II, was confronting a brutal attempt to crush human freedom: the communism that had replaced Nazism as the usurper of Poland's liberties. Once again, he was doing so not with what the world recognized as "power," but with what he understood to be the truth that could set his people free in the deepest sense of freedom: the truth about the dignity, vocation, and destiny of human beings, which he believed had been revealed in Jesus Christ.

And once again, as he spoke, he was interrupted, not by the crudities of Nazi megaphones, but by the spontaneous, rhythmic chant of his people—"We want God! We want God . . ."

THE DRAMA OF A LIFE

The sheer drama of Karol Wojtyła's life would defy the imagination of the most fanciful screenwriter.

Brief months after his country regains its independence, a son is born to Polish parents in a small, provincial town. His mother dies before he is ten. Raised by his father, a pious, retired military officer and a gentleman of the old school, the youngster is the best student in town, an enthusiastic athlete, and an amateur actor. One of his closest friends is the son of the leader of the local Jewish community.

Moving to Kraków with his pensioner father, he enters the ancient Jagiellonian University, but his promising academic and theatrical careers are cut short by World War II. During the Occupation, he is a quarryman, blaster, and manual laborer, walking to work in freezing winter clad only in denims and clogs. Defying the ruthlessness of his country's Nazi occupiers, he joins an underground cultural resistance movement and helps create a covert theater. After the local parish priests have been shipped off to Dachau, he takes his first steps in classic spirituality under the tutelage of a lay mystic who forms young men into "Living Rosary" groups.

His father dies and the young man's vocational struggle intensifies. Is his destiny the stage or the altar? He eventually enrolls in the clandestine seminary run by the heroic archbishop of Kraków, an aristocrat who serves Hans Frank the people's diet of stale bread and ersatz coffee when the haughty Nazi governor-general insists on being invited to dine at the episcopal manse. Surreptitiously studying philosophy and theology at the chemical factory where he still works, the seminarian lives from day to day in a world where yesterday's classmate and fellow altar server becomes tomorrow's martyr to the firing squads.

In the aftermath of the Warsaw Uprising, the Nazis try to forestall a similar eruption of overt resistance by arresting all the young men in Kraków. Our protagonist dodges the Gestapo manhunts, works his way across town, and enters the bishop's residence, where the clandestine seminary is re-formed underground. After his country's "liberation" by the Red Army, he is ordained a priest and sent to Rome for graduate studies in theology. Returning home after a look at the worker-priests of France and Belgium, he begins a ministry to university students that involves innovative worship, intense conversation, thousands of hours in the confessional, and a sharp break from the typical pattern of interaction between Polish priests and their people.

After completing a second doctoral degree, he joins the faculty of the only Catholic university behind the iron curtain, commuting to his classes by overnight train. His lectures are packed by standing-room-only crowds. His first book, on the ethics of married life, raises more than one clerical eyebrow by its celebration of human sexuality as a gift of God for the sanctification of husband and wife. Consecrated a bishop at age thirty-eight, he is elected administrator of the Kraków archdiocese when the incumbent dies and the government and Church deadlock on a new appointment. Attending all four sessions of the Second Vatican Council from 1962 through 1965, he becomes a leader in crafting a new Catholic openness to the modern world and a mainstay in the great conciliar battle to define religious freedom as a basic human right.

Named archbishop of Kraków with the enthusiastic support of the communist government, he causes consternation among the commissars who promoted his nomination by becoming a relentless, sophisticated advocate for the religious and other civil rights of his people. While conducting one of the most extensive implementations of Vatican II in the world, the archbishop, who is named cardinal at age forty-seven, refuses to behave the way senior prelates are supposed to behave: he skis, he vacations with lay people, he kayaks. He also remains a working intellectual, leading doctoral seminars in his residence and delivering scholarly papers at international conferences.

At fifty-eight, he is elected the 264th Bishop of Rome, the first non-Italian pope in 455 years and the first Slavic pope ever. KGB leader Yuri Andropov warns the Soviet Politburo of danger ahead, and his judgment is vindicated when the Polish Pope returns to his homeland in June 1979 and triggers the revolution of conscience that eventually produces the nonviolent collapse of the Soviet empire in east central Europe. The Slav Pope dramatically revitalizes the world's oldest institution, the papacy, through pastoral pilgrimages to every corner of the globe, through an aggressive exploitation of every modern means of communication, and through an endless stream of teaching documents that touch virtually every aspect of Catholic life as well as the most crucial questions on the world's agenda.

He survives an assassination attempt, redefines the Catholic Church's relationship with Judaism, invites Orthodox and Protestant Christians to help imagine a papacy that could serve the needs of all Christians, preaches to Muslim teenagers in a packed stadium in Casablanca, and describes marital intimacy as an icon of the interior life of the triune God. After he faces a series of medical difficulties, the world media pronounce him a dying, if heroic, has-been. Within the next six months he publishes an international bestseller translated into forty languages, gathers the largest crowd in human history on the least Christian continent in the world, urges the Church to cleanse its conscience on the edge of a new millennium, and almost single-handedly changes the course of a major international meeting on population issues. Addressing the United Nations in 1995, he defends the universality of human rights and describes himself as a "witness to hope" at the end of a century of unprecedented wickedness. Two days later, the irrepressible pontiff does a credible imitation of Jack Benny during Mass in Central Park, and the cynical New York press loves it.

As fiction, the story would be too sensational for all but the most romantic tastes. What, then, are we to make of the story as fact? And how can we understand this thoroughly modern man who insists that "in the designs of Providence there are no mere coincidences"?

Paradox

The pontificate of Pope John Paul II has been one of the most important in centuries, for the Church and the world. Some would argue that John Paul II has been the most consequential pope since the Reformation and Counter-Reformation in the sixteenth century. As that period defined the Catholic Church's relationship to an emerging modern world, so the Second Vatican Council and the pontificate of John Paul II have laid down a set of markers that will likely determine the course of world Catholicism well beyond "modernity" and into the third millennium of Christian history.

John Paul II has also been, indisputably, the most visible pope in history. In fact, a case can be made that he has been the most visible human being in history. He has almost certainly been seen live by more people than any man who ever lived. When one adds the multiplying impact of television to the equation, the breadth of his reach into the worlds-within-worlds of humanity becomes almost impossible to grasp.

Yet there is a paradox here: this most visible of men may also be the least understood major figure of the twentieth century. Certainly the judgments about the man and his accomplishment have been, to put it gently, contradictory.

To tens of millions of people, many of whom are not Roman Catholics, he is the great figure of our time, the defender and principal embodiment of a moral force that has led humanity safely through this bloodiest of centuries. In this view, John Paul II is the paladin, the champion, of the cause of human freedom. To others, including many in his own Church, John Paul II is an unyielding authoritarian, out of touch with the aspirations of those he claims to lead and dares to teach, a throwback to a period the Church had putatively put behind it at the Second Vatican Council. Still others, within and without the Church, admire his defense of human rights, his outreach to Judaism, and his dedication to peace while deploring his theology and his moral judgments.

Time named him "Man of the Year" in 1994. Mikhail Gorbachev, who might have been expected to take a somewhat rueful view of the matter, declared that John Paul II was indispensable to the peaceful conclusion of the Cold War. Fidel Castro remarked privately that his first meeting with John Paul II was like being with family. Those who work with him on a daily basis—even those who disagree with certain of his decisions or with his method of conducting the papacy—unanimously testify to his personal sanctity, his kindness, and his seemingly limitless capacity to listen.

Yet journalists of wide experience and historians of literary distinction have heaped opprobrium on him. One of the latter, who admitted that he prays daily for the Pope's demise, charged him with plotting a Rome-Riyadh Axis, an unholy Catholic-Islamic "Alliance for the Repeal of the Enlightenment," in order to conduct a joint *jihad*, a "final war against the godless."[1] A papal biographer described John Paul II as becoming "increasingly emotional and confrontational in his vision of the world and its ills" as he ages, an angry old man incapable of understanding the world he helped to create.[2] Another pair of biographers claimed that he "surrounds the Church with barbed wire."[3] Another veteran journalist has conceded that while "my faith in God is intact . . . my allegiance to the Roman Church has been suspended while I examine this brief Polish interlude in its long history."[4] The London *Independent*, which editorialized in 1995 that John Paul II was the only global leader left in the world, charged eighteen months earlier that his pontificate has been "characterised by intolerance . . . and an authoritarian character that has left him out of touch with many Western Catholics."[5] Inane rumors about John Paul II's alleged intentions (e.g., his putative plans to announce a new dogma, according to which the Virgin Mary is present in the consecrated bread and wine of the Eucharist) have been reported without a blush by sources that consider themselves papers-of-record (in this particular instance, the *Sunday Times* of London).

Why has this most visible of public figures never come into clear focus? Why do the judgments on his accomplishment vary so wildly?

Several reasons, although touching the surface of the problem, are still significant.

In the first instance, Pope John Paul II has always been a man with a deeply ingrained sense of privacy and has only recently begun to reveal certain aspects of his early life and development in published autobiographical reflections.[6] Karol Wojtyła's mysticism is another factor in his reticence. As with other mystics, he would find it virtually impossible to describe his deepest religious experiences, which make him the man he is. Those who have heard Pope John Paul II groaning in prayer before morning Mass in his private chapel know that there is a dimension of Karol Wojtyła's life in which God is his sole companion and interlocutor, in a conversation literally beyond words.

John Paul's Polishness has been a barrier to his being understood in the West. Poles may be admired for their romantic heroism. But a deeply entrenched prejudice, compounded by historical and geographical ignorance, makes it difficult for many Western intellectuals and writers to imagine

Poles in the forward thrust of world intellectual and cultural life. Indeed, the very term "Polish intellectual" strikes too many in the West as oxymoronic. What was once an advantage—John Paul II, the pope from the Slavic borderlands, an indisputably romantic figure—turned rather quickly into a virtual indictment. How could this Pole, this Slav, this man from a country that had dropped out of history, understand freedom, modernity's highest aspiration?

Understanding John Paul II has also been made difficult by the traditions of secrecy and the habits of suspicion that characterize the relationship between many of those who work in the Vatican and those who analyze its activities. The habit of caution ingrained in many officials of the Holy See is not without foundation. Living in a cultural environment in which journalism is even more an inexact science than in other parts of the world, the men of the Vatican have learned, perhaps too well, that silence is often safer than the effort to communicate a point of view. The upshot is that, while things have improved considerably during the pontificate of John Paul II, Holy See public relations remain underdeveloped by most contemporary standards. Combine the modern journalist's working assumption that all public figures are guilty until proven otherwise with habitual Vatican caution, and the net result is coverage that too often begins with the assumption of duplicity on the part of Vatican officials. Although he has made an unprecedented personal outreach to the world media, John Paul II has been regularly caught in the backwash of this unfortunate set of relationships.

But when one probes beneath the surface, the more interesting causes of the contradictory assessments of John Paul II, man and pope, become clearer. John Paul II is frequently perceived in conflicting terms because he is, in fact, a sign of contradiction. His life, his convictions, and his teaching pose an unmistakable challenge to his times, to which he seems in many other respects so well-attuned.

- To a late modernity dominated by the pleasure principle and by personal willfulness, he has insisted that suffering can be redemptive and that obligation is at the core of biblical religion.
- In an intellectual environment in which the human capacity to know anything with certainty is denied, he has taught that universal truths exist, that we can know them, and that in knowing them certain moral duties are laid upon us.
- At a time in which the "personality" is deemed infinitely plastic and in which "human nature" (if its reality is admitted at all) is viewed as a cultural construct, he has defended the idea of a universal human nature and has insisted on the *givenness* of the human condition.
- In a culture in which happiness is identified with talent and its assertion, he has taught that happiness is found in the obedient submission of talent and will to transcendent truth and love.

- Against the temptation to regard utility as the sole criterion for measuring anyone's worth, he has insisted that every human being possesses an inherent and inalienable dignity and value.
- At a historical moment that celebrates the pursuit of self-interest, he has taught that we worship God and we strive for holiness, not because these are "good for us," but because these are things that are to be done.
- In a world that takes history to be the product of impersonal economic and political forces, he has defended the priority of culture and the world-transforming power of the human spirit.

That John Paul II has been a sign of contradiction within the modern world is not much in doubt. But that he has been a pope *against* modernity and its aspiration to freedom, a pope of "rollback" and "restoration," is another matter altogether. Indeed, the countercase can be made: that the "contradictions" embodied by John Paul II are in fact in service to the human happiness that is freedom's goal.

Demonstrating that case requires stepping back from the conventional analysis and looking at this well-known public figure from a different angle—from *inside* the convictions and commitments that make him who he is.

UNDERSTANDING "FROM INSIDE"

In a brief author's introduction to his play *Our God's Brother,* Karol Wojtyła wrote of a "line inaccessible to history" that stands between any man and our attempts to understand him.[7] The "history" that cannot get to the fundamental truths about a human being is "history" understood as documents, statistics, and the other materials of the contemporary academic historian's craft. These are important. They tell us things, some of them quite significant. But they cannot give us an authoritative answer to the questions, "Who *is* he? Who *was* she?" Referring to other biographical efforts and their emphasis on his role as a statesman, Pope John Paul II once remarked, "They try to understand me from outside. But I can only be understood from inside."[8]

What is this "inside," and how might it be approached?

It may help to begin by thinking of Karol Wojtyła as a man who grew up very fast. The traumatic events that shaped his early life could have led him to conclude that human existence is irrational, even absurd. Wojtyła came to a different conclusion. Beginning with his late teenage years under the Nazi Occupation, he gradually came to the conviction that the crisis of the modern world was first of all a crisis of *ideas,* a crisis in the very idea of the human person. History was driven by culture and the ideas that formed cultures. Ideas had consequences. And if the *idea* of the human person that dominated a culture was flawed, one of two things would happen. Either that culture would give birth to destructive aspirations, or it would be incapable of realizing its fondest hopes, even if it expressed them in the most nobly humanistic terms.

Karol Wojtyła's early intuitions about the root of the crisis of the modern age were refined experientially. No pope in centuries has brought to his office such extensive pastoral experience with the real-world problems of ordinary men and women. His convictions were also developed philosophically as Wojtyła participated at the Catholic University of Lublin in a bold experiment at reconstructing the intellectual foundations of modern civilization. Through thousands of hours in the confessional, in hundreds of seminars, books, lectures, and articles, and throughout a pontificate that has addressed virtually every major issue on the human agenda, his fundamental conviction has remained constant: the horrors of late twentieth-century life, whether Nazi, communist, racist, nationalist, or utilitarian in expression, are the products of defective concepts of the human person.

The modern age prides itself on its humanism and declares freedom its noblest aspiration. Though Karol Wojtyła shares both the pride and the aspiration, he believes that neither contemporary humanism nor the freedom it seeks has been given a secure foundation. And the cracks in the foundations are not of interest to philosophers only; they are life-and-death matters for millions. For a humanism that cannot give an adequate account of its most cherished value, freedom, becomes self-cannibalizing. Freedom decays into license; anarchy threatens; and in the face of that anarchy a host of devils, each promising security amid the chaos, is set loose—demons like the supremacy of race (Hitler) or class (Marx), the messianic lure of utopian politics (Lenin), chapter after bloody chapter, the butcher's bill always lengthened by humanity's increasing technological accomplishments.

Very early in his life, Wojtyła began to think about a question of historic consequence: How might we realize our humanity in an age in which the artifacts of our own creativity threaten the very existence of the human project? As he pondered that problem, certain convictions grew in him. One was that the human person is a moral being *as such*: morality is not a culturally constructed and historically conditioned appendage to what is, essentially, a cipher. To be human is *to be a moral agent*. That, in turn, meant that we live in a human universe the very structure of which is *dramatic*. And the great drama of any life is the struggle to surrender the "person-I-am" to the "person-I-ought-to-be." That struggle meant confronting, not avoiding, the reality of evil. Evil had made itself unmistakably manifest—in the world, in such distinctly modern enterprises as the Holocaust and the Gulag Archipelago; in daily life, in the exploitation of one human being by another, economically, politically, or sexually. But evil did not have the final word, because at the center of the human drama is Christ, whose entry into the human condition and whose conquest of death meant that hope was neither a vain illusion nor a defensive fantasy constructed against the fear at the heart of modern darkness.

Karol Wojtyła believed that Christ-centered hope to be the truth of the world.[9]

THE DISCIPLE

To try to understand Karol Wojtyła "from inside" also means to think about him in something other than the conventional "left/right" categories that have shaped the world media's coverage of his pontificate. These are, of course, political categories that date from the French Revolution and have dominated much of modern thought. Though they illuminate some facets of various policy issues, political parties, and ideological tendencies, the "left/right" taxonomy is hopelessly inadequate for getting "inside" John Paul II, the man and the pope. In fact, John Paul seems to defy the rules of this categorization by occupying several positions along the conventional spectrum. Thus we have often read about John Paul II, the "doctrinal conservative" and "social-political liberal."

There are not, though, two Wojtyłas, the "fundamentalist" on matters of Church doctrine and the "social progressive" on political and economic issues. There is only one Karol Wojtyła, a Christian so completely convinced of the truth that Christianity bears that this conviction animates literally everything he does. On one interpretation, the depth of this conviction and its particularity mark John Paul II as "sectarian." John Paul believes, however, that this Christian radicalism commits him to an intense conversation with nonbelievers and with believers of different theological and philosophical persuasions. That conversation has led him to articulate a set of genuinely transcultural moral requirements for the exercise of freedom. As he put it to the representatives of worldly power at the United Nations in 1995, "As a Christian, my hope and trust are centered on Jesus Christ . . . [who] is for us God made man, and made a part of the history of humanity. Precisely for this reason, Christian hope for the world and its future extends to every human person. Because of the radiant humanity of Christ, nothing genuinely human fails to touch the hearts of Christians. Faith in Christ does not impel us to intolerance. On the contrary, it obliges us to engage others in a respectful dialogue. Love of Christ does not distract us from interest in others, but rather invites us to responsibility for them, to the exclusion of no one. . . ."[10]

The universality of Karol Wojtyła's interests and concerns is thus a function of his particular, specific, and radical Christian commitment.

It is important to clarify the meaning of "radical" here, for as it applies to Karol Wojtyła, it does not mean "further left" (on the conventional left/right spectrum) but *deeper*. The English word "radical" (like the French and Spanish *radical* and the Italian *radicale*) comes from the Latin *radix*, "root." To see Wojtyła as a "Christian radical," then, is to try to understand his radicalism as an example of what the American philosopher Alfred North Whitehead once described as the simplicity that lies on the far side of complexity. Wojtyła has never denied the sometimes tortuous complexity of the human condition in the modern world. The Wojtyła difference, so to speak, is that he has not been paralyzed by that complexity. As he worked through those complexities intellectually, he became convinced that some things are, simply, *true.*

In more biblical terms, Karol Wojtyła was seized early in his life by the "more excellent way" of which St. Paul spoke to the Corinthians (*1 Corinthians* 12.31): the way of Christian love, which the apostle described as the greatest of spiritual gifts. And having been seized by this, Wojtyła committed his life to it. To be seized by the "more excellent way"—to be seized, ultimately, by Christ—was a life-transforming truth, to whose lifting-up he committed his own life. From his seminary days, Karol Wojtyła's life has been a continual encounter with those who understand the "more excellent way" and those who do not, with those whose dedication to the "more excellent way" he would like to help deepen, and with those he would like to introduce to it. Nothing in his life happens outside the truth of the "more excellent way." His faith is not one facet of his personality or one dimension of his intellect. His faith *is* Karol Wojtyła, at the most profound level of his personhood.

This intense rootedness can be startling, even disturbing, in a world in which assembling a personality from bits and pieces of conviction—religion here, politics there; morals here, aesthetics there—is one of the hallmarks of modernity. But it is precisely this rootedness that has allowed Pope John Paul II to proclaim, without hesitation or fear of hypocrisy, "Be not afraid." His life, forged in the furnace of the great political and intellectual conflicts of the twentieth century, is an embodiment of that proclamation, just as his teaching is an explanation of the sources of his fearlessness and his public ministry is the action implied by it. The ground on which he makes that proclamation, which is universal in intention, is the conviction that Jesus Christ is the answer to the question that is every human life.

To put it in a single word: to understand Karol Wojtyła "from inside" is to understand him as a *disciple.*

SURPRISES

Now it must be admitted that there is something surprising about the advent of John Paul II, particularly at the end of the twentieth century. This was, after all, the century that was supposed to witness the withering away of religion as a maturing humanity, tutored by science, outgrew its "need" for such psychological props as religious faith. Yet at the millennium, the most compelling public figure in the world, the man with arguably the most coherent and comprehensive vision of the human possibility in the world ahead, is the man who is best described as the compleat Christian.

Much of late modernity assumes that dependence on God is a mark of human immaturity and an obstacle to human freedom. The life of Karol Wojtyła and his accomplishment as Pope John Paul II suggest a dramatic, alternative possibility: that a man who has been seized and transformed by the "more excellent way" can bend the curve of history so that freedom's cause is advanced.

That the Supreme Pontiff is someone aptly described as a Christian radical has also been something of a surprise within the Catholic Church. The surprise is not because the recent history of the papacy has replicated the rascalities and scandals of the Renaissance. Since the sixteenth century Counter-Reformation, though, the exercise of the world's oldest office had been cut to fit a certain template designed primarily by and for the Italians who dominated Vatican life. Brilliant and dedicated Italians, many of them saints, saved Catholicism in the sixteenth century: men like Charles Borromeo, Robert Bellarmine, and Antonio Ghislieri, whom history remembers as Pope Pius V. Over time, however, this historically and culturally conditioned model for the papacy came to be understood as a reflection of God's enduring intentions for the Office of Peter in the Church. And in that model, especially as it evolved after the loss of the Papal States in 1870, the principal jobs of the Roman Pontiff were thought to be the effective management of the Roman Curia, the central bureaucratic machinery of the Catholic Church, and the careful management of the Church's relations with sovereign states, in a diplomacy conducted according to the premises of the modern state system.

The theory had it that the pope should manage the Church's permanent bureaucracy, but the bureaucracy often thought it should manage the pope. For more than four centuries, the curial managers of popes believed, not without reason, that "we know how to do this" (as they often put it) and that wise popes would accommodate themselves to the prevailing methodology. Those who accommodated—and they all did, to one degree or another—were often men of intellectual sophistication and personal sanctity. By agreeing to conduct their office as curial tradition dictated, however, they agreed to a papacy that was more managerial and bureaucratic than evangelical in character.

Karol Wojtyła was an outsider to all this. He had not been acculturated, one might say, to be a pope. But he had been one of the world's most dynamic, innovative, and successful local bishops. And he had been that precisely because he was an evangelist and pastor who was a Christian radical. As he once put it, if the Holy Spirit had seen fit to call the bishop of Kraków to the office of Bishop of Rome and pastor of the universal Church, there must have been something in his experience that was useful for others.[11] Thus the Church, as well as the world, has had to learn to live with a very different kind of pontificate, the most distinctive characteristics of which are expressions of Karol Wojtyła, the disciple who was a product of the Church in the modern world, not of the Roman bureaucracy.

A QUESTION OF RELEVANCE

Because he is, at heart, a Christian disciple, it may seem that Wojtyła's story is of interest solely to Christians, perhaps only to Catholics. Yet the world has not responded to John Paul II as some might have predicted. Moreover, John Paul II has understood himself to be making a proposal to the entire world about the nature of the human person, the moral requirements for human community, the meaning of human history, and the trajectory of human destiny.

That proposal, the public implications of the "more excellent way" that has been the lodestar of Wojtyła's life, comes at a time when the cause of freedom, often taken to be synonymous with the cause of democracy, appears historically triumphant. Closer examination suggests the possibility of a more ominous situation.

The secular argument for human freedom, launched almost three centuries ago under the rubric of "natural rights," has often been reduced to a calculation of probabilities: democracy and the personal freedoms it protects are good not because they have an inherent moral superiority over other forms of organizing society, but because they are the least messy alternative in a world of dramatic differences. Being tolerant, civil, and, in a word, "democratic" is just easier than being cranky and assertive; it keeps the lid on, so to speak. But if the social pressures of plurality and difference become intense, the answer to the question, "*Why* be tolerant, civil, democratic?" cannot simply be "Because it works better." That essentially pragmatic answer cannot be sustained when racial, ethnic, or religious conflict reaches the boiling point. Only a moral commitment to tolerance and democratic civility that is buttressed by norms transcending our immediate circumstances can sustain a commitment to the freedom of the "other" when that "other" becomes threatening. And that is the situation of a world in which "otherness" impinges on us daily, thanks to the transportation and communications revolutions.

Perhaps even more ominously, the Promethean temptation to steal fire from the gods and remake the human condition has reemerged on the edge of a new millennium, not from race- or class-based political fanatics this time, but from science. The very question of who counts as a human being is now being debated in a way our grandparents could not imagine. Is a cloned human being a member of the human community? What about the socially unproductive and the inconvenient, the gravely handicapped, the elderly, the unborn? If the question, "What are these putative people good *for*?" is the only question our cultures and our laws recognize, then we really are living in Aldous Huxley's brave new world, and tyranny cannot be far around the corner.

In these circumstances, John Paul II's proposal about the moral foundations of the free society, based on his distinctive understanding of the nature and dignity of the human person, is assuredly not for-Catholics-only. It has implications for the Pope's fellow Christians, for Jews, for Muslims, for adherents of the other great world religions, and for "all men and women of good will" (as his encyclicals put it). The papacy has traditionally claimed a universal reach. John Paul's pontificate is the first in history in which that claim has been empirically validated. It is a very obscure corner of this planet that has not been touched in some way by the life of this pope and by his proposals for humanity's future.

The Broadness of a Gauge

Modern assertiveness notwithstanding, we are neither self-constituting nor self-defining. Family, education, physique, languages, native culture, friendships, vocation, hobbies, religious and philosophical convictions—these constitute some of the many rails on which our lives run. That all life journeys run along such rails is a given of the human condition, but the gauge of the rails differs.[12] Some lives run along narrow gauges, others along broad. One way to think of Karol Wojtyła's life "from inside" is to think of it as running along a particularly broad-gauged rail bed.

He is an intellectual who is unbeholden to the shibboleths of the professoriat and who has a deep appreciation for untutored popular piety.

He is an accomplished philosopher, recognized as such by peers throughout the world, but he never took a serious course in the subject.

He is a mystic who was a vigorous sportsman for almost seventy years.

He is a celibate with a remarkable insight into human sexuality, especially as viewed from the perspective and experience of women.

He lived from age nineteen until age fifty-eight under totalitarian regimes and has written cogently about the cultural factors that make democracy possible.

He is a Pole with a marked sensitivity toward Jews and Judaism.

He has had a considerable impact on world affairs and the life of the Church while evincing not the slightest interest in management theory or in the conventions of politics.

He is arguably the most well-informed man in the world, yet he rarely reads newspapers.

He has been a notably successful statesman without extensive preparation for the job.

He was blessed with great mentors as a young man, but he is primarily an autodidact who learns quickly from experience.

He has a penetrating insight into those he meets, such that one wants to entrust him with one's decisions, but his signature phrase as a confessor and spiritual counselor has always been "You must decide."

He has demonstrated the ability to rouse the passions of some of the largest crowds in human history, but he has never played the demagogue.

He is a disciple known for the intensity of his love, like the apostle John, who has been called to exercise an office of authority and jurisdiction in the Church, like the apostle Peter.

These striking characteristics have given his life a remarkably rich texture. They reinforce the claim that one cannot get "inside" Karol Wojtyła, Pope John Paul II, if one insists on forcing his thought and action into the usual liberal/conservative categories. He can only be grasped and judged if one approaches him and accepts him for what he says he is: a man of faith, whose faith is who he *is*.

That faith has also given rise, in Karol Wojtyła, to a great hope for humanity.

On the edge of the twenty-first century, Pope John Paul II stood before the representatives of the nations of the world, and having looked into the heart of virtually every great darkness of his time over the course of his seventy-five years, offered an antidote to the fear that had driven his century mad:

> It is one of the great paradoxes of our time that man, who began the period we call "modernity" with a self-confident assertion of his "coming-of-age" and "autonomy," approaches the end of the twentieth century fearful of himself, fearful of what he might be capable of, fearful for the future. Indeed, the second half of the twentieth century has seen the unprecedented phenomenon of a humanity uncertain about *the very likelihood of a future* . . .
>
> In order to ensure that the new millennium now approaching will witness a new flourishing of the human spirit, mediated through an authentic culture of freedom, men and women must learn to conquer fear. *We must learn not to be afraid,* we must rediscover a spirit of hope and a spirit of trust. Hope is not empty optimism springing from a naive confidence that the future will necessarily be better than the past. Hope and trust are the premise of responsible activity and are nurtured in that inner sanctuary of conscience where "man is alone with God" and thus perceives that *he is not alone* amid the enigmas of existence, for he is surrounded by the love of the Creator![13]

To understand Pope John Paul II "from inside" is to understand that, for him, hope for the human prospect is rooted in faith. And that faith is not the assertion of one religious option in a supermarket of possible truths. It is, to his mind, the truth of the world. It is the truth that had seized him in his youth and had formed his adult life. It is the truth to which he is obliged to bear witness.

How Karol Wojtyła came to that understanding, how he deepened it and learned to express and defend it, how he has borne witness to it as Pope John Paul II, and what all that might mean for the Catholic Church and the world in the twenty-first century is the business of this study.

THE SUBJECT AND THE AUTHOR

This book is the culmination of twenty years of studying and writing about John Paul II. I began writing about the Pope shortly after his election, first in magazines and newspaper columns, later in books. One of those books, *The Final Revolution: The Resistance Church and the Collapse of Communism*,[14] was the first sustained argument that John Paul II had played a crucial role in the collapse of European communism and the occasion for our first personal meeting. I was in Rome to lecture on the book's themes and met the Holy Father when he invited me to Mass in his private chapel.

During the course of the next years I found myself in Rome for lectures or conferences numerous times, and the Pope often invited me to his morning Mass, to lunch, or to dinner, usually with other American or Polish friends. In the late spring of 1995, I was in Rome to mark my twentieth wedding anniversary, and in the course of that visit the question of whether I should write a biography of the Holy Father was first broached. In December of that year, when I was in Rome to give the keynote address at an international conference marking the thirtieth anniversary of the Second Vatican Council's *Declaration on Religious Freedom,* the Holy Father invited me to dinner, along with another friend. That evening, in the course of the freewheeling conversation that John Paul's openness invites, the question of a biography came up again. And over roast chicken and a good local wine, the Pope made it clear that he would be grateful if I would take on the task.

In March 1996, I went to Rome to discuss the mechanics and ground rules of the project with the Holy Father, his priest-secretary, and other officials of the Holy See. The Pope agreed that he would make himself available to me on a regular basis, and that in addition to our personal conversations he would answer questions I would submit to him in writing. It was also agreed that officials of the Holy See would be informed of the Holy Father's interest in this work, so that I would have the access I needed to people and materials in order to tell the story adequately.

At the same time, it was clearly understood between us that this would be my telling of his story. The biography would be as authoritative as unprecedented access to the Pope and his closest associates would make it, but it would not be "authorized" in that the Holy Father retained no rights of approval. As I got to know him better, it became evident that John Paul II is too respectful of others ever to have thought of asking for editorial control over someone else's work. Both he and I have understood this, from the beginning, to be a project in which he would cooperate, but for which I would bear full responsibility.

The infallibility with which Catholics believe the Holy Spirit endows the Bishop of Rome in making binding judgments on matters of faith and morals is no guarantee of preservation from errors in matters of personnel, strategy, and tactics, nor is it a warrant of sanctity. John Paul II would be the last to claim that his every judgment has been vindicated by subsequent events. Like every other leader, he deserves to be understood in terms of how he understood the issues and the options available at the time he took a decision. Unlike some others, John Paul II deserves great respect for the painstaking and prayerful way in which he has exercised the exceptional powers of his office. At a time in history when the world historical stage came to be populated largely by leaders who seemed smaller than their responsibilities demanded, he has been a large figure indeed, and not simply because of the power at his disposal, but because of the integrity with which even his most implacable critics concede he has wielded that power.

Melchior Cano, the great Dominican theologian at the sixteenth-century Council of Trent, got it just right when he said, referring to the office of the papacy, that "Peter has no need of our lies or flattery. Those who blindly and indiscriminately defend every decision of the supreme Pontiff are the very ones who do most to undermine the authority of the Holy See—they destroy instead of strengthening its foundations."[15]

That has been the watchword of this project.

I

A Son of Freedom

Poland Semper Fidelis

MAY 18, 1920	Karol Józef Wojtyła is born in Wadowice and baptized on June 20.
AUGUST 16–17, 1920	Red Army invasion of Europe is repelled at the "Miracle on the Vistula."
SEPTEMBER 15, 1926	Karol Wojtyła, "Lolek," begins elementary school.
APRIL 13, 1929	Emilia Kaczorowska Wojtyła, Lolek's mother, dies.
MAY 1929	Lolek's first holy communion.
SEPTEMBER 1930	Lolek enters secondary school.
DECEMBER 5, 1932	Edmund Wojtyła, Lolek's older brother, dies.
FALL 1934	Lolek begins to perform in local theatrical productions.
FEBRUARY 1936	Karol Wojtyła begins intense work with avant-garde theatrical director Mieczysław Kotlarczyk.
MAY 3, 1938	Karol Wojtyła is confirmed.
MAY 27, 1938	Wojtyła graduates from high school and is class valedictorian.
AUGUST 1938	Lolek and his father move to Kraków, where the younger Wojtyła begins an active undergraduate life at the Jagiellonian University.
SPRING 1939	Wojtyła completes unpublished volume of poetry, "Renaissance Psalter."
JUNE 1939	Lolek successfully passes matriculation exams for further studies in Polish philology.
JULY 1939	Karol Wojtyła completes military training with the Academic Legion.

The Marne, Tannenberg, and Verdun; the Battle of Britain and Midway; Stalingrad and D-Day's Omaha Beach—according to the conventional wisdom, these were the decisive battles of the twentieth century. Only Poles and professional historians remember the August 1920 Battle of the Vistula, or, as pious Poles insist, the "Miracle on the Vistula." Yet much turned on this, including the destiny of a three-month-old infant named Karol Józef Wojtyła, born in the small provincial city of Wadowice the previous May 18.

In the summer of 1920, Polish history seemed set to repeat itself in a particularly ugly way. The Second Polish Republic, the first independent Polish state since 1795, was about to be strangled in its cradle as the Red Cavalry of General Semën Budënnyi drove westward out of Ukraine, sweeping all before it. For Poles, it brought back memories of other invasions from the steppes and other preludes to national disaster. For Lenin, who wanted to "probe Europe with the bayonet of the Red Army,"[1] the infant Polish Republic was of no moral or historic consequence. It was simply the highway along which Trótsky's Red Army legions would march to Germany, triggering a revolutionary uprising across all of Europe. To make sure that any resistance would be summarily crushed, the Provisional Polish Revolutionary Committee, the puppet regime to be installed in the wake of the Red Army's inevitable victory, would be led by Feliks Dzerzhínskii, head of the Cheka, the Soviet secret police, the most feared man in Bolshevik Russia.

By August 12, as one historian has put it, "it was clear to most observers in Warsaw that the last desperate week of the resurrected Poland had arrived." The entire diplomatic corps fled, with one exception: Archbishop Achille Ratti, the Pope's representative. A Polish delegation left for Minsk, where they hoped to start negotiations for an armistice or a surrender with the Soviets. Dzerzhínskii was headed for Wyszków, thirty miles from Warsaw, from which he expected to enter a fallen capital on August 17.

But Marshal Józef Piłsudski, who dominated the life of the Second Polish Republic from its inception in 1918 until his death in 1935, was not prepared to concede defeat. Piłsudski's intelligence operatives had detected a gap between the two corps of Trótsky's army. In a daring move, Piłsudski pulled some of Poland's best divisions from the lines on which they were engaged and secretly redeployed them to take advantage of the gap between the Soviet forces. On August 16, the Poles attacked, and by the night of the 17th, the Red Army, which had begun its own attack on Warsaw on the 14th, had been reduced to a rabble of fleeing refugees at a cost of fewer than 200 Polish casualties.[2]

Distracted by that year's calamitous flu epidemic and still reeling from the slaughters of the First World War, western Europe seemed unaware that, but for the Poles, the Red Army might just as easily have been camped along the English Channel as fleeing back into Great Russia. Lenin, though, understood that world history had just taken a decisive turn. In a rambling speech on September 20 to a closed meeting of communist leaders, he went into dialectical dithyrambs trying to explain why "the Polish war . . . [was] a most important turning point not only in the politics of Soviet Russia but also in world politics." Germany, he claimed, was "seething." And "the English proletariat had raised itself to an entirely new revolutionary level." It was all there, ripe for the taking. But Piłsudski and his Poles had inflicted a "gigantic, unheard-of defeat" on the cause of world revolution. At the end of his speech, Lenin swore that "we will keep shifting from a defensive to an offensive strategy over and over again until we finish them off for good." But for now, the westward thrust of Bolshevism had been rebuffed.[3]

Among many other things, Piłsudski's stunning victory meant that Karol Wojtyła would grow up a free man in a free Poland, a member of the first generation of Poles to be born in freedom in 150 years. An experience he would never forget, it became part of the foundation on which he, too, would change the history of the twentieth century.

THE CROSSROADS

The nation into which Karol Wojtyła was born was once the greatest power in east central Europe. The Polish-Lithuanian dynastic union, formed by the marriage in 1386 of the Polish Queen Jadwiga to the Lithuanian Duke Władysław Jagiełło, created a mammoth state that, by defeating the Teutonic Knights, the preeminent military power of the age, at the Battle of Grünwald in 1410, set the stage for 200 years of Poland's growth. A decade after Columbus discovered the New World, Polish rule extended from the Black Sea in the south to the Baltic in the north, and from the German borderlands on the west almost to the gates of Moscow in the east. In those days, France alone exceeded the Polish kingdom in population among the nations of Europe. Polish power and the world-famous Polish heavy cavalry, the winged Hussars, played a decisive role in world history. In 1683, Polish troops led by King Jan III Sobieski halted the Turkish advance into Europe at the epic Battle of Vienna. Sobieski presented Pope Innocent XI with the green banner of the Prophet, captured from the Turkish grand vizier. Along with it came the message "*Veni, vidi, Deus vicit* [I came, I saw, God conquered]."[4]

Poland's subsequent history was less glorious as historians typically measure national accomplishment. Memories of lost grandeur remained alive, though, in the form of an intractable conviction that Poland *belonged* at the European table. That conviction also had much to do with Poles' sense of their location.

A rhetorical convention, Stalinist in origin but widespread in the West, assigns Poland to "eastern Europe." Poles never speak of themselves this way. Poland, for Poles, is in *central* Europe, and any map of Europe will quickly confirm their claim. For Poles, though, this sense of being in the center of Europe is a matter of history and culture as well as of geography.

To be sure, Poland is a Slavic nation, speaking a Slavic language. But the fact that Poles use the Latin, rather than the Cyrillic, alphabet in writing their language is more than an orthographic curiosity. It tells us how to locate the axis of Polish culture.

Throughout its early national history, Poland was in constant contact with the civilization of western Europe. More than a century before the Jagiellonians, during the reign of the Piast dynasty, Polish scholars were to be found in the West of the high Middle Ages. Martin the Pole, a historian, worked in Paris, and the Silesian philosopher Witello was a colleague of Thomas Aquinas.[5] Renaissance Polish humanists like Nicholas Copernicus, Jan Kocjanowski, and Jan Zamoyski all graduated from the University of Padua, then the leading school in Europe; in 1563, Zamoyski served Padua as its rector.[6] Poland's constant interaction with the West was not limited to intellectuals. Kraków's Rynek Głowny, at 650 feet by 650 feet the largest market square on the continent, was a crossroads of European commerce and culture. There, you could buy almost anything, hear almost any European language, meet almost anyone. This was not living on the edges of civilization. It was life in the middle of things.

Being in the center of Europe meant being in the center of Europe's controversies, of which the religious proved the most bloody in the sixteenth century. Poland was not immune to religious conflict, but it was also notable for a tradition of religious toleration that was remarkable for its time. Nowhere else in Europe during the wars of religion was there anything like the pledge made by Poland's leaders on January 28, 1573, that "we who differ in matters of religion will keep the peace among ourselves, and neither shed blood on account of differences of Faith, or kinds of church, nor punish one another by confiscation of goods, deprivation of honor, imprisonment, or exile. . . ."[7] Life is never as simple as declarations, of course, and Norman Davies, a distinguished historian of Poland, argues that while toleration was the formal rule, the spirit of tolerance could be in short supply among individual Poles. The difference, Davies concludes, is that toleration did in fact prevail in Poland, the shortcomings of the people notwithstanding. Poland "was indeed a 'land without bonfires.' There were no campaigns of forced conversion; no religious wars; no autos-da-fé; no St. Bartholomew's Eve; no Thomas and Oliver Cromwell." At the height of its influence as a world power, there were limits to religious freedom in Poland that moderns would find intolerable, but these "limitations . . . were trivial in comparison to the horrors which occurred in most other European countries."[8]

Catholic and catholic

None of Poland's intellectual, cultural, commercial, architectural, and political linkages to the West bears so much on the modern Polish drama as the strongest of the nation's ties to the civilization of Latin Europe: the Roman Catholic Church.

Polish history is generally taken to begin with the baptism of the Piast prince Mieszko I in 966. Mieszko's choice for Latin Christianity over Eastern Christianity, which had been formed in the orbit of Constantinople, decisively shaped Poland's history for more than a millennium. The motives for Mieszko's conversion were not unalloyed; accepting Latin-rite baptism helped him maintain room for maneuver against the ambitions of the Holy Roman Empire.[9] Whatever the complex motivation involved, Mieszko's baptism as a Latin-rite Christian firmly anchored his emerging nation in the culture of the West. Over time, Poland would become perhaps the world's most intensely Catholic nation.

By Mieszko's choice, a Slavic land and people would be oriented toward the Latin West. Thus the very intensity of the Catholicism of this land and people had an ecumenical or universal element built into it. These Roman Catholic Slavs were a bridge between Europe's two cultural halves; they could "speak the language of two spiritual worlds."[10] Poland's Catholicity and its geographic location led to a certain catholicity of cultural temperament.

The fabric of Polish Catholicism had a distinctive texture, and one of its brightest threads was a fidelity to Rome untinged by sycophancy. Yet the Polish experience of "Rome" differed over the centuries. From the Polish point of view, "Rome" could misunderstand, even betray, Polish aspirations—as when the Church failed to support (and in one instance, sharply condemned) Polish patriots' attempts to throw off the yoke of oppression after the final partition of Poland in 1795 had erased "Poland," the state, from the map of Europe. But "Rome" could also stay and defend. During that third and final partition, the Pope's representative refused to leave his post as the vivisection of Poland was completed—just as the apostolic nuncio, Archbishop Ratti, would do in 1920 in the face of the Red Army.

The salt mine at Wieliczka is a metaphor for the special character of Polish Catholicism and its relationship to the national history. Salt has been dug out of the earth at this mine near Kraków since the Neolithic Period, about 3500 B.C. At the deepest level of the mine, 600 feet or so below the earth's surface, is the greatest of a series of chapels carved out of salt by pious miners—the chapel of Blessed Kinga, wife to a thirteenth-century prince of Kraków, Bolesław the Shameful. Six thousand cubic yards of salt were removed to clear the chapel. Five great salt chandeliers hang from the vault, and when their tapers are lit, the impression is of standing inside a diamond lit by the sun. The land above the mine at Wieliczka is flat, a natural invasion route from east and west, across which marauders wrought havoc for centuries. Lodged deep within Polish soil, its ornaments carved from native material and radiating light where one expects darkness, is the steady, beating heart of a great spiritual culture, which often lacked what the world recognizes as power.[11]

The Neighborhood

Poland is not always appreciated this way. Indeed, the suspicion seems widespread that the Poles must, for some reason or other, deserve their bad luck.[12] Yet Poland's curse is neither in the stars nor in the Polish people. It's the neighborhood.

For more than a thousand years, the Polish people and their state have inhabited an enormous flat plain bounded by large, aggressive, materially superior neighbors. Whether they were Teutonic Knights, vassals of the Holy Roman Empire, Prussian soldier-statesmen, or the armies of Hitler's Thousand Year Reich, the Germans were always to the west, and almost always aggressive. German-Polish enmity followed and peaked in World War II, when the Nazis sought to eradicate the Polish nation from history.

The real, enduring passions of Polish antipathy are located eastward, however, toward Russia and Russians. For hundreds of years, Poles tended to think of Russians as "savage exotics living beyond the pale of Christendom." An old Polish joke (which one can still hear today) has it that, should Poland be invaded simultaneously by Germans and Russians, the Polish army should shoot the Germans first, on the ancient principle of business before pleasure.[13] This loathing was reciprocated by Russians, and not merely at the level of popular prejudice. In the seventeenth century, the monastery at Zagorsk, one of the spiritual centers of Russian Orthodoxy, featured a sign that read, "Three Plagues—Typhus, Tartars, Poles."[14] During the eighteenth-century partitions of the Polish state, these feelings of mutual hatred hardened, as the autocratic Russian authorities sought to turn Poles into Russians and the Poles contributed their share to the conspiratorial violence that wracked the czarist empire.

Poland's historic problem of location was often compounded by a certain incapacity for politics. The concept of freedom that entered Poland in the fifteenth century through Kraków's Jagiellonian University was deeply influenced by the philosophy of William of Ockham: freedom is the capacity to assert one's will against the willfulness of others. Over time, this notion made the Poles great freedom fighters, asserting their freedom *against* an enemy, but rather bad at living freedom *for*.[15] There was, for example, the *liberum veto* of the Polish gentry class, by which a single nobleman could block the passage of any piece of legislation. Between 1652 and 1764, when a strong central government might have taken the steps necessary to defend Poland against its predatory neighbors, forty-eight out of fifty-five sessions of the Polish parliament, the Sejm, were dissolved because someone had proclaimed, *Nie pozwalam*, "I disapprove."

Yet Poland's "Noble Democracy," or democracy by the rule of a large gentry class, avoided the worst excesses of royal absolutism, even at the cost of a kind of democratic anarchy. Its deficiencies were not the result of willfulness and selfishness alone. The gentry's moral claim to participation in Poland's governance was captured in the famous phrase, *Nic o nas bez nas*: "Nothing about us without us." The phrase was fanciful when it gave moral sanction to the irresponsible use of the *liberum veto* in eighteenth-century Poland. It would have a different ring to it in 1980, when "Nothing about us without us" became one of the mottoes of Solidarność, the Solidarity trade union and political opposition.

A DIFFERENT IDEA OF "HISTORY"

Poland's location at the crossroads of Latin and Byzantine Europe, its geography, and its repeated experience of invasion, occupation, resistance, and resurrection gave rise to a distinctive Polish way of looking at history. The partitions of Poland in 1773, 1793, and 1795 were unprecedented in modern Europe. A historic state was murdered "in cold blood . . . by mutilation, amputation, and, in the end total dismemberment."[16] Yet the Polish nation survived the destruction of the Polish state, because Poles came to believe that spiritual power was, over time, more efficacious in history than brute force. A nation deprived of its political autonomy could survive as a nation through its language, its literature, its music, its religion—in a word, through its culture. Culture, not politics or economics, was the driving force of history.

Thus history, viewed from the Vistula basin, looked rather different than it did from other vantage points. Poles may have been romantics, but few of them succumbed to the "blood and iron" *Realpolitik* that helped make a charnel house of twentieth-century Europe and paved the way for fascist and communist totalitarianism. Nor did Polish nationalism, for all its patriotic fervor, ever become narrowly xenophobic. Tadeusz Kościuszko sought Polish independence from Russia under a banner that read "For Your Freedom and Ours." The Poles who died at Monte Cassino in 1944 had similar universalist sentiments. As the epitaph in their cemetery in Italy puts it: "We Polish soldiers/For your freedom and ours/Gave our bodies to the soil of Italy/Our souls to God/But our hearts to Poland."[17]

Poles were also skeptical of the fondness for utopian revolutionary violence that became fashionable in Europe in 1789. Their political circumstances—in which national survival was the crucial issue—did not permit too much speculation, much less action, along utopian lines. Yet Poland's relative immunity to this particular modern virus also reflected the conviction that, over history's long haul, the spirit counted for more than what secular realists, including utopian revolutionaries, deemed the facts of the matter. What realists insisted was "reality" did not wholly determine what was "real"—for example, the negation of Poland—if you refused to believe their claims. It was a particularly Polish form of stubbornness with Christian cultural roots. And it served Poland well between 1795 and 1919, the time Poles refer to as their "Babylonian Captivity" or their "Time on the Cross."[18] Without that stubbornness, Poland, the state, might never have reemerged on the political map of Europe.

The Second Polish Republic, the Poland in which Karol Wojtyła grew up, was born at the end of World War I amid immense difficulties. The new state had no internationally recognized boundaries. Seven different currencies circulated in the territory that would eventually settle down as "Poland," and four legal systems were in play. Its industry had been destroyed; half the rolling stock, bridges, and other infrastructure of modern transportation had gone up in smoke during the war. By 1918, half of Poland's agricultural land was uncultivated and a third of the livestock had been stolen by the armies that had fought across the Vistula basin. Influenza was rampant, and starvation loomed until relief shipments arrived from the United States. Few Poles had any experience of operating a modern government.[19] Poland's commitment to the priority of the human spirit in history was severely tested in the new country's first months of independence.

Yet for all these difficulties, "Poland" was a reality, and the Poles had changed the course of world history by repelling the Red Army's westward thrust. It was thus into a free Poland, beset by problems but hopeful about its independent future, that Karol Józef Wojtyła was born on May 18, 1920.

HOME

Wadowice, Karol Wojtyła's boyhood home, was an ancient town, founded in the mid-thirteenth century and located on the River Skawa in the foothills of the Beskidy Mountains. The parish of Wadowice was established in 1325. In 1564, toward the end of the Jagiellonian dynasty, Wadowice was incorporated into the Kingdom of Poland along with the rest of the Duchy of Oświęcim.

In 1819, Wadowice became the center of an administrative district in Galicia and home to a regiment of Austro-Hungarian troops. In the late nineteenth and early twentieth centuries, the town developed a reputation for literary and theatrical activity. With a pre–World War II population of about 10,000, Wadowice counted only a half-dozen automobiles. Horse-drawn carriages were still common, as were peasants in traditional dress. But this was no rural backwater. Its traditional cultural interests and the play of its history oriented Wadowice toward Kraków (Poland's cultural capital) and Vienna, rather than toward Warsaw. Like most other Poles in Galicia, the people of Wadowice harbored no burning antipathy toward the Habsburg Empire, but they were Polish patriots who welcomed the rebirth of an independent Poland after World War I. The elder generation in Wadowice may well have felt that at long last the sufferings of the past were over. Poland would no longer be an exile nation, wandering in the wilderness of history.

The people of Wadowice were small businessmen, lawyers, tradesmen, farmers, and officials of the local provincial administration. They worked in the town's factories, producing biscuits and steel parts. A steam-powered sawmill, two brickyards, and a factory where fertilizer was made from animal bones treated with sulphuric acid completed the town's light industry.[20] After Poland regained its independence, the Austrian barracks was taken over by the 12th Infantry Regiment of the new Polish army, and the regiment's senior

officers became important figures in local society. The soberly dressed towns-
people were in regular contact with the more colorfully clad farmers of the
region. Some of the local poetry, memorized by Wadowice's schoolchildren,
described the hard lives of those who were trying to wrest a living from the
rocky soil of the region. The countryside, the people's Catholicism, and the
world of culture met in the person of "Wawro," a local peasant-philosopher-
sculptor, whose popular primitives—birds, sorrowful Christ-figures, wayside
shrines—were expressions of a simple soul who impressed the better-educated
townspeople because he thought seriously about his art.[21] The contempt with
which modern artists and intellectuals often regard popular piety was not
prominent in Wadowice.

The Second Polish Republic was a heterogeneous affair in which ethnic
Poles were sixty-five percent of the total population.[22] In Wadowice, this pluralism was primarily reflected in the town's large Jewish population, some 2,000
strong. According to Karol Wojtyła's boyhood friend, Jerzy Kluger, the Jews of
Wadowice thought of themselves quite naturally as Poles. More than seventy
years after they first met, Pope John Paul II remembered Kluger's father, a lawyer
and the leader of the Wadowice Jewish community, as a "great Polish patriot."[23]
The Jews of Wadowice were originally German-speaking and had been largely
inculturated into local society; they dressed and spoke like the other people of
the town. Wadowice was not without its ethnic and religious tensions, but it was
also a place where the Polish poet Adam Mickiewicz's description of Jews as the
"elder brothers" of Christians was taken seriously by many local Catholics. Karol
Wojtyła would later write that he "vividly [remembered] the Jews who gathered
every Saturday at the synagogue behind our school. Both religious groups,
Catholics and Jews, were united . . . by the awareness that they prayed to the
same God."[24] Wadowice's Jews, for their part, had recent and good reason to
regard themselves as being thoroughly Polish. Some had fought with Piłsudski's
Polish Legion, in which Kluger's father had been an officer, and others were
serving as officers in the new Polish army.

The military garrison helped contribute to the town's atmosphere of tolerance. At the annual regimental ball, the colonel in command would always
dance the first mazurka with Jerzy Kluger's mother.[25] The local priests were
also committed to religious toleration. Father Leonard Prochownik, who had
served in Wadowice since 1915 and who officially became the town's pastor in
1929, is still remembered as someone whose promotion of interreligious tolerance was responsible for the town's relative lack of anti-Semitism.[26] Kluger's
grandmother Huppert was friendly with the parish clergy, and the local policeman would shoo eavesdroppers away when the Jewish matron and the Polish
pastor, both a little deaf, walked amid the birches and firs of the town square,
carrying on a voluble conversation.[27]

Physically and culturally, the focal point of Wadowice was St. Mary's
Church (more formally, the Church of the Presentation of the Blessed Virgin Mary), located at one end of the long axis of the rectangular town square.

The parish had been part of the town's life for more than 650 years. Every Sunday, both townspeople and those who lived in the countryside packed its Masses, dressed in their best clothes. Inside the main body of the onion-domed church, whose decoration was primarily baroque, worshipers found an elaborate high altar recessed in a chancel and six small altar-shrines, each dedicated to a particular devotion. The baptistry chapel, in which thousands of children were christened over the centuries, displayed a copy of Poland's greatest national icon, the "Black Madonna," which tradition held to have been painted by St. Luke on a table belonging to the holy family of Jesus, Mary, and Joseph. Dark wooden pews that could seat perhaps 200 congregants rested on the church's tiled floor. There was ample standing room, and it was used.

The parish of Wadowice was fortunate in its clergy, men of piety and learning. Father Prochownik's assistant, Father Edward Zacher, was ordained in 1927 and was sent to Rome for graduate studies in theology. After returning to Poland in 1929 and spending two years at Zakopane in the Tatra Mountains, he was assigned to Wadowice as catechist or religion teacher in the two local high schools. Just outside the town, within easy walking distance, was a Carmelite monastery, home to one of the Church's most rigorous religious orders. Its most notable monk had been Rafał Kalinowski. Condemned to death but ultimately dispatched to eight years of Siberian exile for his role in the 1863 Polish Uprising against the czarist empire, Kalinowski entered the Discalced Carmelites at age forty after a period of self-imposed exile in Paris, and died in the "monastery on the hill," as the people of Wadowice called it, in 1907. He would be canonized by John Paul II in 1991.[28]

About six miles farther along the road toward Kraków was one of the great pilgrimage sites in Poland, Kalwaria Zebrzydowska, which would play a large role in Karol Wojtyła's spiritual life as long as he lived in Poland. A vast outdoor shrine, Kalwaria was originally built by the regional governor of Kraków, Mikołaj Zebrzydowski, who in 1600 commissioned a Church of the Holy Cross on the mountain of Żarek—according to one tradition, after his wife had experienced a vision of Christ. When the new church was dedicated in October 1601, Zebrzydowski decided to build another chapel nearby, modeled on the Church of the Holy Sepulcher in Jerusalem, and invited the Franciscan fathers and brothers to look after the shrines. Having been to the Holy Land and sensing a resemblance between its topography and that of his property, the pious nobleman then decided to erect a whole series of chapels on his land, similar to those he had seen in Jerusalem commemorating various scenes from the passion, death, and resurrection of Christ. By 1617, some twenty-four chapels, comprising an extended outdoor version of the traditional Lenten devotion known as the "way of the cross," extended along many kilometers of footpaths through the rolling countryside.

"Zebrzydowski's Calvary" soon became a place of pilgrimage for Catholics from all over Poland, especially during a great outdoor passion play performed each Holy Week. The passion play often drew a hundred thousand pilgrims to Kalwaria Zebrzydowska. The movement of the play from shrine to shrine and the emotional intensity of the event were such that the pilgrims became virtual participants in the drama of Christ's suffering and death. Lasting several days, the passion play included both local actors and volunteer professionals from distant cities and towns, eager to take part in what became a major national ritual.* The site was further expanded by Michołaj Zebrzydowski's son Jan, who, after his father's death in 1620, began a second series of chapels dedicated to scenes from the life of Mary, the mother of Christ. The feast of Mary's assumption into heaven on August 15 soon became the occasion for another great annual pilgrimage to Kalwaria from all over southern Poland.

In the early twentieth century, Kalwaria Zebrzydowska included forty-five chapels, twenty-four constituting the "Path of Our Lord" and twenty-one marking the "Path of Our Lady." Ten chapels common to both "paths" symbolized the intertwined lives of Jesus and Mary. The chapels were imaginatively constructed to convey the meaning of the biblical scene they commemorate. The chapel commemorating Jesus taking up his cross is cruciform in shape, and the chapel in remembrance of Jesus' meeting with his mother en route to his crucifixion is heart-shaped, a reminder to pilgrims that the dying Christ, by giving his mother into the care of the beloved disciple, John, gave her to all his disciples, who would always find a home in the heart of Mary. The Christ-centered character of Kalwaria's Marian piety is most powerfully symbolized by the crossing of the two paths at one of the shrine's largest churches, the chapel of Mary's assumption into heaven. Its location and design anticipated the Second Vatican Council's teaching that Mary, the first of believers, is the first fruit of the redeeming work of Christ.

ROOTS

Neither the elder Karol Wojtyła, a noncommissioned officer in the 56th Infantry Regiment of the Austro-Hungarian army, nor his wife, Emilia, had family ties to Wadowice, the town in which they raised their family after their marriage in 1904.[30]

---

*The passion play at Kalwaria sets the stage in Krzysztof Zanussi's film *From a Far Country*, a fictional drama built around the life of Pope John Paul II. At the beginning of the movie the future pope, a young boy, watches the passion play unfold through the snow-covered hills of Kalwaria Zebrzydowska. One night he becomes separated from his father, who searches for him from tent to tent. He finally locates him in a smoke-filled tent where some of the actors are taking a break; the man who has played Jesus that afternoon is drinking a beer, while the youngster watches him wide-eyed. John Paul II was once asked whether this scene had any tether to history, but before the Pope could answer, his secretary interrupted with a laugh: "Yes, there was *piccolo Carlo*, scandalized because Jesus was drinking a beer . . ." The Holy Father grinned, perhaps a bit ruefully, and said that director Zanussi, a friend, had taken some artistic liberties with his biography.[29]

Karol Wojtyła's family traced its ancestry to the village of Czaniec, which has since disappeared into a suburb of today's Bielsko-Biała, some forty miles southwest of Kraków. Baptismal and marriage records often identify the Wojtyłas as *hortulani*, small farmers, although the parish records of Biała list some Wojtyłas as merchants and include such characters as "Wojtyła the vagabond" and "Wojtyła the beggar" whose relationship to Pope John Paul II's family cannot be established. Maciej Wojtyła, the Pope's grandfather, left Czaniec and moved to the village of Lipnik, where he worked as a guildmaster tailor and farmer. Karol Wojtyła, the Pope's father, was born in Lipnik on August 18, 1879, to Maciej and his wife Anna (née Przeczek), the daughter of a baker. Anna died when young Karol was a boy. Karol's stepsister, Stefania, was born in 1891 of Maciej's second marriage to Maria Zalewska, the daughter of a tailor. Maciej Wojtyła died in Lipnik on September 23, 1923, when his grandson, the future pope, was not yet three and a half.

The earliest extant records of Emilia Kaczorowska Wojtyła's family are also located in the Bielsko-Biała area. Emilia's father, Feliks Kaczorowski, was born in Biała on June 26, 1849, and worked as a saddler. In 1875, he married Maria Scholz, the third daughter of a cobbler. Emilia, their fifth child, was born on March 26, 1884. A year later the family moved to Kraków, where four more children (one of whom died in infancy) were born. Maria Scholz Kaczorowska died in 1897; Feliks remarried and died in 1908 after fathering four more children by his second wife, Joanna. The Kaczorowskis lived at 15 Smoleńsk Street in Kraków, where Feliks operated a saddlery that specialized in upholstering horse-drawn carriages. Emilia is thought to have completed eight grades at a school run by the Sisters of Mercy. Always of somewhat delicate health, she helped manage the household and raise her smaller siblings until her marriage to Karol Wojtyła.[31]

Karol and Emilia's son Edmund, known in the family as "Mundek," was born on August 27, 1906. A handsome young man, he became a fine student and active athlete, remembered for his exceptional personal charm. From 1924 through 1929, Edmund Wojtyła studied at the Jagiellonian University in Kraków, where on May 28, 1930, he was awarded the degree doctor of medical science. He then went to practice his profession at the hospital in Bielsko.[32]

Emilia gave birth to a daughter some years after Edmund. There are no records of her birth, baptism, or death in infancy. Local recollections in Wadowice have it that she lived for several weeks before succumbing. She was presumably baptized privately at home, perhaps by her parents as the Church permits in emergencies, and was likely buried in the local cemetery, although without a headstone, as the custom of the time dictated.[33]

From 1919 on, Karol and Emilia lived with Edmund in an apartment on the second floor of the house owned by Chaim Blamuth at Rynek, 2 (now Koscielna, 7), across the street from St. Mary's Church.[34] There, the couple's third child and second son was born on May 18, 1920. Lolek, as family and friends would call him, was baptized by a military chaplain, Father Franciszek

Zak, at St. Mary's Church on June 20, 1920, and formally given the names Karol Józef, which were reminiscent of the Habsburg monarchy his father had served.*

Lolek's baby photos suggest a chubby youngster with a broad Slavic face. One picture taken with his mother displays a marked resemblance between the two. Endless stories about young Karol Wojtyła's childhood now abound, and it is virtually impossible to separate truth from pious fantasy or creative memory in these matters. The story that Emilia walked him in a pram through Wadowice and told her neighbors, "You'll see, my Lolek will be a great man someday," has been testified to so often that it should perhaps be given the benefit of the doubt.

The elder Karol Wojtyła continued his career as a lieutenant in the Polish army until he was retired on pension with the rank of captain circa 1927.[36] While Lolek was growing up, Emilia, who was skilled in embroidery, took in sewing to help supplement the family's income. The Wojtyła apartment was modest but certainly middle-class, housed in a solid brick structure covered by stucco, and built around a central courtyard, where Emilia would sit and talk with her neighbors while Lolek played. The apartment had several rooms and a kitchen. The extant furniture, china, cutlery, and decorations suggest solidity, piety, and a simple, but hardly impoverished, standard of living. Until Edmund left for Kraków and the university in 1924, it must have been a bit crowded. Personal tragedy would soon reduce the family further.

Karol Wojtyła's boyhood friend Jerzy Kluger remembers the two youngsters playing on the town square, a block from the Wojtyła flat. When they were "about six or seven," Lolek and Jurek Kluger somehow became convinced that the town policeman, Ćwięk, had a wooden sword. One day, when Ćwięk was taking a nap on the square, the boys decided to test their theory by easing the sword out of its scabbard. They lost their balance, tripped, and fell over the startled custodian of law and order—who was presumably more disturbed by the interruption of his nap than by the attempted requisition of one of the symbols of his office.[37] When they weren't playing in town or at home, the boys could swim in the Skawa during summer months or skate and play a primitive game of ice hockey on its frozen surface in the winter. Hiking, for most of the year, was another youthful recreation. Soccer was their favorite team sport. Pilgrims to Wadowice today can see the field on which "Lolek the Goalie" honed his skills, often playing on a team primarily made up of the town's Jewish boys.

On September 15, 1926, Karol Wojtyła began the first grade at the local elementary school, located on the second floor of the town administration building on the market square, a minute's walk from the family apartment. Classes were large, ranging upward of sixty students per classroom. The cur-

---

*Pope John Paul II was once asked whether his father had given him the middle name "Józef" in honor of Piłsudski, the founding hero of the newly independent Polish Republic. The Pope's secretary, Monsignor Stanisław Dziwisz, laughed and said, "Franz *Józef*," emperor of Austria-Hungary from 1848–1916.[35]

riculum included Polish, religion, arithmetic, drawing, singing, and, according to his report cards, "games and exercise" and "handicrafts." Lolek was a gifted student from the start.[38] The carefree innocence usually associated with early grammar school days was not destined to last very long, though. On April 13, 1929, while Lolek was completing the third grade, his mother, who had often been ill, died of kidney failure and congenital heart disease.[39] Emilia Kaczorowska Wojtyła, aged forty-five, was buried from the parish church on April 16 after a funeral Mass celebrated by the pastor, Father Prochownik.

Much has been written about the long-term impact of his mother's early death on Karol Wojtyła. It is frequently suggested, for example, that Wojtyła's Marian piety is displaced maternal affection. Others have gone so far as to argue that his papal teaching on women and Holy Orders reflects a problem relating to women that began with Emilia's death.[40] Such speculations, frequently based on amateur psychoanalysis conducted from afar, are of no use to serious students of Wojtyła's life. Moreover, John Paul's recent autobiographical writings are virtually silent on the subject of his mother, noting only that he "does not have a clear awareness of her contribution" to his religious training, "which must have been great."[41]

While his silence about his mother's death no doubt reflects his sense of privacy, it may also suggest that Karol Wojtyła, as an adult, retained few memories of the woman who died when he was nine years old. In a post-Freudian world, simple explanations can seem like evasions. But one explanation of why the Virgin in Michelangelo's *Pieta* does not look at her dead son is that the sculptor, whose mother died when he was six, did not remember what a mother's gaze looked like. John Paul II's silence about his mother may well indicate nothing other than a relative paucity of memories about her, as one of his closest aides once observed.[42] On a table in his bedroom, in both the papal apartment in the Vatican and at his summer residence at Castel Gandolfo, Pope John Paul II keeps a small photographic portrait of his parents, taken some time after their wedding. That is how he remembers his mother.

Karol Wojtyła had many mentors in his youth and adolescence. The most influential of them was his father.

The elder Karol Wojtyła, universally referred to in Wadowice as "the captain," was a gentleman of the old school and a man of granite integrity whose army career, in the judgment of his superior officers, was based on a combination of intelligence, diligence, dependability, and, above all, honesty.[43] His outstanding characteristic, according to Jerzy Kluger, was that he was a "just man," and he believed he had a responsibility to transmit that commitment to living justly to his son.[44]

Having worked previously as a tailor, Wojtyła served for twenty-seven years in one of the most remarkable creations of the Habsburg Empire, an army that was perhaps the modern world's first great multinational institution. Leading the troops of a polyglot empire, its officers were expected to be multilingual and to speak fluently the language of the men whom they led.[45] Once an aristocratic caste, the Habsburg officer corps was composed of a majority of commoners by the time of Karol Wojtyła's service. And in the European world of the Dreyfus Affair, an environment in which anti-Semitism flourished, the officer corps of the Dual Monarchy included a large number of Jews. It was not without its faults, but judging from the reports filed by Karol Wojtyła's superiors and by Wojtyła's advancement in rank, the army of the Dual Monarchy was an organization in which the character, responsibility, and personal decency for which the young Polish soldier was praised were valued and rewarded.[46]

The captain was not a demonstrative person, but neither was he a recluse. Jerzy Kluger remembers him as neither familiar nor distant, but rather "approachable."[47] He could appear severe to strangers, but he was fair, if strict, in his child rearing.[48] Having completed his elementary and early secondary education before going to work, he was primarily an autodidact. Fluent in German as well as Polish, he taught German to Lolek at home; the future pope would speak the language with an Austrian accent.[49] Karol Wojtyła was also a patriot devoid of xenophobia who was widely conversant with Polish literature, to which he introduced his son. The captain also gave Lolek and Jurek Kluger private lessons in Polish history, which he illustrated with readings of partition-era poets like Cyprian Norwid.[50]

His son also remembers his father as a "man of constant prayer."[51] At night, as in the early morning, young Karol would find his father on his knees silently praying. Father and son read the Bible together and prayed the rosary regularly. But what, in addition to the formulas of prayer, did the captain teach his son about his faith?

Captain Karol Wojtyła, a religious educator by example as much as by admonition and instruction, taught his son that the Church is more than a visible institution. The "mystery of the Church," its "invisible dimension," is "larger than the structure and organization of the Church," which are "at the service of the mystery."[52] By the testimony of the son, it was his father's way of life that first planted in the future pope the idea that the life of faith has first to do with interior conversion.

Pope John Paul II has also written of how impressed he has been, since his youth, by Jesus' saying to his disciples, "Fear not, little flock, it is your Father's good pleasure to give you the kingdom" (*Luke* 12:32). This admonition against fear presumed that there might be things of which the disciples might be afraid: there would be persecutions, there would be hardened hearts. "He did not prepare them for easy success," John Paul II once wrote. But here, he suggests, is the heart of the Gospel: "*The Gospel is not a promise of easy success. It does not promise a comfortable life to anyone. It makes demands and, at the same time, it is a great promise*—the promise of eternal life for man, who is subject to the law of death, and the promise of victory through faith for man, who is subject to many trials and setbacks."[53]

Demand and promise; cross before crown—given John Paul's testimony that this spirituality of redemptive suffering has been the heart of the Gospel for him since he was a youngster, one can see here another imprint of the teaching and example of the most influential religious educator of his early years: his father, the man who first took him on pilgrimage to Kalwaria Zebrzydowska, the year after his mother died.[54]

In his brief autobiographical recollections of his early religious formation, John Paul II wrote that he was "above all" grateful to his father. "We never spoke about a vocation to the priesthood, but *his example was in a way my first seminary*, a kind of domestic seminary."[55] From a priest still awestruck by the gift of priesthood on the golden jubilee of his ordination, there could be no higher praise.

SCHOOLBOY

After completing his elementary education, Karol Wojtyła entered the Marcin Wadowita State Secondary School, an all-boys' junior-senior high school on Wadowice's Mickiewicz Street, in the fall of 1930. Since Emilia's death the previous year, and with Edmund in Kraków completing his medical studies, Captain Wojtyła and his son had established a rigorous daily routine. With school beginning at 8 A.M., they rose early, prayed, and breakfasted together. After young Karol became an altar boy, they often attended the early morning Mass at St. Mary's, which was celebrated at 7 A.M. Mornings were spent in school, and then father and son took their main meal, in the early afternoon, at the bar and restaurant run by Mrs. Maria Banas, near their home; her son Bogusław was a schoolmate of Lolek's and her husband was a friend of the captain. Two hours of play would follow, then homework and a light supper prepared at home by his father, with whom the youngster would sometimes take walks in the evening. The arrangement with the Banas family made life easier for the widower and his son, but it also resulted in one hair-raising incident. A local policeman would drink at the Banases' bar after duty; when he thought he may have had too much, he would put his revolver in the cash drawer and leave it with the Banases for safekeeping. When Karol Wojtyła was about fifteen, Bogusław Banas took out the revolver, pointed it playfully at Lolek, who was about two yards away, and said, "Hands up or I'll shoot!" Somehow the gun went off. The bullet narrowly missed Lolek and shattered a window. Mr. Banas, roused from a nap, burst into the room, took the gun from Bogusław, and returned it to the cash drawer. No one said a word. Everyone knew it had been a very close call.[56]

In 1930, Father Kazimierz Figlewicz, a young priest, came to Wadowice to teach catechism in the elementary and middle schools and was assigned responsibility for the parish altar boys who assisted the priests during Mass. He remembers young Karol Wojtyła as "quite tall, but also somewhat plump," a "very lively boy, very talented, very sharp and very good," who got along well with both his friends and his teachers.[57] Father Figlewicz became Lolek's confessor, the priest to whom he went to confess his sins and receive absolution. The two would also visit and talk outside the private precincts of the confessional, and remained in touch after Father Figlewicz was transferred to the cathedral of Kraków. During the latter part of Lolek's high school years, Father Figlewicz invited him to Kraków for the solemn Holy Week services at the cathedral, which, John Paul II later wrote, made a "profound impression" on him as a youngster.[58] Father Kazimierz Suder, who first knew Karol Wojtyła in the Kraków seminary after World War II, believes that Father Figlewicz was the future pope's "idol."[59] He certainly helped plant the seeds of a priestly vocation in Karol Wojtyła.

In his late elementary and early high school years, Lolek also drew close to his brother, Edmund. They had not seen much of each other while Edmund was studying in Kraków, but after his move to the hospital in Bielsko, home visits were easier and more frequent. Mundek took his younger brother to soccer games, sometimes seating him on his shoulders so that the smaller boy could see better. Lolek, for his part, visited the hospital in Bielsko and put on one-man shows for Mundek's patients. This blossoming friendship between brothers was not to last, though, for on December 5, 1932, Dr. Edmund Wojtyła died, a few days after contracting scarlet fever from one of his patients. He was just twenty-six. It must have been a hammer-blow to Edmund's father and younger brother. Father Kazimierz Suder believes that Lolek was struck even harder by his brother's wholly unexpected death than by the death of his mother.[60] The inscription on Edmund's tombstone in Kraków describes him as "a victim of his profession, sacrificing his young life in the service of humanity."[61] For Lolek, then twelve years old, it was a lesson in God's will, to which he attributed his brother's self-sacrifice when neighbors sought to console him.[62]

The secondary school Lolek attended offered an excellent classical education. Latin and Greek were staples of the curriculum, in addition to courses in Polish language and literature, history, and mathematics. Wojtyła began to study Latin when he was thirteen and developed a fondness for the language that has continued throughout his life; his study of Greek began a year later. Throughout his high school years, he continued to receive top grades, even as his extracurricular activities expanded. He became a member of the Sodality of Mary, a society of young men dedicated to fostering devotion to the mother of Christ, and came to know its chaplain, Father Zacher. During his last two years of high school, he was elected to two terms as the Sodality's president. In the summer of 1937, he completed a mandatory course in military preparedness at a national cadet camp. The final year of high school also included preparations for the sacrament of confirmation, which Karol Wojtyła received on May 3, 1938.

Shortly afterward, the archbishop of Kraków, Adam Stefan Sapieha, visited the Marcin Wadowita Secondary School. Wojtyła, the school's premier student, was chosen to give a welcoming address. He evidently impressed Sapieha, who asked Father Zacher whether he thought they could make a priest out of the youngster. Zacher replied that it didn't seem likely. Wojtyła was set for studies at the Jagiellonian University, where he intended to pursue his literary and theatrical interests. "A pity," the archbishop is said to have replied.[63]

It would not be Karol Wojtyła's last encounter with the aristocratic archbishop who, along with his own father, would have perhaps the most enduring influence on the man he would become.

THE LIVING WORD

When he first disappointed Archbishop Sapieha, Karol Wojtyła, by his own account, had other things on his mind, being "completely absorbed by a passion for literature, especially dramatic literature, and for the theater."[64] It was a passion he had absorbed from his home, his education, and his town, where he had been saturated with Polish Romantic literature and drama. Its themes would shape his thinking for decades to come.[65]

Nineteenth-century Europe was replete with revolutionary literature. The literary patriots who created Polish Romanticism were different. Not only were they poets, novelists, and dramatists rather than pamphleteers; they had a unique view of the revolutionary enterprise. For many political theorists in nineteenth-century continental Europe, "revolution" implied a complete break with the past, with an ancien régime that usually included Christianity as a bastion of the unjust status quo. Polish Romanticism, on the other hand, considered revolution as the recovery of a lost value that had been crucial in the nation's formation. The past was not to be overthrown but recovered as an instrument of national renewal. Polish Romanticism acknowledged Catholicism as the yeast that had given rise to Poland's distinctive national character. To be revolutionary in this singular tradition, then, was to be intensely interested in Christian doctrine and morality.

Karol Wojtyła's first exposure to Polish Romanticism probably came when his father read him the famous trilogy of Henryk Sienkiewicz, in which bold knights charge back and forth across the steppes of the old Polish-Lithuanian Commonwealth, in violent pursuit of glory and defense of faith and fatherland. Sienkiewicz had no pretensions to literary depth. A master storyteller, his fictional account of the days of Poland's grandeur was written to strengthen Polish spirits at a time during the partition when the future seemed darkest. It was almost certainly through Sienkiewicz, for example, that Karol Wojtyła first heard Prior Augustyn Kordecki's epic speech to the defenders of the Jasna Góra (Bright Mountain) monastery at Częstochowa, home of the icon of the Black Madonna. That defense broke the back of the Swedish invasion of 1655, the traumatic period that Polish history remembers as "the Deluge":

It may be that God and His Holy Mother intend to blind the enemy on purpose . . . so that he'd go so far in his lawlessness and rapacity. Otherwise he'd never dare to raise the sword against this holy place . . .

The enemy jeers at us and despises us, asking what's left of our former virtues. And I'll tell him this much: we've lost them all but one, and that is our Faith and the honor we show to the Holy Mother, and that is the foundation on which we can reconstruct the rest . . . [Our enemies] understand what is at stake here . . . [And] if God hasn't blinded them by design, they'd never dare strike at Jasna Góra. Because that day would be the beginning of the end of their supremacy and the beginning of our awakening.[66]

A great popularizer, Sienkiewicz conveyed to a mass audience several key ideas in Polish Romanticism's distinctive view of Polish history: history had a spiritual core; the deterioration of its traditional national virtues had caused Poland's political collapse; reestablishing Polish independence required recovering those virtues as the foundation of a new Polish state. Karol Wojtyła deepened his understanding of this singular way of reading history in his adolescent encounter with the great poet/dramatists of Polish Romanticism, including Adam Mickiewicz, Juliusz Słowacki, and Cyprian Kamil Norwid.

Mickiewicz (1789–1855)—poet, playwright, and political activist—was the defining exponent of Polish Romanticism and the greatest Polish literary figure of his time. Born in Lithuania, he never set foot in Warsaw or Kraków and died near Constantinople. But Mickiewicz was the "posthumous child" of the old Polish-Lithuanian Commonwealth and the indisputable master of Polish literature for the greater part of the nineteenth century.[67] His intellectual life and literary work were full of passion, particularly for Polish independence. And he expressed that passion through a distinctive set of ideas, forged in the tension between the rationalist pride of the Enlightenment and the humility required by faith, between Romanticism's celebration of intuition (the "truth of the heart") and Christian orthodoxy's insistence on objective truth.[68]

In epic poems like *Pan Tadeusz*, in visionary poetic dramas like *Forefathers' Eve* (which had such an emotional impact on its audiences that czarist censors sometimes banned it), and in didactic works like *The Books of the Polish Nation and of the Polish Pilgrims*, Adam Mickiewicz insisted that history had a deep spiritual dimension in which suffering prepared the soul for glory. It was a familiar Christian theme—redemptive suffering as a personal spiritual discipline. For Mickiewicz, though, redemptive suffering was also the national destiny. Partitioned Poland was a Messiah among nations, a suffering servant whose time on Calvary would redeem the world and show it the path beyond Western materialism into a new, more spiritual form of freedom.[69]

Mickiewicz was a political progressive and philo-Semite who interpreted the revolutionary tradition's "liberty, equality, and fraternity" according to his

Christian belief that the Incarnation of Christ, the Second Adam, had made all men equal, irrespective of their convictions about Christ.[70] In the revolutionary transformation of the world as imagined by Mickiewicz, the simple intuitions of the pious and humble were more trustworthy avenues to the truth of things than the speculations of intellectuals or what the worlds of power took to be wisdom.[71]

Juliusz Słowacki (1809–1849) competed with Mickiewicz for the role of spiritual leader of the noncountry of Poland. His drama *Kordian*, quite consciously intended as a rival to Mickiewicz's *Forefathers' Eve*, is another epic about the making of history, illustrated by a series of scene-fragments from the spiritual evolution of its hero, who, offering himself for the sins of his country, stands atop the Alps and opens himself to being martyred by history.[72]

Słowacki was fascinated by the question of how the world must have looked to Adam, the first man, and his literary work was in some respects an effort to imagine the world, its origins, and its destiny afresh. Like other Polish Romantics, he was convinced that partitioned, suffering Poland played a unique role in the drama of world history. In Słowacki's case, this meant that the "Spirit" which had created the world and shaped each succeeding phase of history now resided in Poland. There, it would give birth to a figure who would lead humanity beyond its present sufferings into a new and better future. It was during this last, mystical period in his career that Słowacki wrote a poem about a "Slav Pope" who would be a "brother" to all humanity.[73] The major work of this phase of his life was the unfinished epic *King-Spirit*, a poem that "presents the wandering of the Spirit as it informs . . . leaders, kings, and saints throughout the centuries of European civilization."[74] Here, Słowacki most powerfully displayed that mystical bent in which, according to Nobel laureate Czesław Miłosz, "he raised historical events to cosmic dimensions and saw in history superhuman, mystical forces shaping the fate of mankind."[75] The creative proclamation of *Słowo*, the Word, could bend history in the direction in which the Spirit led it.

Karol Wojtyła memorized *Pan Tadeusz* and acted in *Kordian*, but the most influential of the Polish Romantic poets on his thought was Cyprian Kamil Norwid (1821–1883), who, according to Miłosz, "aspired to be like Don Quixote, a knight of truth."[76] "A man is born on this planet to give testimony to truth," Norwid wrote in an echo of the Gospel of St. John, and the great truth to which witness should be borne was that "Christ had led man out of the realm of fatality and into the realm of freedom."[77] Norwid's poetry was an effort to probe the truth of things through art, and a deliberate rejection of the notion of "art for art's sake."

Norwid also wrote extensively about the dignity of labor and the imperative of respect for workers and their work. Work, he argued, was a result of original sin, man's fall. But "work accepted with love is the highest manifestation of human freedom" and is thus redemptive.[78] On the other hand, Norwid criticized what he regarded as the crass materialism he found in the West, and especially in the United States. Technical progress was spiritually empty; a genuine civilization, a real history, could not be built on this foundation alone.[79]

It is, of course, one thing to read intensely in the classics of a literary tradition, as Karol Wojtyła did at home and at his secondary school. His even deeper immersion in Polish Romanticism came from his participation in the tradition on stage.

Wadowice was proud of its reputation as a regional center of literary culture, including amateur and civic theater. The traditions that had emerged during the period of the partitions—recitations of the poetry of Mickiewicz and Słowacki in private homes, school- and church-based theaters for the performance of the national classics—flourished during the brief life of the Second Polish Republic. Karol Wojtyła eagerly entered into these local literary activities during his high school years. In collaboration with the Moscicka Secondary School for Girls, Wojtyła's high school produced the ancient Greek tragedy *Antigone* in the fall of 1935; Wojtyła played opposite the Moscicka School's leading actress, Halina Królikiewicz, whose father, Jan, was the principal of Lolek's school from 1934 through 1938. Halina and Lolek once convinced a famous actress, Kazimiera Rychterowna, to be the judge of the annual Wadowice high school competition in the recitation of poetry, in which the two youngsters were the chief contestants. Wojtyła chose Norwid's *Promethidion*, which he recited in a manner befitting the poet's quiet intellectuality, while Halina opted for a dramatic poem. Halina won. (In the endless speculation about Karol Wojtyła's possible youthful romances, it is Halina Królikiewicz with whom he is usually linked. Halina, for her part, has denied any serious romantic involvements until her marriage years later. John Paul II wrote in 1996 that, while he had many friends among the girls with whom he went to school and with whom he worked in the theater, he had no special friendship that was an emotional obstacle to his entering the seminary.[80])

In 1937, the schools produced Słowacki's *Balladyna*, a theatrical cocktail in which characters and situations drawn from Polish ballads were mixed with others taken from Shakespeare: *A Midsummer Night's Dream, Macbeth, King Lear,* and so forth.[81] At one performance, Wojtyła played two roles, having had to memorize overnight the part previously played by a youngster who was suspended for a school prank.[82] The quality of this and the three other productions the school mounted in 1937–1938 can be inferred from the fact that the school-based theater of Wadowice went on tour, playing in other amateur theaters in the region and at Kalwaria Zebrzydowska.

The parish also sponsored theatrical performances. Under the direction of Father Zacher, Wojtyła played Count Henryk, the co-lead, in one of the emblematic dramas of the Polish Romantic tradition, Zygmunt Krasiński's *The Undivine Comedy*, which Mickiewicz called "the highest achievement of Slavic theater."[83] In this apocalyptic fable, Krasiński worked through his own dissatisfaction with the options history seemed to have conjured up, between disembodied spirituality and the ruthless materiality of modern, rationalist revolution. The main theme of his fable is that the revolution can only be redeemed by Christ.[84] That Wadowice (and its parish church) would produce a play of such intensity and symbolic complexity tells us something about the cultural climate of the time and place. That a teenager could take on the role of Count Henryk is also instructive.

During these days as a high school actor, Karol Wojtyła met Mieczysław Kotlarczyk, who deeply influenced his thinking about the relationship of the proclaimed word to the dynamics of history.

When they met, Kotlarczyk was teaching history in the girls' high school of Wadowice, where he had been born and raised. His father was a "fanatic for theater" who would "get a theatrical idea at night and wake the whole family to tell them about it."[85] The senior Kotlarczyk ran one of Wadowice's theaters, in which his son played. Mieczysław studied at the Jagiellonian University, deepened his sense of the special qualities of Polish poetry, and did his doctoral dissertation on early nineteenth-century theater criticism. Afterward, he moved back to Wadowice as a teacher.[86] What he really wanted to do was use the family theater as the vehicle for giving theatrical flesh to his distinctive, even radical, ideas about the drama and its relationship to life.

Although the technical aspects of Kotlarczyk's vision would develop over time, certain basic notions were in place during his period in Wadowice. As one of his most accomplished students put it years later, Kotlarczyk was both a "deep Christian believer" and "a man of one idea, the theater," for whom the drama was the most important thing in life because it was a "way of perfection," a means of "transmitting the Word of God," the truth about life.[87] He was seized by the power of words, not simply to communicate an idea, but to elicit an emotion, which was both entirely subjective and entirely objective, or true. Speech, in this understanding, came alive in the intimacy created between the one who spoke and the one who listened. The actor's task was to introduce the listener to that intimacy by minimizing himself to the point where the truth of the spoken word could reach and touch the listener.[88] Kotlarczyk tried to create a "theater of the inner word" in which plot, costumes, the dramatics of performance, and the other accouterments usually associated with theater were stripped to the bare minimum. What happened in the consciousness of the audience, which was made possible by the remarkable, self-denying discipline of Kotlarczyk's actors, was what counted.[89]

For Mieczysław Kotlarczyk, the actor had a function not unlike a priest: to open up, through the materials of this world, the realm of transcendent truth.[90] His "theater of the inner word" would make present universal truths and universal moral values, which stood in judgment on the here-and-now and offered the world the possibility of authentic transformation. This "radical man," "stubborn and fanatical," went to the Salzburg Mozart Festival in 1937 and found it too focused on externals and spectacle. Only when "the word" had absolute priority could the theater be a way of perfection.[91]

In 1936, Kotlarczyk took sixteen-year-old Karol Wojtyła, twelve years his junior, under his wing. Lolek was soon a regular visitor at Kotlarczyk's home, where he and Halina Królikiewicz were tutored by the director in his unique way of articulating a poem or a script. According to Kotlarczyk's sister, Mieczysław would walk up and down the family apartment, reciting a passage of poetry. Lolek would walk behind him, trying, and not always succeeding, to speak the way Kotlarczyk thought things should be spoken. Kotlarczyk would then cast Lolek and Halina opposite each other in performances in his theater.[92]

By the end of his career as a high school actor and occasional director, which his father had encouraged, Karol Wojtyła was involved in something that went considerably beyond the aesthetic and intellectual boundaries of the typical local theater.[93] Kotlarczyk's emerging theories and Wojtyła's immersion in the literature of Polish Romanticism had planted seeds for future reflection about the relationships between emotion and intellect, and between our perceptions of reality and the truth of things. Young Karol Wojtyła had also begun to think about the power of the word to transform history despite enormous material obstacles.

Theater, for Wojtyła, was also an experience of community, the self-disciplined action of a group of individuals who, by blending their individual talents with the talents of others, become something more than the sum of their parts. And the intensity of the theatrical vocation, particularly according to Mieczysław Kotlarczyk, was, perhaps, the beginning of other intuitions to be pursued later. If drama could unveil the deeper dimensions of the truth of things, might there be a dramatic structure to every human life? To the whole of reality?

ALMA MATER: THE JAGIELLONIAN UNIVERSITY

Anti-Semitism began to emerge more publicly in Poland after the death of Józef Piłsudski, the dominant figure in the Second Polish Republic, in 1935. Economic boycotts of Jewish businesses were organized throughout the country and supported by newspapers and politicians maneuvering for position. Another aspiring Wadowice actress, Ginka Beer, left for Palestine after an anti-Semitic disciplinary action forced her out of medical school in Kraków. Lolek Wojtyła and Jurek Kluger visited her before she left. "Have you seen what's happening against the Jews in Germany?" she demanded. "Well, something of the sort is going to happen here. And I can't take it any more . . . it's as if I can't breathe. So I've decided to leave." They walked her to the train station. She remembered years later that, as she left Wadowice, the elder Karol Wojtyła had said to her, "Not all Poles are anti-Semitic. You know I am not!" Eighteen-year-old Lolek was too upset to say anything.[94]

In 1938, Jurek Kluger noticed that his father had added his Hebrew name

to the nameplate of his office, the result of a new discriminatory law in support of the economic boycott. During their senior year of high school, Lolek
and Jurek saw that some of their fellow students were joining anti-Semitic political parties. Fights occasionally broke out in school. Lolek defended his
Jewish friends, and in the ongoing arguments cited Father Prochownik's
insistence that anti-Semites were anti-Christian. One night, a group of rowdies
staged a demonstration in the market square and broke the windows of several shops and houses while yelling, "Economic boycotting is an act of patriotism!" The next day, Gebhardt, the history teacher and a fierce disciplinarian,
came into the classroom strangely ill-at-ease. After a desultory lesson during
which he was mostly silent, he turned to the students and said, "I hope none
of my students are to be numbered among last night's hooligans. I am speaking to you not as a history teacher but as a Pole. What happened has nothing
to do with the tradition of our Fatherland." He then read the class Adam Mickiewicz's 1848 manifesto with its pledge of esteem to the Jewish elder brother
in the faith of Abraham and the promise of a Poland of equal rights for all citizens. The captain was waiting for Lolek after school that day. He gave Jurek
Kluger a rough hug and said, "How is your father? Please give him my regards.
Don't forget, will you?"[95]

Karol Wojtyła, Jerzy Kluger, and their classmates graduated from high
school on May 27, 1938, with Lolek as class valedictorian. At the commencement ball, the new graduates danced late into the night, Karol Wojtyła and
Halina Królikiewicz among them. The good-byes were shadowed by foreboding. That summer, Lolek did his national service on a road construction job in
the town of Zubrzyca Gorna. He later recalled that he spent most of his time
peeling potatoes.[96]

In the summer of 1938, Karol Wojtyła and his father left Wadowice and
moved to Kraków, where Lolek would begin his studies at the Jagiellonian University in the fall semester. They lived in the basement flat of a house originally
built by Emilia's brother at the end of World War I; Emilia's two surviving sisters lived on the top two floors.[97] The house, at Tyniecka, 10, in the Dębniki
district, was nicely located on the south bank of the Vistula, from which there
was a commanding view of Wawel castle and cathedral, beyond which rose the
spires emerging from the heart of Kraków's Old Town. A brief stroll took one
to the Dębniki market square. The parish church of St. Stanisław Kostka,
stolid, working-class Dębniki's sole experiment in art deco architecture, was
also nearby. The university was a twenty-minute walk away, across the Dębniki
Bridge and into the Old Town.

The convenient location aside, the apartment was often referred to by
friends as "the catacombs." The entrance was on the side of the house and
opened into a corridor that divided the flat in two. To the left was Lolek's room,
then his father's; to the right was a kitchen, then a bathroom. It was dark and
damp, and in the winter the old-fashioned, coal-fired tile stoves couldn't keep
the chill out of the air.[98]

Its lack of creature comforts was likely lost on young Karol Wojtyła, who was used to austerity and who was soon involved in the multiple worlds of undergraduate life at the Jagiellonian University. Founded in 1364, the Jagiellonian was one of Europe's most distinguished centers of learning. In 1413, the university's rector, Paweł Włodkowic, had gone from Kraków to the Council of Constance to argue against coercion in the conversion of the pagan Lithuanians.[99] Here was where Copernicus, who would shatter the cosmology of the ancient world, had been educated. Here was where dozens of generations of scholars had pondered the inscription over the entrance to the Great Hall of the university's Collegium Maius—*Plus ratio quam vis*: "Reason rather than force." For six centuries, the Jagiellonian was a crossroads of Christian and humanistic culture. As Karol Wojtyła would write years later, it was difficult to study at such a university without being moved emotionally; its pathways could not be walked "without due piety."[100]

In his freshman year Lolek took a demanding academic load: courses on Polish etymology, phonetics, and inflection and on the interpretation of literary texts; surveys of medieval, modern, and contemporary Polish poetry, dramas, and novels; introductory courses in Russian; and a survey of the grammar of Old Church Slavonic, the historic basis of modern Slavic languages. To continue their undergraduate program, Polish philology students like Wojtyła had to pass two stringent exams at the end of their first year, in Polish grammar and Old Church Slavonic. Both were considered crucial for dealing with the philological challenges ahead.

In the course of these preliminary studies, Karol Wojtyła began to realize "more fully . . . what language is," as he wrote later. He had long been "passionate about *belles lettres* and above all Polish literature."[101] Now he began to grasp something of "the mystery of language itself," that "without language there would be no literature": the human capacity for language made the human world, including the world of literature, possible.[102] Already on his way to being a genuine polyglot, the freshman, powerfully struck by the rich diversity of the world's languages, was eager to delve deeper into their common structures and their singularities. The young philologist, he mused decades later, might well "have ended [up] with linguistics" as a scholarly profession.[103]

Wojtyła also immersed himself in theatrical activities. At the end of the 1938–1939 academic year, he played Sagittarius in a fantasy-fable, *The Moonlight Cavalier*, produced by the experimental theater troupe that would become known as "Studio 39." The play, which featured characters from the Zodiac and some improvisational satire on local personalities and issues, was performed in the courtyard of the Collegium Maius. Poland's leading actor, Juliusz Osterwa, was in the audience. Impressed, he invited the student actors to his apartment afterward and told them to keep in touch.

During the year, Lolek also joined several student groups involved in poetry recitations and became a member of the Circle of Scholars of Polish Studies, a student organization that did literary readings, discussed curriculum reform, and resisted the restrictions on Jews studying at the Jagiellonian. He began taking private lessons in French; his friend Juliusz Kydryński, a fellow actor, had introduced him to the Szkocki family, who lived in Dębniki and whose boarder, Mrs. Jadwiga Lewaj, taught the language, which Lolek wanted to learn to enhance his literary studies. In the midst of this blizzard of activity, Karol Wojtyła continued to write poetry and worked as a volunteer librarian.

In late September 1938, just before beginning his studies at the Jagiellonian, Karol Wojtyła had taken a compulsory six-day military training course in the Academic Legion. On November 28, as Poland began to accelerate its preparations for the trial ahead, he received a letter from the county subprefect of Wadowice, exempting him from active military duty because of his studies. In February 1939, Academic Legion cadets were ordered to take physical education on Tuesdays and Fridays, from 8 to 9 P.M. at a local gym.

The shadows over the Second Polish Republic were growing longer. The previous fall, Jerzy Kluger had left his university engineering studies in Warsaw after a month. An outbreak of violent anti-Semitism at the university drove him back to Wadowice, and his family hoped to be able to send him to England for studies.[104] Lolek and his friends, already striking in their late-adolescent seriousness, became even more so. In April 1939, on Holy Thursday, he went to Wawel Cathedral to watch Archbishop Sapieha conduct the ancient ritual of the washing of feet, in commemoration of Jesus' service to his disciples at the Last Supper. In May he went on a student pilgrimage to the shrine of the Black Madonna at Częstochowa, where parallels between the Swedish "Deluge" of 1655 and the looming Nazi threat must have been on many minds.

In mid-June, Lolek passed the two exams that would permit him to continue his matriculation in Polish philology. On June 24, 1939, he and some friends celebrated the successful completion of their first year of university studies with a party in the home of a classmate, Anna Nawrocka. There was wine and a gramophone and some dancing, but conversation was more important to Lolek and, one imagines, to everyone else.[105] A splendid university career had begun. The odds that it would continue worsened as the summer of 1939 wound down. While Wojtyła put in another round of training with the Academic Legion (a photo of the period shows him with a rifle at "present arms," looking distinctly uncomfortable[106]), Poland's allies hesitated and dithered. The German army intensified its preparations for "Case White." And a hitherto unimaginable negotiation took place in Moscow between Europe's two totalitarian giants.

A SON OF FREE POLAND

Recollections of the early lives of men and women who rise to greatness are always subject to a kind of retrospective filtration by friends and associates. The temptation to find previews of later qualities and accomplishments in youthful characteristics and successes is often irresistible. But every available piece of evidence from his contemporaries suggests that Karol Wojtyła was in fact a model son, student, and friend.

His intellectual gifts were acknowledged by all; he learned quickly what it took others hours to master.[107] He wore his success lightly. There is no record of him provoking jealousies among his peers, in part, perhaps, because he always seemed available to help others work their way through the material they found difficult.[108] He grew up in a culture where piety was regarded as normal, and if he seemed even more pious than others his age, this was not regarded as aberrant, only admirable.

Lolek was in no sense a grind. He had the normal social life of an adolescent of his time and place, with good friends among both boys and girls. An avid sportsman, he would trek for miles in search of better ski runs. He had already shown a contemplative side to his personality, but he had also made and kept friends from virtually every walk of life in his town. With a gift for mimicry, he did impressions of his high school teachers that his friends found irresistibly funny.[109] He had adjusted well to the demanding environment of a major university and a large, culturally assertive city.

His affection and respect for his widower-father were powerful magnets that gave a basic orientation to his moral compass. To some, the captain may have seemed a man who bore the tragedies life had thrust upon him with stoic resignation. The moral lesson the son learned from the father was not Stoic, however, but Christian—the lesson of suffering transformed by faith. His father's life was austere, the son would later recall, but austerity for the elder Karol Wojtyła was not simply a matter of the frugality required by living on a small pension.[110] It was born of convictions about Christian asceticism, and from the unshakable certainty that the true measure of a man was not his wealth but his character.

Lolek also learned from his father that manliness and prayerfulness were not antinomies. Perhaps above all, the captain transmitted to his son an instinct for paternity. He would, later, come to understand this in theological terms: the instinct for paternity and the responsibilities of fatherhood were a kind of icon of God and of God's relationship to the world. Fatherhood meant rejecting the prison of selfishness; fatherhood meant being "conquered by love." That love compelled one to "give birth" in acts of self-giving, as Karol Wojtyła would put these things in the last play he ever wrote.[111]

Karol Wojtyła was the son of a particular time, a particular place, and a unique set of relationships. Those who had taught him to love his country, its history, and its literature had also taught him that there was no room for narrowness in the authentic tradition of his fatherland. Rather, the Polish experience as he learned it was a metaphor for the human condition in the twentieth century: the quest for freedom was a universal aspiration. In the pursuit of that aspiration, truth was more powerful than what the world usually regarded as real power. The human spirit, ordered to truth, was the most irresistible of forces. To understand *that* was to be a son of free Poland.

He was a young man of whom much was expected in the future, in a career that Karol Wojtyła expected to be focused on language, literature, and the theater. History and, he would insist, Providence, had other plans.

2

From the Underground

The Third Reich vs. the Kingdom of Truth

SEPTEMBER 1, 1939	World War II begins as Germany invades Poland.
NOVEMBER 6, 1939	184 Jagiellonian University professors are arrested and deported to Sachsenhausen; Karol Wojtyła begins clandestine studies and underground cultural resistance activities.
FEBRUARY 1940	Lolek meets Jan Tyranowski, who introduces him to Carmelite mysticism and the "Living Rosary" youth groups.
LENT 1940	Wojtyła writes *Job: A Drama from the Old Testament.*
SUMMER 1940	Wojtyła writes *Jeremiah: A National Drama in Three Acts.*
SEPTEMBER 1940	Karol Wojtyła begins work as a quarryman at the Zakrzówek mine.
FEBRUARY 18, 1941	Lolek's father, the elder Karol Wojtyła, dies.
MAY 23, 1941	Wojtyła's parish priests are arrested by the Gestapo.
AUGUST 22, 1941	Mieczysław Kotlarczyk launches the "Rhapsodic Theater."
OCTOBER 1941	Karol Wojtyła begins work at Solvay chemical plant.
NOVEMBER 1, 1941	Wojtyła plays King Bolesław the Bold in the first clandestine production of the Rhapsodic Theater, Słowacki's *King-Spirit.*
FALL 1942	Karol Wojtyła is accepted by the Archdiocese of Kraków as a clandestine seminarian and begins underground studies in philosophy.
FEBRUARY 29, 1944	Wojtyła is struck by a German truck and hospitalized.
APRIL 1944	Jerzy Zachuta, Wojtyła's fellow-underground seminarian, is arrested by the Gestapo and shot.
AUGUST 6, 1944	Archbishop Adam Stefan Sapieha begins an underground seminary in his residence.
JANUARY 1945	The German Occupation abandons Kraków and the Red Army arrives.

NOVEMBER 1, 1946	Karol Wojtyła is ordained a priest by Cardinal Sapieha.
NOVEMBER 15, 1946	Father Wojtyła leaves for graduate theological studies in Rome.
SUMMER 1947	Wojtyła visits France, Belgium, and Holland.
JUNE 1948	Karol Wojtyła completes his first doctorate.

High atop the Wawel, the hill commanding Poland's ancient capital, sits the cathedral church of Kraków. To its north is the Old Town, its immense market square dominated by St. Mary's Church, from whose tower a trumpeter announces every hour of the day. The trumpet call, the solemn *hajnał,* breaks in mid-note, in memory of a thirteenth-century watchman killed by an arrow in the throat while warning the city of an impending Tartar invasion. To the south is the traditional Jewish quarter, Kazimierz. In the fall of 1939, its residents did not yet know the name Oskar Schindler. West of Kazimierz is Skałka, where St. Stanisław, the first bishop of Kraków, was struck down in 1079 by the sword of King Bolesław the Bold.

Site of the coronation of Polish kings and burial place of many of the nation's political, religious, and cultural leaders, Wawel Cathedral has been the magnetic pole of Poland's emotional life for centuries. It had also witnessed a host of invasions and depredations since construction of the present structure began in 1320. Tartars and Swedes had laid waste the country; the Austrians had stripped the Old Town of its fortifications and walls; occupying powers of varying degrees of ferocity had displaced the kings and queens of Poland from the royal castle, atop the "Polish Zion." Now, on September 1, 1939, Wawel Cathedral was about to experience something beyond the imagining of those who had worshiped beneath its gothic vault for centuries.

Karol Wojtyła left his apartment at Tyniecka, 10, in Dębniki early that morning and set out for the cathedral. It was the first Friday of the month and, according to Catholic custom and personal habit, he was going to make his confession to Father Kazimierz Figlewicz and serve Father Figlewicz's Mass. Entering the cathedral in the morning darkness, he walked past the tomb of King Władysław Jagiełło and the silver casket containing the remains of St. Stanisław. Passing the white marble memorial to Blessed Queen Jadwiga, Jagiełło's consort and partner in forming the great Polish-Lithuanian Commonwealth, he came to the altar in the north nave where Jadwiga's relics were venerated. Before the altar's great black crucifix, the young queen was often absorbed in prayer—and from that cross, "according to the traditions of our ancestors" (as an inscription had it), Christ had spoken to Jadwiga about her duty.

During that early morning Mass, other voices, far less gentle, made their presence known in Wawel Cathedral. First came the high-pitched wail of the warning sirens. They were followed by the chatter of anti-aircraft batteries and the explosions of bombs from Luftwaffe aircraft. The congregants scattered, but Father Figlewicz and his server concluded the Mass, if somewhat more rapidly than usual. Then Karol Wojtyła turned to the young priest who was his spiritual confidant and the keeper of his most personal secrets and said, "I've got to go, my father's at home alone." As he ran back across the Vistula, Luftwaffe Stukas began strafing the city's suburbs.

FORGED IN FIRE

World War II, which Poles sometimes describe as the war they lost twice, was an unmitigated disaster for Poland. Six million of its citizens, out of a prewar population of 35 million, were killed in combat or murdered, a mortality rate of eighteen percent. The nation was physically decimated. Poland became the site of the greatest slaughters of the Holocaust. And, at the end, another totalitarian power seized control of Poland's political future.

The experience of the war was decisive in forming the man who became Pope John Paul II. The war's horrors and an unexpected encounter during the Occupation with a lay mystic began to shape Karol Wojtyła's distinctively Carmelite spirituality, which focused on the cross as the center of the Christian life, and indeed the center of human history. It was during the Occupation, and in part because of the Occupation, that his vocational discernment began to bend inexorably toward the priesthood.

The struggle for moral survival between September 1939 and January 1945 provided young Karol Wojtyła with heroic models for living out that priestly vocation. One of them, the Franciscan Maximilian Kolbe, would sacrifice his life for a fellow prisoner in the starvation bunker at Auschwitz. Another was Adam Stefan Sapieha, the archbishop who had thought it a pity that the brightest young man in Wadowice was going to study philology instead of theology.

The Occupation gave Karol Wojtyła his most profound experience of the world of manual labor. The experience would provide grist for his literary mill, even as it would shape the social doctrine of the Catholic Church throughout the world. And it was during the long, dark night of Occupation that Karol Wojtyła began to experiment with cultural activism, the defense of national cultural identity, as a means of political resistance and liberation—a distinctive approach to the politics of revolution that would alter the course of the twentieth century, forty years later.

The war was a trial by fire, a six-year period of unspeakable cruelty broken by acts of unimaginable heroism. As John Paul II wrote in 1995, "Half a century later, individuals, families, and peoples still retain memories of those six terrible years: memories of fear, violence, extreme poverty, death; tragic experiences of painful separation, endured in the absence of all security and freedom; recurring traumas brought about by the incessant bloodshed." The experience of this manmade hell caused some to conclude that life was an absurdity. Karol Wojtyła came to a different conclusion and grew up very fast as a man, a thinker, and a disciple.[1]

KILLING FIELDS

Postwar communist historiography, too often adopted by Western commentators, was given to describing the Second Polish Republic as a buffoon state run by fascist colonels. The truth is more complex.

Interwar Polish governments treated their political opponents with a heavy-handedness that would be unacceptable in developed democracies today. Yet opposition political parties flourished during the 1920s and 1930s and were in their strongest condition by the time war broke out in 1939. The only exception was the Polish Communist Party. But it was liquidated on orders from Moscow, not by Polish colonels. Government attempts to shackle the press usually failed; the judiciary maintained its independence and justice was generally evenhanded; critics of the government maintained their positions on university faculties.[2] The regime, in a word, was not fascist or even semi-fascist.

The cultural situation was more difficult. Marshal Piłsudski, a philo-Semite, subscribed to a theory of Polish nationalism in which there was ample room for cultural and religious diversity. Others insisted, often crudely, that a free Poland had to be ethnically Polish and Catholic. Among those holding this view were many members of the rural clergy. Their prejudices were undoubtedly confirmed when the Primate during the interwar years, Cardinal Augustyn Hlond, SDB, deployed a host of classic anti-Semitic stereotypes in a 1936 pastoral letter and wrote that "it is a fact that the Jews are fighting against the Catholic Church."[3] The attitude Wadowice's priests took toward their Jewish fellow townsmen demonstrates that such sentiments were not universally shared. But anti-Semitism came increasingly to the foreground after Piłsudski's death. The substantial Ukrainian minority was also heavily pressured in interwar Poland, and political violence was close to the surface of public life.[4]

Reborn Poland had its cultural accomplishments as well as its political, ethnic, and religious tensions and discord. Illiteracy was dramatically reduced. The army, in which every young man had to serve, became a great technical training school.[5] Polish intellectual life, particularly in philosophy and mathematics, flourished.[6] The arts experienced an explosion of creativity. Polish Catholic intellectuals became an independent cultural force by articulating a position that challenged both Polish messianism and Polish chauvinism—a development that would have a considerable impact on the future.[7]

Perspective is important here. There was poverty and injustice in interwar Poland, but it cannot bear serious comparison to the wholesale starvation and mass executions that attended the birth and consolidation of the Bolshevik regime in the Soviet Union. Anti-Semitism was not unique to Poland, as American immigration quotas in the 1930s made clear and as Vichy France later demonstrated. Despite the Poles' troubles in establishing a stable modern government, they never fell on each other in an orgy of fratricidal slaughter like their Spanish contemporaries. During the Second World War, Poland was the only occupied country in which the Nazis failed to establish even the bare outlines of a collaborationist regime.[8] That seems to suggest that for all its difficulties, the Second Polish Republic was something its citizens thought worth defending.

Poland's interwar diplomacy had its faults. Its seizure of land from Czechoslovakia while that country was being consumed by the Nazis was a sordid business that also suggested geopolitical woodenheadedness; a Polish-Czechoslovak alliance, pre-Munich, might have set the history of the late 1930s on a different course.[9] In the end, though, no diplomacy, however creative, could have saved Poland from its ancient curse—geography.

Adolf Hitler warned the German army high command in March 1939 that the time had come to resolve the "Polish problem" by military means. On April 1, he decreed that the invasion date would be September 1, and on April 28, he unilaterally abrogated the 1934 Polish-German nonaggression pact. The final decision to invade was taken on May 23, 1939, after the Polish government had refused to buckle under to German demands about incorporating the Free City of Danzig (in Polish, Gdańsk) into the Third Reich, and about the position of German ethnics in Poland.[10] These demands were a smokescreen behind which lay a draconian strategic concept: "Danzig is not by any means the main cause of the disagreement," Hitler conceded privately. "The chief objective is to get new areas for Germany in the east and to control and safeguard new sources of foodstuffs. The question of Poland being spared therefore does not arise."[11]

Within a month of Hitler's May 23 decision, the Wehrmacht high command had given the Führer the operational plans for "Case White," the invasion and conquest of Poland. Mobilization orders were dispatched to the Reich railroads on August 15, as Poles celebrated the Assumption of the Blessed Virgin Mary by pilgrimages to Kalwaria Zebrzydowska, Częstochowa, and elsewhere throughout the country.[12]

A week later, German Foreign Minister Joachim von Ribbentrop was in Moscow to conclude the nonaggression pact that sealed the Second Polish Republic's fate while charting its partition. Two ancient animosities now combined under totalitarian auspices. An intensely Catholic country was about to be dismembered by two radically secularist ideologies. Germany's ancient *Drang Nach Osten*, the "drive to the East," met with Stalin's need for a cushion against what he knew was coming eventually from his putative German "ally." Meanwhile, Poland's Western allies dithered. British Prime Minister Neville Chamberlain gave belated warnings to the German government that his appeasement at Munich the year before rendered ineffectual from the moment they were dispatched.

The Polish war plan, "Plan Z," was not insane. Assuming German thrusts from Silesia and Slovakia and knowing that they could not defeat the Wehrmacht on their own, the Poles created a semicircle of seven army groups along their western and southern frontiers. The idea was to resist the initial attack and then conduct a fighting retreat into Poland's interior, using the country's rivers as defensive barriers against the invaders. By this juncture, it was assumed, Britain and France would have invaded Germany from the West, and Wehrmacht forces would have to be withdrawn to meet that mortal threat. Then would come winter and wet weather; the heavily mechanized German forces would bog down; and the Polish army would go over to the offensive, catching the Germans in an east-west pincer between Poland and its Western allies.

It soon became clear, though, that the large Polish army was unprepared for the rigors of blitzkrieg. The lethal combination of German armor and mechanized infantry and the Luftwaffe's virtually instantaneous control of Polish airspace made the planned fighting retreat impossible. Poland's war plan, though brave, was uninformed by the new realities of warfare.[13] Moreover, the country's geography—that vast, flat plain—made it the ideal testing ground for blitzkrieg tactics. Then, of course, the Poles never anticipated the double stab, from west and east, that the Ribbentrop-Molotov Pact made possible.

In any event, the failure of Poland's British and French allies to honor their pledges by striking at Germany on the ground rendered any Polish strategy moot. The agreement with the British and French involved the Poles holding on for up to two weeks, which would have given the French time to "throw 90 divisions, 2,500 tanks, and 1,400 planes across the virtually undefended Rhine." The Poles held on for twice that time, but, with the exception of a diversionary attack into the Warndt Forest along the Franco-German frontier, the French army did nothing of strategic significance, "while the RAF confined itself to dropping leaflets on German cities."[14] By leaving Poland to its fate, Great Britain and France lost the best chance they had to end Hitler's aggression without a world war.

Despite that betrayal, the Poles contributed mightily to the Allied cause throughout the Second World War. Polish troops fought with the British in Norway and with the British and French in France in the spring of 1940. Poles flying with the RAF were responsible for twelve percent of German losses during the Battle of Britain that fall.[15] The Polish II Corps won the fourth and decisive battle for Monte Cassino in Italy. The Polish 1st Armored Division was instrumental in the Allied breakout from Normandy in August 1944 (in the Battle of the Falaise Pocket, Polish units ran into German formations they had fought in the Carpathian Mountains in 1939).[16] Polish intelligence, which had been cooperating with the Allies before the war broke out, acquired Germany's Enigma coding machine and, with what Churchill's private secretary called "immense courage," delivered it to the British, for whom it was arguably the intelligence coup of the war, allowing the decryption of German military orders.[17] The Poles who fought with the Allies were often dismissively styled as émigrés, particularly after the war. But they were, in truth, Poland torn away from its own soil and its own battlefields. And as such, John Paul II once said, "they constituted the very marrow of the Poland that [was] fighting for the cause of independence: in keeping with the password—For your freedom and ours."[18]

The key date was September 17, 1939. While the French huddled fearfully behind the Maginot Line, paralyzed by memories of the First World War, the Soviet Union invaded Poland from the east. Displaying that delicate moral sensibility for which Soviet diplomacy was always noted, the deputy foreign minister, Vladimir Potemkin, summoned Polish ambassador Wacław Grzybowski to the Kremlin to inform him that "the Polish-German War has revealed the internal bankruptcy of the Polish State." Thus the Soviet Union was obliged to intervene on behalf of "the kindred Ukrainian and Byelorussian people who live on Polish territory."[19] That Stalin had something in mind beyond ethnic peacekeeping was made immediately clear when advancing Soviet forces began shooting the senior Polish officers they captured, a grim preview of the Katyn Forest massacre of May 1940, in which the NKVD, predecessor to the KGB, murdered more than 10,000 Polish officers in cold blood, decapitating the future leadership of an independent Polish military.[20]

On the night of September 17–18, the Polish government fled by car across the Czeremosz River into Romania, accompanied by Cardinal Hlond, the Primate. The next day, the commander-in-chief of the Polish military, Marshal Edward Ridz-Śmigły, followed suit, intending to prosecute the war from France. The result was that no general surrender order was ever issued to Polish troops, and no such surrender ever took place. Warsaw held out until September 27, conceding only when the Luftwaffe and the Wehrmacht's artillery had destroyed the city's water supply and food stocks were gone. A tenacious and fierce Polish underground resistance, linked to the legitimate Polish government that eventually re-formed itself in London, immediately commenced.[21] On October 5, Hitler reviewed German troops at a victory parade in Warsaw. The resistance had planted enough explosives on the reviewing platform to kill the Führer and his entire entourage. The plot failed when a German order removed from the scene the man responsible for detonating the charge.[22]

The fourth partition of Poland had taken place. The Polish state was, once again, extinguished. Its people began a desperate struggle for survival. It was an objective their Nazi captors were determined to deny them.

"POLAND WILL BE ERASED"

Western histories of the Second World War usually focus on the Battle of Britain, the North African and Italian campaigns, D-Day, and the Allied armies' march to the Rhine and beyond as "the story" of World War II, but a persuasive case can be made that east central and eastern Europe were the pivots of the war in Europe. More German casualties were inflicted on the eastern front than in the west, and without such depletions of manpower, the war in the west would certainly have unfolded differently. The centrality of Poland in the continental struggle and the Nazis' own crazed racial theories led to a German occupation of Poland marked by unparalleled brutality. Rousseau's famous charge to the Poles—"If you cannot prevent your enemies from swallowing you whole, at least you must do what you can to prevent them from digesting you"[23]—was tested as never before.

Poland's eastern lands were absorbed into the Soviet Union, while central and western Poland were divided into two spheres of German occupation. Parts of Poland, including Wadowice, were incorporated into the Third Reich. The remainder was styled the "General Gouvernement" and placed under the control of Hans Frank, who took up residence in the royal palace on the Wawel, in Kraków. The rule of law, or anything remotely resembling the rule of law, ceased to exist, and a reign of terror ensued.

Frank, a gangster who fancied himself an intellectual, entered Wawel Castle through a portal bearing the Latin inscription *Si Deus Nobiscum Quis Contra Nos* [If God is with us, who can be against us?]. From the residence of Poland's kings he dispatched instructions to his subordinates designed to demonstrate to the Poles that God, with them or not, was an irrelevancy:

> The Pole has no rights whatsoever. His only obligation is to obey what we tell him. He must be constantly reminded that his duty is to obey.
>
> A major goal of our plan is to finish off as speedily as possible all troublemaking politicians, priests, and leaders who fall into our hands. I openly admit that some thousands of so-called important Poles will have to pay with their lives, but you must not allow sympathy for individual cases to deter you in your duty, which is to ensure that the goals of National Socialism triumph and that the Polish nation is never again able to offer resistance.
>
> Every vestige of Polish culture is to be eliminated. Those Poles who seem to have Nordic appearances will be taken to Germany to work in our factories. Children of Nordic appearance will be taken from their parents and raised as German workers. The rest? They will work. They will eat little. And in the end they will die out. There will never again be a Poland.[24]

In Hans Frank's General Gouvernement, the only penalties for "crimes" or resistance were immediate death or sentence to a concentration camp— and a "crime" could include failing to step off the sidewalk for a passing German patrol.[25] The people were to survive on a 900-calorie-per-day diet. Secondary and higher education were shut down. Poles would only be taught to count to one hundred and to read enough to obey simple instructions. Participation in Polish cultural activities was a capital offense. Kraków's great Słowacki Theater was renamed the Staatstheater and reserved for German use. Performance of the works of Chopin and Szymanowski was forbidden. The

Germans systematically demolished libraries and other repositories of Poland's memory.[26] In Kraków, the statue of the national poet, Adam Mickiewicz, in the Old Town market square was destroyed, as was the monument to the Polish-Lithuanian defeat of the Teutonic Knights in 1410. Wit Stwosz's colossal wood-carved altarpiece in St. Mary's Church was disassembled and taken to Nuremberg.

The Catholic Church became a particular target of Poland's Nazi masters, who understood its role as the historic custodian of the national culture and identity. Decapitating Polish society necessarily involved decapitating the Church. Before the war, the Church had prospered, owning more than a million acres of land, as well as rectories and convents, hospitals and orphanages, small industrial farms and handicraft industries. Twenty million Roman Catholics had worshiped in 5,100 parishes, served by 11,300 priests and almost 17,000 nuns. Now, the Catholic Church in Poland would show that it knew how to suffer.

The Polish nation's view of the Church was indelibly marked by the sacrifices of its clergy during the war. In addition to innumerable laity, 3,646 Polish priests were imprisoned in concentration camps, of whom 2,647 were killed; and 1,117 nuns were imprisoned, of whom 238 were executed and 25 died from other causes. The Dachau concentration camp outside Munich became the world's largest monastery, housing at one time or other 1,474 Polish priests and hundreds from other occupied countries. Some 120 Polish priests were subjected to criminal medical experiments. In late 1939, the leading priests of the diocese of Pelplin, the cathedral chapter, were executed en masse. Bishop Michał Kozal of Włocławek died in Dachau in 1943, where Father Hilary Paweł Januszewski, the former Carmelite prior in Kraków, died in 1945 from typhus he contracted while voluntarily serving the camp sick. Another Kraków priest, Piotr Dańkowski, died in Auschwitz with a log tied to his shoulders on Good Friday, 1942. Alfons Maria Mazurek, prior of the Discalced Carmelite monastery in Czerna, died on August 28, 1944, after being taken from the monastery and beaten to death. The Salesian Józef Kowalski was arrested at Karol Wojtyła's parish in Dębniki in May 1941 and taken to Auschwitz; beaten for refusing to grind rosary beads into the ground with his foot, he was drowned in feces on the night of July 3, 1942.[27]

Shortly after arriving in Bydgoszcz at the beginning of the war the Germans began executing priests in reprisal for the Polish army's resistance. A priest in occupied Poland could be shot for daring to lead a procession around his church without permission. Roadside shrines were wrecked. The German attempt to limit the use of Polish extended even to the confessional; one priest in Chojnice was so severely beaten after hearing confessions in the language of his penitent that he later died in jail.[28] Hans Frank closed Wawel Cathedral, later allowing two Masses a week, celebrated by Father Figlewicz under the supervision of German guards.[29] By the end of the war, something on the order of one-third of Poland's clergy had been murdered outright or had died in concentration camps. And in many cases, it was the most enlightened, assertive priests who perished.[30]

Participation in Catholic youth groups was forbidden and the price of defiance was high, particularly when these groups were involved with the Polish resistance. Wanda Połtawska, a young Catholic resistance courier, spent several years as a medical guinea pig in the Ravensbrück concentration camp, where diseased baccilli were injected into her bone marrow. There, her resistance continued as she discovered "the suicidal courage of people who could act as they chose today because they [knew] that by tomorrow they would be dead."[31] Others in the resistance were more fortunate. Stefan Wyszyński, a young priest noted for his involvement in labor activism, survived one Gestapo arrest and worked underground during the war years. His nom de guerre during his clandestine ministry in Warsaw was "Sister Cecilia," as in "Where is Sister Cecilia saying Mass today?"[32]

Polish life between 1939 and 1945 had a bizarre, even surreal quality. It was not a question of knowing whether you would be alive next year. Given the arbitrary terror meted out by the occupiers, the question was whether you would be alive tomorrow. The pressure was unrelenting: "they" could make as many mistakes as "they" liked; you could make only one. Criminals once thought that way; three months into the Occupation, virtually every Pole thought like that. The official ration was clearly inadequate for survival, so everyone was by necessity an outlaw, living on the black market. When news of the French collapse before the Wehrmacht reached Poland, suicides took place in Warsaw, Kraków, and the manor houses of the Polish intelligentsia. There would be no help. There would be no spring. A seemingly endless winter had set in. Poland was a nation under ice.[33]

THE WORKER

At the outbreak of the war Karol Wojtyła and his father fled their apartment in Dębniki and, with thousands of other Poles, headed eastward, with a battered suitcase. The roads were filled with refugees, many of them Jews, pushing children in prams, the elderly being helped by their grandchildren. Peasants drove their livestock before them. People prayed, sang, cursed. There was no destination, only a desperate desire to avoid the onrushing Wehrmacht. The elder Wojtyła, weak and in poor health, could occasionally ride in a cart or a truck. Lolek and his father sometimes found themselves in a ditch, trying to take shelter from strafing Luftwaffe aircraft. Passing beyond Tarnów, they made it as far as the San River, some 120 miles from Kraków, before they learned that the Russians had invaded Poland from the east. Kraków, even under Occupation, was preferable to summary execution or deportation by the advancing Red Army. Kraków, even under the heel of Hans Frank, was home. They reversed course and walked back.[34]

On their return, they saw the swastika flag flying from Wawel Castle's Sandomierz rampart. In the weeks the Wojtyłas had been in flight, the Germans had imposed themselves with ruthless efficiency. Special shops *Nur für Deutsche*, "For Germans Only," monopolized meat, fresh vegetables, the best bread, the only butter. Leaving the "catacomb" apartment in Dębniki, Lolek discovered that, in frigid temperatures, Poles were forming lines to buy black bread at 4 A.M.[35] In its first stages, though, the Occupation could seem more a distraction than a reign of terror to a high-spirited young man. In mid-September, Wojtyła wrote to Mieczysław Kotlarczyk, still in Wadowice:

> "*Vita Cracoviensis*." [The Kraków life.] Just think, think! It consists of stand-ing in line for bread, or (rare) expeditions to find sugar. Ha! And also of a black longing for coal—and of reading. For us, life [once] consisted of evenings on Długa Street, of refined conversation, of dreams and longings. We dreamt away many an evening until midnight or beyond, but now . . . [36]

In his letter to Kotlarczyk, Lolek also mentioned his attempts to find a part-time job at the Słowacki Theater. The German expropriation of that grand playhouse for their exclusive use quickly ended any hope of openly con-tinuing his acting career. That was a blow, but the brutal face of the terror showed itself in earnest in early November 1939.

According to ancient custom, the Jagiellonian University had opened its doors in October. Some of its professors, perhaps sensing what was coming, began teaching even before the school year officially began. Students, includ-ing Karol Wojtyła, duly registered for their fall courses. It would be a short-lived semester.

A lecture for all professors and academic staff by SS Obersturmbann-führer Müller was announced for the morning of November 6 in the Szujski Hall of the university's Collegium Novum. Some, suspecting a trap, absented themselves, but 184 academics attended, and when Müller entered the lecture hall escorted by a squad of soldiers they knew their fate was sealed. In what SS records referred to as the Sonderaktion Krakau [the Kraków Special Action], the entire group, which included eighteen current or former rectors and fifty deans or assistant deans, was summarily arrested and shipped off to the Sach-senhausen concentration camp, where many eventually perished. The Nazi strategy of cultural decapitation had arrived in force at east central Europe's second oldest university.[37] After the faculty arrests, the Germans looted the Jagiellonian, wrecking libraries and destroying laboratories.[38] Four days before the arrest of the professors, Lolek had written Mieczysław Kotlarczyk about his hopes for an "Athenian Poland," made "more perfect than Athens" by the "boundless immensity of Christianity."[39] That exuberant youthful vision now had to be pursued by clandestine means.

By the beginning of 1942 the Jagiellonian University, in a defiant act of self-preservation, had reconstituted itself underground, operating clandes-tinely with five faculties, including all the departments that had been in oper-ation before the war. During the three years of the university's clandestine existence, 136 professors risked instant death by teaching 800 students (including Karol Wojtyła), often at night in private homes. The atmosphere of the times was captured in a memoir by Juliusz Kydryński, whose family risked arrest constantly by opening their apartment to clandestine scholarship:

"One of the meetings we had arranged was due to take place in an hour. The chairs were all arranged in the room for about thirty people. Then the Gestapo arrived. They were asking for somebody whom we probably knew and they saw all the chairs. My mother said we were preparing for a party. This seemed to satisfy them and they left. But that was a very close thing . . . If the Gestapo had arrived when there were people there . . . I would not be speaking today."[40]

Meanwhile, life had to be sustained at a basic physical level. Mieczysław Maliński, another Dębniki resident whom Karol Wojtyła would soon meet, described the normal conditions of life in Kraków under the Occupation in these grim terms:

". . . Police round-ups, deportation to camps and forced labor in Germany or some other place unknown, beating up by SS men, death shooting in the street—all these things were part of daily life. . . . Shots were frequently heard at night after curfew hours, when the police arrested people who were caught walking the streets without passes, and fired at any who did not stop when challenged. We were hungry for five years without a break, and each winter we were desperately cold."[41]

In the Wojtyła apartment, potatoes were the staple of the diet, dressed up with a bit of onion and margarine.[42] In addition to keeping fed, it was just as urgent for Karol Wojtyła to get an *Arbeitskarte*, a work card, that would permit him to stay in Kraków. Every able-bodied male between fourteen and sixty in the General Gouvernement had to have a job. The alternatives were to be shipped off to a concentration camp or to be summarily executed. For the first year of the war Lolek worked as a store messenger for a restaurant. It was relatively light work, and it suited Wojtyła's interest in continuing his education, his theatrical career, and the cultural resistance activities in which he was becoming involved. While others were "dying of boredom," he wrote Kotlarczyk at the end of 1939, "I have surrounded myself with books, dug in with Arts and Sciences."[43] He also intensified his study of French.[44] At the same time, he read and reread Conrad, Słowacki, Mickiewicz, and Wyspiański on his own, complemented by the Bible, especially the Hebrew Scriptures.[45]

In the fall of 1940, as the Nazis began to interpret their work rules ever more stringently, Karol Wojtyła began almost four years as a manual laborer for the Solvay chemical company. For a year, he walked every day from the apartment in Dębniki to and from the Solvay quarry at Zakrzówek—a thirty-minute hike, but that was no small matter in sub-zero winter weather when he and his friend and fellow quarryman, Juliusz Kydryński, had to make the trek with petroleum jelly smeared over their faces to keep their skin from freezing.

The Zakrzówek quarry, a pit hundreds of feet deep, mined limestone, essential for the production of soda in the Solvay chemical plant located in another Kraków suburb, Borek Fałęcki. Throughout the harsh winter of 1940–1941, in which temperatures dipped to –22° Fahrenheit (–30° Celsius), Lolek shoveled limestone into miniature railway cars at the bottom of the pit, occasionally working as a brakeman on the trains. In the spring he received a kind of promotion, as an assistant to Franciszek Łabuś, a veteran dynamiter. Łabuś took a liking to the young man whose previous experience hadn't prepared him for the rigors of the quarry and offered Lolek some career advice. "Karol, you should be a priest," he told the novice blaster. "You have a good voice and will sing well; then you'll be all set."[46]

Although Karol Wojtyła would later mine his experience of the quarry for his literary, philosophical, and theological purposes, the fact remains that this was hard and dangerous work. Every day, each worker had to fill one of the small tramcars with limestone. The new worker-students couldn't meet this quota, but the sympathetic quarry management could only reduce the quotas. The limestone still had to be broken up and shoveled, hour after hour. The one break each day was for breakfast. Food had to be brought from home and usually consisted of tough bread with jam and ersatz coffee. Lolek and Kydryński sometimes managed to get into a small hut in the pit where there was an iron stove to warm themselves and their coffee briefly. The rules said that they could take only one break for fifteen minutes per day; in practice, they managed to slip away every couple of hours or so to try to get warm. The quarrymen, Kydryński remembered, were good Poles, who didn't scorn the students but rather sympathized with their being forced into this kind of back-breaking work in order to avoid deportation to Germany.[47]

The workday at Zakrzówek lasted from early in the morning until 3 P.M., after which Lolek, dressed in denims and clogs, walked home with whatever he had managed to scrounge at the quarry and elsewhere for his father and himself: some coal, a few potatoes, perhaps some cabbages or peas. The young quarryman's salary, meager as it was, was the family's only income since the Nazis had stopped the captain's pension.

In October 1941, Karol Wojtyła was transferred to the Solvay chemical factory in Borek Fałęcki, a somewhat longer walk from Dębniki but a major improvement in his working conditions. At Borek Fałęcki, he worked in the plant's water purification unit, often taking the night shift. It was easier to read then, in between lugging buckets of lime hanging from a wooden yoke over his shoulders. The plant workers could also take advantage of a modest food service, which fed them a half-liter of soup and a few ounces of bread during their shifts.

Despite the reticence caused by the omnipresent danger of the Gestapo, the working conditions at Borek Fałęcki meant that Lolek could talk with his fellow workers. He sometimes debated religious issues with a man named Mankowski, an atheist and a member of the Polish Socialist Party. Fellow workers also remember Karol Wojtyła praying on his knees at the Borek Fałęcki plant, unafraid of ridicule and seemingly able to tune out the racket around him to concentrate on his conversation with God. On his way home to Dębniki he frequently stopped at the parish in Podgórze run by the Redemptorist priests, to pray or to attend early morning Mass after completing the night shift. "From here," he recalled thirty years later, "I gained the strength to last through the difficult times of the years of Occupation."[48]

During the long nights at Borek Fałęcki, Karol Wojtyła came to a new appreciation of the Marian piety that had long characterized Polish Catholicism. In his early manhood, he later wrote, he thought he ought to "distance" himself a bit from the kinds of devotion to Mary he had encountered as a boy in order to "focus more on Christ."[49] While tending the water purification machinery at the Solvay plant he read the works of St. Louis Grignon de Montfort, an eighteenth-century French preacher, who taught Wojtyła that "true devotion to Mary" was always focused on Christ.[50] Mary was the first disciple; indeed, Mary's fiat ("Be it done unto me according to thy word" [*Luke* 1.38]) and its unique role in the Incarnation of the Son of God had made discipleship possible for others. To be a disciple of Christ was to be like Mary, prepared to dispose oneself utterly to the will of God. Marian piety was authentic when it led beyond Mary to a more intense relationship with Christ, which meant with the Holy Trinity itself. Marian piety was a special path into "the mysteries of the Incarnation and Redemption."[51]

The Zakrzówek quarry and the Solvay factory introduced Karol Wojtyła to a world he had never known before, the world of the industrial laborer, the *robotnik* as he was called in Polish. The kinds of men he encountered—from Łabuś the blaster, to the workmen at the water purification plant who intuitively understood that study was work and covered for him so that he could continue his surreptitious reading uninterrupted—were not the kind of people he had known in Wadowice or in the academic and literary world of Kraków. Although there were some rough customers among them, what struck the young Wojtyła most about these men was their innate dignity, which expressed itself in friendliness and a willingness to help others despite their own hard circumstances. Others would theorize about the nature and aspirations of the urban proletariat. Thanks to four years of breaking rocks at Zakrzówek and hauling buckets of lime at Borek Fałęcki, Karol Wojtyła knew these men, "their living situations, their families, their interests, their human worth" from inside.[52]

From that inside perspective, the young rock breaker began to think more deeply about the meaning of work itself. The Catholic piety with which he had grown up held that backbreaking work was one of the curses of original sin, one of the enduring punishments for Adam and Eve's defiance of God. His experience of the quarry eventually led Karol Wojtyła to a different view. Work, with all its rigors and hardships, was a participation in God's creativity, because work touched the very essence of the human being as the creature to whom

God had given dominion over the earth. Fifteen years later, he tried to grasp this dimension of his experience in the pit at Zakrzówek poetically:

> Listen, when cadences of knocking hammers so much their own
> I transfer into our inner life, to test the strength of each blow—
> Listen: electric current cuts through a river of rock—
> Then the thought grows in me day after day,
> The whole greatness of this work dwells inside a man.[53]

"Inside" man is, of course, a complicated place. Wojtyła's 1956 poem about his experience as a manual laborer is built around the tension between love and anger that was, in his mature view, the warp and woof of work as a specifically human activity. Animals are busy; only people work. We work because we love—our families, our children, all those for whom we work and who depend on our work. Yet work involves wrestling with the unyielding material of the earth, and that wrestling can give birth to what Wojtyła styles

> . . . a fundamental anger
> which flows into people's breath
> like a river bent by the wind.[54]

Anger is also a result of exploitation and the disloyalty of fellow workers. In the world of work, love and anger are inseparable, and to enter into the human experience of work is to live in this unescapable tension, in this "lever of anger and love." The tension is part of the "inner structure" of the world. It is, simply, the way things are.

Life and life's meaning are intensely personal, and even the man who dies tragically (as did a fellow quarryman whose accidental death left a "profound impression" on the young Wojtyła[55]) has transcended the blandness of being a generic *robotnik*, because in his uniquely personal way, he "took with him the inner structure of the world/in which love will explode higher if a greater anger penetrates it."[56] The built-in tensions of work, Wojtyła suggests, find their resolution in the transcendent dignity of the worker, who can never be reduced to a mere unit of production.

A SPIRITUAL MOUNTAINEER

Mysticism is a dimension of religious experience at once magnetically attractive and virtually impenetrable. Mystics write about their experiences, but at the heart of any genuine mystical experience there is something that a third party cannot share. In the Carmelite tradition, for example, the highest level of mystical knowledge is to know that there is nothing to be said about God.

During his second year of life in occupied Kraków, Karol Wojtyła was introduced to this world of intense religious contemplation as a direct result of the Nazi attack on Poland's Catholic clergy.

The parish of St. Stanisław Kostka in Dębniki was led by the Salesian Fathers, a religious community founded by St. John Bosco. It was a dynamic parish in which the Salesians placed great emphasis on youth work. At the risk of their lives, the priests tried to continue this apostolate during the early years of the Occupation, conducting underground catechetical programs for elementary and high school students. The Germans systematically stripped the parish of its clergy, and on May 23, 1941, the Gestapo rounded up all but two of the remaining Salesians, shipping the others to concentration camps, where eleven died, including the pastor, Father Jan Świerc. As the Nazi pressure on St. Stanisław Kostka's youth work increased, the Salesians turned to laymen to lead what had now become a clandestine ministry. The most successful of these lay leaders was a man named Jan Tyranowski, whose confessor once described him as a "spiritual Alpinist."[57]

Born on February 9, 1901, Jan Tyranowski completed elementary school and sufficient years of business school to begin working as an accountant. His nervous disposition did not lend itself to that trade so, like his father and grandfather before him, Tyranowski learned tailoring and supported himself in the family business. Of medium height, with a full head of wavy hair, he sported a brush mustache and was always properly, even elegantly, turned out.

A shy personality with a somewhat delicate constitution, he might have lived a conventionally reclusive life. Then, in 1935, the already devout Tyranowski heard a sermon at St. Stanisław Kostka in which one of the Salesians said, "It's not difficult to be a saint." That simple phrase stuck in his mind, and the tailor of Dębniki began to regularize his spiritual life in a systematic fashion. He also made a vow of celibacy, despite the interest in marriage which at least one woman in the parish had expressed to him. By the time of the Occupation, he was living a daily schedule of prayer and meditation more strict than that observed by many religious orders.[58] A methodical man, Tyranowski wrote out the framework for his meditations in a set of notebooks he kept in a fine, almost calligraphic hand. But he was not dedicated to order and method in prayer as ends in themselves. For Jan Tyranowski, the goal of contemplative prayer was a release from thoughts and images, a certain freedom to simply *be* in God's presence.[59]

Karol Wojtyła met Jan Tyranowski in 1940, perhaps in February, and probably at one of the weekly Saturday meetings of young people at the parish. Tyranowski, a largely self-taught man who had read broadly in Catholic spirituality and whose modest flat on Różana Street contained an impressive library of spiritual classics in several languages, quickly became one of the lay leaders of these discussions.[60] To the young men of Dębniki, Tyranowski could seem rather formal at first, speaking somewhat like a walking catechism text. Yet the gentle tailor-mystic, who had made a considerable study of psychology on his own, somehow managed to communicate to these young men that the points of doctrine they were discussing were not abstractions for him, but the objects of his daily experience.[61] It was a powerful, almost irresistible, quality.[62] After the May 1941 Gestapo raid, the remaining Salesian parish priest at St. Stanisław Kostka asked Tyranowski to begin forming a group of young men who could continue the parish's youth ministry in the absence of the clergy. Thus was born the "Living Rosary," with Karol Wojtyła as one of the first leaders.

The Living Rosary as created by Jan Tyranowski consisted of groups of fifteen young men, each of which was led by a more mature youngster who received personal spiritual direction and instruction from the mystically gifted tailor. Tyranowski met with the entire Living Rosary organization every third Sunday of the month and was also available to any member of a Living Rosary group as needed. As new members joined the program, new groups were formed and a new leader chosen from outstanding members of an existing group. In weekly, hour-long meetings in his apartment, Tyranowski taught his group leaders both the fundamentals of the spiritual life and methods for systematically examining and improving their daily lives. Jan Tyranowski's approach to the interior life included an apostolic dimension. The practice of the presence of God, he taught his young charges, should lead to an intensified life of service to others. Members of the Living Rosary pledged themselves to a life of intensified prayer as brothers in Christ who would help one another in all the circumstances of their lives—as workers, as students (Karol Wojtyła tutored Mieczysław Maliński in Latin after they met in the Living Rosary), in the difficulties of their family lives.

By 1943, some sixty young men, the youngest of whom was fourteen, were involved in the Living Rosary. Four group leaders, or "animators," among them, Karol Wojtyła, were responsible to Tyranowski. All of this was clandestine, the Germans being particularly paranoid about youth groups as possible breeding grounds for anti-Occupation conspiracies. The Gestapo once raided Tyranowski's apartment during a Living Rosary meeting. No one knows what the tailor said, but he evidently convinced the raiders that no conspiracy was afoot and the Germans left.[63]

It was, of course, a conspiracy, but of a different sort. The Living Rosary groups also discussed how Poland might be reconstituted as a Christian society after the war. Those discussions included sharp arguments with representatives of partisan groups advocating violent resistance to the Germans, and, sometimes, Mieczysław Maliński recalled, a member of the Living Rosary disappeared "'into the woods'; occasionally they would return afterwards for a brief spell, and then be heard of no more."[64]

For the young Karol Wojtyła and his friends in the first Living Rosary groups, Tyranowski represented a unique lay combination of personal holiness and apostolic zeal, a kind of life "that was completely unknown to us before." What drew them to him was his ability to "shape souls" by showing how "religious truths" were "not interdictions [or] limitations" but the means to form "a life which through mercy becomes [a] participation in the life of God." To do this with adolescents—with their distinctive combination of self-assurance and self-doubt—was no mean accomplishment. And it seems to have been a matter of personal example as much as formal teaching. As Karol Wojtyła later wrote, his way of life "proved that one could not only inquire about God but that one could live with God."

Tyranowski was the retail apostle par excellence. There was something startling about him, a "sort of strange relentlessness" that created a "bowstring of tension" between the master and his disciples. But it was the relentlessness of love, in which the depth of an individual's conversion to Christ was the key index of achievement.[65]

Leading a Living Rosary group, which meant taking a measure of responsibility for the lives of fifteen other young men, was one important factor in Karol Wojtyła's rapid maturation. In addition, Jan Tyranowski's personal sanctity exemplified the apostolic possibilities of a lay vocation, and helped confirm Wojtyła in the view that holiness did not reside solely inside the sanctuary rail or in the parish priests' house. You did not spend hours with Jan Tyranowski, who, as John Paul II later said, "lived a very personal experience of God," and not conclude that sanctity was everyone's vocation in the Church.[66] Tyranowski also deepened young Wojtyła's experience of prayer. Karol had always prayed. Now he prayed as a means of entering God's presence so that that experience animated every aspect of life, not merely his moments of contemplation.

Tyranowski's most enduring contribution to Karol Wojtyła's life and thinking was to introduce the young student-worker to St. John of the Cross, the sixteenth-century Spanish reformer of the Carmelite order who was declared a Doctor of the Church (Catholicism's greatest acknowledgment of theological creativity) in 1926. The tailor must have sensed that the Spanish mystic's poetry would appeal to young Wojtyła, and that first taste of the literary fruits of Carmelite mysticism soon led to Karol's reading St. John's major theological works: *The Ascent of Mount Carmel, The Dark Night of the Soul, The Spiritual Canticle,* and *The Living Flame of Love.*[67]

Carmelite mysticism is a spirituality of abandonment. The "dark night" is the purification through which the soul must go in order to achieve communion with God. One learns to lay aside the hope for reward and to be drawn forward by God's grace for its own sake. In the dark night, God can seem absent. In the dark night, like Jesus in the desert and on the cross, one abandons every other security and plunges into a kind of radical emptiness, on the far side of which is the intense peace of mystical communion with God himself, a communion of shared "presence," devoid of imagery and concepts. In this spiritual tradition, the living, loving God is beyond the reach of feeling, imagination, or thought. God can only be known in himself when all of our human attempts to "reach" God are abandoned in complete self-surrender, which is an act of complete love.

It was an approach to the human condition as radically opposed to the Nazi will-to-power as could be imagined. Under the tutelage of the unexpected apostle, Jan Tyranowski, and amid the madnesses of the Occupation, the imitation of Christ through the complete handing over of every worldly security to the merciful will of God seized Karol Wojtyła's imagination. Over time, it would become the defining characteristic of his own discipleship.[68]

RESISTANCE THROUGH CULTURE: THE RHAPSODIC THEATER

At the same time that he was getting his first taste of manual labor and taking his first steps in mysticism, Karol Wojtyła became more immersed in theater than he would ever be again.

Karol and his literary friends were determined that the German attempt to stamp out Polish culture would not deter them. In fact, the deliberate effort to decapitate Poland seemed to charge these young actors and authors with an even more intense sense of purpose. In October 1939, a few weeks after returning from his trek to Poland's eastern borderlands, Karol and his Jagiellonian classmates, Juliusz Kydryński and Tadeusz Kwiatkowski, joined by Danuta Michałowska, a high school student passionate about the theater, met at the Kydryńskis' home to recite classic Polish texts, each taking different parts.[69] Two months later, Karol wrote his first play, *David*, which has been lost. A letter to Mieczysław Kotlarczyk described it as a "dramatic poem, or drama, partly biblical, partly rooted in Polish history," in which the apprentice playwright had "bared many things, many matters of my soul."[70]

In the following months, he penned two more biblically inspired dramas. *Job*, written in the spring of 1940, was a meditation on justice in history, provoked by the experience of the Occupation. The play's narrative line follows the biblical story rather closely, with Job's circumstance representing Poland's suffering under the Nazi jackboot—an adaptation of nineteenth-century Polish Romanticism and its identification of dismembered Poland as the suffering "Christ of nations."[71]

In the summer of 1940, the twenty-year-old Wojtyła, who had been reading extensively in the Hebrew Bible, completed *Jeremiah*. The play's inspiration was biblical, but the setting was late sixteenth-century Poland, where the Counter-Reformation Jesuit preacher Piotr Skarga was contending for the nation's soul. Wojtyła paralleled Skarga's fierce sermons on national reform with Jeremiah's biblical prophecies, calling the Kingdom of Judah to repentance. *Jeremiah*, which marked a literary advance over *Job*, mixed historical time with "dramatic time" and ingeniously wove biblical material together with Skarga's preaching and his own script.[72] Thematically, *Jeremiah* continued the young playwright's exploration of the *why* of Poland's suffering.[73]

Another aspect of Karol's intensified dramatic activity involved the famous Polish actor and director Juliusz Osterwa, whom the Nazis had forbidden to practice his craft. Like Mieczysław Kotlarczyk, Osterwa thought of theater as a vocation as well as a career. During the Second Polish Republic he had founded a theater company, Reduta, to bring the classics of the Polish stage to a mass audience. The members of the company lived as a community, in an almost monastic style, and were deeply committed to the ideals expressed in nineteenth-century Polish Romantic literature.[74] Meeting Osterwa through Juliusz Kydryński, Wojtyła soon found himself involved in various of the older actor's projects, including fresh translations of the world's dramatic masterpieces into contemporary Polish. Karol's contribution to this endeavor reflected the quality of the classical education he had received in Wadowice. He prepared a fresh translation of Sophocles' *Oedipus* from the original Greek, while Osterwa was working on *Antigone* and *Hamlet*.[75] Osterwa came to at least one performance that Karol and his friends staged in the Kydryńskis' third-floor apartment at 10 Felicjanek Street: Act Two of Stefan Zeromski's *The Quail*, an examination of love and duty, with Wojtyła in the role of a country teacher and Danuta Michałowska as the teacher's wife coveted by another man, played by Kydryński.[76]

Osterwa seemed to lose interest in Kydryński, Wojtyła, and their friends after they produced *The Quail*. Perhaps the difficulties of performing in an ersatz theater before an audience of thirty people dampened the veteran actor's enthusiasm for underground drama. There also seem to have been artistic tensions between the youngsters and the older man. By the time Osterwa had left Kraków, Karol confessed to being "not as impressed by him" as he used to be. Osterwa's celebrity was getting in the way of the dramatic exploration of the interior life to which Karol and his young colleagues were committed.[77]

Osterwa's departure left a bit of a void, but that would be more than filled in July 1941 when, a month after the German invasion of the Soviet Union, Mieczysław Kotlarczyk came to live in Kraków. Life in Wadowice (which, like Oswięcim, renamed "Auschwitz," had been absorbed into the Third Reich) had become too dangerous for so visible an intellectual as Kotlarczyk. So he and his wife, Zofia, moved into the Wojtyła apartment in Dębniki.* Although Kotlarczyk worked as a tram driver, what he burned to do was put his ideas about a "theater of the word" into practice. This new form of drama was an artistic experiment, but he also saw that it could be "a protest against the extermination of the Polish nation's culture on its own soil, a form of under-

---

*In mid-December another refugee from Wadowice came to live in the apartment at Tyniecka, 10: Maria, Mieczysław Kotlarcyzk's younger sister, then sixteen. The family was afraid that she would die if she was sent away for slave labor; so they sneaked her across the Skawa River in the dead of night and got her to Kraków by train. She lived with Karol Wojtyła and the Kotlarczyks until August 1942, at which point Wojtyła's aunts, the owners of the building, fearful that the Gestapo might take reprisals if the unregistered Maria were discovered, suggested that she move elsewhere. Mieczysław Kotlarczyk got her to Krościenko, where she could obtain the identity card that was unavailable in Kraków to an escapee from the Reich. Karol Wojtyła didn't agree with his aunts and told Maria that, if it were his decision, she could stay. Fifty years later, Maria Kotlarczyk Ćwikla remembers an atmosphere "without fear" in the "catacomb" apartment. It was more like a theater, she recalled, with rehearsals and recitals going on constantly. Her brother, ever the teacher, gave her a bibliography to work through so that she wouldn't waste the year away.[78]

ground resistance movement against the Nazi Occupation."[79] As the Pope later recalled, what came to be known as the Rhapsodic Theater "was born in that room," lent by Karol Wojtyła to the refugee Kotlarczyks.[80]

The key organizational meeting was held on August 22, 1941, in the Dębowski family's apartment at 7 Komorowskiego Street. Kotlarczyk laid out his ideas that afternoon before a group that included Karol Wojtyła, Halina Królikiewicz (who had arrived in Kraków the previous autumn with cabbages and potatoes as barter for rent[81]), Tadeusz Kwiatkowski (Halina's future husband, who was involved in underground literary publishing), Juliusz Kydryński, Danuta Michałowska, the host couple with their daughters Krystyna and Irena, and several others. Kotlarczyk made it clear that this would be very much his enterprise, run according to his principles. He could be stubborn, even fanatical about those principles—over half a century later, Danuta Michałowska, with the affection of mature friendship, would say that "Savanarola was nothing" compared to Mieczysław Kotlarczyk pursuing his vision.[82] No doubt that was part of the reason that he attracted disciples. But his visionary's insistence on doing it his way led to a rift. Kotlarczyk's ideas about the artistic path to pursue differed widely from Juliusz Kydryński's, and these two strong and stubborn men soon came to a parting of the ways.[83]

With Kydryński gone, Kotlarczyk quickly whittled down the August 22 group to the players who would be the core of the Rhapsodic Theater during the war years: the director himself, Krystyna Dębowska, Halina Królikiewicz, Danuta Michałowska, and Karol Wojtyła.[84] Tadeusz Ostaszewski, a sculptor who was Krystyna's fiancé, became the group's stage designer. With the exception of Mieczysław Kotlarczyk, they were all in their late teens or early twenties.

Rehearsals were held Wednesdays and Saturdays, in the late afternoon between the end of work and the beginning of curfew. The young actors often rehearsed in the "catacomb" apartment in Dębniki, sometimes by candlelight when the power had been cut off. On their way to Tyniecka, 10, they walked past posters announcing an ever-increasing list of executions by firing squads, their virtually certain fate if they had been caught.[85]

Their first production took place in the apartment of the Szkocki family, who had befriended Karol Wojtyła during his first year at the Jagiellonian and to whom he had been introduced by Juliusz Kydryński. Fittingly enough, the play was Słowacki's *King-Spirit*, which they performed four times, beginning on November 1, 1941—All Saints' Day in the liturgical calendar. Karol Wojtyła took the role of King Bolesław the Bold, who ordered the murder of St. Stanisław. Supported by Kotlarczyk (but criticized by others), Wojtyła gave the role of the villain a new twist, playing the king as if he were a man preparing himself for confession years after his crime.[86]

The Rhapsodists' program picked up speed in 1942–1943. Another Słowacki poem, *Beniowski*, was given one performance in February. This was followed in March by a poetry cycle written by Jan Kasprowicz, *Hymns*, which the troupe interpreted as a Passion oratorio. *Wyspiański's Hour*, a production assembled from pieces of three Wyspiański plays, was performed four times, once before Juliusz Osterwa, who pronounced himself highly impressed. A similar montage of poems, *Norwid's Hour,* was given three performances, and Mickiewicz's *Pan Tadeusz* was produced twice. The last Rhapsodic Theater production in which Karol Wojtyła participated was Słowacki's *Samuel Zborowski;* he played the title role of a sixteenth-century Polish nobleman rebelling against the establishment of his day. The premiere was on March 16, 1943, and the play was performed three times.[87]

Given the circumstances under which they worked—which included the necessity of constantly changing rehearsal and performance sites to avoid arousing Gestapo suspicions—the Rhapsodic Theater's productivity during the Occupation was remarkable: seven productions in twenty-two formal performances and more than one hundred rehearsals, all of them clandestine. Three more productions were prepared but never performed, including Sienkiewicz's *Quo Vadis* and an adaptation of Dante's *Divine Comedy.*[88] For the members of this unique troupe, underground theatrical activism was not a matter of filling time that would otherwise have been lost to boredom. The young actors of the Rhapsodic Theater "certainly" thought of themselves as involved in a resistance movement, according to Danuta Michałowska and Halina Kwiatkowska.[89] And their purpose was equally clear: "to save our culture from the Occupation" and to help restore the nation's soul, which was a precondition to its political resurrection.[90]

In addition to the lifelong friendships that were formed, the Rhapsodic Theater helped forge the man Karol Wojtyła would become in several ways.

Kotlarczyk's rigorous direction honed his articulation, his timing, and his sense of connection with an audience. A young man who could calmly continue a clandestine performance of *Pan Tadeusz* while Nazi megaphones blasted their propaganda through the streets below was likely to be able to handle himself publicly in virtually any dramatic situation.[91] The themes explored in Kotlarczyk's "inner theater," which deepened Wojtyła's appropriation of the Polish Romantic tradition while stripping it of some of its more messianic excesses, also left their imprint. Słowacki's prominence in the work of the wartime Rhapsodic Theater was not accidental. The poet who sought to remake Poland through the power of *Słowo,* "the word," found a posthumous vehicle for his hopes in Kotlarczyk's conviction that the power of drama lay in the spoken and received word, not in theatrics. This left a deep and abiding impression on Karol Wojtyła, whose literary instincts had already inclined him to the view that "the word" could alter what the world of power thought were unalterable facts, if that word were proclaimed clearly, honestly, and forcefully enough.

This Christian subtext to the Rhapsodic Theater, which reflected the New Testament image of the world created through the Word, the *Logos* who was with God and who was God (see *John* 1.1–3), also found expression in Kotlarczyk's understanding of theater as ritual. In the world according to Mieczysław Kotlarczyk, one did not simply go to the theater to be enter-

tained. Rather, Kotlarczyk deliberately crafted the dramatic method of the
Rhapsodists to evoke sentiments of transcendence and patriotism in a quasi-
liturgical atmosphere.

The word of truth, publicly, indeed almost liturgically, proclaimed was the
antidote the Rhapsodic Theater sought to apply to the violent lies of the Occupation. The tools for fighting evil included speaking truth to power. That was
what Kotlarczyk and his Rhapsodic Theater believed, and lived. That belief and
that experience made an indelible impression on Karol Wojtyła, who would
not forget when, on a different kind of stage, he would confront another totalitarian power in the future.[92]

Some have suggested that, confronted by the horror of Nazi-occupied
Poland, Karol Wojtyła retreated into a religious quietism.[93] In the light of the
evidence, it is clear that he had a decision to make. Some young Poles chose
armed resistance or clandestine sabotage. The evidence makes clear that Karol
Wojtyła deliberately chose the power of resistance through culture, through
the power of the word, in the conviction that the "word" (and in Christian
terms, the Word) is that on which the world turns. Those who question the
choice he made are also questioning that judgment about the power of the
Word and words.

REMORALIZING POLITICS

The Rhapsodic Theater was allied to a broader movement of clandestine cultural resistance known as UNIA [Union], of which Karol Wojtyła was a member. UNIA was founded in 1940 through a merger of three preexisting
underground organizations, complemented by recruits from the now-
proscribed Catholic youth groups and from the nationwide Catholic Action
movement.[94] The new organization was structured territorially and included a
Kraków district organization. UNIA was built by its members recruiting or rec-
ommending new members. After scrutiny by local UNIA leaders, new members took a solemn oath committing themselves to the organization's
principles and to the rules of conspiracy.

UNIA tried to apply Christian moral principles and Catholic social doctrine to public life at a time when there was, officially, no "public life" for Poles.
Its name, "Union," expressed its vision of postwar Poland as a nation in which
differences of ethnicity, religion, and social class would be overcome through
two shared convictions: politics and economics should be guided by the universal moral law, the only legitimate source of public authority, and free individuals should make the common good a priority in their public lives.

In one sense, UNIA was an attempt to articulate a political philosophy
capable of disciplining the talent for divisiveness that had made the history of
Polish politics such a bedlam, leaving the Polish nation so vulnerable to its enemies. In another respect, UNIA was an underground effort to lay the foundations of a new Polish state that would embody in its laws, economy, and public

ethos the communitarian themes of Catholic social doctrine developed by Popes Leo XIII and Pius XI: support for the family as the basic unit of society; the anti-totalitarian principle of subsidiarity, according to which decision making should be left at the lowest level possible in society (rather than absorbed by an omni-competent state); and "self-government," UNIA's term for Catholic personalism and its stress on the inalienable dignity of the individual man or woman created in the image and likeness of God. Those principles, UNIA leaders thought, were a solid foundation for a democratic state, and a barrier against both the radical individualism of one stream of modern political thought and the totalitarian demolition of individuality.

UNIA had a military component, which at full strength numbered some 20,000 members, many of whom saw combat as part of the underground Polish Home Army during the Warsaw Uprising of August 1944. UNIA also sponsored another dangerous form of anti-Nazi activism. Its Council to Help the Jews, code-named "Zegota," delivered false identification papers to some 50,000 Jews trying to escape Hitler's Final Solution, hid some 2,500 Jewish children from Nazi manhunters in Warsaw, and provided regular financial support to approximately 4,000 persons.

UNIA, however, was primarily an instrument of ideological and cultural resistance to the Nazi attempt to erase Poland from the map of history. It maintained an underground Institute of Central Europe for research purposes, and sponsored a number of "columns," attempts to organize and catechize the worlds of labor, culture, youth, and women. The UNIA-sponsored Cultural Union supported a wide range of cultural resistance activities. In addition to lectures and discussions, it published an underground newspaper, *Culture of Tomorrow,* and a Unionist Library Series to replace what the Nazis were systematically destroying. UNIA also supported a number of underground theaters, including the Rhapsodic Theater, Mieczysław Kotlarczyk having been a member of UNIA for some time.

UNIA was a pioneering effort to build what a later generation would call "civil society" from under the rubble of totalitarianism. Its principles of "self-government" and "union" were an attempt to marry the Polish passion for freedom ("Nothing about us without us") to a Catholic-inspired communitarian concept of the common good. History, in the person of Stalin, would determine that UNIA's dreams for postwar Poland were dashed. Its communitarian ideas about a just modern society and a reconstituted European community remained part of the intellectual architecture of Karol Wojtyła for life.[95]

SEMINARIAN IN HIDING

Death was an ever-present reality in occupied Kraków. Before his twenty-first birthday Karol Wojtyła had seen a lot of it. He had witnessed violent death on the refugees' road to Tarnow. His professors, men of culture and distinction, had been summarily arrested and carted off to concentration camps. The

Gestapo had kidnapped the parish priests of Dębniki, many of whom would be subsequently martyred. Kraków's historic and vibrant Jewish life was being systematically destroyed, as Jews were herded into a ghetto, where they died by the thousands, dispatched to the extermination camps or sent to the nearby Płaszów labor camp—where some were saved by being named on what the world would eventually know as "Schindler's list."

Although he had become progressively weaker, the elder Karol Wojtyła, "the captain," was an anchor for his son in these troubled waters. Lolek had his friends, his underground studies, his clandestine theatrical life. He had found a new spiritual mentor in Jan Tyranowski. But his father was the sole surviving member of his immediate family and the last living link to an almost unimaginably simpler past. Father and son continued to share the apartment on Tyniecka Street, and the older Wojtyła attended his son's clandestine plays and dramatic readings.[96] When Lolek began to work at the Zakrzówek quarry, he walked back to town with Juliusz Kydryński, whose mother gave him a late afternoon dinner and then sent something home with him for the captain, who had been bedridden since Christmas 1940.

February 18, 1941, began like any other day during this period. After working at the quarry Karol stopped, as usual, at the Kydryńskis to pick up dinner and some medicine for his father. He hurried back to the Dębniki apartment through the bitter cold, accompanied by Juliusz Kydryński's sister Maria, who would heat up the captain's meal. Entering "the catacomb," Maria turned right into the small kitchen, while Karol went to his father, whose room was at the end of the dark hallway on the left. The captain was dead.

Maria Kydryńska remembers the son in tears, blaming himself for not being present when his father died. He then ran to St. Stanisław Kostka for a priest, who came and gave the deceased man the last rites of the Church. Lolek spent the entire night on his knees beside his father's body, praying and talking with Juliusz Kydryński, who had come to be with him; the orphaned young man later recalled that, despite his friend's presence, "I never felt so alone. . . ."[97]

Father Figlewicz said the funeral Mass on February 22 at the Rakowice cemetery, in whose military section Karol Wojtyła was buried on another bitterly cold day. The Kydryńskis, concerned about the twenty-year-old orphan living by himself, invited young Karol to stay with them. He accepted, moving back to the Dębniki apartment in the late summer of 1941 when Mieczysław and Zofia Kotlarczyk escaped Wadowice and came to Kraków. Juliusz Kydryński remembered this as a period of intense reflection for his friend, who would sometimes pray while lying on the floor in a cruciform position.[98]

Catholicism does not consider the priesthood a career but a vocation, a calling or invitation from God to "put on Jesus Christ" in a singular way. A priestly vocation is thus a complex work of the Holy Spirit whose inner dynamics cannot be reduced to psychological categories. Being orphaned before his twenty-first birthday certainly had its effect on Karol Wojtyła's discernment of a call to the priesthood. That it took almost a year and a half for the decision to mature suggests that considerable interior wrestling went on before the final step was taken. Later in life, when describing these years to friends and colleagues, he would speak of an evolutionary process of gradual clarification or "interior illumination."[99] During 1941 and the first half of 1942, Karol Wojtyła, moved by the humiliation of totalitarian occupation and by the heroism he had witnessed in the face of it, began to sense in himself a "progressive detachment from my earlier plans."[100] The priesthood began to loom larger as a way to live in resistance to the degradation of human dignity by brutal ideology.

There were other influences at work, and a pattern began to emerge from what might otherwise seem a random series of acquaintances. The captain and Lolek had never discussed a possible vocation to the priesthood, but the son would later recall the father's life of prayer and self-sacrifice as "a kind of domestic seminary."[101] The same might be said of the workers at the quarry and the Solvay chemical plant, the heroic Salesians of the Dębniki parish, the Kraków Carmelites with whom he once made a wartime retreat, the Living Rosary and Jan Tyranowski, and the continuing guidance of Father Figlewicz.

Teachers and contemporaries in Wadowice and Kraków had told him that he was bound for the altar. He had always resisted the notion. Now, an idea that would eventually become one of his deepest convictions began to take shape: that in the sometimes baffling designs of Providence, there is no such thing as a mere coincidence. An orphan before his majority; his intellectual gifts and his longstanding bent toward a life of prayer; the hardships he had endured during the Occupation; his passion for the theater—like the people who had touched his life most profoundly, these were not fragmentary incidents in a life, but signposts along a path pointing in the direction of the priesthood. It was not so much a question of his choosing this vocation against others. Throughout the spring and summer of 1942 the conviction grew in him that he had been chosen. And to that election there could be only one response.[102]

In the autumn of 1942, Karol Wojtyła walked to the seventeenth-century residence of the archbishops of Kraków at Franciszkańska, 3, a few blocks from the Old Town market square, and asked to be received as a candidate for the priesthood. The rector of the seminary, Father Jan Piwowarczyk, accepted him, and Karol began to lead a new, double life.

In the first days of the Occupation, the Gestapo had tried to control the seminary, intending to downgrade it to a kind of clerical trade school with no instruction by university-level professors. The seminary, with the agreement of Archbishop Sapieha, simply ignored these instructions. The Gestapo's next move was to ban the reception of new seminarians. The archbishop's response was to hire the young aspirants as "parish secretaries," place them in local parishes, and have them attend classes clandestinely at the Kraków seminary. Raids were frequent. On one occasion five students were arrested, immediately executed by firing squad or dispatched to Auschwitz.

The archbishop then decided to take the seminary fully underground. Candidates would be accepted secretly. They would continue their work, telling no one of their new position. They would study in their free time, occasionally presenting themselves to professors for examination. And in due course, it was hoped, they would complete their studies and be ordained, having managed to avoid the Gestapo in the interim.

Karol Wojtyła was among the first ten seminarians chosen for this extraordinary process of clandestine priestly formation. He continued to work at Borek Fałęcki. Always a reader, he studied during the overnight shift without drawing special attention. He also continued to perform with the Rhapsodic Theater, but Mieczysław Kotlarczyk eventually had to be told that his young protégé's time could no longer be poured so readily into preparing scripts, rehearsing, and performing.[103]

Kotlarczyk passionately disagreed with Karol's decision to become a priest and "tried for days to dissuade him."[104] It was not that Kotlarczyk was anticlerical. On the contrary, he was a devout Catholic. In his visionary's world, though, the most important thing was the theater, where one best served God and Poland. Halina Królickiewicz remembers that it was all a "complicated business because everybody thought [Wojtyła] would become an actor. But we also knew his piety and devotion, so we understood."[105] But it took a while. Wojtyła's friends recruited Tadeusz Kudliński, whom Karol knew and respected from the Jagiellonian student theater group, for an all-night, curfew-breaking, one-on-one debate with Lolek. Kudliński reportedly tried to persuade Karol to remain "in the world" through the Gospel parable of the talents: God had given him abilities as an actor, and it would be burying his talents to refuse to develop them.[106] That argument failing, Kudliński tried the young seminarian's favorite poet, Norwid, himself borrowing from Scripture: "Light does not exist to be kept under a bushel." Karol refused to budge.[107] He had been chosen. He could not decline the gift.

Wojtyła's biggest problem in his early days as a clandestine seminarian was not with his Rhapsodic Theater colleagues, however, but with philosophy, and specifically with metaphysics. Then as now, the intellectual preparation of seminarians included courses in philosophy. One of the books Karol was assigned to read and digest for examination was Kazimierz Wais's *Metaphysics*, a 1926 text written in the dry, dense, highly abstract formulas of early twentieth-century neo-scholasticism. Karol Wojtyła, a literary man, had never encountered anything like this before, and it floored him. But, as he later said, "after two months of hacking my way through this vegetation I came to a clearing, to the discovery of the deep reasons for what until then I had only lived and felt. . . . What intuition and sensibility had until then taught me about the world found solid confirmation."[108]

Put another way, Karol Wojtyła was inoculated against the infection of radical skepticism in the chemical factory at Borek Fałęcki, as watery lime splashed against the pages of *Metaphysics*. There he discovered a "new world of existence" built around the classic conviction, central to the philosophy of Aristotle and Thomas Aquinas, that the world was intelligible.[109] That conviction was the foundation from which he would think philosophically in the future. The war had given him a direct, indeed harsh, experience of reality. Wais, for all the agonies he inflicted, put in place the first building blocks for a philosophical defense of realism—the intelligibility of the world—against radical skepticism and its cousin, moral relativism.

Reality soon imposed itself on the worker-seminarian in other, direct ways. On February 29, 1944, Karol Wojtyła was walking home from a double shift at Borek Fałęcki when he was struck down by a German truck. Mrs. Józefa Florek, seeing the body in the road, jumped off the tram she was riding and found Karol lying unconscious. Shielding him from the traffic, she managed to flag down a car. A German officer got out and told her to fetch some muddy water from a nearby ditch. They cleaned the blood off Karol, and when the officer saw that he was still alive, he stopped a passing lumber truck and told them to take the semiconscious man to a local hospital. When Karol woke up at last he found his head wrapped in bandages and his arm in a cast. He had suffered a severe concussion, numerous cuts, and a shoulder injury. He spent the next two weeks in the hospital, recuperating and pondering the peculiar ways of Providence. That he had survived this incident seemed a confirmation of his priestly vocation.

While living his double life, Karol often went to the archbishop's residence to serve Archbishop Sapieha's morning Mass, a practice he continued after recovering from his accident. One morning in April 1944, his fellow server and another clandestine student for the priesthood, Jerzy Zachuta, didn't show up at Franciszkańska, 3. After Mass, Karol went to Zachuta's home to see what had happened. In the middle of the previous night, the Gestapo had taken his classmate away. Immediately afterward, the name of Jerzy Zachuta appeared on a Gestapo poster listing Poles to be shot.[110] One was taken, the other remained. In the designs of Providence, there are no mere coincidences.

Four months later, on August 1, Poland's capital exploded in the Warsaw Uprising, the desperate attempt by the underground Polish Home Army to rid the nation's capital of the Germans and establish the legitimacy of an independent Polish government before the Soviet army arrived. After two months of indescribably fierce fighting, including pew-by-pew, hand-to-hand combat in St. John's Cathedral, the city fell while the Soviet army sat just across the Vistula, doing nothing; better for the Germans to exterminate the Home Army than to have to do it themselves. Warsaw was then leveled on Hitler's personal order. Nothing more than two feet high was to be left standing.

August 6, the liturgical feast of the Transfiguration, was "Black Sunday" in Kraków as the Gestapo swept the city, rounding up young men to forestall a reprise of the Warsaw Uprising. Archbishop Sapieha immediately called in his underground seminarians, intending to hide them in his residence. Mieczysław Maliński, by now another clandestine candidate for the priesthood, had taken a group of boys out for a hike that afternoon. On their way back they spotted the Gestapo roundup and hid. That evening Maliński, after making provision for his young charges, snuck through fields and neighbors' gardens, working his way back to his home in Dębniki, where he found his family safe. In the early morning hours, there was an ominous knock on the door. The family froze, but it was a priest from the archdiocese, sent by Sapieha to order Maliński to report to the archbishop's residence later that day. When he arrived there, Maliński's first question was, "Is Karol Wojtyła here?"[111]

He was, but it had been a close call. During the sweep the day before, the Gestapo had searched the first two floors of the house at Tyniecka, 10. Karol had remained behind a closed door in his basement apartment, praying for deliverance with heart pounding.[112] Once the Germans departed empty-handed, Irena Szkocka volunteered to help Lolek get across town to the archbishop's, walking a block ahead as a scout. Entering the residence, he was immediately given a cassock to wear; in the event of a raid, Archbishop Sapieha intended to inform the Gestapo that all these young men were his secretaries.

Even asylum created problems. Hans Frank's "Labor Office" began to make inquiries about the Borek Fałęcki worker who wasn't showing up on the time sheets. At the archbishop's request, Father Figlewicz met with the plant director to see what could be done to make Karol Wojtyła "disappear." The director was hesitant to take such a chance, but he must have made arrangements. Inquiries about *robotnik* Wojtyła ceased. As Wojtyła himself would later put it, the authorities "were unable to find my trail."[113]

Father Stanisław Smoleński was the young seminarians' spiritual director and Father Kazimierz Kusak was prefect of studies. With Father Piwowarczyk, who had accepted Wojtyła as a clandestine seminarian, now assigned to a parish, Archbishop Sapieha himself was the rector. Living in daily contact with the archbishop, Karol Wojtyła came to know the man who would be his model of Church leadership for more than half a century.

"AN UNBROKEN PRINCE"

Adam Stefan Sapieha was the scion of a noble Polish-Lithuanian family. His early ecclesiastical career was spent in Rome, where he served as a secretary to Pope Pius X, who personally consecrated him a bishop in the Sistine Chapel on December 17, 1911, giving him a plain gold pectoral cross.[114] Sapieha was a "short man of iron will," a leader with a great natural authority that reflected his innate dignity and strength of character.[115] At his ceremonial ingress into his new see in 1912, he went straight from the railway station to visit a poorhouse, keeping the gentry who had expected to host him for breakfast waiting and causing a flutter among his fellow nobles.[116] In a line of bishops that traced its roots back to the martyred St. Stanisław, he would, in his old age, give new meaning to the tradition that the bishop of Kraków was the final *defensor civitatis*, the ultimate "defender of the city."[117]

The Prince Archbishop, as everyone called him, had not prospered during the reign of Pius XI. These two strong personalities had crossed swords when the future pope was papal nuncio in Poland in the immediate aftermath of World War I, and during Pius XI's pontificate, Sapieha was denied the cardinal's red hat worn by his two predecessors, Albin Dunajewski and Jan Puzyna.[118] A week before Pius XI died in February 1939, Sapieha, pleading ill health and age (he was seventy-two at the time), wrote the pope asking permission to resign—a rarity among bishops in that era. His letter was never answered because of Pius's death. When Sapieha renewed the request to the newly elected Pius XII on a visit to Rome in April of that year, he was refused. The political situation was deteriorating and things were too unstable to risk a change. Sapieha would have to stay in place.

He soon became the "uncrowned king of Poland," or, in the words of John Paul II, an "unbroken prince" who was a "real *pater patriae*" to a nation facing extermination.*

The primate, Cardinal Hlond, having fled in September 1939 with the Polish government, lived in southern France from the fall of 1940 through February 1944, when he was arrested by the Gestapo and taken to Wiedenbrück in Westphalia, where he was liberated by American troops on April 1, 1945.[120] During the entire war, Adam Stefan Sapieha, growing stronger as he grew older, was the unshakable foundation of Catholic resistance to the Nazi Occupation. In ancient Polish custom, the Primate of Poland held the office of *Interrex* during the period between the death of one Polish king and the election of his successor. Archbishop Sapieha was the de facto *Interrex* of Poland for more than five years—the focal point of legitimate authority in a nation being run by gangsters. It was a role he assumed without hesitation.

Hans Frank, evidently looking for some sliver of legitimation, hinted repeatedly that an invitation to dinner at the archbishop's residence would be well-received. Sapieha finally issued the invitation and sat the master of Occupied Poland at the other end of his formal dinner table. The two men were alone. Dinner was then served: black bread, made in part from acorns; jam made from beets (sugar beets for sweetness, red beets for color); ersatz coffee. When Frank stared down the table at his host, the archbishop blandly explained that this was the ration available on the food coupons distributed by the Nazis, and he certainly couldn't risk reprimand or the arrest of one of his servants by dealing on the black market.[121] Hans Frank's reply is lost to history. Presumably he did not press for a second invitation.

Sapieha's natural authority reflected his aristocratic lineage and bearing, but bloodlines alone could not sustain a man in these desperate circumstances. Every night at 9 P.M., the seminarians saw the Prince Archbishop go

---

* *The Unbroken Prince* is the title of a play by Juliusz Słowacki, an adaption of a seventeenth-century drama by Pedro Calderón de la Barca, which tells the story of the martyrdom of Prince Ferdinand of Portugal, who died because he refused to give a Christian town to the Muslims in exchange for his own life.[119]

into his chapel alone, for an hour. It was understood that he was presenting his problems to his Lord, and that he was not to be disturbed.[122]

The problems were grave in the last extreme. His priests were being arrested and shipped off to concentration camps or executed. Parishes had to be assisted in their efforts to help prisoners at the Nazi labor camps, by hiding food in the woods for them. A constant stream of prisoners into Gestapo headquarters across the street from the archbishop's residence had to be defended. Families whose fathers had disappeared needed assistance. So did Kraków's Jewish community, on whose behalf Sapieha made representations to Hans Frank at least twice. The archbishop also ordered baptismal certificates issued to Jews in order to help them escape the Holocaust. There were parents and spouses to be comforted. All of this Sapieha did on his own, cut off from contact with Rome. On two occasions the archbishop tried to warn the Vatican of Nazi plans to exterminate Jews and Polish nationals.[123]

Yet in the midst of the Occupation, Adam Stefan Sapieha planned for the future. A member of the reformist wing of the Polish hierarchy, Sapieha had broken up huge old parishes before the war and created new ones, bringing his priests closer to his people. He had also reformed the seminary, insisting on serious theological instruction. As the war wound down, he began to make plans for a new Catholic newspaper, *Tygodnik Powszechny* [Universal Weekly], to be edited by a young lay journalist, Jerzy Turowicz. The archbishop assigned one of the archdiocese's leading priest-intellectuals, Father Jan Piwowarczyk, the former seminary rector, as "ecclesiastical adviser" to the paper.

Above all, Sapieha was convinced that the revitalization of Polish Catholicism after the war required a well-educated and dynamic corps of priests. So he risked his life in creating the clandestine seminary program during the early years of the Occupation, and he quite literally turned his house over to the underground seminary in the aftermath of Black Sunday, 1944. Both students and faculty joked about being under "house arrest."[124] Life was spartan. Each student had his own bed or cot, but the only other furniture was a common table. What meager personal possessions they had brought with them were stored in suitcases under their beds, in what had once been one of the archbishop's drawing rooms.[125]

At his first meeting with the students the archbishop announced that he was not prepared to wait any longer for the Germans to reopen the seminary. He himself would be the rector. If they were discovered and the Nazis wanted to take reprisals against him, so be it. "We will trust in God's Providence," he concluded. "No harm will befall us."[126]

For a man of his background, and given the ecclesiastical protocol of the time, Sapieha was remarkably available to his young boarders. He would simply show up during recreation, visiting with the students; he tried to have a word with each of them during the course of the day. The students, for their part, came to know the man who would ordain them priests. They could see the depth of his piety, both in his solitary evening prayer and in the long thanksgiving meditations he made after saying his morning Mass.

Under the leadership of Fathers Smoleńksi and Kusak, Sapieha's underground seminary was organized on a full daily schedule. The students got up at 6 A.M. for an hour of private prayer. Mass was celebrated at 7 A.M., with breakfast following. Classes were then held from 8:15 until noon, in another of Sapieha's drawing rooms. At 12 noon, students and faculty stopped to recite the Angelus and an act of contrition. Lunch and recreation in the archbishop's garden followed. In mid-afternoon, the students went to the chapel for fifteen minutes of adoration before the Blessed Sacrament; this was followed by private study. At 6:30 P.M., either Father Smoleński or Archbishop Sapieha would give a conference on a spiritual topic. Dinner was at 7 P.M., with evening prayer and personal devotions at 8:15. Confessions were heard once a week; the students were free to choose their own confessors, among the faculty or from priests brought into the seminary from outside. The academic year began with a three-day retreat, an intensified period of prayer without academic classes, usually led by Father Smoleński. Another major retreat was held in Lent, and briefer retreats took place throughout the year. Guest speakers were invited to enrich the academic curriculum. Juliusz Osterwa came to give the underground seminarians elocution lessons and explain how a sermon should be preached—which, given the typical pattern of clergy/lay relations in the Poland of that era, must have ranked as a considerable innovation.[127]

Later in life, Pope John Paul II remarked somewhat wistfully that he had never had a real experience of the seminary, given the war and its immediate aftermath, but young Karol Wojtyła seemed to have little trouble adjusting to life during his months of "house arrest" at Franciszkańska, 3.[128] His intellectual capabilities were soon apparent to his classmates, as was his piety. The Prince Archbishop himself quickly came to appreciate the talents of the young man from Wadowice who, to Sapieha's way of thinking, was finally where he belonged.

LOSING TWICE: THE COMMUNIST OCCUPATION OF POLAND

As the Red Army's 1st Ukrainian Front drove westward past Dębica and Tarnów, the Occupation prepared to abandon Kraków. Explosive charges were set, and on the night of January 17–18, 1945, the Germans quit the city, blowing up the Dębniki Bridge and breaking the windows in the archbishop's residence.[129] The students set to work the next day cleaning things up at Franciszkańska, 3. Shortly afterward they moved to reclaim the old seminary building near Wawel Castle, which had been occupied by the SS. The seminary was a catastrophe. Its windows had been shattered, the tiled roof had collapsed, the central heating had failed, and the SS's prisoners had kept from freezing by lighting open fires in the rooms. Worst of all were the lavatories, where piles of frozen excrement had to be chopped up and carted away. Karol Wojtyła and Mieczysław Maliński volunteered for this odious task, after which carrying tiles to the roof was a relief.[130]

The young seminarians, having survived the Occupation, might have imagined that a return to normality in a free and independent Poland was at hand. If they did, they were quickly disabused of the notion. For the second time during the Second World War, Poland was about to be sacrificed to a total-itarian power.

The Polish Government-in-Exile in London was denied a significant voice in shaping its country's future. In July 1944, the Moscow-controlled Polish Committee for National Liberation, known in the West as the "Lublin Committee," signed an agreement with the USSR giving the Soviets complete control over law and order in the rear of the advancing Red Army. This set the stage for a reprise of the first days of the Nazi Occupation, as local officials were replaced (often under bogus charges of collaboration), resistance units were broken up or incorporated into Soviet-friendly groups, and anyone disinclined to obey was shot.[131]

What unfolded in the wake of this new occupation took place within new frontiers. At the Tehran and Yalta Conferences, the Western Allies had agreed to move "Poland" some 150 miles west on the map of Europe. Wilno and Lwów would now be in the Soviet Union, albeit in the pseudo-"republics" of Lithuania and Ukraine. Breslau, Stettin, and Danzig were "recovered" from Germany and henceforth known as Wrocław, Szczecin, and Gdańsk. A little more than half the territory of interwar Poland was included in the new Polish People's Republic, and the territory the new Poland lost (approximately 108,000 square miles) was far more than what it gained (some 61,000 square miles).[132] Poland's transplantation westward would cause problems between Polish Catholicism and the Vatican for almost a quarter-century, and helped set the stage for two of the most brutal persecutions of Catholicism in the USSR, in the Lithuanian and Ukrainian Soviet Socialist "Republics."

The war had also drastically altered Polish demographics, and no social class had been spared. The intelligentsia, including the Church leadership, had been gravely weakened. Polish Jewry had been almost completely destroyed in the Holocaust. Combined with the loss of its old eastern lands and the expulsion of Germans from the "Recovered Territories" in what was now western Poland, the net result was the most Polish (and Catholic) Poland in Polish history.[133]

The new rulers brought with them a checkered history. The interwar Communist Party of Poland (KPP) had been a political embarrassment and an ideological concern to Moscow; its incapacity to make headway politically was compounded by its tendency toward ideological deviations. In 1938, during his own Great Purge in the Soviet Union, Stalin liquidated some 5,000 KPP members; others would eventually die in the Gulag.[134] After the German invasion of the USSR in June 1941, however, Stalin saw that a resurrected Poland under communist auspices would suit his purposes and the Polish Workers' Party was born. Władysław Gomułka, who had escaped Stalin's purge of the KPP because he had been jailed at the time by his own government, emerged as First Secretary.[135] While every inch a hard-line communist, Gomułka was also, in his way, a Polish patriot nervous about the impact of Soviet imperialism on the "Polish road to socialism." So he was forced aside in 1948 in favor of Bolesław Bierut, an unreconstructed Stalinist who would cause no migraines in the Kremlin. By mid-1948, reconstituted Poland was thoroughly enmeshed in the Soviet external empire, its defense minister a senior Red Army officer intent on protecting the land bridge to the Soviet-occupied zone of Germany. The new Poland, a putative expression of an ideology that had never gained a foothold among the Polish people, and a state whose geopolitical raison d'être was the security of the Soviet Union, was a product of the Red Army and of pusillanimous Western policy. Poland's "liberation" in 1945 was a euphemism.

All of which made an enduring impression on Karol Wojtyła. Yalta, for him, became something more than the cruel truth that Poland, presumably one of World War II's victors, was in fact a double loser. Yalta was the triumph of a false and inhuman power realism over the moral pledges that the Western allies had made to Poland before and during the war. Yalta was where those who imagined themselves the forces of freedom blinked a second time when confronted by another totalitarian power. World War II had ended not with the reestablishment of freedom and the restoration of the rights of nations, but with communist totalitarianism spread over more than half of Europe and over other parts of the world. Yalta was a grave injustice, and no enduring peace could be built on that kind of foundation. Politics, even world politics, was not a matter of power alone. Moral issues were engaged.

Meanwhile, as Poland was being reshackled by communism—a process Stalin once described as akin to "fitting a cow with a saddle"[136]—Prince Archbishop Sapieha visited the archdiocesan soup kitchen, disguised in a battered old overcoat and hat, to make sure that the soup being served to the destitute doctors, lawyers, professors, and other professionals of "liberated" Kraków was up to his standards. It was.[137]

Ad Altare Dei

Amid the ironies and tragedies of Poland's "liberation," life gradually returned to something approaching normality in the Kraków seminary. The Jagiellonian University reemerged from underground, and Karol Wojtyła completed his third year of theological studies as World War II wound down in the West. He was elected a vice president of the Students' Fraternal Aid Society of the university, an organization that helped distribute Western aid to the impoverished student body. His personal commitment to living in poverty continued to make an impression on his seminary classmates. Sent a new sweater by Mieczysław Kotlarczyk, he gave it away to a beggar who came and asked for him by name.[138]

After a summer vacation on the outskirts of Kraków at the parish in Raciborowice, Karol began his fourth and final year of preordination theology in the fall of 1945, while working as a teaching assistant in undergraduate theology courses. Among his professors was the formidable Father Ignacy Różycki. The demanding theologian noticed that his prize pupil put a small inscription—"To Jesus through Mary," or "Jesus, Mary, and Joseph"—at the top of every page of every paper he submitted. It was a habit Karol had formed years before, and it would continue throughout his writing life. Różycki encouraged Wojtyła's interest in St. John of the Cross. Karol, for his part, continued to teach himself Spanish, a project he had begun the year before using a German-Spanish dictionary as his guide; his goal was to read the Carmelite mystic in the original.[139]

Karol had in fact been wrestling for some time with the question of whether he should enter the Discalced Carmelite monastery at Czerna to pursue a contemplative life in complete withdrawal from the world. At one point in 1945 he finally put the question to the Prince Archbishop, who responded tersely: "First you have to finish what you have begun." Sapieha's brisk conclusion resolved the matter. Over a half-century later, John Paul II would reminisce that, despite his intense interest in John of the Cross, "I don't think I had a very strong vocation to the Carmelites."[140]

Shortly after the war, Karol became aware of the self-sacrifice of Father Maximilian Mary Kolbe in the Auschwitz starvation bunker. The martyred Franciscan, who had given up his life to save a fellow prisoner, a married man with children, became a model of the priest as a man who lives his sacramental condition as an *alter Christus*, "another Christ," by complete self-emptying in service to his people. It was an ideal that was inculcated at the Kraków seminary through communal recitation of the "Litany of Our Lord Jesus Christ, Priest and Victim," a staple of the seminary's piety based on the New Testament's *Letter to the Hebrews*. The Kraków litany, which includes eight invocations of Jesus Christ as the victim of a redeeming sacrifice, drove home to the seminarians that dying-to-self—self-gift or self-immolation—was the crux of any Christian vocation seriously lived, and most especially the vocation of the priesthood.[141] The idea of self-gift would reemerge time and again in Wojtyła's life-work, and would become one of the crucial concepts in his philosophy of the human person and of human moral agency.

THE PRIEST

On February 18, 1946, Adam Stefan Sapieha was created a cardinal by Pope Pius XII. When he returned to Kraków in March, his train was met at the station by a group of students who honored this great hero of the Occupation by lifting his car and carrying it and the new Prince of the Church to St. Mary's Church in the Old Town market square.[142] At a seminary celebration of Sapieha's cardinalate, Karol Wojtyła declaimed a homily by Father Kajsiewicz, a nineteenth-century Polish hero, on the religious meaning of patriotism— hardly a random choice of topic.[143]

In late June and early July 1946, Wojtyła successfully passed examinations in Scripture, dogmatic theology, moral theology, canon law, and catechetics to complete his preordination theology course.[144]

Cardinal Sapieha, who wanted his most talented priests to have an experience of Rome, had decided that Karol should begin doctoral studies in theology at Rome's Pontifical Athenaeum of St. Thomas Aquinas (universally known as "the Angelicum"), in the fall 1946 semester.[145] First, the cardinal would ordain him a priest on an accelerated schedule.

The entire month of October 1946 was an intense month of preparation for priestly ordination. After a six-day retreat led by Father Smoleński, the seminary spiritual director, Karol, having solemnly bound himself to a life of celibacy and to praying daily the Liturgy of the Hours (the Divine Office, or breviary), was ordained a subdeacon by the Prince Cardinal on October 13.[146] A week later, after a three-day retreat made privately, he was ordained deacon by the archbishop on October 20. He then made another six-day retreat in preparation for his ordination to the priesthood, which was scheduled for November 1: the great solemnity of All Saints and the fifth anniversary of the Rhapsodic Theater's premiere performance of *King-Spirit*. While these preordination preparations were taking place, Stanisław Starowieyski, a younger seminarian not yet ordained, whom Sapieha was sending to Rome for his entire course of theological studies, arranged their tickets and passports so that his friend Wojtyła could focus completely on his retreats.

On the morning of November 1, 1946, Karol Wojtyła, the only candidate for ordination that day, processed into the archbishop's private chapel in the episcopal residence at Franciszkańska, 3.[147] The archbishop had already made an indelible impression on Karol's thinking by his example. According to the Church's theology, he would now make an indelible impression on Karol's soul through the act of ordination. The priesthood, as both ordaining prelate and ordinand understood it, was not simply a matter of what one did; it was a matter of who one *is*. His baptism in Wadowice had marked Karol Wojtyła as a Christian. What was about to transpire in the archbishop's chapel would mark him as a priest of Christ.

After the Mass's first Scripture reading, Cardinal Sapieha sat on a faldstool, a small portable throne, in front of the altar. Karol knelt before him, vested in amice, alb, cincture, stole, and maniple. A folded chasuble lay over his left arm, and he held a lighted white candle in his right hand. After the seminary authorities formally testified that he was worthy of Holy Orders, Karol was addressed by the cardinal, who charged him to be "perfect in faith and action . . . well-grounded in the virtue of the twofold love of God and of neighbor." Karol then prostrated himself facedown on the floor, his arms extended as on a cross, while the Litany of the Saints was chanted over him—the Church on earth asking the Church in heaven to come to the aid of the man about to be ordained a priest.[148]

At the end of the litany, Karol rose and knelt before Cardinal Sapieha, who stood in silence and laid his hands on Karol's head in the central act of the rite of ordination. After calling down upon the ordinand the power of the Holy Spirit, the cardinal sat again, took that part of the stole that was hanging behind Karol's left shoulder, brought it over his right shoulder and crossed it over his breast, saying, "Take thou the yoke of the Lord, for His yoke is sweet and His burden light." The cardinal vested Karol in the chasuble, the outermost vestment of the priest celebrating Mass, saying, "Take thou the priestly vestment whereby charity is signified; for God is well able to give thee an increase of charity and its perfect works."

After the Church's ancient hymn to the Holy Spirit, "Veni Creator Spiritus," the cardinal sat again on the faldstool and Karol knelt before him for his priestly anointing. The cardinal anointed the palms of Karol's hands, held open before him, first with the sign of the cross, and then all over, while praying, "Be pleased, O Lord, to consecrate and hallow these hands by this anointing, and our blessing." The cardinal then brought Karol's hands together and one of the assisting priests bound them with a white cloth. Sapieha took a chalice containing wine and water and a paten holding a host. While Karol held his bound hands before him, the cardinal placed the chalice and its covering paten between his fingers so that they touched both sacred vessels, and prayed, "Receive the power to offer Sacrifice to God, and to celebrate Mass, both for the living and the dead, in the name of the Lord."

After Karol's hands were cleansed, he presented his lighted candle to the cardinal as a votive offering. The Mass continued with Father Karol Wojtyła now celebrating the Church's central act of worship with Cardinal Sapieha, exchanging with him the ancient kiss of peace, and joining him in receiving the Body and Blood of Christ in Holy Communion. After Communion, and sitting once again on the faldstool before the altar, Cardinal Sapieha laid his hands on Karol, kneeling before him, while praying, "Receive the Holy Spirit: whose sins thou shalt forgive, they are forgiven them; and whose sins thou shalt retain, they are retained." Unfolding the back half of the chasuble down Karol's back, he then prayed, "The Lord clothe thee with the robe of innocence," and then asked Karol to promise reverence and obedience to himself, as his bishop, and to his successors. After Karol had responded, "*Promitto*" [I promise], the cardinal exchanged with him again the kiss of peace. Then the cardinal, rising with his miter and his pastoral staff, blessed Karol thrice, saying, "The blessing of God Almighty, the Father, the Son, and the Holy Spirit, descend upon you: that you may be blessed in the Priestly Order and may offer propitiatory sacrifices for the sins and offense of the people to Almighty God, to whom belongs glory and honor, world without end."

At the end of the ordination Mass, the cardinal, seated on the faldstool for the last time, addressed the newest priest of the Archdiocese of Kraków in these words: "Dearly beloved son, consider attentively the Order you have taken and the burden laid on your shoulders. Endeavor to lead a holy and godly life, and to please almighty God, that you may obtain His grace, which may He of His mercy be pleased to grant you. Having been ordained a priest, you shall say, after your first Mass, three other Masses: one of the Holy Spirit, one of the blessed Mary ever-virgin, and a third for the faithful departed. And pray also to almighty God for me." The cardinal concluded the rite by reciting the prologue to John's Gospel, ending, "And the Word was made flesh and dwelt among us; and we saw His glory, the glory as it were of the Only-Begotten of the Father, full of grace and truth."

Karol answered, "Amen."[149]

November 2 in the Roman Catholic liturgical calendar is the solemn feast of All Souls, the Church's most intense day of prayer for the dead. Priests are permitted to say Mass three times on All Souls' Day, so Father Karol Wojtyła had not one, but three, "first Masses" on the day after his ordination. He celebrated them in the Romanesque crypt of St. Leonard in Wawel Cathedral. This small crypt-chapel near the royal tombs is one of the oldest and most hallowed parts of the cathedral, dating to the turn of the eleventh century. The newly ordained priest chose it for his first Masses "to express my special spiritual bond with the history of Poland," and to pay tribute to the deceased kings and queens, the bishops, cardinals, and poets, all buried nearby, "who were extremely influential in my education as a Christian and a patriot."[150]

In the presence of a few friends and the mortal remains of King Jan III Sobieski, King Michał Korybut Wiśnowiecki, Prince Józef Poniatowski, and Tadeusz Kościuszko, and wearing the black vestments prescribed for the day, Father Wojtyła offered three Masses for the repose of the souls of his mother, his brother, and his father. The master of ceremonies (the "manuductor," or "guider of hands," as he was called in those days) was his old priest-hero, Father Figlewicz, who led him through the ritual. The altar server was his friend Mieczysław Maliński, who also represented Jan Tyranowski, confined to the hospital in the ninth month of the illness that would take his life the following year; Father Wojtyła was the first of ten priests formed in the tailor-mystic's Living Rosary. The only relative present was Maria Wiadrowska, Emilia's elder sister and the ordinand's godmother. There was no way to print the traditional ordination cards distributed to friends and family. On each holy card Father Karol Wojtyła wrote by hand, *Fecit mihi magna . . . Kraków Nov. 1, 1946*—"He has done great things for me," a verse from Mary's Magnificat (*Luke* 1.46–55).[151]

In the hectic days that followed, Father Wojtyła celebrated Mass at St. Stanisław Kostka in Dębniki and at his home parish in Wadowice. At the Confession of St. Stanisław in the nave of Wawel Cathedral he said Mass for his friends and colleagues in the Rhapsodic Theater and for some of the surviving members of UNIA, whose leadership was under intense pressure from the new communist authorities. Then, on November 11, he baptized his first child: Monika Katarzyna Kwiatkowska, the infant daughter of his friends Halina Królickiewicz and Tadeusz Kwiatkowski. He also found time to attend a Rhapsodic Theater production, but couldn't make an anniversary gathering of his old troupe. His letter of apology to Mieczysław Kotlarczyk was a window into the new ordinand's conception of the priesthood: "Maybe it's God's design that I can't come to this anniversary meeting. That's how I understand it—I should be present in your activity, just as a priest should be present in life in general, should be a hidden driving force. Yes, despite all appearances that is the main duty of the priesthood. Hidden forces usually produce the strongest actions. . . ."[152]

LEARNING ROME

Wojtyła and Starowieyski left Kraków on November 15 and traveled to Katowice, where they boarded a train for Paris. It was the young priest's first time outside Poland. He stared out the windows at places he had known before only from geography books: Prague, Nuremberg, Strasbourg, and finally Paris itself, where the two Poles were guests of the Polish Seminary on Rue des Irlandais. They left almost immediately for Rome on another train, arriving toward the end of November. For several weeks they stayed with the Pallottine priests on Via Pettinari, while arrangements were being completed for their permanent residence at the Belgian College, where the Prince Cardinal wanted them to live. On their first Sunday in Rome, they went to St. Peter's, where Pius XII, carried into the vast basilica on a portable throne, the *sedia gestatoria*, was completing a beatification ceremony.[153]

The rector of the restored Kraków seminary, Father Karol Kozłowski, had told the young priest that it was as important to "learn Rome itself" as to study, and Wojtyła took his advice. Life in Rome could be short on creature comforts in the aftermath of the war, but the city, in those days, was tailor-made for tourists. Today's endless traffic jams were unknown and one could walk or bike everywhere with ease.[154] After getting settled at the Belgian College, Wojtyła explored the catacombs, churches, cemeteries, museums, and parks of the capital of Christendom with fellow students who knew both the sites and their history.[155]

The Belgian College where Wojtyła lived for two years was an intellectually lively environment, full of arguments about the *nouvelle theologie*, the "new theology" associated with the Dominicans Marie-Dominique Chenu and Yves Congar and the Jesuits Jean Danielou and Henri de Lubac, which would later play a significant role in the Second Vatican Council. There were also debates about the worker-priest experiments being conducted in France and Belgium. The cardinal archbishop of Paris, Emmanuel Suhard, had just described his country as mission territory, and pastoral experimentation was in the wind. Wojtyła would meet and talk at the college with Father Jozef Cardijn, founder of the Young Christian Workers movement in Belgium, an attempt to evangelize the workplace that had been launched in the 1920s.[156] Wojtyła's rector was Father Maximilian De Fürstenberg, who, like Cardijn, would later be named a cardinal by Pope Paul VI.

The college was small, with twenty-two resident student-priests and seminarians, among them five Americans. In this polyglot environment Wojtyła could improve his French and practice the German he had learned at home, while beginning to study Italian and English. The good company was a useful distraction from the physical difficulties of life. The college was then located in a handsome four-story building with garden, but its interior left a lot to be desired. It was freezing cold in the winter, blazing hot in summer, and each student's room had only a desk, chair, bed, and sink. Showers were not installed until 1947. The first indoor bathrooms had been put in by the British army at the end of the war. The food, a fellow resident recalls, "was very poor and not so tasty."[157]

The location on the Quirinale was perfect, though. It was a brief walk to the Angelicum, and en route to class Wojtyła often visited the church of Sant'Andrea del Quirinale, which housed the relics of St. Stanisław Kostka, the sixteenth-century Jesuit novice and patron saint of Polish youth for whom his Dębniki parish had been named. Wojtyła was struck by the number of German seminarians in their bold red cassocks who prayed at the tomb of the Polish saint: "At the heart of Christendom, and in the light of the saints, people from different nations would come together, as if to foreshadow, beyond the tragic war which had left such a deep mark on us, a world no longer divided."[158] While getting his first taste of the internationality of the Church, he stayed in touch with his roots, reading the Gospels in Polish every day and often reciting St. John's account aloud, as if it were a rhythmic poem.[159]

During academic breaks, Wojtyła traveled through Italy with colleagues from the Belgian College or with Stanisław Starowieyski. They visited San Giovanni Rotondo in the south during the 1947 Easter vacation and went to confession to the famous Capuchin stigmatic, Padre Pio, who was "a very simple confessor, clear and brief." The greatest impression Padre Pio left on the young priest was at Mass, during which the stigmatic, as the Pope later recalled, "physically suffered."[160] Naples, Capri, Monte Cassino, Assisi, and Subiaco, birthplace of the Benedictine Order and thus of Western monasticism, were other destinations. Later, when they visited Paris, Wojtyła stunned Starowieyski by observing that the overcrowded Paris Metro was a "superb" place for contemplation.[161]

During the summer of 1947, Starowieyski and Wojtyła traveled around Europe with funds provided by Cardinal Sapieha. They met Parisian worker-priests in the French capital and discussed their efforts to evangelize the post-Christian French proletariat—an experience that Wojtyła later remembered as "enormously important," and the occasion for his first article in *Tygodnik Powszechny*, some time later.[162] The two young Poles spent ten days in the Netherlands, admiring "the vigor of the Church . . . its active organizations and lively ecclesial communities."[163] Most of the vacation was in Belgium, where Wojtyła took charge of a mission to Polish Catholic miners near Charleroi for a month. In addition to saying Mass, hearing confessions, and conducting catechism classes, he visited the mines and the miners' families, whose welcome reminded him of his days in the quarry at Zakrzówek and the Solvay chemical plant.[164]

They started back to Rome in late October 1947 and stopped at Ars, home of St. John Mary Vianney, the legendary nineteenth-century *curé*. Ordained despite his deficiencies as a Latinist and a scholar, the Curé of Ars became the most sought-after confessor of his era, spending up to eighteen hours a day in the confessional counseling souls who came to him from all over France. Convinced that the sacrament of penance was an indispensable part of the drama of a Christian life, Karol Wojtyła came away from Ars determined that, in his priesthood, he, too, would make himself a "prisoner of the confessional."[165] It was a conviction strengthened by his observations on the growing gap between the Europe of gothic cathedrals through which he was traveling and the rapidly de-Christianizing Europe that was emerging, either freely or by communist fiat, in the aftermath of the war. The gap, he was convinced, could only be filled by a much more pastorally and evangelically engaged laity.[166]

One such layman lay gravely ill in Poland. Jan Tyranowski had spent exactly one year in the hospital, suffering from what was first diagnosed as tuberculosis, then as a generalized infection, and what may in fact have been a widespread cancer. He had lost an arm to amputation, and he had been unable to attend his mother's funeral. Living Rosary members divided up visiting time, and a priest saw him every day. He took his illness without complaint, spent much of his time consoling others, and in his last hours asked the forgiveness of all whom he might have somehow offended. By all accounts his death, in March 1947, was exemplary: he died smiling at his friends and holding a crucifix to his breast.[167] Distance, budgets, and Karol's responsibilities in Rome made it impossible for his disciple, who was even then pursuing the Carmelite studies to which the tailor-mystic had first introduced him, to come home to Poland for the funeral.

Back in Rome, Father Karol Wojtła's primary task was to complete his doctoral dissertation. He had passed the licentiate (master's) exam in theology in July 1947, with forty marks out of a possible forty. The dissertation, which he had begun sketching in Kraków under the tutelage of Father Różycki, was the final requirement for his doctoral degree.

Father Wojtyła prepared his doctorate during a time of considerable ferment in Catholic intellectual circles. In many European seminaries and graduate schools, efforts were under way to put the Church's classic philosophy and theology, drawn from St. Thomas Aquinas, into dialogue with modern currents of thought. By contrast, the Dominican-led Angelicum, where Wojtyła studied, had positioned itself as the defender of a rigorous neo-scholasticism, a form of Thomism that had been developed from the mid-nineteenth through the early twentieth centuries as an alternative to modern philosophical methods. The intellectual climate at the Angelicum was certainly less adventurous than at other European centers. But if its professors were not so speculative as others, they gave their students a solid foundation in the basics of the Church's theology. Angelicum graduates like Karol Wojtyła, who would later carry out original and creative philosophical and theological work, did so on the basis of having mastered the fundamentals of theology. They knew the tradition they would later engage critically and try to develop. That knowledge was a useful barrier against the temptation to criticize before they had understood.[168]

The leading figure on the Angelicum faculty during Wojtyła's doctoral studies was Father Reginald Garrigou-Lagrange, OP, the undisputed master of traditional neo-scholasticism. After Wojtyła had completed his work and returned to Poland, Garrigou would become embroiled in the fierce theological controversies of the late 1940s, which ultimately led to Pius XII's 1950 encyclical *Humani Generis* and its sharp criticism of some of the exploratory theologies of the time. The temptation to read Garrigou's entire career through the prism of this bitter controversy should be resisted, though. Father Garrigou-Lagrange was a strict traditionalist in his philosophy and his dogmatic theology, but he was also intensely interested in the mystical tradition, and particularly in St. John of the Cross. Deeply concerned about the Church's situation after the war, he tried to develop a new priestly spirituality for a post-Christian Europe, bringing the mystical tradition to life in the world. In this respect, at least, Garrigou was something of a reformer. Moreover, Garrigou's intellectual combativeness was not always mirrored in his personality. His students respected his encyclopedic knowledge. Unlike others in the professoriat, he was accessible to students, who were eager to get into his Saturday afternoon seminar on spirituality. Some of the young priest-students took him for their confessor, perhaps the highest compliment that one priest can pay another.

Father Garrigou-Lagrange became the director of Karol Wojtyła's doctoral thesis, which examined St. John of the Cross's understanding of faith. The Carmelite mystic was the obvious first bond between the venerable French Dominican and the young Polish priest. Wojtyła would also have been attracted to Garrigou's work on priestly spirituality, with its emphasis on contemplation in the world. Garrigou and Wojtyła thought about St. John of the Cross differently, however. For Wojtyła, as for Jan Tyranowski, the Spanish Carmelite's writings mapped the terrain of mystical experience. For Garrigou, John of the Cross was a speculative theologian whose doctrine of faith had to be reconciled with the Church's theology as articulated by Thomas Aquinas.[169] The creative tension between these two approaches was evident in Wojtyła's dissertation, written in Latin and titled *Doctrina de fide apud S. Ioannem a Cruce* [The Doctrine of Faith According to St. John of the Cross].[170]

In his dissertation, Wojtyła emphasized the personal nature of the human encounter with God, in which believers transcend the boundaries of their creaturely existence in such a way that they become more truly and completely themselves. This encounter with the living God is not for mystics only. It is the center of every Christian life. The mystical experience reveals important things about the road to God and about the nature of our communion with God. It teaches us, for example, that the highest wisdom we can achieve is to know that we cannot "objectivize" our knowledge of God, for we do not come to know God as we come to know an object (a tree, a baseball, an automobile). Rather, we come to know God as we come to know another person, through mutual self-giving. As two persons in love come to live "within" each other without losing their own unique identities, God comes to live within us, and we come to dwell, in a sense, "within God," without the radical difference between Creator and creature being lost. This is how Wojtyła interprets St. John of the Cross's dramatic teaching that the goal of the Christian life is to become *Dios par participación*: "God by participation."[171]

Wojtyła's dissertation drew three other conclusions. First, because God cannot be known the way we know an object, there are limits to rationality as an approach to the mystery of God. Reason can know that God exists, but natural reason cannot tell us all the attributes of the God of the Bible. Second, faith is a personal encounter with God. Faith does not allow us to "grasp" who God is intellectually, for that would mean that faith enjoys a position superior to God. Rather, the encounter with God in faith teaches us that this "non-objectifiability" of God is a dimension of God-in-himself. It is the reason we can speak of God as "person" and of a personal encounter with God. Third, Wojtyła concludes that mystical communion, rather than an emotional "high," is an experience of communion, of "being-with," which utterly transcends the conventions of our creaturely existence.[172]

Wojtyła's dissertation also reinforced his convictions about the inalienable dignity of the human person. Given the intensely personal nature of the encounter with God, the human person must enjoy freedom, for an authentic relationship of mutual self-giving can only be entered freely. The certainty that emerges from that relationship is not the kind achieved by completing an algebraic equation. It is the certainty that emerges from the human heart, which can be given intellectual expression but which, ultimately, has its distinctive language of prayer and praise. But it is certainty, nonetheless.[173]

Mysticism, the interior dialogue with a personal yet ineffable God, is not something peripheral to the human condition. It is central to knowing the human person, and the tensions built into the human encounter with the infinite are the key to the drama of human life. We cannot really know others unless we know them as persons called to communion with God. God is part of understanding the human person, and whoever takes God away from human beings is taking away what is deepest and most truly human in us. In drawing these conclusions, Karol Wojtyła, while thinking theologically, defined the line of battle on which, for forty years, he would contest with communism for the soul of Poland.

In his review of the dissertation, Garrigou criticized Wojtyła for not using the phrase "divine object" of God. One assumes that this was an issue between dissertation director and student during the preparation of the dissertation and that Garrigou did not persuade Wojtyła of his point. Whatever the process involved, the fact remains that, in his insistence on not treating God as a divine "object," even by way of analogy, Wojtyła was moving beyond the vocabulary, formulas, and intellectual categories that dominated the Angelicum during his two years there. The Thomism he had learned in Kraków and at the Angelicum—and its core philosophical conviction that the human mind could grasp the truth of things through a disciplined reflection on the world—had given him an intellectual foundation. But it was precisely that, a foundation. And foundations were meant to be built upon.

LESSONS

On June 14, 1948, Father Karol Wojtyła passed his doctoral examinations with high marks and his thesis was given eighteen marks out of a possible twenty by the examiners. His oral defense of the dissertation received the highest grade possible, fifty marks out of fifty. Despite these achievements Father Wojtyła did not receive the doctoral degree from the Angelicum, whose rules required that the dissertation be published before the degree could actually be conferred. The young Polish priest couldn't pay for the printing, so on his return to Poland he resubmitted the dissertation to the Faculty of Theology of the Jagiellonian University, which, after appropriate review, conferred on him the degree of doctor of theology in December 1948.[174]

Leaving the Angelicum in the summer of 1948 and returning to Poland marked the end of Karol Wojtyła's preparation for the life for which he believed he had been chosen.[175]

Events had chiseled him into an early maturity. Having come relatively late to his vocational decision after anticipating living his Christian life as a layman, he was a priest intimately familiar with the lives of ordinary people. He was a Polish patriot, but like his father before him, he was untouched by xenophobia. He knew the special cultural and intellectual connection between his country and the universal Church, even as he thought that his hard-pressed country might have something to offer the West that had betrayed it twice in six years. He had learned totalitarianism from inside. As he later said, "I participated in the great experience of my contemporaries—humiliation at the hands of evil."[176] Yet he had found a path beyond humiliation and bitterness. It had led him to the altar, where he had pledged to spend himself in service to his people.

He was, his seminary confessor remembered, a man "who loved easily."[177] That capacity for love, and all his learning, would now be tested in the daily life of a parish priest in the Polish People's Republic.

3

"Call Me *Wujek*"

To Be a Priest

JUNE 15, 1948	Father Karol Wojtyła returns to Poland from graduate studies in Rome.
JULY 28, 1948	Wojtyła arrives in Niegowić, his first parish assignment.
DECEMBER 26, 1948	Jagiellonian University Faculty of Theology confers the doctoral degree on Wojtyła.
MARCH 6, 1949	Karol Wojtyła publishes his first essay, on the French worker-priest movement, in *Tygodnik Powszechny*.
MARCH 17, 1949	Father Wojtyła is assigned to St. Florian's parish in Kraków to begin a student chaplaincy.
WINTER 1949–1950	Wojtyła organizes courses for engaged couples and completes his play, *Our God's Brother*.
MAY 7, 1950	Wojtyła's poem-cycle, "Song of the Brightness of Water," published pseudonymously in *Tygodnik Powszechny*.
FEBRUARY 2, 1951	*Rodzinka*, Father Wojtyła's "little family" of students, begins to form.
MAY 4, 1951	Wojtyła's "little choir" of university students sings the Gregorian "Missa de Angelis" for the first time.
APRIL 1952	Father Karol Wojtyła is dubbed *Wujek*, "Uncle," by his young friends.
AUGUST–SEPTEMBER 1953	Father Wojtyła's *Środowisko* ["milieu"] takes its first mountain trek and its first kayaking trip.
NOVEMBER 1957	Wojtyła's poem-cycle, "The Quarry," published pseudonymously in *Znak*.
MARCH 23, 1958	Wojtyła's poem-cycle, "Profiles of a Cyrenean," published pseudonymously in *Tygodnik Powszechny*.
DECEMBER 1960	Wojtyła's play, *The Jeweler's Shop*, published pseudonymously in *Znak*.

The Sisters of Nazareth in charge of the Catholic women's dormitory on Kraków's Warszawska Street always locked their building overnight. At 10 P.M. on Easter Saturday, 1952, an accommodating nun opened the door and let five university students—Danuta Skrabianka, Ola Kobak, Danuta Motowska, Wanda Szczpak, and Elśbieta Yacuńska—out onto the dark street. Their friend, Teresa Skawinska, had invited them to Zakopane, in the Tatra Mountains south of Kraków, to see the fields of wild crocuses then in bloom—a Technicolor respite from the gray drabness of urban life in Stalinist Poland.

The plan was to walk quietly across town to the train station, where they would meet several young men, students at the Kraków Polytechnic, whom the girls had met at church activities. Together with a university chaplain, they would take the overnight train to Zakopane, enjoy a day in the crocus fields, and return to Kraków on the Sunday night train, in time for Monday's classes. When they got to the station, though, the boys were nowhere in sight. The only person on the platform was a stranger they didn't recognize until he came closer. It was the priest, their chaplain, dressed in battered old clothes, as they'd never seen him before. One of the Polytechnic students finally ran up and said that the boys weren't going to be able to make it. An exam had been moved up and they had to stay home to study.

The girls now had a serious problem. The dorm was locked so they couldn't go home. And a priest on a train trip with five unmarried young women was clearly impossible. Beyond questions of propriety, the communist regime strictly forbade priests to work with groups of young people. When the train arrived, the chaplain simply said, "Let's get in."

It was a quiet trip to Zakopane. The train was crowded. To talk to a priest without a cassock and call him "Father" would raise a lot of eyebrows—or the suspicions of whatever state security types might be ferreting about. On arriving at the mountain resort, they went to Mass in a small chapel and then walked to Teresa Skawinska's home, where her father, an artist, took them out to see the crocuses.

The flowers were as beautiful as they had hoped, but Danuta Skrabianka wondered how they could talk to their chaplain on the trip home without giving him away or compromising him. Gathering her nerve, she explained her concerns and asked him, shyly, whether they could call him by a fictional family name. The chaplain didn't hesitate. Quoting the most famous line in Henryk Sienkiewicz's trilogy, Father Karol Wojtyła answered the worried college girl: "Call me 'Uncle.'"[1]

HARD TIMES

Karol Wojtyła began his pastoral work as a priest in historical circumstances unprecedented for even so ancient a diocese as Kraków. Nothing that the See of St. Stanisław had ever experienced was quite like the Stalinist period in post-war communist Poland.

Day in and day out, the Church confronted the sneering question, first posed by Stalin at the Potsdam Conference, "How many divisions has the Pope?"[2] The communist regime was not satisfied with dominating every aspect of Poland's political and economic life. Its broader cultural agenda was to inculcate an atheistic ideology and a rereading of Poland's national history that severed the link between Polish nationalism and Polish Catholicism.

During his time in Rome, Father Wojtyła had missed the most chaotic months of the communist accession to power in Poland, which followed hard on the heels of the Red Army's advance in the endgame of World War II. While the political engineers imposed the new Soviet order (by, among other tactics, torturing and murdering thousands of Polish patriots falsely accused of collaboration with the Nazis), the Polish people had to rebuild the country from the ground up. Kraków excepted, every city was in ruins. The rubble had to be cleared away; tens of thousands of corpses buried; the buildings rebuilt; electricity, water, and sewage reestablished; streets repaved. An immense population transfer took place, as a million and a half Poles from that part of prewar Poland now within the boundaries of the USSR were moved to the "Recovered Territories" in the west, from which the German population was largely expelled. Another 2.2 million Poles flooded back into the country from Third Reich labor and concentration camps. An anti-Semitic pogrom took place in Kielce in 1946, likely instigated by the communists. Meanwhile, a two-year-long civil war raged in the woods and mountains as various resistance movements refused to surrender to the new Soviet-controlled regime. World War II didn't really end in Poland until mid-1947 or thereabouts.[3] Shortly afterward, a classic Stalin-era "election" was stage-managed to demonstrate the new regime's alleged popular support.[4]

By July 1948, when Wojtyła was back in Kraków awaiting a parish assignment, a certain stability—of a Stalinist sort—had set in to Polish life. The twenty-eight-year-old priest had come back to a place "where the dawn knock on the door was still expected, where prisons were full and beatings many, where the secret policeman was still his brother's keeper, and where the Great Teacher was neither Christ nor Buddha but the megalomaniac son of a Georgian shoemaker through whom millions had died."[5] This was the world in which Father Karol Wojtyła began his ministry.

It was a world in which the Church's resistance would be led for more than thirty years by the former underground chaplain code-named "Sister Cecilia," Stefan Wyszyński. Father Wyszyński had returned to the seminary in Włocławek in 1945, hoping to pick up the threads of his teaching career, but the Holy See had other plans. In March 1946, Pope Pius XII named Wyszyński the bishop of Lublin. He left the Włocławek seminary on the same day that five of his priest-colleagues returned from Dachau, and was consecrated bishop at the Jasna Góra monastery in Częstochowa on May 12, 1946. His time in Lublin was brief. Just over two years later, on November 12, 1948, Pius XII named Bishop Wyszyński, age forty-seven, archbishop of Gniezno and Warsaw and Primate of Poland.

The new Primate brought a carefully thought-out view of the Church's current situation to his responsibilities. During World War II, he believed, the Polish Church had proven that it knew how to suffer and die. Its task, now, was to show that it knew how to live. The unprecedented shock the Church had suffered during the Occupation meant that it could not withstand a direct confrontation with the new communist regime. Conflict was inevitable, but it had to be managed subtly and in the firm conviction that the Church, not the Party, was the true guardian of Poland's identity. His first tasks, Wyszyński believed, were the full restoration of the Church's pastoral ministry and the spiritual renewal of the country as a whole, which he identified with a deepening of Poland's traditional Marian piety. Wyszyński was dubious as to whether intellectuals, particularly Polish intellectuals influenced by western European currents of thought, could contribute to this process of ecclesiastical renewal. But for all his suspicions of those who lived in a world of abstractions, Wyszyński, a longtime student and exponent of Catholic social doctrine, was himself a social and economic reformer. He was also a Polish patriot and a close student of history whose primary political goal was to prevent the absorption of his country by its gigantic neighbor to the east.

Polish Catholicism in the late 1940s could look back on almost a thousand years of national and ecclesiastical history. The Church knew the transient nature of political regimes. It was also beginning to suspect that its position had been strengthened by its mortal enemies, Hitler and Stalin. The sacrifices and heroism of its clergy during the Nazi Occupation had given the Church immense moral credibility. Stalin, by "moving" Poland westward on the European map, had created the most Polish and Catholic Poland in national history. In the first years of Poland's communist regime, the Church and its leaders came to understand that the Church's immediate tasks were to survive and to revitalize itself, mounting a resistance whenever the communist authorities encroached on nonnegotiable issues of Church identity or ministry. A frontal challenge to the regime would have to wait until later.

All of which, it seemed to Father Karol Wojtyła, required a new pattern of relations between Poland's Catholic clergy and the Polish laity. Poland's priests bore a special responsibility for the Church, but they were not the Church. To survive, to revitalize itself, and to assume an independent role in the new Poland, the Church was going to have to make clear that sanctity and vocational commitment were for everyone, not just for the clergy.[6]

COUNTRY CURATE

Father Wojtyła's first pastoral assignment in 1948 was as curate (assistant pastor, or, in the local terminology, "vicar") at the Church of the Assumption of Our Lady in Niegowić, a village in the foothills of the Carpathians, about fifteen miles east of Kraków, past the salt mine at Wieliczka. Although Cardinal

Sapieha usually sent priests returning from studies to a small parish, to immerse themselves immediately in direct pastoral work, the choice of Niegowić seems not to have been random; the pastor, Father Kazimierz Buzała, was a man in whom Cardinal Sapieha reposed much trust.[7] Perhaps the Prince Cardinal also thought that a rural diet would fatten up the newly minted doctor of theology, who had come back from Rome thinner than ever.[8]

Father Wojtyła walked into his assignment. Having gotten as far as Gdów by bus, he hitched a ride in a cart to another village, Marszowice, where the cart driver showed him a shortcut through the fields to Niegowić. It was harvest time, and the new curate "walked through the fields of grain with the crops in part already reaped, and in part still waving in the wind."[9] On reaching the parish's territory, he knelt down and kissed the ground, a gesture he had learned from his reading about the Curé of Ars. After making a visit to the Blessed Sacrament in the wooden church, Father Wojtyła went to the parish house and introduced himself to his pastor, who welcomed him with kindness and showed him to his quarters.[10]

The accommodations in Niegowić made the spartan Belgian College seem almost luxurious. There was neither electricity nor running water nor sewerage in the region. Recent floods had seriously damaged the district's roads and fields.[11] Cows and chickens wandered among the lime trees. Father Wojtyła unpacked his meager belongings, met the other assistant pastor, Father Kazimierz Ciuba, and got to work.

His primary responsibility was religious education. Traveling by horse cart to the five nearby village schools, he taught religion to elementary school–age youngsters. His parishioners remember him reading books in the cart en route to giving his lessons. The children, evidently, varied from village to village and school to school. As he later wrote, "some were well behaved and quiet, others very lively."[12] The people were friendly, and their willingness to provide his transportation during their own work hours tells something about their commitment to the religious formation of their children. That the new curate had arrived with almost nothing formed another bond with his impoverished parishioners. So did the house-to-house visits he made during the Christmas season for carol singing, tromping through the snow in his cassock and well-worn overcoat.[13]

In addition to celebrating Mass for the parish, Father Wojtyła began to hold himself to the promise made during his visit to Ars, that he would become a "prisoner of the confessional." The confessional, he told a visiting Mieczysław Maliński, was where priests encountered their people in the depths of their humanity, helping the person on the other side of the confessional screen to enter more deeply into the Christian drama of his or her own unique life. If priests stopped doing this, they'd become office managers or bureaucrats.[14] (Shortly after arriving in Niegowić the young curate was supposed to give a talk on what he had seen in France and Belgium to a group of local clergy. Father Wojtyła was late, being detained in the confessional. His priestly elders were off-put by this tardiness, thinking it bad form. They came around when Wojtyła gave a talk several cuts above the usual post-dinner clerical fare.[15])

The new curate's personal charity soon became apparent. Determined to live simply, he gave away what he thought he didn't need. When an old woman complained that she had been robbed, he gave her the pillow and comforter some parishioners had just given him, somewhat to the donors' disgruntlement.[16] As for Father Karol, he went back to sleeping on a bare bed.

The parishioners of Niegowić also discovered that their new assistant pastor was a man of no small plans. In the spring, when the parish was discussing what it might do to mark Father Buzała's fiftieth anniversary of ordination, some rather modest ideas were bruited: paint the fence around the church, tidy things up a bit, and so forth. Father Wojtyła suggested that the best possible present for the pastor would be an entirely new church, which the parishioners could raise the money for and build. Stunned at first, they finally agreed to the proposal. The brick church remains today, the first built at the suggestion of Karol Wojtyła.[17]

The young curate also took his first steps in ministry to engaged couples and newlyweds in Niegowić. During his months there he officiated at thirteen weddings and baptized forty-eight babies.[18] And if the people of Niegowić were simple, their new priest didn't treat them like simpletons. He organized a drama club and directed them in a play, *The Expected Guest*, in which he played the title role of a beggar who turns out to be Christ.[19] Faithful to the memory of Jan Tyranowski, he also organized a Living Rosary group in the parish and formed its young leaders. But this was Poland in 1948, and nothing was simple. The curate's work with the parish young people—including songfests in the fields, discussion groups, and sports—drew the attention of the local communist ferrets. When they tried to intimidate one of Father Wojtyła's youngsters, the priest told the teenager not to worry—"they'll finish themselves off."[20]

Niegowić, he thought, was a "wonderful community," but a rural post was not the kind of ministry Cardinal Sapieha had in mind for Father Wojtyła over the long haul.[21] In March 1949, eight months after his arrival, the curate of Niegowić was transferred to St. Florian's parish in Kraków, a very different kind of setting. There, Karol Wojtyła would develop a pastoral method and form a set of friendships that would endure for more than half a century.

The University Chaplain

St. Florian's Church is a five-minute stroll beyond Kraków's Old Town. One walks through the late thirteenth-century Floriańska Gate, past the 130 gun ports cut into the Barbican (the last remnant of the city's fortifications), and on through Jan Matejki Place, where the Kraków Academy of Fine Arts is located. A newcomer in 1949 would also have noticed what was left of a once-great monument to King Władysław Jagiełło's defeat of the Teutonic Knights, built in 1910 with funds provided by the pianist, composer, and patriot, Ignacy Jan Paderewski. The Nazis, offended at the thought of Germans vanquished by Slavs, had wrecked the monument during the Occupation.[22] A hundred yards or so farther on is St. Florian's. Originally built by the noble Potocki family, the large baroque church, damaged during the war, was rebuilt immediately afterward.

In 1949, the parish was one of the liveliest in the city, counting some of the town's more prosperous citizens and leading members of the Kraków Catholic intelligentsia among its parishioners. Father Wojtyła joined a parish staff that included the pastor, Monsignor Tadeusz Kurowski, and three other assistants, Fathers Czesław Obtułowicz, Józef Rozwadowski, and Marian Jaworski, who would become a close friend.

Wojtyła came to St. Florian's at a time when the communist regime was stepping up its pressure on the Church. In 1947, the communists had formed the "Pax" movement to create a bloc of putatively Catholic opinion subservient to the state. In August 1949, the government issued a decree, allegedly to safeguard freedom of religion, but in fact to tighten its control over the Church. The following year Catholic schools, Catholic Action (a movement for social reform) and other Catholic organizations were declared illegal, and the state took over hundreds of Catholic educational and charitable institutions.

In April 1950, the Church agreed to a nineteen-point modus vivendi with the regime. The accord was not received happily in Rome, where some curial diplomats feared that too much had been conceded. The modus vivendi acknowledged the supremacy of the Pope in matters of ecclesiastical jurisdiction, like the naming of bishops, and permitted public worship, like pilgrimages, outside church buildings. Monastic orders, a constant irritant for communist governments, were also allowed. In addition, the Church was permitted to conduct religious instruction in the state schools, to maintain its chaplaincies in hospitals and prisons, to publish independent journals, and to maintain its control over the appointment of parish clergy and seminar staffs. The Catholic University of Lublin, the only such entity in the Soviet bloc, was also safeguarded. For its part, the Church agreed to urge its people to work for social reconstruction and to oppose "activities hostile to the Polish People's Republic." This modus vivendi would prove short-lived. While it lasted, it created breathing space for the Church while clarifying the ground on which the contest for the future would be engaged.[23]

That ground included the upcoming generation of Poles, and Cardinal Sapieha moved aggressively to bolster the Catholic chaplaincy at the Jagiellonian University. The student chaplaincy had traditionally been located at the St. Anne's collegiate church, a stone's throw from the Collegium Maius in Kraków's Old Town. There, Father Jan Pietraszko had proven immensely successful in attracting students and the Kraków intelligentsia—so successful, in fact, that the chaplaincy had to be expanded. To that end, the Prince Cardinal assigned Father Wojtyła to St. Florian's, where a second center of ministry to students at the Jagiellonian, the Kraków Polytechnic, the Academy of Fine Arts, and other institutions of higher education was to be created. Wojtyła, whose personal pattern of working sixteen- to eighteen-hour days was well-established, energetically took up the challenge. He soon began to attract followers, who found his "naturalness," as one put it, an attractive alternative to the regime-cowed professors at the universities and to the more clerically minded and distant Polish priests they had previously known.[24]

During his years at St. Florian's, Father Wojtyła initiated a series of intellectual, liturgical, cultural, and pastoral innovations that changed the character of student chaplaincy in the Archdiocese of Kraków while rebutting, point-for-point, the effort by Poland's Stalinist rulers to reinvent the country's history and culture.

Given the militant atheism promoted by the regime and the ideological climate inside the university, it was essential to engage students intellectually.[25] Wojtyła, who had begun visiting student dormitories and boardinghouses as soon as he arrived at St. Florian's, making contacts and drumming up trade, started a series of Thursday evening conferences on two basic issues: the existence of God and the spiritual character of the human person.[26] These conferences involved a systematic, step-by-step exploration of Christian doctrine. The point was not the rote memorization of catechism answers as ripostes to communist propaganda; it was to demonstrate that the Church, in the Gospel, had a more compelling answer to the perennial questions of human life than the purveyors of the official state ideology. Christian humanism, in other words, was quietly but unmistakably counterposed to Marxism. The texts of these lectures, written in an extremely dense prose style, were typed clandestinely, mimeographed, and circulated surreptitiously as samizdat.[27] In addition to his own lectures, Wojtyła formed a study group that read its way through the *Summa Theologiae* of St. Thomas Aquinas in the original Latin.[28]

The new chaplain's sermons also began to attract the attention of both students and Kraków intellectuals. Jacek Woźniakowski, the distinguished art historian who was then trying to complete his doctoral degree in art history against communist opposition, remembered Wojtyła's early sermons as a bit heavy philosophically. But the young priest's openness to criticism soon led him to a more accessible speaking style. Woźniakowski found Karol Wojtyła, with whom he would work closely for many years, a very intelligent man who quickly learned new ways of doing things from what was demanded of him.[29] The Countess Potocka, whose family had helped pay for St. Florian's, was another friendly critic. She informed the young chaplain that she wanted to be challenged, confronted, and criticized in sermons; Father Wojtyła followed suit.[30]

Maria Swieżawska, wife of philosopher Stefan Swieżawski and the niece of the Prince Cardinal, was sufficiently impressed by Wojtyła's preaching that she sought him out as a catechist and confessor for her two young daughters. Father Wojtyła came to the Swieżawskis' home, an unusual act for a priest of the time, to give the girls their lessons. He was "never" on time, Mrs. Swieżawska recalled, but she forgave him that because of the remarkable depth of the conferences he was giving at the parish. This was the kind of intellectually demanding Catholic education she wanted for her children, not least because of the regime propaganda that surrounded their lives. It really didn't matter that much if an 8 P.M. appointment actually began at 10:30 P.M.[31]

Jerzy Janik, who had recently completed his doctorate in physics, was another young intellectual, first attracted by Wojtyła's preaching, who became a lifelong friend. After hearing several impressive sermons, he approached Wojtyła and suggested that they get better acquainted on a ski trip. Wojtyła accepted, and soon after was launched upon what would become a half-century-long dialogue with the hard sciences—physics, chemistry, astronomy, and so forth.

After getting established at St. Florian's, Wojtyła began to make his way in intellectual circles beyond the parish and the university chaplaincy. Zofia Morstinowa, whom Jacek Woźniakowski remembered as a "frightfully outspoken, fantastic old woman," presided over a literary salon in which pungent criticism never caused personal wounds. She invited Father Wojtyła to one of her evenings. He arrived wearing a worn-out cassock and seeming a bit awkward socially. His shyness, coupled with the intelligence he displayed when discussing his experiences in France during his graduate studies, made for an attractive mix.[32]

Father Karol Wojtyła had been exposed to the liturgical renewal movement during his graduate studies and now set about implementing some of its ideas at St. Florian's. Wojtyła formed a group to discuss the writings of the Austrian theologian Pius Parsch, which explained the rich texture of the liturgy to Catholics for whom worship was sometimes difficult to connect to daily life. At a time when the Church's musical tradition of chant was generally reserved for monasteries, Wojtyła started a student choir and taught them Gregorian chant so that they could sing various parts of the Mass. He encouraged his students to use daily missals so that they could follow the Mass more intelligently, and he initiated "dialogue" Masses in which the students made the responses usually given only by the altar boys assisting the priest. Given the time and the place, this determination to involve the laity in the liturgy could only have been regarded as boldly innovative.[33]

He also put his theatrical interests into pastoral play at St. Florian's. During Lent, Father Wojtyła directed parish youngsters and university students in medieval "mystery plays," exploring biblical themes in a cycle of dramas performed at the parish. While acting as the dramatic impresario of St. Florian's (and meeting young men and women who would become lifelong friends, like Piotr Malecki and Danuta Plebańczyk), he renewed his contacts with the Rhapsodic Theater, attending performances held in a theater near the parish, participating in post-performance discussions, blessing the marriages of his old colleagues, and celebrating Mass for the Rhapsodists on the troupe's anniversaries. When the Rhapsodic Theater moved to a new home in 1950, politics made an official dedication ceremony impossible. Father Wojtyła offered a silent prayer at the unofficial dedication, as documents relating to the Rhapsodists were cemented into their new theater's foundation.[34]

Perhaps the hardest-fought battle between Church and regime involved family life, for the communists understood that men and women secure in the love of their families were a danger. Housing, work schedules, and school hours were all organized by the state to separate parents from their children as frequently as possible. Apartments were constructed to accommodate only small families, so that children would be regarded as a problem. Work was organized in four shifts and families were rarely together. The workday began at 6 or 7 A.M., so children had to be consigned to state-run child-care centers before school. The schools themselves were consolidated, and children were moved out of their local communities for schooling. A permissive law was passed that regarded abortion as a means of birth control.

Whenever they could, Father Wojtyła and his fellow priests at St. Florian's used the ordinary structures of parish life to combat this assault. Meetings with the parish altar boys, for example, were always held with the parents. Families thus spent time together and could receive religious instruction without the regime claiming that this was an unauthorized Catholic youth group. Wojtyła went much further than adapting traditional structures to new circumstances, though. The regime's threat to Christian family life was unprecedented, so unprecedented pastoral initiatives were required.

In 1950, he launched at St. Florian's the first marriage-preparation program in the history of the Archdiocese of Kraków. In those days, a Catholic couple's only encounter with a priest prior to their wedding might have been to complete the appropriate legal forms and discuss the ceremony itself. Wojtyła set out to create a pastoral program that systematically prepared young couples for Christian marriage and family life through religious reflection, theological education, and a frank exploration of the practical and personal difficulties and opportunities of married life and child rearing. In 1951, when the Prince Cardinal added a chaplaincy to the city's health-care workers to his pastoral portfolio, Wojtyła invited lay associates, doctors and nurses, to help lead the program—a commonplace today that was a bold pastoral stroke in its time.

In working with his young couples, Father Wojtyła didn't shy away from certain topics as unbefitting a priest's attention. In a retreat for students a few years after beginning the marriage preparation program, he would tell them, "The sexual drive is a gift from God. Man may offer this drive to God exclusively through a vow of virginity. He may offer it to another human being with the knowledge that he is offering it to a *person*. It cannot be an act of chance. On the other side there is also a human being who must not be hurt, whom one must love. Only a person can love a person. To love means wishing the other's welfare, to offer oneself for the good of the other. When, as a result of giving oneself for the good of another, a new life comes into being, this must be a giving arising out of love. In this area one must not separate love from desire. If we respect desire within love, we will not violate love . . ."[35]

In twenty-eight months at St. Florian's, Father Karol Wojtyła blessed 160 marriages, an average of more than one each week. His intense conversations with engaged couples left a lasting imprint. He came to believe that "young people are always searching for the beauty in love." They might fall short of the mark, but "in the depths of their hearts they still desire a beautiful and pure love." The university chaplain, in his days at St. Florian's, "learned to love human love," he wrote forty years later.[36]

The most long-lasting impact of the St. Florian's experience on Karol Wojtyła, though, is to be found in the deep personal, spiritual, and intellectual friendships he formed during this period with young laypeople, friendships that have lasted, in some cases, for more than fifty years. These relationships are the clearest window into his style of priestly ministry.

ŚRODOWISKO

Previous popes, talking about their formative years as young priests, would have reminisced about their years at the Accademia, the highly selective Roman school for the Church's diplomats, or their first experiences as seminary professors. In virtually any discussion of his early priesthood, John Paul II will stress the importance of "my *Środowisko*." It is a telling difference.

Środowisko, a term first suggested by Wojtyła himself in the 1960s, is now used as a self-description by a group of some 200 men and women, many of them married couples with grandchildren, which first began to take shape during Wojtyła's university chaplaincy at St. Florian's.[37] *Środowisko* does not translate easily. "Environment" is one possibility, but John Paul II prefers the more humanistic "milieu." In any case, what would later come to be known as *Środowisko* involved the fusing of several networks of young adults and young married couples with whom Father Wojtyła worked. The earliest of these called itself *Rodzinka*, or "little family." A later group of Wojtyła youngsters called themselves *Paczka*, "packet" or "parcel."[38] *Środowisko* saw youth groups evolve into networks of intellectual conversation. Both youngsters and intellectuals got involved in vacation excursions. The word itself may be hard to translate, but that this network of friendships was crucial in shaping the ideas and the ministry of Karol Wojtyła the priest, the bishop, and, ultimately, the pope, is indisputable.

Rodzinka, the "little family" that became the first component of Wojtyła's *Środowisko*, began on the evening of February 2, 1951. It was Candlemas, the feast of the Presentation of the Child Jesus in the Temple, and, by Polish custom, the last day to sing Christmas carols. Danuta Skrabianka, a literature student at the university, was living in the women's dormitory run by the Sisters of Nazareth a block or so from St. Florian's Church. She and some of her friends had previously met a "young, poorly dressed, pious priest" who turned out to be in charge of the parish's chaplaincy to students.[39] When he invited them to help form a parish choir, they agreed to talk about it. Climbing the twenty-three steep stone steps up to the choir loft of St. Florian's, they first espied a pair of bad shoes, then a worn cassock—and then the young priest, who shook hands with everyone and started them singing carols. When they had finished the Christmas anthems, the priest asked them to stay and tried to interest them in Gregorian chant. He also invited them to his 6 A.M. Mass the following Wednesday morning. They came back, and were soon joined by young men from the nearby Kraków Polytechnic, whom the young priest had also invited to join the nascent choir. In those Stalinist days, the habit of discretion was strong. The young people didn't know each other's last names, nor did they, at first, know the priest's name. They began referring to him as "*Sadok*"—a mysterious character searching for God in two novels by Władysław Grabski, *In the Shadow of the Church* and *Confessional*, who decides to become a priest in the second volume.[40]

The student choir began singing at Mass at St. Florian's, and on May 4, 1951, the parish feast day, they sang the Gregorian "Missa de Angelis" for the first time. The Wednesday morning Mass with *Sadok* became a regular feature on their schedules, as did his 8 P.M. Thursday evening conferences, so heavily philosophical in their language that the students were regularly sent scurrying to their dictionaries.[41] Still, they kept coming back. *Sadok*'s rapport with them was such that they didn't want to lose contact.[42]

After a while, this group of young people, fewer than twenty in number, began meeting in homes (where they learned each other's surnames) as well as in church. Interested in putting their convictions into action, they began visiting and seeing to the needs of the blind and the sick who had no contact with the state health system. The glue that held them together was prayer, especially liturgical prayer. Father Wojtyła gave them days of recollection, mini-retreats to mark special occasions during the year. On the feast day of the saint in whose honor they had been named (which, according to Polish custom, they celebrated instead of birthdays) he said Mass for them and attended name-day parties in their homes. Like students everywhere, they were nervous about exams. Father Wojtyła celebrated Mass with them on exam mornings and joined their post-exam parties at night. Deep friendships began to form among the students, who started calling themselves *Rodzinka*, "little family."

The charismatic Father Wojtyła continued to attract followers and *Rodzinka* expanded along family lines. Wojtyła would also suggest bringing in new people, especially youngsters he thought needed friends. The group's friendliness, and the openness that characterized their discussions, were in sharp contrast to the atmosphere at the university and the polytechnic, where no one spoke freely for fear of informers. Without their thinking very much about it, the companionship of *Rodzinka* became an alternative to the hollowness of communist society.[43] After the Easter Week 1952 trip to the crocus fields near Zakopane, Wojtyła's young people all began to call him *Wujek*, "Uncle," a kind of Stalin-era nom de guerre.

Previously, the chaplain's task had been to provide sacramental services to students. Wojtyła, who intensified the chaplaincy's sacramental ministry and involved the students in it liturgically, thought of his chaplaincy as a ministry of "accompaniment," a way to "accompany" these students in their lives.[44] The chaplain's presence couldn't be limited to the sanctuary and the confessional. A really effective chaplaincy, he believed, had to be present to these young lives in the world as well as in the church.

Rodzinka and other Wojtyła-led groups of young people were a de facto underground, a new kind of resistance movement creating islands of free space in a totalitarian sea. *Wujek's* young people didn't think of themselves as heroes or rebels, yet the freedom they had experienced with him and among their friends began to spill over into the rest of their lives. Danuta Skrabianka wasn't allowed to study for her master's degree because she had lived in a dormitory run by nuns. When the authorities seized the dormitory and tried to expel the nuns, Danuta and a friend, encouraged by Wojtyła, went to Warsaw to ask that the sisters not be expelled, even though their bachelor's degrees could have been withheld as a result. And when Stanisław Rybicki, another student, wasn't permitted to make further engineering studies because of his Catholicism, he came to Wojtyła, who told him, "You know, if someone likes science, the science will come to him."[45] As yet another member of *Środowisko* put it, "We could live more freely because we were free inside."[46]

Assigned to complete a second doctorate in the fall of 1951, Wojtyła moved from the parish house at St. Florian's to a church residence at Kanonicza, 21, in Kraków's Old Town. The networks that eventually became his *Środowisko* continued to expand. Many of the old members of *Rodzinka* accompanied him to St. Catherine's Church in Kazimierz for the 6 A.M. Mass he celebrated there daily after his move to Kanonicza Street. The St. Florian's link wasn't entirely broken. *Wujek* said a Mass for students there on the first Friday of every month, preached an annual student retreat in the fourth week of Lent each year, and took *Rodzinka* or his "little choir" of Gregorian singers on excursions into the countryside.

As the young people *Wujek* first met at St. Florian's graduated from university and began their professional lives, the intellectual conversation within the Wojtyła network intensified. A physicists' group formed around Jerzy Janik and provided Wojtyła a way to stay in touch with the world of hard science. For his part, the physicist was fascinated by Wojtyła's explanation of a "way of thinking" he had never encountered before—philosophy, and especially metaphysics, "in which one could speak coherently and in a connected way about everything," from the ski poles they were carrying to God.[47]

After their January 1953 trip and a summer vacation excursion later in the year, they decided to keep the discussion going. Janik recruited the scientists, who began to meet regularly with Wojtyła. Their first project was to read Thomas Aquinas and discuss his concept of nature against the backdrop of what they were doing in their labs and classrooms every day. Wojtyła, who had no formal scientific training, had what Janik called an "instinctive grasp of physics," and was able to "translate" the scientists' ideas into his own vocabulary of philosophy. The physicists were interested in discussing theory, but Wojtyła could also appeal to minds of a more immediately practical bent. A second discussion group, composed primarily of engineers, was initiated by Stanisław Rybicki, an early *Rodzinka* member, and a young man named Jerzy Ciesielski.

Marriage was the most important transition in these young lives, and couples within both Rodzinka and the widening circle of young friends who would become *Środowisko* soon began falling in love. Six of the young men and women who climbed into the St. Florian's choir loft and formed the core of *Rodzinka* later married. Wojtyła celebrated all their wedding Masses, after holding individual days of prayer and reflection for each couple. And he didn't hesitate to challenge when he thought that appropriate. When Teresa Mięsowicz told *Wujek* that she wanted to marry Piotr Malecki ("mystery play" veteran, Wojtyła's first altar boy at St. Florian's, and, by this time, a research physicist who called himself the "enfant terrible of *Środowisko*"), Wojtyła pressed her on the question of whether, at twenty, she wasn't too young. They talked it out, and she persuaded him.[48]

Love, for Karol Wojtyła, was the truth at the very center of the human condition, and love always meant self-giving, not self-assertion. In December 1956, he explored this in a letter to *Środowisko* member Teresa Heydel:

> Dear Teresa,
>
> People like to think that Wujek would like to see everyone married. But I think this is a false picture. The most important problem is really something else. Everyone . . . lives, above all, for love. The ability to love authentically, not great intellectual capacity, constitutes the deepest part of a personality. It is no accident that the greatest commandment is to love. Authentic love leads us outside ourselves to affirming others: devoting oneself to the cause of man, to people, and, above all, to God. Marriage makes sense . . . if it gives one the opportunity for such love, if it evokes the ability and necessity of such loving, if it draws one out of the shell of individualism (various kinds) and egocentrism. It is not enough simply to want to accept such love. One must know how to give it, and it's often not ready to be received. Many times it's necessary to help it to be formed. . . . Wujek[49]

A month later, Wojtyła was still thinking out loud, in another letter to Teresa Heydel, about the nature of love:

> Dear Teresa:
>
> Before I leave for Warsaw I have to tell you a few things (think together with you): 1) I don't want you ever to think this way: that life forces me to move away from the perspective of something that is better,

riper, fuller, to something that is less good, less mature, less attractive. I am convinced that life is a constant development toward that which is better, more perfect—if there is no stagnation *within* us. 2) After many experiences and a lot of thinking, I am convinced that the (objective) starting point of love is the realization that I am needed by another. The person who *objectively* needs me most is also, for me, *objectively*, the person I most need. This is a fragment of life's deep logic, and also a fragment of trusting in the Creator and in Providence. 3) People's values are different and they come in different configurations. The great achievement is always to *see* values that others don't see and to *affirm* them. The even greater achievement is to *bring out* of people the values that would perish without us. In the same way, we bring our values out in ourselves. 4) This is what I wanted to write you. Don't ever think that I want to cut short your way. I want your way. Wujek[50]

When children began to arrive, Wojtyła gave each expectant mother a day of recollection before her delivery. He baptized the babies and came to bless their homes afterward, a practice he continued as long as he lived in Kraków, whatever his responsibilities. "He always had time," Teresa Malecka recalled. "He understood that to baptize means to come home, to be with the family, to bless the baby sleeping in the bed. We didn't have to ask him to do this; he wanted to do it."[51]

Wujek taught his young couples that the sexual expression of their love within the bond of marriage was a beautiful thing, a holy thing, even an image of God. At the same time, he had a very high view of marriage, formed in conversation with "serious people, who gave themselves time to think."[52] What others might regard as heroic decisions and sacrificial commitments (e.g., in observing periodic abstinence according to the rhythm of natural family planning), he saw as logical, or simply right. As his letters to Teresa Heydel suggest, this did not make him an insensitive or authoritarian interlocutor. It did make him a challenging and demanding friend.

THE GOSPEL IN KAYAKS

Wojtyła's *Środowisko* was also noted for its outdoorsmanship, another pastoral innovation in a time and place where priests simply didn't take vacations with young adults and young married couples. *Wujek*, a veteran hiker from his youth in Wadowice, was thoroughly at home in nature. His young friends were avid skiers and kayakers. And so the pastoral method of "accompaniment" frequently took them to Poland's mountains and lakes together.

Wojtyła's ski trip with Jerzy Janik in January 1953 was the first in an annual series that continued to the end of his Kraków years. Wojtyła loved skiing, was good at it, and could be something of a daredevil. In August of that year, Stanisław Rybicki, Zdzisław Heydel, and Jerzy Ciesielski organized *Środowisko*'s first summer trek, to the Bieszczady Mountains in southeastern Poland, once the stronghold of interwar Poland's Ukrainian population, where in 1945–1947 thousands of its villagers had paid with their lives for their belief, as they put it, in "neither Hitler nor Stalin."[53] Sixteen young people participated in the trek. The newcomers were told to call Wojtyła "*Wujek*," since the regime still didn't permit priests to go out with groups of young people. They took an eight-hour train trip to Ustrzyki Dolne, in the far southeast corner of the country, where *Wujek* celebrated his first Mass "in the field" with members of *Środowisko*. The next day they hiked up to Ustrzyki Gorne, which had once been a Ukrainian sheep-grazing region. The group stayed overnight in abandoned, one-room shepherd's huts, because they didn't have good tents or sleeping bags; old blankets and rucksacks were the extent of their camping equipment. Passing some of the overgrown cemeteries and burned-out villages that bore mute witness to the bitter struggle that had taken place in the region six years before, they stayed the next night in a barn that had once been a Ukrainian church. Some wanted to skip the usual group evening prayer around a campfire and turn right in, saying their prayers lying comfortably in the straw. It was Stanisław Rybicki, not *Wujek*, who replied that "Whoever prays lying down, God hears while sleeping." Later in the trek, during a rough hike over difficult terrain, Zdzisław Heydel cracked, a bit sourly, "*Wujek*, one day when you're pope, people will get indulgences for walking this trail with you on a moonless night." For all the youthful camaraderie, though, they allowed *Wujek* his solitude when, toward the end of a day of hiking and conversation, singing and jokes, he would drift back to the end of the line of hikers for an hour or two of prayer alone.[54]

The next month, September 1953, was the first *Środowisko* kayaking trip, the beginning of an annual tradition that Wojtyła cherished and that would continue until August 1978. Kayaking together was the inspiration of Jerzy Ciesielski, an engineer of boundless energy who had first met Wojtyła at St. Florian's and with whom he soon struck up a close personal friendship. Everyone recognized, and accepted, the special bond between *Wujek* and Jurek Ciesielski. A certified instructor in skiing, kayaking, and swimming, Ciesielski, because of his infectious enthusiasm and his willingness to teach anyone anything he knew, was the kind of organizer and leader others didn't resent.[55]

The annual kayak trip was a "vacation-plus" for *Środowisko* and Wojtyła. After Ciesielski had taught him to manage a kayak, *Wujek* always had a two-person boat, and others would join him during the day for conversation or spiritual direction. Mass was celebrated using an overturned kayak as an altar, with two paddles lashed together to form the altar cross.[56] Once, in 1955, the kayakers took part in an international competition on the Dunajec River, which runs through a magnificent gorge along the Polish-Slovak border. *Wujek*'s kayak was punctured at Sromowice Nizne and sank at the finish line in Szczawnica. According to one pious report, only his breviary didn't get soaked.[57]

When the children of *Środowisko* became old enough to join the kayak trip, *Wujek* took each meal with a different family every day, working his way around the entire group. Soccer games were organized between the "married team" and the "youth team," *Wujek*, the former goalie of Wadowice, playing for whichever team was shorthanded. Around the campfire in the evening, the adults would discuss books or, years later, John XXIII's encyclical *Pacem in Terris*.

When he left St. Florian's in late 1951 to work on his philosophy doctorate, Karol Wojtyła left parish life as the term is usually understood. To his mind, though, a priest without a parish was a vocational absurdity. *Środowisko* was his nonterritorial parish. "*Wujek* was one of us," his friend Gabriel Turowski remembered, "but at the same time he was a pastor for the people who rested with him."[58]

Whether to smooth troubled clerical waters over his unconventional lay interactions, or to recruit others to the ministry of "accompaniment," Wojtyła accepted the offer of the editor of *Homo Dei* [Man of God], a Polish priests' magazine, to write an article in 1957 explaining what he and his young friends were up to in the mountains and along the rivers of Poland. But he gave his acceptance an interesting twist by inviting Jerzy Ciesielski to share the platform with him.

Wojtyła's essential point was that the priest's duty to help make God present in the world was not satisfied by his daily celebration of Mass. In addition, "the duty of a priest is to live with people, everywhere they are, to be with them in everything but sin." That was the context for looking at vacations as a pastoral opportunity. Daily Mass took on a special texture on a vacation trek: "Nature, not only human art, participates in the sacrifice of the Son of God." At Mass, a thought for the day could be proposed, then be returned to in the evening, during communal prayer. An excursion, he wrote, had to be a "well-prepared improvisation" in which the priest was ready and willing to talk about everything, "about movies, about books, about one's own work, about scientific research, and about jazz bands . . ." Was this kind of pastoral work, built around vacations with young men and women, a "compromise" of the priesthood (as some were, evidently, suggesting)? Doing it like this might not be for everybody. It certainly was a form of ministry, a way of leading others to Christ, for the man who signed himself, simply, "Priest."

The "Young Engineer" (as Ciesielski pseudonymously signed his piece) described the growth of what would later be called *Środowisko*, and suggested that, in the atheistic-secularist environment in which they found themselves, priests had a special responsibility to help those who want "consciously to create the lifestyle of a modern Catholic." These were men and women who were living busy professional, intellectual, and family lives. They knew one another through church and through meetings in the city. "But we live fully during excursions. They help us look at our problems from a different perspective." He then concluded with a moving tribute to the unnamed *Wujek*, who taught them "to look at all things in the spirit of the Gospel."[59]

In Poland as elsewhere, communism deliberately fostered the fragmentation of society and the atomization of its members, the better to maintain political control and the easier to form "new socialist man." If Jurek Ciesielski and Wojtyła's other young friends found that they were "living fully" when they were with him, it may well have been because *Wujek*'s pastoral strategy of "accompaniment" and his invitation to "look at all things in the spirit of the Gospel" was a compelling communitarian alternative to the artificially created and rigorously enforced anti-community that was being pressed on them in communist Poland.

PERMANENT OPENNESS

Two characteristics constantly recur in *Środowisko* members' descriptions of *Wujek*. The first is what Teresa Malecka describes as his "permanent openness": "We felt completely free with him, without any burden. His presence led us to express ourselves. While he was among us, we felt that everything was all right. . . . We felt that we could discuss any problem with him; we could talk about absolutely anything."[60] That openness was complemented, indeed built around, the second prominent characteristic in Wojtyła's priestly personality: "He had mastered the art of listening," as Stanisław Rybicki puts it. No matter what the subject introduced—religion, daily life, work, children—"he was always interested."[61]

Openness and a seemingly endless capacity for listening were completed by a deep respect for the freedom of others. Dr. Rybicki recalls that, while "I talked to him for hours and hours [I] never heard him say, 'I'd advise you to'. . . He'd throw light on [a problem]. But then he would always say, 'You have to decide.'"[62] He was, in a word, gently forcing judgments and choices.

Wujek's interaction with his *Środowisko* unfolded in a dialectic of intimacy and reserve. No subject was off-the-board. His friends respected him as a priest and experienced him as a priest wholly devoid of clericalism. On treks and kayaking trips, he shared in all the chores, down to lugging kayaks and burying garbage. Yet there was a reserve about him that his friends honored. He was not a "buddy," although he was a close friend, and neither he nor they pretended to a false familiarity. They all called him *Wujek*, but used the more formal form of "you" in speaking with him; he would use the more informal form of "you" after getting to know someone. Stanisław Rybicki summed up this dimension of their relationship, and Wojtyła's style, by observing, "Today, many priests try to be like the kids. We were trying to be like him."[63]

Although Wojtyła seems to have been wholly free of the intellectual's tendency to domineer, his capacity for posing the sharp-edged question made him the center of gravity of a discussion. *Środowisko* conversations were serious, but rather than discussing politics or political philosophy, they would talk about the quotidian moral dilemmas of living under a communist regime: theft from work, petty cheating on stupid bureaucratic regulations, and so forth, discussions in which his friends tended to be harder on their colleagues than he was.[64] There were arguments but rarely major disagreements.

It was not all earnest conversation about serious issues. *Wujek* had an extraordinary memory, and loved to sing songs to the end of the last verse, sometimes leaving others in the choral dust. Puns and situation-jokes were frequent.[65] His memory could be a bit disarming. Trekking along a trail, *Wujek* would recite entire poems or long sections of prose and then demand, "Who's that?" His knowledge of literature was formidable, and he did not hesitate to make critical judgments. When Danuta Rybicka was finally allowed to attend graduate school, one of her professors, Kazimierz Wyka, a pro-regime Catholic, once said that Wojciech Żukrowski, author of *Stone Tablets*, was a "Catholic author," a comment Mrs. Rybicka reported to then-Bishop Wojtyła. "No, he's a writer who's a Catholic," *Wujek* replied. Professors were not to be challenged in class, but the intrepid Mrs. Rybicka brought it up, at which point Professor Wyka asked, "Where'd you get that?" "From Bishop Wojtyła," she replied. "That's okay, then," said the professor, "he knows literature and faith."[66]

Wojtyła's pastoral strategy of "accompaniment" was an attempt to get beyond the pattern of sporadic encounters between priests and young people that frequently resulted in the priest being suspected of prying into the crevices of conscience. "Accompaniment" was a way of "walking with" young adults, of helping them unveil their humanity by living through their problems with them. As a colleague would later put it, Wojtyła "tried to accompany someone else in their problems; he was open to revealing the humanity of another."[67]

In Wojtyła's view, this was the way a priest lived out his vocation to be an *alter Christus*, "another Christ." It was also another expression of his commitment to the spirituality of the Cross. God himself had accompanied human beings into the most extreme situation resulting from bad human choices—death—through his own divine choice to be redeemer as well as creator. That is what happened on the cross of Christ.[68] The cross was the final justification for a pastoral strategy of accompaniment.

Father Karol Wojtyła's distinctive priestly "style" came into sharpest focus in the confessional. Private confession to a priest is a difficult aspect of Catholic sacramental practice for the non-Catholic to understand. Other Christians will ask why personal confession to the living, risen Christ is insufficient. Nonbelievers wonder whether it is seemly to unburden oneself of one's most intimate secrets to someone who might be a virtual stranger. Like other Catholics, Karol Wojtyła believed that confession (the sacrament of penance, or, as it is now known, the sacrament of reconciliation) had been mandated by Christ himself (see *John* 20.19–22). To be a confessor was, in his mind, another way of accompanying the drama of another life.

He was, by the testimony of his penitents, a "fantastic confessor."[69] Confession with Father Wojtyła could last as long as an hour, sometimes even longer. Each confession was an exchange of ideas between two individuals, "not the mass production of Christians."[70] The individuality that Wojtyła fostered in the confessional was another reflection of his "openness to individual paths," his capacity to "enter into others' experiences."[71] Ultimately though, there was no ducking the responsibility of making a decision. "He didn't impose," one penitent recalled, "but he did demand"—that decisions be made as wisely as possible. He believed his penitents and friends had it within themselves to know the truth and live it.[72]

The goal of confession, Wojtyła believed, was not psychic relief from stress or inappropriate guilt, although that could be a helpful by-product. The goal was the sanctification of all of life, which could not be divided neatly into containers labeled "religious" and "other." Moreover, the sanctification received through the regular practice of confession and a lengthy, conversational review of one's life in all its dimensions would lead to vocational clarity. The penitent would come to know what he or she ought to do, as well as who he or she was. A career was not the purpose of life. Life was *vocational*, and one of the confessor's privileges was to help a penitent discern the vocation to which God had called him or her.[73] As he once told Danuta Rybicka, whether one lived in a convent, in marriage, or as a single person in the world, "You have to live for a concrete purpose."[74]

Karol Wojtyła's style as a confessor was another example of his creativity as a minister of the Gospel. The theological manuals from which he had been trained had a highly juridical view of the sacrament of penance. Though the sacrament was, fundamentally, a sacrament of God's mercy, the stress was nevertheless on the confessor as judge.

Wojtyła was, by all accounts, a demanding confessor but in a very different way. The confessor's role in the drama of the human condition was to accompany a fellow Christian and a fellow human being in order to promote the penitent's spiritual discernment. The goal was to deepen one's Christian conviction and insight, not simply to internalize a checklist of moral prohibitions. The rules were there; they were real; they were to be obeyed. But the rules were not arbitrary. They defined the drama because they illuminated the dramatic tension of life, the tension between the person-I-am and the person-I-ought-to-be. The confessor was to be a counselor in the practice of the virtues. The idea, as it happens, was classic Thomas Aquinas. It was given a distinctively contemporary expression in Karol Wojtyła, whose theology and pastoral practice was informed by his experience of the theater and his explorations in the psychological sciences.[75]

THE RICHNESS OF FRIENDSHIP

Środowisko, its people, and their lives were *Wujek*'s bridge to the world where his people were actually living, and trying to do so as mature Catholics. What had begun in the quarry at Zakrzówek and the Solvay plant at Borek Fałęcki was deepened and broadened through the people of *Środowisko*: "He lived our problems," Stanisław Rybicki recalls. "He knew life from this side—the side of people who really have to work for their living."[76]

The networks that eventually became *Środowisko* came into being at the same time Wojtyła's intellectual life was accelerating through his postdoctoral studies and the teaching he began at the Catholic University of Lublin in 1954. The two experiences were mutually reinforcing. *Środowisko* was, in a sense, the empirical tether for Wojtyła's increasing skill at philosophical reflection. "We were an experimental field for his ideas," said Danuta Ciesielska. "We were growing into our lives as families and [into] our professional lives, and he learned from us. But we don't feel proud that we taught him something; it was a mutual exchange."[77]

The ideas that *Wujek* tested with his *Środowisko* are suggested by five themes from his student retreat in 1954:

- There was no dividing life up into the serious and the frivolous, the true and the unimportant. The contemporary tendency to fragment life, or to reduce the question of truth to a secondary issue, had to be resisted. "The method of the Kingdom of God is the method of truth." Because of that "man must be prepared to agree with reality in its totality."
- Christianity was not for the sacristy and the sanctuary alone, nor was it an abstraction. "The Kingdom of God proclaimed by Christ is not merely theory . . . but a call to action."
- Jesus Christ was not God pretending to be man; Jesus Christ was the incarnation of God entered fully into the drama of the human condition. "One man experienced the might of the holiness of God: Jesus Christ. He bore the weight of man's guilt and stood bearing this ballast before God. The awareness of sin on the one hand and of the holiness of God on the other drew Him to sacrifice Himself and to union with God. This explains the mystery of the garden of Gethsemane and of Golgotha. . . ."
- Love is not "fulfilling" oneself through the use of another. Love is *giving* oneself to another, for the good of the other, and receiving the other as a gift.[78]
- The lethal paradox of the age was that, for all its alleged humanism, it had ended up devaluing the human person into an economic unit, an ideological category, an expression of a class or race or ethnicity.

You are great, *Wujek* told his young people, because you are God's creation. Anyone who tries to pull you below that standard is demeaning you.[79] Asked why Father Wojtyła was so attractive to young people, Teresa Malecka answered, simply, "He is a *good* man."[80] His capacity to convince others of their capacity for goodness was a part of that magnetism.

THE NOVICE ESSAYIST

In early 1949, Jerzy Turowicz, the elfin editor of Kraków's Catholic newspaper, *Tygodnik Powszechny* [Universal Weekly], had a visitor, a young priest back from graduate studies in Rome. The priest, Father Karol Wojtyła, whom Turowicz remembered having seen perform in the clandestine Rhapsodic Theater during the war, had an article he had written on the *Mission de France* and the worker-priest movement in that country. Turowicz received him politely but noncommittally. The paper received many submissions from the local clergy and rejected more than a few of them. Turowicz had learned not to expect too much. As he read Wojtyła's manuscript, he got interested, then excited. "Mission de France" appeared on the front page of *Tygodnik Powszechny* on March 6, 1949, a prestigious debut for a novice essayist.

The Prince Cardinal, Adam Sapieha, understanding that the future of the Polish Church required Catholicism to have a strong, intelligent voice in the national culture, had begun making plans for *Tygodnik Powszechny* while the Occupation still held Kraków in its iron grip. The cardinal appointed Father Jan Piwowarczyk, the former seminary rector and one of the outstanding priests of the archdiocese, as "ecclesiastical assistant" to the paper, with responsibility for theological and moral issues and a general oversight of the weekly. *Tygodnik Powszechny* may even have been Piwowarczyk's idea. He had been editor-in-chief of *Głos Narodu* [The Voice of the People], an afternoon daily in Kraków that the archdiocese had taken over from the Christian Democratic Party when the latter fell apart prior to World War II. Piwowarczyk's assistant at *Głos Narodu* was a young journalist named Turowicz, who became editor-in-chief when Piwowarczyk was transferred to a parish in the spring of 1939. Turowicz's editorial tenure was a mere two months. Hans Frank had no intention of permitting a Catholic newspaper in his fief. Now, with the cardinal's enthusiastic support for the project, Turowicz was hired to run the new paper.[81]

The Catholic press's situation in communist-run Poland was not a happy one. There were three groups. The first was the official Church press, sponsored, controlled, edited, and published by diocesan chancery offices or religious orders. The quality was not striking. Then there was what Turowicz dismissed as a "press of Catholics," the papers and magazines published by "Pax" and similar regime-sympathetic groups. The Church refused to recognize these journals as authentically Catholic and discouraged serious Catholics from writing for them. Finally, there was the genuine Catholic press, edited primarily by lay people and recognized as authentically Catholic by the bishops, who would assign them "ecclesiastical assistants." These assistants were working members of the staff, and final editorial responsibility rested with the lay editor.[82]

By reason of its literary quality and intellectual dynamism, *Tygodnik Powszechny* was communist-run Poland's best newspaper, the most reliable source of unfiltered information, and the most open, interesting forum for social commentary. Its seriousness of purpose and its impact within the Polish literary class, Catholic and non-Catholic, was acknowledged by the regime—*Tygodnik Powszechny* was constantly harassed by the state, its content censored and its circulation manipulated by the government's monopoly on newsprint. The communists were also unhappy that *Tygodnik Powszechny*, benefiting immensely from the regime's clumsiness with intellectuals, had on its editorial staff such men as art historian Jacek Woźniakowski and Stanisław Rodziński, a brilliant modern painter (and later rector of the Kraków Academy of Fine Arts), whose religious and political convictions made them unemployable in the state-run universities.

Tygodnik Powszechny had a readership "multiplier" that would have been the envy of any Western magazine from the 1950s through the 1980s. Passed hand-to-hand through a wide network of intellectuals, the paper played a crucial role over the years in linking dissident Catholic intellectuals to their non-Catholic counterparts. With its sister monthly, *Znak* [Sign], it was also Polish Catholicism's link to the intellectual ferment under way in Western European Catholicism. In its pages and *Znak*'s, Karol Wojtyła and others first read in translation the work of Henri de Lubac, Yves Congar, Karl Rahner, and other theologians who would shape the Second Vatican Council. *Tygodnik Powszechny* was, in Turowicz's recollection, the only Catholic paper in the communist world that took theology seriously.[83]

More than a few Polish bishops regarded *Tygodnik Powszechny* as dangerously independent and "liberal," and the paper caused occasional headaches for the Primate, Cardinal Wyszyński. These tensions notwithstanding, *Tygodnik Powszechny* was a refuge of honesty in a swamp of communist and acquiescent-Catholic journalistic mendacity. That it took cultural and intellectual life as seriously as questions of the Church and public affairs marked it as a precious rarity in Catholic publishing for its time and place, or any other, for that matter.

"Mission de France," Father Karol Wojtyła's inaugural essay for the paper, was a critically sympathetic look at the worker-priest movement as an innovative pastoral response to the desperate circumstances of postwar French Catholicism, always a magnet of interest for Polish Catholic intellectuals.

France, he wrote, seemed an anomaly. The Church's intellectual culture was highly developed and the country was sinking into post-Christian paganism. What, he asked, was the "meeting point" between these two phenomena? He found it in the recently devised *Mission de France*, the inspiration of the Abbé Godin, whose book, *France: A Mission Country?*, had brought the archbishop of Paris, Cardinal Emmanuel Suhard, to tears. Godin had moved out of his rectory into typical worker housing in the Paris suburbs, where he had made himself like his parishioners and lived "a full and personal assimilation of the Gospel." The key to the renewal of the French Church, Godin believed, would only come when the French Church's "conceptual riches" were transformed "into values of the apostolate."

What Godin had found in the cities and others had found in rural areas was an "absolutely de-Christianized terrain," where life "no longer has any tie with the Christian religious tradition . . . These are the environments in which the children, seeing the body upon the crucifix, ask: 'Who is that?'" This was, of course, the end result that Poland's new communist masters had in mind for their country.

The most innovative and courageous French Church leaders had "looked reality in the face" and decided the Church must "transform itself into a community which demonstrated to the unbelievers who surrounded them what the Gospel is in relation to life." Priests and committed laity alike had to live out a "spirit of poverty and unselfishness" in the new *Mission de France* worker-priest parishes, and the priests had to engage in manual labor. This was not only a return to the traditions of St. Paul, Wojtyła argued, but a recovery of the idea of the priest as "the man who offers with and through Christ each fragment of the pain of men, of their work, to the Father in heaven."

Wojtyła was also taken with the communal life of the worker-priests ("a great help for the personal experience of the priesthood in all its fullness") and by their commitment to a method of persuasion. The new apostles in France could not presume anything, nor could they impose convictions. Their "endeavor [was] to convince." He also applauded the liturgical reforms, including dialogue Masses, which, by encouraging the people's active participation, made the Mass an instrument of "Christian initiation." Finally, Wojtyła was greatly impressed by the emphasis on a converted (or reconverted) laity in the *Mission de France.* The laity, he insisted, were "responsible for the social realization and continuation of the mystery of the Incarnation." And in doing so, they were not conducting a "resistance, an opposition." Rather, this was a "positive activity," an exercise in the construction of "a new type of Christian culture."[84]

Father Wojtyła's second essay in *Tygodnik Powszechny* was his tribute to Jan Tyranowski, entitled "Apostle." In the years that followed he would contribute essays on Christian anthropology, marital chastity, and other issues to both *Tygodnik Powszechny* and *Znak.* In 1957–1958, he wrote, at Turowicz's request, a twenty-part series entitled "ABCs of Ethics," perhaps his most extended pre-papal effort at presenting serious philosophical and theological issues to a nonspecialist audience in a way that would satisfy the intellectually curious and the philosophically trained. In laying out the basics of a Christian philosophical and theological approach to the moral life, Wojtyła took up some of the more controverted questions between Christians and nonbelievers. Was there a common moral border between the two camps? (Yes, the natural moral law.) Was the moral law a merely human construct? (No, the Nuremberg trials had demonstrated that a transcendent moral law existed.) Was a religiously informed ethics a barrier to human maturity? (No, because holding oneself responsible to God's judgment is an impetus to moral seriousness.)[85]

Tygodnik Powszechny was not only a literary outlet for the young priest-essayist; its people became part of his social and intellectual milieu. Here he could talk about theological and ecclesiastical issues with fellow intellectuals who had also given their lives to the Church, although the great majority had done so as laity. He became friends with the Turowicz family, but over decades of friendship and collaboration, they never addressed each other familiarly. The editor always called him "Father" (never "Karol") and Wojtyła always called Turowicz, in the (virtually untranslatable, but certainly formal) Polish fashion "Pan

Jerzy" or "Pan Doctor Jerzy."[86] Father Wojtyła attended the occasional *Tygodnik Powszechny* office party, and his relationship with the staff was secure enough that there could be real arguments when there were disagreements.[87] It was, in both directions, a happy and productive relationship.

PLAYWRIGHT AND POET

Karol Wojtyła's literary work blossomed in the first dozen years of his priesthood. The war, life in a communist-dominated country, and his expanding pastoral experiences and responsibilities all became grist for his poetic and dramatic mill. By his own choice, he wrote under two pseudonyms—Andrzej Jawień (a common surname in Niegowić), and Stanisław Andrzej Gruda. He wanted, Jerzy Turowicz believed, to make a distinction between his literary work and his writing on religion, faith, morals, and Church affairs, which were always published under his own name, and he thought he had a right to have his work considered on its own merits, rather than as clerical curiosities.[88]

Writers write for an infinity of reasons. Wojtyła's plays and poems were an expression of a conviction that he had formed early and that had intensified throughout his life—that reality could not be grasped by one instrument only. Even after he had become a professional philosopher, a teacher of the subject and a professorial guide for others' philosophical work, he remained convinced that one of the weaknesses of modern intellectual life was the tendency in all disciplines to think that there was only one way to get a grip on the reality of the human condition.[89] This struck Wojtyła as both arrogant and impossible. The depths of the human experience were such that they could be probed only by a host of methods. Literature—in his case, plays and poems—could sometimes get to truths that could not be adequately grasped philosophically or theologically. Like many twentieth-century philosophers, Wojtyła believed that language, either technical or literary, was always inadequate to the reality it tried to grasp and convey. Thus Wojtyła's literary activity was not a hobby. It was another way of "being present" to the lives of others, through the writer's natural medium of dialogue.[90]

Our God's Brother

Karol Wojtyła began writing his first mature play, *Our God's Brother*, at age twenty-five, during his final year in the Kraków seminary. He had long been fascinated by the life of Adam Chmielowski, "Brother Albert," one of the most intriguing figures in modern Polish cultural and religious life, first becoming aware of him during his student days at the Jagiellonian University and during the war.[91]

Born in 1845 in southern Poland, Adam Chmielowski was raised by relatives after his parents' death and spent two years at an agricultural school. At age seventeen, he joined the 1863 partisan uprising against Russian rule and was wounded in battle. His left leg was amputated below the knee in an operation performed without anaesthesia. After the uprising was suppressed, he briefly attended an art school in Warsaw and then went to Paris and Munich, where he studied painting and became an accomplished artist. He held his first exhibition in Kraków in 1870 and established a niche as a thinker about his art. Chmielowski criticized the tendency of the Polish painting of his time to focus almost exclusively on such historical themes as the nation's battles. This "historicism," he believed, led to a kind of nationalistic "hysteria" and rendered Polish painting incapable of being "universal."[92]

In 1880, he tried to join the Jesuits but had a nervous collapse and left the novitiate after six months. Living with his brother, he continued to develop a distinctively modern style of painting and became a lay Franciscan missionary. After resettling in Kraków in 1884, he grew increasingly dissatisfied with his life as an artist. Angered by what he regarded as the municipality's inadequate care for the poor, he became involved with helping the homeless. In August 1887, he put on a simple sackcloth habit, taking the religious name "Brother Albert." A year later he made vows before Cardinal Albin Dunajewski, himself a former partisan. Founding the Albertine Brothers and, some years later, the Albertine Sisters, he devoted the rest of his life to the poor and homeless, while living in radical poverty. Brother Albert died on Christmas Day, 1916. Adam Stefan Sapieha was at his funeral, along with a host of clergy from throughout the city and the region, the mayor of Kraków, and people from every social stratum.[93] His most famous painting, *Ecce Homo* (incomplete, like virtually all of his extant work), is displayed in the Albertine Convent in Kraków. Reprints of it are found in churches and homes throughout Poland.

Karol Wojtyła's plays are not "plays" in the conventional sense of the term, and *Our God's Brother* is certainly not a conventional biographical drama, although it follows the trajectory of Adam Chmielowski's life in broad outline. An example of the Kotlarczyk-Wojtyła "inner theater," the play is an attempt to communicate Brother Albert's struggle to identify and live out his vocation. The play's main "action" takes place in the conscience of Adam Chmielowski, who is "becoming" Brother Albert throughout the drama.[94]

The mainspring of the play's dramatic tension is vocational—the struggle to make oneself into a gift, to abandon ego, in this case illustrated by Chmielowski's struggle to justify his comfortable artist's life as he wrestles with a call to radical poverty and service.[95] There is another level to *Our God's Brother*, though. In the play, through the struggles of Brother Albert, Wojtyła is working out for himself the problem of revolutionary violence. Having returned to a Poland now subject to a communist superpower, he found that the problem posed itself in two ways. How is one to assess the Marxist critique of contemporary industrial society? And how does one determine one's own response to tyranny—a question that both the wartime Occupation and his circumstances in 1948–1950 had pressed on Wojtyła.

These questions are explored in *Our God's Brother* through the dramatic confrontation in the play between "Adam/Brother Superior" (Chmielowski) and a character simply called the "Stranger." There has been considerable speculation about possible models for the Stranger. Pope John Paul II has confirmed that the character is "Crypto-Lenin," an adaptation by the playwright of the never-confirmed legend that Chmielowski and Lenin met, perhaps in Zakopane, while the latter was living in and around Kraków in 1912–1914.[96]

The confrontation between Adam and the Stranger is, on the surface, about tactics, the Stranger charging that the "apostles of charity," like Chmielowski, are really the enemies of the poor. The deeper struggle between the two revolutionaries is for souls. Both men are wrestling for converts, for the allegiance of the poor and the homeless, but the ideologically besotted Stranger, who is not unattractive and certainly not unintelligent, can only see his potential disciples in categories: the *lumpenproletariat*, unfit for revolution; the workers, bearers of the dynamics of history; and so forth.

At the deepest level, the dramatic action in *Our God's Brother* is a struggle over the meaning of freedom, and by extension the meaning of human existence. Adam, in this case voicing the playwright's convictions, does not deny either the injustice of society or the legitimacy of the anger that injustice generates. Yet he comes to believe that the only social transformation truly worthy of the human person runs through the cross, which "transforms a man's fall into good and his slavery into freedom."[97] The resolution of the drama is found in Brother Albert's dying words, spoken as a worker's insurrection has broken out in the city:

> Ah well. You know that anger has to erupt, especially if it is great.
> *[He stops.]*
> And it will last, because it is just.
> *[He becomes even more deeply lost in thought. Then he adds one sentence, as
>   if to himself, though everyone listens attentively.]*
> I know for certain, though, that I have chosen a greater freedom.[98]

This is not religious quietism in the face of injustice and tyranny, nor does the playwright accept that the only alternatives are acquiescence to injustice or priests with rifles. Brother Albert poses a third option: service to the poor in the transformation of culture, which will lead in time to the transformation of politics. It was a point well understood by Poland's communist authorities, who wanted to cut the last line, about the "greater freedom," from the script when *Our God's Brother* was finally performed in Kraków in 1980.[99]

Some twenty-five years before the term was coined, *Our God's Brother* was Karol Wojtyła's first exercise in "liberation theology." The Church, his play suggests, is the true place of freedom in the world, because the Church is a witness to the messianic liberation prophesied by Isaiah, the liberation that would truly liberate human beings in the depth of their humanity.[100] Brother Albert did not defend the Church as such but defended human dignity through the Church and the truths it bore. Compared to Lenin, he did indeed choose the "greater freedom."

Our God's Brother is sometimes taken to exemplify Karol Wojtyła's sympathy for certain aspects of Marxism, or at least of the Marxist critique of modern industrial society.[101] This seems rather stretched. Marxism identified certain injustices of early industrial capitalism. But it was not the only biting critique of the socioeconomic status quo: Pope Leo XIII had made a strong defense of workers' rights in the 1891 encyclical that began the tradition of modern Catholic social doctrine, *Rerum Novarum*. Moreover, Wojtyła flatly rejected Marxism's concept of the human person, its understanding of the dynamics of history, and its violent strategy of social change, as *Our God's Brother* makes abundantly clear. To acknowledge that the anger provoked by injustice was just because the injustice was real hardly constitutes an endorsement, however tepid, of Marxism's analysis of the human condition. The "greater freedom" chosen by Brother Albert was a freedom that the Stranger, Crypto-Lenin, regarded as a swindle of the poor. Karol Wojtyła has never doubted that Brother Albert had it exactly right, and Crypto-Lenin exactly wrong.[102]

The Jeweler's Shop

In *Our God's Brother*, the playwright is working through the mystery of vocational decision by reflecting on a historic figure whose struggle paralleled his own and whose example became a model for his own priesthood.[103] Writing the play was one way to repay Karol Wojtyła's "debt of gratitude" to Brother Albert.[104] *The Jeweler's Shop*, a poetic meditation on the mystery of marriage, was a partial payment of Wojtyła's debt to his *Środowisko*.[105] At the same time, it deepened the playwright's meditation on the human struggle to make oneself into a gift, and in doing so, to live out one's destiny as a creature made in the image of God.

Wojtyła's poetic skills are beautifully deployed as *The Jeweler's Shop* tells the inner story of three marriages. Andrew and Teresa have only a brief life together before Andrew is a casualty of the war, leaving Teresa to raise their infant son, Christopher, alone. Stefan and Anna survive the war, but their marriage has fallen into mutual indifference, and then hostility. Stefan takes love for granted, and thus love withers. Anna, for her part, yearns for a more perfect love, and thus stifles the imperfect love she is called to bring to a greater perfection. Stefan and Anna's difficult relationship scars their daughter, Monica, as growing up without a father has been a burden on Teresa's son, Christopher. As they fall in love, Christopher and Monica carry with them the pain and weight of their family histories. Precisely because of that burden, they also embody the hope of redemption from the accumulated evil of the years, for both themselves and their parents.

Wojtyła's viewpoint as playwright is that of a sympathetic and realistically discerning friend who knows marriage from the inside as much as a celibate can. When *The Jeweler's Shop* was published in the December 1960 issue of *Znak*, with the author identified only as "A. Jawień," readers unfamiliar with the pseudonym would not have had any reason to suspect that the playwright was a priest. They would have recognized the author as a realist, not a sentimentalist, but a realist who found hope in love, which is always stronger than mere sentimentality.

Throughout the drama, Wojtyła gently insists that love and fidelity cannot be reduced to emotions. Their only secure foundation is to be found in the human capacity to reach out and grasp the moral truth of things. A marriage is not an on-again, off-again meeting between two emotional states. Marriage is the reality of two persons who have been transformed by their meeting and their initial gift of self to the other. That transformation remains, even when the emotions that were part of the relationship's beginning have disappeared into history.[106] What is necessary is purifying our emotions and transforming them, over time, into the more solid reality of self-giving love. When Anna, thinking she has reached the end of her endurance with Stefan, tries to sell her wedding ring to the Jeweler, he takes it from her, puts it onto his scales, and then declines:

> This ring does not weigh anything,
> the needle does not move from zero
> and I cannot make it show
> even a milligram.
> Your husband must be alive,
> in which case neither of your rings, taken separately,
> will weigh anything—only both together will register.
> My jeweler's scales have this peculiarity
> that they weigh not the metal
> but man's entire being and fate.[107]

In focusing so intently on self-giving love as the foundation of the unbreakable bond of marriage, Wojtyła was also making a large theological claim—that marriage is the beginning of our understanding of the interior life of God, the Trinity of self-giving persons in which personhood is fulfilled in the absolute gift of self. Marriage, he suggests, is the human experience that begins to make God comprehensible to human beings.[108] We are far, indeed, from a pre–Vatican II Catholic understanding of marriage as, inter alia, a "remedy" for concupiscence. The self-giving love and life-giving generativity of marriage are an icon for Wojtyła of the interior life of the trinitarian God, and of God's interface with the world through the Incarnation of his son.

When *The Jeweler's Shop* was published in *Znak* at Christmas, 1960, some of "A. Jawień's" friends were startled. "We read about ourselves," recalled Stanisław Rybicki. There were "entire sections where I heard Stasek," remembered his wife, Danuta, who also recognized personality traits from other *Rodzinka* friends in the drama. A camping trip incident with the Rybickis—the cry of an owl outdoors at night, initially mistaken as a lost camper crying for help—was re-created at the beginning of the play. When Andrew subsequently asks Teresa to marry him—"Would you like to become forever my life's companion?"—he uses a phrase, "my life's companion," that Wojtyła later attributed to Jerzy Ciesielski, describing his wife, Danuta. And Adam, a mysterious "chance interlocutor" whom Anna meets outside the jeweler's shop, certainly reflects the experience of Father Karol Wojtyła, friend and confessor, who "knew exactly how we lived," who "took part in the love between couples and between parents and their children," and who had lived out with his companions the problems of their lives.[109]

As Pope John Paul II later recalled, he was reworking for dramatic purposes situations that "only those present at the time could recognize."[110] No member of *Środowisko* appears in the play as such, but the character of Monica (interestingly enough, the name of Halina Królikiewicz's firstborn) was based on someone whom the playwright had known personally.[111] Wojtyła had the uncanny ability to remember entire conversations decades after they had happened. He put this capacity to good use in *The Jeweler's Shop*, giving its poetic monologues the ring of truth.[112] In adapting his experiences with his friends and his penitents, Karol Wojtyła was not simply ransacking his remarkable memory for dramatic material, however. He was making an important point, ultimately theological in import, about his friends and the lives they were living: your lives, which seem like so many other lives, are in fact caught up in a great drama of sin and redemption. In that drama, human love will yield to "the pressure of reality" and crumble unless it is completed and perfected in being conformed to a Love that is capable of fulfilling love's longing for absolute fulfillment. The human drama "plays," as it were, within the divine drama, a play of which God himself is both author and protagonist, creator and redeemer.[113]

Poetry

During these early years of his priesthood, Karol Wojtyła discovered that the scientific apparatus of philosophy could limit, even impede, the exploration of human experience. Literature, in crucial respects, was a more supple instrument for delving into the hidden depths of the human condition. Thus Wojtyła would urge his colleague at the Catholic University of Lublin, Stefan Sawicki, to read carefully in the "dark literature" of modernity, such as Camus's *The Plague* or Graham Greene's *The Power and the Glory*.[114] Like his plays, Wojtyła's poetry is a way of "being present" to others in a conversation about the truth of things.

It is not easy poetry, in the original or in translation.[115] Yet his poems display the "voice" of Karol Wojtyła in a privileged way, particularly his insight into human relationships, the struggles of the individual conscience, and the mystical experience.[116] Written in a telegraphic, sometimes elliptical style, the poems oscillate between extreme concreteness and abstraction. They also display a striking capacity to get "inside" the experience and conscience of another—a worker in a modern munitions factory, for example:

> I cannot influence the fate of the globe, I do not begin wars.
> Am I working with You or against You—I do not know.
> I don't sin.
> And it worries me that I have no influence and that I don't sin . . .
> I am preparing the fragments of disaster
> but I do not catch a wholeness, the fate of man is above my
>   imagination . . .
> But is that enough?[117]

Or the Samaritan woman whom Jesus meets at the well in Sichar, reflecting on the meaning of their encounter:

> He suffused me without difficulty
> burst my shame in me and the thoughts I'd suppressed for so long
> as if he had touched a rhythm in my temples
> and all of a sudden carried that great exhaustion in me . . .
> and with such care . . .[118]

Sometimes carefully crafted, at other times written hastily on the margins of official papers and then dispatched "as is" to *Tygodnik Powszechny* (where the editors ran them in the form in which they arrived[119]), Wojtyła's poems were simply the way one wrote about a particular idea or experience. They were the appropriate medium of expression for a certain kind of reflection, even a form of prayer.[120] The experiences that compelled this kind of expression could, for Wojtyła, be drawn from such personal encounters as being a confessor or confirming young people in a mountain village, or from great historical events like the Second Vatican Council or the millennium of Polish Christianity.

While Wojtyła's poetry "fits" within the tradition of contemplative religious poetry, there are few exhortations in it, and even these are delivered in a thoroughly humanistic voice. The poet rarely praises or condemns; he most often describes. This is not, in other words, "Christian apologetics in verse."[121] Yet the poet's optic on the lives on which he is reflecting is profoundly Christian. Against the temptation to see life as a relatively flat terrain in which decency is rather cost-free, Wojtyła almost relentlessly lays bare the dramatic tension to be found in every life. He does not scold, but suggests to his readers that *the* great choice posed to the human person in the modern world is the choice "between sanctity and the loss of [one's] humanity."[122] To know this can be both fascinating and terrifying, for we are dealing here with the sacred. That encounter, Wojtyła insists, is unavoidable, if we want to live authentically and maturely, in touch with the dignity of our own lives and in fellowship with others:

. . . You had better walk the wave! Walk the wave, don't hurt your feet—
the wave will embrace you and in such a way that you would not feel that
    you are drowning.
And then will come He and his own yoke
will put on your shoulders. And feeling it you will awake trembling.[123]

The Engaged Ascetic

Father Karol Wojtyła lived an exceptionally rich experience as a young priest, rich in friends, activities, intellectual and literary creativity. Those riches stood in marked contrast to his personal asceticism.

He never had a bank account, never wrote a check, never had any personal money.[124] He slept on the floor and practiced other forms of self-discipline and self-denial. Possessions meant nothing to him, with the possible exception of the skiing and hiking equipment he accepted from his *Środowisko* friends. Mieczysław Maliński, by now a fellow priest, once threw his friend's rusty old razor away and gave him a new one for a name-day present. If he hadn't thrown the old one out, he was sure Wojtyła would have given the new one away, as he did with most gifts.[125] He always wore an old cassock and old shoes. Looking at him, Maliński remembers, you might think he was a beggar, a *clochard*, a nobody.[126]

Given the expectations of contemporary biography, a writer almost regrets the absence of detractors and critics of his subject. Perhaps even more striking is the fact that Karol Wojtyła's intelligence, creativity, and pastoral success did not attract clerical jealousies. Priests sometimes say that envy is the besetting sin of the Roman Catholic clergy. According to Mieczysław Maliński, Wojtyła was "beyond discussion" in Kraków clerical circles, in part because "his extraordinariness wasn't worn lightly—it wasn't worn at all."[127] The one complaint about him was that he seemed to live according to a personal chronometer set to Wojtyła Standard Time and was almost always late for meetings and appointments, having gotten himself absorbed in his previous engagement or his voracious and incessant reading.

He loved his priesthood and yet spent the bulk of his free time, which turned into a different kind of ministerial time, with laypeople. Friends, once made, were friends forever, and he was always accessible to them. Jacek Woźniakowski remembers him as a great "intuitive" reader of souls.[128] This trait might well have made him into a very dangerous personality, at the least a manipulator of others' lives, at worst a rank demagogue. Disciplined by a life of intense prayer and asceticism, he became instead a great confessor and an accomplished poet and dramatist.

The mid-1950s were perhaps the most difficult years for the Catholic Church in communist Poland. The 1952 Constitution of the Polish People's Republic decreed the separation of Church and state, by which the party meant the subordination of the Church to the state. The regime put increasing pressure on Catholic publications and shut down the junior seminaries.

Large numbers of priests were again arrested (including Father Tadeusz Kurowski, Wojtyła's old pastor at St. Florian's); others were harassed by new taxes.[129] A "patriotic priests'" association allied with "Pax" attacked the bishops and called for the Primate's resignation. Bishop Czesław Kaczmarek of Kielce was arrested, tried, and sentenced to twelve years in prison after a classic Stalinist show trial.

The point of maximum confrontation came in May 1953, when the government announced that the state would henceforth appoint and remove bishops and pastors and require all priests to take a loyalty oath to the Polish People's Republic. Led by Cardinal Wyszyński, the bishops drew the line. In a fiery sermon at St. John's Cathedral in Warsaw, the Primate threw down the gauntlet: "We teach that it is proper to render unto Caesar the things that are Caesar's and to God what is God's. But when Caesar seats himself on the altar, we respond curtly: he must not."[130] The bishops then met under Wyszyński's chairmanship in Kraków and issued an epic statement defending the independence of the Church, which concluded: "We are not allowed to place the things of God on the altar of Caesar. *Non possumus!* [We cannot!]"[131] The regime labeled the memorandum high treason (the euphemism was "an attack on the Constitution"). On the night of September 25–26, 1953, Cardinal Wyszyński was arrested and interned, first in a former monastery in the northwest, later in a convent in the south.

He was released in 1956 when the regime, led again by Władysław Gomułka and facing a Soviet invasion in the wake of rioting and unrest, invited him back to Warsaw. Wyszyński demanded a repeal of the 1953 decree, Bishop Kaczmarek's release from prison, the restoration of the Catholic press, the regularization of Church governance, and a new mixed commission of government and episcopate representatives. Gomułka agreed. Wyszyński—by now an international figure, profiled in *Life* magazine as a symbol of resistance to communism—returned to Warsaw and began to implement the "Great Novena," a nine-year program of pastoral renewal he had devised during his internment to prepare the country for its millennium celebrations in 1966.

By all accounts, Father Karol Wojtyła continued to be utterly uninterested in what passed for "politics" in Poland in the 1950s. The only newspaper he read was *Tygodnik Powszechny,* and who was up or down in the party Politburo or among the local party apparatchiks didn't concern him. But it would be erroneous to conclude that he believed in offering up the Church's suffering to God while eschewing any form of resistance. Like many other Polish priests, he was creating de facto networks of resistance to communism by helping to raise up a generation of Poles who could resist the communist culture of the lie with the truth of their religious and moral convictions. His writing never attacked communism directly. He didn't have to. It was perfectly clear to his readers that Wojtyła was giving expression to a vision of human life and human destiny utterly at cross-purposes with the official ideology.

He was a private man who kept a part of himself for himself—the part where he had his most intense conversation with his God. Yet he was becoming something of a public personality in a city he had come to love.[132] He lived a singularly integrated priestly and personal life that was now sharply focused not on defending the institution of the Church (others had that responsibility), but on defending the dignity of the human person, of whom the Church was a servant. Like Brother Albert, he believed that the Church was the defender of the human person against persecution and humiliation. And as Brother Albert had understood, that was why the Church was the true zone of freedom.[133]

4

Seeing Things as They Are

The Making of a Philosopher

SEPTEMBER 1, 1951	Father Karol Wojtyła begins two-year academic sabbatical.
OCTOBER 1953	Wojtyła begins to lecture on social ethics at the Jagiellonian University.
JANUARY 1954	The Jagiellonian University Faculty of Theology awards Wojtyła his second doctorate.
OCTOBER 12, 1954	Father Wojtyła is appointed to the philosophy department of the Catholic University of Lublin [KUL].
1954–1955 ACADEMIC YEAR	Wojtyła delivers upper-level lectures at KUL on "Act and Experience," discussing the philosophical ethics of Max Scheler, Immanuel Kant, and Thomas Aquinas.
MAY 28–30, 1955	Karol Wojtyła participates in an international kayaking competition on the Dunajec river.
1955–1956 ACADEMIC YEAR	Wojtyła's upper-level lectures at KUL on "Goodness and Value" consider the ethics of Plato, Aristotle, Augustine, Aquinas, Kant, and Scheler.
MARCH 5–10, 1956	Father Wojtyła preaches his annual student retreat at St. Florian's in Kraków.
1956–1957 ACADEMIC YEAR	Wojtyła's KUL lectures on "Norm and Happiness" confront the philosophical ethics of David Hume and Jeremy Bentham.
DECEMBER 1, 1956	Karol Wojtyła is appointed to the Chair of Ethics at the Catholic University of Lublin.
1957–1958 ACADEMIC YEAR	Wojtyła's upper-level lectures focus on sexual ethics, a series that will continue in the 1958–1959 academic year.
1960	Karol Wojtyła's book, *Love and Responsibility*, is published by the KUL press.
1960–1961 ACADEMIC YEAR	Wojtyła's last upper-level lectures treat the "Theory and Methodology of Ethics."

One fall day in 1955, a priest in his mid-thirties walked into the seminary at 3 Mickiewicz Street in Kraków to teach his class in Catholic social ethics. He was not dressed in the usual manner of academia. He wore a leather cap rather than a more formal black hat. His threadbare cassock was covered by a worn, dark green coat, which seemed to have been made from material originally intended for the manufacture of blankets.

Entering the recreation hall where his class was held, he tossed his overcoat over the back of a chair and began to pace back and forth behind the podium, not so much lecturing as unraveling a skein of argument in which theology and everyday life were woven together. He never seemed to tire of looking at an issue, first from this angle, then from that, always trying to get the question just right. Sometimes he would stop, pause, and look out at his students—seminarians from Kraków, Częstochowa, and Silesia—to make sure that they had gotten a point. They were mesmerized by him. He not only dressed like no one else on the faculty, he taught like no one else on the faculty. This was not the transmission of information. This was intellectual exploration.

On this particular day, the professor was reprising some material they had recently covered—perhaps something on the relationship between the individual and the good of society, or the question of social class. In these review periods, called "colloquia," his habit was to press the students to talk freely about what they had heard in his lectures. Since the conventions of the day dictated student reticence, he sometimes had to press hard. In this instance, he wasn't disappointed.

Twenty-year-old Romuald Waldera started to give the professor an earful. He had just come to the seminary from the Law Faculty at the Jagiellonian University, where he had been successfully propagandized by the Marxist theoreticians then riding high. Full of the certainties of adolescence and crammed with Marxist vocabulary, he attacked the professor's ideas and the Church's social teaching so vehemently that several classmates, appalled, started kicking him on the ankle and whispering, "Stop it, they'll expel you." During young Waldera's tirade, the professor kept pacing back and forth on the platform at the front of the hall, his hands behind his back and his head down.

The youngster finally fell back into his chair, sweating, the pent-up frustrations of the past months spent. The room was filled with a heavy silence. Father Karol Wojtyła stopped his pacing, stood at the center of the platform, and proceeded to flabbergast everyone in the room, especially Romuald Waldera: "Gentlemen, if you please, your attention. What your colleague has just said here is evidence that he is beginning to think theologically. . . ."

He then met every one of Waldera's points, never raising his voice, answering each question that had been raised. Other students then got involved, each with his own frustrations: frustrations about the human condition, frustrations about the state of Poland, frustrations with God. Once again, the priest-professor walked back and forth, listening. After each eruption, he calmly suggested a Catholic way of thinking about these problems.

After class was over, Father Wojtyła invited Romuald Waldera to the seminary parlor for a conversation. He had sensed a disturbance in the young man, and he wanted to help. A quarter-century later, Romuald Waldera remembered his professor's kindness, and tried to emulate it whenever he had to deal, as a priest, with the revolutionary hotheads of another generation.[1]

A CHANGE OF PLANS

Cardinal Adam Stefan Sapieha, the unbroken prince, died on July 23, 1951. He was laid out in Wawel Cathedral in a coffin surrounded by candles. His priests came to keep vigil with the mortal remains of the bishop who had led them through the long, dark night of Occupation. Looking into the face of the man who had ordained him and had been one of his models of priestly service, Father Karol Wojtyła might have thought that he had been orphaned, once again. Sapieha was buried in the marble pavement in front of the sarcophagus of St. Stanisław, another defender of the rights of the Church against violence.

Cardinal Sapieha had no immediate successor as archbishop of Kraków. According to the agreement that had been worked out between the Polish episcopate and the communist government, the episcopate (which, for all practical purposes, meant Primate Wyszyński) would consult with the Holy See in Rome and submit the names of proposed appointments to the government. The state could not impose a bishop but it retained veto power. That power was exercised in Kraków after Sapieha's death. The Holy See wanted to appoint Archbishop Eugeniusz Baziak as Sapieha's successor. The government refused to agree. When the Holy See dug in its heels, the Kraków see went unfilled for the next twelve years. From the Church's point of view, however, Archbishop Baziak was the de facto Archbishop of Kraków, no matter what the government thought of the legal situation.

Pope John Paul II remembered Eugeniusz Baziak as a man who had "lived a dramatic life," not untinged by the tragic.[2] Born in 1890, he had been named the Latin-rite archbishop of Lwów on November 22, 1945, just as the historic Galician city was being renamed L'viv and incorporated into the Ukrainian Soviet Socialist Republic. First interned, and then expelled from his see by the Soviet government, Archbishop Baziak had been invited to come to Kraków by Cardinal Sapieha.

Baziak was destined to follow Sapieha at the height of the Stalinist pressure on the Polish Church. One of his priests remembered the time as "the period of most radical oppression, a very difficult period," in which, among other things, the communists were trying to appoint assistant pastors in order to penetrate and control the Church.[3] In these grim circumstances, Archbishop Baziak concluded that his job was simply to "stand there," to protect the institution from penetration by maintaining a position of rocklike intransigence. Unhappily, this precluded the friendly relations that Sapieha, who, as John Paul II said, "found it easy to be a prince," enjoyed with his priests and his people.[4] Eugeniusz Baziak, the Pope recalled, was "a good man with a good heart" who adopted what another contemporary called a "severe, strict" attitude only because he wanted the regime to think that he was not to be trifled with. And he decided that the best way to demonstrate that was to be tough with the people immediately around him.[5] It must have cost him personally. Colleagues who had never seen him relax in his residence or in his chancery office remember the close and warm relationship he had with visitors who came to see him from L'viv.[6]

Archbishop Baziak decided that the vicar of St. Florian's should return to academic life and seek a second doctoral degree by writing a "habilitation" thesis, which would qualify him to teach at the university level.[7] Father Karol Wojtyła disagreed with the plan, which Baziak may have discussed with Cardinal Sapieha before his death. Wojtyła's student chaplaincy at St. Florian's was flourishing, and he had just added to it a ministry to health-care workers. Baziak insisted, and on September 1, 1951, the archbishop gave Wojtyła a two-year academic sabbatical to complete the habilitation thesis. To facilitate the work, and, one suspects, to enforce his decision, he ordered Father Wojtyła to move from the priests' house at St. Florian's to a Church-owned building known as the Dean's House at Kanonicza, 21. Located on one of the Kraków Old Town's most splendid streets, the house took its name from the fact that the members of the cathedral chapter, the "canons" of Wawel Cathedral, once lived there. Wojtyła's old mentor at the Kraków seminary, Father Ignacy Różycki, also lived at Kanonicza, 21. Father Marian Jaworski, a fledgling philosopher who had formerly been assigned to St. Florian's as an assistant pastor, was another resident. In the "Dean's House," Karol Wojtyła had a second-floor bedroom that doubled as his study. The twenty-foot-square room was heated by a tile stove, against which Father Wojtyła stacked his skis. A Remington portable typewriter sat on the marble-topped desk where Wojtyła worked.

Archbishop Baziak, who knew Father Wojtyła's tendency to do the work of three men, told the young priest that he would personally approve Wojtyła's pastoral engagements during his academic sabbatical. Wojtyła began saying his daily Mass at St. Catherine's Church in Kazimierz, accompanied by his "little choir" of *Rodzinka* members. He was also allowed to continue some of the work he had begun with students and returned to St. Florian's during the academic year to lecture on ethics. He gave an annual retreat at his former parish during the fourth week of Lent, and on the First Friday of each month said Mass at St. Anne's collegiate church for university faculty and students. As far as Archbishop Baziak was concerned, though, Father Wojtyła's job was to write his habilitation thesis, earn his degree, and get himself approved as a university professor.

EXPLORING THE TRUTH OF THINGS

Karol Wojtyła brought certain intellectual convictions to the assignment his superior had given him. His struggle with Wais's *Metaphysics* at the Solvay chemical factory during the war had convinced him that, if one probed questions deeply enough, the unity of things-as-they-are, from the lime buckets he carried to the God he worshiped, would reveal itself in due course. Reality itself was the true measure of thought. Thought was ordered to getting at the truth of things, as iron shavings are ordered to a magnet.

Wojtyła held on to this hard-won conviction about the "objective" reality of the world as his philosophical interests matured. When he began to focus more directly on ethics, he came to a further conviction, that the "objective" reality of the world disclosed important things about the virtues, about the pursuit of happiness, and about our moral duties in life. He also came to see that the philosophical analysis of reality and its relationship to the moral life he had been taught at the seminary and the Angelicum was inadequate in the contemporary world. Aristotle and Thomas Aquinas had built their philosophies from the foundation of cosmology. But starting with a general theory of the universe and moving to a theory of the human person didn't leave much room for human freedom, and modern science had falsified many of the assumptions that ancient and medieval philosophers had made about the universe.

Some thinkers concluded from all this that morality was, at best, a matter of pragmatic calculation.[8] Wojtyła disagreed. He thought that, beginning from a different starting point, philosophy could still probe deeply enough into things-as-they-are to help us grasp the way we *ought* to act. The human person's moral experience of life "between" the person-I-am and the person-I-ought-to-be was the stage on which the great moral questions of good and evil, virtue and duty, presented themselves. This was where thinking about the philosophical foundations of morality had to begin.

But how could you begin ethics with an analysis of human experience and avoid falling into the trap of solipsism—thinking about thinking about thinking? How could modernity avoid a cul-de-sac of radical skepticism about the human capacity to know *anything* with certitude?

Reconstructing the foundations of the moral life—that was the problem, posed by his earlier intellectual training and amplified by his pastoral experience, that Karol Wojtyła now brought to his postdoctoral philosophical work. At the suggestion of his former mentor and current housemate, Father Różycki, Wojtyła decided to explore the work of the German philosopher Max Scheler, to see whether Scheler's new style of philosophy could help solve the problem. Wojtyła concluded that it couldn't, entirely, but that there were important things to learn from Scheler nonetheless. That conclusion marked a critical intellectual "turn" in Karol Wojtyła's life.

Max Scheler was born in 1874 and, after a turbulent career, died in 1928. In his time he was thought to be a genius. But he was also a rake and something of a loner in the German academic world. His partly Jewish origins made him suspect to some, as his conversion to Catholicism and his later abandonment of the Church made him suspect to others.[9] Nonetheless, Scheler was one of a number of German thinkers who helped lead a Catholic intellectual revival in and around Munich immediately after the First World War. Dietrich von Hildebrand and Edith Stein were other members of the movement, which was linked to the Polish philosophical scene through Roman Ingarden, a one-time member of the group who had moved on to Lwów.

The original lodestar of all these thinkers had been Edmund Husserl (1859–1938), the founder of the new philosophical method called "phenomenology." Scheler, Ingarden, von Hildebrand, and Stein came to believe that Husserl had abandoned his original commitment, which was to use this new way of doing philosophy to relink philosophical reflection to objective reality. Carrying on where their master had declined to go, each of these thinkers created an original body of work in pursuit of Husserl's original intention.

Despite the movement's complexities of analysis and terminology, understanding the basic program of the phenomenological movement is not difficult. Doing so is essential if one wants to get inside the mind and the thinking of Karol Wojtyła.

Phenomenology is an effort to "bring back into philosophy everyday things, concrete wholes, the basic experiences of life as they come to us."[10] The early Husserl and his later disciples thought that philosophy had come unglued from everyday life, in one of two ways. Empiricists reduced our experience to "sense data, impressions, chemical compositions, neural reactions, etc."[11] Idealists, determined to fit everything into ideal types, forms, or categories, drifted off into a world of extreme abstraction and subjectivism.[12]

These very different approaches to philosophy can be illustrated by a simple yet important everyday human example: girl meets boy. An empiricist will analyze the brain chemistry of a young woman seeing, hearing, and touching a handsome young man. Influenced by Immanuel Kant, an idealist may worry that the young woman's commitment to the second categorical imperative (never use another person as a means) may be wavering in the face of other desires.

The phenomenologist, on the other hand, will be interested in the experience as a whole, the psychological, physical, moral, and conceptual elements moving this young woman. How are these elements related? How is her experience of this boy unique? What is her heart telling her head (and vice versa)? And what does this experience—girl meets boy—tell us about the human condition itself?[13]

It was phenomenology's determination to see things whole and get to the reality of things-as-they-are that attracted Karol Wojtyła. In his habilitation thesis, he asked whether it was possible to create a solid philosophical foundation for the moral life on the basis of Scheler's phenomenology of ethics, and particularly his ethics of value.

Every moral code has to have an answer to the question, "Why be good?" How could that question be answered in a culture habitually suspicious of any answer thought to be traditional ("Because that's the way we do things") or authoritarian ("Because God [or your mother, or the legal system] said to be good")?[14] How is it that moral choices are not just personal preferences? How can a modern man or woman make a binding moral judgment and say, "I *ought* to do this," rather than merely "I'd *prefer* to do this"? How can society discuss questions of how we *ought* to live together if nobody knows where "ought" comes from, and everybody thinks that "ought" is an imposition of someone else's will?[15]

These were not only urgent questions in a communist country. On both sides of the iron curtain, modern culture had raised a critical primary issue: Could modern human beings talk coherently about morality at all?[16] Wojtyła thought that Scheler might help him deal with this question, as part of a "great and necessary effort to find a new way of philosophical thinking." This in turn required Wojtyła to go back to quarrying, although now of an intellectual sort. As Pope John Paul later said, "I had to translate a lot of Scheler so that I could work on him and do a philosophical and theological analysis of his mind."[17]

It was a grind, certainly at the beginning. One day Mieczysław Maliński came to Kanonicza, 21, and Wojtyła complained, "Look at what I've got to cope with . . . I can hardly make it all out, my German is poor, and there are a lot of technical terms I don't know how to translate. Do you know what I'm doing? . . . I've started to make a translation of the whole book—there's nothing else for it."[18] The attempt itself was an important indicator of Wojtyła's philosophical development. That he looked to Scheler as a possible guide, and that he put himself through the backbreaking work of translation so that he could analyze Scheler in his own language, suggests that Wojtyła had become convinced that the answers were not to be found in the neo-scholasticism of Father Reginald Garrigou-Lagrange.

Wojtyła didn't lock himself into intellectual combat with the philosophical method he had been taught, expending his energies in a war of attrition against an entrenched Catholic way of thinking. Certain forms of neo-scholasticism might have been an obstacle to a genuine Catholic encounter with modern philosophy. Wojtyła simply went around the barrier, having absorbed what was enduring about neo-scholasticism—its conviction that philosophy could get to the truth of things-as-they-are. The young priest was open to engaging modern philosophy on its own terms, and would recall years later that wrestling with Kant's second categorical imperative was "particularly important" for his later thinking.[19] (That it was indeed wrestling was nicely conveyed by John Paul II on one occasion when he remarked to guests, "Kant, *Mein Gott!* Kant!") As a confessor, a teacher, a writer, and a man with a wide range of human contacts, he also brought a "natural phenomenologist's" intuition to his analysis of Scheler. The net result would be what Wojtyła would call, years later, a way of doing philosophy that "synthesized both approaches": the metaphysical realism of Aristotle and Thomas Aquinas and the sensitivity to human experience of Max Scheler's phenomenology.

It was Scheler's personalism, which rescued moral philosophy from the dry abstractions of Kantian ethics and restored the pathos, ecstasy, and indeed *ethos* to human life, that Wojtyła found most attractive.[20] Wojtyła also agreed with Scheler's claim that human intuitions into the truth of things included moral intuitions, a certain "knowledge of the heart" that was, nonetheless, real knowledge.[21] Scheler's careful analysis of moral sentiments, especially empathy and sympathy, was also important, for it helped break modern philosophy out of the prison of solipsism—empathy and sympathy necessarily involved an encounter with another.[22] Perhaps above all, Wojtyła appreciated Scheler's attempt to ground morals in an analysis of the realities of moral choosing, rather than in a formal, abstract system like Kant's. The question Wojtyła posed in his habilitation thesis was whether Scheler (and, by extension, the phenomenological method) could do for contemporary Christian philosophy and theology what Aristotle had done for Thomas Aquinas.[23]

The answer, for the young priest, essentially, was "No." The moral act is a *real* act with real consequences, and to Wojtyła's mind Scheler had failed to come to grips with how moral choices actually shape a person. Therefore, in Scheler's system, morality was still suspended somewhere "outside" the human universe.[24] Wojtyła was also critical of Scheler's tendency to emotionalize experience and consciousness, leading to a truncated portrait of the human person. The men and women he had hiked with, talked with, and accompanied in their various moral struggles were more than composites of their various emotional states and experiences.[25]

These were specific criticisms of Max Scheler's philosophy. The more general conclusion of his habilitation thesis, *An Evaluation of the Possibility of Constructing a Christian Ethics on the Basis of the System of Max Scheler*, was crucial for the future of Wojtyła's own philosophical project.[26] Phenomenology, he argued, was an important instrument for probing various dimensions of the human experience. Phenomenology would drift off into various forms of solipsism, however, unless it were grounded in a general theory of things-as-they-are that was resolutely realistic and that could defend the capacity of human beings to get at the truth of things. This, he believed, was crucial if modern men and women were going to be able to understand and live by real moral norms. If the choice was not between good and evil, but only between personal preferences, then all choices were ultimately indifferent and real choice no longer existed. This, in turn, would empty the drama of human freedom of its essential tension and deprive human beings of their most distinctively *human* quality.[27]

The Scheler study was Karol Wojtyła's first sustained attempt to link the realist *objectivity* embedded in the philosophy he had learned in the seminary and at the Angelicum to modern philosophy's emphasis on human experience and human *subjectivity*. In his habilitation thesis and in his later philosophical work, reconciliation, synthesis, and "connection" would be among Wojtyła's principal intellectual traits, enabling him to think through Thomism *and* phenomenology, love *and* responsibility, freedom *and* self-denial—and, years later, democracy *and* public morality, the market *and* solidarity.[28] This synthetic approach also reflected Wojtyła's ongoing pastoral concern and his sense of priestly ministry as a matter of "meeting someone wisely."[29] Wojtyła's openness in his encounter with others was a way to "see" into his philosophy, even for those without formal philosophical training. Other philosophers remembered texts. Karol Wojtyła always remembered persons.[30]

There was also an echo here of Wojtyła's constant rereading of the Gospel of John, in which Jesus tells his disciples, after the multiplication of loaves and fishes, "Gather up the fragments left over, that nothing may be lost" (*John* 6.12). Fragments of a life could be gathered into a whole; fragmented human understandings could be similarly reconnected. It was, and is, an approach to thinking that cuts across the grain of modern intellectuals' antipathy toward synthesis and their passion for deconstruction. It seemed to Wojtyła the only way to account for the many dimensions of the human drama while staying in touch with the great minds who had laid the intellectual foundations of our civilization.

Father Karol Wojtyła's habilitation thesis was read by two Jagiellonian professors, Fathers Aleksandr Usowicz and Władysław Wicher, and by Professor Stefan Swieżawski of the Catholic University of Lublin. This three-man committee unanimously accepted the work and the Council of the Faculty of Theology accepted their recommendation at a special meeting on November 30, 1953. The process for admission to the Theology Faculty seemed complete when, on December 3, Father Karol Wojtyła delivered a lecture that brought together his interests in John of the Cross and Max Scheler: "An Analysis of the Act of Faith in View of the Philosophy of Values." His second doctoral degree was awarded by the Jagiellonian University Faculty of Theology in 1954, but before Wojtyła could be formally named a "docent," the lowest rank of senior faculty member, the faculty was suppressed by Poland's communist regime.[31]

Still, his successful completion of a second doctorate meant that Karol Wojtyła was now qualified to begin a career as a university professor. That career would take him into one of the bolder intellectual enterprises of the mid-century, which was then beginning to unfold, as improbable as it may seem, in a small, harassed university in a medieval town called Lublin.*

THE LUBLIN PROJECT

The Catholic University of Lublin [Katolicki Uniwersytet Lubelski, or KUL] was founded in 1918 by Father Idzi Radziszewski. Oddly enough, one of its midwives was Lenin, who allowed Father Radziszewski to take the library and

---

*Father Karol Wojtyła's academic teaching career began in October 1953, when he took over a course in Catholic social ethics in the Jagiellonian University's Faculty of Theology. When the faculty was suppressed by the regime in early 1954, Wojtyła continued to teach the social ethics course in the school of theology that was quickly organized for seminarians, who now had no university-based theology courses to attend. Like his Jagiellonian course, these seminary courses ran for two hours a week, and Wojtyła taught them throughout the 1950s.

Wojtyła took over the social ethics course almost accidentally. The course had been taught for years by Father Jan Piwowarczyk, the former ecclesiastical assistant at *Tygodnik Powszechny* and a specialist in the field. When he was suddenly assigned to teach the course in 1953, Wojtyła adopted Piwowarczyk's course notes, which were based on the older priest's two-volume book on the subject. Wojtyła added the emendations he thought appropriate, but substantively, the course remained essentially as Piwowarczyk had taught it. As a very junior faculty

equipment of Petrograd's Polish Academy of Theology back to Poland when the priest was trying to get KUL launched.[33] Given a state charter by the Second Polish Republic in 1938, the university was shut down by the German Occupation, with numerous professors imprisoned, tortured, or killed outright. Its state charter, which had never lapsed, permitted KUL to survive the imposition of Stalinism in Poland after the war, and KUL became the only Catholic university behind the iron curtain, a distinction it maintained throughout the Cold War.

The faculty and students of KUL pursued the academic life in a situation of constant confrontation, sometimes cool, sometimes hot, with the communist regime. Between 1953 and 1956, the faculties of law, social science, and education were shut down. Even after the Gomułka thaw in 1956, the student population was kept artificially low, KUL graduates found it difficult to obtain academic positions at other universities, and the KUL faculty had trouble publishing its work.[34] These pressures, meant to marginalize the institution, in fact helped turn KUL into a university with a vocation. At a time when many influential figures in European intellectual life were flirting with Marxism, KUL would defend the unique dignity of the human person against an aggressive ideological opponent while demonstrating that Catholic faith and human reason were allies in that humanistic mission.[35]

In allowing KUL to function, even under pressure, the communist regime in Poland may have imagined the school as little more than an intellectual petting zoo. "They had no idea that something new could happen in such a medieval place," according to Professor Stefan Swieżawski; KUL, to the regime, was the Catholic equivalent of "a Hasidic ghetto."[36] The authorities may also have thought that they were creating another opening for penetrating the Catholic Church. (If so, they covered their bet by setting up a larger rival next door, the Marie Curie-Skłodowska University, named for the Nobel Prize–winning discoverer of radium.[37]) The KUL faculty and student body, and especially the university's Faculty of Philosophy, had very different ideas about what they were doing.

KUL's Faculty of Philosophy was established in 1946, in part as a response to the great hunger for philosophy evident throughout Polish intellectual life.

---

member who had not done extensive work in social ethics, Wojtyła saw no need to reinvent material that had been developed by one of Poland's leading scholars in the field. Copies of the Piwowarczyk notes as developed by Wojtyła were later typed out, duplicated, and circulated as intellectual samizdat under the title *Catholic Social Ethics*.

Catholic Social Ethics is a rather conventional presentation of the Church's social doctrine in the 1950s. Poland's special circumstances gave a sharp edge to some issues. But while he courageously and in some instances bluntly criticized communist understandings of the social nature of human beings and communist ideas of politics and economics, here, too, Wojtyła (who did not think of himself as a specialist in social ethics) broke no new ground. *Catholic Social Ethics* gives us a window into the Polish discussion of these questions between World War II and the Second Vatican Council. Its primary value today is to establish a baseline from which to appreciate the creativity of the social doctrine of Pope John Paul II.[32]

The war and the Nazi attempt to decapitate Polish culture had (as Świeżawski puts it, rather gently) created a "very distinctive spiritual and intellectual situation" in Poland. In the immediate postwar period, philosophy lectures at the reconstituted Jagiellonian University were delivered to overflow audiences.[38] Now, at KUL, lectures in that most abstract of philosophical disciplines, metaphysics, drew standing-room-only audiences, with students sitting on the floors, in the aisles, and on the window sills of the lecture hall.[39] There, they heard different members of the KUL faculty examine the philosophical issues posed by the hard experiences both faculty and students shared—life under Nazi Occupation and in Stalinist Poland.

Everyone who had lived through the brutalities of the Occupation and the imposition of communism had confronted the ancient philosophical question, "What *is* a human being?" in urgent, unavoidable ways. Why had some men and women acted like beasts while others had shown remarkable heroism? What accounted for the fact that, while some people were grotesquely self-serving, to the point of betraying their friends, others were nobly self-sacrificing, laying down their lives for others they may have known only slightly? The only way to get at these problems, the KUL philosophers agreed, was through a deepening of *philosophical anthropology*, the subdiscipline of philosophy that dealt with the nature, circumstances, and destiny of the human person. What is "human nature," and how are we to understand its dynamics? How is that curious blend of matter and spirit, the human person, built? How are we to explain the difference in kind between human beings and other sentient creatures? What, if anything, is the point or goal of life? These questions, hardy perennials in the garden of philosophical inquiry since the ancient Greeks, took on an especially sharp edge at KUL in the late 1940s and the early 1950s.

Convinced that a crisis in modernity's understanding of the human person lay at the root of the century's distress, the KUL philosophers began to sketch out a philosophical initiative that would link together three large sets of questions: *metaphysics* (a general theory of reality, a way of explaining things-as-they-are) and *anthropology* (the nature and destiny of the human person) would meet in *ethics* (the question, "What *ought* we do?"). The KUL philosophers believed that the problem of ethics posed itself in a particularly urgent way because of the new political situation. Communism was not only an unsatisfactory, reductionistic account of things-as-they-are and a crude caricature of humanism; communism's totalitarian politics stripped men and women of their power of choice, of responsibility, and thus of their humanity.

The counter to both communist materialism and communist politics, the KUL philosophers thought, was a more complete humanism that gave a more compelling account of human moral intuitions and human moral action. In proposing to do this without falling into the quicksand of thinking about thinking about thinking, the KUL philosophers set themselves no small task. Indeed, it involved nothing less than recasting the entire direction of philosophy since the Enlightenment. Moreover, it was a project with a distinctive edge, for the KUL philosophers proposed to fight the great political-philosophical battle on Marxism's own ground—the question of the true liberation of the human person.

The KUL project was defined by a quartet of relatively young men who had become professors at KUL because Poland's Stalinist rulers had expelled the older teachers. The four included Jerzy Kalinowski (the dean of the Philosophy Faculty, a specialist in logic and the philosophy of law), Stefan Swieżawski (a historian of philosophy and an exponent of the existential Thomism of Jacques Maritain), Father Mieczysław Albert Krąpiec (a Dominican specialist in metaphysics), and Father Karol Wojtyła (a specialist in ethics). They were later joined by Fathers Marian Kurdziałek (who specialized in ancient philosophy) and Stanisław Kamiński (a specialist in epistemology, or the theory of knowledge).[40] These were very different personalities, with divergent interests and academic specialties. They nonetheless achieved what Swieżawski later called a "rare and exceptionally fruitful collaboration," built around four agreements.[41]

They began with an ancient conviction—they would be radically realistic about the world and about the human capacity to know it. If our thinking and choosing lacks a tether to reality, the KUL philosophers believed, raw force takes over the world and truth becomes a function of power, not an expression of things-as-they-are. A communist-era joke in Poland expressed this realist imperative in a way that everyone could grasp: "Party boss: 'How much is 2+2?' Polish worker: 'How much would you like it to be?'" The political meaning of the realist assumption of the KUL philosophers was later expressed in the famous Solidarity election poster that read, "For Poland to be Poland, 2+2 must always = 4." Human beings can only be free in the truth, and the measure of truth is reality.[42]

The KUL philosophers also agreed to adopt a distinctively modern starting point for philosophical inquiry. Philosophy would begin with a disciplined reflection on human experience rather than with cosmology (a general theory of the universe), as ancient and medieval philosophy and the neo-scholasticism Wojtyła had been taught at the Angelicum had done. Because human beings are the only creatures aware of their own being and capable of wonder at that amazing fact, thinking should begin with the human person, "a remarkable psychophysical unity, each one a unique person, never again to be repeated in the entire universe."[43] The stakes were high here. If philosophy could get to the truth of things-as-they-are through an analysis of human experience, then the path to a reconciliation between Catholic philosophy and the scientific method could be opened while, concurrently, modernity would be free from the dungeon of solipsism.[44] Adopting this starting point was also important in the confrontation with Marxism. There, the serious questions did not involve who understood physics better, but certain very basic issues: What is the human vocation? How do we build

history? Is the redemption of history to be understood in material and political terms, or does history have a transcendent dimension?[45]

Another fundamental agreement among the KUL philosophers was their
commitment to reason. Other thinkers might have had the cultural, economic, and political freedom to speculate about the alleged absurdity of life.
The KUL philosophers, veterans of the cultural resistance against Nazism, had
no such luxury. They had seen the films of Hitler's Nuremberg party rallies;
they had been subjected to more than five years of Nazi propaganda; they had
lived through a brutal occupation. They knew what irrationalism could do if
it got loose in history with sufficient material force. But the KUL philosophers'
commitment to the method of reason was coupled with a determination that
they would not get caught in the endless cycle that the Polish philosopher Wojciech Chudy would later call the "trap of reflection." Rather, their thought
would illuminate what good men and women *ought* to do.

Finally, the KUL philosophers agreed that they would practice an ecumenism of time. If they refused to be imprisoned inside their own consciousness, they also declined to be slaves to contemporaneity. The history of
philosophy had things to teach the present; the past had not been made completely disposable by modernity.[46]

These were men who believed that ideas were not intellectuals' toys. Ideas
had consequences, for good and for ill. The history of the twentieth century's
various torments, proved that defective understandings of the human person,
human community, and human destiny were responsible for mountains of
corpses and oceans of blood. If they could help the world get a firmer pur-
chase on the truth of the human condition, in a way that was distinctively modern *and* grounded in the great philosophical tradition of the West, the future
might be different.

The KUL philosophers were a community of personal and intellectual
friendship. Prior to being a reader of Wojtyła's dissertation on Scheler, Stefan
Swieżawski and his wife, Maria, had known the young priest at St. Florian's in
Kraków, where he had been the catechist and confessor of their two daughters. There was virtually no family anniversary at the Swieżawskis in which
Wojtyła did not participate. He, in turn, acknowledged on many occasions his
great intellectual debt to Swieżawski's book, *Being*. (During his entire tenure
at KUL, Professor Swieżawski commuted to Lublin from Kraków or Warsaw,
the authorities being mysteriously unable to grant him an apartment in the
city where he taught—a perfect illustration of the petty harassment meted out
to the KUL faculty by the Polish communist regime.) Wojtyła also became
close to the Kalinowski family, and was godfather for Jerzy Kalinowski's daughter.[47] Hiking and skiing trips together cemented the bonds of friendship in
more pleasant circumstances than the departmental offices.

The KUL philosophers were also that rarity in academic life, a genuine
team. On virtually every trip Father Wojtyła made to Lublin, he and his colleagues met as a group to talk through the common project in which they were

engaged. Although Kalinowski, as dean, was the initiator of their conversations, this was a gathering of equals who, as John Paul II later recalled, found it a "great advantage" to learn from each other's distinctive perspective and current work.[48]

At the same time there were real arguments and intellectual differences among the KUL philosophers, some of whom (like Father Krąpiec) had combative personalities. Karol Wojtyła's continuing interest in phenomenology and his ongoing investigation of modern and contemporary philosophy raised eyebrows among some of his more traditional colleagues, as did his philosophical and professorial style. He had a generally "unfootnoted" way of doing philosophy—rather "like a peasant," his premier student later noted—and he was far more concerned with mapping the terrain of things-as-they-are than with providing an extensive academic apparatus of citations and cross-references for every proposal or assertion.[49] Father Wojtyła was also singularly free of that professorial *gravitas* usually associated with senior academics in European universities.

To say that the KUL philosophy faculty had its disagreements and, in some respects, its rivalries, is simply to say that it was a faculty of men, not angels. The important thing about the KUL philosophers was the boldness of their intention. They first conceived their project as a response to the peculiar circumstances of their time and place. The range of its reach and its capacity to shed light on the human condition in very different situations would only come into focus when Professor Karol Wojtyła took the most adventurous part of the Lublin project to an audience whose numbers vastly exceeded the readership of Polish philosophical journals.

THE PROFESSOR

Stefan Swieżawski was not much taken by phenomenology himself, his tastes in contemporary philosophy running more to the linguistic analysts. Still, he had studied under the great Polish phenomenologist Roman Ingarden in Lwów, and his appointment as one of the three readers of Karol Wojtyła's habilitation thesis on Max Scheler had convinced him that the young priest's rapid development as a philosopher warranted bringing him into the KUL project. In September 1954, Swieżawski and his wife, Maria, were hiking with their friend Father Wojtyła in the mountains south of Kraków, and Swieżawski "heatedly" urged Wojtyła to join the KUL Philosophy Faculty. Wojtyła may have imagined that his post-habilitation academic work would be in Kraków, but Swieżawski pressed him hard, and within a month the KUL academic senate had agreed to Wojtyła's appointment as a docent in philosophical ethics. After the arrangement had been approved by Archbishop Baziak, Father Karol Wojtyła began commuting to Lublin from Kraków. In November 1956, at the beginning of his third year on the KUL staff, Wojtyła succeeded the Dominican Feliks Bednarski (who had been transferred to the Angelicum) in the

Chair of Ethics in the KUL Faculty of Philosophy, a position he would hold for twenty-two years.

While continuing his student and health-care chaplaincies in Kraków, Father Wojtyła came to KUL every two weeks during the academic year. To save time, he took the overnight train, arriving in Lublin early in the morning. He was sometimes joined on the train by Father Franciszek Tokarz, a professor of Hindu philosophy, who, after getting to know Wojtyła, once betook himself to the Kraków chancery office and said, "Make him a bishop. He is wise, pious, and good. That's the difference between him and me. When I get up in the morning and go out for a cigarette, he's praying. And when I get back he's still praying."[50] The impact, if any, of Professor Tokarz's unsolicited advice is unknown to history, but the two men, whose philosophical interests were vastly different, became friends.

The accommodations for visiting faculty at KUL were not elegant. The transients bunked down in a multiroomed apartment, where the only permanent resident, Stefan Sawicki, a young assistant professor of literature, lived in the kitchen. The apartment included a double room, a triple room, and one single room. Commuting professors used to argue about who would get the single room. Wojtyła never asked for it. Once, when there was no bed free, he slept on a table.[51]

The trains being what they were, Wojtyła was often late for class, rushing to KUL from the station. He told his students that he was operating on "Kraków time," not Lublin time.[52] He donated his salary, anonymously, to a scholarship fund that helped impoverished students pay for their education. His students in the mid-1950s remember his walking around the KUL campus in a frayed cassock and old overcoat. They also remember that he would frequently step into the campus chapel for a moment of prayer between classes or meetings.[53]

Wojtyła was an enormously popular professor, always approachable, in or out of class. His talent for relating theoretical material to the issues of everyday life gave his classes a concreteness that students found attractive. This was someone fascinated by people and the human condition in all its variety, a man capable of fostering a "deeper interaction" with his students than other faculty members. "He was interested in us as persons," as one former student summarized his magnetism.[54] Wojtyła also immersed himself in pastoral work at KUL, hearing confessions and counseling students who came to him with personal problems or for spiritual direction.[55]

His introductory-level courses on general philosophical ethics were delivered without notes. Wojtyła spoke slowly and developed his material through illustrations drawn from the students' own experiences. He used the examples of women in childbirth, soldiers together in combat, and religious celibates to demonstrate how men and women well-known to undergraduates exemplified the giving of oneself in service to others—a key norm in Wojtyła's personalist ethic.[56] This "Law of the Gift" was built into the human condition, he argued philosophically. Responsible self-giving, not self-assertion, was the road to human fulfillment. Wojtyła posed it not only as an ethic for Christians, but as a universal moral demand arising from the dynamics of the human person, who is truly a person only in relationship. A genuinely human existence was always coexistence, a meeting with others wisely.[57]

Wojtyła also taught upper-level philosophy courses for students in the later years of the five-year basic program at KUL, which led to a master's degree. These "monographic lectures" (as the advanced courses were known), delivered from handwritten notes over a year-long cycle, were far more difficult than the introductory course and involved an intense dialogue between Wojtyła and major figures in the Western philosophical tradition: Plato and Aristotle, Augustine and Aquinas, Kant, Hume, and Bentham, and, of course, Max Scheler. In delivering these demanding lectures, which emphasized freedom as the essence of man's spiritual nature, Wojtyła did not simply read his notes to his students. This was a dialogue with the philosophies of others, an exercise in "thinking as contemplation." Sometimes both professor and students would stop "and simply admire the beauty of the text."[58]

The lecture titles illustrated Wojtyła's effort to link philosophical realism (the analysis of things-as-they-are) to a philosophy of human consciousness: a "both/and" approach that demonstrated the lecturer's attempt to present the human reality in as full and rich a manner as possible and his conviction that Western philosophy had gone off the rails when our way of knowing the world got detached from the world itself. In 1954–1955, Wojtyła's monographic lectures dealt with "Act and Moral Experience"—the "structure" of a moral act and how we experience ourselves as moral actors. The principal interlocutors here were Max Scheler and his ethics of value, Immanuel Kant and his ethics of duty, and the Aristotelian-Thomistic theory of potency and action.[59] Wojtyła's synthetic conclusion to this four-way dialogue was another demonstration of his personalism: "The moral values of honesty and courage, through honest and courageous action, become an honest and courageous *person.*"[60]

The next two years of monographic lectures filled in the detail of this framework in conversation with two millennia of Western thinking.[61] His 1955–1956 lectures addressed "Goodness and Value," the possibility of defining an objective measure of moral action, and the way that moral norms grow in us through our moral action. The 1956–1957 lectures took up the issue of "Norm and Happiness." Again, the question was to put an objective moral standard, "given" in reality, into conversation with the experience of happiness that derives from acting well. In 1957–1958 and 1958–1959, Wojtyła worked through questions of sexual ethics in a series of lectures entitled "Love and Responsibility." His 1960–1961 upper-division course was the most abstract of the series, dealing with the "Theory and Methodology of Ethics." Pastoral obligations in Kraków made it impossible for Wojtyła to teach the advanced course in 1959–1960, and after the 1960–1961 series he dropped the course for lack of time.[62]

In addition to his other teaching responsibilities, Professor Wojtyła led a doctoral seminar in philosophical ethics in which his most advanced students began to prepare their dissertations. Even as his pastoral responsibilities in Kraków expanded, Wojtyła tenaciously held on to the responsibility of preparing doctoral candidates, bringing the students to him when necessary. This was the venue in which Wojtyła began to develop philosophical disciples and he enjoyed it tremendously.

The doctoral seminar was often conducted outdoors, in the hills or along mountain trails, Wojtyła sometimes lecturing while seated on a log. He was, according to his students, an excellent seminar leader, refusing to dominate, helping his students learn to think philosophically by gently compelling them to comment on what they were reading or writing. His skills as a listener, honed in pastoral life, were particularly transferable to this kind of teaching. So was his sometimes disconcerting capacity to do two things at once. When the seminar moved to the archbishop's residence in Kraków, Professor Cardinal Wojtyła would handle his correspondence while listening to a presentation and discussion, saying little, but then offering a cogent summary of the discussion in which no essential point was missed.[63]

Wojtyła-the-philosopher refined his distinctively phenomenological way of doing philosophy in the doctoral seminar. Many philosophers think in a linear way: they state a problem, examine a variety of possible solutions, and then, through a step-by-step process of logic, reach and state a conclusion. Wojtyła did not (and in fact does not) think linearly. His method was circular, but in the manner of walking down a spiral staircase, not going round-and-round a closed circle. He, too, would begin by identifying a problem: for example, what constitutes a just act? Then he would walk around the problem, examining it from different angles and perspectives. When he had gotten back to the starting point, he and his students would know a little more, so they would start walking around the problem again, reexamining it from this angle or that, but now at a deeper level of analysis and reflection. This continued through any number of perambulations, never forcing a conclusion before the question had been exhaustively examined from every possible point of view.[64] It was a powerful method of leading a seminar, a situation in which Wojtyła's sharply honed capacity for analysis and making distinctions worked to great effect. Transferred to the printed page, however, it made for very difficult philosophical essays.

Wojtyła's doctoral students were also his researchers. After he became a bishop, and especially after his appointment as archbishop of Kraków, the demands on his time were such that he simply could not keep up with the technical philosophical literature in his fields of interest. The doctoral seminar reviewed articles and books for him, writing summaries of arguments that were then discussed in meetings. The students also marked up the sections of articles or books they thought he should read on his own. Professor Wojtyła told the members of his seminar that this was the first time in the history of KUL that the students were teaching the faculty.[65]

Arguments with the professor were not simply permitted but expected in Wojtyła's doctoral seminar. Debate could get heated, with substantial disagreement and criticism of the teacher by the students. Yet Wojtyła was never regarded as simply another colleague. The relationship between him and his closest student-disciples, however friendly, was always marked by respect. His students wanted to be close to him; he was a thinker and human being they wanted to emulate.[66]

Professor Wojtyła's sense of responsibility for his doctoral students did not cease when they completed their degrees; he also tried to help them get teaching positions. One of his earlier efforts on this front was frustrated. Sister Zofia Zdybicka, an Ursuline nun, had been through both Wojtyła's undergraduate and graduate-level courses in philosophy. He was impressed by her interest in the philosophy of religion, and thought she would make a fine addition to the KUL faculty, where she would have been the first nun appointed to a professorship. This exercise in proto-feminism came to naught when another woman, Sister Zofia's religious superior in the Ursuline community, refused permission for such an innovation. A successor superior agreed at a later date.[67]

When Karol Wojtyła joked with his doctoral students about their teaching him, he was not simply making a pleasantry. Professor Wojtyła learned at KUL as well as taught. Through faculty colleagues at KUL, and especially Stefan Swieżawski, Wojtyła had his first serious encounter with Etienne Gilson's historical rereading of Thomas Aquinas and with Jacques Maritain's modern Thomistic reading of Catholic social ethics, including Maritain's moral defense of democracy as the modern method of government most reflective of human dignity. It was Swieżawski, for example, who introduced Wojtyła to Maritain's *Integral Humanism*, a key 1936 text that later influenced the Second Vatican Council and its approach to the modern world.

Wojtyła's more advanced students, like *Środowisko*, were also a kind of laboratory for his own developing ideas. In 1957, the professor went on vacation with philosophy, psychology, and medical students in the Mazurian Lakes country of northeastern Poland. There he discussed with them the draft of a book he was writing on sexual and marital ethics, which, like his monographic lectures for the next two years, would be called *Love and Responsibility*. The draft text was circulated before the group left for the lake country. Each day a different student prepared a presentation on a given chapter, which the entire group then discussed and debated. According to Wojtyła's student and friend Jerzy Gałkowski, Wojtyła was not only interested in his students' judgment on the book's theoretical soundness, but also wanted to know if what he had written made sense to them practically and humanly.[68]

The conversation was serious, on this and other student outings with Wojtyła. There was something about him that precluded frivolity and pointless chatter. But Father Professor could also join in boisterous student songs around the campfire, including the "Pessimists' Hymn," a provocative line from which had it that "even the laity won't stop the clergy destroying God's work."[69]

RESPONSIBLE LOVE

Professor Karol Wojtyła's work as a philosopher, like his literary activity as a poet and playwright, developed in concert with his work as a priest. Wojtyła did not bracket his pastoral concerns when he stepped up to the lecturer's podium or sat at the professor's desk. His intellectual product was influenced, indeed driven, by his pastoral experience. *Love and Responsibility*, Wojtyła's first book, was one such synthesis of the several dimensions of his life. A philosophical complement to the issues he explored dramatically in *The Jeweler's Shop*, it exemplified Wojtyła's conviction that one could only get to the truth of things by a variety of methods.

Love and Responsibility was, its author remembered, "born of pastoral necessity." Wojtyła's extensive pastoral experience in marriage preparation and as a confessor of young adults had convinced him that the Church's sexual ethic needed development and re-presentation.[70] Young men and women had a right not simply to instruction, but to an affirmation and celebration of their vocations to marriage, which included a vocation to sexual love. With *Love and Responsibility*, he stepped into one of the minefields of contemporary Catholic life.

When the early Church formally rejected the gnostic and Manichaean teachings that the world was inherently polluted, Christianity took a principled stand against the claim that sex was intrinsically evil. Yet the enduring theological influence of St. Augustine, or at least of some of his commentators, cast a Manichaean shadow over Catholic sexual ethics. The Church affirmed marriage as a vocation, included matrimony among its seven sacraments, and taught that the married couple, not the priest presiding at their wedding, were the ministers of the sacrament. But the Church also taught a theory of the "ends" or purposes of marriage that could be taken to (and sometimes did) denigrate sexual love. The primary end of marriage (and, pari passu, sex) was the procreation of children, and the sexual dimension of marital love was relegated to the secondary "ends" of matrimony, which were somewhat primly expressed as "mutual consolation of the spouses" and "a remedy for concupiscence." Combined with the fact that the Church's marriage law adopted a rather impersonal view of sexuality, the net result was a presentation of human sexuality that tended to focus more on legal prohibitions than on love. The Church was thus poorly positioned to respond to the challenge of the sexual revolution and its promise of liberation when it exploded in the developed world after World War II. In due course, this would result in one of the great crises of twentieth-century Catholic life, the bitter debate over contraception that preceded and followed the Second Vatican Council.

Life under communism posed its own challenges to sexual morality and marital chastity. As payback for its 1956 concessions to the Church, the Gomułka regime instituted a permissive abortion law, a direct assault on classic Catholic morality. Youngsters on state-sponsored summer outings were encouraged to experiment with sex as another means to pry them away from the Church. The communist campaign against traditional family life had its own secondary effects on sexual morality, for the linkage the Church taught between marital love and procreation was broken if men and women came to think of children as problems to be solved rather than as gifts to be cherished. Communist materialism also contributed to a cultural climate in which sexuality became morally devalued.

These were the life circumstances that Father Wojtyła's students and his young married friends were confronting. His work in philosophy and theology and his experiences as a confessor and counselor had convinced him that the Church's sexual ethic, properly interpreted, contained essential truths that deepened human happiness when they were faithfully lived out. He had also discovered that the spiritual adviser's "task is not only to command or forbid but to justify, to interpret, [and] to explain" the ethics of marital chastity and sexual love which the Church derived, primarily, from the New Testament.[71] Rules of sexual conduct were important. In a modern cultural climate, though, men and women would not embrace those rules unless they understood them as expressions of fundamental moral truths and as a road map to basic human goods. "Such a good is the person, and the moral truth most closely bound up with the world of persons is 'the commandment to love'—for love is a good peculiar to the world of persons."[72] Wojtyła thus argued that the best way to approach sexual morality was in the context of "love and responsibility." Love is an expression of personal responsibility, responsibility to another human being, and responsibility to God. How, he asked, can men and women become responsible lovers, so that their sexual love embodies and symbolizes a genuine freedom? How can our love become a fully human love?

The "personalist norm," Wojtyła's variant on Immanuel Kant's second categorical imperative, was his entry point for thinking about the ethics of human sexuality. Wojtyła argued that the moral imperative to avoid "using" others is the ethical basis of freedom, because it allows us to interact with others without reducing them to objects by manipulating them. Wojtyła suggested that we avoid "using" each other only when two genuine freedoms meet each other in pursuit of a good they hold in common.[73] I can say, and you can agree, that I am not "using" you (or you me) when my freedom freely encounters your freedom as we both seek something that is truly good, and that we both recognize as good. This encounter of two freedoms is the substance of love, and love is the expression of the personalist norm in all relationships. Loving is the opposite of using.[74]

A commitment to "loving rather than using" had considerable implications for sexual morality. If someone understands his sexuality as simply another function or expression of his personal autonomy—his freedom understood as license—then whatever his knowledge about the biological facts of life, he will miss one of the crucial *moral* facts of life: our sexuality reveals our profound dependence on others. I cannot achieve my destiny by myself, cutting myself off from others by reducing them to pleasure-objects. To achieve my destiny, I must "meet the freedom of another person and depend on it."[75]

Sexual morality transforms sex from something that just happens into something that expresses human dignity. Sex that just happens is dehumanized sex. Sex that is an expression of two persons—two freedoms—seeking personal and common goods together is fully human and fully humanizing.

Wojtyła's key philosophical move, which he adopted from Thomas Aquinas and explored through phenomenological analysis, was to distinguish between a "human act" and an "act of man." An "act of man" is mere instinct. Sexuality as an "act of man" does not rise above the level of animal sexuality, which is also instinctive and wholly impersonal. A "human act," on the other hand, includes a judgment, which gives that act its distinctive moral texture. A "human act" expresses my freely rendered judgment about something that is good. Love is thus the "human act" par excellence, and ought not be reduced to the simple emotion of attraction. Attraction uncoupled from judgment reduces someone else to an object of desire.[76]

The other *person*, not simply the other *body*, is the true object of a sexual act that is a truly human act. And the goal of sexual expression is to deepen a personal relationship, to which the mutual gift of pleasure contributes. In freely giving myself sexually to another as an expression of love, I am being myself in a most radical way, for I am making myself a gift to another in a way that is a profound expression of who I am. The "Law of the Gift"—for Wojtyła, the basic moral structure of human life—is powerfully confirmed by a careful analysis of the ethics of sexuality.

In addition to being a more humanistic approach to sexuality, reconceiving sexual expression as mutual self-donation allowed Wojtyła to transcend the argument about the "ends" of marriage then being fiercely contested in Catholic moral theology. Rather than asserting that either the begetting of children or the communion of the spouses was the "primary end" of marriage, Wojtyła's sexual ethic taught that *love* was *the* norm of marriage, a love in which both the procreative and unitive dimensions of human sexuality reached their full moral value.[77]

Love and Responsibility was an antidote to Manichaeanism and the outline of a personalistic, humanistic response to the claims of the contemporary sexual revolution. There was neither prudery nor prurience in Wojtyła's treatment of sexuality. His analysis of marriage avoided false romanticism and the sterilities of some moral theologies' abstractness. *Love and Responsibility* taught that sexuality was a good, because sexual desire led men and women into marriage, a difficult, but finally helpful, school in which we learn, "in patience, in dedication, and also in suffering what life is, and how the fundamental law of life, that is, self-giving, concretely shapes itself."[78]

Chastity, in this context, is not simply a string of prohibitions. Chastity is the "integrity of love," the virtue that makes it possible to love the other as a *person*. Chaste sexual love is ecstatic, in the original Greek meaning of ecstasy, being transported "outside" oneself. Chaste love involves putting one's emotional center, and, in a sense, one's self, in the custody of another. We are made as free creatures so that we can dispose of ourselves as a gift to others. We are free so that we can love freely, and thus truly. Freedom, not prohibition, is the framework of Wojtyła's sexual ethic.[79]

Love and Responsibility raised a few eyebrows when it was first published in 1960—at which point Karol Wojtyła had been a bishop for two years.[80] Wojtyła recalled that when the French edition was published in 1965, Father Henri de Lubac, one of the great theological inspirations of Vatican II, "strongly emphasized" that the fifth chapter, "Sexology and Morals," had to be retained, which suggests that the author had been told by others in the early 1960s that questions of sexual function and the mutual exchange of pleasure between wives and husbands were beneath his priestly and episcopal dignity. Wojtyła obviously disagreed.[81] If priests and bishops could not speak candidly and humbly about desire and sexual fulfillment with their people, they were defaulting in their pastoral responsibilities. If prudes disagreed, that was regrettable. But it was their problem.

Love and Responsibility was a book about responsible love, not a book about contraception. It discussed marital chastity and sexual ethics within the framework of Wojtyła's philosophical personalism and his defense of Christian humanism as a response to the false humanisms of the time. The truth about the human person was that the heart of the individual drama of our lives is the history of love or its negation. Mutual self-donation in a *communio personarum*, a community of persons, was the moral framework—the *humanistic* framework—in which to ponder the question of birth control.*

Wojtyła affirmed the Church's teaching that the morally appropriate regulation of births takes place through a responsible use of the natural cycle of fertility, rather than through mechanical or chemical means. He did not doubt that natural family planning was a method that required virtue, even heroic virtue, but he argued that it was the only method that met the high standards of human dignity, objectively and personally. Not everyone agreed, to be sure. Still, by locating the natural method of family planning within the broader context of responsible love and mutual self-giving, and by affirming sexual love as an essential expression of the vocation of marriage, Wojtyła's proposal might have given the Church's moral position on "natural" family planning an opportunity to be heard and engaged in a cultural climate in which "natural" was becoming a term of moral, even spiritual, force.

"Love or its negation": that, Wojtyła always believed, was *the* issue posed by the sexual revolution, the unforeseen results of which included the demeaning of women into objects of male sexual pleasure (claims to a "liberation" of both sexes notwithstanding). The Catholic teaching on marital chastity and its

---

* Communio personarum, a Latin term that Wojtyła prefers to any Polish word or its equivalent, is the phrase that best captures Wojtyła's fascination with love and the Law of the Gift: that one can't develop as a human being except by giving oneself, in which, paradoxically, one finds oneself.

relationship to various means of regulating births simply wouldn't make sense, though, unless the Church could present its understanding of "responsible love" in a way that could be grasped by men and women who believed that sexual love was a good. *Love and Responsibility* was intended to make moral sense about human sexuality, in dialogue with the women and men who had invited the author into their lives as "their pastor and their confidant."[82] That it did not succeed immediately, beyond the author's limited readership, would have consequences with which Karol Wojtyła would have to grapple in the not-too-distant future.

5

A New Pentecost

Vatican II and the Crisis of Humanism

JULY 4, 1958	Father Karol Wojtyła is named auxiliary bishop of Kraków by Pope Pius XII.
SEPTEMBER 28, 1958	Karol Wojtyła's episcopal consecration.
JANUARY 25, 1959	Pope John XXIII announces the Second Vatican Council.
DECEMBER 24, 1959	Bishop Karol Wojtyła begins celebrating Christmas midnight Mass in an open field in Nowa Huta.
DECEMBER 30, 1959	Wojtyła submits an essay on the crisis of humanism to the papal commission preparing Vatican II.
JULY 16, 1962	Bishop Wojtyła is elected temporary administrator of the Archdiocese of Kraków.
OCTOBER 11, 1962	Vatican II opens.
NOVEMBER 7, 1962	Bishop Wojtyła addresses the Council on liturgical reform.
NOVEMBER 21, 1962	Wojtyła speaks during the Council debate on revelation.
JUNE 3, 1963	Pope John XXIII dies, and is succeeded on June 21 by Pope Paul VI.
FALL 1963	Bishop Wojtyła enters the Council debate on the Church as the "People of God."
NOVEMBER 1963	"The Church," Wojtyła's poem-cycle on Vatican II, is published pseudonymously in *Znak*.
DECEMBER 5–15, 1963	Wojtyła visits the Holy Land.
DECEMBER 30, 1963	Karol Wojtyła named Archbishop of Kraków by Pope Paul VI.
MARCH 1964	Archbishop Wojtyła's inaugural pastoral letter stresses lay responsibility.
SEPTEMBER 25, 1964	Wojtyła addresses Vatican II on religious freedom.
OCTOBER 8, 1964	Wojtyła speaks during the Council's debate on the lay vocation.

OCTOBER 21, 1964	Archbishop Wojtyła addresses the Council on the Church's dialogue with the modern world.
DECEMBER 8, 1964	Wojtyła makes one of many reports to Kraków on the Council at St. Mary's Church.
JANUARY–APRIL 1965	Archbishop Wojtyła works in Ariccia and Rome on a sub-commission re-drafting the Council document on "The Church in the Modern World."
FEBRUARY 1965	Wojtyła writes on the Council and theologians in *Tygodnik Powszechny.*
APRIL 1965	Archbishop Wojtyła emphasizes viewing the Council "from inside" in another *Tygodnik Powszechny* article.
JUNE 1965	Wojtyła's poem-cycle, "Holy Places," published pseudonymously in *Znak.*
SEPTEMBER 22, 1965	Archbishop Wojtyła addresses the Council on the responsibilities of religious freedom.
SEPTEMBER 28, 1965	Wojtyła speaks at Vatican II on the Christian understanding of "the world" and the problem of modern atheism.
NOVEMBER 18, 1965	Letters of reconciliation exchanged by the Polish and German hierarchies.
1969	Wojtyła's *Person and Act* is published by the Polish Theological Society.

I n early August 1958, as his friends Stanisław and Danuta Rybicki awaited the birth of their first child, Father Karol Wojtyła began a two-week *Środowisko* kayaking trip on the River Lyne in northeastern Poland. Organized by "Admiral" Zdzisław Heydel, the flotilla of kayaks had traveled fifteen miles or so the first day. The vacationers then camped along the riverbank, played soccer, and talked around the campfire. Heydel had left behind in Kraków a detailed daily schedule, so that mail from children and friends who couldn't join the trip could be forwarded to local post offices where the kayakers could pick it up. On August 5, which happened to be the day Stanisław Rybicki, Jr., was born, Wojtyła got a letter ordering him to report immediately to the Primate, Cardinal Wyszyński, in Warsaw.

They took off in two kayaks, Wujek alone in one, Zdzisław Heydel and Gabriel Turowski in another. Turowski, an immunologist, was known to his friends as *"Gąpa"* [dumbbell or dummy] because he would play dumb when State Security called him in for interrogation after his annual refusal to participate in May Day demonstrations. The three men pulled off the river at a spot along the road to Olsztynek, the nearest railroad station, and left the kayaks under a bridge. "Admiral" Heydel tried to flag down a passing car. A milk truck stopped, and Heydel said they'd pay for the gas if the driver got them to Olsztynek. Wujek climbed into the back and sat amid the milk containers. When they got to the station in Olsztynek he slipped into the men's room, put on a cassock, and, as Turowski later put it, "left the men's room a priest again."

When Father Karol Wojtyła arrived in the Primate's office, Cardinal Wyszyński informed him that, on July 4, Pope Pius XII had named him titular bishop of Ombi and auxiliary to Archbishop Baziak, apostolic administrator of the Archdiocese of Kraków. Wojtyła accepted the nomination and went straight to the Ursuline convent in the capital, where he knocked on the door and asked if he could come in to pray. The sisters didn't know him, but his cassock was a sufficient passport. They led him to their chapel and left him alone. After some time, the nuns began to worry and quietly opened the door of the chapel to see what was happening. Wojtyła was prostrate on the floor in front of the tabernacle. Awestruck, the sisters left, thinking that perhaps he was a penitent. Some hours later they came back. The unknown priest was still prostrate before the Blessed Sacrament. It was late, and one of the nuns said, "Perhaps Father would like to come to supper . . . ?" The stranger answered, "My train doesn't leave for Kraków until after midnight. Please let me stay here. I have a lot to talk about with the Lord. . . ."

Having settled matters with the Lord, Father Wojtyła went to talk things over with Archbishop Baziak, who presumably expected his new auxiliary bishop to remain in town. Wojtyła told the archbishop that he had to get back to the River Lyne to celebrate Sunday Mass for his friends. Heydel and Turowski met him on the road to Olsztynek, at the bridge where they had flagged down the truck, and they kayaked back to the campsite. His old friends, stunned by the news, wondered what they should call him. Don't worry, he said, "*Wujek* will remain *Wujek*."[1]

SUCCESSOR OF THE APOSTLES

And so Karol Wojtyła, at thirty-eight, found himself the youngest bishop in Poland.

Speculation about a "master plan" for Wojtyła devised by Cardinal Sapieha and executed by Archbishop Baziak strains credulity. The Church really didn't work that way, and neither did the minds of Sapieha and Baziak. On the other hand, the Prince Cardinal held Father Karol Wojtyła in high regard, and it is certainly plausible to imagine Sapieha telling the exiled archbishop of Lwów about his esteem for the young man he had ordained and whose early ministry he had nurtured. Archbishop Baziak, for his part, must have been impressed by the young professor who, even as he shuttled between Kraków and the KUL philosophy department, continued to expand his local pastoral ministry. Wojtyła was now preaching regularly at the great red-brick Mariacki [St. Mary's] Church that dominates Kraków's Old Town market square. His St. Florian's–based student chaplaincy continued to thrive. And he was conducting an extensive ministry with heath-care professionals, stressing on retreats and days of recollection that the renewal of the Church required the renewal of the laity. Eugeniusz Baziak, who had been through a lot in his life, had evidently come to appreciate the combination of intelligence, piety, pastoral zeal, and internal toughness that Father Karol Wojtyła represented. It also says something about Archbishop Baziak that this very formal, even stern, man was not put off by Wojtyła's entirely different clerical style. Wojtyła's openness may have struck others as alarmingly freewheeling. Eugeniusz Baziak, who could no more imagine himself kayaking with young couples than he could imagine flying to the moon, must have understood that Karol Wojtyła was a priest to the core.

Father Wojtyła may also have represented for Baziak exactly the kind of resistance to communism that the archbishop, who had lived under house arrest for three years in the mid-1950s, thought appropriate in the aftermath of the 1956 Gomułka thaw. Though Wojtyła wasn't agitating on street corners, his teaching and his pastoral work were helping create a generation of confident young Catholics who would embody an ongoing cultural resistance to Marxism—and, by extension, to the usurpation of the Polish state by the Polish United Workers' Party. "The redemption of mankind," Father Wojtyła had told a 1957 conference of Catholic physicians, means "assisting man to achieve the greatness he is meant to possess." That was what communism claimed to do—to liberate humanity for greatness. Father Wojtyła was a magnetic teacher and evangelist who could meet that argument on its own ground and counter it with a more compelling humanism, the liberation of humanity through "union with God," as he put it to the doctors. That was what the Church was for.[2]

After baptizing Stanisław Rybicki, Jr., on August 31, the bishop-elect attended his first meeting of the Polish episcopate at Częstochowa and made a five-day preordination retreat at the Benedictine monastery at Tyniec. There was a bit of a fuss about the ceremony. The bishop-elect wanted a liturgical "commentator" who would explain the lengthy, complex rite to the congregation as it unfolded; Archbishop Baziak refused this concession to liturgical renewal. So Wojtyła got hold of a translation of the Latin ritual and recruited a squadron of women who volunteered to hand-make booklets for those attending the service.[3]

On the feast of St. Wacław (St. Wenceslaus), September 28, 1958, Karol Józef Wojtyła processed into Wawel Cathedral to be consecrated a bishop, receiving the fullness of the priesthood and becoming a successor of Christ's apostles, according to the Church's theology. The cathedral was packed with Wojtyła's friends, academic colleagues, and, of course, the members of his *Środowisko*, none of whom let the wet, overcast day dampen their spirits.

Seated on the archbishop's *cathedra*, or throne, with Father Wojtyła standing before him, Archbishop Baziak began the ceremony by asking that the apostolic mandate, the Pope's authorization for the new bishop's consecration, be read. It was the last historic act of the nineteen-year pontificate of Pius XII, who died eleven days later. Baziak then examined the bishop-elect on his commitment to serving the Church. No one doubted his faith, of course, but it was the Church's ancient practice that her ministers should profess their faith and their commitment publicly, in front of those they were called to serve and govern. Then, the consecration Mass began.

After the first Scripture reading, Father Wojtyła prostrated himself on the floor of the sanctuary while the choir sang the Litany of the Saints over him. At the end of the litany, Wojtyła knelt before Baziak, now seated on a faldstool before the high altar. Amid a deep silence, Archbishop Baziak, assisted by two other bishops, placed the open Book of the Gospels, the yoke of Christ, on Wojtyła's bowed neck, then laid his hands upon Wojtyła's head, as did the two co-consecrating bishops. The archbishop then prayed the consecration preface, asking God that the new bishop be sanctified by "the dew of the divine anointing."

While one of the assisting chaplains bound Wojtyła's head with a long white cloth, Baziak knelt before the altar and intoned the great hymn to the Holy Spirit, "Veni Creator Spiritus." As the choir continued the anthem, Baziak, reseated on the faldstool, anointed Wojtyła with holy chrism, first making the sign of the cross on the crown of his head, then anointing the entire crown, while praying, "May thy head be anointed and consecrated by heavenly benediction in the pontifical order." He then blessed Wojtyła three times, and after cleansing his hands of the chrism with bread crumbs, chanted the prayer of anointing, asking God that the new bishop "may be untiring in his solicitude, fervent in spirit; may he detest pride, cherish humility and truth, and never desert it, overcome by either flattery or fear."

Baziak next anointed the new bishop's hands and bound them with a white cloth. He bestowed upon Wojtyła the bishop's pastoral staff, or crosier, and placed on his right hand a bishop's ring, praying, "Receive the ring, the symbol of fidelity, in order that, adorned with unshakable faith, thou mayest keep inviolable the Spouse of God, His Holy Church." Baziak then took the Book of the Gospels from Bishop Wojtyła's neck and touching it to his bound hands, prayed, "Receive the Gospel, and go, preach to the people committed to thee, for God is powerful to increase His grace in thee, He Who liveth and reigneth, forever and ever." The new bishop replied, "Amen," and exchanged the kiss of peace with Archbishop Baziak and his co-consecrators.

After Bishop Karol Wojtyła had cleaned his hands, Mass continued with the proclamation of the Gospel and Archbishop Baziak's sermon. As the offertory began, Bishop Wojtyła presented his consecrator with three gifts: two lighted candles, two small loaves of bread, and two small barrels of wine. The candles were carried by Zdzisław Heydel, the erstwhile kayaking "Admiral," and Marian Wojtowicz, who later became the first priest in the community founded by Albert Chmielowski. The loaves of bread were presented by Stanisław Rybicki and, according to ancient Kraków custom, a representative of the bakers' guild. The small barrels of wine were offered by Jerzy Ciesielski and Zbigniew Siłkowski, a friend of the new bishop's from Wadowice.

At the end of Mass, Archbishop Baziak placed the twin-peaked miter on the head of the kneeling Bishop Wojtyła. Life then imitated art as sunlight burst through the clouds and the cathedral's stained glass, covering the newly consecrated bishop in a warm glow. Baziak led Bishop Wojtyła to the faldstool, where he sat before his people with miter, crosier, and bishop's ring as the archbishop and the co-consecrators intoned the Church's ancient hymn of thanksgiving, the "Te Deum." As the choir continued the hymn, Bishop Karol Wojtyła rose, walked through the cathedral, and blessed the congregation.

Perhaps it was at this point in the lengthy proceedings that one of Wojtyła's fellow workers from the Solvay plant shouted out, "Lolek, don't let anything get you down!" It was, according to reports, a sentiment "received with sympathy by the congregation and by the new bishop himself."[4]

Bishop Wojtyła chose as the motto on his episcopal coat-of-arms the Latin phrase *Totus Tuus* [completely yours], an adaptation of St. Louis de Montfort's prayer of dedication to the Virgin Mary, which he had first encountered during his nocturnal reading by the dim light of the Solvay chemical plant.

THE YOUNGEST BISHOP IN POLAND

Not everyone thought the appointment of Karol Wojtyła as bishop was a good idea. Professor Adam Vetulani of the Jagiellonian University complained about his "misery" with "cleric-scholars." See what happens, he wrote a friend: "You educate . . . a docent and a 'statesman' emerges." Toasting his young friend, whom he insisted on calling "Bishop Docent Karol Wojtyła," at the post-consecration reception, the curmudgeonly professor could not resist asking "one thing only: may he have adequate strength and time to fulfill the obligations which he has earlier taken upon himself, and for which he has trained through strenuous work for many years."[5]

Professor Vetulani need not have fretted. Bishop Wojtyła continued teaching at KUL, although he came to the campus less often. The doctoral seminar would sometimes meet for six hours at a time, to compensate for the less-frequent sessions, and lectures in his introductory course were taken over by some of his philosophical protégés. His upper-division "monographic lectures" continued until 1961.

In the first months of his episcopacy Wojtyła took on a host of new pastoral responsibilities. Always in demand as a guest preacher and retreat master, he now traveled even more extensively throughout the archdiocese, saying Mass, blessing buildings, ordaining subdeacons and deacons, confirming deaf-mute children, supervising meetings of various deaneries for Archbishop Baziak, preaching to days of recollection or special Masses for various groups of professionals, including doctors, lawyers, and intellectuals.[6]

Ecclesiastical administration has never been Karol Wojtyła's understanding of his episcopal vocation. For him, the episcopate is preeminently an office of preaching and teaching, and in the service of that apostolate in Kraków he was indefatigable. In March 1959, to take but one example, he conducted a day of recollection for the staff of *Tygodnik Powszechny* and preached at retreats for mining engineers, nurses, teachers, lawyers, and physicians. The pace eventually caught up with him. That same month he was diagnosed with mononucleosis, after a blood test that included a difficult biopsy of his bone marrow. The doctor apologized for the discomfort he had caused. The bishop sympathized with the doctor for having had to grind his way through a particularly hard bone.[7]

Wojtyła's preaching and teaching in the period just before and after his consecration as a bishop developed themes of renewal that would soon become familiar throughout the Catholic world. At a colloquium for physicians in 1958, he stressed "God's enormous confidence in the possibilities of man," a confidence to which the Incarnation of the Son of God bore eloquent witness.[8] Later that year, he told a day of recollection for young people that "prayer is the reaction to the mystery that the world carries within itself." Without prayer we cut ourselves off from the depth-dimension of the world.[9] In Łodz, at a 1960 Lenten retreat for college teachers, Bishop Wojtyła taught that grace was "the very joy of existence" and that "the Church is not an organization of Christ, it is an organism of Christ."[10]

His ecclesiastical status may have changed, but other things hadn't— including the Polish regime's determination to make life as difficult as possible for the student chaplaincy at the Jagiellonian University and for the archdiocesan health-care ministry. On October 11, 1959, Wojtyła was scheduled to preach at a Mass for the beginning of the academic year in St. Anne's collegiate church. The regime forbade posting any announcements of the event, except for a small notice in the church vestibule. Yet the church was filled to overflowing, and several professors, including the redoubtable Adam Vetulani, defied the authorities by sitting in the chancel during the service. A few months later, in February 1960, Bishop Wojtyła visited a sanitarium for women run by the Albertine nuns on Zielna Street, meeting and blessing every patient. As a result of his visit, the Albertines noted primly in their diary, they had "difficulties" and "unpleasantness" with the authorities.[11] In addition to these relatively minor confrontations, Bishop Wojtyła began, on December 24, 1959, an annual custom that would long be a burr under the communist saddle—Christmas midnight Mass in an open field in Nowa Huta, the so-called model workers' town outside Kraków, the first town in Polish history deliberately built without a church. Given the freezing winter weather, he wrote some years later, a Christmas Mass for those who had no place else to go that night bore a "striking resemblance in external conditions" to another Christmas, almost 2,000 years before.[12]

It was not all work. The new bishop kept up his kayaking during two-week excursions with *Środowisko* friends in late July and early August of each year. He also skied whenever possible. Karol Wojtyła always loved Christmas and took advantage of the Polish custom of extending the holiday through January to participate in many *Opłatek* celebrations, at which groups of

Polish friends break and share a Christmas wafer while singing traditional carols, most of which the bishop knew by heart. He also kept in touch with the Rhapsodic Theater, celebrating a twentieth-anniversary Mass for the troupe at Wawel Cathedral on September 19, 1961, and pseudonymously publishing an essay on *"Forefathers' Eve* and the Twentieth Anniversary" in *Tygodnik Powszechny*.

THE VICAR CAPITULAR

Archbishop Eugeniusz Baziak died on the night of June 14–15, 1962. Bishop Wojtyła substituted for the deceased archbishop at the ordination of new priests for the archdiocese on June 15. On June 19, he welcomed those who had come for the archbishop's funeral with a richly biblical homily, drawing out a gentler aspect of Baziak's character that those who had seen only his severity might have missed. The late archbishop was like the Gospel figure of the good shepherd, who not only watches, guards, and defends, but who searches for the lost sheep, "and, having found it, returns it to the flock, and rejoices, and is glad. . . ."[13]

The priests and people of Kraków buried Archbishop Eugeniusz Baziak, the exile, in the Bishop Zebrzydowski chapel of Wawel Cathedral, near the great black cross where Queen Jadwiga had prayed. On his tombstone, they gave him in death the title the communists had denied him in life: "Archbishop of Kraków."

A week later, Bishop Wojtyła, en route to a reunion of his former students, stopped at a parish north of Kraków to celebrate Mass. The local priest had just been arrested for saying Mass "illegally" in a temporary building outside the parish church, and Wojtyła wanted to show solidarity with the parish and its imprisoned pastor. He soon had a more formal responsibility in the face of persecution. On July 16, the Metropolitan Chapter, a group of senior priests, elected Bishop Wojtyła "vicar capitular," or temporary administrator, of the Archdiocese of Kraków until a successor to Archbishop Baziak (and, technically speaking, to Cardinal Sapieha) could be appointed and installed. It was a striking vote of confidence in the younger of Kraków's auxiliary bishops— who, two weeks later, honored the principle that *"Wujek* will remain *Wujek"* by taking his annual fortnightly kayaking trip with his young couples and their families. During the trip they discussed the significance of the forthcoming Second Vatican Council, which Pope John XXIII had announced in 1959. Wujek insisted that it would be a watershed in the life of the Church.[14]

After years of preparation, the Council was set to open in Rome on October 11, 1962, but Wojtyła had urgent local business to attend to first. The city's communist authorities were trying to claim the Kraków seminary's building on July Manifesto Street for the Higher School of Pedagogy. Informed of this by the Metropolitan Chapter while he was on a parish visitation in the countryside, the vicar capitular came straight back to Kraków and, to everyone's amazement, asked to see the secretary of the local Communist Party. It was the first such meeting ever and it paid a handsome return. The Higher School of Pedagogy was permitted to use the third floor of the building, but the seminary remained on the first two floors and thus kept control of the building until the nascent pedagogues vacated the premises in the summer of 1979.[15]

There was also a personal matter of grave concern. Dr. Wanda Połtawska, a psychiatrist who had been a great help in preparing *Love and Responsibility*, was stricken with what the doctors diagnosed as terminal cancer. Wojtyła wrote the Italian Capuchin stigmatic, Padre Pio, asking for his prayers. When Dr. Połtawska was X-rayed prior to her scheduled surgery, the cancerous mass had disappeared. It was, Wojtyła believed, a miracle wrought by Padre Pio's intercession, another example of the extraordinary that lay just on the other side of the ordinary.[16]

Now he was ready for Vatican II. Bishop Karol Wojtyła departed for Rome on the evening of October 5, 1962, taking leave of his priests and people, gathered for Mass at Wawel Cathedral, with "great personal emotion" and "great trembling of heart" as he set out on a "great highway from the tomb of St. Stanisław to the tomb of St. Peter."[17] Although he had told his friends that Vatican II would be something rare and important, he could not have foreseen in detail just how crucial the forthcoming Council would be for the self-understanding of the Roman Catholic Church, for its struggle to survive in communist-dominated east central Europe, for the Church's encounter with the modern world—and for the future of the Titular Bishop of Ombi and Vicar Capitular of the Archdiocese of Kraków.

THE GAMBLE OF VATICAN II

There have been only twenty-one general or "ecumenical" councils in the history of the Catholic Church. These gatherings of all the world's bishops in communion with the Bishop of Rome have been held in Asia Minor, northern Italy, France, Germany, and Rome, lasting as briefly as a few months and as long as eighteen years.[18] Ecumenical councils have defined dogma, written creeds, condemned heresy, laid down guidelines for sacramental practice, deposed emperors, fought schisms, and proposed schemes for the reunification of Christianity. No matter where they took place, what they did, or how long they took to do their work, virtually every one of them was steeped in conflict and followed by controversy.[19]

When Pope John XXIII stunned the Church and the world on January 25, 1959, by announcing his intention to call an ecumenical council, Cardinal Giovanni Battista Montini—who would succeed him as pope, bring the Council to a successful conclusion, and suffer through thirteen years of conflict over its implementation—called a friend and said, "This holy old boy doesn't realize what a hornet's nest he's stirring up."[20] Montini was, by nature, a man who worried an issue. In this instance he was prescient.

Pope John planned an ecumenical council unprecedented in the history of the Church. Previous councils had completed their work by issuing creeds, canons, condemnations, or other formal doctrinal decrees, which provided interpretive "keys" to a Council's work. John wanted his Council to be pastoral and evangelical rather than juridical and dogmatic. He envisioned an open conversation in which the world's bishops would relive the experience of Christ's apostles at Pentecost. The Second Vatican Council, in the Pope's mind, would renew Christian faith as a vibrant way of life; it would engage modernity in dialogue; it would issue no condemnations; it would try to give voice again to the pure message of the Gospel. It would, in the now-famous phrase, open the Church's windows to the modern world.

To do all of this without providing authoritative interpretive "keys" to its work was an enormous risk. In many of its leading intellectual and scientific centers, the modern world to which the Church proposed to open itself was closing its own windows on any idea of transcendence. Catholicism had been largely cut off from the pan-Christian ecumenical movement. Its theological life was still shadowed by the Modernist crisis of the late nineteenth and early twentieth centuries. An aggressively atheistic opponent with its own ultra-mundane theory of redemption controlled the destinies of billions of human beings. The Church itself was deeply divided about the possibility of a serious dialogue with modernity. Some senior churchmen believed that any conversation with the political forces let loose in the French Revolution would inevitably lead to Christianity's collapse. Others believed, just as passionately, that the Church's vision of human dignity and human destiny could help direct the modern quest for freedom into productive rather than destructive channels. To take an ancient religious institution into an open-ended conversation about its nature, its worship, its mission, and its relationship to the world under these circumstances was a tremendous act of faith in the power of the Holy Spirit to guide the Church in truth.

There is a familiar telling of the story of how Pope John's great gamble worked out in which the conciliar lines of battle are clearly drawn between good "liberals" and bad "conservatives," the former winning in the end despite the intransigence of the latter. This "Whig" interpretation of the history of Vatican II has important elements of truth in it. The Roman Curia, the Church's central bureaucracy, had become intellectually ossified and too often identified its own concerns with the needs of the universal Church. Catholicism, as Pope John famously put it in his opening address to the Council, had used too much of the medicine of condemnation and too little of the medicine of mercy in its approach to modernity. The Church's theology, its study of Scripture, its worship, and its approach to modern politics all needed development. It is also true that these necessary developments were resisted, sometimes bitterly and with some throwing of sharp elbows, by churchmen who can accurately be described as anti-modern. Politicking certainly had a lot to do with how the Council played itself out, and there were surely identifiable "camps" or parties involved in this. The Council was composed of men, and large gatherings of human beings make decisions through political processes and factions.

All that can be conceded to the Whig or "progressive" interpretation of Vatican II—and yet, Pope John Paul II would insist, that telling of the story still misses the essential experience, the crucial point, of the Council.[21]

Karol Wojtyła attended every session of the Second Vatican Council. He has often spoken about the great "debt" he owes to Vatican II, which had a "unique and unrepeatable meaning for all who took part in it." It was a time of "great spiritual enrichment," shaped by "the experience of a worldwide community."[22] The Council was a "great gift to the Church, to all those who took part in it, to the entire human family. . . ."[23] It was "the seminary of the Holy Spirit,"[24] a time in which Christ's promise to his apostles, "I am with you always" (*Matthew* 28.20), "took on a special freshness."[25] In payment of his personal debt to the Council and in fulfillment of his commitment to its teaching, Karol Wojtyła initiated one of the most extensive implementations of the Council of any diocese in the world.

Given that experience and that testimony, he must be taken seriously when, as archbishop of Kraków and as Bishop of Rome, he has insisted that any interpretation of the Council that does not treat Vatican II as, first and foremost, a profound *spiritual* experience—an "act of love" amid the hatreds of the age, an effort to "enrich" the faith of the Church so that Christians might live an "increasingly full participation in divine truth"[26]—is simply going to miss what was central to the experience of the Council itself. Karol Wojtyła was not, and is not, a naïf. As an active participant in the four sessions (or "periods") of Vatican II and in working groups that refined draft documents between the Council's formal meetings in Rome, he knew a lot about the backstage politics of Vaticanum Secundum, as he and fellow Poles called it. Knowing all that, he still insisted (and insists) that Vatican II can only be understood fully and truthfully if one understands it as a religious event, not a political contest, in which the Holy Spirit, not ecclesiastical factions, was the chief protagonist. Anyone interested in understanding Wojtyła as bishop and as Pope must make the effort to "get inside" Vatican II as he experienced it.

A SON OF THE COUNCIL

The Second Vatican Council gave Karol Wojtyła, who had not been outside Poland since returning from his Roman graduate studies in 1948, a new and very concrete sense of the Church's universality. He came from a country preparing to celebrate the millennium of its baptism. Now, traveling to Rome every fall for the two-month-long Council sessions, he met bishops from churches barely a century old who were debating the future of Catholicism with vigor and insight. It was, he said, "an inspiration" to him, an experience he tried to grasp poetically in verses scribbled on the sides of official Council working documents and mailed off to *Tygodnik Powszechny.*[27] He was deeply moved, for example, by his first extensive contacts with Africans, and by the discovery that they were living the same truth in quite different ways:

> It's exactly You, My Dear Brother, I feel in you an enormous land,
> in which rivers rapidly disappear . . . as sun burns the body like a
>   foundry burns iron
> —I feel in you a similar thought:
> If the thought does not run in a similar way, it separates with the
>   same balance
> truth and error.
> There is joy of weighing these thoughts on one balance,
> thoughts which glitter in your eyes and mine in a different way,
>   although they
> have the same content.[28]

In addition to meeting and working with the world's leading churchmen, Karol Wojtyła also had the opportunity at Vatican II to rediscover old friends and get caught up on more than two decades of their lives. Jerzy Kluger, working in Rome as an engineer, hadn't seen his classmate from Wadowice since World War II had broken out. One day he read in a Roman paper about a speech at the Council by an Archbishop Karol Wojtyła of Kraków. Kluger called the Polish Institute in Rome, where Wojtyła stayed during the Council sessions, and asked to speak to him. Wojtyła was out, but called back on his return and asked his classmate to come over immediately. Kluger worked his way through the purgatorial Roman traffic and entered the Polish Institute. When Wojtyła came downstairs, the two didn't say anything, but simply looked at each other in silence. Then they embraced. When Kluger tried to address the archbishop as "Your Excellency," Wojtyła said, "What do you mean, Excellency? Call me Lolek. . . ."[29]

There were also ancient places to be reencountered or discovered. Wojtyła not only became reacquainted with Rome during the Council, but took Pope Paul's suggestion that bishops try to visit the Holy Land prior to the Pope's own pilgrimage there in 1964. For ten days in December 1963, Wojtyła walked the paths where Jesus had trod, sat on hillsides where Jesus had preached, prayed at the spot when Jesus had died. He went with "several score" of other bishops, who began in Egypt and thus relived the "exodus to the Promised Land which the Chosen People traveled in the Old Testament." In Bethlehem, he wrote the priests of Kraków, "the Polish bishops sang a few Polish Christmas carols" at the grotto of the Nativity, at the request of an aged Polish Franciscan who had worked in Jerusalem for years. The bishops walked on the Temple Mount in Jerusalem, a "holy spot for Christians" because it was the site of "the Temple of the true God, which Our Lord plainly called 'the house of my Father,'" and because "our Redeemer visited this temple many times in his lifetime." The mystic starkness of the Judean wilderness left a lasting impression on Wojtyła, as on so many others. Here he was powerfully struck by the fact that God, in order to redeem the world, had entered history at one time and one place. As he put it in a poem, "You seek out people every-where/But to seek everywhere/You had to stop in some place./This one is chosen by You."[30]

To walk along the Galilean shoreline from which the apostle Peter had set out to fish for men made one kind of impression. The experience of the Council itself deepened Karol Wojtyła's understanding of the Office of Peter—the papal ministry—in the Church. He had seen Pius XII as a young priest-student, but the pope who had nominated him a bishop was a remote figure. Now, working with Popes John XXIII and Paul VI and spending hours every day inside St. Peter's Basilica, just a few hundred yards from the apostle's tomb, he was profoundly struck by what the Office of Peter meant for the Church—and what that office exacted from the man who held it. Once again, poetry was the best way to express what he was learning:

> In this place our feet meet the ground, on which were raised
> so many walls and colonnades . . . if you don't get lost in them but
>   go on finding
> unity and sense—
> it is because She is leading you. She connects not only the
>   spaces of a
> renaissance building, but also spaces In Us,
> who go ahead so very conscious of our weakness and disaster.
> It is You, Peter. You want to be the Stone Floor, so that they will
>   pass over you
> (going ahead, not knowing where), that they should go where you
>   lead their feet,
> so that they should connect into one the spaces which through
>   sight help the
> thought to be born.
> You want to be Him who serves the feet—like rock the hooves of
>   sheep:
> The rock is also the stone floor of the gigantic temple. The Pasture
>   is the cross.[31]

Even as the Council deepened his sense of Rome's meaning as the center of unity for an increasingly diverse universal Church, Karol Wojtyła, according to those who know him best, kept a critical distance from the temptation to regard "Rome" *as* the Church—what some call the virus of *Romanità*. His primary responsibility was in Kraków, and he made use of his regular presence in Rome during the four autumns of the Council to do some business for the home front. In May 1963, between the first and second sessions of the Council, he had unveiled a memorial at Wawel Cathedral to Rafał Kalinowski and Adam (Brother Albert) Chmielowski, making some pointed comments about these two "Polish rebels" whose participation in the 1863 Uprising was "a stage on the road to sanctity." During the second session itself, he convinced all the Polish bishops to sign a petition, or "postulation," supporting the beatification of Brother Albert. Together with the Roman promoter of Chmielowski's cause, he called on Cardinal Arcadio Larraona, Prefect of the Sacred Congregation of Rites, to press the cause of Brother Albert in person.

Then there was the case of Sister Faustina Kowalska, a young mystic who had died in Kraków in 1938. Her "Divine Mercy" devotion was spreading throughout Poland even as her writings were coming under the theological suspicion of certain Roman authorities. The Archdiocese of Kraków was eager to propose Sister Faustina for beatification, and Wojtyła helped clear the doctrinal air with the Roman Curia so that Sister Faustina's cause could be introduced.[32]

Archbishop Wojtyła also kept the lines open between Rome and Poland by regularly visiting the Polish College, the Roman residence for priest-students and seminarians. On one such occasion, a student asked bluntly what the point was of an ecumenical council without a clearly defined objective. The archbishop replied that Pope John, a very insightful student of his times, was deeply concerned about the "cultural deracination" of modernity and thought that the Church had to renew itself in order to preach the Gospel in an age transformed and in some respects distorted by technology. Christian unity, he stressed, was another essential goal of the Council and was central to the Pope's intention in summoning Vatican II.[33]

Finally, Vatican II was a profound intellectual experience for Wojtyła and a stimulus to his work as a philosopher. The debates over the Council's two central dogmatic constitutions, on *The Church* and on *Divine Revelation,* and his work in helping draft the council's seminal *Pastoral Constitution on the Church in the Modern World* were a kind of postdoctoral school of theology that, as a former Council theologian later put it, "nourished his vision of the Church."[34] At the same time, he thought that the Council's vision of the human person would be even more compelling if it were given a deeper philosophical foundation. Out of that concern would come Wojtyła's major philosophical work, *Person and Act.*

By the end of the Council in 1965, the young bishop who arrived in Rome in 1962 as the unknown vicar capitular of Kraków was one of the better-known churchmen in the world, to his peers, if not to the world press. And he was known, not primarily by contrast to the overwhelming personality of his Primate, Cardinal Wyszyński, but as a man with ideas and a striking personal presence in his own right.

Starting Point

On October 11, 1962, surrounded by the Renaissance pomp of a papal court that would soon be a newsreel memory, Pope John XXIII was carried on the *sedia gestatoria* up the center aisle of St. Peter's Basilica to open the Second Vatican Council. The nave of the basilica had been transformed by an army of workers, the *Sanpietrini,* into a giant *aula* or hall where Vatican II's formal sessions would be held. Tiers of seats rose on each side of the center aisle to accommodate more than 2,000 bishops who were participating in the Council—itself an indication of the Church's growth during the past ninety years, since the First Vatican Council (1869–1870) had fit snugly within one arm of the basilica's transept. As befit his youth and relatively humble ecclesiastical station, the Titular Bishop of Ombi and Vicar Capitular of Kraków sat next to the door, about 500 feet from the high altar.[35] The Council was about to begin, but Bishop Karol Wojtyła had already made a striking contribution to the proceedings.

In June 1959, the Ante-Preparatory Commission established by John XXIII had written to all the world's Catholic bishops, superiors of men's religious orders, and theological faculties, asking their suggestions for the Council's agenda. Many bishops submitted outlines of internal Church matters they wanted to discuss. Bishop Karol Wojtyła sent the commissioners an essay—the work of a thinker, not a canon lawyer. Rather than beginning with what the Church needed to do to reform its own house, he adopted a quite different starting point. What, he asked, is the human condition today? What do the men and women of this age expect to hear from the Church?

The crucial issue of the times, he suggested, was the human person: a unique being, who lived in a material world but had intense spiritual longings, a mystery to himself and to others, a creature whose dignity emerged from an interior life imprinted with the image and likeness of God. The world wanted to hear what the Church had to say about the human person and the human condition, particularly in light of other proposals—"scientific, positivist, dialectical"—that imagined themselves humanistic and presented themselves as roads to liberation. At the end of 2,000 years of Christian history, the world had a question to put to the Church: What was Christian humanism and how was it different from the sundry other humanisms on offer in late modernity? What was the Church's answer to modernity's widespread "despair [about] any and all human existence"?

The crisis of humanism at the midpoint of a century that prided itself on its humanism should be the organizing framework for the Council's deliberations, Bishop Wojtyła proposed. The Church did not exist for itself. The Church existed for the salvation of a world in which the promise of the world's humanization through material means had led, time and again, to dehumanization and degradation.

Wojtyła's further suggestions for the Council's agenda continually referred back to this fundamental crisis of the age. The pursuit of Christian unity (through "less emphasis on those things that separate us and searching instead for all that brings us together") was essential to the proclamation of a compelling Christian humanism. A zealous, educated laity was essential if Christian humanism was to penetrate all of society, "especially in those places where priests and clergy cannot fulfill their own mission." The evangelization of modern culture through Christian humanism required priests who could affirm "all things worthy in themselves of being affirmed, even if they do not have an outwardly religious or sacral character."

The sanctification of all of life would happen "indirectly" in some cases, Wojtyła further suggested. Whenever the priest engaged the world of culture or work, he had to present "the sacred in such manner as seems entirely fitting to the men of today." This, in turn, required seminaries that were "not simply professional schools but true academies," preparing priests who could minister to an increasingly well-educated laity. The evangelical action of both priests and laity, and the Church's witness to Christian humanism, would also benefit from an introduction of vernacular languages into the Mass and other sacramental celebrations.[36]

Karol Wojtyła's submission to the Ante-Preparatory Commission reflected the imprint of his first four decades of life: the Nazi Occupation and life in Stalinist Poland; his experiences in the classroom and the confessional; his effort to grasp "God, inscrutable in the mystery of man's inmost life" through his poetry, his plays, and his philosophical essays. There are overtones of Mieczysław Kotlarczyk and the Rhapsodic Theater in Wojtyła's discussion of the relationship of the sacred and the worldly. His experiences with his young couples resonate through his proposals for a lay apostolate that embodies Christian humanism in venues the clergy cannot reach. (One can even hear an echo of kayak paddles on the Mazurian Lakes in Wojtyła's proposal that canon law be changed so that "attendance at Mass on a portable altar . . . fulfill the Church's requirement for Holy Days and Sundays" without special permission.)

What was singular and, to use an abused term in its proper sense, prophetic about Wojtyła's proposal was its insistence that the question of a humanism adequate to the aspirations of the men and women of the age had to be the epicenter of the Council's concerns. There would be much talk before, during, and after the Council about "reading the signs of the times." Here was a thirty-nine-year-old bishop who, having done precisely that, had put his finger on the deepest wound of his century so that it could be healed by a more compelling proclamation of the Gospel.

WORKING THE PROCESS

The Second Vatican Council had a jargon all its own, largely drawn from the Latin that was its official language of business. A bishop was not a "member" of the Council but a "Council Father." On entering the Council *aula* (not hall), he presented his "passport" (not his pass). If he wanted to say something, he did not give a speech; he "made an intervention." In preparing the intervention, he might consult a *peritus* (or theological expert), who could help polish his argument and his Latin. The draft Council documents were not printed in brochures but in *fascicules*. In voting on these documents, a Council Father didn't cast a ballot "Yea" or "Nay," but rather *Placet* (It is pleasing), *Non placet* (It is not pleasing), or *Placet iuxta modum* (It is pleasing but needs changes). Moderators (four cardinals who ran the proceedings) had to be distinguished from the twelve Council Presidents (whose function was never really clarified in four years).[37] The Council met in formal session to hear interventions (usually a dozen or so) in the mornings. A good deal of the real business, and certainly most of the human interaction, of Vatican II took place elsewhere—in, for example, the two coffee bars that were set up inside St. Peter's and immediately dubbed Bar-Jonah and Bar Mitzvah. Lunches, dinners, and seminars, held in hotels, religious houses, or the national seminaries in Rome where many bishops stayed, were other venues where things got talked out in a way that was often difficult, if not impossible, in the *aula*.

It was a rich learning environment for everyone concerned, and the "informal Council" made an important contribution to Vatican II. In later years, some participants would look back critically on the way in which these informal discussions tended to subordinate bishops to theologians and biblical scholars who almost constituted (and in some of their own minds, did constitute) a parallel teaching authority in the Church. Some bishops, Wojtyła included, took advantage of the knowledge of distinguished *periti* without being overwhelmed by them.

The primary historical record of Vatican II is composed of the Council Fathers' formal spoken or written interventions and the sixteen official conciliar documents those interventions helped shape. Bishop (and, in the third and fourth periods of the Council, Archbishop) Wojtyła spoke and made written interventions in all four sessions of Vatican II. Those texts are one way of seeing how he understood the Council from inside.

At Vatican II's first session, in the fall of 1962, Bishop Wojtyła joined in a heated theological controversy about how the Church should understand the relationship between the sources of divine revelation, Scripture and Tradition; it was a topic with considerable ecumenical repercussions, given the classic Reformation maxim, *Sola Scriptura* [Scripture alone]. Wojtyła argued that the entire debate ought to be recast. God himself is the only Source of revelation. By stressing God's *self*-revelation in Scripture and Tradition, rather than treating "revelation" as a matter of biblical or theological propositions, Wojtyła was applying his personalism to the Church's understanding of God and God's relationship to the world.[38]

When the Council Fathers debated the renewal of the liturgy in the first session, Wojtyła made a brief intervention reflective of his own pastoral experience, urging that the revised rite of baptism stress the parents' and godparents' obligation to instruct the child in the faith.[39] In the debate over the nature and mission of the Church, Wojtyła submitted a written intervention urging a more personalistic and pastoral stress on the salvation of souls as the Council worked through the implications of Pius XII's image of the Church as the Mystical Body of Christ. In addition, he wanted the notion of a distinctive lay vocation given higher visibility in any document on the Church. This was a legitimate "demand" of men and women today, and acknowledging it would broaden a "sense of responsibility for the Church" within the Catholic community. Wojtyła stood with the rest of the Polish hierarchy in asking for a separate conciliar document on the Blessed Virgin Mary, a position the Council would eventually reject for theological and ecumenical reasons. In line with the solution that would eventually be adopted (which was to incorporate the Council's statement on Mary into the *Dogmatic Constitution on the Church*), Wojtyła proposed early on that any discussion of Mary speak of her "motherhood" *in* the Church, a maternal care that all the sons and daughters of the Church be conformed to Christ. This kind of Marian theology, he suggested, would also help improve a draft document in which "the Church is presented to us more as a teaching society than as a mother."[40]

In the Council's second session, in the fall of 1963, Wojtyła spoke during the debate on the Church as the "People of God," suggesting that this image be described sacramentally, in analogy to the Incarnation of Christ. The Church was the "People of God," a community constituted by a "supernatural transcendence" that made it unique and that gave it its particular mission in the world—which was to teach the world that its true destiny lay in the completion of history, when God would be all in all.[41] In a written intervention in the same debate, Wojtyła the philosopher argued that the "final cause," the constituting purpose, of the Church was holiness. Every baptized Christian had a vocation to holiness, which was not a preserve of the clergy or hierarchy but the destiny of all whom Christ had "sanctified in the truth" so that they might be "sent . . . into the world" (*John* 17.18–19). The holiness to which Christians were called, Wojtyła wrote, was nothing less than a "sublime sharing in the very holiness of the Holy Trinity," of God himself.[42]

Karol Wojtyła participated in the third (fall 1964) and fourth (fall 1965) sessions of the Council as the Archbishop of Kraków, rather than as a very junior auxiliary bishop. His spoken and written interventions intensified accordingly. In the third session, he submitted a lengthy written intervention "in the name of the Polish episcopate" on Mary's place in the proposed *Dogmatic Constitution on the Church,* and added a personal written intervention arguing that the chapter on Mary should not become the document's last chapter but should immediately follow its first, on "The Mystery of the Church." As Mary had nourished Christ's body as his earthly mother, so she continued to nourish the Mystical Body of Christ.[43]

In the third session, Archbishop Wojtyła forcefully entered the debate on a proposed *Decree on the Apostolate of the Laity.* In a spoken intervention, he welcomed the revised draft text because it properly identified the source of the lay apostolate in the baptismal dignity and responsibility of all Christians, rather than in the fact that some laypeople belonged to specific apostolic movements. Basic sacramental theology, not ecclesiastical sociology, was what gave rise to a distinctive apostolate of lay men and women. The archbishop suggested that this decree would be particularly important for those who, when they spoke about "the Church," "do not seem to be speaking about themselves," but only about priests, nuns, and bishops. Wojtyła went on to recommend a "dialogue within the Church" in which clergy and laity were "opened to each other in complete sincerity." This would promote the evangelical action of the entire Church, because the Church's mission to the world depended on a mission of the Church to itself, in which the members of the Body of Christ mutually enriched one another for the sake of their common witness. Wojtyła also made a strong pitch to include young people and their unique apostolate in any conciliar document on the laity. (In this particular debate, Wojtyła was the only speaker to recognize the presence of women as auditors at the Council, beginning his remarks, *Venerabiles Patres, Fratres, et Sorores . . ."* [Venerable Fathers, Brothers, and Sisters].[44])

In a written intervention on the same proposed decree, Wojtyła argued that the point of a revitalized apostolate of the laity was not to turn the laity into quasi-clerics, concerned primarily with the internal life of the Church. It was to renew the laity as apostles in the world of culture and work. With his friends at *Tygodnik Powszechny* and the Rhapsodic Theater in mind, the archbishop also praised the specific contributions of writers and artists to the evangelization of culture: "they do not just teach, but they also please, by enticing minds and hearts to the truth."[45]

Karol Wojtyła also participated vigorously in the third session's most controversial debate, on religious freedom, in one spoken and two written interventions.

Why was religious freedom so controversial at Vatican II?

Some Council Fathers took a philosophical position that, once its premises were granted, was at least logical. "Error" had "no rights"; states should recognize this so that justice would be served; therefore, the optimum arrangement between Church and state was one in which the state recognized the truth of Catholicism and gave it a privileged place in society. Others, including a vocal French missionary archbishop, Marcel Lefebvre, were convinced that any Catholic endorsement of religious freedom meant endorsing the radical secularizing politics that had been let loose during the French Revolution. Still others worried that a conciliar defense of religious freedom would involve such a dramatic development of doctrine as to suggest that the Church had been gravely mistaken in the past. These concerns not infrequently overlapped in some bishops' minds.

On the other side of the issue were three clusters of bishops. The Council Fathers from the United States had lived an experience in which Catholicism flourished under a constitutionally mandated "separation" between Church and state. They did not think this way of arranging things should be considered inferior to the way things had been done in the Europe of altar-and-throne alliances. A second cluster was composed of those Western European bishops who, for theological and political reasons, were determined to distance the Church from ancien régime nostalgia. Then there were the bishops of east central Europe, many of whom had done time in prisons or under house arrest, who wanted a strong conciliar defense of religious freedom to strengthen them in their struggle against communism.

When Wojtyła entered this debate in the third session, the proposed declaration on religious freedom was an appendix to what would eventually become the Council's *Decree on Ecumenism.* The archbishop of Kraków's first intervention on the subject, on September 25, 1964, addressed religious freedom as an ecumenical issue as well as a Church-state question. Weaving back and forth between the ecumenical and public policy sides of the question, he laid out a sophisticated position, most elements of which would find their way into the *Declaration on Religious Freedom* the following year.

Religious freedom, he began, touched the heart of the dialogue between the Church and the world, because religious freedom had to do with how the Church thought about the human person and the human condition. It was important, therefore, to understand freedom in all its complex richness, and not reduce it to a neutral, indifferent faculty of choice. Freedom, the archbishop of Kraków argued, was freedom *for,* not simply freedom *against.* And what freedom was *for* was truth. It was only by living in the truth that the human person was set free.

This understanding of freedom led, in turn, to two conclusions about society. The first was that the state was incompetent in theology and had no business either authorizing or proscribing religious institutions. The second conclusion was that the communist claim that religion was "alienating," and thus a legitimate target of state animus, was nonsense. The Council "ought to proclaim the full and integral truth about man, who is in no respect alienated by religion, but brought to completion by it."[46]

At the time Wojtyła entered the religious freedom debate, the argument was stalled at the level of Church-state theory—between proponents who were primarily interested in disentangling the Church from altar-and-throne arrangements, and opponents who were convinced that religious freedom was the opening wedge to religious indifferentism and subsequent governmental hostility. By putting the question in a personalist context and by showing how the transcendence of the human person, manifested in freedom, "faces" toward God, the archbishop of Kraków demonstrated that religious freedom could be vigorously defended without reducing "freedom" to a matter of indifference between opinions.

Backstage maneuverings by the opponents resulted in the vote on religious freedom being blocked at the end of the Council's third session. Thus the fourth and final session of Vatican II began in September 1965 with a showdown on religious freedom. Archbishop Wojtyła, as one of the proponents of a new *Declaration on Religious Freedom* (now styled, in Latin, *Dignitatis Humanae*), spoke in the first days of debate, sharpening the point he had made in the third session on the relationship between freedom and truth. It was not sufficient, he argued, to say simply, "I am free." Rather, "it is necessary to say . . . 'I am responsible.' This is the doctrine which is based on the living tradition of the Church of the martyrs and confessors. Responsibility is the necessary culmination and fulfillment of freedom."[47]

Then, perhaps concerned that its opponents would, in defeat, claim that the only "authority" behind the declaration was that of human reason, Wojtyła submitted a written intervention urging that the document make an even stronger case for religious freedom as a matter of God's revealed will for the world and for human beings. The declaration, he proposed, should present religious freedom "substantially as revealed doctrine, which is entirely consonant with sound reason." It was the Council's job to teach divine truth. If that truth was also clear to human reason, as seemed to be the case in states that protected religious freedom, "so much the better." The world expected something more from the Church than what the world already knew itself: "The world is waiting for the doctrine of the Church, that is, revealed doctrine, about these matters. . . ."[48]

The Council Fathers evidently agreed. The final text of *Dignitatis Humanae,* which would help change the history of the twentieth century, reads as follows:

> The Vatican Council declares that the human person has a right to religious freedom. Freedom of this kind means that all men should be immune from coercion on the part of individuals, social groups, and every human power so that, within due limits, nobody is forced to act against his convictions in religious matters in private or in public, alone or in association with others. The Council further declares that the right to religious freedom is based on the very dignity of the human person as known through the revealed word of God and by reason itself. This right of the human person to religious freedom must be given such recognition in the constitutional order of society as will make it a civil right.[49]

Dignitatis Humanae included several points that had been urged by Archbishop Wojtyła, among others. Human dignity involves a "moral obligation to seek the truth, especially religious truth." Knowing the truth involves an obligation to live according to that truth. This obligation to seek the truth cannot be fulfilled unless men and women "enjoy both psychological freedom and immunity from external coercion," for it is by a free "personal assent that men must adhere to the truth they have discovered."[50]

The Declaration then took up Wojtyła's challenge to ground religious freedom as securely as possible for Catholics, in the revelation of God which was the foundation of the Church's life:

> One of the key truths in Catholic teaching, a truth that is contained in the word of God and constantly preached by the Fathers, is that man's response to God by faith ought to be free, and that therefore nobody is to be forced to embrace the faith against his will. The act of faith is by its very nature a free act. Man, redeemed by Christ the Savior and called

through Jesus Christ to be an adopted son of God, cannot give his adherence to God when He reveals Himself unless, drawn by the Father, he submits to God with a faith that is reasonable and free.[51]

Finally, the Council took aim at the kind of regime under which Archbishop Wojtyła and other east central European proponents of religious freedom were forced to live, denouncing governments that "strive to deter the citizens from professing their religion and make life particularly difficult and dangerous for religious bodies."[52] In a parting shot at groups like "Pax" in Poland, which were urging that "secondary" matters such as religious freedom be subordinated to the cause of world peace, the Council Fathers concluded that it was essential, "to establish and strengthen peaceful relations and harmony in the human race," that "religious freedom must be given constitutional protection everywhere. . . ."[53] There could be no genuine peace without freedom. Karol Wojtyła, longtime critic of the division of Europe under Yalta, heartily agreed.

THE CHURCH AND THE MODERN WORLD

While he did important work on religious freedom and, to a lesser extent, on the theology of the laity, Archbishop Karol Wojtyła's primary contribution to the Second Vatican Council involved what eventually became the *Pastoral Constitution on the Church in the Modern World. Schema XIII*, as it was known during the first three sessions, was intended by Pope John XXIII and two of its principal promoters, Cardinal Leo-Jozef Suenens of Belgium (one of the four Council Moderators) and Cardinal Giovanni Battista Montini of Milan (who was elected Pope Paul VI between the Council's first and second sessions), to demonstrate that what the world aspired to and what the world suffered were "the joy and hope, the grief and anguish of the followers of Christ as well," as the final text put it. The Church lived in the world and for the world because "nothing that is genuinely human fails to find an echo" in Christian hearts.[54] That the Council should affirm this seemed not only reasonable, but urgently necessary, to Karol Wojtyła, who had begun his suggestions for the Council's agenda with an analysis of the crisis of modern humanism.

Schema XIII, which would be known after the Council as *Gaudium et Spes*, from the "joy and hope" in its first sentence, had almost as rocky a passage through the Council as the *Declaration on Religious Freedom*. By the time the Council's third session was in its fourth week, in October 1964, members of the Roman Curia were trying to get *Schema XIII* removed from the Council's agenda altogether. Their efforts failed, although even *Schema XIII*'s friends admitted that the draft needed a lot of work. Thus, with the strong support of Pope Paul VI, debate on "the Church in the modern world" began on Tuesday, October 20, after Archbishop Wojtyła had celebrated the daily Mass for the Council Fathers.[55]

Speaking the next day, Wojtyła, who had previously been involved in preparing two major Polish Bishops' Conference memoranda on *Schema XIII*, defended the idea of such a document in the name of a Polish episcopate convinced that *Schema XIII* had a "special timeliness." Men and women of good will were eagerly anticipating what the Council had to say to them. The Council could not disappoint them. There were also those who claimed that the Church had nothing to say to modernity, and they, too, had to be addressed. But the schema had to take account of the many "worlds" that composed "the modern world," which could not be limited to the advanced industrial societies of Western Europe and North America.

Then there was the crucial question of approach. The "'ecclesiastical' mentality" with its "lamentations on the . . . miserable state of the world" should be shunned, as should any sort of magisterial "soliloquy." The document had to reflect a commitment to "dialogue with the world," and had to speak in such a way as to make clear that "the Church is seeking with it the truth and the just solution of the difficult problems of human life." The document should take a cue from good teachers, he argued, adopting a "'heuristic' method [that permits] the disciple to find the truth almost on his own." The Church had a proposal to make to modernity, and it should make that proposal through "the power of arguments" rather than by "moralization or exhortation."[56] In support of just such a revision of *Schema XIII*, Archbishop Wojtyła, in the name of the Polish bishops, submitted more than eighty proposed changes to the draft text during the third session.[57]

By the time the Council reconvened for its fourth and final session on September 14, 1965, yet another draft of *Schema XIII* had been prepared. This final working draft, the foundation of *Gaudium et Spes*, had been hammered out in three lengthy drafting sessions in early 1965 by a subcommission involving key bishops and *periti* (among them, Professor Stefan Swieżawski of KUL).[58] Archbishop Wojtyła actively participated in all three meetings, working in the subgroup that included Archbishop Gabriel-Marie Garrone, the Dominican theologian Yves Congar, and the Jesuit scholars Henri de Lubac and Jean Danielou.[59] De Lubac, reminiscing about the "arduous birth of the famous *Schema XIII*," remembered that he had "worked side by side" with the archbishop of Kraków and that "it did not take long to discover in him a person of the very highest qualities."[60] The regard was mutual. Work on *Schema XIII* was the beginning of a "special friendship" between Wojtyła and de Lubac, the young archbishop being encouraged by the support of the venerable theologian, who prior to the Council had been the object of severe criticism in Rome.[61] But it was the French Dominican, Father Congar, also under suspicion throughout the 1950s for his writings on the nature of the Church and on ecumenism, who left a striking written recollection of Karol Wojtyła as a partner in drafting *Gaudium et Spes*. Congar kept a diary, and its entry for February 2, 1965, describes Wojtyła's work at a meeting in Ariccia, outside Rome:

At the afternoon meeting, which was devoted to discussion of the second chapter, Bishop Wojtyła made a few remarkable comments. "One exclusively considers here," he said, "the problems and questions that have arisen from the new situation of the world. . . . However, the contemporary world also gives some answers to these questions, and it is necessary for us to consider these answers as well, because they conflict with the Church's answers. In the text that has been presented to us, there is no reference to the answers that the contemporary world is offering, and no discussion about the problems that are created because of these conflicting answers."

Wojtyła made a remarkable impression. His personality dominates. Some kind of animation is present in this person, a magnetic power, prophetic strength, full of peace, and impossible to resist.[62]

The debate on *Gaudium et Spes* opened on Wednesday, September 22, 1965. The following Tuesday, September 28, Archbishop Karol Wojtyła gave what some would consider his most memorable speech at the Second Vatican Council. The new "Pastoral Constitution," he suggested, was "more of a meditation" than a statement of doctrine.[63] Which was exactly right, since "its principal concern is the human person," considered in himself, in community, and "in the scheme of all things."

The Church made a unique proposal to the world and its distinctive angle of vision should be more carefully identified in the document: the Church, in dialogue with the world, always looked at history through the prism of the redeeming Cross of Christ. That God had entered the created world to redeem it, Wojtyła continued, has "fixed once and for all the Christian meaning of 'the world.'" The world was not something external to the Church, nor were "creation" and "redemption" somehow extrinsic to the world, its history, and its aspiration. The story of creation and redemption *is* the world's story, properly understood. Telling the world's story as that kind of story, and thus bringing the world to conversion, was the greatest service the Church could do for the world.

Wojtyła agreed with those who argued that the secular world had a legitimate autonomy. From his intense dialogue with scientists back in Kraków he knew, for example, that there was no such thing as "Catholic chemistry" or "Christian physics." There was chemistry, and there was physics, and the truths of these things were true in their own right. These truths, he insisted, always had to be related to *the* truth which the Church knew: the truth of humanity's redemption and its transcendent destiny. Wojtyła thus anticipated and implicitly rejected the notion that a dialogue between the Church and the modern world was one in which "the world sets the agenda for the Church," as the World Council of Churches would soon put it. Genuine dialogue was a two-way street. As the Church opened its windows to the modern world, it ought to call the modern world to open its own windows to the possibility of transcendence.[64]

Archbishop Wojtyła then took up the question of atheism as a pastoral issue, as a part of the Church's "dialogue with everyone." The atheist was totally alone. Solitude from God led to a deep personal solitude, indeed a profound loneliness, that forced men and women "to seek a kind of quasi-immortality in the life of the collective." The Church's dialogue with atheism should begin not with arguments or proofs about the existence of God, but with a conversation about the human person's "interior liberty." In that kind of conversation, the Church might be able to show the atheist a path beyond the radical loneliness and radical alienation that came from rejecting God in the name of liberation from alienation.

The Moderator, Cardinal Döpfner of Munich, interrupted: "Excellency, please finish, your time is up."

With a bow to the Moderator, Archbishop Wojtyła concluded with his personalist principle in its most condensed form—the closer human beings come to God, the closer they come to the depth of their humanity and to the truth of the world. Christian faith is not alienating; Christian faith is liberating in the most profound sense of human freedom. *That* was what the Church should propose to "the modern world."[65]

Gaudium et Spes, the *Pastoral Constitution on the Church in the Modern World*, would retain a privileged place in the thinking and affections of Karol Wojtyła for the rest of his life. He had worked very hard on the development of the text. He had defended the necessity of such an innovative document and its singular synthesis of Christian doctrine and reflection on the pressing problems of the late twentieth century. Thus it is no surprise that two of its sections are among the most quoted citations from the Second Vatican Council in his papal teaching.

In Wojtyła's interpretation of Vatican II, *Gaudium et Spes* 22 was the theological linchpin of the entire Council: "It is only in the mystery of the Word made flesh that the mystery of man truly becomes clear . . . [and] all this holds true, not for Christians only, but also for all men of good will in whose hearts grace is actively present." This was the treasure the Church had to offer to the modern world: a humanism enriched by the human encounter with Christ, who, far from alienating humanity, reveals to it the full truth of its dignity and glorious destiny.

Gaudium et Spes 24, the Council's philosophical and moral linchpin, was the essential complement to the Christ-centered anthropology proposed in *GS* 22: "Man can fully discover his true self only in a sincere giving of himself." The Law of the Gift was the fundamental dramatic structure of the human condition. Living in that drama, rather than by self-assertion, was the road beyond alienation and the path to human fulfillment. This was the truth of the human condition that the Church wished to explore with the modern world—a truth that, for Christians, was confirmed in a definitive way by Christ.

FROM PETER TO STANISŁAW

For Karol Wojtyła, participation in the Second Vatican Council was a public responsibility, not a personal privilege. From the first session of the Council on, he worked hard to keep Kraków informed of what was happening at Vat-

ican II and to give Poles a sense of connection to a great, international
Catholic event. After each session of the Council he gave public lectures and
conferences on what had been happening in Rome to the priests of the archdiocese, to intellectuals, to seminarians and students. He also wrote letters
during the Council to his priests, keeping them in touch with his thinking.
Prior to his departure for Rome for each session, he celebrated a public Mass
and preached on the Council's agenda. (On September 10, 1964, he confessed in Wawel Cathedral that he felt a "certain suspense" about the fate of
Schema XIII.[66])

These efforts touched only certain sectors of the Kraków archdiocese,
though. Wojtyła wanted the whole archdiocese to have a sense of participation in Vatican II, which was fostered in part by special days of prayer he
organized in the parishes, convents, and monasteries of the archdiocese.
Each day during the Council, one institution of the Archdiocese of Kraków
was linked to Rome through a day-long vigil of prayer. As for a sense of connection to the "news" of the Council, that could only be created through the
media. Since the state-run Polish press was wholly uninterested in, if not
downright hostile to, Church matters, Wojtyła had to turn to alternative
media to keep his people in touch.

On November 24, 1962, six weeks after the Council opened, he broadcast
to Poland on Vatican Radio, telling his listeners that the spirit of Vatican II was,
above all, one of spiritual renewal.[67] Wojtyła broadcast twice on Vatican Radio
during the second session. On October 19, 1963, he participated in a radio
program marking the 600th anniversary of the Jagiellonian University, reminding his listeners that the suppressed Faculty of Theology "had undoubtedly
earned a right to be a full participant" in the life of the university and in Polish culture. On November 25, he broadcast on the role of the laity in the
Church and the world. Others might have been tempted to use this topic to
define the ideological divisions among the Council Fathers. Wojtyła chose to
give a lesson in Christian humanism, proposing that "The world was entrusted
primarily [to laypeople] so that they could carry into . . . all the facets of its
existence that which is in the Son of God: truth and love." The lay role in the
Church, he continued, "consists in completing the work of Christ, the Son of
God, in the world, and with the world's help." In doing so lay Christians were
"regaining the world, in all its facets and manifestations, for the Eternal Father.
On the road to this, however, lies an even higher aim: the regaining of man
himself, in his humanity, for the Eternal Father. . . ."[68]

During the third session, on October 19, 1964, the archbishop broadcast
a reflection on the dignity of the human person, noting that the Council documents did not include a special treatise on the human person because "the
person is deeply embedded in the entire teaching of this Council."[69] During
the fourth session, on October 20, 1965, he discussed the *Declaration on Religious Freedom* on Vatican Radio, linking its teaching to the fifteenth-century
rector of the Academy of Kraków, Paweł Włodkowic, who protested the forced

conversion of pagans at the sixteenth ecumenical council, the Council of Constance.[70]

Archbishop Wojtyła also wrote about the Council for *Tygodnik Powszechny*. In March 1964, Wojtyła analyzed the sometimes heated debate on the nature of the episcopate and the role of bishops in the Church. On the disputed question of "collegiality" (i.e., how the college of bishops, as successors of the apostles, shared responsibility for the governance of the Church with the pope, the successor of Peter), the archbishop characteristically took a theological rather than political approach—to strengthen the principle of collegiality was a "strong move toward the realization of universality and solidarity in the Church." The question was not so much "Who's in charge?" but "How does the college of bishops manifest the unity of the Church amidst its splendid diversity?"[71]

In a February 1965 article on "The Council and the Work of Theologians," Archbishop Wojtyła reflected on his experiences with consultors at the recent meeting in Rome to shore up the draft of *Gaudium et Spes*. Theology, he argued, was not a form of "religious studies." Theology began with God's revelation and was always revelation's servant. Theology fulfilled that service in dialogue with other branches of the intellectual life, of which Wojtyła made special mention of the hard sciences. Like the Council itself, theology should focus on "the problems of the contemporary world" and especially the crisis of humanism. How were the men and women of modernity to be "human, reasonable, and free"? That was the great question for theologians and bishops alike.[72]

Two months later, Archbishop Wojtyła addressed an open letter to the editors and staff of *Tygodnik Powszechny*, which summarized his thinking on the meaning of Vatican II as he prepared for its fourth and final session. It was important, the archbishop suggested, to look at the Council from inside as well as from outside. From the outside, the Council could sometimes appear to be a political exercise, a question of which faction in the Church would dominate the Catholic future. If the press wanted to tell the full story of Vatican II, it had to take an "interior" view of the Council as well.

Wojtyła argued that a view "from inside" would treat Vatican II as, above all, "a personalist Council." This intense focus on the human person, evident in both *Dignitatis Humanae* and *Gaudium et Spes*, was neither a "concession" to modernity nor a lapse into subjectivism and relativism. Truth and freedom were always linked, and an emphasis on religious freedom was, at the same time, an "augmentation" of human responsibility. If men and women were truly free to seek the truth, they were ever more obliged to take that search seriously. The relationship of freedom to duty and truth took human beings into the heart of the relationship between creation and Creator.

Then there were the politics of Vatican II. There were, to be sure, debates and votes, as in a legislative body, but something else, something deeper, was going on. The Council Fathers were in constant conversation, and even those who did not speak formally in public nonetheless participated in the evolution of the Council's thinking, through their conversations in and around the

Council *aula*. One couldn't get to the full reality of what was happening at Vatican II simply by analyzing public speeches and votes.

"Differences in points of view play an important role" in the Council, the archbishop wrote, but they should be understood in terms of the distinctive character of the Church, which was not, in its essence, a political community. The bishops constituted an "authentic plurality: a plurality of persons, a plurality of experiences and reflections, a plurality of interior lives, a plurality in the surroundings they represent, a plurality of life in different conditions." What the Council was doing was turning that plurality into a unity, through diversity, contradiction, and opposition.

The same could be said, Wojtyła suggested, about the debates over "authority" at Vatican II. Authority in the Church was a matter of service. It was not about personal privilege, nor was it about power. Moreover, when the issue of authority touched the debate over collegiality, commentators had to understand that they would never get to the truth of the issue if they insisted on pitting the pope against the bishops. The Church was always a matter of the pope *and* the bishops. What Western political theorists called the "separation of powers" was not an ecclesial model of governance.[73]

Archbishop Wojtyła's letter to *Tygodnik Powszechny*, a gentle suggestion that his friends should look more deeply into the spiritual reality of the Council than their Western journalistic colleagues were doing, summed up his experience of Vatican II as, at its irreducible core, a *religious* experience. Having just come through the conciliar battle over religious freedom and the struggle to save *Gaudium et Spes*, Wojtyła could hardly be accused of naïveté about the political facts of life in a complex human event like the Second Vatican Council. Yet he continued to insist that this was only one dimension—indeed, the surface dimension—of what was happening in Rome. The Holy Spirit was preparing the Church for a renewal of its mission in the third millennium. That, he was convinced, was the real story of Vatican II, and it was far more compelling than tales of ecclesiastical intrigue.

SECURING THE FOUNDATIONS

Not even so assiduous a listener as Karol Wojtyła could just sit for hours in the Council *aula*, absorbing a seemingly endless flow of Latin rhetoric. Decades later, Pope John Paul II would admit, a little sheepishly, "You know, I wrote many parts of books and poems during the sessions of the Council."[74] The poems describe Wojtyła's personal and spiritual experience of the Council. At the same time, Wojtyła was also thinking the Council through philosophically—and drafting, in the Council *aula*, what would become his major philosophical project, the study entitled *Osoba y czyn*, or *Person and Act*.[75]

The idea, he later recalled, was first put to him by Monsignor Stanisław Czartoryski, a Cracovian priest, who, after reading *Love and Responsibility*, had told Wojtyła, "Now you must write a book on the person."[76] Wojtyła had a slightly different understanding of what he was doing in *Person and Act*. The point, John Paul II later wrote, was to work out in detail the philosophical issues involved in putting the older Aristotelian-Thomistic "philosophy of being" together with the "philosophy of consciousness" he had analyzed in the Scheler dissertation (i.e., to work out the relationship between the objective truth of things-as-they-are and our subjective or personal experience of that truth).[77] Wojtyła's leading philosophical disciple, Father Tadeusz Styczeń, has a third variant reading on the intention of *Person and Act*. Its purpose, he claims, was to make the philosophical argument for moving from Descartes's *Cogito ergo sum* [I think, therefore I am], which had eventually landed philosophy in the prison of solipsism, to *Conosco ergo sum* [I understand, therefore I am]. This would reconnect thinking-about-thinking to the things that were to be thought and understood.[78]

Still, the book is perhaps best understood as a product of the Second Vatican Council. *Person and Act* is Karol Wojtyła's attempt to give a coherent, intellectually sophisticated, *public* account of the philosophical basis of Vatican II's teaching on freedom and its relationship to truth. Like any complex event, Vatican II can be "read" in a number of ways. Theologians point to two of the Council's dogmatic constitutions, on the Church and on divine revelation, as the core of the Council's teaching. Millions of Catholics, whose primary contact with the Church is at Sunday Mass, "read" Vatican II through its *Dogmatic Constitution on the Sacred Liturgy*. If, however, the Council was the Church's response to a crisis in humanism—a crisis of such magnitude that it was no exaggeration to view it as a genuine crisis of world civilization—then it was clear to Wojtyła that the Council's proposal to the modern world, in its *Declaration on Religious Freedom* and its *Pastoral Constitution on the Church in the Modern World,* needed a clearer philosophical explication.

The Council had ringingly affirmed that the human person, precisely as a *person*, has a right to religious freedom, and that the right of religious freedom is ours so that we may freely meet our obligation to seek the truth—including the ultimate Truth, which is God in his self-revelation. Wojtyła believed it was crucial to demonstrate philosophically that the human search for meaning is directed toward the good, and that the person who seeks the good wants to direct himself to something that is, *objectively,* good. The internal dynamism of our freedom thus impels us to take seriously the question of what is, in reality, *good*—which is also what is *true*.

In *Gaudium et Spes*, the *Pastoral Constitution on the Church in the Modern World,* the Church proposed how the world might achieve its aspiration to freedom and build a civilization characterized by justice, peace, and prosperity through an enriched and deepened concept of the human person. Wojtyła thought that this anthropology had to be put on a more secure philosophical foundation, accessible to everyone no matter what his or her religious disposition. As he wrote to Father Henri de Lubac while finishing the first draft of *Person and Act*:

I devote my very rare free moments to a work that is close to my heart and devoted to the metaphysical sense and mystery of the PERSON. It seems to me that the debate today is being played out on that level. The evil of our times consists in the first place in a kind of degradation, indeed in a pulverization, of the fundamental uniqueness of each human person. This evil is even much more of the metaphysical order than of the moral order. To this disintegration planned at time by atheistic ideologies, we must oppose, rather than sterile polemics, a kind of "recapitulation" of the inviolable mystery of the person. . . .[79]

Person and Act is not a debate with other philosophers and is very light on such scholarly apparatus as footnotes, cross-references, and digressions on the work of others. But that did not make it an easy read. On the contrary, *Person and Act* is an extraordinarily dense work. Wojtyła asked his protégé, Father Styczeń, to review his first draft. The two took a hiking trip into the Tatras to discuss it, and when Wojtyła asked Styczeń what he thought, the younger man puckishly replied, "It's a good first draft. Perhaps it could be translated first from Polish into Polish, to make it easier to understand for the reader—including me."[80] A generation of Kraków clergy joked that the first assignment in Purgatory for priests who misbehaved would be to read *Person and Act*. This density was the result of many factors. Wojtyła's distinctively circular style of thinking made for difficulties, as did the fact that he was writing such a complex work in his spare time. It is also not clear whether Karol Wojtyła has ever found the scientific language to express himself adequately. A close student of his poetry and plays, Anna Karoń-Ostrowska, suggests that the answer is, "No," for there is always something about the truth of things that escapes our ability to express it analytically.[81] *

Person and Act is very much part of the unfinished symphony of Karol Wojtyła's philosophy. Thirty years after its initial appearance, a definitive Polish edition had not been published, although the second and third Polish editions (edited by several of Wojtyła's students and other philosophical colleagues) were major improvements over the first edition; the third edition included several articles by Wojtyła, developing themes in the original work.[82] German (1981), Italian (1982), Spanish (1982), and French (1983) editions, of varying degrees of reliability, have been published. But the most serious problems were with the English translation and edition of the work.

Anna-Teresa Tymieniecka, a former student of Roman Ingarden living in Boston and active in world phenomenological circles, had published several articles of Wojtyła's in *Analecta Husserliana*, the yearbook of phenomenology she edited, thus helping to bring his work to the attention of philosophers around the world. Much impressed by the first Polish edition of *Osoba y czyn*, she proposed publishing a revised and elaborated text of the work in English. Cardinal Wojtyła agreed and worked through numerous revisions and elaborations with Dr. Tymieniecka. The result, according to virtually everyone involved, was a much-improved text. This revised Polish text was then translated into English by Andrzej Potocki and sent to Dr. Tymieniecka in the United States for publication. Several knowledgeable persons close to the process claim that, at this point, Dr. Tymieniecka significantly changed the Potocki translation, confusing its technical language and bending the text toward her own philosophical concerns, to the point where the reader is, on occasion, not really in contact with Wojtyła's own thought.[83] These problems only surfaced after Wojtyła had been elected Pope. At that juncture, he had no time to check through hundreds of pages of text, and appointed a commission composed of Father Styczeń, his old friend Father Marian Jaworski, and Dr. Andrzej Półtawski (a Kraków-based philosopher and the husband of Dr. Wanda Półtawska) to review and correct the revised English translation text that had been prepared by Dr. Tymieniecka.

Person and Act: *The Foundations of Solidarity*

With *Person and Act*, Karol Wojtyła took his intellectual project to a new level by attempting to create a fully developed philosophy of the human person in which his interlocutors were his readers. Despite the extraordinary demands it makes on the reader, *Person and Act* is actually an invitation to a conversation. This, Wojtyła suggests, is how I read the human condition. How does that fit with your own experience?

The book begins with a lengthy and rich introduction in which Wojtyła reflects on the nature of human experience. The author then tries to show how our thinking about the world and ourselves helps us to understand ourselves precisely as *persons*. While it is true that some things simply "happen to me," I have other experiences in which I know that I am making a decision and acting out that decision. In those experiences, I come to know myself, not as a jumble of emotions and sensory perceptions, but as a *person*, a *subject*, or, in the classical term, the "efficient cause" of my actions. Some things don't simply "happen" to me. I am the *subject*, not merely the object, of actions. I make things happen, because I think through a decision and then freely act on it. Therefore, I am *somebody*, not simply something.

Wojtyła then shows how, in moral action, that *somebody* begins to experience his or her own transcendence. Our personhood, he argues, is constituted by the fact of our freedom, which we come to know through truly "human acts." In choosing one act (to pay a debt I have freely contracted) rather than another (to cheat on my debt), I am not simply responding to external conditions (fear of jail) or internal pressures (guilt). I am freely choosing what is good. In that free choosing, I am also binding myself to what I know is good

---

But she refused to take corrections from anyone other than Wojtyła and, moreover, was eager to publish the book quickly to capitalize on the author's election as Pope. Dr. Tymieniecka also claimed that she had Wojtyła's agreement to publish her retranslation as the "definitive text of the work established in collaboration with the author by Anna-Teresa Tymieniecka," although why a truly "definitive text" would (like the edition Dr. Tymieniecka proposed to publish) have two chapter sevens, one of which is labeled "unrevised," was not made clear. In any case, Dr. Tymieniecka went ahead with the publication of the text she had prepared, to the intense aggravation of many of Wojtyła's philosophical colleagues and students. Years of private argument ensued between the Holy See's publishing house, the Libreria Editrice Vaticana, which holds the rights to all of Wojtyła's pre-papal work, and Reidel, the Dutch house that had published the English edition. These resulted in an agreement to publish a corrected English edition. The corrected edition was prepared but has never appeared. Dr. Tymieniecka continues to insist that hers is the "definitive" edition of *Osoba y czyn*, a claim that no serious student of Wojtyła's work accepts. The author himself, whose relative indifference to the fate of his published work is as striking as his unfailing charity, insists, whenever the subject is raised, that Dr. Tymieniecka "must be given credit for initiating the translation."[84]

The very English title, *The Acting Person*, suggests something of the problem with Dr. Tymieniecka's work. *Osoba y czyn* is translated, literally, *Person and Act*: a title that retains the tension between subjective consciousness and objective reality in which Wojtyła is trying to work. "The Acting Person" places most of the stress on the subjective, or phenomenological, side of Wojtyła's analysis—which is the criticism most frequently leveled against Dr. Tymieniecka's reworking of the text. Every other language edition of *Osoba y czyn* retains the tension in the Polish original: thus the German *Person und Tat*, the Italian *Persona e atto*, the Spanish *Persona y acción*, and the French *Personne et acte*.

and true. In this free choice of the good and the true, Wojtyła suggests, we can discern the transcendence of the human person. I go beyond myself, I grow as a *person*, by realizing my freedom and conforming it to the good and the true. Through my freedom, I narrow the gap between the person-I-am and the person-I-ought-to-be.

Freedom, on one modern reading of it, is radical autonomy—I am a *self* because my *will* is the primary reference point for my choosing. Wojtyła disagrees. Self-*mastery*, not self-assertion, is the index of a truly human freedom, he argues. And I achieve self-mastery not by repressing or suppressing what is natural to me, but by thoughtfully and freely channeling those natural instincts of mind and body into actions that deepen my humanity because they conform to things-as-they-are. Empiricists try to find the human "center" in the body or its processes. Kantian idealists try to find it in the psyche, in the structures of my consciousness. Wojtyła leapfrogs the argument between empiricists and idealists by trying to demonstrate how moral action, not the psyche or the body, is where we find the center of the human person, the core of our humanity. For it is in moral action that the mind, the spirit, and the body come into the unity of a *person*.

That person lives in a world with many other persons. So *Person and Act* concludes with an analysis of moral action in conjunction with all those "others" who constitute the moral field in which our humanity realizes itself and transcends itself, or grows. Here, philosophical anthropology touches the border of social ethics—How should free *persons* live *together*? As might be expected, Wojtyła takes a position beyond individualism and collectivism. Radical individualism is inadequate, because we only grow into our humanity through interaction with others. Collectivism strips the person of freedom, and thus of his or her personhood. Once again, Wojtyła suggests, the issue is best posed in "both/and" terms, the individual *and* the common good.

In working out his theory of "participation," Wojtyła analyzes four "attitudes" toward life in society. Two are incapable of nurturing a truly human society. "Conformism" is inauthentic because it means abandoning my freedom. "Others" take me over so completely that my self is lost in the process. "Noninvolvement" is inauthentic, because it is solipsistic. Cutting myself off from the "others" eventually results in the implosion of my self. "Opposition" (or what might be called "resistance") can be an authentic approach to life in society, if it involves resistance to unjust customs or laws in order to liberate the full humanity of others. Then there is "solidarity," the primary authentic attitude toward society, in which individual freedom is deployed to serve the common good, and the community sustains and supports individuals as they grow into a truly human maturity. "It is this attitude," Wojtyła writes, "that allows man to find the fulfillment of himself in complementing others."[85]

He could not have known, when he first wrote about it in *Person and Act*, that "solidarity" would become the banner under which the history of the twentieth century would be dramatically changed.

THE CRISIS AND THE PROPOSAL

Karol Wojtyła's philosophical project will be assessed by professional philosophers for a long time to come. Those who are not professional philosophers but who admire intellectual courage will remain impressed by his effort to bridge the gap that had been opened in the seventeenth century between the world we want to grasp and the intellectual processes through which we wrestle with that world. Philosophy, however, was never an end in itself for Wojtyła. It was always in service to his apostolic, evangelical, and pastoral life as priest and bishop. Leaving the professional assessment of his philosophical accomplishment to his philosophical peers, it thus makes sense to assess the pastoral achievement of Wojtyła's philosophical work.

His first achievement was to demonstrate that a Law of the Gift was built into the human condition. What he would later call the "threshold of hope" was not so much ahead of us as above us, in the dramatic struggle to surrender the persons that we are to the persons we ought to be.[86] That struggle can only be resolved by self-giving. Wojtyła's demonstration of the Law of the Gift can be engaged by anyone patient enough to work through a philosophical argument, and in engaging it, they will meet a concept of goodness with traction, one that does not collapse into a mere "social construct."[87]

Wojtyła's second achievement as a pastorally engaged intellectual was a function of his wide range of interests. His literary training and theatrical experience were joined to a rigorous philosophical analysis to produce a picture of human life as inherently, "structurally" *dramatic*. We are not accidents of biochemistry or history, adrift in the cosmos. We can, as moral actors, become the protagonists, not the objects (or victims), of the drama of life. It was a demonstration with appeal to those living under totalitarian repression and to those oppressed by a sense of powerlessness rooted in nihilism.

Wojtyła also developed a profound critique of the utilitarianism that permeates modern culture—the temptation to measure others by their financial, social, political, or sexual utility to me—by demonstrating the moral fact that our relationship to truth, goodness, and beauty is the true stuff of our humanity. Finally, Wojtyła showed how accepting the moral *truth* involved in the Law of the Gift is not a limit on our freedom or our creativity. Truth makes us free and enables us to live our freedom toward its goal, which is happiness.

The Italian philosopher Rocco Buttiglione, one of the most insightful commentators on Karol Wojtyła's philosophical project, suggests that there is a "hidden theological tendency" in Wojtyła's personalism.[88] His method of analysis, in *Person and Act*, was strictly philosophical, but the inspiration was Christian. It is in God the Holy Trinity, a "community" of self-giving "persons" who lose nothing of their uniqueness in their radical self-giving, that we see confirmed the Law of the Gift and the truth about freedom as freedom-for-self-donation. Wojtyła's philosophy, like every other aspect of his life, was touched by his ongoing dialogue with God in prayer. As his life unfolded, that "theological tendency" in his philosophical thought became more and more explicit.

HOMECOMING

On December 7, 1965, the day before the Second Vatican Council closed, *Dignitatis Humanae* and *Gaudium et Spes* were solemnly promulgated—a moment of great satisfaction for Archbishop Karol Wojtyła. That same day, the mutual excommunications leveled in the eleventh century by the Pope and the Patriarch of Constantinople were lifted by Ecumenical Patriarch Athenagoras and Pope Paul VI, a landmark in ecumenism between Western and Eastern Christianity. For Wojtyła and the Polish episcopate, though, the most dramatic episode at the end of the Council was the letter of forgiveness and reconciliation they sent to the German bishops.

Poland was planning to celebrate the millennium of its Christianity in 1966, an event to which Primate Wyszyński hoped to attract bishops and Catholic leaders from all over the world, including Pope Paul VI. In the closing weeks of the Council, the Polish episcopate dispatched fifty-six letters of invitation to the millennium celebrations to other national episcopates, most members of which were, of course, living in Rome at the time. The November 18 letter to the German hierarchy, which Karol Wojtyła helped draft (and which was discussed with German bishops before it was released), was devoted in large part to a detailed review of the difficult history of relations between the two countries. The Polish bishops recounted the immense sufferings of their own people at German hands, while acknowledging that Germans, too, had suffered from Poles. The letter ended, "We forgive, and we ask your forgiveness."[89]

The Polish bishops' letter was intended to have specific, concrete consequences. By clearing the air between the two hierarchies before the millennium of Polish Christianity, it would help make it possible to regularize the situation of the Polish dioceses in the "Recovered Territories" of postwar western Poland, the permanence of which as *Polish* dioceses the Vatican had refused to acknowledge, given the lack of an international treaty finalizing the new German/Polish border. These practical considerations notwithstanding, though, the letter was a magnificent Christian gesture and a dramatic expression of the oft-cited "spirit of Vatican II." The Church wanted to act as a reconciler in the world. The Church could not be that kind of reconciler without reconciliation in its own household. The Poles would take the lead in reconciling one of the great animosities in the second millennium of Christian history, applying John XXIII's "medicine of mercy" to one of the Church's deepest wounds.

The Polish government, however, saw the letter as an opportunity to try to drive a wedge between the Church and the Polish people, refused to let it be printed in the Polish press, and launched a vicious campaign against the bishops under the rubric, "We do not forget and we will not forgive." Many Catholics, not at all sympathetic to the regime, were shocked by the idea that Poles had any reason to ask Germans for forgiveness in light of the horrors of recent history. On his return from Rome, Archbishop Wojtyła held a meeting with members of his *Środowisko*, some of whom had taken serious exception to the letter.[90] But a private session to sort out the issues among friends was one thing; a public attack was something else.

As part of its anti-episcopate campaign, the regime concocted an "Open Letter from the Workers of the Soda Plant in Kraków to Archbishop Karol Wojtyła," which was published in the December 22, 1965, issue of the daily paper, *Krakowska Gazeta*. It was an obvious, clumsy propaganda exercise. According to the letter that had doubtless been prepared for their (required) signatures, the Solvay plant workers professed themselves "deeply shocked" that the archbishop would talk matters over with German bishops and "make an authoritarian decision on matters of vital interest to our nation." "No one gave a mandate to the Polish bishops to take a position on matters . . . belonging to the competence of other venues," the letter declared. The only body "entitled to make pronouncements in the name of the Polish nation is the government of the Polish People's Republic." As if any further hints about its literary and ideological pedigree were needed, the letter asserted that "the Germans do not have anything to be forgiven for, since the direct guilt for bringing about the Second World War and its bestial course falls exclusively on German imperialism and fascism, and its successor, the Federal Republic of Germany." The "workers" concluded by reiterating their "deep disappointment" at the "uncitizenlike behavior" of their archbishop, especially since he had been a "laborer at our plant during the Nazi Occupation."[91]

Never one to turn down a catechetical opportunity, Archbishop Wojtyła wrote back on Christmas Eve, in a letter that had to circulate as samizdat, since the regime refused to allow its publication.

After noting that he had received a copy of the alleged "workers' letter" only after having first read it in *Krakowska Gazeta*, the archbishop recalled his time at the Zakrzówek quarry and the Borek Fałęcki chemical plant. These years had been a "priceless and vital experience" for him, "the best school of life," and the "best preparation" possible for his present responsibilities. Men who had shared such an experience couldn't have written the kind of letter and made the kind of accusations the archbishop had just read. "A careful reading" of their letter suggested that they couldn't, in fact, have written it if they had been "honestly acquainted . . . with the actual text of the letter of the Polish bishops to the German bishops and with the German bishops' response to this letter."

Any serious person who had actually read the two texts would have to acknowledge three things, he continued. First, these letters grew out of "the deepest principles of Christian ethics contained in the Gospel." Second, the Polish bishops' letter made plain the history of horrors that Poles had suffered at German hands. The German bishops' letter, he pointed out, "accepted this accusation in its full extent, asking first God himself, and then us, to forgive the guilt of their nation." In light of this, the Polish bishops' request for forgiveness "maintains its proportions in accordance with the Gospel." In so long and tangled a history as that of Germany and Poland, it was inconceivable that "people would not have something for which to ask mutual forgiveness." Finally, the Polish bishops had defended the present Polish position in the Recovered Territories, and the Germans had acknowledged that the present generation of Poles living there "considers these lands to be their native region."

Wojtyła concluded with an example of the Christian humanism he had proposed to the Council's Ante-Preparatory Commission in 1959, that he had just helped define at Vatican II, and whose foundations he was trying to secure in *Person and Act:* "When we worked together during the Occupation, a lot of things united us, foremost [among them] a respect for the human being, for conscience, individuality, and social dignity. That is what I learned in large measure from the workers of 'Solvay'; but I am unable to find this fundamental principle in your open letter. . . ."[92]

As had become his custom, Archbishop Karol Wojtyła celebrated midnight Mass on Christmas Eve in the open fields at Nowa Huta. On Christmas morning, he said a private Mass in the chapel at the archbishop's residence for former Solvay colleagues and their families.[93] At a sermon on New Year's Eve at the Mariacki Church in the Old Town market square, he spoke of Vatican II as an encounter with the mysteries of modern history. He then told the congregation that history could not be turned back, no matter what the authorities were trying to do by keeping Nowa Huta officially church-free. And he announced that he had brought back with him, on the highway between the tomb of St. Stanisław and the tomb of St. Peter on which he had first set out in 1962, a stone from Peter's grave, donated and blessed by Pope Paul VI. It would be the cornerstone of the church to be built at Nowa Huta, some day.

The new battle lines in the struggle for religious freedom had been drawn. Although the struggle would intensify over the next thirteen years, the battle would now be fought by Polish Catholics supported by the full weight of a solemn conciliar pronouncement on religious freedom as the first of human rights.

On this front, and on many others, Archbishop Karol Wojtyła now proposed to put the Council he had helped shape into practice.

6

Successor to St. Stanisław

Living the Council in Kraków

MARCH 8, 1964	Karol Wojtyła installed as Archbishop of Kraków.
MAY 1964	Wojtyła's essay, "Reflections on Fatherhood," published pseudonymously in *Znak.*
MAY 7, 1965	Archbishop Wojtyła establishes annual archdiocesan Day of the Sick.
1966	Poland celebrates the millennium of its Christianity.
APRIL 1966	Wojtyła's millennium poem, "Easter Vigil," published pseudonymously in *Znak.*
JUNE 28, 1967	Karol Wojtyła is created a cardinal by Pope Paul VI.
AUGUST 31, 1967	Poland's communist regime shuts down the Rhapsodic Theater.
OCTOBER 14, 1967	Cardinal Wojtyła breaks ground for the Ark Church in Nowa Huta.
FEBRUARY 1968	A commission of Kraków theologians submits its memorandum, "The Foundations of the Church's Doctrine on the Principles of Conjugal Life," to Pope Paul VI.
AUGUST– SEPTEMBER 1969	Cardinal Wojtyła travels through Canada and the United States.
FALL 1969	Wojtyła establishes the archdiocesan Institute of Family Studies.
SEPTEMBER 11– OCTOBER 28, 1969	Cardinal Wojtyła participates in the international Synod of Bishops in Rome.
1970	Wojtyła writes *Sources of Renewal,* a guided tour of Vatican II's documents.
DECEMBER 16–17, 1970	Wojtyła's *Person and Act* is debated at the Catholic University of Lublin.
SEPTEMBER 30– NOVEMBER 6, 1971	Wojtyła participates in the Synod of Bishops on the ministerial priesthood and justice in the world.

DECEMBER 24, 1971	Cardinal Wojtyła celebrates his first Christmas midnight Mass in an open field in Miestrzejowice.
MAY 8, 1972	The Synod of Kraków opens.
AUGUST 16, 1972	Cardinal Wojtyła celebrates Mass at a campsite on Błyszcz mountain, the Oasis movement's "Mt. Tabor."
FEBRUARY 1973	Wojtyła represents the Polish Church at the International Eucharistic Congress in Melbourne, Australia.
APRIL 16, 1974	Cardinal Wojtyła defies the Czechoslovak communist regime by speaking at the funeral of Cardinal Stefan Trochta in Litoměřice.
SEPTEMBER 27– OCTOBER 26, 1974	Wojtyła serves as *relator* of the Synod of Bishops on evangelization.
MAY 1975	Wojtyła's poem-cycle, "Meditation on Death," published pseudonymously in *Znak*.
MARCH 7–13, 1976	Cardinal Wojtyła preaches the Lenten retreat to Pope Paul VI and the Roman Curia.
JULY 13– SEPTEMBER 11, 1976	Wojtyła travels to the United States for the International Eucharistic Congress in Philadelphia.
MAY 15, 1977	Cardinal Wojtyła dedicates the Ark Church in Nowa Huta.
SEPTEMBER 30– OCTOBER 29, 1977	Wojtyła participates in the Synod of Bishops on religious education.
MAY 25, 1978	Cardinal Wojtyła defends the basic human rights of all Poles before tens of thousands of pilgrims during Kraków's annual Corpus Christi procession.

At 9:45 A.M. on March 8, 1964, the head sacristan of Wawel Cathedral ceremonially processed through the great stone structure to the cathedral's west door, carrying a small silver casket with the relics of the martyred St. Stanisław. Outside, in the courtyard, the archbishop-elect was waiting. Karol Józef Wojtyła, vested in *cappa magna* and ermine mozzetta, kissed the reliquary containing the mortal remains of his predecessor, the first bishop of Kraków, and walked up the steps to be installed as archbishop. He was met at the door by the cathedral chapter, a group of senior priests resplendent in medieval fur collars. One of the canons welcomed him with a speech recounting the history of the archdiocese, and the dean of the chapter handed over the keys of the church. As the archbishop-elect walked through his cathedral, stopping to pray at the shrine of St. Stanisław, at the great black cross of Blessed Queen Jadwiga, and in the Blessed Sacrament chapel, he retraced his path of a quarter-century ago, just before Luftwaffe bombs had begun falling on Poland's ancient capital.

Entering the sanctuary, the archbishop-elect sat on a temporary throne as the chancellor of the archdiocese read aloud the Papal Bull naming Karol Wojtyła metropolitan archbishop of Kraków, first in Latin, then in Polish. The archbishop rose, kissed the altar, and was installed on the *cathedra*, the throne or bishop's chair, of Wawel Cathedral, where he sat and received the homage of his auxiliary bishops, the cathedral chapter, the priests of the archdiocese, the seminary professors, the superiors of religious communities, and, finally, the young seminarians, whom he greeted with obvious affection.

Forty-three-year-old Archbishop Karol Wojtyła, the seventy-sixth bishop in an episcopal line reaching back to Poland's origins in the kingdom of the Piasts, then preached to his people about what was happening that day—to him and to them.

It was impossible to enter Wawel Cathedral, he said, "without fear and awe." Here was gathered the "whole of our nation's past," the only foundation on which a truly Polish future could be built. Whenever he entered the cathedral, he said, he felt "something being born." Thus he wished "now to humble myself before the highest and deepest mystery of birth which is in God Himself. I wish to pay the deepest worship of which man is capable . . . to the Eternal Word, the Son born eternally of the Father. . . ."

He was, he said, a son of the Church of Kraków, "which has borne me as a mother bears a son." But if he remained a son, he was also, now, their father, born as their archbishop on this day of installation: "Peter, in the person of Pope Paul VI, has said to me, 'Feed my sheep' . . . These words have tremendous authority; they draw strength from the words of Christ Himself—when He said 'Feed my sheep' to St. Peter, Pope Paul's predecessor. So, my dear ones, I now stand on the threshold of that great reality which is expressed by the word 'Pastor.' And I know that I stand there as of right, that I am not entering by any other way than through the door of the sheepfold whom Christ has appointed, that is to say, through Peter. . . ."

His was an office of service to a local Church that they must build together: "To be a pastor, it seems to me, one must know how to take what one's flock has to offer; in order to take, one must know how to give; one must coordinate and integrate everyone's gifts into a single common good. . . ."

Every episcopal act of coordination and integration had one solemn purpose—to witness to the truth about the human person, about humanity's relationship to God, and about humanity's noble destiny, all of which had been revealed in Jesus Christ. Those who thought themselves the masters of Poland in 1964 had their five-year plans. The archbishop of Kraków had no such scheme. What he had was something "simple and eternal." Because "the things of eternity, the things of God, are the simplest and deepest," there was no need to fret about programs. Rather, "what we must do is to show increased zeal and increased readiness in carrying out the eternal program of God and Christ and adapting it to the needs of our day. . . ." The Second Vatican Council had begun that process of renewal, "but for many of us its decrees are merely written documents. I want to awaken the archdiocese of Kraków to the true meaning of the Council, so that we may bring its teachings into our lives. . . ."

Having defined his only "program" as the Gospel, ever ancient and ever new, the archbishop retired to the sacristy to vest for Mass. The golden chasuble had been given to the archdiocese by Anna Jagiełło, wife of King Stefan Batory. The miter came from Andrzej Lipski, a seventeenth-century predecessor as bishop. The bishop's staff dated from the reign of Jan Sobieski. The chalice used at Mass was from the middle years of the Jagiellonian dynasty. The message of his vesture, like the message of his sermon, was unmistakable: You, the people of this venerable episcopal see, are the inheritors of a great tradition. That tradition is the truth about your past. From that tradition you can build a future worthy of your dignity as free men and women, born free in baptism with the freedom that no one can ever take from you—the freedom of the children of God.[1]

UNEXPECTED CONSEQUENCES

Sociologists of bureaucratic process might have said that a principle of unintended consequences was in effect. Whimsical theologians might regard it as evidence that the Holy Spirit has a wicked sense of humor. However one describes it, Karol Wojtyła's appointment as archbishop of Kraków was influenced by men who quickly realized that they had made a serious mistake.

Archbishop Eugeniusz Baziak died on June 15, 1962. Karol Wojtyła's appointment as archbishop was signed by Pope Paul VI on December 30, 1963, and publicly announced on January 19, 1964. The eighteen-month delay was the result of yet another deadlock over the See of Kraków: this time, between the Primate, Cardinal Wyszyński, and the Polish government. According to the agreement that had been worked out in 1956, the Primate sent the government the names of episcopal nominees who had been chosen by the Holy See (presumably, with Wyszyński's agreement). The government then had three months to cast a veto. If no veto was received during that time, the Primate made the public announcement of a nomination. The formal point of contact in the government was the prime minister, but the real power in such decisions was wielded by the Communist Party's second-ranking figure, Zenon Kliszko. Kliszko was the marshal (or Speaker, in Anglo-American terminology) of the Sejm, the rubber-stamp Polish parliament. More to the point, he was the Party's chief ideologist and the guardian of Polish communist orthodoxy.

In the late fall of 1963, Father Andrzej Bardecki, the ecclesiastical assistant at *Tygodnik Powszechny*, had a visitor. Professor Stanisław Stomma, head of a five-member Catholic micro-party permitted in the Sejm, discreetly asked Father Bardecki if they could take a walk on the Planty, the greensward that surrounds Kraków's Old Town and a pleasant place to talk while avoiding the secret police bugs in the *Tygodnik Powszechny* office. Once the two men were outside, Stomma told Bardecki that he had recently spoken with Zenon Kliszko about the logjam in filling the vacant archbishopric of Kraków. Kliszko, who did not lack ego, was very pleased with himself for having vetoed all seven names the Primate had proposed over the past year and a half. "I'm waiting for Wojtyła," Kliszko said, "and I'll continue to veto names until I get him."

Stomma had thanked the ideologist for sharing this confidence, but had had to work hard to keep himself from laughing. Wojtyła was precisely the candidate Stomma, his fellow Catholic parliamentarians, and priests like Father Bardecki were quietly hoping for.

Why did Kliszko and, according to Father Bardecki, the entire Politburo of the Polish Communist Party, take this line on Wojtyła? How could they misread him so dramatically?

Wojtyła's age may have had something to do with it. The graybeards of the Polish communist leadership would have thought him, at forty-two, a boy, unseasoned, someone who could be manipulated. Then there was his utter lack of interest in politics, as they understood politics. He was an intellectual, a bit abstract, not very knowledgeable about the nitty-gritty of public life, a man who would be satisfied with vague assurances. Kliszko and his comrades must have concluded that this combination of age, intellectuality, and inexperience made Karol Wojtyła the perfect pawn for achieving their longstanding strategic goal—dividing the Polish hierarchy in order to marginalize the Primate and diminish the Church's public influence.

From a distance of thirty-five years, there certainly seems to have been enough counterevidence to have given the comrades pause. There was Wojtyła's demonstrated capacity to attract the loyalty of the young and his links to the Rhapsodic Theater, a suspicious group. He had shown impressive negotiating skills in talking the local authorities out of seizing an archdiocesan seminary building in 1962. A year later, he had successfully called the authorities' bluff when they tried to evict seminarians and faculty from one wing of the Silesian seminary in Kraków, threatening to stand publicly with the faculty on the day of the eviction if the order was carried out; it wasn't.[2] His Christmas midnight Masses at Nowa Huta should have suggested that this was not a man to accept a fait accompli. Then there was his sermon in January 1963 on the centenary of the January Uprising against the Russians—what was this business about the "inner freedom of man"? And his sermon at the unveiling of the memorial to Kalinowski and Chmielowski at Wawel Cathedral, five months later—shouldn't his reference to the holiness of these conspirators, and his reminder to Poles that they had often had "to break through to freedom from the underground," have raised caution flags in the comrades' minds?

If these sermons didn't faze Zenon Kliszko—and if Wojtyła's other experiments in cultural resistance, far from bothering the communists, in fact commended Wojtyła to them—the explanation must be that Kliszko and his colleagues were deluded by their own ideology and propaganda. "Cultural resistance" made no sense to them. In the orthodox Marxist jargon, ideas were "superstructure," ephemera, not the real stuff of power. Let the boyish vicar capitular preach sermons about the "supernatural episcopal responsibility for the people of God" in service to which St. Stanisław had surrendered his life. Let him urge college students to think about their lives vocationally and go to confession regularly. All of this was opium, not only for the masses but for the restive Kraków intelligentsia. Let Wojtyła keep doing what he had been doing, with the authority of the metropolitan archbishop. He would, at the very least, help keep the lid on. Beyond that, there was the delicious possibility that this naïf would let himself be maneuvered into fracturing the unity of the episcopate, by taking positions the regime could manipulate against Wyszyński.

Did Cardinal Wyszyński think that Karol Wojtyła was a vague, abstract intellectual whom the communists could manipulate? That Wojtyła was eighth (or, by some accounts, seventh) among Wyszyński's nominees for Kraków suggests at a minimum that the Primate regarded Wojtyła as too young and inexperienced for the position. In his few years as a member of the Polish episcopate, Wojtyła had never crossed the Primate. But the vicar capitular of Kraków was a great defender of *Tygodnik Powszechny*, and the Primate had had his difficulties with the paper and its independent-minded editors. Wojtyła's sympathy for the reform-minded bishops at Vatican II might also have raised questions in Wyszyński's mind, not so much because of the reforms themselves, but because the Primate thought that Western reformers didn't understand his situation and were absorbed with issues of little relevance to the Polish Church. In any case, Wyszyński clearly didn't know Wojtyła very well. Asked shortly after Wojtyła's appointment what the new archbishop of Kraków was like, the Primate paused, and then said, "He is a poet."

In December 1963, Professor Stomma returned to *Tygodnik Powszechny* and, once again, took Father Bardecki for a walk along the Planty. Zenon Kliszko, he said, had just told him that he had received a nomination letter from Cardinal Wyszyński with Karol Wojtyła's name on it. Stomma was delighted. So was Bardecki. And so, we may assume, was Zenon Kliszko.

Then there was the warden at the prison in Gdańsk, who at the time had a distinguished prisoner. Father Piotr Rostworowski, abbot of the Camaldolese monastery outside Kraków, was doing time for helping smuggle Czech citizens across the Czech-Polish border. When Karol Wojtyła's nomination as archbishop was publicly announced, the warden paid his prisoner a visit and gloated over the nomination. This was "very good news," he told the abbot; Wojtyła was exactly the man the comrades wanted. Four months later the warden, on another visit to the abbot, took a different line. "Wojtyła has swindled us!" he cried.

All of which, Father Bardecki concluded, was evidence that "the Holy Spirit can work his will by darkening as well as enlightening people's minds."[3]

"MY BELOVED KRAKÓW"

Karol Wojtyła lived in Kraków for exactly forty years, including four years as auxiliary bishop, two years as de facto leader of the archdiocese, and fourteen as its archbishop. From the outset, there was a remarkable fit between the city and the man, between the ancient see and the young bishop.

He was a Polish intellectual and Kraków was an intellectual center as well as Poland's longstanding cultural capital. He was a Polish patriot in a city where the nation's history was enshrined in the cathedral church and where he could read the story of Poland's struggle for freedom off the palaces, streets, colleges, churches, and houses he walked by every day. He was a writer living in the cradle of Polish publishing, the city where the first book in Polish had been published. He was, by adoption and conviction, a Cracovian, which meant that he was a European living at the heart of Europe.

He was a priest and bishop in a city of great witnesses to the faith: Stanisław, the model for his successors in the Kraków episcopal line; Piotr Skarga, sixteenth-century preacher of national renewal through spiritual revival; Dunajewski and Puzyna, rebels in 1863 who became bishops and cardinals. This was the city of Brother Albert and the self-sacrificing religious communities he had founded, and the home of Sister Faustina Kowalska, the mystic of divine mercy. It was the episcopal see of Adam Stefan Sapieha, the unbroken prince, and the diocese in which Father Maximilian Kolbe had offered himself in the starvation bunker at Auschwitz. All of this was alive in Kraków in an almost palpable way. And it was alive in Karol Wojtyła, who believed that popular devotion to the saints and a serious Catholic intellectual life reinforced each other.

The man who seemed born to be archbishop of Kraków laid out the basic themes of his episcopate in a pastoral letter to the archdiocese written for Lent, 1964. (Like his other pastoral letters over the years, this one could not be printed but was typed by relays of nuns using six sheets of carbon paper per typewriter, and then hand-delivered to each parish; the mails could not be trusted.[4])

To be the archbishop of Kraków, he wrote, was to know a "profound sense of responsibility," deepened by the "great and eloquent memories of the past" that were alive in the archdiocese. If that sense of responsibility did not engender fear, it was because he had "total confidence in Christ the Lord and in His Mother" and a "sincere trust" in the people he served. Life was not an absurdity, for "God wants all men to be saved and to come to a knowledge of truth. (*1 Timothy* 2.4)" That was both the Church's faith and its mission: to help men and women realize the dignity of their nature and the nobility of their destiny. And in carrying out that mission, he, as their bishop, "the first servant of [the] common good," expected everyone to take "responsibility for that part which the will of God has given him."[5]

Karol Wojtyła, who was created a cardinal in 1967 by Pope Paul VI, at the exceptionally young age of forty-seven, was the first bishop of Kraków in the thousand-year history of the see who was not born to the gentry class. That proved no barrier to his becoming one of the most effective diocesan bishops of his time, and in any place.

PRIORITIES

According to those who worked with him, Cardinal Wojtyła had a distinctive way of approaching problems and decisions. In each instance, he would pose two questions to his collaborators. "What is the truth of faith that sheds light on this problem?" was first. Then, after that had been discussed, "Who can we get—or train—to help?"[6] Wojtyła was running a very large organization as archbishop of Kraków, but this was an organization with a difference. This was the *Church,* and he would govern it like the Church, not like some other kind of institution.

He lived this approach to leadership and problem solving every day. Each morning, after Mass and breakfast, the archbishop disappeared into his chapel, and it was known that he was not to be disturbed. There, alone, a few yards from the spot where Cardinal Sapieha had ordained him a priest, he spent two hours writing at a small desk, facing the Blessed Sacrament in the tabernacle on the altar. It is said that there are theologians who do theology at their desks and theologians who do theology on their knees; the same might be said about bishops and the governance of dioceses. Karol Wojtyła was a bishop who governed his diocese (and did his philosophy and theology) "on his knees"—or at a desk in the sacramental presence of his Lord.[7]

The archbishop often took his most difficult decisions to the shrine at Kalwaria Zebrzydowska, where he would frequently be found walking the grounds, rosary in hand, thinking through a problem in prayer. Every Friday, he left the archbishop's residence (in which his office was also located) and walked across Franciszkańska Street to the Franciscan basilica, where Władysław Jagiełło had been baptized before his marriage to Queen Jadwiga. Walking beneath stained glass designed by his fellow playwright, Stanisław Wyspiański, he went into a side chapel where he prayed the fourteen stations of the cross.

The inspiration for Karol Wojtyła's style and method as archbishop was the Prince Cardinal, Adam Sapieha, whose simple gold pectoral cross Wojtyła wore over a plain black cassock. Photos of Sapieha were prominent in the archbishop's large study.[8] If Sapieha was the model, though, his approach had to be adapted to new circumstances. Twelve years after the Prince Cardinal's death, Kraków was a huge, sprawling diocese of 1.5 million Catholics, including 1,500 priests (771 diocesan and 749 belonging to religious orders), 1,500 nuns, 1,500 brothers (professed members of men's religious orders who were not priests), and 191 seminarians. In fourteen years as leader of this complex community, Karol Wojtyła pursued seven priorities, which disclose a lot about his understanding of the Church and its mission.

Religious Freedom

Thanks to the demographic realities and Cardinal Wyszyński's leadership, Poland's Catholics enjoyed a measure of liberty in practicing their faith that was the envy of their Lithuanian, Czechoslovak, and Ukrainian neighbors, who were actively persecuted. No citizen of a free society would have recognized the Polish situation as one of religious freedom, however, and the modus vivendi that had been worked out with the communist regime did not come close to satisfying the criteria of religious freedom defined by the Second Vatican Council.

The Kraków episcopate had a special historic texture in matters of religious freedom. To be the successor of St. Stanisław was to be the heir of an ancient tradition in which the bishop was the *defensor populi*, the "defender of the people," and the *defensor civitatis*, the "defender of the city" of last resort.[9] Cardinal Sapieha had fulfilled these roles magnificently during the Nazi Occupation and in the first years of Polish communism. Now it was Karol Wojtyła's turn to defend the people and the city, not so much against public persecution (although there were instances of that) but against a state determined to uproot the Polish nation from the soil of Christian culture in which it had been planted. During Wojtyła's episcopate, the struggle for religious freedom centered on two issues: building churches, and the public display of Catholicism, symbolized by the annual Corpus Christi procession.

From 1962 (when Wojtyła was chosen vicar capitular) until 1978, the Archdiocese of Kraków created eleven new parishes and ten new "pastoral centers," transitional units on the way to being fully erected parishes.[10] Every one of these initiatives involved a struggle with the regime.

Parishes could not be legally established or church buildings constructed without the government's permission; according to canon law, no parish could be created without a church building. By denying permits to build churches, the government could effectively choke off the Church's development, which required the formation of new parishes. Wojtyła developed a sophisticated, assertive resistance strategy in the face of regime intransigence and canonical difficulties. An average of thirty requests for building permits were filed with the government in each year of Wojtyła's episcopate, and every year the backlog grew, as previous years' unsatisfied requests were kept pending. While the archdiocese kept pressing the authorities to resolve this growing roster of permits denied or delayed, Wojtyła adopted a parallel strategy of "creating facts" to which the government had to respond. Bracketing the issues in canon law, he and courageous priests would form a parish-without-a-church through the dogged, often door-to-door evangelization of a neighborhood, over a period of months or years. Then, when a living parish had been created, the government would be presented with a fait accompli—"Look, the people want a church, society needs a church."

One focal point for this strategy was Nowa Huta, the model workers' town-without-a-church built by the communists on the outskirts of Kraków. The new town was filled with enormous apartment blocks, some of which contained as many as 450 flats, yet there was no way to pass laterally from one apartment to another down the long axis of a building. If you wanted to visit a neighbor outside the two- or three-apartment module in which you lived, you went down the stairs or elevator, left the building, reentered through another door, and then climbed the stairs or took the elevator up to your neighbor's module. Nowa Huta's apartment blocks were aptly described as human filing cabinets, and the cabinets were deliberately designed to keep the files separated. Churches, places for communities independent of the regime, had no place in Nowa Huta.

The great symbol of the struggle for Nowa Huta's soul was the building of what became known as the "Ark Church," which arose from the field in the Bienczyce neighborhood where Wojtyła had celebrated Christmas midnight Mass since 1959. Permission for building this assertively modern structure—its architecture suggesting the Church as the "ark" in which Mary, Queen of Poland, was saving her people—was finally obtained on October 13, 1967, after years of agitation. The very next day, October 14, Cardinal Karol Wojtyła led a groundbreaking ceremony, swinging a pickaxe and helping dig the first section of the trench for the church's foundation, in which the stone from St. Peter's tomb donated by Pope Paul VI would be imbedded. Ten years of volunteer labor from all over Poland and throughout Europe went into completing the Ark Church. Its exterior was decorated by 2 million small polished stones from the riverbeds of Poland. The interior was dominated by a great steel figure of the crucified Christ forged by the workers at Nowa Huta's Lenin Steelworks. The tabernacle was a gift from the diocese of Sankt Pölten in Austria, and was shaped like a model of the solar system; its decoration included a piece of moon rock, given to Paul VI by an American astronaut. The Dutch had donated the church's bells. The Ark Church was dedicated by Cardinal Wojtyła on May 15, 1977. His sermon at the dedication Mass, attended by pilgrims from Austria, Czechoslovakia, Hungary, Yugoslavia, Germany, Holland, Portugal, Italy, Canada, the United States, England, Finland, and France, put a new definition on the model workers' town. "This is not a city of people who belong to no one," the cardinal insisted, "of people to whom one may do whatever one wants, who may be manipulated according to the laws or rules of production and consumption. This is a city of the children of God. . . . This temple was necessary so that this could be expressed, that it could be emphasized. . . ."[11]

While the Ark Church was the most famous symbol of the war for Nowa Huta, the harshest battle in that war was fought in another Nowa Huta neighborhood, Miestrzejowice.

Father Józef Kurzeja came to see Cardinal Wojtyła in 1970 and, as John Paul II remembered, made a straightforward proposal: "We need a church in Miestrzejowice. Maybe they'll put me in prison, but I'm ready to begin."[12] The cardinal agreed, and Father Kurzeja went to work. He wasn't a terribly good preacher, his assistant remembered, nor could he sing very well, but he was a big, honest man in his mid-thirties whom people wanted to be around.[13] Kurzeja bought a small piece of unoccupied property in Miestrzejowice and built a tiny wooden house, more like a toolshed than a home. There was an altar on the side, and the priest began to attract a congregation by going door-to-door in the neighborhood. With the battle for the Ark Church largely won, the Nowa Huta front line moved to Miestrzejowice, where, in support of Father

Kurzeja's effort, Cardinal Wojtyła began saying Christmas midnight Mass in another open field. On Christmas Eve, 1971, he preached on the text from the Gospel of Luke, "And there was no room for them at the inn . . ." Before thousands of people at an open-air Mass, the cardinal vigorously defended Father Kurzeja: "The priest who shepherds your flock here under the bare sky, who has nothing except your good will and your solidarity, is not seeking any personal goals, any personal gain. What does he want? He wants to teach the Gospel, God's truth, but at the same time humanity's deepest truth. He wants to teach the principles of morality, of God's commandments. Does that not lie within the interests of this new city, Nowa Huta? That people observe the moral law? . . . Does this not lie within the interests of the nation, the state? For that, surely the priest does not deserve punishment. Surely he deserves only praise. . . ."[14]

The authorities didn't agree. Constantly harassed on the street, in his apartment, and at the wooden chapel by State Security, the Słuzba Bezpieczeństwa, and subjected to constant SB interrogations, Father Józef Kurzeja collapsed and died of heart failure at age thirty-nine on August 15, 1976.[15] It was the day after the thirty-fourth anniversary of another martyrdom, Maximilian Kolbe's in the starvation bunker at Auschwitz. Father Kurzeja's vindication, the church in Miestrzejowice, was named St. Maximilian Kolbe and dedicated by Pope John Paul II in 1983.[16]

The annual Corpus Christi procession, a late springtime tradition the communists were determined to eradicate and Wojtyła was determined to preserve, was another focal point in the struggle for religious freedom in Kraków during Wojtyła's episcopate Prior to the war, this great public procession honoring the Eucharistic Body and Blood of Christ went from Wawel Cathedral through the streets of the Old Town to the Rynek Głowny, the market square, around the circumference of which the archbishop of Kraków processed, carrying the Blessed Sacrament in an ancient gold monstrance. Stational altars were erected along the periphery of the Rynek, at which the procession would stop temporarily and the archbishop would preach. Hans Frank had, of course, banned the procession during the Occupation. The communists permitted a truncated procession to leave Wawel Cathedral and process around the courtyard of the royal palace, but the procession was forbidden to enter the city.

After numerous protests from the archdiocese, the restrictions were eased slightly so that the Corpus Christi procession was permitted to come down from Wawel Hill and walk two blocks up Grodzka Street, turning left at Poselska Street for a block before continuing back to Wawel along two blocks of Straszewski Street.[17] Stational altars were set up along this drastically shortened route. Preaching at these stational altars before tens of thousands of Cracovians, on what had become a major patriotic as well as religious event, Karol Wojtyła emerged in the 1970s as a charismatic public personality—and did so just as Poland was becoming more openly restive after the regime shot down strikers at the Gdańsk shipyard in 1970.[18]

Wojtyła had always been seen as an interesting, if demanding, preacher. In these Corpus Christi processions, he began to develop the kind of charisma that can move great crowds. His language became more simple and direct, as he employed some of the lessons he had learned from Mieczysław Kotlarczyk during these annual acts of cultural resistance. But the message was constant even as the medium was refined. This procession in honor of the Eucharistic Christ was a means to give back to the people of Kraków their authentic culture and their rights as citizens.

On June 10, 1971, the first time since the war that the procession had been able to leave Wawel, Wojtyła preached at the fourth stational altar on the impossibility of separating the Polish people from their religious tradition: "We are the citizens of our country, the citizens of our city, but we are also a people of God which has its own Christian sensibility. . . . We will continue to demand our rights. They are obvious, just as our presence here is obvious. We will demand! . . ."[19]

In 1972, his sermon at the first stational altar on Wawel Hill described the annual procession as "a procession . . . of our city, of our whole history" and bluntly told the authorities, "We are waiting . . ."[20] In 1974, before tens of thousands packed into the streets, the cardinal insisted that "We are not from the periphery!" As for the endless delays over building churches, was it part of "the program of the socialist system that people stand for years on end under the open sky" to exercise the rights guaranteed them in their constitution? "What program is that part of?"[21] In 1975, with the procession still forbidden to enter the market square, the cardinal's sermon at the first stational altar included a rare instance of public sarcasm: "I am inclined to think that such actions do not favor the processes of normalization between the Church and the State."[22] His sermon at the first station during the 1977 procession warned the government that "awareness of human rights keeps growing" throughout society and throughout the world: and "these rights are undeniable!" He concluded the 1977 procession with a confession at the fourth station: "I ask forgiveness from Our Lord that—at least seemingly—I did not speak of Him. But it only seems that way. I spoke of our matters . . . so that we might all understand that He, living in the Sacrament of the Eucharist, lives our human life. . . ."[23]

Karol Wojtyła's struggle for new churches and for the restoration of the Corpus Christi procession was about *place*, not in the sense of geography, but of belonging. Buildings and processions were important. The people had a right to worship according to their traditions and convictions, and as Wojtyła put it during the May 25, 1978, Corpus Christi procession, "a nation . . . has a right to the truth about itself."[24] The struggle over *place* transcended questions of buildings and processions, however. The issue was whether the Polish people would have the freedom to be themselves as Christians in what claimed to be a "People's Republic." The Polish communist strategy was to reduce Polish Catholicism to a folk memory. Cardinal Wojtyła's struggle for religious freedom was a struggle to secure room for a living Church, proclaiming the truth about human life and human destiny and living that truth through service to all of society. If that could be secured, totalitarianism would, by definition, have failed.[25]

The Seminary and the Faculty of Theology

Strengthening the priesthood in the Archdiocese of Kraków by reforms in the academic training of seminarians and the continuing education of young priests was the second of Cardinal Wojtyła's pastoral priorities.[26]

As the last man to be granted a doctoral degree by the Jagiellonian University Faculty of Theology, Wojtyła keenly felt the injustice the regime had done when it shut down the faculty in 1954. But this was hardly an issue to be reduced to the offended sensibilities of an alumnus. Closing the faculty was an attempt to rewrite Polish history and a clumsy effort to lobotomize Polish culture. For in addition to being deprived of its legal status, the Faculty of Theology had lost its library and lecture halls, its professors were pressured by the regime, and the government removed all references to the Faculty of Theology from newspapers, periodicals, and guidebooks.[27]

No theology would have meant no education of future priests. Shortly after the shutdown, the expelled professors formed a Faculty of Theology within the Kraków archdiocesan seminary. The governmental expulsion was treated as an arbitrary act rescinding the authority to grant degrees in the name of the state. The faculty retained its authority to grant pontifical degrees under the authority of the Holy See and continued on this academic basis.

That solved the immediate problem of providing for the education of seminarians, but the situation was unjust and Wojtyła frequently criticized the government for committing an act of cultural vandalism. Time and again he pressed the regime to restore the Faculty of Theology to its ancient rights within the Jagiellonian University. Concurrently, he worked in Rome to support the Faculty of Theology, which was granted the status of a pontifical faculty in 1974. On the home front, the cardinal found funds for the Faculty of Theology, defended its facilities against expropriation by the authorities, and planned the creation of its department of philosophy, which he launched in 1976. He also reformed the seminarians' curriculum, bringing them, for example, into the training courses for marriage preparation he established with doctors, psychiatrists, and married couples.[28]

Cardinal Wojtyła was not only interested in the intellectual formation of his future priests, important as that was, but in the formation of real pastors. The secret of pastoral success, he believed, was a priest's holiness and his commitment to the care of souls.[29] In his years as archbishop, Wojtyła met regularly with his seminarians, getting to know each future priest personally. He continued to meet with each class of newly ordained priests throughout the early years of their ministry, sometimes on the ski slopes. In whatever setting, he constantly urged the necessity of a life of deep personal prayer as a good in itself and the essential foundation for pastoral work.

Wojtyła disciplined young priests in a distinctive way. He once had to call in an assistant pastor who had committed what the priest later recalled as a "serious misdemeanor." In a lengthy session in his office, Wojtyła told the curate in no uncertain terms about the gravity of the offense and reprimanded him severely. The cardinal then led the young priest into his chapel so they could pray. The older man knelt so long that the curate became nervous. His train was scheduled to leave shortly to take him back to his parish. Finally, Cardinal Wojtyła stood up, looked at the young man he had just chastised, and said, "Would you please hear my confession now?" Stunned, the assistant pastor went to the confessional, where Wojtyła confessed before him.[30]

Cardinal Wojtyła was also a successful recruiter for the seminary. The number of seminarians studying for the archdiocese increased from 191 in 1962 to 250 in 1978; the number of diocesan priests increased from 771 to 956 in the same period. These were years when vocation recruitment was plummeting in the West and men were leaving the active ministry in great numbers. It is true that, in communist Poland, the priesthood was a stable profession in a small zone of relative freedom, and a passage into the middle class for many sons of working-class people or peasants. It is also likely that recruitment was easier when a bishop, pastor, or diocesan vocation director could appeal to the youthful instinct to be countercultural and defiant. By the same token, the Polish priesthood, lived seriously, was a vocation requiring real courage under communism—the life and death of Father Józef Kurzeja in Miestrzejowice proved that. The government also did its bit to make things difficult, drafting seminarians into the army in the middle of their training to weaken their sense of vocation, and continuing to put pressure on the seminary and the Faculty of Theology. For Cardinal Wojtyła to have increased the quantity and quality of Kraków's priests under these circumstances was a considerable accomplishment. It was not his alone, but he was invaluable to it.

Youth Ministry

As archbishop of Kraków, Karol Wojtyła showed an unusual ease with independent-minded individuals who believed they had a special call from God to undertake a work beyond the Church's normal institutional boundaries. Charismatic personalities tend to make many bishops nervous. Cardinal Wojtyła was willing to tolerate the tension between charismatic individuals and their movements, on the one hand, and the Church's "structure," on the other.

One such individual was Father Franciszek Blachnicki, who had first come to national attention as a temperance crusader. Blachnicki was now the central figure in a youth movement called "Light and Life," which had evolved out of another Blachnicki-led movement, the "Oasis" summer camps for families and young people. Wojtyła had first met Blachnicki at the Catholic University of Lublin in the mid-1950s, where Blachnicki was involved with liturgical renewal efforts at the university chapel. As archbishop of Kraków, Wojtyła extended a mantle of protection over Blachnicki's work with young people, a direct challenge to the regime's attempt to split youngsters from their families.

Like other charismatic personalities, Father Blachnicki had his rough edges. But Wojtyła admired the man who, he later recalled, "in some measure saved Polish youth."[31] And Blachnicki did so not only by creating summer "Oases" that were less morally threatening than the communist youth camps. He did so in the Light and Life movement by sketching a Polish theology of liberation, proposing that Poles overcome their fearful complacency and challenge the regime by "living in the truth:" if enough Poles "plucked up their courage to live by the truth and unmask lies," Blachnicki insisted, "we would already be a free society."[32]

Though Franciszek Blachnicki might have been imprudent at times, Wojtyła shared his analysis of Poland's situation and his pastoral strategy: resistance through the education of young people determined to live a "full-time Christian commitment."[33] Blachnicki's Oasis summer camps and Light and Life meetings were constantly harassed by the authorities, who would swoop down on a campground and decide that the campers' permits were of the wrong sort or had somehow expired. Levying heavy fines against landowners who rented space to Oasis camps was another favorite tactic. In the face of this, the presence of an alternative authority was one form of protection, so Wojtyła spent time during the summers visiting Oasis camps, celebrating Mass, giving talks—and subtly suggesting to the authorities that, if they didn't leave Blachnicki's people alone, they might provoke an embarrassing incident by invading a campsite one day when the archbishop was there.[34]

On August 16, 1972, Cardinal Wojtyła visited an Oasis campsite on Błyszcz Mountain in the Beskid Sądecki range south of Kraków, where some 700 Oasis people were staying. The plan was for the cardinal and his secretary to hike up to the campsite from an adjoining valley, accompanied by Oasis guides. On the way up, the cardinal noticed the darkening skies, heard thunder in the distance, and joked to the guides, "I know three madmen: the first is myself, the second is my secretary, and the third is waiting for us at the summit." When the cardinal asked the third "madman," Father Blachnicki, whether they shouldn't move Mass down to the church in the valley, the charismatic priest insisted that the storm would pass by. It didn't, and the only two umbrellas available were barely sufficient to cover the center of the altar, which had been built out of a rockpile. After Mass they moved down to the valley church for an hour of sharing witness, at which young people told how a Light and Life retreat had changed their lives, and Cardinal Wojtyła thanked them for bringing Vatican II alive in Poland.[35]

Oasis camps and the Light and Life movement were two potent examples of a strategy of informal youth organizing that Wojtyła and his colleagues adopted to get around the regime's ban on formal "Catholic organizations." The catechetical sessions with altar boys and their families he had organized years before at St. Florian's became a diocesan-wide phenomenon. Choirs were another "non-organization" that could easily become a venue for religious education. Cardinal Wojtyła urged students to care for abandoned or neglected Jewish cemeteries—a way of teaching youngsters about a great heritage that had been destroyed, and about what had destroyed it.[36] There were "huge possibilities" for doing things informally, one of Wojtyła's auxiliary bishops, Stanisław Smoleński, remembered. It simply required imagination and nerve.[37] Wojtyła had both and appreciated these qualities in others—a trait that endeared him to his subordinates and set him apart in the episcopate. He was prepared to let all sorts of flowers, some of them quite exotic, bloom, as long as their gardeners were doctrinally orthodox and willing to accept the Church's authority.

Family Ministry

Karol Wojtyła's intense interest in marriage preparation and in ministry to families dated back to his days as a young curate at St. Florian's. Jerzy Ciesielski and other young men and women whom he had helped prepare for marriage, along with friends from his *Środowisko* like Gabriel Turowski, had been involved in various pioneering efforts to create an archdiocesan-wide program of marriage preparation in the early 1960s. As archbishop, faced with the Polish regime's relentless efforts to undermine family life, Wojtyła expanded this form of pastoral care so that it reached into every corner of the archdiocese through a network of lay activists he helped train.

In 1967, Wojtyła organized an intensive, yearlong course on marriage preparation and family life issues in his residence, in which thirty priests and sixty laypeople participated. This multidimensional program explored issues in theology, philosophy, psychology, and medicine, with instructors recruited from all these disciplines and the cardinal himself as a regular lecturer. In 1969, this informal program was transformed into an archdiocesan Institute for Family Studies, which sponsored conferences on such family-related issues as the theology of marriage, human sexuality, child care, and healing post-abortion stress. The institute became the intellectual and training center of the Division of Family Pastoral Care the archbishop had created in the Metropolitan Curia, or central administration, of the archdiocese in 1968.

In the 1970s, the institute, now affiliated with the Pontifical Faculty of Theology, evolved into a two-year program training 250 students each biennium. These students were the seminarians, priests, and lay men and women who became instructors and facilitators in the parish-based marriage-preparation programs the archbishop encouraged every pastor to establish. Each graduate of the course was given a canonical "mission" to do family-care work in a parish by the cardinal himself. In 1974, when the custom of marriage preparation had become well-established throughout the archdiocese, Cardinal Wojtyła mandated a two-month marriage-preparation program prior to every wedding. A 1975 decision by the Polish episcopate lengthened that to a three-month preparation program. In 1974, the cardinal also started an archdiocesan fund to support unwed mothers who rejected abortion and wanted to raise their children themselves. Wojtyła personally encouraged convents to take these young women in and care for them until they had delivered their babies and prepared themselves to raise them as single mothers.[38]

Dialogue with Intellectuals

The Catholic intellectuals of Kraków were enthusiastic about the appointment of one of their own as archbishop. Cardinal Wojtyła, for his part, believed that a personal ministry to intellectuals and their families was an important part of his episcopate. These were the men and women who could develop, throughout the worlds of Polish culture, the Christian humanism he had worked hard to place at the center of the Second Vatican Council.[39]

It was not an easy time to be a Catholic intellectual in Kraków. There were endless harassments over academic degrees. If one finally managed to complete one's studies, few faculty positions were open to qualified scholars who were publicly identified as Catholics. The Church could help them find jobs (at *Tygodnik Powszechny*, for example). But there was the ongoing problem of the surrounding public culture, which constantly worked to "thresh intellectuals from the husk of religious conviction," as one painter put it.[40]

It didn't work. One reason was that *Tygodnik Powszechny* and *Znak* became the focal points of an alternative intellectual community capable of mounting an effective resistance to the pressures of a communist cultural environment. Cardinal Wojtyła's unstinting support for the newspaper, the journal, and their people was a crucial factor in sustaining that resistance.

Unlike bishops who thought of intellectuals as threats, Karol Wojtyła thought of them as friends and allies. The tension in the intellect of this thoroughly modern and culturally literate man who was a completely convinced Christian had been one of the qualities that first attracted young intellectuals during his days at St. Florian's.[41] High ecclesiastical office didn't loosen that tension and the electricity it generated. If anything, it sharpened it.

The Polish Christmas custom of the *Opłatek*, a party or reception in which friends share a Christmas wafer similar to the host consecrated at Mass, gave Cardinal Wojtyła occasions to bring the Kraków intelligentsia into his home for the kind of conversation that was difficult in other circumstances. Each Christmas season, the cardinal sponsored *Opłatek* celebrations for various lawyers, doctors, nurses, writers, and artists. After a brief prayer, rather like a family grace-before-meals, the *Opłatek* wafer would be broken and shared, and a freewheeling conversation began. Personal contact with a cardinal was unusual enough to give these parties a certain tang for the visitors; from the host's point of view, these were occasions when people could speak freely in ways that were simply impossible elsewhere. The cardinal's *Opłatek* celebrations weren't catechetical exercises, but his evident willingness to meet non-Catholics and troubled Catholics at the point to which their own lives had led them had its own evangelical effect, and refuted the regime's repeated claim that Christian faith was alienating and anti-intellectual. No one could take that seriously after talking late into the night with the cardinal archbishop of Kraków in the drawing room of his home.[42]

In 1976 and 1977, Wojtyła's outreach to intellectuals expanded to include the dissident intellectuals of KOR, the "Workers' Defense Committee." Wojtyła and KOR leader Jacek Kuroń, who had been expelled from the Communist Party in 1964, were first introduced in Kraków by Bohdan Cywiński, a Catholic activist with contacts in the more secular world of KOR. A lengthier conversation at Cywiński's Warsaw apartment was, Cywiński remembered, a "typical meeting for the time: the police were outside." The cardinal discussed the general social and political situation with Kuroń and other KOR leaders, whose general view was that the situation was bad but, as Cywiński put it, "stable bad." The workers did seem more willing to challenge their difficult conditions. But there was no intuition among the KOR intellectuals that the political and economic status quo could be changed dramatically, or soon. From Wojtyła's point of view, his contacts with secular dissidents like Kuroń were another facet of his pastoral program—in this instance, an outreach to left-leaning intellectuals who had broken with communism because of their human rights convictions. In addition to the personal contacts, though, these conversations were another link in the chain of cultural resistance.[43]

The Ministry of Charity

Sociologist Rodney Stark argues that one of the reasons the marginal "Jesus Sect" triumphed in the Roman Empire was its religious commitment to care for the sick, the elderly, the blind, the handicapped, and the orphaned. In obeying Christ's command to take care of the least of his brethren, Christianity became a movement that could attract and retain large numbers of converts by offering a more humane way of life.[44] Ever since, Christian communities have sponsored an enormous number of charitable activities and maintained a vast network of charitable institutions: hospitals, nursing homes, homes for orphans and unwed mothers, clinics, institutions for the handicapped and the mentally ill.

None of this was permitted to exist formally in communist Poland, where Catholic charitable institutions and organizations were banned from 1950 on. If the communists would not allow the Church to operate its own charitable institutions, agencies, and programs, then the Church, Wojtyła decided, would make this ban the opportunity to renew parish life in the spirit of the Gospel. Beginning in 1963, each parish established a "Parochial Charity Team" that included permanent members, called "parish guardians," and volunteers. Their task was to identify and care for the sick and needy in the parish's geographic territory, irrespective of religious affiliation; non-Catholics and non-believers were, Wojtyła urged, part of the parish's responsibility. The teams provided food, medicine, and clothing to the needy, nursed shut-ins in their homes, and carried out an extensive home visitation program. To help in this work, the Parochial Charity Team recruited members of other parish organizations—the parish council, the choir, the altar boys, the Living Rosary, Oasis movement families—and cooperated with other parishes and with public agencies like the Polish Red Cross.

In 1965, Archbishop Wojtyła created the Pastoral Ministry of Charity Division in the Metropolitan Curia. In addition to supervising the archdiocesan ministries to the deaf and the blind, this central archdiocesan office coordinated spiritual retreats for the sick and for handicapped children. During the summer, the archdiocese worked with the parishes to sponsor two-week-long retreats for the sick, the handicapped, and the elderly in the countryside (during the communist period, Kraków was notorious for colossal air pollution, a by-product of unfiltered emissions from the Nowa Huta steel mills). The archdiocesan deaneries—clusters of ten or more parishes in a given geographic area—sponsored pilgrimages of the sick to Kalwaria Zebrzydowska and local Marian shrines. College students, seminarians, and nuns were recruited to help mount such pilgrimages. An archdiocesan newsletter, "Helpful Love" (later, "Apostolate of Love"), informed members of the Parochial Charity Teams about new initiatives and methods of care.

Wojtyła urged each parish to develop an educational program that would deepen the spiritual lives of those already committed to charity work and help prepare others for such activity. Participants in such courses took part in retreats organized on a deanery basis; the cardinal regularly visited these retreats and said Mass for the retreatants. His parish visitations always included visits to the homes of the sick and a Mass or other religious service for the local sick in the parish church and a meeting with the Parochial Charity Team. On the occasion of the "Charity Week" observed in Polish parishes since the interwar period, the cardinal issued an annual proclamation to mobilize action on a specific issue during the coming year (thus 1968 was dedicated to the elderly, 1969 to working mothers, 1970 to endangered children, and so forth).

On May 7, 1965, Archbishop Wojtyła announced that the archdiocese would observe an annual "Day of the Sick." These special commemorations and Wojtyła's fifteen annual pastoral letters to the sick were efforts to bring the often marginalized ill and elderly into the life of the local Church. The cardinal also asked the sick to offer their sufferings for the special needs of the archdiocese, for the Church in Poland, and for the universal Church. In illness, he suggested, as in every other time of life, there was a Christian vocation to live out.[45]

Parish Visitation

Cardinal Karol Wojtyła was an intellectual with a deep sympathy for popular piety and a pastor who understood that the center of the Church's life was the parish, not the archdiocesan bureaucracy.[46] As archbishop, he devoted large blocks of time to making lengthy visitations of the parishes of the archdiocese, reminding his people that the parish was not an accidental aggregate of Catholics who happened to live within a certain set of boundaries, but a way to live, locally, Vatican II's universal call to holiness.

Wojtyła's parish visitations lasted several days. In addition to a parish-wide Mass, they often included a celebration of the sacrament of confirmation for the parish youth. The cardinal always celebrated a special Mass for married couples and blessed each couple individually. In addition to talking with the parish clergy, Wojtyła met with the parish religion teachers and the local nuns. If there was a parish cemetery the cardinal visited it, prayed the rosary with parishioners for the souls of their dead, and blessed any new graves. The cardinal also met with different lay groups for discussions about their work, their study, or their charitable activity. The atmosphere he created was that of a retreat, in which conversations longer and deeper than the usual were the norm.[47]

Parishioners appreciated the time and care the cardinal put into his parish visitations, sensing that these were much more than a requirement of church law for him.[48] Cardinal Wojtyła saw them as opportunities to encapsulate in each parish the principal themes and pastoral priorities of his episcopate. Visitations were, in a singular way, what being a bishop was about. As he told the Roman Curia during a Lenten retreat he preached in 1976, each parish visitation was an opportunity to unveil, in a different locale, the seal of dignity that Christ had bestowed on every Christian at baptism.[49]

A DIFFERENT KIND OF ARCHBISHOP

The physical center of Karol Wojtyła's episcopate was the archbishop's palace at Franciszkańska, 3, in Kraków's Old Town, two blocks from the great market square. The archdiocesan offices were on the ground floor. The archbishop's personal quarters, chapel, office, and receiving rooms—which Wojtyła knew well from his days in the underground seminary—were a floor above. High ceilings and parquet floors, subdued pastel walls and sturdy wooden furniture, oil portraits of the bishops of Kraków and paintings of important scenes in Polish history, all gave the residence a feeling of solidity and understated grace.

Karol Wojtyła used a modest, three-room suite for his personal quarters: a small entry hall, a moderately sized private office, and a bedroom barely large enough to hold a single bed, a small desk, three wardrobes, and an old easy chair. Over the door between the entry hall and the office was a portrait of Wojtyła's patron saint, Charles Borromeo, the brilliant theologian-pastor who had implemented the Council of Trent in Milan in the sixteenth century. The bed featured a worn spread and a colorful folk-art pillow. A portrait of Wojtyła's parents was the only photo in the suite.

Archbishop Wojtyła renovated the second floor in 1964–1966, the first restoration in a century. The chapel, located at the top of the great stone stairway leading from the ground floor, was redecorated and a freestanding altar installed. The simple stations of the cross, which had been there since his days as an underground seminarian, remained.

The archbishop rose at 5 or 5:30 every morning and spent the first hour of his day in private prayer. After Mass in the chapel with his secretary and personal staff (and, sometimes, invited guests), he had breakfast in the kitchen and then retired to the chapel, where he spent two hours every morning, between 9 and 11, writing. The period between 11 A.M. and 1 P.M. was reserved for visitors, and the rule was that anyone who wanted to see the cardinal could come. There were no appointments as such. Everyone would arrive at 11 and the cardinal would walk around the room, greeting visitors and fixing the sequence of meetings in his mind. He then invited the first person or group into his receiving office, and the others would wait their turn. Those seen last were often invited to lunch, which was supposed to begin at 1:30 but frequently didn't start until 2 P.M. or 2:15 because the cardinal insisted on seeing everyone who had come to talk. The soup would be getting cold and the younger priests at table might have been getting worried, but Wojtyła would charge into the dining room saying, "The cardinal arrived for lunch at half past one; your watches are wrong."[50] He was not a man to care greatly about food, although he had a sweet tooth and the nuns who cooked for him were reputed to make some of the best *bigos*, a classic Polish stew, in Kraków.[51]

Afternoons and evenings were devoted to more meetings, to visitations around the city or the region, and to reading and study. He had no television, but listened to Radio Free Europe's Polish service on a small radio while shaving in the morning.[52] To make maximum use of his travel time, he had a desk and lamp rigged up in the backseat of his car so that he could read or write while being driven to an appointment.

His energy may have seemed limitless to others.[53] But he paced himself well, never giving any task more time than it needed before moving on to the next. His ability to do two things at once—run a seminar and work through his correspondence, for example—was another factor in his productivity. He also insisted on vacations, kayaking in the summer and skiing in the winter, which he believed were essential to recharging his stores of energy. But according to everyone who knew and worked with him, the mainspring of his daily energy was his constant prayer.

The archbishop lived simply, by deliberate choice. He had neither a bank account nor personal funds, his needs being met by the archdiocese. If a priest or parishioner gave him a gift of money during a parish visitation, he wouldn't even open the envelope, but gave it away the same day to someone in need.[54]

The Archdiocese of Kraków under Karol Wojtyła was not burdened with an extensive bureaucracy.

Four auxiliary bishops served under Wojtyła; Juliusz Groblicki had also been auxiliary to Archbishop Baziak, while Jan Pietraszko, Stanisław Smoleński, and Albin Małysiak were appointed while Wojtyła was archbishop. As a young priest at St. Anne's collegiate church, Pietraszko, nine years older than the archbishop, had developed a following similar to what would become Wojtyła's *Środowisko*. John Paul II remembered him as a "great preacher and teacher" and a "very deep man"; his cause for beatification is under consideration.[55] Smoleński had been spiritual director of the Kraków seminary when young Karol Wojtyła came to live in Archbishop Sapieha's drawing room during the war. Like Pietraszko and Smoleński, the third auxiliary appointed under Wojtyła, Albin Małysiak, was older than the archbishop, having been born in 1917. Wojtyła's auxiliaries were all vicars general, and under canon law his legal deputies in the governance of the archdiocese. There were two archdiocesan chancellors; one who dealt with matters of church law, and a second who was responsible for civil and legal affairs, finance, and administration.[56]

His colleagues frequently said that Cardinal Wojtyła ran the Archdiocese of Kraków like a seminar. Open to new ideas, he wanted to hear what others had to say. He didn't micromanage the archdiocese, and gave subordinates considerable freedom within their own spheres of responsibility. When policy had to be made, he listened carefully to different views and rarely imposed his own solution to a problem, preferring to let a consensus emerge from his colleagues—a consensus that he, of course, helped shape.[57]

Wojtyła expected and accepted criticism from his subordinates, because he trusted them. They, in turn, felt they could be frank with him. In his later years as archbishop, he asked Father Andrzej Bardecki for a critique of a proposed document on secularization that had been prepared for the Polish episcopate. Bardecki read it and sent back a biting memo of criticism, which he later conceded might have been "a little rude" in its choice of vocabulary. Wojtyła read the memo, called the priest in, and said, "You're right. It's not good. But I think you ought to know, Andrzej, that I was the author of that draft; I did it when I was very tired." Bardecki later reflected that virtually any other Polish bishop would have handed a subordinate his head for writing such a critique of a bishop's work.[58]

Wojtyła also knew how to defuse an argument with a staff member. There was occasional tension between the Primate's office in Warsaw and the Pontifical Faculty of Theology in Kraków. On one such occasion, a junior member of the archbishop's staff, Father Tadeusz Pieronek, urging a certain point, said, "Your Eminence, you have to do this." The cardinal replied, "I can't." Father Pieronek began to get angry and said, "You can." The cardinal replied again, "I can't." The priest, now quite agitated, said a third time, "You *can*." At which point the cardinal took off his pectoral cross, held it out, and said, "Here, you rule . . ." Father Pieronek was dumbstruck; the argument was over.[59]

Whenever possible, Wojtyła preferred to talk a problem out rather than issue an edict. Shortly after Vatican II, there was a meeting of the Kraków priests to discuss the question of whether, in the revised liturgy, Holy Communion would be received kneeling, as had been customary, or standing, as was now permitted. The debate, at first heated, eventually grew bitter. The cardinal listened to it all without saying anything. Everyone waited for him to declare himself. When the rhetoric and emotions were spent, Wojtyła got up, went to the podium, and said, "It seems that there are two positions. . . ." He refused to impose a single solution that would have inevitably alienated one faction. His willingness to live with pluralism dissipated the anger and tension among his priests.[60]

There were some things, though, that couldn't be talked through, and they usually involved the regime. In these instances, Wojtyła tended to abandon his "seminar style" of management, acting first and talking later. The creation of de facto parishes to pressure the regime into granting building permits was one instance of this method. There were others. The regime had stalled for years in granting permission for erecting a bronze statue of Cardinal Sapieha, which Wojtyła had commissioned. The statue gathered dust in the Metropolitan Curia. Finally tired of waiting, Wojtyła decided to put it up across Franciszkańska Street opposite the Curia, and issued orders to erect it, explaining that, since it would rest on church property, no permission was needed. The statue was duly erected, draped, and an unveiling was scheduled for a Saturday in May 1976. On the Sunday before the ceremony, the regime's censors cut the archbishop's public invitation to the ceremony from *Tygodnik Powszechny*. The Curia then wrote asking permission of the city authorities for the statue to be set up (where it already was). The permission came in a few days.[61]

Levying heavy taxes on priests was another favorite form of regime harassment. On one occasion, a priest simply didn't have the money to pay his tax and asked the cardinal what to do. Wojtyła suggested that he report to prison. The day he arrived at the jail, the cardinal arrived in his parish, announcing to the thousands gathered outside the church that he was taking over as interim pastor and explaining what had happened. The pastor was released quickly.[62]

In dealing with internal archdiocesan affairs and with the government, Cardinal Wojtyła struck his associates as a man singularly unconcerned about programmatic neatness and tying up loose ends. According to one set of criteria, this made him suspect as a manager. Judged by another standard, it made him a remarkably effective religious leader for whom management was simply one means to his pastoral ends. The ends were what counted.

IMPLEMENTING VATICAN II: THE SYNOD OF KRAKÓW

Having gone to Vatican II conscious of carrying Kraków and its history with him, Karol Wojtyła worked hard to foster a dialogue between the Council and his archdiocese as the epic events in Rome unfolded. In this respect, he began implementing the Council in Kraków long before it formally closed. But this was hardly sufficient payment on the "debt" he always said he owed Vatican II. Something grand was called for.

The idea for the Synod of Kraków matured slowly in the archbishop's mind. In 1966, he and the whole archdiocese were caught up in the nation-wide celebrations marking the millennium of Polish Christianity. Nine years of preparation, the "Great Novena" Cardinal Wyszyński had planned during his house arrest in the mid-1950s, had recatechized Poland and had helped the country reclaim its past, rejecting the shame with which Stalinism had covered everything to do with Poland's historic independence.[63] The archbishop of Kraków now proposed to claim the future, through an ambitious effort at implementing Vatican II.

In the latter part of 1970, as he finished writing *Sources of Renewal,* a guided tour of the Council's texts, Cardinal Wojtyła came to a decision. The best way to deepen the Council's implementation in Kraków was for the archdiocese as a whole to relive the experience of Vatican II through an archdiocesan Synod, a mini-Council on the local Church level. The ninth centenary of the martyr-dom of St. Stanisław provided a ceremonial closing date, so the Synod would end in 1979. Stanisław had been bishop of Kraków for eight years, so the Synod should last that long and would begin its preparatory work in 1971.[64] Diocesan synods were almost always juridical in character, legislative assemblies of the local clergy to provide legal statutes for a local Church. His would be dif-ferent, as Vatican II had been different. This would be a pastoral Synod, an effort to share the experience of collegiality at Vatican II with the priests and people of the archdiocese. The Synod would do some program planning, but first and foremost, it would build Christian community. Cardinal Wojtyła wanted to turn the Church of Kraków into a vibrant evangelical and apostolic movement.[65] That was how the Council could come alive in Kraków, and in concert with, not against, the history of Polish Catholicism he and his people had just celebrated.

The cardinal broached the idea of a Synod to his closest associates in the latter half of 1970. Some of them told him bluntly that it couldn't be done. The canon lawyers, for example, said that a local Synod would have to wait until Rome had completed the new Code of Canon Law. The cardinal explained that what he had in mind was a pastoral Synod, not a juridical one. Wojtyła was, as always, a patient listener, and the skeptics had their say. As his former spiritual director, Stanisław Smoleński, recalled, however, Karol Wojtyła was "very good at getting things done despite obstacles—including the obstacle that 'it's never been done before.'"[66]

After a year of preparation, the Synod was solemnly convened on May 8, 1972, at Wawel Cathedral, with representatives of the entire archdiocese attending. For the next seven years, the Synod was governed by a Central Com-mission, chaired by Bishop Stanisław Smoleński and staffed by Father Tadeusz Pieronek. It met 119 times, assuming ongoing responsibility for the Synod in between its thirteen plenary meetings. All the Synod's major decisions were made in the plenary meetings, in which the delegates included clergy and laity. As the Synod developed, an editing commission began work preparing Synod documents. These were reviewed by the plenary meetings, which could vote "Yes," "No," or "Yes-with-changes," just as at Vatican II. (A local difference in Kraków was that the Central Commission, in reviewing every suggested emendation, addition, or correction, publicly explained why it had accepted, rejected, or modified the proposal.) The Synod of Kraków eventually produced some 400 pages of documents, covering every aspect of the Church's life in the archdiocese. These documents, in turn, were organized under three headings, reflecting the three "offices" or roles of Christ as priest, prophet, and king—three offices in which, *Gaudium et Spes* had taught, the people of the Church who were Christ's Body in the world participated.[67]

The Synod's method of dialogue made the experience of Vatican II come alive for tens of thousands of Catholics throughout the Kraków area. Unlike other Church bodies, the Synod of Kraków did not begin by writing documents. It did not even begin the drafting process for two years, during which some 500 study groups were formed to read through the texts of Vatican II with Cardinal Wojtyła's *Sources of Renewal* as a commentary. These study groups (some fifty of which were still meeting in 1997) were the heart and soul of the Synod of Kraków. They came in all shapes and sizes. Some were located in cloistered convents, others in the seminary; the vast majority of them were parish-based. In them, priests and laypeople, intellectuals and workers, men and women, old people and young people met together to pray, to study the Council's teachings, to compare those teachings with their daily lives, and to suggest applications of the Council's thought in the various ministries of the archdiocese. These reflections and recommendations were brought to the plenary sessions of the Synod by representatives of the study groups.

The study groups were the venues in which the Synod built Christian community according to Vatican II's concept of the Church as a "communion" (*communio*) of believers. In these groups, the archdiocese met the documents of Vatican II organically, as a coherent whole. When it came time to make archdiocesan-wide applications of the Council's teachings, no outside experts were necessary. The people of the archdiocese knew the Council documents themselves, and had learned through years of intense effort to apply Vatican II's teachings to their own particular circumstances. Thus the Kraków Synod helped the archdiocese avoid many of the post-conciliar tensions experienced in other parts of the Church. In Kraków, Vatican II was relived as a religious event aimed at strengthening the evangelical and apostolic life of the Church, not as a political struggle over power within the Church bureaucracy.

Karol Wojtyła left Kraków before the Synod completed its work (although he presided at the Synod's solemn closing on June 8, 1979, as Pope John Paul II).[68] But before his move to Rome, Karol Wojtyła, as archbishop of Kraków, made every effort to help his people relive the experience of Vatican II so that the Council became, as John XXIII had intended, a new Pentecost for the Church—a deepening of faith that led to a revitalization of mission. As a result, Kraków experienced neither anti-conciliar reactionary movements of the Lefebvrist sort nor the deconstruction of Catholic belief and practice that attended Vatican II's reception in other cultures and countries.

The experience of the Synod also taught the people of the archdiocese some things about themselves as citizens. They learned that they could organize and carry out a massive program of study and action, independent of permission from the state. They learned that they could think through the situation of their society, independently. Priests and laity, intellectuals and factory workers learned that they could work together. This experience of *communio*, as Vatican II called it, was also an experience of what anti-communist dissidents in east central Europe later called "civil society." It would have repercussions beyond the imaginings of the communist apparatchiks who kept wondering why all those people were spending so much time talking about Church documents.

THE *Humanae Vitae* CONTROVERSY

First established by Pope John XXIII, the Papal Commission for the Study of Problems of the Family, Population, and Birth Rate was reappointed by Pope Paul VI to advise him on the tangle of issues indicated in its title. For much of the world, though, this was the "Papal Birth Control Commission" and the only issue at stake was whether Catholics could "use the pill." In the highly politicized atmosphere of the immediate post–Vatican II Church, "birth control" became the litmus-test issue between theological "progressives" and "conservatives," even as the issue got entangled in ongoing arguments about the nature and scope of papal teaching authority. When one adds to this volatile ecclesiastical mix the cultural circumstances of the sixties in the West, including the widespread challenge to all established authority and the breakout into mainstream culture of the sexual revolution, it becomes apparent that a thoughtful public moral discussion of conjugal morality was going to be very difficult at this point. In 1968, Paul VI, who thought himself obliged to give the Church an authoritative answer on such a highly charged question, issued *Humanae Vitae*, which instantly became the most controversial encyclical in history and the cause of even further disruption in the Church, particularly in North America and Western Europe. The controversy was inevitable, but it might not have been so debilitating had the Pope taken Cardinal Wojtyła's counsel more thoroughly.

According to the familiar telling of this complex tale, Pope Paul's Papal Commission was divided between a majority that argued for a change in the classic Catholic position that contraception was immoral, and a minority that wanted to affirm that teaching. A memorandum sent to the Pope in June 1966—and journalistically dubbed the "Majority Report"—argued that conjugal morality should be measured by "the totality of married life," rather than by the openness of each act of intercourse to conception. In this view, it was morally licit to use chemical or mechanical means to prevent conception as long as this was in the overall moral context of a couple's openness to children.[69] Another memorandum, dubbed the "Minority Report," reiterated the classic Catholic position, that the use of contraceptives violated the natural moral law by sundering the procreative and unitive dimensions of sexuality. In this view, and following the teaching of Pope Pius XII, the morally legitimate way to regulate conception was through the use of the natural rhythms of fertility, known as the rhythm method.

Pope Paul VI spent two years wrestling with these opposed positions and with the pressures that were being brought to bear on him to take a side. Proponents of the "Majority Report" (which was leaked to the press in 1967 to bring more pressure on the Pope) argued that the Church would lose all credibility with married couples and with the modern world if it did not change the teaching set forth by Pius XII. Some opponents argued that adopting the "Majority Report" position would destroy the Church's teaching authority, as it would involve a tacit admission of error on a question of serious moral consequence. Paul VI eventually rejected the conclusion and moral reasoning of the "Majority Report," and on July 25, 1968, issued the encyclical letter *Humanae Vitae,* section 14 of which began as follows: "Thus, relying on these first principles of human and Christian doctrine concerning marriage, we must again insist that the direct interruption of the generative process already begun must be totally rejected as a legitimate means of regulating the number of children."[70] A maelstrom of criticism followed, as did the most widespread public Catholic dissent from papal teaching in centuries.

Archbishop Karol Wojtyła, well-known to the Pope as the author of *Love and Responsibility,* had been appointed by Paul VI to the Papal Commission, but had been unable to attend the June 1966 meeting at which the majority of the commission took the position later summarized in its memorandum. The Polish government had denied him a passport, on the excuse that he had waited too late to apply.[71] Wojtyła played an important role in the controversy over contraception and in the development of *Humanae Vitae,* nonetheless. The encyclical, however, was not crafted precisely as Wojtyła proposed.

In 1966, the archbishop of Kraków created his own diocesan commission to study the issues being debated by the Papal Commission. The archbishop, soon to be cardinal, was an active participant in the Kraków commission's deliberations, which also drew on the expertise he had begun to gather in the nascent archdiocesan Institute for Family Studies. The Kraków commission completed its work in February 1968, and a memorandum of conclusions— "The Foundations of the Church's Doctrine on the Principles of Conjugal Life"—was drawn up in French and sent to Paul VI by Cardinal Wojtyła.[72]

According to Father Andrzej Bardecki, one of the participants in the Kraków process, Wojtyła's local commission had seen two drafts of a proposed encyclical on the subject of conjugal morality and fertility regulation. One draft, prepared by the Holy Office, the Vatican's principal doctrinal agency, struck some members of the Kraków commission as "stupid conservatism," stringing together various papal pronouncements on the subject while neglecting to mention Pius XII's endorsement of the rhythm method of fertility regulation, or "natural family planning." The alternative draft, which Bardecki remembered as having been sponsored by German Cardinal Julius Döpfner, took the position of the "Majority Report" of the Papal Commission, which involved a serious error in its approach to moral theology, in the judgment of the Kraków theologians. By arguing that conjugal morality should be judged in its totality, and each act of intercourse "proportionally" within that total context, the "Majority Report" and the German draft misread what God had written into the nature of human sexuality, and did so in a way that undermined the structure of moral theology across the board.

Were the only alternatives, therefore, "stupid conservatism" or a deconstruction of the moral theology?

The Polish theologians didn't think so. The Kraków commission memorandum, which reflected the thinking of Cardinal Wojtyła and the moral analysis of *Love and Responsibility*, tried to develop a new framework for the Church's classic position on conjugal morality and fertility regulation: a fully articulated, philosophically well-developed Christian humanism that believers and non-believers alike could engage.

The starting point for moral argument, they proposed, was the human person, for human beings were the only creatures capable of "morality." This human person, male or female, was not a disembodied self but a unity of body and spirit. My "self" is not *here*, and "my body" *there*. As a free moral actor, I am a *unity* of body and spirit. Thinking about the moral life has to be thinking within that unity, taking account of both dimensions of the human person.

The Kraków theologians went on to argue that nature had inscribed what might be called a moral language and grammar in the sexual structure of the human body. That moral language and grammar could be discerned by human intelligence and respected by the human will. Morally appropriate acts respected that language and grammar in all its complexity, which included both the unitive and procreative dimensions of human sexuality: sexual intercourse as both an expression of love and the means for transmitting the gift of life. Any act that denied one of these dimensions violated the grammar of the act and necessarily, if unwittingly, reduced one's spouse to an object of one's pleasure. Marital chastity was a matter of mutual self-giving that transcended itself and achieved its truly human character by its openness to the possibility of new life.

This openness had to be lived responsibly. "The number of children called into existence cannot be left to chance," according to the Kraków memorandum, but must be decided "in a dialogue of love between husband and wife." Fertility regulation, in fulfillment of the "duty" to plan one's family, must therefore be done through a method that conformed to human dignity, recognized the "parity between men and women," and involved the "cooperation" of the spouses. By placing the entire burden on the woman, chemical and mechanical means of fertility regulation like the contraceptive pill and the intra-uterine device violated these criteria. Contrary to the claims of the sexual revolution, such artificial means of contraception freed men for hedonistic behavior while violating the biological integrity of women with invasive and potentially harmful tools. Family planning by observing nature's biological rhythms was the only method of fertility regulation that respected the dignity and equality of the spouses as persons.

The Kraków theologians openly admitted that living marital chastity this way involved real sacrifice, a "great ascetic effort [and] the mastery of self." Education in the virtue of chastity must begin with "respect for others, respect for the body and [for] the realities of sex." Young people had to be taught "the equality of right between man and woman" as the foundation of "mutual responsibility." Pastors who shied away from programs aimed at educating couples in fertility regulation through natural biological rhythms were derelict in their duties, and were complicit in the "grand confusion of ideas" that surrounded sexuality in the modern world. Moreover, the memorandum continued, the pastor did not fulfill his responsibilities as a moral teacher by inveighing against promiscuity. On the contrary, no one could preach or teach persuasively on this subject unless the entire question was put in the humanistic context necessary for the Church's teaching to ring true. It was imperative that pastors work with laypeople in this field, for "well-instructed Christian couples" were better positioned to help other couples live chaste lives of sexual love.

Elements of the Kraków commission's memorandum may be found in *Humanae Vitae,* but Father Bardecki's suggestion that sixty percent of the encyclical reflected the approach devised by the Polish theologians and Cardinal Wojtyła claims too much.[73] *Humanae Vitae* did make references to Christian personalism, to the good of sexual love, and to the duty of responsibly planning one's family.[74] But the encyclical did not adopt in full the rich personalist context suggested by the Kraków commission. Absent this context, with its emphasis on human dignity and on the equality of spouses in leading sexually responsible lives, *Humanae Vitae*'s sharp focus on sexual acts opened it to the charge of legalism, "biologism," and pastoral insensitivity, and left the Church vulnerable to the accusation that it had still not freed itself of the shadow of Manichaeism and its deprecation of sexuality.

Although the charge would likely have been made in any case, the encyclical's failure to adopt the full Kraków context made this indictment more difficult to counter. The Kraków proposal came to the same conclusion as the encyclical on the specific question of the legitimate means of fertility regulation. Kraków, however, offered a more compelling explanation of why this position was better fitted to the dignity of the human person, and particularly to the dignity of women.

The timing of *Humanae Vitae* could not have been worse; 1968, a year of revolutionary enthusiasms, was not the moment for calm, measured reflection on anything. It is doubtful whether any reiteration of the classic Catholic position on marital chastity, no matter how persuasively argued, could have been heard in such circumstances. On the other hand, one has to ask why a position that defended "natural" means of fertility regulation was deemed impossibly antiquarian at precisely the moment when "natural" was becoming one of the sacred words in the developed world, especially with regard to ecological consciousness. The answer is obviously complex, but it surely has something to do with whether *Humanae Vitae* provided an adequately personalistic framework in which to engage its teaching.

The Kraków memorandum also demonstrated that the marital ethic it proposed was not a matter of Catholic special pleading (still less Polish Catholic special pleading); its moral claims could be debated by reasonable people, irrespective of their religious convictions.[75] *Humanae Vitae* did not demonstrate this adequately. The encyclical was a step beyond the "stupid conservatism" that had worried some participants in the Kraków Commission, but it was not enough of a step. Kraków had dealt with the fact that changing cultural conditions required articulating a new context for classic moral principles. Rome remained rather tone-deaf to the question of context. The result was that the principles were dismissed as pre-modern, or just irrational.

The failure to explicate a personalist context for the Catholic sexual ethic, compounded by the politicization of the post–*Humanae Vitae* debate in the Church, had serious ramifications for the Church's effort to articulate a compelling Christian humanism in the modern world. In its first major post–Vatican II confrontation with the sexual revolution—the most potent manifestation of the notion of freedom as personal autonomy—the Church had been put squarely on the defensive. Had the Kraków commission's memorandum shaped the argumentation of *Humanae Vitae* more decisively, a more intelligent and sensitive debate might have ensued.

A CARDINAL IN CONVERSATION

Henry Kissinger believes it to be "an illusion . . . that leaders gain in profundity while they gain experience." High office, because of its endless demands on the officeholder, is an occasion to spend down rather than to build up intellectual capital.[76] Karol Wojtyła has been an exception to the Kissinger Rule since he became vicar capitular of the Archdiocese of Kraków at forty-two—in part, because he has insisted on setting time aside for serious intellectual work. During the years of his episcopate, those two hours each day, writing in the solitude of his chapel, produced numerous philosophical essays and three books, as well as a stream of pastoral letters, sermons, poems, and a play. In addition, the cardinal remained a working intellectual by continuing to hold the Chair of Ethics at the Catholic University of Lublin, although he met students on a reduced schedule.

Karol Wojtyła and Emilia Kaczorowska at their wedding, 1904. *(John Paul II Museum, Wadowice; Adam Bujak)*

Lolek and his mother, 1920. *(John Paul II Museum, Wadowice)*

High school graduation, Wadowice, 1938: Karol Wojtyła is at the far left in the second row; Jerzy Kluger is fourth from the left in the same row *(John Paul II Museum, Wadowice)*

Karol Wojtyła, with a young friend, in the apartment at Tyniecka, 10, during the Occupation, 1941. *(John Paul II Museum, Wadowice)*

The quarry at Zakrzówek. *(Adam Bujak)*

The "unbroken prince," Cardinal Adam Stefan Sapieha. *(Archives of the Archdiocese of Kraków)*

Hiking in July 1953: Father Karol Wojtyła on the right. *(John Paul II Museum, Wadowice)*

Bishop Karol Wojtyła on a parish visitation, 1962. *(Archives of the Archdiocese of Kraków)*

Cardinal Stefan Wyszyński, Primate of Poland, 1966. *(Adam Bujak)*

Kraków, 1966: the procession from Wawel Cathedral to Skałka, site of the martyr-dom of St. Stanisław, with Archbishop Wojtyła in the center. *(Adam Bujak)*

Archbishop Wojtyła ordaining a priest during the millennium of Polish Christianity, 1966. *(Archives of the Archdiocese of Kraków)*

Archbishop Wojtyła after learning of his nomination as cardinal, 1967. *(Adam Bujak)*

Cardinal Wojtyła, celebrating Mass at Kalwaria Zebrzydowska, 1969. *(Adam Bujak)*

Cardinal Wojtyła outside Wawel Cathedral. *(Adam Bujak)*

Inspecting the construction of the Ark Church in Nowa Huta. *(Archives of the Archdiocese of Kraków)*

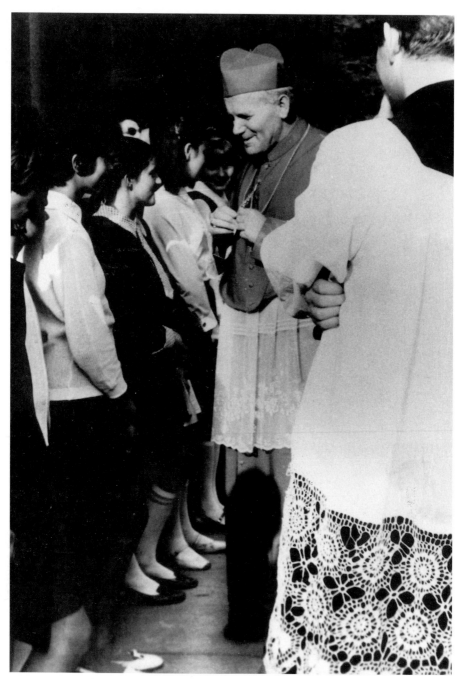

On a parish visitation, 1969. *(Archives of the Archdiocese of Kraków)*

Wojtyła and his secretary, Father Stanisław Dziwisz, on a parish visitation, 1969. *(Archives of the Archdiocese of Kraków)*

Cardinal Wojtyła preaches at the second stational altar during the 1971 Corpus Christi procession in Kraków. *(Archives of the Archdiocese of Kraków)*

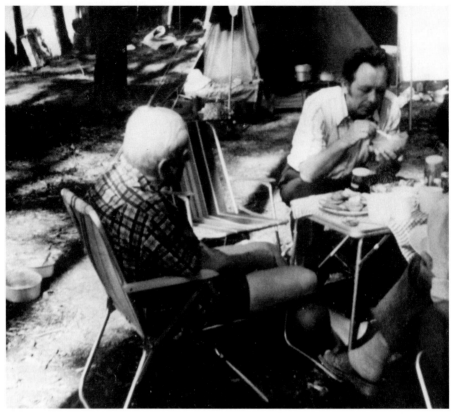

Wojtyła on his last Środowisko kayaking trip, with Gabriel Turowski, 1978. *(John Paul II Museum, Wadowice)*

Cardinal Wojtyła in his kayak, 1978. *(Grzegorz Rybicki)*

The archbishop of Kraków also defied the Kissinger Rule because he was a cardinal in constant conversation.

The discussion groups he had formed as a young priest continued to meet regularly during his years as archbishop. Jerzy Janik remained the cardinal's connection to physicists and others in the hard sciences, while Jerzy Ciesielski and Stanisław Rybicki organized his contacts with engineers. Until the end of his Kraków years he met at least four or five times per year with both the scientists' and engineers' groups, usually for an entire evening at which a paper would be read and discussed.

Cardinal Wojtyła also nurtured an ongoing dialogue with historians, with topics often generated by the need for a deeper understanding of major national or local anniversaries. The millennium of Polish Christianity in 1966 was one occasion for a series of such discussions with historians, as was the 600th anniversary of the Jagiellonian University and the 900th anniversary of the pastoral work of St. Stanisław in Kraków.[77]

And then there were, of course, the philosophers. In addition to his work with KUL students and faculty, Cardinal Wojtyła opened his home to philosophical conversation among thinkers of various schools of thought, serving on one occasion as a respondent to the venerable Roman Ingarden, who read a paper in German on the concept of responsibility.[78] Franciszkańska, 3, also saw a steady stream of visiting artists, musicians, and writers from Poland and abroad. James Michener, a best-selling American writer, stopped by while working on his novel, *Poland*. Wojtyła later taped an interview for a television series Michener was helping produce. After forty minutes on camera, the cardinal surprised the author by asking, "How did I do? Can I land a job in Hollywood? I studied to be an actor as a young man, you know. . . ."[79]

The cardinal kept contact with his literary and theatrical roots in other ways. After the regime closed the Rhapsodic Theater for good in 1967—an action the archbishop protested to the Polish minister of culture, to no avail—Wojtyła helped Mieczysław Kotlarczyk get jobs teaching speech and dramatic theory at the seminary in Kraków and at KUL.[80] In June 1974, Wojtyła hosted a two-day study session in his residence on Catholicism and Romanticism in the work of Zygmunt Krasiński. The problems addressed by "the most controversial of the great bards of Polish Romanticism," he told the conferees, "have not lost their question marks in the contemporary world. . . ."[81] That Krasiński's greatest work, *The Undivine Comedy*, had suggested that only a Christian revolution could address modernity's discontents was not lost on the cardinal's audience.

Tygodnik Powszechny, Znak, and the circle of writers, poets, and intellectuals built around those two publications remained crucial conversation partners for Cardinal Wojtyła. The benefit, Jerzy Turowicz suggests, was mutual: "I have a right to say as his friend that *Tygodnik Powszechny* had an influence on him."[82] Wojtyła used the editors of the paper and the journal as sounding boards for reflecting out loud on Church affairs throughout Poland, the Church-state situation, and modern culture. His oversight of *Tygodnik*

Powszechny and *Znak* was exemplary by their editors' own standards. The archbishop met with the editors every other month to talk over mutual concerns. Later, as the demands on his time increased, these meetings became quarterly but remained real working sessions. The two staffs would come to Franciszkańska, 3, for Mass in the cardinal's chapel, "followed by dinner and a long conversation . . . He listened, but preferred that you'd speak, and he'd take the floor at the end."[83] Not once in his sixteen years as vicar capitular and then archbishop did he ask that something not be printed in *Tygodnik Powszechny*. "There was no censorship," according to editor Turowicz. "We may have asked his advice, but he never intervened on his own initiative" to alter the paper's contents or editorial analysis.[84]

There were arguments, but Wojtyła had the ability, not universal among senior prelates, to work happily with people with whom he did not always agree. During her years at *Tygodnik Powszechny,* the peppery Halina Bortnowska often criticized the more traditional "Wyszyński Church," as she sometimes called it. Wojtyła was far more sympathetic to popular piety, but maintained his friendship with the outspoken young philosopher and writer, whom he asked to edit the revised edition of *Love and Responsibility.*[85]

Then there was politics. The paper's editors, especially Turowicz and Jacek Woźniakowski, didn't agree with the position Wojtyła took at the beginning of his episcopate: that any involvement with local politics would impede his pastoral effectiveness, and that commentary on political matters should be the sole prerogative of Primate Wyszyński. Woźniakowski and others argued that ignoring such matters was impossible, that Wojtyła had to be informed if he was going to be effective, and that even if the newspapers were heavily censored, he should at least look at them to get the regime's view of approved "news" and commentary. Wojtyła reluctantly agreed, and started reading the papers. Woźniakowski said he was "stupefied" at how quickly the archbishop, who had paid absolutely no attention to such things before, caught on, grasped the essentials, learned the arguments and the personalities—and then refused to spend excess time on digging into any more detail than was necessary.[86] The paper's editors were also the archbishop's contacts with the literary world. Prior to his summer vacation, the cardinal asked Turowicz and his wife to recommend books for him to read while on holiday.

On several occasions Wojtyła had to mediate between *Tygodnik Powszechny* and Cardinal Wyszyński. Although he always defended the paper's independence, the cardinal tried to get his friends to see things from the Primate's perspective. "This is a problem of disappointed love," he told them during one discussion. *Tygodnik Powszechny* had vigorously defended Wyszyński in 1953 so "the Primate imagined that you would follow him in his every idea, and you didn't; so he has lived through a period of disappointed love toward you." It was, Woźniakowski recalled, the kind of frank analysis that would not have been forthcoming from other Polish clergy, in talking with lay people.[87]

The regime's continual harassment of the newspaper became enmeshed with the regime's increasing loathing for Cardinal Wojtyła. The communists could not very well vent their displeasure directly on him, but his colleagues were not immune from retribution. In November 1977, the regime started an aggressive anti–*Tygodnik Powszechny* campaign, ostensibly because the paper had cut parts of a statement made by Polish party leader Edward Gierek after his meeting with Pope Paul VI. Gierek's statement had been reprinted in full in all the party-controlled papers, and *Tygodnik Powszechny*'s editors, who had severe space problems, didn't feel required to duplicate the coverage. They had also cut the Pope's statement, which suggested to the editors that the real target of the regime's animus was the paper's protector, Cardinal Wojtyła. Confirming evidence appeared in a few weeks. After a *Tygodnik Powszechny/Znak* editors' meeting with the cardinal on December 21, 1977, Father Andrzej Bardecki was walking home to his apartment when he was set upon by thugs who, if not members of the SB, were at least "inspired" by the SB. They beat him senseless. Cardinal Wojtyła rushed to the hospital the next morning and said, "You replaced me; you were beaten instead of me."[88]

Cardinal Wojtyła's intellectual life was also fired by his continuing connection to KUL. As the 1970s wore on, his protégés, including Father Tadeusz Styczeń and Jerzy Gałkowski, began to assume more of the routine work of the Chair of Ethics and organized Wojtyła's doctoral seminar, which came to Kraków to meet with the Cardinal Professor for two-day sessions. The cardinal paid the expenses of faculty and students alike from the scholarship fund he had set up anonymously at KUL with his modest professor's salary.

On December 16–17, 1970, the KUL Faculty of Philosophy sponsored a debate on *Person and Act* that became an intellectual donnybrook. Among Wojtyła's faculty colleagues, Mieczysław Krąpiec, Jerzy Kalinowski, and Stanisław Kamiński were quite critical of the book. Even the first among the cardinal's philosophical disciples, Tadeusz Styczeń, wasn't sure whether Wojtyła's proposal to bracket questions of philosophical methodology and concentrate exclusively on human moral action could be done.[89] The cardinal gave an oral response to his critics at the end of the conference. His more formal response was the essay, "The Person: Subject and Community," which was published in 1976. There, he suggested that what he and his colleagues had been debating at KUL in 1970 (and ever since) was not a matter for philosophers only: "After twenty years of ideological debate in Poland, it has become clear that at the center of this debate is not cosmology or philosophy of nature but philosophical anthropology and ethics: the great and fundamental controversy about the human being."[90]

The cardinal's friendships with KUL colleagues and students continued to mature in the 1970s. When Jerzy Gałkowski, Tadeusz Styczeń's successor as Wojtyła's teaching assistant, became engaged to Maria Braun, another former student of the cardinal's, the two couldn't imagine having anyone else bless their wedding. The problem was scheduling, and a solution was finally found. Maria's family had a vacation place in the Świętokrzyskie Mountains near

Kielce; on his way to a meeting of the Polish episcopate in Warsaw, the arch-bishop of Kraków stopped en route and the wedding was celebrated on July 6, 1964, in a small country church in Bolimów—at 7 A.M. on a Monday morning. "Adventures weren't unusual with Karol Wojtyła," the bridegroom later put it. Cardinal Wojtyła sometimes visited the Gałkowskis at their home in Lublin on his increasingly rare trips to KUL. Their oldest son was shy as a small boy and once hid under the dinner table when the cardinal arrived. Wojtyła immedi-ately got down with him saying, "Well, if that's where you want to play, that's where we'll play."[91]

As Cardinal Wojtyła's troubles with the regime intensified in the 1970s, he didn't want to force the issue of a promotion in academic rank, which would have to be approved by the government. He retained the rank of docent, the lowest on the academic scale, even while holding the Chair of Ethics at KUL. In 1978, Father Krąpiec, who had been perhaps the most critical of Wojtyła's colleagues in the Faculty of Philosophy, was the rector of the University. Despite their philosophical differences, he wanted to do something for the car-dinal. Krąpiec found a loophole in the university statues that permitted the university to give Wojtyła the title of "Honorary Professor" without government approval. It was further discovered that one privilege of this title is that the scholar who holds it is never retired, so Karol Wojtyła remains "Honorary Pro-fessor" at the Catholic University of Lublin for life.[92]

Ecumenism, or inter-Christian dialogue, was yet another arena of conver-sation for Cardinal Karol Wojtyła. In overwhelmingly Catholic Kraków there were not many opportunities for extensive ecumenical conversation. The city had small Lutheran and Orthodox congregations, and there were a few Mari-avites, members of a small group that had broken with Catholicism in 1906.[93] In January 1963, Bishop Wojtyła participated in the first ecumenical service held in Kraków during the Chair of Unity Octave, an eight-day period of prayer for Christian unity observed in the West since the early twentieth century. In his sermon, he praised the Protestant monks from the ecumenical community at Taizé, France, whom he had met during Vatican II. At dinner that evening in the medieval refectory of the Dominican priory, Wojtyła was seated between a Lutheran pastor and an Orthodox priest, neither of whom had ever set foot in the priory before. The Dominican prior, eager to make his "separated brethren" feel at home, decided that historical reminiscence was in order. He began his welcoming remarks by saying, "The Inquisition quite probably met here once, and now here we are. . . ."[94] Wojtyła, for his part, used to chaff the Dominicans about being served chicken whenever he came to dinner: "Some-times I get Thomistic chicken, sometimes I get ecumenical chicken. . . ."[95]

Wojtyła's commitment to Christian unity and his sensitivity to the position of the minuscule Protestant minority in Kraków expressed itself personally. As a priest and young bishop, Wojtyła always went to Jerzy Janik's home for at least a part of Christmas Eve dinner. There he met another of Janik's friends, a Lutheran lady who had been the physicist's first tutor in English. When the old woman died at age ninety-three, Janik called the cardinal to let him know. Wojtyła said that he'd like to say Mass for her and asked if the Janiks could come on a certain day. The cardinal then asked Janik whether he would go to the Lutheran pastor on Grodzka Street to invite him to the Mass, so that the pastor wouldn't feel pressured by an archiepiscopal invitation. Janik did, and the pastor came and sat with the Janik family in the first pew of the archbishop's chapel at the appointed time. When the cardinal entered the chapel in his Mass vestments, he went straight to the pastor, before going to the altar, and embraced him as a brother in Christ.[96]

REMAINING *Wujek*

Środowisko flourished as Karol Wojtyła continued to live a pastoral strategy of accompaniment during his episcopate in Kraków. He said Mass for his friends and their families as often as his schedule permitted, always preparing a homily. He also gave one-day retreats to *Środowisko* and invited everyone to his residence for Christmas caroling each year. When big decisions had to be made, his friends still wanted to consult with him and he made himself available to them.[97]

He also stayed in touch by letter. Teresa Heydel Życzkowska had written him in the early 1960s with the news that she was finally able to sleep through the night, two years after the birth of her twins. Wojtyła's response was a characteristic blend of the personal and the evangelical:

> Dear Teresa:
>
> You were afraid that I wouldn't be able to read your letter to the end. Well, I not only finished it but I carried its meaning within me for several days, thinking about what to reply. Today, these thoughts crystallized when I was receiving the vows of some sisters. I sense tiredness in your letter, which is easy to understand, knowing your character and your nervous system. On top of this, you always wanted to plan and do everything rationally. And here is the kingdom of irrationality, where normal activity and energy aren't enough; you need to wait things out, some time to do nothing, and, simply, patience—especially since there are two. I realized that, on the one hand, there is always a price we pay for love. On the other, thanks to God, love is returned in that price. What I mean is, the concrete challenge of love cannot be separated from Him; it is always in Him.
>
> I'm sorry you weren't on the kayak trip but we can speak anytime.
>
> For me, the most burdensome things are not our "chores," but our "burdens."
>
> I kiss you and Michael and the twins—especially the one who has my name, who is such a challenge for his parents. Wujek

A tradition Wojtyła had begun for the children of *Środowisko* at the house on Kanonicza Street—a pre-Lenten *Kinderbal*, or children's party—eventually moved to the archbishop's residence. When the children became teenagers,

Wojtyła told their parents that they had to give them a "real party," so the annual *Kinderbal*, now with dancing, moved to the home of Teresa Życzkowska. The cardinal archbishop came and wrote in the Życzkowskis' guest book, "Not much has changed since their parents were doing this—except the music. Wujek."[98]

The children, of course, were not the only ones getting older. Jurek and Jasią Janik were celebrating their twenty-fifth wedding anniversary in 1977, and Wojtyła had promised to say Mass for the couple and a small number of friends in the archbishop's chapel. When the group arrived at the residence the cardinal's secretary, Father Dziwisz, met them and said that he was sorry but the cardinal had come down with the flu and was running a high fever. Janik wished the cardinal a speedy recovery and turned to go. Dziwisz said, "No, no, no, the Mass will not be in the chapel but in his private apartment." So the secretary led them to Wojtyła's three-room suite. The cardinal came out of his bedroom in his vestments, said Mass, gave a sermon directed at the anniversary couple, and at the end of Mass said, "I'm sorry, but I've got a fever and I've got to get back to bed."[99]

As *Środowisko* aged, its people became even more intensely prayerful. Once they had discussed C. S. Lewis's *Screwtape Letters*, an insightful yet humorous exploration of temptation and sin, while kayaking. Now, in 1975, there were long discussions around the campfire about evil and the Christian mystery of suffering. Gapą Turowski had been arrested again that year for declining to participate in the regime's May Day festivities, age and experience had brought pain as well as pleasure, how did suffering fit into God's plan for the world? The regime's increasing anger with the cardinal also began to touch *Środowisko*'s summer holiday. In 1977, at the end of the annual kayak trip, the SB arrived at the campsite soon after the cardinal had left in his car and started checking the identity papers of the *Środowisko* members who had remained: "What was that big car?" they demanded. "Well, it arrived, and then it left," was the reply—no lie, but no information, either. The following year, during what would be *Wujek*'s last kayaking trip, the arrangements were changed. Wojtyła's car drove along the main road toward the kayaking site, followed by his now-regular SB "tail." At a prearranged point, the cardinal's driver sped up, briefly lost the tail, and then quickly turned off onto a small side road that wove back and forth through the fields. Stanisław Rybicki was waiting. *Wujek* jumped into his car, and off they went, the cardinal's car and driver returning to Kraków along the main road, still followed by the SB. The same procedure was used in reverse at the end of the trip, during which state security wasn't seen again.[100]

(The regime's security paranoia could have its amusing aspects. Cardinal Wojtyła was skiing once in the Tatras near the Czechoslovak border and was stopped by the border patrol. The cardinal handed over his papers, but the militiaman, not recognizing him, began to berate Wojtyła: "You moron, do you realize whose identity papers you've stolen? This is going to put you away for a long time." When Wojtyła protested his innocence, the militiaman shot back,

"A skiing cardinal? Do you think I'm crazy?" Wojtyła, who was once asked whether it was becoming for a cardinal to ski and answered that it was unbecoming for a cardinal to ski badly, finally sorted things out with the militiaman's superior.[101])

Cardinal Wojtyła and his friends suffered a tragic, shattering loss in 1970. Jerzy Ciesielski, who had become a docent at the Kraków Polytechnic, accepted a three-year visiting professorship in engineering at the University of Khartoum. He went to Africa alone in 1969–1970, but at the beginning of the 1970–1971 academic year he brought his wife, Danuta, and their three children to Sudan with him. On the night of October 9–10, 1970, he and the three children were en route to the Sixth Cataract of the Nile, on a tour ship that had been made available for visitors from abroad; Danuta had remained ashore in their apartment. Ciesielski had gone below decks to sleep with the two younger children in their cabin while teenage Marysia remained on deck. In a terrible accident, the boat sank and Ciesielski, his son and younger daughter were all drowned. Marysia alone was saved.

Danuta Ciesielska had to wait in Khartoum for the recovery of the bodies, which took some time. She sent a telegram to friends in Kraków, asking them to break the news gently to her father, who had a bad heart. One of these friends got word to Cardinal Wojtyła, then in Rome. When the bodies were finally recovered from the river and cremated, Danuta and Marysia brought the ashes home for burial, a journey which took them through Rome. Wojtyła met them at the airport with a car and driver, celebrated Mass for them, and asked them to delay the funeral services until he could come back to Kraków and celebrate the funeral Mass. Danuta agreed, and the ashes remained in Wojtyła's chapel at Franciszkańska, 3, until their burial at the cemetery in Podgórze, just outside Kraków. The cardinal led the procession into the cemetery. Ciesielski's ashes were carried by his best man, Stanisław Rybicki, Zdzysław Heydel, and two other friends. Jerzy Ciesielski, a "born teacher with a mystic core," was forty-one when he died.[102] As would happen often in Karol Wojtyła's life, a great friend had been taken away.

Cardinal Wojtyła paid tribute in a memorial essay published in *Tygodnik Powszechny*'s last 1970 issue. Jerzy Ciesielski, he wrote, was a living anticipation of the Second Vatican Council and its teaching on the universal call to holiness. If he was an unusual man, it was because for him, his faith "was the normal measure of his duty"—which, he once said, was "to advance toward sanctity." There "was not a lot of 'slippage'" in Jerzy Ciesielski's life, the cardinal recalled. He accepted "all the things that he had been given to do and to experience" as the elements or "materials" of his vocation to holiness.

Within this happy, outgoing man who loved nature and was an accomplished athlete "there was something like a deep underground stream . . . and his life never overflowed beyond its banks." He never doubted that marriage was his vocation. The way he lived that vocation and helped others live theirs had taught his friend, the archbishop, much of what he knew about the expe-

rience of married life as a sacrament. In his work at Vatican II on the lay vocation in the modern world, it was his friend, Jurek Ciesielski, whom he had in
mind.[103]

In his relationship to his *Środowisko*, Karol Wojtyła lived the instinct for
paternity he had learned from his own father, and which he, as a consecrated
and faithful celibate, could live only through such friendships. As his experience of paternity within the family of *Środowisko* deepened, he turned to poetry
and drama to express his insights into this profound human mystery. The
result was his last play, *Radiation of Fatherhood* (never published while he lived
in Kraków) and a brief "quintessence" of this play-poem's thought, the medi-
tative essay, "Reflections on Fatherhood," published pseudonymously by "A.J."
(that is, "Andrzej Jawień") in the May 1964 issue of *Znak*. The play and the
essay are explorations, at once poetic and theological, of the depth meaning
of *Środowisko*.

Critics suggest that *Radiation of Fatherhood* is the most technically accomplished of Wojtyła's dramas. Most readers will agree that it is his most difficult.
The playwright's blending of the medieval European mystery play and
Mieczysław Kotlarczyk's inner theater receives its fullest realization here, as the
play's field of action is entirely "inside" the souls of its three characters and its
chorus.[104]

Radiation of Fatherhood continues Wojtyła's literary meditation on the Law
of the Gift built into the human condition. Thus the character Adam medi-
tates on the hard road to selflessness: to become a father, Adam suggests, is to
be liberated from the "terrible" freedom of self-centeredness and to be "conquered by love."[105] Only in the "radiation of fatherhood . . . does everything
become fully real."[106]

As always, there is a biblical and theological dimension to Wojtyła's "inner
theater." In the Garden of Eden, the playwright suggests in "Reflections on
Fatherhood," the biblical Adam "became lonely of his own free will." That act
of self-exile, that choice for loneliness over self-giving, is the original sin, the
wound in every human heart. Yet original sin is not the whole of the human
story, for even in our self-imposed loneliness we want to be redeemed. And
that is what "entering the radiation of fatherhood" means—overcoming the
choice for loneliness by exercising one's freedom in self-giving love and thus
transcending oneself. We can overcome, Wojtyła the philosopher-poet-
playwright suggests. We *shall* overcome, Wojtyła the Christian disciple believes,
because God has overcome in Christ. That radiation of fatherhood and that
reconstitution of sonship save us from the terror of absolute loneliness.

The harshest face of human loneliness is death, to which Karol Wojtyła
was no stranger. As he matured in the 1970s, he deepened his reflection on
the inevitability of death poetically. Maturity, he wrote, was a circumstance in
which "the surface reaches the bottom," as in a seabed; maturity meant "the
soul more reconciled with the body." Maturity was also fear, and "the love that
transforms fear." But maturity was also tension:

When we find ourselves at the banks of autumn,
awe and love explode in a contrary desire,
awe in a desire to return to what had already been existence
and still is yet—
love in a desire to go to Him, in Whom being find its whole
    future.[107]

For the Christian believer, death means entering into the Paschal Mystery of Christ's death and resurrection. Because we see it all the time, we know what it means to pass from life to death. What will it mean to reverse "the order of passing," to go from death to life? That is a mystery, a "deep script/that has not been read to the end yet." Christ, however, had read that script, tested it on himself, and passed over. And so, while death had in it "something of annihilation," Christian hope beyond annihilation rests in Christ's "passing-over," by which death is not eliminated but conquered. That is the hope inscribed in a Christian soul in the course of a lifetime. Wojtyła's meditation on death thus ends in prayer:

And so I am written in You by hope.
apart from You I cannot exist—
if I put my own "I" above death,
and tear it out of the ground of annihilation,
that is because,
it is written into You . . .[108]

TESTING THE WORLD STAGE

During the 1970s, Karol Wojtyła became one of the best-known churchmen in the world to his peers in the higher leadership of Roman Catholicism.

Wojtyła's election to the College of Cardinals in 1967 intensified his involvement in international Catholic affairs, which had begun at the Second Vatican Council. During the Council, Pope Paul VI had developed a deep admiration for the young Polish bishop. That admiration eventually grew into a feeling of paternal affection that was reciprocated by Wojtyła, who said on several occasions that Paul VI had "been like a father" to him. At an audience on November 30, 1964, the archbishop of Kraków presented the Pope with an album of photos detailing the crowning of Our Lady of Ludzmierz; the Pope, visibly moved by the masses of people in attendance, murmured to his secretary, "This is Poland. Only there is this possible."[109] Earlier in the year, Pope Paul had sent a gift of three bells to St. Florian's in Kraków. The authorities had initially locked them up, but after some discussion they were released as "musical instruments."[110]

In the mid-1960s, the Polish government had indicated to the Holy See that it would be interested in the appointment of a second cardinal in Poland. Polish communist diplomacy was not noted for its subtlety, and the intention to pursue a divide-and-conquer strategy, splitting the Polish Church between Cardinal Wyszyński and a new cardinal, was not missed in the Vatican. The communists, who had already come to the conclusion that Wojtyła had "swindled" them, did not have the young archbishop of Kraków in mind.[111] Paul VI, however, did, and on May 29, 1967, Wojtyła's nomination to the College of Cardinals was officially announced. After protesting the liquidation of the Rhapsodic Theater, attending the doctoral defense of his student and teaching assistant, Jerzy Gałkowski, and spending a quiet day of prayer at Kalwaria Zebrzydowska, Cardinal-elect Wojtyła left for Rome via Vienna, where he visited with that city's archbishop, Franz König (who, at the Council, had thought Wojtyła "a clever boy"[112]).

Wojtyła received his cardinal's biretta from Paul VI in the Sistine Chapel on June 28. That afternoon, he and his secretary had fruitlessly searched around Rome for red socks, considered a proper part of the wardrobe of a prince of the Church.[113] Returning to Kraków on July 9, he told the thousands waiting to greet him outside the cathedral that the honor bestowed on him was a gift from the Pope "for the Church of Christ in Poland, and particularly for the Church of Kraków."[114] That afternoon, at a celebratory luncheon, Professor Adam Vetulani offered a toast to the new cardinal and, repeating his performance nine years before, reminded him that he was still a professor whom the historian hoped would "reap the richest harvest from your academic activity."[115]

Cardinals are members of the clergy of the Diocese of Rome and are given the titular pastorates of Roman churches. Wojtyła's "title" was S. Cesareo in Palatio, a small church just off the Via Porta Latina. Cardinals are also members of "congregations" or "councils" of the Roman Curia, the equivalent of cabinet departments in the world of government.[116] Meetings of these congregations brought him to Rome frequently in the 1970s. But it was his service on the international Synod of Bishops that really introduced Karol Wojtyła to the post–Vatican II world episcopate.

Wojtyła and the Synod of Bishops

The Synod of Bishops was established by Paul VI to give one concrete expression to the theological fact, described by Vatican II's *Dogmatic Constitution on the Church,* that the Catholic bishops of the world constituted a "college" with, and under the headship of, the Bishop of Rome. Wojtyła did not attend the Synod's first meeting in 1967, to which he had been elected by the Polish episcopate. The government, in one of its fits of pique, had denied Cardinal Wyszyński permission to attend, and Wojtyła refused to leave the country without the leader of the Polish Church.[117] In 1969, Cardinal Wojtyła was appointed by Paul VI as a member of the first "extraordinary" or special meeting of the Synod, called to discuss the Holy See's relationship to national conferences of bishops, and relations among the conferences themselves. In one intervention, Wojtyła stressed that the "community" among bishops had to be rooted in a genuine sacramental *communio*, or "communion," and not simply in the sociological fact of their common membership in a rather exclusive club. He was also concerned that commentators in the Catholic and secular press were treating the Synod as a political exercise, a power struggle between Rome and the bishops' conferences. This, he thought, rather missed the essential nature of the Synod, which was an ecclesial reality.[118]

The next meeting of the Synod, in 1971, discussed two topics, the priesthood and social justice. In the discussion on justice, the cardinal emphasized that religious freedom was as much a justice issue as poverty. He also said that justice within the Church demanded that local Churches other than those of Western Europe and Latin America have a say in these debates. During the Synod, on October 17, Pope Paul VI beatified Maximilian Kolbe, the self-sacrificing Franciscan of the Auschwitz starvation bunker. Cardinal Wojtyła gave a French-language press conference on October 13, in which he said that Kolbe's priestly self-sacrifice had consisted not only in offering his life for another, but in the fact that he helped the nine other men condemned with him to die with a measure of dignity. Father Kolbe's spirit of forgiveness, the cardinal concluded, "broke the infernal cycle of hatred."[119] At the end of the 1971 Synod, Wojtyła was elected to the Synod Council, the international committee that prepared the agenda for future meetings. It was a first indication of how high he stood in his brother bishops' esteem.

The 1974 Synod, to which Wojtyła was elected by the Polish episcopate, discussed evangelization in the modern world. Cardinal Wojtyła was appointed its relator, the man who drafted the final report on which the Synod Fathers would vote. During the Synod, the question of evangelization in communist countries and Marxist-influenced societies was discussed. Wojtyła thought the conversation was marred by the naïveté of Western Europeans and Latin Americans for whom Marxism was a "fascinating abstraction" rather than an "everyday reality."[120] The Synod of 1974 ended in a kind of ecclesiastical gridlock. Wojtyła's attempt to write a *relatio* that would satisfy the contending parties at the Synod failed. The Synod fathers, unable to agree on a text of their own, handed the whole business over to a post-synodal commission, which in turn handed all the material generated by the Synod to Paul VI, suggesting that he do something with it. The result was one of the finest documents of Paul VI's pontificate, the apostolic exhortation *Evangelii Nuntiandi*.[121]

The failure of his *relatio* notwithstanding, Karol Wojtyła was reelected to the Synod Council, and thus came to Rome in 1977 for the Synod meeting on catechetics, or religious education. In one intervention, Cardinal Wojtyła said that the regime in Poland was promoting "an atmosphere of anti-catechesis," in which atheism "was imposed as a new state religion" in violation of the principle of religious freedom. In a second intervention, the cardinal noted that "the saints were the best catechists," because effective religious education took place not simply through the transmission of ideas, but through the example of heroic virtue.[122]

The 1977 Synod, which took place under the lengthening shadow of Paul VI's age (the Pope was seventy-nine) and ill health, was an opportunity for senior churchmen to discuss the Church's future. During the four weeks of the Synod and the following two weeks of meetings with the Curia during his *ad limina* visit (the pilgrimage every bishop makes, every five years, "to the threshold of the apostles"), Cardinal Wojtyła met informally with many future papal electors, including cardinals from France, Germany, England, Australia, Italy, the United States, and the Roman Curia. At the end of the Synod, Cardinal Wojtyła was elected to the Synod Council for the third consecutive time. Ten years after receiving the red hat and after extensive contact with his peers, he was one of the most respected bishops in the Church.[123]

Learning the World

Karol Wojtyła became familiar with new parts of the world in the late 1960s and throughout the 1970s. In August and September 1969, he traveled for the first time to Canada and the United States, visiting primarily with Polish communities. Arriving in Montreal on August 28, he followed a relentless schedule. In a packed month, the cardinal visited and preached in Québec City, Ottawa, Calgary, Edmonton, Winnipeg, Toronto, Hamilton, London, and St. Catherine's, before crossing the U.S./Canadian border at Niagara Falls and beginning his exploration of the United States in Buffalo, New York—from which, in fifteen days, he went to Hartford and New Britain, Connecticut; Cleveland; Pittsburgh; Detroit; the Polish-American seminary at Orchard Lake, Michigan; Boston; Washington; Baltimore; St. Louis; Chicago; Philadelphia; Doylestown, Pennsylvania (the "American Częstochowa"); and New York City, before flying to Rome for a meeting of the Council on the Laity on October 2.

In Philadelphia, he was the guest of Cardinal John Krol, a Polish-American for whom he had done a kindness two years before. According to Polish custom, a new cardinal makes a solemn reentry into his hometown after receiving the red hat. Cardinal Krol, who had been elected to the College of Cardinals in 1967 along with Wojtyła, was denied a visa to go to his father's home, so Wojtyła went for him, entering the small village of Siekierczyna in a horse-drawn sleigh.[124] Staying at St. Charles Borromeo Seminary in Philadelphia in 1969, the archbishop of Kraków wanted especially to talk with the African-American students about their experience in the United States, the situation of the black Church, and how they had come to the seminary.[125]

In February 1973, Wojtyła represented the Polish Church at the International Eucharistic Congress in Melbourne, Australia. En route to Australia he stopped in Manila, where his predecessor, Adam Stefan Sapieha, had participated in the 1937 Eucharistic Congress. Wojtyła was struck by the depth of Filipino piety, which reminded him, he wrote in a diary he later published, of Poles at Częstochowa. The cardinal then spent three days in New Guinea, visiting Polish missionaries. The Melanesians, he noted, "have a somewhat different outlook on clothing than we do." It was Wojtyła's first exposure to Pidgin English, a language the polyglot archbishop had never encountered before. After Mass and a meal on February 9, "the natives honored us with their dancing and a kind of pantomime depicting the arrival and killing of the first white missionary on the island." In Australia, in addition to the activities of the Eucharistic Congress in Melbourne, Wojtyła visited Polish communities in Brisbane, Sydney, Adelaide, Perth, Canberra, and Hobart. He also flew to New Zealand for three days to meet the Polish community in Wellington. In each city, there would be a Mass and sermon for the local Poles, in addition to meetings with civic officials, veterans' groups, and Polish cultural associations, and visits to nursing homes, schools, and convents. During a meeting with Polish military veterans in Canberra, the cardinal was presented with a steel statue for the church then being built in Nowa Huta; some of the steel was shrapnel the veterans had kept after it had been extracted from their wartime wounds. Wojtyła liked the freshness, openness, and multicultural diversity of Australia, a completely new world to him. But he confessed in his diary that he thought there had been a bit too much stress on the Church discovering itself in the Eucharist, rather than on the Church discovering Christ.[126]

In April 1974, Cardinal Wojtyła traveled to Litoměřice in Czechoslovakia for the funeral of Cardinal Stefan Trochta, who had spent ten years in communist prisons and eight years as a manual laborer. The Czechoslovak secret police surrounded the church where the funeral was held and the local communists refused permission for Wojtyła, Cardinal Franz König of Vienna, and Cardinal Alfred Bengsch of Berlin to concelebrate the funeral Mass. Wojtyła sat in the pews with the rest of the congregation, came up to communion with the laity, and then defied the authorities by speaking over Trochta's casket at the end of the service. That night, en route to Rome, he stopped in Vienna and said his Mass at 10 P.M. in the Vatican embassy.[127]

In addition to his own travels, the cardinal of Kraków was also becoming a magnet for Church dignitaries who wanted to visit Poland and to meet him. In October 1973, he hosted Cardinal Julius Döpfner, chairman of the German Bishops' Conference, with whom he prayed at Auschwitz and Birkenau.[128] The following year, Wojtyła received visits in Kraków from French and Italian cardinals and bishops from Belgium and Burundi.

In 1976, the international pace of his life quickened. In a striking gesture of confidence in the young Polish cardinal, Pope Paul VI invited Karol Wojtyła to give the annual Lenten retreat to the Pope and the Roman Curia, traditionally held during the first week of Lent. Wojtyła had only a brief time to prepare the twenty-two sermons or conferences he was expected to give in Italian during the retreat. He went to Zakopane, the ski resort in the Tatras, from February 9 to 15, where he was joined from the 12th on by Father Tadeusz

Styczeń. From February 20 to 25, he devoted his morning writing time in his chapel to developing the texts he had sketched in Zakopane while taking occasional ski breaks. Wojtyła left for Rome on March 1 and spent four days at the Polish College, finalizing and polishing his sermons.

The retreat began on the evening of March 7, in the St. Mathilda chapel of the Apostolic Palace. Wojtyła addressed the retreatants—the senior leaders of the Roman Curia—from the front of the chapel. Out of the corner of his eye he could see Paul VI, seated by himself in a small room just outside the sanctuary. As had become his custom during Lent, the seventy-eight-year-old Pope was wearing a hair shirt underneath his white cassock. The archbishop of Kraków began the retreat by reminding his listeners that he came from a persecuted Church where the privilege of going on retreat was sought by far more men and women than the Church could accommodate. He described the atmosphere of an Oasis retreat for teenagers, and gently suggested that these aging (and, in some instances, hardened) veterans of the Church's central bureaucracy try to put themselves in the place of youngsters on an Oasis, who found in their retreat a way "of rediscovering God and themselves, an experience that brings with it a fresh discovery of the meaning of life."[129]

The curial retreat bore a striking resemblance to themes that were being developed in the Synod of Kraków. Its pivot was *Gaudium et Spes* 22, the text that Wojtyła regarded as the theological centerpiece of Vatican II: "it is only in the mystery of the Word made flesh that the mystery of man truly becomes clear." In exploring this Christian humanism with the curial retreatants, Wojtyła, like the Kraków Synod, made extensive use of the "threefold office" of Christ—the prophetic, priestly, and regal "offices" that also belonged to Christ's people in the Church. He examined these aspects of the Christian life through a variety of literary prisms: the Old and New Testaments, Christian classics, contemporary philosophy and theology, and literature. Irenaeus, Augustine and Aquinas, Martin Heidegger and Paul Ricoeur, Henri de Lubac and Karl Rahner, Hans Küng and Walter Kasper, Saint-Exupéry's *Night Flight* and Milton's *Paradise Lost*—all were drawn into Wojtyła's meditations on the glory of man redeemed by Christ. In addition, he made extensive use of his personal and pastoral experience to illustrate his points, speaking movingly about what he had learned of human dignity and the "royal" office of the Christian as a confessor: "When a man goes down on his knees in the confessional because he has sinned, at that very moment he adds to his own dignity as a man. No matter how heavily his sins weigh on his conscience, no matter how seriously they have diminished his dignity, the very act of turning again to God is a manifestation of the special dignity of man, his spiritual grandeur . . . the grandeur of the personal meeting between man and God in the inner truth of conscience."[130]

When Wojtyła's sermons were published by *Znak*, they made a profound impression on his friends among the Kraków intellectuals. The painter Stanisław Rodziński, for example, found in them a theological confirmation of what he had been wrestling with in his own art: the tragedy and madness of a modern world whose definitions of humanism excluded the truth about the spiritual hungers of the human person.[131] Certain men of the Curia may have had a different, if related, reaction. Here was an intellectually astute and articulate pastor who could speak Christian truth to modernity in a dialogue that really would be a two-way street. A sensible world, some of them may have thought, would want to see this man pope. But that, of course, was impossible.

Four months after the curial retreat, Cardinal Wojtyła spent another six weeks in the United States while attending the International Eucharistic Congress held in Philadelphia during the U.S. Bicentennial. His American journey began in Boston, where it had been arranged for him to deliver a lecture in the Harvard Summer School's annual series. After several days in seclusion at the St. Sebastian Country Day School in suburban Boston, practicing his English, Wojtyła delivered a lecture on "Participation or Alienation" to a large audience in Emerson Hall. The Summer School's director, Thomas Crooks, was much taken with Wojtyła, a "dazzlingly impressive man." After the lecture, Crooks hosted a reception for Wojtyła in Lehman Hall, in Harvard Yard. Standing on the steps of the building, Crooks turned to the cardinal and said that, given his position as a prince of the Church in a communist country, something was bound to happen. The cardinal, perhaps thinking of the escalating tensions with the regime in Poland, simply said, "I know."[132] Zbigniew Brzeziński, who "hadn't been in the habit of attending social functions for visiting Polish bishops," was vacationing in Maine. But "for some reason" he could never understand, the Columbia University political scientist and future national security adviser to the President of the United States accepted an invitation to Cambridge to have tea with Cardinal Wojtyła, and came away struck by his combination of "intelligence and calm strength."[133]

After three days in Washington, including a lecture at the Catholic University of America School of Philosophy, Wojtyła arrived in Philadelphia. During the Eucharistic Congress, he stayed at St. Charles Borromeo Seminary again, where, in happy indifference to ecclesiastical protocol, he wandered the corridors at night and dropped into faculty members' rooms to talk about the Church's situation in the United States.[134] The Congress had been organized around the theme, "The Eucharist and the Hungers of the Human Family," and Wojtyła had been chosen to preach at the August 3 Mass dedicated to "The Eucharist and Man's Hunger for Freedom." Acknowledging the bicentennial of American independence and the role of Polish patriots like Tadeusz Kościuszko and Kazimierz Pulaski in securing it, he suggested that freedom was a "test of maturity," a gift and a task that found its fulfillment in goodness, in "loving what is truly good." It would not be the last time he was misunderstood by some Americans as a scold.

The cardinal was, however, concerned about the United States, after a whirlwind tour that touched Chicago; Stevens Point, Wisconsin; Baltimore; Detroit; Orchard Lake, Michigan; Great Falls and Geyser, Montana; Los Angeles; and San Francisco. His friends at *Tygodnik Powszechny* remember him as being "disappointed" by American culture and its tendency to dissipate freedom into shallow license.[135] He may also have been disturbed by what appeared to be a certain flaccidity or insouciance in post-Vietnam American public life about the world situation, and the threats to the human "hunger for freedom" that were still being mounted by an aggressive atheistic ideology. Did America and its leaders understand that the world was facing "the greatest historical confrontation humanity has gone through . . . the final confrontation between the Church and the anti-Church, of the Gospel versus the anti-Gospel"? Wojtyła would never have narrowed this "confrontation," which he insisted "lies within the plans of Divine Providence," to the clash between democracy and communism. There were elements of the confrontation between true and false humanism present within the democracies.[136] Still, communism was one particularly threatening expression of the crisis of world civilization in the late twentieth century. He knew that in his bones. He was going back home to face it.

THE DEFENDER

The confrontation between the Church and Poland's communist masters was a constant war, not a sporadic set of skirmishes. It was always "we" and "they," "us" and "them," for as Pope John Paul II later put it, "the communists tried to be accepted, not just as a political authority, but as a moral authority, as an expression of the Polish nation." The principal obstacle to that was the Church, which the regime "tried to pretend . . . did not exist."[137] The confrontation could not be understood in conventional Western political terms. This was a nonadjudicable struggle. Somebody was going to win and somebody was going to lose.

Karol Wojtyła understood that individual communists may have been, in their own ways, Polish patriots, and he thought that there may have been grains of truths in Marxism's theoretical critique of early industrial capitalism. That was not what was at stake in Kraków. There was no Christian-Marxist dialogue in Poland because Poland's communists were "never sufficiently certain about their principles, or about the reactions of their Soviet masters, for a sustained debate to take place." As the years wore on, they increasingly depended on "policemen rather than . . . philosophers" to sustain themselves in power."[138] And they did so in ways that the archbishop of Kraków, defender of religious freedom at Vatican II, found quite simply unacceptable. As he had said in Rome during the 1977 Synod on religious education, "One can understand that a man may search and not find; one can understand that he may deny; but it is not understandable that a man may have imposed on him the dictum—'It is forbidden for you to believe'."[139]

The mid-1970s were a time of continuing harassment—usually petty, sometimes quite nasty—for the independent-minded in Poland. Students were forced to memorize ersatz poetry, such as "The individual is nothing, the individual is nil. The Party is everything." Elections to student governments were rigged in favor of children whose parents were regime-acceptable. Nonsense holidays—the fortieth anniversary of the Polish-Soviet Friendship Society, for example, or the fortieth anniversary of the International Brigades in the Spanish Civil War—were substituted for ancient religious feasts. The incompetent were promoted over the deserving, if the latter were politically suspect. Qualified students were denied university admission because of the alleged ideological sins of their parents.[140] The Church was not immune to the petulance and paranoia of the authorities. The archbishop's residence at Franciszkańska, 3, was thoroughly bugged, Wojtyła's car was constantly tailed, and when a more vigorous signal had to be sent, an elderly man, like Father Bardecki, was beaten up by SB goons.

It was, as Václav Havel famously described it, a culture of lies, which Karol Wojtyła was well-positioned to challenge.[141] In what presented itself as a "workers' state," he had been a manual laborer; he had maintained a longstanding interest in and relationships with workers; and he was steeped in the imagination of his favorite poet, Norwid, who had tried to understand the world of work and workers in spiritual terms. The friendships he had nourished over the years with his *Środowisko* had given him a detailed understanding of what things were like, day in and day out, for ordinary people in the Polish People's Republic. This intimate knowledge of life within the culture of the lie fed Wojtyła's intellectual challenge to communism and his activism in mounting a sustained cultural resistance against the regime. No adversary could accuse him of not knowing what was happening on the street. He could see, feel, and hear the assault on human dignity he had described to Henri de Lubac as "the evil of our times."[142] That was *the* issue. And it was nonnegotiable.

He was also the custodian of a heritage, the bishop of Kraków as the defender of the people of Kraków. His regime opponents may have dismissed this as mythic twaddle. For him, it was a living, breathing tradition in which he was immersed in his home and his cathedral. As he lived that tradition, he helped provide symbols for his people's rising dissatisfaction with the status quo. Events and struggles that, in other contexts, would have been mere matters of a zoning decision or a parade permit—like the building of new churches or the holding of great public processions—became emblematic of a rising cultural resistance to the communist monopoly on political power, the communist expropriation of Polish history, and the communist "pulverization of the fundamental uniqueness of each human person."[143]

While he was encouraging and leading that resistance, Cardinal Wojtyła also had to cope with a new set of diplomatic initiatives from the Vatican.

The Ostpolitik of Pope Paul VI

Four days after the Second Vatican Council opened, an American U–2 reconnaissance aircraft returned photographs of nuclear-capable Soviet medium-range ballistic missiles at San Cristóbal in southwest Cuba, some fifty miles outside Havana. Pope John XXIII and the tactically brilliant curial diplomat who was his de facto foreign minister, Agostino Casaroli, were deeply shaken by the ensuing Cuban Missile Crisis. In its wake, they began to redesign the *Ostpolitik*, the "eastern politics," of the Holy See vis-à-vis the communist regimes of east central Europe. That process intensified and expanded during the pontificate of Paul VI.[144]

John XXIII, Paul VI, and Archbishop Casaroli were not simply reacting to events. They believed that Pope Pius XII's ban on dealing with communists had exhausted the diplomatic statute of limitations and become imprudent. Attempts to create a new dialogue with the Soviet government actually preceded the Cuban Missile Crisis, as the Holy See sought permission to have Catholic bishops and Russian Orthodox representatives from the USSR attend Vatican II. John XXIII's April 1963 encyclical on world peace, *Pacem in Terris*, was well-received in the Soviet bloc. On his accession to the papacy several months later, Pope Paul VI tried to build on the foundation of conversation his predecessor had laid.

The new *Ostpolitik* was first seriously tested in Poland by Paul VI's eagerness to participate in the millennium celebrations of Polish Christianity in 1966. Casaroli, dressed in a business suit and tie, made a secret trip to Poland to try to negotiate acceptable terms for a papal visit. The government did not flatly refuse, but it set impossible conditions. The regime first proposed that the Pope could go to Wrocław (thus ratifying the post–World War II Polish-German border) but not to Warsaw. And it insisted that Cardinal Wyszyński not have a large role in the visit. When Casaroli explained that these terms were unacceptable, the government's next bid was for a visit of less than twenty-four hours, during which the Pope could fly into Częstochowa for Mass in the evening and leave the next morning. Such furtiveness was also unacceptable. The regime blocked the visit by making it impossible for the Pope to come honorably.[145]

Casaroli, however, was not a man to take "No" for a permanent answer. With the ice broken, he began to visit Poland openly in 1967, consulting local bishops, including Cardinal Wojtyła in Kraków. The Polish government had suggested to the Holy See that the Vatican was only getting Wyszyński's view of matters and encouraged Casaroli's conversations with other bishops. Casaroli came away from these conversations convinced that the picture the Holy See was getting from the Primate and the situation as viewed by the other members of the episcopate was "substantially the same," even if "some aspects of the analysis" were different. With that clarified, and after a pause due to the 1968 Soviet invasion of Czechoslovakia, the Gdańsk shipyard massacre in 1970, and the subsequent change of Polish regime from Gomułka to Gierek, Casaroli and his lieutenants settled down in 1971 to years of shuttling between Rome and Warsaw in search of a legal agreement to regulate the relations between the Holy See and the Polish People's Republic. Since Cardinal Wyszyński was the obvious Polish interlocutor for Vatican officials in this effort, Casaroli did not see Wojtyła again until 1974.[146]

The *Ostpolitik* of Paul VI was based on an analysis of the world situation and a vision of the European future, according to which the division of the continent was a permanent feature for the foreseeable decades ahead. The Soviet Union was a formidable regional hegemonic power, and as long as it remained that, the Berlin Wall was not going to crumble. The Holy See had to be realistic.[147] Realism meant downplaying the role of ideological conflict in international relations, and it was within a state-to-state model of international relations that Archbishop Casaroli was operating. Reform in the communist world would come gradually, and stability was the precondition to reform. The Holy See had to acknowledge the status quo in order to set a baseline for a new relationship with the countries of the Warsaw Pact. As for the future, perhaps a gradually liberalizing East would converge over many decades with a West gradually becoming more social-democratic in its politics and economics.

In the meantime, the hard-pressed Church behind the iron curtain had to survive. To Pope Paul VI and Casaroli, "survival" meant the survival of the Church's sacramental life. That meant priests, and above all, it meant bishops. A medium-term tactical goal of the *Ostpolitik* was to reach legal agreements with Warsaw Pact governments allowing the Church (after a minimum of consultation with the governments involved) to appoint bishops. This strategy, referred to in Italian as *salvare il salvabile*—saving what could be saved—was intended to create what Casaroli referred to as "breathing space" for the Church. Operating that strategy required such tactical concessions from the Church as lowering the temperature of Catholic anti-communist rhetoric, disentangling the Holy See from the West in international politics, and, perhaps most controversially, reining in the underground Church that had been created in east central Europe during the first two decades of the Cold War. Most specifically, this meant stopping the clandestine ordination of priests by underground bishops, which was a thorn in the side of communist governments, particularly in Czechoslovakia.

The underground clergy in Czechoslovakia protested, sometimes bitterly. They were convinced that the Vatican's diplomats, who had no direct experience of communism, were vulnerable to communist manipulation, and they believed that the attempt to get bishops through deals with the communist regime in Prague would end up yielding bishops who were puppets.[148] But the Czechs and Slovaks, among the most hard-pressed Catholics behind the iron curtain, were in no position to carve out an independent path. The Poles were, and they did.[149]

Cardinal Wyszyński's strategy was one of surviving, and ultimately prevailing, by rebuilding and unity. Having lived with it since World War II, the Primate had a rather different view of "real existing socialism" than Archbishop Casaroli, and he feared that the Vatican diplomat's lack of experience with communists would cause exactly the kind of problems he had successfully avoided for two decades.[150] Wyszyński's was not a strategy of endless confrontation. Unlike Cardinal Mindszenty in Budapest, a major figure in the abortive Hungarian revolution of 1956, Wyszyński was moderate in his demands, but extremely immoderate in defending them. His demands were the minimum consistent with the Church's integrity and the dignity of conscientious people: he asked that the Church be allowed to contribute to building Polish society without compromising its principles. The Hungarian prelate, in contrast, made maximum demands, chose direct confrontation— and was crushed. Wyszyński was no less a Catholic and no less devout an anticommunist than Mindszenty. But he was a strategically wiser man. For after Mindszenty was crushed, the Hungarian Church took the road not of compromise, but of surrender.[151]

As a matter of sound strategy, Cardinal Wyszyński was determined to be the gatekeeper in any dealings between any agency of the Church, including the Holy See, and the Polish regime. There could only be one point of reference for Church-state issues or the communists, experts at manipulating cracks into fissures, would gain an advantage. What had worked for two decades internally shouldn't be compromised by the Holy See. Casaroli, for his part, thought that the Polish Primate was a "real prince" and a "great man of the Church" who possessed formidable political skills, including the crucial skill of knowing just where the edge of the precipice was.[152] But he and Paul VI were determined to reach whatever legal agreements could be reached with the Polish government as part of their more comprehensive *Ostpolitik*. The stage was set for continuous chafing between Rome and Warsaw.

Wyszyński and Wojtyła

From the moment his appointment as archbishop of Kraków was announced, Karol Wojtyła was determined not to let a millimeter of distance open between himself and the Primate on Church-state affairs. After he received the cardinal's red hat, Wojtyła intensified his efforts to remain the number two man in the public eye. The two cardinals had, to be sure, differences of style and of analysis. Wojtyła, for example, was more interested in Marxism as an intellectual problem than Wyszyński. But there was never a serious conflict between the two.[153] Which raises the question, was Cardinal Wyszyński a mentor to the younger man he once described, perhaps somewhat dismissively, as "a poet"?

Wojtyła admired Wyszyński's rocklike stance, his incorruptibility, his devotion to duty, and his longstanding commitment to social justice. Bred in the Sapieha tradition, Wojtyła was naturally impressed by Wyszyński as another *pater patriae* in hard times. At the same time, Wojtyła did not hesitate to make his own distinctive sorts of criticisms of the regime, or to pursue his program of cultural resistance through instruments (like *Tygodnik Powszechny*) that Wyszyński sometimes found hard to appreciate. Wyszyński's passion for a unified front sometimes led him to silence dissenting views prematurely; Wojtyła was a man who instinctively tried to hold people of different views together. Wyszyński didn't trust intellectuals and thought that the repository of national honor was the faith of simple people; Wojtyła, who knew full well that intellectuals could and did behave badly at times, was nonetheless committed to a Polish Church that had room in it for both critical intelligence and popular piety.[154] But Cardinal Wojtyła consciously decided, out of both loyalty and tactical prudence, to remain in the Primate's shadow whenever the two appeared together.[155]

At the same time, Karol Wojtyła had his own way of being a bishop, his own reading of the dynamics of contemporary history, and his own sense of the tactics appropriate in the local Church for which he was responsible. Curiously, the cardinal archbishop of Kraków impressed Archbishop Casaroli during the diplomat's visits to Kraków as more of a "theoretician" of the struggle "between communism and the Christian reality" than as a man "interested in concrete political problems," a reticence Casaroli ascribed to Wyszyński's dominance of the Polish Church-state scene.[156] What Casaroli perceived as Wojtyła's "reticence" in fact reflected a different approach to the whole question of the Church's relationship to the world of political power.

Casaroli remembered being impressed by the fact that Wojtyła had never met Edward Gierek, the Polish Communist Party First Secretary "who held the real power." The implication seemed to be that anyone interested in being a real player would have met the other real players. Karol Wojtyła had a different sense of who the "real players" in the Polish drama were. He was far more interested in getting to know the dissidents of KOR, the Clubs of the Catholic Intelligentsia (KIK), the editorial staffs of *Tygodnik Powszechny* and *Znak*, and Poland's leading philosophers, poets, and musicians than in spending time making useless banter with communist leaders, no matter how exalted. Casaroli had noted the difference between Wojtyła and other Polish bishops, in that the Kraków cardinal was "always interested in conversations and contacts" with laypeople. Spending time on these, Casaroli thought, was a "restraint" on "political conversations."[157] In Wojtyła's mind, this hardly constituted a painful tradeoff.

Years later, Cardinal Casaroli remembered being struck by three things: that Poland was the only place in his extensive travels where he had ever heard bishops talking in the blunt realist métier of "reasons of state"; that this rationale—fear of a Soviet intervention—was invoked by Cardinal Wyszyński in appealing for worker restraint during the riots of 1970 following the Gdańsk shipyard shootings; and that Cardinal Wojtyła didn't think in these terms. Which was, of course, precisely the point. Wojtyła did not approach Church-state issues through a form of "realism" that deemed politics a realm of amorality, because he believed that moral judgment, as *the* distinctively human characteristic, could not be excluded from politics.

On Cardinal Wyszyński's part, one can discern a growing respect for Karol Wojtyła. The Primate appreciated Wojtyła's role as mediator with the intellectuals, and knew that the younger man had shown himself a deft negotiator in several local crises in Kraków. He also appreciated Wojtyła's deference to him, which was personally authentic as well as politically essential. Wojtyła's first move, on being named a cardinal, had been to visit Wyszyński. Later that same year, he helped foil yet another government attempt to split the two men, this time using a presumably unwitting Charles de Gaulle as the wedge. When de Gaulle came to Poland on an official visit in 1967, he agreed, under Polish regime pressure, to remove a visit to the Primate from his agenda. When, later in his trip, the General arrived in Kraków, he found Cardinal Wojtyła "otherwise engaged." Le Grand Charles was greeted at Wawel Cathedral by the sacristan.[158] This pattern of deference to the Primate held for more than a decade. During one of Wyszyński's greatest triumphs, the Polish hierarchy's visit to West Germany in September 1978, Wojtyła remained so far in the background that it is difficult to find photographs of him on that historic occasion. Wojtyła even joked about it. Asked what percentage of Polish cardinals skied, he replied, "Forty percent." The reporter said, "But, Your Eminence, there are only two Polish cardinals." "In Poland," Wojtyła replied, "Wyszyński counts for sixty percent."

Wyszyński was usually portrayed in the West as the "hard-liner" and Wojtyła as the "moderate." The truth of the matter is that, in the last several years of his tenure in Kraków, the communist regime hated and feared Cardinal Wojtyła more than it feared Primate Wyszyński. The Primate had not lost his edge, but the moves in that particular dance had become familiar to both partners, and familiarity bred a certain comfort, however strained. With Wojtyła, the regime never knew what was coming next.[159] A man they had imagined to be a quiet intellectual had become a charismatic public personality. His defense of religious freedom was increasingly sharp-edged and struck the regime at its most vulnerable point, its claim to be the true representative of the Polish people. He was a magnet for young people and systematically interposed himself between the regime and youth. And he was ecumenical in his support for dissent, frequently inviting dissident intellectuals, Catholic and otherwise, to his drawing room at Franciszkańska, 3. Here, the regime must have feared, was the man who could realize dissident Adam Michnik's call for a rapprochement between left-leaning anti-communist intellectuals and the Catholic Church.[160]

Those who projected a political reading of Catholic affairs—Wyszyński the "conservative" and Wojtyła the "moderate"—onto Polish Church-state relations missed all of this. The true state of affairs was not lost on the SB, however, nor, one assumes, on its KGB masters. They were terrified that Wojtyła might succeed Wyszyński as Primate.[161] That would turn out to be the least of their worries.

Wojtyła and the Ostpolitik

Karol Wojtyła did not believe in "convergence" between the two halves of a Yalta-divided Europe. To his way of thinking, Yalta was a moral catastrophe;

thus the Yalta system had to go. There could be no compromise with basic injustice, and the Vatican sometimes had to be reminded of that fact.[162]

Cardinal Wojtyła never doubted the good intentions of Paul VI in his *Ostpolitik*, and he certainly knew of the Pope's personal torment, torn between his heart's instinct to defend the persecuted Church and his mind's judgment that he had to pursue the policy of *salvare il salvabile*—which, as he once put it to Archbishop Casaroli, wasn't a "policy of glory."[163] The archbishop of Kraków also believed he had an obligation to maintain solidarity with a persecuted and deeply wounded neighbor, the Church in Czechoslovakia, where the situation had deteriorated during the years of the new Vatican *Ostpolitik*. So Cardinal Wojtyła and one of his auxiliary bishops, Juliusz Groblicki, clandestinely ordained priests for service in Czechoslovakia, in spite of (or perhaps because of) the fact that the Holy See had forbidden underground bishops in that country to perform such ordinations.

The clandestine ordinations in Kraków were always conducted with the explicit permission of the candidate's superior—his bishop or, in the case of members of religious orders, his provincial. Security systems had to be devised. In the case of the Salesian Fathers, a torn-card system was used. The certificate authorizing the ordination was torn in half. The candidate, who had to be smuggled across the border, brought one half with him to Kraków, while the other half was sent by underground courier to the Salesian superior in Kraków. The two halves were then matched, and the ordination could proceed in the archbishop's chapel at Franciszkańska, 3. Cardinal Wojtyła did not inform the Holy See of these ordinations. He did not regard them as acts in defiance of Vatican policy, but as a duty to suffering fellow believers. And he presumably did not wish to raise an issue that could not be resolved without pain on all sides. He may also have believed that the Holy See and the Pope knew that such things were going on in Kraków, trusted his judgment and discretion, and may have welcomed a kind of safety valve in what was becoming an increasingly desperate situation.[164]

As for Poland, it was, in the late 1970s, a curious, hard mixture of the unreal and the brutal. Workers could wryly joke that "We pretend to work and they pretend to pay us," but those police batons on which authority rested were all too real. Amid the "baffling unreality" of late-communist life and the failure of Gierek's regime's "practical materialism"—a desperate effort to improve access to consumer goods that, financed by massive foreign borrowing, was driving Poland ever closer to economic catastrophe—Cardinal Karol Wojtyła had developed an effective and broad-ranging armory of tools of resistance.[165] In doing so, he had quietly led his fellow bishops into articulating a Christian personalist alternative to the false humanism of communism. As they wrote in a 1978 pastoral letter reflective of Wojtyła's thinking, "the spirit of freedom is the proper climate for the full development of the person. Without freedom, a person is dwarfed, and all progress dies."[166] Wojtyła could help lead the bishops to such a statement, not simply by force of intellect, but because he shared his more traditionally minded colleagues' Marian devotion and their dedication to Polish popular piety.

THE MINISTRY OF PRESENCE

By some lights, Karol Wojtyła was not a terribly good manager as archbishop of Kraków. He was, some charged, too interested in dialogue with those who made problems for his plans. He was not a detail-oriented administrator. He didn't fire recalcitrants and replace them with his own people. His respect for older people and his distaste for making a spectacle of anyone led him to leave some men in office whom others would have removed, and caused him to promote priests whom others would have preferred to have seen sidetracked in their careers. He never exacted retribution when others crossed him. Some, taking this as weakness, continued to put obstacles in the way of his efforts.[167] His willingness to take a long-range view of virtually every issue was both a blessing and a cause of problems—he was hard to follow sometimes, his mind and imagination being too many moves ahead of the game as his associates looked over the board.[168]

Yet, in the words of Father Józef Tischner, he was a man of the "big picture whose ideas turned into institutions."[169] Though he paid not the slightest attention to management theory, he was the embodiment of what management experts regard as effectiveness: he had certain well-defined goals, and he accomplished them. Moreover, he accomplished them while drawing intense loyalty and affection from his associates, his subordinates, and his people.

He was a tremendous presence in Kraków. At all levels of society, his people knew they had a bishop who had remained a priest and pastor amid increasing responsibilities and international obligations. Like his namesake, St. Charles Borromeo, he made significant contributions to an ecumenical council and then effectively implemented them in his own diocese. There is every reason to believe that Karol Wojtyła would have wanted to spend the rest of his life in service to his "beloved Kraków."

It was precisely because he had done that so well that he would not be the archbishop of Kraków forever.

7

A Pope from a Far Country

The Election of John Paul II

APRIL 17–24, 1974	Cardinal Karol Wojtyła participates in an International Thomistic Congress in Rome, Naples, and Fossanuova.
JUNE 27, 1977	Giovanni Benelli of Florence, Bernardin Gantin of Benin, and Joseph Ratzinger of Munich are created cardinals by Pope Paul VI.
AUGUST 6, 1978	Paul VI dies at Castel Gandolfo and is buried in St. Peter's Basilica on August 12.
AUGUST 25, 1978	The College of Cardinals elects Albino Luciani as pope; Luciani takes the unprecedented double-name, "John Paul I," and declines the papal tiara at his installation Mass on September 3.
SEPTEMBER 28, 1978	Cardinal Karol Wojtyła celebrates his twentieth anniversary as a bishop with the lay friends of his *Środowisko*.
SEPTEMBER 28–29, 1978	Pope John Paul I dies during the night.
SEPTEMBER 30– OCTOBER 2, 1978	Karol Wojtyła writes his last poem, "Stanisław."
OCTOBER 8, 1978	Cardinal Wojtyła preaches on love for Christ as the prime requisite of a pope at a memorial Mass for John Paul I in Rome.
OCTOBER 13, 1978	Wojtyła's closest friend in Rome, Bishop Andrzej Deskur, suffers a stroke.
OCTOBER 14, 1978	Conclave II opens.
OCTOBER 16, 1978	Karol Wojtyła is elected pope, takes the name "John Paul II," and breaks precedent by addressing the crowd in St. Peter's Square in "our Italian language."

Professor Stefan Swieżawski, the Lublin historian of philosophy, was not an
impulsive man. But he felt a solemn obligation to tell his friend, Cardinal
Karol Wojtyła, something that had come to him during Mass, unbidden and
unwilled, as if it were a kind of revelation. His wife thought her husband temporarily bereft of his senses: "If you insist on telling him this stupidity," she said,
"I refuse to accompany you." So Swieżawski, the man of reason who had dedicated his scholarly life to the history of reasoning, went alone to tell his friend
a truth that had not occurred to him by any logical process of deduction.

It was April 1974. The Swieżawskis and Wojtyła were in the Abbey of Fossanuova, the oldest Cistercian foundation in Italy, southeast of Rome. Settled
in 1133 by monks from the famous French Abbey of Citeaux, Fossanuova was
now hosting several sessions of an international congress marking the 700th
anniversary of the death of St. Thomas Aquinas, who had died in the abbey's
guest house in 1274. Cardinal Wojtyła had prepared a paper on "The Personal
Structure of Self-Determination," which had made a considerable impression
on his scholarly colleagues. His fellow philosophers were also charmed by his
personality. He wandered through a restaurant during a lunch break, talking
with the different language groups that had formed, sitting on the arms of
chairs, asking questions, cracking jokes, clapping friends on the back. Beneath
the groined vaulting in the abbey church, built in the Burgundian style and
consecrated in 1208, the philosophers now met Karol Wojtyła, priest and
bishop, as he celebrated one of the Congress Masses.

It was Eastertime and the cardinal chose to preach on the "two
Thomases." The first was Thomas the Apostle, "Doubting Thomas," who
refused to believe the other apostles that first Easter night when they told him
that they had "seen the Lord." When Jesus appeared again to his friends in the
Upper Room, he had fallen to his knees with the exclamation, "My Lord and
my God" (*John* 20.24–29). The second Thomas was the man in whose memory
the congress was meeting. Thomas Aquinas was a thinker whose enormous
work of scholarship reflected a life lived at the crossroads of faith and reason.
Yet confronted by the reality of the living Christ in a vision toward the end of
his life, he had come to see the magnificent corpus he had written as so much
straw compared to what he now knew by the grace of an intense personal
encounter with the risen Lord. That flash of mystical insight, the preacher suggested, was the beginning of the beatific vision for St. Thomas, the beginning
of his experience of seeing God "face to face," in the glorious light of which
everything else was as nothing.

As Cardinal Wojtyła, preaching in Italian without notes, wove a rich tapestry of reflection, his old friend Stefan Swieżawski had a thought. Or, perhaps
more accurately, a thought came to him. He had known the cardinal for a quarter-century, since the young curate of St. Florian's had become his daughters'
catechist and confessor. Swieżawski had been one of the readers of Wojtyła's
habilitation thesis and had persuaded the young philosopher to join the

Lublin faculty. The two had worked together at the Second Vatican Council. Now, he felt himself "absolutely obliged" to tell his friend what had come into his mind, unexpectedly, during Wojtyła's sermon.

Professor Świeżawski found Cardinal Wojtyła walking amid the small columns in the Romanesque cloister of Fossanuova, outside the sacristy where he had removed his vestments after Mass. There was no one else around. Świeżawski went up to the younger man and told him, "You will become Pope."

Karol Wojtyła did not inquire from whence this remarkable information had come. He simply looked gravely into Stefan Świeżawski's eyes, said nothing, and slowly walked away, absorbed in prayer.

Four and a half years later, an envelope bearing a Vatican postmark arrived at the Świeżawski apartment in Warsaw. The letter inside was handwritten on plain, uncrested paper, dated October 21, 1978, and read in part:

> . . . Well, dear Stefan, your letter reminded me of your words in Fossanuova during a congress in honor of St. Thomas. *Deus mirabilis!* Thank you for your constant help and your presence which have accompanied me for years, including my habilitation at the university. I count on your presence accompanying me in the future. I am aware that in the near future there will be more challenges for me—like exams to pass! I need your prayers and I entrust everything to the hands of Jesus. *Totus tuus!* My greetings to your wife, daughters, and grandchildren.

The signature, in a familiar script, bore the name by which the world would come to know the man Professor Świeżawski had felt obliged to tell of his destiny: "John Paul II."[1]

THE INCREASING BURDEN OF AGE

Pope Paul VI's 1970 apostolic letter, *Ingravescentem Aetatem*, revamped the College of Cardinals and the rules for the election of a pope by setting the maximum number of electors at 120 and decreeing that cardinals lost their right to vote in conclave when they turned eighty. The document's title, "The Increasing Burden of Age," was an apt metaphor for the last years of the fifteen-year pontificate of Paul VI.

On his election in 1963, Pope Paul had dedicated his pontificate to completing Vatican II and implementing it without schism—no small goals, given the contentiousness that always surrounded ecumenical councils and their aftermath. In virtually any other age, Pope Paul's achievement would have seemed monumental. In addition to steering the Council to a successful conclusion, he oversaw what lay Catholics around the world regarded as the primary effect of Vatican II, the most comprehensive revision of the Church's liturgy since the Reformation. Latin was replaced by vernacular languages; new Eucharistic Prayers (the "Canon," or central prayer of the Mass) were intro-

duced; the revised rite of the "sacrament of the sick" made clear that what had
been known for centuries as "Extreme Unction" should not be limited to the
last hours of life; the ritual of the sacrament of penance (now referred to as
the sacrament of reconciliation) was revised, and Catholics were presented
with a variety of ways to go to confession; a comprehensive liturgical and catechetical program for the reception of adult converts, the Rite of Christian Initiation of Adults, restored ancient Christian practices that had lain fallow for
centuries.

Pope Paul also made major structural changes in the Church's governance. He created the Synod of Bishops, a body without precedent in Catholic
history. He dis-established the papal court, disbanding the Noble Guard, the
Palatine Guards, and the Pontifical Gendarmes and stripping the papacy of
most of the vestiges of Renaissance display that had long surrounded it. He
reformed the Roman Curia, making the Secretariat of State the clearinghouse
for all curial business, reconstituting the Holy Office as the Congregation for
the Doctrine of the Faith, and creating new agencies for the laity, for the promotion of justice and peace, for dialogue with Judaism and other world religions, and for dialogue with nonbelievers.[2] Pope Paul also internationalized
the Curia, taking a Frenchman, Cardinal Jean Villot, as his Secretary of State
(the highest-ranking post in the Church's new central administration) and
appointing other non-Italians to key posts throughout the bureaucracy.

Paul VI created dozens of new dioceses, particularly in the Third World,
and vastly expanded the number of native-born bishops in Africa and Asia. He
began to internationalize the practice of the papacy itself, traveling to the Holy
Land and India (1964), the United Nations and New York City (1965), Portugal and the Marian shrine of Fatima (1967), Colombia (1968), the World
Council of Churches in Geneva and Uganda (1969), and Hong Kong, the
Philippines, and Australia (1970). His three meetings with Athenagoras, Ecumenical Patriarch of Orthodoxy, illustrated his ecumenical commitment. So
did the Uganda pilgrimage. After praying at the shrines of twenty-two Catholic
African martyrs he had canonized in 1964, the Pope also prayed at the shrine
of twenty-three Protestants martyred in the same persecution. During the pontificate, considerable theological progress was made in "bilateral" ecumenical
dialogues between Roman Catholics and Anglicans, and between Roman
Catholics and Lutherans. The Pope's social doctrine, embodied in the 1967
encyclical *Populorum Progressio* [The Development of Peoples] and the 1971
apostolic letter *Octogesima Adveniens* (marking the eightieth anniversary of Leo
XIII's *Rerum Novarum)*, was primarily concerned with Third World issues,
including economic development and revolutionary violence.

It was, and remains, an impressive record. Yet as the seventies wore on,
the impression created by the pontificate was not one of dynamism and evangelical reinvigoration but of drift amid unaddressed and grave problems. The
theological divisions in the Church evident at the Council hardened throughout the fifteen years of Paul VI. Archbishop Marcel Lefebvre and his follow-

ers, still bitter at the Council's adoption of the *Declaration on Religious Freedom* and convinced that liturgical reform was Protestantizing Catholicism, attacked Paul's authority in the name of their own concept of authority. By 1976, the situation had deteriorated to the point where the Pope suspended Archbishop Lefebvre from his episcopal functions for ordaining priests without authorization at the seminary he had founded in Switzerland.[3] Along the other end of the theological spectrum, a "progressive" party that had thought itself an irresistible force during the Council continued to press for what it considered a more authentic implementation of the "spirit" of Vatican II, particularly in response to the sexual revolution and the politics of the sixties. Biting criticism from these quarters followed *Humanae Vitae*'s critique of contraception, Paul's 1967 encyclical defending priestly celibacy (*Sacerdotalis Coelibatus*), and the 1976 statement from the Congregation for the Doctrine of the Faith, *Inter Intersigniores*, which confirmed that the Church could only ordain men to the ministerial priesthood. The Council had challenged the Church to deepen its faith, evangelize modernity, and renew its service to the world. Factions in the post-conciliar Church continued to battle over who was in charge.

Meanwhile, a crisis in Catholic elites, influenced by the cultural upheaval of the sixties, followed hard on the heels of Vatican II. Large numbers of priests left the active ministry. Convents, monasteries, and seminaries emptied in the developed world. Catholic universities took a markedly secular turn. The Church in Holland seemed irreconcilably split between the two theological parties, and less bitter but still serious divisions festered in France and the United States. The Church in Latin America was divided along political lines. One faction, accustomed to an alliance with authoritarian governments, was being challenged by another, its politics formed in part by the conviction that Karl Marx could do for Catholic theology in the twentieth century what Aristotle had done for Thomas Aquinas in the thirteenth.

These divisions in the Church were frequently described in political categories and did, in fact, often mirror different economic and political positions. Perhaps without the full awareness of some of the combatants, though, deeper issues of doctrine and theology were being engaged across the ecclesiastical spectrum, involving both what is commonly perceived as the "Catholic Left" and the "Catholic Right."

The distinctive nature of the Church, its mission, its sacramental life, and its ministry were all at stake in the post-conciliar debates over collegiality, papal authority, priestly celibacy, the future of women's religious orders and other forms of consecrated life, and the question of ordaining women to the priesthood. Whether and how doctrine develops was at issue between the Lefebvrists and the defenders of religious freedom. Whether there are absolute moral norms that permit us to say that some acts are always "intrinsically evil" was a core issue between the "Majority Report" of the Papal Commission studying fertility regulation and the teaching of *Humanae Vitae*. In all of this, the Church's long-delayed wrestling with modern intellectual life was being played out.

A Church that Pope John XXIII had hoped to revitalize for mission and service was thus investing extraordinary amounts of energy internally, in a form of ecclesiastical civil war. Concurrently, the political expression of militant atheism, the Soviet Union, took an increasingly vigorous role on the world stage. To churchmen accustomed to thinking in terms of civilizations as well as nation-states, gloomy predictions about the decline of the West, coupled with the drift and division within world Catholicism, made for a very disturbing picture.

Pope Paul VI was a man of deep faith, profound compassion, and acute intelligence. Yet some of his finest personal qualities rendered him incapable of setting a firm course for the post-conciliar Church. As early as 1964, he had struck Archbishop Wojtyła, who esteemed him, as a man "fatigued by love."[4] In the last years of his pontificate, other aspects of his complex personality came into clearer focus.

Giovanni Battista Montini's "infinite courtesy" and magnetic personality were readily displayed in one-on-one conversation.[5] But he lacked a compelling public presence, appearing in large settings and on camera as someone reserved, vaguely uncomfortable, and even tentative. Although he had read seriously in modern French thought, what he found there seemed to reinforce a tendency to worry an issue to death. Paul VI's intelligence led him to see every side of a question simultaneously, and the tension between the certainties in which he was intellectually formed and the ambiguities he had learned from life and from his widespread reading frequently led him into a tar pit of uncertainty. There, he would tie himself in knots over a decision, wanting, as Cardinal Franz König of Vienna observed, to make the best of everything.[6]

He was a man of intense piety, yet the comfort he drew from his deep life of prayer did not seem to offer him assurance or comfort in the conduct of his office. His close aide, Agostino Casaroli, remembered him as "tormented" by some situations and decisions.[7] He publicly berated God for not answering his prayer that his friend, the Italian Christian Democratic leader, Aldo Moro, be spared by the Red Brigades in 1978. Toward the end of his life, he worried that he had not been prudent in some of his judgments as Pope. This was an "agony for him," Cardinal William Baum recalled, for he loved the Church with passionate devotion and was painfully aware that he would have to render an account of his stewardship.[8] This agony included a concern that, in his *Ostpolitik*, he may not have been sufficiently vigorous in defending the persecuted. In any case, the strategy of *salvare il salvabile* was, by definition, an attempt to make the best of a terrible situation in which he could see no good alternatives.

It is sometimes said that Paul VI was a misplaced pope historically—that he would have been perceived as far more successful and that he would have suffered far less personally had he succeeded Pius XII rather than John XXIII.[9]

His unalloyed personal decency, combined with a certain frailty that had dogged him throughout life, made him especially vulnerable to the contentiousness, sometimes rising to bitterness, of the post–Vatican II period. A man dedicated to the Council, he felt the acrimony that followed Vatican II personally.[10] In another historical moment, he might have been a man who could have bent history to his purposes. In the time in which he was destined to be pope, he became the kind of man who is consumed by history.[11] He knew himself to be that, and in his faith, he thought of it as Christian self-sacrifice. From the first day of his pontificate, the papacy was a Calvary for him.[12]

The fifteen-year pontificate of Giovanni Battista Montini raised a hitherto unthought question. Could *anyone*—and particularly anyone formed in the typical pattern of post-Reformation popes—do this job in the extraordinary internal and external circumstances of late twentieth-century Catholicism? From the Italian, and specifically curial, point of view, Montini was the perfectly prepared pontiff.[13] He was the son of a good Catholic family, members of the professional class who had remained loyal to the Holy See after the unification of Italy. He had been trained in the Vatican diplomatic service, was experienced in the ways of the Curia, and had serious intellectual and artistic interests. He had been the successful archbishop of a major Italian see. This was, as Cardinal König put it years later, the "more-or-less normal way" one became a pope.[14] The troubled pontificate of Pope Paul VI thus raised the question of whether the "normal" way worked anymore.

Toward the end of Paul's pontificate, more than one churchman had begun to think that the answer to that question was "No," that the next conclave had to look beyond the hitherto "normal" pattern, and that one man whose combination of personality and accomplishment might promise a revitalized papacy was the archbishop of Kraków, Karol Wojtyła. By 1978, Wojtyła, despite his relative youth, had become one of the most widely respected senior leaders in Roman Catholicism. He was known to be an intellectual of considerable voltage, a man eager to engage contemporary culture and to make the dialogue between Catholicism and modernity a genuine two-way street. He had grappled with and understood modern intellectual life but he was not an ambiguist. Indeed, he probably understood the complexities and ambiguities of real human lives better than most academics, and on the far side of ambiguity he had discovered a new, more securely grounded certainty.[15]

In addition to his intellectual gifts, Wojtyła was a warrior, and a happy one. He was living under increasing pressure from the Polish communist regime. His experience of the Synod of Bishops and his travels had shown him the depth of the divisions within the Church and the threats posed to Christian humanism by other, noncommunist forms of exploitation and cultural decay. Yet he was energized, not paralyzed, by the challenges ahead, even if it seemed that they would last his lifetime and beyond. As he wrote his friend, Henri de Lubac, in 1969, "we have firmly hoped, we will always hope, and we are and will be happy."[16]

This was not a man consumed by history. This was a man determined to shape history through culture. His conviction that "we are and will be happy" was an act of will, indeed an act of faith, made through, not around, suffering, pain, and humiliation at the hands of evil. The combination was very attractive—a man of deep interiority and acute intelligence with an exceptional public personality. But a pope? The common wisdom on that, in the Vatican and among the speculators in the world press, was firmly set: impossible. Fifty-eight-year-old Polish bishops are not elected pope.

THE "SEPTEMBER PAPACY" OF PAPA GIANPAOLO

Giovanni Battista Montini, Pope Paul VI, died at the papal summer residence at Castel Gandolfo, on August 6, 1978. After receiving the sacrament of the sick and his last Holy Communion (the Viaticum, or "food for the journey"), he said his last words in this world, the Lord's Prayer. At the moment of his death, the inexpensive alarm clock young Father Montini had brought back from Poland in 1923 and had used ever since rang spontaneously.[17]

The ritual surrounding the death of a pope followed its usual course. Cardinal Villot, whom Pope Paul had appointed *Camerlengo* [chamberlain] of the Church, officially certified the Pope's death in the presence of three witnesses and the papal master of ceremonies. Paul VI's seals of office—the Fisherman's ring and the lead seal under which his most formal documents had been dispatched—were broken and the papal apartment in the Apostolic Palace sealed. The Dean of the College of Cardinals, the eighty-five-year-old Carlo Confalonieri, former secretary to Pius XI, notified his brother cardinals of the Pope's death and summoned them to Rome. The dean also gave official notification to the diplomatic corps accredited to the Holy See and to heads of state throughout the world.[18]

Pope Paul's body, vested in gold-and-white miter and red chasuble, lay in state at Castel Gandolfo for three days. On August 9, a motorcade bore the deceased Pope to Rome in a plain wooden casket. The cortege stopped briefly at the Basilica of St. John Lateran, the pope's cathedral as Bishop of Rome, where Cardinal Ugo Poletti recited prayers for the deceased with the communist mayor of the city standing beside him. The black Mercedes hearse then drove into St. Peter's Square, stopping just beyond the obelisk, perhaps the last thing that the dying St. Peter (whom tradition says was crucified upside down in Nero's circus) had seen on this earth. Twelve men who had once carried the Pope on his *sedia gestatoria*, the portable throne whose use he had revived after arthritis made it impossible for him to walk in lengthy processions, took the casket from the hearse and bore it into St. Peter's Basilica. It was placed on a bier before the *confessio*, the tomb, of Peter, in front of the papal high altar. Tens of thousands of mourners filed past the Pope's remains in the next two days. On August 12, the funeral Mass was held in St. Peter's Square, the Book of the Gospels resting on top of the cypress casket. Thirteen interfaith and ecumenical delegations attended, in addition to representatives of more than one hundred countries and international organizations. After the Mass, the wooden coffin was placed inside a lead casket, which was placed inside a third, oak casket, and then buried as Pope Paul had specified—not in a sarcophagus, but in the ground in the crypt of the basilica, a few dozen yards from the tomb of Peter.[19]

Cardinal Karol Wojtyła was on vacation when Paul VI died, and returned to Kraków on August 8. Before leaving for Rome on August 11, he wrote to Father Andrzej Szostek, a brilliant philosophy student at KUL, whose doctoral dissertation he had agreed to review and which he praised highly in his letter. He sent a copy of the same letter to the Faculty of Philosophy at KUL asking that, under the circumstances, it be allowed to substitute for his presence at Szostek's defense of his doctoral dissertation.[20] On August 19, in the interregnum between the funeral and the opening of the conclave, Cardinal Wojtyła spoke on Vatican Radio about his memories of Paul VI, recounting the Pope's intense interest in the battle for the church at Nowa Huta and Paul's gift of a piece of St. Peter's tomb for the Ark Church's foundation. On the bier in St. Peter's, Wojtyła said, Paul VI was "in another dimension. He looks at another face."[21]

Because of Pope Paul's age and ill health, his death was not a surprise to the College of Cardinals. Conclave speculation had long been in the air, and by the time the cardinals had gotten through almost two weeks of daily meetings or "congregations" between the funeral and the opening of the conclave on August 25, a consensus had begun to form about the kind of new pope needed. Although a few members of the College thought that Vatican II had been a serious mistake, the overwhelming majority believed that the Council was a great achievement whose promise had not been fulfilled because mistakes had been made in its implementation. What was needed now was a stock-taking to see how implementation of the Council could be improved. As that conversation continued, a further consensus emerged. The Church needed a pope of dialogue, a man of vibrant public personality who would embody Catholicism's openness to the world, and a pope who would set a clearer theological and pastoral direction. This latter concern was not confined to elderly men who found it difficult to adjust to the post-conciliar Church. It was among the important issues for African cardinals, who believed their young churches needed a doctrinally coherent and morally challenging Catholicism in order to evangelize.[22]

One of the Church's newest cardinals had made a lucid analysis of the post-conciliar situation three years before. Joseph Ratzinger, fifty-one, had been ordained archbishop of Munich-Freising in May 1977 and created a cardinal one month later. As a theological adviser to Cardinal Frings of Cologne, Ratzinger had played an important role in the debates that produced several key texts of Vatican II, including the *Dogmatic Constitution on the Church*. Ratzinger was convinced that the Council had many significant achievements to its credit. But the climate in the Church after the Council had become "acrimonious and aggressive." The hallmark of Christianity—joy—seemed singularly absent from many post-conciliar debates. What had happened?[23]

Not everything that had occurred after the Council had happened because of the Council. In Ratzinger's view, the Church had been caught in a "global spiritual crisis of humanity itself or, at least, of the Western world." But the Church had not responded to this crisis as the Council Fathers might have hoped. Had the Council Fathers themselves been trapped by an excessively optimistic reading of what could be done in dialogue with the modern world? Ratzinger thought so. When the cultural climate of the sixties turned from euphoria about the limitless possibilities of evolutionary progress to disenchantment in some quarters and revolutionary enthusiasms in others, the Church, unanchored, had been swept along by the riptides of the times.

The crucial question for the effective implementation of the Council and for the Church's service to the world, Ratzinger believed, was not a matter of redesigning the Church's international, national, and local bureaucracies. The "crucial question" was "whether there are . . . saints who . . . are ready to effect something new and living."[24] Unless the Church's dialogue with modernity was an expression of the universal call to holiness, the Church would inevitably mirror the *Zeitgeist,* the spirit of the age—which at this moment in the self-destructive crisis of humanism was hardly worth emulating.

Cardinal Ratzinger, one of the youngest members of the conclave, had never had the opportunity to meet Karol Wojtyła of Kraków. In the interregnum between the death of Paul VI and the formal opening of the conclave, the fifty-one-year-old Bavarian and the fifty-eight-year-old Pole finally met, and discovered that they had very similar analyses of the Church's situation. Ratzinger, one of the intellectual fathers of *Lumen Gentium* (the *Dogmatic Constitution on the Church*), and Wojtyła, one of the architects of *Gaudium et Spes* (the *Pastoral Constitution on the Church in the Modern World*), found themselves in what Ratzinger later recalled as a "spontaneous sympathy" for each other's sense of what was needed to secure the legacy of Vatican II.[25] Most concisely, *Gaudium et Spes* had to be reread through the prism of *Lumen Gentium* so that the Church could engage the modern world with its own unique message. In Ratzinger's words, the Church must once again "dare to accept, with joyful heart and without diminution, the foolishness of truth." Karol Wojtyła, who would later tell the French writer André Frossard that the most important word in the Gospels was "truth," must have agreed.[26]

A majority of the College, notwithstanding their love for Paul VI, evidently felt that the drift of recent years had to be replaced by a firmer course. A few, including König of Vienna, believed this would best be accomplished by looking outside Italy for a candidate. His view was not widely shared. One of the Italian cardinals told the Austrian, "Look, we know this situation better. We have done it for centuries . . . We know how to do it."[27] The result indicated that, on this point, too, an overwhelming majority of the electors were agreed. At the least, they were unwilling to experiment, given their own innate institutional conservatism and their knowledge of the burdens the new pope would face.

There may have been an emerging consensus on what the Church and the papacy needed, but few cardinals came to Rome in August 1978 expecting to find easy agreement on a candidate. The divisions of the post-conciliar years seemed too deep to permit a quick election, particularly given the requirement that the new Pope be chosen by two-thirds plus one of the cardinal-electors. Then there was the size and plurality of the electoral college; 111 cardinals, more diversified than ever in their nationalities and pastoral experiences, did not seem to promise a quick election.[28] Cardinal Wojtyła, expecting a long conclave, told his secretary, Father Dziwisz, and Father Stanisław Ryłko (a Kraków priest who had just finished his doctorate in Rome and was helping Dziwisz with pre-conclave business), to take some time off. After Wojtyła had entered the sweltering and un-air-conditioned Apostolic Palace, where he and the other electors would be sealed off during the voting, the two priests headed for the beach.[29]

Cardinal-electors swear a solemn oath to protect the conclave's secrecy. Some believe themselves sworn to say nothing about what happened between the time they were locked into conclave and the time they were released. Others believe that their oath of secrecy binds them not to reveal anything about the actual balloting, but that they may discuss other things that happened in the conclave itself. Paul VI was adamant about conclave secrecy, in part because of a concern that a government might attempt to manipulate the electors. The new circumstances he created in *Ingravescentam Aetatem* helped produce leaks about the election of his successor, though. Cardinals eligible to vote, sensing the discomfort of those excluded by the eighty-year age limit, discussed conclave matters with them. These elderly cardinals, not bound by the oath of secrecy, talked to friends and journalists. The conclaves of 1978 were the most heavily reported in history, and sifting through the stories while weighing the credibility of various sources is a daunting business. Nonetheless, the broad outlines of what happened during the conclave of 1978, confirmed by some who participated in the election, seem reasonably clear.

On this account, the Great Elector of the conclave of August 1978—the man who put together the decisive coalition of votes—was Cardinal Giovanni Benelli of Florence. Although Benelli had been a cardinal only since June 1977, he had been Paul VI's principal assistant and virtual chief-of-staff for ten years, wielding great power as *Sostituto* [deputy head] of the redesigned Secretariat of State. Resentments over that, coupled with his relative youth (he was fifty-seven when Pope Paul died), precluded his election as Paul's immediate successor, but he was a man of great self-confidence and formidable persuasive skills. By the time the cardinals entered the Sistine Chapel, at 4:30 P.M. on August 25, and locked the doors of the conclave behind them, Benelli, who shared the consensus view of the qualities required in the new pope, had persuaded many electors to support Cardinal Albino Luciani of Venice, a man barely mentioned in the feverish pre-conclave media speculation.[30]

Cardinal Luciani was elected on the fourth ballot taken on the first day of voting, August 26. It was the fastest conclave since 1939, when Eugenio Pacelli had been elected as Pius XII on the first day of voting. The cardinals had done their work efficiently, but confusion reigned supreme outside. The venerable system of announcing the election through a smoke signal from the chimney of the Sistine Chapel—white for a new pope, black for an inconclusive ballot—failed. Four different signals, of indeterminate color, appeared between 6:22 P.M. and 6:51 P.M. Finally, a loudspeaker announced that the puzzled thousands in St. Peter's Square should look toward the central *loggia* of the basilica, which opens off the Hall of Benedictions above the vestibule or narthex of St. Peter's. At 7:17 P.M., Cardinal Pericle Felici, the senior cardinal-deacon, appeared on the *loggia* and made the announcement in Latin according to the prescribed formula: *"Annuntio vobis gaudium magnum: habemus Papam—Eminentissimum ac Reverendissimum Dominum Albinum, Sanctae Romanae Ecclesiae Cardinalem, Luciani, qui sibi nomen imposuit Ioannem Paulum Primum. "*[31] Fathers Dziwisz and Ryłko, hearing the news on the radio, left the beach and hurried back to Rome.

Albino Luciani was the son of a Socialist Party organizer, a priest in the reformist northern Italian tradition of Antonio Rosmini, a successful preacher and catechist, and an author whose book on religious education, *Catechism Crumbs,* had gone through six editions. While Cardinal Patriarch of Venice, Luciani had published *Illustrissimi,* a charming and insightful book of letters he would have written to famous historical figures, including Mark Twain (a favorite of the new pope's), Charles Dickens, G. K. Chesterton, Pinocchio, the Empress Maria Teresa of Austria, and Jesus.[32] Luciani was a popular bishop who had canceled the gaudy procession of gondolas and other watercraft that typically marked the ingress of a new Patriarch of Venice to his see, avoided the haut monde of Venetian society, and sold the pectoral cross given him by John XXIII to kick off a fund-raising drive for a center for the retarded. He certainly didn't think of himself as *papabile* (a "man with the makings of a pope"). To anyone who suggested otherwise, he quoted a Venetian proverb about dumplings: "You don't make *gnocchi* out of this dough."[33]

Yet this man of simple tastes, deep goodness, considerable catechetical skills, and a winsome shyness elicited a powerfully sympathetic public response in thirty-three days. He used the personal "I" instead of the papal and royal "we" in his audiences. He refused a coronation, began his pontificate with a simple ceremony of installation, and kept as the motto on his papal coat-of-arms the single word that had adorned his arms as a bishop: *Humilitas.* He joked with reporters at his first press conference and had children come up to him in the audience hall during his addresses so that he could quiz them and illustrate his points. Quoting Pope Gregory the Great, he asked the people of Rome to "toss me a life preserver of prayer, lest I drown." At first he declined to use the *sedia gestatoria,* until the crowds that flocked to the public appearances of the five-foot, five-inch-tall Pope complained that they couldn't see him. A pope who radiated hope and Christian confidence was, it seemed, precisely what the world was looking for.

For all the vitality of his public presence, though, John Paul I was a sick man when he was elected. He had had a long history of serious circulatory problems (about which the electors did not inquire during the conclave, and for which he had had no medical treatment since becoming pope). He felt the pressures of the papacy acutely. His unfamiliarity with the workings of the Church's central bureaucracy weighed heavily on him—and on some accounts, he was given little help from the permanent staff in adjusting to his new situation. He had accepted the papacy as an act of obedience to what he believed was the will of God working through his brother cardinals. When the fourth "scrutiny," or ballot, had shown him elected and the *Camerlengo,* the Frenchman Jean Villot, asked him whether he would accept election, he startled his eminent colleagues by saying, "May God forgive you for what you have done." It was, he later explained, a sudden "school memory" that had "popped into my head"—a quotation from St. Bernard of Clairvaux, who had criticized the College of Cardinals for electing a shy, retiring Cistercian monk as Pope Eugene III in 1145.[34] He had not meant to offend the cardinals, but it was, in retrospect, an eerily prophetic statement. Neither Luciani, nor the electors who thought they had found the answer to the Church's post-conciliar crisis by choosing him, could have known that the formal document certifying the Pope's election was a death warrant with a very short due date.[35]

Early on the morning of September 29, 1978, one of the household sisters found Pope John Paul I dead in his bed, where he had been stricken the night before by a massive heart attack. The "September Papacy" was over and the Church was once again plunged into crisis.[36]

ANOTHER INTERREGNUM

On September 28, 1978, Cardinal Karol Wojtyła completed a visitation at the parish of St. Joseph in the Złote Łany [Golden Wheatfield] area of Biała and returned to Kraków, where at 6 P.M. he celebrated Mass at the altar of the Holy Cross of Blessed Queen Jadwiga in Wawel Cathedral. It was the feast of St. Wenceslaus, the twentieth anniversary of his consecration as a bishop, and Wojtyła preached on martyrdom. After Mass, he went to the home of his friends Gabriel and Bożena Turowski for an anniversary party with his *Środowisko.* A big display of vacation photographs from a quarter-century of kayaking and skiing had been prepared. Over it hung a banner reading, "Wujek will remain Wujek." His friends kidded him about how many votes he had gotten at the recent conclave. He wanted to talk about the most recent kayak trip. His friends also thought he was a bit subdued and remembered later that he had made an effort to thank everyone for his or her friendship over the years.[37]

The next morning, September 29, the cardinal was at breakfast at the Metropolitan Curia when the telephone rang. One of the staff took the call and returned, shaken, with the news that Pope John Paul I had died during the night. Wojtyła left the table and went straight to his chapel. Later that morning, he attended a meeting of the governing council of the Faculty of Theology. When the dean, his old friend Father Marian Jaworski, offered condolences on the Pope's death, Wojtyła replied that life's surprises had to be accepted, like everything else, "in a spirit of deep faith."[38] Yet he was clearly shaken himself.

On October 1 he preached at a memorial Mass for the deceased pope at the Mariacki Church in the market square, remembering John Paul I's "freshness and originality" and the fact that he had been elected on the feast of Our Lady of Częstochowa. But Wojtyła was a "different person" that day, Father Stanisław Małysiak remembered. Małysiak had worked with the cardinal for a long time and thought he knew how to read his emotions.[39] This was not simply a eulogy for a deceased pope. This was a man wrestling with himself.

Before leaving for Rome, the cardinal called Jerzy Janik to say that they'd have to postpone a seminar they had planned to hold at the Janik home for a couple of weeks. Janik wished him a safe trip, and couldn't help remembering that, years before, when he and his wife had been out hiking with Wojtyła, Jasią had jokingly said, "Where shall we go when you become pope?" Wojtyła hadn't laughed, but simply said, "We'll go to the Alps or the Apennines."[40]

Cardinal Wojtyła went to Warsaw October 2 for a meeting of the Main Council of the Polish episcopate, thus missing the American evangelist Billy Graham, whom he had given permission to preach in St. Anne's Church. In Warsaw he stayed at the Ursuline convent, where the sisters remembered him as looking very serious.[41] Wojtyła left for Rome at 7:30 A.M. the next morning, along with Cardinal Wyszyński. By 11 A.M. on October 3, the Primate of Poland and the archbishop of Kraków were in St. Peter's Basilica praying at the bier of John Paul I.

In the hours after the death of John Paul I, Karol Wojtyła wrote his last poem.[42] It was titled, simply, "Stanisław," and he wrote it, he said later, to pay "my debt to Kraków."[43] It was about martyrdom as the source of Polish nationhood and unity, and the universal model of the Christian vocation.

The Church, Wojtyła wrote, had bound itself to the Polish land "so that everything the Church binds here should be bound in heaven"; the Church was the root which he and so many other Poles had "let out together into the past and the future." One of the fathers who had given birth to the Church in Poland, and indeed to Poland itself, was his predecessor in the See of Kraków, Bishop Stanisław, in whose martyrdom by the sword of King Bolesław "the nation again was baptized/by the baptism of blood," so that it might "go many times through the baptism of other trials." The word of truth and the blood of martyrs had both nurtured "the soil of human freedom" in Poland, which had first been tilled by the breath of the Holy Spirit. And it was the spirit who "will unite everything/the word . . . and the . . . blood," so that if "the word did not convert, blood will convert."

Poland was a "land of difficult unity," a "land subjected to the freedom of everyone towards all," and, just a century before, a "land . . . torn apart through almost six generations,/torn apart on the maps of the world! and how much more in the fate of its sons!" Yet through this national martyrdom, as in the martyrdom of Bishop Stanisław, Poland was "united in the hearts of Poles/as no other land." The power of the spirit and of the Spirit, confirming the Law of the Gift written into the human heart, was the first truth about history.[44]

It was a poem charged with a sense of valedictory. While he was writing it, his pen broke.[45]

Marek Skwarnicki, a Kraków poet and member of the *Tygodnik Powszechny* staff, was in Rome for a meeting of the Pontifical Council for the Laity when John Paul I died. He attended the funeral, looked at Wojtyła sitting with the other cardinals in the rain outside St. Peter's, and thought, "My God, what will happen if he's elected?" This was not, Skwarnicki insists, a romantic Polish fantasy, but something that had been talked about rather freely in Rome.

In the aftermath of two papal deaths within less than two months, there was renewed discussion of a non-Italian pope. Skwarnicki's own reasoning went something like this. A Western European was unlikely, because the Church there was divided into two post-conciliar factions and electing someone from one would cause trouble with the other. A pope from the Third World—Pironio of Argentina, for example, an Italian ethnic—was a possibility, but more likely in the future. So the question became, where and for whom to look in Europe? Wojtyła was a European "from another world." The Polish Church, the Church of a "praying country," was strong at a time when the universal Church was in crisis, and although Western intellectuals may not have been taken with its popular piety, Polish Catholicism was very much a Church of the "People of God." Wojtyła was known throughout the world and in the Curia. He had been a broker between the Polish bishops and the German bishops, a delicate business deftly handled. König of Vienna knew him and admired him. He was an expert in communism, which was a danger in the Third World, where half of Catholicism lived. Therefore, Wojtyła was *papabile.*

On the other hand, Skwarnicki thought, election as pope would be an emotional earthquake for Wojtyła. The poet remembered how happy the cardinal had been after Luciani's election. Wojtyła certainly didn't want to leave his "beloved Kraków" or his country in a time of need. The Curia knew Wojtyła was a great pastor who did not pay a lot of attention to bureaucratic process; the Polish cardinal knew something about the Curia and found it difficult to imagine himself confronting its entrenched factions and ways of doing things. Wojtyła, who was aware of his own limitations, knew how much his strength drew on Polish high culture, and how much he would miss by being cut off from his intense conversation with poets, painters, scientists, and philosophers.

These thoughts were churning through Marek Skwarnicki's mind when he went to lunch at the Polish College on October 5, nine days before the conclave would begin—on the earliest date possible under Church law.[46] Among the other guests was Jerzy Turowicz, editor of *Tygodnik Powszechny*. Wojtyła seemed "distracted" during the table talk, and Skwarnicki's intuition told him that something was going on. Wojtyła never acted this way.

After lunch, the cardinal invited Turowicz and Skwarnicki to a sitting room where they sat in comfortable armchairs and looked through the windows at the pines of Rome. The cardinal asked Skwarnicki about the recent meeting of the Council for the Laity, but the poet had the impression that Wojtyła, uncharacteristically, wasn't listening to his answer. Then Skwarnicki mentioned that he was leaving for Kraków, but had to be back in Rome for a meeting of the European Council of the Laity on October 20. Wojtyła repeated the date, "October 20," as if it were in some unimaginable future.

The conversation shifted to the subject on everyone's mind, the death of John Paul I. Wojtyła began to describe what had happened to him the day the Pope died. He had been out on his parish visitation and a storm had exploded in the mountains during Mass. As he described the storm, he became unusually emotional. His friends listened in silence, not knowing what he was thinking. He then stopped, concerned that he had become too demonstrative. Shortly afterward, his secretary, Father Dziwisz, opened the door a bit and looked in to remind the cardinal that there was another appointment waiting. Skwarnicki and Turowicz quickly stood up, and the cardinal embraced both of them. This was standard practice with Turowicz, but a first for Skwarnicki. He embraced them so strongly, Skwarnicki remembered, that the two men left the room shaken. It was as if they were saying good-bye, not for a few weeks, but for a much longer time. As they left, Dziwisz said to Turowicz and Skwarnicki, "Pray for Cardinal Wojtyła; pray for his return to Kraków."[47]

Sister Emilia Ehrlich was already doing just that. An Ursuline nun who had worked with Cardinal Wojtyła in Kraków on various projects, including tutoring him in English, she was then doing graduate studies in Scripture in Rome at the Pontifical Biblical Institute. One of the sisters in her convent, an Italian, was praying that Cardinal Benelli would be elected. Sister Emilia was praying that Cardinal Wojtyła wouldn't be.

So, it seems, was Wojtyła. Echoes of that prayer can be heard in a remarkable sermon he preached on October 8, at the Church of St. Stanisław in Rome, at a concelebrated Mass for the repose of the soul of John Paul I led by Cardinal Wyszyński. His text was *John* 21, in which the risen Christ questions Peter along the lakeshore in Galilee:

> When we think about this wondrous summoning of Pope John Paul, then we must return to that first summons, the summons directed to Simon, to whom Our Lord gave the name "Peter." Especially of that definitive summons after the Resurrection, when Christ asked him three times, "Do you love me?" And Peter answered three times, "You know I do, Lord." And Christ asked: "Do you love me *more* than do the others?" . . .
>
> This question was so difficult, so very demanding. And possibly Simon Peter, of all the Apostles, best understood how this question exceeds the scope of a human being. That is why he trembled in answering. He was giving himself up to the love of Him who was asking, when he answered, "Lord, you know that I love you."

... The succession of Peter, the summons to the office of the papacy, always contains within it a call to the highest love, to a very special love. And always, when Christ says to a man, "Come, follow me," He asks him what He asked of Simon: "Do you love me *more* than do the others?" Then the heart of man must tremble. The heart of Simon trembled, and the heart of Albino Luciani, before he took the name John Paul I, trembled. A human heart must tremble, because in the question there is also a demand. You must love! You must love more than the others do, if the entire flock of sheep is to be entrusted to you, if the charge, "Feed my lambs, feed my sheep" is to reach the scope which it reaches in the calling and mission of Peter.

The text of St. John's Gospel continues. Christ speaks enigmatic words, He says them to Peter: "When you were younger, you girded yourself and went where you wanted. But when you grow old, someone else will gird you and lead you where you do not want to go." Mysterious, enigmatic words . . .

And so in this summons, directed to Peter by Christ after His Resurrection, Christ's command, "Come, follow me," has a double meaning. It is a summons to service, and a summons to die. . . .[48]

Five days later, on October 13, personal tragedy struck. Bishop Andrzej Deskur was felled by a massive stroke and rushed to the Policlinico Gemelli, where it seemed at first as if he might not live. Deskur and Karol Wojtyła had been friends since the mid-1940s. They were in the seminary together and, after the war, had many Kraków acquaintances in common; Deskur's brother, Joseph, married one of Stefan and Maria Swieżawski's daughters. Andrzej Deskur had lived in Rome for years and was then serving as President of the Pontifical Commission for Social Communications. Ever since Vatican II, Deskur, one of the few Poles in Rome, had been Wojtyła's guide through the Vatican labyrinth. When he became a senior curial official, his home was the place where, over lunches and dinners, Wojtyła met members of the Curia or could talk with other visiting members of the hierarchy in informal surroundings. Wojtyła went immediately to see his friend, and concelebrated Mass for him the next morning, October 14, at the Polish College. That afternoon, he went back to the Gemelli to visit Deskur, who was badly paralyzed and hardly able to speak. The guide was gone.

Karol Wojtyła left his friend's bedside and went straight to the Vatican, where, after singing the "Veni, Creator Spiritus" with his brother cardinals, he was locked into the conclave.

Meanwhile, Marek Skwarnicki had returned to Kraków and told his colleagues that he was going to Wadowice. He was certain Wojtyła was going to be elected pope, and somebody had to get started on the background story. His colleagues thought he had gone a little crazy.[49]

WHO?

Cardinal Jean Villot, the *Camerlengo* responsible for guiding yet another papal interregnum, was not happy with the leaks from Conclave I in August. He remonstrated with the cardinals before Conclave II, reminding them of the oath of secrecy they had sworn. Thus fewer details about the extraordinary process that produced the first non-Italian Pope in 455 years (and the first Slavic Pope ever) have become public. It is known that Wojtyła occupied Cell 91 in the Apostolic Palace, and that he took a Marxist philosophical journal into the Sistine Chapel to read during the lengthy process of ballot counting; when asked by a chaffing colleague whether that wasn't a bit scandalous, he smiled and replied that his conscience was clear. Pope John Paul II himself has provided one small detail about the conclave. At a certain point in the proceedings, his old rector at the Belgian College, Cardinal Maximilian De Fürstenberg, approached him and asked, in words reminiscent of the liturgy for the ordination of a priest, "*Deus adest et vocat te?*" [God is here, and calling you?].[50]

According to the consensus view that has formed over the years, De Fürstenburg's question became a plausible one because, on the first day of voting, October 15, there was a deadlock between the two principal Italian candidates, Cardinal Giuseppe Siri of Genoa and the Great Elector of Conclave I, Cardinal Giovanni Benelli. Unable to find an alternative Italian, the conclave then moved quickly to elect Karol Wojtyła, who had, according to Cardinal Carlo Confalonieri, received some votes at Conclave I, and who was chosen on the eighth ballot at the end of the second day of Conclave II, October 16. No more plausible political explanation of the election of Pope John Paul II has been proposed. Sifting through rumors and hints of conclave politics does not, however, get to the more interesting, and indeed prior, question—why were the cardinals willing to break with centuries of tradition, and in such a dramatic way?

In human terms, the election of a non-Italian, Polish Pope was possible because many members of the College of Cardinals were in a state of spiritual shock after the death of John Paul I. To have felt, as so many evidently did, that Cardinal Luciani was "God's candidate" (Cardinal Basil Hume's phrase after Conclave I), and then to have him removed abruptly from the scene, could only raise the question, "What is God saying to us here?" John Paul I's death, Cardinal Joseph Ratzinger remembered, led the College of Cardinals to an examination of conscience: "What is God's will for us at this moment? We were convinced that the election [of Luciani] was made in correspondence with the will of God, not simply in a human way . . . and if one month after being elected in accordance with the will of God, he died, God had something to say to us."[51] Cardinal William Baum remembers the death of John Paul I as "a message from the Lord, quite out of the ordinary . . . This was an intervention from the Lord to teach us something." That sense of shock led to a conclave experience that Baum thought was "intensely prayerful" and even "more profoundly spiritual" than Conclave I in August, when there was so much talk about sensing the will of God in the quick and painless election of Albino Luciani.[52] The shock of the September Papacy, so abruptly and unexpectedly ended, created the human conditions for "the possibility of doing something new," Cardinal Ratzinger believed.[53]

The deadlock among Italian candidates was the immediate occasion for doing the hitherto unthinkable. The crucial fact that helps explain the eventual outcome was that Conclave II in 1978 took place in the wake of what the College of Cardinals had to regard as an unambiguous signal that something else, something different, something bold was required of them.

The next question, then, is, why Karol Wojtyła?

Cardinal Franz König had come to Conclave II more determined that ever to press for a non-Italian pope. The day before the conclave began he spoke with his old friend, Cardinal Wyszyński, and said, "The conclave will open tomorrow; who is a candidate for you?" The Primate replied that he didn't have a candidate. König replied, "Well, perhaps Poland could present a candidate?" Wyszyński said, "My goodness, you feel *I* should go to Rome? That would be a triumph for the communists." König answered, "No, not you, but there is a second. . . ." To which the Primate replied, "No, he's too young, he's unknown, he could never be pope. . . ."[54]

König was unpersuaded. Wyszyński had not, evidently, fully measured the degree to which Wojtyła had become a major international Catholic figure. König believed that a pope from behind the iron curtain would help break the "mentality of division" that had set in since World War II, so he set out to persuade others. Their initial response was cool, but the novelty of the proposal began to seem less threatening after the Italian deadlock. The Primate's initial reaction notwithstanding, Wojtyła, as we have seen, was far from unknown. Several cardinals had read his 1976 papal retreat meditations, *Sign of Contradiction*, and had been impressed. The Africans, concerned about doctrinal clarity, knew him to be deeply evangelical man and a man of the Council. He was not a curial cardinal, which was attractive to those who thought a break with traditional patterns of Church governance was essential. Wojtyła was a powerful public personality, which was important in light of the positive public response to the brief pontificate of John Paul I. Then there was the *Ostpolitik* of Paul VI. Its diplomatic achievements were very thin, and the archbishop of Kraków had doubts about the strategy it embodied. But by disentangling the Holy See from its post–World War II alignment with the West, the *Ostpolitik* had made the election of a pope from behind the iron curtain thinkable.[55]

The most compelling thing about Wojtyła's candidacy, though, was his record as a diocesan bishop. Once the psychological break with the presumed inevitability of an Italian papacy had been made, this must have been a crucial factor, and perhaps the crucial factor, in the rapid emergence of Karol Wojtyła as a candidate in Conclave II. He had shown that leadership was still possible amid the post-conciliar tension and confusion and against external pressures. According to Cardinal König, that Wojtyła had "had real pastoral experience," that he had shown how to be a bishop in the post–Vatican II Church—that was what made him *papabile*.[56]

The "break" having been made because of the Italian deadlock, things moved very rapidly. As they did, Primate Wyszyński, now fully convinced, reminded his younger colleague of Christ's challenge to Peter fleeing Rome in Sienkiewicz's *Quo Vadis*, and told Wojtyła, simply, "Accept it."[57] Wojtyła's candidacy became irresistible on the fourth and final ballot on October 16. At approximately 5:15 P.M., the cardinals, who had been keeping their own tallies, were formally told what they already knew—Cardinal Karol Wojtyła had received the votes necessary to be elected pope. At a certain point in the tally, Wojtyła had put his head in his hands. Cardinal Hume remembered feeling "desperately sad for the man."[58] Jerzy Turowicz later wrote that, at the moment of his election, Karol Wojtyła was as alone as a man can be. For to be elected Pope meant "a clear cut off from one's previous life, with no possible return."[59] Cardinal König, who was as responsible as anyone for advancing Wojtyła's candidacy, was "very anxious about whether he would accept."[60]

When Cardinal Jean Villot, who had told the cardinals in his sermon *pro elegendo Pontifice* that they "must elect a bridegroom of the Church," stood in front of Wojtyła's desk and asked, *"Acceptasne electionem?"* there was no hesitation.[61] Karol Wojtyła knew the seriousness of the times and the weight of responsibility that was being laid upon him, but he saw in his brothers' votes the will of God. And so, "In the obedience of faith before Christ my Lord, abandoning myself to the Mother of Christ and the Church, and conscious of the great difficulties, *accepto.*"[62] Then, to the second, ritual question, as to what name he would be known, he answered that, because of his devotion to Paul VI and his affection for John Paul I, he would be known as John Paul II. The College of Cardinals burst into prolonged applause, and the new Pope was taken down a flight of stone steps and into the small dressing room off the Sistine Chapel where three white cassocks, large, medium, and small, had been prepared. The dressing room is sometime referred to as a "crying room," because of the emotion that can overwhelm a newly elected pontiff. By this time, though, Pope John Paul II had shed whatever tears there were to be. He walked vigorously back to the Sistine Chapel to receive the homage of the cardinals and immediately broke his first precedent. When the papal master of ceremonies indicated that he should sit in front of the altar for the ceremony, John Paul II replied, "I receive my brothers standing. . . ."[63]

Outside, at the far end of the Via della Conciliazione, a red-orange full moon was visible from St. Peter's Square, where thousands had gathered. Spotlights swept back and forth across the crowd. At 6:15 P.M., the smoke from the small chimney atop the Sistine Chapel started again and the crowd saw that it was white. A voice crackled over the sound system, *"Prova, prova, prova"* [Testing, testing, testing]; then a big, throat-clearing cough; and finally the announcement, *"È bianco, il fumo è bianco, è veramente bianco!"* [It's white, the smoke is white, it's really white!] Inside, Cardinal Wyszyński was telling the new Pope that God had chosen him to lead the Church into the third millennium, an admonition to which John Paul II would frequently allude in the years ahead. In the square, into which thousands more were pouring as news of an election was confirmed by a telephone call from the conclave to the Vatican press office, Sister Emilia Ehrlich was praying fervently that the man about to appear before the crowd wouldn't be Cardinal Wojtyła: "Everybody else was praying for their cardinal; I was praying that they wouldn't take ours."

Cardinal Felici, who would make the public announcement again, turned to Cardinal König on their way to the *loggia* overlooking the square and asked, "How do you spell his name?" Felici jotted down the answer, murmuring "What a terrible spelling . . ." He came out on the *loggia* and began as he had weeks before: *"Annuntio vobis gaudium magnum: habemus Papam!"* The crowd roared, and then waited. Felici continued: *"Eminentissimum ac reverendissimum Dominum Carolum . . ."*— and then paused to draw out the suspense. Someone in the crowd, thinking the cardinals had elected the eighty-five-year-old Carlo Confalonieri, cried, "They've gone mad!" Felici pressed on, checking his hastily scribbled notes, *". . . Sanctae Romanae Ecclesiae Cardinalem Wojtyła, qui sibi nomen imposuit Ioannem Paulum Secundum."*

At the unfamiliar name, chaotic questioning started in the square. *"Chi è?"* [Who?] was the first thing tens of thousands of people asked. *"È nero?"* an Italian said to Jerzy Turowicz—"Is it a black?" *"È Asiatico?"* someone else asked. Sister Emilia Ehrlich didn't have to ask. She turned very pale, and the man beside her said, "What's the matter? Isn't he good?" "No," she answered, "he's much too good."

It was nothing like August, when the crowd—largely Romans, of course—had been in a festive mood from the moment Felici announced Albino Luciani's election. Now they were restive. Who was this *straniero*? What had the cardinals thrust upon them?

John Paul II, who felt the drama and tension as much as any Roman, stepped to the microphone on the *loggia*, brushed a fussy papal master of ceremonies out of the way, and broke precedent again by addressing the crowd, rather than simply giving them the apostolic blessing in Latin as custom dictated. In a clear, sonorous Italian, he introduced himself to his new diocese:

> Praised be Jesus Christ!
> Dear Brothers and Sisters . . .

The crowd began to cheer, hearing their language, sensing his good will, wanting to encourage him.

> . . . We are all still grieved after the death of our most beloved John Paul I. And now the eminent cardinals have called a new bishop of Rome. They have called him from a far country: far, but always near through the communion of faith and in the Christian tradition. . . .

He had, the British actor Sir John Gielgud once said, a perfect sense of timing. Now, the crowd with him, he let them know him as a man and as a fellow Catholic, making the connection between their native Marian piety and his own:

> . . . I was afraid to receive this nomination, but I did it in the spirit of obedience to our Lord Jesus Christ and in total confidence in his Mother, the most holy Madonna.
>
> I don't know if I can make myself clear in your . . . *our* Italian language. If I make a mistake, you will correct me. . . .

Even louder cheers broke out. There was one last thing to do. The rapport established, a theme had to be proclaimed. No one who knew him could doubt it would be Christian humanism:

> . . . And so I present myself to you all, to confess our common faith, our hope, our trust in the Mother of Christ and of the Church, and also to start anew on this road of history and the Church, with the help of God and with the help of men.[64]

"*Wujek* JUST BECAME POPE!"

Polish television, state-controlled, didn't make the announcement for several hours after word of Wojtyła's election had been received; an official party position had to be worked out. Meanwhile, the news had reached the Metropolitan Curia in Kraków by phone, and as Father Stanisław Małysiak remembers, "went around like spilled water." A huge, spontaneous celebration erupted throughout the city as the story spread. The bells of the Mariacki Church started ringing; then the bells at Wawel Cathedral, including the gigantic Sigismund bell, rung on only the most important Church and national occasions; then, it seemed, every bell in Kraków. People poured into the streets with lighted candles and flowers, waving Polish flags, crying, embracing spontaneously. A photograph of Cardinal Wojtyła was placed on the pedestal of the statue of Adam Mickiewicz in the market square, and a mound of flowers began to form in front of his old residence at Franciszkańska, 3. Within an hour, the Mariacki was filled to overflowing and a Mass was hastily organized.[65]

Stanisław Rybicki was home in bed, sick. His wife, Danuta, was out late, and on coming home, found her husband in tears; "Don't be mad that I'm late," she said. "*Wujek* just became Pope," he replied. They cried together, feeling as if they had lost a member of the family. Then they broke open a bottle of wine they had bought on holiday in Czechoslovakia. Their usual vintage, Red Cardinal, had been unavailable. Now, to toast the election of *Wujek*, they drank what they had found—White Cardinal. On hearing the news, Stanisław Rybicki remembered, he couldn't help marveling, "He went from a kayak to the Barque of Peter. . . ."[66]

Teresa Życzkowska was also home in bed with a terrible cold. Her uncle called and said, "*Habemus Papam*—Karolek!" "Don't be stupid," she replied. Her husband then turned on the radio, and the news was confirmed. "We've lost *Wujek*," she thought, shocked.[67]

In Lublin, Jerzy Gałkowski came home and found his house filled with people in the midst of a party. When he asked what on earth was going on, they told him that KUL had just given the world a pope. Gałkowski brought out the wine and they all sat around the TV, eager to see how the government would play the story—which became, in the hands of the communist spin doctors, a triumph of Polish nationalism.[68]

An old priest came pounding on the door of the Swieżawskis' apartment in Warsaw. Maria Swieżawska answered the door, and the old man blurted out the news. She took her head in her hands; thinking what he would do as pope and what could be done to him, she could only say, "*Jezus Maria! Jezus Maria!*"[69]

In Wadowice, Father Edward Zacher was praying in the local church. One of the younger priests came running over from the parish house and said, "We've got a Pope!" "Who is that?" the pastor asked. "It's Lolek!" said the assistant. The old man blinked, felt his heart pounding, and then shouted, "Thanks to heaven!" He ran over to the parish house, got the news confirmed on the radio, and then ran back to the church to ring its bells. People started pouring out into the streets, and within minutes the church was packed. Father Zacher, who had taught Lolek his catechism, tried to speak. But he couldn't. Emotion choked him, and one of his assistants made the formal announcement.[70] When he got himself under a bit of control, Father Zacher kept saying, with a huge smile, "But he did not keep his word, he did not keep his word." At a celebration marking the fiftieth anniversary of Wojtyła's baptism, Zacher had given his fifth sermon in praise of his former student and said there would be only one more, a sixth, when the cardinal was elected Pope. The cardinal had grunted and said there would be no sixth sermon. Now, Zacher told everybody, "he didn't keep his word for the first time in his life."[71] Later, the old man went to the baptismal registry for 1920. Here, in telegraphic phrases, were recorded the milestones of Karol Wojtyła's Christian life: his baptism, confirmation, priestly ordination, episcopal consecration, nomination as archbishop of Kraków, and election to the College of Cardinals. Now, Father Zacher made yet another entry under the name of "Carolus Joseph Wojtyła": *Die 16 X 1978 in Summum Pontificem electus et sibi nomen Ioannem Paulum II imposuit.*[72]

In Prague, Father Miloslav Vlk, a hard-pressed underground priest, got the news from friends the night of October 16. Since his ordination in June 1968, during the last weeks of Alexander Dubček's Prague Spring, Father Vlk had rarely been able to practice his ministry publicly. The state had suspended his license to work out of a church or to celebrate the sacraments in public. To avoid arrest as a vagrant, Vlk, like many other Czechoslovak priests, had taken a menial job, in his case, as a window washer. So he washed windows by day and conducted a clandestine ministry in homes at night. Wojtyła's election was, for Vlk, a sign of "living hope." He was a fellow Slav who knew the communists' "lies and tactics" and would know what to do to help.[73]

Archbishop Francis Arinze of Onitsha, a forty-five-year-old Nigerian, was in Belfast, Northern Ireland, speaking on behalf of the Irish Missionary Union.

The parish priests with whom he was staying didn't know who Wojtyła was. Arinze had met him at the Synod of Bishops and described him to his Irish hosts as "a happy person, a joyful man, who spoke with clarity and courage." "Now," the African told the Irishmen, "we are going to have a bit of clarity in the Church. We are going to know where we stand, clearly, without being aggressive—but clear." John Paul II, Arinze was convinced, would put a "positive" face on Catholicism again.[74]

World press reaction to Wojtyła's election focused, understandably enough, on the novelty of a non-Italian Pope. John Paul II's Polishness was of intense interest to the media, and swarms of reporters descended on Kraków and Wadowice, looking for the inside story on this pope who had come from such an exotic cultural background and whose pre-papal life was so dissimilar to that of his predecessors. Despite widespread misreporting of Wojtyła's position vis-à-vis the Polish regime (i.e., that he was a "moderate," in contrast to Wyszyński the "hard-liner"), some commentators began to intuit that the election of a Slavic Pope, a Pole, might have unexpected consequences in the Cold War. The KGB agreed, and ordered up a special study on how Wojtyła had been elected and what his papacy portended.

It was an exciting, heady time, those days immediately following the appearance of *un Polacco* on the *loggia* overlooking St. Peter's Square. The discomfort of the last years of Paul VI and the shock of John Paul I's death were quickly dissipated. Enthusiasm about the future was in the air. Millions around the world found it deeply moving that the Polish Church, which had suffered so long and had fought so hard against overwhelming odds, had now been rewarded.

The most penetrating comment came from André Frossard, a French journalist who had converted to Catholicism from the fashionable atheism of the intellectual class. Frossard knew the crisis of humanism from the inside and, as an adult, had struggled out of the slough of skeptical cynicism and found liberation in faith. He believed that humanity was going through "a remarkably fluid period of history, one devoid of any solid moral or rational base, a time of collapsing values and ideologies in which he who wishes to go forward has only one choice left . . . to walk on the water."[75]

Now, on seeing the new Pope and sensing in him the power of a witness, André Frossard wired back to his Parisian newspaper: "This is not a Pope from Poland; this is a Pope from Galilee."

8

"Be Not Afraid!"

A Pope for the World

OCTOBER 22, 1978	Pope John Paul II solemnly inaugurates his ministry as universal pastor of the Church.
OCTOBER 29, 1978	John Paul visits the Marian shrine at Mentorella.
OCTOBER 1978	The KGB and the Central Committee of the Soviet Communist Party commission analyses of Karol Wojtyła's election as pope.
NOVEMBER 1978	The Lithuanian Catholic Committee for the Defense of Believers' Rights is formed.
NOVEMBER 5, 1978	John Paul visits the shrines of Italy's patron saints, Francis of Assisi and Catherine of Siena.
NOVEMBER 12, 1978	Pope John Paul II takes possession of his Roman cathedral, the Basilica of St. John Lateran.
NOVEMBER 20, 1978	John Paul meets with Cardinal Iosyf Slipyi, head of the persecuted Greek Catholic Church in Ukraine.
DECEMBER 3, 1978	John Paul II makes his first Roman parish visitation.
DECEMBER 11, 1978	John Paul urges religious freedom for all on the thirtieth anniversary of the Universal Declaration of Human Rights.
DECEMBER 23, 1978	John Paul II sends Cardinal Antonio Samorè to mediate the Beagle Channel border dispute between Argentina and Chile.
DECEMBER 29, 1978	John Paul appoints Franciszek Macharski his successor as Archbishop of Kraków, ordaining him a bishop on January 6, 1979.
JANUARY 28, 1979	John Paul II addresses the third general conference of Latin American bishops in Puebla, Mexico.
FEBRUARY 25, 1979	John Paul presides at the wedding of a Roman street-cleaner's daughter.
MARCH 4, 1979	*Redemptor Hominis,* John Paul's inaugural encyclical.

Papal coronations once began with the new pontiff enthroned on the *sedia gestatoria*, carried above throngs of Romans and pilgrims. The solemn inauguration of the papal ministry of Pope John Paul II, 264th Bishop of Rome, began on October 22, 1978, with the new Pope kneeling in prayer at the tomb of the apostle beneath the dome of St. Peter's Basilica.

Around the dome's interior, in letters six feet high, is the Latin inscription, *Tu es Petrus et super hanc petram aedificabo ecclesiam meam et tibi dabo claves regni caelorum* [You are Peter, and upon this rock I shall build my Church and I shall give you the keys of the kingdom of heaven (*Matthew* 16.18)]. Karol Wojtyła finished his prayer at the tomb of the Galilean fisherman and processed out to the great square in front of the basilica, preceded by 112 cardinals. There, in the course of a simplified but still splendid ritual, he would explain just what Christ's words to Peter meant in the last quarter of the last century of the second millennium of Christian history.

At the beginning of the rite, Cardinal Pericle Felici placed the pallium—a simple yoke of white lamb's wool, decorated with six black crosses and worn by metropolitan archbishops as a sign of their service and their authority—over the shoulders of John Paul II, formally investing him with the symbol of the power he had received six days before, from the moment he had said, "I accept," in the Sistine Chapel. The College of Cardinals, led by its dean, Carlo Confalonieri, lined up in single file so that each cardinal could pledge fidelity to the new Pope. After the dean had genuflected before the seated Pope and made his obedience, precedent was broken again. For the second cardinal in line was not the next-most senior member of the College, but the Primate of Poland, Stefan Wyszyński. He had just begun his genuflection when John Paul II rose from his throne, bent down, seized the old man, and locked him in a long embrace.

After the cardinals' obedience, the inauguration Mass continued. The first reading, in English, was taken from the fifty-second chapter of *Isaiah* and described Jerusalem's joy at its redemption by the Lord. The second reading, in Polish, was from *1 Peter*. In it, the governors of the Church were admonished to lead by example and by love. The Gospel was from *John* 21. As a sign of the Church's universality, Christ's exhortation to Peter to "feed my sheep" was proclaimed in both Latin and Greek.

At the conclusion of the Gospel, John Paul II—clad in white and gold vestments and wearing a white miter—sat on a portable throne facing a crowd of perhaps 300,000, which had spilled out of St. Peter's Square down the Via della Conciliazione. Red and white gladioli, Poland's national colors, surrounded the altar. To his right were some 300 bishops; to his left, 800 dignitaries from around the globe, representatives of the world of power. With his ingrained sense of timing, he looked out over the vast crowd, above which Polish flags were being rhythmically waved back and forth. An international television and radio audience also waited—including tens of millions of his countrymen, witnessing the first Mass in history on Polish state television. An unaccustomed quiet fell over the huge congregation. What would this unexpected Pope say?

He began with an act of faith, in the words of the man at whose tomb he had prayed, a little more than an hour before:

"You are the Christ, the Son of the living God" (*Matthew* 16.16).

Anyone assuming the Office of Peter in the Church, John Paul said, had to begin this way. Peter's confession of faith on the road to Caesarea Philippi was born of "deeply lived and experienced conviction," but it not an act of his will alone. Faith was a gift, and Christ had called Peter blessed "because it was not flesh and blood that revealed this to you but my Father in heaven" (*Matthew* 16.17). Peter's successor could only begin his own Petrine service "on this day and in this place [with] these same words: You are the Christ, the Son of the Living God."

Salvation history, the new Pope proposed, did not run parallel with human history. Salvation history was human history read in its true depth, against the horizon of its true destiny. Since the Church was immersed in history as a witness to that truth, it was important to understand that Peter's confession was not just about Peter and Jesus. It was the starting point of the Church, and in Peter's act of faith, the history of salvation took on a new, "ecclesial dimension." The story of the Church, a pilgrim in history, was *humanity's* story, rightly understood.

Christ had brought humanity close to "the mystery of the living God." No one else could do this but God's own Son, and he had done it in a way that we could recognize, as one like us. Christ, the Son of the living God, had not only told us about his Father, he had told us "the ultimate and definitive truth" about ourselves. Jesus Christ, John Paul proclaimed, *is* the truth about the human condition. That was what the Church must tell the world, believers and seekers, skeptics and doubters. And so he had a request to make: "Please, listen once again. . . ."

To bear witness to the truth about God and about humanity, Peter had been led to Rome. "Perhaps," John Paul said, "the fisherman of Galilee did not want to come here. Perhaps he would have preferred to stay there, on the shores of the lake of Genesareth, with his boat and his nets." But he was obedient, and he came, and he stayed, obedient to the point of martyrdom, the fullness of Christian witness. Now a new Bishop of Rome had come to the city. Perhaps he, too, would have preferred to remain in another place. Yet he had come to Rome, "full of trepidation, conscious of his unworthiness," to make the witness required of him. He had come to Peter's city prepared to spend out his life in service to the truth that human beings, redeemed in Christ, were so much greater than they imagined.

This new Bishop of Rome was "a son of Poland." Yet "from this moment he, too, becomes a Roman. Yes—a Roman." And he was a Roman not only by office, but because he had been, in a sense, a Roman all along. He was "the son of a nation . . . which has always remained faithful to this See of Rome."

The world might find it odd that a Pole was now Bishop of Rome. The Church should not.

This new Bishop of Rome would not be crowned with the *triregnum*, the papal tiara. Rightly or wrongly, John Paul noted, the tiara had come to be considered a symbol of the Pope's temporal power. Today, after the Second Vatican Council, the Church was not a Church of power, but a Church of evangelical witness. The tiara could express something else, though: the threefold office of Christ as priest, prophet, and king, which Christ had bestowed on the people of the Church, the Body of Christ in time and history. That was what the papacy, and indeed all authority in the Church, was for: "service, service with a single purpose—to ensure that all the People of God share in the threefold mission of Christ and always remain under the power of the Lord." "The mystery of the cross and resurrection" was the only power the Church possessed and the only power the Church should want: "the absolute and yet sweet and gentle power of the Lord," which "responds to the whole depths of the human person, to his loftiest aspirations of intellect, heart, and will." The language of charity and truth, not the language of force, was the Church's language.

This new Bishop of Rome intended to be a servant. And so, before the eyes of the world, John Paul II prayed, "Christ, make me become and remain the servant of your unique power, the servant of your sweet power, the servant of your power that knows no eventide. Make me a servant. Indeed, the servant of your servants."

And the message of this "servant of the servants of God" was the call of Christ to his disciples: *Be not afraid!*

> Be not afraid to welcome Christ and accept his power. Help the Pope and all those who wish to serve Christ and with Christ's power to serve the human person and the whole of mankind.
>
> Be not afraid. Open wide the doors for Christ. To his saving power open the boundaries of states, economic and political systems, the vast fields of culture, civilization, and development.
>
> Be not afraid. Christ knows "what is in man." He alone knows it.

The world, he reflected, was afraid of itself and of its future. To all those who were afraid, to all those caught in the great loneliness of the modern world, "I ask you . . . I beg you, let Christ speak to [you]. He alone has words of life, yes, of eternal life."

The new Bishop of Rome thanked those who had come to share this day—the representatives of the nations, the hierarchy of the Church, priests and religious, pilgrims in their tens of thousands, all those listening or watching on radio and television. He added greetings in English, French, German, Spanish, Portuguese, Russian, Czech, Ukrainian, and Lithuanian. The most heartfelt were those he spoke in Polish, citing the great Mickiewicz, poet laureate of Polish freedom:

My dear fellow-countrymen . . . Everything I could say would fade into insignificance compared with what my heart feels, and your hearts feel, at this moment. So let us leave aside words. Let there remain just great silence before God, the silence that becomes prayer. I ask you: be with me at Jasna Góra and everywhere. Do not cease to be with the Pope who prays with the words of the poet, "Mother of God, you who defend bright Częstochowa and shine at Ostrabrama. . . ."

He appealed first to his fellow Catholics, then to all Christians, for prayer. Finally, John Paul turned again to the world. The world might think that the Pope was only for the Church. The Pope could not think of himself that way. And so he appealed to all humanity, "Pray for me. Help me to be able to serve you. Amen."

When the three-hour inaugural Mass ended, about 1 P.M., John Paul II didn't go directly back into the basilica. In another break with precedent, he walked alone toward the enormous throng in the square. He greeted and blessed a group of handicapped people who had been brought to the Mass in wheelchairs. A small boy broke through the barriers to give him flowers, and an officious Italian prelate tried to shoo him away. John Paul II grabbed the boy and hugged him. Although he couldn't embrace the whole crowd, he could salute them. So he took the great silver papal crosier in both hands and shook it at the cheering throng, as if it were a sword of the spirit wrenched free of the stone in which it had been imprisoned.

When he finally returned to the papal apartment, the cheers continued and he came to the window several times to wave back. They only dispersed when John Paul II sent them home with a laugh: "It's time for everyone to eat lunch," he said, "even the Pope."[1]

DETERMINED TO LEAD

The papacy is unlike any other office in the world, and not simply because of its institutional longevity. The pope is called the "Supreme *Pontiff*," a contraction of the Latin *pontifex*, "bridge builder." A bridge goes from somewhere to somewhere. What does the Supreme Pontiff bridge? He is a bridge between God and humanity; between the Roman Catholic Church and other Christian Churches and ecclesial communities; between the Roman Catholic Church and Judaism; between the Roman Catholic Church and other world religions; between the Roman Catholic Church and the worlds of political, economic, and cultural power; between the center of the Church's unity and the college of bishops dispersed in local Churches throughout the world. As the custodian of an authoritative teaching tradition, the pope is also, according to Catholic theology, a "bridge" between historical humanity and the truth about its origin, nature, and destiny.

To be pope is to take on a task that is, by precise theological definition, impossible. Like every other office in the Church, the papacy exists for the sake of holiness. The office, though, is a creature of time and space, and holiness is eternal. No one, not even a pope who is a saint, can fully satisfy the office's demands. Yet the office, according to the Church's faith, is of the will of God, and the office cannot fail, although the officeholder will always fall short of the mark. That distinction between the office and the man who holds it is a consolation to any pope. According to one distinguished theologian, it is also "unutterably terrible." The office reflects the unity of person and mission in Jesus Christ, of whom the pope is vicar. Every pope, the saints as well as the scoundrels, "stands at an utterly tragic place," because he cannot be fully what the office demands. If he tries to be that, he arrogantly makes himself the equal of the Lord. If he consoles himself too easily with the thought that he must, necessarily, fail, he betrays the demand that the office makes of him, the demand of radical love. The Office of Peter always reflects Christ's words to Peter—that, because of the depth of his love, he will be led where he does not want to go (see *John* 21.18).[2]

Providing leadership to the Roman Catholic Church and being present to all the other communities to which the pope is a "bridge" is an extraordinarily complex task. Its inherent complexity is magnified by the fact that, misconceptions notwithstanding, the pope is not an absolute monarch. During Vatican II, Paul VI once proposed that the *Dogmatic Constitution on the Church* include the phrase that the pope is "accountable to the Lord alone." This was rejected by the Council's Theological Commission, which noted that "the Roman Pontiff is also bound to revelation itself, to the fundamental structure of the Church, to the sacraments, to the definitions of earlier Councils, and other obligations too numerous to mention."[3] Among the latter is his obligation to the truth of things as they are, which is another limit on his authority. A distinguished philosopher, who considers himself an extremely orthodox Catholic, once told a gathering that "If the Pope said that '2+2=5' I'd believe him." Another distinguished philosopher, no less committed to the papacy, gave the far more orthodox reply: "If the Holy Father said that '2+2=5,' I would say publicly, 'Perhaps I have misunderstood His Holiness's meaning.' Privately, I would pray for his sanity." The pope is not an *authoritarian* figure who issues arbitrary decisions by virtue of his own unbridled will. The pope is the custodian of an *authoritative* tradition of teaching, a "magisterium," that defines the boundaries of the Church. He is its servant, not its master.[4]

For Karol Wojtyła, who had long been convinced that truth is liberating, the "limitations" of the papacy were not constraints at all. The truth that binds and frees at the same time was, in his judgment, an instrument for exercising the Office of Peter in service to human freedom. And he intended to exercise that office according to the biblical model of *Luke* 22.32, in which Christ instructs Peter that his special task among the apostles is to "strengthen your brethren."

In the first days of his papacy, more than one observer remarked that John Paul II seemed to have been "doing this all his life." One of the men who elected him, Cardinal William Baum, a close student of Church history, said years later, "I cannot think of anyone who was more prepared [for the papacy] than Cardinal Wojtyła."[5] Cardinal Agostino Casaroli, who would have occasion in the future to be nervous about just how this new-model Pope was conducting his office, confessed in his retirement that "Poland was too small for the large personality of Cardinal Wojtyła . . . [which was] more fitting for a pope."[6] This was not simply a clerical view of a particularly gifted member of the club. The Kraków physicist Jerzy Janik knew his old friend Karol Wojtyła well, and thought that "he was well-adjusted from the beginning to the world-scale."[7] His press spokesman for many years, the Spanish layman Joaquín Navarro-Valls, agreed—John Paul II "felt at ease" in his office from the beginning.[8]

Although this ease was frequently attributed to the skills of an accomplished actor quickly adjusting to a new role, that is not how John Paul II understood it. There was no pause between his ministry as archbishop of Kraków and his ministry as Bishop of Rome, he said, because of his "confidence in the Holy Spirit, who was calling to the See of Peter a cardinal with this experience, with this background"—which must have meant that "this background is useful for the universal Church."[9] The new Pope did not think he required extensive instruction on how to be a bishop from those accustomed to managing popes. He had been a bishop for twenty years and the leader of a historic archdiocese for fourteen. And he was determined to mark visibly the continuity between the two experiences—even if that, too, involved breaking precedent.

Archbishop Bruno Heim, the Church's acknowledged authority on ecclesiastical heraldry, prepared seven sketches of a coat-of-arms for John Paul II. The new Pope declined them all and kept the arms he had borne as archbishop of Kraków: a large capital "M" beneath a cross, representing Mary beneath the cross of Christ, with the Montfort-inspired motto, *Totus Tuus.* Archbishop Heim sniffed that "the practice of using initials is completely opposed to the true heraldic diction and reminds one of the commercial advertisement or trademark."[10] Bishop Jacques Martin, Prefect of the Papal Household, was another offended expert, noting that "the coat of arms of this Polish Pope is far more expressive in its spiritual meaning than in its heraldic conformity."[11] Though it may seem a small matter, it was a declaration of independence by the new Pope and an expression of his conviction that history should note that he had come to the See of St. Peter from the See of St. Stanisław. Every structure in the Vatican that would be built or altered in his pontificate would bear the distinctive, stubbornly nonconformist arms of the former archbishop of Kraków.

He had faced the emotional upheaval of assuming the impossible task of the papacy before and during the conclave that elected him. From the moment he answered Cardinal Villot, "*Accepto,*" he was determined to lead—and to do so in the way he had led since his consecration as a bishop, twenty years before.

EARTHQUAKE IN THE CURIA

John Paul II may have felt at ease in the papacy from the beginning, but some of his collaborators did not feel entirely comfortable with him. If his accession to the papacy was a *terremoto*, an earthquake, then the quake's epicenter was the Church's central administration, the Roman Curia. The world press, the Soviet leadership, and the College of Cardinals were all shocked, in different ways, by the election of John Paul II. The most shocked of all were the Italian priests, bishops, and cardinals of the Curia.

Rome, after all, is an Italian diocese. And if "Italian" was a concept with no political expression until far into the Italian domination of the papacy, the idea that the Roman episcopate was an "Italian" prerogative had real cultural and linguistic meaning for the operation of the Roman Curia. Rome's 2,700-year civic history, and the Roman See's endurance when the city itself had fallen on hard times, were historical realities that gave perspective to the pressures of present-day decision making in a global Church. "We think in centuries here," a classic curial comment, can, in fact, be a helpful attitude in a media-driven age of constant, rapid change.

On the other hand, the Curia, and especially its Italian members, had gotten used to "managing" popes. That proprietary instinct gradually extended to a sense of managing the entire Church, so that local Churches became branch offices of Roman Catholic Church, Inc. In light of Vatican II's teaching on the collegiality of bishops, this was no longer a viable model. Those who "think in centuries," however, can sometimes be late in getting the word of change.

During the last years of Paul VI, it became almost *de rigueur* for journalists to portray the Curia as a nest of ambitious vipers at worst and a den of self-serving rascals at best. Neither image touches the truth of the matter, or the crucial issue that John Paul II faced on his election. One of John Paul's closest associates has said, privately, that of the several hundred figures he had dealt with in the Roman Curia, only one or two could be called scoundrels, a very good percentage in any human organization. The primary problem with the Roman Curia in October 1978 when John Paul II became Pope was not rascality but attitude—an unwarranted, if historically understandable, devotion to "the way we do things here," which many Italian Curialists in particular had come to identify with God's will for the Church. *Gli stranieri*, the foreigners, don't really fit in well here, a very senior curial official once said, quite without embarrassment. A Pope who had his own ideas about how things ought to be done, who had tested those ideas and found them true in direct pastoral practice, was inevitably going to be resented in that kind of environment. Add to this the natural disappointment of "losing" the papacy to *gli stranieri*, and one of the problems confronting John Paul II at the beginning of his pontificate comes into focus.

From the outset, John Paul II showed that he was not a man to be "managed." At his first press conference, he once again broke precedent by walking through the crowd of journalists in the Hall of Benedictions, fielding impromptu questions in English, Italian, French, Polish, and German. When one of the papal "managers" present tried to stop him from descending from the dais, John Paul simply shook him off. Someone asked whether he would go to Poland. "If they'll let me," came the papal response. Another reporter asked whether he would continue to ski. "If they'll let me," the Pope said again.[12] In each case, everyone knew who "they" were.[13] John Paul II was also aware of the strain between his immediate predecessor and certain members of the Curia, and he was determined that "they" would not run, or ruin, his life.

As his Kraków years had shown, he was not a leader given to micromanaging the work of others or summarily dismissing difficult subordinates. He had learned that establishing and pursuing his priorities was a far better way to be a bishop than struggling against a bureaucracy. He, too, could think in centuries, and he knew that certain encrusted aspects of the curial style would eventually fall off the Barque of Peter like so many barnacles. Why waste energy, and why hurt individuals, by forcing change now, as long as the barnacles didn't interfere with the pursuit of the priorities? He was singularly uninterested in bureaucratic intrigues and other institutional trifles, so he could simply ignore many of the things that agitated or obsessed some of his collaborators.

As Pope, Karol Wojtyła could lead the Church and challenge the world by embodying a new, pastorally and evangelically assertive style of papal ministry. Or he could spend his pontificate wrestling with the Roman Curia. Given those options, the only one real choice was to lead, not by fighting an internal war of attrition, but by creating new facts—immediately, by new initiatives, and over time, by new appointments.[14] At the same time, he left no doubt as to who was in charge. He did not ask anyone's permission to keep doing, from the See of St. Peter, what he had been doing in the See of St. Stanisław, just as he hadn't asked permission to visit his friend Bishop Deskur in the hospital immediately after Conclave II ended. Deskur, his former guide through the Roman maze, said that he knew what his role in the new pontificate would be: "My mission now," he said, "is to support the Holy Father with my suffering."[15]

THE ACTIVIST

Even before his installation, John Paul II began to lay out, in word and deed, many of the key themes that would shape his pontificate for two decades.

He had asked the cardinals to remain in conclave with him on October 16, the night of his election. After sleeping in his old cell, 91, he concelebrated Mass with the electors the next morning and, in an address after the liturgy, gave them and the Church a preview of what was coming.

His first task and "definitive duty," he told them, was to complete the implementation of the Second Vatican Council, an "event of utmost importance in the almost two thousand year history of the Church." In that implementation, the leaders of the Church would have to "take once again into our hands the 'Magna Carta' of the Council, the Dogmatic Constitution *Lumen Gentium*, so that with renewed and invigorating zeal we may meditate on the nature and function of the Church, its way of being and acting." This was the strategy he had discussed with Cardinal Ratzinger before Conclave I: the Church's proposal to the modern world had to be distinctively Catholic and Christian if the Church was to fulfill its unique mission "in the paths of life and of history." After pledging himself to implementing the Council's teaching on collegiality through the Synod of Bishops, he committed his pontificate to furthering the "lofty" cause of Christian unity and to developing the Church's mission to help build peace and justice among nations, singling out religious freedom for special attention.[16]

On October 19 he met again with the College of Cardinals in his first formal papal audience, reflecting on the "great courage" it had taken for them to call him to be Bishop of Rome. He recalled that each new cardinal swears to be faithful to Christ "unto the shedding of your blood," and he linked that pledge to the commitment of those countless, unknown Christians around the world "who are still not spared the experience of prison, sufferings, and humiliation for Christ." It was the second explicit reference to the persecuted Church in three days. At the end of the audience another precedent fell. After giving the College his apostolic blessing, he asked then to join him in imparting that same blessing to the whole Church as a sign of their brotherhood and the Church's universality.[17]

On October 20, John Paul II received the diplomatic corps accredited to the Holy See. He stressed that the men and women he was meeting were "not only the representatives of governments, but also of peoples and nations," ancient countries with long histories and new countries full of possibilities. In contributing to human development, the Church recognized a "special richness in the diversity and plurality of . . . cultures, histories, and languages," some of which the Church had helped form. The sometimes tragic history of Poland, he said, had taught him "to respect the specific values of each nation and each people, their traditions and their rights among other peoples." The Holy See had no pretensions to power, as the world understood power. Its aim was to contribute "above all to the formation of consciences." The Church did not need special privileges to do that. Justice, however, demanded religious freedom for all, including the right to worship and the believer's right "to participate fully in public life." Although a brief discourse, it marked the first step in a new papal approach to international politics, in which the conversion of culture was the first priority and religious freedom was the nonnegotiable litmus test of a just society.[18]

The press conference followed on October 21. The Pope thanked the journalists for their extensive coverage of "the really historic labor of the great

Pope Paul VI," for "having made so familiar the smiling face and the evangelical attitude of my immediate predecessor, John Paul I," and for "the favorable
coverage" of the events surrounding his election. It was, he said, "always difficult to read events and to enable others to read them." For his part, he wanted
journalists to find "the help they need from competent" Church bodies. Journalism, he went on to say, was a kind of vocation, a "service which the Church
and humanity appreciate." All the more reason then, to be grateful for the
freedom in which some journalists work: "Think yourselves lucky to enjoy it!"
Once again, without fanfare but also without flinching, another signal had
been sent to the masters of the land from which he had come.

They were not happy with him, to put it gently. The party line, expressed
on TV and in a telegram of congratulations from Poland's communist chief-
tains, was that his election was a great triumph for the Polish nation.[19] John
Paul II quickly replied, in an October 21 telegram to Polish Communist Party
leader Edward Gierek, that the history of the Polish nation had "been bound
up for a thousand years with the mission and service of the Catholic Church."[20]
The regime was, by its own standards, generous with passports for Poles wanting to attend the October 22 inauguration in Rome, but couldn't resist using
even that process for petty harassment, score settling, and minor espionage.
Jacek Woźniakowski and Tadeusz Mazowiecki, two prominent Catholic writers
and friends of the new Pope, were denied passports. The son of one of the
Pope's *Środowisko* friends was told that he could have a passport and the price
of his ticket if he agreed to tell the SB what was happening in his department
at the Jagiellonian University.[21] Polish TV agreed to devote three hours to the
inaugural Mass. John Paul II made sure that the ceremony was exactly that
long, so that the last image transmitted back to his homeland was his blessing
the vast crowd with the papal crosier, not Rome-based Polish communist commentators applying on-site "spin" to the story.[22]

The Polish communist leadership was also the target of sarcasm from its
fraternal socialist ally. At the inaugural Mass, the Soviet ambassador to Italy
turned to Polish President Henryk Jabłoński and acidly observed that "the
greatest achievement of the Polish People's Republic was to give the world a
Polish pope."[23] Giancarlo Pajetta, an Italian communist with much experience
in Poland, tried to put the best face on things by suggesting that "At least our
Polish comrades won't have him breaking their balls any more."[24] He was
wrong about that, too.

On October 23, the day after his installation, John Paul II held an emotional farewell audience for Polish pilgrims in the new Vatican audience hall.
He sent the Polish bishops home with two letters. The first was given to the
Primate with the request that he and the bishops distribute it throughout the
country. In it, he told his countrymen that "it was difficult to think and speak"
of leaving the See of Stanisław for Rome "without a very deep emotion. It seems
that the human heart—and in particular the Polish heart—is not sufficient to
contain such an emotion." Because of World War II and the repression of the

communist years, the Church in Poland had become "the Church of a special witness." Without that witness, "it is not possible to understand why a Polish pope is speaking to you today." How could any of this have happened, he asked—the election of John Paul I on the feast of Our Lady of Częstochowa, his wholly unexpected death, a Polish cardinal called to St. Peter's Chair, his acceptance by the Church—without the finger of God being on it?

He then addressed Cardinal Wyszyński: "Venerable and beloved Cardinal Primate, allow me to tell you just what I think. This Polish Pope, who today, full of fear of God, but also of trust, is beginning a new pontificate, would not be on Peter's chair were it not for your faith which did not retreat before prison and suffering. . . ." When Wyszyński tried, once again, to genuflect before the Pope and kiss his ring, John Paul II, once again, bent down and drew the old man into a tight embrace.[25]

The Primate may have been first among the brethren, but the Pope did not forget his other countrymen—including Poland's communists—in fitting this great drama into a history that, he insisted, had a divine scriptwriter. They were all caught up, he told them, in something much larger than they could understand. It was a patriotism that had "nothing in common with a narrow nationalism or chauvinism." What they were feeling sprang "from the law of the human heart" and bore witness to the nobility of the human spirit, which had been tested harshly "many times during our difficult history."

Leaving was hard, and there was no sense denying it. "But if such is Christ's will, it is necessary to accept it, and therefore I accept it." He asked the prayers of all Poland, then closed with his blessing, "and I do so not only by virtue of my mission as bishop and pope, but also to meet a deep need of my heart." As for his "beloved Kraków," he asked, in a second letter sent to the archdiocese through auxiliary bishop Juliusz Groblicki, that the archdiocese believe that "coming to Rome for the conclave, I had no other desire than to come back among you . . . but Christ's will was different." Perhaps he could come back for the jubilee of St. Stanisław and the closing of the archdiocesan Synod.[26]

Four days later, in his second week as Pope, the pain of separation was still clear in a letter to his cousin Felicja Wiadrowska, the daughter of his mother's sister, Maria:

> Dear Lusia:
>
> God has decreed that I remain in Rome. It is indeed an unusual edict of Holy Providence. These days I think a lot of my parents and of Mundek, but I also think of your mother and father, who were always so good to me . . . You are the only one left living of all my closest family . . . John Paul II[27]

Audiences for the College of Cardinals and for the diplomatic corps accredited to the Holy See were normal papal events, as were a new pope's meetings with old friends and colleagues. But the managers of popes had to adjust quickly to the distinctive cast of characters with whom the new pontiff was engaged—and intended to remain engaged. Jerzy Kluger, his wife and children were invited to stop by and meet his old classmate on October 23. A few days earlier, the managers had first met Sister Emilia Ehrlich. After consoling the nun who badly wanted Cardinal Benelli to become pope—"She was crying because her cardinal wasn't elected and I was crying because mine was."—Sister Emilia had gone back to her studies at the Pontifical Biblical Institute. On the Thursday after Wojtyła's election, a functionary tracked her down there and said, "I don't understand it, but they're telephoning and saying that the Pope wants to see you." Sister Emilia took the bus to the Vatican and presented herself at the Porta Sant'Anna. "They were quite scandalized. They gave me two Swiss Guards, like I was a prisoner, and walked me for quite some distance." When she saw the Pope, Sister Emilia "had a color shock: he came in all in white, and I had never seen him that way." They stood there for a moment, looking at each other, and then Sister Emilia started to cry. The Pope said, "Let's not go soft," and told her that he needed help dealing with the blizzard of requests for the rights to his poetry that had been pouring in from publishers. He wanted her to take care of it and told her that she should "see the Secretariat of State." Sister Emilia didn't know where that was, but set off to find it, no doubt to the further amazement of the managers of popes.[28]

In the weeks after his inaugural Mass, John Paul II regularly broke out of the gilded cage that was now his home and office. On October 29, he went by helicopter to the Marian shrine at Mentorella, cared for by the Resurrectionist Fathers, a group of priests whose nineteenth-century founding was inspired by Adam Mickiewicz. As word of the Pope's visit spread, thousands of people flocked to the shrine from the neighboring areas. John Paul II apologized to the local authorities for causing such trouble, and then explained why he had come. Mentorella, he said, was a place that had "helped me a great deal to pray" during his visits to Rome. Now that he was a Roman, he wanted to come back, because "prayer . . . [is] the first task and almost the first signal of the Pope, just as it is the first condition of his service in the Church and in the world."[29]

A week later, on Sunday, November 5, John Paul, in his new office as Primate of Italy, presented himself to his people at the shrines of Italy's two patrons, St. Francis of Assisi and St. Catherine of Siena. After flying to Assisi, the Pope told an enormous crowd at the basilica that, because he "was not born in this land, I feel more than ever the need of a spiritual 'birth' in it." That was why he had come to Assisi, where St. Francis, the *Poverello*, "wrote Christ's Gospel in incisive characters in the hearts of the men of his time"— the new Bishop of Rome needed his prayers. Returning to Rome that evening, he drove to the church of Santa Maria sopra Minerva, within whose high altar rest the remains of Catherine of Siena. Standing beside the relics of this corrector of popes—the woman who, by force of will, had virtually compelled Pope Gregory XI to return to Rome from Avignon in 1376—John Paul reflected on "how deeply the mission of women is inscribed in the mystery of the Church," and suggested that he would "say many things about this theme" in the future.[30]

On Thursday, November 9, John Paul II met the priests of Rome in the Hall of Benedictions. The following Sunday, November 12, he took possession of his cathedral as Bishop of Rome, the Basilica of St. John Lateran.[31] Or, to put it more accurately, he came to ask his diocese to accept him: "As you welcomed my predecessors throughout the centuries . . . I beg you to welcome me, too." He also had a challenge for the Romans, residents of a city where Catholic practice was often lax: "Go in spirit to the banks of the Jordan, where John the Baptist taught—John, who is the patron saint of this basilica, the cathedral of Rome. Listen once more to what he said, indicating the Christ: 'Behold the Lamb of God, who takes away the sins of the world.' . . . Believe with renewed faith . . . in Christ, the Savior of the world!"[32]

John Paul met with thirteen thousand cheering teenagers on November 29, and asked them to "tell everyone that the Pope counts a great deal on the young."[33] On December 3, the first Sunday free on his calendar, he made his first Roman parish visitation to the church in Garbatello where he had worked during his student days.[34] The following Sunday, he was at the Vatican "parish" church of St. Anne's just inside the Porta Sant'Anna, where he began his homily to "my fellow parishioners" with the words of St. Augustine: *Vobis sum . . . episcopus, vobiscum sum christianus* [For you I am a bishop; with you I am a Christian].[35]

The next day, December 11, the thirtieth anniversary of the Universal Declaration of Human Rights, he urged that "freedom of religion for everyone and for all people must be respected by everyone everywhere."[36] It was a theme to which he returned in his homily at midnight Mass on Christmas Eve, in his World Day of Peace message on January 1, and in his New Year's address to the diplomatic corps on January 12, 1979. During his first two months in office, John Paul II conducted the most assertive papal defense of religious freedom in the thirteen years since the Second Vatican Council had adopted *Dignitatis Humanae.*

The new Pope took his first diplomatic initiative two days before Christmas, 1978, when he sent Cardinal Antonio Samorè to Chile and Argentina to mediate a solution to the Beagle Channel boundary dispute, which was threatening to break out into open warfare. The Holy See had not served as an international mediator since settling the 1885 dispute between Spain and Germany over the Caroline Islands, and some of his more cautious advisers worried that Vatican prestige would suffer if the attempted mediation failed. John Paul had a different view—as he put it to a Vatican diplomat who congratulated him on his courage, "Do you think that, after accepting this office, I could stand by and watch those two Catholic countries go to war?"[37] Samorè's mission, a classic diplomatic shuttle between Buenos Aires and Santiago, was a success. On January 9, 1979, the two countries formally requested Holy See mediation of the boundary dispute and forswore the use of armed force during the mediation. Given the anxiety in the Vatican Secretariat of State, it was only the direct, personal initiative of John Paul II that prevented a small but bloody war.[38]

The Romans, meanwhile, had decided that they loved their new bishop. In his *Urbi et Orbi* message "to the city and the world" on Christmas Day, he had told them that Christmas was the "feast of man." "Every human being . . . unique and unrepeatable" had been given the power to become a child of God, for God, by entering human history in the stable at Bethlehem, had given human nature an unsurpassable dignity.[39] The next day, hundreds of Romans came back to St. Peter's Square. It was a Tuesday, and neither a general audience nor the recitation of the Angelus was scheduled, but the crowd began to clap and call for the Pope. He came to the window shortly before noon, prayed the Angelus with the crowd, and teased them: "I rejoice with you and I wonder why you have come. Perhaps you came to see if the Pope is at home on the second day of Christmas. And then I think you have come because today is a really beautiful day and attracts one outside. But the Pope has to stay at home because he never knows when people are coming to recite the Angelus." The crowd continued to cheer, and the banter continued: "I do not understand what you are saying. You do not have microphones. But I understand that you love the Pope. Thank you and a Merry Christmas to all. . . . Blessed be the name of the Lord."[40]

A few weeks later, yet another precedent was broken. Popes do not usually perform weddings. This Pope, determined to remain a pastor, was different. During the Christmas season, he had visited the Christmas crib or crèche set up by Roman street cleaners near the Vatican. Vittoria Janni, a street cleaner's daughter, asked the Pope if he would perform her wedding. John Paul II smiled and agreed. Vittoria Janni and Mario Maltese were married at a Mass celebrated by the Pope on February 25 in the Vatican's Pauline Chapel.[41] Four days later, John Paul met with 13,000 members of the Italian military, mugged for the cameras in the plumed helmet of a *bersagliere*, and quoted Pascal: "Outside Jesus Christ we do not know what is our life, or our death, God or ourselves."[42] Two days later, he began leading the First Saturday Rosary internationally broadcast on Vatican Radio. Other Roman clergy had usually led the half-hour ceremony of prayer; listener demand caused the change.[43]

On the solemnity of the Epiphany, January 6, 1979, John Paul II conferred episcopal ordination on the man he had named his successor as Archbishop of Kraków—Franciszek Macharski, an old friend, fellow seminarian, and one of the key leaders of the Synod of Kraków. After the ceremony in St. Peter's, at a meeting with the new archbishop and those who had come to Rome with him from Kraków, the Pope presented his successor with the simple gold pectoral cross that Pope Pius X had given Adam Stefan Sapieha in 1911 and which Karol Wojtyła had worn during his fourteen years as archbishop: "This," he said to Macharski, "belongs to the archbishop of Kraków." Macharski, knowing how much the Pope loved the Sapieha cross, had an exact replica made and gave it to John Paul II some months later. The Pope has worn the duplicate Sapieha cross ever since.[44]

Within four months of his election, the nonstop Pope had reinvigorated the world's most ancient office, making clear, by his actions as well as his words, that evangelization and reevangelization were his pastoral priorities. He had demonstrated that he intended to exercise his titles as "Bishop of Rome" and "Primate of Italy" far more directly than his Italian predecessors. He had let the young people of the world know that they were his favorites and his great hope. He had demonstrated his reverence and concern for marriage and family life. He had deftly deployed the traditional diplomatic levers at his command, even as he had begun to reorient the Church's interaction with the worlds of power. His forthright defense of religious freedom sent unmistakable signals throughout the world, and particularly throughout the communist leadership. This was a Pope who would not be bound by the usual rules, who would deliberately bring the pressure of world opinion to bear on behalf of human rights.

CHANGING THE ROUTINE

In addition to doing things that popes simply hadn't done before, John Paul II did them at a pace that was dizzying by the standards of the institutional culture in which he now found himself.

He rose at 5:30 A.M. ("not easily," as he once put it), and after dressing went straight to his chapel for the best part of his day, more than an hour of private prayer, kneeling before a modern crucifix and an icon of the Black Madonna. What he once called the "geography" of his prayer extended beyond the world crises and the concerns of local Churches he brought before the Lord. It included the hundreds of personal prayer requests the household nuns took from his correspondence and typed on sheets they placed inside the top of his prie-dieu.[45] At 7:30 A.M., he concelebrated Mass with his secretaries and other priests, before a small congregation that almost always included invited guests as well as the nuns who cared for the papal apartment. At 8:30 he had breakfast, often with guests invited to stay after Mass.

From 9:30 to 11 A.M., he did his writing. As in Kraków, he often wrote in the chapel, before the Blessed Sacrament, and he retained the lifelong habit of putting a brief prayer at the top of every manuscript page. Here was where he worked on his encyclicals, apostolic letters and exhortations, and audience addresses. In the most important cases, he wrote his own drafts and then sent them out to be reviewed by trusted colleagues. In other instances, he worked from a draft text prepared by the Curia or by other consultants. At 11 A.M., his official appointments, including audiences for different groups, began and lasted for two and a half hours. At 1:30 P.M., he had *pranzo*, lunch, with guests. The most ample meal of the day included an antipasto, a pasta, a meat or fish course with numerous vegetables, a *dolce* (his favorite, visitors noted), and fresh fruit, served with wines and mineral water. When lunch was over, usually before 3 P.M., he took a ten-minute *riposo* and then tried to get some exercise, walking in the Vatican gardens, for example, while the Curia and the rest of Rome took their more ample midday naps. He prayed at least one of the several rosaries he said each day while he walked.

A locked pouch containing documents, correspondence, and other official business came in from the Secretariat of State at 3 P.M. His secretaries sorted it out, and presented what had to be signed or decided to the Pope; sometimes the decision was "We need to study this some more."[46] In the late afternoon, official appointments began again. He met in scheduled, formal audiences with the Cardinal Secretary of State, the Cardinal Prefect of the Congregation for the Doctrine of the Faith, the Cardinal Prefect of the Congregation for Bishops, the *Sostituto* (the deputy chief of the Secretariat of State and the Pope's de facto chief-of-staff), and the "foreign minister," the Secretary of the Section for Relations with States, once each week, and more often if necessary.

Dinner was at 7:30 P.M., usually with guests, and concluded about 9 P.M. Another pouch came in from the Secretariat of State at this point. For the rest of the evening John Paul read, did more writing, conferred with his personal staff, or, when the technology became available, checked the incoming faxes until 11 P.M., when he went to bed.

Relaxation, for John Paul II, did not usually mean music or movies, although he occasionally watched the latter and thought they could be an important stimulus for "creative work," but rather catching up with philosophy.[47] It was impossible to do systematic reading in his discipline, but the man who had left a new volume on Heidegger on his bed stand when he left for Conclave II was rarely without a philosophical title through which he browsed as time permitted.

Amid all the splendor of the Apostolic Palace—the Raphael frescoes, the gilding, the rich tapestries, the omnipresent marble—visitors can be surprised by the simplicity, indeed middle-class conventionality, of the Pope's apartment. His two priest-secretaries shared an office just off the more "public" parts of the papal apartment—the chapel, the dining room, the large and small reception rooms. The Pope's personal office was just beyond the secretaries' room and featured a large icon of the Black Madonna. His bedroom was divided in two by an old-fashioned folding partition or screen. On one side was a small desk, and on the other the bedroom proper, which included a full-sized bed with a simple white counterpane, several freestanding closets, and a large table on which were displayed some of the large books of photography John Paul enjoyed scanning. On the far wall of the bedroom was a map of the Diocese of Rome; over the years, the parishes the Pope visited would be marked on it. There are only two photographs in John Paul's private quarters: a small photograph of the Prince Cardinal, Adam Stefan Sapieha, on the desk in his personal office, and a small, silver-framed photo of his parents, taken shortly after their wedding, on the table in his bedroom.

He tried to make the apartment a home for those who lived there. When a young Zaïrois priest, Father Emery Kabongo, became his second secretary in 1982, the African immediately noticed that John Paul II didn't "act like a big chief," but was "a man with whom you can live." On the day Kabongo arrived from the Secretariat of State, the Pope walked in while the new man was being shown around the office by the first secretary; John Paul greeted him, gave him his blessing, took him into the kitchen to meet the sisters, told him that he was "part of the family," and that "Stanislao [Dziwisz, the first secretary] is your brother." In the six years that he worked for John Paul II, Kabongo never got a lecture from the Pope about how he should do his work. John Paul, he remembered, was never angry at inefficiency or bureaucratic mistakes; his rare displays of anger came when someone who should have known better denied a truth of the Catholic faith. The African also noticed that the Pope arranged his life to have as many contacts with people as possible.[48] All of them were treated with an unaffected naturalness. John Paul, in many ways a man of almost courtly personal manners, did not encourage visitors to kiss his ring, as previous custom dictated, but neither did he embarrass those who wished to make this gesture of deference. His ability to put visitors at ease was amplified by his ability to speak the languages of most of his guests.

John Paul's entire daily routine, according to associates and collaborators, was punctuated by prayer, not simply when he was in the chapel for Mass or the recitation of the Liturgy of the Hours (to which he attached great importance), but constantly—in between meetings, en route to audiences, in a car, in a helicopter, even on the roof. Paul VI had installed a solarium atop the Apostolic Palace, to which John Paul II added a set of modern stations of the cross. He prayed the stations every Friday during the year and every day during Lent. Each week, he received the sacrament of penance and made his confession to a Polish priest. Once, the priest-secretary he had inherited from Paul VI and John Paul I, Father John Magee, couldn't find him anywhere in the papal apartment. It was suggested that he look in the chapel. He looked and didn't see the Pope. It was suggested that he look again—down. There was John Paul II, prostrate before the tabernacle. Whatever the issue, he was, from the beginning, a man who made "all his major decisions . . . on his knees before the Blessed Sacrament," as one of his senior curial aides put it.[49]

John Paul II received a daily news brief, culled from major world papers by the Secretariat of State, written in Italian, and arranged so that he could scan the headlines and then go deeper into a summary of a particular news story or read the story (or opinion column) himself, as he chose. As in Kraków, he learned far more from his ongoing and intense round of daily conversations than he did from what others had decided was "the news." When he first began issuing personal invitations to his private Mass, and to breakfast, lunch, and dinner, the managers of popes were appalled; invitations to "the apartment" had always been managed by the Secretariat of State and the Prefecture of the Papal Household. One Curialist, disturbed by the flood of previously unknown people coming into the Apostolic Palace for audiences or meals with the Sovereign Pontiff, complained, "These halls were once a place of respect, of good taste. Now it's become Campo de' Fiori" (the great open-air market in Rome). That was, in fact, precisely John Paul II's view of the matter. The Church is first and foremost a pastoral reality, and, of course, everything is going on in it at once, just like an open-air market.[50]

In addition to making it clear that Peter's house was the Church's house, John Paul II was determined to preserve a personal sphere of conversation and initiative. As he broke precedent by acting as master of his own chapel and table, he developed methods for maintaining a private correspondence with friends and intellectual interlocutors throughout the world. It was the old Kraków strategy of "creating facts," now applied to a different kind of bureaucratic inertia. The Pope didn't ask permission to keep in touch with the people with whom he wanted to be in personal conversation. He simply sidestepped the Secretariat of State.[51] Similarly, he didn't ask permission to invite Jerzy Janik and his family to Castel Gandolfo the first summer he lived at the papal summer villa there. He simply invited them, and the Janiks came.[52]

The man who made his life work as Pope was the same man who had made his life work as archbishop of Kraków, his longtime secretary, Stanisław Dziwisz. Dziwisz was born in 1939 in Raba Wyżna. The village was near Nowy Targ, on the way to the Zakopane ski resort, and Dziwisz became a first-class skier. Ordained in 1963 by Bishop Wojtyła, Dziwisz spent two years in parish pastoral work south of Kraków before becoming the second secretary (or "chaplain") to Archbishop Wojtyła in 1966, and, shortly after, the principal secretary. Dziwisz later completed his doctoral studies in theology while serving as the Pope's secretary.

The relationship between the two men is perhaps best described as that which every father wants from a son: love and duty without fear or sycophancy. Dziwisz brought complete loyalty, utter discretion, sharp judgment, a puckish sense of humor, and indefatigability to his job. He was by no means a carbon copy of Wojtyła. They came from different social backgrounds (Dziwisz was from a large family in a rural area), had different interests and different tastes, and sometimes read situations differently. When he moved into the Vatican with the newly elected John Paul II, Dziwisz brought with him a simple understanding of his task—to make happen what the Holy Father wanted to happen.

It is the unhappy lot of the papal secretary to have to say "No" to many important people, including many important churchmen, and the resentments that can build up are, if not edifying, at least understandable. Yet Stanisław Dziwisz has not drawn the resentment and wrath of men of rank in the Church the way some of his predecessors have. That is explained, at least in part, by the fact that this son of very humble conditions is a gentleman whose selflessness is known and respected, even by those to whom he has had to say "No."

Within a few weeks of his election, John Paul II's youthfulness, vigor, and confidence in the message he preached seemed to many a new model of the papacy. It actually involved retrieving a venerable concept of the episcopate from the first millennium of Christianity. Then, as one scholar has put it, "many of the Fathers were at one and the same time bishops, preachers, pastors of souls, theologians and spiritual leaders, to say nothing of mystics . . . Each facet of their personality and work interacted with the other dimensions, enriching them."[53] Given the Church's and the world's experience of the managerial papacy, John Paul's evangelical and apostolic approach looked radical indeed. From his point of view, he was simply being what a bishop ought to be, according to the ancient tradition renewed by the Second Vatican Council.

STORM SIGNALS IN MOSCOW

Not everything could be bent to his will. John Paul II thought the Pope should spend Christmas, and especially his first Christmas as Pope, in Bethlehem. The idea caused consternation in the Secretariat of State. Bethlehem was in the West Bank, which had been bitterly disputed territory since the Arab-Israeli war in 1967. The Holy See did not have full diplomatic relations with any of the relevant states. A pilgrimage to Bethlehem couldn't be abstracted from the tangle of issues in which the Holy See was embroiled in the region. The visit would be a logistical nightmare—the Pope couldn't simply arrive in Bethlehem like any other pilgrim. John Paul II finally withdrew the proposal, although he mentioned his desire to be in Bethlehem at his Christmas Eve homily in Rome. His desire to make a pilgrimage to the Holy Land, as he said to more than one visitor over the next two decades, intensified as the years went on.[54]

The idea of an impromptu pilgrimage to Bethlehem also suggested that John Paul II thought of the papacy's relationship to world politics in rather different terms than his predecessors.

John Paul understood that the Holy See's unique status in international law and diplomatic practice was to the Church's advantage. It gave the Church a place at the table in international legal and political institutions and a forum for expressing its moral concerns. Similarly, the independence of the Vatican City micro-state protected the papacy from becoming dependent on any state power. Vatican City State guaranteed the Church's freedom, and in that sense it was an embodiment of religious freedom. For John Paul II, though, the Holy See's international legal status and the independence of the state of which he was sovereign were not ends in themselves, but means for achieving the real goal of the Office of Peter, which was to preach the Gospel and strengthen the brethren, wherever they might be. The rules of the game as understood in international politics could not be allowed to impede that evangelical and apostolic mission. Popes since Leo XIII had learned to engage world affairs through the moral force of their office. John Paul II pressed the Church's disengagement from temporal power in new ways, in what amounted to a redeclaration of the Church's independence to pursue its unique moral role in world affairs without fear or favor.

In their natural fascination with the mediagenic, non-Italian Pope, commentators often missed this deeper, "structural" point about the *terremoto* that was John Paul II. The Soviet leadership, or at least some of the more acute members of the Soviet leadership, understood—and grasped that much more was at stake than what the less-alert comrades thought was another passing episode involving the religious fevers of the endlessly agitated Poles.

Initial Soviet reaction to the news of Karol Wojtyła's election was muted, even somewhat upbeat. The new Pope would pursue the policies of John XXIII and Paul VI, the political weekly *Novoe vremya* suggested. "The lamentable experience of Pius XII shows that anti-communism is a dead end for the Church," and Wojtyła's election should be read as a defeat for the Italian cardinals who wanted to delay the implementation of Vatican II.[55]

This relative good cheer was a matter of publicly treading water. Behind the scenes, the Soviet leadership was in a state of shock. At the time of Wojtyła's election, an "eminent Italian journalist" with good Soviet connections had told Jerzy Turowicz that "the Soviets would prefer Aleksandr Solzhenitsyn as Secretary-General of the United Nations than a Pole as Pope."[56] Yuri Andropov, head of the KGB, understood that things had changed—drastically and for the worse, from his point of view. Just as Andropov had understood the threat that Solzhenitsyn had posed to the Soviet regime, he quickly grasped that the election of Karol Wojtyła spelled serious trouble in the Soviet Union and its external empire.[57] Shortly after the shock of October 16, 1978, Andropov called the chief KGB agent, the *rezident,* in Warsaw and demanded, "How could you possibly allow the election of a citizen of a socialist country as pope?" The *rezident* is said to have suggested that the Comrade Chairman make his inquiries in Rome, not in Warsaw.[58] Andropov then ordered an analysis of the election from Section 1 (Reports) of the First Chief Directorate of the KGB. The report, which reflected the KGB spymaster's view that history worked through plots, concluded that Wojtyła had been elected as part of a German-American conspiracy in which key roles were played by the Polish-American archbishop of Philadelphia, Cardinal John Krol, and Zbigniew Brzeziński, national security adviser to President Jimmy Carter. The goal of the plot was, presumably, the destabilization of Poland as the first step toward the disintegration of the Warsaw Pact.[59] The analysis was almost comical, but the threat analysis was acute.

While Andropov was conducting his inquiry, the Central Committee of the Soviet Communist Party ordered up its own analysis of the political consequences of Wojtyła's election. Prepared by the director of the Institute for the Economy of the World Socialist System, Oleg Bogomolov, and completed less than three weeks after Wojtyła's election, the report described the former archbishop of Kraków as a "right-winger" who had made trouble in Poland while avoiding a frontal assault on communism. Bogomolov correctly identified one immediate problem: Wojtyła's election would likely result in increased Vatican pressure for religious freedom in Warsaw Pact countries. One proposed countermeasure was a quiet warning to the Holy See that a "hostile" campaign for human rights would lead to more repression of religious institutions in central and eastern Europe. Bogomolov also suggested that "it is worth studying the possibility of improving relations with the Catholic clergy in Lithuania, Ukraine, and Belorussia," in order to forestall the kind of moral (or, in Soviet terms, ideological) assault that Wojtyła was likely to launch.[60]

Bogomolov's proposal suggests that Kremlin anxiety over the election of Pope John Paul II was not confined to the possible unraveling of the Soviet position in Poland. Poland was the geographic linchpin of the Warsaw Pact because it was the land bridge to East Germany, the most crucial strategic asset in the external Soviet empire. But if Poland was the linchpin of the *external* empire, Ukraine was the linchpin of the *internal* empire Lenin and Stalin had consolidated on its original czarist base. The repository of Ukrainian nationalism, especially in Western Ukraine (or Galicia) was the Eastern-rite Greek Catholic Church [GCC], which had been persecuted in an exceptionally harsh fashion from the Stalin period on.[61] Nothing terrified the masters of the Kremlin more than the thought of renascent Ukrainian nationalism. No institution was more likely to be the base for such a renaissance than the GCC—and Wojtyła's sympathies with the Greek Catholics of Ukraine were well-known. The Ukrainian-speaking John Paul II's meeting with the exiled Ukrainian Cardinal Slipyi on November 20, 1978, had not gone unnoticed.

Then there was Lithuania, another intensely Catholic part of the Soviet empire where the Church had been brutalized since the country's forced incorporation into the Soviet Union in 1940. Clandestine ordinations, an active underground network of clergy and nuns, and the longest-running samizdat publication in the USSR, the *Chronicle of the Catholic Church in Lithuania* (first published in 1972), had kept the Church alive under religious repression and cultural Russification. Now came a Lithuanian-speaking Pope, a cultural heir of the old Polish-Lithuanian Commonwealth, who shortly after his election dispatched his red cardinal's zucchetto clandestinely to the Marian shrine at Ostrabrama in Vilnius.[62] Within months of John Paul's election, a report to the Soviet Council on Religious Affairs warned that "extremist-minded priests of the Catholic Church" had been at work throughout the Lithuanian Soviet Socialist Republic, launching the Catholic Committee for the Defense of Believers' Rights.[63] Several of the priests involved were soon en route to hard-labor camps in Siberia and another would be murdered in a "road accident" in 1986.[64]

Formed primarily by their experience of Stalin's purge trials, the men who ran the USSR during the Brezhnev era were less interested in the fine points of ideology than their predecessors in the 1920s and 1930s. Marxist-Leninist ideology remained important, though, because it legitimated their rule over the multinational Soviet Union and over its satellites. This was rule in the name of the Dynamics of History, and, according to the Brezhnev Doctrine (created to justify Soviet tanks crushing the Prague Spring of 1968) it could not be, and would not be permitted to be, reversed. This was the context in which the Soviet leadership thought about its relationship to the Roman Catholic Church and analyzed the pros and cons of the *Ostpolitik* of Paul VI. Men like Leonid Brezhnev, Andrei Gromyko, and Yuri Andropov did not believe in any historical "convergence" between a liberalizing communist world and an increasingly social democratic West. They appreciated the *Ostpolitik* because, by lowering the temperature of public confrontation between the Catholic Church and world communism, it permitted the consolidation of the Soviet position in both the internal and external empires, while weakening the hold of an institution they regarded as an implacable historical enemy.

Karol Wojtyła did not come to the papacy with a master plan for dismantling the Soviet Union or its external empire. It would never have occurred to him to think of his responsibilities in those terms. He was determined to give public witness to the truth about the human condition contained in the Gospel of Jesus Christ—and a deliberately evangelical papacy necessarily confronted the counterclaims about human nature, community, and destiny embedded in communism.

John Paul II's refusal to accept the Yalta division of Europe as a fact of life was a frontal challenge to postwar Soviet strategy. That was bad enough, from the Soviet point of view. But a Slavic Pope, capable of addressing the restive peoples of the external and internal Soviet empires in their own languages, was a nightmare beyond the worst dreams of the masters of the Kremlin. Then there were the terms in which John Paul II was voicing his challenge. As he had done when archbishop of Kraków, he avoided direct condemnations of Marxism-Leninism, which would have opened him to the charge of being an ecclesiastical politician allied with the West. At the same time, by relentlessly focusing on human rights, and particularly on the fundamental right of religious freedom, he subtly attacked the heart of the communist project in history—communism's claim to be the twentieth century's true humanism and the true liberator of humanity.

The hopes the Kremlin had invested in the Vatican *Ostpolitik* of the late 1960s and 1970s had been dashed. The new Pope posed a serious threat, not simply to the Warsaw Pact, but to the Soviet Union itself—and did so precisely because he was a witness rather than a politician.

PUEBLA AND CHRISTIAN LIBERATION

At a Christmastime meeting with the College of Cardinals on December 22, 1978, John Paul II announced his wish to travel to Mexico the following month to visit the shrine of Our Lady of Guadalupe near Mexico City and to participate in the Third General Assembly of CELAM, the council of Latin American bishops' conferences.

This first of his pastoral pilgrimages abroad took the new Pope into the heart of one of the most intractable problems of modern Catholicism, the Church's position in Mexico. Violently persecuted by Mexican revolutionaries during the first part of the century, the Church had eventually reached a modus vivendi with the government after World War II. But the state remained officially, indeed constitutionally, anti-clerical, Church-state relations were tense, and in public life "the Church did not exist," as one Mexican church-man later put it.[65] When the Mexican bishops invited John Paul to come to their country during the CELAM meeting at Puebla de los Angeles, there was predictable nervousness in the Vatican Secretariat of State. The Holy See had no diplomatic relations with the Mexican government, which had not issued its own invitation to the Pope. The problem was solved by means of some adroit personal diplomacy.

President José López Portillo's mother and sisters, all of them practicing Catholics, lived in a house within the presidential compound in Mexico City; one of the sisters was the president's confidential secretary. Father Marcial Maciel, the Mexican founder of the Legionaries of Christ, a relatively new renewal movement of priests, encouraged these ladies to encourage the pres-ident to invite the Pope. Their intervention evidently succeeded. President López Portillo overrode the protests of his anti-clerical interior minister and issued the invitation, stipulating only that the Pope would not be received as a head of state and would have to have a visa like any other visitor. Whatever distress this may have caused among the Vatican diplomats, the arrangement was fine with John Paul II.

After Mass and an overnight stop in the Dominican Republic, John Paul II flew into Mexico City on an Alitalia jetliner on January 26, 1979. He knelt, kissed the ground, and rose to be greeted by the President of the Republic, who, sensing the growing public enthusiasm over the Pope's visit, had decided to come to the airport for an "unofficial" greeting, during which he said to John Paul, "Welcome to your home." The motorcade into Mexico City took an hour to cover a little less than five miles. A million Mexicans turned out along the route, throwing a cascade of flowers on the Pope's car. Hundreds of priests and nuns defied a century-old ban, reinforced by the Mexican Constitution, on wearing religious habits in public.[66] After celebrating Mass in the cathedral, the Pope addressed 300,000 Mexicans in Constitution Square. That after-noon, the Pope visited López Portillo at the presidential compound and met the president's mother and sisters. John Paul chatted with the family for half an hour and blessed the small chapel they had built in their house.[67]

If the Pope struck some of those who saw him in Mexico City and Guadalupe on January 26 and 27 as pensive, even preoccupied, it was with good reason. In addressing the CELAM general assembly on January 28, he would be tackling the question of what kind of Church post–Vatican II Catholi-cism would be in Latin America—a question now focused through the intense debate over "liberation theology." The resolution of that question would deter-mine the future of one-half of world Catholicism.

The term "liberation theology" was itself a misnomer, for by the late 1970s a variety of liberation theologies had evolved. Though they differed in styles of analysis and points of prescription, they were animated by several common convictions. They belittled the reformism of Vatican II, which envisioned a gradual transformation of social, economic, and political structures under the impact of Christian humanism's dialogue with modernity, in favor of a more revolutionary strategy that drew on Marxist categories of social and economic analysis. The "sinful social structures" of the established order were to be overthrown through class struggle. In this struggle, the Church, exercising a "preferential option for the poor," would organize small Christian "base communities" where the poor would be taught to comprehend their own victimhood and, inspired by the image of Jesus the Liberator, would take up the task of re-creating society. If this involved violence, then this "second violence" of the poor should be judged as self-defense against the institutionalized "first violence" of the "dominant" social structures.[68]

Although typically understood as an indigenous Latin American phenomenon, the Latin American liberation theologies were, in the main, developed by theologians who had studied in Europe and had brought back to Latin America the "Marxist analysis" then prominent in European faculties. These theologians came from, and returned to, a situation in which the Church had traditionally been allied with social, economic, military, and political power. That model of the Church's relationship to society had been rejected by the Second Vatican Council. The public implication of *Dignitatis Humanae* was that altar-and-junta alliances were not appropriate for the Church; *Gaudium et Spes* had committed Catholicism to activism on behalf of freedom, peace, and justice. The issue, post–Vatican II, was not whether the Church would be engaged with the injustices faced by the Latin American poor, but how.

The theologies of liberation openly advocated a "partisan Church." The Church, in this view, was not so much a communion of believers in which men and women sought to understand one another, exchanged ideas on reconstructing society, and celebrated the sacraments as the pledge of a bond deeper than politics. Rather, the Church, by accepting the class struggle as the fundamental dynamic of history, had to be a partisan actor, "to decide for some people and against others," as one prominent liberation theologian put it.[69] If this meant setting the "people's Church" over against the "hierarchical Church," then that was what justice required. Liberation theologies thus illustrated what happened when Vatican II was pulled apart and politicized. When *Gaudium et Spes* was read through the interpretive filter of "Marxist analysis," the net result was a narrower, less inclusive, more class-based Church—the mirror-image of the narrow, class-based Church the theologies of liberation rightly criticized.

The theologies of liberation had made some important points. The Church in Latin America had been historically deficient in empowering the poor. Too long allied with oligarchy and privilege, it had lost its prophetic edge in dealing with worldly power. Liberation theologies correctly understood that

Catholic renewal would come from the bottom up, and that one effective way to animate that grassroots renewal was to restore the Bible to the people. Linking the Church's liturgy and the celebration of the sacraments to people's daily lives was a prominent theme in the theologies of liberation, as it had been in the classic liturgical movement of the pre-Council years and of Vatican II itself. The delicate task facing John Paul II was to distinguish what was insightful in the liberation theologies' interpretation of Vatican II from what was inappropriate and even unorthodox. And the new Pope had to do this while facing, and he hoped, bridging, the divisions within the Latin American hierarchy.

Puebla, where the CELAM conference was being held, is some eighty miles from Mexico City. John Paul drove there through dramatic scenery, including the volcanoes Iztácihuatl and Popocátepetl, and saw the mountain pass Hernán Cortés had crossed en route to conquering the ancient Aztec capital. More than a million Mexicans came to see the Pope on his way from Mexico City to Puebla. Indians in native costume and parish delegations carrying crosses and portable altars had camped along the roadside during the night with their dogs, horses, and donkeys. The papal motorcade stopped briefly in San Martin, Texmelucan, and San Miguel Xoxtla, where the Pope gave brief, impromptu speeches in fluent Spanish.

Puebla greeted the Pope exuberantly, with balloons, fireworks, and Handel's "Hallelujah Chorus," broadcast over the incredible scene by a small plane with a powerful loudspeaker. The streets of the city were filled to bursting with a crush of people waving Mexican, papal, and Polish flags. Small bands and the city's tolling church bells added to the din. John Paul celebrated Mass on a raised platform built against the wall of the local seminary. The crowd outside chanted, *"Puebla, Puebla, Puebla ama Papa!"* [Puebla, Puebla, Puebla loves the Pope!].[70]

After Mass, John Paul II spoke to the Latin American bishops in a session closed to the public and the press. His lengthy talk, one of the most important of his pontificate, was the mature reflection of a man who had wrestled from young adulthood with the moral question of revolutionary violence as a response to social injustice. In a deeply personal and thoroughly ecclesial address, John Paul II developed the liberation theology implicit in his play *Our God's Brother,* read through the Christian humanism of Vatican II.

He came to them, he began, "as a brother to very beloved brothers," who admired what the bishops of Latin America had accomplished in their first two general assemblies, at Rio de Janeiro in 1958 and Medellín, Colombia, in 1968. Their great strength lay in the fact that they came to Puebla "not as a symposium of experts, not as a parliament of politicians, not as a congress of scientists or technologists, but as . . . pastors of the Church." As pastors, their "principal duty" was to "be teachers of the truth," for the truth was the foundation for all truly liberating human action.

The truth entrusted to bishops was "the truth concerning Jesus Christ," which was the center of the "new evangelization" CELAM was considering at

Puebla. The truth about Jesus Christ was not a theological abstraction, for from it would come "choices, values, attitudes, and ways of behavior" that could create "new people and . . . a new humanity" through a radically Christian life. The basic truth about Jesus Christ remained the truth confessed by Peter: "You are the Christ, the Son of the Living God." *That* was what the Church preached. That was "the one Gospel," and "re-readings" of the Gospel through ideological lenses made an authentically Christian liberation impossible. Among those "re-readings" was one with which they had become familiar in recent years. It was the image of "Jesus as politically committed, as one who fought against Roman oppression and the authorities, and also as one involved in the class struggle. This idea of Christ as a political figure, a revolutionary, as the subversive Man from Nazareth, does not tally with the Church's catechesis . . . The Gospels clearly show that . . . Jesus . . . does not accept the position of those who mixed the things of God with merely political attitudes (cf. *Matthew* 22.21; *Mark* 12.17; *John* 18.26). He unequivocally rejects recourse to violence. He opens his message of conversion to everybody. . . ."[71]

True liberation was found in the salvation offered by Christ, a messianic liberation wrought by "transforming, peacemaking, pardoning, and reconciling love."[72] That was the faith that had formed Latin America, its "religious practices and popular piety." And that was the faith that must "go on animating, with every energy, the dynamism of [Latin America's] future."[73] Any other "re-reading" of the Church emptied the Gospel of its power and the Church of its distinctive character. The "Kingdom of God" could not be reduced to "the mere changing of structures" in society, because a politicized, secularized Kingdom devalued the freedom that every person sought.[74]

Marxism could not do for Christian theology what Aristotle had done for Thomas Aquinas, because Marxism's view of the human person was fundamentally flawed, and that "anthropological error" permeated Marxism's politics and economics.[75] Over against Marxism's materialistic reduction of humanism, the Church proposed the truth that "man is God's image and cannot be reduced to a mere portion of nature or a nameless element in the human city." Christian humanism, "this complete truth about the human being," was the foundation of the Church's social doctrine, in which men and women were not the victims of impersonal historical or economic forces but the artisans of society, economy, and politics.[76]

The bishops' task as pastors and teachers of the truth was to "defend human dignity [as] a Gospel value that cannot be despised without greatly offending the Creator."[77] In defending religious freedom, in protesting coercion and torture, in promoting the right of participation in public life, the Church "does not need to have recourse to ideological systems in order to love, defend, and collaborate in the liberation of man." She only had to look to Christ. A comprehensive liberation of the human family was the Church's cause, because it was the cause of Christ.[78]

The future, as always, was in God's hands. But God had placed that future "with new evangelizing momentum" in the bishops' hands, too. "'Go, there-fore,'" John Paul told his brothers, "'and make disciples of all nations' [*Matthew* 28.19]."

After returning to Mexico City on the night of January 28, the Pope took a call from Cardinal Sebastiano Baggio, Prefect of the Vatican's Congregation for Bishops, who was presiding over the CELAM conference. Baggio told John Paul that his address had been well-received by the bishops. The previously preoccupied and pensive Pope went upstairs to his bedroom humming and was in his usual good humor, joking with his entourage, throughout the rest of his Mexican pilgrimage.

The next day, January 29, he spoke in Cuilapan to more than half a mil-lion Indians from Oaxaca and Chiapas, many of whom had been camping near the ruins of an old colonial-era monastery for days. The Pope was helicoptered into the site, and the Indians, dressed in colorful native garb, brought him gifts, danced and sang, placed numerous brightly embroidered woolen stoles, one by one, on the Pope's shoulders, and gave him a chief's headdress. He was obviously moved, embracing and kissing those who presented him with gifts, taking time to speak with each one individually.

Against the backdrop of a dry plateau bereft of vegetation, John Paul II told the massive crowd that he wanted "to be your voice, the voice of those who cannot speak or who are silenced" in order to "make up for lost time which is often time of prolonged suffering and unsatisfied hopes." Then, his voice rising and impassioned, he blasted the injustices that had warped the lives of the Latin American poor and lit into those responsible for the ongo-ing oppression of the powerless. "The depressed rural world, the worker who with his sweat waters also his affliction, cannot wait any longer for full and effective recognition of his dignity, which is not inferior to that of any other social sector," John Paul insisted. "He has the right to be respected and not to be deprived, with maneuvers which are sometimes tantamount to real spolia-tion, of the little that he has . . . He has the right to real help—which is not charity or crumbs of justice—in order that he may have access to the devel-opment that his dignity as a man and as a son of God deserves. . . . It is nec-essary to carry out bold changes . . . [and] urgent reforms without waiting any longer."[79]

Commentators immediately juxtaposed the Puebla and Cuilapan addresses, the first being the voice of John Paul the "theological conservative" and the second the voice of John Paul the "social and political liberal." It was not hard to detect, beneath those clichés, a further juxtaposition between the "bad John Paul" of Puebla and the "good John Paul" of Cuilapan. The juxta-position made little sense. Everything the Pope had said in his dramatic defense of the poor in Cuilapan was implicit in what he had said in Puebla about Christian liberation. And this view of Christian liberation was not a per-sonal idiosyncrasy; it was based on Vatican II.[80]

John Paul II had important, critical, even radical things to say about social, economic, and political affairs because he was an evangelist who believed that the truth of the human condition had been revealed in Jesus Christ. Reading him from "outside" yielded a split-screen vision of the man and his message, a pattern first established in the wake of Puebla and Cuilapan that continued throughout the pontificate. The Puebla and Cuilapan addresses should have been the first indication that John Paul II and his pontificate could only be read accurately from the "inside." The theology was always first, and politics, like culture and economics, was one of the arenas in which theological truths had implications. It was not an approach that commended itself readily to an international press corps trained to think of politics as the "real world" and theology as a matter of personal taste.[81]

A deeply tanned John Paul II returned to Rome late in the afternoon of February 1 and went straight to St. Peter's to say a prayer of thanksgiving. Karol Wojtyła had long since decided that his destiny was not in his own hands, and once a decision had been made he was not one to fret over what might be. Yet in this first international test of his pontificate, he had to have been concerned about his own capacity to be the kind of public witness he thought a pope should be, and about the way he, a Pole, would be received. Then there was CELAM, for what was at stake at Puebla was nothing less than the legacy of Vatican II in Latin America. Now the answers were in. Many of the Latin American bishops had been grateful for what he had said. The popular response had been overwhelming. Taking off from Mexico City, the Pope had seen the entire city twinkling with flashes of light, as millions of Mexicans held mirrors up to the sun to reflect its rays in his direction. He had successfully tested the possibility of an evangelically and apostolically assertive papacy—a "living encyclical of word and action," as Marek Skwarnicki described it—in very difficult circumstances.[82]

Now, in his first encyclical letter, he would explain the Christian humanism that would be the program of his entire papacy.

PROGRAM NOTES FOR A PONTIFICATE

As the twenty-one epistles in the New Testament suggest, Christian leaders have used letters as teaching instruments from the very beginning of the Church. Scholars date the origins of the modern papal "encyclical," a letter to a specific group of bishops or to the world episcopate, to Benedict XIV's *Ubi Primum* in 1740, although it was Gregory XVI who, in the early nineteenth century, first used the term "encyclical" to refer to these documents. Before the First Vatican Council, encyclicals were largely admonitory, warning against this or that deviant teaching. After Vatican I, Leo XIII used the encyclical as a vehicle for addressing theological issues and the Church's relationship to modern social, political, economic, and intellectual life, as did Popes Pius XI, Pius XII, John XXIII and Paul VI. Benedict XV used the device of an "inaugural encyclical" to declare a halt to the brawling over Modernism that had damaged

Catholic theology and the *communio* of the Church. Paul VI's "inaugural encyclical," *Ecclesiam Suam*, signaled that ecclesiology—the Church's self-understanding and mission—would be the theme of his pontificate.[83]

John Paul II has said that he began work on a letter addressed to the entire Church and to all men and women of good will "immediately" after his election. Like Paul VI, he wanted to announce and explain the great theme of his pontificate through a major teaching document with doctrinal authority, and Christian humanism, as he put it, "was a subject I had brought with me" to Rome.[84] Five months after he arrived, he published the first encyclical ever devoted to Christian anthropology.

When it was released publicly on March 15, 1979, *Redemptor Hominis* [The Redeemer of Man] introduced his new global audience to an analysis of the contemporary human condition that Karol Wojtyła had been refining for thirty years.[85] It was intended to be "a great hymn of joy for the fact that man has been redeemed through Christ—redeemed in spirit and in body."[86] That redemption was intimately linked, Wojtyła had long believed and taught, to the dignity of the human person. Thus *Redemptor Hominis* was meant to "unite the mission of the Church with service to man in his impenetrable mystery."

The encyclical begins on the millennial note that would intensify as the pontificate unfolded. Both the Church and the world are living a "new Advent," a "season of expectation," on the threshold of the year 2000. It would be an anniversary with global implications, for Christ had revealed both the face of God and the truth about the human condition: "Through the Incarnation," John Paul writes, "God gave human life the dimension he had intended man to have from his first beginning."[87]

Here, as throughout his pontificate, the Pope is reminding the Church and the world that the Incarnation tells us something about God and something about ourselves. Satisfying "the fatherhood of God" and revealing the depths of God's love, the Son of God's birth as a man had also confirmed "the greatness, dignity, and value" of humanity, for "man cannot live without love. He remains . . . incomprehensible [to] himself, his life is senseless, if love is not revealed to him, if he does not encounter love, if he does not experience it and make it his own, if he does not participate intimately in it." Love is greater than sin, than alienation, than every human frailty at every time and every place, because "God is love" (*1 John* 4.8). That is the amazing good news—the "Gospel"—that Christianity had to tell the world.

God's love, which gave birth to and sustained the world, could only be encountered in freedom. To be true to its mission, the Church has to be a "guardian" of human freedom. A truly human freedom seeks the truth and is bound by it.[88] Love encountered in freedom, and freedom ordered to truth—this is the essence of Christian humanism. The redeeming, all-conquering love of God is the foundation and the inexhaustible message of the Church's mission of genuine liberation.

In the modern world, the Pope writes, this mission must confront the threat that humanity felt from its own accomplishments. Modern humanity "lives increasingly in fear," and the greatest fear was that of "an unimaginable self-destruction, compared with which all the cataclysms and catastrophes of history known to us seem to fade away." The modern world experienced a threatening lag between its material capacities and its moral character. Because of this, some had come to believe that life was inherently absurd. The Church's response is that God had given humanity "kingship" and "dominion" over the created order. Humanity could master the artifacts it brought into being, if it is understood that true human development involved "being more" rather than "having more."[89]

The answer to humanity's fear of itself lay in rediscovering that human nature is moral and spiritual, not simply material. John Paul gives this ancient theme a distinctively contemporary reading by suggesting that the most compelling evidence for humanity's "soul" is the worldwide human rights movement. In the promotion and defense of human rights, the Church sees the answer to many of the threats that had turned the twentieth century into a time of fear and slaughter: warped ideologies, totalitarian state power, the dissolution of the family, terrorism.

John Paul then defines the great human rights theme of his pontificate. Religious freedom, he insists, is the first of the human person's "objective and inalienable rights." This is not special pleading but a conclusion drawn from a disciplined reflection on human dignity, and it could be engaged publicly by every thoughtful person. Without naming names—without having to—John Paul II then challenges the world from which he had come, the world behind the iron curtain:

> [The] curtailment of the religious freedom of individuals and communities is not only a painful experience but is above all an attack on man's very dignity . . . [It is] a radical injustice with regard to what is particularly deep in man, what is authentically human . . . [A]theism as a human phenomenon is understood only in relation to the phenomenon of religion and faith. It is therefore difficult . . . to accept a position that gives only atheism the right of citizenship in public and social life, while believers are . . . barely tolerated or are treated as second-class citizens or are even—and this has already happened—entirely deprived of the rights of citizenship.[90]

John Paul concludes his inaugural encyclical by revisiting one of the most familiar sentences in St. Augustine's *Confessions*—"You have made us for yourself, Lord, and our heart is restless until it rests in you." Here, he proposes, is the key to unlocking the mystery of modern restlessness, modern fear, and the "insatiability" built into modern materialism. Renewed by Vatican II, the Church has a proposal to make to the world. The restlessness of modern hearts could be calmed, the hungers that burdened our souls satisfied, and the fear that haunted the modern world dispelled, if men and women shared in the prophetic, priestly, and kingly missions of Christ—if they freely grasped the truth, freely worshiped in the truth, and freely served one another and the world in truth.[91]

Redemptor Hominis offered the world a Church in love with humanity, and for the most weighty of reasons—because God had "so loved the world" (*John* 3.16) that He had sent his only son as the *redemptor hominis,* the redeemer of man. Modernity took history very seriously. So did the Church. What the Church brought to this modern passion for history was the conviction that there is, in fact, only one human history—a history filled with God's presence and redemptive promise. In that promise, John Paul proposed, the answer to the fear that haunted humanity at the end of the twentieth century could be discovered, and embraced, and lived in service to the entire world.

9

"How Many Divisions Has the Pope?"

Confronting an Empire of Lies

JANUARY 24, 1979	Soviet foreign minister Andrei Gromyko calls on Pope John Paul II in the Vatican.
MARCH 2, 1979	The Pope moves to strengthen Czechoslovakian Catholicism through a letter on religious resistance to tyranny.
MARCH 19, 1979	A papal letter to Ukrainian Cardinal Iosyf Slipyi anticipates the 1988 millennium of Christianity in Kievan Rus' and defends the principle of religious freedom for all.
APRIL 30, 1979	Archbishop Agostino Casaroli named Pro-Secretary of State of the Holy See.
JUNE 2–10, 1979	John Paul II's first pilgrimage to Poland.
AUGUST 14–31, 1980	Gdańsk shipyard strike gives birth to Solidarity trade union and movement.

In 1966, Poland's communist rulers had been singularly unsuccessful in their efforts to co-opt the millennium of Polish Christianity. The regime hung signs in the streets: *Tysiąclecie Państwa Polskiego* [A Thousand Years of the Polish State]; every church in the country prominently displayed a banner reading *Sacrum Poloniae Millennium 966–1966* [Poland's Sacred Millennium 966–1966]. Other church banners read *Deo et Patriae* [For God and Country]; the regime could only muster a weak *Socjalizm I Ojczyzna* [Socialism and Fatherland]. The churches proclaimed *Naród Z Kościołem* [The Nation Is with the Church]; the regime tried *Partia z Narodem* [The Party Is with the Nation]. To the Church's proud boast, *Polonia Semper Fidelis* [Poland Ever-Faithful], came the sorry counter *Socjalizm Gwarancja Pokoju I Granic* [The Communist Regime Is the Guarantee of Peace and Frontiers].[1]

The regime didn't even try to keep pace with the Church symbolically during John Paul II's return to his homeland in June 1979. Victory Square, scene of many of the Polish communist regime's great public displays, had been transformed by government workers into an enormous liturgical stage for the papal Mass. From it, John Paul would address 1 million of his countrymen live, and tens of millions more on radio and television. The centerpiece of the altar platform was a fifty-foot-tall cross, draped with an enormous replica of a priest's stole, reminding all present that they were witnessing a sacramental representation of Christ's sacrifice on Calvary. Beneath the huge cross, where Mary had stood faithfully by, was a replica of the Black Madonna of Częstochowa.

No hero in Polish history—not King Jan III Sobieski, not Tadeusz Kościuszko, not Józef Piłsudski—had ever entered Warsaw as John Paul II did on June 2, 1979.

Rebuilt Warsaw was a grim, gray place, its skyline dominated by the Palace of Culture and Sciences, a garish communist-baroque confection given to the city by Stalin. The city's grayness too often matched the people's mood. Now, for the Pope, Warsaw had come alive, visually and spiritually. Thousands of pilgrims had been welcomed into the homes of strangers. Every church in the city had remained open overnight to give shelter to those who could not find places elsewhere. The entire route from Okecie Airport to the rebuilt Old City was lined with hundreds of thousands of men, women, and children, five and ten rows deep, waving small Polish and Vatican flags. There was no disorder, only jubilation, as the enormous crowds kept to the places assigned to their parishes by the Church's efficient organizers.

The city had been transformed by homemade decorations. The windows and porches of the drab apartment blocks along the roads John Paul would travel had been turned into shrines and altars bedecked with flowers, flags, and photographs of the Pope. As the papal motorcade moved slowly along the street, bouquets were thrown in the Pope's path while the crowd broke out in songs, cheers, and, in some cases, uncontrollable tears. Many Poles knelt on the roadside as a beaming John Paul II scattered benedictions left and right from the converted truck on which he rode. On June 2, 1979, 3 million Poles, twice the city's normal population, had come to see their countryman, Karol Wojtyła of Wadowice, Kraków, and Rome.

Some 230,000 tickets had been issued for the Mass; 300,000 people had wedged themselves into Victory Square, with another three-quarters of a million or so overflowing into the surrounding streets. It was a brilliantly sunny, hot day. Accompanied by the strains of the papal anthem and the hymn "Gaude Mater Polonia" [Rejoice, Mother Poland], the Pope and Primate Wyszyński walked slowly toward the Tomb of the Unknown Soldier in the square. A young couple gave the Pope a bouquet, which he laid on the tomb before kneeling in silent prayer. He kissed the grave, signed the book of remembrance ("To Poland's Unknown Soldier—John Paul II"), and walked to a tent where he vested for Mass.

Attended by the Warsaw diplomatic corps and by representatives of the Lutheran, Reformed, Orthodox, Methodist, and Baptist churches, the Mass began with a greeting from the Primate, who proclaimed that national unity—a constant theme of communist propaganda—had now, in fact, been achieved: "Holy Father, the capital is united today in prayer, led by the head of the Roman Catholic Church . . . Christ's vicar on earth, apostle of Christ and His Gospel, messenger of truth and love, a son of Poland, chosen by God. . . ."

After the proclamation of the Gospel, a deep silence fell over the tremendous crowd. Polish Communist Party leader Edward Gierek watched nervously from a window in a hotel adjacent to the square. He, and millions of others, wondered: What would he say? What *could* he say?

Karol Wojtyła looked out at a sea of expectant faces, paused—and then gave what may have been the greatest sermon of his life.

Today, he began, he wanted to "sing a hymn of praise to divine Providence" which had enabled him to come home "as a pilgrim." In doing so, he was fulfilling the wish of Pope Paul VI, who had so "ardently desired to set foot on the soil of Poland" that his desire reached "beyond the span of a pontificate." On his election, this Polish Pope had "immediately understood" that he had been chosen in order to fulfill what Pope Paul had been prevented from doing during the millennium celebrations in 1966.

His papal pilgrimage was a continuation of those celebrations, because he had come for the anniversary of St. Stanisław's martyrdom, and that epic event in 1079 had been a fruit of Poland's conversion in 966. St. Stanisław's witness, his resistance to the tyranny of autocratic state power, had become "a special sign of the pilgrimage that we Poles are making down through the history of the Church." He, Pope John Paul II, was a product of that national spiritual journey and the defense of religious freedom that was one of its hallmarks.

Why had a Pole been called to the chair of St. Peter? Was it not because the Poland of today had become, through the terrible trials of the twentieth century, "*the land of a particularly responsible witness*"?

The Poles, he insisted, had a right to think that, to think "with singular humility but also with conviction" that it was to Poland, today, that "one must come . . . to read again the witness of His cross and His resurrection." This was no cause for boasting, however. "If we accept all that I have dared to affirm in this moment, how many great duties and obligations arise? Are we capable of them?"

The crowd began a rhythmic chant, "We want God, we want God. . . ."

It was, John Paul continued, the Vigil of Pentecost, so let us return in our imaginations to the Upper Room in Jerusalem. There, the apostles and Mary waited for the Holy Spirit so that they could be the risen Christ's witnesses to the ends of the earth. Pentecost, the feast of the descent of the Holy Spirit, was *"the birthday of the faith and of the Church in our land of Poland, also."* Just as the apostles, filled with the Holy Spirit, had gone from the Upper Room and preached in foreign tongues, so, too, was Pentecost "the proclamation of the mighty works of God in our Polish language." The mightiest of those works was the human person, redeemed by Christ: "Therefore Christ cannot be kept out of the history of man in any part of the globe, at any longitude or latitude of geography. The exclusion of Christ from the history of man is an act against man. Without Christ it is impossible to understand the history of Poland, especially the history of the people who have passed or are passing through this land. ..." Even those who "appeared to be at a distance, outside the Church," those who "doubted or opposed," lived within the Christian context of Polish history and culture. Anyone who tried to deny this or to uproot it damaged the Polish nation. For Poland and its history—"from Stanisław in Skałka to Maximilian Kolbe at Oświęcim"—could not be understood without reference to Jesus Christ. That was why he had come to Poland: to reaffirm that "Christ does not cease to teach the great cause of man," for Christ was "an ever-open book on man, his dignity, and his rights ..." Today, in Victory Square, he and his countrymen were asking, in the supreme prayer of the Mass, *"that Christ will not cease to be for us an open book of life for the future,* for our Polish future."

The Tomb of the Unknown Soldier bore silent testimony to a truth for which countless Poles had died, that "there can be no just Europe without the independence of Poland marked on its map!" Polish soldiers had fallen on numerous battlefields "for our freedom and yours." Was history thus absurd? No. For that spirit of sacrifice was emblematic of "every seed that falls into the earth and dies and thus bears fruit. It may be the seed of the blood of a soldier shed on the battlefield, or the sacrifice of martyrdom in concentration camps or in prisons. It may be the seed of hard daily toil . . . in the fields, the workshop, the mine, the foundries, and the factories. It may be the seed of the love of parents who do not refuse to give life to a new human being and undertake the whole task of bringing him up. It may be the seed of creative work in the universities, the higher institutes, the libraries and the places where the national culture is built. It may be the seed of prayer, of service of the sick, the suffering and abandoned—'all of that of which Poland is made.'"

All of that, he concluded, was in the hands of the Mother of God—"at the foot of the cross on Calvary and in the Upper Room of Pentecost." All of Poland's suffering and triumph; all of the history of the peoples who had lived on this land, "including those who died in their hundreds of thousands within the walls of the Warsaw ghetto"; all that was what he—"a son of this land . . . who am also Pope John Paul II"—offered to God in this Eucharistic sacrifice.

> . . . And I cry from all the depths of this millennium, I cry on the vigil of
>   Pentecost:
> "Let your Spirit descend.
> Let your Spirit descend,

and renew the face of the earth,
the face of this land."
Amen.[2]

Throughout the Pope's sermon, the crowd responded rhythmically: "We want God, we want God, we want God in the family, we want God in the schools, we want God in books, we want God, we want God. . . ."[3] Seven hours after he had arrived, a crucial truth had been clarified by a million Poles' response to John Paul's evangelism. Poland was not a communist country; Poland was a Catholic nation saddled with a communist state.

Poland's "second baptism," which would change the history of the twentieth century, had begun.[4]

The Post-Constantinian Pope

The modern diplomats of the Holy See are priests whose instinctive first question, on reaching any new assignment, is, "Where are we saying Mass tomorrow?" Yet these priest-diplomats also prided themselves on their realism. Their task, as they saw it, was to maneuver within the boundaries of the possible to defend the Church's interests. Those interests were distinctive: the freedom of the Church to manage its internal affairs, in order to carry out its missions of evangelization, worship, and service. Still, Vatican diplomacy, reflecting the days when the Holy See was a worldly power, had become used to thinking of those distinctive interests much as nation-states thought of their economic or political "interests"—as the subjects of negotiation between sovereign powers, with the results codified in legally binding treaties.

The *Ostpolitik* of Pope Paul VI and his "foreign minister," Archbishop Agostino Casaroli, was a product of this venerable tradition, updated for the late twentieth century. The claims of some of its most vociferously anti-communist critics notwithstanding, the *Ostpolitik* was certainly aimed at defending the Church, its people, and its distinctive interests. But Paul VI and Casaroli, two veteran diplomats, read history and what Vatican II had called "the signs of the times" through rather conventional realist filters.

The *Ostpolitik* of the Vatican, and indeed the character of papal diplomacy as a whole, changed dramatically on October 16, 1978, with Karol Wojtyła's election as Pope John Paul II. The change was not simply a question of tactics—although those changed, too—but of premises. Wojtyła brought a distinctive reading of contemporary history to the papacy. Married to the vision of "the Church in the modern world" he had helped craft at Vatican II, that analysis led to a new model of papal diplomacy.

Karol Wojtyła was a "realist" philosophically, convinced that the human mind could grasp the truth of things and give a coherent account of what it had grasped. Yet his philosophical "realism" did not translate into a "realist" view of international relations, in which the engine of history is understood to be economic and military power. Wojtyła disagreed, as a Christian and an analyst of history's dynamics. As a Christian convinced that the Gospel revealed the truth about humanity and its destiny, he believed that God was in charge of history. This freed the Church to act in history in a singular way. As a Pole who had reflected long and hard on the fact that the Polish nation had survived when the Polish state was abolished, he was convinced that culture drove history, over the long run. The realists were wrong, not because military and economic power were unimportant, but because culture was more important. And the most powerful component of culture was cult, or religion.

Realism in international relations theory read history as a realm of amorality. History was a butcher's block, Hegel had argued. Wojtyła, again, disagreed. In his Christian-Polish view, history was best read through the prism of moral analysis, and viewed through that prism, the subjugation of the nations within Stalin's external and internal empires was a moral catastrophe. Its rectification was the precondition to peace and what Paul VI had called "the development of peoples."

This was not an idiosyncratically "ethnic" vision of modern history. It was another way of taking Vatican II seriously. As his friend Professor Stefan Swieżawski put it, the Council had marked "the end of the Constantinian epoch," in which the Church was a power alongside other political powers.[5] In *Dignitatis Humanae* and *Gaudium et Spes,* the Council had taken the position that the just state was a state with limited, constitutionally defined powers.[6] The loss of the Papal States in 1870, coupled with Vatican II's moral judgment about the just state, implied a new, "post-Constantinian" relationship between the Church and the world of politics, Swieżawski believed. So did Karol Wojtyła.

To be a "post-Constantinian" Church did not mean returning to the catacombs. The Church was the custodian of certain truths about the human condition and those truths had public consequences, so the Church's diplomacy had to continue. But it should now deal with the world primarily through the realm of culture, Wojtyła thought. That meant the forthright defense of basic human and national rights. Witness to the truth about the inalienable dignity and rights of the human person should be the identifying mark of the "post-Constantinian" Church envisioned by Vatican II.

The *Ostpolitik* of the Holy See also changed on October 16, 1978, because Pope John Paul II knew the Church's situation behind the iron curtain as only a native of east central Europe, familiar with the local languages and culture, could. John Paul knew there was something radically different about communist regimes, a point that did not seem fully appreciated by the Vatican diplomats who conceived and executed Paul VI's *Ostpolitik.* All states commit criminal acts sometimes; communist regimes were criminal enterprises by their very nature. The "rule of law" in a communist regime was a fiction; communist regimes committed violent acts and maintained an enormous apparatus of repression on principle. Under a communist regime, terror was a routine way to maintain order, which could give communist regimes an air of invincibility. This Pope, however, had measured communism's weaknesses as well as its apparent strengths. And he knew that cultural resistance could be an effective antidote to the seemingly impregnable position of a criminal state.[7]

The new Pope also believed that his entire life had been a preparation for the Office of Peter and its responsibility to "strengthen the brethren" (cf. *Luke* 22.32). This was not arrogance; he had not sought the position to which he had been elected. But the ease with which he assumed the papacy suggested a calm confidence, built on the foundation of a rocklike faith, that "strengthening the brethren" meant, among other things, revamping the *Ostpolitik* of the Holy See.

His first months in office had signaled this "Wojtyła Difference" in a number of ways.

His inaugural sermon with its antiphon—"Be not afraid!"—and its theme—"Open the doors to Christ!"—was an unmistakable call to a different kind of arms for the persecuted Church behind the iron curtain. So were his frequent references to religious freedom in his first public statements as Pope. So was his Christmas letter to the Church in Kraków, in which he challenged his people and the Polish regime. St. Stanisław, he wrote, was "the patron of moral order in our country." He had defended his society from the evil that threatened it, "and he did not hesitate to confront the ruler when defense of the moral order called for it."[8] Communist censors cut the references to the martyred saint and told Jerzy Turowicz to run a bowdlerized version in *Tygodnik Powszechny*; Turowicz refused. The full text, which could not be published, was then read from all the pulpits of the archdiocese.

John Paul's forthright defense of the persecuted was not limited to the Church in Poland. He moved quickly to strengthen the Church in Czechoslovakia, the hardest-pressed Catholic community in the Soviet external empire. Greeting Prague's Cardinal František Tomášek in the Sistine Chapel during the cardinals' homage immediately after his election, he embraced the seventy-nine-year-old prelate and said, "We are standing very close to one another and will stand closer still, because now the responsibility for you is being transferred to me." The Pope reiterated this "special feeling of nearness" to the Czech Church in a 1978 Christmas message to Cardinal Tomášek and in a letter dated March 2, 1979, marking the 250th anniversary of the canonization of St. John Nepomucene, martyred in 1393 at the hands of the Bohemian King Wenceslas IV. John Paul urged Czechoslovaks to imitate their patron saint's "faith, alive like an ardent flame . . . [which] develops in us such certainties as to make us fearless in the avowal and practice of our religion." In an unmistakable reference to the regime-sponsored "Pacem in Terris" priests (known in Czechoslovakia as the "pax terriers"), the Pope cited the Gospel description of the good shepherd who, "unlike the hireling," goes in search of his sheep, encourages them, and helps them carry their burdens.[9]

The results of John Paul's personal support were impressive. During the next decade, Cardinal Tomášek, who had been quite timid in his relations with the Czechoslovak communist regime and had criticized Catholic participation in the Charter 77 human rights movement, became one of Czechoslovak communism's fiercest and most feared critics. Czechs and Slovaks throughout the 1980s witnessed "this singular spectacle of the [octogenarian] cardinal getting older and tougher at the same time."[10]

The new Pope also reached out to another veteran of persecution, the Ukrainian Cardinal Iosyf Slipyi, in a letter dated March 19, 1979. The letter anticipated the 1988 millennium of Christianity in Kievan Rus', now Ukraine, which marked the beginnings of Christianity among the eastern Slavs. John Paul reminded the Ukrainians, who were "especially dear" to him, that the baptism of Kievan Rus' had taken place when Christianity, later divided into Roman Catholicism and Orthodoxy, was united in faith and communion. The Pope closed by citing the Universal Declaration of Human Rights and its "principle of religious freedom," which guaranteed rights most certainly not enjoyed in practice by the Greek Catholic Church in the Ukrainian Soviet Socialist Republic.[11]

The Soviet foreign minister, Andrei Gromyko, came to the Vatican on January 24, 1979, to take the measure of the new Pope in person. Gromyko, who allowed that the Soviet government "knew the Vatican was in no way isolated from world politics," had had one meeting with John XXIII and five with Paul VI, with whom "questions of war and peace were the main topic." Gromyko's description of his meeting with John Paul II is instructive:

> [The Pope] greeted us and remarked, "I want to underline the importance of contacts for helping to secure peace on earth."
>
> I agreed with him, of course, and then went on to describe some of the major Soviet initiatives designed to achieve that end. "As far as I can judge," I finished, "the Catholic Church accords great importance to strengthening peace, to disarmament, and to the liquidation of weapons of mass destruction. The Soviet leadership believes that this position has great value. As for ideological or religious differences, they must not be allowed to stand in the way of collaboration on this noble goal."
>
> The Pope moved on to the issue of religious belief. "It is possible that the obstacles to freedom of religion have not been removed everywhere." He paused. "According to some sources, something of this sort may be happening in the USSR."
>
> This kind of accusation was nothing new to us. I replied, "Not all rumors deserve attention. The West spreads all kinds of misinformation about the state of the Church in the Soviet Union, but the truth is that from the first day of its existence the Soviet state has guaranteed freedom of religious belief. . . . We have religious people, but that doesn't create problems either for themselves or for Soviet society."
>
> The Pope and Casaroli listened thoughtfully. Then the Pope said, "That's more or less what we thought."
>
> No more was said on the subject.
>
> This first meeting with John Paul II took place before the events of

the early 1980s in Poland, in relation to which the Vatican took up a position that crossed the threshold dividing politics from religion. . . .[12]

John Paul II had a rather different recollection of this encounter. When he raised the question of religious freedom at the beginning of their conversation, the Pope recalled, Gromyko replied that he was a deputy to the Supreme Soviet from Byelorussia and he knew that the churches were full there. What was the Pope making such a fuss about? John Paul, fully aware of the Soviet foreign minister's view that the Church, "by back alleys and back doors . . . encourages ideological unity with the exploiting class," didn't pursue the matter further with such an accomplished liar. The next day he told reporters that the audience was the "most tiresome" he had had as Pope.[13]

He had made his point, however, and it had registered. However they analyzed (and distorted) the matter through their own ideological presuppositions, the Soviets knew that they were dealing with a very different kind of pope.

DEPLOYING ASSETS

Cardinal Jean Villot, the Secretary of State of the Holy See, died on March 9, 1979. This opening at the pinnacle of the Church's central bureaucracy gave John Paul the opportunity to reshape the senior leadership of the Roman Curia, which he did seven weeks later, on April 30. Archbishop Agostino Casaroli was named Secretary of State and given two new deputies. A Spaniard, Archbishop Eduardo Martínez Somalo, formerly nuncio in Colombia, became *Sostituto* or deputy Secretary of State for "ordinary" affairs (i.e., having to do with the internal governance of the Church) and Monsignor Achille Silvestrini, another veteran Vatican diplomat, was named "foreign minister" (technically, Secretary of the Council for the Public Affairs of the Church) to replace Casaroli. Monsignor Audrys Bačkis, a native Lithuanian who had grown up in exile, was named undersecretary to Silvestrini, who was also appointed a titular archbishop.[14]

Given the "Wojtyła Difference" and Casaroli's role as architect of the *Ostpolitik* of Paul VI, Casaroli's appointment as Secretary of State may have struck some as curious. In fact, the appointment was a good example of John Paul II's adroit deployment of the Curia's resources to advance his own agenda.

The Pope and his new Secretary of State did not share a common view of the Church's situation in east central Europe, and Casaroli must have found John Paul II's approach to the Church in the world a challenge to his own longstanding views on how the Holy See's diplomacy should be conducted. Yet the two could work together, because Casaroli was a faithful servant and John Paul II found multiple advantages in having the veteran Italian Curialist as his chief operating officer.

The appointment of Casaroli helped ease the strain of the transition to a Polish Pope for many in the Church's central bureaucracy. Casaroli was widely recognized as the most accomplished member of the Holy See's diplomatic service, and his elevation could be understood as a compliment to his peers and longtime colleagues. In addition, Casaroli was an adept tactician and skillful diplomat who was also a good priest, devoting his free time to a ministry to juvenile delinquents in Rome. John Paul II had no intention of micromanaging the internal affairs of the Church, and Casaroli, very much a man of the system, could be counted on to keep the machinery running according to the broad policy outlines set by the Pope.

Casaroli's promotion also made things more complex for the Soviet Union and its satellites. It was difficult for them to suggest publicly that the Holy See had abandoned its interest in finding common ground when the principal architect of the former *Ostpolitik* had just been elevated to the highest position in the Curia. Moreover, Casaroli had been the key figure in the Holy See's adherence to the Helsinki Final Act in 1975, a treaty the Soviet Union badly wanted in order to secure the Yalta division of Europe (even if getting it had required accepting the human rights guarantees that Casaroli and others insisted on writing into the Final Act).[15]

Casaroli and Silvestrini would continue to negotiate quietly with these regimes and nurture what relationships had been built up over a decade of attempted rapprochement. Meanwhile, the Pope would pursue his far more assertive approach to the problems of the persecuted Church, hammering away publicly on human rights issues, with special reference to religious freedom. The Pope, who believed in "normalization" of relations as a tool for transforming the communist world, deftly deployed subordinates who had been committed to "normalization" as an end in itself. John Paul II, often accused of not being terribly interested in management, in fact knew quite well how to do different things and achieve different goals using the same people who had served his predecessors.[16]

The new order was harder on Cardinal Casaroli than on John Paul II. The cardinal once confessed that "I would like to help this Pope more, but I find him so different." They were, in fact, very different men: a veteran Church bureaucrat and a man who had spent his entire priesthood and episcopate in the front lines of the struggle for religious freedom. John Paul II believed that he should be the voice of those who had no voice. Casaroli believed that such matters could be settled quietly with governments without apparent reference to those voices. Yet Cardinal Casaroli did help John Paul II, who realized the wealth of experience that his Secretary of State brought to his responsibilities and took advantage of that experience, confident of Casaroli's loyalty.[17]

THE RETURN OF THE NATIVE

John Paul II's return to Poland was inevitable. Getting it done was a complicated and difficult business.

In his remarks to the Poles who had attended his inauguration in Rome, the new Pope had indicated that he wanted to return home for the ninth centenary of the death of St. Stanisław, which would also coincide with the closing of the Synod of Kraków. The Polish bishops had raised the question even earlier. In a statement issued the day after his election, the episcopate enthusiastically expressed the hope that their former colleague would come for the Stanisław anniversary in 1979 and for the 600th anniversary of the arrival of the icon of the Black Madonna in Częstochowa in 1982. As negotiations for a papal visit began between the regime in Warsaw and the Vatican, the Polish government gave no public indication of its attitude, in part because opinions among the communist cadres were divided. The upper echelons argued for a generous welcome. Lower-level operatives, perhaps closer to the population's real feelings, expressed grave doubts about the visit's impact. On January 11, 1979, John Paul II tried to move things along by, in effect, inviting himself home, telling the Polish authorities that it was his "duty" to take part in the ceremonies commemorating the anniversary of Stanisław's martyrdom.[18]

Senior Polish party and government officials knew they had no other choice than to agree to a visit. But they were not independent agents, and their Soviet allies were not enthusiastic. Even as Cardinal Wyszyński and Archbishop Luigi Poggi, a key Casaroli aide, pressed Polish party leader Edward Gierek to agree to an official welcome, Gierek was being pressured by Moscow. In his memoirs, the Polish party boss described an angry, indeed bizarre, telephone call he received from Soviet party chieftain Leonid Brezhnev in early 1979.

After Gierek had said that the Polish regime would give John Paul a respectful reception, Brezhnev shot back, "Take my advice, don't give him any reception. It will only cause trouble." When Gierek explained that it was impossible for a Polish government not to receive a Polish pope, the Soviet leader had another idea: "Tell the Pope—he's a wise man—he can declare publicly that he can't come due to illness." After being informed that that, too, was impossible, Brezhnev told Gierek that Gomułka had been a "better communist" because "he didn't receive Paul VI in Poland, and nothing awful happened. The Poles have survived the refusal to admit a pope once; they'll survive it a second time." Gierek insisted that "political reasons" required him to admit John Paul II to Poland. "Well," Brezhnev concluded, "do as you wish. But be careful you don't regret it later."[19]

With Brezhnev temporarily squared away and John Paul's visit now a fait accompli, negotiations between the Polish Church and the government turned to the question of dates. In Poland's liturgical calendar, the feast of St. Stanisław is celebrated on May 8. A papal visit on this date, with its unmistakable overtones of religious resistance to state power, was simply too much for the regime to contemplate. After months of negotiations, a compromise was finally reached. Rather than coming to Poland for two days in May as originally envisioned, John Paul II would come to Poland for nine days in June and visit six cities rather than just Warsaw and Kraków.

In announcing this agreement on March 2, 1979, the state-controlled media warned against the "illusion" that the visit would change the party's leading role in any way or alter the "strictly secular" nature of the Polish People's

Republic.[20] The regime may have convinced itself that, by deflecting the visit from the traditional date of Stanisław's feast, it had won a considerable victory. In fact, the communists had lost a great deal. John Paul happily traded two days for nine, and two cities for six. Moreover, the change of dates from May to June supercharged the visit with religious symbolism. The Pope would arrive in Poland and celebrate his first public mass on the Vigil of Pentecost, the great feast marking the descent of the Holy Spirit on the apostles in the form of "tongues of fire" (*Acts* 2.1–4). As for the anniversary of St. Stanisław's martyrdom and the closing of the Synod of Kraków, the Polish episcopate simply extended the anniversary celebrations for another month (culminating on June 10), and the Archdiocese of Kraków rescheduled the closing of the Synod until the Pope's visit. The ostensible communist triumph in the battle over St. Stanisław turned out to be the very definition of a Pyrrhic victory.

Venues were another contested issue. The communists refused to have the Pope in Silesia, where John Paul wanted to revisit the shrine of the Virgin Mary in Piekary, a pilgrimage he had regularly undertaken as archbishop of Kraków. Silesia, however, was the political fiefdom of Edward Gierek, and the party leader, no matter how resigned to the papal visit, was not about to be upstaged on his home turf.[21] The government also refused to let the Pope into Nowa Huta, an indication of just how stung the communists had been by the Ark Church and the battle for Mistrzejowice. Even with these sites off-limits, the Pope was about to undertake an extensive tour. The itinerary finally agreed upon included the national political capital, Warsaw; the cradle of Polish Catholicism and the country's primatial see, Gniezno; the shrine of the Black Madonna, Częstochowa; and a series of events in Kraków and its environs—Kalwaria Zebrzydowska, Wadowice, Oświęcim (Auschwitz), Nowy Targ (in the highlands), and the Cistercian monastery at Mogiła on the outskirts of Nowa Huta.

The Church and the government also locked horns on how the Polish broadcast media would cover papal events. For thirty years, the regime had stubbornly refused the Church access to radio and television. The Polish episcopate, which had bitterly resented this exclusion from national life, argued that the papal events were of great public interest and ought to be extensively covered for that reason. The regime was being pressed by its comrades in neighboring countries, upset at the thought of their people being able to pick up the Polish broadcasts; the Lithuanian regime sent a fraternal delegation to Warsaw to plead for limiting their scope. Calculating that more extensive TV coverage might cut down on the crowds at certain papal venues, the Polish government finally agreed to national broadcasting of the arrival ceremonies, the papal visit with government officials at Warsaw's Belvedere Palace, the Mass in Victory Square, the visit to Auschwitz and the Mass there, and the departure ceremonies in Kraków. Coverage of the Pope's visits to Częstochowa and Gniezno was limited to regional radio and TV. None of the details of television coverage was settled until the very last minute.[22]

The organizational arrangements for the papal visit, including the enormous task of managing the crowds, were left entirely to the Church—another strategic error by the regime. People who had been told for thirty years that they were incapable of organizing themselves independently of the state or the party could now test that claim empirically. The testing went on in thousands of homes and churches where meals were prepared for pilgrims, marshals trained in crowd control, and decorations made and displayed. Weeks before John Paul arrived, the people of Poland had refuted the claim that only the "vanguard" of society could organize society properly.

SETTING THE STAGE

Whatever the Polish government may have thought it had done in deflecting John Paul's visit until June, the Church and the Pope were determined to honor St. Stanisław's martyrdom according to ancient custom. On May 8, the martyr's Polish feast day, John Paul II issued an apostolic letter, *Rutilans Agmen*, to Cardinal Wyszyński, Archbishop Macharski, and the entire Polish Church. The martyrdom of the bishop of Kraków, one of that "glowing band"[23] of witnesses from which the Church had drawn its strength over the centuries, was still "at the root of the affairs, experiences, and truths" of the Polish nation, he wrote. It was a heritage of which Poland, in her present "peculiar situation," wanted to "remind herself." That act of memory was embodied in 6,000 Polish expatriates from around the world who, led by Cardinal Wyszyński, came to Rome on May 16 for a solemn commemoration of the Stanisław anniversary in the Paul VI Audience Hall. In his opening address, the cardinal pointedly noted that the forthcoming papal pilgrimage would be bracketed by the Pope's visits to the relics of St. Adalbert in Gniezno and St. Stanisław in Kraków, the connecting tissue between them being the papal visit to the shrine of the Black Madonna in Częstochowa.[24] John Paul's itinerary had been built around the three icons that tied Polish national identity most closely to Catholicism.

Two days later, on May 18, John Paul and the Primate led a commemoration of the thirty-fifth anniversary of the decisive World War II battle for Monte Cassino in which the exiled Polish army (including the Pope's classmate, Jerzy Kluger) had figured so prominently. Poland, John Paul said, continued "to live in the orbit of the consequences" of that conflict—an unmistakable reference to the Yalta division of Europe. The war should have taught that it was "only on the basis of full respect for the rights of men and the rights of nations—full respect!" that peace in Europe could be built. That meant the right of a nation "to social life in the spirit of its own national and religious convictions and traditions and to the sovereignty of its own territory." There was no need to add that Polish sovereignty was infringed by Poland's incorporation into a falsely described "alliance" meant to protect a regime deliberately constructed in opposition to Polish convictions and traditions.[25]

Back in Poland, the regime was attempting preemptive damage control. In March, the Polish Communist Party sent out a secret set of instructions to teachers in the country's schools, which were later published in an underground periodical. The instructions suggest the mindset of the regime in the prelude to the Pope's return home:

> The Pope is our enemy. . . . Due to his uncommon skills and great sense of humor he is dangerous, because he charms everyone, especially journalists. Besides, he goes for cheap gestures in his relations with the crowd, for instance, puts on a highlander's hat, shakes all hands, kisses children, etc. . . . It is modeled on American presidential campaigns. . . .
>
> He is dangerous, because he will make St. Stanisław the patron of the opposition to the authorities and a defender of human rights. Luckily we managed to maneuver him out of the date May 8. . . . Because of the activation of the Church in Poland our activities designed to atheize the youth not only cannot diminish but must intensely develop. . . . In this respect all means are allowed and we cannot afford any sentiments.[26]

The Polish regime wasn't completely ham-handed. It refurbished sites the Pope would visit and cooperated with the Church in setting up the papal venues and arranging the necessary public health services for the huge crowds expected. The government also provided extensive communications facilities for the world press. It was taking no chances with its own media, however, and issued detailed censorship directives to Polish journalists, which were promptly leaked to the underground press.[27]

While all this was going on in the name of the Polish state, the Polish nation continued to make preparations for receiving its most distinguished son. Students in a Warsaw dormitory put up a large banner on their building that quoted the Pope on the world's youth: "You are the hope of the world, the Church's hope, my hope." The authorities in charge of the dormitory tried to get the banner taken down. The students, unanimously, refused. Asked later who had told him to remove the banner, the dormitory manager said, "An older man from the Soviet Embassy."[28]

In Kraków, volunteers were decorating the Pope's old home at Franciszkańska, 3, with papal and Polish flags, working hurriedly on a makeshift scaffolding. The night before the Pope arrived, they were still at it late at night when the streetlights suddenly went out. As one participant later put it, "Nobody believed it was just bad luck since ours was the only block without lights." Proving that "we" could be more resourceful than "them," drivers parked their cars across from the archbishop's residence so the volunteers could complete the decorations with the aid of their headlights. No one complained about the dead batteries afterward.[29]

NINE DAYS THAT CHANGED THE WORLD

The idea of "pilgrimage"—a journey to a sacred place for prayer, penance, and almsgiving—is deeply inscribed in the religious imagination of humanity. In biblical times pilgrimages to Jerusalem were common, particularly on the great feasts of Passover, Pentecost, and Tabernacles. Pilgrimages to the Holy Land were a staple of early Christian life, and as the Church expanded throughout the Mediterranean world, other pilgrimage sites emerged, often associated with the relics of the apostles.

The tradition of pilgrimage, reflecting the biblical conviction that God had acted decisively in history at certain specific times and in certain real places, readily transferred to other cultures as the Christian movement grew. Poland was no exception, as the great pilgrimages to the shrine of the Black Madonna at Częstochowa and to Kalwaria Zebrzydowska attested throughout the centuries. From his boyhood days, Karol Wojtyła had actively participated in the Polish pilgrimage tradition. Now, he set out on what one commentator would later call "the most fantastic pilgrimage in the history of contemporary Europe."[30]

In announcing the final itinerary for the Pope's visit in a communiqué dated May 4, the Polish bishops stressed that the Pope was coming at their invitation, and that "the Holy Father's journey has the religious character of a pilgrimage to his native country in the year dedicated to the ninth centenary of the martyrdom of St. Stanisław, Bishop of Kraków. The pilgrimage will traverse the principal places of the saints, sanctified by the blood of martyrs."[31] This insistence on "pilgrimage" as the leitmotif of what was about to happen was not a sop to the government, but an accurate description of John Paul II's conception of his world travels. From the beginning, he was determined that his visits would be structured to convey their pastoral purpose.

The "iconography" of the Pope's trips abroad was established in the Dominican Republic and Mexico in January 1979 and has been maintained ever since. On arriving in a country, the Pope knelt and kissed the ground to express his conviction that God was present in this particular place and with these particular people. The diplomatic formalities were observed but kept to a minimum, as he met with the local head of state and other officials of the government. In traveling through any country, he was never accompanied in his "Popemobile" by political figures, but only by the local bishop and/or the head of the national episcopal conference, who were his hosts. The principal events of any pastoral visit were always liturgical, not political, in character. The impact of any given visit on public affairs was something John Paul II was content to leave to the people of a country, to their religious leaders—and, he insisted, to the Holy Spirit.

June 2—Warsaw

At 10:07 A.M. on Saturday, June 2, 1979, John Paul II walked vigorously down the gangway from the Alitalia 727 *Città di Bergamo*, knelt, and kissed the ground of Poland. Church bells began tolling throughout a country electric with anticipation. Polish President Henryk Jabłoński and Primate Wyszyński made brief statements of welcome. John Paul's response deliberately set the context for the next nine days. The Polish Pope had come home to return to his people their authentic history and culture.

There were proprieties to be observed. John Paul thanked President Jabłoński for the courtesy of his reception and reiterated his hope that his visit would serve "the great cause of rapprochement and collaboration among nations." He praised Cardinal Wyszyński and said that the program for the days ahead would be his response to the Primate's welcome.

Then he addressed his "beloved brothers and sisters," his "dear fellow-countrymen," whom he greeted on this special day "with the same words I used on October 16 last year to greet those present in St. Peter's Square: 'Praised be Jesus Christ!'" That was how he had learned to greet fellow Poles during his life among them, and that was how he came to them now. Poland had been denied its history and its culture by five years of Nazi occupation and thirty-three years of communist hegemony. Now he, a son of Poland, would give his people back what was theirs by birthright.

After a triumphal entry into the capital through streets packed with hundreds of thousands, John Paul was driven along Warsaw's Royal Way to the Old Town. He went first to the Cathedral of St. John, rebuilt after its destruction during the Warsaw Uprising of 1944, in which the Polish Home Army had fought the Wehrmacht hand-to-hand and pew-by-pew, the fighting spilling down into the cathedral's crypt. Once again, he began with a confession of faith: "Praised be Jesus Christ!" And once again, he summoned up the historic memory of his people, whose presence in the cathedral confirmed "the thousand-year right of citizenship that this Church has in the present-day life of the capital, of the nation, of the State." To be in this rebuilt cathedral, he said, was to be reminded of "what Christ once said: 'Destroy this temple, and in three days I will raise it up' (*John* 2.19)." Salvation history was not something that had happened in the past, he claimed; salvation history was the dramatic context in which Poland continued to live out its national life. For did not Polish tradition have it that St. Stanisław, whose martyrdom he had come to Poland to commemorate, once said to King Bolesław, "Destroy this Church, *and Christ, over the centuries, will rebuild it*"? It was in the context of this history, charged with signs of God's purposes, that he was meeting his countrymen today—"the first Pope from the Polish race, on the threshold of the second millennium of the nation's baptism and history."[32]

The reclamation of Polish history continued at the Belvedere Palace, official residence of the Polish president, where John Paul and Cardinal Wyszyński met with President Jabłoński and Communist Party leader Edward Gierek. The Pope's formal remarks were polite but firm. He had come, he said, at the invitation of the Polish episcopate, "which expresses the will of the Catholic society in our motherland." He was grateful to the authorities of the Polish People's Republic for having "also opened to me the gates of my native land." Then, after acknowledging what had been done to rebuild the capital and its royal palace from the ruins of the war, he challenged the moral premise of the totalitarian system.

Poles knew that the state was not an end in itself. Rather, "the *raison d'être of the State is the sovereignty of society, of the nation, of the motherland.*" This was "the terrible historical lesson" of Poland's nineteenth-century history, which had become, in the aftermath of World War I, "a new forge of Polish patriotism." The present Polish state frequently asserted its commitment to "peace [and] co-existence," a communist mantra. That commitment, John Paul insisted, had a "*profound ethical meaning,*" touching the "*objective rights of the nation,*" which included the right "to the formation of its own culture and civilization." The authentic history of Polish culture was one in which there was no place for forced ideological conversions.[33]

As for the present international situation, "peace and co-existence," he said, required an end to "all forms of economic or cultural colonialism." This meant that any alliances into which a state entered had to be engaged on the basis of "voluntary collaboration." The Warsaw Pact was not mentioned; it did not have to be. As for the Church, it did not "desire privileges" but only the freedom to carry out its evangelical and moral mission. That had been the program for thirty years of "a man of rare quality, Cardinal Stefan Wyszyński, Primate of Poland." He had shared the Primate's aspiration when he was archbishop of Kraków, and he would continue to share it. Appealing to the "responsibility" that fell on each of his communist hosts "before history and before your conscience," this "son of the same motherland" made it unmistakably clear that he would be watching: "Permit me to continue to consider [Poland's] good as my own, and to feel my sharing in it as deeply as if I still lived in this land and were still a citizen of this state . . . Permit me to continue to feel, to think, and to hope this, and to pray for this."

It was a hope, and a warning, addressed to men in Moscow as well as in Warsaw. There can be no doubt that it was taken as such.

By the end of the day, the great cross in Victory Square had been dismantled.

June 3—Gniezno

After staying overnight at the Primate's residence, John Paul attended a Mass celebrated Sunday morning, the Solemnity of Pentecost, for tens of thousands of university students, many of whom had kept overnight vigil at Warsaw's collegiate Church of St. Anne and in an adjacent square. In his address, the Pope asked his "young friends" to consider the great question, what is a human being? It was, the Pope suggested, life's most fundamental query, and it raised another, deeper question: "What is to be the measurement for measuring man?" His physical capacities? His technical expertise? The Scripture readings for that day's feast of the Holy Spirit proposed a richer answer: the true measure of the human heart and spirit was "the measurement of conscience," the "measurement of the spirit open to God." The young people of Poland knew that theirs was a country in waiting, but for what? Poland was waiting, the Pope reminded them, as St. Paul had reminded his Romans, "for the revealing of

the sons of God." It was waiting for future "doctors, technicians, jurists, professors . . . in order that in each one of us God Himself should to some extent
be revealed."[34]

Leaving the political capital, John Paul flew by helicopter to Gniezno, the
repository of the relics of St. Adalbert, the first missionary to Poland. Here his
Polish pilgrimage along "the route of the history of the nation"—the road
from Gniezno through Częstochowa to Kraków and the relics of St. Stanisław—
really began.

Gniezno's population was about 60,000. A million Poles filled the plains
outside the city, on which Poland had been baptized a thousand years before,
as far as the eye could see. At the heliport in Gebarzewo near Gniezno, the
Pope addressed representatives of rural Poland and stressed the importance
of religious education for children, whom he prayed would "have easy access
to Christ." Those who denied them that access stood under the "severe" judgment of which Christ had spoken when he said that those who gave scandal to
children would have been better off if millstones had been hung about their
necks and they had been thrown into the sea (see *Luke* 17.2). "Let us meditate
every once in a while on those words," he suggested, before leaving the podium
to work the front lines of the immense crowd, shaking hands, blessing the people, kissing children held up to him by their parents.[35]

At an open-air Mass that afternoon outside the tenth-century cathedral of
Gniezno, with every inch of space along the way from Gniezno Common to
the cathedral taken by an unbroken mass of people, John Paul once again
greeted the Poland that had been "inserted into the mysteries of the divine life
through the sacraments of baptism and confirmation." "In this upper room of
our Polish millennium" they were gathered, he said, like the apostles—in this
instance, to recall again "the mystery-filled date . . . from which we start to
count the years of the history of our motherland and of the Church that has
been made part of it—the history of Poland 'ever faithful.'"[36] The New Testament day of Pentecost had been a day of linguistic miracles. The Scripture read
at Mass had spoken of the apostles preaching in Jerusalem and being heard in
their own tongues by men from all over the Mediterranean world. On June 3,
1979, John Paul said, Poland was living a similar pentecostal experience, which
touched the entire world of the Slavic peoples and their recent history—and
which rendered the Yalta division of Europe moot.

That the Spirit of God continued to speak through all the world's languages was confirmed by the millennium-long experience of the Slavic peoples, with their distinctive tongues. Perhaps, he said, that was why the Holy
Spirit had brought him to the papacy, to "introduce into the communion of
the Church the understandings of the words and of the languages that still
sound strange to the ear accustomed to the Romance, Germanic, English, and
Celtic tongues." Was it not Christ's will "that this Polish Pope, this Slav Pope,
should at this precise moment manifest the unity of Christian Europe," the
result of the "rich architecture of the Holy Spirit?

"Yes," he concluded: "It is Christ's will, it is what the Holy Spirit disposes . . . We shall not return to the past! *We shall go towards the future!* 'Receive the Holy Spirit!' (*John* 20.22). Amen!"[37]

During this stirring homily, John Paul noticed a banner in the crowd: "Father, remember your Czech Church." He interrupted his prepared text to reassure these long-suffering people, and all those who were being prevented from hearing his voice, that he would never forget them.[38]

That afternoon, speaking from the balcony of the archbishop's residence, John Paul defended the spiritual independence of Polish culture. "Christian inspiration," he said, "continues to be the chief source of the creativity of Polish artists," which was where "the soul of the nation is reflected."[39] The Pope also bantered with the enormous crowd. It had been an extremely hot day and the weather became the subject of a papal wisecrack: "In June, ninety degrees heat is as common one hundred fifty miles west of Warsaw as a Polish pontiff."[40]

June 4–6: Częstochowa

Jasna Góra, the "Bright Mountain" shrine of the Black Madonna at Częstochowa, is built atop a limestone promontory rising above the flat plains of the Silesian Basin. More than a million Poles had gathered on the grounds surrounding the shrine on June 4 when John Paul—speaking from the ramparts of the Pauline monastery where the Swedish invasion had been broken in 1655—began his sermon at an outdoor Mass by quoting an epic he had once performed in the Rhapsodic Theater, Adam Mickiewicz's *Pan Tadeusz*: "Holy Virgin guarding bright Częstochowa . . ." That invocation "expressed what then beat and still beats in the hearts of all Poles." For it was to Jasna Góra that every Pole came, physically or in spirit, to bring the "decisive moments" of life, "the occasions of responsibility," to be laid before the Virgin.

His voice breaking with emotion, John Paul said that it was inconceivable that the first Polish Pope in history should not have come to Jasna Góra. How could he not come to "this shrine of great hope," where "so many times I had whispered *totus tuus* in prayer" before Mary's image? How could he not come "to listen to the beating of the heart of the Church and of the motherland in the heart of the Mother"?

Jasna Góra was "the nation's shrine." Here was where one learned what Poland really was and who the Poles really were. Anyone who wanted to "know how . . . history is interpreted by the heart of the Poles . . . must come here" where one heard "the echo of the life of the whole nation in the heart of its Mother and Queen."

Thirteen years before, at the culmination of the celebrations of the national millennium and at the beginning of the new era opened by Vatican II, the Polish nation had reconsecrated itself to Mary, petitioning "for the freedom of the Church in the world and in Poland." He now asked his countrymen's consent "that I, as St. Peter's successor present with you here today, should entrust the whole of the Church to the Mother of Christ with the same lively faith, the same heroic hope" as had been done thirteen years before. "Consent that I should *entrust* all this to Mary. Consent that I should *entrust* it to her in a new and solemn way.

"I am," he concluded, "a man of great trust. I learned to be so here."[41]

The Pope interrupted himself during his homily to imagine out loud what the Italian prelates in his party were saying to themselves: "What are we going to do with this Polish Pope, this Slavic Pope? What can we do?" The crowd burst into ten minutes of "thunderous applause and cheers."[42]

That evening, after praying privately before the icon of the Black Madonna, John Paul met with parish delegations from the Diocese of Często-chowa and with the sick, who had been gathered outside the monastery. Whenever he had met the sick as a priest and bishop, he said, he had felt that his words of compassion were inadequate. But there was "the one reality in which human suffering is essentially transformed": the cross of Christ. On the cross, the Son of God had accomplished the redemption of the world. And it was "through this mystery that every cross placed on someone's shoulders acquires a dignity that is humanly inconceivable." In entering more deeply into the mystery of the cross, suffering was ennobled. And so he asked the sick for a favor: "You who are weak and humanly incapable, be a source of strength for your brother and father who is at your side in prayer and heart."[43]

After celebrating Mass for 6,000 Polish nuns—whom he called a "living sign . . . in the midst of humanity [that] is beyond price"—John Paul participated in a plenary assembly of the Polish episcopate in the Jasna Góra monastery. The meeting presented the Pope with a major challenge. In four days, he had established himself as the authentic spokesman of the Polish nation, as the vast crowd response had made unmistakably clear. He was leaving Poland in less than a week, though, and the seventy-eight bishops he left behind, especially Cardinal Wyszyński, would have to bear the daily burden of defending the free space he had created. How could he continue to speak for Poland without undercutting his brother bishops and the Primate? How could he do so in what was, for him and his former colleagues, a tremendously emotional moment?

The answer was to reaffirm the strategy on which Wyszyński had insisted for more than thirty years: unity. John Paul began his formal address by noting that "the quality that particularly characterizes the Polish Bishops' Conference is that unity which is the source of spiritual strength." That unity had given society a "justified and deserved" confidence in the Church and the Polish episcopate. The embodiment of both that unity and that confidence was the Primate. As Pope, he wanted to say before his brother Polish bishops what he had said to Polish pilgrims in Rome and to the Polish authorities in Warsaw: Cardinal Stefan Wyszyński was "a providential man for the Church and for the motherland."

His own work as a Polish bishop, John Paul continued, had "enabled me to study at close quarters the problems of the modern Church in their universal dimension." Others might think of the Polish case as unique; John Paul saw it as a particular window into the universal crisis of modernity. There *was* something singular about Poland at the end of the twentieth century, though. Faced with that crisis of humanism in an acute form, Poland had responded by intensifying its Christian faith. This was a lesson with resonance far beyond Poland's borders.

The Polish hierarchy had supported, and sometimes saved, the Polish nation in times of crisis. This, he knew, was something difficult for instinctively anti-hierarchical moderns to appreciate. For Poles, "it is simply a part of the truth of the history of our own motherland," the truth that he had come to restore to his people. And as he had written in his last poem, the warrant of that truth was to be found not in argument, but in blood: in "the heritage of the holy martyr bishops Wojciech [Adalbert] and Stanisław."

John Paul then reviewed the teaching of Vatican II's *Dogmatic Constitution on the Church*, which had described the hierarchy as servants of the Church's mission to the world. Church-state relations in Poland had to be dealt with in this evangelical context. "Normality," as John Paul II and the Council understood it, meant the public situation prescribed by Vatican II's *Declaration on Religious Freedom* (which, the Pope noted in an almost acerbic aside, "directly tallies with the principles promulgated in fundamental state and international documents, including the Constitution of the Polish People's Republic"): the freedom of the individual to pursue the truth according to the dictates and demands of conscience, the freedom of the Church to make its evangelical proposal to society, and the freedom of individual believers and of the corporate Church to be servants of society's needs. That was what the Church asked—no more, but also no less. In so asking, it reminded the state that it existed to serve society, not the other way around.

St. Stanisław's life, witness, and death at the hands of arbitrary state power had built a great truth into the foundations of Polish history and culture, John Paul said—the laws promulgated by the state must be accountable to the moral law inscribed by God in nature and on the human heart. The moral law "places an obligation on everyone, both subjects and rulers." Only when this moral law was recognized could the crisis of modernity be resolved. For it was only in recognizing the moral law that "the dignity of the human person [can] be respected and universally recognized."

The anniversary of St. Stanisław, the Pope concluded, also required Poles to think about themselves and their country "in the European context." There was a way in which one could talk reasonably about "Western Europe" and "Eastern Europe," but it was not the way of the iron curtain. "Despite the different traditions that exist in the territory of Europe between its Eastern part and its Western part, there lives in each of them the same Christianity, which takes its origins from the same Christ, which accepts the same Word of God, which is linked with the same twelve apostles." This "spiritual genealogy" was what made Europe "Europe." The unity of the Polish episcopate, so long at the service of the nation and its unity, must now be put at the service of a wider responsibility. For "Christianity must commit itself anew to the formation of the spiritual unity of Europe. Economic and political reasons alone cannot do it. We must go deeper: to ethical reasons."[44]

Later that afternoon, John Paul preached on unity through reconciliation among nations at a Mass for another million pilgrims from Lower Silesia. But to the men in Warsaw and Moscow, the Pope's address at Jasna Góra, by linking Poland's religious freedom and national integrity to the cause of European unity, could mean only one thing. Without ever mentioning the word "Yalta," John Paul II had set himself and the Church against the post-1945 division of Europe. This man was a threat to the entire communist position, precisely because he deployed weapons to which communism was acutely vulnerable.[45]

The ubiquitous Communist Party slogan "The Party Is for the People," continued to decorate buildings throughout the country. A codicil had been surreptitiously added to at least one such banner: ". . . but the People are for the Pope."[46]

June 6–10: Kraków

On June 6, his last day in Częstochowa, John Paul celebrated Mass for seminarians and the novices of religious orders, met with thousands of priests and religious brothers (whom he reminded of the Polish clergy martyred in the concentration camps of World War II), and celebrated a second Mass for hundreds of thousands of miners and other workers from Upper Silesia. Standing on the same ramparts where Prior Kordecki had defied the invading Swedes three centuries before, John Paul looked down into the city of Częstochowa and beyond, to the Bolesław Bierut steel mill and the surrounding colleries of the Silesian industrial basin. The workers hadn't been given a holiday but they had come anyway, the miners dressed in the traditional gold-buttoned black frock coats of their trade and wearing white-plumed black hats. In his homily the Pope asked these manual laborers to remember the poet Norwid ("Work exists . . . for resurrection") and not to let themselves "be seduced by the temptation to think that man can fully find himself by denying God, erasing prayer from his life, and becoming only a worker, deluding himself that what he produces can on its own fill the needs of the human heart. 'Man shall not live by bread alone' (*Matthew* 4.4)."[47]

On the evening of June 6, John Paul II flew into his "beloved Kraków." "He left here with a bag, a toothbrush, and a couple of rolls to eat," a hotel doorman remarked to foreign journalists. "Look at the way he came back."[48] It was a tumultuous homecoming. A vast crowd was waiting in the rain on the great greensward of the Błonia Krakowskie, the Kraków Commons, to greet the Pope at what seemed like an enormous family reunion. He felt, he said, "even closer to you" because of "the separation to which the Lord has called me." During the days ahead, he concluded, he wanted to do "the same things I have always done: proclaim 'the great works of God' (*Acts* 2.11), give witness to the Gospel, and serve the dignity of man. As St. Stanisław did so many centuries ago."[49]

John Paul II drove into his city in an open car, past the exultant faces of men, women, and children he had baptized, confirmed, and counseled, past couples whose marriages he had blessed and whose parents he had buried. When he recognized a face in the throng, he waved and called out a greeting. Arriving first at Wawel Cathedral, he wondered aloud at the "inscrutable designs" of Providence, which had brought him back home to celebrate the completion of the Synod of Kraków in a wholly unexpected way. Then he went to spend the night in his old room at Franciszkańska, 3. Except for a vase of fresh flowers, it had been left exactly as it was when he departed for Warsaw and Rome the previous October 2.

That night, and for the next three nights, the streets surrounding the archbishop's residence and the roofs of nearby houses were thronged with young people—high school and university students and workers, celebrating a kind of papal street festival, clearly to the discomfort of the authorities. The first night, John Paul came out on a balcony and began a dialogue with the crowd, asking, "Who's making all this noise? I haven't heard so much noise since Mexico, where they cried 'El Papa, El Papa.' . . ." The youngsters took the cue and began the rhythmic chant, 'El Papa, *Sto lat*, El Papa, *Sto lat*! [May you live a hundred years!]." They called for a speech, but the Pope explained there wouldn't be any; he had a sore throat. So they sang together, as they would for the next three nights. To locals familiar with Karol Wojtyła's encyclopedic knowledge of Polish songs, what was even more amazing than this unprecedented public dialogue was the fact that during one such impromptu songfest, their former archbishop had to confess publicly, "I don't know this one; it must be new."[50]

When the Pope had first come out in response to the incessant singing and cheers of the crowd, he had stepped onto the window sill so he could be seen better. Unidentified hands held on to the pleats of his cassock to hold him safely on the ledge. "When I was archbishop," he cracked, "I didn't have to hop onto the window sill, and even when I leaned out the window, nobody grabbed my cassock."[51] Later, he pretended to complain over the din: "It's bad enough being the Pope in Rome. It would be far worse being the Pope in Kraków, spending all the time standing at this window with no time to sleep and no time to think."[52] Finally, at midnight, John Paul called off the songfest with the last word: "You are asking for a word or two, so here they are—Good night!"[53]

The next morning, June 7, John Paul went on pilgrimage to Kalwaria Zebrzydowska. There, he said, virtually every problem he had faced as archbishop had "reached its maturity," not in strategic planning but in prayer, amid "the great mystery of faith that Kalwaria holds within itself." Along its paths of

Jesus and Mary, up hills, down ravines, and across brooks, the great shrine "expressed a synthesis of all that is part of our earthly pilgrimage," which had been transformed from darkness to light through the Incarnation of the Son of God. From the woods of Kalwaria he wanted to issue a "simple fundamental invitation" to whoever might be listening: "pray." Pray especially, he asked, "for one of the pilgrims of Kalwaria whom Christ has called with the same words He spoke to Simon Peter, 'Feed my lambs . . . Feed my sheep' (*John* 21.15,19). Pray for me here, during my life and after my death."[54]

From Kalwaria, he went to his birthplace, Wadowice. Leaving his helicopter, he spotted the peaks of the Beskidy Mountains on the horizon, named them one by one, and asked whether he had forgotten any. He hadn't. Thirty thousand people, twice the normal town population, waited for him on the soccer field where he had played goalie and in the square where he and Jerzy Kluger had gotten into trouble with the somnolent policeman, Officer Ćwięk. The native son mingled with his fellow townsmen, shaking hands, blessing children, and singing "Poland Semper Fidelis" along with the local band. "We always had a good band in Wadowice," he remembered aloud. "Before the war it was the band of the 12th Infantry, but you young people wouldn't remember that. . . ."

He was formally welcomed by Monsignor Edward Zacher, his old religion teacher and still the town pastor, who greeted the Pope and the crowd with the words that Cardinal Felici had used in Rome eight months before: *"Annuntio vobis gaudium magnum, habemus Papam!"* The Pope responded by praying for all those who had touched his life here, "beginning with my parents, my brother and my sister, whose memory is linked for me with this city." Most of all, he said, he wanted to give thanks for his baptism on June 20, 1920. Prior to addressing the crowd from the church balcony, he had gone inside, genuflected, and kissed the font in which he had been christened.[55]

John Paul's pilgrimage turned from life to death and from icons of goodness to the great modern icon of evil as he flew by helicopter to the town of Oświęcim and the Auschwitz-Birkenau concentration and extermination camps.[56] From the helicopter pad on the outskirts of town, the Pope was driven to the gate of the Auschwitz concentration camp in a limousine constantly pelted with flowers thrown by the half-million Poles lining the roadway. But this was neither the place nor the moment for smiles. John Paul walked through the wrought-iron entrance gate with its infamously cynical inscription, *Arbeit Macht Frei* [Work Makes You Free], and along the gravel paths separating the red-brick barracks buildings until he came to Block 11. There, in the basement, in Cell 18, Maximilian Kolbe had died a martyr to charity. The Pope knelt in prayer, kissed the cement floor where Kolbe had lain in agony, and then left a bouquet of red-and-white flowers and an Easter candle brought from Rome. Outside Block 11 was the "Wall of Death," against which prisoners were executed by firing squad. En route to praying there with West Germany's Cardinal Hermann Volk, the Pope met and embraced seventy-eight-year-old Franciszek Gajowniczek, whose life Father Kolbe had saved by his self-sacrifice.

A brief helicopter ride then took the Pope a few kilometers to the Auschwitz II extermination camp at Birkenau, where industrial-age mass slaughter had been carried out less than thirty-five years before. An altar platform had been set up over the tracks on which the victims had arrived by train, some to be dispatched immediately to the gas chambers and crematoria, others to rude wooden huts to await execution. The cross on the platform was "crowned" with barbed wire, and from one of its arms hung the striped material used in making prisoner uniforms at the Auschwitz concentration camp.

John Paul II walked through that place of incredible horror slowly, his head bowed, stopping at the monument with commemorative tablets memorializing the Nazis' victims in their twenty languages. He paused for the longest periods at the tablets in memory of the Jewish, Russian, and Polish dead, and then walked back down the tracks, stopping wherever he saw former prisoners dressed in their distinctive striped camp uniforms, to the altar where he celebrated Mass before a crowd estimated at more than a million. His concelebrants were priests and bishops who had been imprisoned in the camps during the war. In his sermon at what he called this "Golgotha of the modern world," he spoke of Father Kolbe's "victory through faith and love" in a place "built for the negation of faith—faith in God and faith in man." This was a place meant "to trample radically not only on love but on all signs of human dignity, of humanity," a place "built on hatred and contempt for man in the name of a crazed ideology." Some may have been surprised that he had come to a "place built on cruelty." But he had "begun his first encyclical with the words 'Redemptor Hominis' and [had] dedicated it to the whole cause of man, to the dignity of man, to the threats to him, and finally to his inalienable rights . . ." So it was "impossible for me not to come here as Pope."

He had come, now, as a pilgrim, to kneel in prayer:

> I kneel before all the inscriptions that come one after another bearing the memory of the victims of Oświęcim in [their] languages: Polish, English, Bulgarian, Romany, Czech, Danish, French, Greek, Hebrew, Yiddish, Spanish, Flemish, Serbo-Croat, German, Norwegian, Russian, Romanian, Hungarian, and Italian.
>
> In particular, I pause . . . before the inscription in Hebrew. This inscription awakens the memory of the people whose sons and daughters were intended for total extermination. This People draws its origin from Abraham, our father in faith (cf. *Romans* 4.12), as was expressed by Paul of Tarsus. The very people that received from God the commandment, "You shall not kill," itself experienced in a special measure what is meant by killing. It is not permissible for anyone to pass by this inscription with indifference . . .

Remembering Auschwitz, he concluded, had to yield a commitment—that the rights of every human person, enshrined in the Universal Declaration of Human Rights written in the shadow of Auschwitz, be honored and respected, along with the legitimate rights of nations to their language, culture, freedom, and development. What had happened at Auschwitz must never be permitted to happen again: "Never one at the other's expense, at the cost of the enslavement of the other, at the cost of conquest, outrage, exploitation, and death . . . Holy is God! Holy and strong! Holy Immortal One! From plague, from famine, from fire and from war, deliver us, O Lord. Amen."[57]

The next day, Friday, the Pope, nursing a sore throat, flew to Nowy Targ in the foothills of the Carpathians to meet Poland's highlanders. Once again, the crowd was estimated at more than a million, and given the mountaineers' splendid native dress, it was the most colorful gathering thus far. Entire parishes had come from the surrounding territory or had trekked across the mountains from Czechoslovakia and Hungary. The altar platform was built of rough-hewn wood, in the local style, and was topped by the wooden statue of the Madonna of Ludmierz, the principal Marian shrine of the Tatra Mountains. The atmosphere was entirely different from that of the afternoon before, the Pope engaging in another informal give-and-take with the mountain people and telling highlander jokes in the local dialect. His homily was a paean to "this beautiful land," to the love for work on the land that had animated Poles for centuries, and to the Polish family. He also challenged the young people present to be "witnesses for Christ," reminding them that the Greek word for "witness" was the basis of the word "martyr."[58] Youngsters from the Light and Life movement had brought huge bread baskets, now filled with Bibles rather than loaves. The Pope helped distribute the books, then led the young people in a vow, sworn on the Bibles, that they would commit themselves to "liberation from the slavery of alcoholism and other addictions, and the slavery of lies and fear."[59] After Mass, the Pope was serenaded by a hundred-piece highlander band, complete with fiddles and shawms, the local bagpipes. On the way to the airport, the highlanders began laying their brilliantly decorated coats under the wheels of the car carrying their departing friend.[60]

That afternoon, John Paul presided over the solemn closing of the Synod of Kraków in Wawel Cathedral. Mass began with a procession involving 1,500 participants in the Synod, after which Archbishop Macharski presented his predecessor with the Synod documents and a commemorative medal. John Paul's homily began with a simple declaration: "Today, the ardent desire of my heart is fulfilled." The Synod he had called to implement the Second Vatican Council fully in Kraków, and to link the aggiornamento of John XXIII to the witness-unto-death of St. Stanisław, had finished its work. He laid the completed documents of the Synod on the sarcophagus of the martyr-bishop.

While the Pope was closing the Synod at Wawel, tens of thousands of young students and workers had been gathering at St. Michael's Church at Skałka for a youth meeting with John Paul that had been scheduled for Friday evening. After a brief prayer service inside the church—the actual site of St. Stanisław's martyrdom by King Bolesław—the Pope came outside to address the young people. The atmosphere was festive and highly charged. Emotions had been building throughout this incredible week, and had now reached a fever pitch of youthful enthusiasm. The Pope was showered yet again with flowers and serenaded by a string orchestra, trumpets, guitars, and a brass band. The youngsters kept shouting *Sto lat, sto lat* to the point where John Paul jokingly asked, "How can the Pope live to be a hundred when you shout him down? Will you let me speak?" Some semblance of order being restored, he simply said, "I love you all."

Formal remarks had been prepared, in which the Pope planned to make a simple request: "Allow Christ to find you. . . . Be afraid only of thoughtlessness and pusillanimity." Perhaps warned that a political demonstration might break out, or perhaps just sensing that things could get out of control and provide the regime with an excuse to crack down on the youngsters, John Paul announced that he wasn't going to give his prepared text, on the grounds that he still had a sore throat and that "the text I had written is not appropriate to the occasion." He could, he said, "improvise in Polish."

Laughter at that wisecrack broke the mounting tension, and the Pope started reminiscing about his days as a young priest. "When I was told that I was to be a bishop, I asked the Primate whether I could still go climbing in the Tatras. He said I could. But now that I am Bishop of Rome, it might be harder. . . ." The youngsters started chanting, "Then stay with us, stay with us. . . ." "Ah, you're wise now," John Paul replied, "but it's too late. Where were you on October 16 [the date of his election]? You weren't there to defend me. Just like Poles, to close the barn door when the horse is gone." Another wave of laughter swept the crowd. The banter back and forth continued until about 10:30 P.M., the Pope mixing jokes with admonitions drawn from his formal remarks and the young people chanting and singing. The atmosphere slowly changed and tension gave way to reflectiveness. Finally, in what may have originally been intended as the beginning of a mass demonstration, several young men lifted up a twelve-foot-tall cross, and tens of thousands of youngsters immediately raised smaller crosses they had been hiding. "It was an eerie, shattering scene," a foreign reporter later wrote, "as the street lights cast shadows on the young faces and the crosses held above them." A single word from the Pope, one misinterpreted signal from this man they were prepared to follow anywhere, could have started a riot in defiance of the government.

John Paul II simply said, "It's late, my friends. Let's go home quietly." And they did. As the papal limousine drove slowly back to Franciszkańska, 3, the guitars played a farewell song. The white-clad figure inside the car covered his face with his hands and wept.[61]

The next morning, after a meeting in his former residence with the faculty and students of the Pontifical Faculty of Theology, the Pope's helicopter took him to the Cistercian abbey of Mogiła on the outskirts of Nowa Huta. Forbidden by the authorities to visit the Ark Church, John Paul threw a bouquet of flowers over it from the window of the helicopter. Hundreds of thousands of Nowa Huta residents had assembled to meet the man who had defended their religious freedom so tenaciously during his episcopate. The parishioners of the Ark Church had wanted the Pope to crown a new statue of Mary, Queen of Poland, for their hard-fought sanctuary; when the authorities struck Nowa Huta from the papal itinerary, the parishioners decided to bring the statue to the Pope in Mogiła. In his sermon, he recounted the drama of the Ark Church and the struggle for a church in Miestrzejowice, returning "in prayer and heart to the tomb of Father Józef [Kurzeja] of holy memory," whose church-building efforts had cost him his life. Surrounded by workers from the Nowa Huta steel mills, John Paul also insisted that "Christ will never approve that man be considered, or that man consider himself . . . merely as a means of production, or that he be appreciated, esteemed, and valued in accordance with that principle. Christ will never approve of it." The cross that had been raised on the spot where the Ark Church now stood was a symbol of the fact that Christ, and Christians, opposed "any form of degradation of man." The building of the church, however great an accomplishment, was only the beginning, though. "You have built the church," he concluded. "Now build your lives with the Gospel."

In the middle of the homily, a voice was heard clearly from the crowd: "Long live the Pope who knows what he is doing."

After a brief rest at Franciszkańska, 3, John Paul visited and prayed at the graves of his parents and brother in the Rakowice cemetery, met with nuns at the Mariacki Church in the Old Town market square, held a reception for distinguished visitors and visiting bishops at his old residence, and attended a concert at the Franciscan Church where he had so often made the stations of the cross. The concert was the premiere of Henryk Górecki's "Beatus Vir," which Cardinal Karol Wojtyła had commissioned as part of the Stanisław anniversary and which the composer himself conducted. Górecki had found the Latin psalm texts for his piece in a missal lent to him by Piotr Malecki, one of the members of Wojtyła's Środowisko and the Pope's first altar boy at St. Florian's; it was the missal Wojtyła had given Malecki in the 1950s. A rehearsal of "Beatus Vir," which Górecki was writing up to the very last minute, was interrupted shortly before the premiere when the woodwinds rushed to a window to serenade John Paul as the Popemobile drove by. For the performance itself, Cardinal Casaroli and Archbishop Paul Marcinkus, the papal trip planner, had decreed that the Pope could not sit at the front of the Franciscan basilica, as had been hoped, but had to sit at the rear. At the end of the performance, Górecki, one of whose legs is shorter than the other, limped down the eighty-yard-long center aisle, tears streaming down his face, to embrace the Pope.[62]

June 10, the last day of the pilgrimage, began with Mass on the Kraków Commons, attended by the largest crowd in Polish history—between 2 and 3 million. The Mass marked the official close of the Stanisław jubilee, and the Gospel text for the day was Christ's great commission to the apostles: "Full authority has been given to me both in heaven and on earth; go, therefore, and make disciples of all nations. Baptize them in the name of the Father, and of the Son, and of the Holy Spirit. Teach them to carry out everything I have commanded you. And know that I am with you always, until the end of the world" (*Matthew* 28.18–20). Here, John Paul said, was a "great mystery in the history of humanity and in the history of the individual human person."

Time was the rhythm of human lives. To be truly human, time, he proposed, must be ordered toward a goal. Otherwise, the human person would disappear along with the ever-receding past. The Gospel text that had just been proclaimed pointed human beings beyond the fragility of time and gave history its rightful nobility. Christ remained with his followers in time and history, immersing them and the world "into the living God," and preparing them for a life without end in the unity of God's own life, "for which earthly life is merely a preface, an introduction." The goal of human life was to be found in "the world of God." This was where men and women discovered "fulfillment in life and in the human vocation."

That vocation demanded to be lived in the interior freedom by which we search for the truth and adhere to it freely. The men and women before him did not live their freedom as strangers in the strange land of modernity. They were the heirs of a tradition that was "a treasure, a spiritual enrichment . . . a great common good." How could anyone throw this away? "Can one refuse Christ and all that He has brought into history?"

Virtually everyone there had received the sacrament of confirmation as a young adult. Now, John Paul said, his people were living a "great 'Confirmation of history,'" a new anointing by the Holy Spirit, in the anniversary of St. Stanisław and its link to the millennium of Poland's baptism. So he had something to ask of them, as he prepared to leave "this Kraków in which every stone and every brick is dear to me," as he prepared to leave "my Poland," which had received him as it had received no other son in a thousand years:

> You must be strong, dear brothers and sisters. . . . You must be strong with the strength of *faith*. . . . Today more than in any other age you need this strength. You must be strong with the strength of *hope*, hope that brings the perfect joy of life and does not allow us to grieve the Holy Spirit.
>
> You must be strong with *love*, which is stronger than death . . . and helps us to set up the great dialogue with man and the world rooted in the dialogue with God Himself, with the Father through the Son in the Holy Spirit, the dialogue of salvation. . . .
>
> When we are strong with the Spirit of God, we are also strong with faith in man. . . . There is therefore no need to fear. . . .
>
> So . . . I beg you: never lose your trust, do not be defeated, do not be discouraged. . . . I beg you: have trust, and . . . always seek spiritual power from Him from whom countless generations of our fathers and mothers have found it. Never detach yourselves from Him. Never lose your spiritual freedom. . . . Never disdain charity, which is "the greatest of these" and which shows itself through the cross. . . .

All this I beg of you: recalling the powerful intercession of the Mother of God at Jasna Góra and at all her other shrines in Polish lands; in memory of St. Adalbert who underwent death for Christ near the Baltic Sea; in memory of St. Stanisław who fell beneath the royal sword at Skałka.
   All this I beg of you.
   Amen.[63]

Lesson in Dignity

Before leaving Poland on June 10, John Paul met briefly with the journalists who had covered his pilgrimage in the world press. At the end of his formal remarks, delivered in French, his voice was trembling and he had to fight back the tears as he said, "I hope, I hope, I hope to meet you again in this country. I hope . . ." The airport farewell ceremony at Balice, outside Kraków, followed a last motorcade through packed streets. At the airport, President Jabłoński tried to salvage something from the wreckage by stating that uncritical allegiance to the heritage of Poland's history and culture would not serve the modern Polish state well. Since the Pope had not suggested any such Polish fundamentalism, the president's remarks, aimed at an audience in Moscow as well as in Poland, evaporated into the late spring air. John Paul listened respectfully and acknowledged, with unintended irony, that the government's agreement to his visit had been an "act of courage."[64] When Primate Wyszyński spoke—"You comforted our hearts with your living faith. . . ."—the Pope, standing on the airport tarmac, could be seen brushing away tears. Then, kissing "the ground from which my heart can never be detached," he boarded a LOT Polish Airlines jet for the return flight to Rome.[65]

   Thirteen million Poles, more than one-third the national population, had seen the Pope in person. Virtually everyone else had seen him on television or heard him on radio. In nine days, the country had lived through what political scientist Bogdan Szajkowski described as a "psychological earthquake, an opportunity for mass political catharsis."[66] Things that people had believed for decades, but could not affirm publicly, John Paul had affirmed. Things they had wanted to say, he had said. Even the way he had said it made a difference, for the Pope had spoken in "a beautiful, sonorous Polish, so unlike the calcified official language of communist Poland."[67] He had always insisted that this was a pilgrimage, though, so its primary effects should have been evident in the realm of the human spirit.

   As they were.

   People felt and acted out the change before they could articulate what had happened to them. Without thinking much about it, they began behaving differently. As Adam Michnik, one of the country's most prominent dissidents and a non-Catholic, wrote, "those very people who are ordinarily frustrated and aggressive in the shop lines were metamorphosed into a cheerful and happy collectivity, a people filled with dignity . . . Exemplary order reigned everywhere."[68] Communism had promised solidarity among the masses and had produced atomization, ill-humor, and distrust. John Paul II had delivered what the comrades promised but had no means of delivering, and had begun to heal the divisions they had deliberately fostered.

Prior to June 1979, it had been quite clear who "they" were: the regime, the petty communist bureaucrats, the thugs of the SB. But it was not clear who "we" were, how many of "us" there were, and whether "we" could trust one another. For tens of millions of Poles, the experience of the papal pilgrimage supplied the answer: "we" are the society and the country is ours; "they" are an artificial crust. By giving his people an experience of their individual dignity and collective authority, John Paul II had already won a major victory from which there could be no retreat. He had begun to exorcise the fear, the anomie, and sense of hopelessness that had previously kept the "we" of society from coalescing.

For Maciej Zięba, a twenty-five-year-old physics student at the time, the pilgrimage was a moment in which "the artificial world around us," the world of lies created by communism, simply collapsed. When he heard John Paul II, playing on the fact that, in Polish, "earth" and "land" are the same word, proclaim in Victory Square, "Come Holy Spirit, renew the face of the earth . . . of *this* land," Zięba knew that something had to change. And that change would begin with himself: "We might have to live and die under communism. But now what I wanted to do was to live without being a liar."[69]

The Pope's old friend and philosophical colleague, Father Józef Tischner, thought that Zięba's experience had been replicated many times over. According to Tischner, people had come to a fundamental decision during the papal pilgrimage: "Let's stop lying." This was at least as much reflexive as conceptual. But instincts are important, and according to Tischner, one result of the papal pilgrimage was a mass, instinctive understanding that moral renewal among "us" had to be the basis for any serious challenge to "them."[70]

There was another, simpler, even primitive, reason for the overwhelming emotion the Pope evoked. It was nicely articulated by an anonymous Polish miner who, when asked why anyone should be religious in a communist state, replied, "To praise the Mother of God and to spite those bastards."[71] No doubt there was a lot of that going on in June 1979. Yet when John Paul said in Kraków that "the future of Poland will depend on how many people are mature enough to be nonconformist," the key word was "mature."[72] And, in fact, there was no contradiction between the desire to "spite those bastards" and John Paul's call to maturity, as demonstrated by the dignified way in which millions of people who very much wanted to "spite those bastards" behaved during the pilgrimage. Under the spell of a different kind of leader, such mass demonstrations of disaffection with a regime could have easily turned into riots. Instead, the character of a pilgrimage was retained, and the result was not bloody cataclysm but a profound experience of social solidarity and community.

The sense of "we" created during the pilgrimage was all the more striking in that one of the more remarked-upon phenomena of the papal homecoming was John Paul's uncanny ability to make individuals think he was talking to them personally. Two miners from Katowice were attending one of the Pope's Masses at Częstochowa, surrounded by a million fellow Poles. One began to make a remark during John Paul's homily when his friend quickly interrupted, "Damn it, don't talk when the Pope's talking to me."[73] Tadeusz Mazowiecki, a leading Catholic intellectual, had a similar experience. He had arranged with a friend whose apartment faced onto the Nowy Świat portion of Warsaw's Royal Way that his elderly aunt could watch the papal motorcade from the friend's balcony. Afterward, the aunt's recollection was that the Pope had stopped to bless her personally.[74] This remarkable sense of one-on-one connection had its own public impact. When John Paul said in Victory Square that Poles had a right to think of their nation as the "land of a particularly responsible witness," millions of Poles, who heard him as if he were speaking to them personally, said to themselves, "Am I being as responsible as I should?"[75]

It was, as Adam Michnik summed it up, a great "lesson in dignity."[76]

The government, Michnik wrote, "heaved a sigh of relief" when John Paul finally left. But, as the Pope had kidded the young people at Skałka in another context, the horse was already out of the barn.[77] The regime had fulfilled its commitment to televise certain of the papal events in typical communist fashion—by showing bits and pieces of the event but not the Pope. It was, a French journalist said, like the telecast of a soccer game in which the cameras showed everything but the ball.[78] The broadcasts also avoided showing the masses of ordinary Poles in attendance; from the way the cameras played over the crowd at Gniezno, one would have thought that the only people attending the Pope's Mass were nuns and pensioners.[79]

Measured by the standards of the previous decades, the government had behaved rather reasonably. Communist rhetoric was kept to a minimum, although there was something almost pathetic about the meeting at the Belvedere Palace, with party leader Gierek talking about Leonid Brezhnev and John Paul talking about God. There were no mass arrests of dissidents, although KOR leader Jacek Kuroń, with a security detail larger than John Paul's, was under virtual house arrest during the visit, presumably to keep him away from the world press. The state-controlled print media published the texts of the Pope's sermons and addresses with a minimum of censorship.[80] Occasional complaints about the number of allegedly political comments from the Pope were voiced publicly by lower-level Communist Party or government bureaucrats. The official line, though, was that the party and the government were "generally satisfied" with the visit.[81] It was a strategy of "grin and bear it," contrived in a fantasy world. The authorities "made believe that those millions of people with radiant faces crowding around John Paul II did not constitute proof of the total fiasco of their thirty-year rule, that they did not constitute proof of the utter collapse of their moral claim to power."[82]

The Western press gave the Pope extensive coverage, much of it favorable but some of it insisting, remarkably enough, that the Pope was strengthening détente with the communist world. Adam Michnik, speaking from the secular left, thought that the Westerners made far too much of what the Polish dissident regarded as a bizarre analogy: between the Pope's return to Poland and the Ayatollah Khomeini's return to Iran. "One can hardly imagine a greater misconception," Michnik wrote.[83] It would not, however, be the last time that the press tried to draw analogies between the "white mullah" and the "black mullahs."

What struck Adam Michnik most forcefully was the Pope's ability to appeal to the consciences of believer and nonbeliever alike. In challenging "dishonorable living," he was reviving an ancient Polish cultural tradition that had lain fallow under communism—"the ethos of sacrifice, in whose name our grandfathers and fathers never stopped fighting for national and human dignity."[84] It was a call to national moral renewal addressed to everyone, and John Paul had done it without sneering at the opposition. For, at the deeper moral level to which he constantly tried to direct his people's reflections, the opponent wasn't communism but their own lethargy, which permitted, by tacit or overt consent, the continued imposition of an alien form of political control on their country.[85]

It was the analysis of *Person and Act*, retooled for a mass audience. Solidarity and opposition were essential dynamics of a mature human life, and freedom to think for oneself should lead to a commitment to the good of others. One thoroughly secular Western correspondent put it simply: "Inescapably, the word for all this is love. [The Pope] receives it from the nation, as only liberators and dictators have taken it in history, but somehow he gives the dangerous gift back again, leaving on one side an intact man and on the other millions of people who go home with a better respect for themselves."[86]

John Paul, though never descending to partisan argument or maneuver, was in fact conducting a kind of national referendum. Before his pilgrimage had barely begun, the results were in.

A revolution of the spirit had been unleashed.

FROM SOLIDARITY TO SOLIDARNOŚĆ

Four hundred forty-eight days after John Paul II flew out of Balice airfield on the outskirts of Kraków, a formerly unemployed electrician named Lech Wałęsa, using a huge souvenir pen topped by the picture of a smiling Pope, a relic of the June 1979 papal pilgrimage, signed an agreement at the Lenin Shipyard in Gdańsk. In it, Poland's communist government agreed to recognize the legality of the first independent, self-governing trade union in the communist world. Its name was Solidarność—"Solidarity." Did the experience of solidarity during John Paul's nine days in June 1979 make Solidarność possible in August 1980?

Edward Gierek's strategy of "practical materialism," as former Wojtyła student Halina Bortnowska once described it, was an economic fantasy that would have eventually crashed in ruins. Trying to salvage the unsalvageable through price increases in July 1980, Gierek managed only to hasten the day of reckoning as worker protests spread throughout the country, culminating in the epic Gdańsk shipyard strike in August 1980—and the birth of Solidarność. But the way things happened in the summer of 1980—the workers' new sense of their own dignity, their patience, their newfound ability to hold a coalition together with dissident intellectuals, their nonviolence, their rhetoric of national moral renewal, the widespread support throughout the population—all this was new in the history of communist-era labor unrest in Poland.[87] According to those who were there and those who have studied the matter since, none of it was imaginable without John Paul II's nine days in June 1979. A moral revolution *then* had set the foundations for a social and political revolution later.[88]

A new sense of self-worth, a new experience of personal dignity, and a determination not to be intimidated any longer by "the power" were by-products of the papal pilgrimage, for nonbelievers as well as believers. If, as historian Norman Davies contends, the pre-Solidarność "essence of Poland's modern experience is humiliation," it was John Paul II who lifted that burden from his people.[89] In doing so, he made a broad-based, nonviolent movement of social self-defense possible.

Józef Tischner suggested at the time of its founding that Solidarność was "a huge forest planted by awakened consciences."[90] Those personal moral compasses had first been formed under very difficult circumstance through the labors of parents, catechism teachers, and clergy. As the Pope's old friend Mieczysław Maliński once put it, the men of the Gdańsk strike were once the children to whom he and countless other Polish priests had given their first religious and moral instruction in freezing churches during Cardinal Wyszyński's Great Novena.[91] The awakened consciences of the Solidarity movement had many fathers and mothers. But it was John Paul II, in June 1979, who sharpened those consciences to a particularly fine edge of purposefulness and gave them permission to exercise the right of moral judgment in public. French political scientist Alain Besançon put it well when he said that, in Solidarity, the people of Poland had regained "the private ownership of their tongues."[92] Those tongues said what they did because they were expressing the convictions of reborn consciences determined to live in the truth.

That commitment to conscience also explains the nonviolence that was a hallmark of the Solidarity revolution. In its sixteen months of freedom, the Solidarity revolution, unique among all the revolutionary upheavals of modernity, killed precisely no one. This was not simply a matter of tactics, the regime having all the guns; it was a matter of principle. The men and women of Solidarity knew the truth to which Adam Michnik gave elegant expression when he said, some years later, that those who start by storming bastilles end up building their own.[93] The revolution that John Paul II inspired reversed a bloody pattern that had gotten itself fixed into European politics in 1789, to the endless anguish of the peoples of Europe.

Another great Slavic moral opponent of communism, Aleksandr Solzhenitsyn, had argued in his 1970 Nobel lecture that the communist culture of the lie and communist violence were closely linked, such that when the lie was dispersed, the violence "will come crashing down."[94] In June 1979, John Paul II, by dispersing the lie, had helped make possible something unprecedented in postwar east central Europe. Poland now had a genuine citizenry, capable of building independent institutions whose very existence would demonstrate the hollowness of the communist system and its dependence on violence for survival.

10

The Ways of Freedom

Truths Personal and Public

APRIL 8, 1979	Pope John Paul II issues his first "Holy Thursday letter" to Catholic priests throughout the world.
JUNE 30, 1979	Fourteen new cardinals are created at John Paul II's first consistory.
SEPTEMBER 5, 1979	The Pope begins four years of audience addresses on the "theology of the body."
SEPTEMBER 29–OCTOBER 1, 1979	History's first papal pilgrimage to Ireland.
OCTOBER 1–7, 1979	The Pope makes his first pilgrimage to the United States.
OCTOBER 2, 1979	John Paul II addresses the 34th General Assembly of the United Nations.
NOVEMBER 5, 1979	The Pope assembles the College of Cardinals for its first consultative meeting in four hundred years.
NOVEMBER 10, 1979	John Paul urges a re-examination of the Galileo case by the Church and by science.
NOVEMBER 13, 1979	The Soviet leadership approves a plan of action to "work against the policies of the Vatican in relation to socialist states."
NOVEMBER 26, 1979	Mehmet Ali Agca threatens to assassinate John Paul II.
NOVEMBER 29–30, 1979	John Paul II visits Ecumenical Patriarch Dimitrios I in Istanbul.
DECEMBER 15, 1979	The Congregation for the Doctrine of the Faith declares that Father Hans Küng cannot be considered a Catholic theologian; John Paul II addresses the Pontifical Gregorian University on theology's contribution to the Church's prophetic mission.
DECEMBER 28, 1979	John Paul names Carlo Maria Martini, SJ, rector of the Pontifical Gregorian University, as Archbishop of Milan.

Father Jan Schotte was worried.

As *Shepherd One*, Pope John Paul II's TWA 727, flew from Boston to New York on the morning of October 2, 1979, Schotte, a former Belgian missionary working in the Vatican's Secretariat of State, had been reviewing the address the Pope would give to the UN General Assembly. Since the complete address was too long to be delivered in its entirety, there would be two texts: a "speaking text" in which certain sections would be bracketed and skipped during delivery, and a full, official text that would be released to the press and published.

The problem was that, in bracketing the sections he thought the Pope could skip over in his verbal presentation, Cardinal Agostino Casaroli had eliminated virtually everything that could be considered a criticism of the Soviet Union and the world's other communist powers—including some of the Pope's references to human rights and religious freedom. Casaroli thought these were the sorts of things that should be dealt with quietly, diplomat-to-diplomat, rather than with public confrontations. Schotte, who had helped develop the papal address, disagreed. To his mind, the Pope's defense of human rights and his moral challenge to totalitarianism were the heart of the matter. Cutting these references from the speaking text would eviscerate the address in the eyes of the world. But junior officials in the Secretariat of State did not normally challenge the judgment of the Cardinal Secretary of State, the Pope's principal adviser.

John Paul II was working in his private cabin during the flight. Schotte brought what he regarded as the now-bowdlerized UN address to him. The Belgian explained the situation, pointed out the Cardinal Secretary of State's proposed cuts from the speaking text, and told the Pope why he thought accepting them would be a serious mistake. Schotte had marked the text, circling those parts that, in his judgment, simply had to be said from the rostrum because they were indispensable to conveying the Pope's message. John Paul II studied the marked and twice-edited text, thought about it, and then agreed with Schotte. He would not accept Cardinal Casaroli's proposed cuts, but would forthrightly discuss the moral foundation of peace—human rights— before the General Assembly.

Custom dictated that the Pope's personal secretary, Monsignor Stanisław Dziwisz, hand him his speaking text when he came to the rostrum—a small thing, but one of the privileges of Dziwisz's office. While various formalities were being attended to at UN headquarters, Dziwisz drew Father Schotte aside and said, "The Holy Father wants you to hand him his papers." Schotte was stunned. When, as ordered, he appeared at the rostrum to hand the Pope the text of his address, more than a few members of the papal traveling party took note. John Paul II had not only taken Father Schotte's advice, but by this simple gesture of gratitude, he had sent a signal to the ever-sensitive antennae of the Roman Curia. Forthright counsel would be expected in this pontificate, in which there would be no trimming on issues of human rights and religious freedom.[1]

RENOVATIONS

In the weeks before his epic pilgrimage to Poland in June 1979, John Paul II continued to renovate the world's oldest continuous institution, the papacy.

On March 31, 1979, he addressed 10,000 boisterous young members of the Italian lay movement, Comunione e Liberazione [Communion and Liberation], which he had supported in Poland and which he hoped might become an instrument for the moral renewal of Italian politics, especially in the Christian Democratic Party.[2] He praised the youngsters for their "generous enthusiasm" and for the "self-sacrifice" involved in living out their ideals. Their belief in Christ was the hope of the Church and the true hope of the world.[3] After his talk, the youngsters wouldn't let him go until he had sung songs and exchanged cheers with them.

On April 8, John Paul wrote a letter to every priest in the world. The letter was dated on Holy Thursday, the day the Church commemorates the institution of the sacrament of Holy Orders at an annual diocesan "Chrism Mass," at which priests renew their vows before their bishop and the holy oils for baptism, confirmation, and the anointing of the sick are blessed. The letter was another initiative in the Pope's personal campaign to reinvigorate the commitment and restore the morale of priests throughout the world.

Poland had been spared much of the turmoil that had shaken the Catholic priesthood after the Second Vatican Council. In his first six months as Pope, John Paul had had to confront the global crisis of the priesthood much more directly. Pope Paul VI had granted more than 32,000 requests from priests who had asked to be released from their vows and returned to lay status—the greatest exodus from the priesthood since the Reformation. Soon after his election, John Paul had stopped the routine granting of these "decrees of laicization." With his Holy Thursday letter, he wanted to rekindle in his brother priests a sense of the religious drama of their vocation.

The priesthood, John Paul insisted, is a vocation, not a career. The priesthood of Holy Orders existed to help others live out the priestly dimension of their Christian lives, to become living sacrifices, "holy and pleasing to God" (*Romans* 12.1). The priesthood was a gift of Christ to the Church and to the individual priest, who acted *in persona Christi,* "in the person of Christ," the good shepherd. "Secularizing" the priestly vocation and way of life emptied it of its unique form of witness: the singular capacity of a priest to enter the drama of another's life, helping direct a fellow human being to God.

Being a man completely "for others," and completely "for the Kingdom," was also the rationale for celibacy, which John Paul described as a unique way of being a parent: "The priest, by renouncing [the] fatherhood proper to married men, seeks another fatherhood and, as it were, even another motherhood, recalling the words of the Apostle [Paul] about the children whom he begets in suffering. These are children of his spirit, people entrusted to his solicitude by the Good Shepherd [and are] more numerous than an ordinary human family can embrace."[4] Married couples, who had taken their own vows, had a right to expect fidelity to vocational vows from their priests. That faithfulness was another way that priests built up the Church.

John Paul closed by asking all priests, and especially "those of you who are doubtful of the meaning of your vocation or of the value of your service," to imagine priestless places:

> . . . think of the places where people anxiously await a priest, and where for many years, feeling the lack of such a priest, they do not cease to hope for his presence. And sometimes it happens that they meet in an abandoned shrine, and place on the altar a stole which they still keep, and recite all the prayers of the Eucharistic Liturgy; and then, at the moment that corresponds to the transubstantiation, a deep silence comes upon them, a silence sometimes broken by a sob . . . so ardently do they desire to hear the words that only the lips of a priest can efficaciously utter. So much do they desire Eucharistic Communion, in which they can share only through the ministry of a priest, just as they also so eagerly wait to hear the divine words of pardon: *Ego te absolvo a peccatis tuis*. So if one of you doubts the meaning of his priesthood, if he thinks it is "socially" fruitless or useless, think on this![5]

On May 15, all the bishops of Italy gathered in Rome for their annual meeting, the first since the Polish Pope's election. The occasion posed another set of delicate "transition" problems for John Paul II.

As Bishop of Rome, John Paul held the ancient titles of "Archbishop and Metropolitan of the Roman Province" and "Primate of Italy." For the first time in 455 years, those titles were in the possession of a non-Italian. As a Pole now resident in Rome, he had come from a land of vibrant Catholicism to a country whose Catholic practice, historically, had been much more casual. Since Italy's unification in 1870, popes had kept a close grip on Italian Church affairs, internally and in relations with the Italian government. This was not John Paul's understanding of ecclesiastical primacy or Church-state relations. The challenge was to demonstrate his concern for the local Church he now led while making it clear that he was not going to micromanage its internal affairs.

He addressed these interlocking issues both theologically and practically, at a concelebrated Mass with the entire Italian episcopate in the Sistine Chapel on May 15. His homily began by reflecting on a paradox of Christian life—and then gently turned the paradox into a challenge to episcopal complacency. Although Christ had promised his followers his peace and urged them not to be troubled, for he would always be with them, Christ's Church grew through trials, suffering, and the witness-unto-death of martyrdom. That was how it had been with the Church in Italy: it was Christ himself, the head of the Church, who had driven Peter and Paul to Rome, where they had confirmed their preaching by the sacrifice of their lives. This was not simply ancient history; it explained why they were all in Rome. They were all players in the drama of salvation history, a script with a divine author.

John Paul then made it clear that they were in charge of the Church in Italy. It was up to them to keep him informed of their "particular problems." The Second Vatican Council had reminded the Church of its responsibility "for the history of human salvation," which unfolded in real, concrete places. He proposed to share that responsibility "in the bond of *collegial union*" with them.[6]

Three days later, on May 18, 1979, he made that commitment to collegial consultation concrete. The President of the Italian Bishops' Conference [CEI], Cardinal Antonio Poma of Bologna, had filled that post for ten years and had asked Paul VI and John Paul I for permission to resign. After requesting that Poma stay on for the first months of the transition, John Paul II had agreed to let the cardinal resign the conference presidency, but this decision, he told his Italian confreres, put him "up against a problem." The CEI's statutes, which had been drawn up during the pontificate of Paul VI, provided that the Pope name the conference president. Demonstrating that he, too, could speak with classic Italian indirection when he had to, John Paul noted that this statute had laid a "difficult task" on him, since he did not "come from the circle of the Italian Episcopate"—all of whose members were acutely aware of that, and some of whom would have resented a president imposed on them by a Pole. At the same time, he wanted to "act in a way that was not contrary to this norm"—which would have seemed a criticism of Paul VI. The solution? He had taken counsel with the heads of the regional conferences of Italian bishops, and the majority had recommended Archbishop Anastasio Ballestrero of Turin as the new president of their national conference. The Pope now confirmed that choice according to the letter of the statute, even as he made clear that the diocesan bishops of Italy should not think of themselves as local franchise managers of a Roman corporation. The Primate of Italy intended to exercise his primacy as an evangelist, not as the chief executive officer of Italian Catholicism.[7]

On June 30, John Paul II held his first ordinary consistory, creating fourteen new members of the College of Cardinals. Among them were the new Secretary of State, Agostino Casaroli; the former *Sostituto*, Giuseppe Caprio; the new President of the CEI, Anastasio Ballestrero; the successor to Albino Luciani as patriarch of Venice, Marco Cé; and two Poles—Franciszek Macharski, John Paul's successor in Kraków, and Władysław Rubin, who had been General Secretary of the Synod of Bishops. The archbishop of Hanoi, Joseph-Marie Trinh văn-Căn, received the red biretta, as did the archbishop of Marseilles, Roger Etchegaray, who would come to Rome five years later as President of the Pontifical Council for Justice and Peace and become one of the Pope's personal diplomatic troubleshooters. One cardinal was named secretly, or *in pec-*

tore. (Twelve years later, at John Paul II's fifth consistory, his name would be revealed: Ignatius Gong Pin-Mei, the bishop of Shanghai, who was then serving a life sentence in a communist prison.[8])

During his first summer in office, the new Pope continued to encourage activist Catholicism in Italy, meeting with the Sant'Egidio Community on July 22. Founded in 1968 by a group of Roman university students, the community, a lay initiative, had taken as its missions the reevangelization of the city and charitable service to the marginalized. The parish church of Sant'Egidio in Rome's Trastevere district was its base of operations and the center of its active liturgical life. Sant'Egidio had helped arrange a meeting between John Paul and Roman students during the previous Lent, a practice the Pope adapted to Rome from Kraków. The community would later become heavily involved in mediating negotiated settlements to civil wars in the Third World. In an audience at the papal summer villa at Castel Gandolfo, John Paul told 600 members of the community that he had "heard that the Church of Sant'Egidio is becoming too small for you. I hope that by remaining faithful to your too-small church, you will arrive at the point where all of Rome becomes too small for you."[9]

His meetings with Comunione e Liberazione (conventionally identified with more conservative Italian politics) and the Sant'Egidio Community (just as conventionally identified with the Italian Catholic "left") were indicators of a principle to which John Paul II held firm throughout his pontificate. If a lay movement was dedicated to a life of serious Christian commitment and "thinking with the Church" (as the classic phrase had it), its politics were its own business. At Vatican II, Karol Wojtyła had promoted the apostolate of lay activism "in the world." As archbishop of Kraków, he had taught that there was no single political expression of the Church's social doctrine, and that lay initiatives "in the world" was the laity's business, not the clergy's. He evidently saw no reason to alter his thinking on this after becoming Bishop of Rome.[10]

Neither had he lost his touch for the unusual or unexpected. In April, he had met an expectant mother at an audience, who asked if the Pope would baptize her baby. He happily agreed, and did so at Castel Gandolfo on August 11. Later that month, he held an audience for competitors in the thirty-third water-skiing championship of Europe, Africa, and the Mediterranean, which was being held on Lake Albano, near his villa. The former-kayaker-turned-Pope, perhaps thinking wistfully about the annual trip he was missing with his *Środowisko* friends, told the athletes that "sports are a real school of true human virtue."[11]

As the first anniversary of his election approached, John Paul II, a man who habitually looked forward, could have looked back on a year in which he had revitalized the papacy stylistically and substantively. He had held firmly to his determination to remain himself in office. During his first summer at Castel Gandolfo, he had invited old lay friends to visit, including Jerzy Janik and his family. The Janiks had driven down from Kraków at the Pope's invitation, expecting, as Professor Janik later said, that they might get a chance to see

John Paul briefly: "the optimists in our family thought we'd be received twice, once in the beginning and once to say good-bye; the pessimists thought we'd be received once." On arriving at the small town in the hills outside Rome, Professor Janik presented himself to the Swiss Guard manning the castello's gate, and when asked his business, simply replied, "We have come to meet the Pope." The guard sent for a nun, who showed them to an apartment a few hundred yards from the gate and told them to wait there for "orders." Two hours later, the Pope called: "Jurek, I was in the garden when you came. Come right over with Jasią and the girls so we can talk." The Janiks went, and got a papal guided tour of the villa: "Now I'll show you where I live. Here's my bedroom, this is the same bed in which Paul VI died. Here's the chapel. . . ." After the tour, John Paul said, "Now, tell me your plans; how can we arrange your stay?" Janik, thinking of the Pope's schedule, replied that, now that they'd seen their old friend, there probably wouldn't be many more occasions to be together. So they planned to see something of Rome and go home. John Paul was having none of it: "No, you can do that some other time. Now you stay here, and we'll have all our meals together and talk."*

A few months before the Janiks arrived, John Paul had started construction of a swimming pool on the grounds of the papal villa. Someone asked about the cost. The Pope replied that he had to get some exercise, and in any event, the pool was less expensive than holding another conclave.[13]

However much it disconcerted the traditional managers of popes, the new papal style was wildly popular. The Rome Tourist Council calculated that John Paul II had attracted more than 5 million tourists in the first six months of the pontificate. When the weather permitted moving his weekly general audiences out into St. Peter's Square in the spring of 1979, there were massive traffic jams as 800 tourist buses jockeyed to discharge their passengers.[14] It was unlikely that this was simply a matter of the new Pope's personal style. John Paul was touching what seems to have been a widespread and deeply felt need for religious leadership, by reenergizing a papal office that some had thought incapable of being a center of spiritual force any longer.

In his first year in office, John Paul II had also made dramatic changes in the time-honored way in which the papacy related to the world of politics and worldly power. Astute observers, not all of them friendly, knew that his triumphant tour of Poland had presaged the emergence of a new, unpredictable, and yet very powerful force on the world stage. Still, it can be argued that nothing John Paul II did in the first year of his pontificate would have a greater impact on the Church and the world in the twenty-first century than the series of weekly catechetical addresses he began at his Wednesday general audience in Rome on September 5, 1979.

---

*Among the things they discussed was the continuation of the series of seminars with physicists and others in the hard sciences that Janik had organized for Karol Wojtyła for twenty-five years. These seminars continued at Castel Gandolfo in the summers of 1980, 1982, 1984, 1986, 1988, 1990, 1993, 1995, and 1997.[12]

BODY LANGUAGE AND GOD-TALK

When Italy completed its unification by capturing Rome in 1870, Pope Pius IX declared himself the "Prisoner of the Vatican" and refused to travel outside the Leonine Wall surrounding the papal properties near St. Peter's Basilica. To maintain contact with the people among whom he had once traveled freely in his carriage, Pius began the custom of the "general audience," at which the pope met and spoke with a large group of pilgrims—in distinction from the "private audiences" popes granted to individual visitors, diplomats, high-ranking clergy, and so forth. In this respect, general audiences were a first effort at papal public relations in an age when public opinion was beginning to carry weight.

The general audience also renovated the ancient tradition of the bishop as a teacher. In the first centuries of the Church, bishops were not primarily administrators (deacons took care of the Church's temporal affairs) but preachers, teachers, theologians, and spiritual guides. Such great thinkers as Ambrose (bishop of Milan), Augustine (bishop of Hippo in North Africa), and John Chrysostom (bishop of Constantinople) worked out major parts of their theologies as preachers and teachers before large congregations of Christians. This was the tradition revived in the papal general audience, although Pius IX and his successors did not view the general audience as the place for imaginative theological exploration, usually limiting themselves to reflections on familiar themes.

John Paul II had something different in mind. In September 1979, he began using his weekly general audience—broadcast throughout the world on Vatican Radio and printed in the six weekly foreign-language editions of *L'Osservatore Romano,* the Vatican newspaper—as a forum for weaving a richly complex theological tapestry based on a single overarching theme. The very idea of a series of "thematic audiences" was another innovation that caused eyebrows to be raised in the Roman Curia: What was *this?*[15] The subject matter was even more explosive. Beginning on September 5, 1979, John Paul II spent four years' worth of general audiences developing an idea he had first proposed in *Love and Responsibility*—that human sexual love is an icon of the inner life of God, of the Holy Trinity.

One Act or Two?

The drama of John Paul's pontificate is often divided into two acts. In Act One, the Pope struggles against communism and is eventually vindicated by the Revolution of 1989 and the collapse of the Soviet Union in 1991. In Act Two, the Pope rejects many aspects of the new freedom he helped bring about, the sharpest confrontation coming at the Cairo World Conference on Population and Development in 1994. There is a grain of truth here. John Paul II certainly spent more time on the affairs of east central and eastern Europe in the first thirteen years of his pontificate than he did afterward. This conventional division of the story into two parts finally fails, though, because it reads the pontificate primarily through the prism of its impact on world politics, which for John Paul has always been a derivative set of considerations. Moreover, dividing the story this way does scant justice to the numerous public initiatives John Paul II took in the 1980s that were global in character, or had little or nothing to do directly with his native region. Most importantly, the "two-act" model of the pontificate of John Paul II fails to grasp the distinctive imagination that Karol Wojtyła brought to the papacy.

As he had written Henri de Lubac in 1968, Wojtyła believed that *the* crisis of modernity involved a "degradation, indeed . . . a pulverization, of the fundamental uniqueness of each human person."[16] Communism was one obvious, dangerous, and powerful expression of this crisis, as Nazism and fascism had been. But the dehumanization of the human world took place in other ways, and it could happen in free societies. Whenever another human being was reduced to an object for manipulation—by a manager, a shop foreman, a scientific researcher, a politician, or a lover—the "pulverization of the fundamental uniqueness of each human person" was taking place. What Wojtyła used to describe to his social ethics classes as "utilitarianism," making "usefulness to me" the sole criterion of human relationships, was another grave threat to the human future. It was not a threat with nuclear weapons, secret police, and a Gulag archipelago, but it was dangerous, and part of the reason was that it was less obvious.

Challenging whatever "pulverizes" the unique dignity of every human person is the leitmotif that runs like a bright thread through the pontificate of John Paul II and gives it a singular coherence. His papacy has been a one-act drama, although different adversaries have taken center stage at different moments in the script. The dramatic tension remains the same throughout: the tension between various false humanisms that degrade the humanity they claim to defend and exalt, and the true humanism to which the biblical vision of the human person is a powerful witness.

In developing his idea of human sexual self-giving as an icon of the interior life of God, John Paul II was working out the implications of the very same concept of human dignity and human freedom with which he challenged communism in east central Europe. In his mind, it was, and is, all of a piece.

A New Galileo Crisis

When he was elected to the papacy, Karol Wojtyła knew that the Church's last effort to address the sexual revolution and its relationship to the moral life, Pope Paul's 1968 encyclical *Humanae Vitae*, had been a pastoral and catechetical failure—however correct he thought it was on the specific question of the morally appropriate means of regulating fertility. *Humanae Vitae*'s teaching on that question had been rejected by vast numbers of Catholics around the world. Many who rejected it felt that their experience of sexual love had been ignored or demeaned by their religious leaders. That feeling of rejection led to the conclusion that the Church had nothing of consequence to say about any aspect of human sexuality.

Paul VI, a deeply pastoral man, had no intention of demeaning the vocation of marriage. But a situation had been created in which anything the Church had to say about human sexuality after the "birth control encyclical" was viewed with suspicion and, in the case of Western elites, with active hostility. Since the sexual revolution sharpened the issues on which the definition of "freedom" was most hotly contested in the developed world, this communications chasm was a crisis of major proportions for the Church. It was another Galileo case, this time involving not arcane cosmological speculations but the most intimate aspects of the lives of the Church's people.

John Paul II believed it was the time to put the entire discussion on a new footing.

The Church had not found a voice with which to address the challenge of the sexual revolution. John Paul thought that he and his colleagues in Lublin and Kraków had begun to do that, in the understanding of human sexuality expressed in *Love and Responsibility* and in the work of the archdiocesan family life ministry under his leadership. Now it was time to deepen that analysis biblically and bring it to a world audience. The results were the 130 general audience addresses, spread over four years, that make up John Paul II's *Theology of the Body*.[17]

The audiences took place in four clusters. The first, entitled *Original Unity of Man and Woman*, began on September 5, 1979, and included twenty-three catecheses, concluding with the general audience of April 2, 1980. Drawing its theme from a phrase in Christ's dispute with the Pharisees about the permissibility of divorce—"Have you not read that He who made them from the beginning made them male and female . . . ?" (*Matthew* 19.4)—*Original Unity* explored some of the most profoundly personal aspects of the human condition through the story of Adam and Eve in the first three chapters of *Genesis*. The second cluster of addresses, *Blessed Are the Pure of Heart*, began on April 16, 1980, and concluded on May 6, 1981, after forty-one catecheses. As the title indicates, its biblical inspiration was the Sermon on the Mount. In exploring "purity of heart," John Paul undertook a lengthy analysis of Christ's saying that "everyone who looks at a woman lustfully has already committed adultery with her in his heart" (*Matthew* 5.28)—a crucial, if widely misunderstood, text for resisting the kind of sexual utilitarianism that turns another person into an object.[18]

The third cluster of audiences in John Paul's *Theology of the Body* began on November 11, 1981, and included fifty catecheses under the title *The Theology of Marriage and Celibacy*. The biblical foundation for this series, which concluded on July 4, 1984, was the dispute between Christ and the Sadducees about the resurrection. What, John Paul asks, does the idea of the "resurrection of the body" to a heaven in which "they neither marry nor are given in marriage" (*Mark* 12.23) tell us about our sexual embodiedness as male and female, here and now?[19] The fourth and final cluster of sixteen addresses, *Reflections on* Humanae Vitae, began on July 11, 1984, and concluded on November 28, 1984.

The 130 texts in John Paul II's *Theology of the Body* did not make easy listening and do not make easy reading. They are highly compact theological and philosophical meditations into which the Pope tried to fit as much material as possible into a fifteen-minute catechetical talk. The difficulties notwithstanding, however, these texts repay careful study. In them, John Paul II, so often dismissed as "rigidly conservative," proposed one of the boldest reconfigurations of Catholic theology in centuries.

Original Unity of Man and Woman

Cardinal Wojtyła had conceived the project that eventually became the first part of the *Theology of the Body* in Kraków. As he recalled years later, he brought his research materials into the conclave that elected Pope John Paul I in August 1978 and worked on the draft texts there.[20] In addition to his pastoral concerns, Wojtyła the philosopher continued to find the fact that God had created humanity male and female a fascinating intellectual puzzle, an "interesting problem" in its own right, as he once put it. What did a humanity that expressed itself through maleness and femaleness tell us about the human condition in general, and about men and women in particular?[21] Then there was the confusion in the Church after *Humanae Vitae*. Something had to be done to explain the Church's sexual ethic in a more persuasive way. Characteristically, Wojtyła decided to write a book about all this. The book he was drafting at Conclave I in 1978 unexpectedly became the material for his general audiences as Pope.

Original Unity of Man and Woman began with the polemics between Jesus and the Pharisees on the question of divorce.[22] Why, John Paul asks, did Christ, in rejecting the Mosaic practice of divorce, put so much emphasis on the fact that God had created human beings as male and female "in the beginning"— a phrase that recurs twice in the biblical story (*Matthew* 19.3–12)? This leads the Pope into the creation stories in *Genesis*, which he treats as profound reflections on enduring truths about the human condition, conveyed through the device of mythic stories about human origins. The first creation story, he writes, links the mystery of man's creation as an "image of God" to the human capacity to procreate ("Be fruitful and multiply. . . ."). The second creation account, emphasizing human self-awareness and moral choice, is the "subjective" counterpart to the "objective" truth in the first account—we are also images of God in our thinking and choosing. From different angles of vision, the two creation accounts testify to the dignity of being human, in which sexuality, procreation, and moral choosing are intimately linked.

John Paul had always liked to do philosophy from the standpoint of Adam in the Garden of Eden: to try to see the world fresh, to recapture the wonder and astonishment that Aristotle believed was the beginning of philosophy.[23] In *Original Unity,* he reflects on Adam's wondrous sense of solitude, which reveals important things about the human condition. Adam's "original solitude," his being-alone, has two meanings. First, he is alone because he is neither an animal nor is he God—this is the solitude of human nature that he shares with Eve and every other human being throughout history. Thinking about this way of being-alone, we come to know ourselves as *persons.* We are different because we are thinking, choosing, acting subjects, not merely objects of nature. With this self-knowledge comes free will, the capacity to determine *how* we shall act. This means, at the most profound level, choosing between good and evil, life and death. In this choosing, we come to know ourselves as *embodied* persons, for there is no human choosing or acting without a body. The body is not a machine we happen to inhabit. The body through which we express who we are and act out the decisions we make is not accidental to who we are.

Second, Adam experiences himself as being-alone because there is no other human creature like him. Thus, for John Paul, the "complete and definitive creation of 'man'" only occurs when God creates Eve, and Adam recognizes Eve as a human creature like himself, although different.[24] His joy at this discovery suggests that this aspect of our "original solitude" is overcome by that remarkable process in which I am genuinely united to another while finding my own identity not only intact, but enhanced.

This, John Paul contends, is what "creation" is for—and that tells us something important about who God the creator is. Men and women are images of God, not only through intellect and free will, but above all "through the communion of persons which man and woman form right from the beginning. . . . Man becomes the image of God . . . in the moment of communion."[25] This yearning for a radical giving of self and receiving of another, which Adam symbolically affirms by recognizing Eve as "flesh of my flesh," is at the foundation of our humanity. It carries with it, "from the beginning," the blessing of fertility, another way human persons are images of God, for procreation reproduces the mystery of creation.

Thus, "from the beginning," our creation as embodied persons and as male and female is a *sacramental* reality, an icon of the life of God. The body makes visible the invisible, the spiritual, and the divine. In the *Genesis* stories, we meet the extraordinary side of the ordinary, this time through our embodiedness and our sexuality.

If our sexuality is built into us "from the beginning," why did Adam and Eve become ashamed of their nakedness? John Paul suggests that "original nakedness," with "original solitude" and "original unity," is the third part of the puzzle of who we are "from the beginning." "Shame" is, essentially, fear of the other, and we become afraid of the other when he or she becomes an object for us. Adam and Eve were not ashamed of their nakedness when they were living in a mutuality of self-giving, in a truly nuptial relationship expressed through their embodiedness as male and female. They were not ashamed when they were living freedom-as-giving. The "original sin" is to violate the Law of the Gift built into us, to turn the other into an object, a thing to be used. And this is a sin, not because God unilaterally and arbitrarily declares it to be so, but because it violates the truth of the human condition inscribed in us as male and female.

Read carefully, the stories of the creation of the human world in *Genesis* reveal that human flourishing depends on self-giving, not self-assertion. Mutual self-giving in sexual love, made possible by our embodiedness as male and female, is an icon of that great moral truth.

Blessed Are the Pure of Heart

John Paul begins the second series of audience addresses in his revolutionary theology of the body with another biblical scene. In the Sermon on the Mount, Jesus is laying out the moral implications of living a life of beatitude—a life that includes "purity of heart"—and says, "You have heard it said, 'You shall not commit adultery.' But I say to you that everyone who looks at a woman lustfully has already committed adultery with her in his heart" (*Matthew* 5.27–28). It has seemed, for centuries, a very difficult, even impossibly high, standard. Yet for John Paul, this text is just as much a "key" to the theology of the body as Christ's reference to our being created male and female "from the beginning."[26]

Sin, the Pope explains, enters the world as a corruption of genuine self-giving, which is motivated by love. When that self-giving is experienced as restraint rather than fulfillment, love decays into lust, and the icon of created goodness (and of the Creator) that was sexual love "in the beginning" is broken. Human beings lose their "original certainty" that the world is good and that we are fit for living in it in communion with others. The difference between male and female, once a source of identity in communion, becomes a source of confrontation. "The world" becomes a place of fear and toil, and there is a basic rupture in the relationship between creature and Creator. The human heart becomes a battlefield between love and lust, between self-mastery and self-assertion, between freedom as giving and freedom as taking—which is often at the expense of the woman, the Pope notes. All of this, to go back to *Genesis*, is the result of acquiescing to the satanic temptation to redefine the humanity built into us as male and female. On this papal reading of the text, "the serpent" in *Genesis* is the first and most lethal purveyor of a false humanism.

Christ's words about the "adultery of the heart" now come into clearer focus. Lust, the Pope suggests, is the opposite of true attraction. True attraction desires the other's good through the gift of myself; lust desires my own transitory pleasure through the use (and even abuse) of the other. The woman at whom a man gazes lustfully is an object, not a person, and sex is reduced to a utilitarian means to satisfy a "need."[27] This "adultery of the heart" can even take place within marriage—not because the object of a man's lust is not his wife, but because the lustful look turns a wife into an object and shatters the communion of persons.[28]

This suggestion of the possibility of adultery-within-marriage set off a firestorm in the world media, which was not assuaged when the Vatican newspaper, *L'Osservatore Romano*, sniffed in response that some of those complaining lacked an "adequate cultural background" to understand what John Paul was saying.[29] Yet the Pope's description of adultery-in-marriage paralleled statements that had been made by feminists for years, and was clearly implied by the theology of the body he had been developing for more than a year. If one assumed that John Paul II was a Polish Manichaean who found sex distasteful and dirty, one might conclude that his reflection on adultery-within-marriage was a particularly odd expression of his neuroses. To those who had taken seriously the Pope's argument that sexual love within marriage is an icon of the interior life of God because it expresses a communion of persons, the Pope's statement about adultery-within-marriage made perfect sense.

The Christian sexual ethic, John Paul taught, redeemed sexuality from the trap of lust. Far from prohibiting *eros*, the Christian ethic liberates *eros* for a "full and mature spontaneity" in which the "perennial attraction" of the sexes finds its fulfillment in mutual self-giving and a mutual affirmation of the dignity of each partner.[30] The "new ethic" of the Sermon on the Mount and Christ's teaching about the beatitude of the "pure of heart" is an ethic of "the redemption of the body," a rediscovery in history of the truth of self-giving as the truth of the human condition "from the beginning."[31]

This ethic did not do away with desire. Rather, it sought to channel our desires "from the heart," so that those desires were fulfilled as they should be— in the communion of persons which is the image of God.[32] "Purity of the heart" is an aptitude, a virtue, the capacity to channel desire toward self-mastery "in holiness and honor."[33] Sexual love lived in "purity of heart" becomes a means of sanctification as the communion of persons is completed in holiness. Christians, the Pope suggests, will find a special motivation for living their sexuality this way, because the human body was the vehicle through which God became man and through which Christ completed the redemption of the world.[34]

There is a nobility and dignity to our being male and female because the self-giving of male and female in sexual love is the visible expression of the interior moral "structure" of the human person.[35] False humanisms imagine human beings to be infinitely plastic and malleable. A true humanism—and a true freedom—recognizes that, because certain truths are built into the human condition, human flourishing depends on living out those truths.[36] Human sexuality, John Paul insists, unveils some of those truths.

The Theology of Marriage and Celibacy

In the Gospel of Mark, the Sadducees, who denied the resurrection of the dead, tried to reduce the notion of resurrection to an absurdity, posing the case of a woman who serially marries seven brothers, all of whom die without giving her children. To which of these seven men, the Sadducees ask, will the woman be married after the resurrection of the dead? Jesus replies that, in the Kingdom of Heaven "they neither marry nor are given in marriage" (*Mark* 12.23). If the resurrection gives men and women the fullness of life promised by God "from the beginning," doesn't Jesus' reply devalue and degrade marriage and sexuality? In the third part of his *Theology of the Body*, John Paul argues that precisely the opposite is the case.

Life in the Kingdom of God is life in perfect self-giving and perfect receptivity. It is life "within" the interior life of God, so to speak, a Trinity of Persons who perfectly give and perfectly receive throughout eternity. "Giving" in the Kingdom is the perfect gift of self to God and the perfect reception of God's self-gift by men and women in their resurrected bodies. "Resurrection" does not mean the loss of our bodies, which would be dehumanizing. It does, in some sense, mean the divinization of our bodies, as we come to resemble the risen Christ, who remains God and man. This "divinization" of human beings is the fulfillment of the nuptial meaning of the human body, an icon of the Law of the Gift built into creation as a reflection of the inner dynamism of God's own life.[37]

Celibacy lived "for the Kingdom" anticipates, in history, life in the promised Kingdom of God, in which there will be "perfect donation" without marriage. Marriage, which has an element of exclusivity built into it, will not be part of a heavenly life in which all the redeemed live in what the Pope terms "perfect intersubjectivity," a modern philosophical image of what Christian tradition calls "the communion of saints."[38] In the world and in history, marriage is a school in which we become fitted for life in the Kingdom by learning to make a complete gift of self to another. The celibate must also become fitted for the Kingdom by learning to make that complete gift of self. Celibacy should be fruitful, leading to spiritual paternity and maternity, as marriage does through the procreation, rearing, and education of children. Marriage and celibacy are two complementary, "conjugal" ways of living a Christian life. Celibacy, lived "for the Kingdom," becomes an icon illuminating the condition that awaits all the faithful in the Kingdom, while marriage is the icon of God's spousal love for his people, Israel, and for the Church.[39]

Marriage, John Paul continues, is in a sense the "most ancient sacrament," for "from the beginning" it was the ordinary reality that revealed the extraordinary fact of creation as an act of self-giving love. In the sacrament of marriage, husband and wife are the ministers of God's grace, and the "language of the body" in marital love is the way in which a couple carries out the "conjugal dialogue" appropriate to marriage as a vocation.[40] For the Christian, conjugal love is also an icon of the redemption, for love between husband and wife has been recognized since New Testament times as an image of Christ's love for his bride, the Church.[41] Marriage gains a new richness of meaning by being understood as the human reality that best mirrors the relationship between the redeeming Christ and the people He has redeemed. God's purposes in creation and redemption are both revealed in marriage.[42] And here the question of divorce, contested throughout Christian history, comes into clearer focus. If a sacramental marriage, an icon of God's creative and redeeming love, is dissoluble, then so is God's love for the world and Christ's love for the Church.*

The Theology of Marriage and Celibacy ends with John Paul's most dramatic celebration of marital love. Sexual love, he concludes, is an act of worship. "Conjugal life becomes ... liturgical" when the "language of the body" becomes the means to encounter, through an experience of the sacred, what God had willed for the world and for humanity "from the beginning." The sexual gift of self, freely offered and freely received within the covenant of marriage, becomes a way to sanctify the world.[44]

Reflections on *Humanae Vitae*

In the fourth cluster of meditations in John Paul's *Theology of the Body*, the Pope asks how the good of sexual love is to be used to promote human happiness. How is sexual love to be lived *chastely*? To bring sexuality within the ambit of the four cardinal virtues of prudence, justice, courage, and temperance, John Paul proposes, is to live a life of sexual love most humanly.

In dealing with these difficult questions, *Humanae Vitae* had put the moral challenge of marital chastity in the rather negative context of "endurance." John Paul's *Theology of the Body* repositions the entire question, asking how various ways of living a life of sexual love fit into the iconography of marriage. The challenge is to live out our embodiedness as male and female—to live sexual love—so that sexual love in marriage becomes the most illuminating possible icon of self-giving.[45]

The Pope begins by teaching that all married couples are called to "responsible parenthood." The issue involved is not merely "avoiding another birth." The truly human challenge is building a family according to the virtue of prudence. Judgments about the number of children they can responsibly raise are judgments a married couple must make "before God" in the tribunal of conscience. Judgments about "fertility regulation" (a better term than "birth control," in the Pope's view) are not judgments that anyone else can make for them. There can be "morally worthy reasons" for limiting fertility; given collapsing birth rates in some societies, there can also be morally worthy reasons for having bigger families than might first seem appropriate to a couple.

If family planning is a grave moral responsibility for everyone living the vocation of marriage, the next question is *how* to regulate fertility and live responsible parenthood, so that the spouses' human dignity is protected and the iconography of married love as mutual self-donation is honored. John Paul argues that it is dehumanizing to transfer mechanical and chemical methods,

---

*This does not, of course, resolve the question of what constitutes a sacramental, and thus indissoluble, marriage. But it does suggest the gravity of what is at stake in this issue.[43]

appropriate to humanity's domination of nature, to the realm of sexual love. Periodic abstinence from sexual activity, using the natural rhythms of the body as the means for regulating fertility, is a more humanistic method of exercising procreative responsibility and living marital love chastely. It is also more in tune with the sacramental character of marriage, for it gives bodily expression to the fact that married couples are the "ministers of the design" that God has built into procreation. Living the virtue of marital chastity, the couple's relationship to the natural rhythms of fertility is ennobled and, from a Christian perspective, becomes a vehicle of grace.[46]

John Paul suggests that what is "natural" is what best conforms to human dignity, to the nature of the human person as an intelligent creature called to maturity through self-mastery.[47] Repositioning the discussion of sexual morality within the broader horizon of a genuine humanism, the first moral question shifts from "What am I forbidden to do?" to "How do I live a life of sexual love that conforms with my dignity as a human person?" Within that context, some things are still not to be done. But they are not to be done because they demean our humanity and damage the communion of persons which sexual love is intended to foster.[48]

Growing into the maturity of self-mastery is not easy. Living marital chastity means thinking of marriage as a vocation to be grown into, as a couple grows in the love "poured into [their] hearts as a gift of the Holy Spirit." A couple's maturation into a communion of persons involves sexual expression and sexual abstinence, ecstasy and asceticism. To remove that tension from married life is to empty it of one crucial aspect of its inherent drama, and its humanity. Truth and love can never be separated in the mysterious, ecstatic, ascetic "language of the body."[49]

A Theological Time Bomb?

The Church and the world will be well into the twenty-first century, and perhaps far beyond, before Catholic theology has fully assimilated the contents of these 130 general audience addresses.[50] If it is taken with the seriousness it deserves, John Paul's *Theology of the Body* may prove to be the decisive moment in exorcising the Manichaean demon and its deprecation of human sexuality from Catholic moral theology. Few moral theologians have taken our embodiedness as male and female as seriously as John Paul II. Few have dared push the Catholic sacramental intuition—the invisible manifest through the visible, the extraordinary that lies on the far side of the ordinary—quite as far as John Paul does in teaching that the self-giving love of sexual communion is an icon of the interior life of God. Few have dared say so forthrightly to the world, "Human sexuality is far greater than you imagine." Few have shown more persuasively how recovering the dramatic structure of the moral life revitalizes the ethics of virtue and takes us far beyond the rule-obsessed morality of "progressives" and "conservatives."

John Paul's *Theology of the Body* has ramifications for all of theology. It challenges us to think of sexuality as a way to grasp the essence of the human—and through that, to discern something about the divine. In the *Theology of the Body*, our being embodied as male and female "in the beginning" is a window into the nature and purposes of the Creator God. Angelo Scola, rector of the Pontifical Lateran University in Rome, goes so far as to suggest that virtually every thesis in theology—God, Christ, the Trinity, grace, the Church, the sacraments—could be seen in a new light if theologians explored in depth the rich personalism implied in John Paul II's theology of the body.[51]

Few contemporary theologians have taken up the challenge implicit in this dramatic proposal. Fewer priests preach these themes. A very small, even microscopic, percentage of the world's Catholics even know that a "theology of the body" exists. Why? The density of John Paul's material is one factor; a secondary literature capable of "translating" John Paul's thought into more accessible categories and vocabulary is badly needed. The "canon" of Church controversies as defined by the media—birth control, abortion, divorce, women in Holy Orders—is also an obstacle to a real engagement with John Paul's thought. John Paul II's *Theology of the Body* is emphatically not made for the age of the twenty-second sound-bite, or for a media environment in which every idea must be labeled "liberal" or "conservative." It may also be the case that John Paul II's theology of the body will only be seriously engaged when John Paul, lightning rod of controversy, is gone from the historical stage. These 130 catechetical addresses, taken together, constitute a kind of theological time bomb set to go off, with dramatic consequences, sometime in the third millennium of the Church.

When that happens, perhaps in the twenty-first century, the *Theology of the Body* may well be seen as a critical moment not only in Catholic theology, but in the history of modern thought. For 350 years, Western philosophy has insisted on beginning with the human subject, the thinking subject. Karol Wojtyła, philosopher, took this "turn to the subject" seriously; John Paul II has taken it seriously as a theologian. By insisting that the human subject is always an *embodied* subject whose embodiedness is critical to his or her self-understanding and relationship to the world, John Paul took modernity's "anthropological turn" with utmost seriousness. By demonstrating that the dignity of the human person can be "read" from that embodiedness, he helped enrich the modern understanding of freedom, of sexual love, and of the relationship between them.

THE POPE OF HUMAN RIGHTS

On October 2, 1979, four weeks after he began his catechetical series on the theology of the body, John Paul II gave one of the crucial public addresses of his pontificate, to the General Assembly of the United Nations at its headquarters in New York. What he had to say about human rights was a direct challenge to the way most UN member states thought about international politics and the pursuit of peace.

In the Land of St. Patrick

En route to the New World, John Paul stopped for two and a half days in Ireland, a once intensely Catholic country showing signs of distancing itself from its historic roots, and a politically divided island where the fever of low-grade civil war, putatively in the name of Catholicism and Protestantism, had persisted for generations. The formal purpose of the visit was to make a pilgrimage to the shrine of Our Lady of Knock in County Mayo, site of a Marian apparition in 1879. John Paul wanted to remind the Irish that, like the Poles, their history and culture could not be understood without Christ. He also had some things to say about violence committed in the name of Christianity.

The first Pope to set foot on Irish soil arrived in Dublin on September 29, an unusually sunny day. At the airport arrival ceremony, John Paul expressed his happiness at being in the Emerald Isle through the prayer known as "St. Patrick's Breastplate." He was, he told the Irish, "happy to walk among you— in the footsteps of St. Patrick and in the path of the Gospel that he left you as a great heritage—being convinced that Christ is here: 'Christ before me, Christ behind me . . . Christ in the heart of every man who thinks of me, Christ in the mouth of every man who speaks of me.'" The first papal Mass in Ireland's fabled Catholic history took place later that day at a site known as the "Fifteen Acres" in Phoenix Park. Public transportation had been suspended for the day, but more than 1.2 million people found their way to the park, where a great cross, 120 feet high, had been raised before a phalanx of sixty flagpoles bearing the white and gold papal banner. In his homily, John Paul challenged the Irish, who had sent so many thousands of missionaries out into the world, to reevangelize themselves: "Be converted!"[52]

After a motorcade through the streets of Dublin, the Pope flew by helicopter to Drogheda, thirty miles or so from the Irish Republic's border with British Northern Ireland. The original plan had been for the Pope, warmly invited by Anglican Archbishop George Simms, to visit the ancient primatial See of Armagh, in Northern Ireland. Fear of violence had made the trip planners settle for a stop in Drogheda, itself a potential tinderbox of historic emotions. There, in 1649, the Puritan conqueror Oliver Cromwell had perpetrated the greatest massacre in Irish history; Drogheda was also the site of the relics of St. Oliver Plunkett, archbishop of Armagh, who was hanged, drawn, and quartered on London's Tyburn Hill in 1681. Some 300,000 people, many of them from Northern Ireland, came to see and hear the Pope, who made an impassioned plea for an end to sectarian hatred and the killing that had been done in its name.

Oliver Plunkett, he said, was not a symbol for revenge: for he had preached by word and deed "the love of Christ for all men. . . . He was indeed the defender of the oppressed and the advocate of justice, but he would never condone violence. . . . His dying words were words of forgiveness for all his enemies." John Paul publicly thanked the Anglican Primate for his invitation, which had been "taken up and repeated by . . . leaders and members of other churches, including many from Northern Ireland."

These invitations proved that, popular and media imagery to the contrary, "The Troubles" in the North were not "a religious war, a struggle between Catholics and Protestants." "The Troubles," he suggested, were a struggle between haters, and Christianity forbade hate. There were injustices to be remedied, but Christianity resolutely forbade "solutions to these situations by the ways of hatred, by the murdering of defenseless people, by the methods of terrorism. . . . The command 'Thou shalt not kill' must be binding on the conscience of humanity, if the terrible tragedy and destiny of Cain is not to be repeated."

Then, to those Cains who may have been listening, he made his most powerful and personal plea: "On my knees I beg you to turn away from the paths of violence and to return to the ways of peace . . . violence destroys the work of justice. . . . Further violence in Ireland will only drag down to ruin the land you claim to love and the values you claim to cherish. . . ."[53] Many of the "violent men" of Northern Ireland would ignore that appeal in the years ahead. But some would trace the more hopeful signs of peace that appeared decades later back to John Paul II's decisive refutation of violence. As elsewhere, the truth of what he said could not be measured by immediate impact, but by the fact that it was the truth.

En route by helicopter to Galway and a meeting with Irish youngsters on September 30, John Paul stopped briefly in Clonmacnois, a great center of scholarship during the Dark Ages that had sent hundreds of missionaries into Europe. The Pope, more alone than he would ever be in Ireland, stood briefly in the extensive ruins of the monastic city and prayed at the tomb of one of the local saints before flying to the Ballybrit Raceway, where 300,000 young people were waiting for him. He told them the same thing, he said, that he had told the young people of Kraków during his years as archbishop: "I believe in youth with all my heart and with all the strength of my conviction." Speaking almost autobiographically, he left them with a testimonial: "Sometimes," he said, "one could have the feeling that, before the experiences of history and before concrete situations, love has lost its power. . . . And yet, in the long run, love always brings victory, love is never defeated. Young people of Ireland, I love you."

Fourteen minutes of boisterous applause, cheers, and singing followed, and stopped only when a priest pleaded for quiet so that Mass could continue.

At Knock, the Pope visited with 3,000 sick, blessed the cornerstones for thirty-four new churches throughout the country, and celebrated Mass for a half-million Irish. He spoke of the Marian apparition (in which, according to local legend, Mary, accompanied by St. Joseph and St. John the Evangelist, appeared to a group of obscure villagers) in particularly poignant terms:

There is something unique and especially Irish in the Marian apparition at Knock.... The Virgin appeared not just to a child or children, but to a group of people representing all ages.... In a land where all the ancient shrines were in ruins or in the hands of the Irish [Anglican] Church, she asked for no new shrine. In a land where the people had known unbelievable hardship and oppression ... she asked for no penance. In a land where devotion was constant and everywhere, she asked for no processions, no pilgrimages. In fact, she asked for nothing at all. In a land known far and wide as a place for talk, she astonishingly said nothing at all. But she came.... When it seemed that everyone else was leaving for Australia or Boston or New York, the mother of Jesus came. And being the proper lady that she was, in a land that held women and marriage and the priesthood in high regard, she brought with her her husband, St. Joseph, and St. John the Evangelist garbed as a prelate. And they also remained silent. Appropriately enough, they came in the rain.[54]

After meeting with the Irish bishops and with seminarians, priests, and nuns at the national seminary at Maynooth, John Paul celebrated the last public Mass of this Irish pilgrimage at the Greenpark Racecourse in Limerick, where a quarter of a million people had gathered on the morning of October 1. He then flew out of nearby Shannon Airport on an Aer Lingus 747 for Boston, where he arrived late that day. The Pope was welcomed at the airport by the president's wife, Rosalynn Carter, and by national security adviser Zbigniew Brzeziński, perhaps thinking back on his spur-of-the-moment decision to attend a Harvard lecture by a visiting Polish cardinal in the summer of 1976. The weather was not kind, but a driving rainstorm failed to prevent a crowd of 2 million from gathering for the papal Mass on Boston Common. With hundreds of thousands of non-Catholics estimated to be present, it was arguably the largest ecumenical service in Christian history. As the Pope approached the altar, thousands of red-and-white balloons were released, Irish Boston's tribute to its Polish guest.[55]

Prior to the Mass on Boston Common, John Paul had met with several thousand priests and nuns at Boston's Cathedral of the Holy Cross. As he was leaving, he spotted the only wheelchair in the church and went to see twenty-six-year-old Jane De Martino, who had been paralyzed in an accident. The Pope held her hand, leaned over and whispered to her, kissed her, and left her with a small box containing a white-and-gold rosary. A Boston policeman who had been standing nearby began to cry. "I've got to get back to church," he said, and walked away.[56]

Speaking Truth to Power

The next morning, John Paul flew to New York. After some mild banter at the airport with Mayor Edward Koch—The mayor: "Your Holiness, I am the mayor." The Pope: "I shall try to be a good citizen."—he was driven in a motorcade to UN headquarters on the East River, where he was greeted by Secretary-General Kurt Waldheim. John Paul II walked into the Secretariat building as if this were something he did every day, projecting vigor, energy, and the quiet strength of a man comfortable in whatever situation he happened to find himself. Smiling and polite, he also conveyed a sense of power—physical power, but also the power of a discerning mind. This was a gracious man unimpressed by diplomatic niceties or flattery. When it came time for him to speak, he was completely at home at the rostrum, animatedly addressing the delegates, guests, and press as if he were back lecturing at Lublin, shifting his position from time to time, now leaning on an arm as if to ponder a point more slowly, then looking up and gesturing as if to say, "Now, listen to *this*. . . ."

John Paul came to the United Nations at a time of increasing anxiety and political agitation about the nuclear arms competition between East and West. The SALT II arms control negotiations were stalled. Anti-nuclear protests were common in the United States and Western Europe, and the "nuclear freeze" movement was just beginning to have an impact on the American public debate. Both diplomatic negotiators and street protesters seemed to share the conviction that nuclear weapons could, somehow, be factored out of the political struggle between NATO and the Warsaw Pact—that sufficient application of will could resolve the weapons dilemma and bring peace, even if the ideological competition remained unresolved. War was caused by weapons, peace was the absence of war, and war could be prevented by arms control. However differently they worked on the issue, diplomats and protesters alike were tacitly agreed on this "realist" reading of the arms race.

John Paul II had a very different idea of how the world politics of the late twentieth century worked, as he was about to make unmistakably clear.

His hour-long UN address opened with the usual Vatican statement on the UN's importance and the Holy See's distinctive role in world affairs. Then the Pope got down to cases, reminding his listeners that, when Christ had appeared before the Roman judge Pontius Pilate, he had said that his mission was "to bear witness to the truth" (*John* 18.37). That was what he, the Vicar of Christ, proposed to do as well. He was addressing them not as another diplomat speaking the language of power according to the club rules, but as a witness to the truth about "man in his wholeness, in all the fullness and manifold riches of his spiritual and material existence."[57]

Politics, he reminded them, was about human beings. *Their* welfare, and nothing else, was the reason for politics, "whether national or international," because any legitimate politics always "comes *from man*, is exercised *by man*, and is *for man*." Any politics that did not hold itself to this humanistic criterion had lost much of its reason to exist; it was a politics that could "come to contradict humanity itself."[58]

Human progress had to be measured by a criterion worthy of human beings, and this meant measuring progress not only by science and technology, but "also and chiefly *by the primacy given to spiritual values* and by *the progress of the moral life.*" The realm of conscience was where the human world showed itself to be most human. When the claims of conscience and moral truth were denied, science and technology had been used to make the world a slaughterhouse. That was why the "fundamental document" of the United Nations, the document that gave it its moral raison d'être, was not the UN Charter but the 1948 Universal Declaration of Human Rights, "a milestone on the long and difficult path of the human race." The cause of peace could only advance "through the definition and recognition of, and respect for, the inalienable rights of individuals and of the communities of peoples."[59]

Respect for human rights meant respect for the dignity and worth of every human being. Thus peace was threatened whenever a politics characterized by the "thirst for power regardless of the needs of others" held sway. This was true among, as well as within, nations. If national "interest" was the sole criterion in international politics and if the concept of "interest" was stripped of moral components, then diplomacy was not an honorable business. Peace required thinking about obligations and duties, not just interests.[60]

Discussing the arms race, John Paul rejected the notion that the danger of nuclear war could somehow be detached from the conflict between communism and its challengers. The threat of war in the modern world did not come from weapons per se. It came from forms of injustice, sometimes deliberately imposed by governments, that attacked human rights, destroyed societies, and thereby threatened the entire international order.[61]

The world was working to define "as least some of the inalienable rights of man," and John Paul wanted to contribute to that discussion by listing those rights he thought it most important to recognize internationally. At the center was "the right to freedom of thought, conscience, and religion, and the right to manifest one's religion either individually or in community, in public or in private." This was central because "the values of the [human] spirit" were the driving force behind the "development of civilization" and the pursuit of peace. Peace required "enabling man to have full access to truth, to moral development, and to the complete possibility of enjoying the goods of culture which he has inherited, and of increasing them by his own creativity."[62]

Injustices in the economic order and in the spiritual order constituted the gravest threat to peace in the world, and a "humanistic criterion" was essential in evaluating social, economic, and political systems. The elimination of exploitation and free participation in economic and political life were the standards by which systems should be judged.[63] Economic, political, and social arrangements that systematically violated this "humanistic criterion" were by their nature threats to peace. So were those spiritual injustices that "wounded the human person in his inner relationship with truth, in his conscience, in his most personal belief, in his view of the world, in his religious faith, and in the sphere of what are known as civil liberties." Civilization had a centuries-long trajectory toward political communities "in which there can be *fully safeguarded the objective rights of the spirit, of human conscience and of human creativity, including man's relationship with God,*" and today's political leaders had to attend to that historical dynamic.[64]

Then, as if to make sure that there was no misunderstanding about who some of the principal perpetrators of "injustice in the field of the spirit" were, John Paul identified as threats to peace those systems that, although signing international human rights agreements, nonetheless created forms of "social life . . . in which the practical exercise of these freedoms condemns man . . . to become a second-class or third-class citizen, to see compromised . . . his professional career or his access to certain posts of responsibility, and to lose even the possibility of educating his children freely."[65] He was speaking to the world from the rostrum of the UN General Assembly as the Supreme Pontiff of the Roman Catholic Church. But he was still Karol Wojtyła of Kraków, and he was determined to bear witness to what Jacek Woźniakowski, Stanisław and Danuta Rybicki, Henryk Górecki, Stanisław Rodziński, and countless others had suffered in their professional lives for the sake of conscience.

Moving toward his peroration, John Paul turned once again to religious freedom as essential to the cause of peace. As Vatican II had taught, denying anyone the freedom to search for the truth and to adhere to it dehumanized that person, for the search for truth was of the essence of our humanity. Religious people, agnostics, and even atheists should be able to agree on this as a matter of common humanistic conviction.[66] No one could reasonably suggest that religious freedom was a sectarian matter.

John Paul II's 1979 UN address was historic in several respects. It contained a powerful diagnosis of the crisis of late modernity, which was far deeper than the conflicts between East and West, between capitalism and socialism, between rich and poor. It was a crisis in the very soul of humanity, and the core of the struggle was spiritual and moral.

Without once mentioning the words "communism" or "Marxism-Leninism," the address was a bold challenge to the Soviet system, and it was understood as such. As former U.S. ambassador to the UN Daniel Patrick Moynihan, who was present, noted, "I can attest from having watched that the Eastern European and Soviet delegates knew exactly what he was talking about, and for once in that chamber, looked fearful rather than bored."[67] But, in the name of humanism, the address also challenged the idea of politics as mere technique—an idea with influential adherents in the West.

The address also marked the point at which the Catholic Church unambiguously committed itself to the cause of human freedom and the defense of basic human rights as the primary goals of its engagement with world politics. That commitment had been implicit in John XXIII's 1963 encyclical *Pacem in Terris* and in the Second Vatican Council's *Declaration on Religious Freedom.* John Paul II had now made it explicit, and his actions in Mexico and Poland, in January and June 1979, had made it clear that the commitment would have public edge. For the Church would defend those rights on the basis of a humanism whose claims could be assessed by every man and woman of good will.

The address also challenged conventional ways of thinking about peace. At the UN, John Paul argued that avoiding war was neither a matter of cutting back on weapons (desirable as that might be) nor a matter of personal peacefulness and charity (as embodied by Mother Teresa of Calcutta, who was awarded the Nobel Peace Prize later that month). Rather, peace was the product of a moral commitment to human freedom, embodied in just political structures, nationally and internationally. Peace and human rights were indivisible. The Church, from John Paul's point of view, made its most effective contribution to peace when it relentlessly defended and promoted human rights, of which religious freedom was the centerpiece.

The delegates to the General Assembly had listened to John Paul's address in silence. No one had wandered about the floor of the General Assembly, as often happened during normal business. However they construed its meaning, the representatives of the worlds of power knew that they had been listening to a force to be reckoned with.

Woo-hoo-woo

The five-day tour of the United States in October 1979 by the man *Time* magazine dubbed "John Paul, Superstar" was a kaleidoscope of events that left powerful memories and a fixed media interpretation of the Pope in its wake.

On the night of his UN address, John Paul celebrated Mass for 75,000 in Yankee Stadium and asked Americans, proud of their open society, to think of openness more comprehensively: "Christ demands an openness that is more than benign attention, more than token actions or halfhearted efforts that leave the poor as destitute as before or even more so." En route to the Stadium, John Paul had stopped briefly at St. Charles Borromeo parish in Harlem and had addressed a small crowd standing on a vacant lot in the South Bronx: "Do not," he begged them, "give in to despair. . . . And do not forget that God has your lives in his care, goes with you, calls you to better things, calls you to overcome."[68]

Tens of thousands of teenagers were waiting for John Paul at Madison Square Garden on the morning of October 3. The scene that followed was unprecedented in the history of the papacy. As the Popemobile (a converted Ford Bronco) drove slowly around the inside of the arena, a band from St. Francis Preparatory School in Brooklyn played the themes from *Rocky* and *Battlestar Galactica* while the Pope reached out to touch the extended hands of exultant teens leaning over the front-row railings. At one point, John Paul started imitating a drummer and then gave a "thumbs up" to the crowd. The young people gave him blue jeans, a T-shirt ("Big Apple Welcomes John Paul II"), and a guitar. The noise was incredible; no Knicks or Rangers crowd at the historic Garden had ever caused such a din. At one point, when the youngsters had temporarily exhausted the names of Catholic youth organizations or local schools to cheer, they started rocking the roof with the rhythmic chant, "John

Paul II, we love you!" The Pope, shaking with laughter, took the microphone and started his own chant: "*Woo-hoo-woo;* John Paul II, he loves you!"

The message, when things finally settled down, was a call to maturity. Each of them, he said, was "approaching that stage in your life when you must take personal responsibility for your own destiny." In making those decisions, he urged, "look to Christ. When you wonder about the mystery of yourself, look to Christ who gives you the meaning of life. When you wonder what it means to be a mature person, look to Christ who is the fullness of humanity." And then, as always with the young, he made an act of faith: "The Church needs you. The world needs you, because it needs Christ and you belong to Christ. . . ."[69]

The next day, at a Mass attended by more than a million in Philadelphia's Logan Circle, John Paul took his homiletic cue from Independence Hall's Liberty Bell and urged Americans to deepen their understanding of freedom. Freedom was ennobled when the free human person chose wisely. Freedom linked to truth, freedom aimed at human flourishing, were inseparable in public life and in personal relationships, including sexual relationships. That was the purpose of the moral norms for living chastity in married life—they enabled the truthful use of freedom for the human flourishing of a marriage.[70]

After reminding the chairmen of the priests' councils from all the dioceses of the United States that "priesthood is not merely a task . . . [but] a vocation, a call to be heard again and again," John Paul flew to Iowa and the American heartland.[71] Des Moines had not been on the original papal schedule, but the Pope had received a handwritten letter from a farmer, Joe Hays, inviting him to visit the country's agricultural center. John Paul agreed, and a frantic five weeks of preparation began. A ten-foot-square banner, in burnt-orange, blue, green, and red, formed the backdrop to the altar platform and had been crafted by fifteen volunteers during a two-week long quilting bee. Speaking under the open Midwestern sky to the largest crowd in the history of Iowa, John Paul took the bounty of the earth as the starting point for the most moving homily of his American pilgrimage, a reflection on the bounty of Christ, satisfying the hungers of humanity in the Eucharist:

> Farmers everywhere provide bread for all humanity, but it is Christ alone who is the bread of life. . . . Even if all the physical hunger of the world were satisfied, even if everyone who is hungry were fed by his or her own labor or by the generosity of others, the deepest hunger of man would still exist. . . . Therefore I say, Come, all of you, to Christ. He is the bread of life. Come to Christ and you will never be hungry again. . . .[72]

A local Protestant minister from Granger, Iowa, told his neighbor, Joe Hays, "You got a Pope who knows how to pope."[73]

John Paul then flew to Chicago, where Polish-Americans in the tens of thousands continually serenaded him with *Sto lat!* [May you live a hundred years!]. "If we keep this up," John Paul cracked, "they're going to think it's the Polish national anthem."[74] In the Windy City, the Pope spoke to all the bishops of the United States, reminding them that holiness must be "the first priority in our lives and in our ministry." Living that holiness through his episcopal vocation, the bishop had to be willing to speak the truth, even in the face of cultural opposition. This, he said, the American bishops had done: in their public statements and conference documents condemning racism; rejecting the culture of divorce; defending the right-to-life of the unborn, the handicapped, and the terminally ill; challenging the sexual revolution; and calling the American nation to live the full truth of its commitment to liberty and justice for all. He also urged them to revitalize the practice of sacramental confession and to foster a renewed sense of reverence in the liturgy, which is "above all 'the worship of divine majesty.'"[75]

After Mass in Grant Park for half a million and a Chicago Symphony Orchestra concert at Holy Name Cathedral, John Paul flew to his last stop in the United States, Washington, D.C., where he was met at Andrews Air Force Base on October 6 by Vice President Walter Mondale. After a brief visit to St. Matthew's Cathedral, John Paul was driven to the White House, where he was welcomed on the North Lawn by President Jimmy Carter with the Polish phrase *Niech będzie Bóg pochwalony* [May God be praised]. Carter and the Pope had been in private correspondence for some time, and while it is unlikely that either Vatican or U.S. policy was much affected by the unprecedented exchange, the very fact of its existence demonstrated how John Paul II's first months in office had changed the papacy.[76] After an hour-long discussion, Pope and President met 6,000 guests on the South Lawn of the White House, where Carter spontaneously created what *Time* later referred to as "one of the most moving moments of his presidency." Speaking man-to-man and Christian-to-Christian, the Georgia Baptist told the Polish Catholic, "As human beings each acting for justice in the present—and striving together for a common future of peace and love—let us not wait so long for ourselves and for you to meet again. Welcome to our country, our new friend." John Paul embraced the President as the guests erupted into prolonged applause.[77]

That afternoon, John Paul spent several hours at the Vatican embassy in Washington discussing the international situation with Carter's national security adviser, Zbigniew Brzeziński. The meeting hadn't been on the official schedule. When Brzeziński, responding to the Pope's invitation, mentioned that there were some family logistical problems that weekend afternoon, John Paul told him to bring his wife and children along. As they were finishing, Brzeziński said that, when he talked to President Carter, he sometimes thought he was talking with a religious leader, and when he talked with John Paul II, he had the impression of talking to a world statesman. The Pope laughed.[78]

John Paul spent Sunday morning, October 7, at the Catholic University of America and in its environs. Prior to meeting with ecumenical leaders and the presidents of Catholic colleges and universities, he celebrated morning prayer and spoke with several thousand American nuns at the National Shrine of the Immaculate Conception. Addressing the Pope on behalf of the Leadership Conference of Women Religious, an organization of nuns known for its assertive feminism, Sister Teresa Kane, RSM, the LCWR's president, said that women ought to be "included in all the ministries of the Church," clearly a reference to the ordination of women.[79] The atmosphere in the huge basilica was electric, but not with unalloyed approbation. Some of those present thought Sister Teresa's speech a courageous act; other nuns regarded it as an exercise in bad manners. The Pope listened. Sister Teresa, dressed in a business suit, came up to the papal throne in the sanctuary, genuflected, and kissed the Pope's ring. Then, as a small group of sisters stood in silent protest of what they regarded as their disempowerment, John Paul took what could have become an ugly moment to a wholly different level, speaking of the consecrated religious life of nuns as a love affair with Jesus Christ:

> Two dynamic forces are operative in religious life: your love for Jesus—and, in Jesus, for all who belong to him—and his love for you.
>
> Thus every one of you needs a vibrant relationship of love with the Lord, a profound loving union with Christ, your spouse. . . .
>
> Yet far more important than your love for Christ is Christ's love for you. You have been called by him, made a member of his Body, consecrated in a life of the evangelical counsels, and destined by him to have a share in the mission that Christ has entrusted to the Church: his own mission of salvation. . . .
>
> Your service in the Church is, then, an extension of Christ, to whom you have dedicated your life. . . . And so your life must be characterized by a complete availability: a readiness to serve as the needs of the Church require, a readiness to give public witness to the Christ whom you love. . . .[80]

Although Sister Teresa Kane's remarks drew extensive and understandable media attention, the Pope's ecumenical meeting with leaders of other Christian communities in the chapel of Trinity College, across the street from the National Shrine, was also newsworthy. In his address, John Paul stressed that issues of marital chastity and public morality, not only questions of doctrine, had to be on the ecumenical agenda. "The moral life and the life of faith," he said, "are so deeply united that it is impossible to divide them."[81] His comments created a considerable discussion in ecumenical circles that would be revisited many times in the future.

The papal visit to Washington concluded Sunday afternoon with Mass on the National Mall for 200,000. His green vestments whipping about him in a crisp autumn breeze, John Paul ended his American pilgrimage where Thomas Jefferson began the Declaration of Independence, with the inalienable right to life. "Nothing," John Paul insisted, "surpasses the greatness or dignity of a human person," and for that reason, the Church "will stand up every time that human life is threatened": by abortion, by child abuse, by economic injustice, by any form of exploitation, by the abandonment of the sick, the elderly, the inconvenient. In doing so, he argued, the Catholic Church was serving the noblest in the American tradition. Had not Jefferson himself stated that "the care of human life and happiness and not their destruction is the just and only legitimate object of good government?" The first Pope to preach in the shadow of the Washington Monument, the Capitol, and the Lincoln Memorial closed by praising all those Americans—members of "other Christian churches, all men and women of the Judeo-Christian heritage, as well as all people of good will"—who were united "in common dedication for the defense of life in its fullness and for the promotion of all human rights."[82]

Authoritarian or Authoritative?

John Paul II's American pilgrimage was lavishly covered in the press, for whom *Time's* cover headline—"John Paul, Superstar"—defined one aspect of that remarkable week: the Pope's personal magnetism. Still, several of the Pope's addresses brought to the surface a question that had been bothering many commentators since Karol Wojtyła's election. How could this passionate and persuasive defender of human rights be so "doctrinaire" in his approach to what had become firmly fixed in the media's corporate mind as *the* issues in contemporary Roman Catholicism—birth control, abortion, divorce, and the ordination of women to the priesthood? *Time* spoke for many when its cover story claimed that the Pope's address to the bishops had reaffirmed "the thought that Christianity is a body of fixed beliefs rather than a faith that ought to be adapted to modern circumstances."[83]

John Paul II clearly thinks this is a false dichotomy. First of all, Christianity is, quite simply, the person of Jesus Christ. The Church, in bearing witness to Christ, adapts its presentation of the basic truths of its faith to the circumstances of the time and culture in which it finds itself. John Paul II's UN address was a good example of this interaction of doctrine and culture. The unchanging biblical truth about the dignity of the human person, put into conversation with modern philosophy and political theory, had yielded a potent defense of human rights and a new form of Christian humanism.

But the Church's doctrine is not infinitely plastic. The Church is the custodian of a body of truths—the "deposit of faith," as it is traditionally called—and if it shaves the edge off those truths it ceases to be the Church. There are, in other words, boundaries. They are important in themselves, because they consist of certain truths, and they are important for the development of doctrine—if there are no boundaries, how could one know whether a proposed development is authentically Christian or not? At the same time, there should be no boundaries to the charity with which the Church proposes the truths of which it is the custodian. The truth, the Pope had told the bishops in Chicago, must always be proposed in love.

To defend the truths of Catholic faith was not to be "doctrinaire," it was to be doctrinally serious. When he articulated those truths as the Bishop of Rome, John Paul was not imposing Karol Wojtyła's personal theological views on Catholicism. He was giving voice to the tradition of which he was the servant, not the master. He was not an authoritarian. He was the voice of an authoritative tradition.

It was not an easy distinction to grasp in a cultural climate like that of the United States, where doctrinal differences within and among religious communities are often regarded as matters of personal lifestyle choice, rather than of truth. It was even more difficult in a media environment in which the bobbing and weaving of politicians was the lingua franca of public discourse, and virtually every "position" was assumed to be negotiable. Grasping the distinction between the *authoritarian* and the *authoritative* is, however, essential to understanding John Paul II's approach to his office and his responsibility.

UNFINISHED BUSINESS

Three weeks after the first anniversary of his election, John Paul launched another experiment in governing the Church.

Although the College of Cardinals is sometimes described as a kind of ecclesiastical senate, in recent centuries it had functioned corporately only when electing a Pope. The only other times that significant numbers of cardinals met together were when the College received new members. But that happened as a result of papal nominations and hardly constituted an exercise in anything but pro forma collegial counsel to the Pope. John Paul wanted to make use of the College as a corporate body more frequently—an idea that had evidently been bruited among the cardinals during their meetings before the conclaves of 1978. The College of Cardinals, he believed, shared with the Pope the special papal *sollicitudo omnium ecclesiarum*: the "care for all the [local] Churches" and for the universal Church. Being a cardinal, in his view, was less a matter of personal privilege than of corporate responsibility for the entire Church, with and under the Pope.[84] So he called the cardinals together for an innovative "plenary assembly" on November 5, 1979, which 120 members of the College attended. It was the first time in 400 years that the College of Cardinals had met for business other than a papal election.

In his opening address, John Paul told the cardinals that, though he had some issues he wanted to discuss, he also wanted them to propose topics for future discussion. In addition to whatever was said in their conversation during these days of meetings, he welcomed written memoranda and proposals. He reflected on some of the recurring problems involved in implementing the Second Vatican Council, which "continues to be the main task of the pontificate." A correct understanding of freedom in the Church, which was always "freedom for" rather than "freedom from," was one issue. So was the need to rebuild a sense of "solidarity" within a Church too often riven by divisions. Solidarity in the Church also meant a more effective sharing of resources between the "rich and free" Church and the "poor and constricted" Church. That solidarity, in turn, should provide the impetus for the renewal of evangelism the

Council had intended to promote. It was time to recover a sense of the fervor and enthusiasm that had marked the experience of Vatican II.

John Paul asked the cardinals' counsel on three specific questions: the restructuring of the Roman Curia, the revitalization of the Pontifical Academy of Sciences, and the sorry state of Vatican finances. The Pope spoke somewhat obliquely on this third, always delicate subject: it is necessary, he said, "to formulate the question of economic resources." The fact was that the Holy See had been running large operating deficits since 1970, and something had to be done to bring expenditures and income into line.

None of these issues, large or small, was resolved by the four-day-long meeting, but a precedent of consultation had been set. A Commission of Cardinals was established to make recommendations about the financial situation.

Five days later, on November 10, the Pontifical Academy of Sciences commemorated the centenary of Albert Einstein's birth. John Paul II addressed the meeting in the first of a series of efforts to bridge the centuries-old gap between the Church and science. The Galileo case was the symbolic opening of that rift, and John Paul did not hesitate to praise "the greatness of Galileo" and to acknowledge that Galileo "had to suffer a great deal . . . at the hands of churchmen and Church institutions." The Pope expressed the hope that "theologians, scholars, and historians, animated by a spirit of collaboration, will study the Galileo case more deeply and, in loyal recognition of wrongs from whatever side they come, will dispel the mistrust that still opposes, in many minds, a fruitful concord between science and faith. . . ."[85]

A week after affirming before scientists that the truth, from whatever source, was the truth, John Paul extended his reflection on reason and faith at his Roman alma mater, now formally known as the Pontifical University of St. Thomas Aquinas, but still called "the Angelicum" by one and all. His lecture discussed the continuing importance for philosophy and theology of Thomas Aquinas, "a master who was deeply human because he was deeply Christian, and precisely because he was so deeply Christian was so deeply human."[86] John Paul suggested that Aquinas's "openness to the whole of reality in all its parts and dimensions" made him particularly important for students today, who had grown up in a fragmented intellectual climate. Such openness to reality as a whole, he said, "is also a significant and distinctive mark of the Christian faith."[87]

Just short of a month later, on December 15, the question of the Church's grasp on truth reoccurred when the Congregation for the Doctrine of the Faith clarified some doctrinal boundaries with one of Catholicism's most famous dissidents, the Swiss theologian Hans Küng, longtime Professor of Catholic Theology at the University of Tübingen in West Germany. Handsome and articulate, Küng had been the first example of a new phenomenon in Catholic life in the years since Vatican II—the dissenting theologian as international media star. Küng had done important work in alerting the Catholic world to what would become key issues at the Council. His doctoral dissertation—which argued for a compatibility, if not identity, between the Catholic understanding of "justification" and the theology of Karl Barth, the foremost Protestant theologian of the century—was a pioneering work in ecumenical theology.[88] In the eyes of at least some of his theological peers, though, Küng's intellectual product had declined in quality over the years.[89] Others worried that he had become so much the media personality that his penchant for making provocative statements was diminishing his ability to contribute to a truly ecclesial discussion inside the Church.[90] Küng himself was admirably frank about his position. On certain issues, including the Church's capacity to make binding and irreformable doctrinal definitions through the exercise of papal infallibility, he did not hold to be true, and he would not teach as true, what the Catholic Church held to be the truth.

On December 15, 1979, the Congregation for the Doctrine of the Faith [CDF] agreed with Hans Küng. He was not teaching what the Church taught, and therefore, according to a formal declaration by CDF, he "could not be considered a Catholic theologian." His ecclesiastical mandate to teach as a "Professor of Catholic Theology" was withdrawn.

The Küng affair was a cause célèbre throughout the Catholic world, especially in theological circles. Much of the media attention focused, naturally enough, on Küng's challenge to the doctrine of papal infallibility defined at the First Vatican Council. The crucial issue, the German bishops wrote in defense of the CDF declaration, was the ancient dogma that the Holy Spirit preserved the Church from fundamental error. Küng affirmed this as a general proposition, but claimed, as the Germans put it, that the Church could make "concrete errors in definitions of faith," even in cases where "the magisterium of the Church had pronounced [the definitions] as irrevocable." CDF had declared this unacceptable, since it called into question the fundamental Christian belief, based on Christian faith in the Holy Spirit, that the Church abided in a truth it could authoritatively articulate. The German bishops—who, as a body, could hardly be accused of theological obscurantism—agreed.[91]

Hans Küng was neither excommunicated nor deprived of his functions as a priest. He continued teaching at Tübingen, but not as a "Professor of Catholic Theology." Over time, he gradually faded from international media prominence. As he was no longer an officially certified Catholic theologian, his continuing dissent from the Church's teaching was of reduced interest.[92]

The same day that the Congregation issued its declaration, John Paul II drove to the Piazza della Pilotta near the Pantheon to meet with the faculty and students of the Pontifical Gregorian University, founded by St. Ignatius Loyola in 1551.[93] John Paul's theme was the special contribution that theology made to the prophetic mission of the Church, its witness to the truth about the human person.

He began by praising the Gregorian's founding generations of Jesuit scholars for having sought "allies" for theology among the arts and sciences.

Natural science had, since those days, become increasingly specialized, but "the fundamental urge to take into account all the progress made by science in things pertaining to man and the context of his life" remained valid for those practicing theology today.

Contemporary theology continued to find allies in other intellectual disciplines, including philosophy. Theology today needed a dialogue with modern philosophy, not simply with the great philosophical masters and systems of the past. "Be not afraid!" John Paul said, applied "to the great movements of contemporary thought." Whatever deepened our understanding of the "whole truth" about the human world deepened our understanding of Christ, the redeemer of that world. To be sure, not every contemporary philosophy could be a collaborator with theology. Some were "so poor or so closed" as to make any real dialogue impossible. Theologians today had to apply the test St. Paul had proposed two millennia ago to the Thessalonians: "Test everything, hold fast to what is good" (*1 Thessalonians* 5.21).

Theology was not religious studies, John Paul continued, standing outside the Church like a neutral observer examining a specimen. Theology was an "ecclesial science" that "grows in the Church and works on the Church." Because of that, its growth, which certainly involved critical and discerning development, had to be based on a "responsible assimilation of the patrimony" of Christian wisdom. A good theological education, he implied, did not begin with critically dismantling the tradition. It began with learning the tradition.

Theology also had to do with holiness.. True theology was an encounter with Christ, and true theological teaching was a way to "convey to the young a living experience of him." Theology did not exist for itself, but for the Church and for "the formation of Christians." Theologians should "do your work for truth courageously and openly, free of every prejudice and pinching narrowness of mind." It was the "excellence of truth," St. Thomas Aquinas had written, not the excellence of their own skills, that theologians ought to love.[94]

Less than two weeks later, on December 28, John Paul appointed Father Carlo Maria Martini, SJ, the Gregorian University's rector, as Archbishop of Milan, perhaps the most prestigious position in the Italian hierarchy. In the wake of the Küng affair, rumblings had been heard about a papal war against theologians. John Paul's address at the Gregorian and the appointment of Martini, an internationally recognized biblical scholar who had led one of the Church's most adventurous theological faculties, should have indicated that such suggestions were overwrought.

PETER AND ANDREW

Shortly after his election, John Paul II called the President of the Secretariat for Promoting Christian Unity, Cardinal Johannes Willebrands, and told him to get busy organizing a papal visit to the Ecumenical Patriarch of Orthodoxy, Dimitrios I, in his ancient See of Constantinople.[95] Since Vatican II, Roman

Catholic and Orthodox delegations had become accustomed to exchanging visits on the patronal feasts of the Sees of Rome and Constantinople (today's Istanbul): June 29, the feast of Sts. Peter and Paul, for the Romans, and November 30, the feast of St. Andrew the Apostle, Peter's blood brother, for the Orthodox. On John Paul's initiative, it was arranged that he make an ecumenical pilgrimage to see Patriarch Dimitrios at the end of November 1979.

John Paul's ecumenical credentials were suspect in some quarters when he was elected Pope. His first year in office quickly put such suspicions to rest. At the Pope's insistence, ecumenical meetings and prayer services became staple features of his world journeys. *Redemptor Hominis* had reaffirmed the Second Vatican Council's ecumenical commitment. Archbishop Meliton of Chalcedon, representing Patriarch Dimitrios, was warmly welcomed to Rome for the celebrations of Peter and Paul on June 29. With his brief visit to Dimitrios, John Paul II gave Roman Catholic ecumenism a decisive orientation eastward.

The Polish Pope had grown up in the borderlands between Roman Catholicism and Orthodoxy. He had studied Old Church Slavonic, the traditional liturgical language of the Slavic Orthodox world and the basis of many modern Slavic languages. Unlike other Polish clergy, he had developed a great respect and affection for Eastern Christianity, its distinctive liturgical forms, and its unique spirituality. He thought of Europe as a cultural unity and frequently invoked the image of Europe as a body that breathed with two lungs, East and West. And by "East" and "West" he meant two distinct expressions of the same culture, not two divided political camps.

More than some of his Catholic collaborators and many of his Orthodox interlocutors, he felt acutely the imperative to do something about the division between Roman Catholicism and its Orthodox sister Churches. His papacy was taking place on the threshold of the third millennium of Christian history. The first millennium, in which great questions of Christian doctrine had been resolved by East and West together, had been a millennium of Christian unity. The second millennium had been the millennium of Christian division: East and West had split in 1054, and Western Christianity had splintered in the sixteenth century. Might at least one of those breaches, the originating breach between Constantinople and Rome, be closed on the threshold of the third millennium?

Throughout his pontificate, this would remain John Paul's great millennial hope. It would cause him personal anguish, require him to absorb insults, and open him to charges of naïveté and betrayal from members of his own communion who had no interest in a "dialogue of love" with Orthodox churches whose leaders, during the communist period in Russia and elsewhere, had been among their persecutors. No amount of resistance would dissuade him from the view that he had an obligation to close the breach between Rome and the East.

He began his active pursuit of this great hope on November 28, 1979, flying to Ankara, capital of Turkey, for a round of diplomatic formalities that, according to Turkish government sensibilities, had to take place before his meeting with Dimitrios. He then flew to Istanbul on the morning of November 29 and was met at the airport by the Ecumenical Patriarch. The two churchmen immediately embraced, the Pope unable to suppress a great smile of satisfaction. At St. George's Cathedral in the Phanar, the seat of the Ecumenical Patriarchate, John Paul reminded his listeners that, amid enormous doctrinal controversy, "these two sister-Churches had maintained full communion in the first millennium of Christian history" and had "developed their great vital traditions" in the bond of unity. It was in "this common apostolic faith" that they were meeting now," in order "to walk toward this full unity which historical circumstances have wounded."[96] Patriarch Dimitrios responded that their meeting was "intended for God's future—a future which will again live unity, again common confession, again full communion, in the divine Eucharist."[97]

That evening, after meeting with Armenian Catholics and Armenian Orthodox, John Paul presided at a concelebrated Mass at the Catholic Church of the Holy Spirit in Istanbul. Patriarch Dimitrios and his synod were present, along with other Christian leaders. The contacts of recent years, the Pope said in his homily, "have caused us to discover again the brotherhood between our two Churches and the reality of a communion between them, even if it is not perfect." Tomorrow, while he would take part in the celebrations of the feast of St. Andrew in the Ecumenical Patriarchate's church, "we will not be able to concelebrate." But communion in prayer "will lead us to full communion in the Eucharist. I venture to hope that this day is near. Personally, I would like it to be very near."[98]

After the Patriarch's celebration of the Divine Liturgy for the feast of St. Andrew the next day, John Paul reiterated his conviction that "full communion with the Orthodox Church is a fundamental stage of the decisive progress of the whole ecumenical movement." At the end of the second millennium, he asked, "is it not time to hasten towards perfect brotherly reconciliation" for the sake of evangelization?[99] Patriarch Dimitrios responded by praising John Paul's "talent for freedom" and announcing the concrete accomplishment of his discussions with the Pope: the opening of a formal theological dialogue between Roman Catholicism and Orthodoxy on the international level.[100]

John Paul flew back to Rome that night, full of "intense emotions," as he put it at the Rome airport.[101] The successor of Peter had joined the successor of Andrew in giving the final blessing at the Latin-rite liturgy for the feast of St. Andrew. The Bishop of Rome had exchanged the kiss of peace with the Ecumenical Patriarch of Constantinople at the Orthodox liturgy for the same feast the following day. It was not full communion, and the Patriarch's comment about full communion being in "God's future" could be variously interpreted. John Paul, however, had made it abundantly clear that full communion was what he was striving for—and sooner rather than later.

SHADOWLANDS

The hard-eyed men in the Kremlin were, presumably, not all that interested in John Paul's views on the theological controversies between Roman Catholics and Orthodox Christians, or in the Pope's imaginative efforts to rebuild the foundations of Catholic sexual ethics. They were, however, deeply interested in, and deeply worried about, John Paul II's impact on world affairs—particularly in Stalin's internal and external empires, the Soviet Union and the Warsaw Pact. An official Soviet report complained that the Vatican had begun to "use religion in the ideological struggle against Soviet lands"—which was, evidently, considered a "more aggressive" approach to relations between the Church and the masters of communist governments.[102]

Something had to be done. On November 13, 1979, the Central Committee Secretariat gave its approval to a proposed "Decision to Work Against the Policies of the Vatican in Relation with Socialist States." The document had been written by a group that included the deputy chairman of the KGB, Victor Chebrikov. Among those approving its plan of action were Mikhail Suslov, keeper of the communist ideological flame, and two men who would eventually become General Secretary of the Soviet Communist Party (and thus leader of the Soviet Union), Konstantin Chernenko and Mikhail Gorbachev.

The planned counteroffensive had six components. The Communist parties of the Soviet "republics" with large Catholic populations—Lithuania, Latvia, Belorussia, and Ukraine—along with state television, the Soviet Academy of Sciences, the Tass news agency, and "other organizations . . . of the Soviet State" were to be mobilized to conduct expanded "propaganda against the policies of the Vatican." Meanwhile, Communist parties in Western Europe and Latin America were to dig out what information they could on local Catholic activism inspired by John Paul II, while concurrently launching their own anti-Vatican propaganda campaigns. The Catholic peace movement, which had come to such prominence in North America and Western Europe, was the third target. The foreign ministry was to "enter into contact with those groups of the Catholic Church engaged in work for peace" in order to "explain to them the policies of the Soviet Union in favor of world peace."

The fourth point in the action plan was ominous, both in the ambiguity of the goal and in the choice of agency for implementing it. In addition to the foreign ministry, the KGB was ordered to "improve the quality of the struggle against the new Eastern European policies of the Vatican." The KGB got further orders in point five: "through special channels" in the West and through the publications it controlled within the communist bloc, the KGB was to "show that the leadership of the new pope, John Paul II, is dangerous to the Catholic Church." The Soviet Academy of Sciences, meanwhile, was to intensify its study of Church activities throughout the world, while improving "the study of scientific atheism."[103]

Two weeks after this virtual declaration of war against John Paul II was approved at the highest levels of Soviet state authority, a young Turkish terrorist recently escaped from prison, Mehmet Ali Agca, sent a letter to the Istanbul newspaper *Milliyet*. He was, he claimed, deeply offended by the Pope's impending pilgrimage to Turkey, a ruse by "Western imperialists" to deploy the "Commander of the Crusades" against "Turkey and her sister Islamic nations." "If this visit . . . is not canceled," Agca concluded, "I will without doubt kill the Pope-Chief. This is the sole motive for my escape from prison. . . ."[104]

The shadowlands surrounding the pontificate of John Paul II were becoming well-populated.

II

Peter Among Us

The Universal Pastor as Apostolic Witness

The Alitalia jet flew north over the Alps, en route to Cologne in November 1980. Entering German airspace, John Paul II's plane was met by an escort of Luftwaffe fighters—perhaps the first time that Karol Wojtyła had seen aircraft marked with the black knight's cross since the days when he had dodged Luftwaffe bombs in Kraków and Luftwaffe strafing on the refugees' road to Tarnów. Prior to his first pastoral pilgrimage to West Germany, many Poles had said that it would be impossible for any Pole, even this Pole, to kiss German soil. The historical memories were powerful enough, but there were also tensions as fresh as the morning's newspapers. More than a few German Catholics professed indifference to the arrival of a Pope they regarded as a reactionary. Others, including leading German theologians, were more openly hostile. Some German Protestants were not enthusiastic, and student radicals had scribbled graffiti throughout Cologne: "Papal visit? No, thanks."

Arriving at the airport, John Paul II walked down the open gangway in the pouring rain, knelt, and kissed the soil of Germany.

Interest, it seemed, was higher than what people had told the pollsters. West German television, which broadcast up to eight hours of papal activities each day for five days, said that the number of viewers broke all previous records. The cameras often took tight shots of the Pope's face, and what Germans saw was not what many had expected. This was not a man asserting himself in an authoritarian fashion. Even during the lengthy Masses, his was not the face of someone presiding over a great public ceremony. It was the face of a man lost in prayer, living in a dimension of experience beyond words. Whatever the Germans expected to see, what they saw and were fascinated by was the face of a mystic.

Nor were they expecting his humor. When schoolchildren at the Cologne airport chanted from a balcony, "*Amo te! Amo te!*" he asked in high good humor, "Is that all the Latin you know?" During a sermon in Cologne, the congregation burst into applause after a particularly effective papal exposition which he completed with a citation from St. Paul; the Pope replied, "I thank you on St. Paul's behalf." Whatever this man was, people began to think, he was no ecclesiastical martinet. Martinets didn't behave this way.

A closed-minded authoritarian would not have told the leaders of the Evangelical Church, custodians of German Lutheranism, that he had come as a pilgrim "to the spiritual heritage of Martin Luther" and that "we have all sinned" in breaking the bonds of Christian unity. A reactionary, and a Polish reactionary at that, would not have acknowledged the Christian debt to the children of Abraham, telling the leaders of West German Jewry that no one could approach Christ without encountering Judaism. And what did the "anti-bourgeois" radicals make of his statement at a meeting with the elderly, whom he described as a treasure demonstrating that "the meaning of life is not confined to making and spending money"?

Many German theologians were not persuaded, but some secular dissenters were a bit shaken. The president of the Bavarian "Voltaire Club" told a Radio Free Europe correspondent that John Paul was complicating the imagery of dissent: "I wish that this Pope might be less lovable and noble as a person. His charisma makes our dialogue more difficult." Others were less polite. A Dutchman walked around dressed as Satan, carrying a sign asking why the Pope, who was working sixteen-hour days, didn't take up manual labor. A young girl, dressed up like Joan of Arc with a noose around her neck, told one and all that she was a feminist and that "the Church, the enemy of women, would like to burn us all at the stake." A dissident priest in Osnabrück kept roaring through a bullhorn, "Pretty words, medals, and rosaries are not enough!" Yet in terrible weather the crowds kept building throughout the pilgrimage. No one, least of all John Paul II, thought that he was resolving the crisis of Catholicism in Germany or the crisis of German culture. But he was touching something in the German soul.

In 110 hours, John Paul II traveled almost 1,800 miles inside West Germany, celebrated seven Masses, gave twenty-four major addresses, spoke to millions live and millions more on television. Perhaps the most memorable moment for the Polish Pope on German soil came outside the Schloss Augustusburg in Brühl. After meeting with public officials, John Paul was escorted to the torch-lit courtyard by President Karl Carstens and Chancellor Helmut Schmidt. A military band dressed in greatcoats and the distinctive German military helmet—familiar sights to Poles of John Paul's generation—stood along a red carpet punctuated by vases of yellow chrysanthemums. After playing various French, Italian, and English marching tunes, they launched into the "Dąbrowski Mazurka," the Polish national anthem, which begins with the words, "Poland is not yet lost. . . ."

John Paul II, walking down the carpet to his Mercedes-built Popemobile, paused briefly and with a catch in his voice, said quietly to his companions, in Polish, "What a moment. It is not lost! Indeed not!"[1]

PETER AND THE APOSTLES

Two years into his pontificate, in addition to redefining the papacy's role in the world of political power, John Paul II was clarifying how it is that the Pope is Peter among the bishops of the Church.

The 1979 *Annuario Pontificio*, the thick, red-bound Vatican yearbook, had described October 22, 1978, as the "solemn inauguration" of John Paul's "ministry as universal pastor of the Church." Some critics chafed at the title—did it suggest that the Church had only one pastor, the Pope, and that the bishops of the Church were deputy pastors or local branch managers? John Paul II's first years in office demonstrated that he read the responsibility of being "universal Pastor" through the lens of *Luke* 22.32, Christ's charge to Peter to "strengthen your brethren." In John Paul II's judgment, that charge had to be interpreted evangelically and literally. The Pope had a duty before Christ to be present to the people of the Church wherever they were. That, in the late twentieth century, was what the traditional papal *sollicitudo omnium ecclesiarum,* the Pope's "care for all the Churches," meant. What was most certainly not meant by that "care" was that the Pope was Chief Executive Officer of Roman Catholic Church, Inc., and the local bishops were simply managers of the branch offices.

There really is no appropriate organizational analogy for the relationship between the Bishop of Rome and the College of Bishops throughout the world. The American governmental model—an executive (Pope) with a legislature (College, or Synod, of Bishops)—does not fit. Neither does the Westminster model: a prime minister (Pope) with a parliament (the College of Bishops, or the Synod of Bishops, or an Ecumenical Council held on a regular basis). The corporate model—CEO (Pope) plus junior executives (the bishops)—is clearly impossible. So is the collective leadership model favored by some authoritarian regimes: the first-among-equals (Pope) who cannot act without authorization from the rest of the politburo or junta (the bishops). None of these analogies sheds much light on the subtle, complex teaching of Vatican II about the relationship between papal primacy and the collegial responsibility of the bishops for the governance of the Church—both of which, according to the Council, Christ willed for his Church, *together.*

The Council had taught that the Pope and the bishops in communion with him share responsibility for the whole Church, although the College of Bishops cannot exercise this authority without its head, the Bishop of Rome. The Pope, precisely as Bishop of Rome, has to exercise a "care for all the Churches." The bishops, precisely because they are in communion with the Bishop of Rome, must exercise a care for the universal Church, beyond the boundaries of their local jurisdiction. Because the Church is not a political community, primacy and collegiality are not a zero-sum game in which primacy diminishes as collegiality increases. Moreover, the meaning of primacy, collegiality, and their relationship is an area where tensions and adjustments will mark the Church's life until the end of time.

The theological term the Council used to characterize the essence of the Church was *communio,* which somewhat inadequately comes into English as "communion." The Church has many other characteristics: it has executive functions, it can legislate, it can conduct judicial proceedings. In its essence, though, the Church is a *communio*—a communion of brothers and sisters in Christ whose relationship to one another is different from any other relationship in their lives, because it is founded on Christ, the Son of God and redeemer of the world, and lived through the sacraments. Husbands and wives, parents and children, pastors and people, consecrated religious and their communities all live this *communio* of the Church in distinct ways.

The way in which the Pope and the bishops were to live it in their relationship to each other was called "collegiality." The theory, at least, was reasonably clear. The bishops, successors of the apostles, formed a "college or permanent assembly" with Peter as their head. Christ willed both the college and the headship as components of the unchangeable structure of the Church.[2] Both had responsibility, in different ways, for "all the Churches." The question was, how should collegiality actually work?

Unlike many other bishops at Vatican II, the Polish hierarchy had lived a real experience of collegiality since World War II. It was a singular experience, given the political realities and the unchallenged authority of the Primate, Cardinal Wyszyński. But it was also genuinely collegial. The Polish bishops had an episcopal conference that met annually, a coordinating committee that could take decisions between meetings of the whole episcopate, and a staff secretariat at a time when such things were not even dreamed of by bishops in other countries. Within the conference, there was real delegation of authority over specific areas of pastoral concern (youth work, student ministry, family ministry, and so forth); there was real sharing of experiences; and there were real debates. When the debates, which were always conducted behind closed doors, were finished, there was also real unity.

This was the experience of collegiality Karol Wojtyła brought to the papacy. Brother bishops worked together, argued issues and strategies, made decisions—and then, when decisions had been made, supported one another. It was a collegiality that strengthened the bishops, the Primate, and the *communio* of the entire local Church. One of his duties as "universal pastor," as John Paul understood it, was to foster that kind of collegiality within other national episcopates, and between the world episcopate and the Holy See.

He would work at it relentlessly for more than twenty years. The results were mixed, but not for lack of will or effort on his part.

COLLEGIALITY AND CRISIS MANAGEMENT

In January 1980, John Paul tried to facilitate a collegial solution to the problems of one of the most contentious local Churches in post-conciliar Catholicism, the Church in the Netherlands.

Dutch Catholicism prior to the Second World War was one of the most vital in the world. The experience of the Nazi Occupation had forced long-antagonistic Dutch Catholics and Protestants to think of each other as unhyphenated Dutchmen, which broke down many old barriers of prejudice. On some accounts, though, it also weakened Dutch Catholics' sense of identification with the institutional Church.

Then came Vatican II. The Dutch bishops participated vigorously in the Council's debates and were eager to promote conciliar reforms when they returned home in 1965. But the Dutch experience of implementing the Council was the opposite of what Karol Wojtyła had fostered in Kraków. Decision-making assemblies were immediately introduced at all levels of the Church, and decisions on implementing the Council were frequently made by people who, for all their good will, simply had not had the opportunity to assimilate the teachings of Vatican II as a whole. Moreover, this virtually instant implementation took place during the mid- and late-sixties, a period of cultural upheaval that hit the Netherlands with particular force.

Consequently, some of the world's most radical liturgical experimentation began in the formerly staid Netherlands. A new "Dutch Catechism" was deemed inadequate by the Congregation for the Doctrine of the Faith [CDF] in Rome. In late 1970 and early 1972, the appointment of two new bishops critical of the prevailing liberalizing trends had caused further rifts in a thoroughly polarized local Church, and between Dutch Catholic leaders and Rome. Radicalization and polarization had gone hand-in-hand with a rapid emptying of Dutch churches during the post-conciliar battles. Yet religious issues remained of great interest to many Dutch, who passionately debated them in the press.

In 1975, Cardinal Johannes Willebrands, President of the Secretariat for Promoting Christian Unity, became Primate of the Netherlands at Paul VI's request, in an attempt to heal the breaches between the factions and between Dutch Catholicism and Rome. Commuting between his Vatican responsibilities and the primatial See in Utrecht, Willebrands failed to make much headway. By the death of Pope Paul, the Dutch Church was deeply, even bitterly divided, and so was its episcopate. Some even feared schism—a formal break with Rome.

In the early fall of 1979, John Paul II was living in the Torre Giovanni, a ninth-century tower and guest house in the Vatican gardens, while the papal apartment in the Apostolic Palace was being renovated. One evening he called a meeting there to talk over the situation in the Netherlands. Those invited included Cardinal Casaroli, Cardinal Willebrands, Archbishop Martínez Somalo, Bishop Jozef Tomko (a Slovak and former official of CDF and the Congregation for Bishops, who had been named General Secretary of the Synod of Bishops in July 1979), and Father Jan Schotte. After the question of what might be done to help the Church in the Netherlands was thrashed around for some time, the Pope suggested, "Why not have a Synod?"

In drawing up the legislation for the Synod of Bishops, Paul VI had made provision for "special assemblies," but this possibility had never been applied to the situation of a local Church. Still, the group decided that this could be precisely the kind of instrument they were looking for: a collegial process of discussion including all the Dutch bishops and the relevant officials of the Curia, presided over by the Pope, in which decisions on matters dividing the Dutch episcopate could be taken without being imposed unilaterally by Rome. John Paul II, who is quite convinced that the Holy Spirit works through the Synod process, may also have been anticipating that this kind of collegial experience would begin to heal the personal rifts between the Dutch bishops and get them functioning more as a team again.[3]

What came to be known technically as the "Particular Synod for Holland" met at the Vatican from January 14 through January 31, 1980. The issues on the agenda were among the most controversial and divisive within the Dutch Church and among the Dutch bishops: liturgy, religious education, seminaries and the priesthood, lay leadership, and ecumenism. The Synod itself was a linguistic nightmare. There were seven Dutch bishops, who had no international language in common; there were seven curial officials, none of whom spoke Dutch and one of whom, Cardinal James Knox, didn't even speak Italian. Father Schotte had to translate everything for everybody. (At one point in the lengthy proceedings, John Paul II leaned over and whispered, "Sometimes your translation is clearer than what the guy actually said. . . .")[4]

After more than two intense weeks of discussion, prayer, and Masses together, the Synod closed with a concelebrated Mass in the Sistine Chapel, during which each of the Dutch bishops signed the document listing the Synod's forty-six conclusions. Something had happened among them. In the sacristy after the Mass, two Dutch bishops, in tears, came up to Father Schotte and said, "Why couldn't we have done this before?"[5] The bishops also agreed to form a special "Synod Council" that would meet annually with the General Secretariat of the Synod of Bishops in Rome, so that the bishops could continue to assess the pastoral situation together and discuss the implementation of the Dutch Synod's resolutions. That Council continued to meet throughout the pontificate of John Paul II.

The Synod established a mechanism for getting the Dutch bishops to function as a conference in facing their pastoral problems. To say that it accomplished more would be to claim too much. Implementation of the Synod's resolutions took place at different rates when the bishops went home. Sharply different visions of the Church and its relationship to modern society continued; so did diverse patterns of seminary education in different dioceses. Yet bishops who had barely been on speaking terms with each other had had to take their own collegiality seriously. Under the circumstances, collegiality-as-crisis-management could claim a modest accomplishment.

Another local Church in crisis, the Greek Catholic Church in Ukraine, presented John Paul II with an entirely different set of problems.

To avoid complications with the papal pilgrimage to Poland in June 1979, the Pope's March 19, 1979, letter to Ukrainian Cardinal Iosyf Slipyi was not publicly released until John Paul had returned to the Vatican. The letter's defense of the 1596 Union of Brest (in which the Ukrainians had declared their allegiance to Rome while retaining their Eastern-rite liturgy), his praise for the millions "who [had] endured sorrows and injustices for Christ" and "demonstrated fidelity toward the Cross and the Church," and his invocation of the Universal Declaration of Human Rights to challenge Soviet attempts to crush the Greek Catholic Church had caused consternation in both the Kremlin and the Russian Orthodox Patriarchate of Moscow, then very much under the Soviet thumb. Those at the Secretariat for Promoting Christian Unity who wanted to avoid anything that might agitate the Russian Orthodox leadership also thought it a mistake. The Patriarchate signaled its displeasure (and, presumably, the Kremlin's) by canceling a Roman Catholic–Russian Orthodox theological colloquium that was to have been held in Odessa. Its "foreign affairs spokesman," Metropolitan Juvenaly, also wrote Cardinal Willebrands, President of the Christian Unity secretariat, demanding an explanation of the "exact meaning" of the Pope's letter and threatening "public criticism" if he and his colleagues were not satisfied with the response.[6]

The Pope, however, was determined to defend the Ukrainians' religious freedom. He knew they had felt betrayed by Paul VI's *Ostpolitik* and his ecumenical outreach to Russian Orthodoxy, and while not endorsing that analysis, he wanted to make clear that he would not downplay religious freedom for the sake of an ecumenical dialogue that was vastly complicated by the Patriarchate of Moscow's entanglement with Kremlin politics. John Paul's March 1979 letter to Cardinal Slipyi was one indication of his concern. So was the Synod of Greek Catholic bishops from throughout the world Ukrainian diaspora he convened at the Vatican on March 24, 1980. Since Slipyi was in his late eighties, provisions had to be made for a successor to maintain the continuity of the Ukrainian Church's leadership—even if most of that leadership would continue to live in exile (primarily in North America and Australia) for the foreseeable future. There were also issues to be discussed: the ongoing Ukrainian effort to have the Major-Archbishop of L'viv named "Patriarch"; the controversy over ordaining married men to the priesthood in the Ukrainian diaspora;[7] support for the hard-pressed underground Greek Catholic Church in Ukraine itself; the ecumenical imperative.

The Synod lasted for four days. At its conclusion John Paul II confirmed the Synod's choice of Myroslav Ivan Lubachivsky, whom the Pope had appointed the previous September as Ukrainian archbishop of Philadelphia, as coadjutor to Cardinal Slipyi with the right to succeed him as Major-Archbishop of L'viv on Slipyi's death. The historic continuity of the Greek Catholic Church in Ukraine had been provided for, but none of the other issues was definitively resolved. Determined to defend the persecuted, John Paul II was equally determined to do what he could to advance ecumenism with Russian Orthodoxy, the largest Orthodox Church in the world. Holding those two imperatives together—a task made even more difficult by Ukrainian passions and indiscretions, on the one hand, and by the curial tendency toward accommodation of the Russian Orthodox, on the other—became one of the most delicate and controversial balancing acts of the pontificate.

Two months later, on May 29, 1980, John Paul met for the second time with the Italian Bishops' Conference at its annual meeting. In the seventeen months since he had become Pope, he had made twenty-nine pastoral visitations to Roman parishes and had gone to more Italian cities—Assisi, Monte Cassino, Canale d'Agordo and Belluno, Treviso, Nettuno, Loreto, Ancona, Pomezia, Pompei, Naples, Norcia, and Turin—than his Italian predecessors John XXIII and Paul VI. He was now in a better position to analyze the Church's situation and to make some recommendations.

Italian Catholic practice may have declined; Italy's high culture may have remained enamored of Marxism; the country's politics may have been corrupted by criminals and paralyzed by urban terrorism; and in the midst of all this, Italian Catholics and their leaders may have internalized a sense of their own marginalization. If so, John Paul had a different view of the matter. The Italians, he insisted to their bishops, were a people "whose religious soul, whose deep Catholic mold, has inspired and left its mark, unquestionably, on the manifestations of everyday life, the forms of piety, family, and civil society, the springing up of charitable institutions, as well as the highest expressions of religious architecture, figurative art, and also literature."

That was what he had seen in his Italian journeys, and that was why he wanted his bishops to get the reevangelization of their country under way. "You . . . are responsible," he told them, "for the Church which is in Italy, independently of the fact whether the Pope is of Italian origin or not. . . ." John Paul specifically discussed Catholic social action, religious education, family life ministry, and youth ministry as urgent pastoral priorities. It was an exceptionally forthright talk in an ecclesiastical environment noted for the widespread use of the subjunctive—and another example of John Paul's determination to move a group of bishops toward a more evangelically assertive understanding of their role.[8]

Two weeks later, on June 13, John Paul sent the Italian Church an apostolic letter, *Amantissima Providentia* [The Most Loving Providence of God], for the sixth centenary of the death of one of Italy's co-patrons, St. Catherine of Siena—a woman noted for her determination to get bishops to do their duty.[9] In August and September he went on pastoral journeys to the Abruzzi region, to Velletria and Frascati, to Siena, to Cassino, Otranto, and Campo Verano. In late November, when a devastating earthquake hit the southern part of the country, the Pope went to express his solidarity with the worst hit areas, including the village of Balvano, where an entire congregation of Sunday worshipers, including many children, had been buried in the ruins of the church.[10] The Primate of Italy who had challenged his brother bishops to reevangelize their country by word and deed fully intended to contribute his part to that effort, even to the point of meeting on June 16 with the Italian Union of Hairdressers.[11]

In his homeland, John Paul continued to build on the momentum created by his June 1979 pilgrimage. On April 5, 1980, a Polish monthly edition of *L'Osservatore Romano*, the Vatican newspaper, was launched under the editorship of Father Adam Boniecki, a Marianist priest. It was another instrument in the struggle to keep his countrymen informed of his activities and views, as the monthly edition (like the weekly editions in English, French, German, Spanish, and Portuguese) would be filled with papal audience addresses and sermons and Church documents.

The Poles were already an assertive force. The Hungarian Church, however, was a different matter. Since the fiercely anti-communist Cardinal Mindszenty had left Budapest as part of the *Ostpolitik* of Paul VI, the Catholic leadership had increasingly accommodated itself to the regime, and the results had been disastrous. While some sixty percent of the country's population was baptized Catholic, only a quarter of those Catholics, at best, were active members of the Church, and only one-third of those "active members" attended Mass regularly. The state/party apparatus managed the appointment of pastors, severely regulated religious education, and controlled Church publishing. In 1976, the average age of Catholic priests was sixty-seven and some dioceses had not ordained a new priest for years.[12]

In December 1978, shortly after his election, John Paul had tried to light a fire under the Hungarian bishops with a personal letter. Four months later, he had met in Rome with the Hungarian Primate, Cardinal László Lékai, the leader of the party of accommodation, during the 400th anniversary celebrations of Rome's Hungarian College. Other Hungarian bishops had visited the Vatican since, and John Paul had been able to nominate bishops for four vacant Hungarian sees. Now, he thought it his "duty" to send another letter, this time to the entire Church in Hungary, on the imperative of religious education. Dated May 1, 1980, the letter began with a reminder that "everyone needs to be catechized," and urged both bishops and priests to take seriously their people's "right to catechesis."[13] It was an attempt to rally the Hungarian Church so that it did not drift into further marginalization, but new energies required local leadership. As John Paul was reported to have said when asked about a possible papal visit to Hungary, "The Pope will visit Hungary when the cardinal has learned to bang his fist on the table."[14]

YOUNG CHURCHES

At the same time as he was working with or attempting to reinvigorate the Dutch, Ukrainian, Italian, and Hungarian bishops, John Paul's eyes were turning south, toward Africa, and his first pastoral pilgrimage to that continent.

No world leader in the last two decades of the twentieth century paid such sustained attention to Africa as John Paul II. After the enthusiasms of decolonization and the controversy over apartheid, Africa became the forgotten continent. The only world institution that insisted that a continent of 450 million people could not be allowed to fall off the edge of history was the Roman Catholic Church.

African Church leaders had been enthusiastic about John Paul's election, which confirmed the Church's universality, and thereby confirmed the place of newcomers like themselves within it. As Nigerian Cardinal Francis Arinze put it later, "Because Africans are new Christians, apart from Egypt and Ethiopia, that feeling of belonging, and not just as second-class citizens, is very important: because in world politics Africa doesn't even rank as second-class, but third-class." John Paul II came to Africa, Arinze believed, to "help people understand that it's not when you become a Christian that counts; [what is important is] that all are in the Father's house."[15] The Pope's image quickly became known throughout the continent; Poles going into the bush found themselves greeted as *nduyu yd Papa*, "brother of the Pope."[16]

John Paul's first African pilgrimage began on May 2 when his Alitalia DC–10 landed at Ndjili Airport near Kinshasa, the capital of Zaire, after a seven-hour flight from Rome.

The Pope was greeted by longtime Zairean dictator Mobutu Sese Seku. The day before, Mobutu had married his longtime consort so that she could greet John Paul in the legal status of a presidential wife. Mobutu had given his people two days' holiday for the papal visit, and the road into Kinshasa was flooded with hundreds of thousands of Africans waving small white-and-yellow papal flags. After kissing the soil of Africa, John Paul announced himself in simple, evangelical terms: "I come to you as a pastor, a servant of Jesus Christ, and the successor of St. Peter. I come as a man of faith, a messenger of peace and hope."

At the cathedral of Kinshasa, he was welcomed by Cardinal Joseph Malula, who had told *Time* magazine before the second conclave in 1978, "All the imperial paraphernalia, all that isolation of the Pope, all that medieval remoteness and inheritance that makes Europeans think the Church is only Western—all [that] makes them fail to understand that young countries like mine want something different. We want simplicity. We want Jesus Christ. All that, all that must change."[17] Now, he heard the Pope he had helped elect tell him and his brother African bishops that Peter had come to Africa for an exchange of testimonies, a sharing of acts of faith. That evening, John Paul met with President Mobutu and other members of the government, stressing the importance of religious freedom for social development. Then he sent both his hosts and the men in the Kremlin a message: "If the problems of Africa find solutions free from any outside interference, that positive achievement will surely have a beneficial effect on the solution of similar problems in other continents." At the Vatican embassy in Kinshasa, the Pope met late that same night with the six archbishops of Zaire and finally paused for his first meal in Africa—bass, shrimp, and local fruit, prepared by the only Italian restaurateur in the city.[18]

The Pope's Mass at the aptly named St. Peter's Church in Kinshasa the next morning was typical of the exuberant liturgies that followed. The Mass was celebrated in French with hymns in Swahili and other local languages and the Lord's Prayer in Latin. In his homily, the Pope argued that monogamy, an issue in a culture accustomed to polygamy, was "not of western . . . origin" but was a basic humanistic concept "of divine inspiration," applicable to all cultures and circumstances. At the same time he praised the African traditions of permanence in marriage, respect for mothers and children, social solidarity, and reverence for ancestors as important for the flourishing of families, and urged the bishops to make marriage preparation a centerpiece of pastoral work in Africa. After meeting with the Zairean episcopate and visiting a cloistered Carmelite convent, John Paul went to the Kinshasa hospital for lepers, where he laid his hands in blessing on each of the patients.[19]

A million Zaireans and Africans from throughout the continent flooded the square in front of Kinshasa's People's Palace on Sunday morning, May 4, as John Paul ordained eight new African bishops—four from Zaire, one from Djibouti, two Burundians, and a Sudanese. After the morning-long ceremony, the Pope met with Zairean students and African intellectuals, but canceled the "evening of culture" that had been arranged for him, in solidarity with the nine persons who had been trampled to death and the eighty others injured in the crush to enter the square—a tragedy of which he had been unaware until informed by President Mobutu in the early evening.[20]

Meeting with Polish missionaries in Zaire, John Paul remarked that he found the process of a new nation's birth, this "sense of a beginning" to be "most fascinating." He then had something to say, if indirectly, to his critics back in Rome: "Some people think that the Pope should not travel so much. He should stay in Rome, as before. I often hear such advice, or read it in newspapers. But the local people here say, 'Thank God you came here, for you can only learn about us by coming. How could you be our pastor without knowing us? Without knowing who we are, how we live, what is the historical moment we are going through?' This confirms me in the belief that it is time for the Bishops of Rome . . . to become successors not only of Peter but also of St. Paul, who, as we know, could never sit still and was constantly on the move."[21]

He left them an image of Our Lady of Częstochowa, "so that you could have in this black continent a likeness of our Black Madonna. It's not the same black as the African one, but still black. And I think that because of that your faithful, your black parishioners, will easily find an understanding of that black Mother of Christ."[22]

After spending the better part of four days in Kinshasa, John Paul II's African pilgrimage continued at an accelerated pace. Brazzaville, the capital of Congo, was given half a day on the schedule for May 5. The officially Marxist government gave everyone a holiday and permitted an open-air Mass, celebrated in temperatures over 100° Fahrenheit.[23] As the Pope drove through Brazzaville, en route to praying at the tomb of the assassinated Cardinal Emile Biayenda, virtually the entire population was in the streets to greet him.[24] The Pope then flew back to northeast Zaire, to Kisangani, to repay the visit that its archbishop, Augustin Fataki Alueke, had paid him in Kraków in 1978. He stayed in a mission house overnight, and celebrated Mass the next morning for hundreds of thousands of Zaireans, paying tribute to the religious and lay missionaries, men and women, who had been murdered in Kisangani and elsewhere in 1964.[25]

Flying to East Africa that noon, John Paul arrived in Nairobi at 4 P.M., where he responded to President Daniel arap Moi's welcome in English and a few words of Swahili. He concluded with the words of the Kenyan national anthem, "May the God of all creation bless our country and nation," and when he repeated the phrase in Swahili, the enormous crowd erupted in cheers. The next day, May 7, produced the most striking visual image of the pilgrimage and the Pope's most memorable statement. Mass at Uhuru Park drew more than a million Kenyans. During the ceremonies, John Paul was given numerous presents, among them a live goat that, as readers of *Tygodnik Powszechny* were later informed, "made itself heard during the service." The unforgettable image was of the Pope, wearing a splendid headdress of ostrich feathers, with a shield in one hand and a spear in the other, seated on a leopard-skin-covered drum. The statement was a simple one, but it expressed the heart of John Paul's Christ-centered humanism: "Christ is not only God, but also a man. As a human being, he is also an African." The vast congregation exploded in applause, at which John Paul added a line: "On my next visit to Kenya I will surely preach my homily in Swahili."[26]

The Pope flew across the continent the next day, landing in Accra, the capital of Ghana. The departure scene in Nairobi, where the crowd had gathered before the Pope's 8 A.M. departure, was another astonishment. The exultant crowd, which had been singing and dancing for hours, knelt in silence as the papal jet climbed into the sky. Half an hour after the plane had disappeared, the crowd, urged by police to leave, remained, still silent in prayer.[27]

John Paul II insisted on an ecumenical meeting in each of his pilgrimages. The meeting in Accra had an international quality, since the Archbishop of Canterbury, Robert Runcie, was in Ghana at the same time. The Bishop of Rome and the head of the Anglican Communion met in the Vatican embassy and later issued a communiqué stating that "time is too short and the need too pressing to waste Christian energies on pursuing old rivalries"—a statement with particular relevance in the African mission fields.[28] After Ghana, John Paul visited Upper Volta (later Burkina Faso) and Ivory Coast (where he had his first major meeting with a large Muslim population) before returning to Rome the night of May 12.

He had delivered fifty major addresses in ten days and had left his traveling party and the reporters covering him gasping in his wake. Halfway through the pilgrimage, the correspondent of the West German *Deutsche Presse Agentur* sent home a dispatch with the title, "The Pope Holds Out." Some of the prelates in the papal entourage seemed to be "at the end of their tether" after five days in Africa, and the journalists were miserable in the tropical heat. "The Pope is the only one not to show any signs of fatigue. When he left the plane in Kisangani, in the midst of the green hell of the jungle in northern Zaire, he looked just as fresh as when he left Rome."

The observant German correspondent thought he had detected the secret of papal resilience in one of John Paul's characteristic personal habits. He could tune out the maelstrom around him, even during prolonged ceremonies, and refresh himself from what could only be described as a kind of inner well: "His eyes are then focused in the distance, as if into another world from which he derives his inexhaustible energy."[29] Believers often talk about the "power of prayer." John Paul, in those moments when he did seem somewhere else, was in fact praying—and recharging his personal batteries for the next encounter, speech, or Mass.

He had enjoyed himself enormously in Africa and was moved and invigorated by the unselfconscious joy of these new Christians.[30] John Paul wasn't above teasing those who were falling behind his ferocious pace. At one point he waved to a German TV crew and said, "How about you guys, are you still alive?" As for his exhausted curial colleagues, he told them, "Don't worry, we'll spend Christmas in the snow for a change, in Terminillo"—a popular ski resort in the Abruzzi. The prelates, accustomed to the traditional pace of the Vatican, were not entirely comforted.[31]

MARS HILL REVISITED

The evangelical freedom lived so spontaneously by Africa's Christians stood in marked contrast to the mood of those Western European Catholics who had become convinced of their irrelevance to modern life. Two and a half weeks after he flew out of Abidjan, John Paul tried to do something about the depressed condition of Catholicism in France.

The occasion for his first pastoral visit to the "eldest daughter of the Church" was an invitation to address the Executive Council of UNESCO, the United Nations Educational, Scientific, and Cultural Organization, headquartered in Paris. It was an opportunity to speak before a world audience on what had quickly become one of the dominant public themes of his pontificate—the priority of culture in shaping the human future. At the same time, a papal address to UNESCO had to be set in the proper pastoral context, and John Paul was eager to challenge a country whose culture he had long admired to retrieve its Catholic roots. The UNESCO address thus took place in between a pastoral visit to Paris and a pilgrimage to Lisieux and the Carmelite convent of the "Little Flower," St. Thérèse, perhaps the most popular of modern Catholic saints.

In a radio and television broadcast to the French nation three days before he arrived, the Pope said he hoped that the "special situation" of French Catholicism since Vatican II was "a question of what are called 'growing pains.'"[32] That hypothesis was tested in four days even more crammed with activities than Africa had been. John Paul arrived in Paris on a Friday morning, May 30, 1980, and by the time he left from Lisieux the following Monday evening, he had given twenty-eight addresses to virtually every sector of French Catholicism. In addition, he met with the Chief Rabbi of Paris and leaders of the French Jewish community, with Muslim leaders, and with public officials including President Valéry Giscard d'Estaing, Prime Minister Raymond Barre, and Jacques Chirac, the mayor of Paris.

John Paul returned time and again to the theme that French Catholics should throw off their sense of marginality, recognize their dignity, and be proud of their Christian heritage, which had done so much to shape what he called "the French genius." His response to President Giscard's welcoming speech on May 30 defined his mission. He had come, he said, to deliver a message of faith: "Of faith in God, of course, but also . . . of faith in man, of faith in the marvelous possibilities that have been given to him, in order that he may use them wisely and for the sake of the common good, for the glory of the Creator."[33]

The French bishops got the same message, forcefully, on June 1. There was to be no retreat into a bunker of solipsism, licking the wounds of recent centuries. Of course there was despair in modern society. But were the bishops not the bearers of "the Gospel and of holiness, which is a special heritage of the Church of France? Does not Christianity belong immanently to the 'genius of your nation'? Is not France still 'the eldest daughter of the Church'?"[34] At the papal Mass at Le Bourget Airport earlier that day, the Pope had been ever more blunt, asking the 350,000 present and the rest of French Catholicism about their fidelity: "Allow me . . . to question you: 'France, eldest daughter of the Church, are you faithful to the promises of your baptism?' Allow me to ask you: 'France, daughter of the Church and educator of peoples, are you faithful, for the good of man, to the covenant with eternal wisdom?'"[35]

Four days of papal exhortation could not reverse trends more than two centuries old, nor could it heal the divisions between left and right in French Catholicism. Eight months after his French pilgrimage, convinced that a new kind of leadership was imperative in the French Church, John Paul would make a daring episcopal appointment in an effort to change the course of modern French Catholic history.

The Pope regarded his UNESCO speech on June 2 as one of the most important addresses of his life. It was very much the product of Karol Wojtyła, philosopher of culture, and included several excursions into technical philosophical language that must have puzzled the delegates who were not simply lost. At one point, John Paul, speaking in French, described the human person as "the only ontic subject of culture" and observed that, because we judge culture a posteriori, by its products, a culture "contains in itself the possibility of going back, in the opposite direction, to ontic-causal dependencies." Within the dense prose, though, John Paul offered a passionate defense of the human spirit and its creativity, on what he described as the "Areopagus," the Mars Hill of the modern world.

As St. Paul had done on the Areopagus of Athens (see *Acts* 17.16–34), John Paul began with a diagnosis of his audience's situation. A growing lack of confidence about humanity's prospects was draining modern life of the "affirmation and joy" essential to human creativity. The answer to this crisis, he proposed, could only be found in the realm of the human spirit, the world of culture, for culture included all those products of human creativity that make us more fully human and that contribute, not simply to our *having* more, but to our *being* more. Culture had a spiritual core, and could not be understood, as Marxists understood it, as a by-product of various economic forces. So he had come to UNESCO to "proclaim my admiration before the creative riches of the human spirit, before its incessant efforts to know and strengthen the identity of man."

The defense of human persons who must be loved, not for their utility but for the grandeur of their "particular dignity," linked the message of Christ and his Church and the modern quest for human dignity and freedom. It was not true, John Paul argued, that religious faith reduced human beings to a condition of immature dependency. The evidence that the religious impulse was of the essence of the "whole man" was right before their eyes: wherever religious institutions had been suppressed and believers had been made second-class citizens, religious ideas and works of art had reemerged time and again. The truth about the "whole man" demanded to be expressed.

The same was true of national cultures. Try as oppressors might, the "sovereignty of society which is manifested in the culture of a nation" could not be completely suppressed, because it was through that cultural sovereignty that the human person "is supremely sovereign."

The challenge before UNESCO was to guard the fundamental spiritual sovereignty of the human person, which expressed itself through the creativity of individuals and the cultures of nations. The delegates should oppose any "colonialism" by which a materially stronger political force tried to subjugate the spiritual sovereignty of a culture. Being able to speak to the leadership of UNESCO, he concluded, fulfilled "one of the deepest desires of my heart." Thus he wanted to leave them with a "cry . . . from the inmost depths of my soul: Yes! The future of man depends on culture! Yes! The peace of the world depends on the primacy of the spirit! Yes! The peaceful future of mankind depends on love. . . ."[36]

The Bishop of Orléans, Jean-Marie Lustiger, listening to John Paul at UNESCO, thought to himself, "Communism is finished." Somebody had finally said that economics did not rule the world, and that culture was the real engine of history.[37]

HARD CASES: BRAZIL AND WEST GERMANY

On June 27, 1980, John Paul II made further changes in the Curia, one of which would have a marked impact on Catholic life in the United States. Cardinal Sergio Pignedoli, whose widely bruited papal candidacy in 1978 turned out to have been a journalistic fantasy, had died. To succeed him as President of the Vatican's Secretariat for Non-Christians, John Paul named Archbishop Jean Jadot, a Belgian who had been apostolic delegate in the United States since 1973. Jadot was replaced in Washington by Archbishop Pio Laghi, who as nuncio in Argentina had helped facilitate the Holy See's mediation of the Beagle Channel dispute.[38] At Laghi's departure audience, John Paul "ticked off on four fingers" his concerns about the Church in the United States to his new Washington representative: the effective proclamation of the Gospel, including the celebration of the sacraments and religious education; the appointment of bishops; the state of religious life in monasteries and convents; and the formation of priests in seminaries.[39] At the same time, Cardinal Władysław Rubin was named Prefect of the Congregation for Oriental [Eastern-rite] Churches; Cardinal Pietro Palazzini, a man with a reputation for getting things done in the languid Roman bureaucracy, was named Prefect of the Congregation for the Causes of Saints, which John Paul wanted to reinvigorate; Bishop Paul Poupard, rector of Paris's Institut Catholique, was called to Rome to head the Secretariat for Non-Believers; and Father Jan Schotte, who had won the Pope's confidence in the first year of the pontificate, was named Secretary of the Pontifical Commission "Justice and Peace."

The next day, John Paul received Orthodox Archbishop Meliton of Chalcedon and a delegation from the Ecumenical Patriarchate in Constantinople, who had come to Rome for the feast of Sts. Peter and Paul. Then, on June 30, John Paul took off for an eleven-hour flight to Brasilia, the modernistic capital of the world's largest Catholic country, where he spent twelve days developing further the meaning of the title "universal pastor."

"John of God"

It was a pilgrimage fraught with difficulties. The Brazilian government, many of whose senior officials were Catholics, and the Church leadership were in conflict over the slow pace of democratization, the continued jailing of political prisoners, and the country's vast disparities in wealth. The government complained to the nuncio that Church leaders failed to condemn the violent left; the bishops responded that the government was doing virtually nothing on behalf of the poor. The Brazilian bishops were unhappy about the way their activities and ideas were reported to the Vatican; some in Rome thought the Brazilian bishops had gone off the theological and political deep end. There were even quarrels about where the pilgrimage would begin. The Brazilians proposed Fortaleza, in the poorest part of the country, where the Pope could inaugurate a national Eucharistic Congress; the Vatican Secretariat of State insisted on Brasilia, lest the government be offended.

None of this augured another papal triumph. Yet somehow, over twelve days, John Paul, who had learned Portuguese in the months prior to his departure for Brasilia and used it throughout Brazil, managed to create a measure of unity in a divided Church and a divided society. Twenty million people saw the Pope in person and tens of millions more saw him on television. Balance, with evangelical edge, was the watchword of the entire pilgrimage.

On the first day, the Pope met with President João Batista Figueiredo, attended an official reception for 2,000 invited guests from the elite of Brazilian society, and then spent a half-hour at the local jail, talking with prisoners.

At a Mass for a half-million youngsters in Belo Horizonte—from the altar platform, the Pope could barely see the end of the vast congregation, which extended down into a valley—John Paul gave Holy Communion to a blind boy, a paralytic girl, two lepers, a Polish nun, two university students, several workers, and a couple marking their sixty-eighth wedding anniversary. There, the youngsters started a chant, "John of God! Our king!" that was soon picked up by others around the vast country—until the Pope met with 150,000 workers in São Paulo, who altered the chant to "John of God is our brother!" There, the Pope denounced "the chasm" between the wealthy and "the majority living in poverty" while preaching that "the class struggle advocated by material ideologies cannot give anyone happiness—it can only be achieved through Christian social justice." John Paul accepted a memorandum on the repression of workers presented by a delegation of Christian trade unionists and addressed to "Our comrade in labor, John Paul II, Christ's worker and our colleague."[40]

In Rio de Janeiro, as the Pope walked through a *favela* teeming with poverty, the people greeted him with a specially composed samba. John Paul took the ring from his finger and gave it to the local parish; it was the ring Pope Paul VI had given him when naming him a cardinal.[41] At São Salvador da Bahia in the poverty-stricken northeast, he urged all those who had influence in Brazilian society—professionals, entrepreneurs, politicians, labor leaders, teachers—to build a "social order based on justice" and a society that recognized the primacy of ethics over technology and the priority of people over things. Deep in the Amazon jungle, where he took part in a waterborne procession of thousands of small craft, the Pope met with local Indian leaders, who charged the government with a policy of virtual genocide. The local authorities had wanted the Indians to perform a dance, but the native peoples had refused, insisting that they were not actors and this was not entertainment. John Paul asked the chiefs for documentation of their plight, which they provided.

In Recife, John Paul publicly embraced the most controversial Brazilian prelate, Archbishop Helder Camara. But the Brazilian bishops had to be reminded of their unique mission as well as encouraged, and so the Pope's four-hour, closed-door address to the episcopal conference was an extensive reflection on the Church's distinct character as a religious community, on Catholic social doctrine, and on the imperative of strengthening Catholic unity. An engaged Church, but not a partisan Church; a Church with a special care for the poor, but not a Church espousing class struggle; a Church of and for the people, but a Church with a doctrine and an ordained leadership; a clergy passionate about social justice, but not clerical politicians or revolutionaries; a Church, to put it simply, of Vatican II in its fullness—that was the Church John Paul urged his bishops to help build in Brazil. Predictably, the address was described by some as "conservative." The more accurate term would have been "evangelical."[42]

In the Land of Luther

Catholicism in West Germany was another hard case for John Paul II, whose first pastoral pilgrimage there took place from November 15 to November 19, 1980.

German theological scholarship had deeply influenced the Second Vatican Council, sometimes described as the Council at which the Rhine flowed into the Tiber. Yet German theology had divided in the post-conciliar years and former allies had become foes, often amid intense acrimony. The country, meanwhile, remained thoroughly secular. Very few West German Catholics attended Mass regularly. Yet theirs was arguably the wealthiest Church in the world, at least in terms of liquid assets. A "church tax" automatically collected by the state for the Church's use had given West German Catholicism vast financial resources. This, in turn, gave the German Catholic development agencies, Adveniat and Miserior, great influence in the Third World, where many bishops depended on German subsidies for their pastoral programs. For all its intellectual accomplishments, though, German Catholicism continued to struggle with a deep-set, if almost never-conceded, cultural inferiority complex. The scars from Bismarck's *Kulturkampf,* which had tried to enforce the notion that a good German was a good German Protestant, had not entirely healed. Since the Second World War, there was the new challenge of an aggressive secularism allied with philosophy, literature, and the arts, and the war itself had left behind a burden of conscience.[43]

Many expected John Paul's five days in West Germany to be something of a disaster. They were not. They even became something of a personal triumph, as previously skeptical or hostile Germans found themselves glued to their televisions, seemingly mesmerized by the personality of a Polish Pope who could say, on his arrival, that he wanted his pilgrimage to "honor the great German nation." Ecumenists were pleased that John Paul went out of his way to mention the 450th anniversary of the Augsburg Confession, the central doctrinal statement of the Lutheran Reformation, as an occasion to intensify efforts toward fulfilling Christ's prayer, "that they may all be one" (*John* 17.21).[44]

The Pope's defense of marriage and the Church's sexual ethic was humanistic rather than authoritarian: just as there was no "trial" life and no "trial" death," there was no "trial" love or "trial" marriage, "for one cannot love only on trial, accept a person only on trial and for a limited time."[45] His address to 6,000 German professors and students at Cologne was a paean to Christian scholarship and the mutual enrichment of faith and reason.[46] He urged the German bishops to strengthen the Church's unity by helping those usually labeled "progressives" to overcome the false dichotomy often posed between an authoritative religious tradition and human freedom, and by helping those alienated by change to understand that "the Church of Vatican II and that of Vatican I and of the Council of Trent and of the first Councils, is one and the same Church."[47]

His old friend and editor, Jerzy Turowicz, reporting on the pilgrimage for Kraków's *Tygodnik Powszechny*, wrote that "the Pope's presence wiped out worn stereotypes [and] changed the image of the papacy and the Catholic Church."[48] It was an understandable exaggeration from a man deeply committed to German-Polish reconciliation and eager to see John Paul's image as an ogre shattered. That, at least, had happened. The people of West Germany saw for themselves a man of transparent faith who had demonstrated his ability to be a "universal pastor" in the midst of painful historical memories. John Paul's first pilgrimage to West Germany did not dramatically change the Church's situation in the Federal Republic, though, nor did it succeed in lowering the level of tension between many German Catholic intellectuals and Rome. As the pontificate unfolded, those tensions would wax and wane. They would never be satisfactorily resolved, and the German-speaking Catholic world (in Austria and Switzerland as well as in Germany) would prove singularly resistant to the teaching of John Paul II.

THE COMMUNITY OF THE FAMILY

The Church's responsibility toward families and family life was the theme of the first General Assembly of the Synod of Bishops held under John Paul II's leadership. Before the Synod opened on September 26, 1980, the Pope made another intervention into world politics on behalf of human rights.

The Priority of Religious Freedom

The occasion was the meeting of the Conference on Security and Cooperation in Europe [CSCE] being held in Madrid. The Helsinki Final Act, signed in 1975, provided for periodic review conferences to monitor compliance, and the Madrid review conference of 1980–1981 became an international forum for holding the Soviet Union and its Warsaw Pact satellites accountable to the human rights guarantees they had signed at Helsinki five years earlier.[49] The human rights situation in the European communist world had not improved since the Final Act was concluded. In fact, it had arguably gotten worse.

On September 1, 1980, the Pope sent a personal letter to the heads of state of the thirty-five Helsinki Final Act signatory nations, soon to meet in Madrid. There was little of the usual diplomatic indirection at the beginning of the document. John Paul got straight to the point: human rights were increasingly recognized around the world as a crucial component of the pursuit of peace, and the Madrid meeting ought to undertake a "serious examination of the present situation" of freedom in Europe, with special reference to religious freedom.

The Pope's letter offered a checklist by which the Madrid review conference could measure whether religious freedom was being honored in practice. Were individuals free to believe and to join a believing community? Could they pray individually and collectively and have places of worship? Were parents free to educate their children in their faith, and to choose religious schools for their children without penalty? Could chaplains and other ministers offer religious assistance in public facilities—hospitals, the military, prisons? Were men and women free to believe without suffering social, political, or professional penalties? Could religious institutions choose their own leadership, manage their own affairs, and educate their own clergy? Was the ministry exercised freely? Were religious communities free to communicate their faith, through the spoken and written word? Could they publish and receive publications and use the mass media? Were they free to perform charitable works in society? Could they freely maintain contact with co-religionists and religious authorities in other countries? No communist country even came close to satisfying these concrete criteria of respect for religious freedom.

John Paul II's letter to the Madrid CSCE review conference was another unmistakable challenge to the Yalta system and to the ideology that, in Soviet eyes, justified it. That it was dated the day after the Polish government had agreed, at Gdańsk, to permit free trade unions only made matters worse from the Soviet point of view. A week later, John Paul gave the screw another twist by announcing the theme of his annual message for the January 1 World Day of Peace: "To serve peace, respect freedom." The Soviet claim that peace could be pursued without reference to human rights and other controverted moral issues—which Andrei Gromyko had so blandly proposed to John Paul in January 1979—was under assault on several fronts.

Synod on the Family

The Synod of Bishops, created by Paul VI during the Second Vatican Council, had experienced both bureaucratic and theological troubles in its first decade. The Synod was neither a continuation of the Council nor a mini-Council, although some imagined it might function that way. The entire world episcopate, with and under the Bishop of Rome, exercises authority over the universal Church, and this authority could not be delegated to a subset of the world's bishops. A smaller gathering of bishops, however representative, could not make binding decisions for other bishops or for the people of the Church. They could only speak in their own name, and while what they said would carry weight, it would not be definitive in terms of doctrine or practice. The Synod's decisions had to be submitted to the authority of the Pope, and then issued with his approval, before they became definitive.[50]

The Synod was not a legislature, but as an expression of the collegiality of the College of Bishops it should be something more than a sounding board. How to make the Synod of Bishops concretely reflect the *communio*, the "communion," of the bishops was an organizational problem from the outset. The first approach adopted, to leave the Synod essentially to its own devices, produced one set of problems. The 1971 Synod document on "Justice in the

World" had gotten into murky theological waters by seeming to equate political activism with evangelism and the celebration of the sacraments as a "constitutive dimension" of the Church. The 1974 Synod on evangelism had deadlocked and failed to agree on a consensus statement.[51]

John Paul II had tried to bring some clarity into the Synod's procedures and to protect it within the Roman bureaucracy by appointing Slovak Bishop Jozef Tomko as General Secretary of the Synod of Bishops on July 14, 1979. Tomko was a veteran curial official who understood how to give the Synod a presence in the internal Vatican bureaucratic process. Tomko had two additional advantages: he was known to be the Pope's man, and the Pope had made it quite clear that he wanted to reinvigorate the Synod, not simply in its meetings but through an entire process of preparation, celebration, and implementation.[52]

The 1980 Synod, on "The Role of the Christian Family in the Modern World," was the first that the new team, John Paul and Tomko, had summoned and prepared, and set the pattern for the Pope's participation in Synods throughout his pontificate. He attended virtually every general session, listening but never speaking, and constantly taking notes.[53] He invited each member of the Synod to lunch or dinner at the papal apartment, and he presided and preached at the opening and closing Masses.

The 1980 Synod discussions demonstrated that the fifteen years after *Gaudium et Spes* and the twelve years after *Humanae Vitae* had not produced agreement among the world's bishops on the crisis of family life in the modern world, or on the Church's marital ethic.[54] Some bishops thought they were being manipulated by the Roman bureaucracy as they formulated the "propositions" the Synod would forward to the Pope, in order for him to prepare a message on the family to the entire Church. Others thought that those bishops pressing for a revision of the sexual ethic defended by *Humanae Vitae* had failed to grasp Paul VI's prophetic stance against the sexual revolution's assault on marriage. Still others thought that the discussions had paid insufficient attention to the real circumstances of family life today. If Synods, as an expression of collegiality, were supposed to build unity within the world episcopate, the 1980 Synod on the Family fell short of the mark.[55]

The deadlocked 1974 Synod on evangelization had resulted in the first "post-synodal" apostolic exhortation, Paul VI's 1975 document, *Evangelii Nuntiandi*. John Paul II decided to adopt this method of completing a Synod with an apostolic exhortation—a new form of papal teaching instrument. On October 16, 1979, he issued *Catechesi Tradendae* to mark the completion of the October 1977 Synod on religious education or catechetics. There is, it should be admitted, an unsettled quality about the device of an apostolic exhortation, a major papal teaching document, as the appropriate conclusion of a Synod. The results of the bishops' discussion, everyone agrees, should be a factor in the life of the Church. But the weight of those discussions, no matter how well-reflected in an apostolic exhortation, tends to be diminished by the very fact of a papal teaching document, which is what the Church remembers about a Synod.

In any case, the same method used in *Evangelii Nuntiandi* and *Catechesi Tradendae* was applied to the Synod on the Family. The new apostolic exhortation, *Familiaris Consortio* [The Community of the Family], was signed on November 21, 1981. Addressing issues which he believes are "still of primary importance," *Familiaris Consortio* is one of John Paul's personal favorites in a pontificate replete with teaching documents.[56]

Familiaris Consortio links the contemporary problems and promise of family life to what had already emerged as a key theme in the pontificate—the true meaning of freedom. The positive "signs of the times"—a greater sensitivity to personal freedom in entering marriage; the high value contemporary culture places on interpersonal relationships; efforts to promote the dignity of women; a worldwide stress on the importance of education—are expressions of the modern quest for a freedom worthy of human beings. The "shadows" over the family—challenges to the natural authority of parents; governmental, social, and cultural interference in parents' rights as educators; the denial or rejection of the blessing of fertility; the exploitation of women because of "machismo" attitudes on the part of men—reflect distorted ideas of freedom.[57] The "shadows" had created a distorted idea of the family as an accidental gathering of individuals who live together because it serves their self-interest to do so.[58] But accidental gatherings have little binding force and can be broken up at will.

In sharp, but thoroughly humanistic, contrast to this thin concept of marriage and the family, John Paul teaches that marriage can never be a mere contract, nor can the family be simply a utilitarian convenience for its members. Since human beings are made "through love" and "for love," and because love is "the fundamental and innate vocation of every human being," this vocation is the heart of marriage and the heart of the family. Confirmed for Christians in the redemption won by Christ's self-sacrificing love, the demands and obligations of family life are liberating, not confining.[59]

In its mission to "guard, reveal, and communicate love," a mission that is a "real sharing in God's love for humanity and the love of Christ the Lord for the Church," the Christian family is a "domestic Church"—one specific, graced way to live the *communio* characteristic of the followers of Christ.[60] In light of this *communio*, John Paul vigorously defends "the equal dignity and responsibility of women with men," while arguing that "the true advancement of women requires that clear recognition be given to the value of their maternal and family role, by comparison with all other public roles and all other professions."[61] Men, for their part, are called to live their fatherhood as an icon of "the very fatherhood of God."[62]

Familiaris Consortio tries to reframe the debate over contraception in this sacramental context, arguing that contraceptive sex violates the iconography of marriage by introducing into a relationship that ought to embody the fruitfulness of love an "objectively contradictory language . . . of not giving oneself totally to the other."[63] John Paul also defends the "inalienable" rights of parents to be the primary educators of their children and argues that other educational agencies must be the servants of parents and families—a point that told against democracies as well as communist countries.[64] Taking a cue from the Synod discussion, John Paul outlined a series of "rights of the family" that the Synod Fathers had proposed and that he promised to study with the idea of eventually issuing a "Charter of Rights of the Family."[65]

Familiaris Consortio disappointed those who hoped or expected that John Paul II would announce doctrinal changes in the Church's sexual ethic, or modifications in dealing with such perennial hard cases as separated or divorced Catholics or Catholics living in common law marriages.[66] That expectation misconstrued the nature of the development of doctrine in the life of the Church. Popes do not simply announce doctrinal changes, as if they were arbitrarily changing what had once been decided just as arbitrarily.

In the microcosm of marriage and the family, the values at stake were the same as in the struggle for freedom from political tyranny, and so was the crucial issue: the "pulverization" of the human person. Viewed from this angle, the 1980 Synod and *Familiaris Consortio* had given an authoritative interpretation to Vatican II's teaching on marriage and the family and had put those two basic human institutions—two schools of self-giving love, and thus of freedom properly understood—at the center of the Church's pastoral agenda.

FATHERHOOD AND MERCY

When he began writing *Redemptor Hominis* shortly after his election, John Paul II did not think of his inaugural encyclical as the first panel of a Trinitarian triptych, a three-part reflection on the mystery of God as Holy Trinity.[67] Christ-centered humanism was to be the driving theme of his pontificate, and *Redemptor Hominis* was intended to announce that to the Church and to the world. Reflection on the dignity of the human person redeemed by Christ led naturally, though, to reflection on the God who had sent his Son to be the redeemer of the human world. And that, in turn, led to a reflection on the Holy Spirit, sent by the Father and the Son to continue the risen Christ's redeeming and sanctifying work. Thus *Redemptor Hominis* "grew" into two more encyclicals, *Dives in Misericordia* [Rich in Mercy] on God the Father, published on November 30, 1980, and *Dominum et Vivificantem* [Lord and Giver of Life] on God the Holy Spirit, published on May 18, 1986.

Dives in Misericordia, the most intensely theological of John Paul's encyclicals, also reflects two personal dimensions of his spiritual life.

Kraków was the center of the "Divine Mercy" devotion promoted by Sister Faustina Kowalska, a Polish mystic who died in 1938 at the age of thirty-three. Through a series of mystical experiences, Sister Faustina believed that she had been called to renew Catholic devotion to God's mercy, which in turn would lead to a general renewal of Catholic spiritual life. The elements of the Divine Mercy devotion she created include celebrating the first Sunday after Easter as Divine Mercy Sunday; the "chaplet of Divine Mercy," a set of prayers asking God's mercy on the Church and the world; and a holy hour in memory of Christ's death, during which the stations of the cross are prayed or Eucharistic adoration is celebrated. The devotion's icon is the "Image of the Merciful Jesus," a painting of Christ clothed in a white garment with two rays emanating from his breast, representing the vision that Sister Faustina had on February 22, 1931. Sister Faustina recorded her mystical experiences in a spiritual diary she kept for four years before her death. As her Divine Mercy devotion spread and the question of her possible canonization as a saint was raised, Sister Faustina's diary was given its first scholarly analysis by Father Ignacy Różycki, Karol Wojtyła's former teacher, his housemate on Kanonicza Street, and the director of his habilitation thesis on Max Scheler.[68]

As archbishop of Kraków, Wojtyła had defended Sister Faustina when her orthodoxy was being posthumously questioned in Rome, due in large part to a faulty Italian translation of her diary, and had promoted the cause of her beatification. John Paul II, who said that he felt spiritually "very near" to Sister Faustina, had been "thinking about her for a long time" when he began *Dives in Misericordia*.[69] That sense of spiritual affinity was deepened by the second personal element that bore on the composition of *Dives in Misericordia*.

John Paul II had also been thinking about fatherhood for a long time. Life with his own father and with the unbroken prince, Cardinal Sapieha, had given him a profound experience of both familial and spiritual paternity. He thought of his own priesthood as a form of paternity. As his intuitions about fatherhood deepened, Karol Wojtyła had made a dramatic claim in his poetic essay, "Reflections on Fatherhood": "everything else will turn out to be unimportant and inessential except for this: father, child, love. And then, looking at the simplest things, all of us will say: could we have not learned this long ago? Has this not always been embedded at the bottom of everything that is?"[70]

Fatherhood—not electrons, protons, neutrons, and all the other apparatus of the atom—was "at the bottom of everything that is." As John Paul II developed this poet's intuition about reality in *Dives in Misericordia*, he opened up new dimensions of classic biblical texts.

Themes from the Hebrew Bible enriched John Paul's reflections on Jesus' preaching of a Gospel of mercy and illustrated the Pope's conviction that Christianity could only be understood through Judaism and its unique role in salvation history. While God's merciful love begins "in the very mystery of creation," the Pope writes, the experience of the People of Israel revealed that "mercy signified a special power of love," strong enough to prevail over "sin and infidelity."[71] Although the Hebrew Bible constantly teaches that God is a God of justice, it also reveals that "love is 'greater' than justice: greater in the sense that it is primary and fundamental."[72] For Christians, that teaching is completed in the mystery of Christ's passion, death, and resurrection, which is the most revelatory icon of the Father's mercy. Here, mercy is shown to be stronger not only than sin, but stronger than death itself.[73]

Christ's parable of the prodigal son (*Luke* 15.14–32) is, for John Paul, a synthesis of the biblical theology of mercy, and demonstrates how the question of a true humanism inevitably opens up the question of God.[74] In John Paul's analysis of this most poignant of New Testament parables, the prodigal son is a kind of Everyman, burdened by the tragedy of the human condition, which is "the awareness of squandered sonship," of one's lost human dignity.[75] The forgiving father, by being faithful to his paternity and going beyond the strict norm of justice, restores to the wayward son the truth about himself, which is the lost dignity of his sonship. True mercy does not weaken or humiliate its recipient. It confirms the recipient in his or her human dignity.[76]

Mercy also has a corporate or social dimension. The powerlessness or alienation humanity often feels in the face of technological progress testifies, John Paul suggests, to the truth to which the Hebrew Bible and the New Testament bore witness: "Justice alone is not enough, if that deeper power which is love is not allowed to shape human life in its various dimensions."[77] One path beyond modern "unease" lies in building societies in which justice is opened to love and mercy, the true fulfillment of human aspirations.[78]

Dives in Misericordia drew far less press attention that *Redemptor Hominis*, which was newsworthy because of its programmatic character and its novelty. But there are many forms of news. Among his encyclicals, *Dives in Misericordia* is the clearest expression of the pastoral soul of John Paul II, and the clearest indication of how that soul was formed by Karol Wojtyła's experience and understanding of fatherhood.

CONVERSION FROM THE HEAD DOWN

Prior to leaving on a 21,000-mile pilgrimage to Asia, John Paul II made what was arguably the boldest episcopal appointment of his pontificate.

Aron Lustiger[79] was born in Paris in 1926, the son of Polish Jews who had immigrated to France the previous decade. During the first year of World War II, young Aron, who was being cared for by a French Catholic family in Orléans and who had received no serious Jewish education, converted to Catholicism and was baptized on August 25, 1940, taking the Christian name Jean-Marie. His mother was deported from France and died in Auschwitz in 1943. After studying literature, philosophy, and theology at the Sorbonne, Jean-Marie Lustiger was ordained a priest in 1954 and served as a chaplain to Catholic students and inquiring nonbelievers at his alma mater for fifteen years. In 1969, he was appointed pastor of the Parisian parish of Ste. Jeanne de Chantal, where his work with students and the elderly continued to attract notice and his homilies drew large congregations of intellectuals.[80]

In 1979, Cardinal François Marty of Paris began to prepare for his succession, asking the priests of the archdiocese to send him memoranda on the qualities required in a new archbishop. A group of his colleagues went to Father Lustiger, put him under virtual house arrest, and said: "Write what we think." Lustiger prepared a lengthy, unsparing report on the state of French Catholicism, and laid out the strategy he and his friends thought necessary to deal with it.

According to this analysis, the Church in France, prior to the French Revolution, had been a "Church of power" allied to the political order and in some respects dependent on it. Then came 1789 and the subsequent Terror, when French Catholicism took the earliest (and, until the twentieth century, the hottest) blast from secular modernity. Reeling from that bloody assault, the Church divided. A restorationist wing sought the return of the ancien régime—at first comprehensively, then, when that proved politically impossible, culturally. Over time, this faction had produced the extremism of Action Française, Petainism during World War II, and, ultimately, Archbishop Marcel Lefebvre's rejection of Vatican II. The counterfaction, seeking an accommodation with secularism and the political left, had eventually given birth to the non sequitur of "Christian Marxism." The bitter battle between these two camps had divided French Catholics for more than 150 years and had drained the Church of its evangelical vigor.

The creativity of Lustiger's analysis lay in seeing that these two factions, far from being polar opposites, were two variations on the same false option, the determination to be a "Church of power." They differed on what form of political power was preferable as a partner for the Church. Both agreed, although they could never admit it to each other, that to be the Church in France must mean to be a "Church of power."

Lustiger disagreed. It was the marriage with power that had made the Church vulnerable to the assault of secular modernity. As for a pastoral strategy, it was impossible to find a satisfactory middle ground between the restorationist and accommodationist factions. The restorationists regarded Vatican II's *Declaration on Religious Freedom* as heresy, while the accommodationists had mistaken the opening to modernity in the *Pastoral Constitution on the Church in the Modern World* as an invitation to cohabitation with Marxism and, later, deconstructionism, both of which led to the collapse of Christian orthodoxy. In these circumstances, Lustiger proposed, the only true option was the evangelical option. The Church must abandon the pretense of power, refuse alliances with any political force, and reevangelize France, not through the mediation of politics, but through the conversion of culture. This meant taking the Gospel straight to the molders and shapers of French high culture, the thoroughly secularized French intelligentsia. The hardest cases should be put first, and France should be reconverted from the head down.[81]

Lustiger later described his memorandum as "very, very radical."[82] In fact, it displayed striking parallels to John Paul II's "culture-first" understanding of history. The two men had never met, but they had a mutual intellectual interlocutor in Jerzy (Georges) Kalinowski. Wojtyła's former Lublin colleague was teaching in France and had introduced Lustiger and the leaders of the French edition of *Communio,* an international theological quarterly, to Wojtyła's *Sources of Renewal* and others of the Polish cardinal's writings in the mid-1970s.[83] Lustiger and the young French intellectuals of the *Communio* circle had a good sense, through Kalinowski, of how Cardinal Wojtyła viewed French Catholicism at the time of his election as Pope: Wojtyła was very admiring, and very critical. That combination of admiration and critical challenge had been clearly displayed in Paris from May 30 to June 2, 1980.

Lustiger is not certain, but it seems likely that his memorandum to Cardinal Marty found its way to Rome. In any event, Jean-Marie Lustiger was named Bishop of Orléans on November 10, 1979. Throughout 1980, the question of a successor to Cardinal Marty dragged on. John Paul was, evidently, wrestling with a decision he must have considered one of his most consequential to date. New leadership, setting a new course for French Catholicism, was clearly needed, but those most frequently mentioned for the Paris post were identified with one or the other of the two main factions in the Church.[84] A possible candidate from outside the episcopate, Dom Paul Grammont, the abbot of Le Bec-Hellouin, had indicated that, at age sixty-nine, he thought he could not accept the assignment.[85] The exception within the current French hierarchy was Lustiger, but he had been a bishop for only a few months and his appointment to Orléans had not been happily received by some French bishops, who correctly perceived in him a profound challenge to business as usual. Then there was the question of biography. Could the son of Polish Jewish parents be the archbishop of Paris?

John Paul dealt with this crucial appointment on his knees, in the chapel in the papal apartment. Finally, the decision was clear. Bishop Lustiger, informed of his appointment to Paris, was aghast. He thought the Pope was taking an enormous risk and asking him to do the same. When he had been told of his appointment to Orléans, he had written John Paul a memo "reminding him who I was and who my parents were." John Paul had gone ahead with the Orléans appointment, and now he went ahead with Paris. Three times, Lustiger was told by Monsignor Dziwisz, the Pope's secretary, "You are the fruit of the prayer of the Pope." That settled the matter for Lustiger, who later said that if he hadn't been certain that the appointment had been the result of intense prayer, in which the Pope had confronted the risks both of them would be taking, he wouldn't have accepted.

France was stunned. John Paul had done the unthinkable. The criticism wasn't limited to Catholics—Jews were not happy with the elevation of a convert who had always said that he still considered himself a son of the Jewish people. Lustiger faced it all squarely, began a systematic canvass of the Paris clergy in some sixty two-hour meetings, and then got on with the job of reevangelizing—or in many cases, evangelizing—France from the head down, preaching every Sunday night to intellectuals and students in Notre-Dame Cathedral and writing a series of popular books.[86]

ASIAN PILGRIMAGE

John Paul further refined the title of "universal pastor" on his next overseas journey, which took him to Pakistan, the Philippines, Guam, Japan, and Alaska during twelve days in February 1981.

With the exception of the Philippines, one of the most intensely Catholic countries in the world, East Asia had been the Church's great evangelical failure in the first two millennia of its history. Christians of all affiliations amounted to approximately one percent of the region's population. Japan had almost exactly the same number of Catholics in 1981 as it had in 1945, despite a major postwar population boom.[87] The papal pilgrimage, built around the beatification of Lorenzo Ruiz, a Filipino missionary who had been martyred in Japan, had two goals. John Paul wanted to demonstrate his respect for the ancient cultures of the Far East. And in the spirit of *Luke* 22.32, Peter wanted to strengthen the brethren farthest from him geographically. To prepare for the trip, he took crash courses in Japanese and Tagalog, the native language of the Philippines, for two hours a day in the weeks before his departure.[88]

John Paul flew from Rome on February 16 in the Alitalia jetliner *Luigi Pirandello*. En route to Manila, a "technical stopover" for refueling had been arranged in Karachi. The euphemism was intended to assuage activist Muslims hostile to the idea of the papal infidel on their soil. The "stopover" lasted four hours. The Pope was greeted at the airport by President Zia Ul-Haq and then driven through streets filled with donkey-drawn wooden-wheeled carts and white-garbed old men pedaling bicycles to a stadium, where he celebrated Mass for 100,000 enthusiastic, impoverished Pakistani Catholics. Leaving from the airport shortly after Mass, John Paul thanked President Zia by noting that "one of the dominant features of the character of Abraham, a prophet recognized by Christians, Muslims, and Jews alike, was his spirit of hospitality."[89]

The wonderfully surnamed Cardinal Jaime Sin, a shrewd, exuberant Chinese ethnic who had been archbishop of Manila since 1974, had submitted three possible Philippine itineraries to the papal trip planners. John Paul had chosen the most demanding. "Let us hope," Sin said with a sigh, "that the reporters can keep up with the front runner in white."[90]

The cardinal had other, and graver, causes for concern. Filipino strongman Ferdinand Marcos and his wife were determined to use the papal visit to bolster their own political position. Imelda Marcos had already tried to seize public credit for inviting the Pope, and had backed down only when Cardinal Sin threatened to have a pastoral letter read in churches throughout the country, explaining that the Pope was coming at the invitation of the bishops and that the Marcoses were lying.[91] Just prior to the Pope's arrival, President Marcos had formally lifted the martial law he had imposed in 1972. Cardinal Sin, for one, was not impressed: "Despite all of Marcos's legalistic attempts to clothe his regime with the veneer of legitimacy of legal democracy, his was a dictatorial rule."[92]

There was something almost comic about the Filipino first couple's behavior during the papal visit. Virtually everything they did to try to impress John Paul was certain to have the opposite effect. The welcoming ceremony at the airport outside Manila was grandiose, with five honor guards, endless salvos from artillery, jet fighters buzzing the field, and schoolchildren dressed in paramilitary uniforms. The Marcoses' reception for the Pope at Malacañang, the presidential palace, was an exercise in garishness. At considerable expense, the residence had been transformed into an elaborate Philippine village for the occasion, and the well-heeled guests were required to dress in national costume. The First Lady used a private jet to fly ahead to each of John Paul's stops in the country, so that she could be seen welcoming the Pope. By the third stop, in Davao, John Paul II, whose patience and courtesy are both legendary, had had enough of the charade and began greeting the local dignitaries as if Imelda simply weren't there. State-controlled Philippine television, meanwhile, kept the Pope in the background and Mrs. Marcos in the foreground, surrounded by her "loving people," as she put it.[93]

John Paul's remarks to the Philippine political elite showed the influence of Cardinal Sin and the pro-democracy Filipino bishops. At the Malacañang reception, the Pope squarely confronted martial law, whose recent formal recision was belied by the government's ongoing behavior. Any alleged conflict between national security and human rights, he said, had to be resolved according to the principle that the state exists to serve human beings and their rights. If the state systematically violated those rights, it was not serving the common good.[94]

Although international media attention focused on the drama between the Pope's human rights concerns and the Marcoses, John Paul's primary concern in the Philippines was the Philippine Church, the strongest Catholic presence in East Asia. His message to the bishops was similar to the message he had delivered in Brazil: defend religious freedom and other human rights, promote social justice, but do not sell the Church's evangelical birthright for the pottage of politics. Bishops and priests best served the well-being of society by forming lay Catholics capable of exercising leadership according to the moral standards set by the Church's social doctrine—a familiar message, delivered not by issuing orders, but by explaining the vision of Vatican II, in which Catholic social action was one dimension of the universal call to holiness. Nowhere else on his world travels to date had John Paul so emphasized the evangelical role of the laity and their responsibility for preaching the faith to their neighbors.[95]

The centerpiece of the Philippine pilgrimage was the February 18 beatification—the last step toward sainthood—of Lorenzo Ruiz and his companions. It was the first such ceremony ever held outside Rome or Avignon. Cardinal Sin had asked that the beatification of the Filipino lay missionary martyred in Nagasaki in the seventeenth century take place in Manila, and John Paul had readily agreed. A million Filipinos came to Luneta Park for the ceremony, at which the Pope was joined by bishops from Australia, Bangladesh, Hong Kong, India, Indonesia, Japan, South Korea, Macao, Sri Lanka, and Taiwan. Breaking into Tagalog from English, John Paul reminded the enormous congregation, the largest Catholic celebration in the history of Asia, of the martyr's words to the Japanese court that would condemn him: "Even if this body would have a thousand lives, I would let all of them be killed [before you would] force me to turn my back on Christ." This son of a Chinese father and a Tagala mother, a husband and father himself, "reminds us that everyone's life and the whole of one's life must be at Christ's disposal." That was "the full meaning" of this first beatification conducted in East Asia, which was intended "to animate all the Christians of the Far East . . . to spread the word of the Lord." It was an invitation with special meaning for the Philippines, who should draw "deep assurance and fresh hope" from the lives of their martyrs. What they were celebrating in Luneta Park, and what the Filipinos were to bring to Asia, was "the love of Jesus Christ, who is the Light of the world."[96]

The trip schedule was typically brutal, sixteen-hour days without breaks. The Pope met families, priest, seminarians, nuns, lepers, university students. He went to some of the poorest shantytowns in the country and to a refugee camp where Vietnamese boat people were living in appalling conditions. At the latter, the government had discreetly removed the barbed wire just before the Pope's arrival. At one stop, a little girl was supposed to hand flowers to the Pope. When he put out his hand to accept them, she changed her mind and hid the bouquet behind her back. The nuns in charge almost fainted in embarrassment; John Paul burst out laughing.[97] Visiting the Catholic radio station Veritas on February 21, he broadcast a message throughout Asia: "Christ and His Church cannot be alien to any people, nation or culture. Christ's message belongs to everyone and is addressed to everyone. . . . [The Church] wants to be, in Asia as in every other part of the world, the sign of the merciful love of God, our common Father."[98] In addition to its other targets, the broadcast was John Paul's first attempt to penetrate China. It would not be his last.

After an overnight stop in Guam, the Pope arrived in Japan on February 23. The contemporary tension between being authentically Japanese and authentically Catholic had almost 400 years of history behind it, dating to the bloody persecutions that destroyed most of Japanese Catholicism in the seventeenth century. National self-consciousness and anti-Catholicism had formed at the same moment in Japanese history. John Paul's pilgrimage to Japan was a modest effort to reopen a long-stalled conversation.

In a rare gesture of regard, Emperor Hirohito met the Pope at the door of the Imperial Palace. It was the first time the emperor, whose religious status in Japanese culture was not ended by his postwar renunciation of divine origin, had ever received the head of another faith.[99] That afternoon, John Paul met with thousands of Japanese teenagers and young adults, not all of them Christian. After the songs and dances that had become customary at these papal youth events, the Pope had a lengthy give-and-take with the youngsters, who asked questions about everything from his faith to his hopes for the modern world. The most moving meeting of the entire pilgrimage had taken place earlier in the day, when John Paul went to visit Brother Zeno, a Polish Franciscan missionary who had come to Japan with Maximilian Kolbe in the 1930s. After the war, Brother Zeno had become a guardian of castaways and orphans, wandering the mean streets of Tokyo, picking up the human refuse from the sidewalks and caring for them. Now over ninety and sick, Brother Zeno could barely hear. When John Paul bent over his bed, the old man asked him whether he was the Polish Pope. John Paul replied that he was, and tears began to roll down Brother Zeno's wasted cheeks. There were no dry eyes in the room as the Pope embraced the aged Franciscan and stroked his head gently.[100] The Japanese newspapers had said for years that Brother Zeno, whose holiness had won him enormous respect rare for a Westerner, "does not have time to die." Now another of "God's brothers," as playwright Wojtyła had styled the self-sacrificing Brother Albert Chmielowski, would die a very happy man.

On February 25, John Paul spoke at the Hiroshima Peace Memorial in Japanese, English, French, Spanish, Portuguese, Polish, Chinese, German, and Russian. The address was built around an antiphon, repeated three times: "To remember the past is to commit oneself to the future." Humanity, John Paul insisted, "is not destined to self-destruction," and the antidote to the threat of war was "a system of law that will regulate international relations and maintain peace." He closed with a prayer in Japanese, asking "the Creator of nature and man, of truth and beauty," to "instill into the hearts of all human beings the wisdom of peace, the strength of justice, and the joy of fellowship."[101]

After addressing scientists and United Nations University students, John Paul left for Nagasaki, the center of Japanese Catholicism, which welcomed the Pope with icy wind and snow. There, he visited the "Hill of Martyrs" where Lorenzo Ruiz and his companions had been crucified, and the house where Maximilian Kolbe—known to the skittish local bishops as "Mad Max" for his impatience in getting on with the conversion of Japan—had lived in the 1930s.[102] At Mass in the cathedral of Nagasaki, he ordained fifteen priests on the first day of his visit. The next day, during Mass at Matsuyama Stadium, he baptized seventy-seven men and women as snow fell on the ceremony.

On the polar route home, the papal plane stopped for refueling in Anchorage, Alaska, where the weather was kinder and 50,000 Alaskans attended an outdoor Mass with the Pope at Delaney Park Strip—the largest crowd in the history of that underpopulated state. A Polish-American had driven a dogsled 600 miles to see John Paul, but didn't have a ticket to the Mass. The dogs made so much noise that the security guards let him in anyway.[103] In his welcoming remarks, Archbishop Francis T. Hurley said that "No future Pope will travel farther from the Eternal City unless he chooses a space ship to the moon—a challenge which many feel would be very tempting to Your Holiness."[104] At the airport, departing for Rome, John Paul rode the last 100 feet to his plane on the runners of Iditarod musher Norman Vaughan's dogsled. "This was great," the Pope said, thanking the driver and his nine huskies.[105]

En route to Alaska, the flight had crossed the international date line and gained a calendar day. With mischief in his eye, the "universal pastor" told an exhausted papal party and press corps, "Now we must decide what to do with the extra day we have been given."[106]

12

In the Eye of the Storm

Months of Violence and Dissent

AUGUST 14–31, 1980	Gdańsk shipyard strike launches the Solidarity trade union and movement.
AUGUST 20, 1980	John Paul II's messages to Polish Church leaders support strikers' demands.
AUGUST 27, 1980	Polish bishops' conference supports strikers' call for independent unions.
OCTOBER 24– NOVEMBER 10, 1980	Crisis over Solidarity's legal registration unfolds.
DECEMBER 2, 1980	Four American churchwomen murdered in El Salvador.
DECEMBER 5, 1980	Planned Warsaw Pact invasion of Poland is halted by Soviet government.
DECEMBER 16, 1980	Pope John Paul II writes Leonid Brezhnev in defense of Polish sovereignty.
DECEMBER 31, 1980	Apostolic Letter, *Egregiae Virtutis*, names Sts. Cyril and Methodius co-patrons of Europe.
JANUARY 15–18, 1981	John Paul meets Solidarity delegation at the Vatican.
MARCH 1981	Bydgoszcz crisis roils Poland; Soviet press intensifies attacks on John Paul II.
MAY 9, 1981	John Paul establishes Pontifical Council for the Family as a permanent curial office.
MAY 13, 1981	Pope John Paul II is shot in St. Peter's Square by Mehmet Ali Agca.
MAY 28, 1981	Cardinal Stefan Wyszyński, Primate of Poland, dies in Warsaw.
JUNE 3, 1981	John Paul returns to the Vatican from the Policlinico Gemelli.
JUNE 20, 1981	John Paul returns to the Gemelli for diagnosis and treatment of viral infection.

JULY 7, 1981	József Glemp is named Primate of Poland.
JULY 22, 1981	Mehmet Ali Agca is found guilty and sentenced to life imprisonment after a three-day trial in Rome.
AUGUST 14, 1981	John Paul leaves the Gemelli to continue recuperation at Castel Gandolfo.
SEPTEMBER 5, 1981	First Solidarity national congress opens in Gdańsk.
SEPTEMBER 14, 1981	*Laborem Exercens,* John Paul's first social encyclical.
SEPTEMBER 25, 1981	Formal written verdict in Agca's trial suggests a plot to assassinate the Pope.
OCTOBER 5, 1981	John Paul II appoints "personal delegate" to govern the Jesuits.
OCTOBER 18, 1981	General Wojciech Jaruzelski becomes First Secretary of the Polish communist party.
DECEMBER 8, 1981	John Paul II blesses icon of Mary, Mother of the Church, the first Marian image in St. Peter's Square.
DECEMBER 11, 1981	John Paul visits Roman Lutheran congregation.
DECEMBER 12–13, 1981	General Jaruzelski declares "state of war" in Poland, imposes martial law, and orders arrest of thousands of Solidarity activists.
DECEMBER 18, 1981	Papal letter to Jaruzelski urges end to violence and creation of a national dialogue.
JANUARY 1, 1982	John Paul's message for the annual World Day of Peace denounces "false peace" of totalitarianism.
MAY–JUNE 1982	Papal visits to Great Britain and Argentina during the Falklands/Malvinas War.

Mehmet Ali Agca, a twenty-three-year-old Turk, left the Pensione Isa on Via Cicerone, near the Piazza Cavour and the Castel Sant'Angelo on the Vatican side of the Tiber. It was May 13, 1981, a glorious spring afternoon, and like 20,000 others, he was going to St. Peter's Square for John Paul II's weekly general audience.

Agca was not a typical pilgrim. Two years before, on February 1, 1979, he had assassinated Abdi Ipekçi, editor of the respected Istanbul daily *Milliyet.* He confessed to the crime, but retracted the confession during his October 1979 trial. On November 23, with his trial unfinished, Agca escaped from the maximum security Kartal-Maltepe prison dressed as a soldier. Three days later, he wrote a letter to *Milliyet* threatening to kill the Pope, if John Paul II should have the temerity to arrive in Turkey as scheduled on November 28. The threat was not carried out and Agca, a wanted man, disappeared into the dark underside of the modern world.

A Turkish court convicted him *in absentia* and sentenced him to death in April 1980, but neither the Turkish authorities nor the international police could find him. Agca, a man from a poor family with no personal financial resources, was traveling extensively that year—Iran, Bulgaria, Switzerland, Germany, and Tunisia for certain, perhaps the USSR as well. In January 1981, he had come to Rome and then spent February in Switzerland and Austria. After returning to Rome for a few days in early April, he had gone to Perugia, registered in a university course, attended one class, and left for Milan, where he booked a two-week holiday excursion to Majorca. During their time on the island, his fellow vacationers almost never saw Agca. He returned to Rome in early May and checked into the Pensione Isa on May 9. A caller had reserved a room for him before his arrival. On May 11 and again on May 12, he went to St. Peter's Square to study the venue.

Along with thousands of pilgrims and Romans, he was back the next afternoon. Walking up the Via della Conciliazione, he crossed into Vatican territory and entered the square, strolling along the Bernini colonnade. The huge piazza was divided into sections by short wooden barricades that formed an impromptu motorway along which John Paul II would be driven in his open-air Popemobile to greet the crowd. Mehmet Ali Agca found a spot just behind a row of pilgrims pressed against one of the barricades, no more than ten feet from where the Pope would pass.

And waited.

THE EYE OF THE STORM

Popes do not have the luxury of putting the rest of the Church and its needs on "hold" while focusing on one set of problems for weeks or months on end. The pope is the eye of a hurricane of activity that never ends. Every day, something is happening, somewhere, that will eventually demand his close attention because of its impact on the life of the Church.

The extraordinary complexity of the pope's task and the exceptional demands it makes on a man's resources of intellect, heart, and spirit were fully displayed in the period between John Paul II's Polish pilgrimage in June 1979 and his twin pilgrimages to the United Kingdom and Argentina during the Falklands/Malvinas War of 1982.

John Paul's first globe-spanning attempts to revitalize Peter's mission to "strengthen the brethren" and his initial efforts to renovate the Church's response to the crisis of humanism in the late twentieth century took place while the nonviolent challenge to communism he had inspired was achieving critical mass in his native land. The beginnings of his *Theology of the Body*; his landmark UN and UNESCO addresses; his pilgrimages to Ireland, the United States, Brazil, Africa, France, West Germany, and East Asia; his historic meeting with the Ecumenical Patriarch of Orthodoxy; his initial efforts to revivify the Italian Church; the Synod on the Family and his second encyclical, *Dives in Misericordia*; the Synods of the Dutch and Ukrainian bishops; his opening attempts to close the breach between science and theology; dozens of episcopal appointments, including such major sees as Milan and Paris—*all* of this

took place during the gestation of Solidarity and the first weeks of its tumultuous sixteen months of freedom.

One day from that period graphically illustrates the multiple pressures
operating on the papacy of John Paul II.

December 2, 1980: As the Vatican watches with deepening concern, the
United States, the European Community, and NATO warn the Soviet Union
against an invasion of Poland that satellite reconnaissance and other forms of
intelligence suggest is imminent. That same day, a Synod of Greek Catholic
bishops from the Ukrainian diaspora reconvenes in Rome and adopts a formal resolution pronouncing null and void the 1946 "L'viv Sobor"—a canonically invalid meeting of Greek Catholic leaders in Ukraine, held under
extreme Soviet duress, which had abrogated the 1596 Union of Brest and
declared the Greek Catholic Church reincorporated into Russian Orthodoxy.[1]
The anti–John Paul II propaganda campaign authorized the previous November now intensifies in the Soviet press, linking the Pope to U.S. President
Jimmy Carter and his national security adviser, Zbigniew Brzeziński, in a plot
to destabilize the USSR.[2]

That same day, three American nuns and a lay worker are raped and murdered in El Salvador—the latest victims in a vicious civil war that had claimed
the life of the archbishop of San Salvador, Oscar Arnulfo Romero, assassinated
while celebrating Mass, eight months earlier. Meanwhile, the situation in
Nicaragua continues to deteriorate, with the Church's leadership criticizing
the human rights record of the new Sandinista regime.

That same day, the encyclical *Dives in Misericordia* is officially published.

December 2, 1980: For John Paul II, another day at the eye of the storm
that was Roman Catholicism, fifteen years after the Second Vatican Council—
a Church in which "dissenting" could mean dissenting for, and from, the truth.

From the late summer of 1980 through the early summer of 1982, John
Paul was confronted by an unremitting series of diplomatic, ecclesiastical, and
personal crises. None of these crises could be temporarily shelved. In dealing
with each, John Paul II remained the universal pastor of a world Church—an
important fact to keep in mind when trying to understand how the hurricane
looked from within the eye.

THE CRISIS OF SOLIDARITY

The fuse that John Paul II lit in Poland in June 1979 burned slowly but steadily.
Fourteen months later, on August 14, 1980, it set off a nonviolent explosion
the result of which, over the next decade, would be the collapse of European
communism.

Birth Pains

The occasion for the explosion was another attempt by the tottering Polish
regime to shore up its *Alice in Wonderland* economics. On July 2, 1980, price

increases of thirty percent to one hundred percent on beef, pork, and high-grade poultry other than chicken were announced. A wave of strikes followed, with the workers' demands focused on economic issues, including the recision of price increases and a cost-of-living wage increase. Local authorities were gradually rolling back the price increases when, on July 9, Communist Party leader Edward Gierek reintroduced the new prices and refused to increase wages. On July 16, train operators in Lublin blocked the railways connecting Poland to the Soviet Union and were joined on strike by other railway workers and by local bakery and dairy employees. The workers now added demands more political in nature. In addition to rollbacks of the price increases, they wanted the government to acknowledge a right to strike, legal immunity for those who had struck, new elections to the official trade union chapters, and direct talks with the government authorities. The Lublin strikes were settled in four days, but a new element had entered the volatile mix. For the first time, workers were beginning to articulate demands for a measure of real freedom. Better-fed servitude would no longer suffice—as a Solidarity poet later put it, "The times are past/when they closed our mouths/with sausage."[3]

The Lublin demands began to be echoed throughout the country. On August 7, Anna Walentynowicz, a crane operator and veteran of the independent trade union movement, was fired from her job at the Lenin Shipyard in Gdańsk. She had been collecting the remains of graveyard candles to make new candles for a memorial to the workers shot down during the 1970 demonstrations in Gdańsk—and was fired for stealing.[4] On August 14, the 17,000 workers at the yard declared an occupation strike. They were led by an unemployed electrician named Lech Wałęsa, who had climbed the twelve-foot-high perimeter fence to get into his old workplace. The shipyard strike committee issued an eight-point program that dramatically raised the political stakes. In addition to economic relief, the workers demanded the creation of a free trade-union movement. They also required a moral accounting from the regime—the erection of a memorial to workers shot down during the 1970 strike at the shipyard.

Attempting to mediate with the local party and government officials, the bishop of Gdańsk, Lech Kaczmarek, suggested that it might help keep things calm if pastoral care were available to the workers. The authorities agreed. On August 17, the first open-air Mass was celebrated in the Lenin Shipyard by Father Henryk Jankowski, Wałęsa's pastor, and attended by 4,000 strikers, with 2,000 friends and family gathered outside the locked gates. At the end of the Mass, Father Jankowski blessed a large cross made by shipyard carpenters. It was immediately raised next to Gate No. 2 as an interim memorial to the victims of the 1970 shootings.[5]

The first strikers' Mass and the raising of the memorial cross gave the Gdańsk strike its distinctive iconography, soon to be familiar all over the world—the workers who defied the so-called workers' state behind barricades decorated with the Black Madonna and other religious symbols. Icons of faith were now the symbols by which Poles could best express the truths John Paul II had preached in June 1979, demonstrate their reignited sense of human dignity, and make clear their yearning for freedom. The Madonna on the shipyard gates, the daily strike Mass, and those rows of strikers queued up to visit open-air confessionals also symbolized the different kind of political struggle in which they were engaged. This was going to be a nonviolent and self-regulating revolution—one that proved Robespierre, Lenin, and the other violent men in the modern revolutionary pantheon wrong.

Many Polish bishops, including Primate Wyszyński, were slow to grasp the significance of what was unfolding in Gdańsk. Bishop Kaczmarek, on the scene, seems to have been an exception. The Primate's sermon at Częstochowa for the feast of the Assumption, August 15, did not directly allude to the Gdańsk strikes but celebrated Marshal Piłsudski's great victory over the Red Army in the 1920 "Miracle on the Vistula." On August 17, in a sermon at Wambierzyce, a Marian shrine in Lower Silesia, the Primate did refer to the nation's "torment and unrest," and to "those workers who are striving for social, moral, economic, and cultural rights." A bowdlerized version of the sermon, eliminating the references to the unrest and highlighting the call for "calm and reason," was broadcast on Warsaw television on August 20. By that time, John Paul II had made his first interventions in the drama, having been briefed on the situation in Gdańsk by his secretary, Monsignor Stanisław Dziwisz, on his return from a well-timed two-week vacation in Poland.[6] At the general audience on August 20, the Pope asked for prayers for "my Poland" and later that day sent a message to Cardinal Wyszyński.[7] Made public three days later, the papal message unmistakably aligned the Church with the Gdańsk strikers' demands: "I pray that, once again, the Episcopate with the Primate at its head . . . may be able to aid the nation in its struggle for daily bread, social justice, and the safeguarding of its inviolable right to its own way of life and achievement." Similar messages were dispatched to Cardinal Macharski in Kraków and to Bishop Stefan Bareła of Częstochowa.[8] On August 21, Bishop Kaczmarek traveled to Warsaw to brief Cardinal Wyszyński and the bishops' conference secretary, Bishop Bronisław Dąbrowski, and to assure them that the strike leaders truly represented the workers.[9]

On August 22, the strikers' position was strengthened when a group of intellectuals organized by Tadeusz Mazowiecki, the editor of the Catholic monthly *Więz* [Link], arrived in Gdańsk to act as advisers at the strikers' request. This was an important example of the class-free social solidarity that John Paul II's 1979 pilgrimage had helped engender, and a by-product of the open conversation between Catholic and non-Catholic intellectuals that Cardinal Wojtyła had fostered in Kraków.[10] The next day, Bishop Kaczmarek, back in Gdańsk, issued a public statement in support of the workers, urging only that the negotiations to begin that day be conducted "with understanding and without hatred."[11]

The talks between a government commission and the Inter-Factory Strike

Committee, representing workers all along Poland's Baltic coast, had moved into a particularly delicate phase when, on August 26, the feast of Our Lady of Częstochowa, Cardinal Wyszyński preached his customary sermon at the Jasna Góra monastery. With the situation still unresolved in Gdańsk, the threat of a Soviet intervention weighing on everyone's mind, and pressure increasing on the Gdańsk negotiators to accept a government-proposed "compromise" that would return things to the status quo, the nation waited to hear what the Primate would say.

The cardinal's sermon bitterly disappointed the strikers. They might have appreciated his appeal for "calm, balance, prudence, wisdom, and responsibility for the whole Polish nation." But they could not understand why, at this moment, he went to such lengths to criticize Polish workers' productivity and to stress everyone's responsibility for the economic catastrophe in which Poland found itself. The sermon's insistence on sovereignty as the absolute precondition to social and economic progress suggested that the Primate's principal concern remained the danger of a Soviet invasion. He simply did not seem to have sensed that a special moment—in biblical terms, a *kairos*—had arrived in Gdańsk.[12]

Once more, John Paul II gently but firmly intervened. At his general audience address the following day, with the world press, the Polish and Soviet governments, and the strikers at Gdańsk all listening to Vatican Radio, he entrusted "the great and important problems of our country" to Our Lady of Częstochowa, whose feast Polish pilgrims and Poles resident in Rome had celebrated the day before. He defended the strikers, arguing that the problems they were forcing onto the agenda were real and could only be resolved by bringing "peace and justice to our country."[13] That same afternoon, the Main Council of the Polish episcopate, meeting in emergency session in Warsaw, took decisive action and issued a lengthy communiqué that strongly endorsed the strikers' demands for an independent trade union, citing the teaching of the Second Vatican Council on the "fundamental rights" of workers to organize.[14] The message was clear—the bishops' conference believed that the strikers should not settle for a return to the status quo, but should hold firm to the demand for independent, non-regime-dominated unions as an essential part of national self-renewal.[15]

In the wake of the Pope's cautious but clear indication of support and the unambiguous statement by the bishops' conference, the strikers held to their position and the government negotiators finally gave in. The agreement signed on August 31 provided for independent self-governing trade unions. The workers' revolt in Gdańsk had refuted the communist doctrine that workers needed a vanguard party to show them their own interests.[16] The terms of settlement, embodied in that single phrase, "independent self-governing trade union," also meant some form of power sharing. And power sharing meant the end of the totalitarian system.

The Solidarity movement had been born.

The Fall 1980 Crisis

The Gdańsk accord was a triumph for the strikers and, at a distance, for John Paul II. But it did not lead immediately to the legal establishment of the "independent self-governing trade union" that had been agreed to. Strikes were spreading throughout the country among steelworkers, miners, and workers in dozens of other state industries.[17] The government and the Polish Communist Party were also in turmoil. Edward Gierek was ousted as party leader on September 5, after suffering a heart attack in the wake of a furious debate in the Polish parliament on the failures of his administration. His replacement as First Secretary, Stanisław Kania, was a former internal security chief who promised the Polish Politburo to "return to Leninist norms" and to implement more effectively the essentially correct policy line of the party.[18]

For all that they ran essentially lawless states, communist regimes were obsessed with the appearance of legality and with juridical process. Legal maneuvers and obfuscations now became the chief tool by which the new Kania regime tried to derail the Solidarity movement. The movement itself had coalesced into a genuine national structure in Gdańsk in mid-September, when delegates from some thirty-five recently created independent unions officially adopted Solidarność, "Solidarity," as the new national union's name. Its connection to John Paul's message in June 1979 was clear to all concerned.[19] Amid the happy chaos of men and women experiencing their first taste of democratic process, the delegates then drafted Solidarity's statutes, which Wałęsa, in order to register the union legally, submitted to the appropriate court in Warsaw on September 24. At this point, though, it was already clear that Solidarity was not simply a new trade union. As one observer wrote, "It was, at the very least, a massive and unique social movement, a movement which was perhaps best described as a 'civil crusade for national regeneration.'"[20]

For that reason, the authorities continued to drag their feet in implementing the Gdańsk accords, and a national warning strike of one hour was called for October 3. In an impressive display of discipline, workers across the country downed tools for precisely one hour, between noon and 1 o'clock. The instructions had been relayed throughout Poland by local Solidarity committees, as the union was still denied access to the national media.[21] The demonstration strike had the desired effect. The party's Central Committee met to review the situation, and after two days of vitriolic argument agreed to internal party reform.

Still, the courts refused to register Solidarity legally and tensions mounted during October. Tadeusz Mazowiecki went to Rome at the beginning of the month to brief John Paul. The Pope had one urgent question: "Will it last? Does this movement have a future?" Mazowiecki assured him that it did.[22] The Polish Bishops' Conference, meeting in Warsaw on October 15 and 16, issued a statement supporting the workers' demands for full implementation of the

Gdańsk accords. Three days later, the Primate met with Warsaw Solidarity leader Zbigniew Bujak and gave him his unconditional support: "I am with you." On October 21, Wyszyński talked with the new party leader, Kania, who had just been taking counsel with the foreign ministers of the Warsaw Pact countries. Two days later, the Primate flew to Rome to attend the closing sessions of the Synod on the Family and to give the Pope his impressions of the situation.[23]

The sluggish communist legal system finally got moving, only to make a serious political mistake. On October 24, Wałęsa returned to the Warsaw Provincial Court, where the judge, Zdzisław Kościelniak, announced that Solidarity was legally registered. But he unilaterally inserted a clause into the statutes recognizing the Communist Party's leading role in society, the socialist system, and Poland's international alliances. Eight million Solidarity members were stunned and angered. Wałęsa denounced the unilateral insertions and said the movement would never accept arbitrarily imposed changes in statutes it had democratically adopted.[24]

The pressure now mounted exponentially inside Poland and throughout east central Europe. The Solidarity leadership demanded that the prime minister meet with them immediately in Gdańsk. Posters that had once read, "We demand the registration of Solidarity" now had an addendum in black crayon: "with unchanged statutes." After meeting with the deputy prime minister, the Solidarity leadership agreed to negotiate with the government in Warsaw, but also set November 12 as the date of a national general strike if the registration impasse was not resolved. On October 28, Czechoslovakia closed its borders to Poland. The next day, party leader Kania flew to Moscow as the Czechoslovak and East German press unleashed a fusillade of bitter criticism against Solidarity in general and Wałęsa specifically. East German party leader Erich Honecker had already written Leonid Brezhnev, urging Soviet action before "socialist Poland" was lost.[25]

The communiqué from the Brezhnev-Kania meeting suggested that Moscow had not yet lost confidence in its man in Warsaw. The Soviets may also have been playing for time. The immediate registration crisis ended on November 10 when the Polish Supreme Court overruled the Warsaw Provincial Court and struck the offensive insertions from the statutes. Solidarity compromised by accepting the addition of language from the Gdańsk accords acknowledging the party's leading role as an appendix to the statutes.

For the moment, a direct, massive, national confrontation had been avoided. Cardinal Wyszyński held a reception for the Solidarity leadership after their day in court, reminisced about his own days as a union chaplain in interwar Poland, and then warned obliquely against pressing demands on which the state could not possibly deliver. The Primate evidently did not believe the threat of Soviet intervention had completely receded. Afterward, Wałęsa and the other Solidarity leaders went to a celebration at a local theater, where the theme song of the evening, a political cabaret tune called "So That

Poland Shall Be Poland," nicely captured the Solidarity movement's intention.[26]

That intention made ongoing confrontation with the Polish regime and its Soviet ally unavoidable. Solidarity—the union that was always more than that, but that could not be the overt political opposition everyone knew it was—could not coexist with a totalitarian state. The Soviet Union's leadership understood this, and had been preparing for some time to make Solidarity go—by force.

A two-day campaign in December 1980 was planned. On the first day, more than a dozen Soviet divisions, two Czech divisions, and an East German division were to move into Poland, followed by nine more Soviet divisions the following day. All this was known to the United States government from satellite reconnaissance, from information relayed by a Red Army general in Moscow, and from information on Soviet troop dispositions and plans delivered at immense personal risk by a well-placed Polish source, Colonel Ryszard Kukliński, a Polish General Staff officer and aide to General Wojciech Jaruzelski, who also served as a liaison to the Soviet commander-in-chief of the Warsaw Pact Joint Command.[27] U.S. national security adviser Brzeziński called John Paul at the Vatican on Sunday night, December 7, to tell him what the Americans had learned and how. Soviet and Warsaw Pact troops moving toward Poland had been in full readiness since Thursday, December 4, and could invade at any time. The expectation was that the intervention would be on Monday, December 8. Satellite intelligence had confirmed that troop movements toward Poland's borders had stopped on the evening of Friday, December 5, but this could have been a pause in the staging of an invasion. Concern that a massive Soviet military intervention was imminent continued throughout the following week.[28]

The Soviet invasion never took place. As was learned only years later, the halt in troop movements on December 5 was a stand-down ordered by the Soviet government.

There were multiple reasons that the Soviets stopped. Polish party leader Kania had told Brezhnev that an invasion wasn't necessary and that the Polish party could not ensure a passive reaction if the Polish people were confronted by Soviet troops. As the Soviet plan, detailed by Colonel Kukliński, included the liquidation of the Solidarity leadership by summary courts-martial and firing squads, this was sage counsel.[29] Poland would never have stood for what its people would have immediately interpreted as a second Katyn massacre.

The international situation also bore on the Soviet decision. The United States' reaction to the 1979 Soviet invasion of Afghanistan had demonstrated that an invasion of Poland would not be handled as gingerly as the 1968 invasion of Czechoslovakia had been. The Carter administration, with national security adviser Brzeziński in the lead, had also made its position on a Soviet invasion of Poland clear by direct and indirect signals. A presidential hotline message was dispatched to the Kremlin, warning of "very grave" consequences for the U.S./Soviet relationship if the USSR invaded Poland. Similar messages were sent through India, where Indira Gandhi was a useful conduit to Brezhnev, and through West German chancellor Helmut Schmidt and French President Valery Giscard d'Estaing. NATO went to a higher level of defense readiness, of which Soviet intelligence was aware. Knowing that it would leak and get to Moscow, Brzeziński sent a memo to the U.S. Department of State listing advanced weaponry the administration was considering selling to China, then on the U.S. "no-sell" list.[30]

The administration had also talked with AFL-CIO President Lane Kirkland about a worldwide trade union boycott of Soviet air transport and shipping, cutting the USSR off from international trade without a formal, state-led embargo. Kirkland was confident that world outrage at a Soviet invasion to crush Solidarity would be so great that the unions could have mounted a de facto blockade of the USSR. Brzeziński leaked the story of the plans for worldwide trade union action to the *Wall Street Journal,* and thence to the Soviet leadership.[31] The incoming Reagan administration, elected the previous month but not yet inaugurated, issued a statement of support for the measures the outgoing administration was taking.[32] Coupled with Kania's assurances, the international costs of an invasion of Poland may well have seemed unbearable to a Soviet leadership already mired down in Afghanistan and preparing to face the challenge of an assertively anti-Soviet Reagan administration.[33]

Blocked in their attempt to impose a military solution on the 1968 Czechoslovakian model, the Soviet leadership decided to liquidate Solidarity by other means.

John Paul II Intervenes

Amid continuing concern about a Soviet military invasion to save "socialist Poland," Pope John Paul II took a bold personal initiative. Papal diplomats had traditionally used the language of indirect suggestion, careful to leave both the Holy See and the government in question a graceful way to retreat from a crisis without losing face. Now, using the discreet language of diplomacy but making his meaning unmistakably clear, the Pope sent an unprecedented letter to Leonid Brezhnev on December 16. Written in French on cream-colored stationery embossed with the John Paul's personal crest, the letter read as follows:

> To His Excellency, Mr. Leonid Brezhnev,
> President of the Supreme Soviet of the Union of
> Soviet Socialist Republics
>
> I address myself to the preoccupation of Europe and the whole world as regards the tension created by the internal events taking place in Poland during these last months. Poland is one of the signatories of the Helsinki Final Act. This nation was, in September 1939, the first victim of an aggres-

sion which was at the root of the terrible period of occupation, which lasted until 1945. During the entire Second World War, the Poles remained side-by-side with their allies, fighting on all the fronts of the war, and the destructive fury of this conflict cost Poland the loss of nearly six million of its sons: that is to say, a fifth of its population before the war.

Having in mind, then, the various serious motivations of the preoccupation created by the tension over the actual situation in Poland, I ask you to do everything you can in order that all that constitutes the causes of this preoccupation, according to widespread opinion, be removed. This is indispensable for détente in Europe and in the world. I think that this can be obtained only by abiding faithfully to the solemn principles of the Helsinki Final Act, which proclaims criteria for regulating the relations between states, and in particular the principle of respect for the inherent rights of sovereignty as well as the principle of nonintervention in the internal affairs of each of the participating states. The events that have taken place in Poland these last months have been caused by the ineluctable necessity of the economic reconstruction of the country, which requires, at the same time, a moral reconstruction based on the conscious engagement, in solidarity, of all the forces of the entire society.

I am confident that you will do everything you can in order to dispel the actual tension, in order that political public opinion may be reassured about such a delicate and urgent problem.

I vividly hope that you will be kind enough to welcome and examine with attention what I have thought it my duty to present to you, considering that I am only inspired by the interests of peace and understanding between peoples.

JOANNES PAULUS PP. II

From the Vatican
16 December 1980[34]

Its stylized, diplomatic language notwithstanding, this was a very tough letter and could only have been read as such by its recipient and his colleagues. What was happening in Poland was a question of "internal events" that were none of the Soviet Union's business. The implicit parallel between any Soviet invasion of Poland in 1980 and the Nazi invasion of September 1939 made clear the moral terms in which John Paul was prepared to define Soviet aggression and the nature of the aggressor. The reference to "solidarity" among "all the forces of . . . society" essential to national moral and economic reconstruction was phrased in terms of an ethical analysis of the situation. But the deliberate linkage to the movement that bore that name, and that could now claim to represent virtually "all the forces of . . . society," was unmistakable. Had the Pope not wanted to signal his nonnegotiable support for Solidarity, he could have chosen other words.

The multiple invocations of the Helsinki Final Act struck the Soviet Union at a point of considerable vulnerability, for the USSR had insisted on the Helsinki Final Act as a ratification of the post-Yalta status quo in Europe. What Brezhnev and the Soviet leadership had imagined as the means for securing

Stalin's external empire was now being turned on them. Its provisions on sovereignty and noninterference (a favorite Soviet dodge in the face of human rights criticism) were being used as counters against Soviet hegemony in east central Europe.

John Paul did not, as so often rumored, threaten to fly to Poland in the event of a Soviet invasion. He was not a man to make threats of this sort. Nor did his letter mention the presence of Warsaw Pact troops all along Poland's borders. He did not have to. He based his case on the national rights embedded in an agreement to which both Poland and the USSR were signatory, the Helsinki Final Act. At Helsinki in 1975, the Soviet Union had been pleased to act as if Poland were an independent nation. John Paul's letter to Leonid Brezhnev was a reminder of that moral, if not yet political, truth—and an assertion that moral truth was a potent factor in politics among nations.

The Spring 1981 Crisis

Further evidence that John Paul II analyzed the unfolding drama of east central Europe in primarily religious and cultural terms came on December 31, 1980, when the Pope issued an apostolic letter, *Egregiae Virtutis* [Men of Extraordinary Virtue], naming Sts. Cyril (826–869) and Methodius (c. 815–885), the first evangelists of the Slavic peoples, as co-patrons of Europe along with St. Benedict, the founder of Western monasticism.

Cyril and Methodius were brothers, born to a noble family in Thessalonica. To evangelize Moravia, Cyril created a Slavonic alphabet and translated the Gospels, the letters of St. Paul, the Psalms, and the Roman liturgy, laying the foundations of Slavic literature. By the time of his death, Methodius had completed the translation of virtually the entire Bible. The written word came to the western Slavs, quite literally, through the Word of God. The heirs of Benedictine monasticism had saved the culture of Western Europe during the Dark Ages; Cyril and Methodius had created the possibility of an enduring culture in east central Europe.

The idea of honoring the two brothers matured over a year. In 1979, John Paul had quite spontaneously asked Bishop Jozef Tomko, "What do you think we can do for Cyril and Methodius?" Tomko's first reaction was to suggest that they might be named Doctors of the Church—the honorary title given to Catholicism's most influential theologians. Then, Tomko remembered, the Pope got this "fantastic look in his eye," the kind he gets "when he has an inspiration," and said: "Co-patrons of Europe." It was, according to Tomko, a "great vision," a powerful symbol of the Church's drive to give back to the peoples of east central Europe their authentic history and culture.[35] *Egregiae Virtutis* was generally interpreted in the West as a pleasant but inconsequential papal gesture of Slavic fraternity. For the peoples of east central Europe, it was another potent example of how Christian images had become the primary symbols of a rebirth of cultural integrity and freedom.

As the first quarter of 1981 unfolded, Solidarity struggled to establish itself and to carry out its self-regulating, self-limiting social revolution. In August 1980, Lech Wałęsa had promised himself that if he lived through the Gdańsk shipyard strike and an independent trade union was recognized by the regime, his first journey abroad would be on pilgrimage to Rome to thank John Paul II.[36] On January 15, 1981, a delegation of Solidarity leaders met at the Vatican with John Paul for private conversation and a public audience. The Pope's public remarks captured his distinctive view of the driving force of history, as he described Solidarity as a movement *for*, rather than against, something.

A commitment to the "moral good of society" was the "cornerstone" of Solidarity's work, he said, and the beginning of any "real progress" in national renewal. This was a different kind of revolution. Its efforts were "not directed against anyone" but "directed *toward*: toward the common good" of national reform. The right to such a national renewal, he concluded with an eye toward Moscow, is "recognized and confirmed by the law of nations."[37]

The delegation returned to the Vatican on Sunday, January 18, for Mass and breakfast in the papal apartment. The Pope's homily concluded with an exhortation that Poles "let their work serve human dignity, let it elevate man, let it elevate families, let it elevate the whole people." Solidarity would serve the "great cause" of freedom if everyone involved were animated by a biblical commitment: "'I come, Lord, I come, Lord, to do thy will.'"[38]

The next time Wałęsa would see John Paul II would be "in an entirely different situation," as he wrote in his memoirs.[39]

The Polish situation heated up again as John Paul prepared to leave for his February 1981 Asian pilgrimage. A ten-day strike in Bielsko-Biała ended on February 6 with the removal of the provincial governor and three of his aides.[40] Three days later, amid continuing unrest over the government's refusal to recognize Rural Solidarity, the farmers' attempt to participate in the national reform movement, Defense Minister General Wojciech Jaruzelski was named premier of Poland, the head of the government, and appealed for a ninety-day strike-free period. That same day, workers began a general strike in Jelenia Góra. A brief ray of sunshine in the ever-darkening Polish economic picture came on February 27, when Western nations agreed to reschedule Poland's external debt, but the political pressure on Poland's communist leaders increased less than a week later. First Secretary Kania and Premier Jaruzelski were summoned to Moscow to meet with virtually the entire Soviet Politburo on March 4.

Three months after backing down from a Soviet military solution to the threat posed by Solidarity, the Soviet leadership had evidently decided that there must be a Polish-imposed solution. Solidarity must go, and the preferred option now was the imposition of martial law by the Polish regime, which would take the international censure to follow. In Jaruzelski, whom the Soviets trusted completely, they believed they had the man for the job.[41]

Two weeks later, another crisis exploded in Bydgoszcz after the SB severely beat Solidarity leaders. A four-hour national strike paralyzed the entire country on March 27, 1981, as tens of millions of Poles defied the regime in the largest protest against a communist government in east central Europe's postwar history. A general strike of indeterminate length in support of Rural Solidarity and to demand punishment of those responsible for the beatings in Bydgoszcz was set for March 31. Workers prepared to occupy their factories, and concerns about a Soviet invasion resurfaced as the "Soyuz 81" Warsaw Pact military maneuvers began around Poland's borders.*

On March 28, John Paul sent a message to Cardinal Wyszyński that urged continued dialogue rather than a confrontation on March 31. There could be no national renewal without the government's agreement to abide by the "principles [that had been] established by mutual agreement last autumn." As for the neighbor to the east, the Pope continued to insist that "Poles have the undeniable right to solve their problems by themselves, with their own efforts." Once again, he knelt spiritually with the Primate "before the image of Our Lady of Jasna Góra, given to us 'for the defense of our nation,' and once again I entrust to her this difficult and important moment in the life of our common country. . . ."[43]

The Pope's message was reinforced by a personal plea for restraint from the Primate to the members of Solidarity's National Coordinating Committee, whom Cardinal Wyszyński (already gravely ill with cancer) called to his residence on March 28. Wyszyński had been a firm supporter of Rural Solidarity, but he believed the national interest required that the general strike not take place as scheduled.[44] On March 29, the Soviet news agency Tass turned up the pressure with a mendacious report that Solidarity was planning a counterrevolutionary coup d'etat, setting up roadblocks, planning the occupation of communications centers, intimidating the police, and so forth. That same night, a government representative showed Cardinal Wyszyński posters that had already been printed of the impending martial law declaration.[45]

On March 30, Wałęsa and the Solidarity leadership agreed to suspend the March 31 strike after reaching a compromise agreement with the government. There would be an investigation into the Bydgoszcz beatings, and those responsible would be punished. Rural Solidarity was not recognized immediately, but the government agreed to act as if it were until the formal registration process was completed. Wałęsa was immediately accused of selling out, and several members of the national Solidarity leadership resigned.[46] Though the "Soyuz 81" military maneuvers the Soviet Union was then conducting around Poland's borders were most likely a Soviet bluff, the threat of Polish-imposed martial law seems to have been real. It was certainly assumed to be real by John Paul II and the Primate, and they acted accordingly.[47]

---

*Several authors have suggested that John Paul II met with the Soviet ambassador to Italy on March 28, 1981, in an attempt to defuse the crisis; one traces the beginning of a secret negotiation with Leonid Brezhnev to this alleged meeting. No such meeting took place. [42]

On April 2, Cardinal Wyszyński met the leadership of Rural Solidarity and told the union members that "Solidarity . . . has authority, so we can say that besides the authority of the Party there is also social authority in Poland." The time would come, he concluded, when "socio-economic demands will not be the only ones achieved by this massive movement. . . ."[48] Leonid Brezhnev agreed. The counterrevolution in Poland was clearly under way. The Soviet Politburo had met the same day, in a session featuring blistering criticism of the Polish comrades. In its wake, Kania and Jaruzelski were summoned to a meeting with KGB head Yuri Andropov and Soviet Defense Minister Dimitri Ustinov, held the next night in a railway car parked on a spur near the city of Brest. Over the course of a six-hour meeting that ended at 3 A.M. on April 4, the Poles were pressed to impose martial law. Jaruzelski later claimed that the Soviets threatened military intervention. In any event, the Poles convinced Andropov and Ustinov that they were in sufficient control of the situation, and would take the actions needed at what they judged to be the appropriate time.[49] A week later, on April 10, the Polish parliament banned strikes for two months.

The spring 1981 crisis in Poland seemed to have receded. On April 26, John Paul II traveled to Bergamo and Sotto il Monte, the home of Pope John XXIII, for ceremonies marking the centenary of the late pope's birth. His sermon at the memorial Mass in Sotto il Monte, attended by many of Angelo Roncalli's relatives, praised John XXIII as "truly a man sent by God," who had "left us an immensely rich and precious heritage" in his deep spirituality and in the work of the Second Vatican Council.[50] The homily also cited John XXIII's concern for family life; two weeks later, on May 9, Pope John's third successor gave concrete form to that shared concern by establishing the Pontifical Council for the Family as a permanent office of the Roman Curia. Four days later, on May 13, John Paul planned to begin a new series of general audiences to mark the ninetieth anniversary of *Rerum Novarum,* the historic encyclical of Leo XIII that was the first chapter in modern Catholic social doctrine. He had concluded the second part of his meditations on the theology of the body on April 29 and May 6 with a catechesis on the ethical responsibilities of artists portraying the mystery of the human body, and a humanistic critique of pornography.

Now, he was about to be confronted by another form of obscenity.

THE MARK OF CAIN

Teresa Heydel Życzkowska and her husband, longtime members of Karol Wojtyła's *Środowisko,* had come to Rome in May 1981 to visit their old friend. They had attended a Mass celebrated by the Pope in the Vatican Gardens on May 9, and another Mass for a Jagiellonian University delegation on Tuesday, May 12. Despite the tensions in Poland, the reunion with *Wujek* had been a happy one, and the Życzkowskis were looking forward to the Pope's general audience, scheduled for 5 P.M. on May 13 in St. Peter's Square.

John Paul II lunched that day with friends, Professor Jerome Lejeune and his wife. Lejeune, a distinguished French geneticist who had identified the chromosomal abnormality that causes Down's Syndrome, was a leader in the international pro-life movement.[51] At 5 P.M., precisely on schedule, the small Popemobile, a jeep, drove through the Archway of the Bells and into the square with a smiling John Paul II standing in the back greeting the crowd. The custom was to make a circuit or two of the square before driving the Pope to the *sagrato*, the raised platform in front of the basilica, from which he would address the crowd. The jeep drove slowly along a pathway that had been created by wooden barriers, over which people would often hold their small children for the Pope to pick up and bless. He had just returned a little girl to her parents and was driving toward the Bronze Doors of the Apostolic Palace when, at 5:13 P.M., Teresa Życzkowska, standing on the other side of the vast open space in front of the basilica, heard something peculiar. Hundreds of pigeons had suddenly flown into the evening air. A fraction of a second later, thanks to the peculiar acoustics of the square, she knew the reason why.

Standing behind the first row of pilgrims at one of the wooden railings, Mehmet Ali Agca had just fired two shots at the Pope from a Browning 9-mm semi-automatic pistol. John Paul was struck in the abdomen and fell backward into the arms of his secretary, Monsignor Dziwisz. The image of the inert Pope, flashed around the world later that day, instantly reminded millions of people of artistic renderings of Christ being taken from the cross.[52] Sister Emilia Ehrlich, in the square for the audience, remembered a line from Wojtyła's last poem, "Stanisław," as the about-to-be martyred bishop of Kraków confronted his assassin: if "the word did not convert, blood will convert."[53]

John Paul was rushed to a nearby ambulance and driven through the Roman evening traffic to the Policlinico Gemelli, four miles away. The drive would ordinarily take twenty-five minutes or more; the ambulance made it in eight. The Pope was conscious throughout the drive, murmuring brief prayers. Later, he recalled that "at the very moment I fell . . . I had this vivid presentiment that I should be saved."[54] At the hospital, John Paul lost consciousness, and for what could have been a disastrous moment, confusion reigned. The call from the Vatican to the Gemelli had simply said, "*Il Papa è stato colpito*," which could have meant any number of things—that the Pope had been "hit" or "struck" or "affected"—involving any number of contingencies: a fall, a heart attack, a stroke, a shooting. The initial decision was to make a preliminary examination in the tenth-floor suite of rooms that was always in waiting for him.[55] Amid the chaos on the tenth floor, it quickly became apparent that the patient, whose wounds could not be seen, was *in extremis*, with rapidly falling blood pressure and a weakening pulse. John Paul was rushed to the ninth floor operating theater and prepped for immediate surgery, as Monsignor Dziwisz administered the last rites of the Church to his unconscious leader.[56]

One of the Gemelli's three chief surgeons, Dr. Francesco Crucitti, had been at a hospital on the Via Aurelia when he learned of the shooting. He jumped into his car, raced across town down the wrong side of a two-way street, talked his way past an irate policeman with a submachine gun, and tore into the Gemelli, where, as he said, an "unknown genius" had thought to call all the elevators to the entrance in anticipation of his arrival. He rode to the ninth floor and was assaulted by nurses and assistants who tore off his clothes and got him into his surgical gown and shoes while he quickly scrubbed up. Another doctor called from the actual operating room, "Blood pressure 80, 70, still falling." Crucitti walked into the operating room, where the Pope was being anaesthetized, and started to work.[57]

Agca's bullet had caused havoc inside the Pope's abdomen. On making his incision, Crucitti first found "blood everywhere," six pints of it, which were suctioned out so that the source of the hemorrhaging—the immediately life-threatening problem—could be identified. With the bleeding stanched and transfusions begun, John Paul's blood pressure and pulse rose, and the surgery could proceed, as Crucitti later put it, "more calmly." On exploring the Pope's abdomen, the surgeon found multiple wounds, some due to direct impact, others to the blast effect of the bullet entering the body. The colon had been perforated and there were five wounds in the small intestine. Some five hours of surgery were required to close the colon wounds, remove twenty-two inches of intestine, and perform a temporary colostomy.[58]

At 8 P.M., a preliminary bulletin was released to the press and to the thousands who were still waiting in St. Peter's Square or who had flocked there since news of the shooting had been broadcast. The statement was mildly reassuring but not definitive. A group of Polish pilgrims had brought to the audience a copy of the Black Madonna (who, as they say in Poland, is always there when something happens). After the ambulance had rushed away to the Gemelli, they took the icon and placed it on the empty chair from which John Paul was to have delivered his catechetical message. A gust of spring breeze blew it over, and a bystander noticed the inscription on the back, which had been prepared days, perhaps weeks, before—"May Our Lady protect the Holy Father from evil."[59] Forty-five minutes after midnight, a second bulletin was issued stating that the surgery had been successfully completed and that the patient's condition was satisfactory. The crowd, which had been praying the rosary in the square for more than six hours, gradually dispersed. Teresa Życzkowska and her husband went back to their hotel to await further news of *Wujek.*

The Patient

John Paul would later say that "One hand fired, and another guided the bullet."[60] It was a confession of miraculous intervention that the most secular soul might have been tempted to concede. Agca, a professional assassin, had fired at point-blank range. Yet the bullet that struck the Pope missed the main abdominal artery by the merest fraction of an inch. Had the artery been struck,

John Paul would have bled to death before being transferred from the Pope-mobile to the ambulance. Moreover, the bullet, which might have paralyzed him, missed his spinal column and every major nerve cluster in its potential path. Agca's shot had evidently deflected off the Pope's finger, which was broken. On exiting his body, the spent bullet fell to the floor of the Popemobile, from which it was eventually recovered. A second shot grazed John Paul's elbow before wounding two American pilgrims.[61]

The Pope remained in the Gemelli's intensive care unit for another four days. He had received Holy Communion on the day after his surgery and began concelebrating Mass from his bed on May 17. On the 14th, when he was coming back into full consciousness, he asked Monsignor Dziwisz if they had said Compline, the closing prayer of the liturgical day, yet. Dziwisz gently explained that it was already the next afternoon, but from that point on, John Paul always prayed the entire Liturgy of the Hours, which was recited for him until he gathered the strength to pray it with Dziwisz or his other secretary, Father John Magee.

On May 17, pilgrims in St. Peter's Square heard a tape-recorded message from John Paul II, determined not to miss his weekly Sunday noontime appointment, which ended: "I am particularly close to the two persons wounded together with me. I pray for that brother of ours who shot me, and whom I have sincerely pardoned. United with Christ, Priest and Victim, I offer my sufferings for the Church and for the world. To you, Mary, I repeat: *Totus tuus ego sum.*"[62]

That same day, Italy voted to expand legalized abortion, against which the Pope had campaigned vigorously.

On the afternoon of May 18, a recovering John Paul II was moved out of the intensive care unit and into his suite on the tenth floor, which included a waiting room, a bedroom, a bath, a second bedroom for Monsignor Dziwisz, and a large meeting room in which the Pope's physicians, whom he took to calling "the Sanhedrin," gathered from time to time to discuss the case.[63] The local team was supplemented by an international group of specialists whom Cardinal Casaroli summoned from West Germany, the United States, France, Spain, and Poland—a prudent decision, given the intense international interest in the Pope's situation, his surgery, and his post-operative treatment. The Pole was John Paul's old friend and fellow kayaker, Gabriel "*Gapa*" Turowski, then the head of transplantation and immunology in the Department of Surgery at Kraków's Copernicus Academy of Medicine.[64] Turowski stayed in Rome three months, "keeping company with a suffering friend" and lending his professional expertise to the case. John Paul wrote Turowski's wife, Bożena, thanking her for lending him her husband. The Turowskis were expecting a grandchild. Every day the Pope asked *Gapa* whether he was a grandfather yet, and when the positive answer finally came, sent a blessing to the baby and the parents.[65]

On May 20, John Paul, who had been fed intravenously since his surgery, had his first meal since his lunch with the Lejeunes a week before. After he ate some soup and an egg, he and Dziwisz said the "Te Deum," the Church's traditional hymn of praise. Three days later, the medical team issued a bulletin stating that the Pope's life was no longer in danger. The good news was shadowed by a mysterious fever whose cause baffled the doctors.[66]

The Pope was an active patient, determined to understand what was happening to him and to have a say in his care. He had Dr. Crucitti explain the anatomy and normal workings of the intestine and the way in which the colostomy compensated for his temporary disability. When the doctors gathered for a consultation in the meeting room of his suite, he would poke fun at them afterward: "What did the Sanhedrin say today? What did the Sanhedrin decide on my behalf?"[67] He was joking, but the joke had edge on it. Part of the struggle of an illness, he once told his doctors, was that a patient had to fight to become "the 'subject of his illness' instead of simply remaining the 'object of treatment.'"[68] The dignity of the human person was not surrendered at the hospital door.

Neither were the responsibilities of the papacy. Another crisis was at hand in Poland, as the Primate, Cardinal Wyszyński, was dying. John Paul had sent Monsignor Dziwisz to Warsaw to visit the gravely ill cardinal on May 11 and 12. Dziwisz had returned with a letter for the Pope in a sealed envelope.[69] Communication had continued by phone. Their last conversation took place shortly after noon on May 25. Wyszyński, in great pain, asked in short gasps of breath for the Pope's blessing. John Paul, as if in homage to what the older man had said and done in his life, said that he blessed the Primate's "mouth and hands."[70] The Primate died on May 28; John Paul said his evening Mass for him. Three days later, he followed the funeral ceremonies by radio, stopping to say his own Mass at the same time as the funeral Mass was being celebrated in Warsaw.

It was another sharp blow for John Paul II. Though Cardinal Wyszyński was not the kind of paternal figure for Karol Wojtyła that Cardinal Sapieha had been, Wojtyła admired Wyszyński immensely. His praise for him after the second conclave in 1978 and during his 1979 pilgrimage to Poland was genuine and heartfelt, not simply honorific or tactical. The Primate, for his part, had come to think of his onetime junior as a providential man for Poland and for the Church. The rise of Solidarity had not been the Primate's finest hour, but in the spring 1981 crisis he had made clear that he thought Solidarity was Poland's future.

While John Paul was mourning the Primate and pondering the question of Wyszyński's successor, the papal doctors were becoming worried about their patient's condition. On May 27, the day before Wyszyński's death, the Pope had difficulty breathing, shortness of breath, and chest pains, in addition to the fever. The situation improved somewhat during the next few days, and the medical team agreed that John Paul could return to the Apostolic Palace on June 3 to continue his convalescence at home. The Pope, for his part, wanted to participate in the solemn commemoration of two ecumenical councils on

June 6 and 7: the sixteenth centenary of the First Council of Constantinople, and the 1,550th anniversary of the Council of Ephesus, which had solemnly ratified Mary's title of *Theotokos*, "Mother of God." It was too much to ask of himself. He could only manage a five-minute appearance and message from the loggia of St. Peter's on June 6. A taped message was sent to the celebrations at the Basilica of St. Mary Major on June 7.[71]

By June 10, his fever was rising close to 104° Fahrenheit (39.5° Celsius) and then falling. He had an infection in his right lung, but that could be treated by antibiotics and did not account for the spiking fever and his failure to regain his strength. Fear for his life once again stalked his staff and doctors. The gray-faced Pope looked terrible. His eyes, sunken in dark sockets, had lost their customary intensity and sparkle—and no one knew what the problem was. A drip feed was begun again, and on June 12, a viral expert was called in for consultation. By June 20, the situation had deteriorated to the point where a return to the Gemelli for more tests was imperative. During the next several days, the Pope had a series of X-rays and a CAT-scan, none of which revealed anything. Finally, the proper diagnosis was made. John Paul's system had been invaded by a cytomegalovirus, which had been transmitted to him through a tainted blood transfusion on May 13. The "second agony," as Gabriel Turowski later described it, was the result of his tremendous loss of blood between the shooting and the surgery. The cytomegalovirus has a twenty-four-hour cycle, and there would have been no problem if the donated pint of blood had been kept for a day. The urgency of the situation at the beginning of the surgery had required the use of freshly donated blood. Once the cause of his persistent illness was clear, John Paul characteristically wanted to know what the virus looked like. The doctors showed him the slide from which the diagnosis had been made.[72]

Since there was no antibiotic remedy for viruses, supportive therapy—intravenous feeding, glucose, painkillers, and fever reducers—were administered until John Paul's body rid itself of the cytomegalovirus. By June 24, his temperature had returned to normal, and the medical bulletin that day reported that, with his cardiopulmonary and digestive systems working properly again, "the general situation shows signs of an overall improvement."[73] During the crisis, his doctors told the Pope that he could not read office-related material and should instead read thrillers or something similar for relaxation. John Paul reread Sienkiewicz's *Quo Vadis* and read Jan Nowak's memoir of the Polish Home Army and the Warsaw Uprising, *Courier from Warsaw*.[74]

THE CONTINUING CRISIS

As John Paul continued to recuperate throughout July from the effects of Agca's bullet and what André Frossard described as the "auxiliary terrorist," the cytomegalovirus, he conducted his office from the tenth floor of the Gemelli, where Cardinal Casaroli; Archbishop Martínez Somalo, the *Sostituto*, or chief-of-staff; and Archbishop Silvestrini, the "foreign minister," were constant visitors. The most urgent issue was the appointment of a successor to Cardinal Wyszyński. Cardinal Casaroli was concerned that, if the Soviets invaded Poland and a Primate weren't in place, the Church would lose the capacity to make its own appointments.[75] The Polish Communist Party congress was scheduled to start on July 14 and Solidarity was planning its first national congress for early September. It was important that a successor be named and installed in time for what were bound to be historic, and potentially explosive, events.

The late Primate's candidate as his successor was his former secretary, Józef Glemp, who had been bishop of Warmia and chairman of the Polish bishops' justice and peace commission since April 1979. The two men had had a close personal relationship, but Wyszyński was not a sentimentalist and affection could not have been his only reason for promoting Glemp as his successor. Glemp held doctorates in civil and canon law, and Wyszyński may have thought that this was what was needed in the next phase of the struggle for religious freedom and civil liberties in Poland: a man who knew how to read the fine print of contracts.

Józef Glemp was appointed archbishop of Gniezno and Warsaw, and thus Primate of Poland, on July 7, 1981, almost six weeks after Wyszyński's death. The relatively lengthy interregnum—given the urgency of the Polish situation—cannot be attributed solely to John Paul's physical condition. This was a decision that evidently involved debate and anguish. To appoint Glemp as Primate of Poland would be to put the man in a difficult, almost impossible, situation. Wyszyński had possessed extraordinary personal authority that could not be transferred, even by papal appointment. Wyszyński had been physically imposing; Glemp was physically unprepossessing. Wyszyński was a master at appealing to popular religious sentiment; Glemp, who was at least as intelligent as the old Primate, lacked his personal touch and thought in bureaucratic rather than populist terms. Wyszyński could appeal for unity within the Church and speak with the authority of a man who had defied the regime with his epic *Non possumus*; faced with an activist younger clergy inspired by John Paul II and Solidarity, Glemp could only invoke the authority of office, and thus inevitably appear to be an authoritarian. Glemp had a lawyer's view of negotiations, which was that they should take place between experts—not the approach that would win him the confidence of workers and intellectual dissidents experiencing their first taste of democratic process inside Solidarity. And finally, although no one could ever say it, everyone knew that, with Cardinal Wyszyński's death, the de facto Primate of Poland was in Rome.

Nonetheless, after weeks of wrestling with the decision, John Paul II chose Bishop Glemp. The new archbishop of Gniezno and Warsaw was a dedicated churchman and a Polish patriot. But his selection as Primate would not be a success—for himself, for the Church in Poland, or for the man who made the appointment.

Three days after Archbishop Glemp's nomination, the Polish Communist Party began a tumultuous four-day congress, at the end of which the Politburo and Central Committee were reshuffled and Edward Gierek was expelled from the party. Stanisław Kania survived, for the moment, but the fundamental contradiction in Polish life remained. The party that insisted on the "leading role" in national life had been rejected by the majority of an increasingly assertive nation.[76]

Toward the end of July, John Paul began lobbying his doctors to reverse his colostomy sooner than they had planned. The medical team had proposed waiting until cooler weather in the fall; there were also concerns about risking another tainted blood transfusion so shortly after the cytomegalovirus had been beaten. John Paul insisted that he was strong enough to withstand the procedure. He told a meeting of the "Sanhedrin" that, while they were the technical experts, he had a right to explain his problems as their patient. Among other things, he didn't want to go back to the Apostolic Palace until he was completely well and could put the entire assassination episode behind him. All his life, he said, he had defended the rights of man; "today," he said, "I myself am 'man.'" Dr. Crucitti was impressed. The Pope had reminded his doctors that they were not oracles, and that an individual knew things about himself that clinicians could not measure with their instruments and tests.[77]

At the end of the meeting, the medical team agreed and John Paul set the date of his operation himself: August 5, the feast of Our Lady of the Snows.[78] The hour-long surgery was successful, and the Pope returned to the Vatican on August 14. The next day, he celebrated the great feast of Mary's Assumption in St. Peter's Square with 50,000 congregants, an unheard-of number during a month when Romans are traditionally anywhere but the broiling, humid Eternal City. That afternoon, at 5:30, John Paul flew by helicopter to his summer residence at Castel Gandolfo, where he remained through September.

On September 5, the first Solidarity Congress opened in Gdańsk. That same day the Soviet Union, never renowned for political subtlety, began a massive military and naval exercise in the Baltic, including landings on the coasts of Lithuania and Latvia. But 896 delegates to the congress, representing 9,484,000 Solidarity members, were not deterred, and their deliberations concluded with calls for free elections to the Polish parliament and to local and regional councils; self-management in industry; and the abolition of the *Nomenklatura* system by which only party members could be appointed to governmental posts.[79] The delegates were in a radical mood. Wałęsa was denounced for excessive moderation, and was reelected head of Solidarity with only fifty-five percent of the vote. The Central Committee of the Soviet Communist Party sent its Polish comrades a letter describing the Congress as a "disgusting provocation."[80]

The Congress had opened with a Mass celebrated by the new Primate, Archbishop Glemp. The following day, John Paul signaled his concern about the Soviet reaction to the Congress, telling a group of Polish pilgrims at Castel Gandolfo that "the right of our nation to independence is a condition for world peace." During the Congress itself, John Paul's "voice" was that of his old Kraków friend and intellectual colleague, Father Józef Tischner, the Congress chaplain. His sermon at Mass before the second day of meetings crystallized the difference between Solidarity and the regime, between the Christian concept of work and its Marxist counterpart, by lyrically evoking the Christian humanism he and Karol Wojtyła had discussed for years:

> . . . We must look at the issue [of work] from above, like looking from the peaks of the Tatras, where the waters of the Vistula have their beginning. The very liturgy of the Mass encourages us to do this . . . This bread and this wine shall become in a moment the body and blood of the Son of God. This has a deep meaning. . . . Were it not for human work, there would be no bread and wine. Without bread and wine, there would not be among us the Son of God. God does not come to us through a creation of nature alone, holy trees, water, or fire. God comes to us through the first creation of culture—bread and wine. Work that creates bread and wine paves the way toward God. But every work has a part in this work. Our work, too. In this way our work, the work of each one of us, paves the way to God. . . .
>
> Our concern is with the independence of Polish work. The word *independence* must be understood properly. It does not aim at breaking away from others. Work is reciprocity, it is agreement, it is a multifaceted dependence. Work creates a communion. . . .
>
> We are living history. A living history means one that bears fruit. Christ has said, "Let the dead bury their dead" (*Matthew* 8.22). Thus, let us do the same. Let us become occupied with bearing fruit. . . .[81]

By resolution of the entire assembly, Father Tischner's sermon was included in the official records of the Congress.

Two weeks later, John Paul II gave authoritative form to many of the themes his friend had preached at Gdańsk, in his first social encyclical.

THE GOSPEL OF WORK

Although it traces its intellectual roots back to mid-nineteenth-century Germany and France, modern Catholic social doctrine really begins with Pope Leo XIII's 1891 encyclical *Rerum Novarum*. Pope Pius XI marked this historic document's fortieth anniversary in 1931 with the encyclical *Quadragesimo Anno;* Pope John XXIII extended the tradition of an anniversary encyclical with his 1961 letter, *Mater et Magistra*. John Paul II had intended to continue the custom on *Rerum Novarum's* ninetieth anniversary, but that fell on May 15, 1981, two days after the attempt on his life. During his convalescence the Pope continued to work on the encyclical, and *Laborem Exercens* [On Human Work] was finally published on September 14, 1981.

In *Laborem Exercens*, John Paul II took the discussion of "the social question" in a more humanistic direction than his papal predecessors, focusing on the nature of work and the dignity of the worker. In this respect, *Laborem Exercens* is the most tightly focused social encyclical in the history of modern Catholic social doctrine. It is also the most personal, as John Paul brought his own distinctive experience as a manual laborer to bear in analyzing the moral meaning of human labor.

The most theologically creative sections of *Laborem Exercens* unfold John Paul's teaching that, through work, men and women participate "in the very action of the Creator of the universe," in fulfillment of God's initial command to "Be fruitful, and multiply, fill the earth and subdue it."[82] In work, human beings are called to "imitate God."[83] Work is a vocation to which human beings have been called "from the beginning."

Work is about who we *are*, as well as what we *do* and produce. Whether they be agricultural, industrial, post-industrial, or artistic laborers, workers are above all *persons*, which means that in work, properly understood, human beings are always *becoming* more, not just *making* more. This spiritual and moral character—this "subjectivity"—gives work its genuine value and gives workers their specific dignity.[84]

Work is hard. And yet in spite of this toil—perhaps, in a sense, because of it—"work is a good thing" for human beings. For in work, John Paul writes, "man *not only transforms nature*, adapting it to his own needs, but he also *achieves fulfillment* as a human being and indeed, in a sense, becomes 'more a human being.'"[85] Work is another signal of transcendence, an ordinary reality on the other side of which is an extraordinary truth about human dignity.

That is why, following the tradition of Catholic social doctrine, John Paul teaches "*the principle of the priority of labor over capital*"[86] and rejects what he terms "economism," which is "considering human labor solely according to its economic purposes." The priority of labor over capital also touches the question of ownership. John Paul affirms the right to own private property, but places it under a social mortgage—property, which is meant to make freedom and creativity possible, must be used for the common good.[87] The worker should be "a sharer in responsibility and creativity at the workbench to which he applies himself."[88] Sharing in decision making and profits are expressions, the Pope concludes, of an economic system that recognizes workers as "a true subject of work with an initiative of his own."[89]

In discussing the "rights of workers," John Paul defends a right to employment, a right to a just wage and appropriate benefits, and a right to organize free associations of workers, which includes the right to strike. These, too, were traditional Catholic themes, as was the Pope's affirmation of the "family wage," that is, one sufficient to sustain a family without both parents working simultaneously. John Paul gave this teaching a modern twist by proposing as an alternative social benefits such as "family allowances or grants to mothers devoting themselves exclusively to their families."[90] John Paul's argument that society will benefit when mothers are primarily engaged in child rearing may have offended proponents of some forms of feminism, but it was based on the experience of the communist attempt to erode family life by requiring both parents to work. In any case the Pope insisted that mothers should not be penalized or suffer "psychological or practical discrimination" if they devoted themselves to raising children for various periods of their lives.[91] The argument, as always, was a humanistic one, and paralleled proposals for flex-time arrangements and generous maternal leave policies.

Catholic social doctrine had always regarded unions as "movements of solidarity," instruments for the promotion of social justice.[92] Unions, the Pope teaches, should not only agitate for better wages and conditions, important as these are, they should promote the "subjective" dimension of work, so that "workers will not only *have* more" but will "realize their humanity more fully in every respect."[93]

Throughout the encyclical, John Paul uses the phrase "the Gospel of work" to suggest that work has a spiritual dimension, born from its participation in God's ongoing creation of the world.[94] Work has been ennobled by Christ, who spent the greater part of his earthly life as a worker.[95] Work touches the mystery of redemption when the worker identifies his or her toil and suffering with the passion and death of the Lord. In doing so, the worker participates "not only in *earthly progress* but also in *the development of the Kingdom of God.*"[96]

As this bold theological ending suggests, *Laborem Exercens* is another chapter in the unfolding book of John Paul II's Christian humanism.[97] *Laborem Exercens* also breathes deeply of the spirit of Cyprian Kamil Norwid, the Polish poet who taught the redeeming power of "work accepted with love [as] the highest manifestation of human freedom."[98] Thus *Laborem Exercens* is the first social encyclical in which a poet was a major theological inspiration.

The encyclical's brief discussion of the world economic situation is perhaps its least persuasive section. "The economy" in *Laborem Exercens* remains the economy of the industrial revolution. The dramatic transformation of the global economy through the computer revolution is not on the encyclical's horizon. The encyclical is also empirically questionable at other points: it deplores the increasing costs of raw materials and energy, many of which would fall over the next decades; it worries that the world is becoming "intolerably polluted" when at least part of the world—the free world—was becoming less polluted than it had been in decades.[99] John Paul's vigorous defense of free associations of workers was, without doubt, a powerful endorsement of Solidarity, but the encyclical's failure to discuss the ways in which unions in free economies can become status quo institutions weakened its analysis of contemporary trade unionism.

When it was issued, *Laborem Exercens* was taken to be the Pope's philosophical defense of the Solidarity movement. It was that, and more. Its enduring value lies in adding a richly textured analysis of the dignity of work to John Paul's comprehensive project of revitalizing humanism for the twenty-first century.

THE AGCA MYSTERY

Mehmet Ali Agca was quickly apprehended in St. Peter's Square on May 13, 1981. Since the assassination attempt, he had been in Rome's Rebibbia prison under interrogation. His trial opened on July 20 at the Palace of Justice, before Judge Severino Santiapichi and a six-man jury. The trial began with a reading of what had been learned during the interrogation. By his own description, Agca was an international terrorist allied with other such terrorists, making no distinction between terrorism of the political left or right. He had said that, although he and he alone had decided to attack the Pope, he hadn't meant to kill him. If he had, he would have expended all his ammunition rather than firing twice with the pistol he admitted acquiring in Bulgaria. Agca's testimony to his interrogators was full of inconsistencies and holes, which the report to the trial did not attempt to sort out. The question before this court was whether Agca had deliberately shot the Pope.

The jurisdiction of the Italian court was challenged by the defense attorney appointed to represent Agca on the grounds that the shooting had taken place on Vatican territory. The court dismissed the challenge, citing the 1929 Lateran Treaty between the Holy See and Italy, which covered just such an eventuality. At this juncture, Agca got up, dismissed his lawyer, and made a brief speech in which he "absolutely" rejected the Italian court's jurisdiction, claiming that he had been "within the Vatican State . . . when I shot the head of the Vatican State." Agca then claimed that he had been tortured during his interrogation, dared the Vatican to act as the independent state it claimed to be, and shouted that he would refuse to cooperate with the trial. When Judge Santiapichi asked whether he would answer questions in court, he said, "I will not answer. I do not recognize this court. This trial is finished, thank you."

Why Agca took this line was not clear. He may have been playing for time. He may have been confused because a planned escape from St. Peter's Square had not worked and he was anticipating an effort to extricate him from Rebibbia prison. He may simply have been recalcitrant. Whatever he may have thought he was doing, Agca's refusal to cooperate, and what amounted to a confession of guilt, simplified the court's task. Agca was found guilty and sentenced to life imprisonment on July 22. At Rebibbia the next day, he told a lawyer that he did not want his right to appeal exercised. Why was another mystery.

The formal written verdict that concludes an Italian trial on a grave crime was handed down by Judge Santiapichi on September 25. The judge concluded from the evidence that had accumulated since May that Agca had not acted alone: "The threatening figure of Mehmet Ali Agca suddenly appeared among the crowd to execute, with almost bureaucratic coolness, a task entrusted to him by others in a plot obscured by hatred." Still, the judge conceded, the "evidence . . . has not permitted us to uncover the identity or the motives of the conspirators . . ." With Agca presumably safe in Rebibbia, inaccessible to those who might want to silence him forever to preserve the secret of their own complicity, the investigation could go forward.[100]

Who was Mehmet Ali Agca? The initial rush to judgment in the Western press had it that Agca was a religious fanatic who had tried to kill the Pope out of sectarian zealotry.[101] A variant on this described Agca as a veteran "Grey Wolf," a member of an ultra-nationalist band of Turkish fanatics with fascist political views who, in the words of columnist Georgie Anne Geyer, "hates the West and Christianity and sought the most effective way to attack them."[102] Still others declared Agca simply mad. None of these initial explanations stood up under closer examination. If Agca was a religious fanatic, why was there no history of piety or serious Islamic religious practice in his background? If he was a dedicated fascist or rightist, why did a note left in his room at the Pensione Isa—evidently meant to be found—say that he had shot the Pope to foster freedom in Afghanistan and El Salvador? Agca's association with groups that could be labeled "fascist" or "rightist" could have been cover for an entirely different ideological sponsor. If he was a madman, how did he manage to travel so extensively and purposefully, and why was he capable of behaving in a perfectly rational manner when he chose to do so?

The question of Agca's identity was clearly connected to the question of why he had shot John Paul.

Virtually every Pole sympathetic to the Pope, and perhaps many who were not, assumed that Agca had been acting on behalf of the Soviet Union, either directly or through a third party. A Soviet connection was the most plausible answer to the obvious question, who benefited? The threat that John Paul posed, not only to the Warsaw Pact but to the internal order of the USSR, had already been made unmistakably clear. The Soviet media, a useful barometer of Kremlin thinking, had turned against the Pope in an increasingly nasty way in early 1981. In March, a Byelorussian journal described John Paul as a "cunning and dangerous ideological enemy" who had been part of a Nazi-Vatican plot to exterminate the Polish people during World War II, and a "malicious, lowly, perfidious, and backward toady of the American militarists" singing to the tune of his "new boss in the White House." This vitriol was explicitly linked to the Ukrainian Synod of 1980. That same month, the journal of the Ukrainian Communist Party Central Committee described the Greek Catholic bishops as a "coven of political corpses . . . who had collaborated with the German occupiers."[103] Agca's connections to Bulgarians in Rome and elsewhere confirmed Soviet involvement for many Poles. No one with any experience of a Warsaw Pact country believed for an instant that any Bulgarian would have acted independently of Moscow.

Inside the Vatican, a similar view was widespread, if never even hinted at publicly. Some imagined a kind of Canterbury scenario, in which Leonid Brezhnev (in the role of Henry II) asks whether no one will rid him of this meddlesome priest, and his agents rush to do his bidding, arranging an assassination attempt on John Paul (in the role of Thomas à Becket). A more sophisticated analysis, aware of the degree to which Brezhnev had deteriorated under the ravages of disease, drink, and drugs, looked to Yuri Andropov and the KGB as the initiators of the plot, which Brezhnev (and perhaps the Politburo) then approved. In this scenario, the Soviet Union would have been the prime contractor, through the KGB. The Bulgarian intelligence service would have been the secondary (or even tertiary) contractor, running Agca and then arranging his escape or, far more likely, his elimination.[104]

There is some evidence indicating that an abortive assassination plot, with Agca as triggerman and Lech Wałęsa as the target, was afoot in Rome during the Solidarity leader's January 1981 visit to John Paul II.[105] Although Wałęsa made a plausible target from the Soviet point of view, he was a different kind of figure, the head of an organization with a number of vigorous and outspoken leaders, one of whom would certainly have replaced him. John Paul II was a target of another order of magnitude. When word of Cardinal Wyszyński's fatal illness became known in Moscow, as it surely was by late March 1981, the possibility of a double blow to the Polish threat emerged. If John Paul were assassinated and if Wyszyński died within a brief time frame, the shock might crush Poland's spirit, containing the threat to the Warsaw Pact and the Soviet internal empire.

As these speculations were being bruited by Poles, Vatican officials, and others, Leonid Brezhnev sent the recuperating Pope a terse message, saying, "I am deeply indignant at the attempt on your life. I wish you a rapid and complete recovery."[106] The Soviet press occupied itself with blaming the entire affair on the United States. John Paul, it charged, was an obstacle to U.S. policy in the Middle East and El Salvador.[107]

There remain any number of loose ends in the papal assassination drama, and the full truth about Agca's sponsorship and the plot that led to his act of attempted murder on May 13, 1981, may never be known with certainty. That Agca acted alone because of religious fanaticism is simply not a credible hypothesis, given what is already known about his finances, his travels, his contacts, his weapon, and his prior personal history. The relevant Russian archives remain closed to researchers, and even if they were opened, one imagines that this would not be the sort of thing that made it into the files. The principals in any Soviet plot, if one existed, are all long dead. Barring an unforeseen documentary breakthrough, the debate over why and at whose behest Mehmet Ali Agca shot the Pope will continue. The simplest, most compelling answer to the question, Who benefited? will keep alive the intuition that the Soviet Union was not an innocent in this business.[108]

Agca's target has no interest in a documented answer. The night before he was shot, John Paul II read a brief passage from the New Testament as part of Compline, the Church's nighttime prayer: "Be sober, be watchful. Your adversary the devil prowls around like a roaring lion, seeking someone to devour" (*1 Peter* 5.8). That brief text was all the answer John Paul required to the question of why he was shot. There is evil in the world, its name is legion, and it acts through human agents. No further explanation was necessary, and none, in fact, would be more interesting or enlightening.

THE JESUIT INTERVENTION

Shortly after returning to the Vatican from his autumn post-operative convalescence at Castel Gandolfo, John Paul II intervened in the internal governance of the Church's most prestigious male religious community, the Society of Jesus. On October 5, 1981, he appointed Father Paolo Dezza, SJ, as his "personal delegate" to govern the Jesuits, with Father Giuseppe Pittau, SJ, as his deputy. This unprecedented act was the culmination of years of tension between the Vatican and the Society and a papal challenge to the Jesuits to renew their distinctive vocation in its fullness.

In accepting Ignatius Loyola's sixteenth-century proposal to form an elite religious community characterized by spiritual fervor, high intellectual capacity, bravery, esprit de corps, self-denying discipline, and fierce loyalty to the papacy, the Catholic Church was taking a considerable risk. Elites cause difficulties in any complex organization—jealousy, factionalism, intrigues, and power struggles. But these difficulties were hardly unknown in the pre–Counter-Reformation Church. The gamble taken on the Jesuits was of a different order: that a self-governing, self-perpetuating, and self-consciously elite corps of clergy would not spin off into a different doctrinal and disciplinary orbit, because it would remain tethered to the teaching authority of the Church by a distinctive vow of obedience to the Bishop of Rome. If that tether ever loosened or was broken, an elite that ennobled the rest of the Church could become a freelancing clique, nominally linked to the Church's authority but convinced that its own superior intelligence and moral rectitude allowed it to carve out its own path.

Every great religious charism in the history of Catholicism carries within it a distinctive temptation. The Franciscan temptation, the inversion of St. Francis of Assisi's loving embrace of creation, is to a saccharine spirituality. The Dominican temptation is to an arid intellectualism, the corruption of St. Dominic's goal of creating an intellectually vigorous company of preachers. Benedictines, following the Rule laid down by St. Benedict in the sixth century, take a vow of stability, which binds them to a monastery for life; the Benedictine temptation is to let stability decay into complacency. The Jesuit temptation is to become a self-authenticating elite that, imagining itself more enlightened than the Church's authoritative leadership, no longer holds itself truly accountable to that authority.

Had this happened to the Society of Jesus in the years since the Second Vatican Council? The international leadership of the Society flatly denied it, but some Jesuits were deeply concerned about the course of their community. They pointed to drastic changes in the formation of young Jesuits since the Council, which they believed had dulled the Society's intellectual edge, substituted laxity in discipline and a suffocating psychologism for the sometimes excessive rigors of pre-conciliar Jesuit life, and condoned lifestyles that were hard to distinguish as those of vowed religious, when they did not fall off the edge into corruptions of various sorts.[109] The Jesuits worried about the Society's post-conciliar direction were committed to the Church's social doctrine, and some of them were among its most able exponents. But they believed that Fernando Cardenal, SJ, had jeopardized his priestly vocation and shown dubious judgment by becoming the head of the Nicaraguan literacy program in the employ of a self-proclaimed Marxist-Leninist regime. They deplored the pro-abortion voting record of Robert Drinan, SJ, a member of the United States House of Representatives from Massachusetts. And they wondered why the Society's leadership did not address this new form of political clericalism.[110] Some of the Jesuit faculties of theology throughout the world, once known for the most rigorous doctrinal orthodoxy, were now pushing the frontiers of theological speculation in a way that was sharply criticized by some of their peers, including fellow Jesuits. Leading Jesuit intellectuals had become accustomed to publicly challenging the teaching of the Church or the wisdom of its official teachers.[111]

Numbers do not tell the entire story of a community, but the change in Jesuit demographics was another cause for concern. There were 36,000 Jesuits in 1965, at the close of Vatican II. Slow recruitment and resignations from the ministry had cut that figure to 29,000 in 1975. The figure would continue to fall worldwide throughout the decade and into the 1980s, even though recruitment accelerated in countries like India. Yet the Jesuits remained a major influence among Roman Catholic religious communities, of both men and women. Historically, they had been leaders, and the direction they had taken since the Council seemed to many others the way to the future. That direction had, after all, been confirmed and enthusiastically endorsed by the Society's 32nd General Congregation in 1974.

On December 11, 1978, the Father General of the Society, Pedro Arrupe, a charismatic Basque who had led the Jesuits since 1965, had his first audience with John Paul II, to pledge the Society's obedience to the new Pope. Ten months later, at the September 1979 meeting of the Jesuit Conference presidents, who met annually to undertake an international review of the Society, John Paul addressed the group at Father Arrupe's invitation. The message was blunt and the reaction was shock. Given the brief time they had together, John Paul said, he could not review all the positive things the Society was doing. What he did say was to the point: "I want to tell you that you were a matter of concern to my predecessors and you are to the Pope who is talking to you." In addition to this unambiguous challenge, the Pope sent Father Arrupe a critical talk John Paul I had intended to give to the Jesuit leadership before his death, saying he agreed with everything in it.[112]

In June 1979, Father Arrupe had begun speaking confidentially to the Society's four general assistants, his most senior advisers, about the possibility of his retirement. He had been elected *ad vitalitatem,* he told them, not *ad vitam* (for as long as he had vitality, not for life), and he felt his energies waning. The assistants discussed the matter among themselves and with the Father General. Six months later, on January 3, 1980, Arrupe met again with the Pope to arrange another meeting, to which he would bring his general assistants to present their thinking about the future of the Society and determine how that fit in with his goals for the pontificate. John Paul agreed, but the meeting was not scheduled.

Father Arrupe continued to ponder resignation. In February 1980, he told his four general assistants that he was at peace with his decision to resign. In the first week of March, he requested a consultative vote on his resignation from the assistants, citing age as the sufficiently grave reason required by the Jesuit constitutions. After a week-long formal discernment, the assistants agreed that Arrupe had sufficient reason for resignation. Their judgment was conveyed to him by the senior assistant, an American, Father Vincent O'Keefe, SJ. According to the established procedures, the eighty-five Jesuit provincials throughout the world were then consulted about the possible resignation, to which they overwhelmingly agreed.

According to the Jesuit constitutions, Father Arrupe was obliged to summon a General Congregation, the supreme legislative organ of the Society, which was the only body that could accept or decline his resignation. Arrupe explained this to John Paul at a private audience on April 18, 1980. Father O'Keefe had been accustomed to accompanying the Father General to papal audiences, but in this instance he was left outside the room while the Pope and the General met. (This made the assistant nervous; Arrupe, O'Keefe later said, while normally an "articulate man," became "like a kid" in the Pope's presence, a phenomenon O'Keefe referred to as Arrupe getting "spaghetti legs."[113]) John Paul expressed surprise that the discussion of resignation had proceeded so far and asked Arrupe where, if anywhere, the Pope fit into this. In the Jesuit constitutions, he didn't, Arrupe explained, although the practice had always been to inform the Pope of plans for a General Congregation and discuss them with him. John Paul then asked Arrupe what he would do if John Paul said he should not resign. Arrupe replied that the Pope was his superior. John Paul concluded the audience by saying that he'd think about the problem and would write Arrupe a letter.[114]

Two weeks later, on May 1, John Paul wrote Father Arrupe asking that he not resign and that he not call a General Congregation, for the good of the Society and the good of the Church. After his return from Africa, the Pope continued, they would establish a dialogue to resolve the problem. Arrupe's general assistants assumed that this meant they were, at last, to get their meeting with the Pope, but this was, evidently, not what John Paul had in mind.

On December 30, three of the general assistants, frustrated by their inability to arrange a meeting with the Pope for Arrupe or themselves, cornered John Paul in the Jesuit residence next to the Church of the Gesú, where the

Pope had just finished his traditional year-end Mass with Rome's Jesuit community. When Father Arrupe brought John Paul into the house to meet the younger Jesuits, three of the assistants interposed themselves, encircled the Pope, and said, "Holy Father, we are Father Arrupe's council; we're the ones who wrote to you, and we hope you're going to have time to meet with him because we are in deep waters." John Paul replied, *"Sarà presto"* [It will be soon]. As the papal party was leaving, Monsignor Dziwisz assured Arrupe that the meeting would indeed be soon. It took place on January 17, 1981, but was inconclusive.[115] Meanwhile, the Italian press continued to speculate about a rift between John Paul and Pedro Arrupe, or between the Vatican and the Society of Jesus, or both.

The two men met again on April 13, 1981. John Paul told Arrupe that he was concerned about what a General Congregation might do without Arrupe as superior. (The proposed 33rd General Congregation would have met to accept Arrupe's resignation, elect his successor—widely assumed to be either Father O'Keefe or Father Jean-Yves Calvez, the French general assistant—and continue on with whatever business it chose.) Paul VI had been deeply concerned about the results of the 32nd General Congregation in 1974, the Pope said, and John Paul evidently believed that the situation might become even more difficult at a new, post-Arrupe General Congregation. Arrupe denied that the 32nd General Congregation had defied Pope Paul, and subsequently wrote John Paul a long letter defending its actions. The meeting closed with John Paul assuring Father Arrupe that their dialogue would continue.[116] A month later, the Pope was shot.

On August 7, on returning from a trip to the Philippines, Father Arrupe suffered a stroke at Rome's Leonardo da Vinci International Airport, and was taken to Salvator Mundi hospital. A blocked carotid artery affecting the left side of his brain and the right side of his body was diagnosed. Father O'Keefe gave the stricken General the sacrament of the sick, sent cables to the Jesuit provincials informing them of Arrupe's illness, and called Cardinal Casaroli to appraise him of the situation. Casaroli asked to see Arrupe. O'Keefe responded that the doctors had said that he must be spared any possible emotional distress for fear of another stroke. On August 10, three of the general assistants went to Salvator Mundi to consult the doctors. When they had been informed that Father Arrupe could understand what was said to him and that he could make a decision, they went to his room and asked whether he wanted to appoint a vicar general with full powers to lead the Society during his illness. Arrupe indicated that he did. "Do you have someone in mind?" he was asked. He pointed to Father O'Keefe. Cardinal Casaroli and the Jesuit provincials were then informed that Father Arrupe had appointed Father O'Keefe as vicar general for the duration of Arrupe's illness, according to article 787 in the Jesuit constitutions.

O'Keefe and the other assistants were called in by Father Arrupe's doctors some two weeks later and informed that, in their medical opinion, Arrupe "should never again hold a responsible position." The doctors said that Arrupe was in a condition to receive Cardinal Casaroli, who picked up Father O'Keefe at the Jesuit generalate, en route to Salvator Mundi. On the ride to the hospital, O'Keefe lobbied Casaroli for permission to call a General Congregation, because the Society could not be governed indefinitely by a vicar general. Casaroli deflected the request. When they got to the hospital, he had O'Keefe read Arrupe a personal letter from the Pope, expressing his sympathy, remarking that they were both convalescents, and wishing him well. On the ride back from the hospital, O'Keefe pressed Casaroli again, saying that he had to write the Pope about the need for a General Congregation. Casaroli said that O'Keefe should write to him, and that he'd keep John Paul informed.[117]

The letter was ready by September 3. It explained Arrupe's incapacity and argued that the vicar general should, in these circumstances, convoke a General Congregation. Since this was exactly what John Paul had asked Arrupe not to do, the letter tried to explain what was, from O'Keefe's and the other assistants' point of view, a new situation. A similar letter was sent to the Jesuit provincials.[118] O'Keefe took the letter to Casaroli, who promised to take it to the Pope and said that everything would be resolved when the Pope returned from his convalescence at Castel Gandolfo, in October.

The resolution was not what Father Arrupe or his general assistants had anticipated. On October 6, Father O'Keefe was running a meeting when Arrupe's secretary came in and said that Cardinal Casaroli had called asking to see Arrupe, who was living in the infirmary at the Jesuit headquarters. O'Keefe asked whether the cardinal had asked to speak to the vicar general as well. The secretary replied, "No, not necessarily." O'Keefe arranged to be called when Cardinal Casaroli arrived, and intercepted the Secretary of State in the infirmary before he could go into Father Arrupe's room. Casaroli said that he wanted to speak to Arrupe privately. O'Keefe waited outside the closed door. After about fifteen minutes, Casaroli called O'Keefe in. The cardinal couldn't understand what Arrupe was saying. O'Keefe, noticing some documents on the coffee table, listened carefully, and then told Casaroli that Arrupe wanted O'Keefe to arrange for the cardinal to meet with Father Paolo Dezza. O'Keefe said he would do that, made Casaroli comfortable in a downstairs parlor, summoned Dezza, and then went back to the infirmary. Arrupe pointed to the documents on the coffee table and told O'Keefe to read them to him. It was John Paul II's letter appointing Dezza, who would be eighty in two months, as his "personal delegate" to lead the Society until further notice, with Father Giuseppe Pittau, SJ, the former rector of Sophia University in Tokyo and the Jesuit provincial in Japan, as his coadjutor or deputy.

The normal governance of the Society of Jesus was suspended and there would be no immediate call for a 33rd General Congregation. O'Keefe was "kind of stunned" and asked Arrupe, "Where do you think this leaves this vicar general?" Arrupe said, "I don't know, you go see Father Dezza." O'Keefe went to see the other general assistants and met that afternoon with Father Dezza, who had known that the papal letter was coming. The immediate question was how to inform the Society. The Jesuit generalate and the Vatican agreed that the news would be embargoed until the end of October, by which point the Jesuits of the world would have been privately informed. A Spanish paper broke the story in the fourth week of October, the Italian press picked it up, and Father Dezza agreed with O'Keefe's suggestion that the embargo be lifted.[119] It was the greatest shock involving the Jesuits since Pope Clement XIV had suppressed the Society in 1773.

The papal intervention infuriated those who were comfortable with the Society's direction under Father Arrupe and who wanted it to continue under Arrupe's successor. The claim that the whole affair was the result of a vast mis-understanding based on a misinterpretation of what had happened at the 32nd General Congregation is not persuasive, though. Life in religious orders was in crisis in the years after the Second Vatican Council, and while John Paul may not have thought that the Jesuits were worse off than others, he believed their influence was so great that a period of reflection was called for.[120] If he had not thought highly of the Society's unique charism and role and its poten-tial for contributing to an authentic implementation of Vatican II, he would not have intervened, he told Fathers Dezza and Pittau.[121]

The intervention was shock therapy, intended to break a pattern of con-frontation within the Society, and between the Society and the Church's high-est authorities, creating conditions for a new relationship of greater trust.[122] John Paul II evidently believed that doing that would be impossible at a 33rd General Congregation led by Father O'Keefe. That Father O'Keefe and Father Arrupe's other principal assistants did not see the need for such dramatic change is clear from their urgent efforts to secure papal agreement to a Gen-eral Congregation while the reins of power in the Society remained in the hands they had been in for years—theirs. Given so fundamental a difference in the perception of the realities, some extraordinary remedy was required, and John Paul applied it in the form of a personal intervention in the Society's governance.

It remained to be seen how the Jesuits would react, and whether the rem-edy would be sufficient to the problems John Paul and others perceived.

STATE OF WAR

Two weeks after Cardinal Casaroli's visit to the Jesuit generalate, Poland's cri-sis intensified again. On October 18, 1981, Stanisław Kania was ousted by the party Central Committee and replaced as First Secretary by the premier, Gen-eral Wojciech Jaruzelski, who now had all the levers of power in his hands as leader of the military, the government, and the party. The crisis deepened in November as wildcat strikes spread throughout northern Poland, protesting the rapidly deteriorating economic situation. On November 21, Leonid Brezh-nev wrote Jaruzelski, arguing that there was "no way to save socialism in Poland" unless "a decisive battle with the class enemy" was engaged.[123]

John Paul II agreed with the first half of Brezhnev's proposition. Meeting in Rome in early November with a group of Solidarity-supporting Polish intellectuals, he had given them hope by telling them that the freedom movement in Poland was irreversible. People who had regained a sense of their dignity would not be mutely acquiescent in public life. Communism was finished. They were in the endgame, for however long that took to play itself out.[124] John Paul and his visitors all intuited that something ugly was in the wind, however, and the meeting broke up earlier than expected. The Solidarity leaders felt they had to get back to Poland before the storm broke, and they left the Pope sharing their sense of foreboding.[125]

While Poland approached what everyone sensed was a dramatic crossroads, John Paul maintained his breakneck pace of work. Between Jaruzelski's appointment as First Secretary on October 18 and the second week of December, the Pope met with thirteen different groups of bishops—from Angola and São Tome, the Sudan, Ghana, Ivory Coast, North Africa, Mali, and five regions of Italy—each making their quinquennial *ad limina* visits to Rome. On November 11, he started his third series of general audience catecheses on the theology of the body, which had been interrupted by the assassination attempt. The first address in the series began with some papal irony: "After a rather long pause, we will resume today the meditations. . . ."[126] John Paul made another attempt to rally the Hungarian Church with a November 12 letter marking the 750th anniversary of the death of St. Elizabeth of Hungary, and signed *Familiaris Consortio*, the apostolic exhortation completing the 1980 Synod on the Family, ten days later.

On December 8, the feast of the Immaculate Conception of Mary, John Paul celebrated Mass at the Basilica of St. Mary Major and renewed the act of consecration by which the bishops celebrating the 1,550th anniversary of the Council of Ephesus in June had commended the world and the Church to Mary. Earlier that day, at the noon Angelus, John Paul had blessed a mosaic icon, *Maria, Mater Ecclesiae* [Mary, Mother of the Church], which he had had affixed to a corner of the Apostolic Palace overlooking St. Peter's Square. It was the first image of Mary among the 153 statues atop St. Peter's Basilica and its flanking colonnades.[127] Three days later, John Paul visited the Lutheran church in Rome to pray with its minister and congregation.

Meanwhile, the economic situation in Poland continued to decay as the tension between Solidarity and the government increased. The currency was virtually worthless; medicines were unavailable; milk and infant formula were difficult to come by.[128] On November 28, the Central Committee of the Polish Communist Party instructed the communists in the parliament to introduce legislation giving the government emergency powers, including the authority to ban strikes. To a Solidarity leadership already stretched to the breaking point between government pressure and its membership's restlessness, this could only appear as an attempt to reverse the gains of August 1980. The leaders deployed the only weapon they had left, threatening a twenty-four-hour general strike if the legislation were introduced, and a general strike of indeterminate length if it were passed. Attempting to get some sort of dialogue going again, Archbishop Glemp sent letters to every member of the Sejm, to General Jaruzelski, to Lech Wałęsa, and to the Independent Student Union urging moderation on all parties.[129] It was too late. Indeed, it had probably been too late on November 4, when Jaruzelski met with the Primate and the Solidarity leader to broach the possibility of a new forum for ongoing dialogue, a "Front of National Accord."

On December 11 and 12, the Solidarity National Coordinating Commission met in Gdańsk to consider its options. Those who tried to make phone calls or use the telex around midnight discovered that that was impossible. General Wojciech Jaruzelski's coup against the nation had begun.

At precisely 11:57 P.M. on December 12, all 3.4 million private telephones in Poland went dead simultaneously. Roadblocks were set up throughout the country and tanks rolled through the streets of Warsaw. Virtually the entire Solidarity leadership was arrested at their Gdańsk hotels. Wałęsa was seized at his apartment, having declined to hide despite warnings of his impending arrest. Jaruzelski, worried that in a slow-motion crackdown the outraged workers would turn their factories into fortresses, had decided to decapitate the movement's leadership, and the Gdańsk meeting of National Coordinating Commission had given him the opportunity to implement it swiftly. Poles waking up early on Sunday morning, December 13, discovered that their country had been invaded and occupied by its own army, assisted by the SB, whose computer at Gdynia had the last known address of every Pole. Four thousand men and women had been arrested overnight.[130]

Since there was no provision for martial law in Poland's communist legal code, what had just been done was technically known as the introduction of a "state of war." That was the phrase General Jaruzelski used when he broadcast to the nation at 6 A.M. Sunday morning, announcing the formation of a governing Military Council of National Salvation. Poles thought that he had gotten that much, at least, right. "The power" had declared war on "the society."

The Primate was informed at 5 A.M. on Sunday morning that Jaruzelski would announce martial law an hour later. Archbishop Glemp was told that he would be free to move around the country, and that if he needed a telephone, he might have the use of one at the office of the Council of Ministers, a mile and a half away from his residence. John Paul had been given the news some four hours earlier, at about 1 A.M., when the Polish ambassador to Italy called with word that Jaruzelski had decided upon "temporary emergency measures."[131] With the phones cut off in Poland, the Pope was unable to reach his bishops or anyone else.

The next evening, a prayer vigil for Poland was held in St. Peter's Square. John Paul addressed the thousands present from the window of his study and used the word "solidarity" six times in thanking them for their concern for his homeland. On Wednesday, at his weekly general audience, John Paul invoked the now-banned union's name twice more, and alluded to Solidarity's informal motto ("So that Poland shall be Poland"), stating that Poland's struggle was for "the right to be itself."[132] The Sunday and Wednesday statements were broadcast on Vatican Radio, now one of Poland's few links to the outside world.

Violence broke out in different parts of the country; Silesia maintained its resistance the longest, and the repression there was the worst. Near Katowice, 1,300 coal miners had barricaded themselves inside the "Piast" mine, where they held out until after Christmas. An attempted assault on the mine on December 16, using tear gas and rubber bullets, had cost the lives of nine miners and four security police personnel. More than forty people were injured.[133] John Paul wrote directly to General Jaruzelski with an "urgent and heartfelt appeal . . . a prayer for an end to the shedding of Polish blood." He concluded with "an appeal to your conscience, General, and to the conscience of all those who must decide this question."[134]

It seems that it was indeed General Jaruzelski who had decided the question. There is no evidence that the Soviet Union was planning military action against Poland in December 1981. Instead, the Soviet leadership declined Jaruzelski's requests for a small contingent of Soviet troops to come into the country after the imposition of martial law (Jaruzelski, no fool, was evidently eager to have the odium spread to his allies in Moscow). Poland was put under martial law in December 1981 not because that was the only way to prevent a Soviet invasion, but because Jaruzelski failed to do what Władysław Gomułka had done in 1956: call the Soviet bluff, which in this instance had been going on throughout the year.

General Jaruzelski was not a traitor. He did not seek Soviet intervention, which hard-liners in the Polish Communist Party would have welcomed, nor did he liquidate the Solidarity leadership when he had them under his control, as the Soviets surely would have done in December 1980 and as Polish party hard-liners likely wanted to do in December 1981. He misread the threat of Soviet military action, and he missed an opportunity to accelerate the process of Poland's freeing itself from the Soviet orbit. The Soviet Union was in no position to intervene militarily in Poland in December 1981. Jaruzelski had a firm enough grip on power that he could have faced down his own hard-line comrades, if it came to that. The only plausible explanation for why he took the course he did, rather than exercising real leadership by facilitating a national dialogue aimed at real change, is that he was what the Pope, the Polish Church, and the Solidarity leadership all thought him to be—a convinced communist.

Karol Wojtyła had always loved the Christmas season. Christmas 1981 was undoubtedly his most unhappy Christmastide since World War II. On Christmas Eve at 6 P.M., a candle appeared in the audience window of the Apostolic Palace—John Paul's participation in a worldwide symbolic gesture of support for Poland launched by two Swiss clergymen, Maurice Graber, a Protestant, and Andre Babel, a Catholic.[135] His traditional Christmas blessing *Urbi et Orbi* concluded with a special greeting to "my beloved fellow-countrymen," and especially to "those who are suffering, who have been taken away from their dear ones, those who are afflicted by depression, even by despair."[136] John Paul's World Day of Peace message for New Year's Day, 1982, denounced the "false peace of totalitarian regimes." That same day, at the Angelus, he thanked all who were praying for Poland and asked that they continue to do so, because what was at stake there was "important . . . not only for a single country, but for the history of man."[137]

He spoke as a Polish patriot, but he was always more than that. His culture-driven view of history gave him an insight into the travail of his country that transcended nationalism. That distinctive angle of vision on events also gave him an intuition of the future that, to many of his beleaguered countrymen, seemed hard to believe. Martial law for them was the end of a dream, or at least a lengthy interruption in their road to freedom. John Paul II saw it as a desperate move by a crumbling regime, and was confirmed in that view by General Jaruzelski's wooden reply on January 6 to the Pope's December 18 letter.[138]

What he had told Solidarity's intellectual leaders in November still held true. He delivered the same message to the diplomatic corps accredited to the Holy See at their annual New Year's meeting on January 16. Because human dignity was "inscribed in human conscience," the quest for freedom was a rising, not a receding, tide in world affairs.[139]

POLITICAL CRISIS/EVANGELICAL SOLUTION

Five months later, John Paul's own diplomatic ingenuity got a serious testing. The first papal pilgrimage to Great Britain had been scheduled to begin in late May 1982. Eight weeks before the Pope was due to arrive in London, Argentina's military dictatorship seized control of the Falkland Islands in the South Atlantic, a British possession for the past 149 years. The Argentines had long claimed that British possession of the islands (which they referred to as "Las Malvinas") infringed on their sovereignty. What Britain saw as an invasion, the Argentine regime saw as the recovery of lost territory it did not propose to leave again. A British battle fleet assembled and set sail for the South Atlantic to eject Argentina from the Falklands by force.

The impending war put John Paul II in an exceptionally difficult position. The planned visit to Great Britain had aroused considerable hopes. The Catholic population of the United Kingdom was enthusiastic. An important ecumenical meeting had been scheduled with Archbishop Runcie, the head of the Anglican Communion, at Canterbury Cathedral. In a longer historical perspective, the visit seemed set to mark an end to hundreds of years of British suspicions about Catholicism and the Vatican. On the other hand, Britain was about to go to war with Argentina, a formally Catholic country, and to make matters even more complicated, Argentina had been the military aggressor in the current Falklands conflict. Vatican diplomats worried that a papal visit to a belligerent power in the midst of active hostilities would jeopardize the Holy

See's neutrality in international politics. The British bishops desperately wanted the visit to go forward and worried that a cancellation would have a terribly demoralizing effect on British Catholics. The Argentine bishops wondered how the Pope could visit a Protestant country making war on a smaller Catholic country. From many Argentines' point of view, the Malvinas conflict was a matter of a Third World country struggling against First World colonialism. Wasn't John Paul II a champion of the Third World and hadn't he spoken forcefully against colonialism?

As the Argentines dug in on the islands and the British fleet continued its arduous voyage south, the papal pilgrimage to Britain seemed impossible—until John Paul II arrived at an ingenious solution. Collegiality among the world's bishops was the first step in his approach. On May 18, at the height of the fighting in the Falklands, and with Cardinal Basil Hume and several other British bishops already in Rome for a last-ditch effort to salvage the papal visit, John Paul summoned cardinals and bishops from Argentina to an urgent meeting. During the next several days, the issues were thrashed out under John Paul's leadership, and the Pope decided that an insuperable political dilemma could only be resolved by an evangelical and pastoral solution. He would visit *both* Britain and Argentina, a strategy advocated by Cardinal Hume, and he would go as an advocate of peace and a messenger of reconciliation.[140] On May 22, the Pope concluded the consultation by concelebrating Mass at the papal altar in St. Peter's with the British and Argentine bishops.

The papal pilgrimage to the United Kingdom was a great success, the Pope visiting Canterbury, Coventry, Liverpool, Manchester, York, Edinburgh, Glasgow, and Cardiff, in addition to London. Meeting Queen Elizabeth II at Buckingham Palace, John Paul assured her of his prayers for the safety of her son, Prince Andrew, a helicopter pilot in the Falklands War. The Pope also had ecclesiastical reconciliation on his agenda. Praising the Reformation-era Catholic martyrs John Fisher and Thomas More at Westminster Cathedral, the Pope remarked that, "In this England of fair and generous minds, no one will begrudge the Catholic community pride in its own history." The next day, John Paul and Archbishop Runcie jointly presided over a prayer service in Canterbury Cathedral, a historic ecumenical first. The Pope and the archbishop signed a Common Declaration of Unity, reviewing the ecumenical dialogue since Vatican II and expressing their hopes for the future. The declaration was, arguably, the high-water mark in post–Vatican II Anglican–Roman Catholic relations.[141]

John Paul left the United Kingdom on June 2, and arrived in Buenos Aires nine days later for a two-day visit. Although the formal surrender did not take place until June 15, it was clear that Argentina would lose the Falklands/Malvinas War. The hurriedly arranged papal visit became an opportunity to offer encouragement to a people suffering a bitter defeat. Archbishop Alfonso López Trujillo, the President of CELAM, had been invited to the May consultation in Rome, and on returning to Colombia had quickly organized a special assembly of CELAM to meet John Paul in Buenos Aires. The papal visit to Argentina was, formally, a pilgrimage to the shrine of Our Lady of Lujan. The CELAM meeting, with bishops from all over Latin America, was intended to make clear throughout the continent that the papal visit was a "crusade for peace." John Paul's role in preventing war between Argentina and Chile three years before helped give credibility to this interpretation of the visit.[142]

The twin visits to Great Britain and Argentina marked the end of two years of continual crisis that had begun with the struggle over Solidarity's legal registration and continued through Agca's assassination attempt, the death of Cardinal Wyszyński, the Pope's difficult recuperation, his intervention in the governance of the Jesuits, the imposition of martial law in Poland, and the beginning of the struggle to sustain the Solidarity movement. For all the difficulties involved, those sixteen days in late May and early June 1982 seemed a fitting coda to this phase of the pontificate. Presented with a dilemma that would have been unresolvable before, the Pope had found an evangelical and pastoral solution to the problem, because he had changed the way the papacy functioned in the Church and in the world.

13

Liberating Liberations

The Limits of Politics and the Promise of Redemption

NOVEMBER 25, 1981	Cardinal Joseph Ratzinger appointed Prefect of the Congregation for the Doctrine of the Faith [CDF].
FEBRUARY 27, 1982	Jesuit provincials meet with John Paul.
MAY 13, 1982	John Paul II visits Marian shrine of Fatima on first anniversary of assassination attempt.
JUNE 7, 1982	John Paul and President Ronald Reagan meet in the Vatican.
OCTOBER 10, 1982	Pope John Paul II canonizes St. Maximilian Kolbe as a martyr.
NOVEMBER 28, 1982	John Paul establishes the Church's first Personal Prelature for Opus Dei.
JANUARY 18–19, 1983	Vatican consultation reviews draft U.S. bishops' pastoral letter on nuclear weapons.
JANUARY 25, 1983	Apostolic Constitution, *Sacrae Disciplinae Leges*, promulgates new code of Canon Law; Apostolic Constitution, *Divinus Perfectionis Magister*, revises process for beatifications and canonizations.
FEBRUARY 2, 1983	John Paul II creates eighteen new cardinals at his second consistory.
FEBRUARY 24, 1983	Emergency Vatican consultation considers risks of papal pilgrimage to Nicaragua.
MARCH 2–9 1983	John Paul visits Central America.
MARCH 25, 1983	The Holy Year of the Redemption opens.
JUNE 16–23, 1983	John Paul's second pastoral pilgrimage to Poland.
JULY 21, 1983	General Jaruzelski formally lifts "state of war" in Poland.
AUGUST 1983	First biennial international humanities seminar at Castel Gandolfo.

SEPTEMBER 2, 1983	33rd General Congregation of the Society of Jesus opens in Rome.
SEPTEMBER 29– OCTOBER 29, 1983	Synod of Bishops considers penance and reconciliation in the Church's mission; Synod's work is completed by apostolic exhortation, *Reconciliatio et Paenitentia,* issued on December 2, 1984.
OCTOBER 5, 1983	Lech Wałęsa awarded Nobel Peace Prize.
OCTOBER 31, 1983	Papal letter to Cardinal Johannes Willebrands marks Martin Luther's quincentenary.
NOVEMBER 16, 1983	John Paul II sends personal letter to Chinese leader Deng Xiaoping, requesting direct contact with the Chinese government.
DECEMBER 27, 1983	John Paul II visits Mehmet Ali Agca in Rome's Rebibbia prison.
JANUARY 10, 1984	Full diplomatic relations established between the Holy See and the United States of America.
JANUARY 26, 1984	John Paul names John J. O'Connor Archbishop of New York.
FEBRUARY 11, 1984	*Salvifici Doloris,* apostolic letter on the Christian meaning of suffering.
APRIL 8, 1984	Cardinal Bernardin Gantin named prefect of the Congregation for Bishops; Cardinal Roger Etchegaray named President of the Pontifical Council for Justice and Peace.
MAY 2–12, 1984	Second papal pilgrimage to Asia.
JUNE 12, 1984	John Paul addresses World Council of Churches in Geneva.
AUGUST 6, 1984	CDF issues *Instruction on Certain Aspects of the Theology of Liberation.*
SEPTEMBER 9–21, 1984	John Paul's first pastoral pilgrimage to Canada.
OCTOBER 19, 1984	Father Jerzy Popiełuszko murdered by Polish state security officers.
MARCH 22, 1986	CDF issues *Instruction on Christian Freedom and Liberation.*

On February 22, 1983, Archbishop Andrea Cordero Lanza di Montezemolo, the apostolic nuncio in Nicaragua, was enmeshed in preparations for a controversial papal visit scheduled to begin in ten days when he got an unexpected phone call from Archbishop Eduardo Martínez Somalo, the *Sostituto* of the Vatican Secretariat of State. "This is urgent," the *Sostituto* said. "The Pope wants to see you, Archbishop Obando, and Bishop Barni right away. Take the first plane." The nuncio protested: "We're in the last stages of organizing the visit." His superior was sympathetic and said, "I'll talk with the Pope and get back to you." Martínez Somalo called back the next day with a one-word instruction: "Come."

The next plane out was to Miami, so the nuncio, Archbishop Miguel Obando Bravo of Managua (the leader of the Nicaraguan Church), and Bishop Julian Luis Barni, an Italian Franciscan missionary who was due to host the Pope in León, flew to Florida and then caught a plane for Rome, where they were met at the airport and taken directly to the Vatican. There, they went immediately into a meeting with John Paul II and his three senior curial officials: Cardinal Agostino Casaroli, Archbishop Martínez Somalo, and Archbishop Achille Silvestrini, the Vatican's "foreign minister." The Curia was worried about a possible catastrophe in Managua.

John Paul immediately got down to business. "Everything seems ready," he said, "but there's a lot of opposition to the visit. Should we cancel it? What do you think?" Montezemolo said that Archbishop Obando and Bishop Barni should respond first, so that what he said wouldn't prejudice their answers. The two bishops reviewed the pros and cons of the visit, but seemed hesitant to offer a definitive recommendation. John Paul then asked Montezemolo again: "What do you think?"

The Pope's representative in Nicaragua said there were three things to consider: "There are possibilities, probabilities, and a certainty. The possibility is that we will make an agreement [with the regime about the visit], and they won't respect it. The probability is that they will try to force something into the program. What is certain is that they will do everything they can to manipulate the Pope in favor of their revolution." John Paul then asked Montezemolo whether, in his judgment and in light of the dangers, he should go. The nuncio replied, "Now we've gotten to the point where canceling the visit would be worse than going ahead with it"—a judgment seconded by Archbishop Obando and Bishop Barni.

It was then about 1 o'clock. The Pope, who had been listening intensely and asking sharp questions, said, "Come back later this afternoon and you'll have an answer." When the three returned, the Pope was occupied with another issue that demanded his attention, but they met with Casaroli, Martínez Somalo, and Silvestrini. Cardinal Casaroli said that the Pope had decided to go. Montezemolo should return to Managua immediately and do everything in his power to deal with "the possibility, the probability, and the certainty."[1]

The veteran diplomats in the Secretariat of State were justifiably nervous about a papal visit to a country with an uncooperative, even hostile, regime. Some of them feared for the Pope's physical safety in Sandinista Nicaragua—things could always get out of control.[2] Christian liberation had become one of the leitmotifs of his pontificate, however, and John Paul II was determined to preach it. If there was going to be trouble in Nicaragua, he would face it when it came. But he would not back down when confronted by threats, implicit or otherwise. That was not part of the job description as he understood it.

No Coincidences

Given John Paul II's role in igniting the Solidarity revolution in Poland and the impact the Polish revolution eventually had on late twentieth-century history, numerous commentators have been tempted to analyze his as a "political papacy." Some depict the Pope as a wily diplomat, carefully negotiating Poland's transition to freedom with its failing communist masters.[3] Others portray a grandmaster of the geopolitical chessboard, the co-creator of a vast conspiracy to bring European communism to its knees.[4] Then there is John Paul II, prophet of nonviolence, whose underground resistance struggle in post–martial law Poland takes its place alongside Gandhi's Indian independence campaign and Martin Luther King, Jr.'s American civil rights movement in the annals of admirable twentieth-century politics.[5]

There is truth in each of these variations on the theme of John Paul II, "political pope." John Paul did in fact display impressive diplomatic skills throughout the 1980s. He did have what seemed an almost clairvoyant view of the path down which history was traveling. He did insist that authentic liberation from totalitarianism could not adopt totalitarianism's violent instruments if it were to remain true to its purposes. In saying what he said and in doing what he did, though, the Pope did not understand himself to be acting primarily as a world political figure or a statesman.

John Paul II's personal answer to the question of how his papacy, and indeed his life, should be understood came in Portugal, at the shrine of Our Lady of Fatima, on May 12 and 13, 1982. He had gone there on pilgrimage on the first anniversary of Mehmet Ali Agca's assassination attempt, to give thanks to God and to Mary for his life having been spared. Arriving in Fatima, the Pope succinctly summarized his view of life, history, and his own mission in one pregnant phrase: "in the designs of Providence there are no mere coincidences."[6]

The assassination attempt itself, the fact that it took place on the date of the first Marian apparition at Fatima, the reasons it took place, his survival—none of this was an accident, just as the other incidents of his life, including his election to the papacy, had not been accidents. And this, he believed, was true of everyone. The world, including the world of politics, was caught up in the drama of God's saving purposes in history. That, to his mind, was the message the Second Vatican Council wanted to take to a modern world frightened by what seemed to be the purposelessness of life. The Church's primary task was to tell the world the story of its redemption, whose effects were working themselves out, hour by hour, in billions of lives in which there were no "mere coincidences."

Politics did have a bearing on this. To carry out its primary task, the Church asked the world for the freedom in which to make its evangelical proposal, and the Church asked that the world consider the possibility of its redemption. That was all the Church asked, but the very asking had public implications, for only a certain kind of state could grant what the Church asked. The Church's basic *evangelical* mission made the Church anti-totalitarian, because the things the Church asked of the world set boundaries on the reach and the pretensions of government.

The Church that evangelizes is always a *public* Church, for evangelization is always a public proposal and both the making of the proposal and its content have public consequences. Yet the Church engages the world not as another contestant for power, but as a witness to the truth about the human person, human community, human history, and human destiny. The Church had not always acted that way, historically. This was the kind of "public Church" envisioned by the Second Vatican Council, however, and the kind of public Church John Paul II, calling himself the "particular heir" of the Council, intended to foster.

John Paul II's evangelically focused view of history and politics helps get into focus his relationship to another salient actor on the world stage in the 1980s, Ronald Reagan, President of the United States.

The Pope and the president held certain common convictions. They both believed that communism was a moral evil, not simply wrongheaded economics. They were both confident of the capacity of free people to meet the communist challenge. Both were convinced that, in the contest with communism, victory, not mere accommodation, was possible. Both had a sense of the drama of late twentieth-century history, and both were confident that the spoken word of truth could cut through the static of communism's lies and rouse people from their acquiescence to servitude.

As a candidate for the presidency, Reagan had watched a news clip of John Paul II's Mass in Warsaw's Victory Square on June 2, 1979, and was deeply moved, according to his aide Richard Allen.[7] John Paul II, for his part, needed no convincing about the truth of President Reagan's most controversial anti-communist statement—the Polish Pope had known for more than thirty years that the Soviet Union was an empire and that its system was evil. President Reagan admired the Pope enormously and wanted him kept fully informed about U.S. intelligence findings in east central Europe. He also recognized that the Catholic Church had its own interests and its own methods in the contest with communism.[8] John Paul, who once described Reagan as "a good President," was nonetheless determined to maintain his freedom of analysis and action. The Church would not become mortgaged to any state's political agenda.[9]

When they first met, on June 7, 1982, John Paul II and Ronald Reagan recognized in each other a parallelism of interests in challenging the Yalta system. But the claim that the two men entered into a conspiracy to effect the downfall of European communism is journalistic fantasy.[10] From the point of view of the Soviet Union, John Paul II had done his maximum damage during his epic pilgrimage to Poland in June 1979, seventeen months before Ronald Reagan was elected president and nineteen months before he took office. Reagan's decision to share U.S. intelligence with John Paul was appreciated, but

John Paul had his own extensive sources of information in east central Europe, and there is no evidence that anything he learned from U.S. satellite photography or other intelligence sources made any fundamental change in his view of a situation or in his action. Stories of the Pope bent over highly classified photographs of Soviet military installations may titillate some imaginations, but they tell us nothing of consequence about the history of the 1980s, hidden or otherwise.[11] There was no "deal" between the United States and John Paul II in which support for Poland was traded for Vatican silence on the emplacement of NATO intermediate-range nuclear missiles in Europe or on U.S. policy in Central America.[12] To suggest that John Paul would consider such tradeoffs betrays a fundamental ignorance about the man's character.

John Paul II and Ronald Reagan were both committed to the liberation of what their generation called "the captive nations." They pursued different paths to the same goal. There was no conspiracy.[13]

THE UNIVERSAL CALL TO HOLINESS

While Poland suffered through General Jaruzelski's "state of war" and John Paul did what he could to support his countrymen, he took several internal initiatives that left large imprints on a Church standing at the threshold of the twenty-first century.

A Unique Partnership

Three weeks before Jaruzelski's coup against Polish society, John Paul made the single most important curial appointment of his papacy, naming Cardinal Joseph Ratzinger, archbishop of Munich-Freising since 1977, as Prefect of the Congregation for the Doctrine of the Faith [CDF].

Ratzinger was born on April 16, 1927, in a village in Upper Bavaria, the youngest of three children. His theological studies took place after the war at a time of great intellectual ferment in German Catholic circles. After ordination to the priesthood, a postdoctoral dissertation on St. Bonaventure, and a year of parish work, Father Ratzinger became one of the youngest and most popular theology professors in Germany and an adviser to Cardinal Joseph Frings of Cologne. Frings was one of the leaders of the party of reform at Vatican II, and Ratzinger helped draft the cardinal's interventions, three of which played significant roles in setting the Council's course at its first session in 1962. In the last phase of the Council, Ratzinger began to be concerned that some thinking about the Church's action in the modern world was getting uncoupled from the *Dogmatic Constitution on the Church*. Returning to Germany and a teaching position at the University of Tübingen, Ratzinger became even more concerned by the radical direction several post-conciliar German theologies were taking, not least in their dalliance with Marxism.[14]

When his intellectual colleagues at the Council, with whom he had helped establish the international theological journal *Concilium*, declined to challenge these trends, Ratzinger and a number of other influential Vatican II theologians (including Karol Wojtyła's friend, Henri de Lubac, SJ) launched another journal, *Communio*, to promote what they regarded as a more authentic interpretation of the Council. The *Concilium/Communio* split was not just an intellectual parting of the ways. Friendships were broken, and in the course of the ensuing polemics, Ratzinger found himself an object of contempt (*odium theologicum*, as it is sometimes called) in the eyes of some former colleagues. Amid these controversies, he produced an *Introduction to Christianity*, based on his 1967 Tübingen lectures, which was thoroughly contemporary in its use of biblical, philosophical, and theological materials. Despite the important differences between the *Concilium* and *Communio* interpretations of Vatican II, both groups understood themselves to be heirs of the Council, and both were clearly opposed to Council rejectionists like the dissident French Archbishop Marcel Lefebvre.

In the space of three months in the spring of 1977, Paul VI lifted Ratzinger out of his academic chair, named him archbishop of Munich-Freising, and created him cardinal. Ratzinger got to know Karol Wojtyła personally for the first time at the conclaves of 1978; the two had been exchanging books since 1974.[15] Shortly after his election, John Paul II, who wanted to make the Bavarian cardinal Prefect of the Congregation for Catholic Education, said to Ratzinger, "We'll have to have you in Rome." Ratzinger replied that it was impossible so soon after his arrival in Munich; "you'll have to give me some time," he told the Pope. When the Prefecture of the Congregation charged with promoting the Church's theological life and defending orthodoxy came open, John Paul asked again and, Ratzinger says, he "could not resist a second time."[16]

For more than a decade and a half, Ratzinger was subjected to caricature as the fierce *Panzerkardinal*, heir of the Inquisitors, or as a gloomy German out of sorts with modernity. In 1996 and 1997, when his attractive personality shone through a book-length interview, it was said that the cardinal had changed.[17] He hadn't. Those willing to look beyond the caricature when Ratzinger was appointed Prefect of CDF could find several important clues to John Paul II's thinking about the Church's post-conciliar theological situation.

First, Ratzinger's appointment indicated that the Pope took theology and theologians very seriously. By reason of his own contributions to theology and his encyclopedic knowledge of the Western theological tradition, Ratzinger was regarded by friend and foe alike as a theologian of the first caliber. Naming a man of this intellectual quality rather than a curial veteran as Prefect of CDF was an expression of the Pope's eagerness to foster a genuine renewal of theology.

Ratzinger's appointment also suggested that the Pope wanted CDF to interact with the international theological community in a thoroughly contemporary way. John Paul did not appoint a medievalist or a patristics scholar as Prefect of CDF. He appointed a theologian who had been deeply and critically engaged with contemporary philosophy and ecumenical theology.

Cardinal Ratzinger was the first man in his position in centuries who did not take Thomas Aquinas as his philosophical and theological master. The Pope respected Thomism and Thomists, but he broke precedent by appointing a non-Thomistic Prefect of CDF. It was a clear signal that he believed there was a legitimate pluralism of theological methods, and that this pluralism ought to be taken into account in the formulation of authoritative teaching.

It made for an interesting partnership. The Pope was a philosopher; the Prefect was a theologian. John Paul was a Pole; Ratzinger was a German. Karol Wojtyła had been one of the intellectual architects of the *Pastoral Constitution on the Church in the Modern World*; a decade after the Council, Ratzinger was one of the sharpest critics of the way that document was being interpreted. Over the course of his pontificate, John Paul II would speak frequently about the twenty-first century as a possible "springtime" for the Gospel after the winter of the twentieth century. During the same period, Cardinal Ratzinger would deepen an alternative view, that the Church of the immediate future would be smaller and purer, not quite a catacomb Church, but certainly not the dominant force in Western culture it once had been. Cardinal Ratzinger seemed to think that the West and its humanistic project had fallen into irreversible cultural decline. The Pope believed that a revitalization of humanism was possible.

If, as one caricature had it, both John Paul II and Cardinal Ratzinger only spoke with people with whom they agreed, they could not have carried on an intense intellectual conversation for almost twenty years. Ratzinger recognized in the charismatic, pastoral Wojtyła a "passion for man" and a capacity to uncover "the spiritual dimension of history," two traits that made the Church's proclamation of the Gospel a powerful alternative to the false humanisms of their time.[18] Wojtyła recognized in the shy, scholarly Ratzinger a contemporary intellectual who was a more accomplished theologian than himself. Together they made a formidable intellectual team.

They had a regularly scheduled meeting every Friday evening, at which Ratzinger reviewed his Congregation's work with the Pope, alone. Before and during lunch on Tuesdays, the two met frequently for more extended intellectual explorations, usually with others. These luncheon discussions could involve a new encyclical or apostolic letter, a broader topic of concern (bioethics, the ecumenical situation, or the various theologies of liberation), or the themes of the coming weeks' general audience addresses. John Paul, whom Ratzinger describes as "happy to have a continuous work to do" amid his inevitably fragmented schedule, refined the later catecheses of the theology of the body and his six-year catechesis of the Creed (1985–1991) over these luncheon conversations, a distinctive feature of his pontificate.[19]

The Revised Code of Canon Law

The revision of the Church's legal system, the Code of Canon Law, was one of three major initiatives that John XXIII announced shortly after his election in 1958. The work of the revision commission was virtually suspended during Vatican II, and serious drafting of the new Code only began in 1966. The drafting process had dragged on for more than fifteen years when John Paul II took a personal hand in the matter and drove the process through to a conclusion.

In February 1982, the Pope called together a group of seven canonical experts from different countries, each of whom had a different view of what had been drafted thus far. At a working lunch, John Paul told the group that he had read the entire draft Code twice, and wanted them to meet with him to go over the entire project, canon by canon, so that he understood exactly what was being said in each of the 1,752 laws and their various subsections. The experts' group met with the Pope fourteen times, in four-hour sessions, between February and November 1982. Once, when a member of the group complained that the others were unfairly criticizing everything in the draft Code, John Paul said that the critics were bringing their own expertise to bear and "that is what they should do."[20]

The 1917 Code of Canon Law was a collection of preexisting Church legislation, much of which imitated civil law. The old Code was divided into sections having to do with "persons," "things," "processes," and "crimes and penalties." In this secular legal context, the sacraments, the center of the Church's spiritual life and worship, were dealt with under "things." John Paul was determined that the new Code would be an authentic expression of Vatican II's vision of the Church. The new Code, after specifying general legal norms, begins with "The People of God," establishes the equality of all believers in baptism, and organizes the Church's law under the threefold "office" or mission of Christ as prophet, priest, and king. This is the framework for the canons governing the Church's teaching office, its mission of sanctification (where the sacraments are properly located), and its structure. Only after these distinctively ecclesial matters have been dealt with does the new Code go into questions of property, offenses and sanctions, and legal processes. In the latter category, seven canons urge that conciliation efforts be made before a formal legal process is undertaken. The new Code does not imagine law as an adversarial process including winners and losers, but aims to achieve reconciliation outside the Church's courts when possible.[21]

The new Code of Canon Law was promulgated by the Apostolic Constitution *Sacrae Disciplinae Leges* [The Laws of Its Sacred Discipline], which John Paul II signed on January 25, 1983. The apostolic constitution, personally written by John Paul, provides a clear insight into his view of law in the Church.[22] The new Code, he insisted, was a service to the Church's mission of evangelization and sanctification. That mission took place through a human community that, like all human communities, needed a structure of law to function properly. Still, the Code was "in no way intended as a substitute for faith, grace, charisms, and especially charity in the life of the Church and of the faithful." These gifts of the Holy Spirit always had primacy in the Church, and the Code's purpose was to facilitate their development in the Catholic community. The Code was based on the Council's concept of the Church as a *communio,* a communion of believers, rather than on the analogy of a state and its citizens.[23]

The revised Code of Canon Law was the first of three major legislative initiatives in the pontificate of John Paul II. The 1988 Apostolic Constitution *Pastor Bonus* [The Good Shepherd], reforming the structures of the Roman Curia, and the revised Code of Oriental Canon Law, promulgated on October 1, 1990, for the Eastern-rite Catholic Churches, completed the triad and gave John Paul's pontificate a unique legislative breadth. The Pope understood all this lawmaking as an expression of his commitment to the full implementation of Vatican II, a point he underlined at the public celebration of the new Code of Canon Law on February 2, 1983.

The celebration took place during John Paul's second consistory for the creation of cardinals. Among the eighteen new members of the College were Jean-Marie Lustiger of Paris, Colombia's Alfonso López Trujillo, Joseph Bernardin of Chicago, Godfried Daneels of Belgium, Józef Glemp, and Julijanus Vaivods of Riga, Latvia. At this consistory, John Paul began his custom of honoring one of the theological elders of Vatican II with the cardinal's red hat. The first named was Henri de Lubac, then eighty-seven years old, to whom he assigned the Roman titular church once held by Cardinal Alfredo Ottaviani, a man on the other side of the theological controversies in which de Lubac was embroiled in the late 1940s.*

Saints for the World

The most visible expression of John Paul II's determination to remind the Church of the universal call to holiness has been his numerous beatifications and canonizations; 805 men and women were declared "blessed" and 205 were declared saints in the first twenty years of the pontificate—far, far more than any pope in history, even considering that groups of martyrs were beatified or canonized together.

The Church does not "make" saints, nor does the Pope. Through the teaching office of the papacy, the Church recognizes the saints God has made. Karol Wojtyła had long been convinced that God is wonderfully profligate in making saints and that God's saint making touches every vocation in the Church. Holiness is not a preserve of the clergy, nor is it reserved for monks and nuns, deliberately removed from the world. Holiness is every Christian's baptismal vocation.

The Christian ideal, for John Paul II, is the martyr: the witness whose life completely coincides with the truth by being completely given to that truth in

---

*The reception of his appointment by some of de Lubac's French Jesuit confreres illustrated the tensions in the Society of Jesus and the personal unpleasantness to which they could lead. When de Lubac's nomination as cardinal was announced, many of his Parisian Jesuit colleagues declared that this was not their affair and declined to help. De Lubac had to ask his young friends of the French *Communio* to help him prepare for his investiture, and they bought his new robes for the consistory. On his return, Cardinal de Lubac was given a reception by his Jesuit brothers, at which only soft drinks were served.[24]

self-sacrificing love. The Pope has regularly reminded the world that the twentieth century is the greatest century of martyrdom—faithful witness unto death—in Christian history. And no martyr of the twentieth century has been, for John Paul, a more luminous icon of the call to holiness through radical, self-giving love than Maximilian Kolbe. Kolbe was the "saint of the abyss"—the man who looked straight into the modern heart of darkness and remained faithful to Christ by sacrificing his life for another in the Auschwitz starvation bunker while helping his cellmates die with dignity and hope.[25]

Kolbe's canonization was set for St. Peter's Square on Sunday, October 10, 1982. But a question had arisen. Father Kolbe was widely regarded as a martyr, but was he a "martyr" in the technical sense of the term—someone who had died because of *odium fidei*, "hatred of the faith"? He had not been arrested because of *odium fidei*, and witnesses to his self-sacrifice had testified that the Auschwitz commandant, Fritsch, had simply accepted Kolbe's self-substitution for the condemned Franciszek Gajowniczek without evincing any particular satisfaction that he was killing a priest. The theologians and experts of the Congregation for the Causes of Saints (the Vatican office that considers beatifications and canonizations) had argued that Kolbe, while undoubtedly a saint, was not a martyr in the traditional sense of the term. At Kolbe's beatification in 1971, Pope Paul VI had said that Kolbe could be considered a "martyr of charity," but this was a personal gesture and the category lacked standing in theology or canon law. Since then, though, the Polish and German bishops had petitioned the Holy See that Kolbe be canonized as a martyr, rather than as a saintly confessor who happened to have died under extraordinary circumstances.

John Paul II appointed two special judges to consider the question from the theological and historical points of view. Their reports were then submitted to a special advisory commission. The majority of the commission concluded that Blessed Maximilian Kolbe's self-sacrifice did not satisfy the traditional criteria for martyrdom, heroic as it undoubtedly was. On the day of his canonization, it was unclear whether Kolbe would be given the accolade of a martyr, as many Poles, Germans, and others wished.

October 10, 1982, a magnificent autumn morning, found a quarter of a million people in St. Peter's Square, where they saw a great banner, a portrait of Father Kolbe, draped from the central loggia. Still, the question hung in the air: Would Kolbe be recognized as a martyr? The answer came when John Paul II processed out of the basilica and into the square wearing red vestments, the liturgical color of martyrs. He had overridden the counsel of his advisory commission, and in his homily he declared that "in virtue of my apostolic authority, I have decreed that Maximilian Mary Kolbe, who following his beatification was venerated as a confessor, will henceforth be venerated *also as a martyr*."[26]

John Paul II was making an important theological point in deciding that St. Maximilian Kolbe was indeed a martyr—systematic hatred for the human person (systematic *odium hominis,* so to speak) was a contemporary equivalent of the traditional criterion for martyrdom, *odium fidei.* Because Christian faith affirmed the truth about the inalienable dignity of the human person, anyone who hated that truth hated, implicitly, the Christian faith. Modern totalitarianism was an implicit form of *odium fidei,* because it reduced persons to things.[27]

Three months after Kolbe's canonization, John Paul II issued another apostolic constitution, *Divinus Perfectionis Magister* [The Master of Divine Perfection]. Dated January 25, 1983, it radically revised the process by which the Church recognized one of its sons or daughters as a saint.

The idea of officially recognized "saints" may seem in conflict with the idea of a universal vocation to holiness in the Church. If everyone is called to be a saint—if, in fact, everyone *must* become a saint, recognized or not, in order to enter heaven—what is the point of singling out particular men and women for devotion? The two ideas in fact complement each other. Every Christian has a vocation. Sometimes this vocation is entirely singular, embodying some previously unexplored or underappreciated aspect of God's design for the Church; the great founders of new religious orders, for example, are examples of saints as God's "prime numbers."[28] At other times, sanctity emerges more organically, as when a mother, father, priest, religious sister, bishop, pope, artist, or scholar lives his or her vocation in an exemplary, but not necessarily path-breaking, way. In both cases, the Church's public recognition of a saint serves the universal call to holiness. God's "prime numbers" are a reminder that there are always new aspects of God's call to holiness to be discerned and lived out. Saintly exemplars of traditional vocations are models of how Christians less fiercely touched by the divine will can achieve sanctity through grace.

Since Pope Urban VIII's reforms in 1625 and 1634, the Church had determined whether someone was a saintly prime number or a saintly exemplar through an adversarial legal process. The burden of proof fell entirely on those promoting the "cause" of the potential saint. Proponents of the cause made their case. An official known as the Promoter of the Faith (more popularly, the "Devil's Advocate") then did everything in his power to question the sanctity of the candidate, who was, so to speak, assumed guilty until proven innocent.[29] The candidate's lawyers replied in turn, in what amounted to a posthumous religious trial.

Divinus Perfectionis Magister changed all this, dramatically. The legal process was replaced by an academic-historical procedure, the Devil's Advocate was jettisoned, and so was the adversarial joust between the Promoter of the Faith and the candidate's defense attorneys. Theological consultants replaced lawyers as the principal figures in the process and a new group, the "college of relators," was given responsibility for determining the truth about a candidate's life by supervising the production of a critical, documented biography (the *positio*). There would still be witnesses to give testimony about a candidate, but the paradigm guiding the whole process would now be a postdoctoral seminar of historians, not a criminal court. The "relator" of a cause had taken the place of both the defense attorney and the Devil's Advocate; scholarship had replaced legal advocacy.[30]

The new procedures were aimed at making the process swifter, less expensive, more scholarly, more collegial (local bishops now had the entire responsibility for assembling all the relevant data on a candidate), and better geared to producing results. The juridical process was not without merit; it protected the Church against transient enthusiasms and false claims of miracles (which are required for all canonizations, and for the beatification of non-martyrs). The new procedures, though, were more attuned to identifying what was distinctive about a life, and trusted the skills of historical scholarship to ensure that what was distinctive was also authentically Christian. The new procedures also took far more seriously Vatican II's vision of the plurality of forms of sanctity in the Church. The legal procedures had risked imposing a kind of abstract uniformity on the universal call to holiness.[31]

The new procedures also reflected something of the Pope's dramatic sensibility, his sense that history is a stage on which God's freedom and human freedom are both in play, in a drama with nothing less than salvation at issue. Karol Wojtyła's pastoral experience had taught him that saints were all around us, and he thought the Church ought to lift more of them up as evidence of life's richly, even fearsomely, dramatic texture. Viewed from one angle, *Divinus Perfectionis Magister* was a radical act of bureaucratic reconstruction. Viewed from inside John Paul II's pastoral intention, it was another papal reminder that our lives are fraught with more consequence than we often imagine.

A "Personal Prelature" for Opus Dei

John Paul's reform of the beatification and canonization process was widely applauded. Far more controversy swirled around another innovation—the establishment of a "personal prelature" to govern the movement known as "Opus Dei," "The Work of God," or, as its members prefer, simply "The Work."

Founded in Spain in 1928 by Josemaría Escrivá de Balaguer, a priest who died in 1975, the movement counts some 80,000 lay members and 2,000 priests worldwide. Opus Dei members include celibate "numeraries," lay men and women who live in Opus Dei centers while working in the world; "oblates," celibates who live outside the centers; and "supernumeraries," married men and women who pursue their own careers and live in their own homes. The Work sponsors universities in Rome, Spain, and Latin America. Its priests provide spiritual direction to Opus Dei members, conduct chaplaincies on or near college and university campuses, and staff other Opus Dei centers, where evangelization of the unchurched is a priority.

The word "controversy" often seemed custom-made for Opus Dei. Its critics charge it with having been a bulwark of the Franco regime in Spain. Few of those critics acknowledge that Opus Dei members played crucial roles in Spain's smooth transition to democracy, as is widely acknowledged by historians.[32] The critics depict the Work as a pre-conciliar and reactionary move-

ment. Members of Opus Dei constantly underscore the movement's emphasis on the lay vocation in the world, a key theme of Vatican II. Even those sympathetic to Opus Dei can find its basic text, a collection of Monsignor Escrivá's
maxims known as *The Way*, less than scintillating. Those same critically sympathetic observers also note that Opus Dei has provided a means of living
their Christian vocation to some exceptionally sophisticated men and women.
Some of the criticism of Opus Dei is undoubtedly motivated by jealousy of the
movement's élan and its prodigious success at fund-raising. It also seems likely
that the defensiveness of some Opus Dei members contributes to charges that
the movement has a secretiveness about it that does not become an ecclesial
organization. The historically minded recognize that many of the things said
about Opus Dei in the twentieth century, especially the charges of being an
elitist fifth column in the Church, were said about the early Jesuits in Counter-
Reformation Europe.

Cardinal Karol Wojtyła had long been sympathetic to the Work and had
spoken to one of its student centers in Rome during the 1970s. Opus Dei's
stress on sanctifying the workplace through apostolically committed professional men and women paralleled his own understanding of one of the key
themes of Vatican II. Thus it was not surprising that, as Pope, John Paul II was
sympathetic to Opus Dei's request that it be recognized as a "personal prelature," a jurisdictional innovation in the Church's governance envisioned by
Vatican II.[33] In the case of Opus Dei, granting the movement's request for this
status meant recognizing it as, in effect, a worldwide, nonterritorial diocese.
The movement's leadership argued that this admittedly innovative arrangement would allow the "prelate" who led it to promote the movement's distinctive spirituality and more effectively deploy its priests across national and
diocesan boundaries.

There was considerable resistance to the idea of personal prelatures in
the Roman Curia and among more than a few bishops. Opus Dei's critics were
fiercely opposed to granting the movement this unprecedented status, which
would effectively remove it from the juridical authority of local bishops. The
Pope was not persuaded by the critics' arguments, and on November 28, 1982,
he issued an apostolic constitution that transformed Opus Dei into the
Church's first personal prelature, naming Monsignor Escrivá's closest associate and successor, Alvaro del Portillo, as its Prelate.[34]

For John Paul, it was another way to underscore his commitment to fostering the universal vocation to holiness.[35] Opus Dei would, however, remain
a subject of controversy throughout the pontificate.*

---

*Another controversy broke out in early 1992 when the Congregation for the Causes of
Saints was completing work on the beatification of Monsignor Escrivá. Critics charged that the
positio for the cause was poorly prepared, taking virtually no account of Monsignor Escrivá's critics, and that the process had been short-circuited by pressure from Opus Dei. John Paul II evidently disagreed that the process had been deficient. He beatified Escrivá on May 17, 1992, in St.
Peter's Square, at a ceremony attended by more than a quarter of a million persons.[36]

CONFRONTATION IN NICARAGUA

To become a saint is the path of authentic human liberation. Other concepts of "liberation" are always current, however, as was evident in the ongoing controversy over the future of the Church in Latin America. In the early 1980s, John Paul II thought that Latin American Catholicism was caught at the intersection of three sets of problems.

First, there was a theological problem: many of the doctrinally unacceptable ideas promoted by liberation theologians were still shaping lives and destinies throughout the continent, and particularly in Central America. These false theological ideas had led in turn to the second set of problems involving the Church's own life as a religious community. In Nicaragua, El Salvador, and Guatemala, a "Popular Church" was self-consciously trying to supplant what it dismissed as the "institutional Church." In Nicaragua, this "Popular Church" was overtly supported by the Sandinista government, which included priests who remained in public office in defiance of orders from their religious superiors. The government was also putting serious pressure on the Church's bishops and pastors. When the revolution led to the scandalous situation of priests supporting a regime that was harassing the Church, the corruption had obviously become acute. Finally, there was the longstanding and frequently brutal persecution in Cuba, where the Castro regime had a rope around the Church's neck.[37]

John Paul's 1979 Puebla address should have made clear what he thought was the right path to a truly Christian liberation of Central America: an engaged Church that was not a partisan Church; a Church that tried to build *communio* out of fragmented and violent Central American societies; a Church that refused to identify the Gospel with the program of any political party; a Church that did not substitute worldly utopias for the Kingdom of God; and, as always, a Church that vigorously defended religious freedom against persecutors of any ideological stripe. That was emphatically not the kind of unified, engaged Church to be found in Central America in the early 1980s.

El Salvador had been caught in a bloody civil war between a military-dominated government and the guerrillas of the Faribundo Marti National Liberation Front [FMLN] since the late 1970s. With virtual legal impunity, the government and the Salvadoran military committed gross human rights violations in their attempt to crush the Marxist-inspired guerrilla movement. The guerrillas were committed to the violent overthrow of the regime and were no strangers to the abuse of persons. A nonviolent "third way," centered on the Christian Democratic Party and its leader, José Napoleon Duarte, himself a onetime victim of the military, struggled to survive. The Salvadoran Church had become polarized and divided in the late 1970s and early 1980s, as the archbishop of San Salvador, Oscar Romero, became an increasingly vocal critic of the regime's human rights abuses. Romero, in turn, had been deeply influenced by Jesuit liberation theologians Jon Sobrino and Ignacio Ellacuría.[38]

As the country descended more deeply into a spiral of violence, Archbishop Romero was murdered at the altar on March 24, 1980, by members of a reactionary death squad acting with at least tacit support from the government. In a telegram to the President of the Salvadoran Bishops' Conference, John Paul II bluntly condemned the "sacrilegious assassination" with his "deepest reprobation."[39] Romero's successor, Archbishop Arturo Rivera Damas, had tried to get a grip on the deteriorating situation. He was outspoken in his criticism of human rights abuses from whatever quarter, but he could not agree with those who, however brave and dedicated in their resistance to rightist violence, ignored the atrocities of the FMLN. He quietly moved the archdiocesan Justice and Peace Commission, which he believed had turned a blind eye to FMLN crimes, out of the archbishop's residence. In doing so, the archbishop reduced the suspicion in which some anti-FMLN political forces held the Church and strengthened his moral authority as a voice against human rights abuses whatever their origin.[40] In a situation essentially out of control in the early 1980s, Archbishop Rivera tried to strengthen the Christian Democratic alternative to both the bloody-minded militarist right and the guerrillas of the FMLN. It would be more than a decade before the guerrillas were defeated and the military brought under effective civilian authority.

For all the horror of El Salvador, though, Nicaragua was the key to the dilemma of authentic Christian liberation in Central America. More than any other place in Latin America, Nicaragua under the Sandinista regime was a laboratory for the various liberation theologies' claims. The Church situation was even more conflicted than in El Salvador. Two priests were actively involved in the government: Miguel D'Escoto, the foreign minister, and Ernesto Cardenal, the minister of culture; a third priest, Father Cardenal's brother, Fernando, a Jesuit, directed the Sandinista literacy program. The archbishop of Managua, Miguel Obando Bravo, a stocky man of peasant background who had originally supported the revolution against the Somoza family dictatorship, had become the Sandinistas' most visible and effective critic after the new rulers failed to deliver on their guarantees of civil rights and political freedoms. The Sandinistas, in turn, actively fomented the "Popular Church" in opposition to the archbishop.[41]

The apostolic nuncio in Managua, Archbishop Andrea Cordero Lanza di Montezemolo, a gray-haired Italian nobleman whose father, an anti-fascist leader in Mussolini's Italy, had been murdered by the Nazis, was one of the most respected figures in the Holy See's diplomatic service. His posting to Nicaragua was an indication of how serious the situation there was thought to be. Montezemolo's initial encounters with the Sandinista leadership, who habitually called him "Comrade Nuncio," verged on the comic, although it was comedy with an ugly edge. Daniel Ortega, head of the Sandinista front and leader of the government, once careened up to the nunciature driving a red sports car, followed by several jeeps full of Sandinista troops armed to the teeth. Archbishop Montezemolo met this curious delegation at the gate and told

Commandante Ortega that he was welcome, but that the soldiers and their guns had to stay outside: "This is an embassy."[42]

Now, the nuncio had to negotiate John Paul's visit to Nicaragua, part of a papal pilgrimage to Central America in March 1983. Archbishop Obando and the bishops of Nicaragua had invited the Pope because, as Obando later put it, "we were convinced that the presence of the Holy Father would work to the advantage of the Church and the good of our people."[43] As Archbishop Montezemolo later recalled, the Sandinistas were not in a cooperative frame of mind.

Their first gambit involved the archbishop of Managua. Commandante Ortega told Montezemolo that "We don't want the Pope to be seen alone with Archbishop Obando." Montezemolo replied that this was hardly possible: "He's the archbishop of the capital city and the president of the episcopal conference." The eventual agreement was that the Pope would always be accompanied publicly by all the bishops of Nicaragua, but this created its own problem. They all couldn't fit into the Popemobile. The nuncio started looking for a bus, but none could be found in Nicaragua. Then Montezemolo heard about a Mexican political candidate who had been campaigning in a bus with the roof cut off. The nuncio made inquiries, and the Mexican government flew it to Managua.

The next problem involved the priests in the government, who had persistently refused their religious superiors' orders to leave political office. Montezemolo told Daniel Ortega that the Pope wanted this business of the priests in government "settled." Ortega replied that "it's a matter of conscience for them; it's not my affair." He then asked what would happen if Fathers D'Escoto and Cardenal were present at, say, the welcoming ceremony at the airport. The nuncio replied that it was possible that the Pope would not greet them, because they were in open disobedience. Ortega seemed uneasy with this, and Montezemolo went off to see the foreign minister, Miguel D'Escoto.

The portly Maryknoll priest was angry and abusive, insisting that "I am the foreign minister of Nicaragua, I must see the Pope, I must travel with the Pope." Montezemolo replied that he was sorry, the Pope never traveled with political figures on his pilgrimages. D'Escoto was enraged. On their way out of the foreign ministry, Montezemolo's second-in-command muttered, "Tomorrow, either the foreign minister or the nuncio will be gone."

Montezemolo then went to see Father Cardenal. At their first meeting in 1980, the nuncio had been struck by Cardenal's tiled office in a rather peculiar building, which turned out to be one of the old Somoza family palaces; Father Cardenal, who impressed Montezemolo as spiritually intense but "very abstract," even disconnected, had explained without blinking, "Oh, this was the bathroom of Mrs. Somoza." After Montezemolo laid out the situation with the papal visit, Cardenal replied, "But I have to be present, the regime and Daniel Ortega want me there." The nuncio answered that he had just seen Commandante Ortega, who had told him that this was a matter of Cardenal's conscience and not Ortega's affair. Cardenal would not budge.

So the question of Ernesto Cardenal meeting the Pope remained unresolved for the moment. Ortega, however, fearful of an embarrassing incident in front of the international press, took care of the volatile D'Escoto. Some days after their meeting, he called Archbishop Montezemolo and said, "Comrade Nuncio, I forgot to tell you the other day that when the Pope is here there is an important international meeting in India to which I must send the foreign minister."[44]

Archbishop Montezemolo was not the only Vatican official having difficulties arranging things in Nicaragua. Father Roberto Tucci, SJ, the chief organizer of the Pope's pilgrimages, was so exasperated at Sandinista troublemaking in late 1982 that he advised John Paul that they would be better off threatening not to go unless the regime accepted some basic conditions, including free access to the sites the Pope would visit and Church control of the organization of the papal Mass in Managua. John Paul, determined to get to Nicaragua and encourage what he regarded as a persecuted Church, told Tucci that he wanted the visit to go through, even if it might be difficult.[45]

Finally, John Paul II arrived in Managua on March 4, 1983. When the papal plane landed, the entire Sandinista government was lined up on the runway, waiting to greet the Pope. Archbishop Montezemolo went up the gangway with the government chief of protocol, and was met at the door of the plane by Cardinal Casaroli, who took the nuncio aside and asked, "Are any of the priests in the government attending?" Montezemolo took the Secretary of State to one of the plane's windows, pointed to the government receiving line, and said, "Look, Ernesto Cardenal is there, but D'Escoto isn't." Casaroli replied, "We have to tell the Pope," so they went to the forward compartment where John Paul was still seated and showed him Father Cardenal from the window. The Pope asked the nuncio what he should do. Montezemolo replied, "Holy Father, it's not for me to give you instructions, but if you don't greet him, they're prepared for that." John Paul said, "No, I want to greet him, but I have something to tell him."

After the welcoming speeches, Daniel Ortega led the Pope toward the members of the government, with Montezemolo walking at the Pope's left. A few yards from the receiving line, Ortega, nervous about the whole business, said to John Paul, "We don't have to greet them, we can just pass by over here." The Pope replied, "No, I want to greet them." Ortega then led the Pope down the line. When they got to Ernesto Cardenal, the minister of culture swept off his beret and genuflected. Gesturing vigorously toward the priest with his right hand, John Paul said, in a warm and friendly voice, "Regularize your position with the Church. Regularize your position with the Church." It was not, as the nuncio recalled it, a reproach, but an invitation.*

---

*The photo of this airport encounter went all over the world and was widely interpreted as a sharp papal rebuke of Cardenal. Under Sandinista censorship no Nicaraguan paper ran the picture until two weeks after the papal visit. Then a local paper asked Ernesto Cardenal what the Pope had said to him. The minister of culture, alluding to the New Testament scene in which the Lycaonians wanted to offer sacrifice to Paul and Silas after Paul had miraculously cured a cripple, told the paper that John Paul had said, "'Don't kneel to me. I am a man like you'" [Acts 14.15]. Those who were there knew better.[46]

The major confrontation came later that morning at the papal Mass in Managua. The Mass venue, a local park, had been one of the controversial issues in the pre-visit negotiations. Montezemolo had suggested putting the temporary stage for the altar at the other end of the park from the permanent stage used for Sandinista rallies, which was decorated with huge posters of César Augusto Sandino, Marx, Lenin, and other revolutionary heroes. Commandante Ortega had said, "No, we can't do that, but we'll arrange things in the right way." Some days later, Montezemolo noticed that the giant posters had been taken down and thought, "Well, that's cooperation." He later discovered that they'd been taken down to be repainted before being reinstalled. When he mentioned this to the Pope, John Paul replied, "Don't worry, when I'm up there with all the bishops, nobody will be looking at the posters."[47] As things turned out, the regime had far more disruptive plans for manipulating the event.

Father Tucci had arrived in Managua a few days before the Pope's arrival, along with Piervincenzo Giudici, a senior Vatican Radio engineer and an expert in sound systems. Giudici had gone to check the papal Mass site and came back shocked. A second sound system—new, powerful, and independently controlled—had been installed. Archbishop Montezemolo asked the government what was going on and received the bland reply, "Oh, we want to be prepared for an emergency."

In the pre-visit negotiations, Montezemolo had insisted that the park be divided into sections and that the sector in front of the altar be reserved for representatives of Catholic associations and movements. When these representatives arrived at the site at 4 A.M., they discovered that the central front section had already been packed with Sandinista supporters, as had virtually all the space near the altar. The people for whom the Mass was being celebrated were corralled far to the rear of the venue, and police fired automatic weapons over the heads of those who tried to get closer to the altar.[48]

Just beside the papal altar was another platform, filled with members of the government and senior Sandinista Party members. Their behavior was less than devout. During the Mass, all nine members of the Sandinista National Directorate, including Daniel Ortega, waved their left fists and shouted "People's Power!"[49] The confrontation became most dramatic during the Pope's sermon. The Sandinistas had secreted microphones into the sector immediately in front of the altar platform, now full of their supporters. Those microphones and the microphones on the altar platform were controlled by Sandinista engineers, using the "emergency" sound system that had been installed days before. At the beginning of his sermon on the unity of the Church, John Paul could be heard by the Catholic loyalists toward the rear. He said later that he knew they could hear him because he saw and heard that they were applauding. But when he reached the point where he explained the impossibility of a "Popular Church" set over against the Church's legitimate pastors, the Sandinista mob in front of the altar became raucous and tried to drown him out. The local engineers turned down the Pope's microphone and turned up the volume on the microphones that had been placed among the agitators.[50] As this was going on, the government officials on the tribune next to the altar platform continued to misbehave. At last, an angry John Paul had had enough and shouted over the mob, *"Silencio!"* A measure of order was finally restored, although at the end of the Mass the Sandinista chief of protocol went to the engineering console and demanded that the Sandinista anthem be played as a recessional hymn.[51] John Paul stood at the front of the platform, took his crucifix-topped crosier by its base, held it high over his head, and waved it back and forth in salute to the hundreds of thousands of Nicaraguan Catholics who had been kept penned at the back of the venue.

The Sandinistas' subsequent claim—that the mob's attempt to shout down the Pope had been a spontaneous reaction—was a clumsy lie. Their attempted desecration of the papal Mass also backfired politically. Father Tucci had convinced the regime to join a regional television hookup, so the debacle at the papal Mass was broadcast throughout Central America. Millions were shocked at the vulgarity of Sandinista misbehavior. When he returned to Costa Rica late that night, the Pope was met by a larger and friendlier crowd than had greeted him the day before. The Sandinista myth began, slowly, to erode.

Over nine days, John Paul visited Costa Rica, Panama, El Salvador, Guatemala, Honduras, Belize, and Haiti, in addition to Nicaragua. In El Salvador, he preached on reconciliation and made a previously unplanned visit to the tomb of Archbishop Romero. In Guatemala, he defended the native population and challenged the repressive measures taken by the government of General Efrain Ríos Montt. In Haiti, he criticized the regime of the Duvalier family. The Pope was attacked for not mentioning the murdered Archbishop Romero in his sermon in El Salvador, and the pilgrimage as a whole was criticized by those who somehow identified the Salvadoran guerrillas and the Sandinistas with the cause of democracy. The hard-pressed Catholic leader of Nicaragua, Archbishop Obando, was pleased, however. He knew that the great majority of his people had been impressed and touched by the fact that the Pope had come to them, and the Sandinistas' behavior at the papal Mass had clarified the situation. As Obando later recalled, "People began to ask, 'Who are they to treat the Church this way?' . . . People who were doubtful about their relationship to the revolution could now see which side they were on, because they saw how [the regime] treated the Holy Father."[52] For his part, the Pope unmistakably signaled his support for the embattled archbishop of Managua by naming him a cardinal in May 1985.

A year after the papal pilgrimage to Central America, José Napoleon Duarte, the Christian Democratic leader, defeated Robert D'Aubuisson, a vicious ex–military officer whom many suspected of involvement in the murder of Archbishop Romero, in a presidential runoff election in El Salvador—an important indication of the Salvadoran people's interest in a nonviolent democratic transition beyond traditional oligarchy. The Sandinista grip on Nicaragua continued, though, and the priests in the government remained defiant. In August 1984, Father D'Escoto and the Cardenal brothers were formally informed by the Holy See that they were in violation of canon law and must leave their government offices. All three refused.

THE INSTRUCTIONS ON LIBERATION THEOLOGY

The Congregation for the Doctrine of the Faith had been working on a statement on liberation theology for some time. Its *Instruction on Certain Aspects of the Theology of Liberation* was issued on August 6, 1984, a week before the Sandinista clergy were ordered to leave office. The *Instruction* had its origins in a 1982 conversation involving John Paul II and Cardinal Ratzinger. The intellectual initiative was John Paul's. He believed that liberation was a great biblical and Christian theme and that the Church had a responsibility to develop an authentic theology of liberation, particularly in light of what was happening in Latin America. Since the question involved the encouragement of sound theology, John Paul charged CDF with tackling the problem.[53]

At the time, the most prominent and accomplished Latin American liberation theologian was Father Gustavo Gutiérrez, so the Congregation studied his work, while examining other representative figures and the "translation" of their teachings into religious education, preaching, and pastoral practice. Bishops from throughout Latin America were consulted and Ratzinger kept the Pope informed of the discussions. As the text of a statement was being developed, it became clear that two things were needed: a critical identification of the problem areas in liberation theology, and a positive elaboration of the theme of Christian liberation. Thus while the *Instruction on Certain Aspects of the Theology of Liberation* was being developed, a decision was made to complement this first, critical reading of problematic liberation theologies with a second instruction that would lay the foundations for a more adequate theology of liberation.[54]

The principal points in the first *Instruction*, which was personally approved by John Paul II, paralleled the Pope's address to the Latin American bishops at Puebla in 1979. Liberation, it stated, was an important Christian theme. Far too many people in Latin America lived in desperate poverty, and the Church had a special responsibility to them. The *Instruction* also acknowledged that there were several varieties of liberation theology, as there were of contemporary Marxism.

Certain themes in some theologies of liberation, however, were clearly incompatible with Christian orthodoxy. The great biblical image of the Exodus could not be reduced to narrowly political meanings.[55] Sin should not be primarily located in social, political, or economic structures, but in human hearts.[56] "Good" and "evil" could not be understood in strictly political categories.[57] Truth was universal, not "partisan."[58] Class struggle was not the chief dynamic of history, and using class struggle models to justify violent revolution against "structural violence" did not square with a Christian view of history.[59]

The Gospel "poor in spirit" were not the Marxist "proletariat."[60] The Church was not a "partisan" Church and did not belong to any one social or economic class.[61] Christ's atoning death on the cross could not be given an "exclusively political interpretation" as a symbol of the oppressed in their fight for a new society.[62] And the Eucharist, the Church's central act of worship, must not be reduced to a "celebration of the people in their struggle."[63] The *Instruction*'s concerns were well-summed-up in one caution raised toward the end of the document: "One needs to be on guard against the politicization of existence which, misunderstanding the meaning of the Kingdom of God and the transcendence of the person, begins to sacralize politics and betray the religion of the people in favor of the projects of the revolution."[64] Christians had a greater freedom to proclaim.

The meaning of that greater freedom was spelled out twenty months later, in the March 1986 *Instruction on Christian Freedom and Liberation*. The deepest meaning of liberation, the second *Instruction* taught, was redemption, since in being redeemed we are freed "from the most radical evil, namely, sin and the power of death."[65] Thus human beings learn the true meaning of their freedom in the Gospel's call to communion with God.[66] Totalitarianism was evil precisely because it violated the radical freedom of the human person before the mystery of God, who "wishes to be adored by people who are free."[67]

Sin, or "alienation . . . from the truth of . . . being . . . a creature loved by God" was the fundamental alienation of this or any other century and the basic obstacle to human liberation.[68] Work for human freedom was a basic moral responsibility of all Christians, according to what the *Instruction* called the "principle of solidarity," for freedom is fulfilled in this world in nonviolent work for the freedom of others.[69] The Church did have a "love of preference" for the impoverished and the unfree, but because it was not a partisan Church, that love "excludes no one," since it was a witness to the God-given dignity of every human being.[70] As for "authentic development" in poor countries, that required open political systems with a "real separation between the powers of the State," which was a safeguard against governmental abuse of human rights.[71]

The claims of some liberation theologians that the earlier *Instruction on Certain Aspects of the Theology of Liberation* misrepresented their teaching was as unpersuasive as the claim by the Brazilian Franciscan liberation theologian Leonardo Boff and others that the later *Instruction on Christian Freedom and Liberation* vindicated their position. The two *Instructions* differed in tone, but they were two complementary parts of a coherent whole that advanced John Paul II's prescription for the crisis of modernity. An authentic Christian humanism, addressing human liberation at its most fundamental level and applying that understanding to the reform of society, was a necessary alternative to the false humanism and false liberation of Marxism. The second *Instruction* was also an important moment in the development of John Paul's social doctrine, with its tacit endorsement of democracy as a way to help liberate the poor from oppression and injustice. This was a theme that John Paul would develop at considerable length and depth in the years ahead. It not only challenged those infatuated with Marxism, but those sectors of the Latin American Church that were too comfortable with the economic and political status quo.

The two *Instructions* further developed John Paul II's and Cardinal Ratzinger's common view of Vatican II, that the social activism mandated by the *Pastoral Constitution on the Church in the Modern World* should be undertaken in a truly ecclesial way, according to the vision of Catholicism as *communio* taught by the *Dogmatic Constitution on the Church*. Because the Church's unique message of liberation through Christ cut deeper than any political analysis, an evangelical Church, bringing the Gospel to life through its social doctrine, was both more authentically Christian and more likely to help liberate men and women from poverty and political oppression.

"He Is Sad . . . He Understands"

Three months after confronting the Sandinistas in Managua, John Paul II faced another challenge to authentic Christian liberation—this time, in his homeland.

The Jaruzelski government's "state of war" and its violent attempt to restore a "normal" situation in Poland was based on four misconceptions. The first was that Solidarity had been hijacked by extremists and that after their removal from the political scene, "people would [come] back to their senses." The second was that, with Solidarity eliminated, it would be possible to re-atomize Polish society while improving the economic situation, which party leaders had convinced themselves was the root of social unrest. The goal, following Hungary, was the "Kádárization" of Poland. The third misconception was that the Church would eventually come around and make a deal with the government over the corpse of Solidarity. The fourth was that the West, driven by bankers' concerns about a Polish debt default, would weaken in its resolve and eventually accommodate itself to the restored Polish order.[72] The first three assumptions illustrate just how badly the regime had misread the moral revolution triggered by John Paul II's June 1979 pilgrimage.

It was impossible to return Poland to the status quo ante August 1980. The country had gone through a moral and psychological trap-gate from which there was no turning back. But it was not impossible for the regime to make life miserable. Poland, during the martial law period (which formally ended in July 1983) and the years immediately following, was in a state of decomposition. Frustrated in its efforts at "Kádárization," the regime slowly lost its grip, "like the slow retreat of a plague." The economy deteriorated even further and life was hard.[73]

By conviction and necessity, much of the Church in Poland during this period adopted a strategy of "resistance through cultural independence," not unlike what some Poles, including Karol Wojtyła, had done during the infinitely worse Nazi Occupation. If Poland, the nation, had been invaded by the Polish state by the imposition of martial law, the Polish Church would tacitly invoke a claim of "moral extraterritoriality." Just as embassies in a foreign country enjoy "extraterritorial" legal status and are considered the sovereign territory of the country represented, the Catholic Church in Poland became a virtual embassy from the Polish nation to itself.

A young Warsaw priest, Jerzy Popiełuszko, became a national symbol of this strategy of cultural resistance. His parish church in Warsaw, St. Stanisław Kostka, was in the Żoliborz district, just off the "Square of the Defense of the Paris Commune," a traditionally left-wing, bohemian neighborhood and one of the few places in Poland where one could find an intellectually respectable Marxist.[74] In January 1982, Father Popiełuszko, thirty-five, initiated a "Mass for the Fatherland" at the Kostka church. It soon was drawing a packed house, with several thousand workers, widows, students, intellectuals, aristocrats, peasants, black marketeers, and even Communist Party members jammed inside, and perhaps 10,000 more congregants outside, often in cold or inclement weather, listening on loudspeakers to Popiełuszko's quiet eloquence.[75] The young priest's message drew out the implications of John Paul's challenge to vanquish evil with good. Popiełuszko insisted on both nonviolence and resistance. Resistance was a moral obligation in the face of "the power," and nonviolence was the Christian way of resistance.[76]

Father Jerzy Popiełuszko confronted his congregants and the thousands who came to hear him from all over the country with choices: "Which side will you take? The side of good or the side of evil? Truth or falsehood? Love or hatred?"[77] The New York Times's Warsaw bureau chief, Michael Kaufman, recognized moral dynamite when he saw it: "Nowhere else from East Berlin to Vladivostok could anyone stand before ten or fifteen thousand people and use a microphone to condemn the errors of state and party. Nowhere, in that vast stretch encompassing some four hundred million people, was anyone else openly telling a crowd that defiance of authority was an obligation of the heart, of religion, manhood, and nationhood."[78]

There were divisions in the Polish Church during and after martial law. Cardinal Glemp had a different set of priorities and a different understanding of the clergy's role than Father Popiełuszko and other activist Solidarity priests. A lawyer, the Primate seems not to have shared John Paul II's view that communism was essentially finished, and acted as if he expected to be negotiating with the likes of General Jaruzelski for perhaps decades to come. Cardinal Glemp was dubious about Solidarity's internal pluralism and uncertain about the Church's responsibilities to non-Catholic dissidents.[79] He had inherited the Wyszyński tradition of the Primate as sole and unquestioned spokesman of Polish Catholicism. Lacking the old Primate's history of heroic resistance, he did not have the personal moral authority to act in that role—which was, in any event, virtually impossible, given the forces that had been let loose in the clergy and among activist lay Catholics during Solidarity's fifteen months of freedom.

Thus the situation in June 1983, when John Paul II arrived in Poland for his second pastoral pilgrimage, was one of sadness, compounded by division. The rebirth of Solidarity was being impeded not only by the regime's thuggery, but by a breakdown of the vibrant solidarity among Poles he had ignited four years before.

John Paul had wanted to come in August 1982 for the 600th anniversary of the Black Madonna of Jasna Góra, but martial law made that impossible.[80] Nor was the Jaruzelski government overly cooperative in making arrangements for the June 1983 visit. The regime wanted to set up the venues so that it would be difficult for the Pope to work the crowds (the argument was that the American CIA would organize an incident and then blame the Polish government). The government also insisted on controlling access to the venues with layer upon layer of security controls; the clear intent was to keep the crowds down, if at all possible. Perhaps the most controversial point was the Pope's desire to meet with Lech Wałęsa. The minister of internal affairs, General Czesław Kiszczak, argued this with papal trip planner Father Roberto Tucci without ever mentioning the Solidarity leader's name. Wałęsa was "that guy" or "the man with the big family." "Why," the interior minister demanded, "does the Pope want to meet with a man who doesn't represent anybody in this country?" During these negotiations, and to the Pope's surprise, Tucci managed to convince the authorities to provide enough radio circuits so that people all over the country could listen to John Paul's addresses simultaneously.[81]

The Pope arrived in Warsaw on June 16, and the contrast between his demeanor in 1979 and 1983 was immediately apparent. As the Pope stood with head bowed and a somber expression on his face during the welcoming ceremonies, an older woman commented to a reporter, "He is sad. You see, he understands." President Henryk Jabłoński didn't. He greeted the Pope saying that "His Holiness's visit testifies to the gradual normalization of life [in] our country." Later that day, at St. John's Cathedral, John Paul made clear what he had signaled nonverbally at the airport, saying that he had come to Poland to "stand beneath the cross of Christ" with all of his countrymen, "especially with those who are most acutely tasting the bitterness of disappointment, humiliation, suffering, of being deprived of their freedom, of being wronged, of having their dignity trampled on." He then thanked God that Cardinal Wyszyński had been spared having to witness "the painful events connected with the date December 13, 1981." The censors cut the phrase from the papal text printed in secular and Catholic newspapers.[82] Tens of thousands of Poles marched from the cathedral past Communist Party headquarters chanting, "So-li-dar-ność, So-li-dar-ność," "Lech-Wa-łę-sa, Lech-Wa-łę-sa," *De-mo-kra-cja, De-mo-kra-cja. . . .*"[83]

The pilgrimage rapidly became the occasion for public, nonviolent political catharsis, but that was not the Pope's primary purpose. He had come, as always, as an evangelist—this time, to break the fever of despair that had weakened the nation since December 13, 1981, and to teach a lesson about the personal moral foundations of cultural resistance. One of the pilgrimage's greatest sermons on this theme came at Częstochowa during a meeting with young people. It began with the Pope loosening the tension in the crowd of more than half a million with an impromptu papal skit. When he appeared on the platform that had been erected on the monastery ramparts, he simply couldn't speak. The crowd's chants of "Long live the Pope!" and "The Pope with us!" made it impossible to hear anything else. After minutes of this, his unmistakable voice finally carried over the din: "I want to ask you if a certain person who came today from Rome to Jasna Góra may be allowed to speak?" A new chant started: "Go-a-head, go-a-head," changing to "Clo-ser-to-us, clo-ser-to-us!" John Paul boomed out again, "Do you hear me? I'm coming closer"—and he started to walk down from the platform along the red-carpeted steps, a Pauline monk staggering behind him with the portable microphone. When he stopped, he was still fifty yards from the first row of the crowd. Yet this little piece of theater reignited the current that had run between him and the crowds in 1979. Now, they were silent; now, he could teach them.[84]

He spoke as one who had known the experience of degradation and humiliation during the Occupation. No one could accuse him of not knowing what his countrymen were experiencing now. And so the Gospel message could be preached in the power of its simplicity: the love of Christ was more powerful "than all the experiences and disappointments that life can prepare for us." Every Pole could live in that love, no matter what the political circumstances, by choosing the "greater freedom" to be found in reforming one's own life, which was the precondition to reforming society. They must "call good and evil by name." That was the way to build "a firm barrier against demoralization." Then he quietly said the unsayable word, speaking of the "fundamental *solidarity* between human beings" as the basis of society and the principle of its "moral and social renewal." "Mother of Jasna Góra," he prayed in conclusion, ". . . help us to *persevere in hope.*" As he walked slowly back up to the platform and into the monastery, the crowd began a last chant, "Stay-with-us, stay-with-us. . . ."[85]

In Kraków, on June 22, he gave Poland two new icons of the "greater freedom" to be sought through moral and cultural resistance when he beatified the "two rebels" he had preached about in 1963, the Carmelite Rafał Kalinowski and "Brother Albert" Chmielowski. The Pope also continued the kind of spontaneous evening dialogue with the Kraków crowds that had been a feature of the 1979 pilgrimage. He was late in returning to the archbishop's residence one evening from an extraordinary, previously unscheduled meeting with General Jaruzelski at Wawel Castle. Cardinal Macharski, as host, told Cardinal Casaroli, Cardinal Jean-Marie Lustiger of Paris, and other dinner guests to begin supper. John Paul eventually came to the table, ate some soup, and then heard a crowd of students calling to him from outside. He got up, went to the window, and had a lengthy back-and-forth with the crowd. After fifteen minutes or so of this, Cardinal Casaroli remarked to the dinner company, "What does he want? Does he want bloodshed? Does he want war? Does he want to overthrow the government? Every day I have to explain to the authorities that there is nothing to this."[86]

John Paul II knew exactly what he wanted and precisely how far he could go. In his formal remarks before meeting privately with General Jaruzelski at the Belvedere Palace in Warsaw, he avoided the point of maximum concern to the Soviet Union—the Christian basis of Europe's cultural unity and the historic travesty of the Yalta division of the continent. But there was no backing off on the message to Poland's rulers. "Social renewal" (a favorite communist slogan) could only begin, he told Jaruzelski and the others, with the "social accords" that had been reached in 1980. Later, those outside the room where the two men met privately heard raised voices, as the Pope pressed Jaruzelski to open a dialogue with the Solidarity leaders he had imprisoned.[87] At a Mass in Warsaw, he returned to the theme of dialogue, insisting that a social order "in which man's fundamental rights will be respected" could only be created on the basis of a dialogue between the governors and the governed.

It was a sharp message to men who claimed that they had been acting to protect Poland's sovereignty from Soviet intervention. As Timothy Garton Ash observed, John Paul was telling General Jaruzelski and his colleagues, "You never tire of proclaiming your sovereignty—okay, then behave like a sovereign power."[88] The message was not that of a man who thought that Jaruzelski had no choice but to do what he did in December 1981.

In his meetings with Jaruzelski and with the Polish episcopate, John Paul made clear that he would not accept a solution in which the Church, in return for its independence, would cooperate with the state through officially recognized Catholic unions or an officially sanctioned Catholic "opposition" party. Some in the Polish Church favored this, and it certainly was an appealing prospect for the regime. The Pope wasn't having any of it. Solidarity had its own integrity and its right to independence. There could be no genuine dialogue, and thus no genuine social renewal, without genuinely independent workers' associations. The Church would not cut a deal with the regime behind Solidarity's back.[89]

As if to drive this point home symbolically, John Paul had insisted on seeing Lech Wałęsa. The regime finally agreed on a "strictly private meeting" at a cabin in the Tatras, to which Wałęsa was helicoptered by his captors. Father Józef Tischner, the former Solidarity congress chaplain, exploded the myth of the "strictly private meeting" with a single, blunt sentence—"There are no private meetings with the Pope."[90] For his part, Wałęsa stressed the language of dialogue in his future public statements. For theirs, the authorities stated that "There will be no dialogue . . . with the former leadership of 'Solidarity.'"[91] The slow-motion decomposition of the regime, and the Polish economy, would continue.

John Paul II could not persuade Jaruzelski and the regime to talk to the opposition, but his eight days in Poland in June 1983 had strengthened the resistance Church, made clear that there would be no deals over or around

Solidarity, and given his countrymen a measure of hope and something to think about for the immediate future. The question, as in Central America, was authentic Christian liberation. The heaviest chains human beings could wear, he had told the Poles, were "the fetters of hatred. . . ." Authentic liberation was cruciform, in the Christian view of the world: "Forgiveness is love's might, forgiveness is not weakness. To forgive does not mean to resign from truth and justice."

Some took this for unexpected mildness, even accommodation. Calling good and evil by name was an explosive force in the world, however. John Paul did not doubt that a Poland mature enough to be nonconformist, confronting the communist culture of the lie with the power of truth, would eventually achieve its liberation—and in a manner worthy of a Christian nation, witnessing to the truth about the dignity of the human person. It was a question of time.

Bishops and the Bomb

John Paul II's distinctive moral-cultural approach to world politics set the context for the Holy See's intervention in the pastoral letter on war and peace being prepared by the bishops of the United States in 1981–1983.

The proposal for such a pastoral letter was a by-product of the nuclear freeze movement, many advocates of which believed that human rights issues should be subordinated to the great goal of reaching arms control agreements. Those agreements, in turn, would lessen the danger of nuclear war, it was argued. This uncoupling of human rights and arms control was evident in the first two drafts of the U.S. bishops' pastoral letter. After the second draft, the Holy See summoned the American bishops and experts responsible for preparing a third draft to the Vatican for an international consultation on January 18–19 with officials of the Curia and bishops and specialists from France, West Germany, Great Britain, Belgium, Italy, and the Netherlands. Cardinal Ratzinger (who chaired the consultation) and Cardinal Casaroli participated for two days. It was an indication that there were theological issues as well as questions of prudential judgment to be sorted out, and that the Pope was seriously concerned about the line the American bishops were developing.

The participants decided that the consultation's results would be synthesized by Father Jan Schotte, CICM, the Secretary of the Pontifical Justice and Peace Commission, and published as "a point of reference and a guide to the U.S. bishops in preparing the next draft of their pastoral letter." John Paul II intended that the synthesis be sent directly to each bishop of the United States without commentary. The President of the National Conference of Catholic Bishops, Archbishop John Roach of St. Paul-Minneapolis, and Cardinal-elect Joseph Bernardin of Chicago, the chairman of the bishops' drafting committee, unilaterally attached to the Schotte synthesis a cover letter explaining that the Vatican consultation had not raised grave questions about the second draft and that serious substantive changes would not be required in the third draft.

This was not an interpretation supported by a careful reading of the document. The synthesis clearly suggested that the pastoral letter's second draft had confused the different levels of teaching authority in the Church, and was apt to promote confusion among Catholics while diminishing the Church's credibility. The Schotte synthesis also suggested that the bishops, as "teachers of the faith," should not "take sides" in policy matters "when various prudential applications are possible." The synthesis urged that a third draft make clear the distinction between the peace of the Kingdom of God and the peace that was possible in this world, and suggested that the bishops' document had erred in proposing two normative traditions of moral reasoning about war and peace in Catholic moral theology, pacifism, and the just-war tradition. Pacifism had been accorded a greater respect in contemporary Catholic theology, but the normative tradition guiding decisions about war and peace remained the just-war tradition.

The consultation and the Schotte synthesis had a considerable effect on the bishops' third draft, which became the basis of the May 1983 pastoral letter, "The Challenge of Peace: God's Promise and Our Response" [TCOP]. Even in its final, revised form, though, "The Challenge of Peace" did not come to grips with the culture-driven understanding of history that John Paul II had been proposing to the Church and the world since his election. The document quoted copiously from various statements of the Pope's, but the analysis of TCOP drew far more from the conventions of American political science and international relations theory than from John Paul's vision of the depth dimension of late twentieth-century history. Even more strikingly, the Americans had not even begun to reckon seriously with what the new human rights resistance in east central Europe meant for both that captive region and the Soviet Union. In contrast to the approach the Pope took in Poland in June 1983, the American bishops' pastoral letter of a month before—hailed at the time as a great challenge to U.S. foreign and military policy—reflected a much less adventurous view of the Church's relationship to the worlds of political power. The U.S. bishops were determined to be "players" in the game. John Paul II wanted to change the game.[92]

The two-year debate over "The Challenge of Peace" did bring to public attention a previously obscure former U.S. Navy chaplain who would become one of John Paul II's bolder episcopal appointments. Bishop John J. O'Connor was auxiliary bishop of what was then called the Military Ordinariate, the "diocese" of U.S. military and diplomatic personnel, when he was appointed to the committee drafting TCOP. In May 1983, O'Connor was named bishop of Scranton, Pennsylvania. The man whom Jeane J. Kirkpatrick once described as the brightest student she had ever had took Scranton by storm and was named the city's "Man of the Year" six months after his arrival.

On October 9, 1983, Cardinal Terence Cooke of New York died after a protracted, heroic, and, by many accounts, saintly struggle with leukemia. Although the Catholic Church in the United States has, technically, no primatial see, New York is undoubtedly one of the two or three most important archdioceses, if not the most important archdiocese, in the United States. Given its position at the center of international communications and finance, New York also looms large in international Catholic affairs. John Paul evidently wanted an archbishop of New York who could take advantage of its bully pulpit and bring a more assertive, culture-challenging voice to the American Catholic scene. Passing over a triad of candidates who reflected the comfortable and, by some reckonings, ingrown mainstream of the U.S. Bishops' Conference, he pulled Bishop O'Connor out of Scranton after less than nine months and, on January 26, 1984, named him archbishop of New York. There, O'Connor quickly emerged as a powerful defender of the Catholic claim to a place for the Church's moral teaching in American public life. The new archbishop also revitalized the pro-life cause in American Catholicism at a point at which some bishops were inclined, by exhaustion or conviction, to move the defense of the right to life of the unborn from the front of their public policy agenda.

Shortly after his appointment to New York, O'Connor was in Rome and went to see the Pope. "Welcome," John Paul said, "to the archbishop of the capital of the world!"[93]

INTELLECTUALS

In August 1983, John Paul II began a biennial series of summer humanities seminars at Castel Gandolfo. Unique in the annals of the modern papacy, these seminars brought Christian, Jewish, agnostic, and atheistic philosophers, historians, and other scholars into conversation with the Pope, for whom serious intellectual exchange remained a passion.

The Castel Gandolfo seminars were a Roman variant on the discussions with academics that Father Józef Tischner organized and Cardinal Wojtyła hosted at his residence in Kraków. During the latter years of these meetings, Wojtyła met Krzysztof Michalski, a doctoral graduate of the Jagiellonian University who was then an adjunct professor of philosophy at the University of Warsaw. In 1981, shortly before the Bydgoszcz crisis, Michalski and Tischner were in Rome and Michalski broached the idea of a new institute that would bring Polish scholars together with their Western counterparts. The Pope was interested, in part because he sensed that difficulties were on the horizon in Poland and he wanted Polish intellectuals to have an outlet to the West. With the Pope's endorsement of the idea and a letter of introduction from Cardinal Casaroli, Michalski and Tischner went to Vienna to discuss the plan with Cardinal Franz König, whose first question was, "Who's going to pay for this?" The Viennese cardinal soon rose to the occasion and the Institut für die Wissenschaften vom Menschen [IWM], the Institute for Human Sciences, was launched prior to the imposition of martial law in Poland. After the "state of war" was declared, Michalski stayed in Vienna to run the institute while

Father Tischner lived in Poland and came to Vienna as circumstances permitted. From the outset, and with John Paul's approval, IWM was intended to be an independent scholarly institution—not explicitly Roman Catholic, neither left nor right politically, a place where serious research and debate could take place on the future of the humanities and their relationship to the free society.

The first Castel Gandolfo conversations organized by IWM were held in August 1983 on the topic, "Man in the Modern Sciences." The participants included such intellectual luminaries as philosophers Hans-Georg Gadamer, Charles Taylor, and Emmanuel Lévinas, legal scholar Ernst-Wolfgang Böckenförde, physicist Carl-Friedrich von Weizsäcker, the German theologians Gerhard Ebeling (Lutheran) and Johannes Metz (Roman Catholic), in addition to Tischner, Michalski, and others. Each participant presented a paper, which was discussed by the group in a meeting room or on a balcony overlooking Lake Albano, with the Pope listening but rarely interrupting. Meals were organized according to language groups, with polyglot John Paul switching from group to group at different lunches and dinners. At the end of the papers and discussions, John Paul II offered a personal summary of the conversation and then commented on its implications.

John Paul had known Emmanuel Lévinas, the French Jewish philosopher of dialogue and intellectual heir of Martin Buber, prior to being elected Pope, and had a great respect for his work. For his part, Lévinas, who had yet to meet John Paul as Pope, wondered how he would be received. John Paul took Lévinas by the hand, and said, "Thank you for wanting to meet with me." The Frenchman was so floored that he was speechless until lunch—when he then asked the Pope what he was doing meeting with Palestinian leader Yassir Arafat.[94] John Paul, for his part, was not above joking with his illustrious guests. A group photograph was to be taken at the end of the seminar. Father Metz, whose controversial "political theology" was widely regarded as one of the inspirations of Latin American liberation theology, was among those shuffling around, not wanting to seem to be pushing themselves closer to the Pope, in the line-up for the photo. John Paul spotted Metz and called out, "You, Metz, a little closer to the Pope!"—at which everyone laughed, including Metz, who did what he was told.[95]

IWM continued to organize the Castel Gandolfo conversations throughout the pontificate. The roster of intellectuals involved was primarily middle European in origin and intellectual temperament, and the general seminar topics and papers reflected dominantly European (and particularly German-oriented) intellectual problems, interests, and preoccupations. Father Tischner once commented on a curious feature of the seminars. It was easier, he said, to invite nonbelievers than Catholics, since the intellectual factionalism in the Church had become so ingrained that if someone from a particular camp were invited, others would be angry.[96]

Despite some limits on their intellectual range, the Castel Gandolfo conversations became one of the trademarks of the papacy of John Paul II. Like his May 1982 creation of the Pontifical Council for Culture as a permanent office of the Roman Curia, the seminars reflected not only his personal interest in the life of the mind, but his conviction that serious intellectual dialogue was crucial to the reconstruction of a genuine humanism for the twenty-first century, and his commitment as Pope to doing something about that.[97]

The Jesuit General Congregation

If John Paul was successful in opening and sustaining a dialogue with some of the Western world's most prominent intellectuals, he was far less successful in applying papal shock therapy to the Society of Jesus, which had been, historically, one of the Church's most intellectually assertive religious communities.

The papal intervention in the internal governance of the Society in October 1981 had not been followed by open revolt, as some expected. Numerous Jesuits wrote John Paul, individually or in groups, to express their dissatisfaction. One group of seventeen, including the eminent German theologian Karl Rahner, wrote that they accepted the Pope's decision, but since he was now acting as their superior, they felt free to tell him that they "could not see the finger of God" in his intervention.[98] Some months afterward, John Paul told his delegate, Father Paolo Dezza, that he admired the way the Jesuits had reacted to his decision.

Until Father Pittau arrived from Japan in late November 1981, Father O'Keefe, the former vicar general, continued, at Father Dezza's bidding, to do exactly what he had been doing before the papal intervention, including running various meetings for the papal delegate, who was eighty and almost completely blind. Father Arrupe's four general assistants remained at the Jesuit generalate, and it was they who suggested to Dezza and Pittau that the Jesuit provincials from around the world be called to Rome so that the delegate and his deputy could tell them what the Pope's concerns and hopes were. Dezza and Pittau agreed and met with the eighty-six provincials at Villa Cavaletti outside Rome in February 1982. The entire group then had an audience with John Paul in the Vatican on February 27.

The Pope's lengthy address was devoted primarily to praise for the Society's distinguished history and its intellectual, missionary, theological, and pastoral apostolates. Brief mention was made of the importance of an "exact interpretation" of Vatican II, of a distinctively priestly engagement with the quest for justice, and of a rigorous "spiritual, doctrinal, disciplinary, and pastoral" formation for aspiring Jesuits. As if to further underscore his confidence in the Society, John Paul asked them to take up with even greater urgency four tasks: ecumenism, inter-religious dialogue, dialogue with atheists, and the promotion of justice. At the end of the address, the Pope indicated that, if things continued the way they had been going, it would "be possible to convoke the General Congregation within this year."[99]

The address was interpreted by those most opposed to the papal intervention in the Society's governance as a virtual apology for what had taken place a mere four months earlier.[100] Fathers Dezza and Pittau evidently continued to assure John Paul and the relevant curial officials that the papally imposed period of reflection was going as hoped, for on December 8, 1982, with the Pope's approval, Dezza convoked a General Congregation, the 33rd in the Society's history, for September 2, 1983. John Paul concelebrated the opening Mass of the Congregation with more than 200 delegates. His homily asked that the delegates keep in mind the influence that the Society had on other religious, on priests, and on the laity—"What you do often has some reverberations that you do not suspect."[101]

The Congregation wasted no time in electing a new Father General. The delegates clearly understood that to elect one of Arrupe's general assistants would have been interpreted as a direct slap at the Pope. On the other hand, they were determined not to elect anyone who might have been identified as the Pope's candidate—for example, Father Pittau or Father Roberto Tucci. Father Dezza was obviously impossible because of age. After four days of internal discussions the delegates had reached agreement, and on the first ballot, in forty-five minutes, elected Father Pieter-Hans Kolvenbach, a Dutchman who had spent much of his life in Beirut and had been rector of the Pontifical Oriental Institute in Rome for the past two years. In filling the posts immediately under the General, the delegates consistently rejected Father Pittau, who before his appointment as deputy to Father Dezza had been a widely respected figure in the Society. The delegates, in other words, were determined to assert their independence, but to do so in a way that would not immediately provoke further anxiety in the Curia or risk another papal intervention.

Pittau, for his part, believes that the papal intervention had the desired effect: greater humility, a willingness to listen to each other more carefully, a relearning of the fundamental characteristics of the Society, a better dialogue with bishops around the world.[102] Father Tucci agrees that the intervention was successful, although he concedes that "Dezza did not change the Order very much." What did change, thanks to Dezza's old connections and diplomatic skills, was the quality of relations between the Curia and the Society. Dezza may also have been able to suggest to concerned Curialists that the concerns about the Society under Father Arrupe had been exaggerated.[103]

Father Dezza once told Father Tucci that John Paul II had "many hesitations" about allowing Dezza to convoke the 33rd General Congregation, but permitted it because he trusted Dezza's opinion that the message intended by the October 1981 intervention had been received and accepted.[104] Father Dezza may indeed have believed that to be the case; subsequent events suggest that his view was too sanguine.

Father Kolvenbach, a man of deep piety, would not prove to be an assertive General—which was, one assumes, no disappointment to the delegates who elected him so quickly. Jesuit training continued along many of the same lines that had raised earlier concerns. Jesuit involvement in partisan political activity in various Latin American venues also continued. Jesuit theologians would, over the years, be at the forefront of various efforts to "inculturate" Catholic doctrine and worship in Asian societies in ways that seemed to some to deny that Jesus Christ was the sole, unique savior of the world. Jesuit universities in the United States continued to weaken their once-distinctive core curriculum and their Catholic identity. The oldest of them, Georgetown, engaged in a lengthy controversy over whether crucifixes in its classrooms violated the university's commitment to pluralism. The Society continued to diminish in numbers, while other religious orders more attuned to John Paul II's vision of the priesthood and religious life grew.[105] If serious change in the direction of Jesuit life and ministry was the purpose of John Paul II's 1981 intervention, it is not easy to see how the intervention can be rated a success.

Among those who applauded the initial intervention, there are critics who claim that the entire story exemplifies one dimension of the pontificate of John Paul II—a failure to complete bold initiatives with sufficient disciplinary follow-through. A more plausible explanation is that John Paul's fault, if one wishes to describe it as such, is to project his own virtues onto others. The intervention in October 1981 was aimed at creating a period of reflection in which the Society of Jesus could look again at the Second Vatican Council, and at John Paul's pontificate as an effort to secure the Council's authentic teaching in the life of the Church. That seems to have been what the Pope, projecting his own spirit of obedience onto men who had taken a special vow of obedience to the Bishop of Rome, hoped for.

That hope did not take sufficient account of the degree of anti-Roman animus that had built up in the Society, nor the fact that the levers of power at the 33rd General Congregation remained in the hands of the legatees of the Arrupe-O'Keefe years. The Jesuits had indeed learned some things during Father Dezza's delegacy, but the learning seemed to have had more to do with repairing broken lines of communication between the Roman Curia and the Jesuit generalate than with such matters of substance as training, theology, social activism, and way of life.

The Jesuit intervention and its aftermath, set against John Paul II's cordial relationship with new renewal movements of priests like the Legionaries of Christ, also suggests that the Pope conceived his role vis-à-vis Catholic religious communities more as a matter of nurturing and encouraging those who were self-consciously orthodox and loyal to the Church's teaching than of disciplining dissidents and bringing them to heel. This is, in part, a reflection of his respect for the freedom of others. It is also an expression of his calm confidence that the authentic spirit of Vatican II will win out over time, because it is far more compelling—indeed, far more radical—than the inadequate or false interpretations that had led to, among other things, the crisis of the Jesuits in the 1970s.

LIBERATION AND REDEMPTION

Karol Wojtyła's lifelong interest in anniversaries and jubilee years derives from his conviction that God's action in history has sanctified time.[106] For Christians, time is not mere chronology; time is the dramatic arena that God chose to enter for the salvation of the world. Anniversaries and jubilees are occasions to bring the depth dimension of history to the surface of Christian consciousness.

According to traditional dating, the 1983–1984 Holy Year of the Redemption marked the 1,950th anniversary of the turning point in world history, the redeeming death of Jesus Christ.[107] Celebrating the anniversary of humanity's redemption was a good in itself. This particular Holy Year was also intended to set human liberation in its proper theological and religious context.

The custom of a jubilee year of pilgrimage to Rome began with Pope Boniface VIII in 1300. By the Renaissance, the practice of holding a special "Holy Year" every quarter-century had become established. Holy Years were held every twenty-five years from 1450 until 1800, when the sequence was broken by the turmoil of the French Revolution and its effects in Europe. The only Holy Year of the nineteenth century was held in 1825. Ninety-year-old Leo XIII revived the custom in 1900 (and reminisced about having attended the Roman celebrations in 1825). Pius XI held a Holy Year in 1933, to mark the 1,900th anniversary of the death of Christ—the precedent invoked by John Paul II in calling a Holy Year for 1983–1984.

The traditional Holy Year pilgrimage to Rome was built around the city's four patriarchal basilicas (St. Peter's, St. Mary Major, St. John Lateran, and St. Paul Outside the Walls), each of which has a special "holy door" that is opened only during the Holy Year and is the pilgrims' portal to the basilica.[108] In striking contrast to other Holy Years, John Paul wanted this Holy Year of the Redemption to be a universal celebration, and asked every diocese in the world to appoint a jubilee church with its own holy door to which pilgrims could come, and which would enjoy the same status as the Roman basilicas. John Paul also extended the reach of the Holy Year in Rome itself, so that pilgrims could satisfy the customary requirements by visiting the catacombs or the Church of Santa Croce in Gerusalemme (the Church of the Holy Cross in Jerusalem, near the Lateran basilica), instead of the patriarchal basilicas.

The Holy Year of the Redemption began on March 25, 1983. On a rainy, chilly afternoon, John Paul II led a procession from the tiny church of St. Stephen of the Abyssinians in the Vatican, through St. Peter's Square, to the narthex of the basilica. There, wielding the golden hammer used by Pius XI in 1933, he knocked three times on the holy door of St. Peter's, which was then opened. John Paul kissed the door jamb and went to the papal altar where Mass was celebrated. In his homily, the Pope stressed that, in entering the holy door of St. Peter's, those present were also symbolically entering "all the Christian communities, whatever their nature and wherever they are in the world, especially in the catacombs of the modern world. The special Jubilee of the Redemption is the Holy Year of the whole Church."[109]

During the Holy Year John Paul II baptized twenty-seven adult converts (mostly from Asia), and celebrated the marriages of thirty-eight couples. He beatified ninety-nine martyrs of the French Revolution and two martyrs of the Chinese revolution of the 1930s. In July, he recognized the public veneration of the fifteenth-century painter Fra Angelico, making official what had long been his popular title: "Blessed Fra Angelico."[110]

The Holy Year had a pronounced ecumenical dimension. On October 31, John Paul wrote a letter to Cardinal Johannes Willebrands, President of the Secretariat for Christian Unity, to mark the 500th anniversary of the birth of Martin Luther. The letter noted Luther's "deep religious feeling," which had shaped a personality "driven with burning passion by the question of eternal salvation." Healing the breach of the sixteenth century between Roman Catholicism and the Lutheran Reformation would require continued historical scholarship, "without preconceived ideas," in order to "arrive at a true image of the reformer, of the whole period of the Reformation, and of the persons involved in it. Fault, where it exists, must be recognized, wherever it may lie." With "a shared interpretation of the past," Lutherans and Catholics would have a "new point of departure" for their theological dialogue. Beginning with what Lutherans and Catholics held in common—"in the Word of Scripture, in the Confessions of faith, and in the Councils of the ancient Church"—that dialogue should continue in a spirit of "penitence and a readiness to learn from listening."[111]

On the Third Sunday of Advent, John Paul visited the Christuskirche of Rome's Lutheran community, where he participated in and preached at an ecumenical Liturgy of the Word.[112] The Lutheran parish had sent out invitations to an "Advent Service with the Bishop of Rome." Standing in the Christuskirche pulpit wearing a plain red stole over his white papal cassock, John Paul said that the Luther quincentenary was "the daybreak of the advent of the rebuilding of our unity and community." That unity, he proposed, "is also the best preparation for the advent of God in our time. . . ." The service closed with Roman Catholics and Lutherans reciting the Apostles' Creed together.[113]

Ecumenical outreach to eastern Christianity also figured prominently in the Holy Year. On April 16, 1983, John Paul II received Karekin Sarkissian, the Armenian Catolicos of Cilicia. A month later, on May 13, Ignatius IV Hazim became the first Greek Orthodox Patriarch of Antioch to pay a formal ecumenical visit to Rome. On June 6, Moran Mar Basileius Marthoma Matheos I, the Catolicos of the Syrian Orthodox Church of India, came to the Vatican and was received by the Pope. On June 30, John Paul met with Metropolitan Meliton of Chalcedon, the representative of Ecumenical Patriarch Dimitrios at the Roman celebration of the solemnity of Sts. Peter and Paul.

A special Holy Year celebration for children was held in the Paul VI Audience Hall on January 8, 1984. John Paul told 8,000 children that they were "a crown for the Child Jesus," and admitted to "something you already know well:

you are the Pope's favorites."[114] Later that month, on January 22, John Paul made the first papal visit to a Gypsy community, at Rome's St. Rita parish.[115]

Penance and Reconciliation

The Sixth Ordinary Assembly of the Synod of Bishops met during the Holy Year, from September 29 to October 29, 1983, to consider "Penance and Reconciliation in the Mission of the Church Today." New forms of religious education and pastoral practice since the Second Vatican Council had helped displace a certain mechanical understanding of sin, confession, and penance from Catholic life, but the post-conciliar period had also seen an unexpected, dramatic, and unwelcome decline in Catholic penitential practice. The long lines of penitents waiting outside confessionals in Catholic churches in the Western world on Saturday afternoons were now a thing of the past. Some pastors had instituted liturgical penance services with "general absolution" granted to the entire congregation, without individual confessions. The decline in penitential practice was linked to the question of what actually constituted a sin. What was the nature of personal moral responsibility, given all that we know of human psychology? Was sin primarily personal or social? Could one sin in such a way as to jeopardize, even cut off, one's relationship with God?

The 221 Synod Fathers discussed these issues for a month. Bishops influenced by liberation theology urged an even greater emphasis on "social sin" and work for justice as the essence of the Church's ministry of reconciliation. Others suggested that something serious had been drained from Catholic life since the Council and called for a renewal of traditional penitential practice. In *Reconciliatio et Paenitentia* [Reconciliation and Penance], the apostolic exhortation that completed the work of the Synod, John Paul II refocused these disputed issues in terms of the personal drama of human freedom.[116]

The wellspring of reconciliation, John Paul writes, is the cross of Christ. Its vertical beam symbolizes the human need for reconciliation with God, and its horizontal crossbeam represents the need for reconciliation within the human family.[117] Because the Church is the Body of Christ, its "central task" is "reconciling people: with God, with themselves, with neighbor, with the whole of creation."[118] One of the ways the Church lives out that ministry of reconciliation is to remind the world of the reality of sin. For reconciliation is impossible without naming the evil that had caused division and rupture in the first place.

A true humanism must recognize that sin is "an integral part of the truth about man" because human beings are moral actors. Men and women can, and do, commit evil acts, and those acts open up a double wound: in the sinner, and in the sinner's relationships with family, friends, neighbors, colleagues, even strangers.[119] To take sin seriously is to take human freedom seriously, John Paul suggests, and that is why the personal character of sin can never be diminished. Psychological, cultural, and social factors condition the way people make their moral choices. Those factors, if strong enough, can constrain freedom and limit moral responsibility. But these facts of life could not be understood in ways that erode a deeper truth—that sin is a result of an act of personal freedom, which is a crucial dimension of human dignity.[120]

Freedom and dignity also set the context in which John Paul discusses the traditional distinction between "venial sin" (an expression of ordinary human weakness that does not involve a grave moral disorder) and "mortal sin" (which severs one's relationship with God until that relationship is repaired by repentance, confession, absolution, and penance). Some post-conciliar theologians had argued that mortal sin was virtually impossible. *Reconciliatio et Paenitentia* teaches that this theory empties the moral life of its inherent drama and denies individual moral acts their seriousness.[121] If we cannot sin greatly because we have no real moral capacity for doing serious evil, how is it that we can live nobly? Isn't the same lack of capacity implied? John Paul asks.

That is why the practice of individual confession is so important, and why Catholics have "an inviolable and inalienable right" to it. The confessional is the arena in which the personal, dramatic quality of the moral life is fully recognized. Confessor and penitent, in "one of the most awe-inspiring innovations of the Gospel," live out the drama of freedom and responsibility in an intensely personal way that cannot be replicated in general confession and absolution.[122] That is why the practice of general confession and absolution should be limited to "cases of grave necessity," as when there are insufficient confessors to hear individual confessions.[123] John Paul's stress on the imperative of individual confession was not a mulish insistence on a traditional practice simply because it was traditional. It was a recognition that the traditional practice embodied deep truths about the nature of the moral life and about human freedom.

On December 27, 1983, John Paul II gave a personal witness to the imperative of reconciliation by celebrating Mass at Rebibbia prison and visiting his would-be assassin, Mehmet Ali Agca, in his cell. Photos of their encounter showed the two men sitting on black plastic chairs, with Agca, dressed in blue jeans and running shoes, listening intensely to John Paul, whose left hand was open and slightly raised in a characteristic gesture of explanation or instruction. Speculation immediately surfaced that Agca had made some sort of confession. What in fact had happened was that the superstitious Turk had told John Paul of his fears that Our Lady of Fatima was going to wreak vengeance on him. The assassination attempt and Agca's escape had been planned so perfectly that Agca was astounded to find himself in prison and had come to attribute the Pope's survival and his imprisonment to a supernatural power. He had read in prison that the assassination attempt had taken place on the anniversary of the apparition at Fatima, and had concluded that the "goddess of Fatima" who had saved the Pope was now going to do away with him. John Paul patiently explained that Mary, whom many Muslims venerated, was the Mother of God, that she loved all people, and that Agca shouldn't be afraid.[124]

Redemptive Suffering

Six weeks after meeting with Agca, John Paul published a moving apostolic letter on the meaning of suffering, *Salvifici Doloris* [Salvific Suffering]. It was an appropriate topic during the Holy Year, because humanity had been redeemed by Christ's suffering. It was an important topic at any time, John Paul wrote, because suffering "seems to be particularly essential to the nature of man." Contrary to some contemporary conceptions, suffering was not accidental or avoidable. Suffering is "one of those points in which man is in a certain sense 'destined' to go beyond himself. . . ."[125]

There was suffering in the world because there was evil in the world.[126] Yet Christianity affirmed the essential goodness of creation. Because evil was "a certain lack, limitation, or distortion of good," suffering was enmeshed with both good and evil, and caught up in the mystery of human freedom. Suffering, in the biblical view, is sometimes a form of punishment, but that punishment is an opportunity for "rebuilding goodness in the subject who suffers," not a form of divine retribution.[127] No merely descriptive account of suffering could adequately address the profound human mystery involved in it. Nor could reason alone tell us that "love is . . . the fullest source of the answer to the question of the meaning of suffering." That required a demonstration, which God had "given . . . in the cross of Jesus Christ," whose suffering as man and as the only begotten Son of God had an "incomparable depth and intensity."[128]

The greatest suffering is death, and death is what Christ conquered by his "obedience unto death," which was then overcome in the resurrection.[129] Suffering in the world continues, but the suffering Christian can now identify his or her pain with Christ's suffering on the cross and enter more deeply into the mystery of redemption, which is the mystery of human liberation.[130] In the encounter with that liberation, the suffering individual discovers new dimensions to life as a vocation.[131]

Salvifici Doloris concludes with a meditation on Christ's parable of the Good Samaritan. Everyone who "stops beside the suffering of another person" is in the position of the Good Samaritan, whose "stopping does not mean curiosity, but availability." Suffering exists "to unleash love in the human person, that unselfish gift of one's 'I' on behalf of other people, especially those who suffer." "The world of human suffering" summons forth "the world of human love." The dynamics of solidarity in suffering are another confirmation of the Law of the Gift written into the human heart.

The World and the Church

The Holy Year did not involve a respite from affairs of state or from the administration of the Church. On January 10, 1984, full diplomatic relations between the United States and the Holy See were announced—an important development after decades of controversy during which presidents from Franklin D. Roosevelt to Jimmy Carter had been reluctant to exchange ambassadors with the Holy See for fear of Protestant backlash.[132] On January 14, the annual papal address to the diplomatic corps discussed the attributes of sovereignty, and described regional or economic alliances, freely entered into, as a form of solidarity. Sovereignty, the Pope proposed, is an expression of a nation's right to the integrity of its culture.[133] The Argentine and Chilean foreign ministers signed a joint declaration about the Beagle Channel dispute at the Vatican on January 23. John Paul met the two diplomats and told them he would visit their countries when the agreement was finalized.[134] Three weeks later, on February 13, the Pope appointed Dr. Jerome Lejeune, who had lunched with him hours before the assassination attempt in May 1981, as his representative at the state funeral of Yuri Andropov, the former KGB director who had succeeded Leonid Brezhnev as General Secretary of the Soviet Communist Party and de facto leader of the USSR. In mid-February 1984, a new concordat between the Holy See and the Republic of Italy, revising the Lateran Treaty of 1929 and reflecting the Church-state teaching of the Second Vatican Council, was completed. Roman Catholicism was no longer considered the official religion of the Italian state, religious education in state schools became optional, and clergy subsidies from the state were to end by 1990. Four days later, the Pope established the John Paul II Foundation for the Sahel, to provide development assistance to drought-stricken sub-Saharan Africa.[135] On Good Friday, 1984, two days before the close of the Holy Year, John Paul wrote an apostolic letter, *Redemptionis Anno* [In the Year of the Redemption], to Catholics living in Jerusalem, describing himself as a pilgrim in spirit to "that land where our reconciliation with God was brought about" and proposing a "special Statute internationally guaranteed" to preserve "the unique and sacred character of the City."[136]

In Poland, the "state of war" was completely lifted on July 21, 1983. A week later, over Church protests, the Sejm tightened the Polish government's grip on public life and expanded the reach of the state security services. Police and demonstrators clashed in Nowa Huta on August 31, Solidarity's anniversary. Six weeks later, on October 5, Lech Wałęsa was awarded the Nobel Prize for Peace, but the government refused him permission to receive it personally. John Paul's telegram of "heartfelt congratulations" suggested that, in honoring the Solidarity leader, the Nobel committee was honoring "the will and the efforts undertaken to resolve the difficult problems of the world of work and of Polish society through the peaceful way of sincere dialogue and the mutual cooperation of everyone."[137] Six weeks later, on November 21, the Sejm created a military "National Defense Committee" with broad "emergency powers." Two days later, the Soviet Union discontinued negotiations for an intermediate-range nuclear arms control treaty after U.S. Cruise and Pershing-2 missiles had arrived in the United Kingdom and West Germany to counter Soviet SS-20s. Weeks after Yuri Andropov's February 1984 funeral, Polish students began demonstrating to demand the restoration of crucifixes in their classrooms; a month later, on April 6, the government agreed. A Church-run foundation began distributing $2 billion in Western aid to private farmers, which had been held in abeyance until the controversy over classroom iconography was resolved.

Eleven days before the end of the Holy Year, Czechoslovakia's eighty-five-year-old Cardinal František Tomášek, continuing to grow older and bolder with John Paul's support, formally invited the Pope to visit Velehrad in Moravia in 1985, for the 1,100th anniversary of the death of St. Methodius. Students who demonstrated in favor of a papal visit were beaten by state security. The government would eventually refuse permission for John Paul II to participate in the anniversary, but the celebration in Moravia signaled the beginning of a new level of resistance in the Czechoslovak Church.

Two weeks before the Holy Year officially concluded on Easter Sunday, April 22, 1984, John Paul announced a major redeployment of personnel at the senior levels of the Roman Curia. Cardinal Bernardin Gantin, formerly President of the Pontifical Justice and Peace Commission, became Prefect of the Congregation for Bishops. Cardinal Roger Etchegaray was taken from his archdiocese of Marseilles and appointed Gantin's successor at Justice and Peace. Cardinal Eduardo Pironio was moved to the Pontifical Council for the Laity from the Congregation for Religious, where he was succeeded by Archbishop Jerome Hamer, formerly Cardinal Ratzinger's deputy at the Congregation for the Doctrine of the Faith; newly appointed Archbishop Alberto Bovone succeeded Hamer as Secretary of CDF. Archbishop Francis Arinze was brought from Nigeria to take over the Secretariat for Non-Christians. Archbishop Andrzej Deskur, the Pope's old friend, who had continued to suffer from the effects of his October 1978 stroke, became President emeritus of the Pontifical Commission for Social Communications, and was succeeded by an American, newly appointed Archbishop John Foley, longtime editor of the Philadelphia archdiocesan newspaper. The appointment of Cardinal Gantin to one of the Church's most powerful posts was both a sign of John Paul II's personal confidence and, like the appointment of Archbishop Arinze, a strong signal of support for the young Churches of Africa. Gantin fully shared the Pope's vision of the Church and the world and would see it applied to the crucial process of nominating bishops, for which his Congregation was responsible, and to the preparation of the *ad limina* visits that every head of a diocese makes to Rome every five years.[138]

Two weeks after the Holy Year formally concluded, John Paul II flew to South Korea on his twenty-first pastoral pilgrimage and second to Asia. After a refueling stop and Mass in Fairbanks, Alaska, he arrived in Seoul on May 3, 1984. After visiting Kwangju, Taegu, Pusan, and the leper colony at Sorokodo, he presided in Seoul on May 6 at the first canonization ever to take place outside Rome. One hundred three Korean martyrs of the mid-nineteenth century were canonized, including Andrew Kim Taegŏn, the first native Korean priest, and Paul Chŏng Hasang, a lay missionary. The next day, John Paul flew to Port

Moresby in Papua New Guinea, where he made papal linguistic history by preaching in Pidgin. A day in the Solomon Islands and two days in Bangkok completed a 23,000-mile journey, the third-longest of the pontificate.

John Paul flew to Switzerland the next month on a six-day pilgrimage. Its key moment was his June 12 address to the World Council of Churches [WCC] at its Geneva headquarters. The WCC had experienced considerable difficulties since Pope Paul VI had spoken in Geneva in 1969. Its Faith and Order Commission had continued to do serious ecumenical theological work and was preparing a major international study on "Baptism, Eucharist, and Ministry." It was politics—East-West politics and their linkage to Third World politics—that had brought the WCC under serious criticism. Russian Orthodoxy's membership in the WCC, and the generally accommodationist attitudes of the central staff in Geneva, had rendered the World Council virtually mute in the defense of persecuted Christians in communist countries.[139] The 1983 WCC Assembly in Vancouver, British Columbia, failed to condemn the Soviet invasion of Afghanistan and adopted a resolution that was a textbook example of positing moral equivalence between the Soviet occupation of that country and Western support for the Afghan resistance.[140] In the Third World, beneficiaries of the WCC's "Program to Combat Racism" had endorsed and in some instances paid for revolutionary violence against the Rhodesian and South African regimes.[141] In 1982, the WCC's Central Committee had cited Australia, Brazil, Canada, Chile, Colombia, Guatemala, Mexico, New Zealand, Paraguay, the Philippines, Puerto Rico, and the United States for abusing ethnic minorities. But the WCC refused to deplore the Sandinistas' destruction of Miskito Indian villages on Nicaragua's Atlantic Coast and the forced relocation of these indigenous people.[142]

John Paul's address emphasized the theological dialogue necessary to build on "the incomplete but real communion existing between us." The quest for Christian unity, he proposed, was not a negotiation but a matter of giving concrete, historical expression to the unity that already existed between Christians through their common baptism. That meant confronting, "in all frankness and friendship," the Catholic Church's conviction that "in the ministry of the Bishop of Rome it has preserved the visible pole and guarantee of all unity in full fidelity to the apostolic tradition and to the faith of the Fathers." "To be in communion with the Bishop of Rome" was to be in communion with the visible ministry of unity and doctrinal fidelity that Christ willed for his Church. This was "a difficulty" for most of the members of the WCC, John Paul conceded, but "if the ecumenical movement is really led by the Holy Spirit," ways would be found to engage the unavoidable question of the Office of Peter in the Church.

Discussing "communion in ecumenical service" to the world, John Paul characteristically stressed religious freedom, which had not occupied a prominent place on the WCC's recent agenda. The Pope also argued that Christian communities must not "preach violence" as a means of social change. Without mentioning the controversies over WCC "justice and peace" activities, John Paul sketched an alternative vision of the Church's action in the world, built on "the defense of man, of his dignity, of his liberty, of his rights, of the full meaning of his life."[143]

The five remaining days of the pilgrimage were difficult. The President of the Swiss Federation of Protestant Churches did not raise ecumenical spirits by asserting that mutual prayer was pointless without Eucharistic fellowship. John Paul tried to rally the Swiss Catholic bishops to more assertive leadership, without notable success. His defense of conscientious objection to military service and his call for a greater openness to immigration were not well-received by the Swiss. Like Germany and Austria, Switzerland would remain among the local Churches most resistant to John Paul II throughout his pontificate.

The third biennial conversation between the Pope and physicists, organized by his old Kraków friend, Jerzy Janik, was held in August. Cardinal Slipyi, leader of the Greek Catholics of Ukraine, died on September 7, 1984. Two days later, John Paul left Rome for a twelve-day visit to Canada, ranging from the Maritime Provinces to Vancouver on the Pacific Coast, with stops in Montréal, Québec, Toronto, Winnipeg, Edmonton, and Ottawa. Bad weather made it impossible for the Pope to meet with native peoples at Fort Simpson in the Northwest Territories; he promised he would return (and did so three years later). Normally placid Canada saw what papal pilgrimage planner Father Roberto Tucci remembered as some of the "most severe" security measures during any papal journey. Terrorist threats in Québec shortly before the Pope's arrival had local police and the RCMP on edge, and 5,000 security forces were assigned to the pilgrimage. At one point, John Paul, frustrated by his inability to touch the crowds because of the police cordon around him, almost shouted, "Leave me a little more room!"[144]

Less than a month later, John Paul II was compelled to meditate again on the mystery of Christian suffering. Father Jerzy Popiełuszko was driving back to Warsaw from Bydgoszcz on the night of October 19, 1984, when three State Security officers stopped his car. They beat him to death, then threw his broken, trussed body into the Vistula near Włocławek. Polish state radio announced the next day that he had disappeared and was presumed kidnaped. Thousands of Poles began to flock to Popiełuszko's church in Żoliborz, where Masses were said every hour. Lech Wałęsa came and pleaded for nonviolence. For ten days, the church and the adjacent streets were packed with tens of thousands of Poles fearing the worst.

Their expectations were confirmed during a Mass on October 30, when it was announced that Father Jerzy's body had been dredged from the Vistula. One of the local priests, Father Antonin Lewek, a friend of Popiełuszko, urged the crowd at the Kostka church to remember Christ weeping over the death of his friend, Lazarus, and not to lash back in anger. Then, Father Lewek recalled, "Something very moving happened . . . Three times they repeated after the priests, 'And forgive us our trespasses as we forgive those who trespass against us. And forgive us our trespasses as we forgive'. . . It was a Christian answer to the un-Christian deed of the murderers."[145]

Ten thousand steelworkers whom Popiełuszko had served as a chaplain signed a petition asking permission from Cardinal Glemp (who had clashed with the young priest on several occasions), to have Father Jerzy buried at St. Stanisław Kostka rather than in the priests' plot of a local cemetery. After a workers' delegation, accompanied by Popiełuszko's mother, met with the Primate on November 1, Glemp agreed to the exception. Solidarity's martyr-priest was buried in his churchyard on November 3, 1984, at a funeral Mass celebrated by the Primate and attended by hundreds of thousands who flooded the streets of Żoliborz. Cardinal Glemp's sermon was, according to one commentator, "dry" and "placatory." The emotion that everyone felt, and the tie to Rome, was voiced by the white-haired senior assistant pastor at the church, who, in his eulogy, praised his younger colleague's heroism, thanked John Paul II "who was so pleased with Father Jerzy's work," paid tribute to Wałęsa and "all those devoted to the idea of solidarity," and then closed with a promise: "One priest has died, but many priests have come forward to take up and carry on this work for the glory of God and the good of the fatherland."[146]

The struggle for Christian liberation continued in the face of, indeed through, death. To this day, the grave of Father Jerzy Popiełuszko remains a place of pilgrimage where that fact of Christian life is remembered.

14

Reliving the Council

Religion and the Renewal of a World Still Young

DECEMBER 4, 1984	Joaquín Navarro-Valls appointed director of Holy See Press Office.
FEBRUARY 27, 1985	Soviet foreign minister Andrei Gromyko unsuccessfully attempts to enlist John Paul II in campaign against the American strategic defense initiative.
MARCH 11, 1985	Congregation for the Doctrine of the Faith issues "notification" on Brazilian liberation theologian Leonardo Boff's book, *Church: Charism and Power.*
MARCH 31, 1985	John Paul II's apostolic letter *To the Youth of the World.*
APRIL 29, 1985	Major reorganization of Curial leadership, begun in 1984, is completed.
MAY 11–15, 1985	Papal pilgrimage to the Netherlands.
MAY 27, 1985	John Paul creates twenty-eight new cardinals at his third consistory.
JUNE 2, 1985	*Slavorum Apostoli,* John Paul II's fourth encyclical.
JUNE 24, 1985	Holy See's Commission for Religious Relations with the Jews issues *Notes on the Correct Way to Present the Jews and Judaism in Preaching and Catechesis in the Roman Catholic Church.*
JUNE 28, 1985	On the twenty-fifth anniversary of the Vatican's Secretariat for Christian Unity, John Paul declares the Catholic commitment to ecumenism "irrevocable."
JULY 5, 1985	Resistance Catholicism in Czechoslovakia is publicly reborn in massive celebration at Velehrad in Moravia.
AUGUST 19, 1985	John Paul II addresses 80,000 young Muslims in Casablanca.
OCTOBER 28, 1985	John Paul marks the twentieth anniversary of *Nostra Aetate* with an address to the International Catholic-Jewish Liaison Committee.

NOVEMBER 24– **DECEMBER 8, 1985**	The Synod of Bishops marks Vatican II's twentieth anniversary.
NOVEMBER 1985– **FEBRUARY 1986**	Philippine "People Power" revolution ousts Marcos regime and demonstrates new form of liberation theology.
JANUARY 31– **FEBRUARY 11, 1986**	John Paul visits India.
APRIL 13, 1986	John Paul II addresses the Roman Jewish community at the Synagogue of Rome.
MAY 18, 1986	*Dominum et Vivificantem,* John Paul's fifth encyclical.
JUNE 30, 1986	Release of letters by John Paul II, Archbishop Robert Runcie, and Cardinal Johannes Willebrands signals grave difficulties in Anglican-Roman Catholic dialogue.
JULY 25, 1986	Cardinal Joseph Ratzinger informs Father Charles Curran that he can no longer be considered a professor of Catholic theology.
OCTOBER 4–7, 1986	Third papal pilgrimage to France.
OCTOBER 27, 1986	World Day of Prayer for Peace brings world religious leaders together in Assisi.
NOVEMBER 18– **DECEMBER 1, 1986**	Longest papal pilgrimage takes John Paul to Bangladesh, Singapore, Fiji, New Zealand, Australia, and the Seychelles.
DECEMBER 27, 1986	Pontifical Justice and Peace Commission issues "At the Service of the Human Community: An Ethical Approach to the International Debt Question."

The Jewish community of Rome may be the oldest in the world with a continuous history, dating back to the days when emissaries from the Hasmonean prince, Judas Maccabee, arrived in the imperial capital. St. Paul's *Epistle to the Romans* was written to a Jewish Christian community that lived in Rome's Trastevere district, before the division between Judaism and the Christian movement hardened toward the end of the first century A.D. The Jews of Rome made numerous converts among the local pagans. By the end of the first century A.D. as many as twelve synagogues served a substantial Jewish population. There were Roman Jewish physicians, actors, shopkeepers, craftsmen, tailors, butchers, and tentmakers (like the former Saul of Tarsus), in addition to the peddlers and beggars satirized by Juvenal and Martial.

Although Christianity's adoption as the official religion of the Roman Empire made life more difficult for the Roman Jews, Jewish life in Rome from the mid-fifth century until the Counter-Reformation was freer than in any other city in Italy, and perhaps in all of Europe. During those years, whether the Roman Jews were harassed or left in relative peace depended on the attitude taken by the reigning pope. Here, too, things were different than in other parts of Europe. The popes tended to apply their anti-Jewish policies less stringently in Rome than zealots did elsewhere, and enforced the laws protecting Jews (who had no civil status anywhere in Europe) more rigorously. During this period, the Roman Jews asked for, and received, papal interventions on behalf of their persecuted brethren in France and other parts of Europe. Conditions in Rome were hardly ideal. Beginning in 1257, Jews were required to wear a special badge and distinctive clothing and were subject to harassment and ridicule during the *Carnevale* that preceded Lent. The Jewish cemetery on the Aventine Hill was desecrated in 1270. Still, the Jews of Rome were not expelled wholesale, as they were from England in 1240, and Jewish scholarship flourished in the city.

The Renaissance was the apogee of Roman Jewish life. Jews could freely engage in banking. Every Pope had a Jewish doctor. Paul III's Jewish physician, Jacob Mantino, was named to a teaching position at Rome's Sapienza University, a rarity in Europe prior to the nineteenth century. This high period was soon followed by rapidly deteriorating conditions during the Counter-Reformation. Talmudic literature was banned in the city, and Jewish intellectual life collapsed. In 1555, Paul IV decreed that a Jewish ghetto be marked out and the Roman Jews were required to live behind its gated walls. During Christian holidays, the gates were closed and the Jews were not allowed out into the city. Jewish men were required to wear a yellow hat, Jewish women a yellow kerchief. Jews were not to be addressed by titles of respect (for example, "Signor"), no Christian could have a Jewish physician, and Jewish commerce and property ownership were restricted. Most Roman Jews were forced to become peddlers, a trade in which they were regularly abused by the city's Christians. Only one synagogue was permitted, although this restriction was evaded by having five synagogues, operating according to different ethnic rites, under one roof. On their own Sabbath, Jews were required to go to churches to listen to sermons urging them to convert. The Roman Jews were not permitted to sing songs of mourning en route to the Aventine cemetery, nor could they erect tombstones there. Roman Jews were now generally worse off than Jews in other parts of Europe.

The Jews of Rome enjoyed a brief period of relative freedom during the Napoleonic occupation of the city, but with the return of the Papal States in 1814, they were once again confined to the ghetto. Though Pius IX had the ghetto walls and gates torn down in 1846, he strictly enforced the proscriptions on Jewish activity. The Roman Jews were emancipated, freed from civil disabilities, and enabled to participate in public life as citizens on an equal footing with their neighbors when the House of Savoy completed Italy's unification by conquering Rome in 1870.

Jewish life in Rome slowly recovered. A splendid new synagogue was built in 1900 to replace the old Cinque Scuole [Five Schools] building, which had burned down. Unlike its Axis ally, Mussolini's Italy was not determined to liquidate Italian Jewry. The Holocaust sufferings of the Roman Jews began in September 1943, when the retreating German army occupied Rome and internal security matters were handed over to the SS. A massive sweep of the city was carried out on October 16. More than a thousand Jews were captured and dispatched to Auschwitz, where they were murdered a week later. From October 1943 until the Allied capture of the city on June 4, 1944, the manhunts continued. A total of 2,091 Roman Jews were killed in the extermination camps, including 281 children. There were also seventy-three Roman Jews killed among the 335 hostages executed in the Ardeatine Caves in retaliation for Italian partisan raids against the German army. Catholic institutions and individual Catholic families saved Jews from the SS roundups. Roman Jews were hidden at Castel Gandolfo, where children were born in the private apartments of Pope Pius XII, which had become a temporary obstetrical ward.[1]

Throughout 1,900 years of a tortured relationship, no Pope had ever set foot in the Synagogue of Rome, although John XXIII had once had his car stopped so he could bless the Roman Jews leaving their Sabbath worship. On April 13, 1986, John Paul II drove from the Vatican, across the Tiber, and down the Lungotevere, to change history. The Bishop of Rome was going to the Synagogue of Rome to meet the Roman Jewish community at their place of worship.

It was, in a sense, the culmination of a journey that had begun in Wadowice sixty years before. As he drove to the Synagogue of Rome, John Paul carried with him his boyhood friendships with Jews, his father's lessons of tolerance, his old pastor's teaching that anti-Semitism was forbidden by the Gospel, his experience of the Nazi Occupation, and his knowledge of the Holocaust. He had developed, among churchmen, a distinctive sensitivity to Jewish pain and the drama of twentieth-century Jewish life. Now, as the protagonist in another episode in that drama, he had a bold proposal to make to the Jews of Rome, and to Jews throughout the world.

Professor Giacomo Taban, President of the Jewish Community of Rome, welcomed the Pope. The Chief Rabbi of Rome, Elio Toaff, spoke of his "intense satisfaction" at John Paul's coming. John Paul responded by underscoring their common faith in the one, true God. For it was "the Lord who stretched out the heavens and laid the foundation of the earth (*Isaiah* 51.16) and who chose Abraham in order to make him father of a multitude of children" who had, "in the mystery of his Providence," made it possible for the ancient Roman Jewish community to meet with the Bishop of Rome and the Church's universal pastor. This was neither a civic meeting nor the ceremonial beginning of a negotiation, the Pope was suggesting. This was a religious encounter between people who should "give thanks and praise to the Lord"—together. Their meeting was taking place not because emissaries between the Holy See and the Jewish Community of Rome had worked out the details, necessary as that had been. This was happening because God wanted it to happen.

His presence in the Synagogue of Rome, he said, marked an end and a beginning. The period of reflection on Jewish-Catholic relations that had begun with John XXIII and the Second Vatican Council had accomplished many important things. "Legitimate plurality" in society had been clearly affirmed. The Church had condemned anti-Semitism "by anyone"—"I repeat: 'by anyone.'" The Council had declared that "no ancestral or collective blame can be imputed to the Jews as a people for 'what happened in Christ's passion.'" The Church insisted that there was no theological justification for discrimination against Jews, and taught that the Jews had been called by God "with an irrevocable calling." The Church had also learned that Catholics could not think about Catholicism without thinking about Judaism. "The Jewish religion," John Paul said, "is not 'extrinsic' to us, but in a certain sense is 'intrinsic' to our own religion. With Judaism, therefore, we have a relationship which we do not have with any other religion. You are our dearly beloved brothers and, in a certain way, it could be said that you are our elder brothers."

To have moved this far in less than three decades was heartening, but it was only prologue. Jews and Catholics were at the beginning of a new road, John Paul proposed. Their "common heritage drawn from the Law and the Prophets" required a "collaboration in favor of man," in defense of human dignity and human life, in defense of freedom and in work for peace. Above all, Jews and Catholics should ponder together the mystery of divine election and Providence that had brought them together as they had not been together in centuries. Jews and Catholics were on the threshold of a conversation that had been interrupted for more than 1,900 years. On that striking note, which challenged Jews and Catholics alike, John Paul closed with prayer—the 118th Psalm, which he recited in Hebrew:

> O give thanks to the Lord for He is good,
> His steadfast love endures forever!
> Let Israel say,
> "His steadfast love endures forever."
> Let those who fear the Lord say,
> "His steadfast love endures forever."
> Amen.[2]

VATICAN II REVISITED

The dramatic transformation of Jewish-Catholic relations was one aspect of Vatican II's legacy coming to fruition. On January 25, 1985, John Paul II announced an Extraordinary Assembly of the Synod of Bishops to celebrate the twentieth anniversary of the Council's completion and to consider its heritage as a whole. The Extraordinary Synod, which would meet from November 24 to December 8, 1985, was intended to re-create the experience of Vatican II for the bishops who were its legatees and to assess how the Council had been received in the Church throughout the world. The adjective "extraordinary" was curial jargon for a Synod Assembly that took place outside the cycle of Ordinary Assemblies. As things turned out, the event and one of its products would justify the use of the term "extraordinary" in other ways as well.

Among the Incas

The day after announcing the Extraordinary Synod, the Pope flew to Caracas at the beginning of his twenty-fifth pastoral pilgrimage outside Italy and his sixth to Latin America. The journey to Venezuela, Ecuador, Peru, and the Caribbean island state of Trinidad and Tobago produced two of the most remarkable scenes of John Paul's pontificate. The first was the papal motorcade into Quito, the capital of Ecuador, on January 29.

The pattern of these Latin American papal welcomes had become well-established—the Pope would be greeted by huge, boisterous crowds lining the highways, waving national and papal flags, throwing flowers in the Popemobile's path. Things were dramatically different this time. According to local custom, respected guests were honored with silence. The Pope drove into Quito along roads lined with hundreds of thousands of Ecuadorans, holding up crosses or religious statues, who were absolutely quiet. What could have seemed eerie was in fact, one reporter remembered, "totally moving."[3]

Five days later, John Paul was in Peru near Cuzco, the ancient Inca capital, to celebrate a Liturgy of the Word, crown the statue of the Blessed Virgin of Carmelo di Paucartambo, and address the native peoples at the Inca fortress of Sacsahuamán. It was bitterly cold with freezing rain. Some of the journalists in the papal party had gotten altitude sickness. The platform for the biblically based prayer service and the Pope's address was set on the ramparts of the Inca fortress. Across a small valley and covering several nearby hills were thousands of impoverished Incas, descendants of one of the great empires of pre-Columbian America. They had come from all over the region to see John Paul; many had camped overnight in harsh conditions. Now they stood silently, looking up at him on the promontory of their ancestors' fortress, in the pouring rain. High among the cloud-covered Andes, it was perhaps the most remote venue John Paul would visit in twenty years, yet the message was similar to what he had told the diplomats of UNESCO in 1980.

He had come, he said, to affirm the people and their ancient culture and to propose how their lives might be more fully human and Christian. The scriptural text chosen for the day was the story of Ruth and Boaz from the Hebrew Bible. It was a story of hospitality and a "lesson of solidarity," which he proposed as the Christian answer to the violent madness of the neo-Maoist Shining Path guerrillas of Peru. Solidarity was at "the other extreme" from ideologies that divided human beings into groups of irreconcilable enemies and that sought the "extermination of the adversary," he said. In contrast to the "radical egotism" of the guerrillas, the Church preached a more radical revolution of faith and conscience that struck egotism at its roots and paved the way for a more just society. Any truly human revolution had to change hearts and souls as well as material conditions.

On the way from Cuzco to Sacsahuamán, he had thought about the Incas' ancestors, who had worshiped the sun as the source of life. The descendants

of those great builders now stood before him, their ancestral culture transformed by the light of Christ. So today, they had come together, the Indians
and the Pope, along a quite different shining path, in the light of the true "sun
of justice and love, Christ our Savior," who was not only the source of life in
this world but of "the life which is stronger than death, the life which never
ends, eternal life."[4]

The Council After Twenty Years

The Incas had not come to Sacsahuamán to debate the correct interpretation
of the Second Vatican Council. But those who were Catholics, and many who
were not, had been touched by the Council, however remotely situated they
were on the Andean altiplano. The way they worshiped, the language in which
they prayed, the religious education their children received, the relationship
of their clergy to the public authorities, the training their priests and nuns
received, their relations with non-Catholic and nonbelieving neighbors—all
of these had been shaped during the past twenty years by the most important
event in Catholic history since the Reformation. Yet for all its indisputable
impact on Catholic life, from St. Peter's Basilica to the smallest hut church outside Cuzco, what Vatican II *meant* was still hotly disputed throughout the
Catholic world.

Twenty years after it had closed on December 8, 1965, the Second Vatican
Council—the event itself and the documents it produced—was already in a
kind of historical twilight. A "progressive" party in the Church, thinking Vatican II rather old hat, was busy imagining a Vatican III that would complete the
rout of traditional Catholicism which it somehow thought to be John XXIII's
intention in summoning the Council. Another party (usually termed "traditionalists") believed that Vatican II and its ill-advised "opening" to the modern
world was responsible for the crisis of Catholic life since 1965. Neither party
seemed terribly concerned with the historical continuity of the Church as the
embodiment of a living tradition. The "progressives" set Vatican II and their
imaginary Vatican III against the Counter-Reformation Council of Trent and
Vatican I. The "traditionalists" (sometimes called "restorationists") set Trent
and Vatican I against Vatican II.

John XXIII had summoned the Second Vatican Council in the hope that
a new experience of the Holy Spirit, a new Pentecost, would create a deeper
unity in the Church. One result of the Council had been intense acrimony, to
the point where Pope Paul VI had wondered aloud whether the Church had
not gone from healthy self-criticism to pathological self-destruction. "Satan's
smoke," he suggested, "had made its way into the temple of God through some
crack."[5]

How was Vatican II's impact to be measured and judged?

World Catholicism had grown since the Council, from fewer than 600 million in 1965 to more than 830 million in 1985. The largest growth had been

in Latin America and Africa. Roman Catholicism had become a majority Third World communion since the Council and would be even more so by the turn of the millennium. In addition, the leadership of Third World Catholicism had become largely indigenous since 1965. Missionary bishops no longer ruled much of Latin America and virtually all of Africa. In Africa, among some of the most vibrant Catholic communities in the world, first-generation Christians, the sons of pagans, now wore the cardinal's red hat.

The Third World's new prominence in international Catholic demographics was not simply the result of growth in the South; it was also due to decline in the North. The continued collapse of Catholic practice in Western Europe, the part of the world Church that was primarily responsible for Vatican II and that might have been expected to have benefited the most from it, was the most striking example of this. On the other side of the iron curtain, by way of contrast, some of the most intensely Catholic communities in the world were to be found—above ground in Poland, underground in Lithuania, Czechoslovakia, and Ukraine. In at least some cases, persecution had strengthened the Church and prosperity had weakened it.[6]

Lay people in unprecedented numbers were now involved in the Church's worship, educational institutions, and administration, but some 100,000 "religious professionals"—priests and nuns—had left their ministries since Vatican II. In the free world, the clergy was becoming grayer and nuns were disappearing. In eastern Europe and Africa, vocations to the priesthood and religious life were at all-time highs. Although the Council had challenged Catholics to convert modern culture from within, even the most enthusiastic proponents of the Council would be hard-put to make the argument that Catholic influence in the cultural and political life of the West was greater in 1985 than it had been in 1965. The institution of the Church was in the greatest turmoil since the Reformation. At the same time new, primarily lay, renewal movements were flourishing as they had not in centuries.

New Ground

When Christianity engaged modernity, certain problems were inevitable. They appeared first among intellectuals—theologians, primarily—and then worked their way through the Church's structures to its worship, educational life, and social ministry. The "crisis" of Catholicism in 1965–1985 thus reprised many of the difficulties of the Churches of the Reformation in the two generations after World War II—which was not reassuring to those who knew that those difficulties had presaged a virtual disintegration of mainline Protestantism in Western Europe and North America.

The "gamble" of Vatican II was not simply that the Council had provided no authoritative "keys" to its interpretation, as previous Councils had done with dogmatic definitions, canons, or condemnations. The gamble was that opening the Church's windows to the modern world would result in an enriched Catholicism and a converted modernity. For the gamble to succeed, the conversation between Catholicism and modern ways of thinking had to be a genuine dialogue. The questions were whether Catholicism was up to the task and whether modernity was even interested.

Ten years after the Council and a decade before the Extraordinary Synod, an ecumenical group of American Christian theologians, meeting in Hartford, Connecticut, signed the "Hartford Appeal for Theological Affirmation," a series of propositions illustrating how the dialogue between Christianity and the modern world had become a monologue, with Christian doctrine dissolving under the impact of its encounter with modernity. The Appeal's purpose was not to abandon Christianity's conversation with modernity but to restore a genuine dialogue, in which the historic creeds of Christianity were partners in conversation, not candidates for derision, deconstruction, and dismissal. The Hartford Appeal, an informal ecumenical initiative, anticipated many of the issues of faith and culture with which John Paul's Extraordinary Synod would have to wrestle:

- Modernity insisted on the superiority of its understanding of the human condition to anything achieved in the past. Catholicism was, by name and conviction, "catholic" or universal. It could not preemptively privilege any one historical period's way of understanding the world, its people, and their destiny.
- Modernity insisted that God-talk was, at best, metaphorical and at worst, irrational. Catholicism taught that the Creed it professed every Sunday was the truth of the world and its history.
- Modernity insisted that Jesus Christ could only be understood through contemporary models of human maturity. Catholicism taught that Jesus Christ was the man for all times, and that no one age's self-understanding could exhaust the full meaning of humanity and divinity that Christ revealed.
- Modernity insisted that all religions were equally valid. Catholicism honored other faiths, but taught that God had revealed himself and his purposes definitively in the life, death, and resurrection of Jesus Christ, changing the world's history and restoring it to its proper trajectory.
- Modernity imagined that salvation was a matter of achieving one's human potential. Catholicism taught that salvation was communion with God, in which our human potential is realized in an unsurpassable way.
- Modernity conceived worship as the self-affirmation of a community and the self-realization of individual worshipers. Catholicism taught that worship was first and foremost a matter of adoring God, who was worshiped because he ought to be worshiped.
- Modernity insisted that hope beyond death was irrelevant to human liberation in this world. Catholicism taught that hope beyond death liberated men and women in the most radical way, and thus made a genuinely liberating transformation of the world possible.[7]

The signatories of the Hartford Appeal, like John Paul II, knew there was no alternative to a Church engaged with modernity. Humanity had gone through an irreversible gate from which there was no return.[8] Religious beliefs could be deeply and firmly held, but those who held them would always be aware of the fact that they had chosen these beliefs, rather than inheriting them as givens of existence. In the cultural circumstances of the late twentieth century, a "Catholic restoration" that denied this was a fantasy. For John Paul and the Hartford signatories, though, the experience of relativity and choice—the experience of being modern—did not mean relativism. A world of relativism was a world without windows or doors, incapable of hearing the signals of transcendence in modern life.[9] John Paul and the Hartford signatories wanted a world with windows and doors, a modernity open to the possibility that humanity was in fact greater than modernity had imagined. Modern men and women, for all their experience of choice, could still know what was true and good, and could choose truth and goodness. Recognizing that should not be impossible for Christians. That, after all, was what "conversion" meant.

The challenge the Second Vatican Council had put before the Church was a challenge of transition, from an authoritarian religious institution to an authoritative religious community. This was not "middle ground" between traditionalists or restorationists, who wanted to reject modernity root and branch, and progressives, whose embrace of modernity had led them to a radical relativism in which the authoritative was inevitably authoritarian. It was new ground.

It was, John Paul believed, what Vatican II had had in mind all along. Exploring that proposition would be the business of the Extraordinary Synod.

THE CONCILIAR POPE

In the months immediately prior to the Extraordinary Synod, John Paul took several initiatives that illustrated the vision of Vatican II and the revitalized Catholicism he hoped the Synod participants would embrace.

Communicating the Message

After more than five years' experience, not all of it happy, with what senior curial officials call "the way we do things here," John Paul seized control of the Vatican press operation and brought it into the communications age. The key decision was his appointment of the first layman, Joaquín Navarro-Valls, as papal spokesman and director of the Holy See Press Office, the Sala Stampa. A sophisticated Spaniard in his late forties and a member of Opus Dei, Navarro had been trained as a psychiatrist, a profession he sometimes jokingly described as good preparation for his new duties. After a period of medical practice, Navarro had become a journalist and chief foreign correspondent for the Madrid daily *ABC*. He was the paper's Rome correspondent and President of the Foreign Press Association of Italy when he was appointed to head the Sala Stampa on December 4, 1984.

In addition to bringing to the Vatican press room an understanding of the Western media that had eluded his clerical predecessors, Navarro quickly established himself in the confidence of the Pope, to whom he had more access than anyone except Monsignor Dziwisz, John Paul's longtime secretary. As a Spaniard, a professional journalist, and a layman, Navarro was another "outsider" chosen by the outsider Pope to help get his message heard by changing (when possible) or circumventing (when necessary) the encrusted institutional filters of the Vatican. Like any gatekeeper, Navarro had his critics, and his access to John Paul made him an object of envy within the Curia. He brought an acute understanding of the Pope's mind and agenda to his work, and by Roman standards, he revolutionized the functioning of the Holy See Press Office.

His clerical predecessors and their curial superiors, including Cardinal Agostino Casaroli, had been initially aghast at John Paul's impromptu in-flight press conferences on his travels, worried that the Pope might make a mistake and that ambassadors would start calling for explanations. Navarro, for his part, encouraged these exercises as ways for the Pope to get feedback and to communicate his message directly. The traditional Vatican approach to information sharing was, essentially, that the less said about anything, the better. Navarro and John Paul disagreed. They thought the world beyond the Leonine Wall should have access to a news briefing about events in the Vatican. The on-line Vatican Information Service was created and began transmitting daily bulletins in January 1991. Politicians use the media as a way to garner votes. John Paul saw what Navarro called the "dialectic with public opinion," available through the media, as an instrument for reformation in the Church and a tool for shaping the world.[10]

As Navarro saw it, this openness reflected a new vision of the Church and the papacy. It came into focus for the papal spokesman at the airport in Bogotá, Colombia, in early July 1986. A ten-year-old boy had somehow burst through the barriers and run up to John Paul. "I know you; you're the Pope," he said. "You're the same one I saw on television." A new presentation of the papacy was essential, Navarro thought, and John Paul had accomplished it through the media. And he had done it not as another ephemeral celebrity, but as a man emerging into a ministry of global presence from the Church and from the priesthood. The Colombian boy had first known this man from television, to be sure. But he had known him from TV as the Pope, and John Paul II, in person, was indeed "the same one."[11]

Catholic/Jewish Relations

Nostra Aetate, Vatican II's *Declaration on the Relation of the Church to Non-Christian Religions*, had opened a new chapter in Catholic/Jewish relations. John Paul II was determined to secure that accomplishment and advance beyond it. Several pre-Synod events illustrated this distinctive dimension of the pontificate and its relationship to the Council.

On February 15, 1985, the Pope received an American Jewish Committee delegation that had come to Rome to celebrate the twentieth anniversary of *Nostra Aetate*. In his address, John Paul emphasized that *Nostra Aetate* was not only "something fitting" in human terms, but ought to be understood "as an expression of the faith, as an inspiration of the Holy Spirit, as a word of Divine Wisdom."[12]

Four days later, on February 19, the Pope received Israeli Prime Minister Shimon Peres, who invited him to visit Israel.

On April 19, John Paul met with the participants in a colloquium on the twentieth anniversary of *Nostra Aetate*, held at his Roman alma mater, the Angelicum. Once again, he suggested that the Jewish/Catholic dialogue was far more than a matter of civic good manners and tolerance. "Jewish-Christian relations," he emphasized, "are never an academic exercise. They are, on the contrary, part of the very fabric of our religious commitments and our respective vocations as Christians and as Jews," who lived in a kind of providentially mandated and unavoidable entanglement.[13]

On June 24, the Commission for Religious Relations with the Jews, the Vatican office responsible for the dialogue, issued a document with the lengthy title *Notes on the Correct Way to Present the Jews and Judaism in Preaching and Catechesis in the Roman Catholic Church*. The document, intended to guide sermons, the Church's Holy Week liturgy, and Catholic religious education at all levels, stressed that "Jesus was and always remained a Jew . . . fully a man of his environment." To present this accurately "cannot but underline both the reality of the Incarnation and the very meaning of the history of salvation, as it has been revealed in the Bible." *Notes* stressed the importance of teaching Catholics the continuing spiritual mission of the Jewish people, who remain a chosen people and whose contemporary faith and religious life can help Catholics better understand aspects of their own faith and practice. Religious education programs, *Notes* taught, should also help Catholics in "understanding the meaning for the Jews of the extermination during the years 1939–1945, and its consequences."[14]

On October 28, 1985, John Paul II received the International Catholic-Jewish Liaison Committee, the official dialogue body. The Pope reiterated that the "spiritual link" between Catholics and "Abraham's stock" established "a relation which could well be called a real 'parentage' and which [Catholics] have with that religious community [i.e., the Jewish people] alone." John Paul praised the *Notes* issued in June, which would "help promote respect, appreciation, and indeed love for one and the other, as they are both in the unfathomable design of God, who 'does not reject his people' (*Psalm* 94.14; *Romans* 11.1). By the same token, anti-Semitism in its ugly and sometimes violent manifestations should be completely eradicated. Better still, a positive view of each of our religions, with due respect for the identity of each, will surely emerge. . . ."[15]

Youth and the Future

In the months before the Extraordinary Synod, John Paul took the occasion of the United Nations' International Youth Year to launch one of the signature initiatives of his pontificate—the World Youth Days that would draw millions of young people on pilgrimage to Europe, Latin America, North America, and Asia.

The idea of World Youth Day, the Pope remembered, could be traced back to his young friends in *Środowisko* and their exploration of the personal and vocational dynamics of adolescence and young adulthood.[16] His early papal pilgrimages, in Italy and abroad, had convinced him that a pastoral strategy of "accompaniment" with young people was as valid for a pope as it had been for a fledgling priest.

He had been impressed by the interest of French youth, supposedly tone-deaf to Christianity, in the Parc des Princes during his first pilgrimage to Paris in 1980. During the Holy Year youth meeting in Rome on Palm Sunday, 1984, the idea of a World Youth Day began to germinate, and John Paul invited the youth of the world back to Rome for Palm Sunday, 1985.[17] Some 250,000 enthusiastic youngsters accepted. It was then decided to mark Palm Sunday, 1986, as the first "official" World Youth Day, and to celebrate it in the different dioceses around the world. Beginning in 1987, and continuing biennially, World Youth Day was celebrated with the Pope at an international venue to which the youth of the world would be invited—Buenos Aires in 1987, Santiago de Compostela in 1989, Częstochowa in 1991, Denver in 1993, Manila in 1995, and Paris in 1997, where the Pope announced that the next World Youth Day would be in Rome in 2000. On the even-numbered "off" years, World Youth Day is celebrated in the dioceses.[18]

John Paul marked the UN's International Youth Year and his Palm Sunday, 1985, meeting with young people in Rome with an apostolic letter, *To the Youth of the World*, which mixed reminiscence, exhortation, and the Pope's phenomenological approach to anything human in fairly equal proportions.

Youth is a special moment in life, he wrote, because it is the time when an identity and a vocation form, when the first serious personal decisions are made. In the unfolding of those decisions, young people discover themselves as moral actors and face the question of their destiny. Like the rich young man in the Gospel story, young people want to know "what must I do to have eternal life?" Thus youth is also a special time of encounter with the mystery of God.

The "fundamental question of youth," John Paul continued, is the question of conscience and its authenticity. Conscience, the measure of human dignity, is, in a sense, the history of the world: "For history is written not only by the events which in a certain sense happen 'from outside'; it is written first of all 'from inside': it is the history of human consciences, of moral victories and defeats." To develop one's conscience authentically is the true measure of a human personality's development.

Youth is also a special time to discern a personal future, a vocation, in which young people try to "read the eternal thought which God the Creator and Father has in their regard." Discovering one's unique person and task is "a fascinating interior undertaking [in which] your humanity develops and grows, while your young personality acquires ever greater inner maturity. You become rooted in that which each of you is, in order to become that which you must become: for yourself—for other people—for God."

And, of course, he wrote to them of sexuality. That God created human beings male and female is a reality that "is necessarily inscribed in the personal 'I' of each of you." The encounter with this reality brings onto "the horizon of a young heart a new experience . . . the experience of love." Do not, the Pope urged, "allow this treasure to be taken away from you!" If preserving the treasure meant being countercultural and resisting the reduction of love to transient pleasure, then be countercultural. "Do not be afraid of the love that places clear demands on people. These demands . . . are precisely capable of making your love a true love."[19]

John Paul II's remarkable rapport with young people began in the "John Paul, Superstar" phase of his pontificate; the "woo-hoo-woo" encounter in Madison Square Garden in October 1979 was a prime example. As the pontificate unfolded, it was no longer possible to view this simply as a variant on the adulation lavished on pop celebrities. Age, Agca's bullet, and the effects of illness made it necessary to think of the Pope as something more than a rock star in a white cassock. Why did this rapport with the young continue, even intensify? Several reasons suggested themselves. The Pope took young people seriously as persons, paying them the compliment of seeing them as people struggling with the meaning of life. When speaking with the young, he did not take the edge off a Christian message he clearly lived himself. Perhaps most importantly, he did not pander to young people, challenging them to settle for nothing less than moral grandeur. At a time in Western history when virtually no other world figure was calling young people to bear burdens and make sacrifices, John Paul touched the youthful thirst for the heroic and related it to the human search for God. It made for a potent style of evangelization.

Ecumenism

From April 22 through April 27, 1985, the ecumenical commissions of sixty-three national bishops' conferences met in Rome to review the quest for Christian unity twenty years after the Council. The goal of ecumenism, John Paul stressed in his address to them on April 27, remained nothing less than "the *full communion* of Christians in one apostolic faith and in one eucharistic fellowship at the service of a truly common witness," which was an expression of the communion of persons between Father, Son, and Holy Spirit.[20]

Two months later, on June 28, John Paul gave a major address to the Roman Curia on the twenty-fifth anniversary of the Secretariat for Promoting Christian Unity. There had been concern in some ecumenical circles about the future of Catholicism's ecumenical commitment, most recently because of curial criticism of *Unity of the Churches: An Actual Possibility*, a book by the German theologians Karl Rahner and Heinrich Fries. The authors described *Unity of the Churches* as a proposal for breaking what they perceived as an ecumenical logjam. Its critics argued that its proposed bracketing of certain theological issues in order to declare the Churches united reduced ecumenism to a matter of negotiation between voluntary organizations.[21] John Paul's anniversary address concluded with the unambiguous affirmation that "*the Catholic Church is committed to the ecumenical movement with an irrevocable decision,* and it desires to contribute to it with all its possibilities." That, he said, was "one of the pastoral priorities" of the Bishop of Rome.[22] The primary aim of his address was to clarify the theological foundations of Catholic ecumenism.

God the Holy Spirit, not human endeavor, is the source of Christian unity, he proposed.[23] Although that Spirit-given unity had never been revoked by God, it had been damaged by human error and willfulness.[24] That was why ecumenism, the effort to rebuild Christian unity, could not be understood like the negotiation of a treaty or a contract. The unity of the Church was given to the Church, once for all, at Pentecost. The ecumenical task was to "recompose" this already given unity in visible form.[25]

Disregarding the questions that still divided Christians in their profession of faith, or "acting as if they were resolved," could not be called ecumenical progress. Being able to say together "this is *true*" was the way Christian unity was most basically demonstrated. That common confession of conviction made the common celebration of the Eucharist possible. Whatever their good intentions, efforts to evade or bracket difficult questions of doctrine and to celebrate prematurely a Eucharistic unity that was not founded on unity of belief demeaned the ecumenical task.[26]

A common confession of the truth of Christian faith "has to be sought in love; Christian truth cannot be assimilated without charity." That required a "reciprocal humility, inspired by love and the cultivation of truth," so that the wounds of centuries were overcome and a full, deep unity was recomposed in doctrine, worship, and service to the world.[27] Every Catholic, John Paul proposed, had a responsibility to help bring about the unity willed by Christ and given to the Church by the Holy Spirit."[28]

It had been twenty-five years since John XXIII had stunned the Christian world by declaring the Roman Catholic Church fully committed to ecumenism. There would be more surprises to come, as the Pope who had come to his office with little ecumenical experience continued to press this cause in unexpected, even radical, ways.

Dissidents

In the months before the Synod, unity within the Catholic Church was also a major issue for John Paul II.

On March 11, 1985, the Congregation for the Doctrine of the Faith [CDF] issued a "notification" that Leonardo Boff's book, *Church: Charism and Power*, was doctrinally deficient. Boff, a Brazilian Franciscan and former doctoral student of Professor Joseph Ratzinger, had applied "Marxist analysis" to the Church and concluded that an ordained hierarchy was a sinful social structure of which the Church should rid itself. This was, obviously, not Catholic theology, and it was hardly surprising that CDF noted that fact. In the context of the Extraordinary Synod, it was also important to note that Boff's vision of the Church was a critique of the *communio* ecclesiology of Vatican II. CDF asked Father Boff to maintain a year of public silence on the questions dealt with in his book in order to reflect upon them more deeply. Boff had been publishing and lecturing widely, and Cardinal Ratzinger, who retained an affection for his former student, hoped that giving his thought a chance to mature, away from the media spotlight, would help Boff grow as a theologian. Boff agreed to what the German press immediately dubbed his "penitential silencing." His views did not change materially, and he eventually left not only the Franciscan order, but the Church.[29]

Rebuilding unity in the face of widespread dissent was on John Paul II's agenda for his first pilgrimage to the Netherlands in May 1985, one of the most difficult pastoral visits of the pontificate.

Whatever its modest accomplishments in attempting to heal the rifts among the Dutch bishops, the 1980 "Particular Synod for Holland" had not successfully restored unity to the Church in the Netherlands, where deep doctrinal, liturgical, and catechetical divisions over doctrine, worship, and religious education remained. The Dutch prime minister himself said that "the word 'Rome' makes some people nervous if not downright suspicious."[30] John Paul's mission was to break through a massive barrier of suspicion and hostility in order to reopen a dialogue between the Bishop of Rome and the Dutch Church.

He could not do it. Three days before the Pope arrived, a mass meeting in the Hague was organized to protest the papal visit; it was not the best augury for what was about to unfold. John Paul's addresses had been prepared in consultation with the Dutch bishops, some of whom wanted him to say things they were unwilling or incapable of saying themselves—a sure prescription for having the Pope instantly labeled an authoritarian.[31] Archbishop Edward Cassidy, the papal nuncio, had helped arrange a meeting between John Paul and representatives of the Church's work in education, the missions, and social action. Grievances were aired, but during the session one speaker departed from her prepared text to attack the Pope personally for an alleged abuse of authority. Afterward, he received her warmly.[32]

In Utrecht, smoke bombs and eggs were thrown at the Popemobile. Posters were displayed offering a bounty on John Paul's life, whose value was set at approximately $6,000.[33] Turnouts were minimal; the weather was awful. A somewhat brighter future seemed possible, however, when an unexpectedly large crowd of young people met with the Pope at Amersfoort on John Paul's last day in Holland, May 15. The coming generation, raised with little or no religious education, seemed to be searching for a message of hope while their elders continued to live out the passions of the sixties.[34] Two years later, a new seminary was opened in the diocese of s'Hertogenbosch, which would produce sixty new priests during the next decade.[35]

After a day in Luxembourg John Paul moved on to Belgium, where things were calmer. At Beauraing, the country's principal Marian shrine, the Pope celebrated his sixty-fifth birthday, his cake decorated with a model of St. Peter's and the towers of the cathedral at Malines.[36] On May 20, at Brussels, John Paul addressed representatives of the European Council of Ministers, the European Parliament, and the European Commission and sketched themes he would develop extensively in the future: the essential unity of Europe, east and west of the Yalta dividing line; the source of that unity in a common European culture; and the Christian foundations of that culture. In pursuing its vocation to unity, Europe would rediscover the dynamism that decades of bloodshed and ideological division had drained from it. Four and a half years before the Yalta division of Europe was resolved by the nonviolent Revolution of 1989, it was a remarkably prescient, even visionary, speech.[37]

Changes in the Team

On April 29, 1985, John Paul announced two more changes at the highest levels of the Roman Curia, completing the major redeployment of personnel that had taken place in April 1984. The way in which one affected party learned of his new position illustrated the singular way in which even senior appointments in the Vatican are handled.

In February 1985, shortly after John Paul had announced the Extraordinary Synod for the twentieth anniversary of Vatican II, Bishop Jozef Tomko, the General Secretary of the Synod of Bishops, got a phone call from Cardinal Casaroli, telling him that the Pope would name him a cardinal at a forthcoming May consistory. Archbishop Martínez Somalo, the *Sostituto* of the Secretariat of State, called two days later, at 9 o'clock at night, and said, in curial code language, "You know what is new? You are Pro of Pro." Tomko, stunned, didn't respond. Martínez Somalo asked, "What is your answer?" Tomko replied that he was happy to be sitting down so that he didn't fall down. He was now Pro-Prefect (until his cardinalate) of Propaganda Fide, which is what everyone in Rome still called the Congregation for the Evangelization of Peoples. As "Pro of Pro," the Slovak was now responsible for missions and evangelization throughout the world, for the nomination of bishops in mission territories, for the oversight of the most explosive growth in the Catholic world, and for monitoring and guiding the sometimes fractious arguments over evangelization in ancient religious cultures. He hadn't been consulted about the appointment. As he later told a mother superior who was complaining about her difficulties moving sisters around, "Yes, you have the rule of obedience, while we have only the obedience."[38]

Tomko's replacement as General Secretary of the Synod of Bishops was the Secretary of the Pontifical Justice and Peace Commission, Bishop Jan Schotte, who was promoted to archbishop.

John Paul II's third consistory, on May 27, 1985, was one of the largest and most internationally diverse of his pontificate, with twenty-eight new cardinals being created. In addition to Tomko and the embattled Nicaraguan, Miguel Obando Bravo, the red biretta went to Myroslav Lubachivsky, leader of the Ukrainian Greek Catholic Church; Paul Poupard, former rector of the Institut Catholique in Paris and founding President of the Pontifical Council for Culture; the Nigerian, Francis Arinze; Juan Francisco Fresno Larraín of Santiago, Chile, a defender of human rights against the Pinochet government; John O'Connor, "the archbishop of the capital of the world"; Bernard Francis Law, the recently appointed fifty-three-year-old archbishop of Boston; Ricardo Vidal, archbishop of Cebu and the Philippines' second cardinal; Simon Lourdusamy, archbishop of Bangalore, India; Louis-Albert Vachon, of Québec; Henryk Gulbinowicz of Wrocław; Adrianus Simonis, the Primate of the Netherlands; Paulos Tzadua, the archbishop of Addis Ababa; and a number of other curial figures and residential bishops. The "elder" of Vatican II named cardinal in this consistory was Pietro Pavan, an Italian specialist in Catholic social ethics who was one of the architects of the *Declaration on Religious Freedom.* John Paul also honored his old friend Andrzej Deskur, who had said that his job in this pontificate would be "to suffer for the Pope," and who received the red hat in the wheelchair to which he had been confined since his stroke, just before Conclave II in 1978. John Paul assigned Cardinal Deskur his own old titular church, S. Cesareo in Palatio.

Encounter in Casablanca

The evolution of World Youth Day added a new rhythm to the Catholic Church's life. But perhaps the most striking papal encounter with young people during the International Youth Year and in the months before the Extraordinary Synod took place on August 19, 1985, with 80,000 Muslim young people at a stadium in Casablanca, Morocco.

This unprecedented event—the first time a Pope had ever formally addressed a Muslim audience at the invitation of a Muslim leader—came on the last day of John Paul's third African pilgrimage and his twenty-seventh pastoral mission outside Italy. It had taken him to Togo, Ivory Coast, Cameroon, the Central African Republic, Zaire, and Kenya, where he participated in the forty-third International Eucharistic Congress in Nairobi.[39] The stop in Casablanca on August 19, a day that began in Nairobi and ended in Rome, was at the personal invitation of Morocco's ruler, King Hassan II, who had invited John Paul to his country during a royal visit to the Vatican. The Pope had thanked the king for the invitation, but asked what he might be able to do in the officially Islamic kingdom. Hassan had replied, "Your Holiness, yours is not only a religious responsibility but an educational and moral one as well. I am certain that tens of thousands of Moroccans, especially the youth, would be most happy if you spoke to them about moral standards and relationships affecting individuals, communities, nations, and religions."[40] John Paul had happily accepted, and the impending visit became the occasion for the first and, as of 1999, the only formal modus vivendi established between the Holy See and an Islamic state. In a letter dated December 30, 1983, King Hassan legislatively decreed that the Church in Morocco could conduct public worship and religious education and that churches and Catholic schools would be tax-exempt. The Catholic Church would enjoy complete control over its internal affairs; priests and sisters would also be tax-exempt; the Church could receive financial contributions domestically and from abroad and could manage its own finances; and Catholic charitable associations were permitted.

John Paul's address to the youth of Morocco, delivered in French, was strikingly simple in style—a précis of his Christian humanism adapted to this unique audience. He had come to meet with them, he began, "as a believer . . . simply to give witness to what I believe, what I wish for the well-being of my brothers, mankind, and what, through experience, I consider to be useful for all." His first thoughts were of God, "because it is in him that we, Muslims and Catholics, believe." God is the "source of all joy," and to give witness to that, Muslims and Catholics prayed, for "man cannot live without praying, any more than he can live without breathing."

Addressing one of the most difficult issues in Catholic-Muslim relations—religious freedom—the Pope proposed that religious faith, not a secular indifference or neutrality toward religion, was the most secure ground for religious liberty: "obedience to God and this love for man ought to lead us to respect human rights," John Paul suggested. That respect required human "reciprocity in all fields, above all in what concerns fundamental liberties, more particularly religious liberty. . . ."

It was their task, he said, to build a more "fraternal world," to "tear down barriers which are sometimes caused by pride, more often by weakness and fear of people." Their generation was challenged to live "in solidarity" with others so that "each people might have the means to feed itself, take care of itself, and live in peace." But "however important economic problems are, man does not live by bread alone." This was the most important witness they could give to the world they were inheriting: the belief that "we are not living in a closed world."

Both the things they had in common and things that made them different should be acknowledged. Together, Christians and Muslims believed in the one, unique, all-just, and all-merciful God, who wanted his human creatures to be saved and to live with him forever. Christians and Muslims also believed "in the importance of prayer, of fasting and of almsgiving, of penitence and of pardon." As for the "important differences" between the two faiths, which centered on the Christian belief in Jesus as the Son of God and redeemer of the world, "we can accept them with humility and respect, in mutual tolerance. There is a mystery here, and God will enlighten us about it one day, I am sure." For now, if Christians and Muslims alike placed themselves "at [God's] disposal and [were] submissive to his will," there would be born "a world in which men and women of living and effective faith [would] sing the glory of God and seek to build a human society according to God's will."[41]

Cardinal Jozef Tomko was in the stadium at Morocco and had no idea what to expect. He watched the crowd, not the Pope, and what he saw was interest and a kind of reverence.[42] The Muslim teenagers of Casablanca had, in fact, listened to the Bishop of Rome with far more interest and respect than had many middle-aged Dutch Catholics.

STRENGTH THROUGH RESISTANCE

The struggle for freedom in east central Europe continued apace in the months leading up to the Extraordinary Synod of 1985.

On February 27, Soviet foreign minister Andrei Gromyko interrupted the Pope's annual Lenten retreat by requesting an audience. John Paul spoke to him, as he always did, "about religious freedom and the liberty of the Church." Gromyko had other matters on his mind: "He was very worried about the American Strategic Defense Initiative," the Pope remembered; "he was looking for the Church's help against the United States."[43] John Paul understood that Gromyko was far more interested in the deteriorating Soviet position vis-à-vis NATO than in anything else and declined to be recruited into an anti-American campaign.[44]

John Paul's campaign for freedom through cultural resistance moved forward during the middle months of 1985. Although the Czechoslovak regime had refused him a visa to attend the celebrations in Velehrad in July for the 1,100th anniversary of the death of St. Methodius, the Pope had ways of making his presence felt. On March 19, he signed a letter to all the priests of Czechoslovakia, reminding them that Methodius, with his brother Cyril, had established the foundations of Slavic culture in their part of east central Europe. Their evangelical activity, by its culture-forming character, touched every sector of life.[45] Methodius's example, he continued, had three lessons for today. The first was "the courage to accept history and humility before the mysteries of Divine Providence," even if the present historical situation makes it arduous, difficult, sometimes painful. . . ."[46] The second lesson was to maintain the religious character of their priestly personality. Both the clergy permitted to function publicly and those forced to work underground were tempted by the pervasive secularization the Husàk regime enforced in their country. Like Methodius, they should all keep in mind that they had been chosen by God for a special mission. The third lesson was responsibility. Like Methodius, they, as priests, must proclaim the eternal consequences of choices made in history. John Paul's hope for the Methodius anniversary was that it would be for the priests of Czechoslovakia "a powerful stimulus to acquire sanctity in order to encounter modern man, who seeks, questions, suffers, and awaits . . . your work of love and salvation in Christ's name."[47]

Cardinal František Tomášek read the Pope's letter to 1,100 Czechslovak priests—one-third of the country's presbyterate—at a massive concelebration in Velehrad on April 11. It was the largest public display of Catholic and priestly solidarity in Czechoslovakia since 1948.

John Paul continued to celebrate Cyril and Methodius's contributions to the religious and cultural history of Europe by dedicating his fourth encyclical, *Slavorum Apostoli* [The Apostles of the Slavs], to their memory.[48] Issued in June, 1985, the encyclical depicts the brothers of Thessalonica as dedicated evangelists concerned for both the unity and universality of the Church. Their missionary work had brought the western Slavs into the history of Europe and into salvation history, such that "the Slavs were able to feel that they, too, together with the other nations of the earth, were descendants and heirs of the promise made by God to Abraham."[49] Coming to Moravia prior to the break between the Christian East and the Christian West, their mission approved by both the Bishop of Rome and the Patriarch of Constantinople, the brothers embodied a love for the unity of the Church, East and West, and a dedication to its universality.[50] Because they created the foundations of western Slavic literary culture, their evangelism was "constantly present in the history and in the life of these peoples and nations," however much it might be ignored by the people and regime of a given moment.[51]

Slavorum Apostoli addressed controverted questions that had arisen since Vatican II and touched areas far from Bohemia, Moravia, and Slovakia. One of these was "inculturation"—the question of how the Gospel is incarnated in indigenous cultures. In the ninth century, some considered Cyril and Methodius's determination to bring the Gospel to the Slavs in their own language a threat to Church unity. The brothers disagreed then, as did John Paul II now. Successful evangelization, John Paul proposed, involved gaining "a good grasp of the interior world" of those to whom one was preaching. Cyril and Methodius had "set themselves to understanding and penetrating the language, customs, and traditions of the Slav peoples, faithfully interpreting the aspirations and human values which were present and expressed therein" in the light of the Gospel. Respect for others' genuinely human values, and commitment to bringing those values to full light through the Gospel, were the twin dimensions of "inculturation" as exemplified by Cyril and Methodius.[52]

Slavorum Apostoli was dated June 2, 1985, the solemnity of the Holy Trin-

ity. A month later, on July 5, the phoenix of the Catholic Church in Czechoslovakia rose from the ashes of Gustav Husak's "normalization" when almost
200,000 pilgrims came to Velehrad for the main public celebration of the
Methodius anniversary. The regime had tried to co-opt the event and turn it
into a conventional communist "peace festival." When the local authorities
welcomed the pilgrims in these ideological terms, the Catholics shouted en
masse, "This is a pilgrimage! We want the Pope! We want Mass!"[53]

The Church in Czechoslovakia had taken new heart in the seven years of
John Paul II's pontificate. Cardinal Tomášek had become a forceful defender
of religious freedom and a supporter of Charter 77, the human rights movement led by Václav Havel. A 1982 instruction from the Congregation for the
Clergy banning priests from participating in partisan politics had helped whit-
tle down the numbers of priests involved in "Pacem in Terris," and had essentially destroyed the organization's influence.[54] Velehrad now brought resistant
Czech and Slovak Catholics together, bridging the country's internal ethnic
division. The anniversary celebration linked popular piety to resistance to the
regime, encouraged the participants to think that they could act together in
defense of religious freedom, and showed them that they could rebuff the
regime's efforts to manipulate them (as in the bogus "peace festival").[55] Resistance Catholicism in Czechoslovakia had begun in earnest.

A CALL FOR AFFIRMATION: THE EXTRAORDINARY
SYNOD OF 1985

Holding an Extraordinary Synod on the twentieth anniversary of Vatican II to
relive the Council experience and review its implementation had been John
Paul's "personal idea," according to Cardinal Joseph Ratzinger, himself a
major figure in the Synod drama. The Council was, in Karol Wojtyła's settled
view, a great gift of the Holy Spirit to the Church that demanded both celebration and deepened reflection.[56] Among other things, that deepened reflection required the entire Church to divest itself of the "liberal/conservative"
political interpretation of Vatican II and to think about the Council as a religious event in which the chief protagonist was the Holy Spirit.

Shortly after the Extraordinary Synod convened on November 24, 1985,
Cardinal Godfried Danneels of Belgium complained at a press conference that
"this is not a Synod about a book, it is a Synod about a Council!"[57] The book
in question was Cardinal Ratzinger's review of the post-conciliar state of the
Church, a lengthy interview with the Italian journalist Vittorio Messori which
had been published in early 1985 under the provocative title *The Ratzinger
Report*. Danneels was right, of course, and Ratzinger would have been the first
to admit it. Years later, Ratzinger said that "it was true and important for Cardinal Danneels to say that we are having this Synod about the Council as fathers
of the Church and not to discuss a book," because *Il Rapporto*, as it was known
all over Rome, was "not the point of departure for the Synod."[58]

There was a sense in which Ratzinger was being too modest, however. *Il Rapporto* was neither the cause nor the substance of the Synod. But Ratzinger's book had given permission, so to speak, for the Synod to debate two questions that had only been discussed quietly in the two decades since Vatican II. Had there been serious misinterpretations of the Council? Were those misinterpretations impeding the Church's reception of Vatican II's teaching, especially on the Church's distinctive nature as a "communion"? By putting these questions openly on the table, *Il Rapporto* was a major factor in setting the intellectual framework in which the Synod's deliberations were conducted and its recommendations framed.

The issues at the Synod were, in large part, those discussed by Cardinals Wojtyła and Ratzinger prior to the conclaves of 1978. The Church's engagement with the modern world had to be distinctively ecclesial, or it would betray Christ's great commission to "go and make disciples of all nations, baptizing them in the name of the Father and of the Son and of the Holy Spirit" (*Matthew* 28.19). That, and nothing less than that, was what the Church was *for*. Christ's commission made the Church a servant of human dignity. It was through Christ that the Church was an agent of liberation. The "Church in the modern world" had to be the *Church* engaging modernity.

A careful reading of the Extraordinary Synod's *Final Report* suggested that, with varying degrees of conviction and enthusiasm, the Synod members agreed that there had been misinterpretations of the Council and that it was necessary to reread Vatican II.

The *Final Report* emphatically affirmed Vatican II as a "grace of God and a gift of the Holy Spirit" that had done great good for the Church and the world. Against such Council rejectionists as Archbishop Marcel Lefebvre, the Synod unambiguously stated that Vatican II was "a legitimate and valid expression and interpretation of the deposit of faith as it is found in Sacred Scripture and in the living tradition of the Church." That the "large majority of the faithful received the Second Vatican Council with zeal" bore witness to the truths it taught.

The Council's reception had, however, been marked by shadows. Some of them were internal, including "partial and selective readings" of the Council and a "superficial interpretation" of its doctrine. Too much time had been spent over the past twenty years in arguing about the Church's internal management, and too little time invested in preaching God and Christ. There were also external "shadows" in play. Among them was an ideologically hardened secularism that was not open to dialogue. This close-mindedness, the *Final Report* stated bluntly, was a manifestation of the "mystery of iniquity" in our day.

What was required was a "deeper reception of the Council," based on a closer reading of its actual texts "in continuity with the great tradition of the Church." The Roman Catholic Church did not begin at Vatican II, and a deeper reception of the Council meant understanding Vatican II's teaching in light of 2,000 years of tradition.

The *Final Report* affirmed that the first task of the Church was to be the Church: "to preach and to witness to the good and joyful news of the election, the mercy, and the charity of God that manifest themselves in salvation history. . . ." There was no triumphalism here; there was even a certain modesty. "The Church makes herself more credible," the Synod fathers wrote, "if she speaks less of herself and ever more preaches Christ crucified." The way of the Church in the world was always the way of the cross. The easy, friction-free convergence between the Church's evangelical proclamation and secular progress that some had read into *Gaudium et Spes* was not the way the Synod fathers thought about "the Church in the modern world."

As for the Church's own renewal, that required what it had always required—saints. The Synod reaffirmed that everyone in the Church was called to holiness, celebrated the new renewal movements as "bearers of great hope," and proposed, like Vatican II, that the laity sanctify all of life through their witness in the family, at work, and in society and culture. One of the more sharply contested "internal" issues at the Synod had been the theological status of national conferences of bishops, a post-conciliar innovation in many parts of the world. The Synod affirmed the practical utility of these institutions as instruments for coordinating pastoral activity, but equally reaffirmed the authority of the local bishop, which could not be delegated to a national conference.

The *Final Report* stressed that ecumenism had "inscribed itself deeply and indelibly in the consciousness of the Church." At an ecumenical prayer service held in the Synod Hall, built into the roof of the Paul VI Audience Hall, the Pope had said flatly that "divisions among Christians are contrary to the plan of God." The *Final Report*, like the Pope, looked beyond the stage of "good relations" with Protestant and Orthodox Christians to a real ecclesial unity, in which "the incomplete communion already existing with the non-Catholic Churches and communities might, with the grace of God, come to full communion."[59]

The Extraordinary Synod had a few surprises, among which was an inversion of roles. The progressives at the Extraordinary Synod were the party of the status quo. "Why does there have to be a change?" one prominent progressive, himself a creator of the liberal/conservative taxonomy of Vatican II, complained. "What's wrong with the way things have been going?" The progressives most inclined to complain about "Rome" and the Roman Curia were also the most vocal defenders of the new curias that had developed in the national conferences of bishops.[60] Of more long-term significance was the fact that ecumenism, long identified with the progressive interpretation of the Council, was "firmly claimed by what is self-consciously the party of orthodoxy" during the Extraordinary Synod, according to one on-site observer.[61] The progressive party seemed content with the ecumenism of rapprochement amid continuing division. John Paul II was pressing a far more radical agenda of ecclesial unity.

The inversion of roles was most pronounced in reaction to a proposal from Cardinal Bernard Law of Boston, adopted in the *Final Report*, that a world catechism or "compendium of all Catholic doctrine regarding both faith and morals" be prepared. The progressive party, failing to see its relevance to modernity, dismissed the idea as impossibly old-fashioned. Bishop James Malone, the President of the U.S. Bishops' Conference, when asked about it, told a reporter, "Don't worry about that; you won't live long enough to see it completed."[62] Bishop Malone turned out to be dramatically wrong. The *Catechism of the Catholic Church*, published in 1992, became an international best-seller. In part, the *Catechism* was a response to concerns that post-conciliar Catholic religious education had become too process-oriented and too little concerned with content. But the Synod's recommendation of a new universal catechism, endorsed by the Pope in his closing address on December 7, touched on a deeper issue with even wider implications. It involved, in fact, one crucial dimension of "the Church in the modern world."

John Paul II saw the Synod, as he had seen Vatican II, as a preparation for the Church's entrance into the third millennium of Christian history. Would the Church cross that threshold confidently and hopefully, convinced that it had a credible proposal to make, or fearfully and diffidently, unsure of itself and the grounds for Christian hope? There was a real question in many Christian communities as to whether Christians could, after 2,000 years, "give an account" of their hope—as they were enjoined to do in the New Testament (*1 Peter* 3.15). Perhaps, many thought, "giving an account" of the Christian proposal was impossible, given the widespread conviction that human beings couldn't know the truth of anything, much less their eternal destiny. Others thought the task was irrelevant, Christianity being "true for Christians" but not something to be proposed to others.

The *Catechism of the Catholic Church* was a clear statement that Catholicism thought it possible to account for its beliefs and practices in a coherent, comprehensive, and accessible way. It could "give an account" of the hope that possessed it and animated it. It could make a proposal to the men and women of this age—that the world understand its story in light of *this* story.

Although the ringing affirmation of the Church's evangelical mission at the Extraordinary Synod of 1985 did not end the divisions in Catholicism by any means, it did mark the end of a period in Catholic history. The Council that had taken the gamble of not providing authoritative keys to its interpretation had been given an authoritative interpretation by the Synod. That process could now continue through further Synod assemblies and the papal "exhortations" that completed an ordinary Synod's work. Certain interpretations of the letter and "spirit" of Vatican II had been tacitly but decisively declared out-of-bounds. The temptation to self-secularization had been identified, which was the first step toward combating it. At least some of the mythology about "liberals" and "conservatives" had been dispelled. That was accomplishment enough for two weeks' work.

ABOVE, NOT OUTSIDE, POLITICS

Two weeks after the Extraordinary Synod concluded, John Paul II sent Cardinal Roger Etchegaray, the President of the Pontifical Justice and Peace Commission, on a special mission to Tehran and Baghdad, visiting the prisoners of war on both sides of the bloody Iran-Iraq war and quietly exploring the possibilities of a settlement.

Etchegaray's visit to the Persian Gulf was the first of several dozen such missions he would make to world trouble spots during the next fifteen years, as one instrument of the Pope's interest in developing a parallel personal diplomacy to complement the normal diplomacy of the Holy See. John Paul and the French cardinal had different views of the meaning of *Gaudium et Spes* and of the post-conciliar Catholic situation in France.[63] But the former archbishop of Marseilles was an adept conversationalist with a capacity for getting along with people whose experiences and views were very different from his own. Recognizing this, John Paul deployed him on missions to a host of conflict-wracked situations, including Lebanon, Mozambique, Angola, Ethiopia, South Africa, Sudan, Namibia, Cuba, Haiti, Central America, Vietnam, Cape Verde, Guinea Bissau, China, Myanmar, Liberia, Rwanda, Burundi, Indonesia and East Timor, and the Balkans, during the next fourteen years.[64]

Cardinal Etchegaray pursued his "parallel diplomacy" as a personal representative of the Pope, rather than as an official Vatican representative—a fine distinction, but one that allowed him to gain access to all parties in a conflict and to serve as a conduit for peacemaking feelers without committing the Holy See to any particular position or mediation strategy. Etchegaray did not think of these missions as diplomatic in the formal sense. He went to the scene of an international or civil conflict, at John Paul's request, to represent the Pope's concern for the people involved. If, as a result of contacts with all parties, he was able to open up lines of communication between them, so much the better.

This was not politics, strictly defined. It was, the cardinal once said, a "reinforcement and extension of the spiritual mission" of John Paul II, who wanted to be present to conflicts as an instrument of reconciliation. John Paul was, Etchegaray suggested, a man "above, not outside, politics." It was, in another Etchegaray phrase, a "politics of presence," which could sometimes do more to get a needed conversation started than formal diplomacy could.[65]

This back-channel work was difficult and risky, and the risks were not limited to Etchegaray's bouncing back and forth across primitive roads sown with land mines in one grim situation after another. In sending the French cardinal on these extracurricular missions, John Paul II was stretching the public mission of the Church far beyond the boundaries to which the cautious diplomats in his Secretariat of State were accustomed. These were risks the Pope and his improbable diplomatic troubleshooter were prepared to take, in order to give the "Church in the modern world" a new kind of presence in some of the most intractable situations of the late twentieth century.

Catholic People Power

While the Extraordinary Synod met in Rome, a different kind of revolution, embodying John Paul II's vision of the Church in the modern world, was unfolding in the Philippines, the only Catholic country in Asia.

Two years after the 1981 papal pilgrimage for the beatification of Lorenzo Ruiz, the Philippine Bishops' Conference stepped up its public criticism of the increasingly repressive Marcos government. A February 1983 pastoral letter, "A Dialogue for Peace," had charged the government with widespread violations of civil liberties and economic mismanagement compounded by massive corruption. The pastoral letter had also complained about priests and nuns being arrested or intimidated because of their work for justice, and had warned Marcos that tensions would increase without basic reforms.

Six months later, on August 21, 1983, Benigno "Ninoy" Aquino, a prominent Marcos opponent returning to the Philippines from exile, was shot in the head and killed at the Manila airport as he stepped off his plane. A month later, a half-million Filipinos took to the streets in protest against the regime. On November 27, which would have been Aquino's fifty-first birthday, the bishops' conference issued another pastoral letter, "Reconciliation Today," which stressed the power of Christian love to transform corrupt politics and emphasized that reconciliation was the essential prerequisite to genuine social change.

The situation continued to smolder through early 1984. In July, yet another episcopal conference pastoral letter, "Let There Be Life," reflected on the Aquino assassination as one example of a culture of violence that the Marcos government had created: "The murder shocked us all as no other killing in recent history," they wrote, "and for many of us it was the one, single event that shook us out of our lethargy and forced us to face squarely the violence that has . . . [become] practically an ordinary facet of our life as a nation. . . ." At the same time, the bishops continued to stress conversion and reconciliation as the road to social change.

In August and September, large public demonstrations marked the first anniversary of Aquino's assassination. In October, an independent commission concluded that Ninoy Aquino had been killed as the result of a military conspiracy. In January 1985, twenty-five men were indicted, including General Fabian Ver, the chief-of-staff of the Philippine armed forces. In July, the bishops' conference issued a "Message to the People of God," condemning the "increasing use of force to dominate people" as a "frightening reality which we as pastors cannot ignore." More anti-Marcos demonstrations followed in September. Six weeks later, on November 3, Ferdinand Marcos agreed to a "snap" presidential election in early 1986, presumably in at attempt to confuse the opposition, in which there were numerous possible candidates. On December 3, a day after all those charged with Benigno Aquino's murder were acquitted, his widow, Corazon, announced her candidacy for president, instantly unifying the opposition.

With the election now set by the government for February 7, the Philippine drama quickly intensified. The regime was doing its best to intimidate voters and to fix the election. An opposition organization of election monitors, the National Citizens' Movement for Free Elections [NAMFREL] had been formed. On December 28, Cardinal Sin and his auxiliary bishops issued a pastoral letter to the Archdiocese of Manila, stressing the Christian duty to vote, pledging their cooperation with NAMFREL, teaching that vote fraud or cheating was a "seriously immoral and un-Christian act," and denouncing violence. Three weeks later, on January 19, 1986, the cardinal, his auxiliaries, and the priests' council of the archdiocese issued a second pastoral letter, "A Call to Conscience," which sharply challenged a "very sinister plot by some people and groups to frustrate the honest and orderly expression of the people's genuine will." No one thought that the cardinal and his associates were referring to NAMFREL.

The entire national bishops' conference issued a pastoral letter on January 25. Its content was telegraphed in its title—"We Must Obey God Rather Than Men." The bishops now said that a "conspiracy of evil" threatened to subvert the election and bring the country to further ruin. Filipinos had a special responsibility, as citizens of the only Catholic country in Asia, to create a morally serious politics and to resist evil nonviolently.

Two days before the election, Corazon Aquino, now universally known as "Cory," put the issue of Philippine renewal in explicitly religious terms: "While I have done everything humanly possible to bring back power to our oppressed people, there comes a point where God's power has to intervene. We cannot win this election without God's help. . . . After we have made a vow to be vigilant and to sacrifice even our lives to dismantle the Marcos regime, we can only pray. We already have our people's overwhelming support, and prayer is all we need right now."

The February 7 voting was a farrago of government-organized fraud and cheating. Days later, the bishops' conference issued a blunt, uncompromising "Post-Election Statement" that denounced the "unparalleled fraudulence" of the election, taught that a government elected on such a basis has "no moral basis" for its claim to power, and said that Philippine people were obliged to correct the injustice done to them by "peaceful and nonviolent means in the manner of Christ." There was considerable nervousness about the Philippine situation in the Vatican Secretariat of State, and the papal nuncio, Archbishop Bruno Torpigliani, was not a man given to endorsing bold action by a local hierarchy against the government to which he was accredited. Cardinal Sin and his fellow bishops courageously went ahead, declared the Marcos government morally illegitimate, and invited the Philippine people to do something about it—nonviolently.

Their extraordinary statement, coupled with the certification of Marcos's victory by a rubber-stamp National Assembly on February 15, galvanized the People Power revolution in the Philippines. At a "victory for the people" Mass celebrated before a congregation of a million in Manila's Luneta Park on February 16, Corazon Aquino publicly called for a campaign of nonviolent resistance against the regime, a call broadcast throughout the country on the Church's Radio Veritas. Six days later, defense minister Juan Ponce Enrile and the vice chief-of-staff of the Philippine armed forces, General Fidel Ramos, broke with Marcos and prepared to take a stand at Manila's Camp Aguinaldo, the military base where the Defense Ministry was located, and Camp Crame, the site of Ramos's headquarters. Enrile and Ramos called Cardinal Sin and asked his help against what they were certain would be an armed attack on their positions by Marcos-loyal troops. Sin asked them whether they were supporting Cory Aquino as the legitimately elected president of the country. They assured him they were. The cardinal then went on Radio Veritas to broadcast an appeal to "all the children of God" to go to the two camps to protect the rebellious defense minister, General Ramos, and the troops they had persuaded to join them.

The revolution now centered on the broad boulevard running between Camps Aguinaldo and Crame: Epifanio de los Santos [Epiphany of the Saints] Avenue, or EDSA. During the next three days, hundreds of thousands of unarmed Filipinos, bringing rosaries, flowers, and sandwiches to the crews of the tanks with which Marcos was threatening the rebels, formed a vast human shield between the government troops and the camps. Young and old, laity and religious, wealthy, middle-class, and poor people all flocked to the EDSA revolution, as a biblical sense of *kairos*—a graced moment of opportunity—transformed people who had been quietly acquiescent for years into nonviolent resisters. "Most of them were scared to death," a journalist wrote later. "But they came anyway. Their spiritual leader had told them to go." Henrietta de Villa, a prominent Catholic laywoman, brought her entire family, including her ten-month-old grandson; this was something, she believed, that "we should all face together."

Radio Veritas was a crucial instrument for the resistance, directing the massive human traffic and maintaining a steady emphasis on nonviolence. When Marcos-loyal troops blew up its transmitter on the morning of February 23, new broadcast facilities were found. Nuns sat on the steps leading to the studios, praying the rosary and shielding the transmitters and the radio staff from Marcos's troops. Cardinal Sin and his associates deftly managed what could have been an explosively violent situation, always stressing on the radio that the revolution on EDSA had to be nonviolent. At 6:45 P.M. on February 24, Enrile and Ramos, both Protestants, held a press conference while standing in front of a statue of the Virgin Mary, and declared that Corazon Aquino had been cheated out of the presidency by governmental election fraud.

Tension continued to mount as Marcos considered his options and the cardinal continued to encourage his nonviolent resisters. EDSA drew more and more people. Crosses were erected at strategic points to divert tanks and armored personnel carriers. Posters and banners with religious mottoes were everywhere, as were the ubiquitous rosaries the crowd pressed on the tank crews. When the United States government made clear that it would not support Marcos any longer, the regime crumbled. Marcos-loyal troops withdrew from the approaches to Camps Aguinaldo and Crame, Ferdinand and Imelda Marcos flew off to a Hawaiian exile, and Corazon Aquino was sworn in as President of the Republic of the Philippines.[66]

Cardinal Sin later wrote that he had been "deeply inspired by the workers' Solidarność and by the way the Church, especially [the] Pope, supported this movement [for] the good of Poland and, ultimately, [for] the good of Europe and humanity."[67] Notwithstanding the extreme caution shown by Archbishop Torpigliani and the criticism Sin received in the Secretariat of State during the months leading up to the People Power revolution, the cardinal felt supported and encouraged by John Paul II. "He understood," the cardinal recalled later, and "he always encouraged me to carry on."[68]

John Paul understood, because what Sin and his associates were championing was the kind of Christian liberation John Paul had been urging since his election. It differed from various Latin American liberation theologies in seven key respects.

The People Power revolution was a broad-based resistance movement against a mendacious, violent, corrupt regime, not an exercise in class struggle. Cardinal Sin and his associates insisted on nonviolence, as did the personal embodiment of the revolution, Corazon Aquino. There was not a hint in the Philippines of a legitimate "second violence" against the "first violence" of "sinful social structures." The EDSA movement, like Polish Solidarity, was a religiously inspired movement of social reform, not a political party, and its appeal, like that of Cardinal Sin and the Philippine bishops, was explicitly religious and moral, not ideological and political. Pastors, not intellectuals, were in command of the situation, and prudent pastoral responsibility, not the testing of theories, drove the revolution on EDSA. The revolution was supported by Catholic renewal movements that were united to the hierarchy and did not imagine themselves to be an alternative "People's Church" over against the "institutional Church."

Cardinal Sin insists that he was acting as a pastor, not a politician, and that his partisanship was moral, not political in the narrow sense of the term.[69] The distinction is important, although it is not always easy to maintain. During the fraudulent election campaign of 1985–1986, Cardinal Sin told a Rotary Club meeting, in response to government charges of untoward political activity by priests, that he was "reminded . . . of the wise man who said that war was much too important a business to be left exclusively in the hands of generals. Might not the same be said of government, that government is much too important a business to be left in the hands of politicians and political scientists?"[70] In situations like Poland or the Philippines, pastors had a moral obligation to defend human dignity against the depredations of evil governments. This defense had public implications, indeed political implications, but it was not partisan in the sense of posing the Church as an alternative contestant within the same power game. It was partisanship in favor of a changed game.

The revolution on EDSA may have looked like a carnival to Western observers, but it was serious business to the people involved. As a former *Wall Street Journal* correspondent and active participant in these events, Araceli Lorayes, put it, "One had only to reflect on how desperate the situation of the mutineers was, on how utterly powerless we all were—both the opposition who were in hiding and the crowd at EDSA—to realize that ultimately we were all in the hands of God." The secular mind of many reporters couldn't grasp that the Philippine revolution's "inner life, its motivating force, was prayer." Lorayes did not claim that the People Power revolution of 1986 was a miracle in the strict sense of the term, an event caused by God's suspension of the laws of nature. But the power of the Holy Spirit, working through very fallible human beings (some of whom, like Defense Minister Enrile, had mixed motivations), had "brought about the deliverance of the Filipino nation from almost certain disaster."[71]

As John Paul II, Cardinal Sin, and hundreds of thousands of Filipinos saw it, their revolution had not only done something good for the Philippines, it had demonstrated something important about the human condition. The depth dimension of history, which was accessible to the eyes of faith, made sense of what was happening on the surface.

THE ENCOUNTER WITH WORLD RELIGIONS

If cautious diplomats in the Secretariat of State were concerned that the Pope and the archbishop of Manila were violating the canons of prudence in the Philippines, curial officials and some bishops around the world wondered whether John Paul was not veering dangerously close to the heresy of syncretism with one of the most innovative initiatives of his pontificate—a World Day of Prayer for Peace, involving non-Catholic and non-Christian religious leaders from all over the globe, which the Pope planned to convene in Assisi in October 1986.

The Pope announced the initiative on January 25, 1986, and the negative reactions were almost instantaneous. Wouldn't bringing world religious leaders together in one setting suggest that the Catholic Church considered all religious traditions equally valid? How could the Pope pray with men and women who venerated a different God, or many gods? The questions involved serious theological issues. Beneath the surface, though, something like the Curialist's complaint that John Paul II was turning the Vatican into "Campo de'Fiori" could be sensed: Why didn't John Paul understand that this kind of thing was simply *inappropriate*?

It was, in fact, the Pope's idea. His predecessors, pondering such a step, might have circulated a memo asking for reactions from the Vatican bureaucracy, where the idea would have died the death of a thousand cuts. John Paul trusted his intuitions. He discussed the possibility with Cardinal Francis Arinze of the Secretariat for Non-Christians and Cardinal Roger Etchegaray. In those conversations, it was decided that Etchegaray's Pontifical Justice and Peace Commission would take responsibility for arranging "the who, what, when, where, and how."[72] The Pope's point, as Etchegaray explained to his colleagues, was that the world's religious traditions had "deep resources" for addressing international world conflict. Their commitment to prayer was one of them.

John Paul understood that this could not mean a universal praying together, which would indeed be syncretism and therefore impossible, for others as well as for him. "Being together to pray" was something different. The task laid on Etchegaray and his colleagues was to "find a formula by which each one could pray in his own way, and then come together with the others." The Justice and Peace Commission staff thought there should be fasting as well as prayer. Archbishop Virgilio Noë, the former papal master of ceremonies then serving as Secretary of the Congregation for Divine Worship, suggested that the event should involve movement in order to convey the idea of a pilgrimage. Putting all this together, John Paul then decided that the World Day of Prayer for Peace would be held in Assisi, where he, too, would be a pilgrim.[73]

The formula was finally hammered out. John Paul would receive the other religious leaders at the Portiuncula, the small chapel located on the plain below the town of Assisi that was St. Francis's favorite church. Each leader would go to a separate site in the town to pray for ninety minutes with those of his followers who were present. Everyone would then walk to the great piazza in front of the basilica of Assisi where a podium would be erected. There, each religious leader would offer a prayer according to his tradition. The Pope would give a closing speech, and afterward the religious leaders would break their fast together.[74]

Meanwhile, as curial muttering about the preparations for Assisi continued, John Paul took off on January 31 for a ten-day pilgrimage to, of all places, India—a country marked by unparalleled interreligious encounters.

In the Land of the Untouchables

The Pope jetted back and forth across the vast subcontinent, beginning in Delhi and visiting Calcutta, Ranchi, Shillong, Madras, Goa, Mangalore, Trichur, Cochin, Ernakulam, Verapoly, Kottayam, Trivandrum, Vasai, Puna, Goregaon, and Bombay. On the day he arrived, he visited the site where Mohandas Gandhi had been cremated in 1948 and preached on the Beatitudes.[75] He went to the State of Assam in the far northeast, which was usually closed to foreigners, and said Mass in a field as the local peasants were herded into wooden pens for crowd control.[76] In Madras, he prayed at the traditional site of the tomb of the apostle Thomas.

Christian service to the poor and abandoned was a constant theme of

John Paul's addresses in Shillong, Madras, Goa, Mangalore, and, of course, Calcutta. There, he met with the living icon of Christian service in India, Mother Teresa, who over the years had brought some 50,000 of the Indian sick out of the gutters and into her "House of the Pure Heart." The friendship between the Polish Pope and the tiny, Albanian-born nun was deep and intuitive; they understood each other "without a lot of words," as one of John Paul's associates once put it. For the Pope, Mother Teresa was a "person-message" for the twentieth century and a living confirmation that the Law of the Gift graven in human nature could be lived in a way that led to the most profound happiness. No one was happier than Mother Teresa, who lived a life of almost unimaginable asceticism surrounded by suffering. Whenever they met (which was usually in Rome), the nun wanted to talk about how her community, the Missionaries of Charity, was expanding: "I have started a house in Russia," or "I have started a house in China." That this community of women religious, living the toughest kind of commitment, was flourishing while other communities were dying made an impression. Even more impressive was the daily witness of the Missionaries of Charity, the serenity with which they lived lives of hardship. John Paul decided that Rome could use some of that witness. As he later recalled, he came back from India determined to establish a hospice run by Mother Teresa's sisters inside the Vatican.[77]

That Mother Teresa's community did its work in India, where Christians were a pronounced minority, gave the Church a position in Indian society that even the most nationalist Hindu had to respect. The reality of Mother Teresa and the Missionaries of Charity in the slums of Calcutta also illustrated a truth about particulars and universals that had applications far beyond India. Mother Teresa was not a particularly winsome expression of a generic human decency. She was a universal role model precisely because she was a radically committed Christian. She and her sisters embodied two universal goods—compassion, and a profound respect for the human dignity of the poorest of the poor—through the "particular" of Catholicism. She was a living refutation of the claim, widespread in the modern world, that a particular commitment narrowed one's horizons.

In Assisi

Arrangements for the World Day of Prayer for Peace were being completed as the summer of 1986 gave way to the autumn. Two renewal groups, the Sant'Egidio Community and the Focolare movement, took responsibility for hospitality and getting things organized in Assisi. The Pope's Angelicum classmate, Bishop Jorge Mejía, then Cardinal Etchegaray's deputy at the Pontifical Justice and Peace Commission, was asked to write an article for the Vatican newspaper, *L'Osservatore Romano*, giving the rationale for the event, which was still causing a lot of grumbling. Mejía's lengthy article patiently explained once again that while "it is difficult to see how we, as Christians, can insert ourselves into the prayer of others" who did not share our faith in the God of Abraham, it remained the case that "being present when another prays, or when many come together to pray, cannot but enrich our own proper experience of prayer." He also added a tart reminder of the kind of world in which those complaining about the papal initiative were living: "In a world where there is too little prayer," he wrote, "the unheard of fact that believers of the different religions find themselves together to pray acquires an exceptional value . . . What better response can we make to widespread secularism, if not this journey, this mutual encounter, for no other reason than to speak to God, each in his or her own way? . . ."[78]

In Mejía's mind, the whole initiative was an example of the "great, great audacity" of his old Angelicum classmate, the man with the faith "to dare to do this."[79] Whether they agreed or not, senior curial officials eventually got the message. The event was going to happen, with or without their approval, and they decided that they had to be there, taking their accustomed positions as members of the Cappella Papale, the "Papal Chapel," in the front of the assembly. Cardinal Etchegaray said that they would, of course, be welcome, but that he couldn't seat them according to the usual arrangements, as it would be bad form to have the first three rows in the piazza filled with cardinals during the closing session. "They were not happy," Mejía recalled.[80]

The World Day of Prayer itself, October 27, 1986, went off with only one hitch. Cardinal Arinze had urged that African animists be included among the religious leaders. One of those who came was very old, and was dressed traditionally, which is to say scantily, in unseasonably cold weather. He fainted, but was revived in time to meet with John Paul during the meal that followed the closing service.

At the meal, John Paul didn't get a chance to eat. He had had commemorative engravings printed for the other religious leaders, which were distributed when the entire group met to break their common fast. Virtually all of the leaders decided that they had to have the Pope autograph their personal copies.[81]

REOPENING AN ANCIENT CONVERSATION

As bold as John Paul's initiatives with world religions were, there has never been any doubt of the singular place the Pope assigns to the Church's encounter with living Judaism. In the months following the Assisi meeting he pressed even further the proposal he set out during his April 1986 visit to the Synagogue of Rome.

One can detect a steady progression in the Pope's thinking about Jews, Judaism, and Jewish-Catholic relations over twenty years. At his very first meeting with representatives of Roman Jewish organizations, on March 12, 1979, John Paul noted that "our two religious communities are connected and closely related at the very level of their respective religious identities." Jewish-

Catholic dialogue, from a Catholic perspective, was a *religious* obligation, and thus all the more demanding.[82] Five years later, in a 1984 address to an audience for representatives of the Anti-Defamation League of B'nai B'rith [ADL], John Paul took the question a step further: "The encounter between Catholics and Jews is not a meeting of two ancient religions each going its own way." Rather, there was a "mysterious spiritual link . . . which brings us close together, in Abraham and through Abraham, in God who chose Israel and brought forth the Church from Israel."[83]

A year later, addressing an ADL colloquium on the twentieth anniversary of *Nostra Aetatae,* John Paul suggested that the Jewish-Catholic dialogue, to be true to its own distinctiveness, had to become more explicitly theological. As Christians pondered more deeply the Jewish roots of Christianity, and as Jews reflected on the ways that the Church, since the days of Peter and Paul, had read the Hebrew Bible and received its Jewish heritage, the Jewish-Catholic dialogue must turn toward "common theological studies."[84]

Seven months after his April 1986 visit to the Synagogue of Rome, John Paul addressed another ADL-sponsored colloquium and suggested that the "mystery of universal redemption" was a kind of common border between Judaism and Christianity. Jewish-Christian dialogue had to address God's saving action in history *now.*[85]

What John Paul II was proposing in these and numerous other texts was nothing less than reconvening the theological conversation between Christians and Jews that had been broken off at the "parting of the ways" in the late first century A.D.

This was a bold vision. It challenged Jewish interlocutors who instinctively thought "theological dialogue" between Catholics and Jews was code for Catholic proselytization of Jews. It challenged Catholics who had never rid themselves of the last vestiges of the belief that God's redemptive action in Christ had superseded, indeed abrogated, the covenant with Abraham. John Paul insisted that the covenant with "Abraham's stock" was irrevocable, and that that was why a renewed theological conversation with Jews and Catholics was religiously essential.

This was easier for Catholics than Jews to acknowledge, theologically. Christian orthodoxy has always affirmed its debt to Judaism, however much Christians may have defaulted in their obligations to the Jewish people. Judaism has no similar or parallel "place" for Christianity in its mainstream self-understanding. Yet some of the twentieth century's greatest Jewish thinkers—among them, Martin Buber, Franz Rosenzweig, and Abraham Joshua Heschel—had explored the question of how Jews should differentiate their understanding of Christians from their understanding of all the other "others."[86] Some vigorously observant Jewish philosophers and theologians had even begun to ask whether Jews did not have a religious obligation to engage in a theological dialogue with Christians.[87]

The dialogue imagined by John Paul II and similarly courageous Jewish thinkers would begin with such problems as religious belief in an increasingly secularized world and move on to the common moral border between Judaism and Christianity—the Ten Commandments—exploring their implications for building free and tolerant societies. These issues would only open the new discussion John Paul envisioned, though. Questions untouched for almost two millennia remained to be examined. How do Jews and Christians understand Jews as an elect people? What do Jews and Christians understand by "covenant" today? How do Jews and Christians understand their common messianic hope for a completion of God's saving work in history?

These were some of the questions at which John Paul was hinting in his historic visit to the Synagogue of Rome and his addresses commemorating the twentieth anniversary of *Nostra Aetate*. That document, to the Pope's way of thinking, had set a foundation. He was now interested in starting to build, and in a way that had never been done since the theological conversation between Jews and Christians self-destructed during the First Jewish War, 1,900 years ago.

LIFE IN THE SPIRIT

Even as John Paul was making this pioneering proposal in Jewish-Christian relations, he was addressing the theological self-understanding of the Christian community. On May 18, 1986, the solemnity of Pentecost, John Paul II signed his fifth encyclical, *Dominum et Vivificantem* [Lord and Giver of Life]. This extended meditation on the Holy Spirit completed the Pope's Trinitarian trilogy of encyclicals, which includes *Redemptor Hominis* and *Dives in Misericordia.*

The idea of one God who is a Trinity of persons, Father, Son and Holy Spirit, is central to Christian faith.[88] Yet it is the Christian doctrine least well-understood by Christians and it often seems utterly baffling to non-Christians—especially to monotheistic Jews and Muslims, to whom the doctrine smacks of polytheism. The confusion and bafflement are not surprising, for the Trinity is, in the strict theological sense of the term, a mystery—a reality that the human mind cannot ever fully comprehend. Encyclicals are not occasions for theological speculation, and *Dominum et Vivificantem* is less a theological argument than an exhortation to the Church to take more seriously the Third Person of the Trinity, the Holy Spirit, in preparing for the Great Jubilee of 2000. John Paul does not discuss the infinitely complex issue of how the Persons of the Trinity are related, or the endlessly debated question, crucial for relations between Western and Eastern Christianity, of whether the Holy Spirit "proceeds" from the Father (the position of Orthodoxy) or from the Father and the Son (the position of Western Christianity since approximately the ninth century). *Dominum et Vivificantem* is written by a theologically informed pastor looking to rekindle devotion to the Holy Spirit in his people, not by a professor seeking to win a debate.

Christ's gift of the Holy Spirit, the Pope writes, is a new way of God's "being with" the world that goes beyond God's self-gift in creation. This is self-giving for the world's redemption, which is carried out in Christ through the power of the Holy Spirit. Meditating on Christ's saying that the Holy Spirit will "convince the world concerning sin and righteousness and judgment" (*John* 16.8), the Pope proposes that the Holy Spirit comes into the world because the world has forgotten its story. The world does not know where it came from, what sustains it, or where its destiny lies, although it assumes that it knows all these things. The sending of the Holy Spirit reveals to the world the truth about itself and its history.

The Holy Spirit, through the Church, must convince the world of its sin, precisely so that the world can recognize its need for redemption. This means, first of all, wrestling with original sin, "which is the principle and root of all the others."[89] God in creation called the world and humanity to communion with himself; humanity refused. The refusal of communion with God is the original, history-determining sin, and it results in the fracture of communion within humanity itself, beginning with Adam and Eve. In calling men and women to communion, God was revealing humanity's true good. Rejecting that invitation, men and women proposed to decide for themselves what constituted good and evil.[90]

The Holy Spirit's work in the world is to reopen consciences so that the world can begin to discover the outlines of its true story. Calling evil and good by their right names is the first step toward conversion, forgiveness, reconciliation, and the rebuilding of communion—within the human family, and between humanity and God.[91] Individuals can refuse to take that step; this is the unforgivable "sin against the Holy Spirit."[92]

The gift of the Spirit continues to meet resistance in the modern world, John Paul writes, just as it did in the world of the apostles. The world's refusal to consider even the possibility of its need for redemption has led to such death-dealing realities of the late twentieth century as the threat of nuclear destruction, indifference to poverty, the disposal of inconvenient life in abortion and euthanasia, and terrorism.[93] On the edge of a new millennium, the Church in the modern world must be, like the Holy Spirit, a "guardian of hope" and an active witness to life against death. In doing so, the Church, in the power of the Spirit, helps restore to the world "the divine sense of human life." In that rediscovery the world relearns its true story. In that recovery, the Holy Spirit renews what is good in humanity and renews the face of the earth.[94]

Dominum et Vivificantem is the longest, most complex meditation on the Holy Spirit in the history of the papal teaching office. As such, it was an important response to the ancient complaint of Eastern Christianity, that the Christian West did not take seriously the doctrine of the Holy Spirit. Six weeks after the encyclical was released, John Paul welcomed a delegation from the Ecumenical Patriarchate of Constantinople to the annual celebration of the feast of Sts. Peter and Paul, and told his Orthodox guests that their theological dialogue "must proceed to the very end: all the way to the altar of concele-bration."[95] When that day of Eucharistic unity arrives, *Dominum et Vivificantem* will be remembered as one of the paving stones along the road to reconcilia-tion between Orthodoxy and Rome.

ANGLICAN DIFFICULTIES

In the immediate aftermath of Vatican II, no bilateral ecumenical dialogue within Western Christianity had more hopes invested in it than the dialogue between Roman Catholicism and the Anglican Communion. Those hopes rested on the historical assumption that there was something fundamentally different about the English Reformation. Unlike the separations with the Lutheran and Reformed Christians of the continent, some proposed, there was no Church-dividing doctrinal difficulty between Rome and the English Church, the division in the sixteenth century having been largely precipitated by a political dispute. This view was reinforced by the nineteenth-century ascendancy of the Anglo-Catholic movement, which insisted that Anglicanism, along with Roman Catholicism and Orthodoxy, was a "branch" of the one Catholic Church. The Anglican–Roman Catholic dialogue also had a long his-tory behind it, including the "Malines Conversations" in Belgium in the 1920s, led by the second Lord Halifax and the Primate of Belgium, Cardinal Desiré Mercier. The memory of those initial explorations of restored unity gave the dialogue, formally established after Vatican II under the auspices of the Anglican–Roman Catholic International Commission (ARCIC), a special sense of possibility.

After a joint preparatory meeting in Malta in 1968, the formal theologi-cal dialogue known as ARCIC-I met thirteen times between 1970 and 1981 and discussed Eucharistic doctrine, ministry and ordination, and authority in the Church. Its final report, also known as ARCIC-I, was submitted to the Angli-can Consultative Council and to the Holy See in 1982. While ARCIC-I was being digested by the relevant authorities, ARCIC-II was launched in 1983 to discuss salvation and the Church as *communio*.

ARCIC-I was submitted to the Congregation for the Doctrine of the Faith for review. In early April 1982, CDF sent a set of "Observations" on the final report to Catholic bishops' conferences around the world. Though the Con-gregation did not have the final word in the matter, its opinion carried con-siderable weight and indicated that the Anglican-Roman Catholic dialogue was heading into troubled waters.

CDF welcomed ARCIC-I as "a notable ecumenical endeavor and a useful basis for further steps on the road to reconciliation," but disagreed with the report's claim that "substantial and explicit agreement" had been reached on several contested issues. Anglicans and Roman Catholics were still disagreed on Eucharistic adoration, on infallibility, on Marian dogmas, and on the mean-ing of the "primacy" of the Bishop of Rome, and it was not clear that genuine agreement had in fact been achieved on the real presence of Christ in the Eucharist, on the Eucharist as sacrifice, on the nature of the ministerial priesthood, and on the structure of the Church. Apostolic succession and divergences in moral teaching seemed not to have been dealt with at all, or only indirectly. The Congregation nevertheless recommended that the dialogue continue, since "there are sufficient grounds for thinking that its continuation would be fruitful."[96]

That hope soon ran up against the problem that would push the possibility of Anglican–Roman Catholic reunion even further into the future—the ordination of women to the priesthood by some Anglican Churches around the world, which had gained international visibility after the practice began in the United States in 1974. The question of "Anglican orders" had been discussed intensely between Anglicans and Roman Catholics since the late nineteenth century. Anglicans claimed they had maintained the apostolic succession despite their break with the Roman primacy. Rome (in the person of Leo XIII) declared in 1896 that Anglican orders were "absolutely null and utterly void," because the ordination rite used since 1552 omitted references to the Eucharist as sacrifice and the relationship between that sacrifice and the priesthood. Both sides had agreed, in ARCIC-I and ARCIC-II, not to reduce the matter to a historical question but to deal with it theologically, examining each other's current beliefs to see if they were compatible. Had it been clear that Anglicans and Roman Catholics believed the same things about the Eucharist and the priesthood today, ways could be found to deal practically with the issues left over by history.[97]

This was precisely what was called into question by the ordination of women in some Anglican Churches. Could this unprecedented practice be reconciled with the notion of an apostolic tradition transmitted from the apostles to the present day? The Orthodox Churches thought the whole idea impossible, precisely because it had no warrant in Scripture or the Church's tradition. The Roman Catholic Church had also reaffirmed that it could not ordain women to the priesthood, in the 1976 CDF Declaration *Inter Insigniores* [Among the Characteristics of the Present Age]. The question raised by the new practice was whether the Anglican Communion held a fundamentally different understanding of priesthood than Orthodoxy and Roman Catholicism. A further question involved the understanding of *communio* in the Anglican Communion, in which some provinces refused to acknowledge ordinations in other provinces.

Cardinal Johannes Willebrands, President of the Secretariat for Promoting Christian Unity, raised the issue of apostolic tradition in a letter to the Anglican and Roman Catholic co-presidents of ARCIC-II in July 1985.[98] Seven months before, John Paul II had written privately to the Archbishop of Canterbury, Robert Runcie, alerting him to the gravity of the issue for the dialogue's future. After reviewing the history of the discussion—the 1975–1976 exchange of letters between Paul VI and Runcie's predecessor, Archbishop

Donald Coggan, *Inter Insigniores*, and the comments by the official Vatican observers at the 1978 Lambeth Conference (the decennial meeting of world Anglican leaders)—the Pope wrote "with all brotherly frankness" that the Catholic Church continued to adhere to the principles and practice of *Inter Insigniores*. The two communions had come a long way in their mutual dialogue and much progress had been made, but John Paul had to tell Runcie that "the increase in the number of Anglican Churches which admit, or are preparing to admit, women to priestly ordination constitutes, in the eyes of the Catholic Church, an increasingly serious obstacle to that progress."[99] The letter ended on a note of hope, that the grace which had brought the two communions thus far would be sufficient to deal with this new problem. The letter was also a warning. The spread of the practice of ordaining women to the priesthood in the Anglican Communion, especially if ratified by the 1988 Lambeth Conference, could do fatal damage to the hopes for ecclesial reunion between Canterbury and Rome.

Archbishop Runcie's formal reply came in a letter eleven months later, dated November 22, 1985. The Archbishop reaffirmed the Anglican commitment to "full ecclesial unity," while noting that no one had ever thought the path to unity would be easy. He "fully" recognized, he continued, that "one such difficulty . . . is the difference in thinking and action about the ordination of women to the ministerial priesthood." Knowing that, he had consulted confidentially with the Primates of the autonomous Anglican Churches (or provinces) around the world, who in turn consulted within their local Churches. That was why he could reply only now to the Pope's letter.

Archbishop Runcie stated that despite differing opinions within his own Anglican Communion, "those Churches which have admitted women to priestly ministry have done so for serious doctrinal reasons," which he proposed to spell out further in a letter to Cardinal Willebrands. Further, the Archbishop proposed that the Anglican Communion and Roman Catholicism undertake a "joint study" of the question, with special reference to its consequences for "the mutual reconciliation of our Churches and the recognition of their ministries."[100]

The Archbishop's letter to Cardinal Willebrands admitted that the Pope had raised a serious caution by affirming "that the Roman Catholic Church believes it has no right to change a tradition unbroken through the history of the Church, universal in the East and the West, and considered to be truly Apostolic." He also frankly acknowledged that "on the Anglican side, there has been a growing conviction that there exist in Scripture and Tradition no fundamental objections to the ordination of women to the ministerial priesthood." At the same time, Runcie conceded that "for so significant a theological development" to be recognized as authentic, there had to be positive reasons "*for* such a development," not simply a lack of reasons against, and that these reasons had to be theological, not simply sociological or cultural. The Archbishop then stated that "the most substantial doctrinal reason, which is seen not only to justify the ordi-

nation of women to the priesthood . . . but actually to require it," was that Christ had redeemed all of humanity, which "must be a humanity inclusive of women if half the human race is to share in the redemption [Christ] won for us on the Cross." Because the priesthood had a "representative nature," with the priest representing the whole saved community of the Church, a considerable body of Anglican opinion held that "the ministerial priesthood should now be opened to women in order more perfectly to represent Christ's inclusive High Priesthood." In a formulation that seemed in tension with his earlier rejection of "sociological" and "cultural" reasons for a change of this magnitude, Runcie went on to say that this argument was "strengthened today by the fact that the representational nature of the ministerial priesthood is actually weakened by a solely male priesthood, when exclusively male leadership has been largely surrendered in many human societies."

Archbishop Runcie said that he did not think it appropriate for some Anglicans to act on this matter unilaterally until there was consensus within the Anglican Communion, and he recognized that "the argument for ecumenical restraint"—that is, the opposition of Roman Catholicism and Orthodoxy—"is also a doctrinal one, because it is only in such a wider perspective that particular churches can truly discern the mind of the whole Church." He regretted the fact that, after 400 years of estrangement had given way to "tangible signs of reconciliation," there was a "new obstacle between us." He could not see the way forward, but then neither had those who had begun the ARCIC dialogue twenty years earlier seen "the end from the beginning."

Cardinal Willebrands's response, seven months later, emphasized two points. First, the break with tradition unilaterally undertaken by Anglican Churches divided among themselves raised grave questions about the Anglican understanding of the Church's nature and its relationship to an authoritative tradition. There were also serious issues of sacramental theology at issue. Christ had taken on human nature to redeem humanity, and he had done so as a man. That, too, was part of salvation history. The priest who celebrated the Eucharist and the other sacraments of the Church did not represent the priesthood of all the baptized. The priest represented Christ, and "however unworthily, he stood *in persona Christi*" [in the person of Christ]. The ministerial priesthood was an icon of the unique ministry of Jesus Christ, God and man. The manhood of the priest was part of that sacramental iconography. To alter that tradition was a "radical innovation" that threatened a sacramental understanding of the priesthood as the visible sign of Christ's enduring priesthood in the Church.[101]

This exchange of letters was publicly released by the Vatican on June 30, 1986, and marked a turning point in the Anglican–Roman Catholic dialogue. From the Roman Catholic point of view, shared by many Anglo-Catholics, the issue was whether Anglicanism was declaring itself a nonapostolic Church, with a fundamentally different understanding of the sacramental nature of the Church and its ministry. Twenty-one years after Vatican II, the real question

was the one that John Henry Newman had been forced to face in 1841: Was Anglicanism the *via media,* the "middle way" between Rome and the continental Reformation it historically claimed to be? Or was it another form of Protestantism, and therefore in principle separated from communion with Rome?[102]

The hope for visible unity between Anglicans and Roman Catholics would continue to fade—despite the ongoing theological dialogue, warm welcomes to Rome for the archbishops of Canterbury and other visiting Anglican leaders, and impressive joint efforts to heal the historical memories caused by the martyrdoms of the Reformation era.[103] The assumptions on which ARCIC-I had been launched had proven to be false, in terms of the contemporary self-understanding of Anglicanism. Because of that, institutional ecclesial reunion seemed very far away indeed.

MOVING ON

Meanwhile, criticism of the World Day of Prayer at Assisi continued. John Paul's annual Christmas address to the Roman Curia on December 22, 1986, defended the "spirit of Assisi," which the Pope said was rooted in the divinely mandated interplay between unity and diversity in history, against those still carping about Assisi's alleged "syncretism."[104] A year after the Assisi meeting, the Sant'Egidio Community wanted to continue the process with similar meetings in the future. Even "the more open cardinals" were opposed, but John Paul II called in the community's chaplain, Monsignor Vincenzo Paglia, and told him "Don Vincenzo, today I fought for you . . . and we won." The process would go forward with an eye toward the Jubilee of 2000, with Sant'Egidio responsible for organizing similar meetings in different world venues.[105]

Another Jubilee note was struck on December 27, 1986, when the Pontifical Justice and Peace Commission issued a document entitled "At the Service of the Human Community: An Ethical Approach to the International Debt Question." The document asked that the entire question of Third World indebtedness and its impact on poverty in the developing world be rethought according to a humanistic ethics, with a variety of policy options ranging from rescheduling of debt payments to debt forgiveness being considered. It was a theme to which both the Holy See and John Paul II personally would return time and again as the Jubilee year drew nearer.

Bleeding Nicaragua

Nicaragua continued in turmoil. On January 21, 1986, Cardinal Miguel Obando Bravo of Managua met UN Secretary-General Javier Pérez de Cuellar to request United Nations assistance against Sandinista persecution of the Church. The cardinal gave the Secretary-General copies of the letters of the Nicaraguan Bishops' Conference to Commandante Daniel Ortega, which outlined a program

of ongoing Sandinista intimidation, including the expulsion of foreign clergy, threats against Catholic lay activists, the closure of Radio Catolica, and the censorship of official Church documents. After his meeting with Pérez de Cuellar, Cardinal Obando took his case to the Interamerican Commission for Human Rights in Washington. The Nicaraguan bishops received messages of solidarity from the bishops' conferences of Brazil, Argentina, Venezuela, and the Dominican Republic; Obando also got a letter of support from Cardinals O'Connor and Law in the United States.[106]

On July 14, the Nicaraguan Bishops' Conference appealed again to fraternal conferences of bishops around the world for assistance against persecution. The situation, they wrote, was "steadily becoming more difficult." There were ongoing, vicious personal attacks on the Pope and the bishops. The clergy was regularly intimidated by the internal security forces. The director of Radio Catolica and a local bishop had been expelled from the country. Mother Teresa had been refused permission to open two hospices. The Church was still barred from television. The journal of the archdiocese of Managua had been confiscated and the Church's printing press requisitioned. Radio Catolica remained off the air. Requests for dialogue with the government went unanswered.[107]

For his part, John Paul II's November 12 message to a Nicaraguan national Eucharistic Congress stressed reconciliation as one of the foundation stones of a free society. "In Nicaragua," he wrote, "the civilization of love must rise strongly and vigorously in a people reconciled, where hatred, violence, and injustice will be no more; a society in which there will always be complete respect for the inalienable rights of the human person and the legitimate freedom of the individual and the family. It is only through a true and deep reconciliation of each one with God and with all mankind that the much desired harmony will be achieved. . . . The mystery of the Eucharist is in no way alien to the building of a new world. Rather it is its principle and source of inspiration, because the Lord Jesus is the foundation of a new humanity that is reconciled and fraternal."[108]

Closing the Curran Affair

In the United States, the case of Father Charles Curran, longtime faculty member of the Catholic University of America in Washington, D.C., drew to its inevitable close in 1986. Father Curran had been the symbolic centerpiece of American Catholic dissent from the teaching of *Humanae Vitae* as a thirty-four-year-old junior professor in 1968, when he helped precipitate an ongoing controversy over the Church's teaching authority. Since then, he had published numerous books and articles taking issue with virtually every aspect of the Church's sexual ethic, while at the same time becoming a tenured faculty member of a Church-chartered institution.[109] The anomaly could not be sustained indefinitely.

The Congregation for the Doctrine of the Faith had sent Father Curran a detailed set of "Observations" on his written work, outlining the points at which he was in opposition to the authoritative teaching of the Church. An exchange of letters followed, in the course of which Curran declined to bring his teaching into conformity with Catholic doctrine. On September 17, 1985, CDF wrote Father Curran again, noting that "the authorities of the Church cannot allow the present situation to continue in which the inherent contradiction is prolonged that one who is to teach in the name of the Church in fact denies her teaching." Father Curran came to Rome for an "informal" meeting with CDF officials on March 8, 1986. In the wake of that meeting, Curran sent a definitive and final letter of response to the original CDF "Observations," dated April 1, in which he again declined to bring his teaching into line with that of the Church, and proposed a compromise in which he would retain his position at the Catholic University of America to teach moral theology, but not sexual ethics.

This was unacceptable. In a letter of July 25, personally approved by John Paul II, Cardinal Ratzinger informed Father Curran that CDF would advise the chancellor of Catholic University that Curran "was no longer . . . considered suitable [or] eligible to exercise the function of a Professor of Catholic Theology." The situation was parallel to that of Father Hans Küng. Father Curran was neither stripped of his priesthood nor forbidden to function as a priest. Nor was he forbidden to publish, make public appearances, or teach in a non-Catholic institution. As Father Curran had made clear in his writings and in his responses to the CDF "Observations," he did not believe to be true what the Catholic Church did, and he was not teaching what the Catholic Church taught about sexual morality. Therefore, CDF concluded, he should not hold the position of a professor of Catholic theology.

Father Curran was suspended from his faculty position in January 1987 and sued the university for breach of contract on February 28, 1987. After complicated negotiations failed to produce an out-of-court resolution satisfactory to Curran, the suit went to trial. Curran lost the suit on February 28, 1989, and accepted an endowed chair at Southern Methodist University in Dallas.[110]

Father Curran claimed, and no doubt truly believed, that he was exercising "responsible" dissent because he publicly disavowed Catholic teaching that had not been infallibly defined. This claim contradicted the teaching of Vatican II, however. The *Dogmatic Constitution on the Church* had made clear that the Church did not live, so to speak, by infallible definitions alone. The authoritative tradition of the Church, articulated by the Church's pastors, was binding on theologians and the people of the Church alike.[111] To suggest otherwise, as Father Curran did, was to create an absurd situation in which Church teaching was either "infallibly defined" or virtually nonexistent. Vatican II had a much more richly textured view of the nature of authoritative teaching than Father Curran.

The Curran affair also illustrated a serious problem in post-conciliar

moral theology that John Paul II would, at some point, have to address in detail. Father Curran believed that lowering the bar of Catholic sexual morality was the pastorally appropriate response to the tangled lives of human beings, who had been struggling with chastity since Moses had been given the Ten Commandments. For John Paul, whose pastoral experience was at least as extensive as that of most moral theologians, defining sin down was not, in the final analysis, pastorally sensitive, because it took the dramatic tension out of life and denied human beings the opportunity for moral heroism. Repentance and forgiveness, not preemptive absolution, was the truer humanism.

Evangelism "Down Under"

Just prior to the Assisi World Day of Prayer for Peace, John Paul made his third pastoral pilgrimage to France, visiting Lyons, Paray le Monial, Dardilly, Ars, Annecy, and the ecumenical monastery at Taizé in October 1986. Founded by Brother Roger Schutz in 1940 to revive Protestant monasticism, Taizé had evolved into an ecumenical monastic community living under a common rule devised by Brother Roger in 1952. Christian unity was one of Taizé's missions. Brother Roger believed that ecclesial reconciliation could only be founded on prayer. The monks of Taizé celebrated an ecumenical Liturgy of the Hours three times every day in the monastery's "Church of the Reconciliation," in addition to sponsoring ecumenical theological research, hosting ecumenical conferences, and bringing together young people from various denominations.

John Paul had a longstanding interest in Taizé's ecumenical and youth work and had participated in several Taizé-sponsored prayer vigils in St. Peter's. He celebrated the place of monastic rest in the lives of all those who were not monks in a brief address to the guests of the monastery on October 5: "Like you, the pilgrims and the friends of this community, the Pope is only passing through. But to pass by Taizé is like stopping briefly at a spring of water: the traveler halts, quenches his thirst, and continues his journey."[112] Speaking to the Brothers of Taizé themselves, John Paul recalled John XXIII's greeting to Brother Roger—"Ah, Taizé that little springtime!"—and expressed the "wish . . . that the Lord may preserve you like a springtime that breaks out and that he may keep you as little ones, in the joy of the Gospel and the transparency of brotherly love."[113]

Three weeks after the Assisi meeting with world religious leaders, John Paul flew to Dacca on the first leg of his longest pilgrimage, a 30,000-mile journey to Bangladesh, Singapore, the Fiji Islands, New Zealand, Australia, and the Seychelles. He was smothered in leis by young women in Dacca and guarded by loincloth-clad natives in the Fijis. At a cricket ground in Sydney, he held hands in a conga line with youngsters in blue jeans. Several days later, he conducted an impromptu question-and-answer session with Australian children by radio while flying from Darwin to Alice Springs, where he also met with Aborigines and urged them to protect their culture. He wore a hard hat in a

Sydney factory and cradled a baby koala bear in Brisbane, both bear and Pontiff looking a little nervous about the damage the former might inadvertently do to the latter's white cassock.[114]

At a candlelight service at the town hall in Adelaide, standing at the opposite end of the globe from Peter's city, the Bishop of Rome lit the first candle of the Advent wreath, which symbolized the Church's four weeks of preparation for Christmas. Throughout his pontificate, John Paul had insisted that he was, above all, an evangelist. He had now brought the message of the Gospel— "the light of Christ which has come into the world and cannot be extinguished"—quite literally to the ends of the earth.[115]

15

Forward to Basics

Freedom Ordered to the Dignity of Duty

JANUARY 13, 1987	Pope John Paul II meets General Wojciech Jaruzelski at the Vatican.
FEBRUARY 20, 1987	The Pope receives Mrs. Muzeyyen Agca, mother of Mehmet Ali Agca.
MARCH 25, 1987	*Redemptoris Mater,* John Paul's sixth encyclical.
APRIL 1–12, 1987	Papal pilgrimage to Chile and Argentina.
MAY 1, 1987	John Paul II beatifies Edith Stein in Cologne.
JUNE 5, 1987	John Paul issues apostolic letter to the bishops of Lithuania on the 600th anniversary of their nation's conversion.
JUNE 7, 1987	The Pope inaugurates a special "Marian Year," to be completed on August 15, 1988.
JUNE 8–14, 1987	Third papal pilgrimage to Poland.
JUNE 25, 1987	Papal audience for Austrian President Kurt Waldheim triggers controversy and special consultation with world Jewish leaders on August 31–September 1 in Rome and Castel Gandolfo.
JULY 8–14, 1987	John Paul hikes in the Dolomites.
SEPTEMBER 10–21, 1987	Second extended papal pilgrimage to the United States.
OCTOBER 1–30, 1987	Synod of Bishops considers lay vocation and mission in the world; Synod's work completed by the apostolic exhortation, *Christifideles Laici,* on December 30, 1988.
DECEMBER 3–7, 1987	Ecumenical Patriarch Dimitrios I comes to Rome on pilgrimage.
DECEMBER 22, 1987	John Paul's Christmas address to the Roman Curia stresses the priority of discipleship over office.
JANUARY 25, 1988	Apostolic Letter, *Euntes in Mundum,* marks millennium of Christianity among the Eastern Slavs.

FEBRUARY 14, 1988	John Paul's millennium message to Ukrainian Catholics, *Magnum Baptismi Donum,* praises Greek Catholic fidelity under persecution.
FEBRUARY 19, 1988	*Sollicitudo Rei Socialis,* John Paul II's second social encyclical.
MAY 7–19, 1988	Pastoral pilgrimage to Uruguay, Bolivia, Peru, and Paraguay.
MAY 20, 1988	Shelter for the homeless opens in the Vatican.
JUNE 7, 1988	John Paul II writes personal letter to Mikhail Gorbachev, indicating openness to a wide-ranging conversation; letter is delivered in the Kremlin on June 13 by Cardinal Agostino Casaroli.
JUNE 28, 1988	John Paul creates twenty-four new cardinals at his fourth consistory and issues the apostolic constitution, *Pastor Bonus,* reorganizing the Roman Curia.
JUNE 30, 1988	Archbishop Marcel Lefebvre illegally ordains four bishops and incurs automatic excommunication.
AUGUST 15, 1988	Apostolic Letter, *Mulieris Dignitatem,* on the dignity and vocation of women.
FEBRUARY 1989	John Paul II counsels Andrei Sakharov in the Vatican.

The limousine drove into the Cortile San Damaso, where General Wojciech Jaruzelski was met by the Prefect of the Papal Household and the liveried Gentiluomini del Santo Padre and escorted inside, past the salutes of the Swiss Guards. It was January 13, 1987, sixty-one months to the day since the Polish communist leader had declared war on his own country through the imposition of martial law. General Jaruzelski rode up the elevator to the third floor of the Apostolic Palace, where he and his escort turned left and walked past a striking set of frescoed maps of the world to the papal apartment. The door opened and the Pole whose claim to lead his country rested on armed force was taken to the library, where he would meet the Pole whose leadership in their fatherland was based on the power of the spirit.

Both men knew who had won.

General Jaruzelski's security police had murdered Father Jerzy Popiełuszko, and other priests had disappeared under strange circumstances. But Father Jerzy had been right: hopes could not be murdered. His grave in the churchyard of St. Stanisław Kostka had become Solidarity's sanctuary, a piece of free Poland. There were many other such sanctuaries throughout the length and breadth of the country, embassies from the Polish nation to itself. One of them was run at the Kolbe Church in Nowa Huta by another resistance priest, Father Kazimierz Jancarz, the chaplain of the Lenin Steelworks and a burly man in his mid-thirties, given to describing himself as "just a proletarian."

Every Thursday evening at 6 P.M., there was a special Mass celebrated at the Kolbe Church, followed by an educational program in which, as Father

Jancarz put it, "We tried to give people back their memory." There might be a debate on the current political situation or a lecture on Polish history. Lech Wałęsa and the intellectual leaders of the legally nonexistent Solidarity came and participated. An unofficial Christian university sprang up at the church in the mid-1980s. For up to six hours every Saturday, the steelworkers of Nowa Huta studied economics, sociology, psychology, "real history," and the fine points of political organizing and public relations with professors from the Jagiellonian University, the Polish Academy of Sciences, and the Kraków Polytechnic. Fifty workers were enrolled each semester, and four semesters got you a "degree." Some 400 workers eventually graduated, including Father Jancarz himself, who "took the program and learned a lot from it."

Then there were the "evenings of independent Polish culture," during which the church basement was used for theater, political cabaret, jazz, symphonic music, or graphic arts exhibits (poster art, in particular, had flourished in post–martial law Poland). The basement had been cleverly constructed, with tunnels leading out into the warren of apartment blocks in Miestrzejowice so that a large crowd could disperse quickly if the authorities wanted to make trouble. There were no announcements of an "evening of independent Polish culture" beforehand. Publicity was by word of mouth. As many as a thousand people attended each evening.

The Jaruzelski regime could harass this kind of cultural resistance, but it could never stop it. The Kolbe Church eventually became Poland's first private television studio, with technicians who had been fired by state TV. As videocams became available, they were used to make films that were distributed underground. Eventually, the "station" at the church got transmitting equipment and started broadcasting, including the first film on the life of Jerzy Popiełuszko.

As Adam Michnik put it, Poland after martial law was not "socialism with a human face"; it was "communism with a few teeth knocked out." The economy continued its slow-motion collapse and the average Pole's material quality of life steadily deteriorated. That was another reason cultural resistance was so important. An independent world of ideas and creativity helped sustain hope in a time of apparent hopelessness. The regime had tried to maintain what the Pope's old friend, Father Mieczysław Maliński, called a "culture of closed mouths." It had failed.

Meanwhile, during its months in prison, the Solidarity leadership had come to conclusions similar to those reached by other democratic dissidents in east central Europe. The reconstruction of "civil society" through culture was the prerequisite to economic and political change. This meant a new type of resistance. Information was a key to effective resistance through culture, and here was another important role for the Polish Church—the Church was a sanctuary of truth telling in a world dominated by lies. Or, as Father Maliński said, "People came to church to find out what the hell was going on in the rest of Poland."

As he walked across the marble floors of the Apostolic Palace to the papal library, General Wojciech Jaruzelski knew he had lost the gamble he had made on December 13, 1981. "Normalization" on the post-1968 Czechoslovakian model would not work in Poland. There could be no reconstruction of Polish society and the Polish economy without the cooperation of the Solidarity leaders, because these were the only men the Polish people trusted. Perhaps Jaruzelski remembered John Paul's counsel in June 1983: talk to these people, don't jail them.

The myth of self-reforming communism died hard. Two weeks after General Jaruzelski met with the Pope, the new leader of the Soviet Union, Mikhail Gorbachev, addressed the Central Committee of the Soviet Communist Party, defended his proposals for perestroika, or "restructuring," and reaffirmed his commitment to the basic principles of communism. Gorbachev came from a different generation than his three immediate predecessors, Comrades Brezhnev, Andropov, and Chernenko. Their formative political experience had been Stalin's purge trials, and they never quite rid themselves of the slightly reptilian look of men who had been parties to betrayal, torture, and murder in their youth. This was not Gorbachev's world, and he looked different, accordingly. But the man whose "nice smile" and "iron teeth" had been praised by no less than Andrei Gromyko still believed in reform communism.

He was not the kind of man to roll the tanks into a "fraternal" Warsaw Pact state to enforce the Brezhnev Doctrine. This gave General Jaruzelski, the Solidarity leadership, and John Paul II more maneuvering room. But neither was Mikhail Gorbachev willing to concede that communism was doomed no matter how much "restructuring" he accomplished. Alchemy could not become chemistry as long as alchemists held on to their basic assumptions about the way the world worked. The same was true of communism. Self-reforming communism, holding on to its delusions about the human person, was as impossible as scientifically serious alchemy.

For those committed to a path beyond communism, like John Paul II, it was essential to prepare the moral and cultural ground on which free societies could flourish. Freedom was not at risk only in east central Europe, however, and communism was not the only threat to the truth about the human person. The cast of characters on the world stage and the structure of history's drama had changed dramatically since Karol Wojtyła had been presented on the loggia of St. Peter's, more than seven years before. But the basic issues remained the same. The basic issues were always the same.[1]

GOSPEL, HUMAN RIGHTS, DEMOCRACY

John Paul II began 1987 with three characteristic personal gestures. On January 12, he baptized forty-nine babies in St. Peter's Basilica. On February 20, he received Mehmet Ali Agca's mother, Mrs. Muzeyyen Agca, in a private audience. And on March 8, he began the annual Lenten retreat he had invited the Father General of the Jesuits, Peter-Hans Kolvenbach, to preach. Lent 1987 would produce one of the most dramatic scenes of the pontificate and would test the well-oiled machinery of papal travels as it had never been tested before.

Latin America, the demographic center of world Catholicism, was in the midst of long-delayed transitions to democratic politics and market-oriented economics throughout the 1980s. John Paul II had been to the continent seven times, an average of once a year. In the third and fourth weeks of Lent 1987, he was on his way to one of the holdouts against democratization, General Augusto Pinochet's Chile, and to an Argentina consolidating its transition to democracy in the wake of a military junta that had massively violated civil liberties and led the country to defeat in the Falklands/Malvinas War. En route to his first destination, an overnight stop in Montevideo, Uruguay, the Pope held one of his impromptu airborne press conferences, walking up and down the aisle of his Alitalia jet and fielding questions in half a dozen languages for three-quarters of an hour.

One reporter asked whether the Church in Chile should play the same role as it did in the Philippines. John Paul didn't hesitate: "I think it is not only possible but necessary, because this is part of the pastoral mission of the Church." General Pinochet's recent remark, that things would be better if the Chilean bishops stopped acting like a political party and "spent ninety percent of their time praying," had not gone over well. John Paul understood that some leaders wanted, as he put it, "to separate us from this mission," namely, the Church's defense of basic human rights. The Pope was having none of it. As he said, the Church could not "let itself die" by abandoning the cause of human rights. Those who said, "Stay in the sacristy and do nothing else" had better understand that.

Then, when a reporter asked whether the Pope expected to help restore democratic politics to Chile, John Paul gave a succinct summary of the relationship between the Gospel, human rights, and democracy: "Yes, yes," he said, "I am not the evangelizer of democracy, I am the evangelizer of the Gospel. To the Gospel message, of course, belongs all the problems of human rights, and if democracy means human rights then it also belongs to the message of the Church."[2] The sequence here was instructive: from evangelism to culture formation to political change.

Chile

General Augusto Pinochet had become President of Chile in a September 1973 military coup that deposed the government of Salvador Allende, an avowed Marxist who had been elected president by minority vote in 1970. The Pinochet dictatorship banned left-wing political parties, "recessed" the centrist parties (including the Christian Democrats), reversed Allende's statist economic policies, and engaged in considerable repression of civil liberties. There were "disappearances" in Chile—perhaps as many as 1,000—and the regime used torture against its leftist enemies. Yet Chile, unlike neighbor Argentina, did not suffer the horrors of a civil war, which in Argentina resulted in as many as 14,000 "disappeared."[3]

The Chilean bishops had been justifiably worried by the Allende government's declared intention to create a Marxist state in Chile and the steps it had taken to do so. By the same token, the bishops, led by Cardinal Raúl Silva Henriquez, SDB, of Santiago, opposed the Pinochet regime's human rights violations from the outset. Cardinal Silva established a "Vicariate of Solidarity" in Santiago to support victims of governmental repression. The cardinal was also a key figure in engaging the Holy See as mediator when Chile and Argentina seemed on the verge of war in 1978. That successful effort, which had been concluded in 1985 with the Treaty of Montevideo, helped set the stage for a papal pilgrimage in 1987. Chileans were grateful for what John Paul II had done in a seemingly hopeless situation.

Cardinal Silva had retired in May 1983. His replacement, Juan Francisco Fresno Larraín, was a compromise choice, a man of deep piety whose appointment, it was hoped, would ease tensions within the Chilean hierarchy. There had been no disagreement among the bishops about the necessity of defending human rights, but there were disagreements about whether this was best done by public pressure or quiet persuasion. Fresno, who was named cardinal in 1985, chose one of the key leaders of the Vicariate of Solidarity, Monsignor Christian Precht, as his deputy (or "pastoral vicar") and became a public advocate of democracy and reconciliation. Shortly after his appointment, Archbishop Fresno established contacts with leaders of the banned centrist political parties, meeting with them individually. In each case he had three questions: What do you expect for the future? What are you prepared to do? What are you willing to give up? The archbishop then brought the opposition politicians together and read them what they already agreed upon. These consensus points became the basis of the "National Accord for Democracy" announced in August 1984.

Some of the Chilean bishops were afraid that a papal visit would strengthen the Pinochet regime. Cardinal Fresno and Monsignor Precht were convinced that the Pope's presence, the preparations for such a visit, and the experience of community it would generate could help revive civil society in Chile, and thus take the country a step closer to democracy. The strategy of the visit reflected the approach John Paul had succinctly summarized during his flying press conference en route to Montevideo.

The basic message would be evangelical and moral—that "Chile's vocation is for understanding, not for confrontation," as Monsignor Precht later put it. Elaborating on this theme in his thirty Chilean addresses, John Paul confirmed the Church in its role as defender of human rights and promoter of reconciliation. At the same time, he was signaling the opposition and the government, each of which included serious Catholics, that a nonviolent transition to the law-governed democracy envisioned in the National Accord was the right path to take.

The second strategic goal for the pilgrimage was to give the Chilean people an opportunity to vote with their presence and their applause on the road they wanted to travel in the future. To leading figures in the Pinochet regime, "reconciliation" was code language for a politicized Church meddling in its affairs. On the other extreme was a leftist opposition that wanted confrontation (violent, if necessary), and that claimed "the people" were uninterested in reconciliation. During the visit, "reconciliation" was the word most applauded in John Paul II's public addresses, and the pilgrimage became an informal plebiscite on Chile's future.

The third goal was to create an experience of civil society by what Monsignor Precht called "reconquering the streets." Chile's streets had been places of repression, danger, and confrontation. The Popemobile's travels through Chile's cities reversed the public imagery of "street life" over the past decade and a half. The street was now a place where Chileans prayed together, rather than a place of riots and police beatings. The papal Mass venues were deliberately set up to mix people together as they hadn't been for years. Once again, as in Poland and the Philippines, the experience of social solidarity, created by a mass public religious event that reclaimed the country's authentic culture, proved a potent antidote to the politics of violence.[4]

John Paul arrived in Santiago on April 1, 1987, and was greeted by President Pinochet, who defended the past thirteen and a half years of dictatorship. The first moment in "reconquering the streets" followed, as the Pope made a triumphal entry into the capital city, where the Chilean Church welcomed him at the cathedral. Later in the day, he went to the top of a hill overlooking the capital and blessed the city, making special mention of those in exile for their political convictions.[5]

The Pope met General Pinochet the next day at the presidential palace, where the two men had a private meeting at which the papal nuncio, Archbishop Angelo Sodano, was present. There were no set speeches; Pope and president had a conversation. Pinochet pressed the Pope: "Why is the Church always talking about democracy? One method of government is as good as another." John Paul politely but firmly disagreed. "No," he said, "the people have a right to their liberties, even if they make mistakes in exercising them."[6] Pinochet later told the nuncio that the Pope's answer had made him reflect more carefully on the issue. For the moment, though, he wanted a photo that would imply a papal blessing on his regime. So Pinochet's entourage maneuvered John Paul onto a balcony of the presidential palace overlooking a courtyard packed with regime supporters, where the two men were photographed together—a vignette misinterpreted and misreported as the Pope conferring legitimacy on the government or somehow soft-pedaling his human rights convictions.[7] That the opposite was the case should have been clear from the Pope's remarks to students in Valparaíso that same day. Speaking in a stadium where Pinochet's opponents had once been detained and tortured, he urged nonviolence while applauding the youngsters' desire "for a society more congruent with man's proper dignity."[8] The choice of venue was not accidental. Neither was the suggestion that change was imperative.

The real confrontation came the next day, April 3. The papal Mass for the beatification of a native-born Chilean, Sister Teresa of Jesus "of the Andes," was about to be held at Santiago's Bernardo O'Higgins Park, with perhaps as many as a million Chileans in attendance.[9] Monsignor Precht, in charge of liturgical services during the pilgrimage, came to the venue early and sensed that something was wrong. The crowd in front of the altar platform wasn't responding as crowds usually did during the warm-up for the Mass. The Pope was told that something seemed amiss and that there might be trouble. His response was simple: "We are going to do everything as planned."[10] During the biblical readings in the first part of the Mass, a riot started in the crowd to the Pope's left. In addition to making it impossible to hear the readings, the rioters started burning tires they had brought into the park. The police were late in responding. When they did charge into the venue, water cannons, beatings, and tear gas compounded the disruption, in which 600 rioters and police were injured. At the height of the chaos, a Chilean government official turned serenely to Father Roberto Tucci, the organizer of John Paul's travels, and said, "It is good this happened, so the Pope will see how these people are"—by which he meant the leftists who were burning tires.

For his part, Tucci, for the first and only time during the pontificate, was thinking seriously of pulling the Pope out of a venue. The combination of burning rubber and tear gas was making it hard for the Pope and others on the altar platform to breathe. But the smoke gradually diminished, the late-arriving police restored a measure of control, and John Paul carried on.[11] Children received their First Communion from the Pope in tears—not from emotion, but from inhaling smoke and tear gas. At the end of the Mass, John Paul deliberately stayed on the altar platform longer than planned, kneeling before the altar, looking out into the park. No one was going to drive him away from such a scene. Cardinal Fresno, mortified, came up to the Pope and said, "Forgive us." John Paul responded, "For what? Your people stayed and celebrated [the Mass]. The only thing you can't do in these situations is give in to the rioters."[12]

On the way back to the nunciature, the streets of Santiago were packed with people trying to show solidarity with the Pope who had refused to give in. Neither Father Tucci nor Monsignor Precht believes that what happened in O'Higgins Park could have taken place without the prior knowledge and tacit acquiescence of the Pinochet regime. The overriding theme of the papal pilgrimage had been reconciliation; the government had to show that Chile was inherently violent in order to justify its own repressive measures. In a police state governed as Chile was in 1987, it was inconceivable that agitators could have brought tires and gasoline into a controlled venue without the regime turning a blind eye. The fact that the riot went on for some time before the police intervened also raised suspicions. Moreover, not a single rioter was ever arrested, despite both the violent police intervention that eventually stopped the riot and the fact that the entire episode had been filmed.[13]

After the Mass and riot at O'Higgins Park, John Paul met opposition political leaders at the Santiago nunciature. The government was not happy with the idea of the meeting, but the nuncio, Archbishop Sodano, had told them that it was good in itself and would be good for the country. In his brief prepared remarks, John Paul stressed that human rights were inalienable, but should be defended without violence.[14] The themes were familiar, but the meeting's impact was considerable. Officially speaking, there was no formal political opposition in Chile. John Paul's meeting with leaders committed to a nonviolent democratic transition demonstrated that the official reality was not, in fact, reality.[15]

Something crucially important for a peaceful transition to democracy had taken place during the papal visit to Chile. Chileans by the millions had "voted" for the proposal that their country's vocation was for understanding, not for confrontation. The streets had been taken back. As Father Tucci said to Monsignor Precht, after watching the attitude of the Chileans in the streets, "This is a country of witnesses, not just curious observers." The Chilean people had experienced something that had not been part of their national life for more than thirteen years: the public mingling of people of different views who were able to be civil because, as Monsignor Precht later put it, "You have to be honest with your father"—in this case, John Paul II.[16] Even the government had learned something. After acting unilaterally for years, it had been forced to cooperate with the Church in arranging the visit. The interaction was itself a kind of reconciliation.[17]

The visit's Chilean organizers thought the Western media, keeping score between the Pope and General Pinochet, missed a lot of this. Monsignor Precht remembered years later that the two principal images of the trip had been the photo of the Pope and General Pinochet on the balcony and "the spectacular" in O'Higgins Park. Both events had involved governmental manipulations that went unreported. The more significant point was that the conceptual structure of the pilgrimage had not been reported. Cardinal Fresno, Monsignor Precht, and their colleagues were convinced that restoring civil society was the precondition to restoring of democracy. The precondition to restoring civil society was national reconciliation. That was what they, and John Paul II, were trying to accomplish in five days.

The Chilean people seemed to have gotten the message. On October 5, 1988, eighteen months after the papal visit, a national plebiscite formally rejected continued military rule. On December 14, 1989, Patricio Aylwin, a Christian Democrat and leader of the opposition's seventeen-party Coalition of Parties for Democracy, was elected President of Chile with fifty-five percent of the vote, against a government candidate who garnered less than thirty percent and a conservative opposition figure who scored a mere fifteen percent. According to the arrangements agreed to between the government and the democratic opposition in early 1989, General Pinochet remained head of the armed forces, but the military's role in Chilean public life was considerably reduced. By the early 1990s, Chile was a stable democracy.

Argentina

Argentina had made its democratic transition in 1983, in the aftermath of the disastrous Falklands/Malvinas War, but the government of President Raul Alfonsín was not completely secure. The armed forces retained considerable political leverage, and the popular commitment to democracy was not so firm as to make a return to military rule unthinkable. Argentina still carried the raw scars of the military regime's "dirty war" against guerrillas and their putative sympathizers during the 1970s, in which torture was widespread and as many as 14,000 *desaparecidos* [disappeared] had paid with their lives for their opposition politics. The situation facing the Pope was further complicated by the fact that the Argentine hierarchy had not been as forthright in its defense of human rights as the Chilean bishops had been.[18] The papal nuncio, Archbishop Pio Laghi, had made extensive efforts on behalf of political prisoners, helping save the life of Jewish dissident Jacobo Timerman (who was exiled to Israel) and repeatedly warning his Argentine audiences that their country contained an "Auschwitz" and a "Gulag." Bishops and lay Catholics had criticized the nuncio's assertiveness.[19]

John Paul faced a difficult situation in the other country he had helped to avoid a war over the Beagle Channel. The Church had to be reconciled within itself, and the bishops had to be called to a more forthright exercise of their responsibilities as public moral witnesses. The importance of human rights had to be stressed without inflaming the restless military and jeopardizing the fragile democracy that had begun to take root. Peace, reconciliation, and the moral foundations of civil society were the primary themes of the thirty addresses John Paul gave during a week-long visit.

On the evening of his arrival, April 6, John Paul met with President Alfonsín and members of the government at Government House in Buenos Aires, where he spoke of the necessity of the state respecting "legitimate freedom of individuals, families, and subsidiary groups."[20] In the port city of Bahia Blanca in agricultural southern Argentina, he warned against "that modern image of greed which is *consumerism*," which he counterposed to "that beautiful virtue of country people, *their solidarity*."[21] In a homily at Viedma, John Paul stressed Christ's "preferential love for those most in need," which the Lord had expressed by "evangelizing the poor" and by "announcing redemption to those in prison, to the blind and the oppressed."[22]

In Mendoza, he insisted that personal conversion was essential to creating a truly civil society.[23] In Tucuman, he cautioned against the nationalism and xenophobia that had almost brought Argentina and Chile to war.[24] At Rosario on April 11, he spoke at length about the lay apostolate in the world and urged Argentine Catholics not to drift to the margins of public life but "to be *light and salt* right where you are."[25] Young people from all over the world, who had come to Buenos Aires for World Youth Day, were urged to be "'workers of peace' by following the ways of justice, freedom and love."[26]

John Paul was sharply criticized by left-leaning political activists and some journalists for not meeting with a group of mothers of *desaparecidos*. His message about the moral foundations of the free society was hardly ambiguous, however. He sharpened its imagery on Palm Sunday, when he spoke at the World Youth Day Mass about the interrogation and torture of Christ before his crucifixion, an image with "*a new reality and eloquence*" today. The local reference was clear to all with ears to hear.[27] Later that day, his words of admonition to the Argentine bishops were also unmistakable: "remain attentive to that which society itself, [however] secularized [or] apparently indifferent, expects from you as witnesses to Christ, as guardians of absolute values. . . ."[28]

The reminder would not have been necessary had the Pope believed those expectations were being met.

"A Daughter of the Jewish People"

Two and a half weeks after his return from Buenos Aires, John Paul began his second pastoral pilgrimage to West Germany. Its centerpiece, and one of the most controversial acts of his pontificate, was the beatification in Cologne on May 1 of a Carmelite nun, Sister Teresa Benedicta of the Cross, more familiarly known as Edith Stein.

The eleventh child of Siegfried and Auguste Stein, Edith Stein was born in Breslau, today's Polish city of Wrocław, on October 12, 1891; it was Yom Kippur, the Day of Atonement. Siegfried Stein, a merchant, died at forty-eight before Edith had celebrated her second birthday. Her mother, a woman of deep Jewish piety, was left to raise seven surviving children and manage a financially troubled lumber business. She thought of Edith, her youngest, as a "last testament" from her husband. A brilliant child who lost her faith in her mother's God in adolescence, Edith remained impressed by Frau Stein's religious devotion.

As she grew, Edith Stein became consumed with a passion for getting at the truth of things. This passion took a decisive intellectual turn when, during her early studies at the University of Breslau, she read the *Logical Investigations* of Edmund Husserl, the founding father of phenomenology. Transferring to the University of Göttingen in order to work directly with Husserl, Edith Stein quickly became one of his greatest students and met the leading figures of the phenomenological movement, including Adolf Reinach, with whose Lutheran family she became close friends. When Reinach was killed in Flanders in World War I, Edith was powerfully struck by the hope with which his young widow accepted his death. It was the young philosopher's first experience of faith mediated by a Christian experience of the cross.[29]

Edith Stein became Husserl's graduate assistant in 1916 and moved with "the Master," as his students called him, to the University of Freiburg, where she received the doctorate in 1917. Her religious wrestling was intensified by the political chaos of Germany's defeat in World War I; she read the New Testament and Kierkegaard and wrote essays on the nature of human community and its relationship to the state. The moment of enlightenment came when she was visiting her friend and fellow phenomenologist Hedwig Conrad-Martius, and her husband. When her hosts went out for the evening, Edith looked through their library for something to read. She chose St. Teresa of Avila's autobiography and quite literally could not put it down. Having stayed up the whole night reading it, she said to herself, on finishing it the next morning, "This is the truth." Edith Stein bought a missal and a catechism, studied them, and asked the local parish priest in Bergzabern, near the Conrad-Martius farm, to baptize her. Impressed by her knowledge of Catholicism, the priest cut short the usual period of instruction. Edith Stein was baptized on January 1, 1922, taking the Christian name Teresa, with the Lutheran Hedwig Conrad-Martius as her godmother. Frau Stein wept when Edith told her of her conversion. Edith continued to attend synagogue with her mother, praying the psalms during the service out of her Latin breviary, and Frau Stein was moved: "Never have I seen anyone pray as Edith did."

Edith Stein had wanted to enter a Carmelite convent immediately after her conversion, but decided to wait in order not to provoke an embittered break with her mother. She taught for eight years at the Dominican high school for girls in Speyer. During this period, she began making fresh translations of Thomas Aquinas and planned a habilitation thesis that would bring phenomenology and Thomism into conversation while qualifying her to teach at the university level.

From 1928 to 1932, Edith Stein traveled extensively throughout Germany, Switzerland, and Austria, sketching a distinctively Christian feminism. It was a pioneering attempt to develop a Catholic understanding of women's vocations in the contemporary world, and a challenge to the Nazi ideology, which claimed that life, for women, was "children, kitchen, and church"—period. She saw the storm clouds that threatened European life and put the question to educated Catholic women sharply: "In the mine fields of today's society, can we justify looking backwards continuously while our adversary wages war against our views?"[30]

As anti-Semitism began to corrupt German public life, Edith Stein struggled with her desire to enter the convent and pursue a contemplative vocation. Her spiritual director and friends continued to insist that she was too valuable to the Church as a public figure and ought to remain in active life. Her brief tenure as a lecturer at the University of Münster was cut short by new anti-Semitic regulations and she turned down an offer of a teaching position in

South America. Finally, on April 30, 1933, she was at prayer in a parish church when she felt that "the Good Shepherd was giving . . . his consent" to her entering the Carmelites. After a wrenching, emotionally draining farewell with her mother and her family, Edith Stein, forty-two, entered the Carmelite convent at Cologne. She was clothed with the habit on April 15, 1934, taking the religious name "Sister Teresa Benedicta a Cruce"—Teresa, Blessed by the Cross.

Her superiors asked her to continue her scholarly and popular writing. She revised her habilitation thesis into her major philosophical work, *Finite and Eternal Being*, and wrote three other books, including *The Science of the Cross*—all the while living the rigorous prayer life of a Carmelite. (On Sundays she would often say, "Thank God, I don't have to write today. Today I can pray.") Edith Stein's mother died on September 14, 1936, unreconciled to her daughter's decision to enter the convent, which she regarded as her final break with the Jewish people. Sister Teresa Benedicta of the Cross made her final vows on April 21, 1938, learning only later that Edmund Husserl had professed his faith in God on his deathbed shortly before. After the Kristallnacht of November 8, 1938, Edith Stein worried that her presence in the Cologne Carmel was endangering the other nuns. The prioress eventually agreed and arranged for her to be transferred to the Carmelite convent at Echt in Holland. She left Cologne on December 31, 1938.

Edith Stein had long had a premonition that her fate and the fate of the Jewish people, whom she believed she had never abandoned, were providentially intertwined. After arriving in Echt, she wrote her last testament. Its conclusion suggests an intuition of what lay ahead, and an embracing of it in "the science of the cross":

> I joyfully accept in advance the death God has appointed for me, in perfect submission to his most holy will. May the Lord accept my life and death for the honor and glory of his name, for the needs of his holy Church—especially for the preservation, sanctification, and final perfecting of our holy Order, and in particular for the Carmels of Cologne and Echt—for the Jewish people, that the Lord may be received by his own and his kingdom come in glory, for the deliverance of Germany and peace throughout the world, and finally for all my relatives living and dead and all whom God has given me: may none of them be lost.

Nazi Germany invaded and occupied Holland in May 1940. The "science of the cross" now became the overwhelming reality of her life. As the SS noose tightened on the Jews of Holland, Edith Stein realized that she was putting her convent in danger. She and her prioress tried to make arrangements for her transfer to a Carmel at Le Paquier in Switzerland, along with her sister Rosa, who had converted to Catholicism after Frau Stein's death and was the lay doorkeeper at the Echt convent. But there was no room for Rosa at Le Paquier, and Edith refused to leave without her. On July 26, 1942, a pastoral letter from the Primate of the Netherlands was read in all the Catholic churches of the country, condemning the deportation of Dutch Jews to the death camps. In retaliation, all Jewish converts to Catholicism were arrested on August 2, including members of religious orders. At 5 P.M., the SS came to the Echt Carmel for Edith Stein and her sister. After stops at Roermond, Amersfoort, and a transfer camp at Westerbork, they were transported east by rail beginning on August 7, arriving at Auschwitz II-Birkenau on August 9. There, at the railroad tracks where fates were instantly decided, Edith and Rosa Stein were selected for immediate execution and died in the gas chambers that same day.[31]

One of the most remarkable women of the twentieth century, Edith Stein was a "paradigmatic figure" for John Paul II, as he once put it.[32] She was a modern woman and a proto-feminist, a first-class intellectual and a converted skeptic. She had found liberating truth in Catholicism, not obscurantism or patriarchy. She was a contemplative who had an active life, and who saw her scholarly work and her intense life of prayer as a service to the world. She was a witness to the truth, who had defied cruel material force with the power of faith. She was a German who had lived the providential entanglement of Judaism and Christianity.

The cause for her beatification had been introduced by the archbishop of Cologne, Cardinal Joseph Frings, in the early 1960s. In 1983, Frings's successor, Cardinal Joseph Höffner, formally proposed that she be beatified as a martyr. Poland's Cardinal Józef Glemp seconded Höffner's proposal. The Congregation for the Causes of Saints eventually agreed to process the cause on the dual grounds of both Edith Stein's virtues and the manner of her death. On January 25, 1987, with John Paul II present, the Congregation made the unprecedented decision to confirm Edith Stein as both a confessor, a woman who had lived a life of heroic virtue, and a martyr.[33]

The decision settled the question of Edith Stein's beatification, for as a martyr, she could be beatified without a confirming miracle. The announcement of her impending beatification launched a controversy in Israel, Western Europe, and North America, however. Some Jewish scholars and organizational leaders, arguing that Edith Stein had died solely because she was a Jew, claimed that this was an attempt to "Christianize" the Holocaust. Others feared that the Pope would use the beatification to launch a new wave of Catholic proselytization. Underlying at least some of the agitation was the suspicion that this was a ploy by the Church to deflect attention from its own historic role in European anti-Semitism. Jewish representatives made their concerns known personally to John Paul.[34] He responded with one of the great sermons of the pontificate, at the beatification Mass in Cologne on May 1, 1987.

Its very first sentence honored Edith Stein in her Jewishness, and in her identification with the ancient biblical theme of redemptive atonement: "Today we greet in profound honor and holy joy a daughter of the Jewish people, rich in wisdom and courage, among these blessed men and women. Having grown up in the strict traditions of Israel, and having lived a life of virtue and self-denial in a religious order, she demonstrated her heroic character on the way to the extermination camp. United with our crucified Lord, she gave her life 'for genuine peace' and 'for the people.'"

The first biblical reading of the Mass had been taken from the Hebrew Bible's book of *Esther*, the story of a daughter of Israel who had prayed for the deliverance of her people from the archenemy Haman. The liturgy of beatification, John Paul said, "places this more than two-thousand-year-old prayer for help in the mouth of Edith Stein, a servant of God and a daughter of Israel in our century." A new "insane ideology" and a new archenemy had arisen, with a "new plan for the destruction of the Jews," to be undertaken "in the name of a wretched form of racism and carried out mercilessly." John Paul then recounted the death of a woman killed precisely because she was a Jew and a Catholic, and who had offered her impending death for the safety of her people:

> On leaving their convent [in Echt] Edith took her sister by the hand and said, "Come, we will go for our people." On the strength of Christ's willingness to sacrifice himself for others, she saw in her seeming impotence a way to render a final service to her people. A few years previously she had compared herself with Queen Esther in exile at the Persian court. In one of her letters we read: "I am confident that the Lord has taken my life for all . . . I always have to think of Queen Esther who was taken from her people for the express purpose of standing before the king for her people. I am the very poor, weak, and small Esther, but the King who selected me is infinitely great and merciful."

The truth that Edith Stein had found and for which she was prepared to die—the truth that had found and possessed her—was not abstract and intellectual, but concrete and personal. Like other modern souls who found religious belief untenable, she had sought the truth in her studies and in her mind. But she found a deeper truth—"not the truth of philosophy, but rather the truth in person, the loving person of God." Her life, in which she "had sought the truth and found God" was a lesson in intellectual openness, an example of true intellectual freedom.

Avoiding no issue, John Paul then took up the question of Edith Stein's conversion and its impact on her relationship with her family and with the Jewish people: "For Edith Stein, baptism as a Christian was by no means a break with her Jewish heritage. Quite on the contrary she said: 'I had given up my practice of the Jewish religion as a girl of fourteen. My return to God made me feel Jewish again.' She was always mindful of the fact that she was related to Christ 'not only in a spiritual sense, but also in blood terms.'" And so, John Paul said, "in the extermination camp she died as a daughter of Israel 'for the glory of the Most Holy Name' and, at the same time, as Sister Teresa Benedicta of the Cross, literally, 'blessed by the Cross. . . .'"

With members of Edith Stein's family, including nieces who remembered her as Tante Edith, present, the Pope then concluded:

> Dear brothers and sisters: We bow today with the entire Church before this great woman whom from now on we may call one of the blessed in God's glory, before this great daughter of Israel, who found the fulfillment of her faith and her vocation for the people of God in Christ the Savior. . . . She saw the inexorable approach of the cross. She did not flee. . . . Hers was a synthesis of a history full of deep wounds, wounds that still hurt, and for the healing of which responsible men and women have continued to work up to the present day. At the same time it was a synthesis of the full truth [about] man, in a heart that remained restless and unsatisfied "until it finally found peace in God." . . . Blessed be Edith Stein, Sister Teresa Benedicta a Cruce, a true worshiper of God—in spirit and in truth. She is among the blessed. Amen.[35]

Two days later, in Munich's Olympic Stadium, John Paul beatified Father Rupert Mayer, a Jesuit who became the first Catholic priest to win the Iron Cross while serving as a World War I chaplain. A popular pastor in interwar Munich, Mayer, who had lost a leg during the war, had taken his ministry to the local beer halls, where on one occasion he met Hitler—whose movement he then denounced as anti-Christian for, among other reasons, its anti-Semitism. Arrested twice for preaching against the regime, he was eventually sent to the Sachsenhausen concentration camp. When his health started to fail, the Nazis shipped him off to a monastery in Bavaria to avoid making a martyr out of a decorated German patriot. Father Rupert Mayer died in 1945, but he had lived long enough to lead the first Corpus Christi procession through the streets of post-Nazi Munich. "So," he cracked, "a one-legged old Jesuit has outlived the thousand-year Reich."[36]

The Nazis' euthanasia program and the corrupt moral reasoning that justified it was also on John Paul II's mind during his German pilgrimage. At Münster, he prayed at the tomb of Cardinal Clemens August von Galen, who had publicly condemned the Nazi policy of performing euthanasia on the mentally handicapped, the elderly, and other "unproductive" members of society. We should not, John Paul warned, be so sure of our immunity to committing similar horrors. When the inalienable dignity of human life was denied and the value of lives was measured according to pragmatic criteria of utility— "Is this life useful?" "Is this life troublesome or bothersome?"—something akin to the Nazi concept of *lebensunwertes Leben*, "life not worth living," was at work.[37] The eugenic impulse remained alive in modernity, as defenses of abortion and euthanasia on grounds of "convenience" illustrated.[38]

In Speyer on the last day of his 1987 pilgrimage, John Paul spoke for the first time of a Europe united "from the Atlantic to the Urals," the positive side of the intuition he had nurtured, since at least 1981, that communism was finished. Ending the artificial Yalta division of the continent did not settle the crucial questions, he suggested. What kind of Europe, reflecting what sort of values, would emerge from the ashes of the twentieth century? Edith Stein, Rupert Mayer, and Clemens August von Galen were all witnesses to a civil Europe rebuilt according to the respect for human dignity embedded in Europe's Christian cultural roots. But there were other possible Europes, some of them horrific beyond imagining. False humanisms wedded to modern technologies had lethal consequences.[39] Europe had learned that about its recent past. It was time to start thinking about the basic issues of the European future.

Two years before the communist crackup in east central Europe and four years before the collapse of the Soviet Union, John Paul II was already focused on the next set of questions: "What kind of freedom?" and "Freedom *for what?*"

SOLIDARITY, AGAIN

The year 1987 marked the 600th anniversary of Lithuania's conversion to Christianity. On June 5, John Paul sent an apostolic letter to the bishops of Lithuania, praising the "great spiritual wealth [of] . . . the Lithuanian Catholic community" and "its centuries-old fidelity to Christ . . ." Three weeks later, he would beatify Archbishop Jurgis Matulaitis of Vilnius (1871–1927), "a great son and pastor of your people." The presence of bishops from all over Europe on that occasion would, he wrote, express the communion between Catholic Churches east and west, which had remained unbroken despite the iron curtain.

The Church in Lithuania knew the meaning of martyrdom. Since 1940, Lithuanians had faced "humiliation, discrimination, suffering, sometimes persecution and even exile, imprisonment, deportation, and death, rejoicing to suffer dishonor for the name of Jesus"; Lithuanians were facing the same trials in 1987. Those trials were a source of strength because the cross, "embraced in union with the redemptive sufferings of Jesus," became "an instrument of grace and sanctification." With that strength, the youth of Lithuania would "become the seed of a great hope" which knew no better name than true freedom.[40]

Having offered a heartfelt papal salute to Lithuania, John Paul turned his attention to the cultural conditions for freedom in his homeland. His third Polish pilgrimage began in Warsaw on June 8 and took him to Lublin, Tarnów, Kraków, the Baltic Coast, Częstochowa, and Łodz. The Pope's June 1979 pilgrimage had ignited the Polish revolution. His June 1983 pilgrimage had helped keep it alive. The week-long June 1987 pilgrimage was intended to prepare the ground for the revolution's victory and identify the basic issues the free Poland of the future would face.

The government, as usual, had made the arrangements difficult. Gdańsk, birthplace of Solidarity, had been the forbidden city during the 1983 pilgrimage. John Paul insisted that it be on the 1987 itinerary or he would not come. The regime had finally agreed. While this negotiation was going on, Poles were rediscovering their own social solidarity in preparations for the Pope's visit.

The new town of Zaspa, a gray imitation of Nowa Huta built on an abandoned airfield outside Gdańsk, was transformed, according to its most famous resident, Lech Wałęsa, into a "living organism . . . a community of people with distinctive personalities and angles of vision," as it prepared to host a papal Mass. The people of Zaspa battled the regime over the design of the altar platform that was to occupy one end of an old runway, which ran between the huge apartment buildings of the development. True to Gdańsk's maritime and religious heritage, Marian Kolodziej, set designer of the Gdańsk Theater and a former prisoner in Auschwitz, had designed the platform as a ship with three masts, "onto whose bridge the Pilot of the Church was to ascend." Hundreds of hours of volunteer labor had gone into building the altar platform when the authorities decided that the masts were too similar to the monument to slain workers built outside the Lenin Shipyard gates as part of the 1980 Gdańsk Accords. After much argument and haggling, work was allowed to resume three days before the Pope arrived.[41]

John Paul minced no words in his response to General Wojciech Jaruzelski's welcoming address at Warsaw's royal palace. Jaruzelski often spoke of his fervent desire for "peace," the Pope noted. Thanks to the experience of the World War during which Poland had suffered so cruelly, the modern world had learned that peace required the effective protection of basic human rights. What was true between nations was also true within them. Peace within Poland required the vindication of human rights. The leaders of the Polish People's Republic must recognize that taking the human dignity of their people seriously was the only path to the national renewal they talked about incessantly. John Paul then offered General Jaruzelski a basic lesson in Catholic social doctrine, which in this case coincided point for point with democratic political theory.

Society, he said, was composed of men and women who were the bearers of inalienable rights. The state existed for the good of society, not society for the state. The human dignity of the members of society demanded that they be permitted to participate in the decisions that shaped their lives. The Pope understood that Poland was living through a difficult economic period. He also understood that there was no resolving the crisis of Polish social and economic life without taking these basic truths into account. Therefore, John Paul wished to commend to the President of the Polish State Council and his colleagues "the following pertinent words of the Second Vatican Council: 'One must pay tribute to those nations whose systems *permit the largest possible number of citizens to take part in public life* in a climate of genuine freedom (*Gaudium et Spes*, 31).'"[42]

Everyone present knew on which side of the Yalta division of Europe those systems were to be found.

Having attended to the representatives of the failing Polish state, John Paul turned to the Polish nation, where hope for Poland's renewal really lodged.

The pastoral context for the Pope's pilgrimage was a National Eucharistic Congress, which he opened in Warsaw on the evening of June 8, 1987, and closed there on June 14, just before departing for Rome. Its theme—"He loved them to the end"—was taken from the Gospel of John, and referred to Christ's love for the apostles with whom he was about to share the Last Supper (see *John* 13.13). The Eucharist, John Paul said in his opening homily, had been instituted at the beginning of "Christ's redemptive hour," which was "the redemptive hour of the history of man and of the world." In that hour, Christ *"reaffirmed the salvific power of love to the end,"* giving his life for his friends and for the salvation of the world. In that, he revealed that "God himself is love."

The Eucharist built community out of cleansed consciences, which were crucial to renewing society. Poles had to free themselves "from [the] inheritance of hatred and egoism." They had to conquer that "way of seeing the world" in which God is a fiction and love is impotence, before they could reclaim their country in genuine freedom.[43]

The next morning, June 9, John Paul flew by helicopter to the Majdanek death camp outside Lublin, site of some of the most odious "medical experiments" of the Holocaust. After praying in silence at the memorial to the camp's victims, the Pope signed the visitors' book with the text from the book of *Wisdom*, "The souls of the just are in the hands of God."[44] He then went to the Catholic University of Lublin to meet Polish academics and tell them that they, too, were crucial to the future of freedom. Standing under a canopy in the medieval-style cloisters of KUL, his former colleagues seated to his right in their academic finery and the students packed into the courtyard before him, he began with a citation from Thomas Aquinas: *Intellectus est quodammodo omnia* [The human intellect is in a certain sense all things]. Everything that exists had been given to the faculty and students of KUL, indeed to all men and women, as an intellectual task. Everything that is, is of interest. Everything that is ought to be examined freely, as a payment on our "indebtedness . . . toward reality in all its diversity . . . *Man owes truth to the world.*" Thus KUL, and all Polish universities, had a crucial mission in the task of national renewal: "Serve truth! *If you serve truth*—you serve freedom. The freedom of man and of the nation. *Serve life!*"[45]

At Mass later that afternoon, John Paul ordained fifty new priests, a small portion of the enormous number of vocations that had flourished in Poland in the 1980s. In his homily, he asked the newly ordained to avoid the dangers of clericalism in the new Poland he was sure was being born: "Your task, my dear new priests, will be to collaborate with lay people aware of their responsibility for the Church, and for a Christian form of life [in society] . . . They have an enormous potential of good will, of competence, of availability for service." The specific, priestly task of the newly ordained was another form of Christian liberation: "To serve God—to serve man: *to liberate* in man the *consciousness* of royal priesthood, *of that dignity* proper to man as a son or daughter of God himself and proper to the Christian of whom it is said that he is 'another Christ.'"

To be a servant of the people meant to be a "servant of the truth which liberates every man," and to remember that "the transcendent power" of the truth belonged, not to them, but to God. "Yes. *To God. Not to us. To God!*"[46]

On the morning of June 10, John Paul was in Tarnów, where he beatified Karolina Kozka, a young peasant girl killed while resisting rape by a Russian soldier in 1914. Her resistance to violence, the Pope said, "speaks of the great dignity of woman: of the dignity of the human person . . . [and] of the dignity of the body. . . ." That was what saints did—they gave witness to the great dignity of the human person by giving witness to Christ. This untutored peasant girl was a reminder that heroic virtue was within every Pole's grasp.[47]

Later that day, John Paul traveled the short distance to Kraków, "my Kraków, the city of my life, *the city of our history.*" Before more than a million Cracovians on the Błonia Krakowskie, he apologized for not stopping longer, explaining that Kraków had decided to share him with the rest of the country a bit more generously than in 1979 and 1983. At a Mass later that day in Wawel Cathedral, he remembered his debt to Father Kazimierz Figlewicz and the debt all Poland owed to the Jagiellonian University Faculty of Theology, which in its exile from the university he had recently named a Pontifical Academy. What, he asked, is Kraków without it? What was Polish culture without it?[48] It was a pointed reminder of a bitter struggle from the past and a marker for the future.

The Pope then went north to the Baltic coast cities where Solidarity had been born, and relentlessly drove home the theme of "solidarity" as the path to national renewal.

He began on June 11 in Szczecin. The Baltic coast, he recalled, had been the site of "important *pacts* between State authorities and the world of work." What had happened to those agreements? "What was the meaning of those pacts?"

In Gdynia that afternoon he was even more direct. Speaking to sailors, fishermen, and other seafaring people at the port city built by the interwar Republic, he began with a lyrical evocation of the meaning of rivers and the sea for Poland: the Vistula which was *"a silent witness of life in Poland through many generations,"* and the Baltic, which, like other seas, spoke to people "in a language that *transcends all limitations.*" Then he made the connections—between these ancient, natural rumors of angels, the difficult present, and the human prospect in a world beyond the Cold War:

> The seas speak to peoples about the need to find themselves together. . . . *It speaks of the need for solidarity,* both between human beings and among nations.
>
> It is an important reality that *the term "solidarity"* was *expressed right here before the Polish sea.* It is a profound reality that was pronounced here in a new way, with a new meaning that concerns its eternal significance.
>
> Here, along the shore of the Baltic Sea, I too pronounce this word, this term "solidarity" (*solidarność*), because it is an essential part of the *consistent message of the Church's social teaching.* . . .

Yes, *solidarity . . . purified struggles*. There should never exist a struggle against another; a struggle that treats people like adversaries and enemies and leads toward destruction. However, *a struggle for the human being and his rights, for his own genuine progress*, is in order: this is a struggle for a more mature way of life. Indeed, human *life* on this earth becomes *"more human"* when it is governed by *truth, freedom, justice and love. . . .*

The hard road to freedom was not blocked only by communism, he reminded them. Communism had exploited the contemporary "disease of superficiality." The answer to that threat was "to work . . . to *re-acquire depth*, that depth which is really the essence of the human person. The politics of a truly free Poland had to be built on the understanding that democracies had souls.[49]

It was Gdańsk's turn the next day. At a Mass for a million workers in Zaspa, John Paul saluted the Hanseatic port as the urban icon of the Polish struggle for freedom. It had not been cost-free; he had prayed earlier at the memorial to the workers shot down in 1970.[50] But it was now time to think of the future.

The 1980 shipyard strike that had brought the world to Gdańsk had been about work and the rights of workers, but the workers' cause did not stop at the right to organize in the workplace. Because work contributed to the common good of society, workers had *"the right to make decisions regarding the problems of the whole society"*—in brief, to political freedom. Freedom, however, was not autonomy. John Paul concluded with a reminder of what solidarity, and Solidarity, were really about: "Solidarity means: *one another*, and if there is a burden, then *this burden is carried together*, in community. Thus: *never one against another*. Never one group against another, and never a 'burden' carried by one alone, without the help of others."[51]

This was the precise opposite of class struggle, a point the Pope reiterated when he addressed the Polish Bishops' Conference in Warsaw on the last day of the pilgrimage, June 14. Twenty years before its 1966 millennial celebrations, postwar Poland had been called to confront the challenge of Marxism and its claim that religion deprived human beings of their humanity. As Polish bishops, they were used to thinking of that challenge as destructive, as it had been. Now was the time, however, to start thinking about the recent past in a different way. The bishops ought to remember the post-1945 period as a creative challenge that had compelled the Church to proclaim, "with a new depth and power of conviction," the Gospel the Church was always called to proclaim: *"the truth concerning God, Christ, and man."*

Communism, albeit finished as a historical force, had left a terrible hangover in the cultures it had infected—the widespread sense that human beings were simply the objects of impersonal economic and political forces. This deeply ingrained attitude was another form of bondage. The Church had to help Poland overcome it, just as it had defended national independence, the right to participation in public life, and the right of religious freedom. That was the new evangelical mission of the Church in the new Poland that was being born.[52]

General Jaruzelski was not pleased with all this. He demanded an unscheduled fifty-five-minute meeting with the Pope before John Paul's departure, and gave an impromptu talk afterward denouncing Western journalistic misrepresentations of the visit. He also took a sideswipe at John Paul, saying to the departing Pope that, after his farewell, "You will take with you, in your heart, its image, but you will not take with you the homeland's real problems." Surely, Jaruzelski went on, the well-traveled Pope "will have noticed how many social ills and misery, injustice and contempt for human rights still exist" around the world. Maybe the Pope should say something about all of that: "May the word 'solidarity' flow from our Polish soil [to] those people who still suffer from racism and neocolonialism, exploitation and unemployment, persecutions and intolerance."[53]

It was an amazing performance, but the recitation of the communist litany of world grievances rang hollow. Jaruzelski could fret about whether the papal pilgrimage would "add to the authority of Poland."[54] It certainly did not add to his authority—which, in John Paul's addresses, was treated as vestigial. Perhaps the general believed in some form of "national compromise" that would, as he put it, improve work and "everyday morality."[55] As John Paul had made clear since June 1979, though, there was no strategic compromise possible with a system built on a radically defective concept of the human person. Things might be improved on the margins. There had been some easing of repression, and Jaruzelski had dangled the possibility of formal diplomatic relations between the Polish People's Republic and the Holy See during the visit.[56] In the endgame, though, this remained what it always had been, a confrontation in which there would be a winner and a loser.

The June 1987 papal pilgrimage to Poland was built on the assumption that the identity of the loser was already clear.

APOSTLES TO "THE WORLD"

In the three months between his third Polish pilgrimage and the opening of a Synod of Bishops to discuss the vocation of the laity, John Paul found himself caught in an unexpected controversy with world Jewish leaders, made his second pastoral pilgrimage to the United States, and took another step toward the reconciliation of religion and science.

The Waldheim Controversy

The controversy involved the President of Austria, Kurt Waldheim, whom John Paul II received in audience in June 25, 1987, nine days after his return from Poland. Waldheim, former Secretary-General of the United Nations, was the democratically elected head of state of a Catholic country with which the Holy See had full diplomatic relations. Not to receive him was a diplomatic impossibility. Waldheim had also been an officer of the army of the Third Reich, and had neither acknowledged nor publicly expressed regret for his role in wartime human rights violations.[57]

For more than eight years, John Paul II's actions had demonstrated his convictions about his international responsibilities. As Bishop of Rome and universal pastor of the Church, he was, by definition, in conversation with everyone, including those whose politics he might locate on a spectrum ranging from unacceptable to reprehensible. To talk with Andrei Gromyko, for example, was neither edifying nor productive, but it was imperative, notwithstanding Gromyko's role in the Gulag system. Given these realities and the great care that John Paul had taken to reach out to Jewish communities around the world, sympathetic observers might well have regarded Waldheim's state visit to the Holy See as an inevitability—regrettable, but given the Austrian president's determination, unavoidable. Yet the Waldheim visit caused a crisis in Catholic-Jewish relations that threatened to disrupt the Pope's impending September visit to the United States and the future of the Jewish-Catholic dialogue John Paul had worked so hard to nurture.

The immediate problem was the Pope's scheduled meeting with American Jewish leaders in Miami during his second U.S. pilgrimage. In the wake of the Waldheim controversy, Jewish leaders threatened to boycott the meeting. Cardinal Agostino Casaroli, in New York on a personal visit, changed his schedule to meet privately with the angry Jewish leaders and see what could be worked out. On his return to Rome, Casaroli recommended that the Pope meet with a representative delegation from American Jewry in an attempt to salvage the Miami meeting and repair relations. John Paul agreed, and meetings were arranged on August 31 and September 1.

Representatives of the Holy See's Commission for Religious Relations with the Jews met with members of the International Jewish Committee on Interreligious Consultations in Rome to discuss the Holocaust, contemporary anti-Semitism, the Church's teaching on Jews and Judaism, and relations between the Holy See and the State of Israel.[58] During the discussion on the moral implications of the Holocaust, the Jewish representatives expressed what a later communiqué discreetly called the "dismay and concern over the moral problems raised for the Jewish people by the audience" for President Waldheim. With equal discretion, the communiqué reported that "the Catholic delegation acknowledged the seriousness of and the Church's sensitivity to those Jewish concerns, and set forth the serious reasons behind the judgment of the Holy See." The conferees also met with Cardinal Casaroli and were received by the Pope at Castel Gandolfo on Tuesday afternoon, September 1, where what diplomats call a "full and frank exchange of views" was had.

While saving the papal meeting with American Jewish leaders in Miami and getting the Catholic-Jewish dialogue back on track, the Rome/Castel Gandolfo emergency session was also the occasion for two new initiatives. The first was a Vatican commitment to prepare an official document on the *Shoah* and its relationship to the history of anti-Semitism. The second was that Vatican representatives made it clear, in the course of the discussion over the Holy See and the State of Israel, that "serious and unresolved" practical problems, not theological objections to the Jewish State, were the obstacle to full diplomatic relations—an important clarification, given the view to the contrary in some Jewish circles.[59]

"Ordered Freedom"

The sixty-seven-year-old Pope took an athlete's holiday in July, spending six days hiking in the Dolomites in northern Italy, saluting startled fellow hikers with his walking stick and staying in a small house owned by the Diocese of Treviso at Lorenzago di Cadore. Low-key Italian security forces helped keep the paparazzi, eager for photos of the Pontiff in distinctly unpapal hiking attire, at bay.

After the brief respite, John Paul went on his second pastoral pilgrimage to the United States, which took him primarily to the South and Southwest. He landed in Miami on September 10, where he was greeted by President Ronald Reagan and met with representatives of priests' councils from across the country. On September 11, he met with Jewish leaders, and later celebrated Mass at Tamiami Park before flying to Columbia, South Carolina. There, he participated in an interfaith prayer service at the University of South Carolina stadium with evangelical Protestants whose grandparents had unblushingly referred to the Pope as the "Whore of Babylon." After a day in New Orleans and meetings with African-American Catholic leaders and Catholic educators, John Paul went to San Antonio for encounters with Catholic Charities workers, seminarians and religious novices, and the Hispanic-American Catholic community. In Phoenix, on September 14, he met with health-care workers and Native Americans before celebrating Mass in the Arizona State University stadium.

A meeting with what were termed "communications specialists" in Los Angeles the next day was an opportunity for the Pope to challenge Hollywood to attend with greater care to the moral health of American popular culture. The challenge did not meet with notable success. John Paul also met in the City of Angels with the National Conference of Catholic Bishops and with representatives of world religions, before celebrating Mass in Dodger Stadium. In Monterey and San Francisco, the Pope visited old Franciscan missions and held encounters with members of men's and women's religious orders and with lay representatives. After a one-day stop in Detroit to meet Polish-Americans and permanent deacons and their wives, the Pope flew to Fort Simpson in Canada, keeping his promise to meet with the native peoples of Canada's northwestern territories. He was back in Rome on September 21, having covered more than 18,000 miles in twelve days.

The pilgrimage organizers at the National Conference of Catholic Bishops were determined that this visit would be more of a "dialogue" between the Pope and the Church in the United States than 1979 had been, but the formula they adopted seemed artificial. While John Paul's journeys always involved meetings with members of different vocational groups in the Church, the 1987 American program seemed almost a parody of affirmative action, dividing the Church into interest groups—clergy, religious, Hispanics, African-Americans, social workers, health-care workers—who were to express their particular concerns to the Pope and hear his response. The assumption that concerns could be put into such neat group categories was misleading and patronizing, and the device of a "representative" reading a carefully prepared address to the Pope, who then "responded" with his own prepared text, seemed, in a word, contrived. It certainly did not make for a real dialogue, and it reinforced the stereotype that John Paul was more interested in instructing wayward Americans than in listening to their distinctive experience of faith.

In fact the Pope had a great interest in and affection for America, as he had demonstrated in the most memorable statement of his 1987 pilgrimage, a paean to "ordered freedom" that impressed some by its feel for the American political experiment:

> From the beginning of America, freedom was directed to forming a well-ordered society and to promoting its peaceful life. Freedom was channeled to the fullness of human life, to the preservation of human dignity and to the safeguarding of all human rights. *An experience of ordered freedom is truly a cherished part of the history of this land.*
>
> This is the freedom that America is called to live and guard and to transmit. She is called to exercise it in such a way that it will also benefit the cause of freedom in other nations and among other peoples. The only true freedom, the only freedom that can truly satisfy is . . . *the freedom to live the truth of what we are and who we are* before God, the truth of our identity as children of God, as brothers and sisters in a common humanity. . . .
>
> At a difficult moment in the history of this country, a great American, Abraham Lincoln, spoke of a special need at that time: "that this nation under God shall have a new birth of freedom." *A new birth of freedom is repeatedly necessary*: freedom to exercise responsibility and generosity; freedom to meet the challenge of serving humanity, the freedom to fulfill human destiny, the freedom to live by truth, to defend it against whatever distorts and manipulates it, the freedom to observe God's law—which is the supreme standard of human liberty—the freedom to live as children of God, secure and happy: *the freedom to be America* in that constitutional democracy which was conceived to be "One Nation under God, indivisible, with liberty and justice for all."[60]

Newton's Anniversary

On returning from the United States, John Paul prepared for an international research conference he had called on the current relations among the sciences, philosophy, and theology. It was held at the Vatican Observatory at Castel Gandolfo from September 21 to 26, 1987, to mark the 300th anniversary of Newton's *Principia Mathematica*. For five days, scholars from around the world debated the broad question of science and religion with special reference to physics: Could current scientific views of time, space, causality, and matter be "exported" to theology in a way that was honest to the canons of science and consistent with Christian orthodoxy? Could philosophy, a discipline in its own turmoil, usefully "mediate" between physics and theology?

When the conference papers were published nine months later, they included a letter from the Pope to Father George Coyne, SJ, director of the Vatican Observatory. John Paul compared the new dialogue between theology and science to the ecumenical movement. What was thought impossible decades ago was now deemed imperative. Science and theology "have begun to talk to one another on deeper levels than before, and with greater openness toward one another's perspectives . . ." The new dialogue, the Pope suggested, should take advantage of the contemporary scientific interest in unifying knowledge, as when physicists tried to devise a "unified theory" of the four basic physical forces. The new dialogue also had to avoid an imposed and artificial "disciplinary unity," which had led both science and theology astray in the past. A definition of common ground that respected the integrity of both dialogue partners was essential, for science could not become theology, nor theology science.

This long-delayed dialogue about basic issues was essential, John Paul concluded, in revitalizing a humanism capable of shaping a truly humane future: "Our knowledge of each other can lead us to be more authentically ourselves. No one can read the history of the past century and not realize that crisis is upon us both. The uses of science have on more than one occasion proven massively destructive, and the reflections on religion have too often been sterile. We need each other to be what we must be, what we are called to be."[61]

The Synod on the Laity

Scientists were not the only laypeople John Paul was calling to rethink their vocation. The Pope's steady emphasis on the universal call to holiness was aimed at getting all the people of the Church to think of themselves in something other than monarchical terms, in order to live in the world as the Body of Christ should live. In the monarchical model that shaped the Catholic imagination for centuries before Vatican II, the Pope is king, the bishops are nobles, the clergy and consecrated religious are gentry, and the laity are peasants. The last have no responsibilities other than obedience and tithes, and when they are not praying, paying, or obeying (as an old saw has it), they are not being the Church in any significant way. That concept, in John Paul's long-settled view, was a serious impediment to implementing the Council's teaching that the Church is a *communio*, a communion of believers, who together form the Body of Christ in the world and who all share, by baptism, in Christ's triple mission to evangelize, sanctify, and serve.

The Council's understanding of the Church as *communio* was largely lost in the agitations over authority and sexual morality that followed Vatican II.

The Extraordinary Synod of 1985 tried to recover that distinctive way of thinking about the Church—that "ecclesiology," in theological terms. Beginning in 1987, John Paul II convened three Ordinary Assemblies of the Synod of Bishops to work out the implications of this *communio* ecclesiology for three "states of life" in the Church: the laity, the priesthood, and the consecrated religious life of those who take perpetual vows of poverty, chastity, and obedience. In addition to helping establish an authoritative interpretation of Vatican II, the Synods on the laity (1987), the formation of priests (1990), and the consecrated religious life (1994) all aimed at renewing the Council's call to sanctity through the three distinct ways that Catholics live that call.[62]

The most far-reaching of the three in its implications for the Catholic future was the Synod on the Laity, which was held from October 1 through October 30, 1987, and completed by the post-synodal apostolic exhortation *Christifideles Laici* [Christ's Faithful Lay People], issued by John Paul II on December 30, 1988.

The Synod itself included 232 bishop-participants and sixty lay "auditors," who addressed the Synod's general assemblies and participated in its language-based small discussion groups. In addition, a layman (Jean-Loup Dherse of France) and a laywoman (Maria da Graça Guedes Sales Henriques of Portugal) were appointed adjunct special secretaries of the Synod.[63] As was his habit, the Pope attended every general session, listening to almost 300 speeches. The Synod celebrated, as well as discussed, holiness among lay Christians. On October 4, John Paul beatified Marcel Callo, a French lay activist in the Young Catholic Worker movement who had been martyred in the Mauthausen concentration camp in 1945, and two Italian women, Antonia Messina and Pierina Morosini, both of whom had been martyred while resisting rape. On October 18, the Pope canonized Blessed Lorenzo Ruiz and fifteen other martyrs of Japan; Ruiz was the Filipino lay missionary John Paul had beatified in Manila in 1981. And on October 25, the Pope canonized Blessed Giuseppe Moscati, an Italian physician who had died in Naples in 1927.

The Synod eventually agreed on fifty-four "propositions." Together with themes from the speeches and small group discussions and the materials prepared by the Synod secretariat before the meeting, these propositions were used by John Paul II to formulate the post-synodal document he issued fourteen months later.

Christifideles Laici laid out a dramatic, even radical, vision of a laity fully living its mission to society and culture as an expression of its full membership in the Body of Christ. Written by a Pope who had once expected to spend his Christian life as a layman, the lengthy document reflects Karol Wojtyła's extensive experience fostering the lay vocation in the world. John Paul's approach to the laity is reminiscent of John Henry Newman. The great nineteenth-century English theologian, asked by his bishop what the clergy should think of the laity, is said to have responded that "we would look rather silly without them." Newman's sharp wit had been papally confirmed by Pius XII's statement that "the laity are the Church," but few in pre–Vatican II Catholicism took that very seriously. One exception was Karol Wojtyła, whose pastoral strategy of "accompaniment" was an expression of his conviction that every Christian was part of the Church's evangelical mission. As he put it in *Christifideles Laici*, "*It is not permissible for anyone to remain idle.*"[64]

There was a special "urgency" about this on the edge of a new millennium, however. The practical atheism of modernity had made clear that the yearning for God in the human heart could never be extinguished. The degradation of the human person had led to a widespread reassertion of human rights. A century of violent conflict had led to a new determination to pursue peace. Modernity badly needed the Gospel message and, precisely because of its contemporary crisis, was open to it.[65]

Every Christian, the Pope insists, is called to a life of holiness in baptism, and for the laity, the call to holiness is "*intimately connected to mission.*"[66] The responsibility given to lay Christians is nothing less than to continue Christ's saving mission in "the world," which is "*the place and the means for the lay faithful to fulfill their Christian vocation.*" The sanctification of "the world"—society, culture, the workplace—is the distinctively "secular" vocation of the laity.[67] The temptation to clericalize the laity by folding their distinctive vocation into that of the ordained priesthood must be resisted, for the sake of the lay vocation's integrity and dignity. It is rank clericalism, the Pope suggests, to propose that the laity can exercise their mission only by becoming priests *manqué*. The laity have the right and obligation to mission by reason of their baptism. Any suggestion that they can only exercise this mission by imitating the clergy demeans the grace of baptism and falsifies the Church as *communio*.[68] In this context, John Paul also stresses the importance of the local parish, which is not a coincidental aggregation of Christians who happen to live in the same neighborhood, but "*the Church living in the midst of the homes of her sons and daughters.*"[69] The parish should be the "place" where believers gather to strengthen their commitment to their mission in the world, "a house of welcome to all and a place of service to all."[70]

"Being the Church" is not something that the laity do on Sunday mornings only, and it is not something that should happen only in a church building. "Being the Church" is something that the laity do in the world all the time, and in every venue of life.[71] Business, the professions, the creative arts, the media, and politics are, for the Pope, all venues in which Christians live the universal call to holiness.[72]

Although he would introduce the term "new evangelization" later, the basic concept, central to the pontificate of John Paul II, is launched in *Christifideles Laici*. The "new evangelization" of the twenty-first century demands a Church that has transcended clericalism. The Church cannot preach the Gospel or witness to the truth about the human person in the modern world if the people and leaders of the Church think of "the Church" as a clerical preserve in which lay men and women occasionally participate. Being a Christian is a full-time occupation. The only reason for the Church's hierarchical structure is to serve that mission and foster the holiness of those called to mission—which is everybody.

Like John Paul's *Theology of the Body, Christifideles Laici* would seem to be a document well in advance of current Catholic thinking. There is a sense in which Catholic clergy and laity alike are unprepared for the kind of Church John Paul II envisions in this bold proposal. If and when the life of the Church catches up with *Christifideles Laici*, that fact will alter the face of world Catholicism, by reviving dimensions of New Testament Christianity among evangelically assertive Catholics who are far more passionate about service than about ecclesiastical power.

HERE AND NOW

Even as he scouted the unexplored terrain of twenty-first-century Catholicism in *Christifideles Laici*, John Paul continued to deal with the Church's mission here and now: its ecumenical commitment, its social doctrine, its defense of human rights, its post-conciliar divisions, its internal structure, and its bishops.

Andrew Visits Peter

Ecumenical Patriarch Dimitrios I of Constantinople came to Rome on a five-day pilgrimage in December 1987 that marked a public high point in John Paul II's attempts to reconcile the millennium-long division of Christianity into East and West. After his arrival on December 3, Dimitrios addressed the Roman Curia and the Lateran University on December 4, and spoke to young Catholics at the Basilica of S. Maria in Trastevere on December 6. The possibility of a Church breathing again with its two lungs, the Pope's favorite metaphor, was powerfully embodied in two liturgical services, a solemn celebration of Vespers at the Basilica of St. Mary Major on the evening of December 4, and a Mass at St. Peter's the following day, the Second Sunday of Advent in the liturgical calendar.

According to the official announcement, the Vespers service was celebrated "with the participation of Ecumenical Patriarch Dimitrios I." Both the Pope and the Patriarch preached. Similar language was used to describe the Mass at St. Peter's: the Mass was "celebrated by Pope John Paul II with the participation of Ecumenical Patriarch Dimitrios I." John Paul met the Ecumenical Patriarch in the atrium of St. Peter's. The two leaders processed into the basilica side by side, preceded by an Orthodox deacon and a Latin deacon, each liturgically vested and carrying the Book of the Gospels. Pope and Patriarch kissed the altar together and, after the Pope had incensed it, were seated together in front of the papal altar for the first half of the Mass, the Liturgy of the Word. It was not a concelebration, so John Paul was liturgically vested while Dimitrios wore his choir robe, the *mandyas*. But it was as close to concelebration as the two "sister Churches" could come at the present moment. The two deacons proclaimed the Gospel in Greek and Latin, the Greek deacon receiving the Pope's blessing before chanting the reading and the Latin deacon receiving the Patriarch's. Pope and Patriarch then kissed each other's lectionaries and blessed the congregation with them. Both men then preached.

The Ecumenical Patriarch referred to the sad fact that "on this propitious day . . . we gather near the Table of the Lord but are not yet able to serve there together," and closed by praying that "the Lord grant that the Church may see his day (cf. *Acts* 2.20), the day of reconciliation, peace, fraternity, and unity." That seemed to put off the restoration of full communion until the Second Coming of Christ. John Paul, in his homily, had a different timeline in mind. He repeated Vatican II's declaration that full communion could be achieved on the basis of the relationship that had existed between Rome and the East before 1054: the traditions of the Eastern Churches would be fully respected in a return to the situation that had obtained before the separation. The fact that the two men could not drink from the same chalice was "a source of bitter suffering," the Pope said. John Paul concluded with the prayer that Christ might "transform our suffering into an incentive to work tirelessly *to restore full communion among us soon,* and to prepare together, in the midst of men on this earth, a 'highway for our God' (*Isaiah* 40.3)!"[73]

After the homilies, John Paul and Dimitrios recited the Nicene-Constantinopolitan Creed together in the original Greek. During the General Intercessions, prayers were offered for both men. At the end of the Liturgy of the Word, Patriarch Dimitrios left the altar for a special place of honor nearby, at the tribune of St. Andrew. As the Patriarch moved away, John Paul embraced him spontaneously. At the kiss of peace, prior to the reception of Communion, John Paul left the altar and went to the Patriarch for the exchange of Christ's peace and another fraternal embrace. After the post-Communion prayer, Dimitrios once again joined John Paul on the altar, where the two men blessed the congregation, John Paul in Latin and Dimitrios in Greek. They then went to pray together at Peter's tomb beneath the altar before processing out of the basilica together and going up to the *loggia,* where they both addressed the crowd outside.[74]

On December 7, John Paul and Dimitrios signed a joint declaration, which affirmed the ongoing theological dialogue between Roman Catholicism and Orthodoxy as an effort "to re-establish full communion between the Catholic Church and the Orthodox Church," and promised cooperation on work for justice and peace throughout the world. Together, they wrote, "we await the day willed by God when refound unity will be celebrated and when full communion will be established by a concelebration of the Lord's Eucharist."[75]

The colorful and emotionally charged liturgical celebrations were a foretaste of what that refound unity would be like. At the end, though, there remained a divergent sense of possibility between the Pope and the Ecumenical Patriarch. John Paul II seemed determined to press for full communion by the end of the second millennium of Christian history—to end a millennium of division by a return to the unity of the first millennium, which he believed essential to the Christian mission in the third. The Ecumenical Patriarch lived in a different circumstance than the Pope. As first among equal Orthodox patriarchs, he could not press any further than the consensus among his patriarchal brethren in Alexandria, Antioch, Jerusalem, Moscow, Athens, Belgrade, Bucharest, and elsewhere allowed. Dimitrios's evocation of the "day of the Lord" as the moment when the Church's unity would be restored seemed not only to reflect his different ecclesiastical circumstances, though, but a different sense of urgency, and perhaps even a different sense of history.

Social Concern

During these months, a second social encyclical was gestating. John Paul II tried to accomplish three things with *Sollicitudo Rei Socialis* [On Social Concern], issued on February 19, 1988. He wanted to mark the twentieth anniversary of Paul VI's social encyclical, *Populorum Progressio* [The Development of Peoples], and to update the Church's social doctrine in light of the accelerating quest for freedom throughout the world and the new, Third World–dominated demographics of world Catholicism. The third aim was bureaucratic: to get the Roman Curia to accept his post-Constantinian view of the Church's role in the world as an authentic development of Vatican II. The first goal was easily accomplished. *Sollicitudo*'s forty citations from *Populorum Progressio* ensured that Pope Paul's encyclical was duly commemorated. But the second and third goals were not easily combined. The result was an encyclical that read like a committee document, some sections of which deflected attention from the originality of the Pope's own analysis and the principal public themes of his pontificate.

That popes have assistance in writing encyclicals is hardly news. Cardinal Eugenio Pacelli, later Pius XII, is generally thought to have drafted Pius XI's stinging 1937 condemnation of Nazism, *Mit Brennender Sorge*. Pietro Pavan (created a cardinal by John Paul II) drafted *Pacem in Terris* for John XXIII, who kept sending the Italian theologian back to his desk with orders to simplify the text until he, the Pope, could understand it. Drafting assistance does not compromise the teaching authority of a papal document, which receives its authoritative "form" from the Pope's signature, an act that completes the project in a definitive way and without which any draft is just that: a draft.[76]

John Paul II's first six encyclicals, on the other hand, read like the statements of a single author who may have sought expert advice (as from the historians consulted in the writing of *Slavorum Apostoli*) but whom one could also imagine sitting at his desk, pen in hand. That *Sollicitudo Rei Socialis* read so differently was the first stylistic clue that a different process had produced this document.

While *Sollicitudo* is John Paul II's encyclical and carries his papal authority, the document was the result of elaborate consultations and discussions within the Roman Curia. John Paul had had a unique experience of the world Church in the first nine years of his pontificate, sensing momentous shifts in the off-ing where others perceived business more or less as usual. His culturally dri-ven view of the dynamics of social change had given him a different view of the way the Church should relate to the world of politics and economics, a vision that challenged traditional curialism and the new politicization advocated by liberation theology. Perhaps the drafting of a social encyclical in broad con-sultation with the Curia would help "teach" this new vision of "the Church in the modern world" to the Roman bureaucracy.

An initial draft of the encyclical was prepared by the Pontifical Justice and Peace Commission. John Paul had told Cardinal Roger Etchegaray and Bishop Jorge Mejía, the commission's two senior officials, that he wanted to com-memorate *Populorum Progressio* and "go further," taking into account what had happened over the past twenty years. The commission had "multiple meet-ings," out of which, according to Mejía, a "synthesis" was prepared and sent to the Pope.[77] John Paul then prepared a schema of major points he wanted to make in a new social encyclical; the Secretariat of State distributed this to other offices in the Curia. The Justice and Peace Commission solicited comments on economic development issues from the world's bishops' conferences. The results of this survey were given to the Pope, as the process of drafting, circu-lating drafts for comments, and redrafting continued throughout the fall of 1987.[78] The deadline for the twentieth anniversary of *Populorum Progressio,* March 26, had long since passed. Work on what was becoming *Sollicitudo Rei Socialis* continued through the first weeks of January 1988, although the encyclical was formally dated December 30, 1987, to meet the anniversary-year goal. Reporters wondered what was going on. The Pope hadn't traveled abroad since his U.S. visit in September, and no travels were scheduled until a May 1988 pilgrimage to Latin America. Joaquín Navarro-Valls explained to the curious press that "the Pope is on a trip to the Curia."[79]

The encyclical was finally released on February 19, 1988. After acknowl-edging *Populorum Progressio,* John Paul surveyed the contemporary world socio-political-economic scene, explored the moral core of "authentic human development," analyzed the moral obstacles to economic and political devel-opment, laid down moral guidelines for political and economic reform, and traced the relationship between development and Christian liberation. In addition, *Sollicitudo Rei Socialis* made several striking innovations in the Church's social doctrine, reflecting the desire to "go further" that John Paul had expressed to Etchegaray and Mejía.

Populorum Progressio had been widely interpreted as favoring state-cen-tered approaches to Third World economic development. *Sollicitudo* defines a personal "right of economic initiative," crucial for both the individual and the common good, and argued that personal initiatives could not be suppressed in the name of "an alleged 'equality' of everyone in society."[80] *Populorum Pro-gressio* had been virtually silent on the relationship between different political systems and the prospects for economic development in poor countries. *Sollicitudo* is resolutely anti-totalitarian and specifically anti-communist, rejecting the claim of a "social group, for example, a political party . . . to usurp the role of sole leader."[81]

Populorum Progressio treated development economics as an independent variable in the life of a society. *Sollicitudo* follows John Paul's "culture-first" approach to social change by arguing that civil society is essential to development. This was spelled out further in a section on human rights and development, a topic that was not prominent in *Populorum Progressio*. Here, John Paul argues that underdevelopment is a function of insecure civil liberties as well as defective economics.[82]

Populorum Progressio stressed the obligations of the developed to the developing world. While forcefully reiterating that moral claim, John Paul II argues that the deterioration of Third World conditions since *Populorum Progressio* is also due to "undoubtedly grave instances of omissions on the part of the developing nations themselves, and especially on the part of those holding economic and political power."[83] Integral human development requires that Third World countries "reform certain unjust structures, and in particular their *political institutions*, in order to replace corrupt, dictatorial, and authoritarian forms of government by *democratic* and *participatory* ones."[84]

These themes were wholly consistent with John Paul's teaching over nine years. The *Sollicitudo* controversy involved the encyclical's description of the world situation, which resembled the attitudes prevalent in many Church social justice agencies. Both "liberal capitalism" and "Marxist collectivism," the ideologies responsible for "the tension *between East and West*," were "imperfect and in need of radical correction." Moreover, "each of the two *blocs* harbors in its own way a tendency toward *imperialism* . . . or toward forms of neocolonialism: an easy temptation to which they frequently succumb, as history, including recent history, teaches." The clash between East and West, transferred to the Third World, was a "direct obstacle to the real transformation of the conditions of underdevelopment in the developing and less advanced countries," and was the result of an "exaggerated concern *for security*, which deadens the impulse towards united cooperation by all for the common good of the human race."[85]

A. M. Rosenthal, former editor of the *New York Times*, wrote in a column that "All good journalists would put the same headline on the story: 'Pope Condemns Marxism and Capitalism Equally; Says Both Are Imperialistic and Sin Against Poor.'"[86] William F. Buckley, Jr., was less restrained, characterizing the Pope's view of the world as "this Tweedledum-Tweedledee view of the crystallized division between the visions of Marx, Lenin, Mao Tse-tung, and Pol Pot over against those of Locke, Jefferson, Lincoln and Churchill."[87] On the other side of the ideological spectrum, the liberal anti-communist *New Republic* editorialized that John Paul had "become an apostle of moral equivalence" who had failed "to tell the whole truth" because of "political considerations."[88]

These condemnations, as well as the welcome the encyclical received from

Catholic economic and political progressives, were exaggerated.[89] No one could seriously argue that John Paul II was unaware of the difference between, say, NATO and the Warsaw Pact; but the encyclical's reference to "two blocs," invited misunderstanding.[90] It is also true that, from the point of view of many Third World Catholics (a vantage point on history that John Paul was trying to get his Curia to understand), both capitalism and communism, or, more broadly, "the East" and "the West," could seem in need of "radical correction." Even so, this failed to address the question of whether what was called "capitalism" in Latin America was another and very old-fashioned form of state management of the economy. Some of the American criticism of *Sollicitudo* was parochial. John Paul wrote as the universal pastor of a worldwide Church, quite aware that his teaching on economic initiative, his rejection of statist development schemes, and his affirmation of democracy was going to be read as a frontal challenge in Moscow, Havana, and Managua, however much it seemed business-as-usual in New York and Washington—a fact that his Western readers might have acknowledged.

Still, it cannot be denied that *Sollicitudo* showed the influence of those Catholic intellectuals and activists who did believe in "moral equivalence" between "the blocs," and the enduring influence in the Curia of Paul VI's *Ostpolitik* and its "evenhandedness" between East and West. That these ideas found their way into an encyclical whose most original elements were far more congruent with John Paul II's thinking was, according to informed observers, the result of the Pope's attempt to use the preparation of *Sollicitudo Rei Socialis* as a means for getting the Curia to think differently about the Church in the modern world. But curial thinking may have had more influence on the encyclical than the encyclical's original ideas had on the Curia.

Confrontation in Paraguay

Although it had been only thirteen months since his last visit to Latin America, John Paul thought another was imperative. In May 1988, the Pope's thirty-seventh pastoral pilgrimage took him to Uruguay, Bolivia, Peru, and Paraguay. The pilgrimage graphically illustrated the concern for the relationship between political corruption and poverty he had written about in *Sollicitudo Rei Socialis.*

General Alfredo Stroessner had been "reelected" to his eighth term as President of Paraguay on February 18, 1988. He had been in complete control of the country since seizing power in 1954, in a coup supported by the now-dominant Colorado Party and the army. The democratic movement that was changing the political landscape of Latin America had reached Paraguay, but Stroessner had shown no willingness to recognize the nascent democratic opposition and no inclination to submit himself and his party to a real electoral contest.

A meeting with an opposition group, the "Builders of Society," had been arranged as part of the Pope's Paraguayan itinerary. On May 11, when John Paul was in Oruro, an extremely poor area of Peru, papal spokesman Joaquín Navarro-Valls was told by a journalist that General Stroessner, in a letter to the papal nuncio, Archbishop Giorgio Zur, had just canceled the meeting with the Builders. The Pope returned to Cochabamba to celebrate Mass at 11 A.M. Afterward, John Paul met with Secretary of State Casaroli; Archbishop Martínez Somalo, the *Sostituto;* and spokesman Navarro. The Pope's message was blunt. If the report from Asunción were true, "We're not going to Paraguay." John Paul went on with his schedule, while the others tried to get in touch with Archbishop Zur through Rome, where Archbishop Silvestrini, the "foreign minister," was in charge in the absence of Casaroli and Martínez Somalo.

The next day, May 12, Navarro decided to try applying public pressure on Stroessner with a simple press release: "For now, I must express my amazement at a provocation without precedent, bearing on the pastoral activity of the Holy Father." The press wanted more, but Navarro replied that the statement spoke for itself. At 7:30 A.M. on May 13—the feast of Our Lady of Fatima and the seventh anniversary of Agca's assassination attempt—the chief of Paraguayan protocol, Ambassador Papalardo, tracked Navarro down in the convent that was headquarters for the papal party in Cochabamba. He said he had read the stories based on Navarro's press release in the morning papers. He then went on a tirade. The Builders of Society were communists who didn't have anywhere near the support of the Colorado Party. Archbishop Rolón (the President of the Paraguayan Bishops' Conference) was an opportunist who wanted to be remembered in history as the liberator of Paraguay. Navarro absorbed all this, replied calmly that this was an unprecedented problem, and suggested that Papalardo meet with the nuncio and Archbishop Rolón to discuss things. The protocol chief could then call Navarro back after lunch to tell the papal spokesman that the situation had been resolved. At 4 P.M., Ambassador Papalardo called to say that everything had been settled and thanked Navarro for his suggestion.

Navarro told Cardinal Casaroli, who told the Pope, who laughed: "So, they're going to let the Pope come to Paraguay. . . ."[91]

It was a masterful use of public pressure through the media to achieve the Pope's ends. John Paul took advantage of his opportunities as soon as he arrived in Paraguay, calling for the "moral cleansing" of the country and declaring, in terms reminiscent of *Sollicitudo,* that "liberty, justice, and participation" were essential in building an "authentic democracy"—presumably a reference to the eighty-nine percent of the vote that General Stroessner had received in February. Stroessner replied in his own sinister way, arresting political opponents before John Paul had left the country and tightening the repression on the Church and human rights activists afterward. But the general's days were numbered. He was overthrown in a military coup less than nine months after the Pope's visit. The coup leader, General Andrés Rodriguéz, called general elections for May 1, 1989, and was elected in what the opposition agreed was a ballot without systematic or widespread vote fraud. Rodriguéz pledged to serve out Stroessner's term, but did not run for reelection. Paraguay enjoyed its first closely contested election in 1993. Throughout the 1990s, the Paraguayan bishops remained champions of democracy under difficult economic and political circumstances.[92]

The Lefebvre Schism

During his pastoral visits, his preparation of encyclicals, and his hundreds of meetings with the world's bishops, another danger weighed upon John Paul II: the possibility of schism within the Catholic Church.

The Pope and Cardinal Joseph Ratzinger had worked hard to reconcile Archbishop Marcel Lefebvre, the dissident Frenchman, without abandoning their commitment to Vatican II. John Paul had met Lefebvre shortly after his election. The Frenchman had told journalists afterward, "He didn't seem like a Pope to me; he had no character."[93] The Pope, who welcomed the Council's liturgical renewal, believed that there should be a place in the Church for those who wanted to use the pre-conciliar rite, as long as they accepted the Missal of Paul VI as the Church's official liturgy.[94] In October 1984, an indult (a canonical permission) had allowed more widespread use of the pre–Vatican II Tridentine rite contained in the 1962 Roman Missal, a decision, it was hoped, that would help reconcile Archbishop Lefebvre and his followers. But Lefebvre's disdain for the revised Roman rite had never been the core of his dissent from Vatican II, which was theological, not simply liturgical.

John Paul II considered *Dignitatis Humanae*, the *Declaration on Religious Freedom*, to be an interpretive key to the entire Council. Archbishop Lefebvre thought that *Dignitatis Humanae* was heresy, and believed that an established Church in an officially Catholic state was the will of Christ. John Paul II had been one of the intellectual architects of *Gaudium et Spes*. The Pope recalled that Lefebvre, whose "theology was quite different," had an entirely different "vision of the Church."[95] Lefebvre's refusal to be placated by the 1984 indult made unmistakably clear his conviction that Vatican II had been a colossal act of irresponsibility and infidelity, of which liturgical change was only the most obvious manifestation.

The French archbishop's dissent became a full-blown crisis on June 15, 1988, when he publicly announced his intention to ordain four new bishops to carry on his work. According to the Church's theology, Lefebvre possessed the sacramental power to ordain bishops, but he had no mandate from the Pope to carry out these ordinations. According to both doctrine and canon law, Lefebvre's ordinations to the episcopate, while canonically illegal, would be sacramentally valid. The result would be a self-perpetuating schismatic Church. Since this was the worst imaginable outcome, Cardinal Ratzinger made every effort to forestall it—despite the fact that, on May 6, Lefebvre had reneged on a formula of reconciliation he had signed the day before and had thrown down the gauntlet, telling Ratzinger privately that he would ordain bishops on June 30. Ratzinger would not compromise on the fact that Lefebvre had to accept Vatican II and the post-conciliar teaching of the Church's magisterium. What could be done, given that acceptance, was to create room within the Church for a reconciled traditionalist movement. That was what John Paul had proposed to Lefebvre at their first meeting, and what Lefebvre had agreed to on May 5.

After a fruitless meeting with Ratzinger on May 24, Lefebvre wrote the Pope on June 2, saying that he was going to proceed with the ordination of bishops because it was "absolutely necessary" for his movement to have "ecclesiastical authorities who share our concerns and [who will] help protect us against the spirit of Vatican II and the spirit of Assisi"—which Lefebvre regarded as interreligious syncretism, pure and simple. Since the purpose of reconciliation was not viewed the same way by the Vatican and his movement, he and his followers believed it "preferable to wait for a more propitious time for Rome's return to the Tradition." He would go ahead with the episcopal ordinations on June 30, while praying that "the Rome of today, infested by Modernism, will again become Catholic Rome." John Paul responded to this extraordinary letter on June 9, urging Lefebvre to return to the path of reconciliation.[96] Lefebvre's response to the Pope's request was to announce publicly his intention to ordain bishops on June 30. On June 29, Cardinal Ratzinger sent a telegram to the archbishop:

> For the love of Christ and of his Church the Holy Father paternally and firmly asks you to come to Rome today without proceeding to the episcopal ordinations on June 30 which you have announced. He prays to the holy Apostles Peter and Paul to inspire you not to betray the episcopate whose charge you have received, nor the oath you have taken to remain faithful to the Pope, the Successor of Peter. He asks God to save you from leading astray and scattering those whom Jesus Christ came to gather together in unity.
>
> He entrusts you to the intercession of the Most Holy Virgin Mary, Mother of the Church.[97]

Archbishop Lefebvre ordained the bishops on June 30. On July 1, Cardinal Bernardin Gantin, Prefect of the Congregation for Bishops, signed a decree stating that Lefebvre had committed a "schismatic act." Therefore, he, the four bishops he ordained, and the retired bishop who had taken part in the ordination ceremony had automatically incurred excommunication. Any Catholic supporting the Lefebvrist schism would incur excommunication as well.[98]

On July 2, John Paul II issued the apostolic letter *Ecclesia Dei* [The Church of God], which created a commission to reconcile those members of the Lefebvrist movement who did not wish to follow the archbishop into schism and to provide for their pastoral care. These reconciled dissidents were assured that they could practice their faith "while preserving their spiritual and liturgical traditions," according to the agreement that had been reached between Cardinal Ratzinger and Archbishop Lefebvre on May 5, and which Lefebvre had renounced the next day.[99]

Archbishop Marcel Lefebvre was, according to Ratzinger, a "very difficult man."[100] In the end, however, it was not his personality but his ideas that drove him into schism. He embodied the most extreme version of the French Catholicism that insisted on being a "Church of power" aligned with a Catholic state. In that sense, Lefebvre was a twentieth-century victim of the French Revolution. When the final choice had to be made, he hated modernity more than he loved Rome.

Reforming the Curia

While he was on his "trip to the Curia," preparing *Sollicitudo Rei Socialis*, John Paul II was completing a reorganization of the Church's central bureaucracy, which he promulgated on June 28, 1988, with the apostolic constitution *Pastor Bonus* [The Good Shepherd].

John Paul's reorganization completed the curial reform begun by Paul VI in 1967. There was only so much change that could be accomplished then, given personalities and interests. What *Pastor Bonus* did, essentially, was to rationalize the curial organization chart now that human circumstances permitted. The "dicasteries" or departments of the Curia were divided into three types— Congregations (which exercise jurisdiction), Councils (which do not exercise jurisdiction but promote certain pastoral activities), and Tribunals (the Church's courts). Nomenclature was simplified (the "Sacred Congregation for the Doctrine of the Faith" became the "Congregation for the Doctrine of the Faith") or changed (the "second section" or "foreign ministry" of the Secretariat of State was renamed the Section for Relations with States; the Secretariat for Non-Christians was renamed the Pontifical Council for Inter-religious Dialogue). Administrative sorting out was not the kind of thing that John Paul relished, but he intervened in the reorganization process at two points, both of which reflected his pastoral priorities.

Curial officials had proposed merging the office for Christian ecumenical dialogue with the office for dialogue with non-Christians and the office for dialogue with nonbelievers, effectively lumping all "non-Catholics" into one dicastery. According to participants in the process, John Paul said "absolutely no" to this, and insisted on maintaining distinct offices for each type of dialogue. It was a concrete demonstration of the centrality of ecumenism in his pastoral strategy. When he put his foot down about the merger proposal, he told the curial planners that "this [ecumenism] is the will of the Church," and that was that. Maintaining three separate dicasteries for these dialogues was also a sign of the Pope's respect for other world religions and other worldviews, which had their own integrity and should not be tossed into one undifferentiated mass of "non-Catholics."[101]

Then there was the question of where the laity fit into the organization chart. Some wanted to create a Congregation for the Laity. But that would seem to place the laity under the jurisdiction of the Holy See—like bishops, priests, theologians, educational institutions, and religious men and women—which John Paul thought violated the theology of Vatican II. So it was decided to create a Pontifical Council for the Laity, as a center for promoting the lay mission "in the world."[102] This office was also assigned responsibility for coordinating the World Youth Days, which quickly began to absorb considerable energies in the Council.

Pastor Bonus was issued at John Paul's fourth consistory, at which he created twenty-four new cardinals. The nomination of a Lithuanian, Vincentas Sladkevičius, and the fact that he was permitted to come to Rome to be invested as a cardinal, was another indicator of change in the Soviet Union, as well as a papal salute to one of the most valiant local churches in Catholicism. A cardinalate for John Baptist Wu Cheng-chung of Hong Kong was another kind of appeal to a different kind of communist power, and a step toward shoring up the Hong Kong hierarchy in light of the city's uncertain political future. Lucas Moreira Neves, the Brazilian Dominican and former curial official who had been named archbishop of São Salvador da Bahia the previous July, received the red hat, as did Washington's James Hickey and Detroit's Edmund Szoka, who would be brought to Rome in 1990 to try to get the Vatican's finances under control. Mozambique and Cameroon received their first cardinals, the Franciscan Alexandre José Maria dos Santos in Maputo and Christian Wiyghan Tumi in Douala. In *Mitteleuropa*, László Paskai, OFM, of Hungary and Hans Hermann Groër, a former Benedictine abbot appointed archbishop of Vienna in 1986 on the resignation of Cardinal Franz König, were named to the College; the shadow of scandal would descend over the Austrian in due course.

Curial personnel changes were also reflected in the nominations. Cardinal Casaroli's two deputies, Archbishops Eduardo Martínez Somalo and Achille Silvestrini (who had been, respectively, *Sostituto* and "foreign minister" for nine years) were named cardinals, with Martínez Somalo becoming Prefect of the Congregation for Divine Worship and Silvestrini the Prefect of the Apostolic Signatura, the Church's appellate court. Archbishop Edward Cassidy, the former nuncio in Holland, replaced Martínez Somalo as *Sostituto* and Archbishop Angelo Sodano, the former nuncio in Chile, took over from Silvestrini as Secretary of the newly renamed Section for Relations with States.

One cardinal whom John Paul intended to appoint died two days before the public consistory: Hans Urs von Balthasar, the great Swiss theologian who was an important influence on John Paul's thinking and arguably the most creative Catholic theological mind of the century. At his funeral, Cardinal Ratzinger recalled Henri de Lubac's description of Balthasar as the most cultured man in the contemporary world. Few thought the claim an exaggeration.[103]

A month before the consistory, John Paul completed another Vatican "reform" that was quite likely closer to his heart than the business dealt with in *Pastor Bonus*. On his return from Calcutta in 1986, the Pope had moved quickly to establish a "house of mercy" in the Vatican, run by Mother Teresa's Missionaries of Charity. The managers of popes had said that this was impossible. How could you introduce the poor and vagrants into the Vatican? What about security? John Paul kept pressing and a solution was finally found—to take over and renovate a building on the edge of Vatican City State, beside the Congregation for the Doctrine of the Faith but still within the Vatican walls. The Pope blessed the cornerstone of the Casa di Accoglienza per i Più Poveri "Dono di Maria" [the "Gift of Mary" House of Welcome for the Poorest] on June 17, 1987, and the facility was opened two days after John Paul's sixty-eighth birthday, May 20, 1988. It includes dormitories for men and women, and can accommodate seventy persons overnight. Two dining rooms and a kitchen feed one hundred homeless people daily.

Ad Limina Apostolorum

On October 24, 1988, John Paul II received the bishops of Michigan and Ohio on their quinquennial *ad limina* visit to Rome. He had now completed some 300 of these meetings with bishops from all over the world in his decade-old pontificate.

In those ten years, he had traveled 360,000 miles and delivered 1,424 addresses in seventy-four countries. During that same period he had also made seventy-eight pastoral visits to cities and towns within Italy and more than 300 pastoral visits to Roman parishes.[104] He had canonized hundreds of new saints and beatified 309 candidates for sainthood.[105] Seven encyclicals, seven apostolic constitutions, more than thirty apostolic letters, and three post-synodal apostolic exhortations had been written. Ambassadors, heads of state, and international organization officials had been received by the hundreds, as had innumerable pilgrims. Amid all this activity, John Paul had invested as much, and perhaps more, sustained personal energy in his *ad limina* meetings with bishops as in any other facet of the Office of Peter.

According to ancient custom and Church law, every bishop who heads a diocese must come to Rome every five years to make a pilgrimage *ad limina apostolorum*: "to the thresholds of the apostles."[106] In modern times, bishops make their *ad limina* visits in national groups or, in the case of larger countries, regional groups, to simplify scheduling and allow more concentrated discussion of local problems. During the pontificate of Paul VI, a bishop's *ad limina* visit involved a brief personal meeting with the Pope and a series of meetings with curial officials. John Paul changed the standard *ad limina* program to give himself more time with the bishops and to give them more time with him, individually and as regional or national groups.

Under John Paul II, every *ad limina* continued to include a personal, one-on-one meeting with each bishop. These sessions lasted from fifteen minutes to a half-hour or more, and sometimes began with the Pope pointing to an atlas on his desk and asking, "And where is your diocese?" The meetings took place without translators (John Paul rarely needed one), and the Pope, an energetic listener, usually did more asking than answering. His hunger for knowledge about the situation of local Churches was insatiable. Though the circumstances of the Church's 2,400 dioceses varied enormously, bishops often had the impression that John Paul, a veteran diocesan bishop in his own right, "knew what you were talking about," one bishop said, when a problem of personnel, finance, or program was brought up.[107] The one-on-one meeting, Pope and bishop, was more intense with John Paul than with Paul VI and more open. Given the privacy of the encounter, this was the opportunity for bishops to tell the Pope precisely what was on their minds, perhaps unburdening themselves of concerns they could share with no one else.[108]

John Paul made three innovations in the *ad limina* program, so that each bishop now had four occasions to be with the pope, instead of just one. John Paul invited each group of visiting bishops to concelebrate morning Mass with him in the private chapel of the papal apartment. He also invited each group to a meal, usually lunch or dinner, at which the region's or country's problems were discussed with only the Pope and his secretaries present. John Paul also began the practice of holding a group meeting with the visiting bishops at which he would give an address. These *ad limina* discourses became another teaching instrument of the papacy and offered an insight into what the Pope thought about the situation of particular local Churches.[109]

John Paul II's expansion of the *ad limina* visit was more than a gesture of courtesy to fellow bishops. It was an unparalleled way for him to get to know the world episcopate. His amazing memory for names and places surprised more than one of the thousands of diocesan leaders he kept meeting every five years. So did his sense of humor. One bishop, who had put on weight since he had last seen the Pope, was asked by John Paul, "Is your diocese growing?" The bishop replied, yes, parishes were expanding. "So is the bishop," said the Pope. The *ad limina* visit was also a way to stay closely informed about the state of the Church throughout the world. In a typical span running from mid-January through late April 1988, John Paul met with bishops from the Netherlands, two regions of West Germany, the Sudan, Kenya, England and Wales, the American Midwest, Benin, Congo, Mali, New Zealand, Mozambique, the American Southwest, Lithuania, Zaire, and Ontario. The Pope received regular reports from the Holy See's nunciatures and apostolic delegations abroad, but the nuncio or apostolic delegate was rarely a native of the country to which he was assigned. Conversations over lunch or dinner with local Church leaders gave John Paul a sense of the nuances of situations and personalities that could not be so easily conveyed in diplomatic dispatches from the field.

The *ad limina* process worked in both directions. Bishops from young Churches in particular were encouraged by the extended attention they received from John Paul. The Africans, for example, believed that no Pope in history had been better informed about their situation, or the world situation, that John Paul II.[110] The feedback system worked particularly well when the cycle of *ad limina* visits from a country coincided with the preparations for a papal pilgrimage to that country. The Nigerian bishops, for example, had been in Rome for an *ad limina* on January 21, 1982. When the Pope arrived in Lagos on February 8, he was thoroughly briefed, and his addresses reflected his intense listening to the Nigerian bishops, two and a half weeks before.[111]

Under John Paul II, the *ad limina* visit was changed from a canonical formality into a genuine exercise of the Pope's *sollicitudo omnium ecclesiarum*, the traditional papal "care for all the Churches." The *ad limina* was also another example of John Paul's determination to take *Luke* 22.32 quite literally and to be Peter strengthening his brethren—in this case, bishops who, for all the honor of their office, were often lonely men carrying a large weight of responsibility.[112]

ALL THE RUSSIAS

For some Poles, "Asia begins at Przemyśl," a city on the far eastern border of today's Poland. The phrase is a not-too-subtle suggestion that, whatever else it might be, Russia is not "Europe." In either czarist or communist dress, the ancient persecutor of Poles was "other" in a way that the historic oppressor to the west, the Germans, was never quite thought to be. Religiously, politically, ethnically, and culturally, Russia and Russians, whether Sovietized or not, were "other" in a way that made it very difficult for many Poles to think of them as fellow Europeans.

Karol Wojtyła was an exception. His interest in the taproots of Slavic language and culture had prepared him to think of the eastern Slavs—Russians, Ukrainians, Byelorussians—as cousins of western Slavs like the Poles, despite their different alphabet. Wojtyła's culturally driven understanding of history also led him to think of Russia as "Europe." Before the eleventh-century division between Rome and the East, Russia had belonged to one of the two lungs with which the Christian culture of Europe had breathed. If Europe was to advance beyond the political and psychological division that Yalta had created, it had to breathe with both lungs again. And this meant, among other things, that Russia had to be part of Europe.

As Pope, Karol Wojtyła nurtured his interest in Russia and the Russians through numerous channels. He read deeply in the writings of Vladimir Soloviev, the late nineteenth-century Russian philosopher and theologian, a prophet of the reconciliation of Eastern and Western Christianity with a marked millennial strain in his thought.[113] John Paul also became familiar with the work of Russian religious thinkers, once convinced Marxists, who had abandoned Marxism between the 1905 and 1917 revolutions while warning both the government and the Russian Orthodox Church about the impending catastrophe: Nicolai Berdyaev, Sergei Bulgakov, and Simon Frank.[114] These thinkers, and the work of theologians like Pavel Florensky and Georges Florovsky, whom he read in French or Polish translations, familiarized the Pope with the religious core of Russian culture and convinced him that Russia had much to give the world.[115] Their interest in Christian unity also confirmed John Paul in his ecumenical instincts eastward, even as they helped him move beyond a Polish-centered view of Russia.[116]

John Paul nurtured personal as well as intellectual contacts with Russians. Meetings with Andrei Gromyko and other Soviet functionaries were one sort of encounter, but the Pope was interested in the kind of exchange that was impossible in the formal, state-to-state discussions favored by Cardinal Casaroli and others of his diplomats. Thus John Paul began to pursue back-channel conversations with knowledgeable Russians, which eventually led him into the heart of the human rights resistance to Soviet communist rule—not as a politician, but as a pastor.

John Paul II and Andrei Sakharov

In 1983, a Polish friend named Maria Winowska had arranged for Irina Ilovayskaya Alberti to be in the front row at one of John Paul's Wednesday general audiences. The daughter of Russian émigré parents, Irina had been raised in Yugoslavia between the world wars. There, she met an Italian diplomat whom she married in 1946. The Albertis were posted to Prague, where Irina got her first direct exposure to communist brutality during the 1948 takeover of Czechoslovakia. This ugly experience rekindled her interest in Russian affairs, and when contacts with new émigrés and Soviet citizens became possible in the later 1950s and 1960s, she pursued them, not knowing quite where they would lead. After her husband's death in 1975, Irina Alberti was asked by Aleksandr Solzhenitsyn, then living in Switzerland, to accompany the Nobel laureate and his family to their new home-in-exile in Vermont as a personal and family assistant. Mrs. Alberti agreed and spent almost four years with the Solzhenitsyns, becoming deeply versed in internal Soviet politics and the varieties of anti-Soviet resistance, émigré and internal, in the process.

Having completed her work with the Solzhenitsyns and having moved back to Paris, she had come to Rome and was going to meet the Pope. It was a brief encounter, but Mrs. Alberti remembers being impressed and deeply moved by this Pole's love for Russia. Moreover, his interest in Russia and the Russians was not simply the interest of a very bright man, a scholar. He was interested "in a human and spiritual way."[117]

The next meeting between the Polish Pope and the daughter of Russian émigrés came a year or so later. Andrei Sakharov, the brilliant Soviet physicist turned human rights campaigner, was on a hunger strike in Gorki, where he had lived in forced internal exile after his 1980 protest against the Soviet invasion of Afghanistan.[118] His wife, Elena Bonner, another veteran human rights activist, was being denied a passport to leave the USSR for a heart operation necessary to save her life. Bonner was an old friend of Irina Alberti's. When Bonner's children came to Rome as part of their worldwide campaign to get their mother released from exile in Gorki, Mrs. Alberti, who knew of John Paul's admiration for Sakharov, arranged for them to see the Pope. It was all done very discreetly. The Vatican Secretariat of State was nervous about a public confrontation with the Soviet regime, but when Mrs. Alberti got word to John Paul that the Bonner children wanted to see him, he immediately responded affirmatively. The meeting was held in a private room off the main floor of the Paul VI Audience Hall, for ten minutes before a general audience. With Mrs. Alberti translating, John Paul told the children that he was aware of their mother's and stepfather's situation, and that he was raising the issue with the Soviet government through diplomatic channels and private contacts. As the Pope was being whisked away by aides, he said to Mrs. Alberti, "Come and see me when you're next in Rome." "How?" she asked. "Talk to my secretary," the Pope said on his way out the door.

This seemed strange, the idea that one could simply ring up the Vatican, ask for Monsignor Dziwisz, and make an appointment with the Pope. But a French Jesuit friend assured Mrs. Alberti that that was exactly what she should do the next time she was in Rome. So having left the audience with the Bonner children convinced that there had been an as-yet-undetermined but "radical" change in her life, Irina Alberti called the Pope's secretary when she came back to Rome in the summer of 1985. This time she was invited to the papal summer villa at Castel Gandolfo, where she and John Paul spent several hours talking about conditions in the USSR, its government, and the real situation of the Churches there. At the end of this session, John Paul invited her to meet again on her next Roman visit.

As a result of international pressure, Sakharov's hunger strike, and Mikhail Gorbachev's accession to power, Elena Bonner was finally given a passport to leave the USSR and seek medical treatment in the United States. She stopped in Rome in December 1985, and Irina Alberti arranged for her to meet with the Pope. It was an "absolutely secret and private meeting," she recalled, as the conditions of Bonner's passport included a prohibition against meeting with public figures, and Sakharov, back in the USSR, was a hostage to Bonner's good behavior. Mrs. Alberti arranged a subterfuge to fool the reporters who were following Bonner everywhere. They were tricked into trailing the Bonner children while Irina Alberti and Elena Bonner drove into the Vatican in a tiny car.

Elena Bonner's meeting with the Pope lasted two hours, and involved an extensive discussion of what life was like in the Soviet Union, based on her experience and Sakharov's. John Paul listened intensely, but also sympathetically, even pastorally. Elena Bonner, a very tough woman, came out of their meeting crying, and said to Irina Alberti, "He's the most remarkable man I've ever met. He is all light. He is a source of light. . . ."[119]

In February 1989, when Sakharov and Bonner were in Rome together, they met privately with the Pope, who fought off interruptions so he could talk with them for another two hours. Sakharov, whom a poll that year would determine to be the most revered man in Soviet history, was being wooed by Mikhail Gorbachev. The General Secretary of the Soviet Communist Party was urging him to run for the Congress of People's Deputies and become a real actor in politics.[120] But Sakharov didn't want any formal participation in politics to be construed as his giving blanket approval to Gorbachev, whom he regarded as a reform communist, or endorsing the Soviet system, which he thought irreformable. The dilemma had been eating at him.[121]

During the meeting with John Paul, Elena Bonner said to her husband, "This may be the only place in the world where you can ask the question that's tormenting you." Sakharov, whom Irina Alberti described as a "theist unsure about his relationship to God," thought a moment, explained the position he was in—and then asked the question that was plaguing him: "By getting into this game, am I directing it onto a better course, or will I be compromised?" It was the first time Andrei Sakharov had gone to confession, so to speak, in his long, difficult, and heroic life.

John Paul thought about it for a while, saying nothing, just listening and reflecting. Then this veteran confessor said to Sakharov, "You have a clear and strong conscience. You can be sure you won't make a mistake . . . I think you can be of use." Sakharov, relieved of the fear that he would be used, went back to the Soviet Union and was elected to the Congress of People's Deputies, where he quickly became the conscience of the reform movement.[122]

The Millennium of Christianity in Rus'

The millennium of the baptism of the eastern Slavs, due to be celebrated in June 1988, presented John Paul II with a complex problem in which his commitments to religious freedom and ecumenism were in tension.

Although Russian Orthodoxy viewed the millennium as its own, the Greek Catholic Church of Ukraine had at least as strong a historical claim to being an heir to the 988 baptism of Prince Vladimir and Princess Olga of Kievan Rus', the proto-state out of which modern Russia and Ukraine eventually emerged. Both Ukrainians and Russians were right, if in different senses, but neither could admit the other's claim. Indeed, Russian Orthodoxy continued to insist that the Greek Catholic Church in Ukraine did not formally exist.

The Pope's dilemma would have become acute if John Paul had been invited to Moscow for the millennium celebrations in June 1988 without the assurance of access to the Ukrainian Catholics and their underground leadership. Patriarch Pimen of Moscow solved the Pope's problem by making it clear that John Paul would not be welcome in Moscow. This brusquely negative reaction was a harbinger of even greater difficulties. The Pope was not to be deterred from marking the millennium and expressing his respect for Russian Christianity, however. On January 25, 1988, he issued an apostolic letter, *Euntes in Mundum Universum* [Going Out into the Whole World], thanking God for the gift of the baptism of Kievan Rus'. That same day, at a service at the Basilica of St. Paul Outside the Walls to mark the end of the Christian Unity Octave, he extended the kiss of peace to "the sister Church of the Patriarchate of Moscow, which has assumed a great share of the Christian inheritance of the land of Rus'."[123]

The Pope did more for the millennium celebration than issue documents and fraternal salutes. The Gorbachev regime had understood that allowing the Orthodox to celebrate the millennium would win favor in the West. The Soviet government would have preferred a celebration in which there would be one or two large public events for elites, with no effect on the general population. By trumpeting all over the world that the Roman Catholic Church was preparing to mark this great moment in Christian and Russian history, John Paul II effectively took that option away from the Soviets. The Pope who was not welcome in Moscow helped make the celebration of the millennium of Christianity a major public, international, and media event, requiring the Soviet government to acknowledge it as a defining reality of Russian history.[124]

Euntes in Mundum was signed on January 25, but not released publicly until March. In the interim, John Paul signed another letter, *Magnum Baptismi Donum* [The Great Gift of Baptism], addressed to Cardinal Myroslav Lubachivsky and all the Catholics of Ukraine, thanking them for their heroic witness to the millennial faith and looking forward to the day when the Greek Catholics of Ukraine could practice their faith publicly. *Magnum Baptismi Donum* was released in mid-April.

The Holy See's delegation to the millennium celebrations in Moscow was led by Cardinal Casaroli and included Cardinals Willebrands (of Christian Unity), Etchegaray (of Justice and Peace), and three experts. A second "Delegation of the Catholic Episcopate" from around the world included the cardinal archbishops of Vienna, Hanoi, Milan, Warsaw, Munich, and New York, as well as Cardinal Vaivods of Latvia, Archbishop Paskai of Hungary (soon to be created cardinal), Bishop Dario Castrillon Hoyos (President of the Latin American bishops' council), and Bishop Gabriel Ganaka (President of the African bishops' council). Cardinal Casaroli spoke at the public celebration for Russian Orthodox leaders, representatives of international organizations, and members of the Soviet government held in the Bolshoi Theater on June 10. Casaroli diplomatically addressed what he described as the "delicate and sensitive" subject of legal protection for religious freedom, preceding this with an appeal to "the realism of the statesman" to recognize that "the religious 'fact,' and that of Christianity in particular, remains an incontestable actuality . . . and cannot be overlooked by anyone whose responsibility it is to confront reality." After appealing to "the realism of the statesman," the cardinal added what John Paul would likely have put first: "Respect for man demands it."[125]

Although the visit of the Holy See delegation was, officially, to the Russian Orthodox Church, John Paul II's decision to name the Cardinal Secretary of State as head of the delegation told the Soviet government that they were very much a focus of Vatican attention on the trip. John Paul had prepared a personal letter to Mikhail Gorbachev, which Cardinal Casaroli was to hand-deliver along with a memorandum outlining the major problems in Soviet-Vatican relations as the Pope understood them, though no meeting with Gorbachev had been scheduled when the Holy See delegation arrived in Moscow. The Pope had also included Joaquín Navarro-Valls in the Vatican group, thinking that there might be need to bring the international media into play. Navarro promptly leaked word of the Pope's letter to Gorbachev to the press while the Holy See delegation stayed at the Sovietskaya Hotel, waiting for word from the Kremlin.

They were due to leave Moscow on Monday afternoon, June 13. With forty-eight hours remaining, they still hadn't heard from Gorbachev, and tension was mounting. Since the Pope's letter could not be delivered by others, Casaroli faced the prospect of returning home with the historic letter in his luggage. At 4 P.M. on Saturday, June 11, a representative of the Soviet foreign ministry called, said that Gorbachev would meet them in the Kremlin at noon on Monday, and apologized for the delay. Gorbachev wanted the Soviet foreign minister, Eduard Shevardnadze, present, and Shevardnadze had been traveling. Navarro asked the foreign ministry man whether he could tell the world press about the impending meeting; the Soviet official replied, "No, just tell them to be at the Spaskaya Tower of the Kremlin at 11:40 A.M." Navarro did so, and the press naturally wanted to know why. Was something going to happen? "Just be there," was the response.

On Monday morning, Cardinal Casaroli was worried about whether he should wear his cardinal's cassock and pectoral cross or a business suit with Roman collar. Navarro said, "Your Eminence, this photo is going to be on the front page of every newspaper in the world . . ." That settled that, and Casaroli donned his cassock. On a hot June morning, he got into his limousine for the drive to the Kremlin wearing a heavy overcoat, so that his red-piped cassock and cross couldn't be seen until he got out inside the Kremlin walls.

The Vatican delegation met Gorbachev in his office directly above Lenin's old lair, which was preserved "as it was." There were some initial pleasantries, during which the General Secretary of the Communist Party of the Soviet Union told Casaroli not to be nervous, since he and Foreign Minister Shevardnadze had been baptized as infants. Gorbachev, who was full of vitality and confidence, also reminisced about an icon that had been hidden in his home behind a portrait of Lenin. Cardinal Casaroli handed the General Secretary the Pope's letter. Instead of putting it aside for later, Gorbachev opened it immediately and read both the letter and the memorandum of outstanding difficulties.[126]

The letter, on the Pope's personal stationery, read as follows:

To His Excellency, Mr. Mikhail Gorbachev

The Catholic Church looks with great respect and affection on the great spiritual patrimony of the Eastern Slav peoples. With great joy, I have wished that cardinals, archbishops, bishops, and prelates representing the

Holy See and the Catholic Church be present at such a great celebration in Moscow.

I have personally followed the events of international life, and first of all the initiatives in favor of peace [that you have taken]. In recent times, my special attention has been drawn to the promising developments created by the encounters and agreements in these last months between the Soviet Union and the United States of America, especially as regards disarmament, which have given such relief to the whole world.

I have learned with great interest what you have expressed in your meeting with Patriarch Pimen and the Synod of the Russian Orthodox Church on April 29 last, and I have noticed what you have said about the life of the religious community being linked to civil society by a common history and nationhood, about the right of believers as citizens to the free expression of their own religious convictions, and about their contribution to society, especially as regards values and the solution of the most demanding problems of society, and in particular the cause of peace.

I have also noticed that you make allusion to the necessity of changing some attitudes taken in the past by state authorities as regards the Church and believers. And with great attention I have noticed the announcement you have made that a new law on freedom of conscience will soon be passed, and will consider also the interests of religious organizations.

I am convinced that your work, Mr. General Secretary, has created great expectations and legitimate hope on the part of believers. Sharing such sentiments, I would like to express to you the confidence I have that Cardinal Casaroli's visit will open new perspectives for the situation of Catholics in the Soviet Union. As my predecessor, Pope Paul VI, expressed to the then-Minister of Foreign Affairs, Mr. Gromyko, I would like to express the hope that the question of the situation of the Catholic Church in the USSR could be more easily approached and satisfactorily resolved through a direct contact between the Soviet government and the Apostolic See. Toward that end, I am enclosing with my letter a *pro memoria* with some indications that I think are useful for a deeper examination of this problem.

The actual solution of these questions corresponds to the expectation of the Holy See and the entire Catholic Church, but also to vast sectors of world public opinion, which looks with great interest to the initiatives you have taken in many aspects of the social life of your country, in the hope that they will also be extended to the sphere of the religious life of persons and communities. Personally, I feel that I should be remiss in my mission as Supreme Pastor of the Catholic Church if I did not take advantage of such a privileged occasion to draw Your Excellency's personal attention to such a point. I do so with confidence that all this will find an echo in your heart.

I wish peace and prosperity to you and to all the peoples of the Soviet Union, to whom go my esteem and very cordial thoughts. Please accept, Mr. General Secretary, the expression of my highest consideration.

From the Vatican
7 June 1988[127]

JOANNES PAULUS PP. II

The historic letter, the beginning of a conversation that would have been inconceivable three years before, spoke for itself. John Paul was open to the most wide-ranging possible dialogue with the Soviet leader. It was now up to Gorbachev to follow through with improved conditions for Catholics within the Soviet Union and improved relations between the USSR and the Holy See.*

As a condition of the Catholic delegations' presence in Moscow for the millennium celebrations, the Pope had insisted that meetings be held with Ukrainian Greek Catholic Church leaders. Willebrands and Casaroli met with two Ukrainian bishops, Fylmon Kurchaba and Pavlo Vasylyk, at the Sovietskaya Hotel on June 10. The Russian Orthodox leadership was unhappy, but was also unable to block the meeting. Meanwhile, officials at the Soviet Council for Religious Affairs continued to insist that the legalization of the Greek Catholic Church in Ukraine was an internal Russian Orthodox affair—a position in con-

---

*Mikhail Gorbachev responded in a long letter, written in Russian, fourteen months later. After referring to his June 1988 conversation in Moscow with Cardinal Casaroli, the Soviet leader wrote, "The hour of new integrity of the world has arrived. For us, this signifies a new approach toward religion and Church, toward the ecumenical movement, toward the role played by the great religions of the world. . . . "

Gorbachev then praised the "personal attitude and activities" of the Pope and the "positive contribution to international life given by the Vatican City State," which he thought especially important "in the sphere of the moral formation of conscience in order to heal the international situation."

Referring to Europe, Gorbachev noted the "creative role of the Vatican in the Helsinki process" and added a personal observation: "I think that, for the first time since the great world tragedy which hit humanity a half-century ago—and of which your homeland, Poland, was the first victim—the world seems to have renewed hope. For some years now, the East/West relations which determined world politics are not worsening but becoming better."

The Soviet leader then wrote that the "cornerstone of our foreign policy [is] the interest of all of humanity . . . for this reason we are learning and we invite everyone to firmly reject the stereotypes of the Cold War and above all the 'figure of the enemy' that continues to characterize some strategic and political concepts. We are opening ourselves to the world and we are convinced that reciprocal openings will permit the creation of a new climate of effective international cooperation, mutually advantageous in the political, economic, and humanitarian spheres, which is necessary for renewal and progress. And this, if you wish, is the symbol of faith. It is a faith in the reason and morality of man, in his limitless spiritual strength, in his capacity to safeguard and to better in a substantial way the life of the world. We call this the new way of political thinking whose essential characteristics I illustrated last December at the United Nations and more recently in the Congress of Deputies of the USSR."

Gorbachev then looked toward his internal situation: "We in the Soviet Union find ourselves today at the vigil of decisions of primary importance . . . to rebuild the common home of the people of the Soviet Union based on economic efficiency, fraternity, and the variety of our numerous peoples which represents the unique historical richness of our country." In the USSR, he continued, "atheists, Christians, Muslims, Jews, Buddhists, and peoples of other religious beliefs live. And we are learning a difficult but necessary task of the harmonious cooperation and of consolidation on the principles of the renewal of our society. The new law on the freedom of conscience which is presently in the phase of preparation will serve to that end."

Finally, Gorbachev hinted at the possibility of diplomatic relations: "I decided to share these reflections with the hope that the contacts already established between us, between the Soviet authorities and those of the highest ranks of the Roman Catholic Church, will continue and obtain even more the form of political dialogue, and that the problems that exist between us will find, little by little, reciprocally acceptable solutions. It could even be that as a result of our common reflections a place may be found for the possibility to arrive at a new level in the relations between the Soviet Union and the Vatican."

Dated August 6, 1989, the letter was signed "M. Gorbachev."[128]

flict with their usual claim that the Ukrainian Catholic Church was not a religious body but a purely "nationalist" or "separatist" organization.[129]

In July, John Paul II took part in two Greek Catholic celebrations marking the close of the millennium year and continued to press for both religious freedom and ecclesial reconciliation. He preached in Ukrainian at a "Moleben" (a special Marian thanksgiving service) held on July 9 at the Ukrainian Pro-Cathedral of Santa Sophia in Rome.[130] The next day, July 10, John Paul was the principal concelebrant at a Divine Liturgy celebrated in the Byzantine-Ukrainian rite at the papal altar of St. Peter's. In addition to Cardinal Lubachivsky, twenty Ukrainian bishops concelebrated along with dozens of Greek Catholic priests. In his homily, the Pope honored the extraordinary courage of the Ukrainian Church under persecution and demanded religious freedom for the Greek Catholics of Ukraine. At the same time, he appealed again for a healing of ethnic, religious, and political wounds:

> "From the Baptism of Rus' began that slow and manifold process of cultural and social maturation which was to have such a deep influence on the formation of the Ukrainian, Byelorussian, and Russian peoples . . . You in particular, people of the Ukrainian nation, how could you forget that the heritage of the Baptism of your ancestors is shared in common with the Orthodox brethren of your people? Besides, how could you overlook the historic bonds which link your nation with those of Byelorussia and Russia? That Baptism made both you and them *members of the same Church.* . . ."[131]

It was a plea aimed at Moscow as well as at the Catholics of Ukraine, underground and in the Ukrainian diaspora around the world. In each of these venues, but particularly in Russia, it would fall on too many deaf ears to make the full reconciliation John Paul sought possible.

THE MARIAN YEAR AND THE DIGNITY OF WOMEN

The 2,000th anniversary of the birth of Christ, which was rapidly approaching, was never far from John Paul II's mind. The Pope decided that the period between the solemnities of Pentecost in 1987 and the Assumption of Mary in 1988 would be marked as a special "Marian Year" devoted to reflection on Mary, Mother of God and Mother of the Church.[132] If, as a pious tradition had it, Mary was a young girl of thirteen or so at the time of the Annunciation (see *Luke* 1.26–38), the Marian Year marked the 2,000th anniversary of the birth of Mary.

By some accounts, Paul VI's declaration of Mary's title as "Mother of the Church" was a sop to theological conservatives at Vatican II. John Paul II had a different view of the matter. This title, he came to think, had profound implications for how the Church should understand itself. Speaking to the Roman Curia on December 22, 1987, in the middle of the Marian Year, John Paul II explained those implications in a way that must have struck many of his listeners as startling, even quite radical.

Mary, he suggested, was the first disciple, for her assent to the angel's message made possible the incarnation of the Son of God. The incarnation had been "extended" in history through the Church, the mystical Body of Christ. Mary's assumption into heaven prefigured the glorification of all who will be saved. Thus Mary provides a "profile" of what the Church is, of how the people of the Church should live, and of what the destiny of disciples will be.

This understanding of the relationship between Mary and the Church challenged the way many Catholic leaders had come to think of themselves and their powers. The "Marian profile" in the Church is, John Paul suggested, even "more . . . fundamental" than the "Petrine profile." Without being divided from it, the "Marian Church"—the Church of disciples—preceded and made possible the "Petrine Church"—the Church of office and authority. Indeed, office in the Church has no other purpose "except to form the Church in line with the ideal of sanctity already programmed and prefigured in Mary. . . ." The two "profiles" were complementary. But the "Marian profile is . . . pre-eminent" and richer in meaning for every Christian's vocation.[133]

The message was unmistakable. Discipleship came before authority in the Church, and sanctity came before power, even the apostolically transmitted priestly power to "bind and loose" sins. This was not Mariology in the service of traditionalism. This was Mariology demolishing the last vestiges of the idea of the Church-as-absolute-monarchy. And John Paul did not hesitate to draw out another implication of the priority of the "Marian Church": "A contemporary theologian has well commented: 'Mary is "Queen of the Apostles" without any pretensions to apostolic power: she has other and greater powers.'"

The theologian was Hans Urs von Balthasar, who had written extensively about the various "profiles" of the one unified Church: the Church of Mary, of Peter, of John, and of Paul. The various rich symbolisms in play here find their unity in Mary and John at the foot of the Cross, which further underscored the institutional point the Pope made. The Curia and the hierarchy existed to serve the sanctification of the Church, a *communio* of believers redeemed by Christ.[134] The Curia and the hierarchy, expressions of the Petrine Church, existed *because* of the Marian Church of disciples. The Marian Church preceding and making possible the Petrine Church—this was not the way many curial officials, not to mention millions of Catholic laity and clergy, were accustomed to thinking about Catholicism. But it was how John Paul proposed that they should.

The theological and pastoral framework for the Marian Year was created by two important papal documents: John Paul's sixth encyclical, *Redemptoris Mater*, issued on March 25, 1987, and his apostolic letter, *Mulieris Dignitatem* [The Dignity of Women], issued on August 15, 1988.

Redemptoris Mater

The title of John Paul II's sixth encyclical, *Redemptoris Mater* [Mother of the Redeemer], links it closely to his first, *Redemptor Hominis* [The Redeemer of Man]. In the Christ-centered history of salvation, John Paul writes, there is one person who united the two great moments of the Holy Spirit, the "overshadowing" at Nazareth in which Christ is conceived by the power of the Holy Spirit and the sending of the Spirit at Pentecost. That person is Mary. Present to her son as mother, she is also present to the Church as mother. And her motherhood is rooted in faith.[135]

John Paul reiterates his teaching on the priority of the "Marian Church" over the "Petrine Church" in *Redemptoris Mater,* and discusses ecumenical issues in this context, with special reference to the Marian piety of Orthodox Christians. To all Christians, East and West, the Pope asks, "Why should we not all together look to her as *our common Mother,* who prays for the unity of God's family and who 'precedes' us all at the head of the long line of witnesses of faith in the one Lord?"[136] If Mary is "Mother of the Church," then all Christians should entrust themselves to Mary "in a filial manner." The Christian "'welcomes' the mother of Christ 'into his own home' and brings her into everything that makes up his inner life."[137]

The Pope also discusses Mary's particular importance for women in terms of the priority of discipleship. If the Marian Church of disciples is "before" the Petrine Church of office, then there is a fundamental, baptismal equality of discipleship in the Church—between women and men, as well as between laity and clergy—that is prior to any distinction of functions. As for contemporary feminism, John Paul argues that Mary "sheds light on *womanhood as such* by the very fact that God, in the sublime event of the Incarnation, entrusted himself to the ministry, the free and active ministry, of a woman."[138] Mary is thus a model for women who will "find in her the secret of living their femininity with dignity and achieving their own true advancement."[139]

Papal Feminism

Throughout his pontificate, there were few questions on which John Paul thought the Church's teaching was more misunderstood than on the question of the dignity of women. *Mulieris Dignitatem,* the apostolic letter of August 15, 1988, with which John Paul closed the Marian Year, was a major effort to remedy that misunderstanding by developing the distinctive feminism implicit in the Pope's *Theology of the Body* and briefly sketched in *Redemptoris Mater.* The public policy implications of this feminism would be drawn out further in John Paul's 1994 "Letter to Women," but the theological and philosophical foundations of his feminism are in *Mulieris Dignitatem.*

To think through a theology adequate to the dignity of women and the contemporary quest for equality means, for John Paul, going back to "the beginning" and to the mystery of humanity as female and male.[140] That we were created in God's image *as* male and female is the *"fundamental inheritance"* transmitted throughout the course of history; that we were redeemed by Christ *as* male and female is the message of the Church.[141]

That evangelical message includes another crucial, divinely ordered truth of salvation history: a woman is to be found *"at the center of [the] salvific event"* which is God's self-revelation to the world. Mary's "Yes" brought a human being, a woman, into *"a union with God that exceeds* all the expectations of the human spirit." Thus Mary's place *"within Christ's messianic service"* confirms that the essence of human dignity lies in radical self-giving, not in self-assertion or claims of autonomy.[142]

The distorted relationships between men and women, including relationships of domination in which the equal dignity of women is denied, is a problem addressed by one part of the contemporary women's movement. John Paul fully shares the judgment that something is wrong here, but insists that the root of this domination is not culture (although cultures transmit it) but sin. Sin fractures the community of persons that God had intended "from the beginning," and which is the ground of the radical equality of men and women as images of God. The liberation of women from these patterns of domination can never be a liberation *against*. It must be a liberation *for*, one that safeguards the distinctive vocation of women and men that results from what the Pope calls their "personal originality" and destiny. "In the name of liberation from male 'domination,'" John Paul writes, "women must not appropriate to themselves male characteristics contrary to their own feminine 'originality.'" Liberation is for the restoration of communion, of free and equal self-giving—the "original unity" of men and women that God intended. Unity and equality-in-diversity, not domination and not androgyny, are what has been inscribed in human nature "from the beginning."[143]

In exploring Christ's relationships with women, John Paul stresses their countercultural quality. He seems particularly taken with the story of the woman caught in adultery, who is left alone by a male world of judges ready to stone her until Jesus intervenes (see *John* 8.3–11). The Pope suggests that the story has a familiar, contemporary ring. When Christ proposes that the man without sin cast the first stone at the woman, "Jesus seems to say to the accusers: Is not this woman, for all her sin, above all a confirmation of your own transgressions, of your 'male' injustice, your misdeeds?" It was, the Pope suggested, a scenario that had repeated itself throughout history: "A woman is left alone, exposed to public opinion with her 'sin,' while behind 'her' sin there lurks a man—a sinner, guilty 'of the other's sin,' indeed equally responsible for it. And yet his sin escapes notice, it is passed over in silence. . . . How often is she abandoned with her pregnancy when the man, the child's father, is unwilling to accept responsibility for it? . . ."[144]

The Christian Gospel, John Paul insists, is a "consistent *protest* against whatever offends the dignity of women." The truth that Christ preaches about self-giving love was experienced by the women he encountered as a liberating truth. That is one reason they were faithful to him throughout his ministry and were with him on Calvary when almost all of his male disciples had fled. Their fidelity confirms the fact that men and women are radically equal in their capability "of receiving the outpouring of divine truth and love in the Holy Spirit."[145]

Picking up a theme from *Redemptoris Mater,* John Paul writes that motherhood is not just a biological reality, but a moral and personal reality with a dramatic religious meaning. For it is through motherhood that humanity was given its savior. "Each and every time that *motherhood* is repeated in human history, it is always *related to the Covenant* which God established with the human race through the motherhood of the Mother of God."[146]

As for the contemporary debate over the vocation to marriage and the relationship of men and women within marriage, John Paul writes that, for Christians, marriage can only be understood on the analogy of Christ the Bridegroom and the Church, his Bride. In this complex symbolism, we find what the Pope terms a "Gospel innovation." For it is in the context of Christ's love for the Church, his Bride for whom he gave up his life, that St. Paul locates the injunctions that wives should be subject to their husbands and that husbands must love their wives. (See *Ephesians* 5.31, 22–23.) There is no contradiction here, John Paul writes, because the counsel to "be subject" was "to be understood and carried out in a new way: as a '*mutual subjection out of reverence for Christ*' (cf. *Ephesians* 5.21)." Previous generations, the Pope believes, had abused the notion of wives being subject to their husbands, but in light of the redemption won for all by Christ, this subjection cannot be understood as "unilateral."[147] Rather, "mutual subjection" to Christ, John Paul is convinced, creates the distinctively Christian context for exercising authority within marriage.[148]

St. Paul had taught that the "more excellent way" and the greatest of the theological virtues was love (*1 Cor.* 12.31b–13.13). John Paul suggests that what he terms the "feminine genius" is the "place" of this more excellent way in the world and the Church. "In God's eternal plan," he writes, "woman is the one in whom the order of love in the created world of persons first takes root." Because love is the inner dynamic of the life of God, women's experience has a unique dignity, and that dignity is to be measured not by the dominating and male order of power, but "*by the order of love,* which is essentially the order of justice and charity." That dignity gives rise to a vocation to love, which can be discerned in the fact that "the human being is entrusted by God to women in a particular way."[149] Here was a basic issue with untold, profound implications for humanity.

Mulieris Dignitatem was John Paul's most developed effort to address the claim from some feminists that Christianity in general, and Catholicism specifically, is inherently misogynist. For all its eloquence, indeed passion, it clearly did not satisfy everyone. Some have a different concept of the "feminine genius." Others may believe that this man, or any man, cannot comprehend the dignity and difficulties of being a woman. For those open to the possibility, though, it is hard to imagine a more imaginative or demanding conception of Christian discipleship for both women and men than that proposed by *Mulieris Dignitatem* and its vision of the Marian Church.

16

After the Empire of Lies

Miracles and the Mandates of Justice

October 11, 1988	Pope John Paul II addresses European Parliament in Strasbourg.
February–April 1989	Polish roundtable negotiations result in partially-free elections on June 4, which are swept by Solidarity.
March 8–11, 1989	Special consultation between the archbishops of the United States and Vatican officials.
June 1–10, 1989	History's first papal pilgrimage to Scandinavia.
July 17, 1989	Full diplomatic relations established between the Holy See and Poland.
August 20, 1989	John Paul preaches at closing Mass for second international World Youth Day at Santiago de Compostela, Spain.
September 12, 1989	Tadeusz Mazowiecki becomes post-war Poland's first non-communist prime minister.
October 6–16, 1989	John Paul's fifth Asian pilgrimage includes a broadcast request for a new opening to China.
November 12, 1989	Pope John Paul II canonizes Saints Albert Chmielowski and Agnes of Bohemia.
November 24, 1989	Open letter from Cardinal František Tomášek firmly aligns the Catholic Church with Czechoslovakia's "Velvet Revolution."
December 1, 1989	John Paul II receives Mikhail Gorbachev at the Vatican.
January 12–17, 1990	Roman Catholic/Russian Orthodox consultation in Moscow fails to resolve the situation of the renascent Greek Catholic Church in Ukraine.
March 1, 1990	The Holy See establishes diplomatic relations with the Union of Soviet Socialist Republics.

April 21–22, 1990	Papal pilgrimage to Czechoslovakia.
August 26, 1990	John Paul's Sunday Angelus address sets the framework for the Holy See's response to the Persian Gulf crisis.
September 25, 1990	Public presentation of apostolic constitution, *Ex Corde Ecclesiae*, on strengthening the Catholic identity of Catholic universities.
September 30–October 28, 1990	Synod of bishops meets to consider training of priests; Synod's work completed by apostolic exhortation, *Pastores Dabo Vobis*, on March 25, 1992.
January 15, 1991	John Paul sends letters to presidents Saddam Hussein and George Bush, urging a negotiated settlement to the Gulf crisis.
March 4–5, 1991	Special Vatican consultation with bishops of countries involved in Gulf War examines the Church's future in the region.
May 1, 1991	*Centesimus Annus*, John Paul's third social encyclical.

S trasbourg had not missed much of European history since its pre-Christian beginnings as a Celtic village. The Franks took it from the Romans in the fifth century and renamed it Strateburgum. The ninth-century alliance between Charles II of the West Franks and Louis I of the East Franks, the Serment de Strasbourg, is the oldest extant document written in Old French. Church-state issues, including rows between the local bishops and the local freemen, roiled medieval Strasbourg. The Alsatian capital witnessed the French Revolution, the Napoleonic wars, the Franco-Prussian War (during which the city endured a fifty-day siege), and two world wars. Between 1870 and 1945, Strasbourg symbolized the struggle for European hegemony between the West Franks and the East Franks, the French and the Germans, as Strasbourg became Strassburg and then Strasbourg again.

Strasbourg symbolized something else in 1988. After eighty years of Franco-German conflict had culminated in a catastrophic Second World War and a Western Europe threatened by Soviet power, men of vision began to imagine a different kind of Europe. Beginning with raw materials and basic industries, they wove together a European economic community as the foundation for a new form of European political community. In 1979, the first elections had been held to a European Parliament elected by general suffrage. Although the Euro-Parliament had limited powers, it represented another step toward the political integration of the continent—or at least its western part. Fittingly, the new European Parliament was located in Strasbourg. The crossroads of conflict had become one of the continent's premier political meeting places.

Large questions remained, however. What *kind* of Europe was being built out of the Common Market, the Council of Europe, the European Parliament, the European Court of Human Rights, and a welter of other transnational institutions, courts, and regulatory agencies? What was the "freedom" these institutions were to serve? How should Europeans live their new prosperity? Who, in fact, was included in "Europe"?

On October 11, 1988, John Paul II came to Strasbourg's Palace of Europe to address the European Parliament. For more than forty years, he had refused to concede that "Europe" was an inherently divided continent and that the iron curtain represented a natural division. Now he had come to Strasbourg to talk with the Euro-parliamentarians about the kind of future he imagined for a Europe no longer divided by a massively defended ideological fault line.

It was time, the Pope proposed, to shed the Stalinist mentality of "eastern Europe" and "western Europe" so that "Europe" would "one day reach the full dimensions that geography and, even more, history have given it." That history included Christianity, the "faith which has so profoundly marked the history of all the peoples of Europe, Greek and Latin, Germanic and Slavic." Beneath their differences, Europeans east and west of the Cold War divide could recognize each other as Europeans, because much of their culture had been formed by Christian values and the humanism that had grown from those values. "Europe" had to "search more intensely for its soul," for the sources of its commitment to unity-amid-diversity, which meant "the equal right of all to enrich others with their difference."

All cultures, he suggested, were efforts to wrestle with the mystery of human life and human destiny—which inevitably raised the question of God. On the threshold of a third millennium, could one really imagine a new Europe "devoid of this transcendental dimension"? Those who thought that "Europe" could be built out of economic, legal, and political mechanisms alone were deluding themselves. Culture remained fundamental, and the new Europe had to decide between two humanisms that were contending for Europe's soul as the Cold War receded into the past.

In one humanism, "obedience to God" was the "source of true freedom," which was always a "freedom for truth and good." In the second, the human condition lacked a transcendent dimension, religion was a "system of alienation," and freedom was conceived as radical, individual autonomy. The secularists claimed credit for democracy, but the deeper historical roots of the modern democratic possibility, the Pope argued, lay in Europe's Christian history. Christ's distinction between the things that are Caesar's and the things that are God's (see *Matthew* 22.21) had helped make limited government possible. By making clear that there was a sanctuary of conscience in every human soul where state power must not tread, Christianity had freed politics from the burden of omniscience. A Christianity living out Christ's distinction between the things of Caesar's and the things of God's was thus a powerful safeguard against the "political messianism [that] most often leads to the worst tyrannies."

For its part, the new Europe of democracies had to recognize that "things of God's," things of the transcendent order, were involved in free societies. Europe had almost been destroyed in the twentieth century, John Paul concluded, not from "inside" its Christian cultural heritage, but "from outside"—when "ideologies [had] absolutized society itself or some dominant group, in contempt of the human person and his freedom."

The new, unifying, "integrated Europe of tomorrow," open to the European Slavic world, had great tasks ahead of it, if it was to reclaim its role as "a beacon in world civilization." It had to reconcile humanity with nature, and peoples with one another. Most of all, it had to reconcile the human person with himself. It had to resist "cultures of suspicion and dehumanization." It had to build a vision of the human future "in which science, technological ability, and art do not exclude, but elicit, faith in God." The humanism born of biblical faith was Europe's historical heritage, and the "best safeguard" of its "identity, liberty, and progress" in the future.[1]

Critics have sometimes said that John Paul II is a man living in another century. They are right, of course. Three hundred ninety-five days before the Berlin Wall was breached and twelve years before the talismanic year 2000, John Paul II was already living in the twenty-first century.

HISTORY ON FAST-FORWARD

What had seemed immutable since World War II—Soviet hegemony over the world's last great political empire, and the rule of communists within the vassal states of that empire—began to change with striking rapidity in April 1988. Consider the events that followed, one after another, almost, it seemed, without pause:

On April 8, the Soviet Union's last imperial adventure was abandoned, as the USSR announced its withdrawal from Afghanistan.

On April 29, Mikhail Gorbachev met with the leaders of Russian Orthodoxy, acknowledged Christianity's role in Russia's history, and pledged that a new law on freedom of conscience would take account of believers' concerns in an officially atheist state.

On June 30, Andrei Gromyko, who had nominated Gorbachev for the post of party General Secretary, was publicly humiliated at a party conference as his erstwhile candidate proposed modest political reforms. Gorbachev stopped short of endorsing competitive political parties in the USSR or revisions of Soviet republican borders. The Soviet inner empire and the "leading role" of the Communist Party were to remain inviolate.

On August 23, demonstrations in the Baltic republics of Lithuania, Latvia, and Estonia protested the 1940 annexation of these once-independent states by the USSR. Less than three months later, on November 16, the Estonian Supreme Soviet declared the primacy of its own laws over Moscow's—the first step toward reclaiming the independence of the Baltic republics.

On December 7, Mikhail Gorbachev announced major cuts in the Soviet military.

Meanwhile, the transformation of east central Europe and the Soviet outer empire accelerated.

On April 25, 1988, a workers' strike in Bydgoszcz signaled that Poland was beginning to come to a boil again. Throughout April and May, workers struck in Nowa Huta and at the Gdańsk shipyards. Their strike demands included Solidarity's legal restoration. Demonstrations followed in Warsaw, Kraków, Lublin, and Łódź, with young workers and students chanting a theme reminiscent of the Pope's 1987 pilgrimage: "There's no freedom without Solidarity." Uppercase or lowercase "s," the papal message had been received.

On May 22, János Kádár, who had ruled Hungary since Soviet tank treads had crushed the anti-communist revolution of 1956, was replaced as head of the Hungarian Communist Party by Károly Grósz, a reformer of a new generation. By reason of necessity, if not of profound democratic conviction, Grósz and his colleagues were prepared to consider the political reconstruction of the country.

On August 16, miners struck in Upper Silesia, and sympathy strikes spread throughout Poland. With nowhere else to turn, the government sought Lech Wałęsa's help to bring things under control. Wałęsa proposed an end to the strikes, and most strikers were back at work by September 3.

On October 10, a major shake-up took place in the Czechoslovakian party leadership.

On November 23, the governmental leadership was reshuffled in Hungary.

Less than two months later, on January 11, 1989, the Hungarian regime announced that opposition political parties would be allowed.

A week after that, on January 18, General Wojciech Jaruzelski announced that Solidarity would be legally recognized once again as an independent, self-governing trade union. The regime had previously tried to entice the Church into being "society's" representative in negotiations to determine new political and economic arrangements in Poland, but the Polish Church refused to play the role the regime imagined for it. That broke the logjam, and Solidarity was once again recognized as the government's interlocutor, seven years after the regime thought it had consigned the trade union/political opposition to oblivion.

On February 6, 1989, the Polish Roundtable negotiations began. The result, two months later, was an agreement to hold semi-free elections. Thirty-five percent of the seats in the parliament would be openly contested, along with the membership of an entirely new upper house, the Senate. The agreement was signed on April 5, with elections to be held on June 4. Solidarity nominated 261 parliamentary candidates. Each of their campaign posters depicted the candidate shaking hands with Lech Wałęsa (who was not running). Underneath the photos, in the Gdańsk electrician's handwriting, was a simple sentence: "We must win."

Election day gave "the society" a delicious opportunity to reject "the power" in the most personal way. Inept to the end, the government had decided that voting would be by deletion. Ballots contained all the candidates' names, and preference was registered by crossing out the names of disfavored candidates. From the Baltic to the Tatras and from Wrocław to Przemyśl, millions of Poles took enormous satisfaction in crossing out the names of the communist candidates, one by one, each stroke of the pen a gesture of disdain for those who had ruled for more than forty years in the name of their superior insight into history.[2]

It was a complete triumph for Solidarity which, after a second round of runoffs on June 18, won every contested Sejm seat and ninety-nine of the one hundred seats in the new Senate. Parliamentary maneuvering now turned to the question of electing a president. On July 19, in an impressive display of political discipline by the fledgling Solidarity parliamentarians, Wojciech Jaruzelski was elected President according to the agreement reached at the Roundtable—by one vote, deliberately shaved that closely by Solidarity tacticians. Solidarity had kept its side of the bargain while demonstrating that Jaruzelski served at its pleasure. Solidarity, not the Communist Party, had real governing legitimacy in Poland.

A month later, on August 24, after Jaruzelski's candidate for prime minister, former interior minister General Czesław Kiszczak, had been unable to form a government, the president invited one of the thousands of Solidarity leaders he had jailed almost eight years before, Tadeusz Mazowiecki, to do so. On September 12, after three weeks of intensive negotiations, the first noncommunist prime minister of an east central European country in forty years took office.[3] Far faster than Solidarity's leadership had thought possible, Poland was firmly set on the road to freedom.

Across the Carpathians, in Czechoslovakia, the regime still tried to maintain its iron grip by repression. Underneath the neo-Stalinist crust, however, a revolution of conscience was gathering critical mass. A most unlikely revolutionary created one of its important public manifestations.

Beginning in December 1987, a pious Moravian farmer, Augustin Navrátil, organized a national petition for religious freedom, his third such effort since 1976. A simple man of stubbornly held convictions, Navrátil became an activist after being offended by the government's removal of crosses and roadside shrines from the Moravian countryside. His first two petitions for religious freedom had landed him in psychiatric hospitals. According to the Czechoslovak regime, anyone who did things like this was certifiably mad. In his third petition, Navrátil expanded his demands. In addition to defining the relationship between Church and state in a free society, the Navrtátil petition demanded free speech, freedom of assembly, habeas corpus, freedom of the press, and the legal enforcement of contracts. What had begun as a religious act of defiance against the regime's atheism had become a rolling, nationwide referendum, with nonbelievers and Protestants joining Catholics in signing the petition throughout 1988 and into 1989. Cardinal Tomášek urged his people to sign the petition because "cowardice and fear are not becoming to a true Christian."[4]

In early 1989, the Czechoslovak regime, refusing to face the facts represented by the 600,000 signatures the petition would eventually garner, sent Augustin Navrátil off for another spell in the psychiatric ward of a prison hospital. On February 21, Václav Havel, the playwright-leader of Charter 77 and the most prominent figure in the Czech human rights resistance, was sentenced to nine months in prison. A month later, on March 25, a peaceful candlelight procession for religious freedom in Bratislava, the capital of Slovakia, was broken up by water cannons, dogs, truncheons, and tear gas. Although the regime imagined that it was decapitating the movement's leadership and terrorizing its followers, Havel's sentencing and the "Good Friday of Bratislava" turned out to be the prologue to the drama that history would remember as the "Velvet Revolution."

"Do Not Be Afraid to Be Saints!"

As the seeds of resistance he had sown in east central Europe began to flower, John Paul II maintained an intense pace of pastoral activity.

Curial Ecumenism

A joint *plenarium* or formal meeting of the Congregation for the Doctrine of the Faith [CDF] and the Pontifical Council for Promoting Christian Unity [CU] was held from January 30 through February 1, 1989. There had been tension between the two dicasteries over their respective responsibilities in ecumenism. CDF, for example, had taken the brunt of the criticism for delays in the Holy See's response to ARCIC-I, the first report of the Anglican-Roman Catholic International Commission. Cardinal Ratzinger's congregation had its own complaints. CDF felt that it was brought into the ecumenical conversation on serious doctrinal issues only at the last minute. Then, if CDF raised objections, it got all the blame without having been part of the process that had brought things to a point of contention. CU, for its part, felt that bringing CDF into the discussion too early narrowed its range of maneuvering room.[5]

Beneath these bureaucratic concerns was a deeper, substantive issue. By virtue of its nature and institutional history, CU was sometimes inclined to see ecumenical dialogue as a form of negotiation. CDF, especially under Cardinal Ratzinger, looked on ecumenism as a mutual exploration of the truths of Christian faith, not a bargaining process in which one side's "gain" was the other's "loss." There is no doubt that John Paul II shared the view that the only Christian unity worthy of the name is unity in the truth. It is equally certain that the Pope's sense of ecumenical urgency was more characteristic of CU than CDF.

In resolving disputes between dicasteries or curial departments, John Paul's approach has often been to suggest, "Why not have a joint plenary?"[6] The Pope not only knew about the tension between CDF and CU, but thought it natural and even good. As he understood it, CU's job was to probe the limits of the possible, while CDF's was to decide whether the probing had gone too far (in terms of premature agreement on an issue) or whether the new terrain being explored had raised new questions.[7] The point of a joint *plenarium*, a joint meeting of the two departments' senior members, was to try to get the two dicasteries to see their built-in tension in that light.

The result of the three-day meeting was a set of internal and unpublished guidelines to govern the interaction between CDF and CU, making sure that CDF was consulted in time about questions of doctrine. The guidelines were subsequently approved by the Pope and tensions eased. Two years later, on March 25, 1993, CU issued its long-awaited *Directory for the Applications of Principles and Norms on Ecumenism*, a manual for ecumenical activity throughout the Church that had been developed in close consultation with CDF. As all parties recognized, though, stress was a natural part of the relationship between the two, and there would be further occasions in which that stress became visible.[8]

The Bishop as Witness and Evangelist

Contentions within the Church were by no means confined to the Roman Curia. For years, tension had been building between the leadership of the U.S. Bishops' Conference and the Holy See.[9] Another special three-day meeting took place in the first quarter of 1989, between the archbishops of the United States and the leaders of the Roman Curia. In the minds of some American bishops, conflicting views of Church governance were the root of the problem. In the view of some authorities in Rome, the question was whether the American bishops and their bureaucracies had absorbed so much of the denominational religious culture of their country that the bishops were losing sight of their unique role.

These issues crystallized in the opening remarks of Archbishop John May of St. Louis, the President of the National Conference of Catholic Bishops [NCCB], on March 8, 1989. Archbishop May noted that, in the contemporary United States, "Authoritarianism is suspect in any area of learning or culture. . . . Therefore, to assert that there is a Church teaching with authority binding and loosing for eternity is truly a sign of contradiction to many Americans who consider the divine right of bishops as outmoded as the divine right of kings." This, the archbishop concluded, was the "atmosphere" in which the bishops of the United States lived and worked.[10]

Cardinal Ratzinger, in response, suggested that what Archbishop May perceived as a uniquely American problem was in fact a difficulty in all modern societies—the inability to distinguish between authoritarian imposition and authoritative doctrine. That incapacity, in turn, was shaped by a defective notion of freedom as personal willfulness. The tendency of modern culture was to turn bishops into moderators of an ongoing discussion, and for a bishop to take an authoritative stand, teaching the mind of the Church, was regarded as "partisan." But the faith is not a "partisan act," Ratzinger argued, and the bishop could not call his people to be witnesses to the truth unless he was first such a witness himself: "It is the hallmark of the truth to be worth suffering for. In the deepest sense of the word, the evangelist must also be a martyr. If he is unwilling to be so, he should not lay his hand to the plow." Bishops, as messengers of the Gospel, had to leave ample room for "intellectual disputation," and had "to be ready to learn and to accept correction." But bishops also had to remember that they were guardians of an authoritative tradition.[11]

In welcoming the Americans to what he hoped would be a "truly open exchange" that would "strengthen our partnership in the Gospel," John Paul said that he was "fully conscious of the challenges you face in bringing the Gospel message to a world that does not readily accept it."[12] Archbishop May, for his part, said that the bishops had come to Rome in part to learn from the Pope: "No one knows more about spreading the Gospel than you do, Holy Father. In your work here in Rome and in your missionary journeys throughout the world, you have carried the good news of Jesus—in a courageous and loving way."[13] No doubt the sentiments of esteem were honestly stated, in both directions. Yet the special meeting would not have been called had the Pope, senior Vatican officials, and at least some American bishops not believed that something was missing—a sense of evangelical possibility, perhaps—in world Catholicism's wealthiest and, in some respects, most influential vineyard. The NCCB leadership admitted to difficulties but not to the basic problem perceived in Rome, which involved the self-understanding of the American bishops as trustees and teachers of a tradition. Although the issue that was the occasion for the special meeting was raised, aired, and discussed, it was not resolved.

John Paul is, as Archbishop May noted, a singularly effective evangelist. It might also have been underscored that he had been that in situations far more various and at least as difficult as those faced by the American bishops. Further, John Paul had become a compelling figure by preaching a demanding Gospel, with compassion but also without compromise, convinced that the Gospel message is entirely pertinent to the crisis of modernity. As Cardinal Ratzinger had pointed out, bishops who thought themselves "moderators" between factions and constituencies were unlikely to imitate that bold evangelical style.[14] That suggested a lost opportunity in a country on the threshold of becoming the world's only superpower.

The People's Book

Closely related to the teaching authority of bishops, and of the Church itself, is the question of biblical authority, which John Paul took up in a major address to the cardinals, bishops, and scholars of the Pontifical Biblical Commission on April 7, 1989. There had been an explosion of Catholic biblical scholarship in the wake of Vatican II and a dramatic increase in Bible study among Catholics.[15] Yet just when the Bible was being restored to the people, those same people were being told, openly or subtly, that only scholars could really understand the Bible. The idea of the Bible as the Church's book, the book of the people, was getting lost.

As the Pontifical Biblical Commission began a multiyear study on biblical interpretation in the life of the Church, the question the Pope wanted to pose was whether a biblical scholarship that largely confined itself to an intense, critical study of the origins of sacred texts risked losing sight of the religious message of those texts.[16] The Pope also suggested that biblical scholars avoid the "trap of reflection" into which contemporary philosophers had fallen—in the case of biblical scholarship, by focusing so intently on the rings of particular trees that the entire forest of revelation and the good news of salvation it contained dropped out of sight. Biblical scholars could not treat the Bible as simply another ancient text to be dissected. If biblical scholars stood outside the Bible looking in, rather than looking at the Bible with the tools of critical scholarship from a position *inside* the believing community, something was awry.[17]

Africa and Scandinavia

Three weeks after defending the Bible as the people's book, John Paul took off on his fifth pastoral pilgrimage to Africa, a nine-day journey to Madagascar, La Réunion, Zambia, and Malawi. On April 30, 1989, before a congregation of more than a half-million in Madagascar, he beatified a native of Tananarive, Victoria Rasoamanarivo (1848–1894), whose evangelical work after foreign missionaries had been expelled from the island had earned her the title "Mother of Madagascan Christianity."[18] On May 2, it was the turn of Jean Bernard Rousseau (1797–1867), who had evangelized La Réunion. In Zambia, John Paul marked the centenary of the country's evangelization. During an ecumenical service in the capital's Anglican cathedral, the Pope urged Anglicans and Catholics to "avoid all forms of competition and rivalry" in evangelizing Africa.[19] In Malawi, he called for dialogue between Christians and Muslims and asked African Catholics "to reject a way of living which does not correspond with the best of your local traditions and your Christian faith." That implicit critique of consumerism, and the Pope's questioning in Zambia of the effects of African indebtedness on economic development, suggested that he was thinking, yet again, of a future beyond the Cold War and its possible effects on Africa.[20]

The pilgrim Pope marked another milestone in early June as he became the first Bishop of Rome to travel to Scandinavia. It was his longest intra-European pilgrimage in terms of distance traveled (some 7,200 miles), and it took him to Norway (0.48 percent Catholic), Iceland, Finland (0.08 percent Catholic), Denmark, and Sweden (1.14 percent Catholic). Ecumenism in lands marked by radical secularism was the pilgrimage theme. In Tromso, Norway, John Paul became the first Pope to preach north of the Arctic Circle, urging Norwegians who, during the summer, lived in perpetual daytime, to be "children of the light." King Olaf V received him in Oslo, as did Queen Mar-grethe II in Copenhagen. Given the exceptionally low religious practice of Swedish Lutherans (perhaps 3 percent) and the minuscule Catholic popula-tion of the country, the congregation of 10,000 in Uppsala for the Pope's Mass was considered a great surprise. Things were more difficult in Denmark, where the country's Lutheran bishops were divided among themselves on whether they would meet with John Paul in the Cathedral of Roskilde. In the event, the Pope was not allowed to speak during the cathedral service, led by Bishop Berthild Wiberg. Afterward, John Paul met the Lutheran bishops willing to do so at Bishop Wiberg's residence, where there was an exchange of addresses by the Pope and Bishop Ole Bertelsen of Copenhagen. John Paul greeted the Lutherans as "esteemed brothers in Christ" and urged that they pray for the day when they could celebrate the Eucharist together.[21]

The Scandinavian pilgrimage bore ecumenical fruit two and a half years later, on October 5, 1991, when an unprecedented ecumenical prayer service took place in St. Peter's Basilica. The occasion was the 600th anniversary of the canonization of St. Bridget of Sweden, venerated by Catholics and Lutherans alike. John Paul II, Archbishop Bertil Werkström, Lutheran Primate of Swe-den, and Archbishop John Vikström, Lutheran Primate of Finland, presided over First Vespers of the Twenty-seventh Sunday of the Year. The Catholic bish-ops of Stockholm and Helsinki participated, as did King Carl Gustaf and Queen Silvia of Sweden. The queen offered one of the biblical readings dur-ing the service. The basilica was darkened at the beginning of the service, which began with the Pope and the Lutheran celebrants processing together to the high altar, accompanied by Sisters of the Most Holy Savior of St. Brid-get, the "Bridgettine" community founded by the saint, all carrying candles. As the sisters put the candles in the semicircular rail surrounding the tomb of Peter below the papal altar, the congregation sang the hymn "O Joyous Light" together. The basilica's lights were then turned on. Intercessions were offered in all the Scandinavian languages, the Pope preached, and the two Lutheran primates gave addresses. It was the first time that Catholic and Lutheran lead-ers had prayed together in St. Peter's.[22]

At lunch the next day, one of the Lutheran leaders asked John Paul whether the fact that two Lutheran archbishops had stood with him at the altar meant that he recognized the apostolic validity of their orders. The Pope paused and said, with a twinkle in his eye, "One could also ask whether the two archbishops, by being there on that altar with me, recognized my primacy." There was general laughter, and the discussion moved on to other questions.[23]

The Meaning of Heroism

After a ten-day vacation in the mountains of northern Italy, John Paul flew to Spain on August 19, 1989, for the second international World Youth Day, being held at Santiago de Compostela in the country's far northwest corner. According to a tradition dating from 813, the relics of the apostle James, martyred in Jerusalem c. A.D. 44, came to rest in Compostela, where the saint was said to have been an evangelist before his death. In the Middle Ages, Santiago de Compostela was the most important pilgrimage site in the world after Jerusalem and Rome. Now, 600,000 young people had come to Spanish Galicia by boat, train, car, bus, airplane, bicycle, and, in the great pilgrimage tradition, on foot. They had come from North and South America, Asia, Africa, Oceania and, as John Paul put it, from "all over Europe, from the Atlantic to the Urals."

During his two days in Santiago, John Paul pressed the message of a Europe beyond the Cold War, recovering its Christian heritage as it rediscovered the roots of European culture, and challenged the generation that would inherit the new Europe to rethink the meaning of heroism.

The young people spent the entire night of August 19–20 just outside the city, singing and praying in vigil on Monte de Gozo, the "Mountain of Joy" from which medieval pilgrims got their first sight of the shrine of Santiago de Compostela. John Paul had spent part of the evening with them. Then, on the morning of August 20, he spoke to them of true human greatness, by reminding the enormous congregation of the dialogue involving Christ, the apostles James and John, and their determined mother, who had asked Jesus that her two sons be given privileged places in the Lord's kingdom. Jesus, in turn, asked the brothers whether they could "drink the cup that I am to drink?" They had replied, "We can" (*Matthew* 20.20–23). They did not know then the full sense of what they had said, John Paul suggested, because they had not yet realized that drinking "this cup" would mean, as it would for Christ, the complete pouring out of their own lives. They had not yet fully realized what Christ had meant when he had said that he "came not to be served but to serve and *to give his life as a ransom for many* (*Matthew* 20.28)."

That, he suggested, was what a pilgrimage to Santiago de Compostela was for. One came to learn what Jesus had meant when he told James, John, and the other ten that "whoever would be great among you must be your servant" (*Matthew* 20.26). Those words were *"the essential criterion of human greatness,"* and they implied "a transformation, *a renewal of the criteria by which the world is governed.*" The young Catholics who were to reevangelize the new Europe would have to do so according to an exacting standard of service.

As he had with James and John, Christ demanded a radical commitment from his followers today. He did not want mediocrity. For a Christian, mediocrity meant measuring one's commitment by a self-devised standard and thinking of anything beyond that as the preserve of the professional saint.[24] Mediocrity was not what the Church and world of the twenty-first century needed. Young people, the Pope knew, wanted to improve the world they had inherited and to do so in freedom. That required not mediocrities, but saints: "Do not be afraid to be saints! This is the liberty for which Christ has set us free . . . *Dear young people, let yourselves be won by him!*"[25]

After World Youth Day, the Pope stopped briefly at the Marian shrine of Covadonga in northern Spain, some 200 miles east of Compostela. There, "with confidence," he laid before Our Lady of Covadonga "the project of a Europe without frontiers . . . that has not renounced the authentic humanism of the Gospel of Christ."[26] Two days later, at his regular Wednesday general audience in Rome, he spoke of Santiago de Compostela as "a privileged beacon of Christian radiation for Europe, this old Europe which is facing an important stage in its unification and the immanence of the third Christian millennium."[27] The new Europe being born from the old Europe needed more than the amelioration of ancient animosities. It needed a soul. World Youth Day 1989, an important moment in the "new evangelization," was meant to help form that soul.

Asia, Again

On September 8, 1989, two days before thousands of East Germans began fleeing west via Hungary and Prague, John Paul received the members of the Joint International Pentecostal/Roman Catholic Dialogue. On September 12, the day that Tadeusz Mazowiecki's cabinet was approved by the Sejm, he met with Indian bishops on an *ad limina* visit (other *ad limina* groups in September 1989 came from Lesotho, Venezuela, and Peru). The Archbishop of Canterbury came to Rome on September 29 for a four-day visit. The joint declaration signed by Archbishop Runcie and the Pope on October 2 acknowledged that "we do not see a solution" to the new obstacles that had emerged in the quest for "visible unity," which both leaders maintained was still their goal.[28]

The day before, on October 1, John Paul had beatified an entire seminary—twenty-six priests and seminarians of the Passionist order martyred in Spain in 1936. In 1963, Paul VI had put a "hold" on beatification and canonization causes from the Spanish Civil War. Virtually all the martyrs had been victims of the Republican forces, but Paul VI did not look favorably on the Franco regime (which had defeated the Republicans) and didn't want to bolster the Spanish dictator's position by beatifications and canonizations of civil war victims. Pope Paul was also concerned that revisiting the recent past would prove divisive in the current Spanish Church.[29] Generalissimo Franco had died in 1975, but John Paul II was, in any event, a pope of a different mind about the martyrology of the modern world. The Church needed to be reminded that it lived in the greatest century of persecution in Christian history. In addition to beatifying numerous victims of the Spanish Civil War, John Paul also beatified martyrs from two other fratricidal conflicts once thought too controversial to touch—the French Revolution and the Mexican "Cristero" uprising of the 1920s. Father Miguel Pro, a thirty-six-year-old Jesuit shot by firing squad in Mexico on November 23, 1927, may have been the first martyr in Church history whose execution was photographed. John Paul had beatified him on September 25, 1988.

The inaugural Mass, October 22, 1978. (*L'Osservatore Romano*)

John Paul II at Mentorella, October 29, 1978. (*L'Osservatore Romano*)

John Paul II celebrates his twentieth anniversary Mass, October 18, 1998, with (*from left*) Cardinals Franciszek Macharski, Bernardin Gantin, and Joseph Ratzinger. (*L'Osservatore Romano*)

On holiday in the mountains. (*L'Osservatore Romano*)

At Uhuru Park, Nairobi, Kenya, with African prelates, September 1995. (*L'Osservatore Romano*)

Ordaining Bishop Stanisław Dziwisz, March 19, 1998. (*L'Osservatore Romano*)

In the papal helicopter, approaching Cherry Creek State Park, Denver, Colorado, August 15, 1993. (*W. H. Keeler)*

Praying at the Hill of Crosses, Šiauliai, Lithuania, September 7, 1993. (*L'Osservatore Romano)*

In the Valley of the Temples, Sicily, May 1993. (*L'Osservatore Romano*)

With Mother Teresa in Tirana, Albania, April 25, 1993. (*L'Osservatore Romano*)

At the grave of Father Jerzy Popiełuszko, Warsaw, June 1987. (*L'Osservatore Romano*)

The Eucharistic Congress Mass in Seoul, South Korea, October 8, 1989. (*L'Osservatore Romano*)

In Brisbane, Australia, November 25, 1986. (*L'Osservatore Romano*)

The World Day of Prayer for Peace, Assisi, October 27, 1986. (*L'Osservatore Romano*)

In Warsaw, addressing General Wojciech Jaruzelski, June 16, 1983. (*L'Osservatore Romano*)

Saluting Nicaragua's embattled Catholics, Managua, March 4, 1983. (*L'Osservatore Romano*)

In Nairobi, Kenya, May 7, 1980. (*L'Osservatore Romano*)

The Mass at Belo Horizonte, Brazil, July 1, 1980. (*L'Osservatore Romano*)

In Maximilian Kolbe's death cell at Auschwitz, June 7, 1979. (*L'Osservatore Romano*)

With an Indian child at Cuilapan, Mexico, January 29, 1979. (*L'Osservatore Romano*)

The Forty-fourth International Eucharistic Congress was held in Seoul, South Korea, in October 1989. John Paul flew there on October 6–7, his fifth pilgrimage to the Far East. In meetings with South Korean President Roe Tae Woo at the Blue House, the Korean presidential residence, John Paul urged greater legal protection and respect for human rights in what would become Asia's second majority-Christian country early in the twenty-first century. As always, the primary thrust of his message was evangelical. At the Congress's closing Mass on October 8, which he concelebrated with 280 bishops and 1,500 priests before a congregation of more than a million, the Pope, who spoke a few sentences in Korean at the beginning of his homily, pointed out that sharing in the Eucharist compelled work for reconciliation. When Christianity had been introduced to Korea two centuries before, it had created a new form of community that abolished the "inviolable class barriers" of traditional Korean society. In an analogous way, Catholics in Korea today were called to try and achieve reconciliation in the face of the "tragic division" of their country.[30]

At the noontime Angelus prayer following the closing Mass, John Paul, speaking in English, broadcast a greeting to the people of North Korea, where there were neither bishops nor priests to serve the Catholic population. In the broadcast, which was heard in China, the Pope made public for the first time his desire to visit the People's Republic of China and his hope for a reconciliation in truth between the underground Chinese Church loyal to Rome and the regime-sponsored Patriotic Catholic Association. Given the tangled complexities of the situation, it was a nuanced statement that bears careful reading:

> In this filial conversation with Mary, our mother [i.e., the Angelus], I also make mention of our brothers and sisters in Christ living in mainland China. . . . Deep within my own heart, there is always present an ardent desire to meet these brothers and sisters in order to express my cordial affection and concern for them and to assure them of how highly they are esteemed by the other local Churches. I am deeply moved when I think of the heroic signs of fidelity to Christ and his Church which many of them have shown in these past years. Through the intercession of Mary, help of Christians, may Christ be their consolation in every trial and in all of life's daily challenges. May the Lord also inspire within them a firm commitment to the delicate task of fostering reconciliation within the ecclesial community, in communion of faith with the successor of Peter, who is the visible principle and foundation of that unity.[31]

John Paul's broadcast from Seoul was a public effort to accomplish what private diplomacy had failed to achieve—an opening to the People's Republic of China. Six years earlier, in 1983, the Pope had sent a letter to Chinese leader Deng Xiaoping. Written in English on his personal stationery, and replete with expressions of John Paul's respect for Chinese culture and its ancient history, the plea for a renewed conversation read as follows:

To His Excellency, Deng Xiaoping

I am of the opinion that the pursuit of the common good of humanity encourages something that is also the object of my own lively desire: a direct contact between the Holy See and the authorities of the Chinese people. . . .

I am moved to this also by the profound responsibility that is proper to my religious ministry as universal pastor of the Catholics of the whole world, which inspires within me a special solicitude toward Catholics who are in China. Men and women, scattered throughout the country, who feel a deep loyalty and love for their own land . . . and who at the same time feel united with the Pope and with the Catholic communities of all the other countries.

It is a bond which, for the religious faith of Catholics, is an essential one, and which, on the other hand, cannot harm the ideal and concrete unity of their own nation or be to the detriment of its independence and sovereignty . . .

[Taiwan] is undoubtedly a long and complicated situation in which the Holy See has found itself, through a series of events, not always dependent on its own will. Nevertheless, I am confident that in the context of a concrete examination of the question it will be possible to reach a positive solution.

From the Vatican   JOANNES PAULUS PP. II[32]
16 November 1983

At Deng's death on February 19, 1997, the letter remained unanswered.

Human rights were an issue in Indonesia, the next stop on the Pope's second-longest voyage (some 23,400 miles in eleven days). The world's fifth-largest country was predominantly Muslim and had been ruled by the Suharto dictatorship since 1966. Catholics were a majority in East Timor, forcibly annexed by Indonesia in 1975 as Portuguese colonialism was collapsing around the world. The Church in East Timor, including the apostolic administrator of Díli, the capital, Bishop Carlos Filipe Ximenes Belo, SDB, had been involved in nonviolent resistance to what the East Timorese regarded as a foreign occupation. Violent opposition had met with brutal Indonesian repression; the site of the papal Mass in Díli on October 12 had seen considerable bloodshed.

It was a very difficult situation. After blessing the new Cathedral of the Immaculate Conception at Díli, John Paul preached on the challenge of being "salt" and "light" for people who had "experienced death and destruction as a result of conflict" and had known what it means to be "the victims of hatred and struggle," in which "many innocent people have died while others have been prey to retaliation and revenge." The Pope did not mention publicly the issue of East Timor's lost sovereignty, as banners supporting East Timorese independence appeared in the crowd of some 80,000 at the Mass. In Jakarta, though, John Paul had told President Suharto and his cabinet that they could not "disregard human rights in a misguided search for political unity."[33] He also urged the Indonesian bishops to be more vigorous defenders of the right of religious freedom.[34]

The Pope returned home by way of the Indian Ocean island state of Mauritius, where he spent the better part of two days. In Curepipe, a magnificent rainbow crowned his last meeting with thousands of rain-soaked pilgrims.[35] He flew back to Rome on October 16 as unprecedented demonstrations broke out against the East German regime in Leipzig.

WORLD WAR II REMEMBERED

John Paul II was acutely aware that the Yalta imperial system had begun to crumble on the fiftieth anniversary of the outbreak of World War II. Reading the Revolution of 1989 through the prism of moral analysis, the Pope began to offer a distinctive interpretation of the past half-century of European and world history as the revolution unfolded.

On August 26, 1989, the feast of Our Lady of Częstochowa, he wrote the bishops of Poland to mark the anniversary of the war that had devastated their homeland. The following day he issued an apostolic letter to the Church throughout the world. Its theme was taken from Psalm 88—"You have laid me in the depths of the tomb, in places that are dark, in the depths." Taken together, these two important texts define the Pope's view of the meaning of World War II and the challenge such a "depth" reading of history poses to the twenty-first century.

It had been, he believed, a war for the future of civilization, and the aggressor against civilization was totalitarianism. "The Second World War," John Paul wrote, "made all people aware of the magnitude . . . which contempt for man and the violation of human rights could reach. It led to an unprecedented marshaling of hatred, which in turn trampled on man and on everything that is human. . . . Many people were led to ask whether, after that terrible experience, it would ever be possible to have any certainty again."[36]

That question of confidence in the human future remained unanswered, fifty years later: "It could be said that Europe, contrary to appearances, is not yet completely healed of the wounds inflicted throughout the course of the Second World War. For this to happen . . . a genuine solidarity is needed."[37] So was an accurate analysis of what had happened in 1939–1945, for only when that truth was recognized could true solidarity be reestablished. Long before 1939, he wrote, "certain sectors of European culture" had tried to "erase God and his image from man's horizon."[38] One result of that erasure was the substitution of false religions in the form of "Nazi paganism and Marxist dogma," two "totalitarian ideologies" with pretensions to "become substitute religions." Contempt for God had led inexorably to contempt for humanity and for individual human lives. The result was a moral abyss, in which twentieth-century Europe had been reminded of the reality of Satan.[39]

The world had a duty to "learn from the past so that never again will there arise a set of factors capable of triggering a similar conflagration."[40] Racism and anti-Semitism had to be rejected completely. Citizens of the new Europe had to learn that "public life cannot bypass ethical criteria." Statesmen had to learn that "respect for God and respect for man go hand in hand." The Church had to learn from the failure of evangelization that had contributed to the disasters of twentieth-century Europe, and to "be vigilant as to the way the Gospel is proclaimed and lived out today." This underscored the importance of the quest for Christian unity.[41]

A crisis of confidence in the human prospect was the enduring legacy of World War II. That crisis of faith remained to be dealt with, even as the political effects of the war were being reversed in the Revolution of 1989. In dealing with it, the Church had to remember that, as "God does not despair of man," so "neither may we despair of man."[42]

Messianic Liberation

When the papal schedulers slated the canonizations of Blessed Agnes of Bohemia and Blessed Albert Chmielowski for Sunday, November 12, 1989, they certainly did not imagine that the ceremony would take place during a political upheaval that would fundamentally alter the landscape of Europe and the politics of the world.

Two and a half months before, on August 22, the Lithuanian Supreme Soviet had unilaterally voided the republic's annexation by the Soviet Union. Although the gesture had no immediate effect, it was a harbinger of the fact that the revolution gaining irresistible momentum in east central Europe would unravel far more than the external Soviet empire. On September 10, Hungary opened its border with Austria to permit the departure of East German refugees to the West. More than 30,000 eventually escaped the German Democratic Republic through this breach in the iron curtain. Three weeks later, on October 1, East German communist leader Erich Honecker permitted 15,000 East Germans who had taken refuge in the West German embassies in Prague and Warsaw to travel to West Germany on special trains—another breach in the once impregnable technological moat dividing Germany and Europe. On October 18, two days after massive demonstrations began in Leipzig, Honecker, who had ruled since 1971, was ousted as party leader and replaced by Egon Krenz.

There was no letup in the demonstrations or the emigrations. On November 5, more than 500,000 rallied in East Berlin on behalf of democratic reforms. Between November 4 and 8, another 50,000 East Germans fled to the West through Czechoslovakia. The East German cabinet resigned and old warhorses were removed from the Communist Party Politburo on November 7 and 8. It was too little reform too late, however, and the new party and governmental leaders knew it. They essentially surrendered on November 9, opening the Berlin Wall for a free exchange of people between East and West.

Berliners danced atop the Wall. By 1 A.M. on November 10, the legendary Kurfürstendam was filled with Germans from both sides of the border blowing trumpets, embracing, dancing—and scarcely believing what was happening. The greatest symbol of the Cold War had fallen.[43]

The canonizations of Albert Chmielowski and Agnes of Bohemia on November 12 gave John Paul II the opportunity to offer a public interpretation of these epic events. In another vivid demonstration that there are no mere coincidences in the designs of Providence, the canonization ceremony in Rome also became the occasion for Czechs and Slovaks to gather their energies for the next phase of the Revolution of 1989.

The canonization of Brother Albert, the first time in history that a playwright had proclaimed one of his characters a saint, could not have been better timed. Brother Albert had quite literally resisted Lenin's temptation and had chosen the "greater freedom" of a life wholly dedicated to God through service to the poor. In doing so, he became an icon of the full meaning of Christian liberation, which transcended politics while infusing it with meaning and value. As John Paul put it in his canonization homily, the reading from Isaiah during the liturgy—"Release those bound unjustly, untie the thongs of the yoke, set free the oppressed, break every yoke" (*Isaiah* 58.6)—was "the *theology of messianic liberation*, which contains what we are accustomed to calling today the 'option for the poor': 'Share your bread with the hungry, shelter the oppressed and the homeless; clothe the naked when you see them, and do not turn your back on your own' (*Isaiah* 58.7)." "This is exactly what Brother Albert did," the Pope concluded. "He took upon himself Christ's yoke and burden; he did not become merely 'one of those who give alms,' but he *became the brother of those whom he served. . . .*"[44]

During the offertory procession of the canonization Mass, when the bread and wine to be consecrated were brought to the altar, two Albertine Sisters presented John Paul with a reproduction of St. Albert Chmielowski's most famous painting, *Ecce Homo*.[45]

Blessed Agnes of Bohemia had died c. 1282. The long gap between her death and her canonization gave John Paul the opportunity to preach about the strange ways of Providence in history, and how the past could shed light on the sometimes-opaque present. Agnes had had to deal with suffering in her life; so had the Catholics of Bohemia, Moravia, and Slovakia today. What had marked Agnes of Bohemia was her willingness to accept "with total confidence the events which Providence permitted, in the certainty that *everything passes away, but [Christ's] truth remains for ever!*" That, John Paul insisted, was "the lesson the new saint gives to you, her dear compatriots," in 1989: "Human history is in continual movement . . . but the Truth of Christ, which enlightens and saves, *lasts, even amid changing events.* Everything that happens on earth is willed or permitted by the Most High so that men and women may thirst or long for Truth, tend towards it, seek it, and reach it!"[46] Even, the Pope implied, forty years of persecution.

Over seven centuries, Czechs had told themselves that something miraculous would happen when Agnes of Bohemia was finally canonized. The first step toward fulfilling that popular prophecy came at the canonization itself. The Czechoslovak government had been reasonably accommodating about passports, and thousands of Czechoslovakians found themselves in Rome at the same time, breathing free air. Men and women of the underground Church who hadn't seen each other for four decades met again in St. Peter's Square. In the rediscovery of old friends and the making of new allies at a weekend of canonization ceremonies, Catholics from all over Czechoslovakia discovered the degree to which their Church had survived the Stalinism of the 1950s and Husákian "normalization" after the Soviet invasion of 1968. There were far more of them than they had imagined. They were stronger than they had thought. They had the recent example of the Poles and the East Germans before them. Reunited because of the long-awaited canonization of Blessed Agnes, they went home to build their own gentle revolution.[47]

SURRENDER

During the Second World War, Henri de Lubac, trying to parse the singular terrors of the mid-century, proposed that "atheistic humanism" was something genuinely new in human affairs. "Everyday atheism" was a common enough phenomenon throughout history. This was different: it was atheism with a developed worldview, a program, a dynamic. Its prophets—Comte, Feuerbach, Marx, and Nietzsche—all taught that the God of Christians was "an antagonist," the "enemy of [human] dignity."[48]

This was a great reversal. The ancient world had experienced biblical religion as a great liberation from Fate. If God had created the world and the men and women who inhabited it, and if each of those men and women had "a direct link with the Creator, the Ruler of the stars themselves," human beings were no longer at the mercy of "countless Powers—gods, spirits, demons—who pinioned human life in the net of their tyrannical wills. . . ." Relief from Fate was no longer the preserve of a small elite with access to the secret of escape from the capricious will of the powers that controlled destinies.[49]

What the biblical revelation proclaimed as a liberation, the prophets of the new atheistic humanism believed was a yoke. "Getting rid of God" was the precondition to "regain[ing] possession of the human greatness" that God cruelly withheld. This was not the atheism of the decadent wealthy or the atheism of despair. This was atheistic *humanism*, on the march in the name of human liberation, and it was at the root of the "great crisis of modern times," de Lubac argued.[50]

The idea of atheistic humanism had had enormous consequences. Mediated through the politics of Lenin, Stalin, Mao, and sundry lesser communist leaders, it had proven something, de Lubac believed: "It is not true, as is sometimes said, that man cannot organize the world without God. What is true is that, without God, he can ultimately organize it only against man. Exclusive humanism is inhuman humanism."[51]

On December 1, 1989, the representative of the world's greatest experiment in atheistic humanism, the Union of Soviet Socialist Republics, came to the Vatican to call on the world's foremost representative of Christian humanism.

It made little difference that Mikhail Gorbachev was a new kind of Soviet leader, neither reptilian in cold-blooded cruelty like his Stalinist predecessors nor imbued with revolutionary ardor like the early Bolsheviks. Perhaps by this time Gorbachev himself had begun to doubt the possibility of reforming communism. Perhaps he had begun to grasp that there could be no genuine perestroika [restructuring] without much greater glasnost [openness]—and greater glasnost meant an end to the Communist Party's monopoly on power. What Gorbachev thought about the immediate future was of no particular consequence on this day, though. History had brought him to the Vatican as the embodiment of one contending power in the great drama of modernity, a representative of the century-long effort to liberate humanity by rejecting God *in principle.*

Close Encounter

Everyone in Rome knew that something epic was afoot on December 1, 1989. The streets were packed with gawking Romans. Skeptical reporters were genuinely excited. Veteran curial *monsignori* leaned out their windows for a look at the President of the USSR and his wife, Raisa, as they drove around St. Peter's Square, down a brief stretch of the Via di Porta Angelica, through the Porta Sant'Anna, and up the gently sloping Vatican hill. The heir to Lenin's revolution and his consort got out of their black limousine in the Cortile San Damaso and were greeted with the honors due a head of state by the Prefect of the Pontifical Household, the *gentiluomini* of the Holy Father, and the Swiss Guard. Then they went inside.

Italian state television had placed cameras throughout the Apostolic Palace so that viewers could watch the Soviet leader's historic progress to the papal apartment. It was evident from the outset that Gorbachev, very aware of the importance of the moment, was ill-at-ease, particularly for a leader who normally exuded robust self-confidence. One seminarian, watching the dramatic scene on television, thought he looked like a man on his way from death row to the execution chamber. A veteran Roman reporter disagreed, thinking that Gorbachev looked more moved and bewildered than frightened. Papal spokesman Joaquín Navarro-Valls, the erstwhile psychiatrist, thought Gorbachev seemed tense, uncomfortable, unsure about how to behave—Should he look stern? Should he laugh?[52]

Whatever his psychological or emotional condition, Mikhail Gorbachev did not, in his first minutes in the Vatican, project the image of a man looking forward to what lay ahead of him—perhaps because he was unsure of precisely what did lie ahead of him. But he must have had some intuition of what this moment meant historically. By the mere fact of his presence at the Vatican, the system he represented was acknowledging that it had been wrong about the relationship between Christianity and genuine humanism, about Christianity and human liberation.

The reporters had been allowed to watch the first moments of encounter between the Pope and the Soviet leader, and it was obvious to those used to such things that John Paul was emotionally involved in what was happening. His first reactions, the veterans said, were usually a tip to what was up, and the Pope gave Mikhail and Raisa Gorbachev the most cordial of greetings.[53] Gorbachev was a man of principle, the Pope believed, someone who would act on his convictions even if they led to results he didn't like.[54] Though Gorbachev might have wanted to "save 'communism with a human face'" (a project John Paul regarded as self-contradictory), a man of principle was someone who could be talked to, understood, and dealt with, in a way that was impossible with men concerned only with power.[55]

The two men went into the Pope's library for a private discussion, using two interpreters (John Paul can read Russian but doesn't speak it): one provided by the Vatican's Secretariat of State, and Valery Kovlikov, a Soviet Foreign Service officer. Both leaders seemed interested in getting to know each other. The Pope pressed the case for religious freedom, as he had done in all his previous meetings with Soviet officials, but he was also taking the measure of his visitor. Who was this man? What did he believe? How did he justify those beliefs?[56]

While Raisa Gorbachev toured the Sistine Chapel (and pronounced Michelangelo's frescoes inferior to Russian icons), the Soviet President and the Pope talked for an hour and a half, a half-hour longer than anticipated. According to Gorbachev, John Paul spoke of his "European creed" and his conviction that the new coming-together of Europe "from the Urals to the Atlantic" should be regarded as a restoration of normality, a return to Europe's true historical course. Among other things, that meant that the West should look on the events of 1989 less as a victory than as an opportunity to recover an aspect of its heritage.[57]

When John Paul II and Gorbachev had finished their private conversation, Raisa Gorbachev was brought in to be formally presented to the Pope. Her husband, now very relaxed, took her by the hand and said, "Raisa Maximovna, I have the honor to introduce the highest moral authority on earth." Then he added, with a chuckle, ". . . and he's Slavic, like us!"[58]

When they came out of the papal library to rejoin their respective parties and make formal statements, no one in the room was immune to the excitement of the moment. It was electric, and even the veteran reporters felt themselves caught up in it.[59]

John Paul's hands were trembling with emotion when he came to the podium to deliver his formal address of greeting. It gave him, he began, "particular pleasure" to welcome the Soviet president, his wife, foreign minister, and entourage, to the Vatican. A gentle history lesson, coupled with a reflection on the great drama being played out that day, immediately followed. The millennium of the baptism of Rus', which had been celebrated a year before, had been a reminder of the "profound mark left . . . on the history of the peoples who on that occasion received the message of Christ," John Paul noted. "I am pleased to consider your visit, Mr. President, against the back-drop of the Millennium celebration and, at the same time, to look upon it as a promise-filled sign for the future. . . ."

Next came the issue closest to his heart—religious freedom. With his beleaguered Lithuanian and Ukrainian flocks in mind, but speaking so as to make clear his concern for the religious freedom of all, he was polite but pointed: "The events of past decades and the painful trials to which so many citizens were subjected because of their faith are widely known. In particular, it is well known that many Catholic communities are today eagerly awaiting the opportunity of reestablishing themselves and of being able to rejoice in the leadership of their Pastors." It was thus time to make good on "the repeatedly affirmed decision of your Government to proceed with a renewal of internal legislation" on religious freedom so that Soviet practice might be brought "into full harmony with the solemn international commitments to which the Soviet Union has . . . subscribed." It was the precise argument he had made to Leonid Brezhnev in his historic letter of December 16, 1980, urging Gorbachev's predecessor not to invade Poland. This time, it was the human rights provisions of the Helsinki Final Act, rather than its security guarantees, that were in play. In any case, it was his "expectation"—which was identical with "the expectations of millions of [Gorbachev's] fellow-citizens"—that "the law on freedom of conscience soon to be discussed by the Supreme Soviet will help to guarantee to all believers the full exercise of the right to religious freedom," which was the "foundation" of all other freedoms.

At the end of a century of slaughter, John Paul looked forward to the birth of a new humanism, a new "concern for man," that would in turn give birth to a "universal solidarity." Solidarity would be stillborn, however, if the lesson of World War II was forgotten: "If fundamental ethical values are forgotten, fearful consequences for the fate of peoples can result and even the greatest of enterprises can end in failure." Their meeting, he concluded, was not simply unusual. It was "singularly meaningful: a sign of the times that has slowly matured, a sign that is rich with promise."[60]

Mikhail Gorbachev had been working on his own formal remarks up until the last minute. When Joaquín Navarro-Valls had asked for an embargoed copy the afternoon before (the Soviets having already been given the text of the Pope's address), he was told that Gorbachev's statement wasn't finished.

The Soviet leader was not to be outdone in defining the exceptional quality of the moment. "A truly extraordinary event has taken place," he began, an event "made possible by the profound changes that are taking place in many countries and nations." Seventy years of fierce anti-Vatican Soviet propaganda came to an abrupt halt when Gorbachev freely conceded that the Holy See was working "to promote solutions to common European problems and to create a favorable external environment enabling nations to make their own independent choices." The Soviet president then declared Holy See–USSR diplomatic relations a virtually completed matter, with "the formalities" to be sorted out in short order by the diplomats of both parties. Gorbachev also pledged to deliver on his promise of a new law on religious freedom, and concluded, "Within the sphere of the movement of perestroika we are learning the difficult but indispensable art of global cooperation and consolidation of society on the basis of renewal."[61]

The last sentence was reminiscent of the stilted vocabulary of the past. But Mikhail Gorbachev wasn't through yet. In an impromptu and unexpected coda that caught everyone by surprise, he invited the Pope to visit the Soviet Union.

It was another electric moment, and some reporters thought that John Paul's failure to accept, spontaneously and on the spot, was a great lost opportunity. The Pope, keenly aware of ecumenical sensibilities, knew he would have to be invited to the USSR by the Russian Orthodox Church. The Soviet president, familiar with the historic relationship between his office and that of the Patriarch of Moscow, may well have thought that the Patriarchate could be brought around, so to speak. Before that could happen, though, Gorbachev had fallen from power and the USSR had ceased to exist.[62]

A Providential Man?

In trying to understand John Paul II's statement that Mikhail Gorbachev was a "providential man," a description he has used on many occasions with colleagues and friends, it is important to remember the theological lens through which the Pope perceives all of reality. In dealing with President Gorbachev, John Paul did not cease being Karol Wojtyła, the man for whom everything takes place inside the horizon of his conviction that Jesus Christ is the answer to the question that is every human life. That included the life of Mikhail Sergeyevich Gorbachev. Dealing with Gorbachev, John Paul was a pastor who was also fulfilling a statesman's role, not a statesman who was a pastor when he returned to the sanctuary.

John Paul also met Gorbachev as a Pole, intensely aware that this Russian, unlike all of his predecessors, czarist or communist, had permitted Poland to assert its freedom and sovereignty. It seemed to others that Gorbachev had no other choice in the summer of 1989. Given his own domestic problems, he was in no position to reassert the Brezhnev Doctrine in east central Europe. That does not seem to have been the view of John Paul or his Polish colleagues in the Vatican. It may be that the Pope, who had gotten completely beyond a traditional Polish view of the Great Power to the east culturally and spiritually, had not fully done so politically.[63]

John Paul respected Gorbachev as a politician willing to take risks on behalf of what he believed to be the truth of things, and as a man who had come to understand that the human person, not the collectivity, had to be at the center of public concern.[64] That respect did not extend, as some commentators have suggested, to a sympathetic papal appraisal of Gorbachev's plan to maintain the Soviet Union in its post–World War II form.[65] The Pope fully understood that the "union" that made up the USSR had been imposed and maintained by often-brutal force. The destinies of two of Catholicism's most hard-pressed local churches, in Lithuania and Ukraine, were also involved. The Baltic republics were clearly different from Great Russia, culturally and historically. A similar argument could be made for the historical distinctiveness of Ukraine, although this was a much harder case to make to Russians, and especially to the Russian Orthodox Church. Given Orthodoxy's eastern Slavic origins in the lands around Kiev, an independent Ukraine would be a serious blow to the historic claims of the Patriarchate of Moscow.[66] In any event, the Pope who had defended the "rights of nations" from the beginning of his pontificate was not likely to become a proponent for the world's last multinational empire.

Mikhail Gorbachev, who allotted little more than a page in his 700-page memoirs to an account of his December 1, 1989, meeting with Pope John Paul II, may indeed have been a "providential man." Yet even within a morally focused analysis of late twentieth-century history, Gorbachev seems more likely to appear as the instrument of a Providence he never understood than as the conscious servant of a higher design. However Gorbachev, the man and the statesman, is finally assessed, the historical meaning of his meeting with the Pope will become clearer as the event recedes into the past. This was an act of surrender.

The curtain had been run down on the drama of atheistic humanism. As a plausible proposal for the human future, it was finished. That was what Mikhail Gorbachev's coming to the Vatican meant.

St. Agnes's Gentle Revolution

The unraveling of communism in Czechoslovakia began on Friday night, November 17–18, 1989, along Národní třída [National Avenue]—which runs from the Vltava River toward Wenceslaus Square in Prague's Old Town. With the permission of the authorities, 50,000 students marched up Národní třída toward the square to commemorate the fiftieth anniversary of the death of Jan Opletal, a student murdered by the Nazis. The connections between oppressors past and present could not be denied, however, and some anti-regime slogans were chanted. About halfway to their destination, the nonviolent students were confronted by the truncheons and white helmets of the state police and the red berets of a state anti-terrorist squad. Surrounded, the students tried to talk to the troops. Some handed out flowers to the red berets, while others lit candles, sat on the pavement, and with raised arms chanted, "We have bare hands." After what seemed hours of mounting tension, the white helmets and red berets attacked without warning. Men, women, and teenagers were beaten unconscious. No one was killed, but hundreds were hospitalized.

The *masakr*, as it was immediately dubbed, galvanized the nonviolent revolution that overthrew Czechoslovak communism. On November 19, Václav Havel convened the meeting that created the umbrella resistance organization, Civic Forum. Shortly after, a similar coalition, Public Against Violence, was formed in Bratislava under largely Catholic leadership. Massive evening demonstrations began in Wenceslaus Square, where Father Václav Malý, a thirty-nine-year-old priest who had stoked boilers in the basement of the Meteor Hotel when the government took away his license to live his vocation publicly, served as master of ceremonies. On the night of November 24, he read the enormous crowd a message from the aged cardinal whose name they cheered in the chilly evening air, using the familiar diminutive—"Frantši Tomášek! Frantši Tomášek!"

> Citizens of Bohemia, Moravia, and Slovakia:
>
> I must not remain silent at the very moment when you have joined together in a mighty protest against the great injustice visited upon us over four decades. . . . We are surrounded by countries that, in the past or presently, have destroyed the [prison] bars of the totalitarian system. . . . We must not wait any longer. The time has come to act.
>
> . . . Let us fight for the good by good means. Our oppressors are showing us how short-lived the victories of hatred, evil, and revenge are. . . .
>
> I also want to address you, my Catholic brothers and sisters, joined by your priests. In this hour of destiny for our country, not a single one of you may stand apart. Raise your voice again: this time, in unity with all other citizens, Czechs and Slovaks, members of other nationalities, believers and unbelievers. Religious liberty cannot be separated from other human rights. Freedom is indivisible. . . .[67]

Four days later, on November 28, the Czechoslovak Communist Party agreed to relinquish its monopoly on power. By December 7, Prime Minister Ladislav Adamec had resigned. On December 10, Gustav Husák was out as president, too. After three weeks of intense negotiations, Václav Havel was installed as President of Czechoslovakia on December 29. According to Václav Benda, a leading Catholic intellectual in Civic Forum, the regime contacted Cardinal Tomášek early in the negotiations to request that he act as mediator between the opposition and the government. Demonstrating that he was not only getting older and tougher at the same time but cagier, too, Tomášek refused. For him to act as mediator would split the opposition and give a kind of legitimacy to the regime. By putting the Church irrevocably on the side of the people, Tomášek sustained the opposition's broad-based coalition.[68]

In St. Vitus Cathedral, atop Prague's castle promontory, Hradčany, a "Te Deum" was sung on December 29 to celebrate Havel's installation as president.

One of the erstwhile playwright's aides, still amazed at what had happened, said, "St. Agnes had her hand under our gentle revolution."[69] After the last six weeks, no one was inclined to disagree.

A nonviolent revolution had swept away Stalin's external empire in less than six months and had established democratic regimes rather than a new reign of terror. Conscience had proven stronger than coercion, once conscience had been rallied in sufficient numbers.[70] Those who participated in the Revolution of 1989 knew that the key figure in creating that revolution of conscience had been Pope John Paul II.

THE NEW DEAL

Throughout the *annus mirabilis* of 1989, John Paul moved quickly to seize opportunities presented by the new deal in east central Europe and the USSR.

On July 17, full diplomatic relations between Poland and the Holy See were announced.

On July 25, Father Tadeusz Kondrusiewicz was named the Apostolic Administrator of Minsk in the Byelorussian Soviet Socialist Republic, with responsibilities for the pastoral care of Roman Catholics throughout Byelorussia. Bishop-elect Kondrusiewicz's curriculum vitae illustrated the trials of Polish families expelled eastward during World War II. He had been born in 1946 in Grodno, in what would soon be known as "Belarus," but had grown up in Kazakhstan. At the time Kondrusiewicz was named bishop, he was a priest of the Archdiocese of Vilnius in Lithuania, the only place he could study for the priesthood in the USSR of the 1970s.

On October 5, the Ukrainian Catholic bishops' Synod met in Rome. Two weeks later, the Vatican "foreign minister," Archbishop Angelo Sodano, was in Moscow for negotiations over the future of the Greek Catholic Church in Ukraine. The Moscow Patriarchate of the Russian Orthodox Church proposed a de facto dissolution of the Ukrainian Catholic Church. Those valuing their eastern liturgy more than their communion with Rome would become Orthodox, and those valuing communion with Peter over their Eastern-rite liturgy would become Roman Catholic. This was clearly unacceptable. In meetings with President Gorbachev, Foreign Minister Shevardnadze, and chairman of the Council for Religious Affairs Yuriy Khristoradnov, Archbishop Sodano reiterated John Paul's insistence that the new Soviet law on freedom of conscience recognize the legality of the Greek Catholic Church in Ukraine. The Soviets finally agreed, but insisted that the "practical aspects" of the legalization be worked out through a tripartite negotiation involving the Holy See, the Moscow Patriarchate, and the Soviet government. This negotiation was to take place "in the context of closer ecumenical dialogue" between the Russian Orthodox and Roman Catholic Churches.

If past history were any measure, the Patriarchate of Moscow would use the threat of a fracture in that "context" to prevent too many concessions to the Greek Catholics of Ukraine. Given what they evidently assumed to have been the durability of the Gorbachev regime and the USSR, the Holy See and the Pope agreed to this formula, which was not received happily by the Ukrainian diaspora or by the Ukrainian Catholic Church *in situ*. By late October 1989, the Greek Catholics of Ukraine were conducting massive demonstrations in L'viv, and on October 29 they peacefully took over the largest church in the city, the Church of the Transfiguration.[71]

The reemergence of the underground Greek Catholic Church in Romania went more smoothly. On December 30, Archbishop Francesco Colasuonno, a veteran Vatican diplomat, began a nine-day mission there, during which he attended the first meeting of the country's Latin-rite and Greek Catholic bishops since 1950. On January 6, 1990, Romania's interim government confirmed that the decree of December 1, 1948, forcibly uniting the Greek Catholic Church of Romania with the Romanian Orthodox Church, was abrogated, and that the Greek Catholics of Romania would enjoy full religious freedom.[72]

In the wake of Archbishop Sodano's October 1989 meeting in Moscow and President Gorbachev's visit to the Vatican in December, a joint Roman Catholic–Russian Orthodox conference met in Moscow from January 12 to 17, 1990, to try to resolve the situation of the Greek Catholic Church in Ukraine. The Holy See delegation was led by Cardinal Willebrands, President of the Pontifical Council for Promoting Christian Unity, and the Orthodox delegation by Metropolitan Filaret of Kiev, an implacable foe of the Ukrainian Catholics. Although official announcement of the meeting's results stated that "substantial agreement" had been reached on the situation of the Greek Catholic Church in Ukraine, the results of the January meeting were again unsatisfactory to the Ukrainian Catholics.

The Russian Orthodox had played their ecumenical ace and insisted on a statement that "Uniatism" (on the model of the 1596 Ukrainian Catholic "Union of Brest") was not the way to reunite the Churches. The Ukrainians took this as an indirect repudiation of their experience. Although the meeting agreed that the Greek Catholics could recover some of their churches, it also tried to confine their activities to the "canonical territory" of the Roman Catholic Church, an ambiguous formulation the Ukrainians regarded as a brake on their freedom of action. Moreover, the Orthodox refused to recognize the existing underground Greek Catholic hierarchy and insisted that any hierarchical structures for the Greek Catholic Church in Ukraine (such as dioceses and parishes) only be established by consensus agreement between the Holy See and the Moscow Patriarchate—which for the Ukrainians was another Vatican infringement of the freedom, guaranteed by the Union of Brest, they had suffered grievously to defend. Despite the Ukrainians' unhappiness, John Paul ratified the agreement. In what seemed an attempt to meet at least some Ukrainian Catholic concerns, though, he added formal reservations about the "historical judgments" the agreement had made about the Union of Brest, and noted the danger of misinterpreting certain aspects of the agreement.[73]

On February 6, 1990, John Paul appointed Ján Chryzostom Korec, SJ, the Bishop of Nitra in the Slovak portion of Czechoslovakia. The Vatican newspaper blandly stated that "until now he has been rector of the seminary in Bratislava"—a bit of bureaucratese that masked one of the great personal dramas of the resistance Church in east central Europe. Korec had been secretly ordained a bishop in 1951 at age twenty-seven, while working in a Bratislava warehouse wrestling oil barrels. He managed to function as a bishop clandestinely until 1960, when he was arrested and sentenced to twenty-seven years in prison. Released during the Prague Spring of 1968, he was shipped back to jail in 1974. International protests forced his release. He then worked in Bratislava as an elevator repairman, night watchman, and factory hand while continuing his underground ministry as a bishop and writing numerous small books of theology and spiritual reflection. In an attempt to assuage the Husák regime, Paul VI had asked him in 1976 to cease his underground episcopal activity, and particularly his clandestine ordination of priests. Korec obeyed—and watched the repression continue. In the late 1980s, he had emerged as one of the key leaders in the Slovak Catholic resistance. His appointment to a residential bishopric was a sign of confidence and gratitude on the part of a Pope who, as archbishop of Kraków, had had his own reservations about Vatican *Ostpolitik* in Czechoslovakia and who had done his share of clandestine ordinations to the priesthood.

On February 14, the Holy See and Hungary established full diplomatic relations, immediately after Cardinal Mindszenty's remains had been returned to his country and reburied during an enormous funeral Mass in Esztergom, the primatial see. In his letter to Hungarian Cardinal László Paskai for the occasion, John Paul wrote of Mindszenty that "he wore the crown of thorns."[74]

On March 1, the Holy See established full diplomatic relations with the USSR. Archbishop Franceso Colasuonno was named the Holy See's first nuncio in Moscow.

And on March 14, John Paul named twelve new bishops—seven for the Latin-rite Church and five for the Greek Catholic Church—in Romania.

What It Was About

While commentators in the West scrambled for an explanation of what had happened in east central Europe so rapidly and unexpectedly—the majority settling on economics as the cause of the Warsaw Pact's collapse—John Paul tried to bring these events and their implications for the future into clearer focus. On January 13, 1990, at his annual meeting with the diplomatic corps accredited to the Holy See, John Paul gave the assembled diplomats a challenging reading of the history they had all just witnessed. "The irresistible thirst for freedom," he said, had "brought down walls and opened doors." The diplomats would also have noted that the "point of departure" for the Revolution of 1989 "has often been a church." Step by step, "candles were lit, forming . . .

a pathway of light, as if to say to those who for many years claimed to limit human horizons to this earth that one cannot live in chains indefinitely. . . ." The great capitals of the region—Warsaw, Moscow, Budapest, Berlin, Prague, Sofia and Bucharest—had become "stages on *a long pilgrimage towards freedom*": a freedom made possible, in the final analysis, because "women, young people, and men have overcome their fear. . . ."[75]

The next task, he proposed, was to secure the victory of conscience in the rule of law, which must recognize human dignity as the source of rights. Law should build the kind of home worthy of men and women who were free moral agents, and that required "respect for transcendent and permanent values." When man made himself "the measure of all things," he "became a slave to his own finiteness." The rule of law in the new Europe had to be built with "reference to him from whom all things come and to whom this world returns."[76]

On February 14, the Pope began a series of brief prayer meditations at his general audiences, intended to help prepare for a pilgrimage to Poland the following year, called the "Jasna Góra Cycle." The February 21 meditation recalled King Jan III Sobieski's message to Pope Innocent XI on winning the Battle of Vienna in 1683: "I came, I saw, God conquered." That, John Paul suggested, was precisely what had happened in east central Europe: *Deus vicit*, "God conquered."[77] On March 28, he gave thanks "for the fact that the precariousness of lies has been manifest," and he thanked Mary, Queen of Poland, "for all those for whom truth has become strength"—the truth that triumphed over lies.[78] Later meditations in the series would link 1939 and 1989 more closely, reflecting on the betrayal of Poland by the USSR and its Western allies, the anniversary of the Warsaw Uprising, and the extermination camp at Auschwitz. The imperative of social solidarity, and the capacity to "differ nobly," were lessons to be drawn from the present and the events of a half-century ago.[79]

Similar themes marked John Paul's dramatic pilgrimage to a newly free Czechoslovakia in April 1990. The two-day visit, during which the Pope also visited Velehrad and Bratislava, began on April 21 in Prague. St. Vitus Cathedral was packed with bishops, priests, and laity, many from the underground Church. Hundreds of those present, especially among the older clergy, had suffered years of imprisonment in labor camps. All of them, the Pope said, had won a "victory of fidelity": *"fidelity to Christ crucified* in the moment of your own crucifixion"; fidelity to the Holy Spirit "who led you through darkness"; fidelity to *"Peter's successors and to the successors of the apostles, the bishops";* and *"fidelity to the Nation,* which is particularly expressed in solidarity with the persecuted and in frankness with those who seek the truth and love freedom." Their task, now, was to build a free Church *"on the basis of what you have brought to maturity during the years of trial."*[80]

John Paul was not the only man in Prague that day who thought that 1989 should be read in a different way than statesmen were accustomed to reading history. The Pope's fellow playwright, Václav Havel, now President of Czechoslovakia, put it brilliantly in his welcoming address to the Pope at the Prague airport on April 21:

> Your Holiness,
> My dear fellow citizens,
>   I am not sure that I know what a miracle is. In spite of this, I dare say that, at this moment, I am participating in a miracle: the man who six months ago was arrested as an enemy of the State stands here today as the President of that State, and bids welcome to the first Pontiff in the history of the Catholic Church to set foot in this land.
>   I am not sure that I know what a miracle is. In spite of this, I dare say that this afternoon I shall participate in a miracle: in the same place where, five months ago, on the day in which we rejoiced over the canonization of Agnes of Bohemia, when the future of our Country was decided, today the head of the Catholic Church will celebrate Mass and probably thank our saint for her intercession before him who holds in his hand the inscrutable course of all things.
>   I am not sure that I know what a miracle is. In spite of this I dare say that at this moment I am participating in a miracle: in a country devastated by the ideology of hatred, the messenger of love has arrived; in a country devastated by the government of the ignorant, the living symbol of culture has arrived; in a country which until a short time ago was devastated by the idea of confrontation and division in the world, the messenger of peace, dialogue, mutual tolerance, esteem and calm understanding, the messenger of fraternal unity in diversity has arrived.
>   During these long decades, the Spirit was banished from our country. I have the honor of witnessing the moment in which its soil is kissed by the apostle of spirituality.
>   Welcome to Czechoslovakia, Your Holiness.[81]

VARIANT READINGS

Cardinal Agostino Casaroli was not persuaded by this talk of miracles, and in the spring of 1990, he set out to analyze the events of 1989 from the perspective of the architect of the Vatican's *Ostpolitik*.

In a lecture on March 17 in Parma, Casaroli argued that the "Helsinki process"—the negotiations leading up to the Helsinki Final Act of 1975, the Final Act's human rights provisions, the subsequent compliance-review meetings, and the dynamics this process had set loose in communist countries—had been primarily responsible for the changes in east central Europe. It was an intriguing argument, but it was striking that the Secretary of State never suggested that the purpose of the whole Helsinki exercise, from the Soviet point of view, had been to ratify the boundaries of the external empire acquired by Stalin at the Tehran and Yalta Conferences during World War II. John Paul II's basic metaphor for the post–World War II Europe—"Yalta"—was noticeably absent from the cardinal's lecture. Casaroli also proposed that the Helsinki process had introduced the notions of the "human person" and "peoples" as "principles" of international relations, giving traction to the claim that human rights matters were not "internal affairs" but the legitimate concern of all. Yet even as he made these important points, Casaroli described Soviet and Warsaw Pact countries' behavior during the Helsinki process almost clinically, as if profound moral issues were not at stake throughout.[82]

On June 2, Cardinal Casaroli was awarded an honorary doctorate by the Pontifical Theological Academy in Kraków. On this occasion, which followed John Paul's two-day pilgrimage to Czechoslovakia and President Havel's suggestion that he was witnessing a "miracle," the cardinal defended the *Ostpolitik* even more directly. From the beginning of his contacts with communists, Casaroli said, he had been convinced that their "experiment" had no future, because it was utopian. The cardinal did not say that he and Paul VI had therefore regarded the Cold War division of Europe as a temporary arrangement. Casaroli gave John Paul due credit as a "powerful support" for those working to secure human rights behind the iron curtain. At the same time, the cardinal praised Mikhail Gorbachev as a man who "ran to the rescue to repair by democratic means the mortal wounds on the socio-political, moral, and economic levels inflicted on peoples during the long dictatorship"—a description of Gorbachev's achievements and methodology that few Russian democrats would have accepted in mid-1990.[83]

Cardinal Casaroli quite rightly suggested that one always had to "ask if and up to what point human deeds and events, even the most marvelous ones, can have a 'natural' explanation, while taking place under the vigilant eye and the external action of the Lord of nature and of history."[84] But the cardinal's rather bloodless analysis of the high politics of 1989 and his relative lack of attention to the moral revolution that had made 1989 possible missed something that President Havel's evocation of a "miracle" seemed to catch.

Cardinal Casaroli's state-centered analysis could not reach the far more interesting questions posed by the rapidity, style, and result of change in east central Europe in the second half of 1989. Why had this happened *when* it did? *How* had it happened through nonviolence (with the one exception of Romania)? And why had it produced, in the main, democratic regimes instead of new authoritarian ones? Havel knew why. And as he had made plain at the airport in Prague, the Czechoslovak president knew that John Paul II was the indispensable man in shaping the revolution of conscience that had preceded and made possible the nonviolent political Revolution of 1989.

New Things

John Paul II's third social encyclical, *Centesimus Annus* [The Hundredth Year], was issued on May 1, 1991. Written to mark the centenary of Pope Leo XIII's *Rerum Novarum, Centesimus Annus* gave the Church and the world John Paul's mature reflection on the causes and meaning of the Revolution of 1989, while looking ahead toward the "new things" of the twenty-first century and creatively developing the Church's social doctrine.

That there would be a centenary encyclical to celebrate *Rerum Novarum* was a given. In it, John Paul wanted to tackle questions of contemporary economics. So he had said to his classmate, Bishop Jorge Mejía of the Pontifical Council for Justice and Peace, "Perhaps we should hear some economists." Mejía took the hint and, to help prepare the intellectual ground for drafting the encyclical, Justice and Peace invited a group of distinguished economists of various schools to a meeting at the Vatican on November 5, 1990.[85] After a morning session at the Pontifical Council's offices, the economists were driven to the Apostolic Palace, where John Paul II hosted them at a working lunch. Bishop Mejía led the discussion, drawing comments from each of the economists invited. John Paul II questioned the scholars "very sharply, though certainly pleasantly," Professor Robert Lucas recalled. Lucas found himself impressed with the Pope's "intelligence and seriousness" and with his "complete lack of ceremony and pomposity."[86] After their luncheon discussion with the Pope, the economists returned to the Pontifical Council to continue the debate.

In due course, a "synthesis" to guide the drafting of the centenary encyclical was developed by the Pontifical Council.[87] John Paul studied this and circulated it among his intellectual interlocutors, including the Italian philosopher Rocco Buttiglione, who had known Cardinal Wojtyła in Kraków and had published the best study of John Paul's pre-papal intellectual project, the 1982 volume, *Il Pensiero di Karol Wojtyła* [The Thought of Karol Wojtyła]. Out of these conversations, John Paul decided that the new encyclical should make more use of the personalism central to his philosophical studies than the curial "synthesis" had, and ought to reflect more closely the empirical realities of today's world economy. It then became clear that these two concerns could be combined, so that the encyclical's moral analysis of the economy would emerge out of John Paul's philosophy of moral action. The result was an encyclical that did not deal with economics from the top down, in terms of macro-aggregates, but from the bottom up. It would attempt a description of "the economic person" as one dimension of "the acting person," the moral agent created with intelligence and free will, both of which must have something to do with economic life. John Paul had not read deeply in technical works of economics, nor did he think it the Church's business to prescribe technical solutions to economic issues. He was an accomplished philosopher of the human person, though, and the conversations that led him to write *Centesimus Annus* in his distinctively personalist fashion clarified the linkages among the Church's social doctrine, his own philosophical work, and the world of the twenty-first century.[88]

What Happened?

Centesimus Annus begins with a tribute to Pope Leo XIII, whose creative application of Catholic moral principles to the social, economic, and political "new things" of the late nineteenth century created what John Paul calls "a lasting paradigm for the Church."[89] *Rerum Novarum*'s principal themes—the dignity of work and workers; the right to private property and the responsibilities that entailed; the right of association, including the right to form trade unions; the right to a just wage; and the right to religious freedom—remained a part of the Church's intellectual heritage.[90] Leo XIII had also made a "surprisingly accurate" forecast about the collapse of socialism, which both he and John Paul regarded as inevitable because of socialism's "fundamental" error about the nature of the human person.[91] That "anthropological" error, compounded by atheism, had led to immense human suffering.[92]

With this analysis as background, John Paul turns to the question of why 1989 had happened, when it did and how it did. As he had argued on many previous occasions, culture—not economics, and not superior material force—was the engine of history. That was the truth that explained the *why,* the *how,* and the *when* of 1989.

There were other factors, to be sure. One was "the violation of the rights of workers" by a system that claimed to govern in their name. Resisting "in the name of solidarity," working people had "recovered and, in a sense, rediscovered the content and principles of the Church's social doctrine," which had led them to resist "by means of peaceful protest, using only the weapons of truth and justice." This, too, was another refutation of the Marxist creed, for "while Marxism held that only by exacerbating social conflicts was it possible to resolve them through violent confrontation," the Yalta division of Europe was overcome by the nonviolent commitment of people who "succeeded . . . in finding effective ways to bear witness to the truth," rather than by another war.[93]

Economic inefficiency was another key factor in the crisis of real existing socialism, and reflected socialism's "violation of the human rights to private initiative, to ownership of property and to freedom in the economic sector." Marxists who thought that economics explained culture ended up destroying the economies they built. Subordinating culture to economics meant suppressing the most urgent questions in life, and this could only lead to social disintegration.[94]

The deepest cause of socialism's collapse, however, was the "spiritual void" it created. Marxism had tried to "uproot the need for God from the human heart." What it had demonstrated was that this couldn't be done "without throwing the heart into turmoil."[95]

Christian humanism, which reflected the permanent truths built into human nature, could speak to the turmoil in the human heart that atheistic humanism had created. In doing so, it had given people back their authentic cultures. When enough people had recovered enough conscience to say "No" to the communist lie, the lie, and communism, crumbled. That, John Paul suggested, was what had happened in 1989—and why.

The Free Economy

John Paul did not attempt to outline a "Catholic economy" for the post–Cold War world, explicitly stating that the Church's social doctrine "has no models to present."[96] Rather, *Centesimus Annus* explores the questions one might have expected from the author of *Person and Act* and *Laborem Exercens*: What kind of person uses the free economy? How does that activity contribute to the economic common good? How does it serve the human good? *Person and Act* had analyzed the basic structure of moral action. *Laborem Exercens* had explored the experience of work in depth. *Centesimus Annus* achieved a real breakthrough in Catholic social thought by applying these analyses to the "free economy," considered as an expression of human creativity and an arena of moral responsibility. In that sense, *Centesimus Annus* "institutionalized" the moral insights of *Person and Act* and *Laborem Exercens*.[97]

From *Rerum Novarum* through *Populorum Progressio*, Catholic social doctrine had focused primarily on the just *distribution* of wealth—because all wealth comes from the earth, one moral issue is how to distribute it justly. John Paul reaffirms that, because God had given the whole earth to all its inhabitants, the earth's goods had a "universal destination."[98] Now, however, there is a new kind of wealth: in developed countries "*the possession of know-how, technology, and skill*" has more to do with wealth than natural resources do.[99] Catholic social doctrine, the Pope implies, had not taken sufficient account of this important "new thing." Moreover, there was the question of the human economic actor and what he or she brought to the mix. "Value" and "wealth," John Paul argues, are the products of human work, human creativity, human initiative.[100] If work, creativity, initiative, value, and wealth define what an economy is, the first responsibility of the Church is to encourage men and women to make good use of their creativity in order to create wealth and value. The "wealth of nations" resides not so much in the ground as in the human mind, in human creativity.[101]

Because John Paul II's personalism and his theory of moral action made him empirically sensitive to what was actually happening in contemporary economic life, *Centesimus Annus* made a decisive break with the materialism that had characterized some aspects of prior Catholic social doctrine. That, and John Paul's "culture-first" approach to analyzing public life, also meant that, with *Centesimus Annus*, Catholic social doctrine abandoned any quest for a "third way" between or beyond capitalism and socialism. Socialism was dead, and there were many forms of capitalism in the world (another insight that John Paul brought to Catholic social doctrine). The questions for the future were what kind of "free economy," based on what kind of understanding of the "acting person"? The encyclical's moral evaluation of capitalism read as follows:

> Can it perhaps be said that, after the failure of Communism, capitalism is the victorious social system, and that capitalism should be the goal of the countries now making efforts to rebuild their economy and society? . . .
> The answer is obviously complex. If by "capitalism" is meant an economic system which recognizes the fundamental and positive role of busi-

ness, the market, private property and the resulting responsibility for the means of production, as well as free human creativity in the economic sector, then the answer is certainly in the affirmative, even though it would perhaps be more appropriate to speak of a "business economy," "market economy," or simply "free economy." But if by "capitalism" is meant a system in which freedom in the economic sector is not circumscribed within a strong juridical framework which places it at the service of human freedom in its totality and sees it as a particular aspect of that freedom, the core of which is ethical and religious, then the reply is certainly negative.[102]

In the wake of *Centesimus Annus*, defenders of "Christian socialism" tried to argue that "Capitalism A" existed only in textbooks.[103] That was both empirically and textually implausible: empirically, because examples of "Capitalism A" could be found in various Western European and North American countries; textually, because John Paul II had clearly drawn on those examples of "real existing capitalism"—no one of which seemed to him completely sufficient, to be sure—in framing his endorsement of "Capitalism A." By the same token, it is simplistic and misleading to say that *Centesimus Annus* endorses capitalism, period. The encyclical, for example, cannot be taken to endorse libertarianism. John Paul clearly believes that the energies unleashed by the market should be tempered and channeled by law and by the public moral culture of a society. *Centesimus Annus*, while marking the end of "real existing socialism," offers a profound challenge to all forms of "real existing capitalism."

The Free and Virtuous Society

Centesimus Annus also pushed forward the Church's analysis of the complex texture of the free society.

In a striking innovation, John Paul teaches that "society," like the individual, has a "subjectivity." That subjectivity expresses itself in voluntary associations—"various intermediary groups, beginning with the family and including economic, social, political, and cultural groups which stem from human nature itself and have their own autonomy."[104] Nurturing voluntary associations is a crucial part of developing and maintaining the free society. The "subjectivity of society" is one of the most potentially fruitful concepts in the encyclical, and one hopes that Roman Catholic and other intellectuals will develop it further.

The encyclical's positive attitude toward the "free economy" was another reflection of the Pope's "culture-first" approach to Catholic social doctrine. The "modern business economy," John Paul writes, "has many positive aspects" for its "basis is human freedom exercised in the economic field, just as it is exercised in many other fields."[105] The actual functioning of a successful business is one paradigm for the Pope's stress on solidarity as a crucial social virtue. For a successful business requires "the ability to foresee . . . the needs of others and the combination of productive factors most adapted to satisfying those needs." It also requires "the cooperation of many people working towards a common goal." *"Initiative and entrepreneurial ability"* are essential in identifying a need, planning and organizing a business to meet it, and taking prudent risks—and all of those qualities must be affirmed in a culture if a modern economy is to succeed.[106]

The "free economy" is not only to be shaped by culture, but must be directed by law—which means by the State. But there are limits to what the State can do in setting the legal framework for the "free economy," and those limits have to do, again, with the freedom of the human person. The State, for example, "could not directly ensure the right to work for all its citizens unless it controlled every aspect of economic life and restricted the free initiative of individuals."[107]

Centesimus Annus also challenges stereotypes about poverty and the poor. Poverty in the modern world, John Paul argues, is primarily a matter of exclusion from the world of productivity and exchange.[108] We should think of the poor, the Pope urges, in terms of their potential, and justice demands that their potential be given the opportunity to fulfill itself.[109] In the free society, John Paul writes, it is primarily the task of culture to promote "trust in the human potential of the poor and consequently in their ability to improve their condition through work or to make a positive contribution to economic prosperity."[110] Welfare systems that promoted dependency were clearly excluded by such a moral principle.[111]

Centesimus Annus, it must be emphasized, is not an "economic encyclical," but an encyclical about the free and virtuous society. No existing society exemplifies the comprehensive vision John Paul II lays out. It is beside the point to argue whether this is an encyclical about the American system, although *Centesimus Annus* did intend to open a new papal dialogue with the United States. It is, in fact, a challenge to all.

Truth and Democracy

Atheistic humanism may have been a dead letter, but John Paul detected on the horizon a new secularist ideology that posed a serious threat to the future of freedom. The caution he raised on this front gave rise to another controversy about *Centesimus Annus*, and set the context for the Pope's commentary on the post–Cold War world throughout the 1990s.

In John Paul's comprehensive view of the human condition, questions of "ought"—moral questions—emerge at every juncture. That conviction put John Paul on a collision course with theorists of democracy for whom democratic politics was by definition value-neutral. The Pope did not avoid the confrontation, stating his position unambiguously, even bluntly.

If democracies believed themselves so vindicated by the collapse of communism that they could ignore their own moral-cultural foundations, they were in serious danger, not from without, but from within. One finds, the Pope notes, frequent suggestions that "agnosticism and skeptical relativism are the philosophy and the basic attitude which correspond to democratic forms of political life." Those who believe that they know the truth are sometimes suspect as democrats, for they "do not accept that truth is determined by the majority, or that it is subject to variation according to different political trends." Concerns about democracy's future are better directed elsewhere, John Paul argues, for if "there is no ultimate truth to guide and direct political activity, then ideas and convictions can easily be manipulated for reasons of power." Twentieth-century history, he concludes, had shown how "a democracy without values easily turns into open or thinly disguised totalitarianism."[112]

It was a theme that John Paul had been developing for almost thirteen years, but the last word stung. Surely, critics said, the Pope was not suggesting that the countries which had successfully defended freedom from two twentieth-century totalitarianisms now risked emulating the evil systems that had been defeated or had collapsed?

That was precisely what he was suggesting, but with a crucial difference. A new form of tyranny, all the more dangerous for not recognizing itself as such, was encoded in those secularist ideologies that sought to banish transcendent moral standards from public life. The danger was not all that difficult to imagine. If a democracy did not recognize such a transcendent moral standard, the only way to resolve conflict within it was the exercise of raw force by one faction (imposing its will through legislation or by more violent means) over another. The aggrieved faction, in turn, would regard the imposition of a solution as a violation of its basic rights. The net result would be the dissolution of the democratic political community.

This was, or used to be, a matter of basic democratic theory. The grim experience of Weimar Germany—a splendidly constructed democratic edifice resting on a wholly inadequate moral-cultural foundation—was thought to have illustrated it. John Paul seemed to think that the point was being forgotten, particularly in the West.

The 1990s would vindicate that judgment, and he would return to the theme of truth-and-democracy in two other major teaching documents.

A Statement of Faith and Hope

Throughout the pontificate, *Laborem Exercens* remained John Paul's personal favorite among his three social encyclicals. But *Centesimus Annus* is destined to be the most debated of the three well into the twenty-first century. The breadth of issues it addressed, its personalist reading of economics, and its distinctive cultural approach to history combine to assure it a considerable audience— even as its readers continue to differ on its implications for specific public policy issues. The encyclical was a bitter disappointment to Catholic socialists and to advocates of a "Catholic third way," some of whom invested considerable energy in the 1990s trying to explain that the encyclical did not say what it plainly said. Those curious interpretations notwithstanding, *Centesimus Annus* set a course that no future social encyclical can ignore. In that sense, it redirected the trajectory of Catholic social doctrine even as it commemorated its origins.

Beyond the quarrels of theologians and commentators, *Centesimus Annus* was well-received because it was an extraordinary statement of faith and hope. At the end of a century in which humanity had become afraid of what it might be capable of doing, John Paul spoke a word of faith in freedom, and in the human capacity to order public life in decency and justice. His proposal was all the more compelling because it was not the product of optimism but of a transcendent hope, born of faith in God, and in the human person God had created with intelligence and free will—a moral agent capable of building a truly free and virtuous society.

WAR IN THE GULF

The Pope's anticipation of an extended post–Cold War period of rationality, dialogue, solidarity, and the peaceful settlement of international disputes was badly jarred, and the Holy See's capacity to act in the new world disorder severely tested, when Iraqi dictator Saddam Hussein invaded Kuwait on August 2, 1990, commenced a reign of terror, and attempted to annex the oil-rich desert sheikhdom as Iraq's nineteenth province.

According to one senior Vatican diplomat, the Holy See's "framework-setting response" to the Persian Gulf crisis was John Paul II's Sunday Angelus address of August 26, 1990.[113] The Iraqi invasion of Kuwait, the Pope said, involved "a serious violation of international rights and of the United Nations' Charter, as well as of principles of ethics which must govern life among peoples." Because of it, trust was eroding among nations, the "international order, built up at the cost of painstaking effort and the sacrifice of many human lives" was threatened, and the probable economic consequences on poor countries were severe. John Paul prayed that political leaders might find a "just solution to the current problems" while at the same time trying to bring peace to the peoples of the whole Middle East.[114] From that point on, as one of its architects later said, the Holy See's "diplomatic action was aimed at resuming international order through peaceful means," while underlining "other cases of international illegality" in the region, including "Lebanon and the Holy Land," on the principle that longstanding problems should not be forgotten in the attempt to resolve this crisis.[115]

Throughout the fall, as a United States–led coalition of Western and Arab states built up its forces in the Gulf, the Pope made more than a dozen public and private appeals for a peaceful resolution of the conflict. Perhaps the most dramatic was his *Urbi et Orbi* address "to the city and the world" on Christmas Day, 1990. Written in a kind of blank verse, one part of the message struck an almost apocalyptic note:

The Light of Christ
is with the tormented Nations of the Middle East.
For the area of the Gulf, we await with trepidation
for the threat of conflict to disappear.
May leaders be convinced
that *war is an adventure with no return!*[116]

Soon after New Year's Day, 1991, as the UN-set deadline for an Iraqi withdrawal from Kuwait approached and Saddam Hussein continued to dig in his forces, the Pope and the Holy See realized, in the words of Vatican "foreign minister" Archbishop Jean-Louis Tauran, that "the international community was going to reinstitute order through war."[117] In light of that appraisal, John Paul took three more initiatives. On January 4, he wrote a letter to the foreign ministers of Europe, meeting in Luxembourg, urging another effort at a negotiated settlement; the apocalyptic tone was, once again, prominent in the Pope's letter, which referred to "the imminence of an armed confrontation with unforeseeable but certainly disastrous consequences," and argued that "dialogue and negotiation prevail over the recourse to instruments of devastating and terrifying death."[118] On January 11, the Pope sent a message to UN Secretary-General Javier Pérez de Cuellar, supporting the Secretary-General's last-minute mission to Baghdad to find a negotiated settlement, and expressing the hope that "ultimately dialogue, reason, and law may prevail and thus choices with disastrous, unforeseeable consequences may be avoided."[119]

Finally, on January 15, John Paul sent appeals to Presidents Saddam Hussein and George Bush through the Iraqi and American ambassadors to the Holy See.[120] His message to Saddam asked the Iraqi president to make a peace initiative, which "cannot fail to bring you honor before your beloved country, the region, and the whole world." The message to President Bush repeated the Pope's "firm belief that war is not likely to bring an adequate solution to international problems and that, even though an unjust situation might be momentarily met, the consequences that would possibly derive from war would be devastating and tragic. We cannot pretend that the use of arms, and especially of today's highly sophisticated weaponry, would not give rise, in addition to suffering and destruction, to new and perhaps worse injustices." John Paul acknowledged that the American president had "clearly weighed all these factors," but reiterated his "hope that, through a last-minute effort at dialogue, sovereignty may be restored to the people of Kuwait and that international order which is the basis for a co-existence between people truly worthy of mankind may be reestablished in the Gulf area and in the entire Middle East."[121] At 7 o'clock that night, Archbishop Tauran received the U.S. ambassador to the Holy See, Thomas P. Melady. The two men discussed Rwanda and Burundi, in which they both had longstanding interests. The Gulf situation was not mentioned.[122]

The next day, January 16, John Paul II telephoned President Bush to say that, while he was still praying for a peaceful resolution of the conflict, he hoped the Allies would win and that there would be few casualties if it came to war.[123] With combat imminent, John Paul seemed to be making a plea for restraint in the conduct of the war, while underlining that the Holy See recognized that a gross violation of justice and international law had taken place in the invasion of Kuwait. Evidently, there was some concern that this point was getting lost in the Pope's insistent appeals for a negotiated settlement.

At 1:10 A.M. on January 17, Archbishop Tauran got a phone call from a reporter asking him whether he was aware that the air war in the Gulf had begun. At the same time, Italian President Francesco Cossiga called the new Pro-Secretary of State, Archbishop Angelo Sodano, with the same news.

During the air war of January-February 1991 and the brief ground war of February 24 to 28, John Paul II made twenty-five more appeals for a just peace in the Gulf. On March 4–5, the Pope convened a meeting of bishops from all the countries involved in the Gulf War, including the seven patriarchs of the Catholic Churches in the Middle East, representatives from the episcopates of Belgium, France, Great Britain, Italy, North Africa, and the United States, officials of the Roman Curia, and Cardinal Carlo Martini, President of the Council of European Bishops' Conferences.[124] The Pope and his diplomats had decided that it was time to start thinking about the postwar period and the Church's position in the Middle East.[125] As it happened, the political aftermath of the war John Paul had resisted for so long helped to create the possibility of a dramatic diplomatic breakthrough he had sought for years.

An Assessment

In addition to vindicating international law and the moral principles that gave it force, the Holy See's concerns during the 1990–1991 Gulf crisis included the precarious position of the minority Christian communities throughout the Middle East (many of which were under extreme pressure from Arab and Islamic states) and the future of negotiations over the status of the Holy Land, which had been a major issue in Vatican diplomacy throughout the twentieth century.[126] John Paul II's convictions about a Church engaging world politics through moral witness and persuasion also influenced the Pope's initiatives during the crisis. John Paul did not believe that the Pope's role in such a crisis was to conduct a public review of the classic criteria legitimating a just war, and then give a pontifical blessing to the use of armed force if those criteria had been met. The Church's mission in world politics was to teach the relevant moral principles that ought to guide international statecraft. Beyond that, it was the responsibility of statesmen to make prudential judgments on the question of when nonviolent means of resolving a conflict and restoring order had been exhausted.[127] In this sense, John Paul's constant appeals for a negotiated solution to the Gulf crisis, and his efforts to keep the Holy See in dialogue with all the parties to the conflict, fit the pattern of his entire pontificate.

Other factors entered into the Holy See's analysis and diplomacy. Neither

John Paul personally nor the Vatican institutionally had the kind of relationship with the new Bush administration that had existed with the Reagan administration. Under President Reagan, Vatican officials and the Pope himself had been regularly briefed and consulted about American thinking and policy in world affairs. Officials of the Holy See complained during the Gulf crisis and afterward that U.S. Secretary of State James A. Baker, III, never stopped in Rome during his frequent shuttles to the Middle East and the Persian Gulf in 1990–1991. (That Baker's 687-page memoir does not mention John Paul II once suggests that the Vatican complaint was not groundless, and that the Bush administration had a very different view of the Holy See's role in world affairs than its predecessor.[128])

U.S. Ambassador Melady had been provided by the U.S. Department of State with a series of talking points laying out the Bush administration's case. In his memoirs, Ambassador Melady does not suggest that he pressed that case vigorously with Vatican officials. Rather, he raised questions about the attacks on U.S. policy that appeared in *L'Osservatore Romano*, the semi-official Vatican newspaper, and in *Civiltà Cattolica*, a Jesuit-edited journal with historic linkages to the Holy See's Secretariat of State.[129] The net result was that senior officials of the Holy See did not seem persuaded that the United States and its coalition allies had exhausted every peaceful possibility of resolving the conflict.[130] Some thought that President Bush had decided on a violent ejection of Saddam Hussein from Kuwait at the beginning of the crisis. The U.S. administration's failure to consult broadly and regularly with the Vatican, despite the access that was available, had a considerable impact on Vatican perceptions of American intentions and policies, and thus on the positions taken by the Holy See.

Making the situation even more complex inside the Vatican was the fact that the Secretariat of State itself underwent a major change in leadership during the Gulf crisis. Cardinal Agostino Casaroli had retired as Secretary of State on December 1, 1990, and was succeeded by the former "foreign minister" and nuncio in Chile, Archbishop Angelo Sodano. Sodano was succeeded as Secretary of the Section for Relations with States by Archbishop Jean-Louis Tauran, a French veteran of the Holy See's diplomatic service who had been Sodano's deputy. Sodano was not experienced in Persian Gulf or Middle Eastern affairs, unlike Tauran, who had spent years in Lebanon, and was not likely in his first weeks in office to be a center of initiative. The Holy See entered the most heated phase of the Gulf crisis with a new diplomatic leadership that, in addition to dealing with the political complexities of the situation, had to cope with a Catholic patriarch in Baghdad, Rafaël Bidawid, who had publicly defended the Iraqi aggression in Kuwait and was given to telling the press during his frequent visits to Rome that Saddam Hussein was a "real gentleman."[131]

Years after the Gulf War had ended, with the Iraqis expelled from Kuwait but with Saddam Hussein still in power in Baghdad and still causing grave problems domestically and internationally, senior officials of the Holy See argued that John Paul II had been "prophetic" in his claim that war would not solve the problem in the Persian Gulf.[132] That was certainly true at one level of analysis. Given the obligation to see a just war through to a morally satisfactory political conclusion, though, an equally plausible case could be made that it was not the use of force to expel Saddam from Kuwait that rendered the Pope's statements prophetic, but the Bush administration's failures in the endgame of the war, which were caused in part by its phobia about long-term U.S. involvement in reconstructing a post-Saddam Iraq.

For centuries, the Catholic Church had been one of the chief institutional custodians of the just-war tradition of moral reasoning, which since the days of St. Augustine had attempted to direct the use of armed force to morally worthy political goals. The quality of the Catholic debate during and after the Gulf crisis raised serious questions about the degree to which that tradition was still "received" in Catholic thinking. Some months after the war, the Jesuit editors of *Civiltà Cattolica* published an editorial suggesting that no modern war could satisfy the tradition's criteria for a just use of force. The article was so confused conceptually and so misinformed empirically that a notable Jesuit scholar of the just-war tradition labeled parts of the editorial a "willful defiance of the facts" while shredding its argumentation.[133] Another distinguished historian of the just-war tradition, reflecting on the papal addresses during the Gulf War and other developments in Catholic just-war thinking, argued that the Church had, in effect, turned the tradition inside out. Contingent judgments about possible outcomes now outweighed the classic tradition's overriding moral concern that justice be done, to the point where "resort to force is effectively questioned or denied even when there is a just cause."[134] John Paul II was sufficiently concerned that his appeals for peace were being interpreted as declaring pacifism the Church's normative moral position that he felt compelled to say, on February 17, 1991, "We are not pacifist at any cost."[135] There is no doubt, however, that the Pope's apocalyptic rhetoric about the possible effects of armed force in the Gulf was used by those who argued against military intervention on just-war or pacifist grounds to buttress their position.

Just-war reasoning involves rigorous empirical analysis, which was sometimes lacking in the Holy See's approach to the Gulf crisis. The assumption that more "dialogue" could coax Saddam Hussein into withdrawing from Kuwait and making restitution for the wreckage he had caused was never very persuasive, given what was already known about his grisly internal record in Iraq (using poison gas, for example, to kill 5,000 men, women, and children in the Kurdish town of Halabja) and his evident willingness to shed blood wholesale in his catastrophic war with Iran.[136] Nor did Holy See proposals for negotiation seem to take sufficient account of the likelihood that delays in military action heightened the chance that Iraq could deploy weapons of mass destruction. Exaggerated predictions of the direct effects of military action in the Gulf have already been noted.

It was curious that the Holy See, perhaps the single most consistent proponent of international security institutions in the twentieth century, should have found itself opposing the United Nations during one of the very few broad-based "collective security" exercises in living memory. A plausible case could be made that, in the Gulf crisis, the UN functioned precisely as the Holy See had urged it to function for decades. Yet the Holy See was broadly perceived as being in opposition. Further, the record it established in the Gulf crisis did not help the Holy See make its argument for "humanitarian intervention" in the Balkan turmoil that was soon to unfold in the wake of Yugoslavia's political disintegration.

Had the Secretariat of State undertaken a more rigorous empirical analysis of the situation, and had classic just-war categories been more evident in John Paul's public addresses, the Pope's appeals for peace might have elevated the international debate, as he had done so effectively in the past.[137] John Paul's difficult search for a language to express his sense of a pope's appropriate role in such a crisis, combined with the problems of transition in the Secretariat of State and the U.S. failure to consult adequately with the Holy See, lead to the conclusion that the Vatican's performance in the Gulf War crisis between August 1990 and March 1991 did not meet the high standards set in the previous twelve years of the pontificate.

FROM THE HEART OF THE CHURCH

As in any other crisis, John Paul II had numerous other issues to contend with during the pre–Gulf War debate, the war itself, and its aftermath. He received bishops from India, Brazil, the Philippines, South Korea, Bolivia, Vietnam, Taiwan, and eight regions of Italy on *ad limina* visits to Rome. A meeting with representatives of the Brazilian Bishops' Conference was held on March 8–9, 1991, to review with leading members of the Roman Curia the themes discussed during the Brazilians' 1990–1991 cycle of *ad limina* consultations. On August 17, John Paul sent a letter of congratulations to Brother Roger Schutz for the fiftieth anniversary of the ecumenical monastery at Taizé. Ten days later, on August 27, Mr. and Mrs. Lech Wałęsa came to visit at Castel Gandolfo; the same day, a three-day meeting to prepare for a special Synod of Bishops for European episcopates on both sides of the former iron curtain began.[138] On September 14 the Pope met with the dissident Chinese physicist and pro-democracy activist Feng Lizhi, after addressing a meeting of astrophysicists at Castel Gandolfo. On September 28, John Paul received a group of ex-Lefebvrist monks who had been reconciled to Rome through the Ecclesia Dei Commission. The Eighth Ordinary Assembly of the Synod of Bishops met in October 1990. Germany was reunified on October 3, and on October 16 John Paul sent a telegram to Mikhail Gorbachev, congratulating him on winning the Nobel Peace Prize.

On October 8, John Paul received the credentials of Hans-Joachim Hallier, the new ambassador of united Germany, telling him that "the Second World War . . . came to an end on October 3."[139] On November 8, Cardinal

Alfonso López Trujillo, the former Secretary-General and President of the Latin American bishops' council, was named President of the Pontifical Council for the Family; several months later, over lunch, John Paul urged the Colombian cardinal to organize a series of seminars for the world's bishops on married life and bioethics.[140] The Pope delivered a blistering critique of the Mafia during a four-day pastoral visit to Naples and Campania from November 9 to 13, coming back to Rome in time to receive Soviet President Gorbachev on his second visit, which took place on November 18. Gorbachev had been memorizing Bible verses to drop into their conversation.[141] On December 9, Lech Wałęsa was elected President of Poland. A week after that, and in defiance of orders from his religious superiors, a young priest named Jean-Bertrand Aristide was elected President of Haiti. On January 18, Archbishop Camillo Ruini, a former seminary professor serving as Secretary-General of the Italian Bishops' Conference, was named the Pope's vicar for the diocese of Rome, succeeding the retiring Cardinal Ugo Poletti. On January 20, the Polish bishops' letter marking the twenty-fifth anniversary of *Nostra Aetate* was read in all Polish churches. President Wałęsa made a state visit to the Vatican on February 5. Father Pedro Arrupe, SJ, was buried on February 8.

During this same exceptionally busy period, John Paul took up the question of Catholic universities in an apostolic constitution that seemed likely to shape Catholic intellectual life well into the twenty-first century, and perhaps beyond.

Ex Corde Ecclesiae

Karol Wojtyła's piety about the university and what it represents in the world of human culture dates back to his student days at the Jagiellonian in Kraków. It intensified during his years on the faculty at Lublin, in part because Lublin represented an oasis of truth in a desert of lies. Six months after his election as pope, in April 1979, John Paul had issued the apostolic constitution *Sapientia Christiana* [Christian Wisdom], regulating the universities and faculties that receive a special charter from the Holy See and are thus deemed "pontifical universities" or "pontifical faculties." Now, in 1990, he issued another apostolic constitution, *Ex Corde Ecclesiae* [From the Heart of the Church], to chart the future of all Catholic institutions of higher education, the great majority of which are not "pontifical." The apostolic constitution was signed on the solemnity of the Assumption, August 15, and was publicly presented at a press conference on September 25, 1990.[142]

Ex Corde Ecclesiae was an initiative of the Curia's Congregation for Catholic Education, which believed it necessary to complete the work of *Sapientia Christiana*. John Paul II had "real input" into the writing and rewriting of the document, according to a senior official involved in the process.[143] Its opening section bears the distinctive personal mark of Karol Wojtyła's thinking about the nature of a Catholic university, which ought to be the repository and defender of "a kind of universal humanism [that is] . . . completely dedicated to the research of all aspects of truth in their essential connection with the supreme Truth, who is God." This was not a burden, for all knowledge was a reflection of Christ the *Logos*, the Word through whom the world was created, and who "alone is capable of giving fully that Wisdom without which the future of the world would be in danger."[144]

There had been major changes in Catholic universities and colleges since Vatican II, and *Ex Corde Ecclesiae* was an attempt to give direction to their future evolution. To Catholic universities and colleges whose sense of Catholic identity had become attenuated, or who were unclear about the distinctive character of a Catholic institution of higher education, the document urged retrieving the idea that the Catholic college or university is part of the mission of the Church. As the document's title indicated, these were institutions that had grown "from the heart of the Church," and their life should reflect that. *Ex Corde Ecclesiae* also tried to rebuild the relationship between Catholic institutions of higher education and bishops, who "should be seen not as external agents but as participants in the life of the Catholic University."[145]

These ideas about the nature and mission of the Catholic university were then concretized in eleven "norms."[146] The most controversial of them in some countries stated that "Catholic theologians, aware that they fulfill a mandate from the Church, are to be faithful to the Magisterium of the Church as the authentic interpreter of Sacred Scripture and Sacred Tradition." This was a specification of Canon 812 in the new Code of Canon Law, which stated that "it is necessary that those who teach theological disciplines in any institute of higher studies have a mandate from the competent ecclesiastical authority"— which in most instances meant the local bishop. *Sapientia Christiana* had made it clear that theologians at pontifically chartered faculties must have this "mandate." *Ex Corde Ecclesiae* extended the requirement of the mandate to theologians in all Catholic colleges and universities, who were required to make a profession of faith according to a formula established by the Congregation for the Doctrine of the Faith in 1989.[147] Specific local norms for the application of these general norms were to be developed by the national conferences of bishops.

Ex Corde Ecclesiae was well-received in Spain and Latin America, where the "mandate" was not thought a problem and where ecclesiastical authority and instruments (like diplomas and degrees) were regarded as credentials in civil society. In France and Italy, the apostolic constitution's description of the mission of the Catholic university was also well-received, but there was resistance to devising local applications of the norms, on the theory that the Catholic character of the institution was assured by the spirit of the individuals in it, not by legal structures. The question *Ex Corde Ecclesiae* raised, even for institutions where that was true today, was how that character was to be preserved over time as faculties, administrators, and intellectual fashions changed.[148]

The most negative reaction to the "mission" section of *Ex Corde Ecclesiae* and its norms came from the United States. The dominant tendency among American Catholic higher education leaders and the theological community was to frame discussion of the document in terms of Vatican interference with their institutional autonomy and academic freedom. This reaction grew out of a particular history.

Catholic colleges and universities in the United States had been built, in the main, at a time when the Church considered itself an enclave against the wider culture. When Vatican II challenged the Church to engage the modern world, it may well have seemed to many Catholic educators that the choice was between being an enclave and emulating American elite educational institutions.[149] The intention of the Catholic college and university presidents who met for a crucial 1967 planning session at Land O'Lakes, Wisconsin, was to move Catholic higher education into the ranks of the country's culture-forming leadership, and institutional autonomy from Church supervision was considered essential in that effort. But the Land O'Lakes meeting overestimated the amount of Catholic capital available to be drawn on in this process, and looked to elite American colleges and universities for models of "independence" at the precise moment when those schools were in intellectual and moral turmoil. The resulting effort to sever the legal control that had been exercised by bishops or religious orders over Catholic colleges and universities effectively, if unintentionally, cut these institutions loose from their intellectual moorings in the midst of a major cultural crisis. Twenty years after the Land O'Lakes meeting, there were important changes in the thinking of some American Catholic higher educators, and an increasing awareness that something had gone seriously awry in Catholic higher education in the United States since Vatican II. *Ex Corde Ecclesiae* was intended to help advance this reflection even further, but confusions about academic excellence and academic freedom in a distinctively Catholic context impeded the document's reception.[150]

The debate over the Catholic identity of Catholic colleges and universities would continue throughout the pontificate.[151] Granting its entanglement with a host of other issues and concerns, that debate was, at bottom, another expression of John Paul II's conviction that, after the death of the empire of lies, the crucial question for free societies old and new was the relationship between freedom and truth. It was a theme he would pursue tirelessly, even relentlessly, in the years ahead, as he sought to apply the lessons of the Revolution of 1989 to the emerging world of the twenty-first century.

17

To the Ends of the Earth

Reconciling an Unreconciled World

DECEMBER 7, 1990	*Redemptoris Missio,* Pope John Paul II's eighth encyclical.
APRIL 13, 1991	John Paul establishes three apostolic administrations in the Soviet Union.
JUNE 1–9, 1991	The Pope's fourth pastoral visit to Poland.
JUNE 28, 1991	At his fifth consistory John Paul creates twenty-three new cardinals.
AUGUST 14–15, 1991	John Paul addresses third international World Youth Day, in Częstochowa, Poland.
OCTOBER 2, 1991	Ecumenical Patriarch Dimitrios I dies, and is succeeded on October 22 by Ecumenical Patriarch Bartholomew I.
NOVEMBER 28– DECEMBER 14, 1991	The Special Assembly for Europe of the Synod of Bishops meets in Rome.
JANUARY 13, 1992	The Holy See recognizes the independence of Croatia and Slovenia.
MARCH 25, 1992	Polish hierarchy re-organized.
MAY 13, 1992	The Pope announces that a World Day of the Sick will be observed annually on February 11, feast of Our Lady of Lourdes.
JULY 15, 1992	John Paul has surgery for the removal of a benign intestinal tumor.
SEPTEMBER 21, 1992	The Holy See establishes full diplomatic relations with Mexico.
OCTOBER 9–14, 1992	John Paul participates in fourth general conference of Latin American bishops in Santo Domingo.
OCTOBER 31, 1992	John Paul II receives report of the papal commission on the Galileo case and urges new dialogue between science and religion.
DECEMBER 5, 1992	The Pope asserts a "duty" of "humanitarian intervention" in cases of impending genocide.

DECEMBER 7, 1992	Public presentation of the *Catechism of the Catholic Church*.
JANUARY 12 AND 15, 1993	John Paul declares the "hour of the laity" in Polish Catholicism and rejects a partisan Church in two *ad limina* addresses to Polish bishops.
FEBRUARY 10, 1993	During his tenth African pilgrimage, John Paul condemns persecution of Sudanese Christians in address at Khartoum.
APRIL 9, 1993	John Paul writes the Carmelite nuns living in a convent just outside the Auschwitz concentration camp, asking them to continue their ministry in a new location.
APRIL 25, 1993	The Pope ordains four new bishops in Albania.
MAY 8–10, 1993	John Paul makes his most vigorous protest against the Mafia during three-day pilgrimage to Sicily.
JUNE 17–24, 1993	Roman Catholic/Orthodox consultation in Balamand, Lebanon, attempts to repair ecumenical divisions of post-communist period.
SEPTEMBER 4–10, 1993	Papal pilgrimage to Lithuania, Latvia, and Estonia.

In the second half of the second Christian millennium, no incident had done more to sustain the image of the Catholic Church as an authoritarian enemy of human progress than the seventeenth-century Galileo case, in which the pioneering Florentine scientist was condemned by the Church for holding and teaching Copernicus's theory that the sun, not the earth, was the center of the solar system. Galileo, who would spend the last eight years of his life under house arrest, was forced to make a humiliating public retraction—after which he is said to have muttered, "*Eppur' si muove*" [Yet it moves . . .].

As a cultural myth, the Galileo affair had affected far more than the Church's relations with modern science. Scratch the surface of any controversy involving Catholics and modern intellectual, social, or political life, and "Galileo" was sure to be played as a trump card by the Church's opponents. Careful historical investigation had shown that the entire affair was far more complicated than, say, the Marxist playwright Bertolt Brecht had made it out. At the time of the controversy, for example, the heliocentric theory was not well-established and Galileo was in fact challenging the scientific consensus of his time. No amount of historical research, however, could explode the myth of Catholicism's incompatibility with modern science and freedom of inquiry. Only the Church could do that—or try to.

John Paul II, fellow graduate with Copernicus of Kraków's Jagiellonian University, was determined to try. The truth demanded it. So did the evangelization of the twenty-first century.

On July 31, 1981, John Paul had established a study commission to reexamine the entire Galileo case. Under the leadership of Cardinal Paul Poupard, President of the Pontifical Council for Culture, its research on the theological, biblical, scientific, historical, and legal questions involved was brought to a conclusion in 1992, the 350th anniversary of Galileo's death. On October 31, 1992, John Paul met with the members of the Pontifical Academy of Sciences in the Sala Regia of the Apostolic Palace to accept the commission's report. Members of the diplomatic corps, a bevy of cardinals and other high-ranking Church officials, and the members of the Pontifical Council for Culture were present for what all expected to be a historic event.

Cardinal Poupard reported on the interdisciplinary research done during the past eleven years on the difficult relationship between Galileo, a sincere Christian believer, and the Church. The Commission noted that St. Robert Bellarmine, one of the leading theologians of the day and a bulwark of Catholic orthodoxy, had urged prudence in thinking through the relationship between what seemed persuasive (if not irrefutable) scientific evidence, on the one hand, and what were thought to be basic (although possibly reformable) theological propositions arising from the Bible, on the other. In circumstances like this, Bellarmine proposed, it was much better "to say that we do not understand, rather than affirm as false what has been demonstrated." That, Cardinal Poupard continued, Galileo's judges had not done. "Incapable of dissociating faith from an age-old cosmology," they believed, sincerely, "that the adoption of the Copernican revolution . . . was such as to undermine Catholic tradition, and that it was their duty to forbid its being taught." In this, the cardinal said, they had been seriously mistaken. "This subjective error of judgment, so clear to us today, led them to a disciplinary measure from which Galileo 'had much to suffer.'" Turning to the Pope, whose words in 1979 he had just quoted, the French prelate then concluded, "These mistakes must be frankly recognized, as you, Holy Father, have requested."

John Paul thanked Cardinal Poupard for the commission's work. Its conclusions, he said, "will be impossible to ignore in the future." An objective error had been made, which had to be recognized and repented, no matter how complex the subjective motivations involved. The Church had just done that. But now what? What had been learned from this experience?

It could not be blithely assumed, the Pope said, that something like this would never happen again. The Church was not going away, and neither was science. The possibility could not be excluded that "one day we shall find ourselves in a similar situation, one which will require both sides to have an informed awareness of the field and of the limits of their own competencies."

History, literary studies, biblical interpretation, philosophy, and theology had all had to reexamine their procedures and their age-old assumptions because of the scientific method. But science, too, had things to reflect upon in light of the developments of the last several centuries, John Paul suggested. Science was not simply a matter of empirical facts. In describing "the data of experience" and drawing conclusions from it, scientists made use of concepts that were beyond the empirical. Scientists needed philosophers, just as philosophers had come to recognize that they needed scientists.

The same lesson applied to the Church and theology. In confronting

scientific advances, theologians and pastors "ought to show a genuine boldness, avoiding the double trap of a hesitant attitude and of hasty judgment"
about new scientific discoveries. It was essential for theologians "to keep
themselves informed of scientific advances in order to examine . . . whether
or not there are reasons for taking them into account in their reflection or
for introducing changes in their teaching." At the same time, the Pope proposed, everyone should recognize that the Galileo affair had become a "sort
of myth" which had helped to "anchor a number of scientists of good faith
in the idea that there was an incompatibility between the spirit of science
and its rules of research . . . and the Christian faith." That, in turn, had led
to "a tragic mutual incomprehension," based on the notion of "a fundamental opposition between science and faith."

That could not be true, for as Pope Leo XIII had written, "Truth cannot
contradict truth." If that seemed to be happening, a mistake had been made
somewhere. There were different ways of knowing the truth about the human
person and the human place in the cosmos. A genuine humanism respected
that diversity, and celebrated the plurality of intellectual methods necessary to
probe the human condition in its marvelous complexity. Science and theology
were "two realms of knowledge" that should not regard themselves as locked
inexorably in opposition. The Church recognized that. The question now was
whether science did.

The Galileo case had compelled the Church to examine its conscience
and to recommit itself to the ancient Christian conviction that all genuine
knowledge was welcome, because it shed light upon the mystery of the human
person the Church existed to serve. The challenge for the twenty-first century,
John Paul suggested, was for the experimental sciences to commit themselves
to a genuinely humanistic perspective, in which the full truth of the human
condition, including the spiritual dimension of experience, was part of the
conversation about the greatest mystery in the universe—the mystery that is
every human life.[1]

STEADY COMPASS

In the years immediately following the 1991 collapse of the Soviet Union, it
quickly became a truism that the post–Cold War world was an uncharted
wilderness without benchmarks or guideposts. Like every other institution on
the planet, the Church faced a confusingly diverse international situation.

The world's leading powers shied away from maintaining order in the
Balkans and in the Lakes Region of central Africa, where hundreds of thousands
died because there was no persuasive answer to the question of why the victors
in the Cold War should put their sons and daughters in harm's way. Nothing had
yet taken the place of bipolarity and containment as a matrix for thinking about
the new world disorder and devising policy for bringing order out of chaos.

Among academics and pundits, the collapse of communism was generally agreed to have been the result of its misguided economics, which had made it impossible for the Soviet Union and its satellites to compete in a world dominated by the silicon chip and the fiber-optic cable. This was, ironically, an essentially Marxist answer to the demise of Marxism, and illustrated just how deeply economic determinism had entered into the thinking of Western scholars and commentators.

Within the victorious democracies, the meaning of the end of the Cold War was never publicly defined—in part, for fear of aggravating an aggrieved Soviet Union during its collapse, and thus jeopardizing the reunification of Germany within the Western alliance; in part, because the cluster of politicians who succeeded the leaders of the 1980s lacked the historical imagination to see the parallels between 1945 and 1989/1991. Without a compelling public proclamation of freedom's victory over tyranny, tens of millions of Western Europeans and North Americans were left wondering what the struggle of the previous forty-five years had been about. This deficiency in public understanding, in turn, fueled two post–Cold War instincts in the established democracies: to withdraw from world politics into domestic concerns, and to think of freedom as liberation from any traditional moral code, rather than as a method for seeking the truth and conducting public life in ways that advanced the common good.[2]

Just as he had had a different view of the nature of the Cold War than most politicians and international relations specialists, Pope John Paul II had a different view of the world's post–Cold War situation.

In the Pope's mind, the fundamental crisis of modernity remained unresolved. The inalienable dignity of the human person was still threatened in the post–Cold War world, by new authoritarians, retooled ex-communists (or "post-communists," as they were known in central and eastern Europe), and utilitarians. Then there was the question of the moral structure of the free society. As *Centesimus Annus* should have made clear, John Paul passionately believed in the free society. His encyclical had, in fact, offered a more detailed blueprint for building and sustaining such a society than was on offer anywhere else. To the Pope's way of thinking, though, the free society was threatened by the drift toward what Zbigniew Brzeziński called the "permissive cornucopia."[3] Unbridled material appetites, John Paul believed, were another form of tyranny.

Just as culture had been the key to defeating communism, culture would be the key to building a twenty-first century capable of fulfilling the aspirations of those who had struggled so long against communist tyranny. Free economies and democratic political communities were crucial components of the post–Cold War free society. As *Centesimus Annus* had argued, though, neither the free economy nor democracy was a machine that runs by itself. Both needed the foundation, boundaries, and discipline provided by a vibrant public moral culture if freedom was to fulfill itself in genuine human flourishing.

John Paul's compass was unaffected by the atmospheric turbulence of the post–Cold War 1990s. Jesus Christ remained the answer to the question that was every human life. And that was an "answer" with large public consequences.

THE EVANGELICAL IMPERATIVE

John Paul II's charter for the Church of the third millennium was his eighth encyclical, *Redemptoris Missio* [The Mission of the Redeemer], which he signed on December 7, 1990, to mark the twenty-fifth anniversary of Vatican II's Decree on the Church's Missionary Activity.[4] The post-conciliar Church had been divided over the question of what kind of mission the Church had. John Paul insisted that the Church didn't simply *have* a mission. The Church *is* a mission.[5]

In the world as a whole, the Christian movement claimed some 2 billion members, of whom approximately 1 billion were Roman Catholics. Measured numerically, the twentieth century had seen the greatest expansion of Christianity in history. For example, in 1900 there were about 2 million Catholics in Africa; by the end of the century there were almost 100 million.[6] Yet Christianity's development had not kept pace with population growth. During the twentieth century, Christians decreased slightly as a percentage of total world population, from 34.4 percent to 33.2 percent.[7] Some areas of the world—notably the Indian subcontinent and East Asia—remained essentially unevangelized.

In the wake of Vatican II, however, various Catholic theologians had suggested that the Church's mission *ad gentes*, "to the nations" of the unevangelized, was over. Some argued that evangelization today was simply work for justice. Others proposed that, in a post-colonial world, a Christian mission *ad gentes* was cultural imperialism: to evangelize was to impose, and the Church should go to the non-Christian world to learn from the faiths of others, not to teach the faith of which it was a bearer. An even more radical faction saw Jesus as simply one embodiment of a generic divine will-to-redeem that appeared in different forms in different cultures. Jesus was the redeemer for Christians, but other great world religious figures filled that "role" in other cultures.[8] In this intellectual atmosphere, it was not surprising that the post-conciliar period had seen a shrinking of Catholic missionary efforts around the world, at precisely the time when evangelical Protestantism and Islam were assertively seeking converts in Africa, Asia, and Latin America.

Catholic thinking had traditionally held that Christianity was the "ordinary" means of salvation, while God could make provision for "extraordinary" exceptions. Some Catholic thinkers were now proposing that Christianity was the "extraordinary" path. *Redemptoris Missio* was, among other things, an attempt to correct this inversion. It was also much more.

Like any encyclical of such ambitious scope, *Redemptoris Missio* grew from several roots. One was an international congress on the theme of "salvation today," held in early 1988 at the Church's Roman missionary university, the

Pontifical Urban University. Cardinal Jozef Tomko, who had been Prefect of
the Congregation for the Evangelization of Peoples (the curial department
responsible for Catholic missions throughout the world) since 1985, decided
to stage what he later termed a "provocation" at the congress.[9] In his opening
address, Tomko confronted the entire range of proposals made by many theologians of Christian mission during the past generation. The cardinal tried
to raise questions from the vantage point of missionaries, who often found
themselves considered irrelevant—if not downright imperialistic—by "missi-
ologists," theologians of the Church's mission. What was the point of preaching Jesus Christ if Christ was not the redeemer of the world, through whom
all human beings would be saved? Why give one's life to the proclamation of
the Christian Gospel if it was simply one among a variety of possible forms of
God's revelation? How could a real dialogue with world religions take place if
Christians were unconvinced of the truth of the Gospel they preached? If evangelization was simply the promotion of justice in society, who needed a
Church? Cardinal Tomko's address caused sufficient controversy that an entire
book of essays was organized to refute it.[10] The cardinal had brought to the
surface a host of interrelated issues that, clearly, needed attention.

    "It's about time," John Paul said to Tomko, "that I say something about
all this."[11]

The Church as a Mission

While sorting out theological confusions about Christian mission and dealing
with controversies about the relationship of Christ and the Church to God's
saving will for all humanity were two purposes of *Redemptoris Missio*, it would
be a mistake to think of the encyclical as a corrective. It is, rather, a reminder
to the entire Church that every Catholic has a missionary vocation because, as
the Pope puts it, *"the Church is missionary by her very nature."*[12] The universal call
to holiness includes a universal call to evangelize. Christianity is good news that
demands to be shared, and to share Christ with others is the best possible thing
that individual Catholics and the Church can do for the world.[13] Moreover, a
radical sense of the evangelical imperative is necessary for revitalizing the
Church itself, for *"faith is strengthened when it is given to others."*[14] The impending third millennium ought to remind Catholics that the Church's mission, a
continuation of the mission of Christ himself, "is still only beginning."[15]

    That mission, John Paul writes, grows out of the twin doctrines that define
Christianity: the doctrine of God as Trinity, and the doctrine of the Incarnation—Jesus Christ as God-made-man for the salvation of the world. Because
God is a Trinity of self-giving Persons, the Church must be a community of self-
giving missionaries, teaching all nations God's self-revelation in Jesus Christ.
The Pope does not deny that there are saving elements in other world religions, but he insists throughout the encyclical that "God's revelation becomes
definitive and complete through his only-begotten Son," Jesus Christ.[16] Nor

can one disentangle "Jesus" from "Christ," such that Jesus appears as one manifestation among others of God's word to the world: "Jesus is the Incarnate Word—a single and indivisible person. One cannot separate Jesus from the Christ. . . . Christ is none other than Jesus of Nazareth; he is the Word of God made man for the salvation of all."[17]

This uniqueness gives Christ "an absolute and universal significance."[18] Whatever is true in other religions tends toward the truth revealed in Jesus Christ and reaches its fulfillment in him. The salvation offered by Christ is offered to all, even to those who have not explicitly heard Christ's Gospel or who do not formally belong to his Church. Because God wills that his salvation be offered to all, "it must be made concretely available to all," John Paul urges. That is the reason for the Church's mission to the nations. At the same time, he concedes, "many people do not have an opportunity to come to know or accept the Gospel revelation or to enter the Church." They are not necessarily lost. For them, "salvation in Christ is accessible by virtue of a grace which, while having a mysterious relationship to the Church, does not make them formally part of the Church but enlightens them in a way which is accommodated to their spiritual and material situation. This grace is from Christ; it is the result of his Sacrifice and is communicated by the Holy Spirit."[19] Whoever is saved, is saved through Jesus Christ.

If all can be saved by the mysterious workings of grace beyond the formal boundaries of the Church, why worry about mission? The encyclical offers six reasons. The Church *is* a mission by its very nature, and to lose that missionary imperative is to break with the Church of the New Testament. Christian mission is one form of obedience to the great commandment of love for one's neighbor. Christian mission is a fulfillment of our duties to others, who have a right to know about Christ so that they might have the option to believe. Christian mission strengthens unity among Christians, and impels them to deepen that unity so that the scandal of Christian division is less an obstacle to the proclamation of the Gospel. Christ has saved us, and our willingness to share his Gospel with others is an index of the degree to which we have truly understood and grasped the import of that.[20] Finally and most importantly, this is what God requires of us. Like the good shepherd who seeks out the lost sheep (see *John* 10.1–18), the Church that continues the good shepherd's mission must be missionary.[21]

To those who ask, "Who, then, is to be evangelized?" John Paul has a direct answer: everyone. That evangelization takes different forms. One is the pastoral care of the evangelized people of the Church. Another is the "new evangelization" of those who have fallen away from Christian faith or who were poorly instructed. Then there is the mission *ad gentes*, to those places "in which Christ and his Gospel are not known," or where local Christian communities are too immature to take up the challenge of mission. *Redemptoris Missio* is primarily concerned with this third form of Christian mission. The Pope suggests three criteria for developing it in the third millennium.

The first is geographic. The great failure of Christian mission in the first two millennia of Christian history is Asia, and thus it is to Asia that the mission *ad gentes* "ought to be chiefly directed."[22] The second criterion is demographic. There are new human worlds and environments in late modernity that demand the Church's missionary attention—among them John Paul notes the new "megalopolises" or massive urban areas of the developing world, young people, and migrants and refugees in traditionally Christian societies.[23] The third criterion is cultural. The mass communications media, human rights associations and advocates, the feminist movement, movements to protect children, the environmental movement, the world of science, and international legal and political institutions are the "modern equivalents of the Areopagus," waiting for a compelling proclamation of Jesus Christ as the answer to humanity's most urgent questions.[24] In dealing with them, as in dealing with ancient cultures formed by venerable religious traditions, the Church's method, the Pope insists, must be the method of freedom: "*The Church proposes; she imposes nothing.* She respects individuals and cultures, and she honors the sanctuary of conscience."[25]

Christian mission in the post–Cold War world will be lived out, John Paul suggests, in various ways. The first is example: the truth of Christianity is often more powerfully revealed by the quality of Christian lives than by explicit teaching, though the latter must complete the former.[26] People who have seen love in action may be more disposed to consider the teaching that God himself is love. In situations like India, the witness of the Missionaries of Charity is a great good in its own right and a first step toward planting the Church in that particular culture. John Paul also mentions the martyr as the most powerful witness to the truth of Christian faith.[27] Ecumenical cooperation and interreligious dialogue are two other "paths of mission." A growing unity among Christians aids the Church's witness to non-Christians, as does a serious conversation with other religious traditions in which both parties acknowledge that truths are at stake.[28]

The Pope affirms "inculturation," the effort to "translate" Christian truth claims into the idiom of a local, non-Christian culture, which must be guided by two principles: compatibility with the Gospel and communion with the universal Church. Any "inculturation" that empties the Gospel of its distinctiveness is not inculturation but accommodation. One way to test whether that is happening is to determine whether the proposed "inculturation" sets local expressions of Christian truth against the universal Church and its center of unity in the Office of Peter.[29] As for the relationship between evangelization and the pursuit of justice and peace, the Church's primary task and greatest contribution in the "development of peoples" is the formation of consciences. By "offering people an opportunity . . . to 'be more' by awakening their consciences through the Gospel," the Church serves human liberation. In that "being more," men and women will come to recognize their human dignity, the rights that flow from it, and the solidarity that ought to characterize relations among peoples and nations.[30]

The Countercultural Pope

John Paul's encyclical on Christian mission was of considerable interest in Third World mission territories, but in the developed world *Redemptoris Missio* received far less attention than *Centesimus Annus,* which was published four months later.[31] By conventional journalistic standards, *Centesimus Annus* was much more newsworthy, given its analysis of the collapse of communism, its detailed examination of the free economy, and its early warning signals about the new threats to democracy. Yet a case can be made that *Redemptoris Missio* is the most consequential of John Paul's encyclicals for both the Church and the world.

Redemptoris Missio is part of John Paul II's attempt to make the Second Vatican Council irreversible in the life of the Church. If the Council's primary aim was to renew the Church for service to the world, *Redemptoris Missio* is a deeply conciliar meditation on the greatest service the Church can provide the world: to tell the world its true story, the story of creation and fall, redemption, salvation, and sanctification. In *Redemptoris Missio,* the New Testament Church meets the Church of the third millennium—for which Vatican II, the Pope insists, was a providential preparation.

Redemptoris Missio also proposed a fresh response to certain misunderstandings. To those who insist that Christian evangelization threatens civil peace and understanding among world religions, John Paul replies that a Church which "imposes nothing" and which "honors the sanctuary of conscience" is a Church in service to all. To those Christians who believe the Church has "outgrown" evangelism and should concentrate its efforts on social change, the Pope replies that the Church ceases to be the Church when the Church ceases to preach Jesus Christ. To secularists convinced that a maturing humanity will outgrow the "need" for religion, John Paul replies that, at the end of the second millennium, "God is preparing a great springtime for Christianity, and we can already see its first signs."[32] To those offended by the very idea that some religions are true and others false, John Paul replies that the Church honors whatever truths are to be found in world religions and cultures. All truths in this world point toward the one great truth about the world, revealed by God in Jesus Christ—the world has come from God and, through the sacrifice of Christ, is destined to be consummated in God, who wills the salvation of all humanity.

Redemptoris Missio is countercultural in several other ways. John Paul insists that pluralism is more than plurality, the sheer sociological fact of religious differences. Genuine pluralism, he suggests, is plurality transformed into an orderly, truth-seeking conversation among people of divergent religious beliefs. By the same token, *Redemptoris Missio* implies that tolerance is not a matter of avoiding differences but of engaging differences respectfully, in the conviction, as one commentator put it, "that our deepest differences make all the difference, in this world and the next."[33] To those who fear that any such encounter between world religions will automatically lead to fanaticism and even religious war, John Paul replies that Christian evangelism is essential to civil society and to peace, because the civil society capable of sustaining genuine tolerance must be built upon a profound respect for the inalienable rights of human persons. Those who believe it to be the will of God that they respect the convictions of neighbors who have different convictions about God's will are more likely to respect human rights, defend religious freedom, and protect the "sanctuary of conscience" in a free and civil society.[34]

Redemptoris Missio and *Centesimus Annus* are not two dramatically different encyclicals, one meditating on an "internal" Church matter (Christian mission) and the other dealing with "the world." Both encyclicals envision a Catholicism that proposes truths, but imposes nothing. *Redemptoris Missio* reminds the Church what that proposal is, and why making it is imperative. *Centesimus Annus* spells out the public dimensions of the proposal, while reminding the Church that its fundamental public task is the formation of consciences, not political scheming or economic planning. Both encyclicals, together, define a Catholicism for the third millennium that is evangelically assertive *and* in service to the good of the whole human race. The two, John Paul insists, go together. And that is a teaching with great significance for the world beyond the boundaries of the Catholic Church. Because how Christians conceive their mission "to the world" will have much to do with how almost 2 billion human beings think about the shaping of a new century and a new millennium.

ECUMENICAL FRACTURE

The Holy See's first attempt to seize the opportunity presented by the Soviet government's new attitude toward religious freedom was poorly managed, putting John Paul's great hope for an ecumenical rapprochement with Orthodoxy in jeopardy and further complicating Rome's relations with the Greek Catholic Church in Ukraine.

As 1990 gave way to 1991, the situation was, admittedly, complex in the extreme. Seventy years of state atheism, periods of intense religious persecution, and massive population transfers before, during, and after World War II had dramatically changed the Catholic "topography" of the Soviet Union. The Gorbachev initiative on religious freedom, and the Soviet government's insistence that pastoral care for Catholics in the various Soviet "republics" not be guided by bishops in other countries (such as Poland), had made it possible to begin to regularize Catholic life in the Ukrainian Soviet Socialist Republic, where John Paul had reorganized both the Latin and Greek Catholic dioceses. At the same time, the new Vatican ambassador to the Soviet Union, Archbishop Francesco Colasuonno, had discovered a "surprising vitality" in Catholic life in Russia and Kazakhstan, where Latin-rite Catholic communities of German, Polish, Lithuanian, and Ukrainian origin had recently received legal recognition from their local governments, under the new Soviet law on religious freedom that President Gorbachev had promulgated on October 1,

1990. Something had to be done to regularize the situation of these newly recognized communities, and to provide bishops for them and the more than 1.5 million Latin-rite Catholics in the Byelorussian Soviet Socialist Republic.[35]

Responsibility for sorting all this out fell to the Holy See's Secretariat of State, which was in direct consultation, through Archbishop Colasuonno, with the Soviet government. The eventual solution involved the establishment of a metropolitan archdiocese of Minsk-Mohilev in the Byelorussian SSR with suffragan dioceses in Pinsk and Grodno.[36] At the same time, pastoral care for Catholics in Russia, Siberia, and Kazakhstan was regularized, not by creating full-fledged dioceses, but by establishing three "apostolic administrations," which the revised Code of Canon Law defined as "a certain portion of the people of God which is not erected into a diocese . . . due to particular and very serious reasons. . . ."[37] The "very serious reason" in this case was the extreme sensitivity of the Russian Orthodox Patriarchate of Moscow to anything that seemed to imply establishing a normal Catholic hierarchy and structure on the historic territory of Russian Orthodoxy. The apostolic administrations were to be located in Moscow, Novosibirsk, and Karaganda, with a bishop capable of serving the sacramental needs of Catholics in those areas appointed as "apostolic administrator" for each.[38]

As the Church's universal pastor, intimately familiar with the suffering of Christians throughout the Soviet Union, John Paul was fully committed to providing adequate pastoral care for the Catholics in Russia, Siberia, and Kazakhstan. He was also determined to make every effort to heal the ecumenical breach of the eleventh century between Rome and Orthodoxy—and that required taking account of the concerns and fears of Orthodoxy's largest Church, in Russia.[39] The Vatican's hope was that the establishment of apostolic administrations rather than dioceses in historically Orthodox territories with significant Catholic populations would meet the pastoral needs of the Catholics and the sensitivities of the Patriarchate of Moscow.

Precisely the opposite happened, as far as the Patriarchate was concerned.

That the Russian Orthodox leadership was not consulted in advance about the creation of three apostolic administrations in European Russia, Siberia, and Kazakhstan was understandable. The Holy See had spent much of the twentieth century disentangling the Church from the necessity of "clearing" such arrangements, and the appointments of bishops, with political and other authorities. Given that history, there was real reluctance to backtrack by seeking the de facto approval of another Christian communion for regularizing Catholic life and providing normal pastoral care for Catholics. Perhaps an exception ought to have been made in this instance—not by letting the Patriarchate of Moscow vet the appointment of bishops as apostolic administrators, but by informing Russian Orthodoxy's leaders of the Holy See's concerns and its ecumenical reasoning in considering the possibility of creating apostolic administrations rather than canonically erected dioceses. Given the Patriarchate's historic entanglement with the Soviet government, though, this could have seemed a step backward toward seeking governmental approval for normal Catholic life. In any event, there was no prior consultation about the idea of apostolic administrations.

To make matters worse, Metropolitan Kyril of Smolensk, head of the Moscow Patriarchate's department of "external affairs" (which included ecumenical relations), had come to Rome at the invitation of Cardinal Edward Cassidy, President of the Pontifical Council for Promoting Christian Unity, after the two had met in Australia during the February 1991 general assembly of the World Council of Churches. In late March 1991, Kyril was warmly welcomed in Rome by Pope John Paul II, by Cardinal Angelo Sodano, the Secretary of State, and by other officials of the Holy See. He went back to the Soviet Union enthusiastic about his Roman reception but completely in the dark about the impending establishment of the apostolic administrations. Nothing had been said to him.

In the weeks between Kyril's visit and the April 13 announcement of the new apostolic administrations, John Paul II had urged the Secretariat of State and Cardinal Sodano to, as one participant in the discussion recalled, "make sure that the Patriarchate is informed well ahead, before these appointments are announced." The Pope was clearly concerned that everything possible be done to put the creation of apostolic administrations in the best possible light for the Moscow Patriarchate—these necessary provisions for the pastoral care of Catholics in fact demonstrated Catholicism's ecumenical commitment. Unfortunately, John Paul's order to inform the Patriarchate "well ahead" of time was not carried out.

Archbishop Colasuonno, the nuncio in Moscow, told Cardinal Cassidy later that he had tried to meet with Russian Orthodox Patriarch Aleksy ten days before the April 13 announcement but was not given an appointment. Evidently, neither Colasuonno nor his Roman superiors regarded the issue as urgent enough to keep pressing until Patriarch Aleksy agreed to receive the nuncio. Nor did the Secretariat of State seem to believe that the announcement should be delayed until after the Patriarch had been informed, despite the Pope's clear concern that Aleksy not be caught by surprise. The Secretary of State, who had been present when the Pope made plain his wish that Aleksy be informed "well ahead" of the announcement of the apostolic administrations and the bishops, did not ensure that his subordinates heeded the Pope's urgent desire to avoid what Aleksy and his associates might regard as a confrontational fait accompli.[40]

The Moscow Patriarchate reacted with fury to the April 13 announcement of the three apostolic administrations and the appointment of bishops to lead them—a reaction intensified by widespread and erroneous reports that the Pope had created new Catholic "dioceses" in Russia and Kazakhstan.[41] He hadn't. But given the fact that the Patriarchate had been caught completely by surprise, precise canonical distinctions were of little consequence. Metropolitan Kyril, responsible for Russian Orthodoxy's ecumenical relations with

Rome, was particularly embarrassed and angered. He had come back from Rome in March praising the reception he had received in the Holy See. Now he felt betrayed.

That anti-Roman elements in the Patriarchate of Moscow quickly seized this opportunity to magnify their campaign against any rapprochement with what they termed the "first Rome" need not be doubted. Moreover, it seems that no one in the higher leadership of Russian Orthodoxy—the "third Rome," as it understood itself—shared John Paul II's intense sense of ecumenical urgency. There is little or no evidence that any Orthodox leader tried to contain the damage done by the announcement of the apostolic administrations before Patriarch Aleksy had been notified. One can also understand the sense of urgency that seems to have motivated the Secretariat of State. In the first quarter of 1991, no one knew how long the thaw in the USSR would last. For the first time in seventy years, the government wasn't interfering in anything the Catholic Church was doing. Traveling Russian Orthodox officials were still required to report back to the government's Council on Religious Affairs, so any discussion of the changes with Metropolitan Kyril during his Roman visit would inevitably have involved the Soviet government at second-hand. Therefore, why not get Catholic structures in place while the situation was fluid, in case it would later freeze up again?[42]

Yet the considered judgment must be that the creation of apostolic administrations in Russia and Kazakhstan was poorly handled by the Holy See's diplomats. There may well have been a storm of criticism from the Patriarchate of Moscow no matter how or when the announcement was made, but the Secretariat of State's failure to carry out the Pope's instruction about informing the patriarch made an even more vitriolic reaction possible. This, in turn, deflected attention from the Patriarchate's false charge that the new apostolic administrations were instruments for "proselytizing" Russian Orthodox. The entire affair put severe strains on Roman Catholic–Russian Orthodox ecumenical relations for the next two years, strengthened the position of the Patriarchate of Moscow in the ongoing negotiations over the Ukrainian situation, confirmed the ancient suspicions of both regime-friendly and traditionally anti-Roman Russian Orthodox, and vastly complicated the worldwide Roman Catholic dialogue with the Orthodox Churches. It also gave the Patriarchate of Moscow an excuse for refusing to participate in the special European Synod John Paul had called for the fall of 1991, which he envisioned as a major step toward realizing his vision of a Europe breathing again with two lungs.[43]

TENSIONS IN POLAND

Two months after this controversy erupted, John Paul returned to Poland for the first time since communism's collapse. The nine-day visit in June 1991 took him to Koszalin, Rzeszów, Przemyśl, Lubaczów, Kielce, Radom, Łomża, Białystok, Olsztyn, Włocławek, Płock, and Warsaw. The crowds were large, but the pilgrimage was generally regarded as the least successful of the Pope's visits to his native land.

There seemed to be a disconnection between the people's expectations and the Pope's intentions. Poles expected John Paul to share their sense of liberation, but the Pope's addresses tended to focus on the pitfalls of a freedom detached from moral norms. Although the theme chosen for the visit—the Ten Commandments as the moral basis of a civil society capable of sustaining democracy—touched issues John Paul had begun to develop in *Centesimus Annus*, the encyclical and its celebration of the free society was barely referred to during the pilgrimage. As a result, what should have been heard as a papal proposal for living freedom nobly was often perceived as scolding and nay-saying. Poles wanted to celebrate their new freedom with the man to whom they attributed a major role in their liberation. The prescient Pope, already focused on the difficulties ahead, was somewhat out of sync with the popular mood.[44]

The Polish Church was trying to find its own voice in the new situation and having difficulty doing so. With the forty-two-year state of emergency over, the Church's hierarchy had had to change, virtually overnight, from being guardians of a fortress to agents of dialogue and evangelization. A Church forged in resistance had to take up the task of democratic culture-formation, in circumstances in which the moral issues were no longer so neatly divided between "us" and "them." Few Polish bishops and priests had grasped John Paul's concept of a Church in which the clergy were primarily focused on the formation of consciences and public moral culture, leaving the practical application of Catholic social doctrine to an educated Catholic laity. A Church that had sustained itself through decades of crisis by demanding unity-through-uniformity suddenly found itself exploring the boundaries of unity within legitimate diversity—within the Church itself, and in different proposals for how the Church should address social and political issues. Three days after the visit concluded, John Paul's successor, Cardinal Macharski, put it well when he said that the Church, no longer the *defensor civitatis*, the "defender of the city," had to learn how to be the *defensor hominis*, the "defender of the human person" in the previously unknown circumstances of a democracy.[45]

It was not as if the problems the Pope foresaw didn't exist. In the newly feisty Polish media and among secular intellectuals, one frequently encountered the idea that democracy meant a suspension of debate over public moral norms—or, as one writer put it, democratic Poland should be "a state with a neutral *Weltanschauung* [worldview]." This was widely perceived by critical churchmen as one of the first and most noxious imports from the West.[46] That idea, in turn, had fueled a raging national debate over abortion, in which neither the official Church nor its opponents had acquitted themselves very well. A permissive abortion law had been promulgated by the Gomułka regime in the mid-1950s as part of its assault on Catholic morality; it was as certain as anything that the Polish Church would press hard for laws protective of the unborn in post-communist Poland. Unlike John Paul, however, the Polish bishops did not frame the abortion issue as a question of the public moral foundations of democracy. Church leaders, by and large, simply instructed their people that abortion was an abomination to be rejected on the authority of the Church. Catholic voices, like *Tygodnik Powszechny*, that might have been expected to explain John Paul's teaching—that a freestanding "right" to abortion on demand was incompatible with a democratic society based on the protection of basic human rights and the rule of law—were muted or ineffective. The independent Polish press and Polish secularists, both of whom saw the abortion issue as a matter of personal liberty, raised the specter of an ecclesiastical "black tyranny" replacing the recently jettisoned "red tyranny" of communism. Neither the official Church nor its opponents nor the Solidarity-led government seemed capable of arguing the abortion issue as an inherently public question. Everyone involved debated it as an issue of individual autonomy.

Ethnic and ecumenical tensions also marred the visit. St. Teresa's Church in Przemyśl, near the Polish-Ukrainian border, had been seized from Greek Catholic Poles of Ukrainian origin in 1946 and eventually given to the Carmelites. It had been returned to the Greek Catholics for five years in January 1991, until Latin-rite protesters forcibly reversed a decision John Paul had endorsed. For perhaps the first time in his life, John Paul was angry with the Carmelites he had once hoped to join.[47] The alternative was to build a Greek Catholic cathedral in the formerly vacant Greek Catholic Diocese of Przemyśl, to serve as the seat of a new Greek Catholic bishop, Ivan Martyniak. Things were so unsettled in Przemyśl because of ancient animosities between the local Poles and Ukrainians that the Polish bishops had felt compelled to issue a statement on February 28, reminding the irate Latin-rite locals that Bishop Martyniak was "being sent by the Holy Father" and deserved a "worthy entrance" into his See.[48] For their part, the Greek Catholics were upset that their restored diocese had been made subordinate to the Latin-rite Primate in Warsaw, rather than to the Major-Archbishop of L'viv in Ukraine.[49] Cardinal Lubachivsky brought several thousand Ukrainian Catholics to Przemyśl for the papal Mass, but the Pope's hopes for a definitive reconciliation between Latin-rite Polish Catholics and Greek Catholic Poles of Ukrainian origin was not fulfilled during the visit.

Even the Solidarity-led government managed to make difficulties for John Paul. At the end of the visit, the Pope had hoped to spend a few days privately in his beloved Tatra Mountains. The government, caving in to press carping about the cost of the visit and complaining that the Pope didn't understand the pressures democratically elected leaders were under, did not encourage a papal respite in the Tatras. John Paul, who canceled his plans for a brief mountain holiday, was offended and hurt.[50]

The 1991 papal pilgrimage to Poland was not adequately prepared by the Polish Church. The Pope seems not to have been adequately briefed on the dynamics of the new political and cultural situation. The "Ten Commandments" theme, unobjectionable in itself, was not well-suited to the psychology of the moment. And the Polish Church lacked the media resources to meet the challenge of a Polish press that, in dealing with public figures, was beginning to imitate the Western media in assuming guilt and hidden agendas until proven otherwise. John Paul himself would later muse on whether he had not underestimated the degree of damage that communism had done to the culture of his homeland. He also knew that the Polish bishops had made his task in June 1991 more difficult by their heavy-handed approach to post-communist politics, and he may have suspected that his own approach to democratic Poland needed refinement.

The 1991 pilgrimage created a new image of John Paul II in the Western press—the angry old man, incapable of understanding the world he had helped bring about.[51] It was a crude caricature. What could have been described as papal passion in defense of basic human rights was dismissed as the fierce anger of a disappointed lover embittered by his rejection. John Paul II, as anyone who knew him could well attest, was not a man given to bitterness. The inadequacies of the trip's preparation, and the public context set by the poor performance of much of the Polish hierarchy in the previous year, helped give the caricature a certain plausibility among commentators for whom freedom is defined almost entirely as independence from moral authority.[52]

Six years later, John Paul II would find his voice during a pilgrimage to Poland that swept away many of the unhappy memories of the 1991 visit. For the moment, though, the fourth papal pilgrimage to Poland was another trial in a difficult year.

EUROSYNOD 1991

In advancing the new evangelization, John Paul first turned his attention to the "old continent," Europe.

Archbishop Jan Schotte, General Secretary of the Synod of Bishops, had been in England in early 1990 to talk about the Vatican's view of the new Europe. In the course of an informal discussion about how the Church might best grasp the opportunity created by the collapse of the Berlin Wall, Schotte floated the idea of a pan-European Synod of Bishops. Cardinal Basil Hume of Westminster liked it. On his return to Rome, Schotte mentioned his discussion with Cardinal Hume to the Pope. John Paul handed the Belgian prelate a sheet of paper, dated December 24, 1989, on which he had begun jotting down his own ideas for just such a meeting.[53]

The Pope announced the Special Assembly for Europe of the Synod of Bishops at Velehrad, in Moravia, on April 22, 1990, during his dramatic trip to newly free Czechoslovakia. Reporting on the announcement, *Le Monde* described the impending Eurosynod as John Paul's proposed "reconquest of the European mind." A commentator in the Manchester-based *Guardian* suggested that the Pope had emerged "as one of the few European leaders with an indisputably hegemonic project," which was the formation of "a political movement based on belief in God, simultaneously rejecting both irreligion and materialism."[54] The evangelical thrust of the Pope's initiative was lost in these and other commentaries. On June 5, during a special consultation in Rome to begin planning for the Eurosynod, he tried to make his intentions clear again, in an address to the forty-seven churchmen present that was a distinctive reading of the history of European civilization and a portrait of the mind of Karol Wojtyła, European.

History Lesson

Those who had lived through the stirring events of the past months—the fall of the Berlin Wall, the liberation of captive nations, the collapse of the "bloc" system, the end of the Cold War—must have sensed that they were passing through "a divine *kairos*," a special moment when God's power within history was palpable. This, John Paul began, was the way that history ought to be read: "in depth." Only that kind of reading could illuminate the "new situation [that] is dawning in the life of the Nations" of Europe.

Christianity's European presence dated back to the first missions of the apostles. A large part of what the Pope termed "*the great evangelization*" of the continent had spread from Rome, but there was another "important focal point" to Europe's evangelization: Constantinople. For a millennium, the Gospel had come to Europe through that diversity-in-unity John Paul styled "*Rome—Byzantium.*" Only after the eleventh century did evangelization, and the formation of Europe's distinct cultures, involve a divided Christianity.

In addition to shaping national cultures, John Paul continued, the evangelization of Europe contributed to the development of a transnational "*humanist culture*," born from the encounter between biblical religion and ancient Greek philosophy. Married to Roman law, this triad—Jerusalem, Athens, Rome—created what we recognize as "European civilization." The "humanist culture" of Europe began to change several hundred years ago, John Paul argued, when the belief in God that had shaped its understandings of the cosmos and the human person was replaced by a culture built around subjective human consciousness. Man, the "knowing subject," now fully occupied "the center of things." And there, the Pope observed, "he has remained, alone," his loneliness intensified by the breach between science and religion and by the rise of Marxism. There was a deep paradox in all this. The biblical view of creation as intelligible, the biblical view of the human person as having "dominion" over creation, and the biblical view of history as purposeful had shaped the cultural foundations that eventually made what moderns know as "science" possible.

In any case, forgetting God had had tremendous public consequences. Indeed, the very awfulness of twentieth-century European history had created an evangelical opportunity. European man had been forced to acknowledge what the Pope termed "*the other side of a civilization* he was inclined to think superior to all others."

Auschwitz, the Pope insisted, was not the end of Europe's civilizational story. But it revealed the depths of depravity to which men who had forgotten God could descend. Nazism had been "completely vanquished," but one of the victors in that struggle had been yet another totalitarian power. It, too, had finally fallen, thanks to a "*resistance . . . based on the inviolability of the rights of man*," including the centrality of the "*right of freedom of conscience and of religion.*" The human rights resistance that had swept away the communist system posed a fundamental challenge to those who read a secular trajectory in Europe's civilizational history. The events they had all just lived through had demonstrated the exact opposite of the secularist claim: "*religion and the Church have shown themselves to be among the most effective means to liberate man from a system of total subjugation.*"

Far from providing the Church with a chance to gloat, however, this ought to compel a serious examination of the Christian conscience, John Paul said. If Christians had been faithful to the Gospel, would the horrors of the twentieth century have taken place? All the more reason, then, to resist the notion that post–Cold War democratic public life in Europe could "be detached from the values of Christian faith and morals."

The Churches of Europe, East and West, had lived through extraordinary experiences in the past fifty years. Those experiences could only be adequately understood within a concept of history that left room for God and for the workings of God's providence. That was what had made Europe "Europe." And that was what the bishops of Europe, John Paul thought, ought to be considering at the Eurosynod—how to "translate" their countries' recent experiences of God's hand at work in history into a new European Pentecost, one that would take what was best in modern European culture and reconnect it to its most authentic roots, which were Christian.[55]

The Difficulties of Different Expectations

That the Eurosynod could not meet in 1990 made it far more difficult for it to be the energizing evangelical experience for which John Paul hoped. But in order to balance the Synod's membership between the two reunited halves of the continent, bishops had to be appointed to vacant dioceses in central and eastern Europe, and that took time. If the Synod had met in 1990, the ratio of bishops would have been 3:1, West to East. Delaying the Synod until the late fall of 1991 allowed for more equal representation. It also meant that the Synod was meeting a full two years after the *kairos* that John Paul had hoped would ignite the new evangelization of the old continent. During that period, much had happened.

Yugoslavia's collapse into bloody chaos and the inability of the European powers to do anything about it had raised more questions about the concept of a common European home. Transitions to democracy in east central Europe had caused considerable economic dislocation and a lot of dis-

gruntlement. Every newly democratic east central European state was struggling with how to render justice to the victims of the state security services and
to officials complicit in serious injustices. Democratic "normality" in the new
democracies had turned out to mean "normal" divisiveness—a particularly bitter pill after the remarkable unity displayed by the anti-communist resistance
in 1989. The Soviet Union had come apart at the seams, and no one knew what
was coming there next. Western Europe moved quickly to take advantage of
investment opportunities in the new democracies (no small matter, to be sure,
in the reconstruction of east central Europe), but Western Europeans and
their political leaders seemed largely uninterested in the ongoing drama east
of the Elbe River.

Sadly but almost inevitably, by the time the 137 members of the Synod
finally convened on November 28, 1991, much of the energy generated by the
Revolution of 1989 had dissipated.

The Synod met for two and a half weeks. For the first time in Synod history, representatives of other Christian communities participated as "fraternal
delegates." Despite the ecumenical innovation and the Pope's high expectations, it quickly became evident that the bishops had come to the Synod with
different sets of expectations. The new archbishop of Prague, Miloslav Vlk,
believed the Synod ought to have challenged the preconceptions of both
groups of bishops. The bishops of the new democracies should have gotten
beyond an attitude of "We've been martyrs, we don't need you," and the bishops from the established democracies should have looked for some lessons in
the testimony of churchmen who had sustained the faith in very trying circumstances. Yet the problem, as Vlk saw it, was that virtually none of the Westerners understood communism, which meant that they couldn't grasp what
their newly liberated brothers had gone through.[56]

Cardinal Jean-Marie Lustiger of Paris also thought that the bishops were
having problems understanding one another's experiences. The Western bishops were "too conscious of their own superiority," while the bishops from east
central Europe were profoundly conscious of their recent persecution and
reluctant to be led by others. "They wanted to tell what had happened to them
and the Western bishops found it difficult to listen," as Lustiger put it. At the
same time, the Westerners were confronting problems the bishops in the new
democracies could barely imagine—the temptations of material abundance,
which meant being tempted by good things, not simply by evils.[57]

Cardinal Jozef Tomko agreed that there was a communications problem,
based on bishops who had lived "two different realities." But the 1991
Eurosynod, he insisted, was intended to be an "exchange of spiritual gifts," and
at that level he thought it had succeeded. The Western Churches began once
more to "realize that these [other European] Churches were now free," and
the Churches in the new democracies began to realize, like the West, "both
how needy they were and how rich they were in faith." Tomko believed there
was also a rediscovery of old truths at the Eurosynod. Western Churches,

focused for centuries on the intellectual challenge of modernity, "rediscovered the importance of traditional religion and traditions like the family and the Bible" in sustaining the faith. Everyone involved, East and West, was compelled by the Eurosynod to focus on the cross as the center of Christian life. Meeting modern martyr-confessors helped one to rediscover "the old mysteries of the Church in the light of new realities."[58]

Then there was the question of Vatican II. The Western bishops admired the tenacity of their colleagues from behind the former iron curtain, but many found it difficult not to think of the central and eastern Europeans as men who had dropped out of history—and who needed instruction in how to be "the Church in the modern world," according to the Western European understanding of the Council. The bishops from many formerly communist countries were justifiably nervous about the assumption that the Western European model of conciliar implementation applied to everyone—not least because of the continued decline of Catholic adherence and practice in Western Europe. This tension left open the question of precisely what kind of help the Churches in the new democracies should seek from the West in forming new institutions like national bishops' conferences and in rebuilding their seminaries.[59]

Western bishops were tempted to think that their colleagues in the new democracies should go through an accelerated course in post-conciliar theology and pastoral practice. Men like Prague's Vlk felt that the Council had to be implemented there in light of the very distinctive pastoral problems of post-communist societies. The most important issues, Vlk believed, were the re-creation of real Christian community, a new pattern of collaboration between clergy and laity, and fostering lay initiative. Then there was the question of reconstituting public moral culture. Life under communism had been, in a sense, living in black-and-white; "normality," Vlk said, was "shades of gray."[60] Perhaps there was something to be learned from the Western Churches in this regard, but these institutions were hardly exemplars of a robust public Catholicism.

The refusal of the Orthodox Churches, and particularly the Russian Orthodox Church, to participate in the Synod was another frustration for John Paul II's ecumenical agenda. It also provided the occasion for the Synod's most dramatic moment. Though most Orthodox leaders had refused the Pope's invitation to participate, one exception was the newly elected Ecumenical Patriarch of Constantinople, Bartholomew I, who sent a "fraternal delegate" to the Synod, Metropolitan Spyridon Papagheorghiu of Venice, the chief Orthodox leader in Italy. On the evening of December 7, 1991, during an ecumenical prayer service at St. Peter's Basilica in which all the Synod members participated, Metropolitan Spyridon attacked the Eastern Catholic Churches in union with Rome (the "Uniates") for what he termed their "violent" reoccupation of churches in Ukraine and Romania, and charged Rome with setting up "parallel missionary structures" in Russia itself (i.e., the new apostolic administrations). Catholic-Orthodox relations were at a low ebb thanks to

Roman aggression, the Metropolitan concluded. The Synod members and Protestant participants in the ecumenical service were stunned by Spyridon's public attack on Catholicism and the Pope inside the basilica, and the Metropolitan's remarks were followed by an embarrassed silence.

John Paul rose and, without a word, drew Metropolitan Spyridon into an embrace—the ancient kiss of peace.

The 1991 Eurosynod opened new conversations, gave the bishops present a new experience of the unity-within-diversity of European Catholicism, and began a process for reforming the structure of the pan-European bishops' conference to include bishops from behind the collapsed iron curtain. It was not, however, the historic, evangelically energizing event John Paul II had hoped it would be. The asymmetries between the Churches remained great, and too much time had passed since the *kairos* moment of 1989 for that experience of Providence at work in history to bridge the gap between Churches separated for a half-century. The Synod's closing *Declaration* pledged the Church's solidarity with efforts to further reunite once-divided Europe, but the bishops returned to their various homes primarily focused on local concerns and affairs.[61] The most visible, concrete steps toward redeeming the Synod's pledge would be taken by John Paul II personally.

In a World Without a Soviet Union

Six months before the Eurosynod convened, John Paul made his second pilgrimage to the shrine of Our Lady of Fatima in Portugal, on the tenth anniversary of Mehmet Ali Agca's assassination attempt. After stops in Lisbon and the Azores Islands, he arrived in Fatima on May 12 and met the eighty-four-year-old Sister Lucia dos Santos, the sole survivor of the three children who had experienced the Marian apparition in 1917. On May 13, the tenth anniversary of the shooting in St. Peter's Square, he publicly gave thanks to Mary for the liberation of east central Europe from communism, and for his own deliverance from death a decade before.

John Paul celebrated his fifth consistory for the creation of new members of the College of Cardinals on the eve of the feast of Sts. Peter and Paul, June 28, 1991. Three prominent Catholic witnesses under communism received the red hat. Two were from the newly liberated parts of Europe: Alexandru Todea of Romania and the redoubtable Slovak Jesuit, Ján Chryzostom Korec. The third confessor-cardinal was Ignatius Gong Pin-mei, the bishop of Shanghai, who was revealed as the cardinal named secretly (*in pectore*) at John Paul's first consistory in 1979. Weeks short of his ninetieth birthday, the man known in the West as "Cardinal Kung" (according to the pre-communist transliteration of his name) came to Rome to be invested before returning to his retirement home in Stamford, Connecticut. The Chinese government that had jailed and then exiled him refused him permission to come to Shanghai in his new dignity.

New curial cardinals were prominent in John Paul's fifth consistory:

Angelo Sodano, Pio Laghi, José Sánchez, Edward Cassidy, Virgilio Noè, and Fiorenzo Angelini.[62] The Americas received five new cardinals: Nicolás de Jésus López Rodriguez of Santo Domingo, Antonio Quarracino of Buenos Aires, Anthony Bevilacqua of Philadelphia, Roger Mahony of Los Angeles, and Juan Jesús Posadas Ocampo of Guadalajara.[63] The archbishops of Armagh (Cahal Daly), Berlin (Georg Sterzinsky), and Turin (Giovanni Saldarini) became members of the College, as did John Paul's vicar for the Diocese of Rome, Camillo Ruini, and the archbishop of Kinshasa, Zaire, Frédéric Etsou-Nzabi-Bamungwabi. There was no intellectual father of Vatican II honored in the consistory of June 1991, but John Paul did give the red hat to the eighty-nine-year-old Paolo Dezza, SJ, his personal delegate to govern the Jesuits in 1981–1983.

On August 14–15, 1991, John Paul was back in Poland briefly as a million young people, including as many as 70,000 from the Soviet Union, came to Częstochowa for the third international World Youth Day. En route to the Jasna Góra monastery and the shrine of the Black Madonna, John Paul stayed overnight in Kraków and celebrated Mass in the Old Town market square. He stopped briefly in his hometown, Wadowice, where he consecrated a new parish church and met with his high school classmates. Speaking to the towns-people after the Mass, he remembered those Jewish friends who had been lost in the Holocaust:

> Nor can I forget that among our classmates in the school of Wadowice and in its high school there were those who belonged to the Mosaic religion; they are no longer with us, just as there is no longer the old synagogue next to the high school. When a [memorial] stone was [unveiled] in the place where the synagogue used to be, I sent a special letter through one of our classmates [Jerzy Kluger]. In it we find the following words: "The Church, and in her all peoples and nations, are united with you. Certainly first of all your people feel your suffering, your destruction—here we recall how close it is to Auschwitz—then they want to speak to individuals and people, and to all of mankind, to admonish them. In your name this warning cry is also raised by the Pope, and the Pope who comes from Poland has a special reason for this because, in a certain way, he experienced all this with you in our homeland. . . ."[64]

The World Youth Day Mass on the solemnity of the Assumption, August 15, had a special flavor. 'It was the first such celebration, the Pope noted, in which there was a large representation from eastern Europe. Wasn't that, he asked, "a great gift of the Holy Spirit?" This was "your hour," he told the young-sters. Building a "civilization of love" in the world of tomorrow depended on "the commitment of the Christian generation of today," and their willingness to make decisions for the common good. On their shoulders rested the responsibility for defending religious liberty, the "personal dimension of devel-opment," the family, a genuine pluralism of mutual enrichment, and the environment. They were not alone. Christ, the Holy Spirit, and the Virgin of Jasna Góra were with them, helping to create a young, evangelical Church, conscious of its mission: "Receive the Holy Spirit, and be strong! Amen!"

The response was thunderous applause—after which the Pope spontaneously joked that he didn't need such applause, but they evidently did, and in any case the "Most Holy Mother" appreciated it, too, as a token of their joy.[65]

The next week the Pope was in Budapest when an attempted coup against Mikhail Gorbachev collapsed and accelerated the Soviet Union's political disintegration. During his five days in Hungary, John Paul tried to rally a Church whose leadership had played a less-heroic role during the last decades of communism than had other episcopates in east central Europe. At the cathedral in Esztergom, he prayed at the tomb of Cardinal Mindszenty and later met with another stadium full of youngsters in Budapest. On August 23, back in Rome, the Pope sent a telegram to President Gorbachev, extending his "fervent good wishes," thanking God for "the happy outcome of the dramatic trial which involved your person, your family and your country," and expressing the wish that Gorbachev would be able to resume his "tremendous task for the material and spiritual renewal of the Soviet Union."[66] It was not to be. The day after the Pope's telegram, Gorbachev resigned as General Secretary of the Communist Party of the Soviet Union, breaking the party-government link that had defined "democratic centralism" since the days of Lenin. Even that dramatic change was too little, too late. Less than four months later, the Union of Soviet Socialist Republics ceased to exist.

Changes were being rung ecumenically, as well. On October 2, 1991, Ecumenical Patriarch Dimitrios I died. Three weeks later, the Holy Synod of the Patriarchate of Constantinople elected Metropolitan Bartholomew Archondonis of Chalcedon as his successor. The election of the fifty-one-year-old Bartholomew—who had studied at the Ecumenical Institute of Bossey near Geneva and at the University of Munich, who had earned a doctoral degree in canon law at Rome's Pontifical Gregorian University, and who had had extensive contacts with Roman Catholic leaders—raised expectations that progress could be made in advancing John Paul's great hope for healing the breach between Rome and Constantinople. In his congratulatory message to the new Ecumenical Patriarch, John Paul stressed his fervent wish for "collaboration in view of the reestablishment of full communion between our Churches."[67] Bartholomew had not been elected because of any emerging consensus on the ecumenical imperative within the Holy Synod of Constantinople, however, but because of his youthful vigor and what was hoped would be his capacity to handle the often uncooperative Turkish government. Moreover, intra-Orthodox divisions severely circumscribed his room for maneuver. This would become especially evident in the new Ecumenical Patriarch's testy relationship with the Patriarch of Moscow, Aleksy II, whose assertiveness as a representative of Orthodoxy increased even as the Soviet Union collapsed and then disappeared.[68]

The animosities with which Bartholomew had to contend were made evident in Belgrade, the capital of Yugoslavia, three weeks before Ecumenical Patriarch Dimitrios died. There, on September 8—which John Paul had asked Catholic bishops around the world to designate as a special day of prayer for peace in Yugoslavia—Serbian protesters marched outside the Vatican embassy with placards denouncing the "Vatican Satanic State." As Yugoslavia continued to unravel, the Serbs maintained that Catholic support for the independence of Croatia and Slovenia, two constituent "republics" within Tito's quasi-federalist structure, was aimed at disempowering Orthodox Serbia.

The Holy See's diplomats were, in fact, trying to determine just what was going on, and why, in the crumbling Yugoslav federation. On August 8, 1991, the Vatican "foreign minister," Archbishop Jean-Louis Tauran, had gone on a special mission to Yugoslavia at the Pope's request. On his return, he told John Paul, "Holy Father, 'Yugoslavia' doesn't exist anymore. When I was in Zagreb [the Croatian capital] I felt as if I were in Vienna, and when I was in Belgrade I felt as if I were in Istanbul."[69] The cultural differences within the Yugoslav federation were simply too great, and absent the force of a communist regime to hold things together, conflict was inevitable.

The Holy See would have preferred a "federal" solution to Yugoslavia's future, if in a much looser federation than Tito had managed to impose. The Vatican view, according to Tauran, was that "nationhood" did not always have to be expressed in statehood, and the social-ethical principle of subsidiar-ity—leaving as much decision making as possible at local levels—suggested federal solutions to complex ethnic and racial problems. But when the Serb-dominated federal Yugoslav army attacked Croatian nationalists in Vukovar (a city on the Croatian/Serbian border) in September 1991, the Vatican's judgment was that the federal Yugoslav army had become an aggressor against one portion of the Yugoslav population. Absent European Commu-nity [EC] intervention to "name the aggressor" and stop the attack on fellow Yugoslavs, it began to seem as if independence for Slovenia and Croatia was a way to stop the war.[70] On January 13, 1992, the Holy See sent notes to the governments in Croatia and Slovenia, recognizing the independence they had declared on June 25, 1991, then suspended while EC negotiators attempted to find a peaceful solution, and finally redeclared on December 23 while applying for admission as independent states to the EC. The Holy See notes indicated, as had previous diplomatic contacts, that this recogni-tion was contingent upon Croatian and Slovene assurances that the new gov-ernments would be democratic and would respect minority rights.[71]

Serbian Orthodox Patriarch Pavle sent a letter to Orthodox leaders around the world, charging that "the origin of the conflict in Yugoslavia and in the Balkans and not only in this region is the insistence with which the Church of Rome considers the Balkans, which are inhabited mainly by people of Orthodox religion, as a missionary territory."[72] The Patriarch's letter did not address the question of aggression by the federal Yugoslav army. French Pres-ident François Mitterand was also unhappy, alleging a pro-Croatian alliance between John Paul II and German Chancellor Helmut Kohl, and telling Archbishop Tauran three times that the Holy See's recognition of Croatia and Slovenia was responsible for the breakup of Yugoslavia. Tauran, who explained on each occasion that the federal army's aggression had made independence seem a means of stopping the war, was well aware of France's traditional alliance with Serbia, and thought that Mitterand's pique was due in part to the buddy system among socialists.[73]

Over time, the argument that independence for Croatia and Slovenia would end the war in those republics was borne out—albeit far sooner in Slovenia than in Croatia. The violence attendant on the disintegration of the Yugoslav federation did not stop, however, and the locus of ethnic slaughter shifted to Bosnia-Herzegovina. Two years later, in 1994, John Paul, who may have come to wonder whether the rapid recognition of Slovene and Croatian independence was entirely wise (since it had freed the Serbian-dominated Yugoslav army for aggression elsewhere in the shattered federation), would try a private initiative to get all parties to the ongoing conflict into conversation.[74]

Advances could be made elsewhere in post-communist Europe. On March 25, 1992, John Paul reorganized the entire Polish hierarchy, establishing thirteen new dioceses, raising eight dioceses to the rank of metropolitan archdiocese, establishing Łódź as an archdiocese without suffragan sees, reshaping the metropolitan "provinces," transferring fourteen bishops to new positions as heads of dioceses, appointing seven new bishops, and transferring fourteen auxiliary bishops. The Pope also changed the character of the office of Primate of Poland, which had, under Cardinals Wyszyński and Glemp, been synonymous with the position of President of the Polish Bishops' Conference. The Polish primacy had historically belonged to the archbishop of Gniezno; Gniezno had been joined to the archdiocese of Warsaw in a "personal union" by having one man serve as archbishop of both Gniezno and Warsaw. John Paul dissolved the "personal union" between the archdioceses of Gniezno and Warsaw, appointed a new archbishop of Gniezno (Bishop Henryk Muzyński of Wrocławek, the Polish bishops' leader in the Jewish-Catholic dialogue), but allowed Cardinal Glemp—as "Custodian of the relics of St. Adalbert"—to retain the title of "Primate of Poland" during his lifetime. Glemp, of course, remained archbishop of Warsaw.[75]

The canonical details and medieval titles notwithstanding, this massive reshuffling was an attempt to bring the Polish episcopate's structure into line with Vatican II and to facilitate the new evangelization. Poland's vibrant Catholicism needed more bishops, especially given the challenges of democracy. The office of Primate after Cardinal Glemp's tenure would become essentially honorific, it would not be assumed that the Primate was necessarily the President of the Polish Bishops' Conference, and the Polish bishops could choose their leadership like any other national conference of bishops. That, it was thought, would foster a more assertively evangelical Polish episcopate.

Pastoral outreach to the sick had always been a hallmark of Karol Wojtyła's ministry as priest and an expression of his Christian humanism. On May 13, 1992, the eleventh anniversary of his own suffering at the hands of a would-be assassin, John Paul announced that the Church throughout the world would observe February 11, the feast of Our Lady of Lourdes, as a special World Day of the Sick.[76] In Rome, the day would be observed during the following years by a papal Mass for the sick in St. Peter's Basilica, with patients on wheelchairs and gurneys surrounding the high altar, the tomb of Peter, and Bernini's bronze baldachino. At the end of the service, during which John Paul often preached on illness as part of the human vocation and a call to deeper conversion, the basilica lights were dimmed. Ten thousand candles were lit inside red and orange tulip-shaped containers and held aloft by all those attending, while the "Lourdes Hymn" was sung in various languages.

Europe was not the only locus of John Paul's diplomacy in the early 1990s. On September 21, 1992, the Holy See reestablished full diplomatic relations with the Republic of Mexico, after a hiatus of 132 years. The politics within Mexico's ruling political party, the PRI, had clearly changed since 1979. John Paul's two visits to the country, in 1979 and 1990, had also had an impact. By demonstrating the kind of popular support for the Church that the government could not ignore, they had reinserted Mexican Catholicism into the living history of the nation. Recognition of the Church as an institution with a public role had followed, as had constitutional reforms and a "new way of thinking" between political and Church leaders, who could now see themselves as involved in common tasks in the fields of education and social service. Anti-clericalism remained a problem in some sectors of Mexican society, but John Paul's defense of religious freedom as a basic human right had made a considerable difference in attitudes.[77]

Two months after the restoration of diplomatic relations, John Paul beatified twenty-five martyrs of the Mexican Revolution, killed between 1915 and 1937. For the Church in Mexico, the past was now open as well as the future.

PRIESTS FOR A NEW MILLENNIUM

Every great reform movement in the history of the Catholic Church has required a reform of the priesthood. The "new evangelization" was, in John Paul's view, no exception. Even before coining that phrase as the theme for the Church's transition into the third millennium of its history, the Pope had begun reforming the priesthood. Each of his pastoral pilgrimages around the world included a meeting with local priests, and strengthening the ministerial priesthood was a regular topic in his addresses to local bishops on their *ad limina* visits to Rome. In the mid-1980s, the Congregation for Catholic Education began a series of evaluative "apostolic visitations" of seminaries throughout the world. These led to recommendations for reforms in the training of priests and provided a preliminary exploration of the terrain to be mapped at a Synod of Bishops in 1990. At a more personal level, John Paul sought to strengthen the priesthood, which some observers believed had been relatively ignored by the Second Vatican Council, through an annual series of letters to priests around the world. The letters were issued on Holy Thursday, the beginning of the Easter Triduum and the feast on which the Church celebrates the institution of the priesthood by Christ at the Last Supper.[78]

The Holy Thursday letters are a distinctive form of papal teaching, combining biblical and theological reflection with meditations drawn from John Paul's rich personal experience of the priesthood.[79] The letters touched a wide variety of topics: the priesthood as an experience of being with Christ in the "Upper Room" and in the Garden of Gethsemane; the priesthood as an extension of Christ's work of redemption; the importance of pastoral ministry to young people; the life and ministry of St. John Mary Vianney, the Curé of Ars; Marian piety and the life of priests; the ordained priesthood lifting up, "in the person of Christ," the priesthood of all the baptized; the pastoral care of the family; women in the lives of priests. Though the letters are clearly meant as a means to encourage the Pope's brother priests, the fact that John Paul deemed them necessary reflected his sense that the Roman Catholic priesthood had fallen into crisis in the years after the Second Vatican Council.

Rereading a Crisis

In 1970, there were 448,508 Catholic priests around the world. Twenty-five years later, despite a considerable growth in the world's Catholic population, that number had dropped to 404,750. Almost 46,000 priests had left the active ministry. Recruitment to seminaries had plummeted in the developed world, and seminaries themselves had experienced conditions ranging from confusion to turmoil since Vatican II. Discipline among the clergy faltered, and while statistical evidence demonstrated that malfeasance among Roman Catholic priests was no more severe (in absolute and relative terms) than among the clergy of other Christian denominations or among professionals in society, scandals involving priests were evils in themselves and another barrier to recruitment and reform within the presbyterate.[80]

Celibacy and authority are conventionally taken to be the roots of the post-conciliar crisis of the Catholic priesthood. The suggestion is that the crisis will be resolved when Latin-rite Catholicism ordains married men to the priesthood and adopts a more congregational, less episcopal (and papal) style of leadership and decision making. Throughout his pontificate, John Paul attempted to reform the priesthood on the basis of a different judgment. The roots of the crisis of the priesthood, he believed, went much deeper into the subsoil of both Church and society, and involved the Church's sometimes bracing, sometimes disorienting encounter with modern culture.

While pressures on family life in the late twentieth century, the sexual revolution, and the attractions of a consumer society all had had a bearing on the crisis, the Pope suggested that an even more profound challenge came from four ideas. An unconscious rationalism had made biblical revelation seem, at best, a noble fiction. A closed individualism had made it very difficult for men and women to form binding and enduring relationships; the resulting loneliness was one cause of hedonism and the frantic pursuit of pleasure. A kind of practical atheism had drained life of its mystery. And the distortion of freedom into an assertion of the individual's will-to-power had uncoupled freedom from truth.[81]

Absorbed into the Church from the wider culture, these four ideas had had a powerful and often corrosive effect on priests' understanding of their ministry, on recruitment to the priesthood, and on priestly formation in seminaries. In John Paul's view, the path to reform lay in revitalizing the idea of the ministerial priesthood according to Vatican II's teaching on the universal call to holiness. That reform, with specific reference to how priests were trained, was the agenda of the Eighth Ordinary General Assembly of the Synod of Bishops, which met in Rome from September 30 through October 28, 1990.

Men for Others

The work of this Synod was completed by the post-synodal apostolic exhortation *Pastores Dabo Vobis* [I Shall Give You Shepherds], which took its title from the prophetic literature of the Hebrew Bible (*Jeremiah* 3.15). Issued on March 25, 1992, *Pastores Dabo Vobis* is quite likely the longest papal document ever written: 226 pages in the original Vatican edition. Given the seriousness of the crisis in the priesthood, the exhortation is strikingly positive and relaxed. Like the Synod whose work it incorporated, *Pastores Dabo Vobis* describes itself as an address "on the formation of priests." It is also John Paul's most comprehensive statement on the nature and function of the Catholic priesthood. Like *Christifideles Laici*, the 1988 exhortation on the vocation of lay Christians, it provides an authoritative "key" to interpreting Vatican II.

Lifting up the distinctive vocation of the ministerial priesthood, which in turn ennobles the priestly character of all baptized Christians, was very high on John Paul II's teaching agenda in *Pastores Dabo Vobis*. The roots of that distinctiveness, he insists, can only be understood theologically and biblically. When Jesus told his fellow townsmen in the Nazareth synagogue that Isaiah's messianic prophecy was being fulfilled in their midst because he had been consecrated by an anointing with the Holy Spirit, he was describing the essence of the new kind of priesthood he was bringing into the world—a priesthood of perfect mediation between God and humanity. This was something new in salvation history and is, according to John Paul, "absolutely necessary" for understanding the nature of the Church's ordained ministry, which is a unique participation in the priesthood of Christ.[82]

To be a priest, then, is not to perform a task or play a role, but to become an *alter Christus*, "another Christ," a personal continuation of the mediating priesthood of Jesus himself. Ordination does not simply authorize the priest to conduct certain types of ecclesiastical business. It "configures" him to Christ in a unique way.[83] That configuration confers a solemn obligation to serve the Christian community. Service is the way the priest's unique sacramental authority becomes an image of "Christ the Priest."

The image of Christ the Good Shepherd reveals the specific form of holiness that must inform the priesthood—the holiness of "pastoral charity."[84] The priest's "headship" of a local Catholic community is not defined by power. Christian "headship" consists in being a servant, a man suffused with pastoral charity—one who makes a "total gift of *self to the Church*, following the example of Christ."[85]

John Paul analyzes the "vocation crisis" and the dynamics of vocational discernment in a distinctly countercultural way. Discerning a priestly vocation, he proposes, is not a matter of deciding on a worthwhile career. It is the fruit of "an *inexpressible dialogue between God and human beings*, between the love of God who calls and the freedom of individuals who lovingly respond to him."[86] A priestly vocation begins with God, not with an individual. It is a summons from God, not a means of advancing ambitions within the Church. Priesthood conceived as a means of "empowering" individuals is utterly foreign to John Paul II's and the Council's thinking on the subject. So is any notion of the priesthood as membership in a clerical caste.[87]

At the same time, the "call" to the priesthood is heard in the Church and judged by the Church. No one can claim a "right" to be ordained on the basis of a personal discernment alone. The Church, through the local bishop, decides whether a "call" is authentic.[88] The bishop and his priests, for their part, have a serious pastoral obligation to preach and teach about the priesthood as a possible vocation.[89] But this is not a responsibility of priests and bishops alone: "*all the members of the Church, without exception, have the grace and responsibility to look after vocations.*"[90]

Pastores Dabo Vobis makes priestly training more rigorous by stressing the centrality of spiritual formation and a demanding academic formation in philosophy and theology. In many countries, John Paul writes, priests serve the most well-educated laity in the history of Christianity. Priests who lack intellectual maturity and an ongoing interest in theology will not be able to make the Gospel "credible to the legitimate demands of human reason."[91] Priests should study theology as a discipline "ordered to nourishing the faith," he writes, for theology is, at bottom, a means of fostering a deeper personal and communal relationship with Jesus Christ. Theology can "know" many things, but what theology should seek to know above all is Jesus Christ.[92] As for the seminary, it should be conceived, the Popes suggests, on the biblical image of Christ, who, after calling his apostles, took them aside to give them a special period of teaching and formation.[93] That this has not always been the experience of seminaries goes without saying. That it ought to be the image informing the seminaries of the third millennium is John Paul's evangelically centered proposal.[94]

Thinking in Centuries

One of the most interesting and least commented-upon facets of John Paul II's pontificate has been his exceptional success as a recruiter of priests: "the best vocation director the Church has ever had," as one curial cardinal put it.[95] While there has been no scientific survey on the subject, the cardinal's praise seems borne out by experience, at least of an anecdotal sort. Seminaries today are replete with young men who quite frankly say that John Paul's personal example was instrumental in leading them to discern a priestly vocation. Why is an interesting question, the answer to which suggests another countercultural facet of John Paul's personality and accomplishment.

A clue can be found in an observation from one former seminary rector: "a man will give his life for a mystery, but not for a question mark."[96] On this analysis, the confusions about priestly identity that had followed Vatican II had raised so many questions about the nature and function of the priesthood as to make it a very unattractive proposal for many young men. By reviving the idea of the priesthood as a sacral vocation rather than an ecclesiastical function, John Paul has given young men a challenge to heroism that many have found compelling.

John Paul's impact on the future of the Roman Catholic priesthood during the next two generations or so has been more than a matter of breathing new life into an ancient idea—the priest as *alter Christus*, "another Christ." It has also been a matter of persuasion by personal example. To Archbishop Edwin F. O'Brien, the Pope's "personal witness of priesthood has integrated and spiritually enriched his theological statements," and has been "of utmost importance" in making the priesthood a compelling possibility over against the myriad possibilities of making a success of one's life in the world.[97] That personal witness has also provided at least an existential answer to those wondering whether the "gift and mystery" of the priesthood, as John Paul described it in his vocational memoir, is worth the sacrifice of family life and personal independence it involves. Karol Wojtyła has lived an immensely rich human experience as a celibate priest under a vow of obedience.

The reform of seminaries envisioned in *Pastores Dabo Vobis* will take longer to realize. Contrary to popular imagination, the Roman Catholic Church is not governed like a well-run army, in which a decision at the top of the chain of command is quickly and efficiently transmitted to and carried out at the corps, division, regiment, battalion, company, and platoon levels. Local bishops who have not been persuaded by the vision of a new evangelization, or who are unsympathetic to the theology of priesthood in John Paul's apostolic exhortation, or who are unwilling to challenge entrenched seminary faculties can impede or block a full implementation of the document's prescriptions. Nor has John Paul II's view of ordained ministry been eagerly embraced by many theologians on seminary faculties. As that generation of intellectuals fades from the stage, a new generation, less scarred by the post-Vatican II battles, may be willing to look afresh at John Paul's ideas and prescriptions and see in them a path beyond the clericalism the older generation rightly criticized. Again, there is at least anecdotal evidence to suggest that this process is already under way. Seminaries that have embraced *Pastores Dabo Vobis* and whose faculties teach the theology of priesthood on which it is based tend to be growing, while seminaries resistant to John Paul's reform are either static or dying. That growing seminaries self-consciously attuned to the Pope's vision can be found in two countries where the crisis of the priesthood was most acute—the United States and Holland—is interesting, if not definitive.

The impact of *Pastores Dabo Vobis* will only be measured accurately sometime in the middle of the twenty-first century. That it set in place a reference point that demands attention is conceded by virtually all but its most implacable critics.

RETURN TO THE GEMELLI

John Paul had been experiencing occasional intestinal discomfort for some time when his physician, Dr. Renato Buzzonetti, sought the advice of Dr. Francesco Crucitti, who had performed the life-saving surgery on the Pope on May 13, 1981. After examinations in the Apostolic Palace, Crucitti decided that in-hospital tests were necessary, and during his Angelus address to the crowd in St. Peter's Square on Sunday afternoon, July 12, 1992, the Pope announced that he was leaving for the Policlinico Gemelli later that day and asked for prayers. Further testing revealed a growth in the large intestine, and John Paul was operated on early in the morning of July 15. During the four-hour procedure a large, benign tumor was removed, along with some stones from the Pope's gall bladder. Laboratory tests on the tumor revealed a small "center" of atypical but nonmalignant cells. The surgery was completely successful, no further therapy was required, and John Paul was out of bed and sitting in an armchair the next day.[98] He met what he often called his Angelus "appointment" with Romans and pilgrims on Sunday, July 19, through a tape-recorded message. Leaving the Gemelli on July 28, the Pope continued his recuperation at Castel Gandolfo and three weeks later flew to Lorenzago di Cadore in the Dolomites, where he stayed in a cottage for more than two weeks of convalescence and holiday before returning to Castel Gandolfo on September 2.

Despite the seventy-two-year-old Pope's reasonably rapid recovery from major surgery, this episode launched a series of speculations about his health and his imminent demise that would intensify throughout the 1990s. Some of this may have been the result of conscious or unconscious assumptions that John Paul had fulfilled his historic role in the collapse of communism; some of it, from the Pope's detractors in the Church and in the press, was, it ought to be admitted, a matter of wishes fathering thoughts. The traditional silence of the Holy See on such matters had created a working assumption among Vatican reporters that the Church bent or obscured the truth when making statements about the Pope's health. Nothing that press spokesman Joaquín Navarro-Valls, himself a trained physician, could do could shake this conviction in the minds of some journalists.

Interest in the Pope's health, and in details of it that undoubtedly struck curial officials and the papal apartment as no one's business but the patient's, was inevitable. Yet the greatest health crisis in the history of the modern papacy—John Paul's lengthy convalescence from Agca's assassination attempt—had not generated the raft of rumors about a "failing" Pope that followed John Paul's colon surgery in 1992 and his subsequent health problems. The relative lack of rumor-mongering in 1981 was due in part to Cardinal Agostino Casaroli's initiative in bringing in an international group of consultants to review the work of the local physicians and to make recommendations. Casaroli's prudence had given the entire process public credibility. Cardinal Angelo Sodano, Casaroli's successor and the only man in a position to make such a decision, evidently saw no need to convene such a body in this instance, nor did he do so in later cases. A different result followed the return to the traditional practice.

On October 9, 1992, John Paul II flew to the Dominican Republic, where the fourth general conference of CELAM, the council of Latin American bishops' conferences, was meeting to mark the fifth centenary of the evangelization of the Americas, begun with Columbus's voyage in 1492. The Columbus quincentenary launched an intense controversy in Europe and the Western Hemisphere over the heritage of colonialism in North, Central, and South America. John Paul saw the occasion in explicitly evangelical terms, and tried, once again, to link the Church's work for justice and development in Latin America to the Church's primary task of evangelization. As at Puebla, the Pope stressed the obligation to work for justice and the importance of doing so as the Church, not as a partisan political actor imposing a Catholic "model" of development.[99] And, as at Puebla, much of the commentary on the Santo Domingo address misread this as papal quietism.

At Santo Domingo John Paul also proposed a Pan-American Synod that would bring the CELAM bishops together with bishops from North America to consider the new evangelization in hemispheric perspective. The Pope's imagination was fired by the idea of one hemisphere with one (admittedly complex) history of evangelization—far more fired, in fact, than the imagination of virtually any local bishop in the New World. Latin Americans feared that, in any Pan-American Synod, their concerns would simply be overwhelmed by the rich bishops from *El Norte*. The North Americans found it hard to think of their pastoral situation as analogous to the Latin Americans'. John Paul continued to push the Pan-American idea during the 1990s, convinced that the evangelization of the Americas 500 years earlier had created an imperative for common reflection and action.[100]

THE SYMPHONY OF TRUTH

On October 11, 1992, the thirtieth anniversary of the opening of the Second Vatican Council, John Paul II signed the apostolic constitution *Fidei Depositum*

[The Deposit of Faith], promulgating the new *Catechism of the Catholic Church* mandated by the Extraordinary Synod of Bishops in 1985. *Fidei Depositum* and the *Catechism* were formally presented by the Pope at a special Vatican ceremony on December 7, 1992, attended by the College of Cardinals, curial leaders, the diplomatic corps, and representatives of bishops' conference doctrine committees from around the world. During the ceremony, the Pope gave copies of the *Catechism* to two children, representing the world's young people.[101] The *Catechism*'s logo, used in all language editions, was taken from a Christian tombstone in the Catacombs of Domitilla in Rome. The late third-century carving depicts a shepherd under a tree, holding a pastoral staff and a flute while tending a sheep: Christ the Good Shepherd, leading the flock by the authority of his staff, draws them to the shade of the tree of life by the melody of what John Paul calls, in *Depositum Fidei*, the "symphony of faith." That ancient image sums up the purpose and content of the thoroughly contemporary *Catechism of the Catholic Church*.

Oversight responsibility for developing the new *Catechism* had been given in 1986 to a commission of twelve cardinals and bishops chaired by Cardinal Joseph Ratzinger. The actual drafting work was done by an editorial committee of seven diocesan bishops, whose editorial secretary, Father Christoph Schönborn, an Austrian Dominican teaching at the University of Fribourg, was responsible for synthesizing the drafts of individual sections into a coherent whole. Father Schönborn and Cardinal Ratzinger had previously worked together on the theological journal *Communio* and on the International Theological Commission.

The *Catechism* went through nine drafts, all of which were first prepared in French. Bishops around the world were consulted throughout the drafting process, and the editorial committee's work was continually reviewed by the oversight commission. John Paul followed the work closely, according to Schönborn, but rarely gave direct comments on the draft. One exception, widely noted, was the catechism's discussion of the morality of capital punishment, but that was not the only occasion when the Pope took a personal interest in a specific topic. Still, John Paul's influence on the text of the *Catechism of the Catholic Church* is best described as indirect. He influenced the *Catechism* through his teaching, which, Schönborn notes, was "often the basis of a *Catechism* text" even when a direct citation was not made. The editorial committee had decided that, within the *Catechism*, direct quotations would only be made from the most authoritative sources: Scripture, Council documents over the centuries, important writings from the Fathers of the Church and the saints. John Paul II's encyclicals, apostolic letters, and apostolic exhortations are cited more than the teaching documents of any other pope, but those 135 citations do not measure the full scope of his influence on the text.[102]

The *Catechism of the Catholic Church* is not structured in the question-and-answer format familiar to Catholics from pre–Vatican II catechisms or to Lutherans from Martin Luther's *Small Catechism*. The commission and editorial committee decided to return to a more traditional narrative format, following the division of material adopted by the catechism of the Council of Trent. After a very brief prologue, the *Catechism* is divided into four parts.

The first is an explication of the Apostles' Creed, the ancient baptismal creed of the Church of Rome. The second is built around the Church's seven sacraments, celebrations of the mystery of God's saving presence in the world. The third, structured around the Ten Commandments, describes the moral life as a journey toward the summit and goal of human existence, happiness with God forever. The fourth, often regarded as the most lyrical part of the *Catechism*, discusses Christian prayer using the three professions and seven petitions in the Lord's Prayer, given by Christ to his disciples (see *Matthew* 6. 9–13). The *Catechism*, in brief, takes both Catholics and interested others on a basic tour of the Christian life: What does the Church believe? How is that belief publicly celebrated in the community's worship? How is that faith, confessed in the creeds and celebrated in the sacraments, to be lived? How does the individual deepen the life of faith through prayer?

Within each part, the *Catechism* is further subdivided into sections, chapters, articles, and numbered paragraphs. The numeration of the paragraphs is continuous throughout, for a total of 2,865 paragraphs in over 700 pages—a challenging but not indigestibly massive book. The narrative is broken at numerous points by boxed sections that provide concise summary statements of the material discussed at greater length just above. The *Catechism* is also extensively cross-referenced so that the studious reader can work backward and forward through the text, which was deliberately designed to elicit a sense of the "symphony" of faith.

The *Catechism* draws heavily on the Hebrew Bible and the New Testament, citing Scripture thousands of times—far more than any other authoritative source. The documents of the Second Vatican Council are cited almost 800 times, eight times more than the next most frequently cited council, Trent. *Lumen Gentium* and *Gaudium et Spes* are the two most frequently quoted Vatican II texts. In addition to citing canon law, papal teaching, and the prayers of the liturgy, the *Catechism* also draws on the wisdom of theologians and other Church writers, ranging from "Anonymous" (author of *An Ancient Homily for Holy Saturday*) to St. Thomas More (whose letter to his daughter Margaret from the Tower of London, shortly before his execution, describes More's conviction that God's providence is fully and finally in charge of history). St. Augustine is the most frequently cited theologian, in a list that draws most heavily on the Fathers of the Church, east and west. John Henry Newman, John Vianney, and Thérèse of Lisieux are among the modern figures quoted. In addition to Thérèse, women cited include Catherine of Siena, the fifth-century pilgrim Egeria, Elizabeth of the Trinity (a French contemplative beatified by John Paul II in 1984), Joan of Arc, Rose of Lima (the only Catholic author from the New World in the index of citations), and Teresa of Avila.

The final phases of the *Catechism's* gestation were marred by a controversy over the English translation of the text, which delayed the publication of the English edition for more than a year. Quarrels over the acceptable limits of "inclusive" language seem, in retrospect, minor compared to the achievement of the *Catechism* itself. Christoph Schönborn, who was named a bishop during the last year of the drafting process, argues that the "symphonic element" in the *Catechism* is the key to the whole edifice. The *Catechism* is not a matter of 2,865 bricks "put together in a vague, incoherent way." Rather, the attempt was to create what Schönborn calls "a beautiful, coherent expression of the unity of faith," in which the truth of particular doctrines becomes clearer because of their relationship to the entire structure.[103] That was important in itself, because the Catholic faith had always thought of itself as an integrated, unified whole. It was also important as the Church's statement of its confidence in the human capacity to know the truth of things on the threshold of the new millennium.

The *Catechism of the Catholic Church*, as John Paul put it in *Fidei Depositum*, is for "every individual who asks us to give an account of the hope that is in us (*cf. 1 Peter* 3.15) and who wants to know what the Catholic Church believes."[104] It was, at the same time, a challenge to some of the dominant intellectual currents of the late twentieth century—the cluster of ideas and assumptions often identified with "deconstruction" and "postmodernism."

Postmodernism claims that the origins of religious or moral traditions are irretrievably lost and that contemporary men and women have no access to the sources of what their ancestors had believed to be true. The *Catechism* claims that, whatever difficulties contemporary historical scholarship has with a "return to the sources," Christianity's origins are present in a living way because Christ—who is *the* source, the fountain of truth—is always present in and to his Church. Postmodernism claims that plurality is an absolute, and that coherence of conviction—agreement about the truth of things—is impossible over time or between cultures. The *Catechism* states its firm conviction of the unity of faith over space and time, and proposes that every human being is capable of hearing a saving word of grace from God, no matter what the cultural or historical circumstances.[105] Postmodernism claims that there is no such thing as *the* truth; there is only *your* truth and *my* truth. The *Catechism* argues that truth is essential food for the human soul and that we cannot live without the truth. Postmodernism claims that whatever knowledge exists is incoherent; there is no way in which all of reality can be coherently understood. The *Catechism* solemnly and joyfully confesses the coherence of Christian faith as an explanation of how things are, how things came to be, and how the world's story will be completed.[106]

The *Catechism*'s reception was a surprise to the project's critics and even its most hopeful supporters. Within a few years of its publication, more than 8 million copies were in print worldwide. By the end of the 1990s, the *Catechism* was available in forty-four languages, in six CD-ROM versions, and over the Internet on the Vatican Web site. Notwithstanding what some skeptical religious education professionals and bishops may have thought, millions of men and women in very different cultures wanted to know what the Catholic Church had to say about its belief and practice. The *Catechism* sold well in France, where its positive reception was one indicator of progress in the new evangelization, The Philippines received the *Catechism* enthusiastically, as did the bishops of India. The German-speaking world, Schönborn reports, was "rather difficult," but there, too, one could find "islands of deep interest in the *Catechism*, of good work with the *Catechism*." The *Catechism*'s reception in the United States frankly surprised its drafters. When the English edition was finally available in 1994 sales were robust, with 2.3 million copies of the trade edition and several hundred thousand copies of the mass market paperback sold. Shoppers grew accustomed to seeing, nestled among the thrillers and romances on sale at supermarket checkout counters, copies of the *Catechism of the Catholic Church.*[107]

Many bishops, priests, and religious educators, of course, welcomed the *Catechism*, which was formally intended as a guide to local catechisms and teaching materials. Its reception made clear that it was not simply a set of guidelines, however, for the *Catechism* quickly established itself throughout the world as a popular instrument by which Catholics could tell their children and neighbors (and, when necessary, remind their clergy, their religious educators, and, in some instances, their bishops) just what the Catholic Church believed and taught. In a late twentieth-century environment where Catholicism was no longer learned through the slow absorption of a Catholic culture, the *Catechism* also proved an invaluable tool for giving young people a view of the Church's doctrine and practice as a whole, and became a staple of the seminary pre-theology programs mandated by *Pastores Dabo Vobis* for those beginning priestly formation later in life.

Skeptics at the Extraordinary Synod in 1985 had doubted whether the *Catechism* would ever be completed. It was ready in six years, despite some rough patches along the road. Critics of the proposal said that Catholics were no longer interested in "conceptual" approaches to religious education. The exceptional sales of the *Catechism* proved the critics mistaken. Others worried that the *Catechism* would be a book "against" the Council. The 785 citations from the documents of Vatican II made unmistakably clear what John Paul wrote in *Fidei Depositum*—the *Catechism* is a product of the Council, and the Council understood as a coherent whole.

Three weeks after the *Catechism* was promulgated with *Fidei Depositum*, the Galileo case was brought to a close. The two events may seem dissimilar, but they ought to be considered together. Opening a new dialogue between religion and science and presenting a comprehensive narrative of the "symphony of faith" were, for John Paul II, two moments in a single evangelical project. What the Church proposed to the world was that the Word of God, the *Logos* who became incarnate in Jesus of Nazareth, was the agent of creation's purposefulness and the guarantor against the ultimate absurdity of life. In Christ, the heavens and the earth—origins, experience, destiny—were linked together. That was the good news the Church had to tell the twenty-first century: *this all fits together*, in a symphony of truth with a divine composer.

EUROPE, AGAIN

As 1992 gave way to 1993, controversies and opportunities in post-communist Europe continued to occupy a considerable place on John Paul II's agenda.

"Humanitarian Intervention"

On December 5, 1992, the Pope addressed the International Conference on Nutrition being held at the headquarters of the UN's Food and Agricultural Organization in Rome. Although John Paul did not mention the crisis unfolding in Somalia, where U.S. troops were preparing to land in an attempt to enforce the minimum of public order necessary to deal with widespread hunger and starvation, the Somali situation formed an unmistakable backdrop to the Pope's remarks.[108] Hunger, the Pope proposed, could no longer be considered a natural condition, nor was it a by-product of overpopulation. The contemporary problem was not production but food distribution, which was impeded by natural disasters, corrupt and violent politics, and protectionism. "Every day, hunger causes the deaths of thousands of children, elderly people, and members of the more vulnerable groups."

It was a "duty of justice" to remedy this, John Paul urged. "Wars between nations and domestic conflicts should not sentence defenseless civilians to die from hunger for selfish or partisan motives." The principle of noninterference in a country's domestic affairs did not apply in these circumstances. Therefore, the Pope argued, "the conscience of humanity, supported by provisions of international humanitarian law, asks that humanitarian intervention be obligatory where the survival of populations and entire ethnic groups is seriously compromised. This is a duty for nations and the international community. . . ."[109]

That "humanitarian intervention"—meaning military intervention by outside powers to rescue threatened populations—could be morally justified in situations of impending genocide was not very much in dispute. But on whom did the "duty" of "humanitarian intervention" fall? The "international community" was more a fiction than a reality, lacking both a government that could enforce its will and instruments of military intervention. The United Nations had shown itself incapable of dealing with situations like that of Somalia, where great-power intervention was the only available remedy. Was John Paul suggesting that a "duty" of "humanitarian intervention" now lay on the world's major powers, and particularly on the world's sole superpower, the United States? If so, what did that portend for the future of international institutions, which the Holy See had supported ever since World War II? If not, what did it mean to assert a "duty" when one could not identify the party on whom the duty fell?

John Paul's FAO address was a powerful plea for human solidarity and an important challenge to certain enduring "realist" shibboleths about world politics after the Cold War. As an examination of the serious moral and political issues involved in "humanitarian intervention," it raised more questions than it answered. By doing so, the FAO address may have inadvertently contributed to the kind of policy paralysis that had, as the Pope rightly observed, led to "unacceptable" situations and avoidable calamities.[110]

The "Hour of the Laity" in Poland

John Paul forcefully addressed some of the issues of how to be a "public Church" in a democratic Poland when the Polish bishops came to Rome in two groups in January 1993 for their *ad limina* visits.

Those Polish churchmen nostalgic for a return to the 1920s and 1930s— or even to the sureties of the struggle against communism—were quickly told that historical rollback was impossible. On January 12, at the outset of his first *ad limina* address to his fellow Poles, John Paul simply and bluntly told the bishops that they were living in "a new phase of history" which posed "new challenges" for evangelization. Above all, the Pope insisted, fidelity to Christ's command to "proclaim the Gospel to every creature" (*Mark* 16.15) in the new Polish situation meant recognizing that "the hour of the laity has struck for the Church." Poland's Catholic people now had "to assume the role in the Church which is rightfully theirs by virtue of the sacraments of Baptism and Confirmation." That was what implementing the Council meant in the new Poland. The laity must, as *Lumen Gentium* had put it, "make the Church present and fruitful in those places and circumstances where it is only through them that she can become the salt of the earth." To help make that possible, the Polish bishops had to create diocesan and parish-level structures of consultation with the laity, support lay renewal movements, and revive Catholic Action as a movement for strengthening civil society.

Then, having tried to consign clericalism to the Polish past, John Paul took up the most difficult issue of the public Church's presence and style in the new Poland: the legal status of abortion. The new evangelization included a defense of the dignity of human life from conception to natural death, and this, too, was primarily a task for the laity. As for legislation, the Church—laity, priests, and bishops—had to learn to make the case for the right to life of the unborn in explicitly public terms: "It is not a question of imposing Christian principles on everyone, as some people have objected, but of defending a fundamental human right, that is, the right to life. . . ."[111]

The Church's role in national political life dominated the Pope's *ad limina* address to a second group of Polish bishops, including Cardinal Józef Glemp, on January 15. The new evangelization, he began, included "among its essential elements" the social doctrine of the Church. A Catholicism confined to "the walls of the churches" was inconceivable, in Poland or anywhere else. But the evangelization of culture was one thing, and the clericalist direction of politics was another. Deepening the nation's understanding of freedom was not and could not be a matter of the Church becoming a partisan political actor.

The ancient Polish tradition of the Church as defender of the nation was one in which the Church was "not a competitor or partner in the game of politics" but rather "the guardian of the moral order and a critical conscience." Living that tradition faithfully meant some very specific things in the new Poland, John Paul said: "The Church is not a political party nor is she identified with any political party; she is above them, open to all people of good will, and no political party can claim the right to represent her." It was not the bishops' mission to be directly engaged in political affairs: "It is the laity's task to be directly involved in the area of politics, motivated by a sincere concern for the common good of the society in which they live." Post–Cold War dissatisfactions with democracy's sometimes dubious political results could not become an excuse for Catholic laity to avoid engaging in public life and the political arena, which was "their duty in conscience as well as one of the tasks deriving from their vocation." As for the country's historical tendency to indulge in divisive politics (which, as John Paul knew full well, had opened the doors to a return of ex-communists to political power), Poles had to "learn to dialogue with one another in truth and with respect for their own dignity and that of their counterparts, who, although differing, are not enemies."

Eighteen months after the difficult June 1991 pilgrimage, John Paul II had found his voice again in addressing his fellow Poles.

The Auschwitz Convent

Three months after the Polish *ad limina* visits, on April 9, 1993, the Pope sent a letter to the Carmelite nuns living in a convent just outside the walls of the Auschwitz concentration camp, asking them to move to another location in Oświęcim or to return to their mother convent.

The Auschwitz convent controversy was one of the most painful and unedifying of the late twentieth century. In late 1984, a small community of Carmelite nuns had moved into an abandoned building on the border of the concentration camp—Auschwitz I, as it was known, in distinction from the extermination camp at Birkenau, known as Auschwitz II. Protests from Jewish leaders followed. After lengthy conversations in Geneva between Catholic officials from throughout Europe and world Jewish leaders, it was agreed in 1987 that a new interfaith information and education center would be built outside the Auschwitz-Birkenau complex and that the cloistered Carmelite nuns, whose stated purpose was to give up their lives in prayerful reparation for what had been done in the camps, would move to the new center. It was further agreed that "there will . . . be no permanent Catholic place of worship on the site of the Auschwitz and Birkenau camps," so that "every one will be able to pray there according to the dictates of his own heart, religion and faith."

That seemed to settle matters. In Poland's difficult circumstances in the late 1980s, however, the decisions were not implemented promptly and new charges of anti-Semitism were raised. By the summer of 1989, the situation had once again reached a boiling point, with frequently strident charges and countercharges. The Carmelites were not inclined to leave; nationalistically inclined Polish Catholics saw the international Jewish protests against the convent as an attack on Catholicism itself; Jewish protests at the convent site triggered counterprotests by local Poles and further exacerbated tensions. On July 14, 1989, seven Jews wearing striped concentration camp uniforms and led by New York Rabbi Avraham Weiss climbed over the convent fence and began banging on the convent's doors and windows, demanding that the nuns abandon the convent. Construction workers making repairs on the second floor of the building dumped water on Weiss and his followers and eventually dragged them away from the site. The police nearby, who had done nothing to stop the demonstrators, did nothing to stop the workers, either, nor did the nuns and a priest who was present. Weiss said that the police had turned their back on Jews "just like your Church did 50 years ago." Two days later, Weiss's group was allowed into the courtyard of the Metropolitan Curia at Franciszkańska, 3, in Kraków, where they tacked an appeal to Cardinal Macharski on the door, stating that they had come in peace but saying that "as proud Jews we announce—stop praying for the Jews who were killed in the *Shoah*, let them rest in peace as Jews." At a later meeting with an archdiocesan official, Weiss's group charged that the Catholic Church sought to "remove the Jewish character of the *Shoah* and give it a Christian character." Weiss and his group returned to the convent the same day, climbed over the fence again, and staged a six-hour demonstration.

In the wake of the Weiss incident, Cardinal Macharski suspended efforts to implement the agreement on the new center, saying that it was "impossible for me to create the center as I had planned . . . [in] this climate of aggressive demands and uncertainty."[112] Macharski was sharply criticized by Catholic and Jewish leaders; whatever some of the latter's discomforts with Weiss's antics, it took a measure of courage to disagree publicly with him. Cardinal Glemp made matters even worse on August 26 when he gave a sermon at Częstochowa that dredged up anti-Semitic stereotypes about Jewish control of the mass media and included a wholly unacceptable *diktat*: "We have our faults with regard to the Jews, but today one would like to say: my dear Jews, do not speak to us from a position of a nation raised above all others and do not present us with conditions that are impossible to fulfill."[113] Glemp's sermon touched off another firestorm of protest from Jews and Catholics. Within three weeks, the Primate appeared to accept the necessity of fulfilling the Geneva agreement and moving the convent, in the context of the new information center.[114]

The Vatican finally intervened on September 19, in a statement from Cardinal Johannes Willebrands, responsible for the international Jewish-Catholic dialogue. The statement made clear that John Paul II supported the nuns moving from their present location and promised financial support for the new information and education center. That intervention broke the fever that had been building since the Weiss incidents and set the stage for what most of the parties involved now hoped would be a speedy and peaceful resolution of the dispute, which was threatening to damage the entire fabric of post–Vatican II Jewish-Catholic relations.[115]

By 1993, despite the completion of the new center, the nuns had not yet moved. With new protests mounting and some Jewish groups threatening to boycott the mid-April commemoration of the fiftieth anniversary of the Warsaw Ghetto Uprising, John Paul II intervened again, with a personal letter to the Carmelites. He reminded them of Thérèse of Lisieux's description of their common Carmelite vocation: "to be love itself in the heart of the Church." That was what they had wanted to be in their convent. But it was "now . . . the will of the Church [that] you should move to another place in this same Oświęcim." Each sister must decide, as "a matter of free will," whether she would continue to live in this Carmelite community in its new setting, or return to the group's mother convent.

There was still a place for the nuns in the human and Catholic reckoning with all that Auschwitz represented, though:

> "Oświęcim—and all that is connected with it as the tragic heritage of Europe and all humanity—remains a task for the Carmelites. . . . How the future will grow from this most painful and tragic past largely depends on whether, on the threshold of Oświęcim, "the love which is greater than death" will stand watch. You, dear sisters, in a particular way, are entrusted with the mystery of this redeemed love—this love which saves the world. . . ."[116]

Władysław Bartoszewski, the eminent Polish historian and a veteran of the Jewish-Catholic dialogue, described the Auschwitz convent controversy as "a struggle between two powerful and contradictory symbols" touching deeply on the "collective memory" of Jews and Poles and the related issue of national identity. "Since the war," he wrote, "Auschwitz has played a central role in the formation of Jewish identity and an only slightly lesser role in the formation of the Polish equivalent. The issue was not the presence of a few nuns praying in an old dilapidated building. It was about Jews and Poles being able to preserve two separate, conflicting, and essential views of history grounded in the same place."[117]

There were other issues engaged, some as elevated, others far less so. Both communities' leaderships showed a troubling incapacity to distance themselves from their radicals. Ugly forms of anti-Semitism of the sort that had once been thought consigned to the past were revived. The depth of anti-Christian animus among some Jews came to the surface of public debate. Rabbi Weiss's confusion of prayers for the dead with postmortem proselytization betrayed a deep confusion. So did the actions and statements of Poles who could not bring themselves to understand why Auschwitz had such a singular meaning for Jews. Questions of responsibility for the *Shoah* were also lurking just below the surface. The charge that Catholics were trying to give the *Shoah* a "Christian character" was fueled by intense suspicions that the purpose of any such maneuver was to deny any Christian responsibility for the fate of Europe's Jews.

At the root of it all, however, a grave theological issue was being raised. To many Jews, prayer at Auschwitz was blasphemy because Auschwitz was unredeemable—an absolute evil. In the Christian view of history and reality, no place is, in principle, unredeemable. There is no place where, as the Pope put it to the nuns, the "love which saves the world," the "love which is greater than death" should not "stand watch." What the Auschwitz controversy really confirmed was the imperative of the intensified theological conversation between Jews and Catholics for which John Paul II hoped.

Honoring the Martyrs

Two weeks after writing the Carmelites of Oświęcim, John Paul flew across the Adriatic Sea on April 25, 1993, to Albania, which longtime communist dictator Enver Hoxha had once bragged was "the only *really* atheistic state in the world"—a project he tried to impose with relentless brutality. After a brief stop in the capital, Tirana, where he was greeted by the world's most famous Albanian, Mother Teresa of Calcutta, the Pope went to Shkodrë in the small Balkan country's northwest, where he ordained four bishops. One of them, Archbishop Frano Illia, had been condemned to death by Hoxha's regime exactly twenty-five years earlier. The last catacomb had been opened.

Some of the spadework for the Albania pilgrimage had been done even as communist rule was crumbling in 1991. Monsignor Vincenzo Paglia, the ecclesiastical adviser to the Sant'Egidio movement and another of John Paul II's back-channel diplomats, went to Tirana and met with Ramiz Alia, a veteran communist and Hoxha's successor, then struggling to remain politically viable in a rapidly democratizing Albania. Paglia convinced the president to permit the restoration of the Tirana seminary and the Shkodrë cathedral. The first construction site in post-communist Albania was the seminary, on which the public relations–conscious Paglia hung a large, yellow-and-white Vatican banner. It was, he thought, a way of saying, "We're back!"[118]

From September 4 to 10, 1993, John Paul went to the newly independent Baltic republics of Lithuania, Latvia, and Estonia. It was the first visit by a pope to lands formerly belonging to the Soviet Union. For John Paul, the Lithuanian journey in particular was a pilgrimage to another land of martyrs. Between 1945 and 1955, four bishops, 185 priests, and 275,000 Lithuanian Catholic laity had been arrested and imprisoned or deported to concentration camps in Siberia. No Lithuanian bishops had been allowed to attend Vatican II. The cathedral in Vilnius was turned into a gallery for third-rate art; the Church of St. Casimir, nearby, became a museum of atheism.[119]

The most moving event during the papal pilgrimage to Lithuania was the Pope's walk through the Hill of Crosses in Meškuičiai, outside Šiauliai. The first crosses had been erected on the hill during the anti-Russian insurrection of 1863. A hundred years later, some 10,000 crosses of all shapes and sizes had been erected in protest of another form of imperialism. The communists loathed this symbolic linkage of their stranglehold on Lithuania with the czars', and began to clear the site as if they were clearing a dense forest. One by one, clandestinely, the crosses returned. By the time Lithuania recovered its independence, virtually every inch of the hill was covered with crosses. A simple wooden prie-dieu had been set up for John Paul amid this forest of crosses. He knelt there in prayer, head bowed and eyes covered by his right hand, remembering (as he later said in Vilnius) those buried without any cross over their graves, like the Lithuanian martyrs lying under the frozen tundra of Siberia.

The Pope's address to the "world of culture" in Riga, Latvia's capital, was seized upon by members of the Catholic left who had been uneasy with *Centesimus Annus,* and who now suggested that the Pope was retracting his carefully stated appreciation of the free economy. He had done nothing of the sort. Instead, he had reiterated three staples of Catholic social doctrine: that the Church's social doctrine was neither a political program nor an economic program; that no form of capitalism today fully satisfies the moral criteria of Catholic social doctrine; and that the social doctrine of the Church is not a "third way" between capitalism and socialism. Even more oddly, John Paul's reference to the "kernel of truth" in Marxism—its condemnation of the exploitation of workers—was taken in some quarters to suggest that the Pope was not the principled anti-communist he had long been thought to be. The suggestion was wholly implausible. Those making it rarely noted that John Paul, having acknowledged the "kernel of truth," immediately reminded his listeners that Pope Leo XIII had also condemned worker exploitation, on the grounds of a conviction alien to Marxist thought—that *"the center of the social order is man,* considered in his inalienable dignity as a creature made 'in the image of God.'"[120]

BEGINNING AGAIN WITH ORTHODOXY

The 1991 creation of the three apostolic administrations in Russia and the appointment of bishops to fill them had created a deep-freeze in Catholic-Orthodox relations. The seventh plenary session of the Joint International Commission for the Theological Dialogue Between the Roman Catholic Church and the Orthodox Church, held in Balamand, Lebanon, from June 17 to 24, 1993, tried to achieve a thaw, to set ground rules for the relations between Orthodox and Catholics in eastern Europe, and to reignite the conversation John Paul passionately hoped would heal the division of the eleventh century before the jubilee year of 2000. A modest thaw was all that could be accomplished.

The Balamand meeting had been postponed for a year at the request of the Orthodox participants, reflecting the deep divisions within and among their own communities over the future course of what Rome and Constantinople continued to call a "dialogue of love." When the Joint Theological Commission finally met at Balamand in June 1993, six of the fifteen Orthodox Churches that were participants in the dialogue were not represented. There were different reasons for their absence, but in some cases absence presaged further difficulties downstream. After a week of discussion, the commission agreed on a text entitled "Uniatism: Method of Union in the Past, and the Present Search for Full Communion."

As the title suggested, the meeting had dealt with the most burning issue on the ecumenical agenda from the Orthodox perspective—the continuing existence of Eastern-rite Churches, which had, over the past four centuries, entered into full communion with the Bishops of Rome while retaining their Byzantine liturgy and style of internal governance. The largest of these "Eastern Catholic Churches," also known as the "Uniates," was the Greek Catholic Church in Ukraine, which had a large public presence and was marked by robust vitality in the post-communist period.*

What came to be known in ecumenical shorthand as the "Balamand Document" tried to deal with this tangled web of historical grievances by affirming that the "Uniate" option could no longer be a way of achieving full reconciliation between "sister Churches" *and* that the Eastern Catholic Churches had the right to exist and to meet the spiritual needs of their members. Catholics and Orthodox agreed that, as they both shared the same faith, there should be no organized attempt at conversions. In cases where individuals exercised their religious freedom by joining a different communion, there should be no rebaptism, since Catholics and Orthodox recognized the validity of each other's sacraments. The Eastern Catholic Churches were also encouraged to join the Catholic-Orthodox ecumenical dialogue.[122]

Reactions to the Balamand Document were mixed. Addressing an Orthodox delegation that came to Rome in late June 1993 for the feast of Sts. Peter and Paul, John Paul II described the document as a "new step" that should help everyone involved, Orthodox, Latin-rite Catholic, and Eastern Catholic, to "live together in a single region, to continue their commitment to the dialogue of charity, and to begin or to pursue relations of cooperation" in pas-

---

*The history of "Uniatism" is extraordinarily complex and the emotions involved were intensified by various nationalisms. The historic attitude of Orthodoxy toward the "Uniates" was that they were impermissible and offensive Roman missionary salients into historically Orthodox lands. That attitude endured even after Vatican II and the ecumenical initiatives of Pope Paul VI and Ecumenical Patriarch Athenagoras had made clear that Roman Catholicism recognized the Orthodox as "sister Churches" with valid sacraments and a valid ministry. The fact of a vibrant "Uniate" Church in Ukraine (and in Romania) was also a living, and unwelcome, rebuke to those local Orthodox Churches that had played less than heroic roles under communism and had acquiesced in communist governments' attempts to crush the Greek Catholics. But the Orthodox insisted that the "problem of Uniatism" had to be addressed and resolved before the Roman Catholic-Orthodox theological dialogue could go any farther.[121]

toral service.[123] Ecumenical Patriarch Bartholomew also welcomed the document, although he took the occasion of a Vatican delegation's annual visit to the Phanar for the feast of St. Andrew in November 1993 to describe the statement as a "condemnation of Uniatism" and said that the Orthodox in the territories in question tolerated "an abnormal . . . situation" until such time as "the Uniate Churches finally realize where they belong."[124] Even granting the Ecumenical Patriarch's difficulties in pursuing an ecumenical agenda in light of intra-Orthodox tensions, it was not the most gracious statement imaginable.

Those tensions were obvious in the response to Balamand from the Orthodox Church in Greece, which did not send representatives to the meeting. One influential bishop, Metropolitan Christodolous of Dimitrias, denied that "Uniatism" could exist without "proselytism to the detriment of the Orthodox" and suggested that Eastern Catholics would use the document's defense of religious freedom as a ruse behind which to forward an aggressive contra-Orthodox agenda. The theologically influential monastic community of Mount Athos went even farther. In a December 1993 letter to Ecumenical Patriarch Bartholomew, they denied that the Roman Catholic Church was a "sister Church" possessing the means of salvation, and argued that true Orthodox could never recognize either the validity of the Catholic Church's sacraments and priesthood or the pope as the canonical Bishop of Rome without an explicit Catholic renunciation of Rome's heresies. News of what the Balamand Document had described as the "radically altered perspectives and attitudes" in both Catholicism and Orthodoxy during the past decades had evidently not reached Mount Athos, where the monks held fast to the view that the Orthodox Church was the only true Church in an absolute and exclusive way. Another Greek Orthodox theologian and member of the international commission, Father Theodore Zissis, claimed that the Orthodox at Balamand had signed the document "out of charm and polite carelessness." Zissis objected to the use of the word "Catholic" to describe the Roman communion and also denied that Rome and Constantinople were "sister Churches" with mutually recognized and valid sacraments. Catholicism, to Father Zissis, was heretical—period.

The Romanian Orthodox Church formally accepted the Balamand Document, and one of its bishops, Metropolitan Nicholas of Banat, said that the mutual recognition of Orthodox and Catholics as "sister Churches" required the Orthodox to think of the Eastern Catholics as "sister Churches," too. But other Romanian Orthodox bishops were not so accommodating. A year before Balamand, the Patriarchate of Bucharest had published a ritual for receiving "schismatic Roman Catholics and others" into the Orthodox Church; the ritual for the reception of Catholics included a prayer of expiation asking Christ to free the ex-Catholic "from the sleep of the deceit of heresy that leads to perdition." The attitude encoded in that prayer led many Romanian Orthodox leaders to think of Balamand as a sellout. The Greek Catholic leadership of Romania was far from enthusiastic about Balamand. In a letter to Pope John

Paul, Bishop Gheorghe Guțiu, speaking for the entire Greek Catholic hierarchy, defended the historical accomplishments of the Eastern Catholic Churches, and put the recent relationship between Romanian Orthodox and Romanian Greek Catholics in the sharpest terms: "They have remained the oppressors, we the oppressed; they were collaborators with communism while we were the victims of it; they the attackers and we the defenders even up to this very day."

Ukraine had been the reactor core of the meltdown in Catholic-Orthodox relations since the collapse of communism. As the resurgent Greek Catholic Church there became a vital public presence, Ukrainian Orthodoxy split into three bitterly divided factions, Russian Orthodoxy's historic claims were thrown into jeopardy, and Ukrainian nationalism was energized by the resurgent Ukrainian Catholics, the largest Eastern Catholic Church to emerge from the catacombs. Many Greek Catholics in Ukraine were offended by the Balamand Document's dismissal of "Uniatism" as a failed method. Some Ukrainian Catholics argued that what the Orthodox dismissed as "proselytism" was often a case of Ukrainian Orthodox believers freely joining the Greek Catholic Church because it was now publicly possible to do so, or because of their dismay with Orthodoxy's fragmentation in Ukraine. The head of the Greek Catholic Church, however, took an open, positive approach to the document. In an August 1993 letter to Cardinal Cassidy, Cardinal Myroslav Lubachivsky praised Balamand's description of Catholicism and Orthodoxy as sister Churches with the same faith, the same sacraments, and the same apostolically transmitted ministry, as well as the document's defense of religious freedom, its teaching that ecclesiastical division is contrary to the will of Christ, and its recognition that the "Uniate method" in the past had been based on a genuine wish to fulfill Christ's desire for the unity of his Church.[125]

Balamand was, Cardinal Edward Cassidy suggested, about as far as the Catholic Church could go without betraying its own self-understanding. It was now up to local Eastern Catholic and Orthodox communities to settle their problems peacefully on the ground. The resolution of these historic grievances, the cardinal argued, would only come when these communities had learned to live and work together.[126] But Orthodoxy's difficulties in dealing with its own history were a serious obstacle to grassroots reconciliation.

John Paul II's vision of Rome and Orthodoxy reconciled on the threshold of the third millennium was one of the most powerful signs that he was living imaginatively in the future. The inability of some of Catholicism's Orthodox interlocutors to read the past in anything but the most partisan terms, and the rivalry that had begun to emerge between Ecumenical Patriarch Bartholomew in Constantinople and Patriarch Aleksy II in Moscow, was making the Pope's vision ever more difficult to achieve. Within two years, however, John Paul, determined to pursue the new evangelization with, rather than against, Orthodoxy, would make his boldest proposal yet to what he continued to insist were the "sister Churches" of the East.

THE POPE AGAINST TERROR

Four months before the Balamand meeting, which was so profoundly influenced by the Church's experience of persecution under communism, John Paul had confronted one of the new faces of post–Cold War persecution on his fifty-seventh pastoral pilgrimage and ninth to Africa.

The itinerary began on February 3, 1993, in Benin, home of Cardinal Bernardin Gantin, Prefect of the Congregation for Bishops and one of the Pope's closest collaborators. Benin, like central and eastern Europe, was recovering from Marxism, and John Paul praised its people's efforts to build free institutions. After two days in Benin, which included a meeting with Muslims in Parakou, the Pope flew across the continent to Uganda. John Paul visited AIDS patients in a hospital in Kampala, announced that a Special Assembly of the Synod of Bishops for Africa would be held in Rome in April 1994, and celebrated Mass at the shrine of the Ugandan Martyrs canonized by Paul VI in 1964. The decision to hold the African Synod in Rome rather than in an African locale was criticized in the press, particularly in Europe. Cardinal Francis Arinze, the Nigerian head of the Pontifical Council for Inter-religious Dialogue, had a different memory of the decision. The Pope had asked all the African cardinals to come to Rome to discuss the Synod's location. Some had argued for Rome; others for Africa. John Paul said, "Let's do both," which is what eventually happened. The Synod itself was held in Rome, and the post-synodal apostolic exhortation was signed and promulgated in three African cities. "When I read that the Roman Curia had pickpocketed the Synod out of the hands of the poor Africans, I smiled," Arinze remembered. "They didn't have any idea. If we had wanted it only in Africa, that's what we would have had."

Arinze's analysis shed interesting light on what the African bishops were looking for from a Synod that had been bruited for a decade and a half. To hold the Synod in Rome meant that the Pope would be present every day—and the Africans wanted that. It also meant that the leaders of the Curia would be present every day—the Africans also wanted that, so there would be a more open, two-way communication between Africa and the Curia. Finally, Arinze and others thought the African Synod would be taken much more seriously if it were held in Rome: "If it had been in an African country," Arinze said, "the media would have shown the Pope coming down from the plane. And after that they would have shown the woman washing the baby in dirty water in a village, and the children playing in trees, and monkeys in the forest, and some primitive people. They tell us precious little about the Pope's meeting with intellectuals at the university. They show only things they think are funny and enjoyable for Europeans. We want to be taken seriously. We have much more to share than that."[127]

The most dramatic moments of the pilgrimage came in Sudan, a country ruled by Islamic radicals whose fierce persecution of Christians in the south of the country included selling Christian women and children into slavery and crucifying Christians who publicly professed their faith. The depredations of the Khartoum regime had led to armed resistance. Rebels controlled considerable portions of the south of the vast country and engaged the government in a brutal civil war. Several Sudanese bishops had discouraged John Paul from coming to their country. Some said that it would be inappropriate to greet government leaders whose hands were dripping with blood. Others feared an outbreak of anti-Christian violence by Muslim activists.[128] John Paul thought it his duty to defend persecuted Christians, and a nine-hour visit to Khartoum was finally agreed upon.

The Pope kissed the ground at Khartoum airport, and began his address at the arrival ceremony with a frank statement of concern: "When people are weak and poor and defenseless, I must raise my voice on their behalf. When they are homeless and suffering the consequences of drought, famine, disease and the devastations of war, I must be close to them. . . . " He had come, he said, on behalf of "*justice and peace for all the citizens of this land,* without reserve, regardless of their religion, social standing, ethnic background or color." More and more Africans, he suggested, were becoming aware that "society must become more democratic, more respectful of legitimate differences, more stable through the rule of law, reflecting universally recognized human rights." The peoples of Africa were no longer content to be free in the technical sense of belonging to independent states. External colonialism had been consigned to the past. It was now time to shed the internal colonialism imposed by corrupt, authoritarian governments.[129]

John Paul's visit to Sudan and his forthright defense of religious freedom did not measurably affect the ongoing persecution of Christians there.[130] The nine-hour pilgrimage to Khartoum did help put the issue of the post–Cold War persecution of Christians on the international agenda, however.[131] Perhaps even more importantly, it gave a boost to the morale of Christians and those Muslims who opposed the Sudanese government's Islamic radicalism and the influence on it of the leader of the country's Muslim Brotherhood, Hassan Turabi.[132]

Terrorism against Christians in radical Islamic states was one face of an unreconciled post–Cold War world. There were other forms of terrorism, and one of them was very much on John Paul's mind three months later when, on a three-day pilgrimage to Sicily in May 1993, he made his most vigorous public protest against the Mafia. It was the Pope's 109th extended pastoral visit in Italy and his third to Sicily. After traveling to Trapani, Erice, and Mazara del Vallo on the island's western coast, he came to Agrigento, on Sicily's southern shore. On Sunday, May 9, at an outdoor Mass celebrated in the famous "Valley of the Temples" against the backdrop of the ancient Greek Temple of Concord, what the ever-discreet *L'Osservatore Romano* described as a "visibly agitated Pope" demanded that the Sicilians live their faith not simply by "interior personal assent," but also by "*condemning evil with conviction*" and by denouncing the "*culture of the Mafia*, which is a culture of death, a profoundly inhuman, anti-Gospel foe of human dignity and civil harmony."[133] In spontaneous remarks at the end of Mass, he made a passionate plea for a new Sicily:

> Dearly beloved, my wish is that, as the deacon just said, you may go in peace and find peace in your land. . . . In the wake of so much suffering, you have the right to live in peace. Those who are guilty of disturbing this peace have many human victims on their conscience. They must understand that killing innocent human beings cannot be allowed. God once said, "You shall not kill." No man, no human association, no mafia can change or trample on this most sacred right of God. . . . In the name of the crucified and risen Christ, of Christ who is the Way and the Truth and the Life, I say to those who are responsible for this: "Repent! God's judgment will come some day!"[134]

The Pope's blunt assault on Sicily's criminal culture dominated the three days of the visit, as John Paul counterposed Christian solidarity to "the recurring chains of hatred and revenge" in Trapani, where he also described "those forms of *organized crime* that deaden and ruin consciences" as the products of satanic temptation. In Mazara del Vallo, he urged the local priests, seminarians, and religious sisters to "heal this island of the scourge of the Mafia."[135]

Seventeen days later, on May 27, 1993, a car bomb killed five persons, including two children, and destroyed priceless works of art at Florence's Uffizi Gallery. John Paul immediately sent a telegram to Cardinal Silvano Piovanelli, the city's archbishop, condemning "this act of inhuman violence and unprecedented savagery."[136] In July, bombs were set off at the Pope's Roman cathedral, the Basilica of St. John Lateran, and at the venerable Roman church of S. Giorgio in Velabro. Though no group ever claimed responsibility, no one believed the timing was accidental.

The bombings, like the papal visit to Sicily that seemed to have triggered them, took place during a time of exceptional turmoil in Italian public life. The often informal, sometimes extralegal arrangements that had shaped Italy's politics during the Cold War were breaking down under the pressures of their own long-term implausibility, the desire for political and legal revenge, and a new world situation. As Bishop of Rome, John Paul had committed himself to the reevangelization of Italy. At the same time, and as part of the very same process, he declined to play the same assertive role in Italian domestic politics as his twentieth-century papal predecessors. Italy, too, was to be reconverted "from the head down," through the reevangelization of culture, rather than through the manipulation of politics.

If there was going to be a public struggle for the character of the new, post–Cold War Italy, Italy's Polish Primate intended to be involved. The new evangelization demanded action to reconcile an unreconciled society. That, among many other things, demanded a forthright challenge to the "culture of death."

18

The Threshold of Hope

Appealing to Our Better Angels

AUGUST 12–15, 1993	Fourth international World Youth Day in Denver, Colorado.
OCTOBER 5, 1993	*Veritatis Splendor,* John Paul II's tenth encyclical.
NOVEMBER 11, 1993	John Paul breaks shoulder.
DECEMBER 30, 1993	"Fundamental Agreement" between the Holy See and the State of Israel is signed.
JANUARY 15, 1994	John Paul criticizes the idolatry of nationalism in annual address to the diplomatic corps.
APRIL 8, 1994	Rededication of Sistine Chapel completes restoration of Michelangelo's frescoes.
APRIL 28, 1994	John Paul falls and fractures femur; artificial hip joint implanted on April 29.
MAY 13, 1994	Convent for contemplative nuns opens in the Vatican.
MAY 22, 1994	Apostolic Letter, *Ordinatio Sacerdotalis,* on women and the ministerial priesthood.
JUNE–AUGUST 1994	In twelve audience and Angelus addresses, John Paul tries to re-shape the international debate on family planning and population issues prior to the third international conference on population.
SEPTEMBER 5–13, 1994	The World Conference on Population and Development meets in Cairo.
SEPTEMBER 7, 1994	Papal pilgrimage to Sarajevo cancelled.
OCTOBER 19, 1994	John Paul II's book, *Crossing the Threshold of Hope,* is published.
NOVEMBER 11, 1994	"Common Christological Declaration" with the Assyrian Church of the East ends 1,500 years of theological estrangement.
NOVEMBER 26, 1994	At his sixth consistory John Paul creates thirty new cardinals.
DECEMBER 13, 1994	John Paul writes *Letter to Children* throughout the world.

As a helicopter ferried John Paul II to Denver's Mile High Stadium on August 12, 1993, for the opening of the first World Youth Day in North America, no one aboard knew quite what to expect.

A year before, skeptics on the U.S. Bishops' Conference staff had warned that there would be little interest in such an event because "pilgrimage" was a foreign notion, unattractive to young Americans. Some even suggested that the Pope himself was a liability whose presence would make it harder to mount a successful gathering. In the months before World Youth Day, the U.S. press had been full of speculation about the difficulties John Paul II would have with America's "cafeteria Catholics," determined to pick and choose for themselves among the Church's doctrines and moral teachings. The senior assistant attorney general of Colorado worried out loud that allowing a papal Mass in a state park would open the door to a demand for park space from the Ku Klux Klan and goodness knows who else. Sierra Club environmentalists and animal-rights activists had complained about the Mass's impact on the local wildlife. Disenchanted local Catholics in Denver had called a press conference to "disinvite" the Pope to their city.

More than a few U.S. bishops were among the doubters about World Youth Day '93. The bishops staunchly promoted Church programs for teenagers, urged their priests to work with youngsters, and supported Offices of Youth Ministry in their chanceries, but many of them thought "youth ministry" was virtually impossible. The culture, the music, the lifestyle of the teenagers of the 1990s struck them as alien; so did young people's struggles with drugs and sex. Between the bishops and restless, contemporary American youth there seemed to be a chasm that few Church leaders thought it possible to bridge. Whatever had happened in Rome, Buenos Aires, Santiago de Compostela, and Częstochowa during the first four international celebrations of World Youth Day, things were going to be different in Denver, because America was different.

This episcopal skepticism extended to some of John Paul's recent judgments, for it was the Pope who had pressed to hold a World Youth Day in the United States and who had chosen Denver over Cleveland, Minneapolis–St. Paul, and Buffalo as the venue. The majestic Rockies, some thought, must have attracted the mountaineering pontiff. Few seem to have considered that it was precisely Denver's secularity, its self-conscious modernity, and its sense of living on the cutting edge of the high-tech future that recommended it to John Paul, eager to take World Youth Day into the heart of the contest to define the free society in the 1990s.

As the event itself drew closer, it began to look as if the skeptics would be surprised, at least by the numbers. The bishops' conference staff's original expectations of a mere 60,000 registrations had been more than tripled, as over 200,000 young people from all over the world had registered. But what kind of reception would they give the Pope, who, according to pre-event press coverage, was widely perceived by Americans as a moral scold, out of touch with the national temper?

Mile High Stadium had witnessed frenzy during games played there by the city's beloved football team, the Denver Broncos. It was about to experience something wholly unprecedented.

The weather was not cooperative. It had rained much of August 12, and the youngsters who had walked from one pre–World Youth Day event to another, and then out to the stadium, were tired, hungry, and frustrated. They began to feel a little bit better as they wedged themselves into their assigned seats and all sorts of stadium-like behavior began. Some were especially struck by the sight of several hundred American bishops, dressed in red-piped cassocks and skullcaps, doing "the wave" with the crowd. Spirits began to lift. The crowd sang the World Youth Day '93 theme song, "We Are One Body," over and over, led by the Irish pop singer Dana. The rain continued.

As the papal helicopter approached the stadium in the twilight, those inside, including John Paul II, could see that Mile High was filled beyond its normal capacity. Ninety thousand youngsters, half-again as many as the skeptics had predicted for the entire four-day event, had somehow crowded into the seats and onto the stadium's playing field for the opening ceremony. The rain stopped, as if on cue. But it was the noise that was beyond anyone's imagining as the young people chanted time and again, "John Paul Two, we love you!" When the helicopter began its descent, the pilot, a combat veteran of the Vietnam War, had to fight to keep the chopper under control. The turbulence created by the youngsters' cheers, the pilot later said, was buffeting the aircraft so strongly that it was causing instability. It was an eerie sensation. Here, against the magnificent backdrop of the Rockies and on a wholly different kind of mission, the atmospheric disturbance caused by the cheers for the Pope reminded him of what it had been like to be under fire during the war.

An American television reporter told her cameraman that this was being stage-managed for maximum visual effect. All these kids were Vatican plants brought in to show support for the Pope. The cameraman just laughed: "Sure, a stadium full of plants."

Even before John Paul had arrived at World Youth Day's first event, Denver had passed beyond the trap gate of cynicism. In a phrase that would become familiar to millions around the world, it had crossed the threshold of hope.[1]

THE "BIG SURPRISE"

When things finally settled down after the tumultuous welcome for the Pope, John Paul began a multilanguage roll call of the countries represented in Mile High Stadium, which set off another barrage of noise-storms. The roll call had become a World Youth Day [WYD] tradition, and it got the same enthusiastic response in Denver as it had in other venues. In his opening remarks, though, the Pope made sure that everyone knew that something was different this time. As in previous World Youth Days, he reminded the crowd, they had come together as pilgrims, not tourists, but this "stupendous setting in the heart of the United States of America" was not a traditional pilgrimage site. Rather, WYD '93 had come on pilgrimage to the modern world, embodied in a self-consciously contemporary city surrounded by natural splendor. That meant, John Paul said, that he and his young friends were "searching for the reflection of God, not only in the beauty of nature but also in humanity's achievements and in each individual person."

Secular modernity imagined that its heart was an empty shrine. Modern men and women thought they had outgrown the "need" for religious faith. But that could not be. For the modern world had been constructed by human beings whose lives were an open question. Humanity could not flourish in a world of empty shrines, which was an inhuman world. So World Youth Day had come to Denver, John Paul said, to make possible a "real encounter with Jesus Christ." In that encounter, the world's beauty was fully appreciated, solidarity was built on a secure foundation, and men and women were initiated into an "intimate communion with God himself, in a love that goes beyond all limits of time and space, to eternal, unassailable happiness."

It began to rain again during the Pope's opening address, but the electric atmosphere wasn't dampened as tens of thousands of youngsters huddled under colorful ponchos, umbrellas, and the giant signs—"*Willkommen*," "*Bienvenidos*," "*Benvenuti*," "Welcome"—that had greeted John Paul. At one point, the Pope ad-libbed an apology for his "long, too long" speech—and got an ear-splitting chorus of "No" in response. John Paul had also departed from his prepared text at the airport arrival ceremony earlier that day, and in a more pointed way. Replying to welcoming remarks by President Bill Clinton, the Pope noted that the United States had been founded on the assertion of certain self-evident moral truths about the human person, including every human being's inalienable right to life. All the "great causes" led by the United States in the post–Cold War world, John Paul said, "will have meaning only to the extent that you guarantee the right to life and protect the human person." Interrupted several times by the cheers of the few hundred youngsters who had been permitted to attend the airport ceremony, the Pope finally stopped reading his text, paused, and asked, "You are crying for what the Pope says, or against?" "For!" they shouted back.[2]

The next night, Friday, August 13, Mile High Stadium became a great outdoor arena for reliving the experience of Christ's passion and death during a floodlit celebration of the stations of the cross: fourteen commemorations of the events of Good Friday that begin with Jesus condemned to death by Pontius Pilate and end with his entombment. At the conclusion of the stations, the great pilgrim's cross that had been given to the young people of Denver in Rome on Palm Sunday, 1992, and that had visited some forty American dioceses in the year and a half since, was solemnly raised by a dozen teenagers in polo shirts and jeans, behind the pitcher's mound on a field normally occupied in August by Denver's baseball team, the Colorado Rockies. John Paul then addressed the youngsters in a live message broadcast on the stadium's enormous scoreboard.

They had just participated, he said, in a biblically based reflection on the human capacity for injustice. Jesus, "accused before a judge who condemns more out of fear and cynicism than out of conviction," became a "victim of human pride and corrupt justice." In doing so, Christ had become "the image of what human beings are capable of doing to others when their hearts are hardened and the light of conscience is dimmed." Love, however, had proven stronger than cynicism, fear, injustice, and even death itself. Christ had forgiven his torturers from the cross, and that forgiving love, John Paul said, "reaches out to everyone without exception," filling the world with "life-giving grace."

To look into the face of the suffering Christ was also to meet and adore "the Lord raised up between earth and heaven." Suffering became redemptive when united to the self-sacrificing suffering of Christ. Therefore, John Paul urged, "take courage in the face of life's difficulties and injustices. Commit yourselves to the struggle for justice, solidarity, and peace in the world. Offer your youthful energies and your talents to building a civilization of Christian love." That was what one learned from walking the way of the cross, "the mystery . . . at the center of the Church's life." [3]

The Pope had given himself a break for some hiking in the Rockies on Friday afternoon, before the stations of the cross. When he arrived at the St. Malo Retreat Center near Estes Park, Colorado, his host, Denver Archbishop J. Francis Stafford, expected that the seventy-three-year-old pontiff might take a nap of an hour or so. The archbishop certainly wanted one himself. Twenty minutes after the papal bedroom door had closed, John Paul was back in the main part of the house, calling out, "So where is the archbishop of Denver?" The two went off along the park's hiking trails. Underneath his cassock, John Paul wore a pair of white sneakers with gold shoelaces, given him by some teenagers the day before.[4]

As at previous World Youth Days, Denver's closing Mass, in Cherry Creek State Park on Sunday morning, was preceded by an all-night prayer vigil. A quarter of a million youngsters, with sleeping bags, water bottles, and backpacks, hiked fifteen miles from downtown Denver to the park on Saturday afternoon, August 14. They made an impression as they walked en masse through the city. "I'm not a Catholic, and to a cynical old lawyer like me this is just wonderful," said one man, Jerry Valentine, who gave water to the pilgrims as they walked past his home. The heat and the distance were too much for some, who took advantage of the aid stations scattered along the route. The Sudanese youngsters who carried the World Youth Day pilgrim cross on the last leg of the trek to the park said they felt fine; they walked at least this far lots of days.

During the early evening, the pilgrims got settled in their assigned sections of the park, in territory usually inhabited by prairie dogs, coyotes, rabbits, deer, and owls. There was a bit of rain, but the meteorology contributed to the drama—John Paul arrived at the site just as a spectacular sunset broke through the cloud cover. The Pope spoke from a stage about the size of an American football field. Enormous TV screens scattered throughout the park brought him into closer contact with his young audience. The message did not lack edge.

"In the modern metropolis," John Paul said, "life . . . is often treated as just one more commodity to be organized, commercialized and manipulated according to convenience." The drama of the moral crisis of modernity was that so many people refused to recognize the threat posed to life by reducing it to a commodity. Thus young people today had to make a special effort to keep open the dialogue with God and with moral truth that takes place in the conscience, "the most secret core and sanctuary of a person." There, they would also encounter Jesus Christ, whose gift of divine life was "the only true and realistic hope" of a humanity on whom the shadows of a culture of death were lengthening. That was why he asked them to pray that night: "Maranatha! 'Come, Lord Jesus!'"

John Paul's unstinting message changed what the press had begun to describe as a "Catholic Woodstock" into a night of serious reflection. The Pope, whose sense of audience remained acute, didn't want to close on a note of unrelieved solemnity. Leaving the stage, he looked at his digital watch and said that he hoped to meet them the next day, "and for the moment he says to all of you, 'Good night.'" Make it, he finished, "a night of singing, of joy, of sacred joy. . . . *Adios!*"[5]

The next morning, the Pope was helicoptered back to the park. Looking out the window, he saw the largest crowd in the history of Colorado, more than 500,000, with downtown Denver and the Rockies in the background. It was the solemnity of the Assumption of Mary, and John Paul greeted the great congregation accordingly: "In the name of Jesus Christ and his Blessed Mother, I say to you . . . good morning!" It was a blistering hot, dry day. Fourteen thousand people were treated for dehydration, and a fire truck provided by a courteous local government showered pilgrims on the edges of the venue during the Pope's sermon.

During it, John Paul continued to press the challenge of the previous night. The world, he suggested, could not wait for the young to become leaders in some ill-defined future. It needed their witness now. That meant entering the "never-ending battle being waged for our dignity and identity as free, spiritual beings," and challenging the "culture of death" that tried to crush their desire to live life to the full. "Do not be afraid to go out on the streets and into public places," he urged, "like the first apostles who preached Christ and the good news of salvation in the squares of cities, towns, and villages. This is no time to be ashamed of the Gospel. . . . It is the time to preach it from the rooftops."[6]

After Mass, John Paul said good-bye in English, Spanish, Italian, French,

German, Portuguese, Polish, Russian, Lithuanian, Croatian, Arabic, Tagalog, Swahili, Korean, and Vietnamese before departing for Stapleton International Airport and his return flight to Rome. In response to Vice President Al Gore's farewell remarks, John Paul said that he had come to Denver as "a pilgrim of hope" who believed that young people were capable of greatness. His hope was strengthened whenever he met the young because "the longing present in every heart for a full and free life that is worthy of the human person is particularly strong" in youth. Revisiting the history lesson he had proposed to President Clinton three days before, the Pope concluded with a prayer that "America will continue to believe in its noble ideals" and would thereby fulfill its destiny as "one nation, under God, with liberty and justice for all."[7]

The Impact

During the Cherry Creek State Park closing Mass, John Paul II had embraced Denver's Archbishop Stafford and said quietly, "Thank you for making this historic event for the whole Church possible." A year later, in September 1994, Archbishop Stafford brought the "John Paul II Choir" that had been formed for WYD '93 to Assisi, Florence, and Rome. The Pope invited the group to an early morning Mass at Castel Gandolfo, where he told them that the event of the previous August "still lives on in my heart as one of the highlights of my pontificate."[8] "Historic event" and "highlight" were high praise from a man who had played such a large role in Church and world affairs for more than fifteen years. The long-term impact of the Denver World Youth Day can only be measured in the mid-twenty-first century, after succeeding decades have shown how John Paul's challenge actually shaped a quarter-million young lives. But its immediate effect was substantial.

Few, if any, Catholic initiatives since the Second Vatican Council have given so many Catholics a sense of themselves as members of the *communio* of a genuinely universal Church as John Paul II's World Youth Days. That was certainly one impact of Denver, and particularly for the young American pilgrims. Young people by the thousands also experienced a deeper connection to the Church's sacramental life. A standing joke during World Youth Day '93 was that the lines outside the impromptu confessionals set up around the various venues looked like the lines at pizzerias or the other fast-food haunts of modern teenagers. It was a rough analogy, to be sure, but there is no doubt that many, many young people received the sacrament of penance for the first time in a long time during WYD '93. One participant also sensed a "renewed interest, awareness, and awe for the Real Presence [of Christ] in the Eucharist." Catechesis through a sacramental experience of "the mysteries," a practice as ancient as first-century Christianity, was revived in Denver during World Youth Day.[9]

Vocations to the priesthood and consecrated religious life were also clarified and reinforced. Two years passed before Dennis Garcia, a New Mexican teacher and participant in WYD '93, finally made the decision to enter the seminary and study for the priesthood. But it was World Youth Day, he believed, that had planted the seed. Moreover, "the courage and vivacity of the youth, together with John Paul II, gave me the courage to finally say, 'Yes.'"[10] Garcia, it seems likely, was not alone.

The city and county of Denver were also direct beneficiaries of World Youth Day—and not simply in terms of the multimillion-dollar economic benefit bruited by the local press. Something unmistakably calming took place in the Mile High City between August 11 and 15, 1993. The Denver metropolitan area had been experiencing a crime wave during the spring and early summer months leading up to WYD '93. Yet during the five days of the event itself, the downtown and Capitol Hill neighborhoods, typically high crime areas, experienced a dramatic reduction in criminal behavior.[11] For five days at least, a self-consciously secular city was caught up in and transformed by the power of youthful Christian witness. Many Denver citizens, skeptical at best about the Catholic Church and its purposes, were compelled to reconsider because of what they had seen on the streets of their own neighborhoods.

The bishops of the United States were also changed by the Denver World Youth Day. Those who had thought the Pope's moral challenge could not be heard in the American cultural context had to think again, as did those who felt that youth ministry was simply impossible. John Paul had demonstrated that young people could be reached through what Archbishop Stafford called a "language of presence." The Pope had taught his American bishops that being young is a time designed by God for searching and that their job as bishops was to be present to that search.[12]

The bishops also learned something about the vitality of Catholicism in America as a whole. The lack of interest in World Youth Day expected by some in the bishops' conference staff was dramatically falsified by the experience of tens of thousands of Catholic families across America who prepared their youngsters for the pilgrimage to Denver, helped pay their way, and, in short, made the entire event possible. Some things, evidently, were going right for the Church in the United States.[13]

World Youth Day '93 also caused some rethinking in the American press. The *Washington Post*'s E. J. Dionne, Jr., wrote shortly after the event that he had had "trouble recognizing the Church I've belonged to all my life in a lot of [the] coverage" of World Youth Day. The press's obsession with debates over sexual morality left readers and viewers "clueless as to why so many people continue to belong to the Church." Religious people, he concluded, "are owed a little more respect than that which is shown by the assumption that all they care about is sex and nothing but sex."[14] Peter Steinfels of the *New York Times* was another critic of his professional colleagues. The obsessive media focus on dissent and abortion, he wrote, "obscured" the Pope's message. If his colleagues had paid closer attention to John Paul's "underlying moral analysis" and his defense of "universally valid principles of morality," Steinfels wrote, they would have discovered that the Pope had been speaking to a widespread American disquiet about the cheapening of life.[15]

John Paul II came back from WYD '93 with a more complex and hopeful view of the American situation than he had brought from Rome. He had been vindicated in his judgment that this celebration of a Gospel for the young could be taken into the very center of the secular "metropolis," as he had called it. The Pope had also gotten a very different reading on American youth than he may have been receiving from the U.S. bishops. John Paul still had high hopes for a new evangelization and a new Catholic vitality coming *ex oriente*, from the Church east of the old Cold War divide. After the experience of WYD '93, the Pope understood that there were also great possibilities *ex occidente*, out of the West.[16]

Cardinal John O'Connor of New York thought that World Youth Day '93 had been a "watershed experience" in the American perception of John Paul II and in the Pope's experience of the United States.[17] John Paul seemed inclined to agree. In his annual Christmas address to the Roman Curia on December 21, 1993, he called Denver the "big surprise" of 1993, took a gentle jab at the American bishops for their lack of confidence before the event, and put the entire episode in an evangelical framework. It was "not the first time," he reminded the prelates, "that the young people expressed so vigorously their desire to carry the Gospel into the new millennium. Christ is the Way, the Truth, and the Life . . . So how can one say that they like slogans such as 'Christ—yes, the Church—no!'? Rather do not many of them 'go counter' to anti-Christian propaganda? This has obviously amazed and even embarrassed some of the media prepared to witness a great contestation. *This was even a surprise to the American Episcopate*, which has realized that it is not alone in its evangelizing mission but is supported above all by young people, the builders of the future. . . ."[18]

For months to come, guests at John Paul II's table were struck by the only photograph displayed in his dining room. Set on a sideboard, it showed the Pope, rosary in hand, looking out his helicopter window at the vast crowd waiting for World Youth Day's closing Mass at Cherry Creek State Park.

MORAL TRUTH AND THE DRAMA OF FREEDOM

Less than two months after John Paul left Denver, he published his long-expected tenth encyclical on October 5, 1993. *Veritatis Splendor* [The Splendor of Truth], which addressed "fundamentals of the Church's moral teaching," immediately established itself as one of the major intellectual and cultural events of the pontificate.[19]

A Crisis of Culture

The Second Vatican Council had spent little time on moral theology.[20] Yet despite the Council's relative lack of attention to the subject, there was widespread agreement at the time that a renewal of Catholic moral theology was necessary. Few issues after the Council generated such passion and public controversy as the direction of that renewal.

The manuals used to teach moral theology in Catholic seminaries and graduate theological faculties had seemed to more than a few theologians, priests, and bishops to be excessively legalistic ("casuistic" was the technical term). Moral theology's connection to dogmatic theology and spirituality had also become attenuated, as thinking about the moral life had come unstuck from the Church's thinking about the new life of grace it lived in Jesus Christ. Pre-conciliar moral theology's primary reference point was the Ten Commandments, not the Sermon on the Mount—which was not to suggest that the Decalogue was wrong, but that its injunctions ought to be perceived in a distinctively Christian context. The Beatitudes and the Ten Commandments had to be put back together, it was thought. The moral life ought to be reconceived as a life of growth in the happiness of virtue, by which we become fitted for our destiny—eternal life within the light and love of God the Holy Trinity.

Pre-conciliar Catholic moral theology also had intellectual difficulties with conceptualizing human freedom. Because of that, the moral life tended to be portrayed as a struggle between my will and God's will, and the question in any situation became, "*How far can I go* before I butt into an obligation being imposed by that stronger will?" Grace, prayer, and the enlightenment of the soul by the Holy Spirit were all underplayed, even neglected, in what the pre-conciliar moral theology manuals tended to depict as a great wrestling match between my will and God's commands.[21]

The Council's call for a development of Catholic moral theology was fully warranted. The controversy that erupted after Vatican II had to do with the nature of that development and its relationship to the sources of Catholic moral theology in the Bible, the early Fathers of the Church, and St. Thomas Aquinas. The combatants were usually portrayed in "liberal" and "conservative" categories. Deeper and far more interesting questions were being debated than could be captured by those labels.

Should the morality of an action be judged primarily by the character of the act itself, or by a calculation that stressed a person's intentions and the consequences of an action? What was the relationship between a Christian's basic decision for Christ—the "fundamental option," as some post-conciliar theologians called it—and the specific sins that all Christians commit in the course of their Christian lives? Was there a moral "law," inscribed in human nature and in the dynamics of moral choosing, that could be known by reason? Were some acts, by their very nature, intrinsically evil, always and everywhere, without exception? Was freedom a morally neutral characteristic of the will, capable of attaching itself legitimately to any object? Or should freedom be understood as freedom for excellence, a means by which human beings grow into goodness by choosing good?

In its struggle with the meaning of freedom, the Catholic debate on moral theology touched some of the most controverted questions of public life in the late twentieth century. *Veritatis Splendor* was formally addressed to the bishops of the Catholic Church and was intended to set a framework for the future development of an authentically Catholic moral theology. But *Veritatis Splendor* was not simply, or even primarily, John Paul's forceful entry into the intramural wars of Catholic moral theologians. Rather, it is best read as a crucial moment in the Pope's quest for a new humanism, a reminder to men and women of the grandeur of the truth to which they can conform their lives and fulfill their destinies.

Making Moral Sense

If *Veritatis Splendor* is not for Catholics only, neither is it a papal scolding of wayward, willful sinners. John Paul II is too experienced a pastor to think that the polymorphous perversities of the late twentieth century are very original. They aren't, as a brisk reading of *Genesis*, concentrated on the story of Sodom and Gomorrah, will readily attest. There *is* something new in the late twentieth century, though—the inability of educated people to make moral sense to one another.

What passes for moral argument on the edge of the twenty-first century is too often vast confusion. Terms like "right" and "wrong," "virtue" and "duty" are bandied about with no common understanding of what they mean. One group's abomination is another's basic human right. What some consider acts of mercy, others regard as homicides for the sake of convenience. When it comes to moral argument, the modern world too often plays the role of that classic cynic, Pontius Pilate, with his dismissive question, "'Truth'? What is 'truth'?" (*John* 18.38). Pilate, and many self-consciously modern people, think that question is the end of the debate. In *Veritatis Splendor,* John Paul suggests that it is really the beginning.

The widespread notion that freedom can be lived without reference to binding moral truths is another unique characteristic of contemporary life. From Mount Sinai (where the Ten Commandments were understood to be the moral conditions for Israel living its freedom) to the U.S. Declaration of Independence (which staked the American claim to independent nationhood on certain "self-evident" moral truths), it had been widely understood that freedom and truth had a lot to do with each other. No more. And the uncoupling of freedom from truth, led in one, grim direction. Freedom, detached from truth, becomes license, and license becomes freedom's undoing. Without any common understanding of moral truth, life is reduced to the assertion of everyone's will-to-power. That, in turn, leads to chaos. And since human beings fear chaos above all, they will reach for the chains of tyranny to bring order back into life. Freedom untethered from truth is its own mortal enemy.

The idea that every human being creates his or her own truth—what is true "for me"—is yet another crucial factor in contemporary moral confusions. The modern or "postmodern" variation on this perennial temptation is the claim that every moral system is a cultural construct "all the way down." I may think that I value freedom and that "freedom" has some objective meaning. In thinking that, according to postmodern theorists, I am deluding myself, for my concept of "freedom" is as "culturally constructed" as someone else's claim that child sacrifice is a grand idea.

Against such deconstructions of the moral drama of the human condition, John Paul II in *Veritatis Splendor* insists that we are truly free and that our freedom is the condition for any serious concept of "morality." At the same time, the Pope argues that freedom has a built-in trajectory, a dynamism that produces in every human person an aspiration to goodness and excellence. *Veritatis Splendor* begins with a lengthy papal meditation on the Gospel story of the rich young man who comes to Jesus and asks, "Teacher, what good deed must I do, to have eternal life?" (*Matthew* 19.16). For centuries, Catholic commentators had dealt with the rich young man as a kind of poster boy for vocations to the priesthood. To John Paul II, he is Everyman, asking the question that haunts, or inspires, every human life—what good must I do to fulfill my eternal destiny?

Truths with Consequences

To those who object that the essence of the modern human condition is its plurality, John Paul says, you are right—and that is precisely why we have to think more seriously about the possibility of moral truths and their relationship to living in freedom. Moreover, the Pope argues, a genuine public conversation about these issues is a real possibility. In an intellectual climate dominated by relativism, John Paul raises the stakes considerably in *Veritatis Splendor* by insisting that there is a universal moral law built into the human condition—a law that provides the "grammar" for serious moral conversation among people of different cultures and life experiences. This understanding of the rootedness of the moral life in a universal human nature is, the Pope further suggests, the foundation on which a new humanism capable of defending human dignity can be built.

The encyclical's insistence that there are intrinsically evil acts (because there are, in the technical terminology, "exceptionless moral norms") also takes the reader beyond scholarly quarrels and into crucial public issues. To the argument that certain dubious acts can be justified by their consequences or because more good comes out of them than evil, John Paul insists that one can never do evil in order to do good. As for the claim that no act, in and of itself, is always-and-everywhere evil, the Pope counters that homicide, genocide, slavery, prostitution, trafficking in women and children, and abortion are always gravely wrong, because by their very nature they do grave damage to victims and perpetrators alike.

John Paul also tackles the argument that pastoral sensitivity requires a less sharp-edged sense of the reality of evil and its effects in the complexities of individual human lives. Modern moral theologies of "consequentialism" and "proportionalism" may well have been motivated by genuine pastoral concerns. But their intense focus on intentions and outcomes has deflected attention from the moral nature of specific acts and how they shape the character of those who do them. One result, ironically, has been to make it more difficult to condemn radical evil in a century pockmarked by its lethal and brutalizing consequences.

The Pope also argues that recognizing the moral reality of intrinsically evil acts has important public implications for the free society.

Human beings are demonstrably unequal in their physical, intellectual, and aesthetic capabilities, but the equality of all persons before the law is a bedrock principle of democracy. How are we to square self-evident inequality with our commitment to legal and political equality? The answer, John Paul suggests, lies in a concept of equal moral responsibilities. Recognizing that everyone is equally responsible before the moral norms prohibiting intrinsic evil is the sturdiest foundation for defending the principle of equality before the law.[22] The same can be said for maintaining the civil society essential to democratic political life. The bonds of civil friendship are more securely formed by a sense of mutual moral obligation arising from commonly accepted moral standards than from merely contractual obligations.[23] Postconciliar Catholic moral theologies that downplayed or virtually denied the significance of intrinsically evil acts inadvertently reinforced the relativist tendencies of the culture of "I did it my way." Dubious accounts of the moral life in their own right, these moral theologies were also unhelpful in reconstructing the moral foundations of the free and virtuous society.

There was yet another irony in the post-conciliar history of Catholic moral theology, and *Veritatis Splendor* faces it squarely.

Many Catholic moral theologians who had vigorously criticized the preconciliar "manuals" for their rigidity and legalism never made a radical break with the cause of that rigidity and legalism—the identification of freedom with willfulness, and the opposition between law and freedom that results from thinking of the moral life as a struggle between God's will and mine. The basic, wrongheaded question remained in place—"How far can I go?" Some of the new moral theologies, by shifting the center of moral analysis from the moral act to the actor's intentions and the act's consequences, lowered the bar of Catholic morality by saying, in effect, "You can go farther." But that drained the moral life of its inherent drama and rewards, and failed to resolve the intellectual problem of freedom and its relationship to truth and goodness.[24]

A lax version of the old manuals' legalism could not be considered a major improvement in Catholic thinking about the moral life. Genuine renewal in moral theology will come, the encyclical suggests, from retrieving and developing the idea that freedom, informed by reason, is ordered to the truth and finds its fulfillment in the goodness—the *beatitude*—of human flourishing, not in winning a few more skirmishes in the battle between God's allegedly arbitrary will and mine.

The truth about the drama of the moral life and about freedom is revealed, John Paul concludes, by the example of those prepared to die rather than do what they know is wrong. The witness of martyrs is a powerful counter to the claim that the dignity of freedom lies in doing things my way. The martyr teaches us that freedom is truly personal and truly liberating when it seeks the good and rejects evil, even to the point of death. Not everyone is called to be a martyr. Everyone is called to be a witness to moral truth, and "witness" is the original meaning of the term "martyr."[25]

The threshold of hope, the threshold of human dignity, is not crossed by lowering the bar of the moral life but by reaching higher—and then, if one has failed, by reaching higher again.

Controversies Continued

John Paul first announced his intention to address "more fully and more deeply the issues regarding the very foundations of moral theology" in a 1987 apostolic letter, *Spiritus Domini* [The Spirit of the Lord], issued to mark the 200th anniversary of the death of St. Alphonsus Liguori, the influential eighteenth-century moral theologian. Thus *Veritatis Splendor* was at least six years in the making.

Its completion had to await the publication of the *Catechism of the Catholic Church*—which, as John Paul notes in his encyclical, "contains a complete and systematic exposition of Christian moral teaching."[26] Given the magnitude of the two projects, it seemed appropriate to make a full, positive presentation of the Catholic understanding of the moral life first, in the *Catechism*. That, it was thought, would help set the context for a more sharply focused reflection on the foundations of moral reasoning, for a critique of the difficulties in contemporary moral theology, and for an analysis of the relationship between the fundamentals of Catholic morality and the crisis of modern culture.

Several papal commissions were involved in preparing *Veritatis Splendor.* During the drafting process, John Paul consulted with bishops and theologians around the world. Their influence on the final text of the document is not difficult to detect. The encyclical's critique of the idea of freedom-as-willfulness and its emphasis on freedom-for-excellence parallels the work of Servais Pinckaers, a Belgian Dominican and professor of moral theology at the University of Fribourg in Switzerland. The extensive references to St. Augustine and the themes from St. Bonaventure reflect longstanding interests of Cardinal Joseph Ratzinger. The nature of moral action and the philosophical and theological exploration of "intrinsically evil" acts had engaged the attention of Tadeusz Styczeń, SDS, and Andrzej Szostek, MIC, John Paul's colleagues at the Catholic University of Lublin. As in any papal document, the theologian of the papal household, in this instance the Swiss Dominican Georges Cottier, was certainly consulted.

Yet *Veritatis Splendor* is very much John Paul II's encyclical, conceptually as well as formally. Its first part, on Everyman's quest for the goodness that will lead to eternal life, reflects themes from the dramatic anthropology Karol Wojtyła had been unfolding since his days in the Rhapsodic Theater. His Lublin experience had helped him understand key issues in the crisis of contemporary moral philosophy. His struggle against communism had deepened his conviction that tyranny was best resisted by free persons acting according to consciences informed by moral truths. He had been developing the theme that the truth-and-freedom nexus was crucial for the future of democracies old and new since the late 1980s. Thus the suggestion that *Veritatis Splendor* is to be read not as a genuinely papal document, but as the hybrid product of various "Vatican theologians" (as some critics put it) is not persuasive. John Paul II was the intellectual driving force behind the production of *Veritatis Splendor,* from the outset and throughout the process. The further suggestion that the Pope wanted to invoke his charism of infallibility in the encyclical and had to be talked out of it by Cardinal Ratzinger is also false, according to Ratzinger himself.[27]

Press coverage of the encyclical predictably stressed the Pope's reaffirmation of classic Catholic sexual morality, although in fact these issues were barely referenced in *Veritatis Splendor;* it was not clear why reporters thought it newsworthy that the Pope continued to think that fornication was wrong.[28] In the months just prior to the encyclical's publication, speculation was rife about a papal "declaration of war" on theological liberals, as a German theologian, Professor Norbert Greinacher of Tübingen, put it. Greinacher was reacting to Italian press reports based on the leak of an alleged draft of *Veritatis Splendor.* The British Catholic press further confused matters by reporting that "underlying the document . . . is the principle of papal authority"—which was either a banality, or a serious misreading of John Paul's understanding of the issues at stake.[29] Another British Catholic weekly had it that the Pope had been forced to revise the entire encyclical because of adverse reactions to the leaked "draft."[30] That the Pope was tackling questions of crucial importance for free societies was rarely remarked in the prepublication attempts to determine just what theologians the Pope allegedly had in his sights.

After the encyclical's publication, John Paul received regular reports on both the positive and negative reaction to *Veritatis Splendor.*[31] The German-speaking theological world was particularly critical, arguing that the Pope was right in what he rejected but claiming that no responsible theologian was writing or teaching the specific theory of "fundamental option" (i.e., that a person's life-orientation was of greater moral consequence than certain individual acts, no matter how evil in themselves) criticized by the encyclical.[32] Similar criticisms were heard from American theologians. Charles Curran stated flatly that "the encyclical does not portray the true picture of Catholic moral theology today."[33] Lawrence Cunningham of Notre Dame described *Veritatis Splendor* as "this generation's *Humani Generis*" and charged that it attempted to impose one theological school's views on the entire Church.[34] Nicholas Lash of Great Britain made the same charge, although in this instance about the imposition of "one school of moral philosophy."[35]

Many theologians critical of the encyclical took it primarily as a papal gambit in the struggle for intellectual power within the Church. The encyclical's effort to strengthen the moral foundations of the free society went largely unremarked.[36] Nor did the critical Catholic theological response to the encyclical seriously grapple with the Pope's suggestion that the "new" moral theology was a variant on the legalism it so sharply criticized. An opportunity for a genuine development of theology may have been delayed by essentially political responses to an encyclical aimed at getting Catholic moral theology to think, again, about goodness and beatitude as the horizon of the moral life.

Several prominent Protestant moral theologians and Jewish moral philosophers seemed more inclined to give the encyclical a serious, even sympathetic reading. One American Lutheran, Gilbert Meilaender of Oberlin College, concluded a respectfully critical essay by writing that he was "hard pressed to imagine an equally serious statement on the nature of theological ethics issuing at this time from any major Protestant body." Ironically enough, if Protestant theologians wanted "to keep alive the questions of the Reformation and the centrality of the language of faith" in moral theology, they had to be in conversation with *Veritatis Splendor*.[37] Hadley Arkes of Amherst College wondered why some of the theologians critical of the encyclical had not grasped what was going on in modern culture: "Over the past twenty-five years," Arkes wrote, "every taxi driver knows [that] our universities have become seminaries in a new orthodoxy of moral relativism." This, Arkes continued, was very bad news for democracies. We value our own freedom and respect the freedom of others because we understand ourselves and those others as moral agents, capable of understanding right and wrong. What the modern world had forgotten, and what John Paul II had tried to reinstate, was "the connection between freedom and its moral ground," the foundation on which claims to freedom were coherent and persuasive.[38]

In Defense of Freedom

Veritatis Splendor's framework for the future development of Catholic moral theology will continue to shape Catholic life well into the twenty-first century and perhaps beyond. A younger generation of scholars now has a series of authoritative reference points with which to contend. More than their teachers, this younger generation seemed willing to wrestle with the encyclical's suggestion that the conciliar generation of Catholic moral theologians had redefined the rules of moral legalism within the same inadequate game. The response to the encyclical, particularly in North America, suggested that these younger Catholic philosophers and theologians would find sympathetic interlocutors among Protestant and Jewish thinkers whose communities had first experienced the corrosive effects of moral subjectivism and relativism.

Veritatis Splendor ought to have spurred a worldwide Catholic theological debate about the "natural law" and its relationship to Christian faith, and about the nature and goal of freedom. It should also have prompted a self-critical reflection on the relationship between what theologians were teaching and what priests and catechists, in their efforts to "translate" the theologians' work into pastoral life, were doing. Yet the response to the encyclical from too many Catholic moral theologians was characterized more by dismissal (and, in some instances, contemptuous dismissal) than by serious critical engagement. Catholic critics could not even bring themselves to concede what some Protestant commentators readily recognized: that John Paul had courageously taken on a set of issues of utmost importance for the culture of the free society. This failure suggested a curious blindness in those who wanted to construct theologies in tune with the signs of the times.

In public terms, the human dilemma John Paul was addressing in *Veritatis Splendor* was an ancient one, although it had been exacerbated by the modern crisis of confidence in the human ability to know the truth of anything: How is freedom to be lived so that freedom does not destroy itself?[39] *Veritatis Splendor* is a proposal to the post–Cold War world at large, in which John Paul, far from seeking to demean freedoms newly won or successfully defended, tried to reconnect freedom to the good of human flourishing. The encyclical is a defense of freedom, because it is for freedom's sake that the moral culture of the free and virtuous society must guard against freedom becoming self-destructive.

Veritatis Splendor was also part of John Paul's comprehensive program to implement the Second Vatican Council. It takes up the mandate of the *Decree of Priestly Formation* to develop the Church's moral theology, and does so by a method recommended by many of the great theological fathers of Vatican II: *ressourcement*, the recovery of foundational theological themes from the Bible, the theology of the first Christian centuries, and medieval scholarship. *Veritatis Splendor* is just such an exercise in retrieval, reclaiming the venerable notion of freedom as linked to truth and goodness that had gotten lost in the fourteenth and fifteenth centuries under the influence of the philosophy called "nominalism" and its equation of freedom with raw willpower. In this respect, *Veritatis Splendor* is a good example of a pattern that can be found throughout the pontificate of John Paul II, in which the Pope takes up a problem that had not been addressed in the years immediately following the Council and tries to solve it while simultaneously building for the future. *Veritatis Splendor* should not be regarded as merely a corrective to things that had gone wrong in the recent past, though. Its corrective "reach" is centuries long and aims at fostering a renewal of moral theology in the future. Catholic moral theology, John Paul suggests, has to get back beyond the fourteenth century in order to be prepared for the twenty-first. So did a modern world that the late medieval nominalists and, later, the Enlightenment, had taught to think of freedom as willpower.[40]

Veritatis Splendor's opening reflection on the rich young man's dialogue with Christ and its concluding meditation on St. Paul's injunction to the Galatians—that Christ "has set us free for freedom" (*Galatians* 5.1)—are not pious padding to the "real" encyclical. They are an integral part of John Paul's reflection on the drama of moral decision. So are his reflections on martyrdom as the paradigm of living freedom in the power of the truth. The "voice" in *Veritatis Splendor* is primarily that of a pastor, concerned that the power of grace and truth given to the Church through the cross of Christ is being nullified. That pastoral concern extends beyond the Catholic Church and the Christian community to men and women struggling with the demands of freedom, whatever their religious convictions. In *Veritatis Splendor*, the Pope spoke to everyone who aspires to choose the excellent, not simply the expedient, in exercising his or her freedom. He did so in the conviction that choosing the good, not simply choosing "my way," is the index of the genuinely human.[41]

SOLIDARITY IN A SEASON OF EXCLUSION

On November 11, 1993, a month after *Veritatis Splendor* was published, John Paul had just finished addressing a group of workers from the Rome-based UN Food and Agricultural Organization when he slipped on a newly installed piece of carpeting in the Hall of Benedictions atop the atrium of St. Peter's Basilica and fell down several steps. In pain, he nevertheless worked the crowd with his left hand on his way out of the hall, while trying a pun— "*Sono caduto ma non sono scaduto.*" [I've fallen, but I haven't been demoted.] An X-ray revealed a broken shoulder and the Pope spent the night at the Policlinico Gemelli, where the break was set and a cast put on to immobilize the broken joint until it healed. The tumble didn't appreciably slow down John Paul's schedule, but it did change his work habits. For the first fifteen years of the pontificate, he had followed his Kraków practice of doing his writing by hand in the morning, usually in the papal apartment chapel, before the Blessed Sacrament. When the broken shoulder made writing impossible for a while, John Paul called in Monsignor Stanisław Ryłko, who had returned to Rome from Kraków and was working in the Secretariat of State. Monsignor Ryłko brought his laptop computer with him and sat beside the Pope while John Paul dictated what would become his 1994 *Letter to Families*.[42] When they had finished a session, Ryłko corrected any typos and printed out the text for the Pope, who could then make revisions. It proved such an efficient way of doing business that, even after his shoulder healed, John Paul used it for much of his written work, including his homilies and books.[43]

On January 15, the Pope held his annual New Year's meeting with the diplomatic corps accredited to the Holy See. Seated in two rows along both long sides of the magnificent Sala Regia in the Apostolic Palace, beneath frescoes of the Battle of Lepanto by Giorgio Vasari, the diplomats were dressed in a variety of garbs, ranging from Old World diplomatic formal (white tie and tails) to African native traditional. Their dean, Ambassador Joseph Amichia of Ivory Coast, congratulated the Pope on completing his fifteenth year in office, noted that there were fifty armed conflicts under way around the world as they met, and expressed the corps's gratitude to John Paul for his interventions on behalf of peace. The Pope, seated on a small throne and wearing the red state mozzetta and a broad, embroidered stole, thanked the African diplomat for his greetings, wished everyone a happy New Year, conducted the *tour d'horizon* of world affairs that was standard on these occasions—and then made his sharpest critique of the ideology of nationalism in a pontificate noted for its defense of nations' cultural rights.

Civil war in Angola, ethnic violence in Burundi, the implosion of Zaire, authoritarianism in Nigeria, Gabon, Congo, and Togo, the conflicts devastating Somalia and the Sudan, religious radicalism in a destabilized Algeria, and the ongoing ethnic conflicts in the Caucasus and Bosnia-Herzegovina were each noted in the Pope's review of 1993. John Paul said that he hoped the impending Synod for Africa would "help the Catholics of those regions . . . to look around themselves and learn to see in every African the human being which he is, and not just his ethnic identity." Europe, for its part, was witnessing a reaction to individualism in the revival of "the most primitive forms of racism and nationalism." In Bosnia-Herzegovina, for example, "the most iniquitous forms of extremism are still being seen," while "the peoples are still in the hands of torturers without morals."

At the root of both the African and European traumas, John Paul asserted, were "*exaggerated forms of nationalism.*" The issue was not a proper love of country or a determination to defend its identity. The issue was "a rejection of others because they are different, in order more easily to dominate them." This was nothing less than a "new paganism: the deification of the nation." That was bad enough in itself, as 1993 had demonstrated in blood. But the twentieth century ought to have made clear that it could lead to even worse: "History has shown that the passage from nationalism to totalitarianism is swift, and that, when States are no longer equal, people themselves end up no longer being equal. Thus the natural solidarity between peoples is destroyed . . . and the principle of the unity of mankind is held in contempt."

Against those who regarded the Rwandas, Burundis, and Bosnias of the late twentieth century as regrettable but unavoidable examples of the way things simply are in some places, John Paul threw down a flat challenge: "The Catholic Church cannot accept such a vision of things." The universal reach of the Christian mission made the Church conscious of the fundamental identity of all human beings *as* human beings, and required the Church to defend that common human identity against anyone who challenged it in the name of nation, ethnic group, or religion. With an eye toward ancient and contemporary history and the churnings in the new democracies of eastern Europe clearly in mind, John Paul issued an evangelical warning to Catholics and Orthodox: "Every time that Christianity—whether according to its Western or Eastern tradition—becomes the instrument of a form of nationalism, it is, as it were, wounded in its very heart and made sterile."

Idolatrous nationalism was not what the world expected or deserved after the Cold War. The turn into the new century and millennium should be a "season of . . . solidarity between East and West, between North and South." In the Christmas season, in which the "unheard-of tenderness of God is offered to all mankind," it was past time to listen to an invitation the world had ignored in 1993—the invitation to "the *boldness of brotherhood*." That was what the Bishop of Rome wished for the entire world in 1994.[44]

The moral unity of the human race was one of the principal leitmotifs of the pontificate throughout the 1990s, and John Paul's January 1994 New Year's address to the diplomatic corps was the toughest, most challenging articulation of that theme yet. The use of a family concept—brotherhood—as a metaphor for transcultural and international political responsibility was not without its own difficulties. It was, after all, family- and clan-like politics that were making such a mess out of Africa, southeastern Europe, and the Caucasus. As the Pope continued to explore a new vocabulary to express his convictions about the post–Cold War world, he also continued to insist that politics, even world politics, remained an arena of moral judgment and action. If invoking the image of a global "human family" helped remind his listeners of that reality—if Serbs and Bosnians, Hutu and Tutsi, Armenians and Azeri began to understand that their common humanity provided a basis for escaping the death spiral of genocidal violence—then perhaps it was worth the danger of misinterpretation.

THE HOLY SEE AND ISRAEL: FUNDAMENTALLY AGREED, AT LAST

On December 30, 1993, two weeks before the Pope's New Year's address to the diplomatic corps, the Holy See and the State of Israel signed a "Fundamental Agreement" that set the foundations for regularizing the Church's legal position in Israel and provided for full diplomatic relations between the two parties.

The Fundamental Agreement was widely regarded as one of the diplomatic master strokes of John Paul II's pontificate and a historic turning point in Jewish-Catholic relations. It was both. It was also, as the Duke of Wellington famously said of Waterloo, a "damn near-run thing." That it was accomplished at all was due to the initiative of John Paul II, the vagaries (or, as the Pope would insist, the providential coincidences) of history—and a remarkable back-channel negotiation that saved the historic agreement at a moment when it seemed about to unravel.[45]

The Burdens of History

Officials of the Holy See understandably stress the continuity of their Middle East policy and the unchanging character of their basic diplomatic interest in the region, which is to secure the Church's legal position in Christ's native land, the theater of the redemption of the world. Since the Muslim conquest of Jerusalem in A.D. 638, defending that interest had been a considerable challenge involving different forms of intervention. Negotiations with the local Muslim authorities were one early strategy. Attempts at forcible reconquest came later with the Crusades. From the sixteenth century on, the Holy See adopted a "bilateral way," in which treaties between European powers and the Ottoman Empire, generally involving commercial issues, included guarantees of the minimal conditions necessary for Christian access to the holy places.

Maintenance of the Church's legal rights in the Holy Land continued to dominate the Holy See's Middle East concerns during the late nineteenth and early twentieth centuries, which saw the rise of the Zionist movement, World War I, the Balfour Declaration of British support for the creation of a Jewish homeland in the region, and the League of Nations mandate to Britain in the aftermath of the war. In the Holy See's view, the League mandate and the creation of mandatory Palestine had internationalized the question of the Holy Land and the holy places. That view did not change when the United Nations became the regional legatee after World War II.

The UN's 1947 plan for the partition of British mandatory Palestine, embodied in Resolution 181, provided for two territorial, national states joined by an economic union, and a direct international administration for Jerusalem, including religious freedom for all the city's residents. Resolution 181 also provided for religious freedom in the Jewish and Arab states being carved out of mandatory Palestine, guaranteeing the rights of Muslims in the Jewish state, Jews in the Arab state, and Christians in both. Acting primarily through Latin American countries, the Holy See was involved in crafting the religious freedom provisions of Resolution 181, which the Arab invasion of the new State of Israel and the subsequent Arab-Israeli war made politically, if not legally, moot.

Israel's War of Independence in 1948–1949 left the Catholic Church in the Holy Land in a diminished and difficult situation. Jerusalem was divided by the armistice line, with the Old City, including the Church of the Holy Sepulcher, most of the major shrines, the seat of the Latin-rite Patriarch, the Franciscan *Custos* (responsible for the maintenance of the shrines), the seat of the apostolic delegate, and Bethlehem in Jordanian hands. Many Arab Christians had fled or had been expelled during the war, including much of the Arab Christian elite; parishes had been decimated; the local Church in Israel was cut off from the Holy See's representative on the other side of the green line. The Church's time, energy, and meager resources were absorbed in assisting refugees and displaced persons, rebuilding a modicum of infrastructure, and trying to maintain contact with Rome. Catholicism in the new State of Israel, a religious minority within an ethnic minority suspected of being a potential enemy of the state, was frightened and cowering—a Church incapable of engaging the new Israeli society or of thinking through the relationship between the new political situation and the old questions of the Holy Land. The majority of Israel's citizens had bad memories of European Catholicism. The remnant Catholic Church felt alienated and suspect. The situation was thoroughly confused and very difficult.

The 1967 Six-Day War, the Israeli reconquest of Jerusalem, and the subsequent redivision of the region along new armistice lines changed the Church's situation in one crucial respect. To the Holy See, it now seemed as if the 1,300-year-old question of the Holy Land was about to be settled bilaterally between two belligerent powers, Israel and Jordan, rather than as a matter of international concern in which international legal issues were engaged. The idea, for example, of creating Jerusalem as an internationally administered special zone (a *corpus separatum*, or "separate body," in international legal terms) had not been the Holy See's initiative. It was an international proposal with which the Holy See was comfortable in 1947, as it seemed a solution that met the legitimate concerns of all parties at the time. Now, amid the changed politics of the situation, the Holy See continued to insist that the status of Jerusalem and the other holy places involved rights and interests that touched so much of humanity that they could not be resolved unilaterally or as part of a territorial settlement between two belligerents. That international interest, the Holy See insisted, was what remained valid about UN Resolution 181. The *corpus separatum* was a dead letter; no one in the 1960s thought that internationalizing a zone respected the rights of those who lived there. But the Holy See continued to insist that a response to the situation that took account of the legitimate concerns of Christians, Jews, Muslims, and all who valued the great cultural patrimony of the holy places had to be devised at the international level. The principle of international guarantees was what the Holy See wanted to defend. *How* those guarantees were concretely expressed was the business of diplomats and their political masters.

At the same time, the Secretariat of State of the Holy See was beginning to understand that Israel, unlike any other state in the Middle East, was a democratic society that aspired to live by the rule of law and the standards of justice. So it was possible to engage Israel as the Holy See engaged other modern, democratic societies. Moreover, the holy places under Israeli control since 1967 were more open to pilgrims of all faiths than they had been in centuries.

Still, the Church's situation in the place of its origin remained unsettled and precarious. A broadly written Israeli law against Christian missionary activity, adopted by the Israeli Knesset on December 27, 1977, seemed to jeopardize the entire Catholic position in the Holy Land. There were no ongoing serious contacts between officials of the Holy See and the government of the State of Israel. The Camp David peace process, beginning in 1977, intensified concerns about a bilateral "solution" to the question of the holy places, even as it held out welcome prospects for some measure of peace. As the 1970s gave way to the early 1980s, the situation seemed, in a typical Middle Eastern paradox, frozen into volatility.

Changing the Context

John Paul II was hardly unaware of the history he had inherited on his election in 1978. Pius X had told the founder of Zionism, Theodore Herzl, that the Church could not "encourage this movement." No Pope had ever referred publicly to the "State of Israel." The Holy See did not have diplomatic relations with the Jewish state. And while this did not mean that the Holy See did not "recognize" Israel—the Holy See could hardly be accused of not "recognizing" the United States prior to the establishment of full diplomatic relations in 1984—John Paul was aware, from his friend Jerzy Kluger and many others, that the absence of full diplomatic relations was regarded by Israelis and by Jews around the world as a depreciation of the State of Israel and a failure to fulfill the promise of the new Jewish-Catholic relationship envisioned at Vatican II. He knew that the Vatican bureaucracy and the Middle Eastern Catholic hierarchy included men who had neither internalized the Council's teaching on Judaism nor reconciled themselves to a sovereign Jewish state. The well-informed Pope was also aware that, in Israel itself, more than a few Jewish intellectuals and government officials believed the Holy See could not have full diplomatic relations with Israel for theological reasons. Full diplomatic relations would require an unthinkable alteration in the Church's doctrine about the Jews and Judaism in which, or so they imagined, Jewish dispossession of the Holy Land was a core tenet.

In that sense, at least, the question of the Holy See's relationship to the State of Israel could not be disentangled from the broader question of the revolution in Jewish-Catholic relations John Paul was proposing—the reconstitution of a theological conversation broken off more than 1,900 years before. As an abstract matter, the papal diplomats were right. There was no logical linkage between the Jewish-Catholic theological dialogue and the Holy See's diplomatic relations (or lack thereof) with the State of Israel. But John Paul touched the deeper crux in grasping that, whatever the objective realities might be, many, even most, of the Jewish interlocutors he wanted the Church to engage regarded the question of diplomatic relations as part of the overall question of Jewish-Catholic relations. That was how they experienced the issue. And so, at a profoundly human level, that was indeed a part of the issue.

There were other dimensions to the difference Karol Wojtyła brought to sorting out this tangled web. Since he had not been part of the Vatican diplomatic process in the Middle East prior to his election, he was able, as Pope, to look at issues with a fresh eye and to see how once-legitimate concerns might have hardened into shibboleths. He was a longtime defender of the rights of nations who understood the relationship between the Jewish catastrophe of the Holocaust and the founding of the State of Israel. He had never harbored doubts about the legitimacy of Israel.[46] Above all, John Paul was acutely aware that a *kairos,* a special, providential moment, was at hand in the ancient entanglement of Jews and Christians. That conviction did not drive the negotiations that led to the Fundamental Agreement. It did shape the context in which the negotiations leading to the Fundamental Agreement came about.

John Paul II signaled his willingness to take a fresh look at the Middle East early in his pontificate, in an October 5, 1980, homily at Otranto on Italy's Apulian coast. Reviewing the Second Vatican Council's teaching on the abiding character of God's covenant with the Jewish people and the Church's appreciation for Islam's faith in the God of Abraham, the Pope then surveyed in broad strokes the recent history of the Middle East. He related the founding of the State of Israel—the first papal usage of the phrase—to the "tragic experiences connected with the extermination of so many sons and daughters" of the Jewish people in the Holocaust, while at the same time noting "the painful condition of the Palestinian people . . . a large part of whom are excluded from their land." The torments of Lebanon were also on John Paul's mind in Otranto, as was Jerusalem.[47]

Largely unremarked at the time, John Paul's Otranto address set the strategic framework for the Holy See's Middle East policy in the 1980s and 1990s, according to Monsignor Luigi Gatti, the official responsible for the region in the Secretariat of State's "foreign ministry."[48] Vatican II's *Nostra Aetate* had established the new interreligious context. Religious freedom for all would be the primary human rights concern, and thus the primary diplomatic concern. The Church would pursue a historic religious reconciliation in which, as John Paul put it, Jews, Christians, and Muslims would "feel as brothers, no one superior, no one in the debt of others."[49] And historical facts—like the fact of the State of Israel, the fact of Palestinian nationalism, and the fact of Lebanon's disintegration—would be faced squarely. The era of euphemisms was past.

Less than a year later, according to Jerzy Kluger, John Paul II authorized his old friend to initiate private, informal discussions with Israeli diplomats in Rome to clarify the issues involved in moving toward full diplomatic relations. Kluger, an Italian citizen, was also authorized by the government of Israeli Prime Minister Menachem Begin to speak on its behalf. One immediate result of these discussions was a papal telegram of good wishes to the President of Israel on Rosh Hashanah, the Jewish New Year, in October 1981. John Paul, by Kluger's account, also used his Wadowice classmate as a sounding board for thinking out loud about the history of relations between Catholics and Jews and the relationship of that history to the question of diplomatic relations. The two friends agreed to disagree about John Paul's meetings with Palestinian leader Yassir Arafat, which Kluger sharply criticized. Jerzy Kluger's private diplomatic explorations do not seem to have led in any direct way to the negotiations that eventually produced the 1993 Fundamental Agreement between the Holy See and Israel. But like the Otranto address, the Kluger initiative confirms how early in the pontificate John Paul had these questions on his mind. And the conversations Kluger opened may have helped begin to change attitudes among habitually skeptical Israeli politicians and foreign ministry officials.[50]

John Paul's own actions during the early- and mid-1980s—his regular meetings with Jewish groups in Rome and on his pastoral pilgrimages, his condemnations of terrorist attacks on synagogues in Vienna and Rome, his 1982 meeting with Israeli foreign minister Yitzhak Shamir, his numerous commemorations of the twentieth anniversary of *Nostra Aetate,* his historic visit to the Synagogue of Rome in April 1986—helped break down that skepticism even further. And the 1987 Vatican statement that there were "no theological reasons in Catholic doctrine that would inhibit" full diplomatic relations between the Holy See and Israel should have laid that false issue to rest. But old habits of mind die hard, and not only in the Vatican.[51]

Further groundwork for negotiations between the Holy See and Israel was laid in April 1990, when John Paul appointed Archbishop Andrea Cordero Lanza di Montezemolo as apostolic delegate in Jerusalem. Montezemolo, who had demonstrated his ability to handle delicate situations while nuncio in Nicaragua during the 1983 papal pilgrimage there, was also the son of an Italian victim of the Nazis, which helped ease his relations with his Israeli interlocutors. That John Paul would not have told his new representative in Israel of his desire to address the full range of issues between the Holy See and the Israeli state—including the Church's legal status in Israel, diplomatic relations, and the ongoing question of international legal guarantees for preserving the special character of Jerusalem—seems very unlikely. Strategic thinking within the Vatican's Secretariat of State had also begun to shift. Perhaps the multilateral approach had run its course. Perhaps, it was thought, the Holy See could continue to press its position on international legal guarantees for the holy places while reaching a bilateral agreement with Israel on the Church's legal position there. In any case, by the summer of 1991—after the Persian Gulf War but before the Madrid peace conference called in its wake—Montezemolo was telling associates in Israel that he had a mandate from the Pope to pursue a bilateral negotiation with Israel.

The "John Paul II difference" had created the conditions for the possibility of dramatic change. Events now began to move rapidly.

The Negotiation

In August 1991, Archbishop Montezemolo began to work out the blueprint for negotiations with Father David-Maria Jaeger, OFM, a Franciscan priest teaching canon law at his order's seminary in Jerusalem.

Jaeger, then thirty-six, had been born in Tel Aviv, the son of an Israeli father and a Brazilian mother of Jewish heritage. The Jaegers were a mildly observant family and young David was sent to state-run religious schools. As a teenager, he became intellectually convinced of the truth of Christianity and sought to become a Catholic. But he could find no Catholic priest willing to baptize an eighteen-year-old *sabra,* a native-born Israeli. So Jaeger was baptized an Anglican and then presented himself in Nazareth to the Latin-rite patriarchal vicar for Israel, saying, "Okay, now you can receive me as a Protestant convert." Jaeger got involved in Church-state issues in Israel in 1977, working informally with the apostolic delegate. He also helped launch a program on Christians in the Holy Land at the ecumenical Tantur Institute for Theological Studies, just outside Jerusalem, and began to work as the Jerusalem correspondent of the London-based international Catholic weekly, *The Tablet*. Having completed neither high school nor college, the autodidact and polyglot Jaeger entered the Franciscans in 1981 and was sent to Rome for studies. He was dispensed from the prescribed basic course, having taught himself theology during his work at Tantur and elsewhere, and received the bachelor's degree in theology after being examined by a specially appointed pontifical commission in the spring of 1983. After making his solemn vows as a Franciscan in September 1985, he was ordained a priest on March 19, 1986—the only native-born, Hebrew-speaking Israeli to be ordained since the independence of the State of Israel. After completing doctoral studies in canon law in Rome he returned to Jerusalem to teach, and successfully defended his doctoral dissertation—on the role of papal diplomacy in securing Christian legal rights in the Holy Land—in 1989.

Father David Jaeger was quite possibly the only man in the world with the requisite skills the Holy See needed in the impending negotiations with the State of Israel. He was a native Hebrew speaker whose work had given him an intimate knowledge of Israeli law. He had a doctorate in canon law and was an expert on the vastly tangled legal history of the Holy Land. He had extensive, personal, on-site experience with the problems to be resolved. He was a tough-minded negotiator whose commitment to the security of Israel could not be questioned. And he was a priest who, from the Secretariat of State's point of view, could be trusted with the Church's interests.

Jaeger insists that the blueprint for negotiations he developed in the summer of 1991 with Archbishop Montezemolo was not driven by the Madrid peace conference process, but had its own logic and integrity, based on the longstanding positions of the Holy See. The next "real event" in the process, as he puts it, came on May 20, 1992. Archbishop Montezemolo led a Holy See delegation, including Jaeger, to the Israeli foreign ministry in Jerusalem to work out the text of the announcement, to be made a few months later, of a "Bilateral Permanent Working Commission of the Holy See and the State of Israel." It was a serious meeting, and Jaeger suggests that journalistic renderings of this and other events—"A two-car convoy bearing diplomatic license plates entered the parking lot of the foreign ministry, carrying a bevy of black-clad clergy hiding behind dark glasses and being whisked away . . . ," as he once put it—miss the real drama of what happened, which was substantive.

The announcement itself was not difficult to devise. Jaeger drafted it on a yellow legal pad, the two heads of delegation signed it, photocopies were made, and in the confusion, Jaeger ended up with the original. The real argument had to do with defining the bilateral commission's agenda. The Holy See insisted that there could be no announcement without an agreed agenda. Jaeger returned to the foreign ministry on July 15 for what he later called "the toughest of the many tough meetings I took part in." The Israeli position had been that everything was negotiable—Church-state relations, legal and property issues, taxation questions, and so forth—once diplomatic relations were fully established. The Vatican delegation, for its part, knew that Israel badly wanted diplomatic relations with the Holy See, and both sides knew that diplomatic relations were the only trump card in the Holy See's negotiating hand.

The idea that had begun to be floated in the Vatican in 1991 now came back into play. Why not make diplomatic relations one item on a list of issues to be discussed and resolved by the bilateral commission—"the menu," as Archbishop Montezemolo came to call it. The Holy See position at the crucial July 15, 1992, meeting was simply put: "You have a whole menu of items you want to discuss; so do we. Why not discuss them all together?" The leader of the Israeli delegation, Ambassador Moshe Gilboa, finally agreed, despite strong objections from his delegation's legal advisers.

The real breakthrough that made the Fundamental Agreement possible thus came from a change in longstanding Israeli policy, authorized by the government of Yitzhak Shamir. Shamir's ambassador to Italy, his former press secretary Avi Pazner, had made the establishment of diplomatic relations with the Holy See a personal project. Through his direct access to his old friend, the prime minister, Pazner had pressed the case for a change in policy. Foreign minister David Levy wanted to make his mark by solving a continuing irritant in Israel's foreign relations. Shamir, well-known for his acid remark about Poles imbibing anti-Semitism with their mother's milk, had come to understand that John Paul II did not fit his stereotype. Several factors, which John Paul would likely regard as another example of providential noncoincidences, combined to change what had long been the bipartisan Israeli position—that nothing would be negotiated with the Holy See until after diplomatic relations were established.

With a full agenda agreed upon, the bilateral commission was announced on July 29, 1992, and the serious work of negotiation began.

The Holy See's representatives made three decisions at the outset of the negotiation, which their Israeli counterparts accepted. The first was to begin by seeking a shorter agreement on broad norms and general principles, rather than a comprehensive Church-state treaty or concordat. With that shorter agreement in place, further negotiations could take place on practical legal, financial, and property issues. It was anticipated that this first agreement on principles would carry with it an interim degree of diplomatic relations, which the Holy See assumed had begun de facto with the formation of the bilateral commission. At the outset, neither side expected that full diplomatic relations were achievable in the short term, but there were a variety of arrangements that could be way stations en route to full diplomatic exchange at the ambassadorial level.

The second decision was to divide the work of negotiation between a "plenary level," led by the deputy foreign ministers of both parties, and an "experts level," where most of the detailed work would be done. Plenary meetings would only be called to ratify results achieved at the experts level, or to settle questions the experts couldn't resolve. The expert-level meetings would be led on the Holy See's side by Archbishop Montezemolo and his delegation. Ambassador Gilboa and his successors would lead the Israeli experts team.

The third decision was to seek reciprocity in meeting sites, in order to establish experientially that these were negotiations on the international plane between two subjects of international law. It was agreed that the plenary meetings would shift between the Vatican and Israel, while the experts' meetings, which would all be held in Jerusalem to save on expenses, would shift between the Israeli foreign ministry and a Catholic institution, which in practice was usually the Ratisbon Institute.

The negotiation at the experts' level began with a week-long meeting on November 2, 1992. One of the first things that had to be done was to clarify for the Israeli team who their negotiating partners were, and what they represented.

The Israeli diplomats had some idea of the "Holy See" as a subject of international law, and knew that the "Holy See" is usually referred to, in shorthand, as "the Vatican," as is Vatican City State. But there was confusion over the fact that the Holy See is not identical with Vatican City State. According to diplomatic custom and international law, the Holy See is the international legal embodiment of the ministry of the Bishop of Rome as universal pastor of the Catholic Church. The independence of the Vatican City micro-state helps guarantee the independence of the Holy See as a sovereign actor in world affairs. Still, other states exchange ambassadors with the Holy See, not Vatican City State, and the Holy See, not "the Vatican," participates in international legal and political organizations like the United Nations and its affiliated agencies. The Holy See, not Vatican City State, was Israel's negotiating counterpart.[52]

As if this were not enough to sort out, the laws of the Ottoman Empire and the states that succeeded it (like Israel) had no provision for something called "the Catholic Church." The only legal entities were the local leaders of various local Christian Churches—Armenian, Latin-rite Catholic, Greek Catholic, Greek Orthodox, Maronite, Melkite, and so on. Israeli law did not recognize an organic entity called "the Catholic Church" as having legal personality, and thus being a subject of law.

The two problems intermeshed when the question for the Israelis became, "What is the relationship of this entity called 'the Catholic Church' to our negotiating partner, the 'Holy See'?" A treaty or agreement would be made with the "Holy See." But what did that have to do with "the Catholic Church" or with the various Catholic entities in Israel? It was explained that the Holy See wasn't present to talk about itself, but to talk about the legal position of the Catholic Church in Israel. The Holy See didn't have interests of its own that it was trying to secure by legal agreement. And if the negotiation couldn't talk about "the Catholic Church," there really wasn't anything to talk about. After what amounted to a crash course in sacramental theology, ecclesiology, canon law, and international legal history, the Israelis finally agreed to talk about "the Catholic Church." But doubts remained, and would threaten the negotiation again at the final hour.

The Back Channel

By September 1993, the Fundamental Agreement was slowly taking shape. But the experts' meetings had been difficult, several legal technicalities remained to be settled, and so did the question of diplomatic relations. Both sides now had to confront what David Jaeger later called "the quiddity of the whole thing." Given the radical changes in the Middle East since the Gulf War and the fact that Israel was negotiating diplomatic relations with Arab states like Morocco, Tunisia, Oman, and Qatar, the government of Prime Minister Yitzhak Rabin, which had taken office in July 1992, decided that it could settle for nothing less than full diplomatic relations with the Holy See. Israel now wanted to accelerate the process and make the Fundamental Agreement the occasion to move quickly to full diplomatic relations. This concern was communicated to what an Israeli diplomat later described as "the highest level" in the Vatican. The Holy See delegation was thinking along parallel lines. Phasing in diplomatic relations would seem to diminish the genuine accomplishments of the Fundamental Agreement, which were giving the Catholic Church the kind of legal status in Israel that it enjoyed elsewhere. Hesitance about full diplomatic relations, it was also thought, would reinforce those elements in Israeli political and bureaucratic circles that continued to insist that the Holy See could never establish full diplomatic relations with a sovereign Jewish state for theological reasons. It was not clear, however, that the Holy See delegation's view was shared at all levels of the Vatican Secretariat of State. Sensing, rightly or wrongly, that there was foot dragging in the Vatican, the Israelis made it clear that the negotiation for the Fundamental Agreement—including full diplomatic relations—had to be completed by the end of 1993 or everything on "the menu" would have to be reexamined.

At this crucial juncture, a back-channel negotiation brought the Fundamental Agreement to a successful conclusion.

The back channel was the work of Father David Jaeger and Shlomo Gur, a forty-three-year-old career Israeli diplomat then assigned to the office of Deputy Foreign Minister Yosi Beilin. The back channel had first been opened during the difficult experts-level negotiations between late December 1992 and early January 1993. Gur got a call from an Israeli journalist, who said that an Italian journalist friend needed a contact within the negotiations. Gur agreed, and the Italian journalist turned out to be the Rome correspondent of the Milan daily *Corriere della Sera*, an old friend of David Jaeger. Gur then got a call, at home, from Jaeger, who said that he, too, would like to talk to Gur. The two agreed to meet at the Jerusalem Plaza hotel, where Jaeger appeared, for the first and only time in the back-channel negotiation, in a Roman collar.

The two men, Israelis of the same generation but of strikingly different experiences, hit it off personally, and a freewheeling, open, and blunt conversation ensued. They met, according to their recollections, some twelve to fifteen times more in the fall of 1993, usually in the lobby of the Jerusalem Hilton. Both now laugh at subsequent press speculation about secret flights to European capitals. They trusted each other completely and their trust was vindicated: there were no leaks. Nor was there any posturing as they talked frankly, exchanging ideas and finally drafts of a complete Fundamental Agreement.

Neither delegation to the experts' meetings knew about the back channel. Gur and Jaeger would reach agreement on an issue, then communicate it to their principals in Jerusalem and Rome: Yosi Beilin and Foreign Minister Shimon Peres for the Israelis, Monsignor Gatti, Monsignor Celli, Archbishop Jean-Louis Tauran (the Vatican "foreign minister"), and Cardinal Angelo Sodano, the Secretary of State, for the Holy See. The Israeli delegation to the experts' meetings knew that Gur had a Holy See interlocutor. They didn't know it was David Jaeger, who was sitting across from them at the negotiating table. The Holy See delegation was unaware of the back channel, whose confidentiality the principals were determined to protect. In October, in the middle of the back-channel negotiation, Beilin and Tauran met in New York in an emergency, private session to resolve a crucial, deal-breaking issue that Gur and Jaeger had identified. Beilin was so concerned to keep the negotiation going through the back channel that, having reached agreement with Tauran, he resolved the matter on his own authority, saying that he would square things with Peres later.

The Jaeger-Gur back channel worked because of the trust between Shlomo Gur and David Jaeger, the good relationship that had been established between Claudio Celli and Yosi Beilin (the formal heads of the plenary-level meetings of the bilateral commission), and the commitment of Luigi Gatti to achieving an agreement that met the Holy See's longstanding concerns. When the back channel produced a complete draft Fundamental Agreement acceptable to the principals, another crucial factor entered into play: the professional discipline of both sides' diplomatic services. When the heads of the experts-level delegations were informed by their principals that agreement had been reached in a back channel, both Archbishop Montezemolo and Ambassador Eitan Margalit accepted the process without demur.[53]

The Jaeger-Gur back channel was a classic negotiation of its sort, authoritative but noncommittal, as Gur later described it. Issues were resolved without the kind of feints common in negotiations. Proposals could be floated and discussed without fear of compromising a position downstream. Nothing was official until the principals had agreed. If they didn't, it would be as if nothing had happened, officially. It seems unlikely, and perhaps even impossible, that the Fundamental Agreement between the Holy See and Israel would have been achieved without it.

Endgame

In December 1993, it remained to bring the negotiation to a final, successful conclusion and close the deal.

The last substantive point to be thrashed out brought both parties back to the question of what constituted "the Catholic Church" for the purposes of the Fundamental Agreement. The Israelis wanted to define "the Catholic Church" as the several local Churches of different rites existing on its territory. David Jaeger, as he later put it, was "absolutely opposed" to locking in any definition that reduced the meaning of "the Catholic Church" in Israel to the currently existing institutional expressions of Catholicism. Other Eastern rites might want to establish a presence in the Holy Land. New educational, charitable, or pastoral institutions might be formed. In any case, from a theological point of view, "the Catholic Church" was more than an enumeration of presently existing institutions, and Jaeger was determined that the Fundamental Agreement should reflect that.

The issue was resolved by a final back-channel negotiation between Jaeger and Shlomo Gur, after which the experts-level negotiators finally agreed, amid considerable wrangling and with the aid of legal opinions Jaeger had gotten from Israeli and American friends, to insert the phrase "inter alia" [among other things] into the agreement's text, which finally defined "the Catholic Church" and "the Church" as "including, *inter alia*, its Communities and institutions." At the same time, and as part of the back channel's final, comprehensive package, the Israelis agreed to insert "inter alia" into the agreement's definition of "the State of Israel" and "the State," so that these entities were jointly understood to include all institutions established by law in Israel (including the Municipality of Jerusalem, for example), and not simply the central government.

During the entire negotiation, John Paul had insisted on keeping the local Eastern-rite Catholic and Orthodox leaders informed, and Archbishop Jean-Louis Tauran had briefed various Arab governments about the process. At the very end, Cardinal Sodano, who was responsible for making the final recommendation to the Pope, decided on a further consultation with a special commission of six cardinals, including Cardinals Ratzinger, Casaroli, Laghi, and Silvestrini. Briefed beforehand on the negotiation, and in some instances lobbied by men involved in the process, the cardinals' commission unanimously recommended acceptance of the draft Fundamental Agreement, with some minor retouches that caused no problems for the Israeli negotiators.

Finally, the Holy See sent a formal query to the Latin-rite patriarch of Jerusalem, Michel Sabbah, and to two Eastern-rite Catholic patriarchs.[54] The query took the form of two questions: Is the Fundamental Agreement something to be done in itself? Should it be done now? The answers came back: Do it, and do it now.

At last, on December 10, 1993, the Fundamental Agreement was initialed by Archbishop Montezemolo and Ambassador Margalit at the Israeli Foreign Ministry. Settling the arrangements for the formal signing ceremony became another negotiation. The Israelis wanted to sign in Rome, for maximum media exposure. The Holy See replied that the only diplomatic agreements it signed in Rome were with Italy, and that the custom was to sign in the country of destination. An appropriately Solomonic decision was finally devised. The plenary commission would be reconvened to approve and sign the agreement, and according to the principle of reciprocity there would be two meetings—a meeting in Rome on December 29 to approve the Fundamental Agreement formally, and a meeting on December 30 in Jerusalem to sign it. Since he was the Vatican chairman of the plenary commission, Monsignor Claudio Celli, rather than Archbishop Montezemolo, signed for the Holy See. Celli came equipped to the historic event with a personal letter of authorization from John Paul II, a break from the custom of a Vatican diplomat's authorizing letter coming from the Cardinal Secretary of State. The Pope was determined that the Fundamental Agreement be signed in the most solemn way possible, invoking all the authority of his office.

Aftermath

More than a year and a half of intense negotiation had produced a concise document. Its distinctive preamble sets the Fundamental Agreement in the appropriate historical and theological context, beginning with a mutual recognition of "the singular character and universal significance of the Holy Land" and acknowledging "the unique nature of the relationship between the Catholic Church and the Jewish people," including their recent "process of reconciliation and growth in mutual understanding." In Article 1, both parties recommit themselves to "upholding" the universal "human right to freedom of religion and conscience," which the State of Israel also commits itself to "observe," that is, as a precise legal obligation.[55] Article 2 pledges "cooperation in combating all forms of anti-Semitism and all kinds of racism and of religious intolerance"; a second paragraph in the article reiterates the Holy See's "condemnation of hatred, persecution and all other manifestations of anti-Semitism directed against the Jewish people and individual Jews, anywhere, at any time, and by anyone." In addition to the religious freedom obligation in Article 1, Articles 3, 10, and 12 constitute the core of the Fundamental Agreement, by establishing a structure for follow-on negotiations to give legal meaning to Israel's recognition of "the right of the Catholic Church to carry out its religious, moral, educational, and charitable functions, and to have its own institutions, and to train, appoint and deploy its own personnel in the said institutions for the said functions to these ends." Article 14 commits both parties to prepare for full diplomatic relations, which would come into being at the ambassadorial level when the Fundamental Agreement had entered into force—in practice, in the next several months.[56]

The standard diplomatic formula at the end of the Fundamental Agreement—"Signed in Jerusalem, this thirtieth day of the month of December, in the year 1993, which corresponds to the sixteenth day of the month of Tevet, in the year 5754"—was, in this instance, a reminder of what Shlomo Gur had felt during the negotiations: that he and his secular Israeli colleagues, as well as their Holy See counterparts, "were carrying two thousand years of Jewish-Christian history, very complicated, on our backs."

That history, and its contemporary expression in the Holy Land, could not be overcome by the simple fact of a completed agreement. Confusions continued about precisely what the State of Israel had entered into an agreement with. At dinner the night of the formal signing in Jerusalem, Foreign Minister Peres indicated that he thought the agreement was with another small state, Vatican City. More seriously, the Fundamental Agreement was not happily accepted by the local Catholic leaders, despite their responses to the query posed by the Secretariat of State just before the agreement was completed.

On the day after the signing, members of the Holy See delegation met with local Catholic prelates to explain the agreement in further detail and to lay out what was foreseen in the next set of negotiations about the Church's legal "personality," property, and so forth. The local churchmen were quite critical, often disguising their own complaints about the agreement by attributing them to "the people" or "what the people are saying." When they were reminded of the Pope's personal involvement in making the final decision after examining the agreement in detail, there was silence. Then one of them said, "We respect the Holy Father, but the Holy See must also respect the people." It was a response that did not augur an easy course in the future.[57]

The Holy See was neither well-prepared nor well-staffed for the follow-on negotiations, whose successful completion was essential to making Catholicism present to Israeli society as it had never been before. Budget-driven decisions to place the Holy See's nunciature in Old Jaffa rather than in northern Tel Aviv and to limit its staff made it difficult for the Holy See's representatives to engage in an ongoing, sustained way with the elite of Israeli society and their diplomatic counterparts from other nations. The decision to use untrained, inexperienced negotiators from the local Churches in the follow-on negotiations slowed their progress. So did the fact that some Israeli bureaucrats and politicians remained as recalcitrant as some local churchmen. Ignorance about the Church, a pervasive Israeli secularity (exemplified by Yosi Beilin's comment to Claudio Celli at their first meeting, that he, Beilin, had never really thought about the question of Jerusalem having a religious dimension before), and typical bureaucratic sluggishness dragged out the follow-on negotiating process. It took almost four years to complete the first and most crucial text, the "Legal Personality Agreement" for Catholic institutions in Israel, which was signed on November 10, 1997.[58]

In the years after the Fundamental Agreement was completed, it also became clear that the new relationship between the Holy See and Israel, welcome as it was, could not by itself change other realities of the region. The numbers of Christians in the Holy Land continued to dwindle after the 1993 Israeli/Palestinian accords, due largely to Arab Christian migration under economic, political, and religious pressure. For the first time in history, the prospect loomed of a Holy Land without living Christian communities—which meant Christian holy places reduced to the status of museums. On November 6, 1995, Afif E. Safieh, director of a new "Office of the Representative of the Palestine Liberation Organization to the Holy See," was received at the Vatican, in what was widely understood to be the first step toward diplomatic relations with a future Palestinian state. Seven weeks later, at Christmas, PLO chairman Yassir Arafat, celebrating the holiday in a Bethlehem now under the control of his Palestinian Authority, came close to blasphemy by proclaiming it "the city of the Palestinian Jesus."[59] As for Jerusalem, the Secretariat of State was sufficiently concerned about its future that it issued a formal diplomatic note in May 1996, reiterating the Holy See's call for an "international juridical instrument" for "the protection of the holy city's identity," irrespective of how the question of sovereignty was eventually resolved.[60]

Those for whom the Fundamental Agreement was to be the first step toward an entirely different mode of Catholic interaction with Israeli society and culture were as disappointed in the years immediately following the Fundamental Agreement as those who had expected a reasonably prompt completion of the remaining issues on the bilateral negotiating agenda. The disappointments could not change the fact that the Fundamental Agreement was—as its preamble suggested and as those involved in its negotiation sensed during their often difficult work—a historic and irrevocable milestone in the relationship between the Jewish people and the Roman Catholic Church. The seeds firmly planted by the Fundamental Agreement would, the negotiators believed, germinate in time.

The Pope's Role

Like other epic events, the completion of the "Fundamental Agreement Between the Holy See and the State of Israel" has attracted myth-making of various sorts.

It is sometimes said that the Madrid peace conference following the Persian Gulf War forced the Holy See to change its policy on diplomatic relations with Israel. The Gulf War certainly changed the regional and international politics of the Middle East, but the Pope's desire for a new course vis-à-vis Israel was evident to his associates long before the Gulf War. The Holy See's crucial decision to pursue full diplomatic relations in the context of a broader "menu"

of issues was made before the Madrid conference convened. The Israeli negotiators made the crucial policy reversal by agreeing to deal with "the menu"
rather than making the negotiation of every other item on it dependent on
the establishment of full diplomatic relations. The Gulf War and the Madrid
peace conference created conditions for accelerating a course on which the
Holy See was already launched. They did not create the new course.

Two U.S. ambassadors to the Holy See, Thomas P. Melady and Raymond
Flynn, have suggested that U.S. diplomatic interventions at the Vatican were
instrumental in getting the negotiations that resulted in the Fundamental
Agreement started. Diplomatic representations indicating that the Bush and
Clinton administrations would look favorably on full diplomatic relations
between the Holy See and Israel were certainly undertaken, as were numerous
informal conversations with Vatican officials. But there is no evidence that the
U.S. position had any serious impact on either the Pope's decisions or those of
his diplomats. The Fundamental Agreement itself was warmly applauded by
American officials. But according to Holy See officials involved in the process,
the Fundamental Agreement was not significantly influenced by American lobbying.[61]

Roman journalists and Vatican observers have also speculated that John
Paul II, determined to get the bone of the diplomatic relations issue out of the
throat of the Jewish-Catholic dialogue, finally put his foot down and told his
subordinates to make the deal. Those involved in the negotiation deny that
such an incident ever occurred, and the scenario ill-fits the evidence and the
record of John Paul's II's style of papal management. At no time during the
actual negotiation, according to Father Jaeger, did John Paul ever "condition"
other issues by insisting on the absolute priority of achieving full diplomatic
relations. The Pope, too, was committed to the negotiation's achieving success
on the full "menu" of issues. In this sense, at least—his concern for securing
the Church's legal position in the Holy Land—his policy was in continuity with
that of his predecessors.

Yet there can be no serious doubt that John Paul had a decisive impact on
the achievement of the Fundamental Agreement. He made the basic decision
to pursue full diplomatic relations with Israel—which, as one of his negotiators later put it, "No one else would have had the courage to do." That decision was based on his sense of justice as well as on his acute sensitivity to the
fact of Jewish pain and its relationship to Catholicism. The decision having
been made, he typically left the details of its implementation to others, while
continuing to confirm that the course he had chosen should be pursued to a
successful conclusion. A "successful conclusion" was not limited to the issue of
full diplomatic relations with Israel, although that question understandably
drew the most public and media attention.

Several objectives seem to have intersected in the unified mind and imagination of John Paul II. There were the Church's historic interests in the Holy
Land, which had to be defended. There was his intuition of Jewish pain and

his theological commitment to getting the long-delayed theological dialogue between Jews and Catholic under way again. Both involved solving the problem of diplomatic relations. For that act would respond persuasively to the pain caused by the perception of "nonrecognition," demonstrate the Church's millennial commitment to beginning a conversation of a radically different sort with the Jewish people, and irrefutably demonstrate that Catholicism had no theological "problem" with the State of Israel and with living Judaism. At the same time, the achievement of diplomatic relations would help secure the Church's legal position in the theater of the redemption. John Paul saw a whole where many others, including officials of the Holy See and Israeli politicians and diplomats, saw only fragments and pieces.

Given the hangover of historic prejudices and the cautiousness of the Holy See's professional diplomats, the Fundamental Agreement simply would not have happened without its being widely understood throughout the Vatican that such an agreement, in all its dimensions, was the Pope's intention, in which his considered judgment coincided with the desire of his heart. Everything else—including the formal negotiations and the back channel—depended on this.

Sistine Intermezzo

In April 1994, and for the first time in centuries, the world saw Michelangelo's *Last Judgment* as the artist had painted it.

The Florentine genius's Sistine Chapel ceiling frescoes, which covered more than 8,000 square feet, had been restored, one twelve-inch-square section at a time, between 1980 and 1990. Cleaning away more than 400 years of dirt, grime, incense and candle residues, and pigeon droppings had revealed a brilliant array of forgotten golds, greens, and violets, and details of shading long obscured. A similarly painstaking process of restoration, begun in 1990 and completed over four years, now revealed the richly textured blues of the *Last Judgment*, achieved in part by Michelangelo's mixing ground lapis lazuli with his paints.

In addition to authorizing the restoration of the frescoes, which caused considerable controversy in some artistic circles, John Paul made sure, when it came time to clean the *Last Judgment*, that the restorers removed about half the leggings, breechcloths, and other drapings with which prudish churchmen had hidden Michelangelo's nudes, years after the masterpiece had been completed (the remaining drapings were left in place for historic reasons).[62] With the restoration finished, the Pope wanted to underscore theologically the truths Michelangelo's frescoes expressed. The occasion was a Mass marking the restoration's completion, which John Paul celebrated in a scaffolding-free Sistine Chapel on April 8, 1994, the Friday after Easter Sunday.

The timing, he suggested, was eminently appropriate, for Michelangelo's *Last Judgment* revealed "*an extraordinary Christ* . . . endowed with an ancient beauty that is somehow detached from the traditional pictorial model." To stand before this massive fresco during Easter Week was to *"stand before the glory of Christ's humanity,"* which, in the Second Coming, would penetrate "the depths of the human conscience [while] revealing the power of the redemption." The *Last Judgment* was an icon, in which *"Christ expresses in himself the whole mystery of the visibility of the Invisible."*

Christianity had had a long, bitter struggle over icons, the Pope recalled, until the issue was settled in their favor by the last ecumenical council of an undivided Christian Church, the Second Council of Nicaea in 787. The defeat of those who wanted to ban icons from public worship and private devotion was a defense of the Church's sacramental intuition about all of reality—that the extraordinary lay just on the other side of the ordinary, through which the extraordinary was revealed. Icons and paintings like the *Last Judgment* are not simply works of pictorial art; each is, "in a certain sense, like *a sacrament of Christian life, since in it the mystery of the incarnation becomes present* . . . the Mystery of the Word made flesh is reflected in a way that is ever new . . ." and both the artist and those who "participate" in his art by seeing it are "gladdened by the sight of the Invisible."

Michelangelo, the Pope continued, had been courageous enough to admire God the Father at the moment of his creation of the human race, and to transfer the visible, corporeal beauty of Adam to God himself. It was, John Paul said, "an extraordinary piece of artistic audacity," which, some might argue, verged on blasphemy. Yet we can "recognize, *in the visible and humanized Creator, God clad in infinite majesty."* Michelangelo had taken humanity's desire to see the divine as far as it could possibly go, artistically. Images had "intrinsic limits" in expressing divinity, but "everything which could be expressed has been expressed here."

John Paul then linked the Sistine ceiling and the *Last Judgment* to the theology of the body he had been developing for a decade and a half. Because of the incarnation of the Son of God, Christians can and must say that the human body is the *kenosis,* the outpouring in self-giving, of God. Far from being prudish about the body, Christians ought to understand that *"the great humility of the body must be expressed so that what is divine can be revealed."* At the same time, Christians must understand that *"God is the source of the integral beauty of the body."*

The Sistine Chapel was *"the sanctuary of the theology of the human body."* By bearing witness so magnificently to "the beauty of man created by God as male and female," Michelangelo's frescoes also conveyed *"the hope of a world transfigured,* the world inaugurated by the Risen Christ." Within the mystery of God and his creative purposes, the human body was revealed in all its splendor and dignity.[63]

The *New York Times* correspondent found it surprising that, in this remarkable homily and standing before Michelangelo's undraped nudes, John Paul "appeared not the least embarrassed, despite his frequent reaffirmations of the Church's conservative teachings on sexuality."[64] It was not "despite" the Church's moral teaching on sexuality, however, but precisely because of it that

John Paul celebrated Michelangelo's work as a "testimony to the beauty of man," whose physicality and sexuality, understood in the context of creation and redemption, were icons of the life of God. By reducing the body to an object, the sexual revolution had betrayed itself. An appeal to the better angels of our sexual nature might yet redeem the promise of a sexuality in which men and women deepened their intuition of the mysterious border between the ordinary and the extraordinary, the embodied and the divine.

In the months ahead, the debate over the meaning of human sexuality moved from the splendor of the restored Sistine Chapel to the less edifying arena of a major international conference.

CONFRONTATION AT CAIRO

The 1994 confrontation between Pope John Paul II and the administration of U.S. President Bill Clinton over world population and family planning issues was inevitable, and could have been foreseen as early as the summer of 1992.

Governor Clinton and his vice presidential running mate, Senator Al Gore, ran in 1992 on the most radical "social issues" platform in American history, committing themselves to federal funding of abortion on demand at any time during pregnancy, deploring "explosive population growth in the Third World," and pledging the use of federal tax dollars to fund "greater family planning efforts" in U.S. foreign aid programs. On the day President Clinton was inaugurated, January 20, 1993, he signed five executive orders widening the U.S. government's involvement with, and funding of, elective abortion. Four days later, the Vatican newspaper, L'Osservatore Romano, published an editorial charging that the "renewal" Clinton had promised in his campaign "comes by way of death [and] by way of violence against innocent beings."[65] It was the first salvo in what would become the most serious confrontation ever between the Holy See and the United States government.

The confrontation was international in scope. The Clinton administration's full agenda for the September 1994 World Conference on Population and Development in Cairo was ambitious, and was shared by officials of the United Nations Fund for Population Activities [UNFPA] and by major international nongovernmental organizations such as the International Planned Parenthood Federation. It sought nothing less than to define sexual expression, devoid of any connection to marriage or procreation, as a freestanding personal autonomy right under international law, and, in this context, to define a legally enforceable universal human right to abortion on demand. This was, in part, what politicians call "payback." The 1984 world population conference at Mexico City, heavily lobbied by the Reagan administration and inspired by the grim example of communist China's policy of coercive abortion for state-defined population-control purposes, had stated flatly that abortion was not a legitimate means of family planning. In addition to reversing their defeat at Mexico City, the UN officials, European politicians, and American-led nongovernmental organizations that supported the Clinton administration's approach to Cairo were also engaging in one of the distinctive features of post–Cold War international politics—the use of international institutions and international law to achieve political goals that could not be reached by normal democratic procedures at home.

The difficulties the Holy See would have in this struggle were aptly illustrated by a meeting between Archbishop Jean-Louis Tauran and U.S. Undersecretary of State Timothy Wirth, a former U.S. senator and longtime population-control supporter now occupying the "global affairs" desk at the Department of State. Undersecretary Wirth's office ordinarily featured a "condom tree" as a desk ornament. The tree was removed for Archbishop Tauran's visit on November 16, 1993, but little else was achieved. Wirth began talking with Tauran about the widespread problem of children having children in the United States and around the world. The archbishop, eager to identify some common ground, agreed that this was indeed a problem, and one that underlined the importance of cooperation between the Church and governments since moral education was surely part of the solution. This Undersecretary Wirth refused to concede. The issue was biological information, period— "Young people have to know about their bodies," was his summary statement. Moral considerations and moral education were irrelevant.[66] Wirth's attitude was not unique in an administration that seemed to think of population control as the answer to any number of problems. The administrator of the U.S. Agency for International Development, J. Brian Atwood, had defended a new five-year, $75 million grant to the International Planned Parenthood Federation on the grounds that overpopulation was the "core" of the recent chaos in Somalia, in which U.S. troops were then embroiled. How a country of 7 million inhabitants with a territory considerably larger than California could be considered "overpopulated" was not clear. Atwood's claim illustrated just how confused the question of "overpopulation" had become.[67]

The View from the Papal Apartment

For John Paul II, the impending confrontation at the World Conference on Population and Development focused several aspects of the crisis of humanism in the 1990s through a single lens.

As Catholicism had understood for millennia, along with other great world religions, abortion was an intrinsically evil act that killed a child and did grave damage to its mother, its father, the abortionist, and society as a whole. Abortion, the Pope insisted, was not an issue of sexual morality but of human rights. The moral locus of the abortion debate was the ancient injunction against killing the innocent, not the next commandment in the Decalogue, enjoining chastity. To declare this grave wrong a "right" not only debased the language, it threatened the legitimacy of international law. The Pope's distinctive feminism, as well as his extensive pastoral experience, also suggested that abortion on demand—abortion regarded as one item in a long list of family planning options—was very bad for women and for the relations between women and men, as it provided a technological "solution" to the irresponsibility of predatory males. The Church's extensive, worldwide experience in providing health and counseling services to women caught in the dilemma of unwanted pregnancy suggested that the relationship between the quest for women's equality and abortion on demand was not as simple as some insisted.

The American-led push for an internationally sanctioned right to abortion at the Cairo conference was also located in a disturbing historical context. As the nascent democracies of east central Europe emerged from under the rubble of totalitarianism, the Pope had urged them not to live their new-won liberties according to the thin notion of freedom as autonomy, which he had quickly recognized as the new threat to the free society. Now, it seemed as if an alliance was being forged by the world's only superpower, UN agencies, some European governments, and a well-funded group of powerful nongovernmental organizations in order to enshrine this defective notion of freedom in international law, in the name of "reproductive rights." This was a battle that had to be joined.

The universal pastor of an increasingly Third World Church was aware of yet another dimension to the problem. The Cairo conference threatened to be another example of First World countries imposing their policies and their understanding of morality on Third World countries, using the threat of decreased foreign assistance as a weapon. That, in turn, led to yet another form of corruption at the United Nations, an institution in which the Holy See continued to invest significant hopes.

This was not another public policy disagreement between the Holy See and a national government. It was the crucial human rights issue of the 1990s, and it was being played out on a global stage. In every cultural history, a great, defining question often emerges. The question of slavery was that kind of issue in the nineteenth-century United States, as the question of the Jews was in Germany in the 1930s. For John Paul II, the abortion issue was not one issue, but *the* issue for the emerging world culture that would sustain, or corrupt, the free societies of the future. Once the premise was granted that some lives were expendable, there was a lethal logic that led in due course to infanticide, euthanasia, genetic manipulation, and coercive reproduction policies. That was what was happening in advanced industrial democracies, where the manipulation of life was being legitimated by intellectuals who insisted that there are no moral truths built into the human condition.[68] And these matters were inescapably political, because they engaged what Aristotle had once defined as the central question of politics: How ought we to order our lives together?

At stake in the forthcoming Cairo conference was who "we" were, in that venerable formulation.

An Argument Joined

On March 19, 1994, John Paul sent a personally signed letter to every head of state in the world and to the Secretary-General of the United Nations. It began by noting the Church's support for the UN's current "International Year of the Family," and the "duty" of "civil authorities . . . to strive to promote the harmonious growth of the family," a fundamental human institution whose flourishing involved serious issues of morality and spirituality. That was why, the Pope continued, he had found the proposed draft document for the Cairo conference *"a disturbing surprise."* There was "reason to fear that it could cause a moral decline resulting in a serious setback for humanity. . . ."

Economic development was the issue of primary concern to most of the world, and development was supposed to be a co-theme of the Cairo conference. Yet development issues had been "almost completely overlooked" in the Cairo draft document, which seemed far more interested in promoting a "totally individualistic" idea of human sexuality, to the extent that "marriage now appears as something outmoded." Who, John Paul asked, was authorized to do such a thing? *"The family is part of the heritage of humanity!* Moreover, the Universal Declaration of Human Rights clearly states the family is 'the natural and fundamental group unit of society' (Article 16, 3)." It was more than ironic that, in a year dedicated to the family, the family should now be proposed as something dispensable.

The proposed "general international recognition of a completely unrestricted right to abortion" was another grave moral issue raised by the Cairo draft document. The document "leaves the troubling impression of something being imposed: namely a lifestyle typical of certain fringes within developed societies, societies which are materially rich and secularized." This was imperialism of a new and very dangerous sort.

Finally, John Paul asked the heads of state to think about the future. The draft document was holding up to young people the model of a "society of 'things' and not of 'persons.'" Self-mastery, self-giving, and a sense of responsibility were deemed "notions . . . belonging to another age . . ." The world's leaders were depriving the young of "reasons for living" because they were failing to teach "the duties incumbent upon beings endowed with intelligence and free will."

Population and development were indeed serious issues, John Paul concluded. They could not be seriously addressed without a "sense of the sacredness of life" and an understanding of the human "capacity for love and self-sacrifice." That, at bottom, was what was missing in the Cairo draft document.[69]

The day before his letter was formally dispatched, John Paul met with Mrs. Nafis Sadik, the Pakistani head of the UN Fund for Population Activities, who would play a large role at the Cairo conference. John Paul gave her a lengthy memorandum of objections to the Cairo draft document, and tried, as he said later, to explain to her the Church's teaching: "She didn't want to discuss it."[70]

Years later, Nafis Sadik would describe an angry, belligerent Pope to journalists, a description of Karol Wojtyła that made little sense to anyone who had ever known or worked with him. On the evidence of her own testimony, Mrs. Sadik misrepresented both the work of the agency she headed and the implications of the Cairo draft document in her conversation with the Pope, going so far as to suggest that the UNFPA was not involved with abortion.[71] Mrs. Sadik's conclusion about her forty-minute discussion with John Paul—"He doesn't like women. I expected a little more sympathy for suffering and death"—was simply bizarre.[72]

The following week, every ambassador accredited to the Holy See was called to a briefing at which Cardinal Sodano, the Secretary of State, Cardinal Etchegaray, the President of the Pontifical Council for Justice and Peace, Cardinal Alfonso López Trujillo, the President of the Pontifical Council on the Family, and Archbishop Tauran explained Vatican objections to the Cairo draft document in detail. What the diplomats call a "full and frank exchange of views" was not, evidently, desired in some quarters. The U.S. embassy to the Holy See had recently received a message from Undersecretary of State Timothy Wirth's office, reiterating that U.S. policy at Cairo was to promote an unrestricted abortion right, but suggesting that this need not be mentioned to the "host country" if its reaction might be negative.[73]

Abuse in New York, Surgery in Rome

The confrontation now moved to New York, where the third meeting of the preparatory commission for the Cairo conference (Prep-Com III, in the jargon) met from April 4 to 22, 1994. Undersecretary Wirth and his international allies took no chances that open debate might result in substantive changes in the draft document for Cairo. The chairman of Prep-Com III, as he would be of the Cairo conference itself, was Dr. Fred Sai, usually introduced as "the representative of Ghana," but in his non-UN life, the President of the International Planned Parenthood Federation. When Monsignor Diarmuid Martin of the Pontifical Council for Justice and Peace, a Holy See delegate to the meeting, criticized the proposed draft document for its ethical shallowness, Dr. Sai berated him publicly from the chair and complained that the Vatican was trying to foist its notions of sexual morality on the world. Sai's remarks were loudly applauded by a gallery packed with population-control activists. At an earlier session in preparation for the Cairo conference, Prime Minister Gro Harlem Brundtland of Norway had criticized what she regarded as the obstructionism of the Vatican, "a small state with no natural inhabitants." The United States Catholic Conference, a registered nongovernmental organization at the UN, was denied space to hold a seminar in the UN, and organizers of the event were forbidden to post notices of the meeting.[74]

Prep-Com III produced a genuinely radical draft document for Cairo. Only six of 118 pages were devoted to the conference's ostensible topic of "population and development." The rest of the document adumbrated a lifestyle revolution sanctioned and enforced by international law. "Marriage" was the dog that didn't bark in the Cairo draft document. Indeed, the only time the word "marriage" appeared in the document's chapter on "the family" was in a passage deploring "coercion and discrimination in policies and practices related to marriage." The document did speak about "the family in its various forms," but it said nothing about the importance of families rooted in stable marriages for the physical and mental well-being of children. Nor did the draft document discuss the natural and moral bond between parents and children and its importance for achieving such important goals as better education and health care for the young. The document also severed the moral relationship between parents and teenagers by treating sexual activity after puberty as a "right" to be exercised at will, and by suggesting that state-based population and "reproductive health care agencies" be the primary counselors of young people coming to grips with their sexuality.

The document was full of Orwellian euphemisms: coercive state family planning policies became "fertility regulation"; abortion on demand was transmuted into "safe motherhood" and "reproductive rights." Even more ominously, the draft document mandated a large-scale program of state coercion in the service of "reproductive rights" and family planning. States were mandated to override parental prerogatives in the education of adolescents and to ensure that health-care providers had the proper "attitudes" toward their teenage patients. Governments were instructed to "use the entertainment media, including radio and television soap operas and drama, folk theater, and other traditional media" to advance the draft document's program of action. They should also introduce programs to "reach men in their workplaces, at home, and where they gather for recreation," while adolescent boys "should be reached through schools, youth organizations, or wherever they congregate." There was to be no area of life—home, workplace, gym, ballpark—into which state-sponsored propaganda on what the document termed "reproductive rights and reproductive health" did not reach. Those who had thought that this approach to public policy had been consigned to the trash heap of history in 1989 were, evidently, mistaken.[75]

Two days after Prep-Com III closed in a crushing defeat for the Holy See, John Paul beatified a woman whose life and death stood in sharpest contrast to the Cairo draft document's image of marriage and the family. Forty-year-old Gianna Beretta Molla, a pediatrician and mother of three, was two months pregnant with her fourth child when a fibrous tumor developed in her ovary. She had three choices. Surgical removal of her ovary and uterus would save her life but kill her unborn child. The tumor alone could be surgically removed and the unborn child aborted, and she could probably bear more children later. Or the tumor could be removed while attempting to save the pregnancy—an option that posed serious risks to her own life. She chose to save her unborn child, and instructed the surgeon to operate in such a way that the pregnancy was saved. The tumor was successfully removed, but as Dr. Molla knew, she now faced a dangerous delivery. A few days before the birth, she told her doctor, "If you have to choose, there should be no doubt. Choose—I demand it—the life of the baby." Gianna Emanuela was born on April 21, 1962. Gianna Beretta Molla died of complications from the birth on April 29, 1962 and was beatified on April 24, 1994, in the presence of her husband and children, including thirty-two-year-old Gianna Emanuela.

Four days later, on the night of April 28, John Paul fell in his bath. After remaining in the papal apartment overnight, he was taken to the Policlinico Gemelli the following day, where an artificial hip joint was surgically implanted to compensate for the damage done to his femur in the fall. The surgery was not completely successful. John Paul II, who had led a physically vigorous life for almost three-quarters of a century, would never walk easily again.

It took some time, but the Pope eventually grew used to his new physical circumstances, prodding visiting friends with the cane he now used, pretending it was a pool cue or a rifle, and twirling it, almost like a vaudevillian, before audience crowds and participants in his monthly First Saturday rosary in the Paul VI Audience Hall. He even joked about his difficulties. After it had taken him some time to walk several dozen yards to the presider's table at a Synod meeting in October 1994, he looked at the assembled bishops and remarked, quoting Galileo's muttered comment about the earth's rotation around the sun, *"Eppur' si muove"* [Yet it moves . . .].[76] Nonetheless, growing older and accommodating himself to new physical limits was not an easy business for John Paul II. "I used to be a sportsman, you know," he said wistfully on one occasion, leaning heavily on his cane.[77]

In the immediate aftermath of his hip surgery, John Paul read his personal history, as he read all of history, through the lens of his conviction that there were no coincidences in Providence. In this instance, the noncoincidence was between his pain and the confrontation over the forthcoming Cairo conference. A Christian grappling with the mystery of the cross, he reflected aloud on all this on May 29, at his first Sunday Angelus address in St. Peter's Square after his return from the Gemelli. After thanking Christ and Mary for the "gift of suffering," which he had come to understand as "a necessary gift," he described his recent thoughts: "I meditated on all this and thought it over again during my hospital stay. . . . I understood that I have to lead Christ's Church into this third millennium by prayer, by various programs, but I saw that this is not enough: she must be led by suffering, by the attack thirteen years ago [i.e., Agca's assassination attempt] and by this new sacrifice. Why now, why this, why in this Year of the Family? Precisely because the family is under attack. The Pope has to be attacked, the Pope has to suffer, so that every family and the world may see that there is . . . a higher Gospel: the Gospel of suffering, by which the future is prepared, the third millennium of families, of every family and of all families."

That, John Paul concluded, was the witness he wanted to make "in the presence of the world's powerful ones."[78]

From May 29, 1994, on, the way of the cross would ever more visibly mark the pontificate of John Paul II.*

Meanwhile, President Bill Clinton was under severe criticism from the Catholic leadership of the United States. Although Timothy Wirth continued to insist that "we have no fight with the Vatican," the Undersecretary of State himself undertook a tour of the U.S. hierarchy, focusing particularly on the cardinals; it would not be unrealistic to suggest that he was looking for a weak link in the chain of opposition to the Clinton administration's Cairo policy. He did not find one. Instead, a letter from the six resident U.S. cardinals, cosigned by the President of the U.S. Bishops' Conference, was hand-delivered to the White House on May 29. The letter deplored the administration's "promotion of abortion, contraception, sterilization, and the redefinition of the family," and urged the President to reverse the "destructive" American agenda for Cairo. The following month, the bishops' conference as a whole adopted a resolution in which the prelates, "as religious leaders and U.S. citizens," declared themselves "outraged that our government is leading the effort to foster global acceptance of abortion."[80]

President Clinton was in Rome in early June and spoke with John Paul on June 2 in the Vatican. After the audience, the President met with a group of American seminarians and told them that he had had a wide-ranging review of the global situation with the Pope. It seemed to many present an implausible description of what had just transpired, given John Paul's passionate concern about the Cairo conference.

On June 19, the executive board of the newly organized and lay-dominated Pontifical Academy for Life, an international group of physicians, medical ethicists, and philosophers, issued a declaration on the Cairo conference. At its heart was a judgment the Academy regarded as beyond reasonable scientific dispute: "From conception to the last moment of life, it is the same human being that develops and dies." That biological fact led to certain moral judgments: "We affirm that every member of the human species is a person. The care owed to every individual does not depend on either his age or the

---

*Throughout the summer, John Paul continued to wrestle with the meaning of his new physical difficulties. During his summer holiday in the mountains of Val D'Aosta, his friend and student, Father Tadeusz Styczeń, sensed this. One day during the vacation, Styczeń said that he didn't agree with the canon law that required bishops to submit their resignations at age seventy-five. To be a bishop was to be a father, and fatherhood could only be revoked by death. The comment triggered something in John Paul II, who remarked that God could revoke that mission by death or incapacity. Over the week-long holiday, Styczeń thought that his mentor was reliving the meditation on Christ's agony in the garden of Gethsemane which, as Cardinal Karol Wojtyła, he had preached to Pope Paul VI and the Curia in 1976. In that meditation, he had suggested that Christ's most intense suffering during the Passion was in the realm of the spirit—in the struggle, intensified by phisical suffering, to hand everything over to the will of the Father. By the end of the vacation, Styczeń remembered, John Paul had passed through this particular dark night, come to grips with his new situation, and was renewed in his resolve to carry on his mission.[79]

infirmity he may suffer. . . . Personal rights are *absolutely inalienable*. The fertilized human egg, the embryo, the foetus, can be neither donated nor sold. It cannot be denied the right to progressive development in its own mother's womb. No one can subject it to any kind of exploitation. No authority, not even that of the father or mother, can threaten its life."[81]

An extraordinary consistory of all the world's cardinals, held on June 13–14, issued a statement, proposed by New York's Cardinal John O'Connor, expressing solidarity with the Pope's teaching on the nature and rights of the family, "and his insistence that the family be free of coercion, particularly in regard to questions of procreation." The "failed social policies of many developed nations," the cardinals concluded, "should not be foisted on the world's poor."[82]

The Pope's Campaign

Eight days later, on June 30, John Paul began a sustained public campaign in the court of world opinion, aimed at rallying an opposition to the political juggernaut that those who had run Prep-Com III now planned to unleash in Cairo. It was not a voluble campaign and had none of the trappings of either democratic politics or international advertising blitzes. It consisted of twelve ten-minute audience addresses, at the weekly general audience or the Sunday Angelus. There was no shouting. But by identifying the ethical errors of the Cairo draft document and by defining a moral alternative to the libertinism it embodied, the Pope set in motion another resistance movement, this time international in scope, that would prove to have considerable potency.

Many of the themes were familiar and echoed earlier audience addresses and papal documents. Some addresses broke new ground, by developing John Paul's feminism and by confronting recurring falsehoods about Catholic sexual ethics. In both cases, the addresses clarified what the Pope thought was at stake in Cairo.

The June 12 Angelus address stressed the right to life as *the* basic human right and the foundation of any meaningful platform of human rights.[83]

At the June 19 Angelus, John Paul proposed that "marriage as a stable union of a man and a women who are committed to the reciprocal gift of self and open to creating new life" was not a sectarian notion but "an original value of creation." Losing this truth was a "danger for all humanity."[84]

During his June 22 general audience, John Paul sketched the outlines of his distinctive feminism. He insisted that women not be reduced to being objects of male pleasure, defended the equal human dignity of women, and argued that "the equality and diversity of women must be recognized" in civil society and the Church.[85]

At the June 26 Angelus, John Paul proposed that sexuality has a "language of its own at the service of love and cannot be lived at the purely instinctual level."[86]

On July 3, the Pope reminded the world that the characteristics of marriage —unity of persons, communion of life, and fidelity—were the characteristics of a covenant, not merely a contract.[87]

At the July 10 Angelus, John Paul argued that stable marriages were crucial for the welfare of children, who were supposed to be one of the Cairo conference's primary concerns.[88]

In his July 17 Angelus address, the Pope confronted a prime anti-Catholic canard, reminding the world that the Church does not teach an "ideology of fertility at all costs." Rather, it proposed an ethics of marriage in which the decision whether or not to have a child "is not motivated by selfishness or carelessness, but by a prudent, conscious generosity that weighs the possibilities and circumstances, and especially gives priority to the welfare of the unborn child."[89]

The July 24 Angelus address rejected coercive or "authoritarian" family planning programs as violations of a married couple's basic human rights.[90]

Children, the Pope taught on July 31, are a gift to be welcomed, and may never be exploited for the parents' "interests or personal gratification."[91]

The public dimensions of the abortion issue were the topic at the August 7 Angelus. No just state could authorize a private right to lethal violence for private purposes. The foundations of public justice were undermined when the state did not recognize the unborn child's moral claim to protection.[92]

The August 14 Angelus address returned to feminism. Discrimination against women in "workplace, culture, and politics" must be eliminated in the name of an "authentic emancipation" that brings the "feminine genius" into full play in public life.[93]

And at the August 28 Angelus, the Pope wrapped up the series on a philosophical note. Radical individualism, he argued, was inhuman and dehumanizing, and so was a "sexuality apart from ethical references." What the Cairo conference should promote was a "culture of responsible procreation."[94]

While he was conducting this brief course in the ethics of sexuality and family life, John Paul was urging his press spokesman, Joaquín Navarro-Valls, to get into the public debate. "You should say clearly what we think," was Navarro's instruction from the Pope about the role he was to play before and during the Cairo conference.[95] But to whom was Navarro supposed to speak? Not only, he assumed, to the people who had rigged Prep-Com III and abused the Holy See delegation there. The alternative was to take the case to the world. Navarro started a series of briefings at the Vatican press office, which soon led to another skirmish with the United States. On August 25, Vice President Al Gore, who would lead the U.S. delegation during the early days of the Cairo conference, gave a speech at the National Press Club in Washington in which he stated that "the U.S. has not sought, does not seek, and will not seek to establish an international right to abortion."[96] On August 31, Navarro pointed out that the Cairo document's definition of "reproductive health care" as including "pregnancy termination" had been a U.S. initiative. "The draft document, which has the United States as its principal sponsor, contradicts, in reality, Mr. Gore's statement," Navarro concluded.[97] It was an unprecedented rebuke to a public official. John Paul was not displeased with this departure from the Vatican's conventional diplomatic reticence.[98]

The Cairo Conference

The image of the Cairo conference as a clash between the United States and the overwhelming majority of world opinion on the one side, and an isolated, prudish, and mysogynist Vatican on the other, was shattered in the first hours of the conference itself. On September 5, Prime Minister Benazir Bhutto of Pakistan—unmistakably a woman, unmistakably Harvard-educated, and unmistakably a major political figure—took to the rostrum during the opening statements to defend the "sanctity of life" and to condemn the Cairo draft document for trying to "impose adultery, sex education . . . and abortion" on all countries."[99] The charge that a narrowly sectarian Holy See was holding up consensus on the conference's final report, which was to be drawn up on the basis of the draft document developed at Prep-Com III, lost whatever remaining credibility it had. It was now time for a serious negotiation.

Five days of impasse followed, as the delegates tried to reach consensus on the final report's abortion language, its discussion of the family, and its approach to adolescent sexuality.[100] The United States began to retreat from its previously stated position that the final report must support abortion on demand as a means of family planning. Meanwhile, anti-Catholic bias was freely vented by delegates and nongovernmental organization activists alike. When Gail Quinn, an American member of the Holy See delegation, tried to explain the Vatican's objections to some proposed abortion language in the draft final report, she was booed and hissed. Dr. Sai, the conference chairman, did nothing to stop the abuse, and had to be reminded by the delegate from Benin that free speech was sacrosanct at UN conferences. Later, while walking past two U.S. representatives in a delegates-only section of the conference center, Quinn heard one of the Americans say to the other, "There goes that bitch." Colombia's Miguel Trias, the head of a government-sponsored family planning organization, complained to the press that "these Latin American countries are trying to make the Vatican happy. But in 2,000 years the Vatican has never been happy."[101]

Press reports of Vatican defeats notwithstanding, the Holy See had achieved a great deal during the first week of the Cairo conference. The final report being negotiated now stated, unambiguously, that "in no case should abortion be promoted as a method of family-planning." The centerpiece of the U.S. approach to Cairo—the definition of abortion on demand as an internationally recognized basic human right—had been abandoned, as the Americans and their allies had to concede that there was no international consensus behind their position. The strong-arm tactics deployed at Prep-

Com III did not work in Cairo. The revised final report now recognized the rights and responsibilities of parents toward their teenage children, and the worst of the Orwellian language about "family structure" had been pared from the document.[102]

The defeat of the Clinton administration and its international allies at the Cairo population conference was certainly not the result of the Holy See's efforts alone. As at the previous Bucharest and Mexico City world population conferences, Third World countries were worried by what they perceived as the eugenic agenda lurking behind First World–dominated family planning programs. Political leaders in Latin America, Asia, and Africa understood that it was their populations, not, say, Norway's, that were to be brought "under control." The resistance of Islamic, Latin American, and some African countries to the libertinism enshrined in the draft document produced by Prep-Com III was also an interesting sign for the future. One need not admire every aspect of life in these societies to note the importance of their tacit recognition that the "permissive cornucopia" was not the goal of genuine human development.[103] Truly radical feminists, and of the most secular sort, had also opposed the Cairo draft document prepared at Prep-Com III. In the non-governmental organization forums that surrounded the Cairo conference, they held mock trials of the World Bank, the International Planned Parenthood Federation, and the UNFPA, charging them with oppressing women through coercive state-sponsored birth control programs.

All of these factors, in addition to the Holy See's interventions, helped shift the controlling paradigm at the Cairo population conference from "population control" to "the empowerment of women." This was a change of potentially historic consequence. If the new paradigm of women's empowerment could be wedded to a revitalization of the family and a reaffirmation of the distinctively maternal power of women, rather than to the sexual revolution as lived in the developed world, something very different would be afoot in the international politics of the twenty-first century. Such an outcome was by no means assured, and many would regard it as improbable, but that it could even be imagined was one important result of the Cairo population conference—and one that had been virtually inconceivable in January 1994.[104]

It seems extremely unlikely that the Cairo conference would have played out as it did absent John Paul II's insistent campaign throughout the preceding months. The Pope's refusal to concede the Church's irrelevance to the debate in accordance with the prepared political script had been crucial in shaping the conference's dynamics and its outcome. Moral argument, it turned out, was capable of rallying an effective resistance to the imposition of certain First World lifestyles on the rest of humanity, through international law and foreign aid.

No one doubted that similar struggles would take place in the future. By appealing to the better angels of a universal human nature through the power of the word, though, John Paul had forced the moral core of the population argument onto the center of the world stage, changed the nature of the public debate, and helped shift the framework of discussion from "controlling" population to empowering women.

And that, in turn, had changed the course of the Cairo population conference.

THE CHURCH AS SPOUSE

During the months of debate leading up to the confrontation at Cairo, John Paul II fulfilled a longstanding desire to reconfigure one part of the rhythm of Vatican life by opening a convent for contemplative prayer, and issued *Ordinatio Sacerdotalis*, perhaps the most controversial apostolic letter of his pontificate, which reiterated that the Church could not ordain women to the ministerial priesthood. The two events may have seemed utterly disconnected. In fact, both involved the ancient New Testament teaching that the Church is the Spouse of Christ, an image that had decisively shaped the Church's sacramental imagination about the world, and indeed about all of reality.

Constant Prayer

In addition to the house of mercy he had established in Vatican City under the care of Mother Teresa's Missionaries of Charity, John Paul was eager to create a house of contemplative prayer inside the Vatican walls. Prayer, the Pope had long preached, was not only necessary for the ongoing conversion of one's heart and for obtaining the grace of God, prayer was also essential for accurately reading the "signs of the times" and in devising appropriate pastoral programs in response to them.[105] The Church's pastoral action, like its service to the world, was ultimately rooted in contemplation. The steady, constant, contemplative prayer of consecrated and cloistered men and women whose entire lives were acts of intercession was a particularly powerful expression of the Church's continuous self-gift to Christ, her Spouse, who returned the Church's love through grace. That was what the Church believed, and John Paul thought that conviction should be embodied inside the Vatican itself.

Work on a convent for cloistered nuns was begun in 1992 and completed in 1993 in the gently sloping grounds above the Governatorato, the residence and offices of the governor of Vatican City State. On May 13, 1994, the thirteenth anniversary of Agca's assassination attempt, the first group of eight nuns, Poor Clares, moved into the Monastero "Mater Ecclesiae," named for Mary, Mother of the Church. The two-story convent, built of brick faced with limestone and nestled against the Leonine Wall, welcomed nuns from the original Poor Clare community in Assisi and from convents in Croatia, Nicaragua, Rwanda, and the Philippines. "Constant prayer next to Peter," as *L'Osservatore Romano* put it, would be offered by an international community of women born in Bosnia-Herzegovina, Canada, Italy, Central America, East Asia, and central

Africa.[106] A different group of nuns would occupy the convent every five years. The Poor Clares were chosen to be first because theirs was the oldest order of women contemplatives in the Church, and because 1993 was the eighth centenary of the birth of St. Clare of Assisi.

St. Clare had written eloquently on the consecrated virgin as a bride of Christ. In the Catholic sacramental imagination, the spousal relationship of the Church to Christ touched every member of the Church, not only those vowed to poverty, chastity, and obedience. The New Testament image of the Church as the Bride of Christ had played an important role in John Paul's theology of the body, in which the Pope had reflected at length on how the spousal character of Christ's relationship to his Church (suggested by St. Paul in *Ephesians* 5.22–33) shed light on contemporary questions of human sexuality, marriage, and celibacy. Nine days after the opening of the Monastero "Mater Ecclesiae," one classic expression of the Church as the Bride of Christ, an intense controversy involving the relationship of this spousal imagery to the priesthood broke out when John Paul signed the apostolic letter *Ordinatio Sacerdotalis* [Priestly Ordination] on Pentecost Sunday, May 22, 1994.[107]

The Ordinatio Sacerdotalis *Controversy*

The question of whether women could be ordained priests had been debated in the Catholic Church since the mid-1970s, influenced by contemporary feminist theory, by theological speculations about the nature of the priesthood, and by the Anglican Communion's acceptance of women as priests. The Catholic debate on the question was limited almost exclusively to North America and Western Europe. In those parts of the world, acceptance in most academic theological circles required a judgment in favor of the ordination of women by the mid-1980s at the latest.

Paul VI had responded to the early phase of the Catholic debate through a declaration, *Inter Insigniores* [Among the Characteristics], issued in October 1976 by the Congregation for the Doctrine of the Faith [CDF]. Its key sentence read as follows: "The Sacred Congregation for the Doctrine of the Faith judges it necessary to recall that the Church, in fidelity to the example of the Lord, does not consider herself authorized to admit women to priestly ordination." In defense of that judgment, *Inter Insigniores* noted the constant tradition of both Catholicism and Orthodoxy, the biblical fact that Christ (who, in so many other respects, was countercultural in his approach to the women of his time) did not call women to be among the Twelve, the continuation of Christ's practice by the apostles, and the significance of Christ's manhood for those who stand in his place as his priests. Those who act in the Church *in persona Christi*, "in the person of Christ," must be able to represent Christ iconographically as the bridegroom and Head of the Church, the document argued.[108]

Inter Insigniores fueled, rather than settled, the Catholic debate. During the 1980s and early 1990s, the arguments grew more intense and, in some respects, more radical. Some feminist theologians and activists frankly admitted that they were no longer interested in ordination to the priesthood as it existed, but were intent on disassembling the hierarchical structure of the Church as a whole.[109] Finally, John Paul told a group of cardinals and bishops whom he had invited to lunch that he had been thinking about the debate and had come to a conclusion. As Cardinal Joseph Ratzinger later recalled, the Pope said, "I must speak about this. I have the responsibility to clarify this and to clarify it in a definitive way."

Given the failure of CDF's 1976 document to render what was regarded as a definitive judgment, the Pope knew that this had to be a pontifical statement. He did not think a long document was necessary, as the key theological points had been made in *Inter Insigniores*. What was needed was a clear, decisive statement that the debate was about an impossibility. Cardinal Ratzinger and the Congregation for the Doctrine of the Faith were charged with developing the document, and since it was a personal text of the Pope's there was a close and intense collaboration in the drafting between the Congregation and the papal apartment. The presidents of the national bishops' conferences most affected by the debate met in Rome to discuss a draft of the proposed apostolic letter and to offer recommendations. Then John Paul gave the letter "its final form," as Ratzinger put it, and the document was released on May 29, 1994.[110]

Ordinatio Sacerdotalis was, as John Paul wanted, a brief document. It reviewed Paul VI's statements on the question of women and the priesthood, including a 1977 address in which Pope Paul had said that the Church's tradition was a reflection of the "theological anthropology" given to the Church by Christ as part of her "fundamental constitution."[111] John Paul added to his predecessor's defense of the tradition by noting another biblical fact, which he interpreted in terms of his distinctive feminism: "The fact that the Blessed Virgin Mary, Mother of God and Mother of the Church, received neither the mission proper to the apostles nor the ministerial priesthood clearly shows that nonadmission of women to priestly ordination cannot mean that women are of lesser dignity, nor can it be construed as discrimination against them."[112] *Ordinatio Sacerdotalis* also addressed the question of "empowerment" raised by feminist theologians and others, stating that "the hierarchical structure of the Church is totally ordered" to the "holiness of the faithful," rather than to the exercise of power. That was why *Inter Insigniores* had taught, following *1 Corinthians*, that "the greatest in the Kingdom of Heaven are not the ministers but the saints."[113]

Nonetheless, some had continued to argue that the question of the ordination of women was open to debate or that the Church's tradition was a matter of discipline rather than of doctrine. Thus, John Paul wrote, he had to speak: "Wherefore, in order that all doubt may be removed regarding a matter of great importance, a matter which pertains to the Church's divine constitution itself, in virtue of my ministry of confirming the brethren (cf. *Luke*

22.32) I declare that the Church has no authority whatsoever to confer priestly ordination on women and that this judgment is to be definitively held by all the Church's faithful."[114]

In his commentary on *Ordinatio Sacerdotalis*, Cardinal Ratzinger emphasized that this was "not a new dogmatic formulation" but rather "a doctrine taught by the ordinary Papal Magisterium in a definitive way; that is, proposed not as a prudential teaching, nor as a more probable opinion, nor a mere matter of discipline, but as certainly true." That meant, in the practical order, that the teaching required the "full and unconditional assent of the faithful," and that teaching the contrary was "equivalent to leading consciences into error."[115]

The debate intensified, rather than abated, in the wake of *Ordinatio Sacerdotalis*. Cardinal Carlo Maria Martini of Milan said that "the papal document was decisive: it does not admit of either rebuttal or reformability. That is absolutely clear." But Martini went on to say that the truth involved was not a "truth of faith," as it did not concern a matter of revelation. Martini also suggested that the future discussion of women's "absolutely necessary and irreplaceable" mission in the Church should focus on the diaconate, which, the cardinal said, "the Pope does not mention and therefore does not exclude." In Germany, Rita Waschbüsch, president of the prominent lay organization the Zentralkomitee der Deutschen Katholiken, argued that it was impossible for the Pope or anyone else to close discussion of a subject that continued to be debated throughout the Church, but proposed that the conversation should now focus on how women could exercise a fuller mission in the Church as "presently" constituted. The hint of an alternatively constituted Church in the future seemed to suggest that the doctrinal message of *Ordinatio Sacerdotalis* had not been received. Criticism of the apostolic letter was most dramatic in the United States. "Priests for Equality," an organization claiming 4,000 members, issued a statement arguing that *Ordinatio Sacerdotalis* "is not infallible, does not enjoy the consultation of the 2,500 bishops of the Church, and most certainly does not express the sentiments of the faithful." The statement concluded with an apology for "the insensitivity of our Pope." Ruth Fitzpatrick, national coordinator of the Women's Ordination Conference, asked how a papal mandate could stop people from thinking: "That seems to be the real breach of divine law." Similar criticisms were heard from the Women in the Church Committee of the Conference of Religious in England and Wales, which claimed that its vision of a "Church of real inclusivity in all its ministries and Church structures" was shared by groups in Ireland and Australia.[116]

A Question and an Answer

Given the misrepresentation and misreading of the nature and substance of John Paul's teaching in *Ordinatio Sacerdotalis*, the next step in the controversy followed inexorably. During the firestorm of debate occasioned by the apostolic letter, a bishop sent a *dubium*—a question requesting an authoritative response—to the Congregation for the Doctrine of the Faith. Formally stated, the query read as follows:

> *Dubium*: Whether the teaching that the Church has no authority whatsoever to confer priestly ordination on women, which is presented in the Apostolic Letter *Ordinatio Sacerdotalis* to be held definitively, is to be understood as belonging to the deposit of faith.[117]

Less formally, and according to Cardinal Ratzinger's recollection, CDF had received a query from a bishop who had said, in effect: How am to understand all this? The Pope says he has spoken in a definitive way, but the theologians say he hasn't. Some bishops have been giving the impression that the teaching is, indeed, not "definitive." The Holy See had to clarify whether the teaching is definitive or not. CDF, the bishop concluded, had a duty to give an answer.

The *dubium*, according to Ratzinger, led to a "difficult discussion" involving the members of the Congregation and John Paul. The difficulty did not have to do with the substance of the teaching of *Ordinatio Sacerdotalis*, which all concerned believed to be true, definitive, and part of Christ's constituting will for the Church. The discussion was "difficult," Ratzinger remembered, "because the implication of the word 'infallible' is *tutti terremoto* [an earthquake for everyone]. So there were initially different voices, even among the cardinals. All were in agreement that *it is so*. The only question was how to say it better, [and on this people had] different opinions."[118]

The solution the Congregation finally accepted, and the reply John Paul personally approved, was published over Cardinal Ratzinger's signature on October 28, 1995:

> *Responsum*: In the affirmative.
> This teaching requires definitive assent, since, founded on the written Word of God and from the beginning constantly preserved and applied in the Tradition of the Church, it has been set forth infallibly by the ordinary and universal Magisterium (cf. Second Vatican Council, Dogmatic Constitution on the Church *Lumen Gentium*, 25, 2). Thus, in the present circumstances, the Roman Pontiff, exercising his proper office of confirming the brethren (cf. *Luke* 22.32), has handed on this same teaching by a formal declaration, explicitly stating what is to be held always, everywhere, and by all, as belonging to the deposit of faith.[119]

CDF's answer to the bishop's question was that the teaching of *Ordinatio Sacerdotalis* was to be definitively held by all Catholics because it had, throughout the centuries, been constantly taught by the bishops of the Church in communion with the Pope. This teaching constituted an infallible instance of the "ordinary and universal Magisterium" (or teaching authority of the Church), as that had been defined by Vatican II in *Lumen Gentium* 25. John Paul II was not personally exercising the infallibility of the papal office in *Ordinatio Sacerdotalis*. He was teaching definitively what the Church's "ordinary" teaching authority had already defined as a matter of the "deposit of faith" through its constant tradition.[120]

This set off another bruising controversy, centered on the question of whether CDF and John Paul were not unilaterally expanding the scope of infallible teaching. The "deposit of faith" was composed of truths the definition of which was protected by the charism of infallibility given by the Holy Spirit to the Church's teaching authority, the bishops in communion with the Bishop of Rome. Could the Pope identify as belonging to that "deposit" matters to which neither the bishops in ecumenical council nor the Pope had previously applied the term "infallible"? How could an admittedly noninfallible act (such as the issuing of an apostolic letter or the approval of a CDF *responsum*) nevertheless identify an infallible teaching that was to be definitively held as part of the constitutive truths of Catholic faith? The question of the ordination of women became enmeshed in the complex argument the First Vatican Council had intended to settle by its definition of papal infallibility but clearly had not—the question of the nature and means of exercising the Church's highest teaching authority.

The rhetoric in some of the post-*responsum* commentary was high. British theologian Nicholas Lash, the Norris-Hulse Professor of Divinity at Cambridge, accused the Pope of a "quite scandalous abuse of power," which would likely "undermine the very authority the Pope seeks to sustain."[121] Hans Küng charged the Pope and Cardinal Ratzinger with making "every effort . . . to scare, to repress, to forbid discussion." The German dissident group "We Are the Church" released a petition, signed by 1.5 million German Catholics, calling for the ordination of women.[122] Father Richard McBrien of the University of Notre Dame said that it was "utterly irresponsible for the Vatican to say something that doesn't quite mean what it seems to mean." Did John Paul mean to suggest, he asked, that those who disagreed with *Ordinatio Sacerdotalis* were heretics who were thus by definition "outside the Church"?[123]

The post-*responsum* debate helped clarify some of these issues. Father Avery Dulles, SJ, often regarded as the very model of theological carefulness among Catholic thinkers in the United States, sorted through the question of the teaching's authoritative status in a lecture to the bishops of the United States in June 1996. The doctrine taught by *Ordinatio Sacerdotalis* was infallible, Dulles said, not because of the apostolic letter or the CDF *responsum*. That was beyond CDF's competence, and John Paul had decided not to exercise his power to define the doctrine by a statement directly invoking his infallible teaching office. Rather, the apostolic letter and the *responsum* had drawn on a "classical theological method" by appealing to a wide range of sources, including the Word of God in Scripture, the constant tradition of the Church, and the "ordinary and universal magisterium" as described by Vatican II. The weight of those sources, Dulles argued, "strongly supports the Holy See in the present instance." John Paul had authoritatively identified a truth infallibly taught over two millennia by the "ordinary and universal" teaching authority of the Church.[124]

At the same time as Dulles was defending *Ordinatio Sacerdotalis* and the CDF *responsum*, the Catholic Theological Society of America was adopting the first draft of a report that flatly dissented from the apostolic letter's teaching and from the understanding of teaching authority in the *responsum*.[125]

An Opportunity Missed?

The terms, direction, and, in some instances, verbal violence of the dissent from *Ordinatio Sacerdotalis* and the CDF *responsum* suggest the possibility that the original decision made by John Paul and his theological advisers—to issue the apostolic letter as a papal confirmation of *Inter Insigniores* rather than to make a more developed statement of why the spousal nature of the Church meant that the Church could not ordain women to the ministerial priesthood—was a strategic error.

John Paul II had laid the foundations for such a developed statement throughout his pontificate. His development of the Church's teaching on the body, which held that maleness and femaleness were not biological accidents but revelations of deep truths about the human condition that directly touched God's redemptive purposes for the world, was a rich resource that simply had not existed when CDF issued *Inter Insigniores* in 1976. Brought to bear on the controversy over women and ordination, the theology of the body would have challenged what Hans Urs von Balthasar once described as contemporary "monosexism," a leveling-out of the meaning of sexual differentiation that had ominous implications for Church and society and that had distorted the debate over women's ordination since its inception in the 1970s.

The Pope's 1987 Christmas address to the Curia on how the "Marian Church"—the Church of disciples rooted in Mary's unambiguous "Yes" to God's call—preceded and made possible the "Petrine Church" of authority and office had set a foundation for getting the Catholic debate about the priesthood out of the post-Vatican II rut of political categories. With *Pastores Dabo Vobis*, it held out the welcome prospect of rethinking the ministerial priesthood for the twenty-first century as a service that ennobled the baptismal priesthood common to all Christians.

John Paul's defense of the dignity of women and the distinctive "feminine genius" in *Mulieris Dignitatem*, the feminism he would continue to develop in his public statements on the Cairo population conference, and his stated commitment to amplifying the unique mission of women in the Church could have been drawn on to illustrate why the reservation of priestly ordination to men could not be adequately understood according to the canons of contemporary ideological politics. A more developed statement than *Ordinatio Sacerdotalis* could also have clarified the question of justice and demonstrated why the

Church's tradition could not be properly understood as an injustice to women.[126]

Given the passions engaged by this issue and the cultural confusions those passions reflected, it might well have been impossible for any reiteration of the Church's tradition, no matter how developed, to have lifted the level of the debate substantively. Still, the brevity and character of *Ordinatio Sacerdotalis*, which led inexorably to the CDF *responsum*, reinforced the public perception that this was an issue to be understood as a pawn in an ongoing ecclesiastical power struggle, not an issue of doctrine that touched core Catholic perceptions about the sacramental nature of reality.[127]

That was a loss, not only for the peace of the Church, but for a modern world in which the sexual revolution and certain forms of gender feminism had devalued human sexuality and the crucial importance of our being created male and female. John Paul's intense effort to develop a new humanism on the threshold of the new millennium was thus impeded, not by the content of *Ordinatio Sacerdotalis*, but by the kind of debate the apostolic letter inadvertently reinforced.

A PAPAL BESTSELLER

The fall of 1994, for John Paul II, was marked by two disappointments, a major personal triumph, a largely unnoticed but significant ecumenical breakthrough—and a special appeal to the children of the world.

Blocked in Sarajevo

The first major disappointment was the cancellation of a planned papal pilgrimage to Sarajevo. The world seemed to want to forget the city's slow-motion destruction under relentless shelling. In and out of season, the Pope had worked to keep Sarajevo before the world's attention.

Earlier in the year, John Paul had tried another back-channel approach to revive his constantly frustrated initiatives in the former Republic of Yugoslavia. He sent Monsignor Vincenzo Paglia, the ecclesiastical adviser to the Sant' Egidio Community, on a private mission to Zagreb, Sarajevo, and Belgrade. Paglia was to try to arrange a papal pilgrimage to Croatia, Bosnia, and Serbia. Croatian President Franjo Tudjman, a Catholic, and Bosnian President Alija Izetbegović, a Muslim, agreed immediately. At Paglia's third meeting with Serbian leader Slobodan Milošević, the president of the rump of Yugoslavia had agreed to a visit without conditions. Even Bosnian Serb leader Radovan Karadžić, one of the principal instigators of the shattering of Sarajevo, had agreed to the Pope's coming to the Bosnian capital.

But then things began to unravel, and John Paul's visit to Belgrade was blocked by a majority of the Holy Assembly of Bishops, the highest authority of the Serbian Orthodox Church. Patriarch Pavle and his four counselor-bishops, all of whom favored the visit, could not convince the rest of their brethren. The Belgrade portion of the papal pilgrimage had to be dropped. As Joaquín Navarro-Valls put it delicately at a press conference on August 3, "the Holy See has been told that the time is not yet ripe." At the same press conference, however, Navarro announced that Father Roberto Tucci, SJ, the impresario of John Paul's travels, and Archbishop Francesco Monterisi, the nuncio in Bosnia-Herzegovina, would soon leave for Sarajevo to "examine the possibility of a visit by the Holy Father to Sarajevo in the near future."[128]

The Sarajevo visit was not to be, at least this time. On September 7, days before he was to depart, the visit was canceled for what the Vatican termed "security reasons." Those were certainly real. Though John Paul was not a man to fret about his own safety, there were concerns about the danger to civilians that would be posed by an attack on him during the visit. The Pope was bitterly disappointed about the cancellation, speaking of his "great inner suffering" at having to defer the visit when he announced the postponement at the general audience on September 7. The next day, the feast of the birthday of Mary, John Paul offered Mass in the courtyard of the papal villa at Castel Gandolfo for the relief of the people of Bosnia-Herzegovina, and read the sermon he was supposed to have given that day in Sarajevo. It was an impassioned plea for an end to the "fury of destruction."[129]

On September 10–11, John Paul did go to Zagreb for the 900th anniversary of the archdiocese. A week and a half later, though, continuing difficulties with his hip forced him to defer for a year a visit to the United States. The cancellation immediately set off a fresh round of rumors and media speculations than the Pope was *in extremis.*

In Conversation with the World

Stories of a disabled, diminished Pope were soon overrun by one of the most remarkable publishing events of the 1990s—the October 1994 release of John Paul's book *Crossing the Threshold of Hope*, which quickly became an international bestseller.

Threshold began with a television interview that never happened. To mark the fifteenth anniversary of the pontificate in October 1993, Italian Radio and Television had proposed that John Paul be interviewed live by a journalist, Vittorio Messori; the Italian broadcast would then be shared with major networks around the world. The Pope accepted, but scheduling conflicts in September 1993 made it impossible to bring the project to completion in time to meet the October broadcast deadline. After a few months, Messori got a phone call from Joaquín Navarro-Valls, one of the principal promoters of the broadcast interview. Navarro had a message from the Pope: "Even if there wasn't time to respond to you in person, I kept your questions on my desk. They interested me. I didn't think it would be wise to let them go to waste. So I thought about them and ... responded to them in writing. You have asked me questions, therefore you have a right to responses. ... I am working on them. I will let you have them. Then do with them what you think is appropriate."

In April 1994, Navarro met with Messori at the Italian journalist's home and gave him a large white envelope. It was John Paul's answers to Messori's questions, prepared as a book manuscript, with the title *Crossing the Threshold of Hope* handwritten by the Pope on the folder containing the results of this unprecedented act of papal authorship. John Paul indicated that the title was only a suggestion and that the editors could do what they thought right. Messori, Navarro, and the others involved in getting the manuscript published wisely decided to leave the title exactly as the Pope had written it. John Paul reviewed and approved the lightly edited manuscript, which was published simultaneously in the major world languages in October 1994.[130]

Popes had written encyclicals, apostolic letters, apostolic exhortations, and homilies, but no pope had ever written a book that was essentially a conversation with the reader about his own experience of Christian faith and his hopes for the world. Predecessor popes might have worried about how the authority of such a book would fit into the taxonomy of papal documents. John Paul evidently thought that that could be left to the theologians to work out. Here was another opportunity to clarify, in a very personal way, the proposal he had been making for sixteen years. The question of what it meant for a pope to be doing such things could be sorted out later. More than a decade and a half into his pontificate, John Paul II was still governing the Church as an outsider, at least insofar as the traditional managers of popes were concerned.

Substantively, *Threshold* contained no surprises for those who had been following John Paul's published papal texts. To others, who were accustomed by now to thinking of Karol Wojtyła as an authoritarian seeking to impose a rigorous Polish form of Catholicism on the universal Church, *Threshold* was a revelation. Emphatically and unmistakably, this was a Pope in conversation, a man living the teaching he had laid down in *Redemptoris Missio*: "The Church proposes; she imposes nothing." His descriptions of his own struggles in prayer; his autobiographical reflections on the fate of his Jewish schoolmates in Wadowice, on his vocational discernment, on learning "to love human love" through his first experiences as a young priest with those preparing for marriage; his deep ecumenical hopes; his profound sense of the twentieth century as a century of martyrs; his passion to reinstill hope into humanism in the face of modern fear—all this bespoke a richly human and humane sensibility, not the cast of mind of a doctrinaire scold.

For all its popular appeal, *Crossing the Threshold of Hope* was neither generic "spirituality" nor popularized philosophy. Rather, it was another expression of Karol Wojtyła's core conviction that Jesus Christ is the answer to the question that is every human life. That answer, he believed, spoke to the depths of the world's fear at the end of a terrible century:

> . . . *Someone exists who holds in His hands the destiny of this passing world; Someone who holds the keys to death and the netherworld* (cf. *Revelation* 1.18); *Someone who is the Alpha and the Omega of human history* (cf. *Revelation* 22.13)—be it the

individual or collective history. And this Someone is Love (cf. *1 John* 4.8, 16)—Love that became man, Love crucified and risen, Love unceasingly present among men . . . He alone can give the ultimate assurance when he says, "Be not afraid!"[131]

In a modern world that had once feared God's existence and now feared what humanity might be capable of in a world without God, to encounter that Love was to cross the threshold of hope.[132] That, his book suggested, was what John Paul II had been proposing all along, in multiple variations on a single great theme.*

Aging into the Future

Although there were elements of autobiographical retrospection in *Threshold*, the Pope continued to look toward the future even while he visibly aged.

On November 11, as his book was breaking to the top of the best-seller lists, John Paul II signed a "Common Christological Declaration" with the Assyrian Church of the East, whose members live in Iraq, Iran, Syria, Lebanon, India, North America, and Australia. It was the latest in a series of ecumenical agreements with smaller Eastern Churches long divided from Rome—and, in the case of the Assyrian Church of the East, which had broken with the rest of Christianity at the Council of Ephesus in 431, divided from every other Christian communion as well. The Common Christological Declaration recognized that the same faith in Christ could be expressed in different formulas and affirmed that Catholics and Assyrians are "united today in the confession of the same faith in the Son of God." This breakthrough in a 1,500-year-old dispute was entirely the accomplishment of John Paul II's pontificate, and presaged even greater cooperation and perhaps ecclesial reunion in the future, as the Assyrians began to plan common projects with the Iraq-based Chaldean Catholic Church, including a common catechism and joint priestly formation.[134]

Even as his ecumenical hopes with Orthodoxy were being frustrated on a number of fronts, John Paul had made steady progress in resolving centuries-old theological disputes with a group of ancient Eastern Churches, once called "monophysite" or "pre-Chalcedonian," but now usually known as the Oriental Orthodox Churches. These Churches broke with the rest of a unified Christianity over the definition of Christ's "two natures" at the Council of Chalcedon in 451. Yet a patient series of bilateral ecumenical dialogues with these communions resulted during John Paul II's pontificate in declarations with the Armenian Apostolic Church, the Coptic Orthodox Church, and the Syrian Orthodox Church, in which both parties stated that their faith in Christ,

---

*By 1998, *Crossing the Threshold of Hope* had been published in forty languages, and several million copies had been sold. John Paul used the first royalty payment from the book to rebuild shattered churches in the former Yugoslavia.[133]

despite verbal differences in formulation, was "the same." Though there was no formal declaration as such when the Patriarch of the Ethiopian Orthodox Church came to Rome in June 1993, John Paul had said that Catholics and Ethiopian Orthodox shared "the same" faith in Christ. The dialogue between Roman Catholicism and the Oriental Orthodox Churches could now move on to questions of the nature of the Church and of ecclesiastical jurisdiction.[135]

These ecumenical achievements were the result of several factors: the maturing of bilateral theological dialogues; the pressures on small Churches living in an Arab and Muslim sea (a circumstance which could make Rome seem like a protector rather than an ancient foe); large-scale immigration to the West and the desire of these Churches to maintain their own identity amid the pressures of assimilation.[136] Whatever the complexities of motivation, the result was that disputes dating to the first half of the first Christian millennium were being resolved on the threshold of the third.

The Catholic Church of the twenty-first century was further defined by John Paul's sixth consistory for the creation of cardinals, held on November 26, 1994. Miloslav Vlk, the former Prague window washer who had conducted his ministry underground for years because of communist repression, and Jaime Ortega y Alamino, the archbishop of Havana who was still contesting for Cuba's future with one of the world's last communist regimes, received the red hat, as did Vinko Puljić, the forty-nine-year-old archbishop of Sarajevo. John Paul broke precedent by raising the General Secretary of the Synod of Bishops, Jan Schotte, to the cardinalate. Belarus received its first cardinal in Kazimierz Świątek, the eighty-year-old archbishop of Minsk-Mohilev; a veteran of ten years in the Gulag Archipelago, he had celebrated Mass lying on his back in a prison bunk in order to avoid suspicion. Mikel Koliqi, a ninety-two-year-old Albanian who had spent twenty-one years in communist labor camps and twenty-three years in communist prisons, was named cardinal, as were two venerable figures from the Vatican II generation of theologians, the German Jesuit Alois Grillmeier and the French Dominican Yves Congar, who was too infirm to attend the consistory. It was a thoroughly international consistory, with new cardinals from Lebanon, the Czech Republic, Japan, Chile, Scotland, Mexico, Indonesia, Cuba, Belgium, France, Switzerland, Uganda, the United States, Peru, Québec, Spain, Bosnia, Madagascar, Vietnam, Ecuador, Belarus, and Germany being inducted into the College along with four Italians. John Paul's sixth consistory guaranteed that the conclave to choose his successor would be the most multinational in history.

The Pope closed a year of controversy with a December 13, 1994, *Letter to Children.* John Paul wrote of his own memories of Christmas, and of the importance of First Communion; he recalled child martyrs and child visionaries as exemplars of the "Gospel of children." At the close of this International Year of the Family, with all the contention that had caused, he wanted to ask children for something that no other world leader had requested during "their" year—their prayers. Children, he wrote, "instinctively turn away from hatred and are attracted by love." That was why he asked the children of the world to "take upon yourselves the duty of *praying for peace*." The prayers of children had enormous power, and that was a model for grown-ups, who ought to pray with the simple and complete trust of the young.[137]

John Paul concluded his letter by asking the world's children to be missionaries of love. The previous month, placing a ring on the fingers of the men he had just created cardinals, he had reminded them of the necessity of bearing witness even to shedding their blood. The two statements may have seemed dramatically different. To the Pope's mind, being a witness to love and giving oneself completely to the truth were two dimensions of life on the far side of the threshold of hope.

19

Only One World

Human Solidarity and the Gospel of Life

APRIL 10–MAY 8, 1994	Special Assembly for Africa of the Synod of Bishops meets in Rome; Synod's work completed by apostolic exhortation, *Ecclesia in Africa*, issued in September 1995.
JUNE 13, 1994	The College of Cardinals discusses the jubilee year of 2000.
SEPTEMBER 29, 1994	Ambassador Shmuel Hadas, Israel's first ambassador to the Holy See, presents credentials to John Paul II.
OCTOBER 25, 1994	The Holy See establishes "official relations" with the Palestine Liberation Organization.
NOVEMBER 10, 1994	Apostolic Letter, *Tertio Millennio Adveniente*, on the Great Jubilee of 2000.
JANUARY–DECEMBER 1995	John Paul II issues fifteen public appeals for peace in Bosnia-Herzegovina.
JANUARY 14, 1995	On Radio Veritas Asia, John Paul urges all Chinese Catholics to "seek paths of communion and reconciliation."
JANUARY 15, 1995	In Manila, John Paul II gathers the largest crowd in history for the closing Mass of the fifth international World Youth Day.
MARCH 25, 1995	*Evangelium Vitae,* John Paul's eleventh encyclical.
MAY 25, 1995	*Ut Unum Sint,* the first papal encyclical on ecumenism.
JUNE 27–29, 1995	Ecumenical Patriarch Bartholomew I visits the Vatican.
JUNE 29, 1995	John Paul II issues his *Letter to Women* throughout the world.
SEPTEMBER 4–15, 1995	Fourth World Conference on Women meets in Beijing.
OCTOBER 4–9, 1995	John Paul's third extended pilgrimage to the United States.
OCTOBER 5, 1995	John Paul II addresses the Fiftieth General Assembly of the United Nations.
NOVEMBER 12, 1995	An apostolic letter marks the fourth centenary of the Union of Brest.

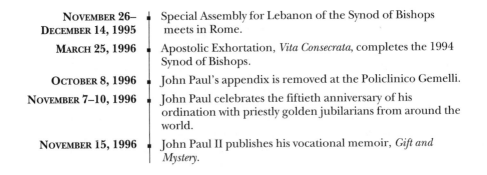

NOVEMBER 26– **DECEMBER 14, 1995**	Special Assembly for Lebanon of the Synod of Bishops meets in Rome.
MARCH 25, 1996	Apostolic Exhortation, *Vita Consecrata*, completes the 1994 Synod of Bishops.
OCTOBER 8, 1996	John Paul's appendix is removed at the Policlinico Gemelli.
NOVEMBER 7–10, 1996	John Paul celebrates the fiftieth anniversary of his ordination with priestly golden jubilarians from around the world.
NOVEMBER 15, 1996	John Paul II publishes his vocational memoir, *Gift and Mystery*.

On the morning of June 13, 1994, as they gathered for the fifth extraordinary consistory of the pontificate, more than one member of the College of Cardinals thought that the Pope was on the verge of making a serious mistake. There were several items on their two-day agenda, but it was the first day's topic, preparations for the Great Jubilee of 2000, that had caused considerable controversy within the College and the Curia.

Earlier in the year, the Pope had sent the cardinals a twenty-three-page memorandum, "Reflections on the Great Jubilee of the Year 2000," and asked for their written responses. The memo proposed five initiatives leading up to and celebrating the turn of the millennium—a series of regional Synods for Asia, the Americas, and Oceania, to be held in Rome; a great ecumenical meeting of all Christian communions; an international meeting of Christian, Jewish, and Muslim leaders; an updating of the Church's "martyrology," bringing thousands of witnesses to the faith onto the official roster of martyrs; and an examination of the Church's conscience in order "to acknowledge the errors committed by its members and, in a certain sense, in the name of the Church."

On forty previous occasions, John Paul had directly or indirectly acknowledged the errors of Catholics throughout history: errors in interreligious relations, errors in the Church's relationship to its own reformers, errors in the Church's treatment of indigenous peoples, errors in its treatment of women, errors that had contributed to the East-West break of 1054 and to the intrawestern fracture of the sixteenth-century Reformation. The Pope was now proposing a general examination of conscience of far greater magnitude—and proposing to do it publicly for all the world to see. The cardinals were worried.

Cardinals from the new democracies of central and eastern Europe were concerned that a public admission of past errors might revive anti-Catholic propaganda in countries that had just been freed from the burden of communist anti-Catholicism. Third World cardinals, representing local Churches often less than 200 years old, were not terribly interested in the tangled history of Catholic Europe. Other cardinals were concerned about the historical methodology of any such self-examination: Did it make sense to judge the

deeds of churchmen in the fourteenth century, who may well have been acting according to their best lights, by the standards of the twentieth? Still others, including Bologna's outspoken Cardinal Giacomo Biffi, had raised a
theological caution. The members of the Church were certainly all sinners,
but in acknowledging that, it was important to remember that the Church
itself, as the Body of Christ, was without sin. Some veteran members of the
Roman Curia thought that this initiative, like others in the pontificate of John
Paul II, was simply an inappropriate thing for a pope to do.

In his opening address to the consistory, John Paul quickly deflected any
attempt to blame the jubilee memo on unnamed papal staffers by making two
personal references to "the memorandum sent to each of you." This was his
document, he stood behind it, and it represented his best thinking on the subject, which he now laid out in further detail.

The Pope spoke at length about the Second Vatican Council as the "high
point" of the Church's preparation for the third millennium. Between 1994
and 2000, any authentic preparation for the jubilee year "must have the application of the Council's directive as its basic criterion." Ecumenism was also
high on John Paul's millennium agenda. The quest for Christian unity was one
of the Church's basic obligations en route to the jubilee year, and in meeting
it, "mutual accord between the Catholic West and the Orthodox East" was "perhaps the greatest task. *We cannot come before Christ, the Lord of History, as divided
as we unfortunately have been during the second millennium.*"

The new martyrology, the Pope continued, reflected Vatican II's emphasis on the universal call to holiness. John Paul knew there had been criticism
of the number of beatifications in his pontificate. If some present had difficulties with this, he gently suggested, they should complain to the Holy Spirit
rather than about the Pope, for "the great number of beatifications vividly
reflects the action of the Holy Spirit and the vitality flowing from him in the Church's
most essential sphere, that of holiness." The Church's devotional and liturgical life was still historically unbalanced, with too little attention paid to examples of sanctity from the young Churches evangelized in the second
millennium.

At the end of the address he squarely faced the most difficult issue raised
by his pre-consistory memorandum: the cleansing of the Church's conscience
as it turned into a new millennium. Conversion, John Paul said, was an essential part of the preparation for 2000: "As she faces this Great Jubilee, the
Church needs '*metanoia,' that is, the discernment of her children's historical shortcomings and negligence* with regard to the demands of the Gospel." This was not
ecclesiastical political correctness. It was obedience to Christ's desire that his
Church be evangelical and united. Cleansing the Church's historical conscience was essential if the Gospel were to be preached credibly.

The cardinals listened and then broke into language-based discussion
groups to think more about the Great Jubilee. It was a busy time and they were
busy men. The year 2000 was half a decade away. Did it really require all this

attention now? At the end of the extraordinary consistory, the cardinals issued two statements. The first urged the nations of the world to clarify the international law of humanitarian intervention in light of the butcheries in Rwanda. The second supported John Paul's campaign to sharpen the moral focus of the Cairo population conference.

As for the Great Jubilee of 2000, there did not seem to be much of a sense that this was a moment of great opportunity. Behind closed doors, various cardinals had expressed their concerns about aspects of the Pope's proposed program, including cleansing the Church's conscience in public. Observers were hard put to suggest that the College of Cardinals left the consistory on June 14, 1994, on fire with enthusiasm about the Great Jubilee of 2000.

Five months later to the day, John Paul II personally ignited the universal Church's preparation for the Great Jubilee. There was a *kairos,* a providential opportunity, to be seized and he was determined to seize it. The enthusiasm of busy prelates who sometimes had difficulty seeing epic historical opportunities amid their quotidian concerns would follow in due course.[1]

SANCTIFYING TIME

A millennial theme emerged in the first hours of John Paul II's pontificate. Shortly after his election, Cardinal Wyszyński had said to him that he must "lead the Church into the third millennium."[2] John Paul's inaugural encyclical, *Redemptor Hominis,* had spoken about the time leading up to the year 2000 as a "new Advent,"[3] and the impending jubilee had shaped the agenda of the Extraordinary Synod of 1985. In the wake of the cardinals' meeting of June 1994, John Paul offered the Church and the world the most developed statement of his millennial vision in the apostolic letter *Tertio Millennio Adveniente* [The Coming Third Millennium], which was signed on November 10 and issued on November 14, 1994. In his most lyrical papal document, the Pope suggested that the year 2000 was the interpretive "key" to his entire pontificate.[4]

The Axial Moment

Tertio Millennio Adveniente begins with a precise definition of what the turn into the third millennium means. What is on the horizon, John Paul writes, is nothing less than the 2,000th anniversary of the axial moment in history: the Incarnation in human flesh of the Son of God, the Word through whom God the Father had made the universe.[5] The Incarnate Son had shown the world the face of God the Father. At the same time, Christ, the redeemer of the world, shows us the true face of humanity.[6] Thus the year 2000 has universal significance. It is, one might say, the 2,000th anniversary of the unveiling of true humanism.

The Incarnation of Christ is the axial point of human history for another reason. In the Incarnation, the great human search for God was satisfied—and by God himself, God in search of humanity, "God who comes in Person to speak to man of himself and to show him the path by which he may be reached." Christianity is not a blind search for the divine, but the human "*response of faith* to God who reveals himself." In that response, men and women come to know themselves as "the epiphany of God's glory," as creatures "called to live by the fullness of life in God."[7] The Incarnation speaks to the human yearning for a destiny that transcends the limitations of time, space, and death: Christianity is "the religion of 'dwelling in the inmost life of God,'" as St. Paul had told the Corinthians. And that is a dwelling without end, made possible by the self-emptying of the Word of God in his Incarnation, birth, life, and sacrificial death.[8]

With the Incarnation, John Paul writes, "eternity entered into time" and the truth about time was revealed: time is not flat chronology but richly textured drama. Conversely, when the Son of God, while remaining the second Person of the Trinity, entered history, he took time upon himself, and then, as it were, lifted it up into the very life of God—Father, Son, and Holy Spirit. From all of this, the Pope writes, there came "*the duty to sanctify time.*" Jubilees came from this concept of sanctified time, which the Church had learned from its Jewish roots. In Christianity, as in Judaism, jubilees were times of liberation linked to a messianic hope. The final liberation of humanity, still in the future, would be messianic in character—the completion of God's saving work in history through the definitive establishment of God's Kingdom.[9] To mark the 2,000th anniversary of the commencement of that Kingdom in the life, death, and resurrection of Christ, the Church would celebrate the year 2000 as the "Great Jubilee."[10]

The Great Jubilee, John Paul immediately continues, is a preparation for a "*new springtime of Christian life,*" a moment of evangelical possibility in the wake of a century of winter. The year 2000 should be marked, not by millenarian frenzy, but by a new spirit of attentiveness. The entire purpose of the Great Jubilee is to get the Church to listen to "what the Spirit is suggesting to the different communities," from the smallest families to the largest nations.[11]

A Church of Pilgrims and Penitents

Jubilees were traditional times of pilgrimage in which the Church relived "the journey of Christ through the centuries."[12] For his own part, the Pope signaled his "fervent wish" to visit Sarajevo, Lebanon, Jerusalem, and the Holy Land in the years leading up to the Great Jubilee. During the jubilee year itself, he proposed "to visit the *places on the road taken by the People of God of the Old Covenant,* starting from the places associated with Abraham and Moses, through Egypt and Mount Sinai, as far as Damascus, the city which witnessed the conversion of St. Paul."[13]

Jubilees were also times of repentance. The deepest form of human liberation—liberation from the grip of sin and its effects—requires the acknowl-edgment and confession of sins. Confession leads to forgiveness, and forgive-ness gives birth to the joy characteristic of jubilee years. Thus, John Paul writes, "it is appropriate that, as the Second Millennium of Christianity draws to a close, the Church should become more fully conscious of the sinfulness of her children, recalling all those times in history when they departed from the spirit of Christ and his Gospel, and instead of offering to the world the witness of a life inspired by the values of faith, indulged in ways of thinking and acting which were truly *forms of counter-witness and scandal.*"[14]

Vatican II had affirmed that the Church is, at the same time, holy and always in need of purification. In times of jubilee, that consciousness should be more acute in the Church, and it should be particularly sharp at a millennial jubilee. John Paul illustrates the point with a metaphor from Rome's Holy Year tradi-tion: "The Holy Door of the Jubilee of the Year 2000 should be symbolically wider than those of previous Jubilees, because humanity, upon reaching this goal, will leave behind not just a century but a millennium. It is fitting that the Church should make this passage with a clear awareness of what has happened to her during the last ten centuries."[15] Christian sinfulness had led to divisions within Christianity. That was why the preparation for the Great Jubilee of 2000 had to be a time of intensified ecumenical work.[16] The Church's sons and daughters also had to repent the times when they gave way "*to intolerance and even the use of violence* in the service of truth." Turning from the errors of the past, the Church should deepen its commitment to what Vatican II had taught in its *Declaration on Religious Freedom*: "The truth cannot impose itself except by virtue of its own truth, as it wins over the mind with both gentleness and power."[17]

The Church of the twentieth century also had accounts to clear. It is delu-sory, the Pope argues, to blame moral relativism, or the religious indifference of late modernity, or the loss of a sense of transcendence on some impersonal process called "secularization." Christians had to look into their own hearts and consciences to see how they had contributed to the religious crisis of the late twentieth century "by not having shown the face of God." The Church also had to repent the ways in which some of its sons and daughters had failed to read the dangers inherent in modern totalitarianism, to the point of acqui-escing in massive violations of human rights. And a reckoning was needed with the various ways in which the Church had failed to live out the great promise of Vatican II.[18]

As it was confronting its failures, the Church ought to reflect more deeply on the great spirits it had helped nurture, and foremost among these were the martyrs. It was imperative that Christians understand that, as John Paul put it, "at the end of the second millennium, *the Church has once again become a Church of martyrs.*" The witness of modern martyrs, a great ecumenical sign, must not be lost. The Church of the martyrs, now in glory, had achieved the unity that Christ willed for his Church. That, John Paul suggests, is a great lesson for the Church on earth.[19]

The Program of the Great Jubilee

The Pope laid out a trinitarian program for celebrating the Great Jubilee of 2000. There would be three years of preparation, each dedicated to one of the persons of the Trinity and one of the theological virtues: 1997 would be the year of reflection on Jesus Christ and a year devoted to strengthening the faith and witness of Christians; 1998 would be dedicated to the Holy Spirit and the virtue of hope; 1999, given to reflection on God the Father, would also be the year to meditate on the virtue of love, for God himself is love.[20]

The aim of the jubilee year itself would be "*to give glory to the Trinity*, from whom everything in the world and in history comes and to whom everything returns." Thus the Great Jubilee would help the Church experience, in an anticipatory way, its destiny—life forever within the light and communion of God the Holy Trinity.[21] That was why the Great Jubilee ought to be marked by a "*meeting of all Christians*," to be prepared "in an attitude of fraternal cooperation with Christians of other denominations and traditions." Such a meeting, John Paul hoped, would be open "to those religions whose representatives might wish to acknowledge the joy shared by all the disciples of Christ."[22]

The Great Jubilee grew out of the fact that the Church had endured for two millennia. But, as John Paul writes, the Church endures in order to grow in witness to the truth, in service to the world, in proclamation of the good news of Jesus Christ—in a word, in mission. The Great Jubilee, the Pope concludes, must be celebrated by looking ahead, to a new springtime of evangelization in which the Church proposes to billions of unevangelized human beings the true story of their origin and astonishing destiny.

John Paul II had little doubt that civilization was in crisis, but his millennialism, in *Tertio Millennio Adveniente*, was not of the apocalyptic sort. Everything necessary for salvation had been done in history, he had mused to dinner companions on one occasion. But much more remained to be done for the human condition, and Christ would do it in and through the Church. The possibility of springtime following a winter of crisis—that was how the Church should look at the century that was ending and the century that lay ahead.[23]

More than sixteen years after his election, the lodestar of the pontificate of John Paul II remained the Incarnation of the *redemptor hominis*, Jesus Christ, and the truth about the human condition revealed in Christ remained John Paul's proposal to the world. Many things had changed since the College of Cardinals had done the unthinkable on October 16, 1978. This had not.

TEMPORALITIES

At the extraordinary consistory in June 1994, Cardinal Edmund Szoka, President of the Prefecture for the Economic Affairs of the Holy See, was able to give his fellow cardinals some welcome financial news. In its 1993 fiscal year (which coincided with calendar year 1993), the Holy See had enjoyed its first surplus after twenty-three straight years of deficits—the worst of which, in 1991, amounted to more than $87 million, or almost 101,000,000,000 Italian lire. FY 1993 ended a decade of Vatican red ink that totaled more than $540 million. Things had been turned around when what some Curialists call "the way we do things here" was changed. By many reckonings, it was none too soon, and not just fiscally. In addition to all the red ink, the Holy See's reputation for financial probity had suffered in the early 1980s.

Vatican wealth is vastly exaggerated in the public imagination. The Holy See's net assets, which are estimated to be between $1 billion and $2 billion, are in fact rather modest—in 1994, smaller than the endowments of thirty-two U.S. colleges and universities.[24] The ocean of red ink the Holy See generated during the 1970s and 1980s was an unforeseen result of the Second Vatican Council. A considerable expansion of the Church's central bureaucratic machinery and the creation of new institutions like the Synod of Bishops had increased expenses tremendously, while income had failed to keep pace. Accounting changes added to the deficit, as the costs of Vatican embassies abroad and Vatican Radio were moved from the separate Vatican City State budget to the Holy See budget, reflecting the fact that these costs involved services to the universal Church.

The Pope had discussed this problem with several extraordinary consistories of cardinals. The 1981 discussion led to the formation of a "Council of Cardinals to Study the Organizational and Economic Problems of the Holy See," often called the "Council of Fifteen," the most active members of which included Cardinal John Krol of Philadelphia and Cardinal Joseph Höffner of Cologne. The Council tried to rationalize the Holy See's budgeting and accounting procedures, which were wholly inadequate by modern standards. Shortly after this, scandal threatened to overwhelm the Institute for the Works of Religion [IOR], a bank that, although not technically part of the Holy See, is widely and not altogether inaccurately referred to as the "Vatican Bank." Its American head, Archbishop Paul Marcinkus, had had no international financial experience when he was appointed to IOR by Archbishop Benelli, chief-of-staff, or *Sostituto,* to Pope Paul VI. Inexperience, compounded by naïveté and overextension (Marcinkus was also governor of Vatican City and, prior to Father Roberto Tucci, the impresario of John Paul II's international travels), led the American archbishop into difficulties with Italian financier Robert Calvi and his Banco Ambrosiano in Milan. Thinking he was helping a friend gain time to work his way out of a financial jam, Marcinkus gave Calvi letters indicating IOR support for the Banco Ambrosiano, while at the same time getting a letter from Calvi stating that IOR was not responsible for Ambrosiano's activities. Only Marcinkus's letter to Calvi was given to Ambrosiano's creditors, however. It looked to some like fraud, but to those who knew Marcinkus, it was indicative of his naïveté. When Calvi's $1.2 billion empire imploded in 1982, there was considerable fallout. Calvi was found hanging, dead, from Blackfriars Bridge in London on June 18, 1982, and thirty-three fraud convictions were eventually obtained in Italian courts. Although the Vatican continued to deny any malfeasance, Cardinal Casaroli negotiated a settlement with the Italian government in 1984 in which IOR paid $244 million to the Ambrosiano creditors as settlement of all present and future claims. Archbishop Marcinkus, whose difficulties may have included opposition from veteran Curialists to the presence of a powerful American in the Vatican, eventually retired from the IOR in 1989, his ecclesiastical career finished.[25]

Reform of the Holy See's financial practices accelerated in 1990 when Cardinal Edmund Szoka, the archbishop of Detroit since 1981, was appointed President of the Prefecture for the Economic Affairs of the Holy See. Cardinal Szoka, who was determined to "professionalize the operation" and to demand "complete transparency" in light of the Ambrosiano fiasco, helped introduce modern accounting and budgeting methods to the Vatican, and by force of personality and will brought resistant dicasteries into line.[26] When Szoka arrived, the prefecture had no computers. The annual audit and the Holy See consolidated financial statement took sixteen months to complete after the close of the fiscal year. After getting the operation computerized (with help from U.S. Catholic foundations) and hiring some badly needed staff, Szoka cut that to five months.[27] Now, auditors from Ernst & Young review the work of the in-house auditors on contract. The consolidated financial statement and annual audit report are published in five languages (Italian, English, French, German, and Spanish) after review by an oversight committee of fifteen cardinals.[28]

Cardinal Szoka gradually brought the expenditure side of the ledger under control by professionalizing Vatican accounting and limiting budget increases to the inflation rate, thus lowering operating costs in real terms. The long-term problem would not be solved until income was increased, however, and to this end Szoka proposed, and John Paul approved, a meeting of the presidents of the national episcopal conferences, which was held in Rome on April 8 to 9, 1991. This particular configuration of bishops had never met before. That innovation, and the fact that the subject was money, made the traditional managers of Vatican finance nervous. But Cardinal Szoka believed that bishops' conferences, and through them, the local bishops, were the key to solving the Holy See's income problem. In the cardinal's mind, at issue was Canon 1271 in the revised Code of Canon Law, which stipulated that the bishops were obligated to support the universal ministry of the Holy See. The record indicated that they were not doing enough.

Szoka, not a man to mince words, explained the financial situation bluntly to the conference presidents. Cardinal Rosalio José Castillo Lara, SDB, the Venezuelan President of the Administration of the Patrimony of the Apostolic See and another Vatican financial reformer, spoke on the obligations of Canon 1271.[29] Though no assessments were levied and the bishops were asked to "solve this at home," a sufficient number of conferences were cooperative enough that income increased substantially. The Holy See's statements showed a modest surplus in FY 1993.[30] Still, a June 1996 letter to all the world's bishops from the "Council of Fifteen" noted that "the implementation of Canon 1271 thus far, unfortunately, has only been partial."[31]

Throughout his seven-year tenure at the *Prefettura*, Cardinal Szoka, who was appointed President of the Pontifical Commission for Vatican City State—and thus governor of Vatican City—in October 1997, met with John Paul as needed to review the budgets and audits of various offices, and to go over the annual Holy See audit and consolidated financial statement. According to Szoka, the Pope's grasp of the major points is quick, but there is no lengthy discussion of details.[32] John Paul willingly leaves auditing and budget-making details to others whom he trusts.[33]

Direct financial support of the Pope from the laity comes via the annual "Peter's Pence" collection, which is separate from the Holy See's operating budget. Its income rose from $27.5 million in 1983 to $67 million in 1993. The funds are primarily used by John Paul to bolster the Church in poor countries. It is not unusual for the IOR to get a call from the papal apartment in the morning, saying that the Pope needs a certain number of envelopes containing $20,000 or $50,000 by noon—gifts to bishops from Africa, Latin America, and Asia coming on *ad limina* visits or for other business. John Paul also takes gifts of money with him to poor Churches on his foreign travels. During the hardest days of martial law in Poland, the Pope made personal financial contributions to support the families of Solidarity leaders through a relief effort operated at St. Martin's Church in Warsaw's Old Town.[34]

The Papal Foundation, founded in 1987 and headquartered in Philadelphia, is another vehicle for supporting the Holy See's activities and poorer local Churches around the world. In November 1987, Cardinal John O'Connor of New York, Cardinal John Krol of Philadelphia, and Archbishop Theodore McCarrick of Newark met with prominent American lay leaders at the Vatican embassy in Washington to discuss the Holy See's financial difficulties. The proposal that emerged from the meeting was to establish a U.S.-based foundation, an endowment whose income would support the Pope's work. Regional fund-raising events to create the endowment were held throughout the United States. Within the first ten years, over $37 million in cash contributions had been received. The Papal Foundation's investments had a market value of $44 million in June 1998. Governed by a board composed of all resident U.S. cardinals and lay trustees chosen by the cardinals, the Papal Foundation made $8.2 million in grants between 1990 and 1997. Grants in the foundation's first years focused on capital improvements in the Holy See, including modernizing Vatican Radio and the Vatican printing works, which helps prepare catechetical materials for developing countries. John Paul II has used the foundation to rebuild churches and Catholic institutions in the former Soviet Union (including seminaries in Ukraine, Lithuania, and Latvia), to support the 1994 Synod for Africa and the beleaguered Church in Sarajevo, to create centers for needy children in the Third World, to help drought victims in North Korea, to build missionary chapels in Ivory Coast and an AIDS hospice in Chile, and to support the work of the Pontifical Academy for Life. The substantial sums raised by the Papal Foundation testified to the impact the Pope had made on American donors of considerable means.

ASIA: TRIUMPH AND TENSIONS

Strengthening solidarity with the world's most populous and least Christian continent was the focus of John Paul's pontificate in early 1995. The year began with a 20,000-mile pilgrimage to the Philippines, Papua New Guinea, Australia, and Sri Lanka, during which the Pope tried, again unsuccessfully, to open a bridge to the People's Republic of China [PRC]. The terms in which the papal offer of dialogue was made suggested a new Vatican strategy for dealing with the divided Church in China and the recalcitrant PRC government.

The Largest Gathering in Human History

In January 1995, international World Youth Day was celebrated for the first time in Asia, in Manila. At the prayer vigil on the night of January 14, John Paul engaged in some banter with more than a million youngsters. They began a rhythmic chant of "Lolek, Lolek," the Pope's boyhood nickname. John Paul said, half-chidingly, "Lolek is not serious." The youngsters stopped. "But John Paul II is too serious," the Pope continued. "We need something in the middle. Yes, in the middle there was Karol . . ." John Paul laughed and a thunderous new chant began, "Karol! Karol!"[35]

The following morning, what was likely the largest crowed in human history gathered for the closing Mass of World Youth Day '95. A Japanese company, using overhead photography to calculate the number of persons per acre, estimated a minimum of 5 million people and suggested that there may have been as many as 7 million. The crowds were so dense that it was impossible to use the Popemobile to drive John Paul into the venue as planned. Arrangements were quickly made to helicopter him to the area where Mass would be said.[36]

Eighteen months later, John Paul was still amazed at what had happened in Manila: "I've never seen so many people in my life," he told Henrietta De Villa when the Philippine ambassador presented her credentials.[37] But WYD '95 had its dark side.

Just prior to the Pope's arrival, firefighters rushed to a Manila apartment, near the Vatican embassy where John Paul was to stay. Inside the smoke-filled apartment, the firemen found smoldering chemicals, a computer diskette containing plans for assassinating the Pope and blowing up a dozen 747 jumbo jets over the Pacific, sufficient materials to build a large pipe bomb, maps of the Pope's expected routes through Manila, and priests' cassocks. The two men who had rented the apartment, Ramzi Ahmed Yousef and Wali

Khan Shah, escaped but were eventually arrested. Ramzi Yousef, one of the leading figures in world terrorism, was convicted in the 1993 bombing of the World Trade Center in New York. In a separate trial, he and Khan were convicted of conspiring to kill 4,000 people in the 747s they had planned to destroy by planting explosive chemicals in the planes' lavatories.[38] Given the opportunity, Yousef and Khan would certainly have tried to kill John Paul II in Manila.

On January 16, the Pope flew from Manila to Port Moresby, the capital of Papua New Guinea. There, John Paul beatified Peter To Rot, a lay catechist and father of three children who was murdered by Japanese troops in 1945 after resisting their persecution of Christians and attempts to reintroduce polygamy. John Paul began his beatification homily in Pidgin, continued in English, but then switched back to Pidgin while reminding the congregation of what the thirty-three-year-old catechist had told those threatening him: "I have to fulfill my duty as a Church witness to Jesus Christ." A new Church, first catechized at the beginning of the century, had given its proto-martyr to the universal Church on the edge of the third millennium.[39]

Australia celebrated the first beatification of a native daughter on January 19 when John Paul beatified Mother Mary MacKillop, foundress of the Sisters of St. Joseph of the Sacred Heart, in a liturgy celebrated on Randwick Racecourse in Sydney. Mary MacKillop was born in 1842 to immigrant Scottish parents whose ancestors had survived centuries of anti-Catholic persecution. The religious community she founded, known in Australian vernacular as the "Brown Joeys" from the color of their habit, was dedicated to education and works of charity. In addition to primary schools, the sisters established orphanages, homes for the elderly, and homes for "girls in danger"—in short, as the postulator of her beatification cause wrote, for "the friendless of all ages." The Irish clergy of her time were not accustomed to assertive Scottish women, and Mary MacKillop was once illicitly excommunicated for what he claimed was "disobedience" by an irascible bishop, who lifted the excommunication a week before he died.[40] Mother Mary MacKillop's grave became a place of pilgrimage after her death in 1909. After a lengthy investigation of her life, the beatification process was finally completed and evidence for the miraculous cure of a cancer-stricken woman through Mary MacKillop's intercession was accepted in 1993.[41]

In his beatification homily, John Paul recalled that Mary MacKillop had not been afraid to reckon with the desert of Australia's vast outback. Today, the Pope suggested, "the Christian community is faced with many modern 'deserts': the wastelands of indifference and intolerance, the desolation of racism and contempt for other human beings, the barrenness of selfishness and faithlessness . . ." Saints were people who saw richness where others saw only emptiness: *"They teach us to see Christ as the center and summit of God's lavish gifts to humanity,"* which could be discerned all over Australia. That was why Catholicism recognized sanctity in Mary MacKillop, and in all the others the

Church canonized and beatified—the blessed were those who taught those around them to see the truth about human life and human solidarity.[42]

The Travails of a New China Strategy

World Youth Day '95 coincided with the twenty-fifth anniversary of Radio Veritas Asia. On January 14 John Paul visited the Catholic station's Manila headquarters for a commemorative ceremony. There, he broadcast a special message to all the Catholics of China, urging them "to seek paths to communion and reconciliation" among themselves. The English-language broadcast was a delicately balanced attempt to facilitate two new sets of relationships: between persecuted Catholics in China and those who were cooperating in various ways with the Chinese regime-approved Patriotic Catholic Association [PCA], and between the PCA's bishops, clergy, and laity and the Bishop of Rome.[43]

Chinese communist persecution of the Catholic Church after Mao Zedong's 1949 victory had been brutal. The first phase involved expelling foreign missionaries from the country; there were 5,496 missionaries in China in 1947, but only 723 in 1952 and twenty-three in 1957. In the second phase, the Maoist regime tried to create a schismatic Catholic Church, loyal to Beijing and separated from Rome—the "Patriotic Catholic Association," formally established in 1957. The third and ongoing part of the persecution was the bloodiest: to try to destroy every person of influence who remained loyal to the Church and refused to cooperate with the PCA, through outright execution or condemnation to the *laogai*, the Chinese Gulag.[44] In June 1958, three months before his death, Pius XII condemned the PCA. For the next several decades, it was assumed that there were two Catholic communities in China—a true Church, underground, and numbering perhaps 6 to 10 million adherents, and the false PCA, which by the 1990s was reckoned to have 10 million congregants.

In the early 1990s, Cardinal Jaime Sin of Manila, himself a Chinese ethnic, began to explore privately the possibility of a new conversation with the People's Republic of China. After a PRC cultural affairs office was established in the Philippine capital, the cardinal asked the Chinese diplomats to his home for "some good Chinese food." During dinner, Sin casually mentioned that he would like to go to China to visit his relatives; what he really wanted to do was assess the Church's situation. An invitation was extended and the wily Philippine cardinal went to the PRC. There, he found clergy and laity from the Patriotic Catholic Association pressing slips of paper into his hand, asking Sin to tell the Pope that they loved him and were praying for him. The Curia was not altogether pleased with Sin's personal initiative, but John Paul, to whom Sin reported on his experiences, never said a critical word to him.[45]

Even before making his own investigation of the situation, Sin had begun preparing for a different kind of Catholic future in China. In the 1980s, he founded the Lorenzo Ruiz Institute in his diocese to train Chinese-ethnic Filipino seminarians. When China was open, there would be priests, graduates of the institute, ready to go. Meanwhile, the seminarians lived in a Chinese architectural ambience, polished their language skills, immersed themselves in their ancestral culture, and, after ordination, worked as priests in Chinese parishes in the Philippines. In setting up the institute, the cardinal believed he was implementing the Pope's constant injunction to the Philippine bishops during their *ad limina* visits to Rome: "Gentlemen, you cannot stay home. Gentlemen, you cannot just keep the faith for yourselves; it is good news that you must share with others."[46]

John Paul had sent Cardinal Roger Etchegaray on a personal diplomatic exploration of China in 1993. Etchegaray came back convinced that the situation was far more complex than the "true Church/false Church" dichotomy suggested. Many, perhaps most, of the PCA bishops were in communion with Rome in their hearts, he believed.[47]

The French cardinal's judgment coincided with a new pattern of thinking in the Holy See, where the key officials on China included Cardinal Jozef Tomko, in charge of the Church's worldwide missionary efforts, and Monsignor Claudio Celli, then serving in the Secretariat of State as the equivalent of a deputy foreign minister. According to their analysis, the Catholic situation in China in the 1990s was not strictly analogous to the Church's former position in east central Europe under communism. In China, religion had always been a state affair. When the great Jesuit missionary Matteo Ricci first came to China in 1583, the mandarins asked him how he, a simple man, could approach God—in China, only the emperor could do that. Post-1949, the Vatican analysis continued, the Communist Party had become the new emperor, rather easily assuming the historic cultural role of manager of all Chinese religious activity. The mistake the communists made, according to Cardinal Tomko, was to "try to impose the handbook of Lenin" on Chinese Catholicism: they had tried to create a national Church as Lenin and his heirs had eventually created a regime-acquiescent Russian Orthodoxy. But Catholicism was not Orthodoxy, and there was no tradition of "national Catholicism" in China, which had always understood itself as in communion with Rome.

Over time, Vatican officials believed, the traditional Roman loyalty of Chinese Catholics who had aligned themselves with the Patriotic Catholic Association had reasserted itself, often clandestinely. The evidence for this lay in cooperation between PCA members and underground Catholics countrywide, and in statements of submission and fealty that many PCA bishops had managed to smuggle to John Paul II in Rome. That some PCA clergy publicly prayed for the Pope at Mass suggested that something significant had changed, even if others continued to toe the party line publicly—a practice that infuriated the underground Church and its leaders, who remained under relentless regime pressure.[48] The Church had sometimes encountered this before. However unfairly, the heroic witness of the politically recalcitrant, by its effect on both the less-heroic and the regime, was helping make reconciliation within the Church and a new position vis-à-vis the government possible.

A careful reading of this analysis also suggests that two other considerations were in play. Vatican officials today are acutely aware that the Holy See's decision in the seventeenth and eighteenth centuries to proscribe traditional Chinese devotions (including the veneration of ancestors) as inherently superstitious and incompatible with Catholicism was quite probably a serious misreading of the spiritual resources of an ancient culture. Born of ignorance, it was an error that had cut off vast evangelical possibilities, and key officials of the Holy See seemed determined that such a grave misreading of Chinese culture not happen again. That determination, coupled with the judgment that Marxism in China is an anomaly that cannot fundamentally alter an ancient civilization in a mere half-century, suggested a new, if complex and delicate, strategy: to promote reconciliation between the underground Church and the PCA while pressing the Chinese government for religious freedom and resisting Beijing's insistence that nothing could be resolved until the Holy See broke diplomatic relations with Taiwan. Such a strategy, it was hoped, would keep faith with the heroic and persecuted underground Church while opening up new lines of conversation with those millions of PCA members who, Vatican officials believed, were fully in communion with Rome in their hearts.

In the context of this new strategy, fifteen PCA priests, nuns, and laity were invited to Manila for World Youth Day '95. The instruction to Manila from Rome was that the PCA members should be treated "as friends," although the priests ought not say Mass in public.[49] Seven months later, when John Paul met with the ten bishops of Taiwan on their *ad limina* visit, he spoke further of "reconciliation," making three things clear: he honored the witness of the underground Church and intended to defend it; he believed that the expressions of fealty he had received from PCA bishops, clergy, and laity were authentic; and he judged that reconciliation within Chinese Catholicism was everybody's responsibility, not a question of one group submitting to another:

> I know that many are wondering how this reconciliation can come about. All need to move; all have to turn towards Jesus Christ, who calls us to unity and to communion. Everyone must discover the steps that can lead to reconciliation. Everyone must bring along his whole self, his past, his moments of courageous witness and his moments of weakness, his present sufferings and his hopes for a better future. What we are speaking of is a long and difficult journey. The goal is clear enough, but the path leading to it seems still obscure. We need to invoke the light of the Spirit, and to let ourselves be guided by his inspiration.
>
> Please assure the priests, religious and lay members of your local Churches in Taiwan of my deep affection in the Lord. At the same time, I renew the assurance of my love, encouragement, and good wishes to all the Catholic members of the greater Chinese family. If these brothers and sisters of ours already pray for the Pope and in some way recognize in him the special ministry of Peter, how much longer will it be before he can embrace them and confirm them in faith and unity?[50]

For its part, the Beijing government showed little interest in a new relationship with the Holy See. While continuing to insist that the Vatican sever diplomatic relations with Taiwan, the PRC stepped up the pressure on the underground Church in various regions of the country. Anti-Catholic government policy frequently overlapped with the regime's one-child-per-family policy and led to further persecution. In December 1996, John Paul's "Message to the Church in China," marking the seventieth anniversary of the consecration of the first Chinese bishops by Pope Pius XI, continued to urge fidelity to the Bishop of Rome and reconciliation among divided Catholics. The Pope also asked the Chinese government what it was so afraid of: "The civil authorities of the People's Republic of China should rest assured: a disciple of Christ can live his faith in any political system, provided that there is respect for his right to act according to the dictates of his own conscience and his own faith. For this reason I repeat to the governing authorities . . . that they should have no fear of God or of his Church. Indeed, I respectfully ask them, in deference to the authentic freedom which is the innate right of every man and woman, to insure that those . . . who believe in Christ may increasingly contribute their energies and talents to the development of their country."[51]

That explicit challenge did not result in a change in government policy. Two Chinese bishops personally invited by the Pope to a 1998 Synod for Asia were refused passports by the regime. In his homily at the Synod's final Mass, John Paul diplomatically expressed the hope that, "as the People's Republic of China gradually opens to the rest of the world, the Church in China will also be permitted to have more contact with the universal Church."[52] The Holy See's "foreign minister," Archbishop Tauran, was more blunt. "One struggles to understand the reason put forth by the Chinese authorities" for denying the bishops passports, he told an Italian newspaper. That there were no formal diplomatic relations between Beijing and the Holy See was a nonissue: "For many years the Holy See did not have diplomatic relations with the United States or England or Mexico, and bishops from those countries could freely come to Rome."[53]

Tauran further suggested that "the Catholic Church is not extraneous to Chinese history." But despite John Paul's private and public efforts to open a conversation, China's communist rulers seemed determined to keep the Church extraneous to any history they directly controlled. Meanwhile, amid criticism from some underground Church members and Chinese émigrés, the Pope continued to urge reconciliation on his divided Chinese Church, anticipating the day when Catholics could play a free role in the building of a new China. Concurrently, he made provision for the immediate future of Hong Kong and Taiwan. In 1996, prior to the British colony's reversion to Chinese rule, the hierarchical succession was assured in Hong Kong when John Paul named a sixty-four-year-old Salesian priest, Joseph Zen Ze-kiun, as coadjutor to Cardinal John Baptist Wu Cheng-chung. In 1998, Taiwan was given its first cardinal, Paul Shan Kuo-hsi, SJ.

THE GOSPEL OF LIFE AND THE FUTURE OF FREEDOM

Issued in March 1995, John Paul's eleventh encyclical, *Evangelium Vitae*, actually began at the fourth plenary meeting of the College of Cardinals, held from April 4 to 7, 1991, to discuss threats to the dignity of human life.

A lecture by Cardinal Joseph Ratzinger had located the heart of the problem in the philosophical nihilism of contemporary Western high cultures: when a "freedom of indifference" dominated society, the dignity of life was seriously imperiled. Ratzinger cited the example of Weimar Germany as a cautionary tale. If moral relativism was legally absolutized in the name of tolerance, basic rights were also relativized and the door was open to totalitarianism. Nazism had not found it difficult to violate the most basic human rights in a society that no longer knew how to make public arguments for absolute values.[54] Abortion, euthanasia, and the manipulation of life for eugenic or experimental scientific ends were thus not "Catholic" issues; they were civilizational issues. The cardinals, agreeing that a cultural turning point had been reached, adopted a closing declaration that asked the Pope "to give an authoritative voice and expression . . . to the Church's Magisterium in regard to the dignity of human life."[55] It was, in effect, an invitation to write an encyclical. John Paul accepted.[56]

The drafting process began with the Pope writing a letter to every bishop in the world, asking their suggestions for the forthcoming document. John Paul also got counsel from bishops with long public experience in pro-life activism, like New York's Cardinal John O'Connor.[57] More than four years of consultation resulted in a 48,000-word encyclical, *Evangelium Vitae* [The Gospel of Life], which John Paul signed on March 25, 1995. It was the feast of the Annunciation, the solemn annual celebration of the Incarnation of the Son of God, who entered history as an unborn child through the consent of Mary of Nazareth.

New Things to Say

The encyclical begins with a survey of contemporary threats to the dignity of human life, which John Paul sums up in the phrase "the culture of death," continues through a biblical meditation on life as a divine gift, discusses the relationship of the moral law to civil law, and explores the ways in which every sector of the Church ought to involve itself in promoting a civilization at the service of life. But more than sixteen years into a pontificate that had vigorously defended the inviolability of human life in hundreds of different cultural settings, it was reasonable to wonder what more John Paul could possibly say about abortion, euthanasia, and other threats to innocent life. In fact, *Evangelium Vitae* broke new ground in historical analysis, doctrine, moral teaching, and the practical application of moral norms to the complexities of democratic politics.

Evangelium Vitae should be read as the third panel in John Paul's triptych of encyclicals about the moral foundations of the free and virtuous society. In 1991, *Centesimus Annus* had celebrated the opportunities that lay before the new democracies of east central Europe and elsewhere, while cautioning against the idea that democracy could be value-neutral. In 1993, *Veritatis Splendor* had deepened the Pope's moral analysis of the democratic prospect by linking the recognition of absolute moral norms to democratic equality, the defense of the socially marginal, the just management of wealth, integrity in government, and the problem of self-interest and the common good in a democracy. Now, *Evangelium Vitae* argued that democracies risked self-destruction if moral wrongs were legally defended as rights.

John Paul's language is unsparing. Democracies that deny the inalienable right to life from conception until natural death are "tyrant states" that poison the "culture of rights" and betray the "long historical process . . . that once led to discovering the idea of 'human rights.'"[58] This was not the kind of critique of democracy popes had mounted in the nineteenth century. That was a critique from outside the democratic experiment, looking in with a deeply skeptical eye. This was a critique from inside. A Church that had identified law-governed democracies as the best available expression of basic social ethics was trying to prevent democracies from self-destructing. John Paul, a longtime critic of utilitarianism, was trying to alert democracies old and new to the danger that reducing human beings to useful (or useless) objects did to the cause of freedom.[59]

Evangelium Vitae also put an unmistakable imprint on well-traveled ground by the solemnity of its teaching on three specific questions. The direct and voluntary killing of the innocent, abortion, and euthanasia are declared gravely immoral; a similar formula is used in each instance; and each declaration of grave immorality is footnoted to *Lumen Gentium* 25—in which the Second Vatican Council confirmed the infallibility of the "ordinary, universal Magisterium" of the world's bishops in communion with the Bishop of Rome.[60]

The appeal to *Lumen Gentium* 25 was used to avoid another bruising controversy over papal infallibility—this time, over whether the Pope could infallibly define specific principles of natural law unless those principles were taught in Scripture. There were widespread press reports that, once again, Cardinal Ratzinger had had to talk John Paul out of invoking the infallibility of the papal office in *Evangelium Vitae*.[61] Ratzinger himself denies that this was the case. According to the cardinal, John Paul had asked the Congregation for the Doctrine of the Faith for its "suggestions . . . about what is possible in this area" and had waited for the congregation's response. "There was never an opposition," Ratzinger insists, "because the Holy Father wanted to be informed about the precise possibilities. He did not take a decision before our suggestions. It was a good collaboration. He wanted to give a very strong formulation, and he was always open to how this should be done. In the collaboration between the Holy Father and our congregation it was decided that this [i.e., the solemn formulas and citations of *Lumen Gentium* 25] was the way corresponding to the tradition of the Church."[62] Different formulations were evidently tried at different stages of the drafting process, and Ratzinger said at the press conference presenting the encyclical that one draft text did invoke papal infallibility for purposes of making an explicit, dogmatic definition. As the cardinal later made clear, this was part of an ongoing discussion process. The interpretation put on it, of a more intellectually sophisticated Ratzinger convincing John Paul that he was overreaching, was a journalistic invention.

The striking development in *Evangelium Vitae* was on capital punishment. The Church's tradition, based on the Bible, had defended capital punishment not only in terms of societal self-defense but as just retribution for an evil done and as a deterrent against future crime. The *Catechism of the Catholic Church* had reviewed this classic reasoning while seeming to narrow the scope of the death penalty's justification to societal self-defense: if nonlethal means were available to protect society from an aggressor, they ought to be used.[63] Now, John Paul narrowed the criterion of social self-defense in cases of "absolute necessity" even further, suggesting that "today . . . as a result of steady improvements in the organization of the penal system, such cases are very rare, if not practically non-existent."[64] The *Catechism* was subsequently revised in its definitive Latin edition to cohere with the encyclical's teaching, which seemed to reflect Karol Wojtyła's experience of, and loathing for, the state's power of execution. It was an issue on which the Pope had strong personal feelings, but it had not matured to the point where the consensus that had been cited in *Evangelium Vitae*'s teaching on abortion and euthanasia could be invoked. The encyclical's silence about the traditional arguments from retributive justice and deterrence seemed likely to fuel further debate on the issue.[65]

Evangelium Vitae also had new things to say about the relationship between the moral law and democratic pluralism, and about the moral responsibilities of legislators. On the moral status of laws permitting abortion and euthanasia, John Paul II is uncompromisingly blunt: "Abortion and euthanasia are . . . crimes which no human law can claim to legitimize. There is no obligation in conscience to obey such laws; instead, there is *a grave and clear obligation to oppose them by conscientious objection*."[66] The methods of civil disobedience were not spelled out. Nonetheless, this was an unprecedented papal challenge to laws passed, or legal situations created, according to the canons of democratic procedure.

The Pope also teaches that no one can licitly take part in a political campaign favoring such laws, nor can any legislator licitly vote for such laws. There was a difference, though, when a conscientious legislator faced a particular kind of legislative situation: "When it is not possible to overturn or completely abrogate a pro-abortion law, an elected official, whose absolute personal opposition to procured abortion was well known, could licitly support proposals aimed at limiting the harm done by such a law and at lessening its negative consequences at the level of general opinion and public morality."[67] The encyclical seemed to support the efforts of pro-life American public officials, like Pennsylvania Governor Bob Casey and Illinois Congressman Henry Hyde, to work incrementally for the full legal protection of the unborn, while flatly rejecting the claim of New York Governor Mario Cuomo that bringing his "personal opposition" to abortion into the public square was a violation of the separation of Church and state.[68]

A Different Kind of Response

Hans Küng thought the entire exercise another example of John Paul's authoritarianism. "The voice in the document is not that of a good shepherd but of a spiritual dictator," Father Küng opined in a press statement. *Evangelium Vitae* proved the Pope's "dogmatic coldness and unrelenting rigorism."[69] But this time Küng was in a clear minority. And it was not simply Catholic bishops who lined up to praise *Evangelium Vitae. Newsweek,* one of the three leading U.S. news weeklies, devoted a cover story to the encyclical, which religion editor Kenneth Woodward praised as "the clearest, most impassioned and most commanding encyclical" of the pontificate, one that would be John Paul's "signature statement" in history.[70] Paperback editions of the encyclical soon appeared in bookstores and supermarket checkout counters. Protestant and Jewish scholars were complimentary, and moral theologians who had been highly critical of *Veritatis Splendor* found many things to praise in *Evangelium Vitae.*[71] The encyclical evidently spoke to a widespread concern that the use of abortion for "family planning" and campaigns in favor of euthanasia bespoke a general coarsening, even cheapening, of life that ought to be resisted somehow.[72] It would be claiming too much to suggest that John Paul's deeper analysis of the "culture of death" was seriously engaged by the public in the older democracies, but his defense of the dignity of life, even on such bitterly controverted public policy issues as abortion and euthanasia, struck a chord. Perhaps, he mused to guests, things had gotten bad enough that attention could now be paid.[73]

   Evangelium Vitae had implications for the Church, too. If, as the encyclical strongly suggested, the "Gospel of Life" was, in fact, the Gospel—if the issues the encyclical addressed were not peripherals, but were at the core of Christian belief—then *Evangelium Vitae* would eventually reshape the ecumenical dialogue between Roman Catholicism and those liberal Protestant communities whose views on the moral issues involved were quite different. Post–Vatican II ecumenism had downplayed these divergences to concentrate on what were considered central theological issues, such as justification, ministry, sacraments, and authority. *Evangelium Vitae* suggested that such bracketing was inappropriate and that unity in the truth included unity in moral truth on issues of this gravity.[74]

   The encyclical's combination of passion and nuance may have helped account for its generally positive and thoughtful reception. On the question of medical treatment of the terminally ill, for example, John Paul reiterated the classic Catholic position that allows for a family and physician to discontinue medical treatment when, as *Evangelium Vitae* puts it, "medical procedures . . . no longer correspond to the real situation of the patient either because they are by now disproportionate to any expected results or because they impose an excessive burden on the patient and his family." Pain relievers that sometimes shorten life could be licitly used, provided that the purpose of providing them is to relieve pain and not to hasten death.[75] This moderation and moral realism, stated with compassion, made it more difficult for critics to accuse John Paul of pastoral insensitivity or mindless rigorism on a whole range of issues—although, as noted, Hans Küng and others tried.

The London-based *Independent*, not infrequently a critic, had editorialized in the wake of the Pope's Manila triumph that John Paul II was the "only truly global leader left" on the world stage.[76] The response to *Evangelium Vitae* helped clarify the nature of that leadership. John Paul did not stand out among the world figures of the 1990s simply because he was so striking a personality and they were so bland. The Pope's leadership, and the public response to it, was a matter of substance. He was raising questions that millions of men and women around the world recognized as some of the gravest on the human agenda for the twenty-first century. They may not have agreed with his answers, but his steady insistence on the centrality of moral questions to human flourishing and his willingness to defend unpopular positions under attack had given his leadership an integrity, even a nobility, that was sorely lacking among the politicians of the mid-1990s.

In pressing those questions in an appeal to "all people of good will," who were among the addressees of *Evangelium Vitae*, he was affirming human solidarity, and the possibility of a common conversation about the human future in a season of division and irresponsibility.

THE UNITY OF CHRISTIANS

On May 25, 1995, two months after signing *Evangelium Vitae*, John Paul issued yet another encyclical, *Ut Unum Sint*, on the imperative of Christian unity. Its title [That They May Be One], commemorated the last words of Pope John XXIII, who died in 1963 with Christ's priestly prayer for his disciples on his lips.[77]

For sixteen years, John Paul II's ecumenical activism had embodied the vision articulated by Vatican II in *Lumen Gentium*, 8—the Catholic Church was necessarily involved with all Christians, who were in some fashion related to Catholicism by their baptism. No matter what they might think of the Catholic Church, the Catholic Church thought of them as brothers and sisters in Christ. Other Christian communions might regard ecumenism as tangential, even optional. At Vatican II, Catholicism had declared itself irrevocably committed to ecumenism because of its own self-understanding.

But was there anything further to be said, given what had been said and done already? John Paul evidently thought so, and the encyclical—which was the Pope's personal initiative, according to Cardinal Edward Cassidy, President of the Pontifical Council for Promoting Christian Unity—deepened the Catholic concept of ecumenism while making what was arguably the boldest papal offer to Orthodoxy and Protestantism since the divisions of 1054 and the sixteenth century.[78]

The first new thing about *Ut Unum Sint* was the unmistakable set of signals it sent throughout the Catholic Church. Those who thought ecumenism a Vatican II fad that would mercifully fade away were unquestionably informed that they were mistaken. The first encyclical ever dedicated to ecumenism made clear that Catholicism's ecumenical commitment was irreversible. The encyclical also challenged those who had grown comfortable in the grooves of post-conciliar ecumenical dialogue. *Ut Unum Sint* asks the ecumenical professionals to recover a sense of the urgency of their task. Christian disunity made it even more difficult to proclaim the Gospel and to bridge the chasms of race, ethnicity, and nationalism that were dividing a conflicted and dangerous world. If Christians could not repair the unity of the Church, they were poorly positioned to advance the unity of the human race. John Paul asked Catholics throughout the world to reignite the commitment to ecumenism that had burned high during the heady years right after Vatican II, but had dimmed since.

Ut Unum Sint was also notable for the degree to which John Paul focused his ecumenical attention on Orthodoxy. With the Great Jubilee rapidly approaching, the Pope was determined to make every possible effort to close the breach of the eleventh century before the end of the twentieth. In the face of the Orthodox opposition and criticism he had experienced throughout the 1990s, the encyclical continues to stress that the Orthodox are "sister Churches" with whom the Catholic Church seeks "full unity in legitimate diversity."[79] The model for how that full communion might be lived could be found in the experience of the first millennium. Then, "the development of different experiences of ecclesial life did not prevent Christians . . . from continuing to feel certain that they were at home in any Church, because praise of the one Father, through Christ in the Holy Spirit, rose from them all, in a marvelous variety of languages and melodies . . . The first Councils are an eloquent witness to this enduring unity in diversity."[80] The suggestion was clear: Why could Catholicism and Orthodoxy not return to the status quo ante 1054? This assumed there were no Church-dividing doctrinal issues remaining between Rome and the East, but that seemed to be John Paul's conviction, notwithstanding some Catholic and Orthodox views to the contrary.

The encyclical also discussed the pursuit of Christian unity with the communities of the Reformation, but at less length and with less a sense of possibility than was evident in the Pope's appeal to Orthodoxy. John Paul praised the progress that had been made in bilateral theological dialogues since Vatican II, but his list of the remaining unresolved issues suggested the magnitude of the task ahead: they included such basics as the relationship of Scripture and tradition, the nature of the Eucharist, the apostolic and priestly ministry, the teaching authority of the Church, and Mary as an icon of the Church. Justification by faith, often regarded as the central question between Rome and the Reformation traditions, was not mentioned, perhaps in anticipation of a long-anticipated joint statement on justification by the Catholic Church and the Lutheran World Federation.

World Protestantism had changed dramatically since Vatican II. The communions with which many of the bilateral dialogues had been conducted were dispirited and declining in the developed world. The growth in Protestantism among evangelicals and pentecostals posed entirely new questions for the ecumenical conversation between Catholics and Protestants. Those questions were not addressed by *Ut Unum Sint*, and many evangelicals in the United States, who deeply admired *Evangelium Vitae* and were eagerly promoting it in their communities, felt somewhat ignored.

The boldest initiative in the encyclical was John Paul's proposal that Orthodox and Protestant Christians help him think through the kind of papacy that could serve them in the future. The ministry of the Bishop of Rome, he writes, had been intended by Christ as a ministry of unity for the entire Church. History, human error, and sin had made that ministry a sign of division. For some Christians, John Paul freely admits, the memory of the papacy "is marked by certain painful recollections. To the extent that we are responsible for these, I join my predecessor Paul VI in asking forgiveness."[81] Despite these memories, Christians of different communions were coming to understand the importance of a unifying ministry at the service of the universal Church, and some seemed willing to rethink the question of the "primacy" of Peter's successor in terms of that kind of unifying ministry. John Paul felt a "particular responsibility" to advance this discussion, "heeding the request made of me to find a way of exercising the primacy which, while in no way renouncing what is essential to its mission, is nonetheless open to a new situation."[82] This was an "immense task" which Christians could not ignore, and which he frankly concedes, "I cannot carry out by myself."

Therefore, he asks, "could not the real but imperfect communion existing between us" set the foundation on which Christian leaders and their theologians could work with him to explore the kind of papacy that could serve the needs of all?[83] The Bishop of Rome, 941 years after the decisive split between Rome and the East, and 478 years after the division of western Christianity in the Lutheran Reformation, was asking his separated brothers and sisters to help him redesign the papacy for the third millennium as an office of unity for the whole Church of Christ.

In this daring proposal, John Paul was suggesting yet again that Orthodox, Protestants, and Catholics alike stop thinking about the quest for Christian unity on the model of a labor negotiation. In a negotiation between a union and a company, the goal—a contract—does not exist; it has to be created, often through a zero-sum exercise in which one side's gain is another's loss. That is not, John Paul insists in *Ut Unum Sint*, the situation of divided Christianity. The goal—the unity of the Church willed by Christ—*already* exists, as a gift to the Church from Christ. The ecumenical task is to give that unity fuller theological expression and more complete ecclesial form amid legitimate diversity.[84] Christians don't create Christian unity. Christ creates the unity of the Church, and ecumenism's task is to bring that already given unity to expression in history.

Despite its historical uniqueness and the bold offer it contained, *Ut Unum Sint* did not receive the extensive media attention given *Evangelium Vitae*. That seemed to reflect the widespread editorial judgment that the pursuit of Christian unity is a matter of internal Church housekeeping, and thus of little consequence for the human future. But this, one commentator argued, was a serious misjudgment: "In a world increasingly marked by resurgent religion, notably Christianity and Islam, the ecumenical reconfiguration of 1.8 billion Christians is a matter of enormous world-historical import."[85] *Ut Unum Sint* could not make that reconfiguration happen by itself. It did secure the ecumenical imperative in the heart of a Church with a billion members.

A Vision Ahead of Its Time

The boldness of John Paul's ecumenical offer in *Ut Unum Sint* was not matched by the creativity of the responses it received.

The deepest difficulties in the Western ecumenical dialogue were graphically illustrated a month before *Ut Unum Sint* was signed. On April 4, 1995, Dr. Konrad Raiser, Secretary-General of the World Council of Churches, gave a lecture at Rome's Centro Pro Unione, proposing what he termed a "paradigm shift" in ecumenism. At the end of the second millennium, a "de facto apartheid between rich and poor," and a "progressive degradation of the whole ecosphere" required an "urgent reordering of the ecumenical agenda." It was time, Raiser argued, to "close the books over our past struggles and to concentrate all our energies on addressing together the life and survival issues of today and tomorrow in the light of the Gospel of Christ." That was the contemporary ecumenical imperative.[86]

The ecumenical movement as conceived since the 1910 Edinburgh Missionary Conference—the reunification of Christianity on the basis of agreed doctrine and practice—was over, according to the head of the World Council of Churches, the institutional heir of the 1910 initiative. Ideologically driven politics were what mattered. Battling global warming was of more consequence for the Churches than debating how we are justified before God; international income redistribution was a more urgent Christian task than celebrating the Lord's Supper together. Insofar as it reflected widespread sentiment within the leadership of the communions represented at the World Council of Churches, Konrad Raiser's address in Rome may be viewed in the future as having marked the end of the old ecumenism. The ecumenical movement described by

Ut Unum Sint was now the only global ecumenical movement still committed to the movement's original goal.[87]

A month after *Ut Unum Sint*, Ecumenical Patriarch Bartholomew I visited Rome for the feast of Sts. Peter and Paul and participated in the solemn Mass celebrated by the Pope at the papal altar in St. Peter's Basilica on June 29. During the Liturgy of the Word, Bartholomew and John Paul were seated beside each other on identical presidential chairs set before the high altar. The Gospel was chanted in Latin and Greek, and both Pope and Patriarch preached homilies. The impending Great Jubilee framed John Paul's sermon and prompted a question from the successor of Peter to the successor of Andrew. In Luke's Gospel, John Paul reminded Bartholomew, the first disciples' mission was described in these terms: "'He sent them on ahead of him, two by two' (*Luke* 10.1)." Was there not a lesson for them in the text? Did it not "suggest that *Christ is also sending us out two by two* as messengers of the Gospel in the West and in the East?" "*We cannot remain separated!*" the Pope insisted. Unity was Christ's will, and unity was what the evangelization of the new millennium required.[88]

Ecumenical Patriarch Bartholomew did not reply directly to the Pope's poignant query. His homily suggested that he was not prepared to commit himself publicly to the proposition that the only questions separating Orthodoxy and "Old Rome" involved issues of jurisdiction, as *Ut Unum Sint* had proposed. The Common Declaration signed by the Pope and the Ecumenical Patriarch on the evening of June 29 noted that a "common witness of faith" was "particularly appropriate on the eve of the third millennium." But its statement that the Great Jubilee would be celebrated "on our pilgrimage toward full unity" seemed to indicate that John Paul's millennial vision of a reunited East and West was not going to be realized according to his timetable.[89]

Personal witness and symbolic acts of reconciliation continued to advance John Paul's ecumenical agenda. The Good Friday way of the cross celebrated by the Pope at Rome's Colosseum took on a new ecumenical cast in the mid-1990s. The 1994 meditations for each station had been prepared by the Ecumenical Patriarch. The 1995 meditations were written by Sister Minke de Vries, Prioress of the Sisters of Grandchamp, a community of nuns in the Reformed or Calvinist tradition, and the 1997 meditations were prepared by Karekin I Sarkissian, Catholicos of All Armenians and head of the Armenian Apostolic Church, with whom the Pope signed a Common Christological Declaration in December 1996.[90]

John Paul also worked to defuse centuries-long religious animosities in east central Europe. Plans for the May 1995 canonization of Jan Sarkander, a Catholic martyr during the religious wars of the early seventeenth century in Moravia, had triggered a bitter response from Czech Protestants. Letters protesting the canonization were sent to the Pope and Cardinal Cassidy by Protestant leaders convinced that Jan Sarkander had been involved in the forcible Catholicization of Protestant areas. Cassidy and the Pope replied that careful scholarly investigation had shown that Sarkander had never been involved in violence against Protestants, and that the canonization was meant to honor Sarkander's fidelity to his priestly vocation at the cost of his life.

The situation remained volatile until John Paul arrived in the Czech Republic on May 20. At the arrival ceremony, he offered special greetings to "my beloved brothers in Christ, the representatives of the various Churches and Christian communities," and emphasized that he had come to Bohemia and Moravia "as a pilgrim of peace and love." That afternoon, speaking to young Czechs at the Marian shrine of Svatý Kopaček, he told them that Sarkander's martyrdom "takes on extraordinary *ecumenical eloquence*" speaking to all separated Christians of their mutual "responsibility for the sin of division" and of the importance of prayer for the forgiveness of sins. "*Indeed, we are in debt to one another,*" he concluded, and recognizing that indebtedness was the beginning of reconciliation.[91] Throughout his pilgrimage to Bohemia and Moravia, the Pope asked forgiveness for the wrongs Catholics had committed in the history of the Czech lands, and forgave Protestants for the harm they had done to Catholics. Two months later, on a pilgrimage to Slovakia during which he canonized three priests martyred in the wars of religion, John Paul added to his itinerary a July 2 visit to a monument in Košice, in order to honor Calvinists martyred in 1687 for their refusal to be forcibly converted to Catholicism.[92]

By 1997, a difficult, even bitter, situation had been turned around, thanks to John Paul's efforts and the local leadership of Prague's Cardinal Miloslav Vlk, who had publicly praised the Christian witness of the pre-Reformation reformer and Czech national hero Jan Hus, burned at the stake by Catholics in 1415. When the Pope returned to the Czech Republic in late April 1997, one of Hus's twentieth-century heirs, Pavel Czerny, head of the Evangelical Church of the Bohemian Brethren, participated with John Paul in an ecumenical service at Prague's St. Vitus Cathedral marking the millennium of the martyrdom of St. Adalbert, the first evangelist of Bohemia. At the April 27 service, the Pope praised the common witness to Christ of Protestants and Catholics under communist persecution. In that witness, he said, would be found the courage to forgive and to break down "the barriers of mutual suspicion and mistrust . . . in order to build a new civilization of love" in the new Czech democracy.[93]

The Anglican–Roman Catholic dialogue continued to demonstrate that it was easier to break down centuries-old prejudices than to break through to theological agreement. When the Archbishop of Canterbury, George Carey, came to the Vatican in December 1996, John Paul admitted, in remarks to the archbishop and his entourage, that "the path ahead may not be altogether clear to us." Still, he continued, "we are here to recommit ourselves to following it." He then invited his "brothers and sisters of the Anglican communion" to "reflect on the motives and reasons of the positions I have expressed in the exercise of my teaching office." *Ordinatio Sacerdotalis* was one of those "positions"; so was the invitation to think through an exercise of the papal primacy that might serve Anglicans. John Paul evidently thought the invitation had not been answered very satisfactorily.[94]

The stalemate in the Anglican–Roman Catholic dialogue, Orthodoxy's inability to respond with a united voice to John Paul's steady pleas for a millennial reconciliation, and the abandonment of a theologically grounded ecumenism implied in Konrad Raiser's 1995 lecture—these hard facts of ecumenical life in the 1990s, coupled with the probability that few Catholics had internalized *Lumen Gentium*'s vision of a Catholicism ecumenically engaged with everyone, suggest that *Ut Unum Sint* expresses a vision ahead of its time, a vision for the long haul of history. John Paul recognizes that there may have been some romanticism in the immediate post-conciliar years about the possibilities of full ecclesial reconciliation within the West and between East and West. But *Ut Unum Sint* requires Roman Catholicism to pursue that goal faithfully and doggedly, in the conviction that this is what Christ wills for his Church. It would not be an easy road to travel. John Paul II insisted that it must be traveled, nonetheless.

"A Voice for the Marginalized and Voiceless": The Beijing Women's Conference

Another challenge to the unity of humanity had to be faced when, on September 4, 1995, the Fourth World Conference on Women opened in the Great Hall of the People in Beijing. John Paul II had been preparing for it for almost a year.

The Pope's annual message for the World Day of Peace on January 1, 1995, was on the theme "Women: Teachers of Peace." Looking at what he termed "the great process of women's liberation," John Paul noted that "the journey has been a difficult and complicated one and, at times, not without its share of mistakes. But it has been substantially a positive one, even if it is still unfinished, due to the many obstacles which, in various parts of the world, still prevent women from being acknowledged, respected, and appreciated in their own special dignity."[95] Seven months later, in a personal *Letter to Women*, the Pope insisted that "this journey must go on!"[96] That the journey continue in ways that met the needs of women unlikely to get much attention in international meetings was the Holy See's strategic goal for the Beijing conference.

The Pope began to lay out the substantive framework for the Holy See's participation at Beijing well in advance of the meeting. In February 1995, he started a series of fifteen Sunday Angelus addresses that further developed his distinctive feminism. These addresses continued through the summer months and touched on philosophical issues (e.g., the equality of personhood between women and men and the complementarity and reciprocity built into sexual differentiation) and practical questions (e.g., the urgent need for women's education, equity for working mothers, political opportunities for women, and the full participation of women in the Church's life and mission).[97] John Paul's

1995 "Letter to Priests" for Holy Thursday stressed the importance of women in a priest's life, suggesting that "in order to live celibacy in a mature way, it is important for the priest to develop deep within himself the image of women as sisters." The ordained priesthood, he insisted, "*must guarantee the participation of everyone*—men and women alike—in the threefold prophetic, priestly, and royal mission of Christ."[98]

On May 26, John Paul met with Mrs. Gertrude Mongella, a Tanzanian and Secretary-General of the forthcoming Beijing conference. At the end of what the Pope remembered as a very cordial meeting, quite different from his session with Mrs. Nafis Sadik prior to the Cairo population conference, the Pope gave Mrs. Mongella a formal message, stressing that real solutions to the "suffering, struggle and frustration that continue to be a part of all too many women's lives" had to reflect the truths contained in the Universal Declaration of Human Rights. The Pope vigorously defended women's active involvement "in all areas of public life," and urged that the Beijing conference call on "all countries to overcome situations which prevent women from being acknowledged, respected, and appreciated in their dignity and competence." John Paul also urged the conference to "draw attention to *the terrible exploitation of women and girls* which exists in every part of the world." As for the sexual revolution and its effects on women, the Pope hoped the conference would reflect on the ways in which the sexual revolution had increased burdens on women by giving license to male "promiscuity and irresponsibility." The dilemma of unwanted pregnancy should not be met not by abortion, but by "a radical solidarity with women" in crisis, and a recognition that "there will never be justice, including equality, development, and peace, for women or for men, unless there is an unfailing determination to "*respect, protect, love, and serve life—* every human life, at every stage and in every situation."[99]

Mrs. Mongella was impressed and said to the press afterward, with reference to the Beijing women's conference, that "if everyone reasoned like he did, perhaps these kinds of meetings would no longer be necessary."[100]

In his June 29 *Letter to Women*, John Paul tried to speak to women in a multitude of different cultural, religious, economic, and political circumstances. He frankly acknowledged that the world was heir to a history and a "conditioning" that has been an obstacle to the progress of women." "Women's dignity has often been unacknowledged and their prerogatives misrepresented; they have often been relegated to the margins of society and even reduced to servitude." This had led to a "spiritual impoverishment of humanity." The causes of what the world called sexism were complex, but "if objective blame, especially in particular historical contexts, has belonged to not just a few members of the Church, for this I am truly sorry."

As women and men looked toward a new millennium, John Paul wanted to highlight the problems of contemporary motherhood, in itself and in relationship to economic life: "Certainly much remains to be done to prevent discrimination against those who have chosen to be wives and mothers." He also stressed the urgent need for "*real equality* in every area: equal pay for equal work, protection for working mothers, fairness in career advancement, equality of spouses with regard to family rights," and full political rights. Educational opportunity for women had to be promoted, as did far better women's health care. Were this to be done, the distinctive "feminine genius" he had described in *Mulieris Dignitatem* would help the family, society, and the Church rediscover the truths that authority is service and that empowerment is for the sake of self-giving.

The Pope who had urged the full expression of women's gifts in the Church made sure the Holy See's delegation to Beijing reflected that commitment. Fourteen of its twenty-two members were women. One of them, Dr. Janne Haaland Matlary, a Norwegian political scientist, had converted to Catholicism in 1982 after having disentangled herself from the radical skepticism about truth that dominated the academic culture in which she was being trained.[101] Another, Kathryn Hawa Hoomkamp, was a former Nigerian minister of health who had been imprisoned for nine months after a military coup.[102] The head of delegation was not a Vatican diplomat, but the Learned Hand Professor of Law at Harvard University, Mary Ann Glendon, a fifty-seven-year-old legal scholar specializing in comparative family law and international human rights law. All three of these accomplished professional women were mothers.

Monsignor Claudio Celli, the Undersecretary for Relations with States, told the Holy See delegation to the Beijing conference at a pre-meeting briefing that they should "try to be a voice for the marginalized and voiceless." It was not going to be easy. Mary Ann Glendon, a professional who knew how to cut through the thickets of international legal documents, was not happy with the draft document that had been prepared for Beijing. It had some sensible things to say about equal opportunity, education, and economic development. But the overall impression created, she later recalled, was unreal: "Reading the drafts, one would have no idea that most women marry, have children, and are urgently concerned with how to mesh family life with participation in broader social and economic spheres. The implicit vision of women's progress was based on a model . . . in which family responsibilities are avoided or subordinated to personal advancement. When dealing with health, education, and young girls, the drafts emphasized sex and reproduction to the neglect of many other crucial issues. The overall effect was like the leaning tower of Pisa: admirable from some angles, but unbalanced, and resting on a shaky foundation."[103]

Joaquín Navarro-Valls, the Holy See press spokesman who was another member of the Beijing delegation, was also worried. Ten days or so before the conference opened, he met with John Paul, Cardinal Sodano, and Archbishop Tauran to review the situation. Navarro's assessment was blunt: "We're dead. We have two, maybe three countries with us." The talk turned to diplomatic options, with Cardinal Sodano describing the many meetings he had already had with ambassadors and UN officials. The Pope acknowledged what Sodano had said, and then added two new ideas. "We have to pray more," was the first, directed to everybody. The second was a suggestion for Navarro: "If you get in trouble, go to the people."[104] It was good advice, and as things worked out, it made a difference at Beijing.

Taking the Argument to the People

The opening ceremonies on September 4 in Beijing reminded Mary Ann Glendon of the conference documents themselves. They were "an odd mixture of the sublime and the silly. . . . Mistresses of ceremonies who appeared to be on loan from the trade show commissariat presided in sequined evening gowns over a program that mingled ballet dancers and hula-hula girls, a performance by a Chinese women's philharmonic orchestra and a parade of fashions, world-class gymnastics and a martial arts display where the women vanquished all the men."[105] The serious business then got started, and the Holy See delegation settled down to eighteen-hour days of seemingly endless negotiating.

Professor Glendon's opening statement on September 5 specified the problems the Holy See had with the conference's draft report and program of action. The documents almost never mentioned marriage, motherhood, and the family except as obstacles to women's self-realization and occasions for violence and exploitation. Sexual and "reproductive health" matters dominated the section on women's health, and virtually no attention was paid to the health problems most of the world's women suffered from: nutritional deficiencies, poor sanitation, tropical diseases, infant and maternal mortality and morbidity, and access to basic health care. Economic inequality was discussed solely in terms of women and men, with the economic problems caused for women by family dissolution and unjust economic structures getting slight attention. Glendon argued that "effective equality" for women would be an illusion without recognizing and supporting women in their roles as mothers. There could be no progress for women, men, or humanity at the expense of children or the underprivileged. It was time to move from aspiration to action on an agenda of basic reforms that would touch the lives of the overwhelming majority of the world's women.[106]

It seemed reasonable enough, but there were soon signs of trouble. Holy See interventions at working sessions were being gaveled out of order. The threat of foreign aid losses was weighing heavily on Third World delegations who had asserted their independence at Cairo. And in any case, the Cairo coalition wouldn't work in Beijing because the Holy See's positions on the advancement of women were at cross purposes with the policies of several Islamic states.[107] Five days into the conference, things took a serious turn for the worse when a minority coalition dominated by the European Union [EU] and including Canada, Barbados, South Africa, and Namibia began pressing the sexual rights and abortion agenda that had been rejected at Cairo, and which the United States, at least overtly, was not trying to get adopted at Beijing.[108] When others rose to protest this agenda they were sometimes ignored by the chair. In one session, a delegate from Slovakia finally called out in frustration, "Why don't you recognize Slovakia? I am in a red dress, I am eight months pregnant, and I have been standing here waving my sign for half an hour!" The chair declined to recognize her.[109]

The EU coalition's determination to salvage Cairo at Beijing blocked agreement on everything else. Mary Ann Glendon thought the coalition was taking positions that would do serious damage to international human rights. The Europeans were trying to undermine the preferential support many states provided to families with children by broadening the definition of marriage, and by implicitly rejecting the Universal Declaration of Human Rights' statement that "motherhood and childhood are entitled to special care and assistance." The coalition wanted to strip the Beijing final document and program of action of every reference to religion and ethics, and eliminate any recognition of parental rights and responsibilities in education from the section on children. Coalition members also tried to argue that the "human dignity" principle at the heart of the Universal Declaration was inimical to the pursuit of equality.[110]

Glendon and her Holy See colleagues began to see what was happening. European and other governments, thinking that a conference on women was of no great consequence, had used delegation appointments as consolation prizes for the radical population controllers and feminists who had lost so badly at Cairo. These delegations, in turn, were determined to make Beijing the occasion to win what had been lost at Cairo. The time had come to take advantage of John Paul's instruction to Navarro: "If you get in trouble, go to the people."

It was to the Holy See's considerable advantage that its head of delegation was one of the world's leading authorities on the Universal Declaration of Human Rights and on European constitutional and family law. Mary Ann Glendon talked with the head of the EU coalition, a Spaniard, and asked her why she was proposing a program that was against not only the Universal Declaration but her own country's constitution. The Spaniard "didn't have a clue," Glendon recalled later; neither did other coalition members.[111] Glendon and Joaquín Navarro-Valls then met on Friday night, September 8, put together a one-page press release summarizing the coalition's agenda and its self-contradictory character, and faxed it to every major newspaper in Europe.[112] The story broke on Sunday, and on Monday questions were being put to now-embarrassed governments in several European parliaments. The governments, in turn, began to take Beijing seriously, sending new instructions to retreat from the agenda the EU coalition had been pressing. The case had been taken to the people through the media and the results were what John Paul had expected. "The people" had shown more moral sense than those who had devised the Beijing agenda.[113]

With the EU coalition defeated, the question now became whether the Holy See could accede to the final report and program of action. Some within the delegation, and some Catholics who participated in the parallel non-governmental organization conference outside Beijing, argued that the documents' concept of the human person was still so defective that they should be rejected outright. Mary Ann Glendon and others had a different view. The matter was thoroughly debated within the Holy See delegation before a summary of the arguments was faxed to the Vatican. On Friday morning, September 15, the last day of the conference, John Paul's decision was received back by fax: "Accept what can be affirmed, and vigorously denounce what you cannot accept." That was what Mary Ann Glendon did, in a closing statement that welcomed the conference's sections on the needs of women living in poverty, on improving literacy and education, on ending violence against women, and on the importance of women's access to capital, land, technology, and employment. Then Glendon blasted the documents' "exaggerated individualism," which had compromised commitments made in the Universal Declaration of Human Rights. Surely, she said, "this international gathering could have done more for women and girls than to leave them alone with their rights!"

The Beijing documents, she concluded, were at odds with themselves in some ways. But the Holy See continued to hope that "the good for women will ultimately prevail," because "women themselves will overcome the limitations of and bring out what is best in these documents."[114] It was an appropriately feminist ending to a conference at which the Holy See delegation, following the Pope's lead, had been a populist voice for many of the women too often ignored by the Western women's movement.[115]

On the Underside of History

John Paul II continued to hope in Africa during a decade in which one American foreign policy analyst suggested that the continent be allowed to fall off the edge of history in a form of international political triage, and a British historian proposed reviving colonialism as the only answer to Africa's crisis of crises.[116] The Pope's intense interest in bringing Africans into the mainstream of the universal Church and of world affairs was embodied in a Special Assembly for Africa of the Synod of Bishops, which met in Rome from April 10 to May 8, 1994. John Paul's broken hip had made it impossible for him to celebrate the Synod's closing Mass at St. Peter's, at which Cardinal Francis Arinze presided as the Pope's legate. The Pope was determined, though, to issue his post-synodal apostolic exhortation, *Ecclesia in Africa* [The Church in Africa] in person, and in Africa.

Part of the rationale for holding the Synod in Rome was that a Vatican venue would compel the Roman Curia, whose senior members would be rubbing shoulders for a month with over 200 African bishops, to take the Synod—and Africa—more seriously. In this sense, the Synod for Africa was another mission of the Pope to his central bureaucracy. Everyone agreed that the "celebration" phase of the Synod, which included the release of *Ecclesia in Africa*, ought to be held in Africa itself. Where, though? The Pope and his advisers thought the celebration should be continent-wide in scope. On September 14, 1995, John Paul flew to Yaoundé, the capital of Cameroon, the first stop in a week-long celebration that continued in Johannesburg, South Africa, and Nairobi, Kenya.

Ecclesia in Africa was signed in Yaoundé, which Cardinal Arinze thought was symbolically important in itself: "It's usually 'given at St. Peter's,' or 'given at Castel Gandolfo.' A major document that is 'given at Yaoundé, in Cameroon, on 14 September, Feast of the Triumph of the Cross, in the year 1995, the seventeenth of my pontificate'—that is something exceptional."[117] For the first time in 2,000 years of Christian history, Africa had been the site of a teaching document of the papal magisterium.

Even by the standards of a pontificate not noted for the brevity of its texts, *Ecclesia in Africa* was lengthy. One crucial section dealt with "inculturation," the ongoing debate about how basic Christian doctrine could be communicated through distinctively African religious practices and categories of thought. The two criteria that had guided John Paul's teaching on "inculturation" were reaffirmed. Any local "inculturation" of doctrine and practice, including worship, must be compatible with the Christian message, and in communion with the universal Church. Moreover, syncretism had to be avoided.[118] At the same time, *Ecclesia in Africa* urged African bishops' conferences to work with universities and Catholic institutes to set up study commissions "for matters concerning marriage, the veneration of ancestors, and the spirit world, in order to examine in depth all the cultural aspects of problems from the theological, sacramental, liturgical, and canonical points of view."[119] As Cardinal Arinze pointed out later, "One hundred years ago, even fifty years ago, if anyone had raised the question of ancestor veneration and said the Church should look into what can be done about it, that person would not have received much welcome. At that time it was simply regarded as pagan, and was rejected and condemned. Today, we see there are elements in it that are good and that Christianity shouldn't jettison."[120] It could, for example, be a way to begin teaching the Christian doctrine of the Communion of Saints, the Church now living in glory with the Trinity.

Ecclesia in Africa was not widely discussed throughout world Catholicism, but in Africa it became the basis for a new conversation between bishops and their people. As the 1990s unfolded, though, Africa continued to suffer: sixty missionaries were killed on the continent in 1997, and the Church had to bear a new burden of guilt as priests were involved in ethnic massacres in Rwanda.[121] John Paul refused to concede Africa's marginality or hopelessness. In March 1998, he flew to Nigeria, vigorously denounced the human rights abuses, authoritarianism, and corruption of the country's military junta, and beatified Nigeria's first candidate for sainthood, Father Cyprian Michael

Iwene Tansi, who had been Cardinal Arinze's teacher and had died in 1964. More than a million Nigerians attended the beatification ceremony in Oba, held in sweltering heat. Mass was celebrated in English, with different parts in Igbo, Efik, Tiv, Hausa, Edo, and Yoruba. John Paul, insisting in his homily that "Christ is . . . a part of the history of your own nation on this continent of Africa," challenged the Nigerians to build a very different kind of society from the one in which they were living. The "key to resolving economic, political, cultural and ideological conflicts," he preached, "is justice." And *justice is not complete without love of neighbor. . . .* This reconciliation is not weakness or cowardice. On the contrary, it demands courage and sometimes even heroism: it is *victory over self rather than over others.* It should never be seen as dishonor."[122]

Archbishop John Onaiyekan of the Nigerian capital, Abuja, said afterward that "the visit of the Pope comes to us like a redeeming factor in a situation where we have been having so much bad news."[123] That seemed to sum up John Paul's impact on Africa. He had strengthened the faith of new Christians by the millions and made them feel like brothers and sisters in the household of Catholicism. That, in turn, had reminded the world that Africa and Africans remained players in the human drama.

Central America, Again

Central America was another region that had been largely forgotten during the 1990s, as the wars of previous decades ended and democratic regimes tried to take root in Nicaragua, El Salvador, and elsewhere. John Paul II returned to Central America in February 1996 on an eight-day pilgrimage that took him to Guatemala, Nicaragua, and El Salvador prior to a brief visit to Venezuela.

That things had changed in Nicaragua was evident on the road into town from the Managua airport on February 7. Thirteen years after his confrontation with the Sandinistas, John Paul found himself facing a billboard en route to the capital: "Welcome, Holy Father, to Your Nicaragua." It was signed, "Daniel Ortega."[124] The former chief of the Sandinista directorate, then attempting a political comeback, evidently thought that a cordial greeting to the Pope would help. The greeting was appreciated, if with a certain sense of irony, but Ortega's welcome had no discernible effect on boosting his political fortunes.[125]

John Paul mused on the difference between 1983 and 1996 during an in-flight press conference en route to Guatemala City on February 5. In 1983, "going to Nicaragua was like a somersault," he said. "But we survived. Then everything changed. Now Ortega himself writes that there is no problem; everything has changed. He does not remember that the last time it was not so easy to meet the people. So goes the world." A journalist asked about criticism of the recently appointed archbishop of San Salvador, Fernando Sáenz Lacalle, and about the possible canonization of the murdered Archbishop Oscar Romero. John Paul replied that the new archbishop had once been

Romero's confessor, and that "if the cause for canonization moves ahead, it will be handled in the usual way." Several months later, the Pope appointed Monsignor Vincenzo Paglia, the ecclesiastical adviser to the Sant'Egidio Community and one of John Paul's back-channel diplomats, as the "postulator" or director of Romero's cause. In 1982, Paglia had given the Pope a biography of Romero and said, "This bishop is the Church's bishop, not the Left's bishop."[126]

WITNESS TO HOPE

On October 4, 1995, John Paul arrived in the United States for the pastoral visit and UN address that had had to be postponed the year before.

Addressing the United Nations General Assembly in October 1979, John Paul II had exuded physical vigor, vitality, and a sense of command. Sixteen years later, a frailer Pope, slightly hunched in his posture, walking far more slowly, and showing an occasional tremor in his left hand, arrived at the General Assembly rostrum to speak to the delegates and the world on the UN's fiftieth anniversary. His sense of command was, if anything, more palpable on October 5, 1995. He was no longer a historic curiosity. By the reckoning of admirers and critics alike, he was one of the dominant figures of the twentieth century, a maker of contemporary history. Before a global television audience, he had some things to say about what that century had meant, and what a new century and a new millennium might bring.

Universals and Particulars

As in 1979, his theme was the universality of human rights, but his address was less a philosophical reflection than an analysis of "what the extraordinary changes of the last few years imply, not simply for the present, but for the future of the whole human family." Since he had last spoken to the UN, a "global acceleration of that quest for freedom which is one of the great dynamics of human history" had vindicated the hope he had expressed in 1979. "Men and women throughout the world, even when threatened by violence, have *taken the risk of freedom*." The fact that this had happened in so many cultures and circumstances was the empirical answer to those who were arguing that the human yearning for freedom was not universal.

The global character of the human rights movement, he continued, empirically confirmed that there is a universal human nature and a universal moral law. The "moral logic" built into human beings was the basis for genuine dialogue between individuals and peoples. If the world wanted "a *century of violent coercion* to be succeeded by a *century of persuasion*," dialogue was imperative. And the "universal moral law written on the human heart is precisely [the] kind of 'grammar' which is needed if the world is to engage this discussion of its future."[127]

The universality of human nature and human rights then led the Pope to discuss particularity and its discontents. History, he suggested, had shown that men and women came to an understanding of their common human nature through the experience of being part of a particular family and a particular nation. There was an unavoidable tension between universality and particularity, two poles of the human condition. That tension, John Paul continued, could be "singularly fruitful" if "lived in a calm and balanced way" that recognized the "rights of nations." Those rights were, in the first instance, cultural. Not every nation could be a sovereign state. But every nation, as a cultural subject with a specific history, had a right to respect and protection: "no one—neither a State nor another nation, nor an international organization—is ever justified in asserting that *an individual nation is not worthy of existence.* . . . History shows that in extreme circumstances (such as those which occurred in the land where I was born) it is precisely its culture that enables a nation to survive the loss of political and economic independence." A national culture, in other words, had a spiritual quality. And it was the human spirit that had, over time, proven itself the most potent force in world affairs.

Recent history had shown that "the world has yet to learn how to live with diversity." "Difference" was still perceived as a threat. When "amplified by historic grievances and exacerbated by the manipulations of the unscrupulous, the fear of 'difference' can lead to a denial of the very humanity of 'the other,' with the result that people fall into a cycle of violence in which no one is spared, even the children." That was happening in Bosnia, in Rwanda, and in Burundi, even as they met. That was why the world had to learn that difference was enriching, for "different cultures are but different ways of facing the question of the meaning of human existence. . . ."[128] And at the heart of every culture was its distinctive approach to "the greatest of all mysteries: the mystery of God."

Religious freedom and freedom of conscience were thus "the cornerstones of the structure of human rights and the foundation of every truly free society." Religious freedom, like every other form of freedom, had an object, a goal—living in the truth. Truth, in turn, was freedom's great protector: "Far from being a limitation upon freedom or a threat to it, reference to the truth about the human person . . . is, in fact, the guarantor of freedom's future."[129]

The twentieth century was drawing to a close enmeshed in a great paradox. The century had begun with humanity full of self-confidence and certain that it had come of age. It was ending with a world full of fear. Human beings were afraid of themselves, afraid of what they might be capable of, afraid of the future. At the turn of the millennium, in order to make possible "a new flourishing of the human spirit, mediated through an authentic culture of freedom . . . *we must learn not to be afraid,* we must discover a spirit of hope and a spirit of trust."

This was not, the Pope quickly added, optimism. This was hope, a hope nurtured "in that inner sanctuary of conscience where 'man is alone with God' and thus perceives that *he is not alone* amid the enigmas of existence. . . ."[130] Optimism was a matter of psychology; hope was a theological virtue informed by faith. In order to conquer fear "at the end of this century of sorrows," he suggested, even politicians and diplomats had to "regain sight of that transcendent horizon of possibility to which the soul of man aspires."[131]

Hope required a secure foundation. For him, as for all Christians, that foundation was Jesus Christ, in whose "Death and Resurrection were fully revealed God's love and his care for all creation." That particular conviction led to a universal hope, for it was precisely because Christians believed that God had become part of the history of humanity in Jesus Christ that "*Christian hope for the world and its future extends to every human person.*" That was why Christian faith led not to intolerance, but to respectful dialogue with other religious traditions and to a sense of responsibility for all of humanity.[132]

And that, finally, was why he was at the United Nations. He was not in the General Assembly hall as a one more player in the politics of nations. He had come, he said, because he was a "witness to hope":

> We must not be afraid of the future. We must not be afraid of man. It is no accident that we are here. Each and every human person has been created in the "image and likeness" of the One who is the origin of all that is. We have within us the capacities for wisdom and virtue. With these gifts, and with the help of God's grace, we can build in the next century and the next millennium a civilization worthy of the human person, a true culture of freedom. *We can and we must do so!* And in doing so, we shall see that the tears of this century have prepared the ground for a new springtime of the human spirit.[133]

Captivating New York, Challenging Baltimore

The Pope's third extended pilgrimage and sixth visit to the United States had begun the evening before, with a service of evening prayer in the magnificent gothic cathedral of Newark, New Jersey.

Aides to President Bill Clinton, who had met the Pope at the Newark airport, had proposed to the papal trip planners that the president escort John Paul up the center aisle of Sacred Heart Cathedral. It was explained, politely but firmly, that the Pope would enter the cathedral as he entered every church in the world—by himself, in order to greet his people as a religious leader. The president was seated in the cathedral's first row, where he heard John Paul begin his homily by referring to "the extraordinary human epic that is the United States of America." When the service was completed, President and Mrs. Clinton strode down the center aisle, working the crowd as if it were a campaign rally. John Paul left for Newark Archbishop Theodore McCarrick's residence through a side door, pausing for several moments of prayer at the cathedral's Blessed Sacrament chapel.[134]

The following evening, after his General Assembly address and a lunch at the Vatican's Permanent Observer Mission to the UN, John Paul went across the Hudson River to Giants Stadium, home to New York's professional football teams, for an evening Mass attended by more than 70,000 members of the Newark archdiocese. It had been raining heavily all day and security regulations dictated that no one could bring an umbrella into a papal venue. Members of the enormous congregation had waited for John Paul for as long as seven hours in a driving autumn storm. Their enthusiasm, televised all over the country, completed the change in the media storyline that had begun in Denver in 1993. Alienated Catholics would not have done what the people of the Newark archdiocese did on October 5, 1995.

The Pope's Newark homily stressed the multiethnic heritage of Catholicism in America and the need for social solidarity. His description of an American character trait suggested that he had been studying the history of American democracy: "Early Americans were proud of their strong sense of individual responsibility, but that did not lead them to build a radically 'individualistic' society. They built a community-based society, with a great openness and sensitivity to the needs of their neighbors." Close to the New Jersey shore, he noted, "there rises a universally-known landmark which stands as an enduring witness to the American tradition of welcoming the stranger, and which tells us something important about the kind of nation America has aspired to be." The Statue of Liberty was a reminder that "the United States is called to be *a hospitable society, a welcoming culture.*" Today, he continued, it was the unborn child who was the "stranger" to be welcomed and brought into the circle of society's protection, along with the immigrant, the poor, the elderly, the handicapped—all those "others" he had defended at the UN.

The papal Mass on Friday at Aqueduct Racetrack was celebrated for the people of the Diocese of Brooklyn. In his homily, the Pope returned to one of his favorite themes, the necessity of a culture that cherished the family and a legal system that protected it.[135] That afternoon, John Paul visited the New York archdiocesan seminary in Yonkers, where he celebrated evening prayer with the faculty and students. On Saturday, October 7, the monthly papal First Saturday rosary was prayed in St. Patrick's Cathedral, after which the Pope blessed the new offices of his UN representatives. The Mass in New York's Central Park earlier Saturday morning provided several of the pilgrimage's most striking images.

The park's fifty-acre Great Lawn had been transformed into a kind of sylvan cathedral. It was, the *New York Times* reported, "a morning of ethereal beauty, with gray mists moving in veils over park woodlands touched by russet and yellow-gold, and treetops swaying like waves rolling on a green sea."[136] Four choirs and soloists from the city's opera companies provided music for the Mass.

John Paul began his homily be referring to the 1993 Denver "surprise" once again, but quickly began playing to his audience: "I know this is not Denver; this is New York! The *great* New York!" They cheered, and the onetime student actor proceeded to play the theater capital of the world as if he had spent his life on stage. His homily was a celebration of the human love he had learned to love through his first contacts with young couples preparing for marriage. Every genuinely human love, he said, "is a reflection of the Love that is God himself, to the point where the First Letter of St. John says, 'The man without love has known nothing of God; for God is love' (*1 John* 4.8)."

That theme led into a reflection on the first three joyful mysteries of the rosary, which commemorate the annunciation to Mary, her visit to her cousin Elizabeth (the mother of John the Baptist), and the first Christmas. Suddenly, the Pope, who had loved Christmas since he was a small boy, took off from his prepared text and started speaking about one of his favorite Polish Christmas carols—which then he began, spontaneously, to sing: "In the silence of the night, a voice is heard: 'Get up, shepherds, God is born for you! Hurry to Bethlehem to meet the Lord.'" The huge congregation roared its approval once again. The Pope, cocking his head to one side, waited for the applause to die down, put his hand to the side of his face, assumed an expression of wonderment, and remarked, "And to think—you don't even know Polish." They applauded even more boisterously. As one visitor told him two months later, it was a perfect imitation of the American comedian, Jack Benny.

But this was not comedy, though there was ample laughter. His Polish Christmas carol conveyed, he said, the same message as a carol everyone in Central Park knew, "Silent Night." That message was that the Son of God had become a human being so that men and women could become holy. "It is," John Paul concluded, "a song to help us not to be afraid."[137]

On Sunday morning, October 8, the Pope flew to Baltimore, Maryland, the first Catholic diocese in the independent United States. On a crisp, clear autumn morning, his homily at Mass in the city's baseball stadium, Camden Yards, was a call to read the signs of these particular American times carefully: "Christian witness takes different forms at different moments in the life of a nation. Sometimes, witnessing to Christ will mean drawing out of a culture the full meaning of its noblest intentions, a fullness that is revealed in Christ. At other times, witnessing to Christ means challenging that culture, especially when the *truth about the human person* is under assault."

One hundred thirty years ago, John Paul reminded them, Abraham Lincoln had asked in his Gettysburg Address "whether a nation 'conceived in liberty and dedicated to the proposition that all men are created equal'" could "long endure." That, John Paul said, was a question for every generation of Americans. For "democracy cannot be sustained without *a shared commitment to certain moral truths about the human person and human community.*" All Americans, he concluded, must remember that "freedom consists not in doing what we like, but in having the right to do what we ought."[138]

Hosted by Baltimore's Cardinal William Keeler, John Paul had lunch with local poor people at "Our Daily Bread," an archdiocesan soup kitchen next door to the Basilica of the Assumption, the first cathedral in the United States and a treasure of Federal period American architecture. At a meeting later that afternoon in the city's newer Cathedral of Mary Our Queen, the Pope defended the right of Americans to bring religiously based moral arguments into public debate, recommitted the Church to interreligious dialogue with Judaism and Islam, and made a pointed historical linkage in the debate over abortion and euthanasia. Baltimore's late archbishop, Cardinal Lawrence Shehan, had become a public hero for defending the civil rights of black Americans in the early 1960s against vocal and sometimes ugly opposition. When the cardinal had done that, the Pope said, "he was expressing a moral truth about the equal dignity before God of all human beings." That same conviction "should compel all of you today to *defend the right to life* of every human being from conception to natural death, to care for and protect the unborn and all those whom others might deem 'inconvenient' or 'undesirable.' That *moral principle is not something alien to America, but rather speaks to the very origins of this nation!*"[139]

An Argument from Inside

John Paul's 1995 visit to the United States was arguably the most successful of his American pilgrimages. The press, perhaps chastened by the criticism that senior journalists had raised about the media's performance at World Youth Day '93 in Denver, was less focused on the "canon" of dissent (contraception, abortion, divorce, women as priests) and more willing to take seriously John Paul's oft-repeated argument that America had to rethink its relationship to its historic moral foundations. There was also some healthy skepticism, this time, about instant opinion polling and what it revealed about Catholic views of the Pope and the "canon." As columnist and television commentator Paul Gigot wrote early in the visit, "Imagine a *Washington Post*/ABC poll on the Second Coming: 'Ninety percent of Americans agree he should come, but a third have doubts about his timing.'"[140]

The Pope's UN address was almost uniformly well-received. The *Wall Street Journal* editorially praised John Paul for filling the "empty vessels" of contemporary public discourse about behavior and responsibility. The UN speech, the *Journal* noted, was "no mere collection of sentences." It was, rather, "an *argument* . . . that makes the innate dignity of the human person the fulcrum of existence—for families, communities, and nations . . ."[141] The *Baltimore Sun*, a paper with a very different political orientation from the *Journal*'s, was similarly impressed with the Pope's claim that "we do not live in an irrational or meaningless world." John Paul's proposal, that a culture of genuine freedom and a civilization worthy of the human person could be built in the next century, was "more than happy talk" because it was based on what the Pope had called "the truth that is written on the human heart, the truth that can be known by reason and can therefore form the basis of a profound and universal dialogue among people about the direction they must give to their lives and their activities." These were, the *Sun* concluded, "encouraging words in an age that sorely needs encouragement" amid a pervasively "gloomy, deterministic view of life."[142]

The far more positive reaction that John Paul received in the United States in 1995 was due to several factors. Unlike 1987, the 1995 pilgrimage was not organized conceptually around the concerns of the American bishops' conference staff. The times were also different. Confronted by baffling issues with an unmistakable moral core, the public and the press seemed ready for more assertive moral leadership than was being provided by American politicians. Perhaps most significantly, John Paul's addresses made arguments from inside the historic experience of the United States. This was not an outsider lecturing Americans on their failings by citing alien norms. This was a religious and moral leader drawing on great themes from American history to challenge Americans to live up to standards they had set for themselves. That approach framed the entire visit, from Newark cathedral on October 4 to the departure ceremony at Baltimore-Washington International Airport on the evening of October 8. The key themes of the message were not dramatically different than in 1987. But the framework was, and it made a considerable difference.

TWA, which had reconstructed the first-class section of a Boeing 767–300 jet as a papal suite for the Pope's return flight to Rome, offered an elaborate dinner menu that included rack of lamb, beef Wellington, quail, halibut, and pheasant. Father Robert Tucci's instructions to those planning papal menus on these trips, that the rules should be "no ice, no spice," were overridden by the airline's wish to be as hospitable as possible. John Paul had some soup, a cold seafood platter, asparagus, strawberries, and a glass of champagne, and went to bed without watching *Apollo 13*, *A River Runs Through It*, or *Field of Dreams*, the three films being offered.[143] It had been a good week, he was tired, and, as always, there were things to do in Rome the next day.

THE GIFT OF CONSECRATION

Shortly after returning from the UN and the United States, John Paul began a series of Sunday Angelus reflections on the documents of Vatican II, thirty years after the beginning of the Council's fourth session. Following a pattern that had governed his interpretation of the Council since the mid-1960s, the addresses began with a meditation on *Lumen Gentium*, the Dogmatic Constitution on the Church, as the key to the Council. They immediately continued with a reflection on *Gaudium et Spes*, the Pastoral Constitution on the Church in the Modern World.[144] On November 8, 1995, there was a solemn commemoration of the thirtieth anniversary of *Gaudium et Spes* in the Synod Hall.[145]

On November 12, the Pope issued an apostolic letter marking the fourth centenary of the Union of Brest, which had brought the Greek Catholics of Ukraine into full communion with Rome. Even as he continued to press for a new relationship with Russian Orthodoxy, the Greek Catholic Church in Ukraine was never far from John Paul's mind and heart. This new letter stressed the historic reality of Ukrainian Catholicism as a Church of martyrs and asked Greek Catholics, while giving thanks to God for their historic fidelity to Peter's successor, to "understand that today this same fidelity commits [the Greek Catholic Church] to fostering the unity of all the Churches." The fidelity of the past, which had so often led to persecution and martyrdom, must be "a sacrifice offered to God in order to implore the hoped-for union" of Catholicism and the Christian East at the end of the second millennium.[146] Honoring contemporary martyrs while opening a new ecumenical dialogue was a delicate balance to strike, a hope perhaps easier to annunciate than to realize.

Another situation that seemed condemned to irresolution was Lebanon, which John Paul had tried to keep before the world's attention since his Otranto address in October 1980. If the world declined to take the travail of Lebanon seriously, the Church had to, because of the historic Christian linkage to a land where Christ himself had walked. A Special Assembly for Lebanon of the Synod of Bishops met from November 26 through December 14, 1995. In his closing homily at a solemn Mass in St. Peter's on December 14, the Pope cited Luke's Gospel on Christ's preaching in Lebanon. He urged that the Beatitudes the Lord had spoken near Tyre and Sidon—and especially the last, "Blessed are you when men hate you . . . on account of the Son of Man! Rejoice in that day, and leap for joy, for behold, your reward is great in heaven" (*Luke* 6.17–23)—be a "*fundamental program*" for the six Catholic communities of different rites in the divided country. In reconstructing the country, he concluded, "Put love above all things!"[147] The Synod's concluding message also urged the restoration of national independence and sovereignty.[148] It was another hope that seemed destined to frustration in the foreseeable future, thanks to the bloody politics of the region and the ambitions of Syria.

That the world thought some situations hopeless had never seemed to John Paul a reason for the Church to remain silent. He had issued fifteen public appeals for peace in Bosnia-Herzegovina in 1995, and had continued to call the world's attention to the tribal slaughter in Rwanda and Burundi. The Pope also tried to focus international public attention on places that tended to fall off the historical stage, like Sierra Leone and the Sudan.[149] In January 1996, the Pope sent Archbishop Claudio Celli on a special humanitarian mission to North Korea. A month later, Cardinal Roger Etchegaray was off to Jakarta, Indonesia, to try to find a diplomatic solution, by back channel if necessary, to the continuing troubles in East Timor. Three weeks before Etchegaray departed, the Pope could note one diplomatic success. On February 1, he received President Ernesto Zedillo of Mexico on a historic first official visit by a Mexican head of state to the Holy See.

"How Is the Pope?"

Although John Paul ordained fourteen new bishops in St. Peter's on January 6 and baptized twenty infants in the Sistine Chapel the next day, his UN address and his American pilgrimage in the fall of 1995 had reminded the world of his health problems. Asked by visitors and friends how he was feeling, the Pope sometimes replied with a wry joke: "Neck down, not so good." Those who worked with him and those who saw him over lunches and dinners found him as intellectually alert as ever. But visitors would also note that he tired earlier in the evening. The inadequacy of his hip replacement surgery in April 1994 continued to cause him pain. His difficulties walking meant that he was getting less exercise, which in turn led to putting on weight. A form of Parkinson's disease, causing a tremor in his left arm and hand, was diagnosed in 1994.[150] Physical limitations were not easy for John Paul. He had been physically vigorous his entire life, and it was difficult to adjust to a situation in which his body no longer did what he asked it to do. The tremor in his arm and hand was not only physically annoying; to a man with both an acute sense of public presence and a deeply ingrained sense of privacy, it was an embarrassment. His profound conviction that his life was in the hands of another authority, coupled with his disinclination to cut down his official schedule or the time he took for reading and writing, could make him seem an impatient patient, sometimes disinclined to look to medication for relief. He made occasional concessions in scheduling. Beginning in 1995, his *ad limina* address to visiting groups of bishops was given to each bishop as a personal letter after their group Mass with the Pope in his private chapel, rather than being read to them in a group audience. He would go to bed a little earlier some evenings. Yet the pace remained intense, even with these adjustments. Close colleagues also noted that, even in dealing with the worst situations, he never lost his sense of humor. Joaquín Navarro-Valls, his press spokesman, once asked him, "Do you cry?" John Paul replied, "Not outside."[151]

As a physician and psychiatrist, Navarro found the Pope a striking combination of two human archetypes, the abstract, rational philosopher and the daringly emotional poet. Either set of characteristics, the Spaniard thought, was difficult to find in high degree in a balanced and healthy personality. The singular thing about John Paul was that he was both, and without any apparent psychological conflict. For such an intense personality, he was remarkably normal.[152]

John Paul's health was a legitimate issue for the press, but the story was more often treated luridly than sympathetically. The sometimes fanciful coverage was not helped by a reversion (which Navarro could not prevent) to the classic curial style, in which any public discussion of papal health was deemed inappropriate. Nor was the suspiciousness of the Vatican press corps assuaged by the decision of the Secretariat of State and the Pope's personal physician not to bring in international teams of specialists for consultations during John Paul's colon and hip surgeries, as Cardinal Casaroli had done in 1981 when the Pope was shot. Casaroli's decision had created a sense of transparency that suggested that the Vatican was not hiding anything about the Pope's medical situation. Absent the window provided by international consultation, the old assumption—however unjustified—inevitably recurred.[153]

For all the occasionally wild speculations in the world media, the public seemed not to be disconcerted by a physically weaker John Paul II. If anything, the Pope's health difficulties provoked a sense of concern that Cardinal John O'Connor of New York found amazing. He would be walking down the street, the cardinal once said, "and people stop and ask me, 'How's the Pope?'" That they were aware and concerned—that the proverbial man-in-the-street knew he had a Pope, whether he was Catholic or not—struck the archbishop of the media capital of the world as something significant.[154]

A More Excellent Way

On March 25, 1996, John Paul issued a post-synodal apostolic exhortation, *Vita Consecrata* [The Consecrated Life]. In addition to completing the work of the ninth Ordinary Assembly of the Synod of Bishops, which had met from October 2 to 29, 1994, *Vita Consecrata* was the final panel in the Pope's triptych of post-synodal exhortations on the three "states of life" in the Church, which had begun with *Christifideles Laici* (on the laity and the distinctive lay mission in the world) and continued with *Pastores Dabo Vobis* (on the priesthood and priestly formation), documents intended to provide "keys" to the authentic interpretation of Vatican II and its implementation in the twenty-first century.

Consecrated men and women—those who take perpetual vows of poverty, chastity, and obedience—are one percent of the Catholic Church throughout the world—1 million men and women in a billion-member community. Yet for almost two millennia Catholic Christianity has considered the consecrated life, or what many Catholics refer to as "religious life," to be in some sense the center of the Church's life and mission. Discussion at the Synod, in which 245 bishops participated along with theologians and auditors from men's and women's religious orders, was predictably focused by the difficulties that many religious communities of priests, brothers, and sisters had experienced since Vatican II, and how those difficulties were to be interpreted. In Africa and Asia, communities of consecrated life were growing, sometimes rapidly. In Western Europe and North America, vocations to the consecrated religious life had dropped sharply since the Council and many religious communities were rapidly aging. Some argued that the failure to recruit young men and women to this admittedly challenging way of life had more to do with secular lifestyles and theological dissent in post-conciliar religious orders than with the age-old problems of living poverty, chastity, and obedience in community. Many of the leaders of the major religious communities vehemently disagreed with this analysis. The net result was a paradoxical Synod. The pre-Synod phase was the most successful in history, with the Synod secretariat receiving the largest number of written responses to the proposed agenda ever. Some participants believed that the Synod itself failed to ignite the kind of theological discussion hoped for, in part because of the ongoing argument over whether (and if so, how) the post-conciliar renewal of religious life had gone wrong.[155]

If the Synod discussions themselves dealt largely with problems, *Vita Con-secrata* took an entirely different approach, focusing on the opportunities to renew religious life in the twenty-first century and encouraging consecrated men and women in vocations that John Paul described as being "at the very heart of the Church."[156] The exhortation is richly biblical and draws extensively on the Eastern Christian theology of beauty to portray the consecrated life. The technical Greek theological term is *philokalia*, or "love of the divine beauty," and the Pope suggests that that distinctive love is the spiritual path to be followed by those living the evangelical counsels of poverty, chastity, and obedience through a vowed and consecrated life.[157] The central New Testament icon for the consecrated life is thus the story of the Transfiguration, in which Peter, James, and John are awe-struck by the radiant, transfigured face of Christ on Mount Tabor (see *Matthew* 17. 1–9). Consecrated men and women, John Paul suggests, are those who have given their lives completely to contemplating that beauty and proclaiming it, through radical withdrawal from the world or active service in it.[158]

The Pope uses other biblical images to describe the meaning of the consecrated life. Jesus' anointing at Bethany by Mary, the sister of Martha and Lazarus (see *John* 12.1–7), is "a sign of [the] *unbounded generosity*" that should characterize a religious life given completely to Christ and his Church.[159] The presence of Mary, Christ's mother, and the apostle John at the foot of the cross expresses the discipleship that is the heart of religious life.[160] Then there are the Virgin Mary and the apostle Peter together in the Upper Room, waiting for the descent of the Holy Spirit (see *Acts* 1.13–14): Jesus' mother represents the "spousal receptivity" of the Church to God's grace; Peter embodies one aspect of that receptivity's fruitfulness, the ordained ministry.[161]

John Paul deployed these powerful biblical images to underscore a crucial point. The consecrated life cannot be judged by the usefulness of what consecrated persons do, as measured by society's criteria of utility. Consecrated life must be understood and measured by a different standard—the Law of the Gift built into the human condition and confirmed by the cross. The dramatic self-abandonment of men and women who give up everything—including, in some cases, an active life in the world—in order to devote themselves entirely to Christ is the most radical form of discipleship possible, and it is its own validation. Lives completely given to Christ without any prospect of earthly reward embody the Church's conviction that the Kingdom of God is already present in history in an anticipatory way, and express the Church's faith that death does not have the final word in the script of the human drama.

The witness of the vows also speaks to "the world." The vow of obedience is a countercultural challenge, demonstrating that freedom and obedience are complements.[162] The vow of poverty is a prophetic challenge to "the idolatry of anything created."[163] Chastity not only challenges contemporary hedonism but is "a witness to the power of God's love manifested in the weakness of the human condition. The consecrated person attests that what many have believed impossible becomes, with the Lord's grace, possible and truly liberating."[164] For these reasons, the consecrated life teaches the entire human family important things about the human condition and about true humanism.[165]

How, then, should the consecrated life be understood in relationship to the other "states of life" in the Church? In the wake of *Vita Consecrata,* a controversy broke out over the English translation of the Latin term *praecellens,* which the English text published by the Holy See translated as referring to the "objective superiority" of the consecrated life. The French and Spanish texts translated *praecellens* as "objective excellence" while the German text translated it as "objective perfection." When the Libreria Editrice Vaticana, the Holy See's publishing house, publishes a multilanguage text, each is considered official, so the debate over the precise meaning of *praecellens,* and what it might mean to think of the consecrated life as "objectively superior" to other forms of Christian life, was bound to continue.[166] One commentator familiar with the internal debate over the translation noted that, whatever else it might mean, to speak of the "objective superiority" of consecrated life "has nothing to do with consecrated persons being 'holier' than priests or laity. Rather, [John Paul] confirms the Christian tradition that the consecrated life is 'the most radical way of living the Gospel on this earth, a way which may be called *divine,* for it was embraced by him, God and man, as the expression of his relationship as the only begotten Son with the Father and the Holy Spirit.'" Moreover, the "objective excellence" of consecrated life "confers a specific responsibility on consecrated men and women," whose mission is to remind the rest of the Church to keep its gaze fixed on the beauty of the Lord, to seek the peace of Christ which is to come, and to strive for the happiness that can only be found in the abandonment of self to God.[167]

Responses to *Vita Consecrata* fell along the fault line in post-conciliar religious life that the Synod had tried to address. Those comfortable with the path taken in recent decades by many religious communities, especially of women, tended to regard the exhortation as badly out of touch. Those who thought the renewal mandated by the Council had been badly distorted and religious life deconstructed as a result were encouraged. That it was the latter groups who were growing in the late 1990s while the former got smaller and older suggested that *Vita Consecrata* would play a large role in the Catholicism of the twenty-first century.[168]

Fifty Years a Priest

John Paul II celebrated the fiftieth anniversary of his priestly ordination by inviting all the world's other priests marking golden jubilees to join him for several days of celebration and reflection in Rome in November 1996.

A month before, there had been yet another flurry of rumors that the Pope's health was rapidly deteriorating. After a period of occasional abdominal discomfort accompanied by a mild fever, John Paul's appendix was removed at the

Policlinico Gemelli on October 8. The following Sunday he concelebrated Mass in his suite's chapel, waved to visitors from a window of the Gemelli, thanked them for coming to what he now jokingly referred to as "Vatican Number Three," and broadcast his Sunday Angelus back to St. Peter's Square from the hospital.[169] Handmade get-well cards from the children of friends were returned with a handwritten note on them—"Thanks. JP II." He left the Gemelli on October 15 and resumed his normal schedule at "Vatican Number One."[170]

Sixteen hundred priests and some ninety bishops accepted John Paul's invitation to share their golden anniversaries together in Rome. What might, in other circumstances, have become a festival of clericalism was instead a moving experience of international priestly solidarity and a reminder that the Church at the end of the second millennium had once again become a Church of martyrs. The celebrations opened in the Paul VI Audience Hall on the evening of November 7, with evening prayer and a program of testimonies. The most moving was from Father Anton Luli, an eighty-six-year-old Albanian Jesuit who had spent forty-two years in communist prisons or labor camps, often under grotesque physical torture. Asked how he withstood the suffering and could forgive his torturers, he once said that, under torture, "Christ was with me, giving me extraordinary strength and joy. It was a tremendous priestly experience, for which I am grateful to God. . . . They could take everything else away from us, but they could never tear from our hearts the love of Christ and of our brothers." In the years since Albania's liberation from communism, Father Luli had become known, simply, as "the saint." Men and women came from all over the country to have him hear their confessions. To the Pope and the jubilarians, he said that "the Lord asked me to live nailed to a cross—and, with my arms spread out in the service of denial, to celebrate my Eucharist, my priestly ministry, through every form of chains and suffering."[171] At the end of his stirring address, Father Luli and John Paul embraced while his fellow priests thundered their gratitude in applause.

The celebrations concluded with a golden jubilee Mass in St. Peter's on Sunday, November 10. The 1,600 visiting jubilarians processed into the basilica wearing stoles embroidered with the papal coat-of-arms, a gift from John Paul II. The procession took almost forty-five minutes, and the concelebrating jubilarians filled an enormous semicircle in front of the altar as well as perhaps one-fifth of the basilica's nave. The high altar was surrounded by a splendid display of red, white, and gold flowers, combining Poland's colors with those of the Holy See. Wearing brilliant red vestments and a gold miter, John Paul was greeted by tremendous applause from the more than 10,000 present when he arrived at the altar after another lengthy procession. Visitors and pilgrims sometimes find the behavior of congregations at great papal liturgies a bit disconcerting, orderliness not being a natural habit in Rome, even in church. Guests at this magnificent Mass were struck by an atmosphere of remarkable good cheer, decorum, and reverence. Romans who had become somewhat jaded by familiarity with priests, bishops, cardinals, and popes seemed to sense that they were participating in a great act of thanksgiving for lives faithfully spent out in devotion to others.

The antiphon for the responsorial psalm after the Mass's first reading had been carefully chosen: Christ's words to Peter at the Last Supper in *Luke* 22.32, "I have prayed for you that your faith may not fail; and when you have turned again, strengthen your brethren," summarized John Paul's concept of the papacy in a single New Testament verse. The image of the Last Supper also framed the Pope's homily. Every time a priest celebrated Mass, he said, he relived the experience of the institution of the Eucharist and the priesthood of the new covenant, and of Christ's washing his apostles' feet. All of that, the Pope suggested, should remind every priest, every day, that "he is *a servant of the mystery of Redemption* . . . called to serve all [his] brothers and sisters." To be a servant, he repeated as he had done so many times before, was the essence of the ministerial priesthood.[172]

Just before the final blessing, a "Magnificat" composed for the occasion by Giuseppe Liberto was sung by a 130-member choir drawn from various parts of Sicily and supported by ten instrumentalists; the congregation joined in the antiphon, *Magnificat anima mea Dominum* [My soul proclaims the greatness of the Lord]. After Mass, the jubilarians, who had been joined as concelebrants by 116 cardinals from all over the world, processed out to special seats on the *sagrato*, the platform in front of the basilica, for the Sunday Angelus and a musical program. The crowd was so large that it spilled out of the vast square and down the Via della Conciliazione. On the square itself, just in front of the offices of the Congregation for Bishops, an enormous multicolored balloon inscribed in Italian and Polish, "*Auguri Santo Padre! Najlepsze Życzenia, Ojcze Święty!*" [Best wishes, Holy Father!] was waiting. John Paul appeared on the loggia outside St. Peter's in white cassock and red cape. After leading the Angelus, he gave a brief address to the entire Catholic presbyterate:

> *I am thinking* at this moment *of all the priests in the world.* Of priests who are elderly and sick: I go to visit them in spirit, and to pause beside them with fraternal sympathy. I am thinking of young priests in the first years of their ministry, and I encourage them in their apostolic zeal. I am thinking of parish priests who are like "fathers of families" in their respective communities. I am thinking of missionaries who are committed on the five continents to proclaiming Christ, the Revealer of God and Savior of mankind. I am thinking of priests in material and spiritual difficulty, and also all those who have unfortunately given up the commitment they made. I pray for support and help for them all from the Lord.
>
> I embrace you, dear priests scattered throughout the world, as *I entrust you to Mary*, Mother of Christ the Eternal High Priest, Mother of the Church and of our priesthood.[173]

As the gaily striped balloon lifted off into the brisk autumn air, the orchestra and chorus of Italian Radio and Television played Haydn's "Te Deum" and other pieces. Bands from the Italian Carabinieri and Police played the "Pontifical Anthem," the Italian national anthem, and the triumphal march from Verdi's *Aida*. The program concluded with a hymn, "The Tree of Faith and Peace," which was sung by a Catholic, a Jew, and a Muslim as John Paul released five doves as a sign of peace.

John Paul then had lunch with the College of Cardinals in the new Vatican guest house, the Domus Sanctae Marthae [St. Martha's House], where future papal electors would live during a conclave. His vitality that afternoon, as he visited with every table and talked with his luncheon guests after a two-and-a-half-hour Mass and a forty-five-minute Angelus-*cum*-anniversary celebration, suggested that rumors about his rapidly declining health were exaggerated. If any of the Church's princes had come to Rome anticipating something more dramatic than the anniversary celebrations, they were mistaken.

The fiftieth anniversary of his priestly ordination also prompted the Pope to write a brief memoir, *Gift and Mystery*, in which he reflected on the influences that had led him to the priesthood, reminisced about the first years of his work as a priest, and offered a series of brief meditations on the theology of the priesthood. A half-century of experience, he wrote, had confirmed him in the conviction that to be an effective priest meant above all to be a holy priest. Programs were important, pastoral planning had its place. But holiness was the way in which the priest could become a "leaven of fraternity" in a world constantly in need of solidarity.[174]

20

A Reasonable Faith

Beyond a Century of Delusions

APRIL 7, 1994	Pope John Paul II hosts Holocaust Memorial Concert in the Paul VI Audience Hall.
FEBRUARY 22, 1996	Apostolic Constitution, *Universi Dominici Gregis*, revises rules for papal elections.
MARCH 21–23, 1996	John Paul's first pilgrimage to unified Germany.
JUNE 15, 1996	Major re-organization of Curial leadership begins.
SEPTEMBER 19–22, 1996	Fourth papal pilgrimage to France.
OCTOBER 14–18, 1996	Negotiations between the Holy See and the Government of Vietnam in Hanoi.
DECEMBER 4–6, 1996	The Archbishop of Canterbury, Dr. George Carey, visits Rome.
APRIL 4, 1997	Holy See press release reports 2.9 million "hits" on the Vatican website in its first three days of operation.
APRIL 12–13, 1997	John Paul goes on pilgrimage to Sarajevo.
MAY 10–11, 1997	John Paul visits Lebanon.
MAY 31–JUNE 10, 1997	The fifth extended papal pilgrimage to Poland.
JUNE 1997	Patriarchate of Moscow cancels planned meeting between Patriarch Aleksy II and Pope John Paul II.
AUGUST 21–24, 1997	John Paul participates in sixth international World Youth Day in Paris.
SEPTEMBER 5, 1997	Mother Teresa of Calcutta dies.
OCTOBER 31, 1997	John Paul addresses Vatican-sponsored symposium on "The Roots of Anti-Judaism in the Christian Milieu."
NOVEMBER 16–DECEMBER 12, 1997	Special Assembly for America of the Synod of Bishops meets in Rome.
JANUARY 21–25, 1998	History's first papal pilgrimage to Cuba.

FEBRUARY 21, 1998	Pope John Paul II creates twenty new cardinals at his seventh consistory.
MARCH 16, 1998	The Holy See's Commission for Religious Relations with the Jews issues "We Remember: A Reflection on the *Shoah.*"
APRIL 19–MAY 14, 1998	Special Assembly for Asia of the Synod of Bishops meets in Rome.
MAY 18, 1998	Apostolic Letter, *Ad Tuendam Fidem.*
MAY 21, 1998	Apostolic Letter, *Apostolos Suos.*
MAY 25, 1998	John Paul becomes longest-serving pope of the twentieth century.
MAY 30, 1998	A half-million members of renewal movements celebrate the Vigil of Pentecost with the Pope in St. Peter's Square.
MAY 31, 1998	Apostolic Letter, *Dies Domini.*
JUNE 25, 1998	Holy See releases text of joint Lutheran/Roman Catholic statement on doctrine of justification.
OCTOBER 11, 1998	John Paul II canonizes St. Teresa Benedicta of the Cross (Edith Stein) in St. Peter's Square.
OCTOBER 15, 1998	Public presentation of John Paul's thirteenth encyclical, *Fides et Ratio.*
OCTOBER 18, 1998	Pope John Paul II celebrates the twentieth anniversary of his papacy at outdoor Mass in St. Peter's Square.
MAY 7–9, 1999	John Paul II in Romania.

Their meeting had been billed as a historic encounter of aging warriors, both of whom had, as one observer put it, "power, charisma, intellectual force, and a clear agenda." Forty-five minutes into history's first papal pilgrimage to Cuba, such exercises in moral equivalence had been overrun by reality. In their exchange of opening remarks, President Fidel Castro demonstrated that he had power, understood as brute force, but little else. John Paul II—older, frailer, and less rhetorically fervid than the gray-bearded revolutionary who greeted him at Havana's José Martí International Airport—exemplified the power that comes from speaking truths long denied or repressed. It was no contest.

On the hot, humid afternoon of January 21, 1998, the Cuban president, dressed in a double-breasted blue suit instead of his usual military fatigues, greeted the Pope at the base of the rampway of his jet. After John Paul kissed the soil of Cuba, held up to him in a container carried by four local children, the two men made their way slowly along a red carpet to a dais with two chairs, where an awning had been erected to protect them from the elements. Fidel Castro, addressing not only the Pope, but the largest international audience he had enjoyed in decades, welcomed John Paul, saying that "the land you have just kissed is honored by your presence." The rest of his twenty-five-minute address, beginning with its second sentence, was a bitter jeremiad about Cuba and Cubans as the victims of history.

The native peoples of the island had been "annihilated" by colonizers; those who managed to survive were turned into slaves or prostitutes. More than a million Africans had been torn from their homelands to replace the Indians as chattels. Somehow, a Cuban nation was formed, but its fight for independence had involved a "holocaust" comparable to Auschwitz. Even today, Cubans were the victims of a "genocide," a program of "total economic suffocation" caused by the imperial wickedness of "the mightiest economic, political, and military power in history." In resisting that brutal hegemon, Castro said, modern Cubans were like the martyred Christians of ancient Rome, choosing death "a thousand times" rather than the surrender of conviction.

As for the revolution he led, it, too, was an innocent victim. Nothing that the Pope would see during his pilgrimage—the reduction of one of the world's most beautiful cities to a Caribbean Sarajevo, the poverty, the crumbling buildings, the empty pharmacies, the hospitals whose remaining windows were held together by tape, the militarization—was the revolution's fault. Nor could the revolution be blamed for what had happened to some of the churchmen John Paul would meet. If there had been "difficulties" between the regime and the Catholic Church in the previous forty years, "the revolution is not to blame." Blame was for others, above all for the United States. Cubans were victims.

When his turn came, John Paul rose with difficulty from his chair, walked to the podium, and speaking quietly, even gently, told the people of Cuba the truth about their history and about themselves.

It was the "Lord of history and of our personal destinies" who had brought him to "this land which Christopher Columbus had called 'the most beautiful that human eyes have seen.'" He knew their aspirations; his hope was that his presence might encourage everyone to make those aspirations a reality. Do not think of yourselves as victims, he urged: *"you are and must be the principal agents of your own personal and national history."*

Some things had clearly changed in Cuba in the previous forty years, but not the character of "this noble people who thirst for God and for the spiritual values which in the 500 years of her presence on the island the Church has not ceased to dispense." And so he wanted to say to believers and nonbelievers alike what he had said at the very beginning of his pontificate: "Do not be afraid to open your hearts to Christ. Allow him to come into your lives, into your families, into society. In this way, all things will be made new."

His prayer for Cuba was a simple one: "that this land may offer to everyone a climate of freedom, mutual trust, social justice, and lasting peace. *May Cuba, with all its magnificent potential, open itself to the world, and may the world open itself to Cuba,* so that this people, which is working to make progress and which longs for concord and peace, may look to the future with hope."[1]

John Paul did not mention the Castro regime or the Cuban communist revolution—nor would he, not even once, during the next four days. He had come to give back to the people of Cuba their authentic history and culture. There was no need to make reference to the men who had reduced their island to penury. That was the past; that was an aberration. He had come to tell the truth about the past and present, to spark hope for the future, and to inspire Cubans to be the protagonists of their destiny.

THE PRIORITY OF CULTURE

Even as he became physically frailer in the second half of the 1990s, John Paul II continued to sharpen one of the distinctive themes of his pontificate—that culture is the driving force of history.

It was a lesson he had first been taught by his father and by his early reading of the classics of Polish Romanticism. Seven decades of intellectual reflection and personal experience had refined and deepened an analysis that cut straight against the grain of the modern delusions that politics and economics are the motors of historical change. The collapse of European communism in 1989–1991 had vindicated the claim that culture drives history. Now, in the late 1990s, John Paul vigorously applied his "culture-first" view of historical change to the reevangelization of Western Europe, to securing the foundations of freedom in the new democracies of east central Europe, and to the liberation of Cuba.

Germany: The Long History of Faith

John Paul's third pastoral visit to Germany, from June 21 to 23, 1996, brought him to one of the lands that had been most resistant to his message for almost eighteen years, and took place in the wake of a public controversy over one of contemporary Catholicism's most difficult pastoral problems: the situation of divorced-and-remarried Catholics who wished to lead full sacramental lives, including the reception of Communion. The controversy pitted leading German bishops against the Congregation for the Doctrine of the Faith and the German bishops' former episcopal colleague, Cardinal Joseph Ratzinger.[2] But perhaps sensing that the difficult question of the divorced-and-remarried could only be engaged properly by a community secure in its profession of faith, John Paul II chose not to address this controversy during his first pilgrimage to a united Germany. Rather, he stressed the new evangelization of a country with a long Christian history and painful memories of the recent past.

At a Mass for the Archdiocese of Paderborn on June 22, John Paul reminded the thousands gathered at the Senne Military Airport that they were the heirs of a religious and cultural legacy that dated back to the meeting in Paderborn in 799 between Charlemagne and Pope Leo III. That world was long past, but it had left an indelible cultural imprint on European civilization. As all Germans faced the challenges of a unifying Europe, they ought to remember, the Pope urged, that "unity . . . cannot depend solely on a commonality of material interests." Rather, it had to be based on "agreement regarding fundamental goals and moral concepts, on a common cultural heritage, and, last but not least, on solidarity of mind and heart." Without the Christian faith, John Paul continued, "Europe would have no soul." That was why Christians were called to "foster the spirit which will unite and shape the Europe of the future." This was a responsibility that "we . . . must assume above and beyond borders."

As for the immediate situation of the German Church, John Paul used an image from the Gospel of the day—Christ reassuring the apostles in a storm-tossed ship on the Sea of Galilee (*Matthew* 8.23–27)—to make an urgent plea: "Do not be downcast and resign yourselves to the storm and the sea! Instead, be united in hope and find strength in your common faith! Remember the long history of the Christian faith of this country! Never allow this faith to become weaker or more feeble! . . . On board the ship of the Church, fear and complaints must never gain mastery of our hearts." That was a Gospel imperative and a lesson from Germany's modern martyrs, who had died resisting Nazi tyranny. A martyrology, the Pope continued, was not simply a historical record, "it is an exhortation." The Second Vatican Council, the World Day of Prayer for Peace, the World Youth Days, the new recognition of heroic virtue in marriage—all of these, John Paul claimed, were fruits of the witness of the martyrs of World War II, who had given the Church "*a better understanding of herself* and of her duty in the world."[3]

At an ecumenical Liturgy of the Word celebrated later that day in Paderborn Cathedral with Catholic, Lutheran, Reformed, and Orthodox Christians, John Paul spoke about the enduring historical consequences of St. Paul's mission to Europe. The same Holy Spirit who had inspired St. Paul—and missionaries like Patrick, Boniface, Cyril, and Methodius, who had brought the Gospel out of the Mediterranean world and into central, northern, and eastern Europe—had strengthened those Christians who had resisted the Nazis in witness to the Gospel, including the Protestant martyrs Dietrich Bonhöffer and Helmuth Count Moltke. And it was the same Spirit who would inspire the new evangelization of the first undivided Germany in almost a half-century.

After the ecumenical service, John Paul went to the Collegium Leoninum in Paderborn to have dinner with the Catholic bishops of Germany, the leaders of what some senior Vatican officials regarded as among the weakest local Churches in the world. Bishop Karl Lehmann of Mainz, the German bishops' president and one of the principal figures in the controversy over divorced-and-remarried Catholics, welcomed the Pope, who then addressed the bishops at length. Seven months before, he recalled, they had celebrated the thirtieth anniversary of the letters of forgiveness and reconciliation exchanged by the Polish and German hierarchies at the end of Vatican II. That was the kind of example the Church should set for the Europe of the twenty-first century. The Church's primary role in the process of European unification should be to strengthen Europe's soul in "brotherliness, mutual understanding, and cooperation" by witnessing to those virtues in its own life, challenging the rampant relativism of modern culture by defending the truth about human dignity, human rights, and human duties.

The Pope also discussed the evangelization of the vast numbers of unchurched men and women in the former East Germany, suggesting quietly but pointedly that this was also an opportunity for the Church in the former West Germany to reevangelize itself in a "second conversion." The new evangelization, he continued, required a Church that presented itself "as a stronghold of joy in the faith and of trust in the future"—which would not be the message German Catholicism communicated if the self-examination called for by Vatican II deteriorated into the kind of "destructive criticism of institutions" that sapped evangelical energies.[4]

On Sunday, June 23, John Paul flew to Berlin. After a meeting with German President Roman Herzog at Bellevue Castle, the Pope went to the Olympic Stadium to celebrate Mass and beatify two martyrs of the Nazi era, Fathers Bernhard Lichtenberg and Karl Leisner.

Lichtenberg had served at St. Hedwig's Cathedral in the German capital and was an outspoken opponent of the Nazis. His regular evening prayer services at the cathedral, a little more than half a mile from Hitler's chancellery, always included prayers for Jews, persecuted Christians, and the deceased soldiers of all combatants. Arrested by the Gestapo in May 1942, he was sentenced to prison, but the Nazis, thinking his continued presence in Berlin a threat, shipped him to Dachau. Already ill, he died en route, in a cattle car, on November 5, 1943. Karl Leisner had become active in Church youth work as a seminarian, taking youngsters on camping trips to Belgium and the Netherlands so they could discuss the Church's faith without Nazi harassment. Arrested for criticizing Hitler, he was eventually sent to Dachau in December 1941. There, three years later, now gravely ill, he was clandestinely ordained a priest by a French bishop, a fellow prisoner. After the camp's liberation in May 1945, Father Karl Leisner was sent to a sanitarium near Munich, where he died of tuberculosis on August 12, 1945.

In his homily, John Paul noted that the beatifications were taking place in the stadium where, sixty years before, "the Nazi regime wanted to use the celebration of the Olympic Games for the triumph of their inhuman ideology." Today, in that same venue, the Church was thanking God for the victory of her martyrs. For Bernhard Lichtenberg and Karl Leisner, martyrdom "was no accidental stroke of misfortune." Rather, it was the "inevitable consequence of a life lived in following Christ." Like the two new blesseds, German Catholics today were called to "bear witness to life" and to "resist the culture of hatred and death, regardless of the guise which it may assume." That required a Christianity that refused to become "conformist and complacent," that declined to sacrifice its independence to any State, and that did not confuse material with spiritual wealth.[5]

At the Sunday Angelus after the beatification Mass, John Paul announced that there would be a second Eurosynod of Bishops in 1999, thanked the Polish bishops who had come to Berlin for the beatification, paid tribute to the Polish priests and intellectuals who had died in concentration camps in Germany during the war, and remembered the thousands of Polish women tortured by medical "experiments" at Ravensbrück (whose survivors included his friend and colleague in the Kraków family ministry, Dr. Wanda Połtawska).[6]

After meetings later that day with the Central Committee of German Catholics and the Jewish Central Council, John Paul had a private meeting with German Chancellor Helmut Kohl. The two men then went to St. Hedwig's Cathedral, where the Pope prayed at Blessed Bernhard Lichtenberg's tomb. Finally, under spotlights, Pope and chancellor walked together through the Brandenburg Gate from east to west, crossing what had once been the murderous no-man's-land surrounding the Berlin Wall. It was a scene that reduced to graffiti the skinhead and gay demonstrations against the Pope that had taken place earlier in the day.

Late that night, Chancellor Kohl, who had previously shared some of his countrymen's skepticism about John Paul II, called his friend, the Italian philosopher Rocco Buttiglione, in Rome. Kohl was excited: "This is the greatest man of the second half of the century, perhaps of the entire century," he told Buttiglione. "And you know, he even draws a bigger crowd than I do!"[7]

Surprises in France

Reevangelization through the restoration of cultural memory was also the strategy John Paul adopted in two visits to France in the late 1990s.

The first, in September 1996, marked the 1,500th anniversary of the baptism of Clovis, King of the Franks—and through him, the baptism of France. Like other great historical events, Clovis's baptism and its effects on the nascent French nation were full of ambiguities; read through the filters of modern secularism, those ambiguities set loose a tremendous controversy in French intellectual circles prior to the Pope's pilgrimage. Expectations were low. To the surprise of many, great crowds in the hundreds of thousands came to Tours, Reims, Saint-Laurent-sur-Sèvre, and Sainte-Anne-d'Auray. At the jubilee Mass in Reims, John Paul, who had asked France sixteen years before whether she was still faithful to her baptismal vows, asked the men and women of 1996 to read their history through the story of French sanctity. French Catholic history had its dark periods, marked by infidelity and confrontation. But every trial, the Pope insisted, "is an urgent call to conversion and holiness. . . . It is when night envelops us that we must think of the breaking dawn, that we must believe that the Church is reborn each morning through her saints."[8]

The unexpectedly positive response to John Paul's 1996 pilgrimage suggested that something was stirring in the French soul. World Youth Day 1997, held in Paris from August 18 to 24, confirmed that suspicion and may have marked a turning point in contemporary French religious history.

Like their American counterparts before World Youth Day '93 in Denver, many French bishops were skeptical about WYD '97. But Cardinal Jean-Marie Lustiger of Paris saw the event as a dramatic opportunity to demonstrate, before the entire French nation, that this was now a Church committed to the reevangelization of France through a new evangelization of culture. During the Pope's four days in Paris, John Paul's contacts with French public authorities were kept to the minimum required by protocol and good manners: a brief welcoming meeting with President Jacques Chirac, and a brief pre-departure meeting on August 24 with Prime Minister Lionel Jospin. Wherever John Paul appeared in Paris between August 21 and August 24, it was in an explicitly ecclesial context. The message was clear. This was not a "Church of power," but a Church of the Gospel, whose witness to Christ compelled a defense of the rights of man.

The rhythm of WYD '97 followed a pilgrimage model that Cardinal Lustiger had first encountered during his days as a student chaplain at the Sorbonne, where Monsignor Maxim Charles was reviving the tradition of student pilgrimages with a group of young intellectuals who later became friends and collaborators of Father Lustiger. These pilgrimages—first to the Cathedral of Notre-Dame, later to Chartres—were inspired by the French liturgical theologian Louis Bouyer, who had written that every significant Christian event should recapitulate Holy Week and Easter, the core of Christian experience. On every student pilgrimage, no matter at what time of the year, young people would "relive" Holy Week from Palm Sunday through the Easter Vigil. That template was adopted for WYD '97 to great effect.

The first official day of the youth festival, which happened to be a Tuesday, re-created Palm Sunday, as the great World Youth Day cross was solemnly carried on a blazing hot afternoon through a crowd of perhaps 500,000 young people—from the Eiffel Tower, down the Champs de Mars, to the front lawn of the Ecole Militaire, where a platform had been built for the opening Mass. Thursday, August 22, when John Paul II first met the participants in WYD '97, was "Holy Thursday." During the welcoming ceremony, the Gospel reading was the account of Jesus washing his disciples' feet (*John* 13.1–15)—a text explicated in a written papal homily read to the young people in their language-based catechetical groups the next day. On Friday, hundreds of thousands of teenagers and young adults relived Good Friday by making the stations of the cross at dozens of venues all over Paris. On Saturday night, a candlelight vigil was celebrated at the Longchamp racecourse, as the Pope baptized twelve young converts from every continent. After this re-creation of the Easter Vigil came the closing Mass on Sunday morning, which turned out to be the largest in French history, with more than a million gathering at Longchamp.

The massive turnout far exceeded the expectations of even the most optimistic of Cardinal Lustiger's associates. Arriving in Paris early in the week, visitors were told that there might be 250,000 young people, with a crowd of perhaps 500,000 for the closing Mass. At least twice that many youngsters turned out, and the outpouring of interest from French teenagers lured many vacationing Parisians back to the city to see what, exactly, was going on. It also stunned the French press, and perhaps more than a few French bishops.

The two local "icons" of WYD '97 were drawn from the modern history of French Catholicism: St. Thérèse of Lisieux and Frédéric Ozanam, founder of the worldwide charitable organization, the St. Vincent de Paul Society, whom John Paul beatified in a nationally televised Mass from Notre-Dame on August 22. The choice of patrons was not accidental. Both were young Catholics: Thérèse had died at twenty-four, Ozanam at forty. Thérèse was a contemplative and a woman who had made original contributions to theology.[9] Ozanam was an intellectual in an age of radical skepticism, a democrat free of the ancien régime longings of many French Catholics of his day, a servant of the poor, a devoted husband and father, and a thinker whose writings on the just society prefigured modern Catholic social doctrine. The message being sent by this iconography was unmistakable. Sanctity is possible in modernity. Youthful enthusiasm can be drawn to Christ. Catholic faith can nurture a free society (liberty), human dignity (equality), and human solidarity (fraternity).

Cardinal Lustiger drove this point home on French national television the night WYD '97 ended. Asked by a middle-aged interviewer how he explained the extraordinary response to World Youth Day, the cardinal suggested that it was a question of generations. The interviewer belonged to a generation that had grown up in the Church, had lost its faith in 1968 or thereabouts, and had been fighting its parents, so to speak, ever since. These young people, Lustiger continued, grew up empty. They had found Jesus Christ and wanted to explore all that that meant. Do not, he concluded, read their lives through your experience. They do not think being Christian and being engaged, intelligent, compassionate, dedicated people are mutually exclusive. Or, as the Pope had put it in his farewell homily at Longchamp: "Continue to contemplate God's glory and God's love, and you will receive the enlightenment needed to build the civilization of love, to help our brothers and sisters to see the world transfigured by God's eternal wisdom and love."[10] In the capital of a particularly skeptical and anti-clerical Enlightenment, a new enlightenment of culture, capable of rebuilding the foundations of the free society, was being proposed.

It had been a week full of the unexpected. The Basilica of Sacre Coeur may never have witnessed anything like the scene there on August 21, with the flags of Canada, Barbados, Malta, Malaysia, Kenya, Panama, and the United States being waved over a congregation of thousands of singing, cheering young people. One catechetical session featured evangelical-style "testimonies" and songs led by a young Hispanic-American, born without arms, who played the guitar with his feet. Parisians smiled and were helpful to Anglophone visitors. A technological "cathedral of light" was created by spotlights at Longchamp during the baptismal vigil. All week long, the concelebrating bishops wore brilliantly colorful liturgical vestments designed by French couturier Jean-Charles de Castelbajac, who not only donated his own time but paid for the materials and labor. There was also political silliness. On Saturday, John Paul made a private visit to the grave of his old friend Jerome Lejeune, the French geneticist who had been a prominent pro-life advocate. Officials of the French Socialist Party immediately started complaining publicly about the Pope's inserting himself into the French debate over abortion. It was, to put it gently, ironic: politicians, in the name of "tolerance," condemning an old man for visiting the grave of a friend.

The unexpected, even stunning, success of World Youth Day '97 had another parallel to WYD '93 in Denver. Some time after the event, the chief of the Paris police told Archbishop Jean-Louis Tauran, the Vatican's "foreign minister," that there "had not been a single incident" with the young people at WYD '97. This was "inconceivable" at a mass gathering of the young for a concert or a soccer game, the veteran policeman said.[11] Once again, something remarkable had happened at a World Youth Day. The youngsters attending were probably not aware of it, but their participation in WYD '97 profoundly challenged the secularist and materialist delusions that had shaped much of modern European culture. French history—modern European history—was not, it seemed, defined solely by the secular revolution of 1789 and the student revolt of 1968.

In Tune in Poland Again

John Paul's June 1997 journey to his Polish homeland took place under several dark clouds.

One was the memory of his 1991 pilgrimage. Widely regarded as the Pope's least successful visit to his native country, it had helped create the international media caricature of the angry old man, incapable of understanding the world he had helped create. The second was Poland's recent political history. In September 1993, a coalition led by ex-communists (or "post-communists," as they were known) won the national parliamentary elections and took power in the Polish Sejm. Two years later, on November 19, 1995, Aleksander Kwaśniewski, the youthful, mediagenic founder of the post-communist Democratic Left Alliance, defeated Lech Wałęsa for the Polish presidency. Wałęsa's erratic behavior since his election to the presidency in December 1990 made his dismissal by the electorate understandable, just as divisiveness within the old Solidarity coalition had made the post-communists' 1993 parliamentary victory understandable.[12] But the fact that it was understandable made it no less disconcerting. The icon of the Solidarity revolution had been displaced by a former communist apparatchik of notably elastic principles, who would certainly try to manipulate the papal visit for his own partisan advantage.

There were also worries about the Pope's health. Poles who had been in Rome in 1996 and early 1997, knowing how little their countrymen had seen of John Paul since his physical condition had weakened, were worried about the shock effects of wall-to-wall television coverage of the forthcoming pilgrimage—would people think the Pope had come home to die, or even to bid Poland farewell? The Polish bishops, many of whom were still trying to find the kind of public voice John Paul had urged on them during their 1993 *ad limina* visits to Rome, were concerned about turnouts at the various papal events and fretted about the reception the Pope would get from the feisty Polish press.

But the Polish Church, or at least some of its most active elements, had learned some things since 1991. The June 1997 pilgrimage was far better prepared than its predecessor. Thoughtful Polish spokesmen for the pontificate conducted a year-long campaign in the media, among intellectuals, and within the Church to prepare the ground for the Pope's visit.[13] In 1991 there was no Polish Catholic press agency. By June 1997 a highly efficient Katolicka Agencja Informacyjna was in place, guided by one of the rising leaders of the Polish episcopate, Bishop Józef Życiński of Tarnów, a forty-eight-year-old philosophical disciple of John Paul II. Prior to the visit KAI published an informative 114-page media guide, which described the current Polish religious situation with commendable candor and helped interpret the Pope's thought to the local and foreign press. Throughout the eleven days of John Paul II's June 1997 pilgrimage, a squadron of young media professionals, several of them Dominican priests, equipped with cellular phones and pouring out press releases on state-of-the-art computer equipment, helped get the story out much more intelligently than had been done six years before. The results were notable throughout the world press.

The social psychology of 1997 in Poland was different, too. As the president of the Znak publishing house, Henryk Woźniakowski, put it, eight years of democratic and capitalist busyness had made the Poles eager to experience, once again, a "liturgical rhythm" in their lives. Poles had also been wrestling with precisely the kinds of public moral questions John Paul had identified in 1991. What were thought to be ominous and premature warnings in 1991 seemed, by 1997, strikingly prescient.[14]

Those who expected another visit from that mythical papal scold were sorely disappointed. Between May 31 and June 10, 1997, John Paul preached a message of encouragement, affection, and challenge in more than two dozen carefully crafted major addresses. "Every return to Poland," he said on his arrival in Wrocław on May 31, "is like a return to the family home, where the smallest objects remind us of what is closest and dearest to our hearts."[15] To Poles frustrated by the bitter political wrangling that had just produced a new constitution satisfying no one, the Pope urged taking a longer historical view. What Poles were living today—a free Church in a free and reasonably secure state—hadn't happened in Poland for centuries. Make this the occasion, he suggested, to deepen the foundations of civil society, which is the precondition to sustaining democracy. Think of citizenship as a vocation to enliven every sphere of life, including politics and economics, with the leaven of the Gospel. Look to your roots as a source of the virtues necessary to make the free society work. Be proud of what your entrepreneurial spirit has accomplished.

The June 1997 pilgrimage regalvanized the electric field of affection that had flowed with such potency between the Pope and his Polish audiences in 1979, 1983, and 1987. John Paul II in 1979—young, sonorous, taking steps two at a time—was one kind of heroic figure. John Paul II in 1997—older, moving far less easily, with a tremor in his arm, but still exuding both iron determination and goodness—was another, perhaps even more heroic, national icon. Whatever his physical difficulties, he had clearly not lost his sense of timing and delivery.

At Gorzów Wielkopolski in the western part of the country, a crowd of 200,000 had been anticipated; 400,000 attended a Liturgy of the Word in a square beside the Church of the First Polish Martyrs. After his homily, John Paul spontaneously recounted Cardinal Wyszyński's prediction that the newly elected Polish Pope would lead the Church into the third millennium. He was "getting more advanced in years," he said, and hoped that those present would "ask God on your knees . . . that I am able to meet this challenge." The crowd erupted into a chant of "We will help you! We will help you!" It was, ironically, the phrase used by workers answering a challenge from the newly installed Communist Party leader, Edward Gierek, in 1970. John Paul answered with a bit of papal whimsy—"I recognize the words, but I hope it will be better this time."

At Częstochowa on June 4, a congregation of half a million began chanting "Long live the Pope!" after the Gospel reading. To which John Paul replied, "He does, he does, and he grows older."

On June 6, Mass was celebrated in a splendidly decorated venue at the ski resort of Zakopane, in the Pope's beloved Tatra Mountains. The mayor of the city, in traditional Polish highlander dress, knelt before the Pope to thank him for "freeing us from the 'red slavery' and for teaching us how to eradicate from our Polish homeland all that is degrading, humiliating, and all that enslaves us." After the Mass, when the tough, craggy Polish mountain people began to sing John Paul an old folk song about a highlander going into exile ("Mountaineer, why do you leave your beautiful hills and silvery brooks?"), those present and those watching on television were hard put to find a dry eye among the half-million present, including the Pope.

John Paul, who seemed to observers to get stronger as the visit unfolded, continued to work the crowds masterfully. When hundreds of thousands of youngsters in Poznań began to chant *Sto lat!* [May you live a hundred years!], he retorted, "Don't flatter the Pope so much; you'd better think about Paris [and the upcoming World Youth Day]!" At Kraków's collegiate Church of St. Anne, on June 8, John Paul spent forty minutes walking through a packed crowd of Poland's intellectual and cultural leaders, greeting old friends (often by nickname, like *Gapa* Turowski), inquiring after wives, husbands, children, and grandchildren. The proper, middle-aged academics stood and applauded the entire time.

Kraków was determined to welcome the Pope grandly. The city's streets were filled with red-and-white (Polish), yellow-and-white (papal), and blue-

and-white (Kraków) banners. Stores sported papal flags and portraits of the Pope. The churches remained open all night for confessions before the June 8 canonization of Blessed Queen Jadwiga, which took place on the Kraków Commons, the Błonia Krakowskie, to which somewhere between 1.2 million and 1.6 million Poles walked that Sunday morning through streets closed to cars and buses, singing and carrying banners announcing every conceivable Catholic organization. The massive, spontaneous procession was a reminder of how colorful Catholicism can be. In addition to laity in all modes of dress, ranging from teenage grunge to highlander formal (complete with fur-trimmed black hats), there were black-robed Benedictines; white Dominicans and Camaldolese; brown Franciscans; gray Albertines; prelates, priests and seminarians displaying scarlet, violet, purple, green, and black sashes; and nuns in a variety of elegant, full habits. It was the second largest gathering in Polish history, topped only by the papal Mass on the same spot in 1979.

The June 1997 pilgrimage, like its historic predecessor eighteen years before, was much more than spectacle. John Paul had a proposal to make, and in his addresses he spelled out his distinctive vision of the priority of culture over politics and economics, while developing his vision of the "public Church" as the shaper of culture.

The June pilgrimage was deliberately filled with images of Poland's Christian past. Rather than pious nostalgia, this was remembering in the service of the present and future. "Fidelity to roots," John Paul insisted, "does not mean a mechanical copying of the past. Fidelity to roots is always creative. . . . Fidelity to roots means, above all, the ability to create an organic synthesis [between] perennial values, confirmed so often in history, and the challenge of today's world: faith and culture, the Gospel and life." The Jadwiga canonization, which Karol Wojtyła had sought for decades, afforded the greatest temptation to forget present and future in a binge on Poland's glorious past. The Pope, instead, focused his June 8 canonization homily on the fourteenth-century queen as a model for the Poland of tomorrow: Jadwiga the queen, for whom power was a matter of public service; Jadwiga the diplomat, working to build a community of nations in east central Europe; Jadwiga the patroness of culture, who endowed the university that bears her dynastic name with her golden scepter; Jadwiga, born to wealth and privilege, whose "sensitivity to social wrongs was often praised by her subjects." The message to Poland's new democracy could not have been clearer. You have inherited a great cultural tradition, and it is that tradition which will enable you to build a genuinely free society worthy of the half-century of sacrifice you made in the name of freedom.

At the commemoration of the Jagiellonian University theology faculty's 600th anniversary that same afternoon, John Paul sent another signal about the Church's relationship to politics. The Pope minced no words about the "dramatic struggle for existence" that the Faculty of Theology had gone through under the communists. Fighting this battle was a defense of the integrity of the intellectual life, a defense of culture, and a defense of the nation. By contending for theology's place in the academy, the Church was defending a form of inquiry that had made its "contribution to the development of Polish learning and culture" for centuries. A culture cut off from transcendent reference points could not serve the human good, because it could not know the truth about the human person.

The Pope's anniversary address at St. Anne's, which did not mention the politics of the present moment once, seemed to be saying to all concerned, inside and outside the Church, that while politics was undoubtedly important, the nurturance of culture, especially in the life of the mind, was far more important. Some may have thought that the upcoming parliamentary elections would decide Poland's future. John Paul suggested that his country's future really depends on "a lively awareness . . . that man does not create truth; rather, truth discloses itself to man when he perseveringly seeks it." That is what universities are supposed to do. That is why universities are, over time, of more consequence to a nation than parliaments. And that was why the Church, embodied in her universal pastor, was reflecting with Poland's intellectual and cultural leaders on the meaning of true humanism, the "integral notion of the human person" that was so important for the life of the mind, rather than telling them for whom to vote.

In Gniezno, five days before, John Paul had delivered a similar message about the free society's dependence on a vibrant and morally serious culture to the presidents of Poland, the Czech Republic, Slovakia, Hungary, Lithuania, Ukraine, and Germany—all new (or newly united) democracies. Politics, he reminded them, was not just a matter of winning elections. *Realpolitik*, imagining politics to be a realm of amorality, had given Europe "this sorely-tried century." The birth of a new Europe capable of responding "to its age-old vocation in the world" depended on a European rediscovery of the continent's ancient "cultural and religious roots."[16]

Pre-pilgrimage seminars had explored the question of what kind of Poland the Pope would visit. The pilgrimage also addressed the question, "What kind of Church should succeed the Wyszyński Church, the Church of anti-communist resistance, in democratic Poland?"[17]

The kind of Church John Paul II proposed in June 1997 was not reticent about Poland's historic Catholicism. In the Pope's vision, Catholicism and the public virtues it inculcates are the best, and perhaps the only, available cultural foundation for a Polish democracy that is prosperous, free, and virtuous. This, in John Paul's mind, should also be a Church that has learned Vatican II's teachings on the lay vocation in the world, on the Church as a public (not partisan) actor, and on the priority of culture over politics and economics in the dynamics of a free society. In the vigorous, culture-forming Church John Paul sketched in June 1997, there is no clericalism, in the sense of priests or bishops usurping political judgment. The Polish episcopate functions as a public conscience, not as a collection of political bosses delivering votes to a particular party. Ecumenism and interreligious dialogue are seen as goods in themselves and essential to nurturing civil society. And the realm of culture, not the maneuverings in the Sejm, is where the Church's leadership focuses its primary attention.

The alternative Church, which is more aptly described as nationalist rather than "conservative," is exactly the opposite. Intensely clerical, it longs for a national political party tied to the hierarchy, and a large, paternalistic state. Ecumenism and interreligious dialogue have only one purpose: the conversion of the wayward. The most visible embodiment of the nationalist Church in the Poland of the late 1990s was Radio Maria, which attracted some 3 million daily listeners (primarily women over sixty) and took the view that democratic Poland after 1989 was worse off than at the height of Stalinist persecution. Radio Maria provided a useful foil for Polish secularists who pointed to its broadcasts and said, "Here is the real Polish Catholicism"—narrow, bigoted, anti-Semitic, xenophobic, authoritarian.

In twenty-six formal addresses during his June 1997 pilgrimage, John Paul had a word of encouragement or praise for virtually every Catholic movement or initiative in Poland. He simply ignored Radio Maria, not mentioning it once. On June 5, after a particularly offensive Radio Maria analysis of one of the Pope's texts, his spokesman, Joaquín Navarro-Valls, issued an official statement that the head of Radio Maria, Father Tadeusz Rydzyk, spoke only for himself, not for the Pope, the Holy See, or the Polish bishops. For those with eyes to see and ears to hear, nothing could have been clearer. Whatever his pastoral sympathies for Radio Maria's listeners, John Paul II was determined that his vision of the Polish Church of the future not be compromised by any hint of accommodation to the nationalist Church's agenda.

Prior to the Pope's arrival in Poland, the scent of a valedictory had been in the air. Eleven bracing days later, speculation had already begun about another papal pilgrimage, to the Baltic Coast and the lakes where Karol Wojtyła used to kayak. The pilgrimage had made clear that the Church of John Paul II and Vatican II—a Church living as the conscience of a national culture—was the only viable Church for Poland's future.[18] So the great Polish experiment would continue. Could a democratic polity and a free economy be built and sustained on the basis of an intact Catholic culture? By giving Poles and Poland a living past rather than a nostalgic past during his June 1997 pilgrimage, John Paul II had not only kept the question alive, he had given impetus to a positive answer.

Italy

No Pope in centuries has taken the titles "Bishop of Rome" and "Primate of Italy" as seriously as the Polish Pope. By the end of 1996, John Paul II had undertaken 127 pastoral visits throughout Italy to more than 250 different locales, and had delivered 858 addresses, homilies, and reflections while traveling almost 43,000 miles inside the country. In addition, he had made 249 pastoral visits to Roman parishes, in each of which he had preached, celebrated Mass, and visited with local congregants.

In March 1994, John Paul concelebrated Mass at St. Peter's tomb with the Permanent Council of the Italian Bishops' Conference to open the nine-month "Great Prayer for Italy"; in December of that year, at the shrine of Loreto, he closed the novena at another concelebration with the bishops of Italy. The entire nine-month program of intensified prayer for the new evangelization of the country was built around the theme of the Pope's March 16 homily in the crypt of St. Peter's: that the history of Italy for the past 2,000 years could not be understood without understanding the country's heritage of Christian faith and culture. The new, post–Cold War Italy, he proposed, should take its rightful place in the new, post–Cold War Europe in fulfillment of this heritage.[19] In 1995–1996, his vicar for Rome, Cardinal Camillo Ruini, launched a reevangelization "Mission to the City," which began with young people distributing the Gospel of Mark, door-to-door, throughout Rome. On September 27, 1997, the Pope spoke to thousands of young Italians at a National Eucharistic Congress in Bologna. After a warm-up by singer Bob Dylan, John Paul picked up the theme of the folk artist's most famous song, telling the young people that what was "blowing in the wind" was the Holy Spirit: "You asked me," he said, "*How many roads* must a man walk down before you call him a man? I answer you: *one!* There is only one road for man and it is Christ, who said, 'I am the way.' He is the road of truth, the way of life."[20]

This papal participation in the new evangelization of Italy paralleled John Paul's efforts to "broaden the Tiber" between the Vatican and the Quirinale, between the Church and the Italian State. According to one knowledgeable analyst, Italian high culture had been dominated by Marxism since the Second World War, despite the fact that the levers of government were controlled by the Christian Democratic Party. In helping to bring down European communism, John Paul had not only removed a political threat, but had destroyed an alternative "Church" and had broken its grip on the imagination of the young. Statism's demise in Italy had also had its effects on the religious situation. In a society in which the state takes all the risks, a secular cast of mind flourishes; by emphasizing prudent risk taking and personal responsibility, the market economics favored by most major political parties in the Italy of the 1990s, had helped create a social situation open to reevangelization.[21] The net result of these two trends was a new openness to Catholicism in Italian culture, which John Paul had tried to seize. As one prominent Italian businessman put it, John Paul was showing a new Italy how it is possible to be a proud, practicing Catholic in the modern world, where many Italians had assumed for decades that secularism was synonymous with success.[22]

That John Paul II should have forged a friendship and collegial working relationship with an intensely Catholic Italian philosopher (and, later, political leader) like Rocco Buttiglione was not surprising. John Paul was also raising questions that the Italian secular left could not ignore. Massimo D'Alema,

General Secretary of the Democratic Party of the Left, the more mainstream of the two parties that had emerged from the collapse of the Italian Communist Party, told reporters in 1997 that the one book on his bedside table was *Crossing the Threshold of Hope*. D'Alema, the one-time *Wunderkind* of Italian communism, claimed to have been impressed by John Paul's analysis of communism's collapse and by the Pope's insistence that the society of the future had to be built around "a quest for values . . . a spirituality." In Italy, D'Alema believed, and indeed throughout the world, John Paul had "an influence greater than the Church," because he articulated universal values in a way that "moves beyond the borders of the Catholic Church." That, he suggested, was particularly interesting to men and women of the left who were looking for a way beyond "the borders of a class culture" and a class-driven or economic analysis of history. It was an analysis that avoided the fact that John Paul had emerged from the heart of the Church and understood himself to be teaching the Church's doctrine. It was, however, a step beyond the instinctive anticlericalism of the Italian left's past.

D'Alema's recognition of what he called "the failure of the attempt to liberate man in a purely materialist way" and his quest for "the ethical and spiritual motivations of political action" was a modest breakthrough in Italian cultural politics, for which John Paul could take indirect (and, through *Threshold*, some direct) credit.[23] As the politics of the Italian left began to mirror the libertinism of the Scandinavian and North American left on the life issues and the sexual revolution, there would undoubtedly be new tensions between Italian social democrats and the culture-forming Church of John Paul II. But a new conversation had been opened because of John Paul II's emphasis on the priority of culture. Its importance became even more evident in October 1998 when Massimo D'Alema became prime minister of Italy.

APPOINTMENT IN HAVANA

John Paul's culture-first strategy of evangelization and social change got its toughest test in the second decade of his pontificate when the seventy-seven-year-old Pope fulfilled a longstanding wish to visit Cuba in January 1998.

The Dance

Cuban Catholicism had never been driven underground like the Church in Ukraine or the greater part of the resistance Church in Czechoslovakia during the communist period in those countries. But it had been persecuted in the early days of the revolution, and even after the persecution eased, the Cuban Church had been systematically frustrated in its efforts to reach out to Cuban society. As the impending collapse of European communism, and of Cuba's welfare provider, the Soviet Union, put increasing pressure on the Castro regime, Church leaders in Cuba became more assertive and the regime seemed open to exploring new avenues of conversation as it sought a way out of its isolation. In 1988, New York's Cardinal John O'Connor had gone to Havana to honor the memory of Father Félix Varela, a nineteenth-century hero of the Cuban struggle for independence who had died in exile in New York City. As O'Connor entered Havana's cathedral to celebrate Mass one evening, he was met with tremendous applause and bombarded with small pieces of paper on which were written the names of political prisoners whose families hoped he might take up their cases with the government. O'Connor gave the names to Castro when they met for four hours, at the dictator's request and according to his nocturnal habits—from 11:30 P.M. until 3:30 A.M. The New York cardinal, prepared to give as good as he got in exchanges with the volatile Castro, evidently made an impression on the Cuban leader. Cardinal Roger Etchegaray, President of the Pontifical Council for Justice and Peace, broached the question of a papal pilgrimage to Cuba on another visit to Havana in 1988. A formal invitation from the Cuban bishops followed, and plans began to be laid.

In late 1989, the Cuban bishops, impressed by events in Europe, wrote Castro and urged him to give up dictatorial power. The Cuban leader flew into a rage, denounced the bishops as counterrevolutionary collaborators, and denied permission for unloading a $500,000 printing press that had been shipped to the island from Germany for the Church's use.[24] Planning for a papal visit continued through a period of intensified repression, which was curiously combined with two changes in regime practice. In 1991, the Cuban Communist Party agreed to admit believers to its ranks, and in 1992 it declared the Cuban state officially "secular," rather than "atheist." At the 1992 World Environmental Summit in Rio de Janeiro, however, Castro accused the Cuban bishops of collaborating with the hated U.S. government, and the papal visit was called off.

In 1993, the Cuban bishops issued a pastoral letter that deplored the sorry state of the island's economic, social, and moral life. The bishops warned that many Cubans were living in "internal exile," their aspirations fixed on things that could only be obtained outside Cuba, like freedom and consumer goods. The letter also blamed the regime for the mass exodus of refugees and urged that exiles be permitted to contribute to solving Cuba's problems. John Paul strongly endorsed the bishops' initiative, which outraged the Cuban government. In 1994, seeking to strengthen the local Church's hand further, John Paul named the fifty-eight-year-old Archbishop of Havana, Jaime Ortega y Alamino, who had been imprisoned as a seminarian in one of Castro's labor camps, a cardinal. Castro permitted Ortega to attend the November 26 consistory to receive the red hat. The dance between Rome and Havana continued, with the Pope sending unofficial personal representatives to the island (prominent among them, Boston's Cardinal Bernard Law) and Castro receiving them.[25]

Archbishop Jean-Louis Tauran was in Cuba from October 25 to 28, 1996.

Castro kept him waiting until midnight for a meeting and then subjected him to a three-hour harangue, but the conversation was open again at the official level. The following month, Castro attended the World Food Summit being held in Rome and was received by John Paul II in a private audience on November 19. Castro formally invited the Pope to visit. John Paul thanked Castro for permitting him to accept the longstanding invitation of the Cuban Bishops' Conference.

Planning for the visit continued throughout 1997. The Pope and the Holy See were determined to make the visit the occasion to resolve several of the Church's most severe problems in Cuba. There was a shortage of pastoral workers, because the regime was blocking the entrance of priests and nuns willing to work on the island. Complete lack of access to the media meant that the Church had no way to present itself to Cuban society. The proscription on the Church distributing humanitarian aid, which it could nevertheless receive, made the Church a collection agency for the regime. And the fate of the 900 or so remaining political prisoners in Castro's notorious prisons remained to be resolved. None of these issues had been settled, and crucial logistical questions about public access to papal events in Cuba remained open, when papal spokesman Joaquín Navarro-Valls flew to Havana in October 1997, three months before the Pope was due to arrive.

Navarro was instructed by Cuban officials to call Castro "Commandante." He declined, saying that he would address Cuba's president as "Mr. President"—a small but important signal that the Holy See was not going to play on the regime's ideological ground. When the papal spokesman was ushered into the Cuban leader's office at 7:45 P.M., Castro immediately said, "Tell me about the Pope." Navarro answered, "Mr. President, I envy you." Castro asked, "Why?" "Because," Navarro replied, "the Pope is praying for you every day, praying that a man with your formation will find his way back to God." The voluble Castro was, for once, silent. Navarro proceeded to describe John Paul's normal day, stressing that his hour of private prayer before his 7:30 A.M. Mass was the best part of the day for him. Listening to this, Navarro recalled later, Castro looked like a man rediscovering old things from his childhood.

It was then time to get down to the business of the papal visit. Navarro was blunt. "Mr. President," he began, "the Holy Father is coming to Cuba on January 21. This is a fact. It's not a possibility any longer. It is in the interest of Cuba that this visit be a great success. Cuba should surprise the world." Castro said that he liked that, particularly the idea of "surprising the world." Navarro then explained just what surprises he had in mind, and asked that the two men reach an agreement on what they understood by "success."

The first request was that Christmas 1997 be celebrated as a public holiday for the first time since the Revolution. Castro replied that this was very difficult, since it was the middle of the sugarcane harvesting season. Navarro said, "But the Pope would like to thank you publicly for doing this when he arrives at the Havana Airport. . . ." Castro eventually conceded, saying, "It might be just for this year," to which Navarro replied, "Fine, the Pope will be grateful to you. We shall let next year take care of itself."

Then there was the matter of the stalled visas for priests and nuns who wanted to work in Cuba. Castro said that things had already begun to move on this, but that it would take months to process the visas. Navarro replied, "But they're needed *now*, to help prepare the people for the visit." Castro asked, "How many do you need?" Navarro, thinking that he was taking a shot in the dark, answered, "Half of those on the waiting list." A few days later, fifty-seven visas were granted: exactly fifty percent of those on the waiting list.

Attendance at papal events was another issue. The regime was resisting giving people time off from work, saying that it couldn't grant a holiday for religious purposes. Navarro asked Castro, "Mr. President, how many heads of state have come to Camagüey or Santa Clara? Your government is providing an official courtesy to a head of state, not a religious holiday. . . ." Castro agreed to give the local people six hours off on the day of the Pope's visit.

The meeting ended at 2:45 in the morning. The atmosphere, Navarro recalled, had been pleasant, even intimate, with Castro determined to show himself a gentleman. Hosting a Pope in Cuba was a completely new experience for him and for his country, and he wanted to do what he could to ensure the success the two men had agreed to pursue at the outset of their discussion. Castro had been particularly insistent on one point: "The Cuban revolution has never been anti-Catholic. You won't find a single drop of a priest's blood shed here, unlike the Mexican revolution or the Spanish civil war." Whatever its empirical merits, the claim itself, Navarro thought, shed light on Castro's personality. When they had finished their business, Castro walked Navarro to his car, exchanging jokes and reminiscing about his meeting with the Pope in Rome. It had been, the Cuban said, like a family gathering. Navarro left feeling certain that Castro had decided to do whatever he could to make the papal visit work.

Other Cuban officials had to be cajoled into cooperation, though. Navarro also met with Caridad Diego, the head of religious affairs for the Cuban government and a hard-liner. When the conversation turned to the question of public access to the papal Masses, Ms. Diego tried to be soothing: "Don't worry, Joaquín," she said, "the squares will be full." "I know, Caridad," Navarro replied, "but with your people or mine? Remember Managua in 1983: Ortega stacked the crowd and the world saw what kind of guy he was." Caridad Diego then started complaining about the price of buses and trucks, but finally agreed that the government would find enough transportation to get seventy-five percent of the people who wanted to come to the events. Navarro immediately said that he could get the money from one of the German Catholic development agencies, Adveniat or Miserior, to which Ms. Diego replied, "We're not that poor."

Diego and Navarro also argued about television coverage of the visit. The Cuban government was happy to provide facilities for foreign television reporters at extortionate prices, but inside Cuba it proposed limiting TV coverage of papal events to a closed-circuit hookup with a feed into the foreign press center in Havana. Navarro replied that "Cuba will look ridiculous," giving the world press a "virtual Pope" who could not be watched by the Cubans. Excuses about a lack of facilities could not be taken seriously. "You have twenty-four-hours-a-day TV on May 1," the well-briefed Navarro reminded Caridad Diego, "and you gave blanket coverage to the reinterment of Che Guevara. . . ."[26] The issue wasn't settled until the day before John Paul arrived, when it was finally agreed to do national television broadcasts of the arrival and departure ceremonies and the closing papal Mass in Havana, with regional TV coverage of the papal Masses in Santa Clara, Camagüey, and Santiago.

Libertad! Libertad!

Prior to the Pope's arrival on January 21, 1998, the inevitable question was what difference his visit to Cuba would make. The arrival ceremony at José Martí Airport settled that. For the first time in forty years, Fidel Castro and his revolution were not the center of public attention. Another revolution, a Christian revolution that sought to restore to Cuba's people their authentic history and culture, was being proposed. Castro, who throughout the visit combined a striking deference to the Pope with continuous anti-American propaganda, seemed to sense this. After the exchange of addresses, at which Castro had told the Cubans that they were historical victims and the Pope had quietly told the island's people that they must be the architects of their own destinies, John Paul began to walk with difficulty to his Popemobile for the drive into Havana. For a split-second, Castro seemed to act as if he, too, should climb in with the Pope. Then he stepped back. For the next four days, Cuba belonged to another revolutionary. That experience falsified the claim visitors saw spray-painted on walls all over the country—"Fidel is the revolution. The revolution is Cuba." Not any longer.

After a triumphant entry into the Cuban capital, the Pope spent the night in Havana. From there, he flew back and forth to Santa Clara, Camagüey, and Santiago during the next three days. The themes of his major addresses were masterfully orchestrated to build one on another: from the family and the integrity of education, through the reinterpretation of Cuban history, and on to a full-throated call for a reborn Cuba restored to history and to the international community.

At the first papal Mass, in Santa Clara on Thursday, John Paul confronted the Cuban regime's monopoly on education, insisting that the state did not have the right to take the place of parents, who "should be able to choose for their children the pedagogical method, the ethical and civic content, and the religious inspiration that will enable them to receive an integral education." That, said the Pope, quoting the Cuban poet-revolutionary José Martí, was how the children of Cuba could "grow in humanity . . . with all and for the good of all." As for the past that the Castro revolution had tried to uproot, John Paul offered a different history lesson: "*In Cuba, the institution of the family has inherited the rich patrimony of virtues* which marked the Creole families of the past. . . . Those families, solidly founded upon Christian principles, were true communities of mutual affection, joy and celebration, trust and security, and serene reconciliation. . . . *Cuba, care for your families, in order to keep your heart pure!*"[27]

At the Plaza Ignacio Agramonte in Camagüey on Friday, January 23, John Paul was met by 200,000 cheering teenagers, each of whom had been systematically propagandized by the regime's atheism their entire lives. Under a blistering hot Caribbean sun, they sang, danced, jumped up and down, waved Cuban and Vatican flags that had been hand-pasted onto small sticks, and heard John Paul, speaking from an altar built atop a socialist-realist bas-relief of Fidel Castro and Che Guevara, urge them to be the protagonists of their own personal and national stories: "*Happiness is achieved through sacrifice.* Do not look outside for what is found inside. Do not expect from others what you yourselves can and are called to be or to do. Do not leave for tomorrow the building of a new society in which the noblest dreams are not frustrated and in which you can be the principal agents of your own history." And there was another history lesson. Ignacio Agramonte, the Cuban revolutionary hero in whose honor the plaza in which they were meeting was named, was in fact a man "motivated by his Christian faith [who] embodied the values by which men and women are distinguished as good: honor, truthfulness, fidelity, the love of justice . . . *in the face of slavery, he defended human dignity.*"[28] As in Santa Clara, the Pope arrived looking tired, and those present wondered how he could make it through a lengthy ceremony. As he would do throughout the visit, he drew energy from the crowd, and got stronger as an event wore on.

That evening, John Paul spoke to an audience composed primarily of regime-approved intellectual and cultural figures at the University of Havana. The Pope was weary and his presentation was not vigorous, but the audience, including major government leaders, sat like students being instructed by a venerable professor. After praying at the grave of Father Félix Varela in the university's Great Hall, he evoked the memory of this beloved "teacher of teachers" and hero of the Cuban independence struggle to illuminate the Christian revolution he was proposing. Many Cubans, John Paul noted, considered Father Varela *"the foundation stone of the Cuban national identity,"* the "best synthesis one could find of Christian faith and Cuban culture," and the man who had taught his countrymen to think well—by thinking freely. The Pope then gave the cultural screw another twist: "He also spoke of democracy, judging it to be the political project best in keeping with human nature, while at the same time underscoring its demands." Those included an education that stressed freedom for responsibility, and a civil society capable of sustaining the rule of law. No one present, including Fidel Castro and Caridad Diego, needed to be reminded that neither of these historic attributes of Varela's hoped-for Cuban culture was very much in evidence in the Cuba of 1998.

Félix Varela's vision of the free and just society had been the fruit of his faith, which could still inspire an authentic renewal of Cuban culture and society today. Christian conviction, not ideology, had been the source of his personal virtues, his patriotism, and his enduring impact on Cuban culture. He had died, John Paul concluded, with the Creed on his lips "and a fervent prayer for the good of my country" in his heart.[29]

Without mentioning the current Cuban regime, John Paul had laid out the framework for its replacement by an authentically Cuban system of freedom, in four historically acute paragraphs.

That night, the Central Committee of the Cuban Communist Party met in emergency session. The following morning, Fidel Castro's brother Raul, second-in-command in fact if not in name, unexpectedly showed up for the Pope's Mass in Santiago, which was being held against the backdrop of the Sierra Maestra, the romantic center of the Castro revolution. There, Raul Castro witnessed the first public display in forty years of Cuba's national icon, the small statue of Our Lady of Charity of El Cobre, which was processed around the venue atop a gray Toyota truck to the ecstatic cheers of the crowd of a quarter-million—many of whom had been funneled to places far away from the papal altar by blue-clad security forces. At the beginning of Mass, Raul had to listen to a blunt denunciation of "false messianism" by the archbishop of Santiago, Pedro Meurice Estíu, whose welcome to the Pope included a biting critique of those "Cubans who have confused the fatherland with a single party, the nation with the historical process we have lived through during the last few decades, and culture with an ideology."

John Paul's homily extended his Cuban history lesson, recounting the process of Christian evangelization and culture-formation that "has continued to forge the characteristic traits of this nation." He unwound a list of Cuban cultural and political heroes who, throughout the centuries, "chose the way of freedom and justice as the foundation of their people's dignity," and then made a plea for the release of political prisoners. As for the future, the Church, he insisted, *"does not seek any type of political power in order to carry out her mission."* The Church sought something else—"to be the fruitful seed of everyone's good by her presence in the structures of society." By defending religious freedom, "the Church defends the freedom of each individual, of families, of different social units, which are living realities with a right to their own sphere of autonomy and sovereignty." It was another frontal assault on the still-unnamed Cuban regime, and the crowd responded with chants of *Libertad! Libertad!* John Paul then crowned the statue of La Caridad of El Cobre as Queen of Cuba, reminding everyone present that El Cobre had been the first place in Cuba to free its slaves, and that the father of Cuban independence, Carlos Manuel de Cespedes, had made the first Cuban flag from the canopy of his family's altar, prostrating "himself at the feet of Our Lady before beginning the battle for freedom."[30]

It was another call to arms, but arms of a different sort. During the crowning, shouts of *Viva! Viva!* echoed back from the Sierra Maestra. Raul Castro, perhaps wondering what temporary insanity had inspired his brother to permit the saying of what had not been said in Cuba for forty years, flew back to Havana. So did John Paul, who spent the evening at a prayer service for patients of a local leprosarium.

What the regime called Revolution Plaza and the Church called by its pre-Castro name, José Martí Plaza, was bracketed by competing revolutionary icons for the closing Mass of the papal visit on Sunday, January 25. A steel profile of Che Guevara dominated the facade of one building. Across the plaza, on another high-rise, was a ten-story-tall picture of the Sacred Heart of Jesus, complete with the inscription, *Jesucristo En Ti Confio* [Jesus Christ, In You I Trust]. Fidel and Raul Castro, Caridad Diego, and virtually the entire higher echelon of the Cuban party apparatus and government were present for the Mass, which was attended by more than a million Cubans who punctuated the liturgy and the Pope's homily with chants of *Libertad! Libertad!* Visitors who had decided they could see more by watching the Mass on a hotel television noticed one oddity. The regime-controlled television network described the proceedings in a straightforward fashion, while one of CNN's correspondents announced that the Mass, the homily, and indeed the entire papal visit proved that "Catholicism and communism can co-exist."

John Paul took the occasion of his last major public address in Cuba to criticize the U.S. economic embargo, thus reiterating a longstanding Holy See position that economic embargoes are, as a general rule, unjust, because those who feel the pain are not those in charge of the government whose policies an embargo seeks to change. It was one sentence in a half-hour homily, the rest of which demonstrated the fatuousness of claims about the coexistence of communism and Catholicism. Cuba's problems, the Pope insisted, were the result of a system that denied the dignity of the human person. John Paul vigorously defended religious freedom again, urging neither a sacred state nor an atheistic state, but a state "which enables every person and every religious confession to live their faith freely, to express that faith in the context of public life, and to count on adequate resources and opportunities to bring its spiritual, moral, and civic benefits to bear on the life of the nation." No communist state had ever done that. A Cuban government that did permit this kind of free Church in a free civil society would, by definition, be neither communist or totalitarian.

The Pope's affirmation of the Church's duty to defend "the concrete human person" in the face of "any injustice, however small" was met by a long burst of applause. When it died down, John Paul improvised a comment: "I am not against applause because when you applaud, the Pope can take a little rest. But there is still a page to go." Even Fidel Castro laughed. But he did not seem amused when the crowd kept chanting, "The Pope is free and wants us all to be free." To which John Paul replied, "Yes, he lives with that freedom for which Christ has set us free."

Cuba, the Pope concluded, "*has a Christian soul*" that had brought her "*a universal vocation.*" It was not the vocation that had brought the Cuban army to Africa in the 1970s. It was a vocation to "overcome isolation . . . to open herself to the world." "*This is the time to start on new paths*," not because the welfare paymaster had collapsed in Moscow, but because "these are times of renewal which we are experiencing at the approach of the third millennium of the Christian era." He then commended "this people so close to my heart" to the Queen of Cuba, La Caridad of El Cobre, that she might "obtain for her children the gifts of peace, progress, and happiness."[31]

Beyond Canossa

The materialist delusion that had ruined so many lives in the twentieth century was amply displayed in Fidel Castro's Cuba during the papal pilgrimage—ironically, in the utter collapse of the materials of modern life on the island. Very few people took seriously Castro's claim that the crumbling buildings, semiclad children, anorexic prostitutes (many of them professional women desperate for income to feed their families), rusting vintage automobiles, and closed-down housing projects evident all over Havana were the results of the economic embargo. They were the artificial products of the Castro revolution itself. The average worker's wage in Cuba in January 1998 was eight dollars a month; doctors might make as much as twenty. Milk cost more than a dollar a quart, when available, and by government order was rationed only to children under seven. Cooking oil was rationed to a liter every month. The party elite and the army excepted, the entire population was living outside the law, simply to survive.

Everyone involved with the papal pilgrimage understood that rebuilding Cuban Catholicism in these grim circumstances would be a colossal job. The Church claimed that perhaps forty percent of the population was Catholic, down from seventy percent in 1958 but no mean achievement under the conditions of the intervening years. Still, visitors at the papal Masses saw that even those who attended and participated so enthusiastically required basic religious education: priest-commentators explained each segment of the Mass to the huge crowds before it took place. John Paul's gift to Cardinal Ortega of a cornerstone for a new archdiocesan seminary at the closing Mass was a symbol of the need to reevangelize the entire island.

The dance between the regime and the Church continued throughout 1998. Two hundred fifty political prisoners on the list submitted to the government in January by Cardinal Angelo Sodano were released within the next several months; some were required to emigrate, to Canada. Seventy others were refused release on the grounds that, as the regime put it, "there cannot be nor will there be immunity for the enemies of the homeland nor for those intent on destroying Cuba." The regime also began to limit some prisoners' access to the priests, deacons, and nuns who worked as prison chaplains. On June 9, 1998, John Paul met in Rome with all thirteen of Cuba's bishops to review the situation. The visit signaled the regime that things ought to be moving faster.[32]

In public terms, John Paul's 1998 Cuban pilgrimage created openings in which the free institutions of civil society can grow over time. Cuba's underground, independent trade unions were encouraged by the visit, as were independent journalists and Cuban human rights activists, whose ranks grew to include members of professional associations. The visit also strengthened the spirits of Cuba's evangelical Protestants, one of whose pastors told a visiting American that "the Pope has done everything just right. This is a *kairos* and things can never be the same again."[33] Two days after his return to Rome, John Paul told his weekly general audience of his hope that "the fruits of this pilgrimage for our brothers and sisters on that beautiful island will be similar to the fruits of [his 1979] pilgrimage to Poland." Given the still-fragile condition of the Cuban Church, and the fact that Castro's political opponents had, virtually without exception, been murdered or exiled, the communist crackup in Cuba would undoubtedly take time. By creating the first mass experience of genuine pluralism on the island in forty years, however, John Paul may well have set in motion a chain of events that will have the same effect in Cuba that his revolution of conscience had in east central Europe.

More than one on-site observer of the visit suggested that Fidel Castro, whose appearance often varied between wistful and haunted, looked like a man who wanted, somehow, to go to confession, to the one man in the world to whom his ego would allow him to confess. Although that did not happen, as far as is known, in a formal, sacramental sense, the very fact of the Pope's visit and the response it generated among the Cuban people was a living refutation of the theme of one of Fidel's legendary revolutionary writings: "History will absolve me." Here were two men who had given their lives to two claims about the truth—and one seemed to sense that the other had made the right choice. John Paul knew that his successor would be a Catholic; Fidel Castro had no reason to be confident about the communist future of Cuba.

Some even imagined the entire visit as analogous to the Emperor Henry IV asking absolution of Pope Gregory VII at Canossa in 1077. But that was not quite right. John Paul was not claiming the power to depose tyrannical rulers and Castro was no Christian prince. The Pope's five days in Havana had demonstrated something that went far beyond Canossa. On the edge of the third millennium, the Church's proposal, as John Paul always described it— the proposal of the truth about the human person found in the Gospel—had a power of sparking national renewal far greater than the power of the anathemas popes had once wielded.[34]

That was the linkage between Poland 1979 and Cuba 1998.

Unresolved Issues

As the three-year preparation period for the Great Jubilee of 2000 formally opened on the First Sunday of Advent, December 1, 1996, John Paul II continued to address several knotty problems where progress had been difficult to come by during his pontificate.

Vietnam

Marxism-Leninism may have been finished as a historically viable proposal for the ordering of modern societies but the totalitarian delusion remained in power in several locales. John Paul had worked for years to improve the Church's situation in Vietnam and to open a dialogue with the country's communist rulers. Vietnam had made impressive economic progress since the end of the Second Indochina War in 1975, and normal diplomatic relations had been resumed with the United States in 1995. But it was still a country where a native Christian evangelist could be sentenced to three years in prison for "propagating religion illegally" by teaching a Bible class to ten adults.

John Paul had dramatically signaled his concern for the Church in Vietnam when he canonized 117 Vietnamese martyrs of the seventeenth, eighteenth, and nineteenth centuries at a great outdoor ceremony in St. Peter's Square on June 19, 1988. Cardinal Roger Etchegaray was in Vietnam three times at John Paul's request—once in 1989 and twice in 1990—to convey the Pope's support to the local bishops and to explore what kind of conversation might be possible with the government. In addition to the continuing repression of Christians and their communities, the appointment of bishops was a chronic problem. For ten years after the 1988 death of Archbishop Philippe Nguyen Kim Dien, an outspoken critic of the government-sponsored Catholic Committee for Solidarity, the government refused to allow the appointment of a new archbishop of Huê. The appointment was finally made in March 1998, at the same time as a five-year logjam over the appointment of a new archbishop for Ho Chi Minh City (the former Saigon) was broken. Exiled Archbishop Francis Xavier Nguyen Van Thuan, then serving as vice president of the Pontifical Council for Justice and Peace in Rome, had been denied an entry permit to attend the ordinations of two new Vietnamese bishops the year before.[35] Several bishops were denied passports and thus could not attend the Vietnamese *ad limina* visit to Rome in December 1996.[36]

Seven rounds of negotiations took place between officials of the Holy See and officials of Vietnam's bureau for religious affairs between 1990 and 1998, although there was an eighteen-month break between early 1995 and the resumption of talks in October 1996. According to Archbishop Claudio Celli, the principal Vatican negotiator at the time, the Holy See, in addition to pressing the government to ease restriction on bishops, priests, and seminarians, made it known that it was "available for diplomatic relations." The initial response was that that was impossible "for historical reasons"—the Church's identification with French colonialism and with the former South Vietnam's American ally. Celli, observing that Vietnam now had diplomatic relations with both France and the United States, asked his government counterpart whether the Holy See was more responsible for Vietnam's post–World War II difficulties than France or America. After all, the Vatican representative said, "We didn't bomb you." "You didn't bomb us," the Vietnamese vice minister for

Religious Affairs retorted, "because you have no planes." Celli was not sure whether the Vietnamese official was joking or not. These were, he recalled, "*very* difficult negotiations."[37]

Even while negotiations were under way and some progress was being made on seminaries and the appointment of bishops, the government censored the Vietnamese-language edition of the *Catechism of the Catholic Church*, omitting those sections that dealt with human rights and human dignity, the Christian's role in society, and the pursuit of the common good.[38] Despite the difficulties, popular piety remained strong. In August 1998, tens of thousands of Vietnamese Catholics came to the Marian shrine of La Vang in central Vietnam for the 200th anniversary of a Marian apparition there.[39] Their fidelity, the changing world economic and political situation, and pressure from younger communist party members eager to reconnect with the world eventually led the government of Vietnam to take a new position. In the first months of 1999 it agreed to a joint study, with the Holy See, of the possibility of diplomatic relations—the essential precondition to any papal visit to their country, from the Vietnamese point of view.

Sarajevo and Beirut

On the weekend of April 12 and 13, 1997, John Paul was finally able to go on pilgrimage to Sarajevo. Arriving at the Bosnian capital's airport on the afternoon of April 12, he described himself as a *"pilgrim of peace and friendship"* come to urge a rejection of the *"the inhuman logic of violence."*[40] After the arrival ceremony, the Pope was driven to Sacred Heart Cathedral, where he presented Cardinal Vinko Puljić with the oil lamp he had had hung and kept lit in St. Peter's Basilica as a reminder to pilgrims of Bosnia's suffering and of the imperative of solidarity with those under brutal attack. Preaching in Serbo-Croatian at a Vespers service for the priests, nuns, religious brothers, and seminarians of Bosnia, the Pope spoke of Sarajevo as a "martyr-city" still "scarred by a violent and crazed 'logic' of death, division, and annihilation." He thanked the priests who had remained with their people during the worst of the war, urged all to make *"a profound examination of conscience"* as the prelude to a "decisive commitment to reconciliation and peace," and asked that special care be taken to "encourage the young, who have often been . . . forced by the harshness of conflict to grow up much too soon."[41]

Snow was falling, and John Paul was visibly chilled, at the Mass in Koševo Stadium on Sunday morning. One of the papal masters of ceremonies had to hold an umbrella over the shivering Pope to keep the snow off him during the liturgy. A determined John Paul once again responded to the congregation of tens of thousands and seemed to grow stronger as the Mass unfolded.

His homily theme, chosen for a city that had often had good reason to think itself forgotten by the world, was that the people of Sarajevo always "have an advocate with God . . . Jesus Christ the righteous!" It was the Second Sunday of Easter, and he reminded them of what Christians had just celebrated during Holy Week. As Christ had had to suffer, so had they; as he had risen, so, now, must they: "*Sarajevo, Bosnia-Herzegovina, arise! You have an advocate with God! His name is Jesus Christ the righteous!*" Who else but Christ, he asked, could be "an advocate for all these sufferings and tribulations" before the throne of God? "Who else can fully understand this page of your history, Sarajevo? Who else can fully understand this page of your history, O Balkan nations, and of your history, O Europe?" Who else, he asked, could give them the peace that is "born of love," and move them to forgiveness and reconciliation?[42]

Just prior to the Pope's arrival, Bosnian security forces found a large bomb, built from twenty anti-tank mines and more than fifty pounds of plastic explosive, hidden under a bridge John Paul was scheduled to cross during his visit. The bomb was dismantled, but it had been another brush with violent death for the seventy-seven-year-old Pope. Local police and Western intelligence agencies said that the bomb seemed to have been the work of an Iranian-controlled terrorist network.[43] Three weeks later, on May 3, John Paul received the credentials of the new Iranian ambassador to the Holy See.

After beatifying the first Gypsy in history, Ceferino Jiménez Malla, on May 4, the Pope fulfilled a longstanding desire to visit another shattered city when he flew to Beirut on May 10, 1997. In Harissa, north of Beirut, John Paul met with Lebanese Catholic youth at the Basilica of Our Lady of Lebanon, where he signed the post-synodal apostolic exhortation that concluded the Special Assembly for Lebanon of the Synod of Bishops. In a French address to the young Lebanese, the Pope urged them to "let yourselves be seized by Christ," and thus break out of the cycle of ethnic and sectarian violence that had destroyed so much of their country's patrimony. After the lengthy address the Pope began joking with the young people he had called "the treasure of Lebanon": "Now I must tell you that you have followed my address attentively. And I must tell you that I have also paid attention to you: are they reacting at the right moment? Are they applauding when they ought to? This is how I knew. So you have passed your examination!"[44]

Mass on Sunday, May 14, was celebrated outdoors before a congregation of hundreds of thousands in and around the esplanade near Martyrs' Square and the Beirut naval base. The liturgy was primarily in French, with some Arabic. The patriarchs of the Eastern Catholic Churches in Lebanon concelebrated with the Pope. The Gospel was proclaimed in the Byzantine style, and during the offertory procession of bread and wine to the altar Maronite hymns were sung. John Paul, preaching in French, stressed his long desire to come to Lebanon and the love he had for Lebanese Muslims and Druze, for Christians of other communions, and for the Catholics of the six different rites present in the country: Maronite, Melkite, Armenian, Chaldean, Syrian, and Latin. He vigorously defended the historic mission of Lebanon as a country that had once shown that "different faiths can live together in peace, brotherhood, and cooperation" and that "people can respect the rights of every individual to religious freedom." That was wholly appropriate, for it was Christ himself who had first brought the Gospel to what was now Lebanon, whose people had been aware of the history of salvation for more than 2,000 years. Noting that Martyrs' Square had also been called "Freedom Square" and "Unity Square," John Paul urged those present to make their recent experience of martyrdom the occasion not to further divide their country, but to restore it in freedom and unity.

On the flight from Rome to Beirut, a reporter had jokingly asked the Pope whether, in light of the dangers of a terrorist attack, John Paul shouldn't give everyone on the plane general absolution. Given the political circumstances and the numbers of people involved, Beirut might have been expected to be a scene of frenzy on Sunday. In fact, those present remember it as characterized by a remarkable calm.[45] For some months afterward, guests in the papal apartment in the Vatican noticed a Lebanese tablecloth, decorated with embroidered cedars, on the Pope's dining room table. Like the "martyr-city" of Sarajevo, what he had termed "martyr-Lebanon" was a country he was determined the world would not forget.

CELEBRITY AND SANCTITY

The contemporary cult of celebrity, in which fame is a function of ephemera— wealth, beauty, social position, the endless attentions of the paparazzi and the international tabloid press—was another threat to the development of a new humanism for the new millennium. Self-absorption and self-indulgence, transformed into a shabby notoriety, were in conflict with the self-giving required by the Law of the Gift built into human nature, and with the message of Christ and the cross.

On the surface, the juxtaposition of the deaths of two famous women in the late summer of 1997 was entirely coincidental. For years, the world had anticipated the death of eighty-seven-year-old Mother Teresa of Calcutta, who died on September 5. No one had expected the violent death five days earlier of Diana, Princess of Wales, killed in an automobile wreck in Paris. John Paul II saw a link between the two events: "It was providential," he told lunch guests at the end of September, "that Mother Teresa died at the same time as Diana." A Pole present volunteered that what seemed a coincidence had in fact illustrated the contrast between the hollow beatification that comes from modern secular celebrity and the true holiness of discipleship. John Paul, whose compassion for the family of the late Princess of Wales was as obvious as his admiration for Mother Teresa, did not disagree. Still another guest suggested that Mother Teresa was a "person-message" for our times, and the Pope agreed. She had embodied many of what he regarded as the central themes of his pontificate—the defense of life, the defense of the family, concern for the poor, the dignity of women, the human rights of the humblest of men and women. She had been a real "sister of God," as St. Albert Chmielowski had been a "brother of our God," John Paul said. The death of the saintly Albanian nun with whom he had enjoyed an intuitive, mutual understanding had "left us all a little orphaned." [46]

Both Diana and Mother Teresa were "personalities." Their lives and deaths illustrated a point John Paul had been making throughout the half-century of his priesthood: true human greatness is found in a personality that points beyond itself, as Mother Teresa's did in pointing to the poor she served, each of whom, she once said, was Jesus in a particularly "disturbing disguise." Wealth, beauty, and position need not be insuperable obstacles to happiness, but they can only become instruments of grace when they are surrendered to the logic of the cross, to the demands of self-giving. On the eve of the third millennium, the royal way to human happiness remained the way of self-abnegation—the way of the cross.

In reminiscing about Mother Teresa weeks after her death, John Paul remarked, "I hope she will be a saint." Even before her September 13 funeral Mass there were calls from around the world for an instant canonization. The Pope, determined not to let doubts be cast on the results by taking shortcuts, was content to let the process run its course. He seemed to have few doubts about its eventual outcome.[47]

The Travail of Dialogue

During 1997 and 1998, the first years of preparation for the Great Jubilee of 2000, the ecumenical dialogues with the Orthodox and Lutheran Churches, in which great hopes had been invested, ran into difficulties. And a new controversy was ignited after the Holy See issued its long-anticipated statement on the Catholic Church and the Holocaust.

A Non-meeting and a Boycott

The Roman Catholic dialogue with Orthodoxy experienced a particularly difficult period between the spring and fall of 1997. Hopes for a long-awaited meeting between Patriarch Aleksy II and Pope John Paul II in June 1997 were dashed, and in a way that further complicated Rome's dialogue with the Ecumenical Patriarch of Constantinople, Bartholomew I. The tangled web of missteps, misapprehensions, and misjudgments that led to several embarrassing outcomes illustrated just how complex the Roman Catholic–Orthodox dialogue had become. Ongoing tensions between Russian Orthodoxy and the renascent Greek Catholic Church in Ukraine, and intra-Orthodox tensions between world Orthodoxy's largest Church, headed by Aleksy, and the claims of Ecumenical Patriarch Bartholomew, were the primary factors involved in the cancellation of John Paul's meeting with Aleksy. The difficulties in making the meeting happen also illustrated how hard it is to get everyone moving in the same direction at the same time, even at the higher echelons of a small and disciplined bureaucracy like the Roman Curia.

According to Cardinal Edward Cassidy, President of the Pontifical Council for Promoting Christian Unity [CU], the question of a meeting between John Paul and Aleksy in June 1997 was first broached in Moscow in December 1996 at a meeting between representatives of CU and the Orthodox Patriarchate of Moscow. The meeting was to take place during the Second European Ecumenical Assembly in Graz in southern Austria. In the wake of this discussion, Cardinal Cassidy asked the Pope if he would be willing to go to Vienna to meet Aleksy before or during the Graz meeting. John Paul said he would, and CU started organizing the meeting on what was understood by all parties directly involved to be a confidential basis, with no public discussion until things had been finalized. But there was a leak in Moscow, a Greek Orthodox archbishop in Vienna was told that the meeting was all set (it wasn't), and the archbishop reported what seemed to be afoot to Ecumenical Patriarch Bartholomew.

Bartholomew was very unhappy that this had been arranged without his having been informed. Cardinal Cassidy told him that he had not been informed because, in fact, nothing had been settled and the Holy See was still unsure whether the meeting would take place. The Ecumenical Patriarch then informed Cassidy that if the Pope were to meet Aleksy but not him, he would take that very badly. Cassidy said that the Pope would be very happy to meet with him, but that the Ecumenical Patriarch may have gotten the wrong idea. The Pope was only going to go to Vienna for part of a day, and as the plans had evolved to date, the Pope and Aleksy would have a private meeting, a public meeting, a joint prayer service, and lunch, all in a monastery—that was it. Bartholomew said that if there was going to be a meeting between the Pope and Aleksy in Vienna, and he, Bartholomew, was going to be in Graz (a plan of which the Holy See had been unaware), then he, too, must meet with the Pope. Cassidy, after consulting with John Paul, said, fine, they'd delay the Pope's departure until the afternoon so that he and Bartholomew could meet. The Ecumenical Patriarchate responded that that was impossible, that Bartholomew had to meet John Paul before, not after, Aleksy. Before when? CU asked. The Ecumenical Patriarchate replied that it could be a half-hour, even fifteen minutes, before Aleksy arrived. The Pope and Cassidy thought that that would be ridiculous. As Cassidy later put it, it would hardly serve Bartholomew's wish to underline his role as first-among-Orthodox-equals to rush in, say hello, and then rush out, with Aleksy then arriving, accompanied by the world media. John Paul came up with another idea. Since Bartholomew was flying to Vienna on a private plane, why couldn't he stop in Rome on the way so that he could be received properly and the two men could talk and have lunch together? The Ecumenical Patriarch declined. He had already been to Rome, John Paul hadn't returned the visit, so he could not come to Rome again. This seemed to exhaust the possibilities, and the Ecumenical Patriarchate was informed that the Holy See was sorry, but there seemed to be nothing left to do. Bartholomew I then canceled his visit to Graz even after Cardinal

Cassidy had insisted that the Pope's meeting with Patriarch Aleksy hadn't been finalized.

As indeed it hadn't. There had been laborious discussions over the joint declaration that John Paul and Aleksy would sign; the most difficult issue remained the question of what the Orthodox regarded as "proselytism" by Greek Catholics in Ukraine. Property issues involving churches in Ukraine also remained to be resolved, the Holy See arguing that it was moving things along as fast as possible, and Moscow disagreeing.

While negotiations on these questions continued, there was another stumble. At the end of the International Eucharistic Congress in Wrocław, Poland, on June 1, 1997, Cardinal Achille Silvestrini, Prefect of the Congregation for Oriental Churches, announced to the world press that the meeting between John Paul and Aleksy would in fact take place. This unintentionally violated CU's solemn promise to the Patriarchate of Moscow that there would be no statement or even public reference to such an event until the Patriarchate's Synod had held its June 11 meeting. In the wake of that session, the Patriarchate canceled the Vienna meeting between Patriarch Aleksy and the Pope. In a television interview in Moscow, Patriarch Aleksy publicly blamed the Holy See for the cancellation. Cardinal Cassidy, while acknowledging that problems remained, believes that the more serious reason for the cancellation was that Patriarch Aleksy couldn't get the full agreement of his Synod to his meeting with the Pope. Orthodox opposition to the meeting, Cassidy was convinced, was the reason the encounter in Vienna never took place.[48]

But that was not the end of this embarrassing sequence. After, and presumably because of, the failure to reach agreement on Bartholomew's meeting the Pope prior to what turned out to be the meeting with Aleksy, the Ecumenical Patriarchate of Constantinople informed the Holy See that, for the first time in a quarter-century, it would not be sending a delegation to the annual celebration of the feast of Sts. Peter and Paul in Rome on June 29. Weeks later, having been criticized by some of his metropolitans for not sending representatives to Rome, Bartholomew remarked that this had all been just a "passing cloud." It was an unprecedented rebuke, nonetheless. Cardinal Cassidy was then asked by several American bishops what should be done about Ecumenical Patriarch Bartholomew's scheduled visit to sixteen U.S. cities in October, in which numerous ecumenical events were planned. Cassidy talked to the Pope, and John Paul said that the plans for the ecumenical meetings with Bartholomew should go ahead "as if none of this had ever happened." Moreover, John Paul said, a Roman delegation would be going to the Ecumenical Patriarchate as usual, on November 30, for the feast of St. Andrew.[49]

The delegation was received cordially by Patriarch Bartholomew, who had, however, raised further, substantive questions about the future of the Roman Catholic–Orthodox dialogue during his American tour. In a lecture at Georgetown University in Washington, D.C., on October 21, 1997, Bartholomew claimed that, during the second millennium, the "divergence" between Orthodoxy and Rome had "continually" increased, so that today the obstacles to the restoration of full communion could not be reduced to "a problem of organizational structures [or] jurisdictional arrangements." Something "deeper and more substantive" blocked the way to communion between East and West: "the manner in which we exist has become ontologically different."[50] That formulation, radically different from the vision John Paul II had articulated in *Ut Unum Sint*, seemed to suggest that there were essential, possibly even unbridgeable, differences between Catholicism and Orthodoxy. Two days later, Bartholomew participated in an ecumenical service with Cardinal William Keeler in Baltimore, praying with men whom, he implied at Georgetown, he regarded as heterodox, but whom he now described as brothers in Christ.

Ecumenical officials at the U.S. Bishops' Conference were later told by members of the Patriarch's staff that Bartholomew had made major changes in his Georgetown address at the last minute, eliminating, for example, an attack on Uniatism (which would have meant, in practice, the Greek Catholics of Ukraine), and that there hadn't been a chance to "fix" all the language in the address before it was delivered. The suggestion was that Catholics should watch what the Ecumenical Patriarch did (as in the joint prayer service in Baltimore) as well as what he said (as in the address at Georgetown).[51] Even those who sympathized with Bartholomew's difficulties with the anti-ecumenical factions in Orthodoxy were left wondering just how full communion could be imagined with an Orthodoxy that thought itself to be living an "ontologically different"—which was to say, essentially different—experience of the Church and the sacraments than did Roman Catholics. Four months later, after an intra-Orthodox meeting of twelve Church leaders in Istanbul, Ecumenical Patriarch Bartholomew told the Belgian daily *La Libre Belgique* that Catholicism and Orthodoxy would "be entering the third millennium without regaining unity."[52]

John Paul II cordially welcomed the Orthodox delegation that attended the celebration of Sts. Peter and Paul in Rome in June 1998, and Catholic ecumenists appreciated the positive things the delegation leader, Metropolitan Jean de Pergame, said about *Ut Unum Sint*. Late in 1998, progress seemed possible on at least one front when Patriarch Teoctist of the Romanian Orthodox Church announced that he would welcome a pilgrimage by John Paul II to Romania, which in May 1999 became the first majority-Orthodox country the Pope visited. Despite this development, and several more encouraging statements by Ecumenical Patriarch Bartholomew in 1998 and early 1999, the hard fact remained that the Pope's visionary hope of closing the breach between Rome and the East by the turn of the millennium was not going to be realized.

In fidelity to Vatican II and to his sense of *kairos*, John Paul had bent every possible effort in that direction—too much so, according to critics in Ukraine and elsewhere. No one, though, could reasonably claim that John Paul II's efforts had been reciprocated by the majority of Orthodoxy's leaders.

Remembrance

In twenty years of meetings with Jewish communities at the Vatican and in every corner of the world, John Paul had persistently, vigorously, and unambiguously condemned the *Shoah,* the Holocaust of the European Jews during the Second World War. Perhaps his most eloquent statement had come during a meeting with Jewish leaders in Warsaw, on June 14, 1987, when he described the Holocaust as a universal icon of evil:

> Be sure, dear brothers, that . . . this Polish Church is in a spirit of profound solidarity with you when she looks closely at the terrible realization of the extermination—the unconditional extermination—of your nation, an extermination carried out with premeditation. The threat against you was also a threat against us; this latter was not realized to the same extent, because it did not have time to be realized to the same extent. It was you who suffered this terrible sacrifice of extermination: one might say that you suffered it also on behalf of those who were in the purifying power of suffering. The more atrocious the suffering, the greater the purification. The more painful the experience, the greater the hope. . . . [Because] of this terrible experience . . . you have become a loud warning voice for all humanity, for all nations, all the powers of this world, all systems and every person. More than anyone else, it is precisely you who have become this saving warning. I think that in this sense you continue your particular vocation, showing yourselves still to be the heirs of that election to which God is faithful. This is your mission in the contemporary world before all the peoples, the nations, all of humanity, the Church. . . .[53]

In the years that followed this dramatic statement, John Paul had tried to meet Jewish concerns about the Carmelite convent in Oświęcim, and worked to keep the memory of the *Shoah* alive in the center of world Catholicism. On April 7, 1994, he had hosted a Holocaust Memorial Concert in the Paul VI Audience Hall. The Royal Philharmonic Orchestra was conduced by Gilbert Levine, a Brooklyn-born American Jew whom John Paul had befriended after he became music director of the Kraków Philharmonic in 1987. The Pope sat in the audience hall side by side with the chief rabbi of Rome, Elio Toaff, and Italian President Oscar Luigi Scalfero. Rabbi Toaff had brought his congregation with him, the first time that many had been inside the Vatican except as tourists. Two hundred Holocaust survivors from twelve different countries attended, along with diplomats from all over the world.[54]

John Paul's call for the Church to cleanse its conscience on the edge of the third millennium certainly included a reckoning with anti-Jewish Christian prejudice and its historical effects during Christianity's first 2,000 years. At a Roman theological symposium on "The Roots of Anti-Semitism in Christianity," sponsored in October 1997 by the Theology-History Commission of the Committee for the Great Jubilee of 2000, the Pope acknowledged that "erroneous and unjust interpretations of the New Testament regarding the

Jewish people and their presumed guilt circulated for too long" and had "contributed to a lulling of consciences" among Christians. The results were clear in living memory. During World War II, "when Europe was swept by the wave of persecutions inspired by a pagan anti-Semitism that in its essence was equally anti-Christian," there had been a failure of "spiritual resistance" by too many Christians. The past had to be revisited, he concluded, in order to purify memories and to prepare a future in which it would be universally recognized that "anti-Semitism is without any justification and is absolutely condemnable."[55]

During the 1990s, as John Paul continued to underscore his abhorrence of the Holocaust and his determination to come to grips with the history of Catholic anti-Jewish prejudice, the Holy See's Commission on Religious Relations with the Jews worked on the official Catholic document on the *Shoah* that had been promised during the emergency meeting between Catholic and Jewish leaders in 1987, in the wake of the papal audience for Austrian President Kurt Waldheim.[56] Eleven years later, on March 16, 1998, *We Remember: A Reflection on the* Shoah was finally published. Another controversy immediately ensued.

We Remember described the *Shoah* as an "unspeakable tragedy" and a "horrible genocide" before which "no one can remain indifferent, least of all the Church, by reason of her very close bonds with the Jewish people and her remembrance of the injustices of the past." The document acknowledged that, while "the Jewish people have suffered much at different times and in many places" because of their "unique witness to the Holy One of Israel and to the *Torah*," the Holocaust "was certainly the worst suffering of all." The fact that it took place "in countries of long-standing Christian civilization" demanded an examination of conscience on the relationship between the Nazis' "Final Solution" and "the attitudes down the centuries of Christians toward the Jews."

Nazi ideology, the document argued, "refused to acknowledge any transcendent reality as the source of life and the criterion of moral good." Nazi anti-Semitism was also fueled by "pseudo-scientific" theories of racial superiority and inferiority and by "extremist forms of nationalism." All three of those planks in the ideological platform of German National Socialism—its atheism, racism, and violent nationalism—were anti-Christian as well as anti-Jewish. Thus, the document proposed, a distinction had to be made between this kind of racist anti-Semitism, which rejected "the constant teaching of the Church on the unity of the human race and on the equal dignity of all races and peoples," and the longstanding "sentiments of mistrust and hostility" that were the basis of Christian "anti-Judaism." Nevertheless, "it may be asked whether the Nazi persecution of the Jews was not made easier by the anti-Jewish prejudices imbedded in some Christian minds and hearts." Did historic anti-Jewish prejudice make Christians "less sensitive, even indifferent, to the persecutions launched against the Jews by National Socialism . . . ?"

We Remember urged that Christians who had risked their lives to rescue Jews during the *Shoah* not be forgotten. The fact that some resisted, however, did not alter the fact that "the spiritual resistance and concrete action of other Christians was not that which might have been expected from Christ's followers." Retrospective moral judgment on what others should have done under the extreme conditions of life in a totalitarian state was not an easy business, the document suggested. Still, the *Shoah* and the failure of Christian witness during it had left a "heavy burden of conscience" on Christians today that required making "an act of . . . *teshuvah*," or profound repentance, "since, as members of the Church, we are linked to the sins as well as the merits of all her children." Finally, the Church wished "to turn awareness of past sins into a firm resolve to build a new future in which there will be no more anti-Judaism among Christians or anti-Christian sentiment among Jews, but rather a shared mutual respect, as befits those who adore the one Creator and Lord and have a common father in faith, Abraham."

Critics of the document compared it unfavorably to a 1995 statement of the German Bishops' Conference, which admitted a "co-responsibility" for the tragedy of the Holocaust, and a 1997 French bishops' statement that had asked Jewish forgiveness for Christian failures in the defense of Jews during the German occupation of France. A lengthy footnote in *We Remember*, defending Pope Pius XII's actions during the war, was heavily criticized; the executive director of the World Jewish Congress, Elan Steinberg, welcomed the "positive elements [in] the document" while deploring "the gratuitous defense of the silence of Pius XII." The document's sharp distinction between Nazi anti-Semitism and Christian anti-Judaism also came under fire, as critics argued that *We Remember* did not take sufficient account of how historic Christian anti-Jewish prejudices had created the cultural conditions for acquiescence, tacit or overt, to Nazi anti-Semitism; Efraim Zuroff of the Simon Wiesenthal Center in Jerusalem essentially dissolved the distinction by charging that the document "does not unequivocally take responsibility for the teachings of the Church that created the atmosphere that ultimately led to the Holocaust, and to the participation of numerous 'believing' persons in that crime." Still others made the document the occasion to engage in innuendo about John Paul II's activities during the Occupation. Rabbi Arthur Hertzberg described the wartime Karol Wojtyła as "a quiet young man who stayed out of trouble." Rabbi Hertzberg, who had evidently not studied Wojtyła's wartime activities very closely, nonetheless had "little doubt that he looks back on that period of his life and wishes he hadn't lived quietly."[57]

The blunt reaction of Meir Lau, a Holocaust survivor and the Ashkenazic chief rabbi of Israel, that *We Remember* was "too little, too late" was not universally shared among Jewish leaders. Rabbi Jack Bemporad, a longtime leader in the Jewish-Catholic dialogue in the United States, called the document "spectacular," while Rabbi David Rosen, the Jerusalem representative of the Anti-Defamation League of B'nai B'rith and its co-representative to the Vatican, took a measured line: the document was "a very important statement, but . . .

disappointing in some respects." No criticisms were registered of John Paul's preface to *We Remember*, a letter to Cardinal Edward Cassidy, chairman of the Holy See's Commission on Religious Relations with the Jews, which described the *Shoah* as an "unspeakable iniquity" and an "indelible stain on the history of the century that is coming to a close." But the Pope's "fervent hope" that *We Remember* "will indeed help to heal the wounds of past misunderstandings and injustices" did not seem likely to be realized in the near term.

No fourteen-page document could have satisfactorily analyzed the complexities of 2,000 years of Jewish-Christian relations and their bearing on as complex a historic reality as Nazism. The gist of the critical reactions to *We Remember*—that the Church had not "gone as far" as had been expected—suggested that the document suffered from a different kind of omission than its critics had identified.

Had it framed the entire question of Catholicism and the *Shoah* with a careful theological explanation of why the Church's remembrance of, and repentance for, the past failures of its sons and daughters was a religious duty rather than a response to political or public pressure, *We Remember* might have helped deepen the entire debate about Christianity and the *Shoah*. The discussion of the Church and the Holocaust had too often become an exercise in which one side's "concession" was regarded as another's "gain." This was precisely the model beyond which John Paul was trying to take the Jewish-Catholic dialogue. That intention did not seem sufficiently accounted for in drafting *We Remember* or among the officials of the Secretariat of State who did the final editing. Thus the deeper disappointment of *We Remember* was that it failed to set what will assuredly be a centuries-long discussion on a new, more theologically sophisticated, and more religiously compelling foundation.

Justification by Faith

During the mid-1990s, there was widespread expectation that years of ecumenical dialogue between Lutherans and Roman Catholics would result in a joint declaration on "justification by faith," the core issue of the Lutheran Reformation. In that declaration, it was anticipated, the two communions would acknowledge that, whatever the disagreements of the sixteenth century, they shared common convictions about justification by faith today. And while they might express those convictions somewhat differently, the question of justification should no longer constitute a Church-dividing issue. Such a joint declaration would mark one of the great accomplishments of modern ecumenism.

On June 25, 1998, the text of a *Joint Declaration on the Doctrine of Justification* was released by the Pontifical Council for Promoting Christian Unity. At a press conference, the Council's president, Cardinal Edward Cassidy, stressed the *Joint Declaration*'s statement that it represented "a consensus on basic truths concerning the doctrine of justification," and on the relationship of faith to good works, in the scheme of salvation. That same day, however, the Holy See issued a *Response of the Catholic Church to the Joint Declaration of the Catholic Church and the Lutheran World Federation on the Doctrine of Justification*, which had been jointly prepared by the Congregation for the Doctrine of the Faith and the Pontifical Council for Promoting Christian Unity.

The *Response* suggested that further clarification on the doctrine of justification and its relationship to other basic truths of Christian faith was required. The second part of the *Joint Declaration* had laid out the ways in which Lutherans and Catholics understood aspects of the doctrine of justification differently. In the *Joint Declaration*, for example, Lutherans stated that, from their perspective, "sin still lives" in human beings immediately after their conversion and baptism. As the *Response* indicated, this was not a position that Catholics could accept, even as a distinctive Lutheran interpretation of a common understanding of justification, for it seemed to deny that God acts through the sacraments in ways that really change a person. It was necessary, the *Response* said, for this and other matters to be more thoroughly clarified.

Lutherans were not happy with what seemed, at least through media reports, to be Catholic reneging. One ecumenical veteran went so far as to suggest that the Holy See had "betrayed" Lutheran and Roman Catholic theologians, and predicted that it would take decades to reestablish the trust that had been shattered. Cardinal Cassidy wrote Dr. Ismael Noko, Secretary-General of the Lutheran World Federation [LWF] on July 30, reiterating—and underlining in his letter—that "there is a consensus in basic truths on the doctrine of justification." Cassidy suggested that the reaction to the *Response* in some Lutheran circles had been exaggerated, and that there were in fact "very few" clarifications required. Cassidy's letter also stated that these clarifications "do not negate" the consensus on "basic truths of the doctrine of justification," that the Church was prepared "to affirm and sign the Joint Declaration," and that there were no "major problems" impeding "further study and a more complete presentation" of the truths of the doctrine of justification.

Dr. Noko wrote the executive committee of the LWF on August 20, enclosing Cassidy's letter, which, he said, "introduces a new perspective on how to read, understand, and interpret" the *Response*. At its meeting of November 13–14, Noko indicated, the LWF executive committee would try to determine what the next Lutheran step in the now-threatened process should be. Meanwhile, as a result of private discussions between Cardinals Cassidy and Ratzinger and key Lutheran theologians and officials, the Holy See had proposed that the issue be resolved by attaching an agreed "annex" to the *Joint Declaration*. The annex would clarify in a definitive way the concerns that had been raised in the *Response* while emphasizing that those concerns did not invalidate the consensus on "the basic truths of justification."

The annex was eventually hammered out, and the necessary clarifications were made on the questions of the enduring human propensity to sin, on human cooperation with God's saving grace, and on the necessity of locating the doctrine of justification within the broader scheme of Christian belief. A further "Official Common Statement" by the Lutheran World Federation and the Catholic Church made clear what the two partners understood the *Joint Declaration* to mean: "The teaching of the Lutheran Churches presented in this *Declaration* does not fall under the condemnations of the Council of Trent. The condemnations in the Lutheran Confessions do not apply to the teachings of the Roman Catholic Church presented in this *Declaration*." After Pope John Paul II gave his personal agreement to the clarifications in the annex, it was announced that the *Joint Declaration* would be signed by Lutheran and Roman Catholic representatives in Augsburg on October 31, 1999—Reformation Sunday.

The process had been much more difficult than anticipated. But Cardinal Ratzinger believed that the difficulties during the summer of 1998 would lead, over time, to a deepened theological dialogue. What had seemed for several months to be a new crisis in the most theologically developed of the ecumenical dialogues turned out to be the unexpected prologue to a historic accomplishment.[58]

RESTRUCTURING

John Paul II's preparations for the Great Jubilee of 2000 and for the Church's life in the twenty-first century were organizational as well as theological. In February 1996, he revamped the rules for the election of a pope. Several months later, John Paul began the third major reorganization of curial personnel in the pontificate, a process that continued through 1998. At the same time, several major episcopal appointments and the Pope's seventh consistory for the appointment of new cardinals signaled the kind of leadership he hoped would make possible a springtime of evangelization and witness in the first decades of the new millennium.

Electing a Pope

On February 22, 1996, Bernini's bronze masterpiece, the "Altar of the Chair" in the apse of St. Peter's Basilica, was ablaze with three-foot-tall tapers, an annual spectacular marking the feast of the Chair of St. Peter. That same day, John Paul signed the apostolic constitution *Universi Dominici Gregis* [The Shepherd of the Lord's Whole Flock], which made several important changes in the way papal elections would be conducted in the future.

John Paul designed *Universi Dominici Gregis* so that the rules governing future conclaves would reflect the fully internationalized situation of the post–Vatican II College of Cardinals and the exigencies of a contemporary papal election. Reams of commentary since the "year of three popes" in 1978 had created the image of a papal conclave as, essentially, a political exercise. John Paul, no naïf about ecclesiastical politics, nonetheless wished to foster conditions under which the inevitable politics involved in electing a pope would be of a different character than the politics of a party convention. The politics of a papal election, according to *Universi Dominici Gregis*, should have the character of a religious retreat, marked by a common sense of purpose and moral responsibility, under the judgment of God.

The conclave to elect John Paul II's successor will be in his debt in one very human way: it will be far more comfortably situated than its predecessors. For centuries, the Apostolic Palace had been carved up into cubicles during the interregnum between a pope's death and the opening of the conclave to elect his successor; the cardinal-electors lived during the conclave in these makeshift roomettes, all of which were furnished with chamber pots but few of which had running water, until their work was finished. Now, with the completion of a new Vatican guest house, the thoroughly modern Domus Sanctae Marthae [St. Martha's House] behind the Paul VI Audience Hall, more suitable quarters, featuring two-room suites with private baths, were available. The first major change mandated in *Universi Dominici Gregis* was the use of the Domus Sanctae Marthae as the cardinal-electors' residence and refectory during the conclave. The actual election would continue to take place in the Sistine Chapel—a place, John Paul wrote, "where everything is conducive to an awareness of the presence of God, in whose sight each person will one day be judged."[59]

As in the past, access to the cardinal-electors during a conclave would be strictly limited to the requisite conclave staff. John Paul underscored that the electors should have no contact "with persons outside the area where the election is taking place" (i.e., the Sistine Chapel, the Domus Sanctae Marthae, and the various places where conclave liturgies were celebrated). A contemporary note was struck when *Universi Dominici Gregis* ordered that the conclave areas should be swept by "two trustworthy technicians" to prevent bugging. The cardinal-electors themselves were strictly forbidden from making audio or visual recordings of the proceedings.[60]

Previous conclaves had been authorized to choose a pope by one of three methods: *inspiration* (in which a cardinal or group of cardinals proclaimed their belief that God had already chosen one of their number, to which the rest of the conclave would assent by acclamation); *delegation* (in which the entire conclave delegated the election to a committee on whose members all would agree); or *election* (technically styled *"scrutiny"*), which in practice was the method invariably used. In *Universi Dominici Gregis*, John Paul II suppressed the methods of inspiration and delegation. Inspiration, he wrote, was "no longer an apt way of interpreting the thought of an electoral college so great in number and so diverse in origin." The second proscription, of election by delegation, was explained in terms redolent of Karol Wojtyła, philosopher of moral agency: delegation "by its very nature . . . tends to lessen the responsibility of the individual electors, who . . . would not be required to express their choice personally." Thus future popes would be elected by secret ballot, which "offers the greatest guarantee of clarity, straightforwardness, simplicity, openness, and, above all, an effective and fruitful participation on the part of the cardinals who . . . are called to make up the assembly which elects the Successor of Peter."[61] John Paul retained Paul VI's restriction of the electoral franchise to those cardinals who had not reached their eightieth birthday before the pope died, although its octogenarian members would participate in pre-conclave meetings of the College of Cardinals.

Following longstanding custom, *Universi Dominici Gregis* establishes that the election of a new pope requires two-thirds of the votes of the cardinals present in the conclave, if the number of electors is equally divisible by three; if not, a majority of two-thirds-plus one is necessary.[62] But if, after thirty-four ballots over thirteen days, the conclave fails to elect anyone by two-thirds majority, the document provides for a valid election by absolute majority, if an absolute majority of the cardinal-electors agree to the procedure. At this juncture, the cardinals are also permitted to limit candidates to the two who had received the highest number of votes on the last ballot conducted under the two-thirds rule.[63]

This was an innovation and there were critics. One American commentator suggested that the new procedure created incentives for a majority unable to command a two-thirds consensus to hold fast to its candidate, refusing compromise, until the majority-election provision became operative.[64] That might indeed be the case if a conclave were simply an exercise in wielding political power. But John Paul, who once described himself as "firmly convinced that the Holy Spirit guides the conclave," did not believe that the process of electing a pope could be understood by analogy to democratic politics.[65] As for the new procedure itself, which the Pope said was deliberately designed with the special religious character of the conclave in mind, it is difficult to imagine the circumstances in which a bare majority of electors could hold intransigently to its position after thirteen days of conclave, thirty-four ballots, and the special days of prayer, consultation, and "exhortations" (preached by senior members of the College of Cardinals) mandated by John Paul after the thirteenth, twentieth, and twenty-seventh inconclusive ballots. No conclave had taken more than four days since 1831. Given the expectations of the Church and the world, it is not easy to think that a conclave could be dragged out for the better part of two weeks, even in the more agreeable quarters at the Domus Sanctae Marthae. John Paul's new rules did make it impossible for an intransigent minority, composed of one-third-plus-one of the electors, to block the election of a candidate who was clearly the overwhelming favorite.

Universi Dominici Gregis also included several personal touches. John Paul's rules were written to ensure that popes would be permitted to die with the dignity befitting any human being.[66] It was strictly forbidden to photograph or film the pope "either on his sickbed or after death, or to record his words for subsequent reproduction." If it was necessary to photograph the dead pope for "documentary purposes," doing so required the permission of the Cardinal Camerlengo, the administrator of the Holy See during the interregnum, who was forbidden to "permit the taking of photographs of the Supreme Pontiff except attired in pontifical vestments."[67]

In addition, John Paul tried to make certain that his longtime secretary,

Stanisław Dziwisz, would not suffer the fate of Paul VI's secretary, Pasquale Macchi, who was rudely ejected from the Vatican less than twenty-four hours after Pope Paul's death and found himself living in a Roman guest house. According to *Universi Dominici Gregis*, the "personnel who ordinarily reside in the private [papal] apartment can remain there until after the burial of the Pope."[68] It was a small, but telling, gesture of appreciation, and another break with local custom.

So was a paragraph largely ignored in the commentary on *Universi Dominici Gregis*, which laid down that the electoral rules John Paul had defined and the pre-conclave procedures he had prescribed were to be observed in full, "even if the vacancy of the Apostolic See should occur as a result of the resignation of the Supreme Pontiff. . . ."[69] No Pope had resigned since 1294, but that did not preclude the possibility in the future—in, for example, an instance of extreme disability. If the Petrine ministry was a service, not a personal privilege, then John Paul evidently believed that the possibility of a papal resignation should be considered in devising the rules of succession.

Universi Dominici Gregis was also criticized for retaining the College of Cardinals as the electoral body for choosing the Pope. Since Vatican II, proposals that popes be elected by a Synod of Bishops or by the presidents of the national episcopal conferences had been bruited. John Paul disagreed. In his judgment, the College of Cardinals combined "in a remarkable synthesis" the two aspects of the Office of Peter. The Pope was the Bishop of Rome and the cardinals were formally members the Roman clergy because of their titular pastorates in and around the city. The Pope was the universal pastor of the Church, and the composition of the College, in which 120 electors were drawn from every continent, reflected that universality. A millennium of experience, he concluded, had confirmed the wisdom of this unique body as the papal electoral college.[70]

Personnel as Policy

The appointment of bishops to major sees often demonstrates how personnel often is policy, in the Church as in the world. That adage of management theory was amply confirmed in crucial appointments John Paul made to two of world Catholicism's most important local Churches in the mid-1990s. On April 13, 1995, fifty-year-old Christoph Schönborn, OP, the auxiliary bishop of Vienna and general editor of the *Catechism of the Catholic Church*, was named coadjutor archbishop of the Austrian capital, and succeeded as archbishop on September 14, 1995.* On April 8, 1997, sixty-year-old Francis George, OMI,

*The term of Schönborn's predecessor, Cardinal Hans Hermann Groër, OSB, had been wracked by charges of sexual misconduct with young men decades before, when Groër was responsible for a Benedictine school. Those charges had further divided a badly split Austrian hierarchy and further debilitated the Church's life in Austria. In February 1998, Schönborn and three other Austrian bishops publicly announced that they had come to the "moral certainty" that the charges against Groër were true. Schönborn publicly apologized "for everything by which my predecessor, and other Church dignitaries, have wronged people entrusted to them." The archdiocese of Vienna, he pledged, was "prepared to offer help to all those who thus have suffered injury," including financial support for therapy.[71]

who had served as archbishop of Portland, Oregon, for only eleven months, was named the new archbishop of Chicago. Archbishop George succeeded Cardinal Joseph Bernardin, whose witness as he approached death the previous autumn had been a moving experience for millions throughout the United States.

Surface appearances and background suggested two very different men. Schönborn was the son of one of Europe's most distinguished families; George was a son of the American middle class. Schönborn, a tall man, carried himself with aristocratic ease; George, a slighter figure, was a polio survivor who wore a leg brace and walked with a limp. Beneath the surface there were great similarities between them, which illustrated John Paul's concept of a twenty-first-century bishop. Both men had had considerable experience as teachers. Both were serious intellectuals, at home in contemporary philosophy and theology and well-grounded in the Church's doctrine—which, as Archbishop George insisted at his first Chicago press conference, was neither "liberal" nor "conservative," but true. Both were committed to the model of the bishop as evangelizer, both were comfortable dealing with the media, and both enjoyed the give-and-take of debate. They were both men in whom friends and visitors sensed the kind of serenity that comes from intense prayer, yet they were good company, sharp listeners as well as able conversationalists, and devoted priests devoid of clericalism.

John Paul's third major reorganization of senior curial personnel further internationalized the Church's central bureaucracy and brought men with extensive pastoral experience and demonstrated intellectual interests into positions of leadership. On June 15, 1996, Dario Castrillón Hoyos of Colombia was appointed Prefect of the Congregation for the Clergy in the summer of 1996. Ordained a bishop at forty-two, he had served as Secretary-General of CELAM, the council of Latin American Bishops' Conferences, from 1983 to 1987, and had been a diocesan bishop for seventeen years. A week later, on June 21, John Paul appointed the Chilean Jorgé Arturo Medina Estévez, bishop of Valparaiso, as Prefect of the Congregation for Divine Worship. In August 1996, the host of World Youth Day '93, Denver Archbishop J. Francis Stafford, was called to Rome to become President of the Pontifical Council for the Laity. (Stafford's successor in Denver was the first American archbishop of Native American background, Charles J. Chaput, a Capuchin.)

The reorganization continued in 1997 with the appointment of a Mexican, Bishop Javier Lozano Barragán of Zacatecas, as President of the Pontifical Council for the Pastoral Care of Health Workers, and was completed in the first half of 1998. Cardinal Roger Etchegaray became the full-time President of the Committee for the Great Jubilee of 2000; promoted to the rank of cardinal bishop, he received the titular see of Cardinal Agostino Casaroli after the former Secretary of State died at age eighty-three on June 8, 1998. Etchegaray's successor as President of the Pontifical Council for Justice and Peace, Archbishop Francis Xavier Nguyen Van Thuan, wore a pectoral cross made of wood and electric wire, a relic of his thirteen years in a Vietnamese prison camp. In June 1998, John Paul accepted the resignation of one of his closest collaborators, Cardinal Bernardin Gantin of Benin, who had been Prefect of the Congregation for Bishops for more than fourteen years; the courtly African remained dean of the College of Cardinals. Gantin's successor was a Brazilian Dominican, Cardinal Lucas Moreira Neves, who had served as Secretary, or deputy head, of the Congregation for Bishops in the 1980s before returning to his native country in 1987 as archbishop of São Salvador da Bahia and Primate of Brazil. The Church's central leadership was further internationalized by the appointment of Bishop Stephen Fumio Hamao of Yokohama as President of the Pontifical Council for the Pastoral Care of Migrants and Itinerant People and José Saraiva Martins, a Portuguese curial official, as Pro-Prefect of the Congregation for the Causes of Saints.

In the midst of this curial rearrangement, John Paul also reorganized the papal household to meet the demands of the impending jubilee year. Centuries of precedent were broken when the Pope appointed an American, Monsignor James Harvey, as Prefect of the Papal Household. Harvey, a native of Milwaukee, had previously served in the Secretariat of State as head of the English section and then as Assessor for General Affairs (the deputy to the *Sostituto*, the de facto papal chief-of-staff). In order to link the work of the Prefecture, which is responsible for all papal audiences, public and private, more closely with the work of the papal apartment, John Paul appointed Monsignor Stanisław Dziwisz, his secretary, as Adjunct Prefect of the Papal Household. Both Monsignor Harvey and Monsignor Dziwisz were named bishops, as was another longtime papal collaborator, Monsignor Piero Marini, the Master of Pontifical Liturgical Ceremonies. John Paul ordained all three men to the episcopate in St. Peter's Basilica on March 19, 1998. In one of the most touching ceremonies of the pontificate, he thanked all three for their help over the years. A special word of gratitude went to Monsignor Dziwisz, whom he had ordained a priest thirty-five years before, for "sharing my trials and joys, hopes and fears" during the entire pontificate.[72] These unprecedented arrangements, which raised eyebrows among the traditional managers of popes, brought out the puckish sense of humor that John Paul and Stanisław Dziwisz share. On the day the changes were publicly announced, Dziwisz, the man closest to Karol Wojtyła for more than thirty years, called Harvey, who now ranked above him on the formal organization chart, and said, "I want you to know that I'm very good at taking orders." Some days later, the Pope and Monsignor Harvey were walking toward an audience when John Paul, who was well aware of the internal muttering about an American Prefect of the Papal Household, started musing in Italian in a quiet voice, *"Il Prefetto . . . Americano . . . impossibile!"* [The Prefect . . . an American . . . impossible!] . . . *"Un Aggiunto . . . Polacco . . . peggio ancora!"* [A Deputy Prefect . . . Polish . . . even worse!].

Three weeks after announcing these household changes, John Paul held his seventh consistory for the election of new members of the College of Cardinals. Twenty men received the red hat; the Pope named another two *in pectore* [in his heart], whose names were not publicly revealed. Among the new cardinals were Archbishops Schönborn of Vienna and George of Chicago; the new curial department heads Dario Castrillon Hoyos, Jorgé Medina Estévez, and J. Francis Stafford; and the archbishops of Palermo, Genoa, Mexico City, Toronto, Lyons, Dar-es-Salaam, Madrid, and Belo Horizonte in Brazil. A retired Polish missionary bishop in Zambia, Adam Kozłowiecki, SJ, received the red hat at age eighty-six, as did five veteran curial officials and the bishop of Kaohsiung, Taiwan's first cardinal.[73]

AN EPISTOLARY SUMMER

On May 25, 1998, a week after his seventy-eighth birthday, John Paul II became the longest-serving Pope of the twentieth century, passing Pius XII, who had served nineteen years and seven months. Pius's major teaching documents had all been issued by the eleventh anniversary of his election, and in the last years of his pontificate he had been something of a recluse. John Paul's twentieth year on the Chair of Peter was marked by a flurry of teaching documents and a pace of activity that, although somewhat slowed by his physical difficulties, continued to exhaust men thirty years younger.

Boris Yeltsin, President of the Russian Federation, came to the Vatican on February 10 for a fifty-minute talk with the Pope and reiterated Mikhail Gorbachev's invitation to John Paul to visit Russia. Absent an invitation from the Russian Orthodox Church and given the Pope's ecumenical commitments, no such pilgrimage was possible. Yeltsin and his family were charmed by John Paul, with whom the Russian president discussed both the internal Russian situation and security issues in Europe. For his part, the Pope emphasized the importance of the Great Jubilee of 2000 being celebrated in fidelity to both the Church's "lungs," East and West.[74]

John Paul made another effort to reach out to German-speaking Catholicism in a June pilgrimage to Austria, his eighty-third apostolic visit outside Italy. In an address to local political leaders and the diplomatic corps in Vienna, he noted that Austria had gone from being a "border country" to a "bridge country," with close links to the new democracies of east central Europe. This should not be understood, the Pope suggested, as an "opening to the east" so much as a "Europeanization of the entire continent." John Paul also stressed that the new Europe had to come to grips with the roots of anti-Semitism, some of which, he said, had not yet been pulled out. The Pope addressed the divided Austrian Church passionately: "The heart of the Bishop of Rome beats for all of you!" he said in his June 19 homily in Salzburg cathedral. "Do not abandon the flock of Christ, the Good Shepherd! Do not abandon the Church! . . . The Pope is counting on you to give a Christian face once again to the old Europe." John Paul's former student and successor at Lublin, Father Tadeusz Styczeń, thought that the Pope had "never been more transparent" than during his 1998 Austrian pilgrimage. He was now, visibly, living the way of the cross, and while that had always been at the center of his spiritual life, what had once been masked by his great vitality was now unmistakably evident.[75] Four months after the visit, an October 1998 national meeting of delegates of Austrian Catholics in Salzburg voted resolutions in favor of ordaining married men to the priesthood and women as deacons, allowing the divorced-and-remarried to receive Communion, individual conscience decisions in matters of contraception, and accelerated procedures for men who wanted to leave the ordained ministry to marry.[76] The Pope's concern for the reevangelization of Europe was not prominently featured in the Salzburg resolutions.

Just prior to the Pope's Austrian pilgrimage, the Vatican community was rocked and John Paul suffered a personal loss when Colonel Alois Estermann, who had just been installed as commander of the Swiss Guards, was murdered in his Vatican apartment, along with his wife, by a disgruntled guardsman. Estermann had jumped into the Popemobile on May 13, 1981, to shield a stricken John Paul from any further shots, and the Pope felt a special affection for the eighteen-year veteran of the Guards. The murderer, Cedric Tornay, who committed suicide after shooting Estermann and his wife, had acted, according to papal spokesman Joaquín Navarro-Valls, in a "moment of madness." The journalistic rumor mill ground out any number of lurid speculations about the murder/suicide, but months later Navarro's analysis remained unshaken by evidence of any other motive.[77]

The Church's campaign for John Paul's "culture of life" could claim a success on June 25, 1998, when Portuguese voters upset the pollsters' predictions by rejecting a law that would have permitted abortion on demand through the tenth week of pregnancy.[78] Six weeks later, on August 17, Norma McCorvey was received into the Catholic Church. As plaintiff "Jane Roe" in the U.S. Supreme Court's 1973 *Roe* v. *Wade* decision, McCorvey had been the leading symbol of the abortion license in the United States for more than two decades.

In 1991 (*Redemptoris Missio* and *Centesimus Annus*) and 1995 (*Evangelium Vitae* and *Ut Unum Sint*), some Catholics joked that they were members of the "Encyclical-of-the-Month Club." July 1998, in those circles, was known as the "Apostolic-Letter-of-the-Week Club," as John Paul issued three major documents addressing the integrity of theological teaching, the special character of Sunday, and the role of national conferences of bishops.

Ad Tuendam Fidem [In Protecting the Faith] was published on June 30 in order, as John Paul put it, to "fill a gap" in canon law. Since 1989, teachers of Catholic theology had been required to affirm a "Profession of Faith" by which they pledged to teach as true what the Catholic Church taught to be true. The 1983 Code of Canon Law, however, had not fully specified the procedures to be taken in dealing with those who violated what they had sworn to uphold and teach. *Ad Tuendam Fidem* filled the gap by making three additions in the relevant canons. It was a bit of legal housekeeping, primarily of interest to canonists. Of considerably more interest, though, was a commentary on the Profession of Faith which the Congregation for the Doctrine of the Faith issued concurrently with *Ad Tuendam Fidem*. The commentary discussed three levels of authoritative teaching: truths held to be divinely revealed (e.g., the truths of the Creed); truths linked to revelation by "logical necessity" (e.g., the condemnation of euthanasia in *Evangelium Vitae*) or by "historical necessity" (e.g., the legitimacy of a papal election); and truths taught by the "ordinary magisterium" of the Pope and the bishops, even if they have not been formally defined. The tripartite schema was not an innovation, but the commentary also included examples of each level of authoritative teaching. One example used to illustrate a truth of the second level (i.e., a truth linked to revelation by historical necessity) was Leo XIII's 1896 declaration that Anglican ordinations were invalid. This immediately touched off an ecumenical controversy with Anglicans and a theological controversy within Catholicism. Months later, it remained unclear whether the examples used in the commentary had been as carefully thought through as the commentary's description of the three levels of authoritative teaching.[79] The documents were released without a press conference; neither bishops nor their doctrinal advisers were given any advance information about the apostolic letter or the commentary. The result was that what ought to have been presented as an effort to ensure the integrity of theological teaching on Catholic campuses was reported as another skirmish in an ecclesiastical power game.

Dies Domini [The Day of the Lord] was signed on May 31, Pentecost Sunday, and released on July 6, 1998. An apostolic letter "on keeping the Lord's Day holy," it was far more than an admonitory warning to Catholics who were lax in their Sunday Mass attendance.[80] *Dies Domini* was in fact a complement to *Laborem Exercens*. The 1981 encyclical had analyzed the "Gospel of work." The 1998 apostolic letter discussed the sanctification of time through keeping the "Lord's Day" as a day of worship, leisure, rest, and recreation.

Sunday, John Paul writes, is the "Easter which returns week by week." As such, it is the day that recalls the creation of the world, anticipates the completion of the world's story in the Kingdom of God, and draws our attention to "the true fulcrum of history," the resurrection of Christ.[81] The modern institution of the "weekend" meets the human need for rest. But only a day kept as the "Lord's Day" can fully meet the parallel human need for celebration.[82]

The breadth of horizon provided by the "Lord's Day" enables human beings to rest and celebrate in a fully human way, because it reflects the "seventh day of creation," the day on which God did not "look to new accomplishments" but enjoyed "the beauty of what [had] already been achieved." Chief among those achievements was the human person, "the crown of creation," with whom God wants to "enter a pact of love." The "Lord's Day," John Paul suggests, discloses the "nuptial shape of the relationship which God wants to establish with the creature made in his own image."[83] By reminding us of our origins and destiny, and by relating that destiny to the liberation won by the risen Christ, the "Lord's Day" teaches us, week in and week out, that we are greater that we can imagine.

In this context, the obligation of Sunday worship is not an arbitrary law imposed by the Church but "an indispensable element of our Christian identity," John Paul writes. For Sunday is not only the first day but the "eighth day," the day after the Sabbath, the day that looks forward in anticipation to the day without end, eternal life in communion with God.[84] As such, it expresses who we are in the most profound sense of our created and redeemed humanity.[85] The "law" of Sunday Mass attendance is the juridical expression of a law inscribed on the human heart.

The third apostolic letter released in July 1998, *Apostolos Suos* [His Apostles], was an effort to guide the development of national conferences of bishops, a post–Vatican II innovation in the Church's life. Once again, the headlines set the letter in a political context: "Pope Tightens Grip by Rome On Its Bishops," as the *New York Times* had it.[86] Once again, the deeper issues were minimized if not ignored.

The question of where national bishops' conferences and their attendant bureaucracies "fit" into the theology of the Church was not a simple one. The college of bishops cannot delegate its teaching authority to any subset of bishops. On the other hand, the Council had urged the formation of national conferences so that the bishops of a country or a region could support one another in their pastoral work. The question was what kind of teaching authority these national conferences had, in addition to their role as pastoral resources for individual bishops.

Apostolos Suos teaches that national conferences of bishops cannot substitute themselves for the individual authority of local bishops and that their authority as corporate entities can only be exercised in a binding way when what they teach is confirmed by the Bishop of Rome. This was not, as widely reported, an attempt to "rein in" bishops' conferences. It was an expression of a basic theological truth taught by Vatican II, that the college of bishops exercises its authority under the authority of its head, the Pope. If the Church, as the Council taught, is a *communio* or "communion," then the question of the relationship of national conferences of bishops to the Bishop of Rome cannot be understood as one in which the conferences' "gain" is the papacy's "loss." Precisely the opposite is true, at least as Vatican II understood the relationship between bishops and the Bishop of Rome in the *communio* of the Church. On this understanding, it is the relationship of the college to its head that confirms the college in its authority. A careful reading of *Apostolos Suos* suggested that national conferences, far from resisting a close working relationship with Rome, should actively seek to have their most authoritative statements approved and ratified by the Holy See. That, according to the theology of Vatican II, was how those statements participated in the teaching authority vested in the Pope and the college of bishops.[87]

THE ASTONISHING HOLY SPIRIT

In its *Dogmatic Constitution on the Church*, the Second Vatican Council had taught that charismatic gifts, "special graces" given by the Holy Spirit to individuals or groups, were a source of holiness in the Church.[88] The tremendous expansion of renewal movements throughout world Catholicism in the years since Vatican II seemed to John Paul to confirm this teaching, and to provide empirical evidence that the Council had been inspired by the Holy Spirit to prepare the Church for an evangelically vigorous third millennium.[89]

As in past centuries, the explosive growth of movements inspired by charismatic individuals had caused tensions with the institutional Church, as parishes and dioceses tried to find a place for renewal groups that sometimes didn't fit easily into established patterns of doing the Church's business. Karol Wojtyła had been willing to live with that tension as archbishop of Kraków, and encouraging renewal movements had been one of the leitmotifs of his pontificate. The Pope invited members of these movements from around the world to come to Rome for the Vigil of Pentecost to celebrate a new moment of "ecclesial maturity," gathered together around Peter, the symbol of the Church's unity. On May 30, 1998, half a million accepted, spilling out of St. Peter's Square, down the Via della Conciliazione toward the Tiber, and into the rabbit warren of streets near the Vatican, in the largest celebration of the Church's charismatic element in Roman history.[90]

Testimonies were given by Chiara Lubich, founder of the Focolare movement, which takes fostering the unity of the human race as its mission; Kiko Argüello, leader of the Neocatechumenal Way, which is dedicated to the evangelization of the unchurched and the reevangelization of those poorly educated in their faith; Jean Vanier, founder of the L'Arche Community, which works and lives with the mentally handicapped; and Monsignor Luigi Giussani, founder of Comunione e Liberazione, an Italian-based renewal movement that had spread throughout the world.[91] In his address, John Paul spoke of their meeting in frankly biblical terms. It was, he said, "as though what happened in Jerusalem 2,000 years ago were being repeated this evening in this square. . . . The Holy Spirit is here with us! It is he who is the soul of this marvelous event of ecclesial communion."

As for the tensions that had been experienced between the movements and the institutional Church during the past thirty years, that was normal. "An unexpected newness . . . is sometimes disruptive," leading to "prejudices and reservations" by some institutional leaders and "presumptions and excesses" in some movements. All of that, the Pope declared, should be understood as a "testing period," in which the truth of what seemed to be Spirit-inspired charisms was being verified by the Church's teaching authorities, the bishops in communion with the Bishop of Rome. Now, John Paul concluded, "a new stage is unfolding," in which renewal movements would bring the "mature fruits of communion and commitment" to the Church and the institutional

Church would be renewed by the vibrant Christian life being lived in movements that hadn't emerged out of the Church's standard structures. "The institutional and the charismatic" were both essential to the Church's constitution, and if the charismatic element was subject to the pastoral judgment of the bishops, the institutional Church always had to remember that "whenever the Holy Spirit intervenes, he leaves people astonished. He brings about events of amazing newness; he radically changes persons and history."[92]

How, precisely, the new renewal movements and communities would eventually be fitted into the Church's legal and institutional structure was an issue for the twenty-first century. Nothing quite like this had ever happened before: these lay-led movements, some of them including men and women who had taken permanent vows of poverty and celibacy while continuing to work professionally in the world, were neither traditional religious orders nor religious societies of the sort found in every Catholic parish. Throughout the Church's history, it had been the popes, rather than the local bishops, who had encouraged charismatically inspired renewal movements.[93] That pattern was replicated by John Paul II, with consequences for the Church in the third millennium that are sure to be profound, and likely to be surprising.

Be Not Afraid, Again

Pope John Paul II's twentieth anniversary, October 16, 1998, fell in the middle of an extraordinary week. The previous Sunday, October 11, the Pope canonized Blessed Edith Stein, St. Teresa Benedicta of the Cross in her Carmelite name, before an enormous congregation of Romans and pilgrims from Poland, Germany, France, the Netherlands, Spain, the United States, and elsewhere. One of the concelebrating priests, a member of the Eastern-rite Melkite Church, was the father of Teresa Benedicta McCarty, the little girl miraculously saved from a lethal overdose of medicine by the intercession of Edith Stein.

In presenting what he termed "this *eminent daughter of Israel and faithful daughter of the Church* as a saint to the whole world," John Paul was lifting up the example of a woman whom he described to dinner companions as a "synthesis" of the twentieth century and its troubled quest for a genuine humanism.[94] Edith Stein, John Paul said in his homily, knew that "the love of Christ and human freedom are intertwined, because *love and truth have an intrinsic relationship.* The quest for truth and its expression in love did not seem at odds to her; on the contrary, she realized that they call for one another . . . St. Teresa Benedicta of the Cross says to us all: *Do not accept anything as the truth if it lacks love. And do not accept anything as love which lacks truth!* One without the other becomes a destructive lie."[95]

This daughter of Israel and of Catholicism had died in the gas chambers of Auschwitz-Birkenau after dismissing the suggestion of rescue: "Why should I be spared," she had asked. "Is it not right that I should gain no advantage from my baptism? If I cannot share the lot of my brothers and sisters, my life, in a certain sense, is destroyed." Thus, John Paul said, when the Church of the third millennium celebrated the feast day of St. Teresa Benedicta of the Cross, Edith Stein, "we must also remember the *Shoah,* that cruel plan to exterminate a people—a plan to which millions of our Jewish brothers and sisters fell victim. *May the Lord let his face shine upon them and give them peace* (cf. *Numbers,* 6.25)."[96] With the canonization of Edith Stein, John Paul seemed to be suggesting, a remembrance of all the Jewish martyrs of the *Shoah* had become part of the annual liturgical rhythm of Catholic life.[97]

The following Sunday, October 18, John Paul marked his twentieth anniversary as Pope and the fortieth anniversary of his consecration as a bishop at another outdoor Mass in St. Peter's Square. The celebration was organized by the Diocese of Rome. Some forty cardinals, 100 bishops, and 800 priests, many from Roman parishes, concelebrated the Mass with the Pope. Vested in a magnificent green and gold chasuble, a gift from the churches of Rome, John Paul preached to more than 100,000 congregants on a text from that Sunday's assigned Gospel reading: "When the Son of man comes, will he find faith on earth?" (*Luke* 18.8).

That, the Pope said, was the question that had challenged every Bishop of Rome for almost 2,000 years. It was a question inextricably intertwined with the question Christ had asked Peter after the resurrection: "Do you love me?" (*John* 21.17). That was what Christ had asked the archbishop of Kraków on the afternoon of October 16, 1978. The question put to Karol Wojtyła that day had been "Do you accept your election?" The evangelical question embedded in that legal formula was Christ's: "Do you love me?"—a question at once magnetic and terrifying, for to love Christ meant to walk his way of the cross.

"After twenty years of service in the Chair of Peter," John Paul said, "I cannot fail to ask myself a few questions today. Have you observed all this? Are you a diligent and watchful teacher of faith in the Church? Have you sought to bring the great work of the Second Vatican Council closer to the people of today? Have you tried to satisfy the expectations of believers within the Church, and that hunger for truth which is felt in the world outside the Church?"[98]

The very asking of those questions, after twenty years, was a moving testimony to the Pope's humility and his enduring sense of responsibility. When children from a Roman parish brought him gifts after Mass and he embraced each of them in turn, the emotion of the moment overflowed—the children were crying, the Pope was shedding tears, and so were thousands in the square. The athletic, vigorous John Paul II of twenty years before had passed into history. Those watching saw something even more compelling: a man who had so evidently spent his life out in service to his Lord was still asking, "Have I loved enough?"

Later in the week, in response to a dinner guest's anniversary congratulations, the Pope said, with a sense of wonderment, "Twenty years the Pope . . . forty years a bishop. . . ."[99]

Prophet of the Twenty-first Century

The canonization of Edith Stein and an emotionally rich twentieth-anniversary celebration were the bookends of a week that also saw the publication of John Paul's thirteenth encyclical, *Fides et Ratio* [Faith and Reason], which was released at a press conference on October 15. The timing could not have been more appropriate.

It was the first major papal statement on the relationship between faith and reason in almost 120 years. The First Vatican Council had taught in 1869–1870 that human beings could know the existence of God through reason, and Leo XIII's 1879 encyclical, *Aeterni Patris*, had proposed the philosophy and theology of Thomas Aquinas as the model for a synthesis of faith and reason. But much had happened in world civilization since the late nineteenth century—not least, philosophy's drastically diminished confidence in its capacity to know the truth of things.

What the Pope describes as philosophy's "false modesty" had precluded its asking the large questions—Why is there something rather than nothing? What is good and what is evil? What is happiness and what is delusion? What awaits me after this life?[100] In addition to demeaning philosophy's true vocation, which was to be a servant of the truth, this "false modesty" had also opened the door to a culture dominated by various kinds of human hubris: an instrumental view of other human beings, a false faith in technology, the triumph of the will-to-power. The lethal effects of those forms of false pride pockmark the twentieth century.[101] It is long past time, John Paul suggests, for philosophy to recover that sense of awe and wonder that directs it to transcendent truth. The alternative is another century of tears.

Philosophy ordered to transcendent truth is also crucial for religion, John Paul argues. Ancient Greek philosophy helped purge religion of superstition. The temptation to superstition is perennial, though, and sometimes takes the form of the claim that faith is not subject to rational analysis. In today's cultural climate, that has meant stressing faith as solely a matter of feeling and experience.[102] Citing St. Augustine, John Paul flatly rejects such "fideism": "Believing is nothing other than to think with assent. . . . Believers are also thinkers: in believing, they think and in thinking, they believe. . . . If faith does not think it is nothing."[103] On the edge of a twenty-first century that seems destined to be heavily influenced by resurgent religious faith, this call to a reasonable faith looms large indeed. If faith and reason do not work together, a revival of religious conviction will not provide a secure foundation for human dignity. For that dignity is ultimately grounded, John Paul is convinced, in the human capacity to know the truth, adhere to it, and live it.

To those "postmodern" theorists willing to allow religion a place at the table of intellectual life because religious truth is one possible truth among others, John Paul says, "No, thank you." Unless thinking is open to what *Fides et Ratio* terms the "horizon of the ultimate," it will inevitably turn in on itself and be locked in the prison of solipsism. The marriage of ancient Greek philosophy and Christian theology in the early centuries of the first millennium taught a wiser lesson: human beings can know what is true, what is good, and what is beautiful, even if we can never know them completely. Recovering that sense of confidence, John Paul asserts, is essential to reconstituting a true humanism in the third millennium. The path to a wiser, nobler, more humane twenty-first century runs through the wisdom of the first centuries of encounter between Jerusalem and Athens.

The tragic separations of reason and faith, science and religion, philosophy and theology have been the fault of both philosophers and theologians, according to the Pope. When theologians demean reason and philosophers deny the possibility of revelation, both are diminished, humanity is impoverished, and the development of a true humanism is frustrated. "Faith and reason," John Paul writes, "are like two wings on which the human spirit rises to the contemplation of truth."[104] We can be sure, he suggests in *Fides et Ratio*, that we will need to fly with both wings in the millennium ahead. The quest for truth is an instinct built into us. And the grandeur of the human person, the Pope concludes, is that we can choose "to enter the truth, to make a home under the shade of Wisdom and dwell there."[105]

Twenty years after beginning his pontificate with the clarion call, "Be not afraid!" John Paul II continued to preach a Gospel of courage in *Fides et Ratio*. "Be not afraid of reason," the encyclical proposes. Be not afraid of the truth. For the truth, dispelling delusions, will set humanity free in the deepest meaning of liberation. The Pope of freedom, the Pope of a new humanism, had remained faithful to his vision for twenty years. Confounding the expectations of skeptics and enemies alike, he had made the Catholic Church the premier institutional defender of human rights and human reason. In doing so, he had helped create the possibility of a more humane future, and had become the prophet of the new century about to unfold.

EPILOGUE

The Third Millennium

To See the Sun Rise

On the evening of November 13, 1994, Pope John Paul II and five guests gathered in a small salon in the papal apartment to ponder the mysteries of chosenness.

The occasion was the premiere of a one-woman play written and performed by Danuta Michałowska, an original member of the Rhapsodic Theater. Miss Michałowska had been struck by the fact that St. Augustine, writing about his fondness for Virgil's *Aeneid*, had expressed pity for the woman Aeneas had left at Jupiter's command. But what about the woman Augustine himself had left behind, the concubine with whom he lived for years, who had borne his son, Adeodatus, and who is never named in Augustine's *Confessions*? The imaginative attempt to think herself back into the situation of this woman-without-a-name, caught up in the mystery of God's providential design for Augustine and trying to understand her place in that design, became Danuta Michałowska's play—*I Without Name*.

Prior to the performance, Miss Michałowska had visited the Roman Basilica of St. Paul Outside the Walls. Hearing a stir and thinking it might be the beginning of a Mass, which she wanted to attend, Danuta Michałowska found herself on the periphery of a small funeral, with a casket, a priest, and perhaps twenty people. Sitting behind the congregation she thought of the funeral of her woman-without-a-name, whom she had taken to calling "Elissa" (the name of Aeneas's lover), and imagined that it would have been something like this— a death unnoticed by history, a small group, a slightly shabby ceremony. Remembering the tears she had shed while writing her play, Miss Michałowska began to pray for the woman-without-a-name, her "Elissa"—and then heard the priest officiating at the funeral say, "Let us pray for Elissa . . ."

November 13 happened to be Augustine's 1,640th birthday. After Miss Michałowska had performed *I Without Name* for the Pope and his guests, John Paul hosted a supper for the playwright-actress and the small audience. His old friend's play had moved him. He had had, he reminisced, a similar sense of being marked by God—of having the finger of God on his life. It was not the kind of chosenness one would necessarily seek out. In addition to its gifts, there was an awesome, even terrible, quality to chosenness. It involved strange roads, odd circumstances, the unexpected and the tragic. Like Augustine and the woman-without-a-name, he had understood that he was not, in the final analysis, in charge of his own life.

What had happened to him, and to the lives that had touched and shaped his own, had happened for a reason. As it had to Augustine and to "I without name."[1]

By the Numbers

Numbers cannot disclose the truth of a man's life "from inside." But numbers can illustrate the scope of a man's activity. The numbers involved in the pontificate of John Paul II are staggering.

By October 16, 1998, the twentieth anniversary of his election, Karol Wojtyła had served as Pope for longer than all but ten men in history. In two decades, he had made eighty-four foreign pilgrimages and 134 pastoral visits inside Italy, traveling 670,878 miles, or 2.8 times the distance between the earth and the moon. During 720 days of pilgrimage outside Rome, he had delivered 3,078 addresses and homilies while speaking to hundreds of millions of men, women, and children, in person and through the media. No human being in the history of the world had ever spoken to so many people, in so many different cultural contexts. He had made more than 700 pastoral visits in Rome itself, to prisons, universities, religious institutes, convents, seminaries, nursing homes, hospitals, and 274 of the diocese's 325 parishes.

At his twentieth anniversary, his written magisterium included thirteen encyclicals, nine apostolic constitutions, thirty-six apostolic letters, fifteen other formal letters to particular persons or groups (including his groundbreaking letters to women and to children), nine post-synodal apostolic exhortations, 600 *ad limina* addresses, and thousands of audience discourses. The *Insegnamenti di Giovanni Paolo II*, the printed record of his teaching, cover ten linear feet of shelf space in libraries. John Paul II was also responsible for promulgating two new codes of canon law and the *Catechism of the Catholic Church*, the first instrument of its kind in more than 400 years. In 144 ceremonies celebrating the universal call to holiness, he had beatified 798 men and women and canonized 280 new saints.

In two decades, he presided over and actively participated in five Ordinary Synods of Bishops, one Extraordinary Synod, and six Special Synods. In addition, he met constantly and at length with the world's bishops during their quinquennial *ad limina* visits to Rome.

Between October 1978 and October 1998 he held 877 general audiences attended by 13,833,000 people, and received an additional 150,000–180,000 each year in special group audiences. Assuming an average of five private audiences per day, the total of these more intimate personal encounters easily tops 15,000—and this does not include his daily conversations with guests at lunch and dinner, in the papal apartment or during his pilgrimages abroad.

In seven consistories he had created 159 new cardinals. At his twentieth anniversary, 101 of the 115 members of the College eligible to vote in a conclave were his nominees. During that same period, he also named some 2,650 of the Catholic Church's approximately 4,200 bishops.

During the first twenty years of his pontificate, the Holy See established diplomatic relations at the ambassadorial level with sixty-four countries and restored such relations with six others, bringing to 168 the total number of countries with which the Holy See enjoyed full diplomatic exchange.

John Paul II had reshaped the Church's institutional face by his 1988 reorganization of the Roman Curia and by creating new entities to meet new needs, including the John Paul II Foundation for the Sahel in 1984, the Populorum Progressio Foundation for Latin America in 1992, and two Pontifical Academies, for Life and for the Social Sciences, in 1994. The Pope also inspired the creation of the John Paul II Institute for Studies on Marriage and the Family at the Pontifical Lateran University. By 1998, the John Paul II Institute had affiliates in Washington, D.C., Mexico City, and Valencia. The influence of these advanced academic centers on Catholic moral theology was already being felt on the Pope's twentieth anniversary, and it seemed likely that that influence would expand in the twenty-first century to touch dogmatic theology, philosophy, and related fields.[2]

These numbers and institutional facts tell a story of remarkable personal energy. Inside the numbers, it can be argued, is an even more impressive story of accomplishment that will shape the life of the Catholic Church—and the innumerable worlds-within-worlds of humanity that the Catholic Church touches—well into the third millennium of Christian history.

THE IMPACT

To assess a papacy before its conclusion is a difficult business. The task is slightly less daunting in this instance, because John Paul II's pontificate has been a series of variations on the one great theme he announced at his installation and in his 1979 inaugural encyclical, *Redemptor Hominis*: Christian humanism as the Church's response to the crisis of world civilization at the end of the twentieth century. As he prepared to lead the Church into the celebration of the Great Jubilee of 2000, eight historic accomplishments of the pontificate of John Paul II could be identified.

John Paul II radically recast the papacy for the twenty-first century and the third millennium by returning the Office of Peter to its evangelical roots. The world and the Church no longer think of the pope as the chief executive officer of the Roman Catholic Church; the world and the Church experience the pope as a pastor, an evangelist, and a witness. John Paul II broke the modern papal mold he inherited, not simply by being the first Slavic pope in history and the first non-Italian pope in centuries, but by living the kind of papal primacy envisioned in the New Testament: Peter as the Church's first evangelist, the Church's first witness to the truths revealed in the life, death, and resurrection of Jesus Christ. It is very difficult to imagine a twenty-first-century pontificate that deliberately returns to the bureaucratic-managerial papal model that reached its apogee in the pontificate of Pius XII. John Paul II has decisively renovated the papacy for the twenty-first century by retrieving and renewing the evangelical primacy of Peter's office in the first-century Church. Here, perhaps, is the most telling example of John Paul II, the radical—the man of bold innovation for whom change means returning to the Church's roots, which he believes are expressions of Christ's will for his Church.

This dramatic renovation of the papacy was not accomplished by personal fiat or by reason of a singular personality, but by a Pope who is self-consciously the heir and legatee of the Second Vatican Council. To grasp the pontificate of John Paul II "from inside" means recognizing that John Paul has sought to secure the legacy of Vatican II as an epic spiritual event—the Council at which the Catholic Church, guided by the Holy Spirit, came to grips with modernity by developing a theologically enriched sense of its unique mission in and for the world.

No two conciliar texts have been so frequently cited in the teaching of John Paul II as sections 22 and 24 of *Gaudium et Spes*, the Council's *Pastoral Constitution on the Church in the Modern World*. The Pope's debt to Vatican II, his profound conviction that the Council must be understood in religious rather than political or ideological terms, and his understanding of the Council's proposal to the world are synoptically captured here. In *Gaudium et Spes* 22, the Council Fathers taught that Jesus Christ reveals the face of God *and* the true meaning of human existence; in *Gaudium et Spes* 24, the Council taught that the meaning of human life was to be found in self-giving, not self-assertion. The Law of the Gift written into the human heart is an expression of the self-giving love that constitutes the interior life of God—Father, Son, and Holy Spirit. To live the Law of the Gift is to enter, by way of anticipation, into the communion with God for which humanity was created from the beginning. Here, *Gaudium et Spes* told the modern world, is a destiny greater than you can imagine. And it is yours because you are greater than you think you are.[3]

In John Paul II's understanding of the Council, everything else Vatican II did—its exploration of Christian personalism, its definition of the Church as a *communio* of believers, its renovation of the Church's worship, its dialogue with science, democracy, and the sexual revolution, its defense of religious freedom as the first of human rights—is a further explication of these two great themes: Christ, the redeemer of the world, reveals the astonishing truth about the human condition and our final destiny; self-giving love is the path along which human freedom finds its fulfillment in human flourishing. In implementing Vatican II in Kraków, and in twenty years of a pontificate inspired by the conviction that God intended the Council to prepare the entire Church for a twenty-first-century springtime of evangelization, Karol Wojtyła has worked to secure the legacy of Vatican II as the Council of freedom—in the conviction that freedom is the great aspiration *and* the great dilemma of humanity on the edge of a new century and a new millennium. The properly evangelical response to the problem of freedom, he believes, is to be found in service. One great service the Church can do the modern world is to remind it that freedom is ordered to truth and finds its fulfillment in goodness. That was what Christ meant when he said that knowing the truth would set human beings free (see *John* 8.32). That is what the Church should propose to the late modern world as the means to realize its great aspiration.

That, he was and is convinced, is what Vatican II was for.

That conviction inspired John Paul II's public accomplishments. His crucial role in the collapse of European communism cannot be understood as the accomplishment of a deft statesman. It can only be grasped "from inside" as the achievement of a courageous pastor, determined to speak truth to power and convinced that the word of truth, spoken clearly and forcefully enough, is the most effective tool against the tyranny of totalitarianism. By inspiring the revolution of conscience that made possible the nonviolent Revolution of 1989 against Marxism-Leninism, John Paul helped restore the political freedom of his Slavic brethren behind the iron curtain. At the same time, he challenged broadly accepted understandings of the dynamics of history. History, he helped demonstrate, is driven by culture, and at the heart of culture is cult, or religion. By lifting up the witness of hundreds of thousands of Christian confessors against communist tyranny, the pontificate of John Paul II demonstrated in action that Christian conviction can be the agent of human liberation.

The "priority of culture" was a lesson the Pope also applied to the quest for freedom in East Asia and Latin America, to considerable effect, and it was the challenge he posed to democracies old and new in the wake of the communist crackup. If culture is the engine of history, then free economies and democratic political communities must be built upon the foundation of a vibrant public moral culture, capable of disciplining and directing the tremendous human energies set loose by freedom. In challenging the freedom of indifference and proposing freedom for excellence in the encyclicals *Centesimus Annus, Veritatis Splendor,* and *Evangelium Vitae,* John Paul reconfigured the Church's social doctrine and scouted the terrain of public life in the twenty-first century, in which science and technology will make certain that questions of what constitutes human life and membership in the human community dominate the world's social and political agenda. Freedom is always a fragile commodity. Its most secure foundation, John Paul has suggested time and again, is a recognition of the dignity of the human person as the bearer of rights endowed by God.

The Christian humanism of Vatican II also inspired John Paul's unprecedented and historic initiatives in search of Christian unity, in quest of a new relationship between the Catholic Church and living Judaism, and in dialogue with other world religions.

With the pontificate of John Paul II, the Catholic Church entered the ecumenical movement for the duration, and in doing so reshaped the contours of the quest for Christian unity. While some veterans of the twentieth-century ecumenical movement were abandoning the search for a unity rooted in a common faith, the Pope urged that the only unity worth pursuing was unity in the truth Christ had bequeathed to his Church. Concurrently, John Paul gave ecumenism a new public thrust, suggesting that Christianity's defense of the unity of the human race was threatened by the Church's failure to live fully the unity that was Christ's gift to his people. Following Vatican II, John Paul argued that the *communio*, the "communion," of the Church had never been completely broken and that all Christians were in a true but imperfect communion with each other and with the Catholic Church, whether they acknowledged that or in fact rejected it. The ecumenical task is to express this abiding unity and communion in a fuller way. How to do that, he suggested, required Protestant and Orthodox Christians to think, with their Catholic brothers and sisters, about what it means for the Office of Peter to be a ministry in service to the Church's unity.

John Paul II has received numerous accolades for his dramatic initiatives in Catholic-Jewish relations, but perhaps without their full import being generally recognized. In the twenty-first century, Catholics and Jews stand on the edge of a new theological conversation, of a range and depth unimaginable in more than 1,900 years. If the future of freedom depends on a recognition of the dignity of the human person created by God, then the witnesses to that truth—the communities that call Abraham their father in faith and that take the Ten Commandments as their fundamental moral code—must deepen their mutual understanding of what it means to be an elect people, called to live as a light to the nations. If, sometime during the third millennium, faithful Jews and Christians begin to talk with each other again about election, covenant, and their common messianic hope, it will likely be recognized that the seeds of that reconvened conversation were planted by the pontificate of John Paul II, in response to the Second Vatican Council's teaching in *Nostra Aetate*.

The World Day of Prayer for Peace at Assisi in 1986 was the most visible expression of John Paul's conviction that all truth is related to the one Truth, who is God. That conviction also undergirded his initiatives with Islam, which holds a distinctive place within the tradition of Abraham, his dialogue with religious leaders like the Dalai Lama, and his approach to other great world religions. Respect for the religious convictions of others without compromising one's own convictions seems, to many secular people, an impossibility. Unless that possibility can be created, the world of the twenty-first century, shaped as it will be by resurgent religious forces, is destined for serious conflict. Previews of that conflict were evident throughout the pontificate of John Paul II, in the Balkans, Sudan, the Middle East, the Indian subcontinent, and southeast Asia. By insisting on religious freedom as the source and safeguard of all human rights, John Paul exemplified an alternative to sectarian violence and state-enforced secularism in situations where the deepest convictions of human beings are in conflict, not conversation.

Finally, the historic accomplishment of John Paul II must be measured in its impact on hundreds of millions of human lives, considered one by one and "from inside." For twenty years, the Pope has inspired men and women, young and old alike, to live out the consequences of the challenge he preached at his papal installation: "Be not afraid!" At the end of the eighth decade of a century of fear, some were surely inclined, on October 22, 1978, to dismiss this as the most fragile romanticism. They were mistaken. That summons to live without fear, to live beyond fear, so transparently evident in the life of Karol Wojtyła, changed innumerable individual lives. By doing so, John Paul changed the course of history.

Taken together, these eight achievements—the renovated papacy, the full implementation of Vatican II, the collapse of communism, the clarification of the moral challenges facing the free society, the insertion of ecumenism into the heart of Catholicism, the new dialogue with Judaism, the redefinition of interreligious dialogue, and the personal inspiration that has changed countless lives—make it plausible to argue that the pontificate of John Paul II has been the most consequential since the sixteenth-century Reformation. As the immediate post-Reformation period and the Council of Trent defined the Church's relationship to an emerging modern world, it is reasonable to suggest that Vatican II as authoritatively interpreted by the pontificate of John Paul II has defined the Church's relationship to whatever is coming after "the modern world."

No one knows whether, in the long view of history, Vatican II will be judged a reprise of the Fifth Lateran Council (1512–1517), a reforming Council that failed in its mission, or by analogy to Trent (1545–1563), a reforming Council that shaped Catholicism and the world for almost half a millennium. There is great and enduring good to be found in the texts of Vatican II. Whether the Council is remembered centuries from now as a great achievement or a disappointing failure will depend on how those texts are transformed into the actual life of the Church.[4]

Given the threats to human dignity that human ingenuity and wickedness are certain to create, it must be hoped that John Paul II's heroic effort to secure the Council's legacy will make it more likely that historians of the future will look on Vatican II as another Trent, not another Lateran V. The false freedom of indifference and self-assertion that characterizes much of the developed world at the beginning of the twenty-first century may prevail over the freedom for excellence proposed by John Paul. If so, the Church will survive, believers are convinced. But what the Pope characterized at the United Nations in 1995 as "one of the great dynamics of human history"—the human quest for freedom—will be in the gravest jeopardy.[5]

THE CRITIQUES

On his twentieth anniversary in 1998, and despite an outpouring of affection and esteem, it remained an open question whether the Catholic Church itself had grasped the significance of the pontificate of John Paul II.

Some argued that the Pope's inclination to "run the Church like a seminar" (as one veteran Curialist put it) was responsible for the sluggish response of the Roman bureaucracy and many of the world's bishops to John Paul's initiatives. Others charged that the Pope, whose office was intended to serve the unity of the Church, was in fact the cause of great divisiveness in Catholicism. There was no question that John Paul had become a figure of contempt to many Catholic intellectuals. Well before his papal jubilee, the man who had been the great "progressive" hope in 1978 had become the target of progressive intellectual animosity, even if that animosity was sometimes tempered by respect for his public accomplishments as a defender of human rights. Beyond these critical assessments by intellectuals and activists lay the fact that world Catholicism had barely begun to come to grips with John Paul II's vision of an evangelically assertive and culture-forming Church of disciples, who lived the universal call to holiness in witness to the world and were supported in that mission by ordained ministers who understood their vocation in terms of service, not of power.

The Conventional Critique

Vigorously promoted by the world media and deeply influenced by the political interpretation of Vatican II as a contest for power between good "liberals" and bad "conservatives," the conventional critique of John Paul II, from inside as well as outside the Church, is well-known. On this reading, John Paul has been an authoritarian, a centralizer of power who has blocked the implementation of Vatican II's call for a recovery of collegial responsibility in the Church. More often than not, this alleged authoritarianism is attributed to the Pope's Polish roots. The conventional critique also depicts John Paul II as intellectually repressive, a misogynist unsympathetic to the concerns of contemporary women, and a virtual Manichaean whose "rigid" sexual morality has rendered the Church's sexual ethic ridiculous in the eyes of its people, especially married couples.

Ultimately, history, and the Lord of history, will judge whether there is merit to this depiction of John Paul II. History's judgment will have to consider certain facts, which raise serious questions about this familiar critique.

That John Paul II understands himself to be a man of the Second Vatican Council is indisputable, on the public record. That he has spent more time in conversation with the Church's bishops than any Pope in modern history (and perhaps in all of history) is also a matter of record. So is the fact that he has devoted vast personal energy to the Synod of Bishops. The Synod process is surely open to refinement and improvement, as are the processes guiding the selection of bishops and their quinquennial *ad limina* visits to Rome. But the charge that John Paul II is out of touch with the world's bishops is highly implausible. Whether the bishops report fully and accurately the concerns and conditions of their local Churches is for them to judge. Others can only note that the Pope has made himself available to his brothers in the episcopate in an unprecedented way, and has done so because he understands this to be a central part of his task.

A subtler variation on the conventional critique suggests that the pontificate of John Paul II has so identified the Church with the papacy that the net result has been to diminish the initiative of the world's bishops, priests, and laity. A charismatic Pope in a hierarchical organization like the Catholic Church—and in a media age—certainly raises the bar of expectation for virtually every other person in a position of formal authority in the Church. But there is a deeper, theological question at stake here, an issue posed to the Church by contemporary history.

The Office of Peter, as Catholicism understands it, is what Hans Urs von Balthasar has called the "external reference point" for the Church's interior unity. That interior unity is not ethnic, linguistic, or political-philosophical, like the unity of a nation-state. The unity of the Church is founded on the celebration of the Eucharist and the participation of the Church-in-the-world in the communion of saints who are already with the Lord in glory. As Catholicism becomes more manifestly a world Church, embodying the truth it bears in a rich diversity of cultures, it can be argued that the Church has even greater need of a visible, authoritative, external reference point for its unity than in its first two millennia.[6] John Paul II has demonstrated the importance of that "external reference point" for the Church's vitality and its unity-amid-plurality in venues from Seoul to Rio de Janeiro, from Kinshasa to Kraków, and from New York to Anchorage.

The charge of intellectual repression must contend with the fact that John Paul II's has been a pontificate of great theological and philosophical creativity, beginning with *Redemptor Hominis* and the *Theology of the Body* and continuing through *Dives in Misericordia* and *Veritatis Splendor* to *Tertio Millennio Adveniente* and *Fides et Ratio*. Even a cursory reading of John Paul's texts discloses a far greater openness to modern and contemporary intellectual methods and insights than was evident in previous papacies. That the Pope, a working intellectual, has been critical of certain fashions in post-conciliar

Catholic theology and philosophy has undoubtedly made many Catholic intellectuals unhappy. But here, too, history will have its say.

The twentieth century has, in the main, been a very bad century for intellectuals, and especially for intellectuals attracted by the allure of power. Heidegger and Sartre, two immensely influential philosophers, illustrate the point in their respective attractions to Hitler's Germany and Stalin's Soviet Union. We cannot know how the future will judge John Paul's critiques of post-conciliar theology's dalliance with Marxism, and his challenge to the sorry public effects of philosophy's entrapment in the prison of solipsism. For the moment, those who are not professional academics cannot help wondering why a man should be thought intellectually obtuse for judging Marxism fatally flawed, or for thinking that human beings can know the truth of things, however imperfectly. As for repression in the direct, personal sense, very few Catholic theologians have in fact been disciplined during this pontificate (public action was taken against six in twenty years), and those who have been were treated far more mildly than in the past.[7] The same can be said for wayward bishops. Thirty-five years after Vatican II, John Paul II's intellectual critics, and in some instances his avowed enemies, remain firmly in control of most theological faculties in the Western world. If this is repression, it is repression of a very inefficient sort.

The generation of theologians who were so influential during and immediately after the Council may feel its intellectual hegemony and ecclesiastical influence threatened by the teaching of John Paul II. If that is the case, an irony should be noted. This fear of losing control of the Church's intellectual agenda puts these theologians in the same position as the much-maligned guardians of Catholic intellectual orthodoxy in the 1940s and 1950s, whose influence on the pre–Vatican II Church the theologians of the 1960s and 1970s vigorously deplored.

The charge that John Paul II is a misogynist or, more mildly, is insensitive to women's concerns is flatly denied by women who have known Karol Wojtyła for decades, many of whom find the suggestion "completely crazy," as one professional woman put it.[8] In terms of the public record, this charge must also contend with the Pope's extensive discussion of the contemporary status of women in *Familiaris Consortio, Mulieris Dignitatem, Christifideles Laici,* and the 1995 *Letter to Women,* and with the Holy See's positions at the World Conference on Women at Beijing.

For almost two decades, John Paul II has been developing a distinctive Christian feminism. Such a feminism, he argues, is far more securely anchored in the Bible and in the theology of the "Marian Church" than in the sexual revolution of the 1960s. The Pope's insistence that, "from the beginning," women and men were created distinct and yet equal, is, to be sure, a profound challenge to those feminists for whom "gender" is a cultural construct of no real significance. Yet here is another irony: John Paul II takes the female embodiedness of women far more seriously than some schools of contemporary feminism.

In the Pope's view, being a woman is not an accident of biology or a construct of culture. It is an icon of a deep truth about the human condition and about the Creator's intention for the world. Concurrently, John Paul's theological reflection on how the "Marian Church" of faith—the Church of disciples—precedes and makes possible the Petrine Church of office gives a certain theological priority to what he has called the "feminine genius" in the life of discipleship. Virtually none of these aspects of John Paul's response to the contemporary women's movement has been given serious consideration by his critics. If the Pope's teaching on the unique vocation of women is adequately received by Catholicism, a most interesting and Church-transforming debate will ensue in the twenty-first century.

The charge of Manichaeanism or a papal deprecation of human sexuality has to contend with John Paul's innovative theology of the body, in which the Pope argues that our sexuality is greater than the sexual revolution imagines. John Paul's portrait of sexual love as an icon of the interior life of God has barely begun to shape the Church's theology, preaching, and religious education. When it does, it will compel a dramatic development of thinking about virtually every major theme in the Creed. For the moment, though, the burden of proof lies with those who argue that John Paul's exposition of the Church's sexual ethic demeans sexual love. A careful reading of the *Theology of the Body* and its exploration of the "nuptial" character of God's relationship to the world suggests the opposite.

The conventional critique of John Paul II, which so often misrepresents his thinking, does so because it misses the relationship between tradition and innovation, the stable and the dynamic, in the Church. The stable elements that can seem static in Catholicism either reflect the Church's inner dynamism, or create an impetus to the unfolding of new, dynamic elements in Christian life. The canon of the Bible is fixed forever, but Scripture is not a dead record of the past. Scripture enables the Word of God to be received freshly by every generation of Christians. The sacraments are not merely traditional rituals, repeated because previous generations of Christians performed them. The sacraments enable contemporary Christians to live the great mysteries of the faith—the life, death, and resurrection of Christ—anew. The purpose of authority in the Church is not to impede creativity, but to ensure that Christians do not settle for mediocrity. Authority is meant to help the individual Christian hold himself or herself accountable to the one supreme criterion of faith, the living Christ. Doctrine is not excess baggage weighing down the Christian journey. Doctrine is the vehicle that enables the journey to take place at all.[9]

To understand John Paul's commitment to preserving the purity of doctrine and the tradition of the Church, one must grasp the distinctive Christian understanding of "tradition." Tradition, which in its Latin root (*traditio*) means "handing on," begins, not with human invention, but inside the very life of God, the Holy Trinity. That "handing on"—the radical self-giving that mysteriously enhances giver and receiver—took flesh in the life of Christ and

continues in the Church through the gift of Christ's Spirit.[10] On this understanding, tradition, the living faith of the dead, must always be distinguished
from traditionalism, the dead faith of the living.[11] That John Paul's has been
a papacy rooted in tradition is certain. That it has been a papacy of traditionalism is belied by the evidence.

The Restorationist Critique

There is another critique of the pontificate of John Paul II that bears careful
examination, though it rarely receives public attention. It is mounted by those
who, in this pontificate, hoped for a "Catholic Restoration" that would return
the Church to the style and sureties of the age of Pope Pius XII. This critique
should not be confused with the radical rejectionism of Archbishop Marcel
Lefebvre and other anti–Vatican II intransigents. The restorationists affirm the
Council, but argue that its implementation has been impeded by a failure to
reassert theological, organizational, and pastoral discipline in the Church.
That failure, the restorationists charge, jeopardizes the Council's achievements and leaves the Church vulnerable to the corrosive acids of late modern
life. While they are reluctant to say it publicly, more than a few Catholic restorationists believe that John Paul II has not reversed the breakdown of Catholic
discipline that began in the years after the Council.

On this critique, and employing the "triple mission" of Christ that Karol
Wojtyła used to organize Vatican II's teaching in *Sources of Renewal,* John Paul
gets high marks for "priest" and "prophet" and low, even failing, grades for
"king." No major religious order, the restorationist critics charge, has been
reformed in this pontificate. The quality of the Church's worship has continued to deteriorate. The Pope has failed to appoint sufficient numbers of bishops capable of defending doctrine and enforcing discipline. Bishops'
conferences and the enormous expansion of local Church bureacracies have
sapped religious authority and replaced it with bureaucratic power—which,
restorationists argue, was a crucial part of the post–World War II decline of
mainline Protestantism in Western Europe and North America. In sum, these
critics contend, Karol Wojtyła's "seminar" style of management is wholly
unsuited for the papacy, however well it may have worked in Kraków.

It is true that Wojtyła, as a manager of large organizations, has never been
the kind of man who deliberately and without regrets gets those opposed to
his plans out of his way. It is also true that, as archbishop of Kraków and Bishop
of Rome, Wojtyła's has not been a "kingly" exercise of authority. And it is true,
further, that there has been a price to be paid for this. But it may not be the
price suggested by the restorationists.

John Paul II has most certainly not micromanaged the Roman Curia. He
was elected as an outsider to the world of the Church's central bureaucracy.
He has conducted his papal office as an outsider to this world and its assumptions about "the way we do things here." And he will die as an outsider to the

papal model favored by many curial veterans. This deliberate decision to govern as an outsider will strike many as a great gift to the Church and the world. The Pope's relative lack of attention to managing his bureaucracy—at least as measured by the practice of his predecessor, Paul VI—has created the time and space in which to conduct an evangelical papacy of great intellectual creativity and public impact. The price that has been paid for this achievement is that John Paul will leave behind him a central administrative apparatus in which a minority of the personnel have internalized the dynamic teaching of his pontificate and its authoritative interpretation of Vatican II. That among the minority are some of the key leaders of the Curia is also true. The fact remains, though, that John Paul II has not invested significant, sustained energy in ensuring that his vision of an evangelically assertive, culture-forming Church of disciples is understood and shared throughout the various levels of the Roman bureaucracy.

On the other hand, the restorationist critics must, or should, concede that no one man can do everything, and that John Paul's choice to conduct a dramatically different kind of papacy was intentional and serious, rather than a reflection of personal weakness. The restorationist critique, like the conventional critique, also has to contend with certain facts that have been established by this pontificate. Primary among them are the unavoidable reference points that John Paul II has put in place for twenty-first-century Catholicism.

Redemptor Hominis has committed the Church to the steady development of a Christian humanism for the third millennium. *Redemptoris Missio* has made it clear that the Church of the future, living its evangelical mission in the world, will be a Church that proposes rather than imposes. The *Catechism of the Catholic Church* has specified in detail what the content of that proposal is. *Veritatis Splendor* has set the framework for the authentic development of Catholic moral theology and its address to the human quest for freedom. *Centesimus Annus* (amplified by *Veritatis Splendor* and *Evangelium Vitae*) provides a model of the free, prosperous, and virtuous society that is far more carefully thought through than many other visions of public life. *Ut Unum Sint* has made Vatican II's commitment to ecumenism irreversible. *Christifideles Laici* and the theology of the priesthood in *Pastores Dabo Vobis* make it far more likely that the Church of the future will come to grips with the twin dangers of a clericalized laity and a laicized ordained ministry. *Mulieris Dignitatem* and the *Letter to Women* have set the course for the Church's engagement with the women's movement of the twenty-first century. The Pope's theology of the body has offered the first compelling papal response to the sexual revolution. These reference points will remain in place long after the pontificate of John Paul II. They cannot be avoided. They are, now, part of the living tradition of Catholicism.

The restorationist critics argue that John Paul's episcopal appointments have been, in general, weak. No doubt there have been mistakes made in the appointment of bishops, as there are in any pontificate. Given the available personnel, however, there are limits to what a Pope can do in this regard. An overall judgment on this crucial aspect of the pontificate must take account of bold, unconventional appointments that would have been unlikely under a more bureaucratically minded and "kingly" Pope: Carlo Maria Martini in Milan, Jean-Marie Lustiger in Paris, John O'Connor in New York, Giacomo Biffi in Bologna, Francis George in Chicago, Józef Życiński in Lublin, Norberto Rivera Carrera in Mexico City, and Miloslav Vlk in Prague are eight of the more prominent examples. Such nominations, it should also be said, would have been virtually impossible under the more "democratic" model of choosing bishops favored by proponents of the conventional critique of John Paul II.

Karol Wojtyła's personal experience of the Polish Episcopal Conference may have given him a certain romantic view of these institutions—an instance where the conventional critique of the Pope's Polishness (shared, in this case, by restorationists) has some merit. Even here, though, the facts do not coincide with the alleged "authoritarian" and "centralizing" trends the conventional critique deplores and the restorationists would welcome. John Paul II has rarely intervened in the work of national bishops' conferences—and then only when a conference has shown itself incapable of rectifying a situation on its own. In doing so, the Pope has made clear that he is exercising the traditional papal *sollicitudo omnium ecclesiarum* [the care for all the Churches], not acting as a chief executive officer disciplining refractory or unproductive branch managers.

Similarly, the Pope's commitment to the Synod of Bishops as an authentic expression of Vatican II has led him to sanction what some would regard as a less-than-satisfactory Synod process and to invest thousands of hours of his own time in listening to Synod interventions that have not been of uniformly high quality. The critics must recognize that the Pope himself is aware of these defects and is convinced, as he once put it, that "what happens to and among the bishops during the Synod can be more important" than the immediate, concrete results.[12] This is not to suggest that the process couldn't be improved, but it does indicate a deliberate strategy on the Pope's part, not a diffident acquiescence to the status quo.[13]

As for the charge that John Paul has failed to reform any major religious order—a charge embodied in what restorationists perceive as the sadly failed Jesuit intervention of 1981–1983—this, too, can be understood as part of a conscious strategy. One can question the wisdom of the strategy, but John Paul has chosen to nurture what is healthy and growing among religious orders, even if that will take decades and centuries to flourish, rather than to divide the Church further by intervening massively in the internal affairs of religious communities. The Pope's personal influence in attracting men and women to existing religious orders will also have its effects in older religious communities over time, as will his vigorous support of new movements, communities, and orders, in which he recognizes the work of the same spirit (and Spirit) that gave birth to religious orders in the past.

Reforming the liturgy has not been a priority for John Paul II because, as the Pope himself reports, his own experience of the post–Vatican II liturgical renewal has been very positive, both in Poland and in Rome.[14] One may also assume that the relative lack of attention to this question also reflects the fact that the Church's bishops have not pressed this on the Pope as a major concern.[15] The numerous movements aimed at "reforming the reform" of the liturgy that have been launched in recent years suggest, however, that this may well be an issue for the next pontificate.

A Crucial Theological Point

The Pope's method of governance was once described in these terms by a close collaborator: "He has a very deep respect of persons. He is patient, waiting with some situations until the moment comes when nobody feels offended. People mistake his respect for persons as weakness. It isn't. He also respects competence. When he gives a responsibility to an office, a congregation, or an individual, he lets them do it. This doesn't mean he is weak. He trusts his collaborators, and he is not a worrier. He is neither afraid of making a decision nor does he force a decision if the situation is not mature."[16] That trust in collaborators can, as we have seen, result in the Pope's plans being frustrated at times. Still, even his critics concede that if a "good manager" is someone who sets priorities and, all in all, gets them accomplished, John Paul II has been a good manager.[17]

In a 1994 letter to a Polish priest, John Paul mused that more than a few Polish churchmen disapproved of the social doctrine in *Centesimus Annus* and concluded with a papal shrug: "But what can we do?"[18] What can a Pope do—if, that is, the Pope is committed to dialogue, to proposing rather than imposing? What he can do, of course, is what John Paul has done: keep proposing, keep making arguments, keep the seminar going until, as Cardinal Jozef Tomko put it, the situation "matures." That has been Karol Wojtyła's method of leadership throughout his life. In judging it, the reader should recognize that it is based on a profound theological conviction.

The Italian philosopher Rocco Buttiglione once put that conviction in these terms: "For John Paul, the ideal is the martyr, the witness, a life coinciding with the truth. That is how he understands his pontifical service. That is what he wrote in the poem 'Stanisław': 'The word did not convert, blood will convert.' He always prefers to be offended than to offend. [On the other hand] no offense could bring him to accept as true what he considers to be false. . . . The center of it all," Buttiglione concluded, "is the idea of the person: the rights of truth and the rights of the person must be reconciled. These rights can enter into an opposition: the person can make the decision to struggle against truth. Then what can we do? Can we impose truth by force? The way of Jesus Christ was to give witness to truth, not through the blood of the offenders or the sinners, but through his own."[19]

That conviction is the foundation of John Paul II's method of leadership through witness and persuasion.

DIFFICULTIES AND IMPOSSIBILITIES

Beyond the conventional and restorationist critiques, there have been things on which history has not been willing to yield, even to so relentless a proposer as Pope John Paul II.

John Paul's major investment in ecumenism has yielded rather modest concrete accomplishments. The willingness of some World Council of Church leaders to abandon the classic ecumenical quest for unity-through-doctrinal-agreement and the broader trend this represents in the WCC's Protestant members has made advances in healing the western Christian fracture of the sixteenth century more difficult. So have the Anglican Communion's internal disagreements over how, or even whether, Anglican Churches are apostolically constituted—the crucial issue in the Anglican decision to admit women to the ordained ministry. The difficulties in concluding the Lutheran–Roman Catholic dialogue on justification suggest that even the most theologically sophisticated ecumenical conversation faces major obstacles in dealing with the accumulated heritage of a half-millennium of division.

Few Orthodox leaders have responded generously or imaginatively to John Paul's great hope, to heal the breach of the second millennium between Rome and the Christian East before the beginning of the third millennium. Here, John Paul II's prophetic sense of urgency may have run ahead of his-toric possibilities. Ancient Orthodox animosities over the "Uniates," Orthodox suspicion of change, Orthodoxy's historic entanglements with state power, and Orthodoxy's difficulties in coming to grips with its performance under com-munism have combined to make the Catholic-Orthodox dialogue far more complex in the 1990s, pushing ecclesial reunion "around the altar of concel-ebration" (as the Pope once put it) into a seemingly distant future. This may well rank as the single greatest disappointment of John Paul's pontificate. But the Pope may also have laid the foundation for a reconciliation he would not live to see.

At the same time, one should note that the fifth century Christological con-troversies that divided Roman Catholicism from the small Oriental Orthodox Churches have all been resolved, explicitly or implicitly, during John Paul's pon-tificate. Of considerable consequence for the future, John Paul's vigorous defense of the right-to-life and his vibrant public witness to Christian truth have helped strengthen the Church's dialogue with evangelical Protestants, the rapidly growing sector of world Protestantism in Latin America, eastern Europe, Africa, and Asia. One veteran of Catholic ecumenism described the 1996 visit to the Pope by Dr. Nilson Fanini, President of the World Baptist Fellowship, as evidence of "unbelievable" change on this front.[20] The indepen-dent American theological initiative, "Evangelicals and Catholics Together," has developed a joint statement of commitment to public moral renewal and a joint statement of belief about the meaning of salvation, both of which would have been difficult to imagine without the ecumenical witness of John Paul II.[21]

John Paul's hopes for the future of interreligious dialogue have also run up against considerable historical barriers.

The Pope's reconfiguration of Catholic relations with Judaism is a solid accomplishment. His 1986 visit to the Synagogue of Rome and the 1992 Fundamental Agreement between the Holy See and the State of Israel are historic landmarks in Catholic-Jewish relations. Because of these advances, which build on the achievement of Vatican II, Catholics and Jews are now primed to reopen the theological conversation as they have not done since about A.D. 70. The question remains whether there is sufficient interest in such a conversation among practicing, religiously committed Jews. The controversy that broke out, once again, during the October 1998 canonization of Edith Stein suggested that a positive answer to that question could not be taken for granted.

The Pope's 1985 meeting with Muslim youth at Casablanca was a major event in thirteen centuries of Catholic-Islamic relations. As John Paul suggested on that occasion, Catholics and Muslims can make common cause on certain moral issues. Real progress in the international Catholic-Muslim dialogue hits a barrier of large proportions, however, with the issue of religious freedom, which for John Paul II has always been the crucial issue in the Church's relations with civil authority. At the beginning of the third millennium, there were 2 billion Christians and 1 billion Muslims in the world, with Catholicism and Islam both claiming about a billion adherents. With evangelical Protestantism, Catholicism and Islam are the most assertive, culture-forming religious communities in the world. Whether the dialogue that John Paul has tried to foster can help Islam develop a Qu'ran-based theory of religious freedom is a large question with immense implications for the twenty-first century. In the short term, attempts to move toward such a dialogue have been seriously impeded by Islamic persecution of Christians in Africa, the Middle East, southwest Asia, and southeast Asia.

John Paul encountered a host of difficulties in his efforts to open a line of dialogue with the rulers of the People's Republic of China. Public requests and private initiatives alike were ignored or rebuffed for years. Religious leaders attract followers in Asia when those leaders are witnesses, according to Philippine Archbishop Oscar Cruz, and the Pope's witness in and to Asia has created new openings for the Church in the area of Christianity's great missionary failure.[22] Perhaps that is one reason that the leaders of the PRC were reluctant for so long to deal with John Paul II—they know that a vibrant Church and totalitarian politics cannot coexist indefinitely. However their reasoning may run, fifteen years of rebuffs to the Pope's request for a new dialogue must rank as one of the serious frustrations of the pontificate.

As for democracies old and new, it remains an open question how seriously John Paul's vision of the free, virtuous, and prosperous society has been engaged in Europe or in the Americas. In that sense, it is difficult to make the case that the Pope has made as measurable an impact on the world-after-communism as he did on the world he faced in October 1978. Still, the intellectual framework of a Catholic approach to the social, economic, and political life of free societies has been put into place. As the cultural contradictions of late modernity mount, particularly under the impact of the revolution in biotechnology, a proposal for how to live freedom-for-excellence in public life will be available—if the people of the Catholic Church and their religious leaders internalize it, and have the faith to act on it.

The pontificate's success in strengthening the Church's diplomatic position around the world has not been matched by a parallel development in the Holy See's approach to international institutions and its address to international issues and crises after the collapse of communism. A Church that has vigorously challenged the corruptions of national governments has tended to take a mild public stance toward the corruptions and incapacities of the United Nations and its affiliated agencies—except when the UN system engages in an assault on human rights, as at the Cairo World Population Conference. Papal and Holy See human rights rhetoric continues to reinforce the UN-sanctioned pattern of describing virtually every desirable human good as a "human right," a practice that some Catholic thinkers say confuses the core rights essential to human dignity. John Paul's papacy has not clarified the moral criteria for the legitimate use of armed force in the defense of those basic rights, nor have the Pope or the Holy See helped develop a morally and politically defensible approach to "humanitarian intervention," despite describing such interventions as imperative in certain circumstances. The foundation for a development of the Catholic Church's thinking about the international public life of the twenty-first century has been laid by the "post-Constantinian" pontificate of John Paul II, but others will have to build a sturdy structure of moral and political analysis on that foundation.

THE SUCCESSION

Speculation about John Paul II's successor intensified from 1994 on. Such speculation is natural, although it usually tells one more about the speculator than about the future. The Pope himself set the formal framework for electing his successor in the 1996 apostolic constitution, *Universi Dominici Gregis*. Beyond that framework, and without engaging in idle surmises about individual candidates, certain realities bearing on the next papal succession were reasonably clear at John Paul's twentieth anniversary, even as it seemed ever more likely that the Pope would lead the Church through the Great Jubilee of 2000 and fulfill what he believes to be the mission given him in 1978.

That John Paul broke the mold of the bureaucratic-managerial papacy will certainly bear on the deliberations of the conclave that will elect his successor. The world and the Church have expectations of a pope that were simply not in place in 1978. The world expects a witnessing pope, not a bureaucrat or an impossibly distant, ethereal figure. The Catholic Church has a new and powerful presence in the world because John Paul II has touched consciences in a way that political leaders cannot. That ability to appeal to conscience *is* papal leadership on the world stage in the twenty-first century, and it is a quality that papal electors cannot ignore in pondering the succession. The Church also has new expectations of a pope. John Paul has reshaped the primacy in a decisively evangelical direction while avoiding the iron cage of bureaucracy. The qualities necessary to carry on his ministry of "presence" to the Church throughout the world will have to be taken into account when considering his successor. Taken together, these two sets of expectations suggest that the Italian and curial hope for a return to pre-Wojtyła "normality" is likely to be frustrated.[23]

In *Universi Dominici Gregis,* John Paul made unmistakably clear his conviction that papal conclaves cannot be understood on the model of democratic electoral politics. Theologically, that means that the Holy Spirit is the supreme protagonist of a conclave. At the same time, the Holy Spirit works through human instruments, the cardinal-electors, who must measure the fit between the historical circumstances and the *papabili,* the men-who-might-be-pope, as best they can. These electors cannot help being aware of the dramatic reconstruction of the papacy John Paul II has achieved, and the new expectations it has created. Many will be aware that John Paul was able to revitalize the papacy because he had been the evangelically successful bishop of a local Church. Some will likely conclude that, insofar as any man can be prepared to be the Successor of Peter, that form of preparation has once again proven sound.

The cardinals will also have to take account of the major challenges facing the next pope in weighing candidates for the office. In a world of resurgent religious conviction, the Catholic defense of religious freedom and the Catholic commitment to culture-formation through proposing rather than imposing will have to be vigorously promoted, in dialogue with Orthodoxy, Protestantism, Judaism, Islam, and other world religions. Cloning, stem-cell research, and other developments in biotechnology are among the developments that will raise previously unimaginable moral questions in the years ahead. What had seemed the assured triumph of democracy in the early 1990s now looks far more fragile. The values of Christian humanism will have to be applied to public life in a world in which new forms of authoritarianism will undoubtedly emerge. Within the Church itself, the rich and diverse teaching of John Paul II remains to be digested, and facilitating that process will loom large as a task for the next pontificate.

These realities, and the fact that the electoral college for the next conclave will have the lowest percentage of Italian electors in a very long time, make it likely that nationality will have no significant role in choosing the next Bishop of Rome.[24] Given the expectations the Church and the world now have of the pope, nationality is neither a major asset nor a crippling liability. It is almost an irrelevance—which is precisely the way things ought to be. And that, too, is a historic accomplishment of the pontificate of John Paul II, preparing the Church for a new millennium.

THE LONG-DISTANCE DISCIPLE

As he aged, John Paul II's rhetorical style became simpler and purer, the distillate of decades of prayer and reflection. Some things about John Paul did not change, though, even as he became frailer physically. Friends and visitors found that the Pope's most recent encounters with pain and suffering had deepened his convictions that God is in charge of his life, that everyone has a place in the great cosmic drama of creation and redemption, and that the world's various melodies have a divine composer—even the melodies piped by discordant flutes. He remained a man with a profound sense of *kairos*, convinced that everything has its time, that time tests ideas and projects, and that one shouldn't accelerate that testing process artificially. He did not demand measurable results from every intellectual and pastoral initiative he had taken. In some cases, he was content to know that he had planted certain ideas in the life of the Church, ideas that would flower many years after his death. "It is the 'turning point' that is the most important," John Paul once wrote, "as when a train enters a switch where an inch decides its future direction."[25] Still, on those rare occasions when he looked back rather than ahead, Karol Wojtyła could detect the truth of what his old friend and fellow philosopher Father Józef Tischner had once said of him: that he was a man whose "ideas turned into institutions."[26]

Approaching the completion of his eighth decade, he remained a Carmelite at heart. The deepest meaning of prayer, he once wrote, could only be understood by reflecting for a long time on a passage from St. Paul's letter to the Romans:

> For the creation waits with eager longing for the revealing of the sons of God; for the creation was subjected to futility, not of its own will but by the will of him who subjected it in hope; because the creation will be set free from its bondage to decay and obtain the glorious liberty of the children of God. We know that the whole creation has been groaning in travail together until now; and not only the creation, but we ourselves, who have the first fruits of the Spirit, groan inwardly as we wait for adoption as sons, the redemption of our bodies. For in this hope we were saved (*Romans* 8.19–24).

His was the prayer of a joyful man and a witness to hope, who believed and wanted to affirm before the world "*the value of existence, the value of creation and of hope in the future life.*"[27] He was utterly convinced that "evil . . . is neither fundamental nor definitive," but he had also learned that the joy a Christian experiences from knowing Christ's ultimate victory over evil intensifies one's awareness of evil's enduring power in the world.[28] Life, and the daily papal duty of bringing the world's suffering before the Lord in prayer, had deepened his Carmelite intuition that all roads to the truth eventually wind their way to Calvary, to the cross. And Calvary was, and remains, a lonely place.

Like many Christians his age, John Paul II in his late seventies experienced something of the loneliness that Danuta Michałowska had explored dramatically in *I Without Name*. Even as he entered more fully into the experience of Christ's abandonment on the cross, the hope he drew from the Easter victory that lay beyond that singular, redemptive abandonment made him a more compelling public figure. A different kind of loneliness—the loneliness of the autonomous, self-asserting self—haunted the world of the late twentieth century. Freedom understood as willfulness had not led to a net increase in the sum total of human happiness. Willfulness had, in fact, made millions even lonelier, living alone with their rights but with little else. Analyzing this frigid cultural climate, philosopher Alasdair MacIntyre concluded that the world was waiting not for Godot, "but for another—doubtless very different—St. Benedict."[29] And that is as good a description as any of what Karol Wojtyła had become on the edge of a new millennium: a man whose lifelong experience of forming communities out of the loneliness of modernity, from the "little family" of *Rodzinka* and the "milieu" of *Środowisko* to the largest crowds in human history, had been given global scope through the mysteries of chosenness.

The antidote to despair amid the sundry madnesses of late modernity, the Pope had long proposed, was the experience of a community of self-giving love in which we learn the destiny that awaits us on the far side of loneliness—life within the community of God, Father, Son, and Holy Spirit. That is what St. Benedict had done in forming monastic communities in what history knows as the "Dark Ages." That is what Karol Wojtyła did throughout his distinctively twentieth-century life.

If the Church of the future knows John Paul II as "John Paul the Great," it will be for this reason: at another moment of peril, when barbarisms of various sorts threatened civilization, a heroic figure was called from the Church to meet the barbarian threat and propose an alternative. In the case of Pope Leo the Great (440–461), the barbarians in question were Attila and his Huns. In the case of Gregory the Great (590–604), the barbarians were the Lombards. In the case of John Paul II, the barbarism threatening civilization has been a set of ideas whose consequences include barbarous politics—defective humanisms that, in the name of humanity and its destiny, create new tyrannies and compound human suffering.

A yearning for the absolute, it seems, is built into the human condition. When fragments of truth are absolutized by barbarians, the world's suffering begins to take on the aspect of the demonic.[30] That is what happened at Auschwitz and in the Gulag Archipelago. That is what happens when utility becomes the sole measure of human life. Against the new barbarisms set loose in the world by absolutized fragments of truth, Karol Wojtyła preached a consistent message, a thoroughly Christian humanism, throughout more than fifty years of priestly ministry: you are greater than you imagine, and greater than the late modern world has let you imagine. By demonstrating, not merely asserting, that faith can transform the world, John Paul II helped restore a spiritual dimension to a history that had become flat, stale, and, as a consequence, brutal.

During almost eighty years of personal pilgrimage to what his former student Halina Bortnowska once described, simply, as "the place he really wants to be," Karol Wojtyła came to resemble G. K. Chesterton's description of Thomas More: "he was above all things, historic: he represented at once a type, a turning-point and an ultimate destiny. If there had not been that particular man at that particular moment, the whole of history would have been different."[31] And, like More's, John Paul II's historic qualities have not been generically humanistic, but specifically religious, in origin. They have been, in a word, Christian qualities.

The Yugoslav dissident Milovan Djilas once said that what most impressed him about John Paul II was that he was a man utterly without fear. That fearlessness is not Stoic, nor is it a consequence of Karol Wojtyła's "autonomy" as someone independent of others. It is an unmistakably Christian fearlessness. In Christian faith, fear is not eliminated but transformed, through a profound personal encounter with Christ and his Cross—the place where all human fear was offered by the Son to the Father, setting us all free from fear.[32] All popes are in some sense men of mystery. That has to do, finally, not with the mysteriousness of the office and its history, but with the Mystery that popes serve. The encounter with that Mystery—the truth of the world revealed in the life, death, and resurrection of Jesus Christ—is the source of Karol Wojtyła's witness to hope. That is the hope that can enable the Catholic Church of the twenty-first century to propose and practice the Gospel of God's devotion to humanity, in what John Paul II believes can be a springtime of the human spirit.

———————

Piotr and Teresa Malecki, longtime members of Karol Wojtyła's *Środowisko*, were staying in the papal villa at Castel Gandolfo in the late summer of 1997 as the Pope's guests. Their bedroom was just below his, and before dawn each morning they knew by the thumping of his cane that he was up and about. One morning, at breakfast, the Pope asked whether the noise was disturbing them. No, they answered, they were getting up for Mass anyway. "But *Wujek*," they asked, "why do you get up at that hour of the morning?"

Because, said Karol Wojtyła, the 264th Bishop of Rome, "I like to watch the sun rise."[33]

Notes

PROLOGUE
The Disciple

1. Conor Cruise O'Brien, *On the Eve of the Millennium: The Future of Democracy Through an Age of Unreason* (New York: Free Press, 1994), pp. 11–12. O'Brien's summary appraisal is unsparing: "I frankly abhor Pope John Paul II" [p. 16].

2. Tad Szulc, *Pope John Paul II: The Biography* (New York: Scribner, 1995), p. 422 and following.

3. Carl Bernstein and Marco Politi, *His Holiness: John Paul II and the Hidden History of Our Time* (New York: Doubleday, 1996), p. 508.

4. David Willey, *God's Politician: Pope John Paul II, the Catholic Church, and the New World Order* (New York: St. Martin's Press, 1992), p. xiii.

5. "The Pope must make his church more catholic." *The Independent*, August 3, 1993, p. 15.

6. See John Paul II, *Crossing the Threshold of Hope* (New York: Alfred A. Knopf, 1994), and *Gift and Mystery: On the Fiftieth Anniversary of My Priestly Ordination* (New York: Doubleday, 1996).

7. "Introduction" to *Our God's Brother*, in Karol Wojtyła, *The Collected Plays and Writings on Theater*, translated with introductions by Bolesław Taborski (Berkeley: University of California Press, 1987), p. 159.

8. Author's conversation with Pope John Paul II, March 7, 1996.

9. On the dramatic structure of the moral life and the centrality of Christ in the human drama, see Kenneth L. Schmitz, *At the Center of the Human Drama: The Philosophical Anthropology of Karol Wojtyła/Pope John Paul II* (Washington, D.C.: CUA Press, 1993), pp. 86, 146.

10. John Paul II, "Address to the Fiftieth General Assembly of the United Nations Organization," October 5, 1995, 17.

11. Author's conversation with Pope John Paul II, March 20, 1997.

12. The image is from Hans Urs von Balthasar, "Pentecost Sermon," in *You Crown the Year with Your Goodness* (San Francisco: Ignatius Press, 1989), pp. 135ff.

13. John Paul II, "Address to the Fiftieth General Assembly of the United Nations Organization," 16 [emphasis in original]. John Paul II habitually highlights phrases and words in his texts, underlining them in manuscript. These highlights are then transposed into italics in the printed version of his texts. It can make for a somewhat jarring style, but replicating it is essential for getting the flavor and the rhythm of the Pope's prose.

14. New York: Oxford University Press, 1992.

15. Cited in John Jay Hughes, *Pontiffs: Popes Who Shaped History* (Huntington, Ind.: Our Sunday Visitor Publishing Division, 1994), p. 11.

CHAPTER 1
A Son of Freedom: Poland *Semper Fidelis*

1. Isaac Deutscher, *The Prophet Armed: Trótsky 1879–1921* (New York: Vintage Books, 1965), p. 466.

2. The main lines of this brief account of the Battle of the Vistula are taken from Richard M. Watt, *Bitter Glory: Poland and Its Fate 1918–1939* (New York: Simon and Schuster, 1979), pp. 142–149.

3. See Document 59, "Political Report of the Central Committee RKP(b) to the Ninth All-Russian Conference of the Communist Party," in *The Unknown Lenin: From the Secret Archive*, ed. Richard Pipes (New Haven: Yale University Press, 1996), pp. 95–115.

4. Norman Davies, *God's Playground: A History of Poland, Volume I* (New York: Columbia University Press, 1982), p. 486; hereinafter, Davies, *Volume I*.

5. Ibid., p. 79.

6. Ibid., p. 151.

7. Ibid., p. 160.

8. Ibid., pp. 199–200.

9. Ibid., p. 63.

10. Rocco Buttiglione, *Karol Wojtyła: The Thought of the Man Who Became Pope John Paul II* (Grand Rapids: Eerdmans, 1997), p. 1.

11. See Buttiglione, *Karol Wojtyła*, chapter one, for an important discussion of history "viewed from the Vistula."

12. See Radek Sikorski, *Full Circle: A Homecoming to Free Poland* (New York: Simon and Schuster, 1997), p. 21.

13. For "savage exotics," see Davies, *Volume I*, p. 386.

14. Ibid., p. 456.

15. Author's interview with Wojciech Giertych, OP, June 10, 1997.

16. Davies, *Volume I*, p. 511. Enlightenment wits, confident of their cultural superiority, had their fun while Poland was murdered. Thus Voltaire had it that one Pole was a charmer, two Poles was a brawl; but three Poles, "Ah, that is the Polish Question." [Ibid.]

17. Cited in *The Spectator*, January 25, 1997, p. 30.

18. See Norman Davies, *Heart of Europe: A Short History of Poland* (Oxford: Oxford University Press, 1984), p. 159.

19. For these and other difficulties in the early days of the Second Polish Republic, see Watt, *Bitter Glory*, pp. 79ff.

20. Tadeusz Karolak, *John Paul II: The Pope from Poland* (Warsaw: Interpress Publishers, 1979), p. 10.

21. Ibid., p. 22. Wawro was the embodiment of the artist who lives out of, rather than against, local popular culture, and as such he may have influenced Karol Wojtyła's later thinking about the relationship of popular piety to high culture. [Author's interviews with Marek Skwarnicki, June 4, 1997, and Father Kazimierz Suder, July 14, 1997.]

22. See Davies, *Heart of Europe*, pp. 118, 120. Ukrainians were fifteen percent of the population of the interwar republic, Jews nine percent, Byelorussians five percent, and Germans two percent. [Ibid.]

23. Author's interview with Jerzy Kluger, March 15, 1997; author's conversation with Pope John Paul II, March 20, 1997.

24. John Paul II, *Crossing the Threshold of Hope*, p. 96.

25. Author's interview with Jerzy Kluger, March 15, 1997.

26. Ibid., and author's interview with Father Kazimierz Suder, July 14, 1997.

27. Author's interview with Jerzy Kluger, March 15, 1997.

28. Cardinal Karol Wojtyła memorialized Rafał Kalinowski in a 1963 sermon, "Two Rebels," reprinted in the Kraków weekly, *Tygodnik Powszechny*, no. 33 (1963).

29. Author's conversation with Pope John Paul II, January 22, 1997; see also A. Kijkowski and J. J. Szczepański, with the collaboration of K. Zanussi, *From a Far Country: The Story of Karol Wojtyła of Poland* (Santa Monica, Calif.: ERI/NEFF, 1981).

30. The loss of church records during World War II and the problems of memory have caused certain unresolvable confusions about the early married life of the Wojtyłas. According to military records searched by a German writer, Karol Wojtyła was assigned to the 56th Infantry Regiment (a unit of Polish troops officered by Austrians) in Wadowice after being drafted into the Austro-Hungarian army in 1900. After a year of service there he was transferred to Lwów (L'viv, in today's Ukraine). In 1904 he was transferred back to Wadowice and, at that juncture, married Emilia Kaczorowska. This reconstructed sequence, however, contradicts the account of Wojtyła's stepsister Stefania, who had it that the marriage took place while the young soldier was assigned to quartermaster duties in Kraków. Stefania also believed that Karol and Emilia Wojtyła lived in Kraków for some time before moving to Wadowice. [See Adam Boniecki, MIC, *Kalendarium*, "Family," translated by Irena and Thaddeus Mirecki et al.; manuscript copy obtained by the author.] Father Kazimierz Suder, a seminary classmate of Pope John Paul II and pastor of the church in Wadowice, assured me that the Wojtyłas had been married at the Church of Sts. Peter and Paul in Kraków, located along the Royal Way between Wawel Castle and the great market square, which served as the military church of the city. [Author's interview with Father Kazimierz Suder, July 14, 1997.]

31. These details are taken from Boniecki, *Kalendarium*, "Family."

32. Ibid.

33. Author's interview with Father Kazimierz Suder, July 14, 1997.

34. European usage would call this the first floor.

35. Author's conversation with Pope John Paul II, January 22, 1997. To be technically precise, Francis Joseph was emperor of Austria from 1848 to 1916 and King of Hungary from 1867 (when he divided his empire into the Dual Monarchy) until 1916.

36. A personal questionnaire completed by Karol Wojtyła at the Jagiellonian University indicated that his father had retired "about 1927," and the extant military records show him on the retired officers list as of the 1928 issue of the *Officers' Annual*. [Boniecki, *Kalendarium*, "Family."]

37. Author's interview with Jerzy Kluger, March 15, 1997.

38. Boniecki, *Kalendarium*, "School Years."

39. The cause of death was listed as myocarditis nephritis in the parish register. [Ibid.]

40. Tad Szulc, in *Pope John Paul II*, simply asserts that the Pope's "cult of Mary flowered from his mother's death: the natural identification" [p. 66]. That Emilia's death was the beginning of an alleged difficulty relating to women is one of the leitmotifs of Bernstein/Politi, *His Holiness*. John Paul II seems to have a different understanding of his Marian piety, which he described as serious but rather conventional, prior to his later encounter with the works of St. Louis de Montfort. See *Gift and Mystery*, pp. 28–30.

41. John Paul II, *Gift and Mystery*, p. 20. A 1939 poem that must be considered part of Wojtyła's juvenilia, "Over This Your White Grave," is a reflection on the loss of Emilia and is included in *The Place Within: The Poetry of Pope John Paul II*, translated by Jerzy Peterkiewicz (New York: Random House, 1994), p. ix.

42. As John Paul II told the French writer André Frossard, "My father was admirable and almost all the memories of my childhood and adolescence are connected with him." [André Frossard and Pope John Paul II, *Be Not Afraid!* (New York: St. Martin's Press, 1984), p. 14.]

43. Boniecki, *Kalendarium*, "Family."

44. Author's interview with Jerzy Kluger, March 15, 1997.

45. In 1904, forty-seven percent of the officers were familiar with Czech, thirty-four percent with Hungarian, nineteen percent with Polish, and fifteen percent with Serbo-Croatian, in addition to the German that was the army's lingua franca. The army recognized ten official languages; officers and noncoms had to be able to use the language that was used by twenty percent or more of a given unit. See Istvan Deak, *Beyond Nationalism: A Social and Political History of the Habsburg Officer Corps 1848–1918* (New York: Oxford University Press, 1990), pp. 99ff.

46. Karol Wojtyła, Sr., was also a man of courage; in the early days of World War I, he was awarded the Iron Cross with Wreath.

47. Author's interview with Jerzy Kluger, March 15, 1997.

48. Ibid.

49. Ibid.

50. Gian Franco Svidercoschi, *Letter to a Jewish Friend* (New York: Crossroad, 1994), p. 15; hereinafter, *Letter*.

51. John Paul II, *Gift and Mystery*, p. 20.

52. John Paul II, *Crossing the Threshold of Hope*, pp. 142–143.

53. Ibid., p. 104 [emphasis in original].

54. Author's conversation with Pope John Paul II, September 10, 1996.

55. John Paul II, *Gift and Mystery*, p. 20 [emphasis in original].

56. Recounted by Bogusław Banas in Mieczysław Maliński, *Pope John Paul II: The Life of Karol Wojtyła* (New York: Seabury, 1979), pp. 274–275.

57. Boniecki, *Kalendarium*, "School Years," citing a reminiscence published by Father Figlewicz in the Kraków Catholic weekly, *Tygodnik Powszechny*, shortly after the election of John Paul II.

58. John Paul II, *Gift and Mystery*, p. 25.

59. Author's interview with Father Kazimierz Suder, July 14, 1997.

60. See Frossard and John Paul II, *Be Not Afraid!*, p. 14, and Jonathan Kwitny, *Man of the Century: The Life and Times of Pope John Paul II* (New York: Henry Holt, 1997), p. 38.

61. Boniecki, *Kalendarium*, "School Years."

62. Kwitny, *Man of the Century*, p. 39.

63. This episode has been recounted numerous times, most authoritatively by the subject himself in *Gift and Mystery*, p. 5.

64. Ibid., p. 6. Several of Karol Wojtyła's youthful poems were published in 1999 under the title *Renesansowy Psalterz* [*Renaissance Psalter*] (Kraków: Białykruk, 1999).

65. Author's interview with Anna Karoń-Ostrowska, April 8, 1997.

66. Henryk Sienkiewicz, *The Deluge, Volume I*, translated by W. S. Kuniczak (New York: Copernicus Society of America/Hippocrene Books, 1991), pp. 764–765.

67. Czesław Miłosz, *The History of Polish Literature*, 2d ed. (Berkeley: University of California Press, 1983), p. 232; hereinafter, *History*.

68. Ibid., pp. 221–222.

69. See ibid., p. 226.

70. George Huntston Williams, *The Mind of John Paul II: Origins of His Thought and Action* (New York: Seabury, 1981), p. 58.

71. See Miłosz, *History*, p. 226.

72. Author's interview with Marek Skwarnicki, June 4, 1997.

73. Author's interview with Danuta Michałowska, April 22, 1997.

74. Miłosz, *History*, p. 241.

75. Ibid., p. 240

76. Ibid., p. 271.

77. Ibid., p. 273.

78. Ibid., p. 273–274.

79. Author's conversation with Marek Skwarnicki, June 4, 1997.

80. See *Gift and Mystery*, pp. 5–6; the story of the poetry competition is from the author's interview with Halina Kwiatkowska, November 8, 1998.

81. Miłosz, *History*, p. 235.

82. Kwitny, *Man of the Century*, p. 46; Boniecki, *Kalendarium*, "School Years."

83. Miłosz, *History*, p. 245.

84. Ibid. The text of *The Undivine Comedy* may be found in *Polish Romantic Drama: Three Plays in English Translation*, Harold B. Segel, ed. (Ithaca: Cornell University Press, 1977).

85. Author's interview with Danuta Michałowska, April 22, 1997.

86. Ibid.

87. Ibid.

88. See Buttiglione, *Karol Wojtyła*, p. 21.

89. Ibid.

90. Ibid., p. 22.

91. Author's interview with Danuta Michałowska, April 22, 1997. See also Bolesław Taborski, "Introduction" to Wojtyła, *The Collected Plays*, p. 6.

92. Kwitny, *Man of the Century*, p. 45.

93. Jonathan Kwitny was simply mistaken in claiming that the elder Karol Wojtyła was uninterested in his son's burgeoning theatrical career. [*Man of the Century*, p. 43.] Asked whether his father had attended his performances, Pope John Paul II seemed surprised by the question and replied that his father had never opposed his activities in the theater, "so of course he came." [Author's conversation with Pope John Paul II, December 11, 1996.]

94. Svidercoschi, *Letter*, p. 28; Kwitny, *Man of the Century*, pp. 46–47; O'Brien, *The Hidden Pope*, p. 124.

95. Svidercoschi, *Letter*, pp. 30–32.

96. Boniecki, *Kalendarium*, "School Years."

97. Ibid.

98. Author's interview with Maria Kotlarczyk Ćwikła, July 12, 1997.

99. Williams, *The Mind of John Paul II*, p. 31. As Pope, Karol Wojtyła would make numerous references to Włodkowic as a precursor of modern human rights theory; cf., among many examples, his "Address to the 50th General Assembly of the United Nations Organization," p. 6.

100. Karol Wojtyła, "The Problem of the Constitution of Culture Through Human Praxis," in *Person and Community: Selected Essays* (New York: Peter Lang, 1993), 264.

101. Pope John Paul II, *Curriculum Philosophicum*, unpublished autobiographical memorandum provided to the author.

102. John Paul II, *Gift and Mystery*, p. 7; John Paul II, *Curriculum Philosophicum*.

103. Ibid. Pope John Paul II wrote about this fifty years later:

"The word, before it is ever spoken on the stage, is already present in human history as a fundamental dimension of man's spiritual experience. Ultimately, the mystery of language brings us back to *the inscrutable mystery of God himself.* As I came to appreciate the power of the word in my literary and linguistic studies, I inevitably drew closer to the mystery of the Word—that Word of which we speak every day in the *Angelus,* "And the Word was made flesh and dwelt among us" (*John* 1.14). Later I came to realize that my study of Polish language and letters had prepared the ground for a different kind of interest and study. It had prepared me for an encounter with philosophy and theology." [John Paul II, *Gift and Mystery*, pp. 7–8 (emphasis in original)].

104. Svidercoschi, *Letter*, pp. 38–39.

105. The details of Karol Wojtyła's first year at the Jagiellonian University are taken from Boniecki, *Kalendarium*, "University," which also reports that years later, when Anna Nawrocka had cancer, Cardinal Karol Wojtyła arranged for her to receive medicines from the United States that were unavailable in Poland at the time.

106. See Adam Bujak and Michał Rożek, *Wojtyła* (Wrocław: Wydawnictwo Dolnośląskie, 1997), p. 25.

107. Author's interview with Jerzy Kluger, March 15, 1997.

108. Ibid.

109. On young Karol Wojtyła's gifts as a mimic, see O'Brien, *The Hidden Pope*, p. 81.

110. John Paul II, *Gift and Mystery*, p. 20.

111. *Radiation of Fatherhood*, in Wojtyła, *The Collected Plays*, pp. 355, 341.

CHAPTER 2
From the Underground: The Third Reich vs. the Kingdom of Truth

1. Pope John Paul II, "Message on the Fiftieth Anniversary of the End of the Second World War in Europe," *OR* [EWE], May 17, 1995, p. 1.

2. See Watt, *Bitter Glory*, p. 461.

3. Quoted in Szulc, *Pope John Paul II*, p. 41.

4. See Norman Davies, *God's Playground: A History of Poland, Volume II* (New York: Columbia University Press, 1982), p. 426; hereinafter, Davies, *Volume II.*

5. Watt, *Bitter Glory*, p. 456.

6. Davies, *Volume II*, p. 427.

7. Ibid., p. 222.

8. Watt, *Bitter Glory*, p. 456.

9. See ibid., pp. 386, 458.

10. *The Times Atlas of the Second World War*, John Keegan, editor (New York: Harper & Row, 1989), p. 38.

11. Cited in James Oram, *The People's Pope: The Story of Karol Wojtyła of Poland* (San Francisco: Chronicle Books, 1979), p. 43.

12. The chronology here is taken from Gerhard Weinberg, *A World at Arms: A Global History of World War II* (New York: Cambridge University Press, 1994).

13. For the Polish war plan and the comparative conditions of the opposed forces, see Watt, *Bitter Glory*, pp. 415–418.

14. Adam Zamoyski, *The Polish Way: A Thousand-Year History of the Poles and Their Culture* (New York: Hippocrene Books, 1994), p. 357. The diversionary attack is described in Watt, *Bitter Glory*, p. 430.

15. Zamoyski, *The Polish Way*, p. 359.

16. See John Keegan, *Six Armies in Normandy* (New York: Viking, 1982), pp. 262–292.

17. Weinberg, *A World at Arms*, p. 50. Weinberg claims that Polish intelligence provided British and

French cryptographers with copies of Enigma in July 1939, which renders the British/French inactivity two months later even more pusillanimous.

18. Pope John Paul II, 24th Jasna Góra Cycle Meditation, at the General Audience of August 8, 1990.

19. Watt, *Bitter Glory*, p. 435.

20. Memorials to this massacre are found in many Polish churches today, the Blessed Virgin cradling the head of a Polish officer, in the back of whose skull is a bullet hole.

21. These details of the endgame are taken from Watt, *Bitter Glory*, pp. 438–439. For a firsthand view of the events of September 1939, see also Jan Nowak, *Courier from Warsaw* (Detroit: Wayne State University Press, 1982).

22. Zamoyski, *The Polish Way*, p. 360.

23. Cited in Davies, *Volume I*, p. 369.

24. Quoted in James Michener, *Poland* (New York: Fawcett Crest, 1983), p. 451.

25. Davies, *Volume II*, p. 441.

26. Author's interview with Danuta Michałowska, April 22, 1997. Miss Michałowska, at the risk of her life, helped hide books on Polish history and literature spirited away from a library in Kraków's Old Town.

27. Memorandum from Cardinal Franciszek Macharski to the author, June 17, 1997. The causes for the canonization of Fathers Dańkowski, Januszewski, Mazurek, and Kowalski are proceeding.

The Soviet occupation of eastern Poland also added to the martyrology of Polish clergy, as priests from these regions were shipped off to the Gulag or executed. In *Gift and Mystery*, John Paul II recalled the case of Father Tadeusz Fedorowicz of the archdiocese of Lwów, who had "of his own free will gone to his Archbishop to ask if he could accompany a group of Poles being deported to the East. Archbishop Twardowicz gave his permission and so Father Fedorowicz was able to carry out his priestly mission among his fellow countrymen dispersed throughout the territories of the Soviet Union, Kazakhstan in particular" [p. 38].

28. See Sikorski, *Full Circle*, pp. 100, 107, 120.

29. John Paul II, *Gift and Mystery*, p. 26.

30. George Blazynski, *Pope John Paul II: A Man from Kraków* (London: Sphere, 1979), p. 9.

31. Wanda Połtawska, *And I Am Afraid of My Dreams* (London: Hodder and Stoughton, 1987), p. 112.

32. See Andrzej Micewski, *Cardinal Wyszyński: A Biography* (San Francisco: Harcourt Brace Jovanovich, 1984).

33. Alan Furst, *The Polish Officer* (New York: Random House, 1995), is a fine fictional evocation of the atmosphere of the Occupation, to which I owe the image of an entire nation forced to think like criminals.

34. On the flight from Kraków, see Svidercoschi, *Letter*, pp. 43–46.

35. Ibid., pp. 52–53.

36. Boniecki, *Kalendarium*, "Years of Occupation."

37. Karolak, *John Paul II*, pp. 45–50. International protests compelled the Nazis to release some of the Jagiellonian faculty members the following year. Some of those released died shortly after their return from Sachsenhausen.

38. Oram, *The People's Pope*, p. 50.

39. Boniecki, *Kalendarium*, "Years of Occupation."

40. Quoted in ibid.

41. Maliński, *Pope John Paul II*, pp. 28, 50. Maliński was then attending an engineering school, which the Occupation permitted to remain open in order to train Poles in low-level skills that would serve the Third Reich.

42. Author's interview with Maria Kotlarczyk Ćwikla, July 12, 1997.

43. Boniecki, *Kalendarium*, "Years of Occupation."

44. Ibid.

45. Ibid.

46. John Paul II, *Gift and Mystery*, p. 10.

47. Cited in Oram, *The People's Pope*, pp. 52–56.

48. Boniecki, *Kalendarium*, "Years of Occupation."

49. John Paul II, *Gift and Mystery*, pp. 27–28; John Paul II, *Crossing the Threshold of Hope*, p. 213.

50. John Paul II, *Gift and Mystery*, p. 29.

51. John Paul II, *Crossing the Threshold of Hope*, p. 213.

52. John Paul II, *Gift and Mystery*, pp. 21–22.

53. *"Tworzywo"* ["Material"], from *Kamieniołom* ["The Quarry"], in Karol Wojtyła, *Poezje i dramaty* (Kraków: Znak, 1979), p. 44; translated by the author and Marek Skwarnicki.

54. Ibid.

55. John Paul II, *Gift and Mystery*, p. 9.

56. *Pamięci towarzysza* ["In memory of a fellow worker"], from *Kamieniołom* ["The Quarry"], in Karol Wojtyła, *Poezje i dramaty*, 2nd rev. ed. (Kraków: Znak, 1998), p. 57; translated by the author and Marek Skwarnicki.

57. See Janusz Kawecki, "Alpinista Duchowy," in *Źrodło*, March 9, 1997, pp. 8–9.

58. Author's interview with Michal Szafarski, SDB, April 9, 1997.

59. Author's interview with Father Mieczysław Maliński, April 12, 1997.

60. For an examination of the chief intellectual influences on Tyranowski, see Williams, *The Mind of John Paul II*, pp. 77–81.

61. See Buttiglione, *Karol Wojtyła*, pp. 28–29.

62. Mieczysław Maliński describes his first encounter with Jan Tyranowski and the tailor's unique personal style of overcoming adolescent resistance in *Pope John Paul II*, pp. 9–20.

63. Author's interview with Michal Szafarski, SDB, April 9, 1997.

64. Maliński, *Pope John Paul II*, pp. 28–31.

65. Karol Wojtyła, *"Apostoł," Tygodnik Powszechny* n. 35 (1949). This tribute to Jan Tyranowski was Karol Wojtyła's second published essay.

66. Author's conversation with Pope John Paul II, September 10, 1996.

67. John Paul II, *Crossing the Threshold of Hope*, p. 142.

68. See Pope John Paul II, "Master in the Faith: Apostolic Letter for the Fourth Centenary of the Death of St. John of the Cross," issued December 14, 1990.

69. Boniecki, *Kalendarium*, "Years of Occupation."

70. Taborski, "Introduction," in Wojtyła, *The Collected Plays*, p. 4; Boniecki, *Kalendarium*, "Years of Occupation."

71. See Taborski, "Introduction to *Job*," in Wojtyła, *The Collected Plays*, pp. 19–24.

72. Taborski, "Introduction to *Jeremiah*," in Wojtyła, *The Collected Plays*, p. 81.

73. Ibid., p. 91. Taborski's introductions to his translations of *Job* and *Jeremiah* are indispensable for grappling with Wojtyła's methods and intentions in these early works, located as they are on the borderline between juvenilia and mature literary product.

74. Taborski, "Introduction," in Wojtyła, *The Collected Plays*, p. 4.

75. Ibid., p. 5.

76. Ibid., p. 4; Oram, *The People's Pope*, p. 61.

77. Boniecki, *Kalendarium*, "Years of Occupation."

78. Author's interview with Maria Kotlarczyk Ćwikla, July 12, 1997.

79. Cited in Taborski, "Introduction," in Wojtyła, *The Collected Plays*, p. 6.

80. Author's conversation with Pope John Paul II, September 30, 1997.

81. See Kwitny, *Man of the Century*, p. 56.

82. Author's interview with Danuta Michałowska, April 22, 1997.

83. See Kwitny, *Man of the Century*, pp. 71–71, for details of this split, based on Danuta Michałowska's recollections.

84. Boniecki, *Kalendarium*, "Years of Occupation." Danuta Michałowska, Halina Królikiewicz, and Krystyna Dębowska would all go on to make the theater their careers.

85. Boniecki, *Kalendarium*, "Years of Occupation."

86. According to the recollection of Danuta Michałowska; see Kwitny, *Man of the Century*, p. 72.

87. On these performances, see Taborski, "Introduction," in Wojtyła, *The Collected Plays*, pp. 7–9.

88. As related by Mieczysław Kotlarczyk in Boniecki, *Kalendarium*, "Years of Occupation."

89. Author's interviews with Danuta Michałowska, April 22, 1997, and Halina Kwiatkowska, November 8, 1998.

90. Ibid.

91. Tadeusz Kwiatkowski remembered the impact of this incident twenty-one years later: because Wojtyła refused to concede to the power of the megaphone, "Mickiewicz did not take up the war of shouting. When the barker finished her glorification of German atrocities, Mickiewicz was announcing the reconciliation of Soplica with the Keymaster. I looked at the faces of the assembled guests. The same thought animated all of us. We all felt we were sons of this nation, a nation which over the course of centuries was often betrayed, but which will not succumb to terror." [Boniecki, *Kalendarium*, "Theological Studies."]

92. The Rhapsodic Theater continued after the war until it was shut down in 1953 at the height of Stalinism in Poland. Reopening in 1957, it survived until 1967 when the communist regime once again closed its doors. The fiftieth anniversary of the founding of the Rhapsodic Theater was marked by the publication of a fine collection of commemorative and historical essays, illustrated by wonderful if grainy old photographs: ". . . *trzeb dać świadectwo": 50-lecie powstania Teatru Rapsodycznego w Krakowie* was edited by Danuta Michałowska, to whom I am most grateful for providing me with a copy.

93. See Garry Wills, "All the Pope's Men," *The New Yorker*, December 2, 1996, pp. 107–113, and the quotations from Rabbi Arthur Hertzberg in Paul Elie, "John Paul II's Jewish Dilemma," *New York Times Magazine*, April 26, 1998, p. 38.

94. The preexisting underground groups included "Warszawianka," whose members included men who had served in the prewar administration of the Second Polish Republic; "Grunwald," another Warsaw-based organization, more blue-collar in character; and "Nowa Polska," which had been formed in and around Kraków under the leadership of Jerzy Braun, a Catholic philosopher and writer.

95. Information on UNIA was provided in a memorandum to the author from Juliusz Braun (a member of the Polish parliament and nephew of UNIA leader Jerzy Braun), translated by Professor Kazimierz Braun. Juliusz Braun also kindly provided me with several documents reflecting UNIA's ideological position and postwar proposals. In addition, Mr. Braun sent me a reprint of an article in French by Konstanty Regamey, another UNIA leader, which stressed that, among the "unknown aspects of the Polish resistance," was the widespread interest underground in articulating a new political philosophy for postwar Poland. The Polish resistance, in other words, was not only "against" the Occupation but was striving to set in place the foundations "for" a new Poland.

96. Boniecki, *Kalendarium*, "Years of Occupation."

97. Szulc, *Pope John Paul II*, p. 117.

98. Cited in ibid.

99. Author's conversation with Bishop Stanisław Ryłko, December 10, 1996.

100. John Paul II, *Gift and Mystery*, p. 34.

101. Ibid., p. 20.

102. Ibid., p. 3.

103. Author's conversation with Pope John Paul II, December 16, 1998.

104. Danuta Michałowska, quoted in Kwitny, *Man of the Century*, p. 78.

105. Author's interview with Halina Kwiatkowska, November 8, 1998.

106. Ibid.

107. As recounted in Kwitny, *Man of the Century*, p. 78.

108. Frossard and John Paul II, *"Be Not Afraid!,"* p. 17.

109. John Paul II, *Curriculum Philosophicum.*

110. John Paul II, *Gift and Mystery*, p. 42–43.

111. See Maliński, *Pope John Paul II*, pp. 63–69.

112. Svidercoschi, *Letter*, p. 77.

113. Boniecki, *Kalendarium*, "Theological Studies."

114. The pectoral cross, suspended from the neck by a chain, is, with the episcopal ring and staff (or crosier), one of the bishop's signs of authority in Catholic vesture. A world beyond the imagination of either pontiff or aristocratic bishop would become familiar with this particular pectoral cross decades later.

115. Author's interview with Father Kazimierz Suder, July 14, 1997.

116. Author's interview with Stanisław Rodziński, June 9, 1997.

117. Author's interview with Cardinal Franciszek Macharski, April 10, 1997.

118. Cardinal Puzyna cast the last imperial veto in a papal conclave, blocking the election of Cardinal Mariano Rampolla in 1904 on instructions from the Emperor Francis Joseph. In the aftermath of this anachronism the conclave rules were changed and the right of imperial veto abrogated.

119. Author's interview with Bishop Stanisław Smoleński, April 9, 1997; author's conversation with Pope John Paul II, September 10, 1996; author's interview with Henryk Woźniakowski, November 6, 1998.

120. B. Stasiewski, "Hlond, Augustyn," *New Catholic Encyclopedia*, volume 7, p. 41.

121. Author's interview with Sister Emilia Ehrlich, OSU, March 21, 1997.

122. Author's interview with Father Kazimierz Suder, July 14, 1997.

123. Author's interview with Bishop Stanisław Smoleński, April 9, 1997; Buttiglione, *Karol Wojtyła*, pp. 30–31.

124. Author's interview with Bishop Stanisław Smoleński, April 9, 1997.

125. Boniecki, *Kalendarium*, "Theological Studies."

126. Ibid.

127. Maliński, *Pope John Paul II*, p.74.

128. Author's conversation with Pope John Paul II, September 10, 1996.

129. John Paul II, *Gift and Mystery*, p. 13.

130. Maliński, *Pope John Paul II*, p. 85.

131. See Davies, *Volume II*, p. 471.

132. Ibid., p. 489.

133. Ibid., p. 491.

134. Ibid., p. 545.

135. On Gomułka, see ibid., pp. 547–548.

136. Davies, *Heart of Europe*, p. 3.

137. Author's interview with Sister Emilia Ehrlich, OSU, March 21, 1997.

138. This last incident took place after the seminary had been restored to its old quarters near Wawel Cathedral, after the Occupation. See Boniecki, *Kalendarium*, "Theological Studies."

139. Ibid.

140. Author's conversation with Pope John Paul II, September 10, 1996.

141. The "Litany of Our Lord Jesus Christ, Priest and Victim" is reprinted in full in John Paul II, *Gift and Mystery*, pp. 108–114.

142. See ibid., p. 18.

143. Author's interview with Father Kazimierz Suder, July 14, 1997.

144. Boniecki, *Kalendarium*, "Theological Studies."

145. The Athenaeum, staffed then as now by Dominicans, would later become the Pontifical University of St. Thomas Aquinas, and was known to everyone under either configuration as "the Angelicum," or, more informally, "the Ange," in distinction from the Jesuit-led Pontifical Gregorian University, "the Greg."

146. The subdiaconate was abrogated by Pope Paul VI in 1972. In 1946 the subdiaconate was considered the first of the Church's "major orders," although it was not regarded as part of the sacrament of Holy Orders, which encompasses ordination to the offices of deacon, priest, and bishop. After the abrogation of 1972, the functions of the subdeacon were assumed by the lay ministries of reader and acolyte. Eastern-rite Catholic Churches have continued the order of subdeacon.

147. Wojtyła's classmates, including Kazimierz Suder, were ordained priests the following Palm Sunday. [John Paul II, *Gift and Mystery*, p. 41.]

148. Fifty years later, Pope John Paul II remembered the impact of this moment on his subsequent priestly ministry: to lie helpless on the floor indicated the candidate's "complete willingness to undertake the ministry being entrusted to him," his willingness to be a "floor" on which others might walk in faith. The "ultimate meaning of all priestly spirituality" was this commitment to spend oneself completely in service to others. [John Paul II, *Gift and Mystery*, pp. 45–46.]

149. The rite of the ordination of priests has changed considerably since 1946, and the ceremonial books of that era are not easy to come by. I am very grateful to Father Vincent McMurry, SS, who lent me the booklet containing the rite in Latin and English which he had given to his mother at his own ordination in 1949. [*The Ordination of a Priest* (Paterson, N.J.: St. Anthony's Guild, 1948).] I have modified the booklet's translations of the Latin somewhat to reflect certain current usages.

150. John Paul II, *Gift and Mystery*, p. 48.

151. Boniecki, *Kalendarium*, "Theological Studies."

152. Ibid. Shortly after his ordination, Father Wojtyła is said to have declined to baptize an orphaned Jewish child being cared for by Christian foster parents, explaining that there was still hope that the child might be claimed by Jewish relatives who would raise the little boy in the Jewish tradition. [See Yaffa Eliach, *Hasidic Tales of the Holocaust* (New York: Vintage Books, 1988)]. Pope John Paul II has said that this is, in fact, "a legend," adding that "I simply don't remember doing it." The Pope did not suggest, however, that such a decision would have been out of character for him. Indeed, it would have been entirely in character. "But I cannot remember such an incident," he concluded. [Author's conversation with Pope John Paul II, December 16, 1998.]

153. John Paul II, *Gift and Mystery*, p. 51.

154. Author's interview with Archbishop Jorge M. Mejía, November 13, 1996.

155. John Paul II, *Gift and Mystery*, p. 52.

156. Cardijn was a critic of the worker-priest movement, telling one of Wojtyła's Belgian College fellow students that "a worker does not want a priest to become a worker, but to be essentially a priest for them, too. A worker-priest can never be a *real* worker, because at any moment he can stop being a worker." [Letter to the author from Canon Gustaaf Joos, July 11, 1998.]

157. Letter to the author from Canon Gustaaf Joos, February 8, 1998.

158. John Paul II, *Gift and Mystery*, p. 53.

159. Boniecki, *Kalendarium*, "Theological Studies." Wojtyła reported the practice in a letter to Mieczysław Kotlarczyk.

160. Author's conversation with Pope John Paul II, December 13, 1997. During this conversation the Holy Father did not mention the legend that Padre Pio had predicted Wojtyła's election as pope during his confession. The Holy Father's emphasis on the brevity, clarity, and simplicity of Padre Pio as a confessor tells against the legend which, if true, John Paul would quite properly have regarded as a private matter.

161. Subiaco and Paris: Boniecki, *Kalendarium*, "Theological Studies."

162. John Paul II, *Gift and Mystery*, p. 55.

163. Ibid.

164. Ibid., p. 56.

165. Ibid., p. 58.

166. Ibid., p. 56.

167. Author's interview with Michal Szafarski, SDB, April 9, 1997.

168. Author's interview with Archbishop Jorge Mejía, November 13, 1996. Mejía studied at the Angelicum at the same time as Karol Wojtyła. He rightly cautions against reading that situation through the lens of today's expectations about the character of a graduate theological education. Judged by those standards, the Angelicum was not an "exciting" intellectual environment; some of its professors were excellent, and others were rather dull. But by giving its students a firm foundation in the tradition, the Angelicum, for all that it lacked the intellectual sparkle of more adventurous faculties of its era, armored its students against faddishness in their intellectual lives.

Another student living at the Belgian College at the time, Gustaaf Joos, remembered decades later that Roman theology students knew that "the exploratory edge of theology was located more in Paris and Louvain." [Letter to the author from Canon Gustaaf Joos, July 11, 1998.]

169. See Buttiglione, *Karol Wojtyła*, pp. 44–53, for an analysis of Wojtyła's dissertation and its relationship to the thought of Garrigou-Lagrange, whose shortcomings as well as gifts Buttiglione frankly recognizes.

170. English edition: Karol Wojtyła, *Faith According to St. John of the Cross*, translated by Jordan Aumann, OP (San Francisco: Ignatius Press, 1981).

171. See Buttiglione, *Karol Wojtyła*, pp. 46–47.

172. Ibid., p. 51.

173. See Buttiglione, *Karol Wojtyła*, p. 53.

174. Boniecki, *Kalendarium*, "Theological Studies." One of the Jagiellonian reviewers of the dissertation, Father Władysław Wicher, while impressed with the work, complained that Wojtyła had spent too much time making his own arguments and too little analyzing St. John's texts: he was "too much a dialectician, too little a philologist." It was a complaint similar to Garrigou's, if along a different axis of criticism, and suggests again that Wojtyła was not simply parroting back the formulas of his traditional Thomistic mentors.

175. His companion, Stanisław Starowieyski, spent his life as a missionary in Brazil, where he died in the 1980s.

176. Author's conversation with Pope John Paul II, January 16, 1997.

177. Author's interview with Bishop Stanisław Smoleński, April 9, 1997.

CHAPTER 3
"Call Me *Wujek*": To Be a Priest

1. Author's interview with Danuta Rybicka, April 19, 1997.

2. See John Colville, *The Fringes of Power: Downing Street Diaries, Volume Two: 1941–April 1955* (London: Sceptre, 1987), p. 322.

3. Davies, *Heart of Europe*, pp. 4, 80–81; Zamoyski, *The Polish Way*, pp. 370–371.

4. See Zamoyski, *The Polish Way*, p.370.

5. Blazynski, *Pope John Paul II*, p. 59.

6. See John Paul II, *Gift and Mystery*, pp. 53–54, 69–70.

7. Author's interview with Cardinal Franciszek Macharski, April 10, 1997.

8. Boniecki, *Kalendarium*; Kwitny, *Man of the Century*, p. 109.

9. John Paul II, *Gift and Mystery*, pp. 61–62.

10. Ibid., p. 62.

11. Szulc, *Pope John Paul II*, p. 159.

12. John Paul II, *Gift and Mystery*, p. 62.

13. See Maliński, *Pope John Paul II*, p. 95.

14. See ibid., p. 96.

15. Boniecki, *Kalendarium*, "1948."

16. Karolak, *John Paul II*, p. 85.

17. Ibid., p. 86; see also John Paul II, *Gift and Mystery*, p. 63, in which the author characteristically ignores his own role in this small rural drama.

18. Boniecki, *Kalendarium*, "Theological Studies."

19. Taborski, "Introduction to *Our God's Brother*," in Wojtyła, *The Collected Plays*, p. 150.

20. Bernstein and Politi, *His Holiness*, p. 77.

21. John Paul II, *Gift and Mystery*, p. 63.

22. The great statues of the Grunwald Monument were reconstructed in 1976.

23. Grażyna Sikorska, "Poland," in *Conscience and Captivity: Religion in Eastern Europe*, Janice Broun, ed. (Washington, D.C.: Ethics and Public Policy Center, 1988), pp. 178–179.

24. Author's interview with Piotr Malecki, April 9, 1997.

25. See John Paul II, *Gift and Mystery*, p. 64.

26. See ibid., pp. 63–64.

27. I am grateful to Mrs. Danuta Rybicka for providing me with a copy of one of these texts, *Rozważnia o Istocie Człowieka*, a November 1951 series of Wojtyła lectures on the nature of the human person.

28. Boniecki, *Kalendarium*, "1949."

29. Author's interview with Jacek Woźniakowski, April 11, 1997.

30. Author's interview with Krzysztof Zanussi, March 25, 1996.

31. Author's interview with Maria Swieżawska, April 7, 1997.

32. Author's interview with Jacek Woźniakowski, April 11, 1997.

33. See Boniecki, *Kalendarium*, "1949," "1950," "1951"; author's interviews with Danuta Rybicka, Piotr Malecki, and Teresa Malecka, April 9, 1997.

34. Michałowska, "... *trzeba dać świadectwo*": *50-lecie powstania Teatru Rapsodycznego*, photo #18.

35. Boniecki, *Kalendarium*, "1954."

36. John Paul II, *Crossing the Threshold of Hope*, p. 123.

37. Letter to the author from Danuta Ciesielska, April 15, 1997.

38. Author's interviews with Danuta Rybicka and Teresa Malecka, April 19, 1997.

39. Author's interviews with Danuta Rybicka, April 19, 1997.

40. Author's interview with Danuta and Stanisław Rybicki, April 19, 1997.

41. Author's interview with Stanisław Rybicki, April 19, 1997.

42. The St. Florian's church bulletin announced that, the young people themselves having asked for a series of conferences for their own benefit, the parish priests had agreed; anything the priests were thought to have initiated would have been forbidden by the state authorities. [Ibid.]

43. Author's interview with Teresa Malecka, April 9, 1997.

44. Author's interview with Bishop Stanisław Ryłko, December 11, 1996.

45. It did, twenty years later, when Rybicki was appointed an assistant professor at the Kraków Polytechnic, having continued his studies privately in the interim. [Author's interview with Stanisław Rybicki, April 19, 1997.]

46. Author's interview with Teresa Malecka, April 9, 1997.

47. Author's interview with Jerzy Janik, July 17, 1996.

48. Author's interviews with Piotr and Teresa Malecki, April 9, 1997. Told of Dr. Malecki's self-description, Pope John Paul II laughed and said, "I think not so *terrible* . . . " [Author's conversation with Pope John Paul II, September 30, 1997.]

49. Correspondence provided to the author by Teresa Heydel Życzkowska, November 9, 1998.

50. Ibid. [emphasis in original].

51. Author's interview with Teresa Malecka, April 9, 1997.

52. Author's interview with Halina Bortnowska, April 7, 1997.

53. Davies, *Heart of Europe*, p. 80.

54. Author's interviews with Teresa Heydel Życzkowska, April 19, 1997, and Jerzy Janik, July 17, 1996.

55. Author's interview with Jacek Woźniakowski, April 11, 1997.

56. Author's interview with Piotr Malecki, April 9, 1997.

57. Boniecki, *Kalendarium*, "1955."

58. Author's interview with Gabriel Turowski, June 10, 1997. Details of the kayak trips are taken from Dr. Turowski's manuscript memoir, "*Wieli Wujek na Kajakach*," ("Great Uncle in Kayaks"), which he coauthored with his wife, Professor Bożena Turowska, and kindly gave me during our interview.

59. Danuta Ciesielska, the widow of Jerzy Ciesielski, kindly shared with me the original copy of her husband's and then-Father Wojtyła's contributions to the May–June 1957 issue of *Homo Dei*.

60. Author's interview with Teresa Malecka, April 9, 1997.

61. Author's interviews with Stanisław Rybicki, April 9, 1997, and June 5, 1997.
62. Author's interview with Stanisław Rybicki, June 5, 1997.
63. Ibid.
64. Author's interview with Danuta Ciesielska, April 9, 1997.
65. Author's interview with Piotr Malecki, April 9, 1997.
66. Author's interview with Danuta Rybicka, June 5, 1997.
67. Author's interview with Stefan Sawicki, April 15, 1997.
68. See Hans Urs von Balthasar, "On Vicarious Representation," in *Explorations in Theology IV* (San Francisco: Ignatius Press, 1995), p. 421.
69. Author's interview with Karol Tarnowski, April 12, 1997.
70. Ibid.
71. Ibid.
72. Ibid.; author's interview with Karol Tarnowski, November 5, 1998.
73. Ibid.
74. Author's interview with Danuta Rybicka, June 5, 1997.
75. On the Thomistic understanding of the sacrament of penance, see Servais Pinckaers, OP, *The Sources of Christian Ethics* (Washington, D.C.: Catholic University of America Press, 1995), p. 233.
76. Author's interview with Stanisław Rybicki, June 5, 1997.
77. Author's interview with Danuta Ciesielska, April 9, 1997.
78. See Boniecki, *Kalendarium*, "1954."
79. Ibid.
80. Author's interview with Teresa Malecka, April 9, 1997.
81. Author's interview with Jerzy Turowicz, July 19, 1996.
82. Ibid.
83. Ibid.
84. All citations from Wojtyła's article on the *Mission de France* are taken from the French translation of the Polish original, which may be found in Karol Wojtyła, *En Esprit et En Vérité* (Paris: Le Centurion, 1980).
85. See *"De l'origine des normes morales," "La loi naturelle,"* and *"Le problème de la vérité et de la miséricorde,"* in Wojtyła, *En Esprit et En Vérité*, pp. 111–113, 123–125, and 129–130.
86. Author's interview with Jerzy Turowicz, July 19, 1996.
87. Ibid.
88. Ibid.
89. Author's interview with Archbishop Marian Jaworski, July 10, 1996.
90. See Stanisław Baranczak, "Playing and Praying," *The New Republic* (December 4, 1987), p. 48; author's interview with Anna Karoń-Ostrowska, April 8, 1997.
91. Author's conversation with Pope John Paul II, January 22, 1997.
92. Author's interview with Stanisław Rodziński, June 9, 1997.
93. See Taborski, "Introduction to *Our God's Brother*," in Wojtyła, *The Collected Plays*, pp. 147–148.
94. See ibid., pp. 150–155.
95. Professor Stanisław Rodziński suggests that, for Chmielowski, this was not a matter of abandoning art but of coming to the service of God and humanity *through* art. [Author's interview with Stanisław Rodziński, June 9, 1997.]
96. Author's conversation with Pope John Paul II, January 22, 1997.
97. Wojtyła, *Our God's Brother*, p. 263, in *The Collected Plays*.
98. Ibid., p. 266.
99. Author's interview with Marek Skwarnicki, April 19, 1997. Mr. Skwarnicki, a distinguished poet and longtime contributor to *Tygodnik Powszechny*, was deputed by Pope John Paul II to oversee the premiere of *Our God's Brother* and of course refused to cut the final sentence.
100. See *Isaiah* 58.6. This text was cited by Pope John Paul II in his homily at the canonization of St. Albert Chmielowski, on November 12, 1989.
101. See, for example, Mark Lawson, "The Pope's Other Self," *The Tablet*, December 14, 1996, p. 1643; Jonathan Luxmoore and Jolanta Babiuch, "Did Karol Wojtyła See and Rescue the Good in Marxism?" *National Catholic Register*, January 26–February 1, 1997, p. 7. Both of these articles were inspired by Krzysztof Zanussi's film version of *Our God's Brother*, which was premiered in Kraków during John Paul II's visit to the city on June 8, 1997.
102. *Our God's Brother* had a difficult history after Wojtyła completed it and read sections of it to the editors of *Tygodnik Powszechny*. [Author's conversation with Pope John Paul II, January 22, 1997.] The play was then virtually lost, and certainly unknown, for almost thirty years. Shortly after Karol Wojtyła's election as pope, Juliusz Kydryński brought his copy of the manuscript, which was evidently in bad shape, to Jerzy Turowicz, who gave it to his colleague Marek Skwarnicki for an opinion. Skwarnicki had no doubts. The play had to be published immediately, finished and polished or not, because the "problematic" with which it dealt was too urgent to permit a delay. After some difficulty persuading John Paul II of this (he claimed the play really wasn't finished and was understandably concerned about his work), the Pope finally agreed and the play was printed in its entirety in the Christmas 1979 issue of *Tygodnik Powszechny*. Under Skwarnicki's personal supervision, it was then produced at Kraków's Słowacki Theater in 1980. [Author's interview with Marek Skwarnicki, April 19, 1997.]
Krzysztof Zanussi's film of *Our God's Brother* illustrates some of the difficulties of producing a compelling presentation of Wojtyła's plays "outside" the context of the "inner theater" in which they were written. The inner dialogue that Wojtyła and his mentor, Mieczysław Kotlarczyk, intended to facilitate "between" the

actor and the audience does not transfer easily to film or to theatrical environments whose audiences have not been prepared for such a different kind of dramatic experience.

103. John Paul II, *Gift and Mystery*, pp. 31–33.

104. Ibid., p. 33.

105. A literal translation of the title, which would also reflect more accurately one of the play's central images, would be *In Front of the Jeweler's Shop*. Both the Taborski translation of the play into English and the 1988 film use the title *The Jeweler's Shop*, which I have adopted here to avoid confusions.

106. See Buttiglione, *Karol Wojtyła*, p. 257.

107. Wojtyła, *The Jeweler's Shop*, in *The Collected Plays*, pp. 297–298.

108. See Buttiglione, *Karol Wojtyła*, p. 265.

109. Author's interview with Stanisław and Danuta Rybicki, July 17, 1997.

110. Author's conversation with Pope John Paul II, September 30, 1997.

111. Ibid.

112. Author's interview with Stanisław Rybicki, June 5, 1997.

113. Wojtyła's notion of the dramatic structure of reality and of God's relationship to the world is similar to, although not derived from, the theology of the Swiss thinker Hans Urs von Balthasar. One difference between the two is that Wojtyła's "dramatic" intuition was formed in considerable part by his experiences on stage and as a playwright; Balthasar's came from a deep reading of the European dramatic tradition. For a brief description of Balthasar's conception of creation and redemption as a "Theo-Drama," see Angelo Scola, *Hans Urs von Balthasar: A Theological Style* (Grand Rapids: Eerdmans, 1995), pp. 65 ff.

114. Author's interview with Stefan Sawicki, April 15, 1997.

115. Wojtyła's literary colleagues believe that the German and Italian translations of his work best convey the texture and meanings of the Polish originals, which is sometimes lost in the commercially available English translation. [Author's interviews with Halina Bortnowska, April 7, 1997, and Marek Skwarnicki, April 19 and June 4, 1997.]

116. Author's interview with Anna Karoń-Ostrowska, April 8, 1997.

117. *"Robotnik z fabryki broni"* [The armaments factory worker], from *Profile Cyrenejczyka* [Profiles of a Cyrenean], in Wojtyła, *Poezje i dramaty*, p. 54; translated by the author and Marek Skwarnicki.

118. *"Późniejsze rozpamiętywanie spotkania"* [Later recollection of the meeting], from *Pieśń o blasku wody* [Song of the brightness of water], in Wojtyła, *Poezje i dramaty*, p. 32; translated by the author and Marek Skwarnicki.

119. Author's interviews with Halina Bortnowska, April 9, 1997, and Jacek Woźniakowski, April 11, 1997.

120. Author's interview with Marek Skwarnicki, April 19, 1997.

121. Buttiglione, *Karol Wojtyła*, p. 242.

122. Ibid.

123. *"Zanim jeszcze potrafiłem rozróżnić wiele profilów"* [Before I could discern many profiles], from *Profile Cyrenejczyka*, in Wojtyła, *Poezje i dramaty*, p. 50; translated by the author and Marek Skwarnicki.

124. Author's interview with Bishop Stanisław Ryłko, December 10, 1996.

125. Author's interview with Mieczysław Maliński, April 12, 1997.

126. Ibid.

127. Ibid.

128. Author's interview with Jacek Woźniakowski, April 11, 1997.

129. Father Kurowski's arrest may have had to do with the fact that he was also an official of the archdiocesan chancery, where the secret police believed evidence of Soviet complicity in the Katyn massacre of 1940, first given to Archbishop Sapieha during the war, might be hidden. [Author's interview with Father Stanisław Małysiak, April 18, 1997.]

130. Cited in Jan Nowak, "The Church in Poland", *Problems of Communism* 31 (January–February 1982), p. 7.

131. See Broun, *Conscience and Captivity*, pp. 333–334, for excerpts from this historic memorandum.

132. Author's conversation with Pope John Paul II, January 22, 1997.

133. Ibid.

CHAPTER 4

Seeing Things as They Are: The Making of a Philosopher

1. Boniecki, *Kalendarium*, "1955."

2. Author's conversation with Pope John Paul II, September 10, 1996.

3. Ibid.; author's interview with Father Stanisław Małysiak, April 18, 1997.

4. Ibid.

5. Ibid.

6. Author's interview with Father Stanisław Małysiak, April 18, 1997.

7. The custom of a second doctoral dissertation to qualify for appointment to a university faculty is unknown in North American academic life but is the norm in Europe. "Habilitation" is from the Latin *habilitas*, "aptitude."

8. For an analysis of the consequences of this conclusion, see Edward T. Oakes, SJ, "The Achievement of Alasdair MacIntyre," *First Things* 65 (August/September 1996), pp. 22–26.

9. See Robert F. Harvanek, SJ, "The Philosophical Foundations of the Thought of John Paul II," in *The*

Thought of Pope John Paul II, ed. John M. McDermott, SJ (Rome: Editrice Pontifica Università Gregoriana, 1993), p. 2.

10. Michael Novak, "John Paul II: Christian Philosopher," *America* 177: 12 (October 25, 1997), p. 12.

11. Ibid.

12. Ibid.

13. The example is adopted from ibid.

14. See Schmitz, *At the Center of the Human Drama*, p. 32.

15. On this point, see Alasdair MacIntyre, *After Virtue* (Notre Dame: University of Notre Dame Press, 1981).

16. See Schmitz, *At the Center of the Human Drama*, p. 33.

17. Author's conversation with Pope John Paul II, December 11, 1996.

18. Maliński, *Pope John Paul II*, p. 110.

19. John Paul II, *Curriculum Philosophicum*, p. 3.

20. See Buttiglione, *Karol Wojtyła*, pp. 54ff.

21. See John H. Nota, SJ, "Phenomenological Experience in Karol Wojtyła," in McDermott, ed., *The Thought of Pope John Paul II*, p. 198.

22. See Buttiglione, *Karol Wojtyła*, p. 57.

23. John Paul II, *Curriculum Philosophicum*, p. 4.

24. Author's interviews with Karol Tarnowski, April 12, 1997, and Andrzej Szostek, MIC, April 14, 1997.

25. See Buttiglione, *Karol Wojtyła*, pp. 58–59.

26. The dissertation and later Wojtyła writings on Scheler may be found in Karol Wojtyła, *Zagadnienie podmiotu moralności* (Lublin: Catholic University of Lublin Press, 1991). The Scheler dissertation has been translated into German and Spanish (see Schmitz, *At the Center of the Human Drama*, p. 154, note 44 for bibliographic references) and Italian (see Buttiglione, *Karol Wojtyła*, p. 54, note 17, for bibliographic reference).

27. See Buttiglione, *Karol Wojtyła*, pp. 58–59.

28. Author's interview with Father Józef Tischner, April 23, 1997. See also Rocco Buttiglione, "Toward an Adequate Anthropology," *Ethos*, special edition no. 2 (1996), pp. 237–246.

29. Author's interview with Father Józef Tischner, April 23, 1997.

30. Ibid.

31. See Boniecki, *Kalendarium*, "1953," "1954."

32. See John M. Grondelski, "Social Ethics in the Young Karol Wojtyła: A Study-in-Progress," *Faith and Reason* 22 (1996), pp. 32–33.

That the course material was essentially Piwowarczyk's was confirmed by me by Bishop Stanisław Ryłko, to whom I had put the question of the material's authorship and who subsequently raised the issue with Pope John Paul II. The response I received was that Wojtyła had "elaborated it [Piwowarczyk's text] but the material was not his [i.e., Wojtyła's]." (Author's interview with Bishop Stanisław Ryłko, November 25, 1997.) Thus Jonathan Kwitny is mistaken in his claim [see *Man of the Century*, pp. 135–142] that *Catholic Social Ethics* is a major and previously unknown Wojtyła text. *Catholic Social Ethics* is not a book, but a set of lecture notes based on a two-volume book, and Wojtyła was not the principal author of the notes, as he himself freely concedes.

33. Oram, *The People's Pope*, p. 82.

34. Author's interview with Sister Zofia Zdybicka, OSU, April 14, 1997.

35. See Buttiglione, *Karol Wojtyła*, p. 38.

36. Author's interview with Stefan Swieżawski, April 7, 1997.

37. Oram, *The People's Pope*, p. 82.

38. Stefan Swieżawski, "Introduction: Karol Wojtyła at the Catholic University of Lublin," in Wojtyła, *Person and Community*, p. ix.

39. Author's interview with Stefan Swieżawski, April 7, 1997.

40. Ibid.

41. Swieżawski, "Introduction," in Wojtyła, *Person and Community*, p. xii.

42. Author's interview with Tadeusz Styczeń, SDS, April 14, 1997.

43. Swieżawski, "Introduction," in Wojtyła, *Person and Community*, p. xiii.

44. See Buttiglione, *Karol Wojtyła*, pp. 58–62.

45. Author's interview with Cardinal Joseph Ratzinger, September 12, 1996.

46. These four points are adapted from Swieżawski, "Introduction," in Wojtyła, *Person and Community*, pp. xii-xiii.

47. Author's interview with Sister Zofia Zdybicka, OSU, April 14, 1997.

48. John Paul II, *Curriculum Philosophicum*; author's interview with Sister Zofia Zdybicka, OSU, April 14, 1997.

49. Author's interview with Tadeusz Styczeń, SDS, April 14, 1997.

50. Author's interview with Sister Zofia Zdybicka, OSU, April 14, 1997.

51. Author's interview with Stefan Sawicki, April 15, 1997.

52. Author's interview with Sister Zofia Zdybicka, OSU, April 14, 1997.

53. Ibid.

54. Author's interview with Halina Bortnowska, April 7, 1997.

55. Author's interview with Sister Zofia Zdybicka, OSU, April 14, 1997.

56. Ibid.

57. This position anticipated Wojtyła's later, sympathetic encounter with the work of the philosophers of dialogue, such as Martin Buber and Emmanuel Levinas. See John Paul II, *Crossing the Threshold of Hope*, p. 36.

58. Author's interview with Halina Bortnowska, April 7, 1997. For the centrality of freedom in Wojtyła's monographic lectures, see Schmitz, *At the Center of the Human Drama*, p. 55.

59. See Schmitz, *At the Center of the Human Drama*, p. 42.

60. Ibid., p. 49 [emphasis added].

61. See ibid., pp. 50ff.

62. The definitive text of the monographic lectures is Karol Wojtyła, *Wykłady lubelskie* (Lublin: Catholic University of Lublin Press, 1986). For analysis and commentary, see Schmitz, *At the Center of the Human Drama*, pp. 30–57, and Jarosław Kupczak, OP, *The Human Person as Efficient Cause in the Christian Anthropology of Karol Wojtyła*, unpublished STD dissertation (Washington, D.C.: Pontifical John Paul II Institute for Studies of Marriage and Family, 1996), chapter two.

63. Author's interview with Halina Bortnowska, April 7, 1997. When it was pointed out to him that others might take this as a mark of disinterest or disrespect, Wojtyła replied, "Oh, really?" and explained that it was easier for him to concentrate when he was working this way. This capacity for doing two things at once, and both well, is frequently remarked by Wojtyła's students and colleagues from the 1960s and 1970s.

64. Offered this once as a description of his intellectual method, Pope John Paul II agreed that it was a reasonable depiction of the way his philosopher's mind worked. [Author's conversation with Pope John Paul II, December 11, 1996.]

65. Author's interview with Jerzy Gałkowski, April 14, 1997.

66. Ibid.

67. Author's interview with Sister Zofia Zdybicka, OSU, April 14, 1997.

68. Author's interview with Jerzy Gałkowski, April 14, 1997.

Wojtyła wanted to travel to the University of Louvain in Belgium, as well as to France and Switzerland, to further his research on sexual ethics. The President of KUL approved the proposal and, in early 1958, got the Ministry of Higher Education to agree to the trip. But the government denied Wojtyła a passport, so he never went. [Boniecki, *Kalendarium*, "1957."]

69. Author's interview with Jerzy Gałkowski, April 14, 1997.

70. John Paul II, *Curriculum Philosophicum*; Henri de Lubac, "Love and Responsibility," in *Theology in History* (San Francisco: Ignatius Press, 1996), pp. 581–583.

71. "Author's Introduction to the First Edition (1960)," in Karol Wojtyła, *Love and Responsibility* (San Francisco: Ignatius Press, 1993), p. 16.

72. Ibid.

73. See Buttiglione, *Karol Wojtyła*, p. 91.

74. See ibid., pp. 90–91.

75. Ibid., p. 95.

76. Ibid.

77. Ibid., p. 99.

78. Ibid, p. 105.

79. On this point see John M. McDermott, SJ, "The Theology of John Paul II: Response," in McDermott, ed., *The Thought of Pope John Paul II*, p. 60.

80. *Love and Responsibility* was first published in Polish by the KUL Press. A French edition was published in 1965, an Italian edition in 1968, and a Spanish edition in 1969. See Buttiglione, *Karol Wojtyła*, p. 83, note 1, for bibliographic information.

81. John Paul II, *Curriculum Philosophicum*.

82. Wojtyła, *Love and Responsibility*, pp. 13, 9.

CHAPTER 5

A New Pentecost: Vatican II and the Crisis of Humanism

1. Author's interviews with Stanisław and Danuta Rybicki, June 5, 1997; Gabriel Turowski, June 10, 1997; and Bishop Stanisław Ryłko, September 29, 1997; Boniecki, *Kalendarium*, "1958."

In a large archdiocese like Kraków, it is customary for the archbishop to have one or more assistant bishops, known as "auxiliary bishops." In the Catholic understanding of the episcopacy, a bishop is regarded as "married" to his diocese, so there can be only one bishop of one see at any one time. But since every bishop has to be a bishop of somewhere, auxiliary bishops are given "titular sees," dioceses that have long since disappeared into the mists of history (in North Africa, for example, where Ombi is located) or that have been suppressed when the Catholic population shifted and a new diocese had to be erected elsewhere (such as Walla Walla, Washington). Assignment to a titular see is meant to indicate that the episcopate is not an honorific and that the bishop's primary task is the care of the people of the Church.

2. Boniecki, *Kalendarium*, "1957."

3. Ibid., "1958."

4. Ibid.; author's interviews with Stanisław and Danuta Rybicki, April 19 and June 5, 1997; Blazynski, *Pope John Paul II*, p. 69.

The rite for the consecration (now called ordination) of a bishop has changed since the Second Vatican Council. I have retained the translation given to participants in a pre–Vatican II episcopal consecration to convey some of the flavor of the ritual of that era.

5. Boniecki, *Kalendarium*, "1958."

6. A "deanery," composed of numerous parishes, was an administrative subdivision of the archdiocese.

7. Boniecki, *Kalendarium*, "1959."

8. Ibid., "1958."

9. Ibid.

10. Ibid., "1960."

11. Ibid.

12. Ibid., "1965."

13. Ibid., "1962."

14. Ibid.; author's interview with Teresa Życzkowska, April 19, 1997.

15. Boniecki, *Kalendarium*, "1962."

16. Author's conversation with Pope John Paul II, December 13, 1997.

17. Boniecki, *Kalendarium*, "1962."

18. The Counter-Reformation Council of Trent met in three discontinuous sessions, the first of which began in 1545 and the last of which ended in 1563.

19. St. Basil, one of the Church Fathers who had a tremendous influence on the early Councils, nonetheless complained of the "shocking disorder and confusion" of conciliar arguments and deplored the "incessant chatter" that overwhelmed the Church when councils met. [See Joseph Cardinal Ratzinger, *Principles of Catholic Theology: Building Stones for a Fundamental Theology* (San Francisco: Ignatius Press, 1987), pp. 368–369.]

20. Antonio Fappani and Franco Molinari, *Giovanni Battista Montini Giovane: Documenti inediti a testimonianze* (Turin: Marietti, 1979), p. 171.

21. There is another interpretation of the Council that continues to draw adherents. In this view, the Council was fundamentally misconceived. The Holy Spirit preserved the Church from fundamental error. But in the opinion of some self-consciously orthodox Roman Catholics, the Council, in its eagerness to engage the modern world, failed to articulate the truths of the faith against their contemporary detractors. But Pope Paul VI and, emphatically, Pope John Paul II have insisted that the Council was a Spirit-guided event for the renewal of the Church, even as their actions and teaching have suggested that the keys to the authentic interpretation of Vatican II needed clarification.

22. Karol Wojtyła, *Sources of Renewal: The Implementation of Vatican II* (San Francisco: Harper and Row, 1980), p. 9.

23. John Paul II, *Crossing the Threshold of Hope*, p. 157.

24. Ibid., p. 159.

25. Wojtyła, *Sources of Renewal*, p. 10.

26. Boniecki, *Kalendarium*, "1962"; Wojtyła, *Sources of Renewal*, p. 15.

27. Author's conversation with Pope John Paul II, March 20, 1997.

28. "*Murzyn*" [The Negro] from *Kościół* [The Church], in Wojtyła, *Poezje i dramaty*, p. 63; translated by the author, Sister Emilia Ehrlich, OSU, and Marek Skwarnicki.

29. Svidercoschi, *Letter*, pp. 83–86.

30. "*Pustynia judzka*" [The Judean desert], from *Wędrowka do miejsc świętych* [Journey to the holy places], in Wojtyła, *Poezje i dramaty*, p. 71; translated by the author and Marek Skwarnicki. Wojtyła's letter to the priests of Kraków on his trip to the Holy Land is in Boniecki, *Kalendarium*, "1963."

31. "*Posadzka*" [Stone floor], from *Kościół*, in Wojtyła, *Poezje i dramaty*, p. 63; translated by the author, Sister Emilia Ehrlich, OSU, and Marek Skwarnicki.

32. See Boniecki, *Kalendarium*, "1965."

33. See Maliński, *Pope John Paul II*, pp. 180–184.

34. Author's interview with Cardinal Joseph Ratzinger, September 12, 1996.

35. John Paul II, *Crossing the Threshold of Hope*, p. 158.

36. *Acta et Documenta Concilio Oecumenico Vatican II Apparando: Series I (Antepraeparatoria), Volumen II: Consilia et Vota Episcoporum ac Praelatorum—Pars II: Europa*, pp. 741–748.

37. A whimsical reflection on all this may be found in Robert McAfee Brown, *Observer in Rome: A Protestant Report on the Vatican Council* (Garden City, N.Y.: Doubleday, 1964), pp. 131–136, from which some of these example are drawn.

38. See *Acta Synodalia Sacrosanti Concilii Oecumenici Vaticani II, I–3*, p. 294. [Hereinafter *Acta Synodalia . . .*]

39. See *Acta Synodalia I–2*, p. 315.

40. See *Acta Synodalia I–4*, pp. 598–599.

41. See *Acta Synodalia II–3*, pp. 154–157.

42. See *Acta Synodalia II–4*, pp. 340–342.

43. See *Acta Synodalia III–2*, pp. 178–179; see also Avery Dulles, SJ, "Mary at the Dawn of the New Millennium," *America* 178:3 (January 31, 1998), p. 9.

44. Boniecki, *Kalendarium*, "1964."

45. See *Acta Synodalia III–4*, pp. 69–70, 788–789.

46. Wojtyła synthesized these two conclusions in a subsequent written intervention on the issue:

. . . it is a matter of greatest importance for the existence and the work of the Church in the modern world that each and every person's right to exercise his religion be strictly observed, and that by virtue of this same right, Catholic parents be able to instruct their children in Christian truth. Moreover, this civil right is grounded not just in a principle of toleration, but in the natural right of every person to be familiar with the truth, which right we must set alongside the Church's right to hand on the truth. [See *Acta Synodalia III–2*, pp. 530–532.]

In this same written intervention, Wojtyła proposed taking the discussion of religious freedom as a civil matter out of the *Decree on Ecumenism* and inserting it in the proposed document on the Church and the modern world. This solution was not adopted, as the "appendix" on religious freedom to the *Decree on Ecumenism* was broken loose entirely and, in its civil aspect, dealt with in a separate conciliar declaration, a move Wojtyła came to support.

47. See *Acta Synodalia IV–2*, pp. 11–13. The "liberalism" here was that Continental European ideology whose components historically included anti-clericalist resistance to Church privileges under the ancien régime. In this historical-cultural context, "religious freedom," having been identified with the program of extreme anti-clericals, could be, and often was, taken to be constitutional cover for what was in fact a deep anti-Christian bias.

48. See *Acta Synodalia IV–2*, pp. 292–293.

49. *Dignitatis Humanae*, 2.

50. Ibid., 2, 3.

51. Ibid., 10–11.

52. Ibid., 15.

53. Ibid.

54. *Gaudium et Spes*, 1.

55. See Henri Fesquet, *The Drama of Vatican II* (New York: Random House, 1967), p. 395.

56. See *Acta Synodalia III–5*, pp. 298–300.

57. See ibid., pp. 680–683 and *Acta Synodalia III–7*, pp. 380–382.

58. *Schema XIII* was the only conciliar text drafted in a modern language: French. The French text, and Italian, English, German, and Spanish translations, were distributed to the Council Fathers along with the official text, which was in Latin. The text put the Vatican's Latin scholars through some hurdles, as they had to create Latin expressions to describe everything from nuclear deterrence to motorists running traffic lights.

On Wojtyła's involvement in the preparation of *Gaudium et Spes*, see J. Grootaers, *Actes et Acteurs à Vatican II* (Leuven: Leuven University Press, 1998), pp. 105–129.

59. All four would be created cardinals: Garrone and Danielou by Paul VI, de Lubac and Congar by John Paul II. Wojtyła felt a special gratitude toward Garrone; see John Paul II, *Crossing the Threshold of Hope*, p. 159.

60. Henri de Lubac, *At the Service of the Church* (San Francisco: Ignatius Press, 1993), p. 171.

61. John Paul II, *Crossing the Threshold of Hope*, p. 159. Henri de Lubac's memoir of the controversies of the 1940s and 1950s may be found in *At the Service of the Church.*

62. From the unpublished diary of Cardinal Yves Congar, OP, *Journal du Concile*: in *Ut Unum Sint, Bulletin de liaison de la Province de France*, 575, November 1994, pp. 180–181. I am grateful to the Very Reverend Maciej Zięba, OP, Provincial of the Polish Province of the Dominicans, for providing me with this text.

63. The neologism "Pastoral Constitution" had been devised for *Gaudium et Spes* to satisfy those who said that the term "Constitution" should be reserved for Council texts that were specifically doctrinal in content and those who wished *Gaudium et Spes* to have the kind of teaching "weight" that its initial sponsors had hoped for it. It is some indication of the tensions provoked by *Gaudium et Spes* that the very title of the final text, "Pastoral Constitution on the Church in the Modern World," was given a footnote, which explained what a "Pastoral Constitution" was and how the two parts of the document (a theological meditation on "The Church and Man's Vocation" and a practical discussion of "Some More Urgent Problems") related to each other.

64. On the need for the world to also open its windows, see Peter L. Berger, "For a World with Windows," in *Against the World for the World*, Peter L. Berger and Richard John Neuhaus, eds. (New York: Seabury, 1976), and Richard John Neuhaus, *The Catholic Moment* (San Francisco: Harper and Row, 1987).

65. See *Acta Synodalia IV–2*, pp. 660–663.

In the fourth session, Archbishop Wojtyła also submitted written interventions on *Gaudium et Spes*. One was a set of proposed textual emendations. The other, perhaps his most lyrical intervention at the Council, revisited themes he had developed in *Love and Responsibility*. He was particularly insistent on the necessity of a dialogue with married couples about marital chastity and the morally appropriate method of regulating births. Marriage was "the school of love and charity," he wrote, "and it is necessary that love and charity, not simply doctrine, be made clear by the Church." [See *Acta Synodalia IV–3*, pp. 242–243.]

66. Boniecki, *Kalendarium*, "1964."

67. Ibid., "1962."

68. Ibid., "1963."

69. Ibid., "1964."

70. Ibid., "1965."

71. Karol Wojtyła, "*A propos du Concile*," in Wojtyła, *En Esprit et En Vérité*, pp. 219–221.

72. Karol Wojtyła, "*Le Concile et le Travail des Théologiens*," in Wojtyła, *En Esprit et En Vérité*, pp. 227–230. This text was the transcription of a broadcast by Archbishop Wojtyła on Vatican Radio on February 12, 1965.

73. Karol Wojtyła, "*Le concile vu de l'intérieur*," in Wojtyła, *En Esprit et En Vérité*, pp. 231–240.

74. Author's conversation with Pope John Paul II, March 20, 1997.

75. The currently available English translation of *Osoba y czyn* is entitled *The Acting Person* (Dordrecht: D. Reidel Publishing Company, 1979). For reasons to be explained below, *Person and Act* is preferable as an English title, and will be used throughout.

76. John Paul II, *Curriculum Philosophicum*, p. 7.

77. Ibid.

78. Author's interview with Tadeusz Styczeń, SDS, April 14, 1997.

79. Cited in de Lubac, *At the Service of the Church*, pp. 171–172.

80. Author's interview with Tadeusz Styczeń, SDS, April 14, 1997.

81. Author's interview with Anna Karoń-Ostrowska, April 8, 1997.

82. By "definitive edition" I mean a final text that has been prepared with the author's close involvement—which, in this instance, has been impossible. So it seems likely that the third Polish edition, and the translations that will be made from it, will be the "definitive" renderings of *Osoba y czyn*. [See Karol Wojtyła, *Osoba y czyn: oraz inne studia antropologiczne*, ed. Tadeusz Styczeń, Wojciech Chudy, Jerzy W. Gałkowski, Adam Roziński, and Andrzej Szostek (Lublin: KUL Press, 1994).] This edition contains an introduction by Rocco Buttiglione which is available in English in Buttiglione, *Karol Wojtyła*, pp. 352–380.

83. To take one important example, *Osoba y czyn* makes extensive and untranslated use of the Latin word *suppositum*, a key Thomistic term to describe the human person as the subject of being and acting. The Tymieniecka retranslation never uses *suppositum* and translates the Latin into English in different ways at different points in the text. See Kupczak, *The Human Person as an Efficient Cause in the Christian Anthropology of Karol Wojtyła*, p. 122, note 9.

84. Author's conversation with Pope John Paul II, September 30, 1997.

Dr. Tymieniecka's explanation of, and commentary on, the process that led to the Reidel publication of *The Acting Person* may be found in *Phenomenology Information Bulletin* 3 (October 1979), pp. 3–52. I discussed the problems of the English edition of *The Acting Person* with Tadeusz Styczeń, SDS (interview, April 14, 1997), Andrzej Szostek, MIC (interview, April 14, 1997), and Andrzej Połtawski (interview, April 23, 1997). See also the discussion in Schmitz in *At the Center of the Human Drama*, pp. 59–60, n. 6.

85. Wojtyła, *The Acting Person*, p. 285.

86. See Schmitz, *At the Center of the Human Drama*, p. 86.

87. Author's interview with Karol Tarnowski, April 12, 1997.

88. Buttiglione, "Towards an Adequate Anthropology," p. 243.

89. See Boniecki, *Kalendarium*, "1965"; author's interview with Cardinal Franz König, December 11, 1997.

90. Author's interviews with Piotr and Teresa Malecki and Danuta Ciesielski, April 9, 1997.

91. Boniecki, *Kalendarium*, "1965."

92. Ibid.

93. Ibid.

CHAPTER 6

Successor to St. Stanisław: Living the Council in Kraków

1. On Karol Wojtyła's installation as archbishop of Kraków, see Maliński, *Pope John Paul II*, pp. 192–199; also Peter Hebblethwaite and Ludwig Kauffman, *John Paul II: A Pictorial Biography* (New York: McGraw-Hill, 1979), p. 62.

2. Boniecki, *Kalendarium*, "1963."

3. This account of Wojtyła's nomination as archbishop of Kraków is taken from the author's interview with Father Andrzej Bardecki, July 11, 1996, supplemented by material from Boniecki, *Kalendarium*, "1962" and "1963." The story of Cardinal Wyszyński's comment on the "poet" was told me by Father John Hotchkin, who heard it from Wyszyński's host on the occasion of the remark, Bishop Ernest Primeau.

4. Letter to the author from Bishop Alfred Abramowicz, January 6, 1998. Abramowicz was executive director of the Catholic League for Religious Assistance to Poland from 1960 to 1990, and remembered that the needs of the Polish Church were utterly basic during the 1960s and 1970s: among other things, typing paper and carbon paper. The latter was essential because the regime would usually refuse permission for mimeographing Church documents.

5. See "*Lettre pastorale*," in Wojtyła, *En Esprit et En Vérité*, pp. 215–218.

6. Author's interview with Bishop Stanisław Smoleński, April 9, 1997.

7. Author's interview and tour of the archbishop's residence with Cardinal Franciszek Macharski, April 10, 1997.

8. Ibid.

The bishop's "cassock," with its shoulder cape, is technically a "simar," not a cassock. But as "cassock" is the far more commonly used term, I use it here and in describing papal vesture later.

9. Author's interview with Cardinal Franciszek Macharski, April 10, 1997.

10. Memorandum of November 4, 1997, by Cardinal Franciszek Macharski, prepared at the author's request.

11. Boniecki, *Kalendarium*, "1977."

12. Author's conversation with Pope John Paul II, January 22, 1997.

13. Author's interview with Father Władysław Gasidło, June 11, 1997.

14. Boniecki, *Kalendarium*, "1971."

15. At a memorial Mass for Father Kurzeja in Miestrzejowice on September 13, Cardinal Wojtyła preached a moving homily:

> We feel in our human way that he did not just depart, that he is not just buried. We feel . . . that he . . . has been incorporated like a cornerstone into the building of this church, into the building of this community which is the living Church in Miestrzejowice: like a cornerstone. And this is the most magnificent thing that can be said about him . . .

I know his secret. I can even repeat the words . . . he spoke to me in 1970 . . . He knew what he was asking for. He knew that this matter would cost him dearly . . . he even added in jest, "if I have to suffer for this cause, even if I have to go to prison, it will only do me good . . ." I remember his words and I will not forget them to the end of my life. Because these words, said then in jest, indicated the price of his sacrifice. [Boniecki, *Kalendarium*, "1976."]

16. Author's interview with Father Władysław Gasidło, June 11, 1997.
17. Memorandum to the author from Cardinal Franciszek Macharski, November 4, 1997.
18. Author's interview with Henryk Woźniakowski, April 10, 1997.
19. Boniecki, *Kalendarium*, "1971."
20. Ibid., "1972."
21. Ibid., "1974."
22. Ibid., "1975."
23. Ibid., "1977."
24. Ibid., "1978."
25. For a discussion of the public/political meaning of the Corpus Christi procession from a cultural-anthropological point of view, see Jan Kubik, *The Power of Symbols Against the Symbols of Power: The Rise of Solidarity and the Fall of State Socialism in Poland* (University Park, Pa.: Pennsylvania State University Press, 1994), pp. 89ff.
26. Author's interviews with Bishop Stanisław Smoleński (April 9, 1997) and Father Stanisław Małysiak (April 18, 1997).
27. Letter to the author from Cardinal Franciszek Macharski, April 20, 1998.
28. On December 8, 1981, Pope John Paul II created the Pontifical Academy of Theology in Kraków with three faculties: theology, philosophy, and Church history. [Historical data on the Faculty of Theology, the Pontifical Faculty of Theology, and the Pontifical Academy of Theology: from a memorandum prepared for the author by the rector's office of the Pontifical Academy of Theology, April 8, 1998, at the request of Cardinal Franciszek Macharski.]
29. See John Paul II, *Gift and Mystery*, pp. 88–90.
30. See Blazynski, *Pope John Paul II*, pp. 160–161.
31. Author's interview with Bishop Stanisław Ryłko, December 11, 1996.
32. Cited in Grażina Sikorska, *Light and Life: Renewal in Poland* (Grand Rapids: Eerdmans, 1989), pp. 116–117.
33. Author's interview with Father Stanisław Małysiak, April 18, 1997.
34. Author's interview with Bishop Stanisław Smoleński, April 9, 1997.
35. See Sikorska, *Light and Life*, pp. 62–63.
36. See Nowak, "The Church in Poland," p. 11.
37. Author's interview with Bishop Stanisław Smoleński, April 9, 1997.
38. See Władysław Gasidło, *Duszpasterska troska Kardynała Karola Wojtyły o rodzinę* (Kraków: Archdiocese of Kraków, 1996), for a detailed historic account of family ministry in the archdiocese by a former director of the Department of Family Pastoral Care. The sketch above is based on the author's interview with Father Gasidło, June 11, 1997.
39. Author's interview with Bishop Stanisław Ryłko, December 11, 1996.
40. Author's interview with Stanisław Rodziński, April 11, 1997.
41. Ibid.
42. Ibid.
43. Author's interview with Bogdan Cywiński, November 14, 1998; see also Jacek Kuroń, *Wiara i wina: do i od komunizmu* (Warsaw: Nowa, 1990).
44. See Rodney Stark, *The Rise of Christianity* (New York: HarperCollins, 1997), p. 161.
45. Information on the charitable work of the Archdiocese of Kraków under Cardinal Wojtyła's leadership was provided in a memorandum to the author from Cardinal Franciszek Macharski, November 4, 1997.
46. Author's interview with Cardinal Edmund Szoka, September 4, 1996.
47. Author's interview with Henryk Woźniakowski, April 10, 1997.
48. Ibid.
49. Karol Wojtyła, *Sign of Contradiction* (New York: Seabury, 1979), pp. 144–145.
50. See Oram, *The People's Pope*, p. 120.
51. Author's interview with Teresa Malecka, April 9, 1997.
52. Author's interview with Jan Nowak, May 13, 1998.
53. One evening, during the May 1978 visit to Kraków of Cardinal William Baum of Washington, D.C., Cardinal Wojtyła announced to his guests that they were going to sleep late in the morning: until 7:30 A.M. The cardinal's secretary, Monsignor James Gillen, muttered, "That's *late*?" To which Cardinal Wojtyła replied, "Who can sleep later than 7:30?" [Author's interview with Cardinal William Baum and Monsignor James Gillen, November 5, 1996.]
54. Author's interview with Bishop Stanisław Ryłko, December 11, 1996. Bishop Ryłko was told this by Pope John Paul II's personal secretary, Monsignor Stanisław Dziwisz, who as his secretary in Kraków had accompanied Cardinal Wojtyła on all visitations.
55. Author's conversation with Pope John Paul II, September 30, 1997; memorandum to the author from Cardinal Franciszek Macharski, June 17, 1997. Bishop Pietraszko died in 1988, at age seventy-seven.
56. The Catholic Church worldwide is organized into ecclesiastical "provinces," clusters of dioceses under the supervision of an archdiocese. The ecclesiastical province of Kraków during Wojtyła's episco-

pate included the "suffragan," or smaller, dioceses of Kielce, Tarnów, Częstochowa, and Katowice. The archdiocese at the center of an ecclesiastical province is referred to as the "metropolitan see"; hence the Kraków central administration, or Curia, was (and is) called the "Metropolitan Curia."

Wojtyła organized his Metropolitan Curia in functional divisions. A Division for Clergy handled priest personnel matters, while the Division of Education was responsible for overseeing religious instruction in the archdiocese, and the Pastoral Division handled chaplaincies (such as the chaplaincies to university students and health-care workers). The Division of Family Pastoral Care and the Pastoral Ministry of Charity Division were created by Cardinal Wojtyła. The Pontifical Faculty of Theology was also considered a "division" of the Metropolitan Curia. The archdiocesan tribunal, the court for church legal matters, functioned under one of the chancellors. By contemporary standards, this was a very lean organization, with most divisions having perhaps five priests and laity as staff.

Finances were always challenging. The archdiocesan patrimony was in lands and buildings. But the communists occupied the buildings, which therefore could not produce rental income. At the same time, the archdiocese had to maintain the properties and pay for repairs—even those it had not authorized. Thus the pastoral work of the archdiocese as a whole had to be funded primarily through financial assistance from its parishes. A collection was taken up on the first Sunday of every month for the seminary and the Faculty of Theology. The Metropolitan Curia itself was supported by a collection taken up on the third Sunday of the odd-numbered months of the year. Other collections supported foreign missions and building maintenance, to which the priests of the archdiocese also contributed twenty percent of any offerings given them by the people at Christmas. Special boxes in churches received donations for the home for single mothers.

In one bizarre expression of communist "legality," the Church, which in the Polish People's Republic was not a legal entity (and, therefore, theoretically could not own property), nonetheless had to pay taxes on properties in its patrimony and on its income, at a rate of forty percent of unexpended receipts during a calendar year. Neither the archdiocese nor its parishes, lacking legal "personality," could have banking or checking accounts. Everything was done on a cash basis. During Wojtyła's episcopate, no program was ever dropped because of a lack of funds. The cardinal himself gave all his income—lecture fees, publication royalties, Mass stipends or other gifts from his people or from foreign visitors—to support his pastoral initiatives, especially the seminary and Faculty of Theology, the Institute for Family Studies, and the home for single mothers.

[Details on archdiocesan organization are taken from the author's interview with Father Stanisław Małysiak, April 18, 1997. Information on finances was provided in memoranda to the author of March 31, 1998 and May 20, 1998 from Monsignor Bronisław Fidelus, who was Wojtyła's vice chancellor for economic and financial matters.]

57. Author's interview with Father Andrzej Bardecki, July 11, 1996; Bishop Stanisław Smoleński, April 9, 1997; and Father Stanisław Małysiak, April 18, 1997.

58. Author's interview with Father Andrzej Bardecki, July 11, 1996.

59. Author's interview with Father Józef Tischner, April 23, 1997.

60. Author's interview with Father Stanisław Małysiak, April 18, 1997.

The cardinal took a similar approach to official permissions for publication. In the wake of the Council, the Znak publishing house was eager to get books by some of the leading conciliar theologians into print in Polish translations. The rules of the day said that if a book had had a *nihil obstat* and an *imprimatur* (official Church approval) in its original form then it should have another *nihil obstat* and another *imprimatur* in the translated edition. Cardinal Wojtyła was perfectly happy to grant the *imprimatur* for Znak's publication of translated works by Karl Rahner and Edward Schillebeeckx, but there was a problem. He had inherited from Archbishop Baziak an archdiocesan reviewer (the *censor librorum*, as he was known) of a different generation and theological sensibility; this older priest, who was responsible for granting the *nihil obstat* (which was supposed to precede the bishop's granting of an *imprimatur*) began to cause difficulties, complaining in one instance that Rahner had "muddled things." The cardinal, as a colleague remembered, was "not a man to make old people suffer," so he wasn't prepared to fire the reviewer. He found another way.

Calling the man in, he said that he understood there were some problems. Did you, he asked, find anything against faith or morals? No, the old priest replied; but Rahner had such a queer way of expressing things. The cardinal asked, well, why not let the readers decide? Yes, yes, said the old man, but I don't *like* what Rahner is saying. Well, in that case, said the cardinal, why not issue the *nihil obstat* indicating that the *censor librorum* disagrees with the views expressed, which are not against faith or morals. The old man finally agreed; Wojtyła had preserved his elderly subordinate's dignity while getting the needed job done. [Author's interview with Jacek Woźniakowski, April 11, 1997.]

61. See Blazynski, *Pope John Paul II*, p. 95.

62. See ibid., pp. 161–162.

63. See Davies, *Volume I*, p. 19.

Easter Vigil–1966 is Karol Wojtyła's poem-cycle for the millennium of Polish Christianity; see *The Place Within*, pp. 121–140.

64. Author's interview with Cardinal Franciszek Macharski, April 10, 1997.

65. Author's interview with Father Stanisław Małysiak, April 18, 1997.

66. Author's interview with Bishop Stanisław Smoleński, April 9, 1997.

Information on the structure and method of the Synod of Kraków was provided in a memorandum to the author by Bishop Tadeusz Pieronek, April 8, 1997.

67. Thus under the rubric of "The People of God's Participation in the Prophetic Mission of Christ," there were Synod documents on evangelization, the family as domestic church, catechetics, theological studies,

religious communities, and missionary activity. The sacraments and the sanctification of time were explored in seven documents under the rubric of "The Participation of the People of God in the Priestly Dignity of Christ." Finally, under the rubric of "The Participation of the People of God in the Royal-Pastoral Service of Christ," the Synod produced documents on family, children, young people, charitable activity, social renewal, contemporary culture, the structure of the archdiocese, and Mary in the life of the archdiocese. Further Synod documents discussed special concerns or ministries in the archdiocese: ecumenism, the major seminary, the ministry to the sick, environmental protection, and anti-alcoholism.

In adopting this "threefold-office" framework for its reflection, the Synod followed Cardinal Wojtyła's lead in *Sources of Renewal*, in which Wojtyła had used the three "offices" of Christ as an interpretive key for organizing the entire teaching of Vatican II. *Gaudium et Spes* 24 had taught that "man can fully discover his true self only in a sincere giving of himself"; it was by participating in the three "offices" of Christ, Wojtyła suggested, that the Christian embodied the Law of the Gift inscribed in human nature in a distinctively Christian way. In exercising the priestly office, men and women gave themselves to God in worship; thus the importance of active participation in the Church's liturgy. Christians exercised the prophetic office by freely giving themselves to the truth; obedience to the Word of God and to the teaching authority of the Church was, therefore, an embrace of one's responsibility toward the gift of truth. And mature Christians shared in the royal office of Christ by growing in self-command: "Every Christian who conquers sin achieves the royal self-dominion that is proper to human beings; by doing so he shares in the *munus regale* [royal office] of Christ and helps bring about Christ's kingdom"—this, another variant on Christian humanism, was the Church's answer to atheism and its demands for moral "autonomy."

68. Nor did Cardinal Wojtyła complete the Provincial Synod for the Archdiocese of Kraków and its suffragan dioceses of Kielce, Tarnów, Katowice, and Częstochowa, which he formally launched in 1975 after two years of consultations and preparation. He received the final document of the Provincial Synod on June 22, 1983, on his second trip to Poland as Pope. [See *Pierwszy Synod Prowincji Krakowskiej* (Kraków: Archdiocese of Kraków, 1994).]

69. The "Majority Report," and a history of the process sympathetic to its perspective, may be found in Robert Blair Kaiser, *The Politics of Sex and Religion* (Kansas City: Leaven Press, 1985). For a different reading of the issues and the majority/minority "reports," see Janet E. Smith, *"Humanae Vitae": A Generation Later* (Washington, D.C.: Catholic University of America Press, 1991), and Janet E. Smith, "*Humanae Vitae* at Twenty: New Insights into an Old Debate," in *Why* Humanae Vitae *Was Right: A Reader*, Janet E. Smith, ed. (San Francisco: Ignatius Press, 1993).

70. I use here the translation prepared by Janet E. Smith in "*Humanae Vitae*": A Generation Later, p. 282.

71. Author's conversation with Pope John Paul II, December 16, 1998. Tad Szulc's suggestion that Wojtyła deliberately missed the crucial vote on the papal commission in June 1966 is without foundation in fact (see *Pope John Paul II*, p. 254).

72. "*Les Fondements de la Doctrine de l'Eglise Concernant Les Principes de la Vie Conjugale*," in *Analecta Cracoviensia* I (1969), pp. 194–230.

73. See Szulc, *Pope John Paul II*, p. 255.

74. *Humanae Vitae*, 7–10.

75. Carl Bernstein and Marco Politi's claim that "the sexual philosophy of Wojtyła and his flock of Polish Catholics became the rule for the universal Church" suggests a lack of familiarity with the argument of both the Kraków memorandum and *Humanae Vitae*, as well as with the processes by which documents such as the latter are developed; see *His Holiness*, p. 113.

76. Henry Kissinger, *White House Years* (Boston: Little, Brown, 1979), p. 54.

77. John Paul II, *Curriculum Philosophicum*, p. 10.

In 1963, in response to questions that had been raised, Bishop Wojtyła authorized an investigation of the remains of St. Stanisław with an eye to clarifying the circumstances of his death. The results of the examination by forensic specialists were congruent with the traditional story, that the bishop had been martyred by a blow to the skull.

78. Author's interview with Andrzej Połtawki, April 23, 1997.

79. James Michener, *Pilgrimage* (Emmaus, Pa.: Rodale Press, 1990), p. 74.

80. The letter of protest is in Boniecki, *Kalendarium*, "1967." On Kotlarczyk, see Kazimierz Braun, *A History of Polish Theater, 1939–1989: Spheres of Captivity and Freedom* (Westport, Conn.: Greenwood Press, 1996), pp. 142–143.

81. Boniecki, *Kalendarium*, "1974."

82. Author's interview with Jerzy Turowicz, July 19, 1996.

83. Ibid.

84. Ibid.

85. Author's interview with Marek Skwarnicki, April 19, 1997.

86. Author's interview with Jacek Woźniakowski, April 11, 1997.

87. Ibid.

88. Author's interview with Father Andrzej Bardecki, July 11, 1996.

89. The two agreed to do a book together on this debate. Wojtyła wrote his essay, and then was elected Pope; Father Styczeń never got his essay done. Wojtyła's essay was finally published in 1982 as a small book, *Człowiek w polu odpowiedzialności* [Man in the field of moral responsibility] (Rome-Lublin: John Paul II Institute, 1991).]

90. Karol Wojtyła, "The Person: Subject and Community," in Wojtyła, *Person and Community*, p. 220. The notes to this essay include a complete list of the papers presented at the 1970 KUL conference, and some

(uncharacteristically) sharp criticism of several critics by the author, one of whom, he suggests, has simply "misinterpreted the basic idea in *The Acting Person*" [note 5].

91. Author's interview with Jerzy Gałkowski, April 14, 1997.

92. Author's interview with Tadeusz Styczeń, SDS, April 14, 1997.

93. Precise numbers of Protestants are unavailable because the Polish government did not maintain statistics on religious denominations. See *Polska* (Warsaw: State Learned Publishing House, 1974), p. 367.

94. Author's interview with Father Andrzej Bardecki, July 11, 1996.

95. Author's interview with Wojciech Giertych, OP, April 18, 1997.

96. Author's interview with Jerzy Janik, July 17, 1996.

97. Author's interview with Teresa Malecka, April 9, 1997.

98. Author's interview with Teresa Życzkowska, April 19, 1997. The letter just above was provided to the author by Teresa Heydel Życzkowska, November 9, 1998.

99. Author's interview with Jerzy Janik, July 17, 1996.

100. Author's interview with Stanisław Rybicki, July 11, 1997.

101. See Blazynski, *Pope John Paul II*, p. 74.

102. Author's interview with Jacek Woźniakowski, April 11, 1997.

103. Karol Wojtyła, "A Remembrance of Jerzy Ciesielski," in Karol Wojtyła, *I Miei Amici* (Rome: CSEO Biblioteca, 1979), pp. 45–53. The cause for Jerzy Ciesielski's beatification as a model Christian husband and father now lies before the Congregation for the Causes of Saints in Rome. In September 1998, Ciesielski's ashes were reinterred in the Church of St. Anne in Kraków.

104. See Taborski, "Introduction to *Radiation of Fatherhood*," in Wojtyła, *The Collected Plays*, p. 323.

105. Wojtyła, *Radiation of Fatherhood*, in ibid., p. 355.

106. Ibid., p. 341.

107. *"Myśli o dojrzewaniu"* [Thoughts on maturing], from *Rozważanie o śmierci* [Meditation on death], in Wojtyła, *Poezje i dramaty*, pp. 91–92; translated by the author, Sister Emilia Ehrlich, OSU, and Marek Skwarnicki.

108. *"Nadzieja, któa sięga poza kres"* [Hope reaching beyond the limit], from *Rozważanie o śmierci*, in ibid., p. 97; translated by the author, Sister Emilia Ehrlich, OSU, and Marek Skwarnicki.

109. Boniecki, *Kalendarium*, "1964."

110. Ibid.

111. Author's interview with Cardinal Agostino Casaroli, February 14, 1997.

112. Author's interview with Cardinal Franz König, December 11, 1997.

113. Wojtyła continued to wear a simple black cassock as cardinal, putting on his more elaborate vesture only for ceremonial occasions. After the ceremony in the Sistine Chapel, he told his secretary that he really wasn't worried about having made a sartorial gaffe; "I watched all the other cardinals and two others had black socks." [See Blazynski, *Pope John Paul II*, p. 71.]

114. Boniecki, *Kalendarium*, "1967."

115. Ibid.

116. During his eleven years as a cardinal, Wojtyła served on the Congregation for the Oriental Churches (1968–1973), the Congregation for the Clergy (1968–1978), the Congregation for the Sacraments and Divine Worship (1972–1978), and the Congregation for Catholic Education (1974–1978), and acted as a consultor to the Council on the Laity.

117. Boniecki, *Kalendarium*, "1967."

118. Boniecki, *Kalendarium*, "1969."

119. Michael O'Carroll, *Poland and John Paul II* (Dublin: Veritas Publications, 1979), pp. 65–66.

120. Cited in Jonathan Luxmoore and Jolanta Babiuch, "John Paul II and the 'Praxis of the Cross,'" *National Catholic Register*, July 13–19, 1997, p. 6.

121. The 1974 Synod was the first significant struggle within the Church's world leadership over the theologies of liberation being developed in Latin America. Interestingly enough, it was the Latin Americans, representatives of a continent in which the Church had been long identified with political power of a conservative sort, who now argued for an evangelization linked to liberation movements of the left; the ideological focus had shifted, but the entanglement of the Church's mission with political power continued. The claim that Wojtyła and others disagreed with this approach because their concept of evangelization was excessively otherworldly suggests a certain ignorance about the kind of cultural resistance in which Wojtyła was engaged in Poland: a form of activism that oppressors took very seriously, but that preserved the integrity and unique mission of the Church. [For a view of the 1974 Synod favorable to the proponents of liberation theology, see Peter Hebblethwaite, *Paul VI: The First Modern Pope* (New York: Paulist Press, 1993), pp. 626–627.]

122. Boniecki, *Kalendarium*, "1977."

123. For these meetings and Wojtyła's election to the Synod Council see ibid.

124. Author's interview with Archbishop John Foley, December 12, 1996.

125. Ibid.

126. See ibid.

127. Boniecki, *Kalendarium*, "1974"; memorandum to the author from Dominik Duka, OP, March 21, 1998.

128. Boniecki, *Kalendarium*, "1973."

129. Wojtyła, *Sign of Contradiction*, p. 6.

130. Ibid., pp. 142–143.

131. Author's interview with Stanisław Rodziński, April 11, 1977.

132. Letter to the author from Thomas Crooks, January 17, 1998.

Wojtyła's visit to Harvard certainly increased his exposure among Western intellectuals, but it hardly constituted his introduction to the world intellectual scene, as Carl Bernstein and Marco Politi suggest in *His Holiness*.

133. Author's interview with Zbigniew Brzeziński, February 7, 1997.

134. Author's interview with Archbishop John Foley, December 12, 1996.

135. Author's interview with Marek Skwarnicki, June 4, 1997.

136. These remarks are cited on the editorial page of the *Wall Street Journal*, November 9, 1978, and attributed to Wojtyła's "last speech in the U.S. in September 1976, as quoted in the *New York City News* (an interim strike newspaper)."

137. Author's conversation with Pope John Paul II, September 10, 1996.

138. Davies, *Volume II*, p. 553.

139. Cited in Blazynski, *Pope John Paul II*, p. 120; the citation is from an article of Wojtyła's in the Vatican newspaper, *L'Osservatore Romano*, in February 1976.

140. These examples are taken from Sikorski, *Full Circle*, pp. 39–41, 44, 145.

141. See Havel, "The Power of the Powerless," in Havel et al., *The Power of the Powerless: Citizens Against the State in Central-Eastern Europe* (Armonk, N.Y.: M. E. Sharpe, 1985), pp. 23–96.

142. Cited in de Lubac, *At the Service of the Church*, p. 172.

143. Ibid.

144. Author's interview with Cardinal Agostino Casaroli, February 14, 1997.

145. Author's interview with Cardinal Agostino Casaroli, February 14, 1997; author's interview with Andrzej Micewski, November 14, 1998.

146. Author's interview with Cardinal Agostino Casaroli, February 14, 1997.

147. Author's interview with Cardinal Luigi Poggi, September 19, 1997.

148. As in fact it did. Author's interview with Cardinal Miloslav Vlk, December 5, 1997.

149. For more detail on the *Ostpolitik*, its historical background, and the situation in Czechoslovakia, see my book, *The Final Revolution*, pp. 59–76, 85–90, 96–102, 159–190.

150. Wyszyński, for example, worried about the "credulity" of Casaroli in his first encounters with Poland's communist leaders, according to the Primate's official biographer. See Micewski, *Cardinal Wyszyński*, p. 278.

151. I am indebted to Rocco Buttiglione for drawing this telling contrast, in an interview on January 21, 1997.

152. Author's interview with Cardinal Agostino Casaroli, February 14, 1997.

153. Ibid.

154. I am indebted for this point to Jacek Woźniakowski, in our interview of April 11, 1997. Woźniakowski, an intellectual of impeccable credentials who was often on the other side of arguments with Wyszyński, nevertheless agreed with the Primate that too many Polish intellectuals had "behaved dreadfully" during the communist takeover of the universities in the late 1940s, by their acquiescence to the imposition of the regime's ideology and the subsequent corruption of university life.

155. Cardinal Franciszek Macharski, Wojtyła's successor as archbishop of Kraków, observed once that his old friend and predecessor, a remarkably photogenic man, had only become so after his election as Pope, when he was not deliberately keeping himself in the background of great public events. The cardinal's observation was borne out by a survey of the photographs in Franciszkańska, 3, where Wojtyła, in pictures in which the Primate is also present, looks very unphotogenic indeed.

156. Author's interview with Cardinal Agostino Casaroli, February 14, 1997.

157. Ibid.

158. See Blazynski, p. 91.

159. This judgment was shared by Cardinal Casaroli, when I proposed it to him in our interview on February 14, 1997.

Wojtyła's friend, Dr. Stanisław Rybicki, who was working in the public water supply office in the mid-1970s, remembers a political-education lecturer saying, "We have to fight Wyszyński, but we're not afraid of him. But we're afraid of Wojtyła; who knows how to deal with him?" Rybicki's wife, Danuta, had a similar experience in 1976. A lecturer from the Warsaw Institute of Marxism-Leninism came to the school in Kraków where Mrs. Rybicka was teaching to speak about "the battle against the Church and religion." The lecturer made a striking concession that Danuta Rybicka remembered more than two decades later: "Sometimes we have to admit that we think in six-year plans and the Church thinks in millennia . . . but [in this instance] we want Wyszyński to live as long as possible because we don't know how to deal with Wojtyła." [Author's interview with Stanisław and Danuta Rybicki, June 5, 1997.]

160. Michnik's 1977 book, *The Church, the Left, and Dialogue* (which could only be published in Paris), was a major break with the tradition of left-leaning intellectual anti-clericalism in Poland. See Adam Michnik, *The Church and the Left*, edited, translated, and with an introduction by David Ost (Chicago: University of Chicago Press, 1993).

161. Author's interview with Cardinal Agostino Casaroli, February 14, 1997.

162. During the 1978 Corpus Christi procession, for example, Wojtyła issued his sharpest challenge to the regime on the question of the Church's public presence in society while being accompanied by Vatican negotiator Archbishop Luigi Poggi. See Boniecki, *Kalendarium*, "1978."

163. Author's interview with Cardinal Agostino Casaroli, February 14, 1997.

164. Author's conversation with Pope John Paul II, December 11, 1996; author's interview with Bishop Stanisław Ryłko, January 18, 1997.

165. On "baffling unreality," see Davies, *Volume II*, p. 625; the phrase "practical materialism" was used by Halina Bortnowska in her interview with the author on April 7, 1997.

166. Cited in Oram, *The People's Pope*, p. 113.

167. Author's interviews with Halina Bortnowska, April 7, 1997; Father Stanisław Małysiak, April 18, 1997; and Bishop Stanisław Smoleński, April 9, 1997.

168. Author's interview with Bishop Stanisław Ryłko, December 12, 1996.

169. Author's interview with Father Józef Tischner, April 23, 1997.

CHAPTER 7
A Pope from a Far Country: The Election of John Paul II

1. Author's interview with Stefan and Maria Swieżawski, April 7, 1997.

Wojtyła's lecture at the International Thomistic Congress, "The Personal Structure of Self-Determination," may be found in Wojtyła, *Person and Community*, pp. 187–195.

2. The "Holy Office," charged with safeguarding the purity of doctrine, had long been premier among the departments of the Roman Curia. In the revised organization chart of Paul VI, it, too, was now subordinate to the Secretariat of State. Paul VI was, of course, a product of the Secretariat of State (in which he had served for thirty years) and his reform of the Curia certainly rationalized its functions according to a more modern style of management. But it was not without interest that the Curia was now led by an operational bureaucracy rather than by a theological agency.

The revision of the Holy Office went beyond the issue of nomenclature to the question of function. As Pope Paul put it in his document on curial reform, "Since charity banishes fear, it seems more appropriate now to preserve the faith by means of an office for promoting doctrine. Although it will still correct errors and gently recall those in error to moral excellence, new emphasis is to be given to preaching the Gospel."

3. See Hebblethwaite, *Paul VI*, pp. 670–674, on Paul VI viewing Lefebvre as his greatest cross; the reporting is based on the Pope's conversations with Jean Guitton.

4. Boniecki, *Kalendarium*, "1964."

5. See the comment of Cardinal John Wright in National Catholic News Service, *Nights of Sorrow, Days of Joy* (Washington, D.C.: NC News Service, 1978), p. 36.

6. Author's interview with Cardinal Franz König, December 11, 1997.

The suggestion that Paul VI was the "first modern pope" is certainly not true in terms of Montini's intellectuality. He was the first pope to have read modern philosophy and theology seriously. But his own intellect was decidedly classical, as his constant references to Augustine illustrate. [See Hebblethwaite, *Paul VI*, p. 697.]

7. Author's interview with Cardinal Agostino Casaroli, February 14, 1997.

8. Author's interview with Cardinal William Baum, November 5, 1996.

When one of his secretaries, Father John Magee, said that the aging pope, who had been lamenting the loneliness of having had virtually all his friends predecease him, could look forward to a grand reunion with them in heaven, Paul VI suddenly became serious and said, "*Caro*, we must never presume on the mercy of God, we have to pray for it. It is not certain that I will go to Paradise. I have to ask God's forgiveness and mercy—and so do you. Lord, remember me when you come into your kingdom." [Hebblethwaite, in *Paul VI*, p. 695; the incident is taken from a memoir by Magee.]

9. Henri de Lubac thought of Paul VI when visiting the tomb of Hadrian VI, the Dutchman who was the last non-Italian pope before Karol Wojtyła; the inscription on the tomb reads *Proh dolor! Quantum refert in quae tempora vel optimi cujusque virtus incidat!*, which the French Jesuit translated, "Alas! What a huge difference it makes when a man of consummate virtue happens to live at the wrong time!" [de Lubac, *At the Service of the Church*, p. 159.]

10. See "The Crisis of Pope Paul VI," *Catholic World Report*, July 1998, pp. 58–60. In this interview, Father Walter Abbott, SJ, who worked in the Curia under Paul VI, suggests that, by 1973, the Pope was close to an emotional breakdown over dissent in the Church.

11. See Hans Urs von Balthasar, *Tragedy Under Grace: Reinhold Schneider on the Experience of the West* (San Francisco: Ignatius Press, 1997), p. 244.

12. Author's interview with Cardinal Franz König, December 11, 1997. On the night before his election in 1963, Montini had told König that he would refuse election because he was in "complete darkness" and didn't know what he would do as pope. [Ibid.]

13. See the memorial address to Paul VI on the centenary of his birth by Cardinal Agostino Casaroli, *L'Osservatore Romano*, November 24–25, 1997, pp. 6, 8.

14. Ibid.

15. That capacity for engaging modernity with both conviction and compassion was well-displayed on March 18, 1977, when Wojtyła delivered a philosophical lecture on "The Problem of the Constitution of Culture Through Human Praxis" at Sacred Heart University in Milan. The category "praxis" was, of course, central to Marxist theory; and Wojtyła, too, understood human action as "the most direct route to understanding the *humanum* in its deepest plenitude, richness, and authenticity." But any theory of human action that thought of "the modification of the world as the sole purpose" of human effort was dangerous because it reduced the human being to "an epiphenomenon, a product." Marxism thus did to human beings precisely what Marx accused capitalism of doing: reducing the person to a commodity. The answer to this, Wojtyła argued, was to reclaim the transcendence implied in human action, such that through the cultures that our action creates, people "become more human, and not merely acquire more means." See Wojtyła, *Person and Community*, pp. 263–275.

16. Cited in de Lubac, *At the Service of the Church*, p. 172.

17. See *Nights of Sorrow, Days of Joy*, p. 36.

18. Another ritual, less ceremonial and certainly less edifying, was also observed. The Pope's longtime

secretary, Monsignor Pasquale Macchi, was ejected from the Vatican and found himself living in a Roman guest house the day after Paul VI died.

19. Details here are taken from *Nights of Sorrow, Days of Joy*.

20. The text of the letter is in Boniecki, *Kalendarium*, "1978." Father Szostek, who got his degree, told me that Wojtyła was the only one of the three readers to whom he had sent his dissertation, on the possibility of universal moral norms, who had read the whole thing. [Author's interview with Andrzej Szostek, MIC, April 14, 1997.]

21. Boniecki, *Kalendarium*, "1978."

22. Author's interviews with Cardinal William Baum, November 5, 1996; Cardinal Joseph Ratzinger, September 12, 1996; Cardinal Francis Arinze, November 9, 1996; Cardinal Franz König, December 11, 1997; and Cardinal Bernardin Gantin, December 13, 1997.

23. Joseph Ratzinger, "On the Status of Church and Theology Today," in Ratzinger, *Principles of Catholic Theology*, p. 370.

24. Ibid., p. 377.

25. Author's interview with Cardinal Joseph Ratzinger, September 12, 1996.

26. On the "foolishness of truth," see Ratzinger, *Principles of Catholic Theology*, p. 393. Wojtyła and "truth" as the center of the Gospel: author's interview with Tadeusz Styczeń, SDS, April 14, 1997.

27. Author's interview with Cardinal Franz König, December 11, 1997.

28. The geographic breakdown of the conclave was as follows: Europe, fifty-six (including twenty-seven Italians); Latin America, nineteen; Asia and Oceania, thirteen; Africa, twelve; North America, eleven. The youngest electors were Cardinal Jaime Sin, the archbishop of Manila, who would turn fifty on October 31; Cardinal Antonio Ribeiro of Lisbon, who had just turned fifty in May; and Cardinals Joseph Ratzinger of Munich-Freising and William Baum of Washington, who were both fifty-one. The oldest electors were Cardinal František Tomášek of Prague, who was seventy-nine, and Cardinal Joseph Trin-Nhue-Khuê of Hanoi, who was seventy-eight. Three cardinals could not participate in the conclave because of illness: Bolesław Filipiak of Poland, Valerian Gracias of India, and John Wright of the United States.

29. Author's interview with Bishop Stanisław Ryłko, February 21, 1997.

30. Cardinal Luciani was better known in Latin America than in North America or even in parts of Western Europe, thanks to a visit he had made to Brazil in 1976. His host on that occasion, Cardinal Aloisio Lorscheider, OFM, may have played a significant role in attracting Latin American votes to the Luciani candidacy. One observer also speculates that Cardinal Confalonieri, while not present in the conclave itself, had been influential in building support for Luciani during the interregnum, when he presided over the daily meetings of the College of Cardinals. [See Peter Hebblethwaite, *The Year of Three Popes* (Cleveland: Collins, 1979).]

31. "I announce to you a great joy: we have a Pope—the Most Eminent and Reverend Lord, Albino Luciani, Cardinal of the Holy Roman Church, who has taken the name John Paul the First."

The College of Cardinals is divided into three "orders." The majority of the College is composed of "Cardinal Priests," residential bishops around the world who become titular pastors of Roman parishes. Cardinals resident in Rome as heads of Vatican offices are styled "Cardinal Deacons" and are also given titular Roman pastorates, frequently of ancient centers at which the early Church dispensed charity, the responsibility of deacons. A small group of six cardinals, including the Cardinal Secretary of State and others whom the Pope particularly wishes to honor, are named "Cardinal Bishops" and are the titular heads of six "suburban" dioceses in the vicinity of Rome. Since John XXIII, all cardinals are bishops (unless they have been dispensed from this requirement by the Pope, as some elderly theologians honored by John Paul II by being named to the College after their eightieth birthdays have been); the fact that the College is divided into these three "orders" has historical and honorific significance, but is of no serious practical import.

32. Albino Luciani, *Illustrissimi: Letters from Pope John Paul I* (Boston: Little, Brown, 1978).

33. See *Nights of Sorrow, Days of Joy*, p. 83; cited in ibid., p. 87.

34. Cited in ibid., pp. 92, 95.

35. For details of the illness of John Paul I and a persuasive refutation of the charge that he was assassinated by conspirators (variously alleged to have been Freemasons, the Mafia, the KGB, the CIA, his Vatican colleagues, or some combination thereof), see John Cornwell, *A Thief in the Night: The Mysterious Death of John Paul I* (New York: Simon and Schuster, 1989).

36. In an interview on RAI-TV in Italy on September 27, 1998, Bishop John Magee, who in 1978 was one of John Paul I's secretaries, confirmed that it had been one of the household sisters who had found the Pope dead. Cardinal Jean Villot, thinking it unseemly that a dead Pope should be found by a nun, told the press that it had been Magee who had discovered that the Pope had died. Villot was also the source of the unsubstantiated story that the Pope had died while reading *The Imitation of Christ*, a classic of Catholic piety. Conspiracy theorists have made much of these inaccuracies. The truth is that Villot was reacting to an unprecedented crisis according to what Curialists call "the way we do things here." His rearrangements of the facts were not meant to hide wicked or illegal behavior—there was none—but to protect an image he, and many other curial officials, thought essential to the papacy.

37. Author's interviews with Gabriel and Bożena Turowski, June 10, 1997; and Stanisław and Danuta Rybicki, April 19 and June 5, 1997.

38. Boniecki, *Kalendarium*, "1978."

39. Ibid.; author's interview with Father Stanisław Małysiak, April 18, 1997.

40. Author's interview with Jerzy Janik, July 17, 1996.

41. Graham in Kraków: see Martin, William, *A Prophet with Honor* (New York: William Morrow, 1991), p. 490. Wojtyła in Warsaw en route to Rome: author's interview with Sister Zofia Zdybicka, April 14, 1997.

42. Luigi Accattoli is mistaken in claiming that John Paul II has continued to write poetry as Pope. Asked in 1995 whether he still wrote poems occasionally, the Pope told his spokesman, Joaquín Navarro-Valls,

"No, this is a closed chapter in my life." John Paul II confirmed that "Stanisław" was his last poem in several conversations with the author. [See Luigi Accattoli, *Karol Wojtyła: L'uomo di fine millennio* (Milan: San Paolo, 1998), p. 159.]

43. Author's conversation with Pope John Paul II, March 20, 1997.

44. "*Stanisław*," in Wojtyła, *Poezje i dramaty*, pp. 103–106; translated by the author, Sister Emilia Ehrlich, OSU, and Marek Swkarnicki.

Pope John Paul II dedicated this poem to his successor, Cardinal Franciszek Macharski, on appointing him archbishop of Kraków on December 29, 1978, and gave Macharski the autograph copy. [Author's conversation with Pope John Paul II, October 23, 1998.]

45. Author's interview with Bishop Stanisław Ryłko, March 20, 1997.

46. Conclave I in 1978, by contrast, had opened on the last date possible.

47. Author's interview with Marek Skwarnicki, April 19 and June 4, 1997. Skwarnicki's complete account of this encounter may be found in his book, *Podróże po Kościela*, 2d ed. (Paris: Editions du Dialogie, 1990), pp. 234–235.

48. Boniecki, *Kalendarium*, "1978."

49. Author's interview with Marek Skwarnicki, April 19, 1997.

50. John Paul II, *Gift and Mystery*, p. 59.

51. Author's interview with Cardinal Joseph Ratzinger, September 12, 1996.

52. Author's interview with Cardinal William Baum, November 5, 1996.

53. Author's interview with Cardinal Joseph Ratzinger, September 12, 1996.

54. Author's interview with Cardinal Franz König, December 11, 1997.

55. Author's interview with Cardinal Agostino Casaroli, February 14, 1997.

56. Author's interview with Cardinal Franz König, December 11, 1997.

57. Author's interview with Father Stanisław Małysiak, April 18, 1997. According to Father Małysiak, Pope John Paul II mentioned this comment to a group of Poles with whom he was dining shortly after Conclave II.

In his April 8, 1994, homily at a Mass marking the completion of the restoration of Michelangelo's Sistine Chapel frescoes, John Paul II recalled that Cardinal Wyszyński had said to him, in that same chapel during Conclave II, "If they elect you, I beg you not to refuse." [See *L'Osservatore Romano*/English Weekly Edition (hereinafter *OR* [EWE]), April 13, 1994, p. 9.] The two renderings, of course, are not incompatible; the Primate may have said both.

58. Cited in Hebblethwaite, *The Year of Three Popes*, p. 156.

59. Jerzy Turowicz, "*Habemus Papam*," in *The Shepherd for All People*, ed. Bolesław Wierzbianski, translated by Alexander P. Jordan (New York: Bicentennial Publishing Commission, 1993. The citation is from Turowicz's first report on the conclave to *Tygodnik Powszechny*.

60. Author's interview with Cardinal Franz König, December 11, 1997.

61. Villot's sermon "for the election of the Pope" was given on October 14, 1978, just before the cardinals were sealed into the conclave. [See *OR* (EWE), October 19, 1978, p. 1.]

62. John Paul II recalled the words by which he accepted his election in his homily at the Mass celebrating his twentieth anniversary as Pope: see *OR* [EWE], October 21, 1998, p. 1.

63. See Szulc, *Pope John Paul II*, p. 281.

64. The original text may be found in *Insegnamanti di Giovanni Paolo II, 1978*. The details of the announcement of Wojtyła election are taken from the author's interviews with Cardinal Franz König, December 11, 1997; Sister Emilia Ehrlich, February 21, 1997; Monsignor Edward Buelt, January 14, 1997; and Jerzy Turowicz, July 19, 1996. See also Turowicz, "Habemus Papam," pp. 3–4.

65. Author's interview with Father Stanisław Małysiak, April 18, 1997.

66. Author's interview with Stanisław and Danuta Rybicki, June 5, 1997.

67. Author's interview with Teresa Życzkowska, April 19, 1997.

68. Author's interview with Jerzy Gałkowski, April 14, 1997. Five days after the election, the "liberal" communist journal, *Polityka*, opined that the new Pope came from a country "which is building a socialist system . . . on the basis of cooperation between Catholics and Marxists" and saw the election as "a special example of a creative and fruitful co-existence between non-believers and Catholics." [Cited in Karolak, *John Paul II*, p. 146.]

69. Author's interview with Maria Swieżawska, April 7, 1997.

70. See Oram, *The People's Pope*, p. 182.

71. Karolak, *John Paul II*, pp. 133–134.

72. Author's interview with Father Kazimierz Suder, July 14, 1997. Father Zacher's insert reads, "Elected Supreme Pontiff on 16 October 1978 and took the name John Paul II."

73. Author's interview with Cardinal Miloslav Vlk, December 5, 1997.

74. Author's interview with Cardinal Francis Arinze, November 9, 1996.

75. Frossard and John Paul II, *"Be Not Afraid!,"* p. 8.

CHAPTER 8

"Be Not Afraid!": A Pope for the World

1. Details of the inauguration are taken from *Nights of Sorrow, Days of Joy*. An English translation of the inaugural homily may be found in *Origins* 8:20 (November 2, 1978). The original is in *Insegnamenti di Giovanni Paolo II, 1978*. I have modified the NC News Service translation for greater accuracy.

The phrase "Open the doors to Christ!" is another echo of St. Louis de Montfort, Karol Wojtyła's mentor in Marian piety, whose work he first read on the night shift at the Solvay chemical plant during World War II; see Benedetta Parasogli, *Montfort: A Prophet for Our Time* (Rome: Edizioni Montfortane, 1991).

2. The analysis is from Hans Urs von Balthasar; see "Rome—The Ministry: The Office," in *Tragedy Under Grace*, pp. 206–220; the quotes are from this text.

3. Cited in Patrick Granfield, *The Limitations of the Papacy: Authority and Autonomy in the Church* (New York: Crossroad, 1987), pp. 62–63.

4. On the distinction between the "authoritarian" and the "authoritative," see Neuhaus, *The Catholic Moment*, pp. 126–130.

5. Author's interview with Cardinal William Baum, November 5, 1996.

6. Author's interview with Cardinal Agostino Casaroli, February 14, 1997.

7. Author's interview with Jerzy Janik, July 17, 1996.

8. Author's interview with Joaquín Navarro-Valls, December 18, 1997.

9. Author's conversation with Pope John Paul II, March 20, 1997.

10. Quoted in Hebblethwaite, *The Year of Three Popes*, p. 195.

11. Jacques Martin, *Heraldry in the Vatican* (Gerrards Cross, Buckinghamshire: Van Duren, 1987), p. 258. John Paul II did agree to lighten the blue field on his arms and to change the color of the cross from black to gold. The Vatican newspaper, *L'Osservatore Romano*, reflecting the curial, rather than papal, view of this symbolic contest of wills, noted that the design "does not conform to the customary heraldic model." [*OR* (EWE), November 23, 1978, p. 4.]

12. Cited in Andrew M. Greeley, *The Making of the Popes 1978: The Politics of Intrigue in the Vatican* (Kansas City: Andrews and McMeel), pp. 230–231.

13. At the end of this itinerant press conference, a former staff member of the *L'Osservatore Romano*, Lamberto De Camillis, who was blind because of diabetes, was introduced to the Pope and said, "Your Holiness, I offer you my blindness so that you may see the needs of humanity." The Pope embraced him. [*OR* (EWE), November 2, 1978, pp. 4, 8.]

14. Author's interview with Joaquín Navarro-Valls, December 18, 1997.

15. Every Sunday, when the Pope is in Rome, Deskur (confined to a wheelchair) has lunch with John Paul II, who always visits his old friend for lunch on his name-day, November 30. [Author's interview with Bishop Stanisław Ryłko, January 18, 1997.]

16. John Paul II, "Urbi et Orbi Message," *OR* [EWE], October 26, 1978, pp. 3–4. This is one of the last discourses of John Paul II to be published with the Pope's voice speaking in the traditional papal "we." Evidently, the word went out from the papal apartment that this practice was now banished—another declaration of independence by the neophyte Pope.

17. John Paul II, "To the Cardinals," *OR* [EWE], October 26, 1978, p. 5.

18. John Paul II, "Il servizio della Chiesa all'umanità," *Insegnamenti di Giovanni Paolo II, 1978*.

19. The telegram of congratulations from party leader Edward Gierek, Polish President Henryk Jabłoński, and Prime Minister Piotr Jaroszewicz was a classic example of late-communist rhetorical style:

> For the first time in ages, a son of the Polish nation—which is building the greatness and prosperity in its Socialist motherland in the unity and collaboration of all its citizens—sits in the papal throne . . . [the son] of a nation known throughout the world for its special love [for] peace and for its warmest attachment to the cooperation and friendship of all peoples . . . a nation which has made universally recognized contributions to human culture . . . We express our conviction that these great causes will be served by the further development of relations between the Polish People's Republic and the Apostolic Capital. [Cited in Szulc, *Pope John Paul II*, p. 287.]

20. Cited in Bernstein and Politi, *His Holiness*, p. 186.

21. On denial of passports, see Christopher Bobinski, "Polish prospects," *The Tablet* 232:7217 (November 4, 1978), p. 1060. The subornation of petty espionage was related to me by a close friend of Wojtyła's.

22. Author's interview with Archbishop Jan Schotte, CICM, May 10, 1991.

23. Author's interview with Monsignor Andrzej Bardecki, July 11, 1996.

24. Cited in Michael Ledeen, *Freedom Betrayed*, (Washington, D.C.: AEI Press, 1996), p. 35.

25. A statue of this remarkable scene is now in the courtyard of the Catholic University of Lublin, where Wyszyński was once bishop and Wojtyła once taught.

26. John Paul II, "Two Messages to Poland," *OR* [EWE], November 9, 1978, pp. 3, 9.

27. Boniecki, *Kalendarium*, "Family."

28. Author's interview with Sister Emilia Ehrlich, OSU, February 21, 1997. The question of approving translations of the new pope's poetry and plays was finally given over to a commission under the aegis of the Libreria Editrice Vaticana, the Holy See's publishing house.

29. John Paul II, "Address at Mentorella," *OR* [EWE], November 9, 1978, p. 1. The original text is in *Insegnamenti di Giovanni Paolo II, 1978*; the Vatican translation brings *annuncio* into English as "announcement," but "signal" is probably closer to the Pope's meaning here.

30. John Paul II, "Address at Assisi" and "Address at S. Maria sopra Minerva," *OR* [EWE], November 16, 1978, pp. 6, 7.

31. St. John Lateran is the cathedral church of the Diocese of Rome and one of Rome's four "patriarchal basilicas," the others being St. Peter's, St. Mary Major, and St. Paul's Outside the Walls. St. Peter's, also known as the "Patriarchal Vatican Basilica," belongs, so to speak, to the whole Church and to the Pope as its universal pastor; St. John Lateran is the pope's cathedral church in his specific character as Bishop of Rome. The Lateran Palace, next door to the basilica, houses the offices of the Vicariate of Rome, the administrative center of the diocese, which is headed by a Cardinal Vicar appointed by the Pope as his delegate for running the day-to-day affairs of the diocese.

32. John Paul II, "Homily at St. John Lateran," *OR* [EWE], November 23, 1978, pp. 6–7.

33. John Paul II, "Address to Audience for Young People," *OR* [EWE], December 7, 1978, p. 11.

34. Boniecki, *Kalendarium*, "Theological Studies."

35. In the course of his homily the Pope cited the entire text from Augustine's Sermon 340: "While I am frightened by what I am for you, I am consoled by what I am with you. For you, in fact, I am a bishop, with you I am a Christian. The former is the name of an office, the latter of grace; the former is a name of danger, the latter of salvation." The full text of the homily in translation is in *OR* [EWE], December 21, 1978], p. 11; the Italian original is in *Insegnamenti di Giovanni Paolo II, 1978.*

36. Cited in Bernstein and Politi, *His Holiness*, p. 188.

37. Author's interview with Cardinal Pio Laghi, November 5, 1996. Cardinal Laghi, then an archbishop, was apostolic nuncio in Argentina at the time.

Argentina and Chile had requested Holy See mediation in their dispute shortly after John Paul II's election. But disagreement over the precise wording of the letter that the two governments would send to the Holy See, formally requesting its services as mediator, caused a crisis. In mid-December both countries were mobilizing their armed forces and the Argentinians sent an aircraft carrier into the Beagle Channel. It was widely assumed that, in any armed confrontation, Argentina would prevail because of its 4:1 advantage in military manpower. But there would have been a lot of bloodshed in the process, given the character of the two military governments involved. In the south of Chile, red crosses were being painted on the roofs of hospitals and schools, in anticipation of air raids, as Christmas approached. [Author's interview with Cardinal Angelo Sodano, December 13, 1996; then-Archbishop Sodano was the apostolic nuncio in Chile at the time.]

38. Author's interview with Cardinal Angelo Sodano, December 13, 1996.

39. John Paul II, "Christmas Message *Urbi et Orbi*," *OR* [EWE], January 1, 1979, p. 1.

40. "An Unscheduled 'Angelus' with the Pope," *OR* [EWE], January 1, 1979, p. 12. The Angelus is a devotion containing three biblical texts about the Incarnation of Christ, three "Hail Marys," and a concluding prayer. The Pope, from the window of his apartment overlooking St. Peter's Square, customarily prays it with pilgrims on Sundays at noon.

41. The Pope's homily at the wedding is in *OR* [EWE], March 5, 1979, p. 8.

42. John Paul II, "Address to Italian Military," *OR* [EWE], March 12, 1979, p. 11.

43. "Pope's Rosary Broadcast by Vatican Radio," *OR* [EWE], March 12, 1979.

44. Author's interview with Cardinal Franciszek Macharski, April 10, 1997.

45. On the "geography" of the Pope's prayer, see John Paul II, *Crossing the Threshold of Hope*, pp. 19–26.

46. Author's interview with Archbishop Emery Kabongo, September 20, 1998. Archbishop Kabongo, prior to his ordination as a bishop, served as a papal secretary from February 1982 until January 1988.

47. Author's interview with Bishop Stanisław Ryłko, November 25, 1997.

48. Author's interview with Archbishop Emery Kabongo, September 20, 1998.

49. Author's interview with Archbishop Jean-Louis Tauran, March 14, 1997.

50. The news summary was described for me by Monsignor James Harvey, then the Assessor of the Secretariat of State, and later Prefect of the Papal Household. The remark about "Campo de'Fiori" was related to me by Joaquín Navarro-Valls in an interview on December 18, 1997.

51. Author's interview with Joaquín Navarro-Valls, December 18, 1997.

52. Author's interview with Jerzy Janik, July 17, 1996.

John Paul II did something else to Castel Gandolfo that bears his personal imprint. In the chapel at the papal villa, Pius XI (the former apostolic visitator and nuncio in Warsaw) had had two large murals painted on the side walls flanking the sanctuary. One was of Prior Kordecki and the defense of Częstochowa against the Swedish "Deluge" in 1655. The other was of the Battle of Warsaw in 1920, the "Miracle on the Vistula," and featured another heroic priest, Father Ignacy Jan Skorupka, and maps of the troop movements in Piłsudski's epic victory. They had been covered up during the pontificate of Paul VI. John Paul II had the paintings, "which in a certain sense had prepared the way for a Polish Pope," uncovered. [Memorandum to the author from Bishop Stanisław Ryłko, September 15, 1998.]

53. Pinckaers, *The Sources of Christian Ethics*, p. 258.

54. Author's conversation with Pope John Paul II, January 16, 1997.

55. "Official Soviet Reaction to the New Pope," RL 251/78 (Radio Liberty Research).

56. Author's interview with Jerzy Turowicz, July 19, 1996.

57. On Andropov and Solzhenitsyn, see David Remnick, *Resurrection: The Struggle for a New Russia* (New York: Random House, 1997).

58. Felix Corley, "Soviet Reaction to the Election of Pope John Paul II," *Religion, State and Society* 22:1 (1994), p. 41. Andropov's evident assumption that something might have been done to prevent Wojtyła's election suggests that Paul VI's concerns for the security of the conclave, which some dismissed at the time as excessive, may not have been entirely without foundation. On this point, see also Vladimir Bukovsky, *Jugement a Moscou: Un dissident dans les archives du Kremlin* (Paris: Laffont, 1995), pp. 213–214.

59. Ibid.

60. Ibid.

61. For a detailed study of this persecution, arguably the most intense in the twentieth century, see Bohdan R. Bociurkiw, *The Ukrainian Greek Catholic Church and the Soviet State (1939–1950)* (Edmonton: Canadian Institute of Ukrainian Studies Press, 1996).

62. Szulc, *Pope John Paul II*, p. 283. Vilnius (the Polish "Wilno") was the birthplace of Józef Piłsudski; both Adam Mickiewicz and Czesław Miłosz had attended the university there.

63. Cited in Corley, "Soviet Reaction to Pope John Paul II", p. 46.

64. See Michael Bourdeaux, *The Gospel's Triumph over Communism* (Minneapolis: Bethany House, 1991), pp. 134–148. Copies of the *Chronicle of the Catholic Church in Lithuania*, a detailed record of persecution and resistance, were clandestinely shipped in a plain wrapper to Brooklyn, New York, where they were translated and distributed by Lithuanian Catholic Religious Aid, a volunteer organization.

65. Author's interview with Archbishop Norberto Rivera Carrera, November 21, 1997.

66. "Mexican Priests, Nuns, Defy Ban on Wearing Church Garb in Public," *Seattle Times,* January 28, 1979.

67. Author's interview with Marcial Maciel, LC, February 19, 1998.

68. An overview of the common threads running through the various liberation theologies at the time of John Paul II's address to CELAM from the perspective of a sympathizer to the liberation theology project may be found in Phillip Berryman, "Latin American Liberation Theologies," *Theological Studies* 34:3 (September 1973).

69. Gustavo Gutierrez, cited in Richard John Neuhaus, "Liberation Theology and the Captivities of Jesus," *Worldview,* June 1973, p. 48.

70. See ibid.

71. John Paul II, "Address to the Third General Assembly of CELAM," in *Puebla: A Pilgrimage of Faith* (Boston: St. Paul Editions, 1979), pp. 100–101.

72. Ibid.

73. Ibid., p. 101.

74. Cf. ibid., pp. 106–107.

75. The analysis of the "anthropological error" in Marxism in John Paul II's Puebla address is similar to that of the Pope's colleague in the drafting of *Gaudium et Spes,* Henri de Lubac; see de Lubac, *The Drama of Atheistic Humanism* (San Francisco: Ignatius Press, 1995); the first French edition of de Lubac's work was published in 1944.

76. John Paul II, *Puebla: A Pilgrimage of Faith,* pp. 109–110.

77. Ibid., p. 113.

78. See ibid., pp. 117, 120.

79. John Paul II, "Address in Cuilapan," in *Puebla: A Pilgrimage of Faith,* p. 146.

80. Thus the editors of the *New York Times* were factually mistaken when they criticized the Pope's "disappointing" speech at Puebla for telling the Latin American bishops that "they must confine themselves to the pulpit and the altar," as were the *Manchester Guardian* editors who accused John Paul of promoting "the old argument that the Church must avoid temporal disputes focusing on man's soul." [*New York Times,* January 30, 1979; *Manchester Guardian Weekly,* February 4, 1979.] These confusions persisted for decades. In 1997, for example, Jonathan Luxmoore wrote of a Pope who, in Latin America, "appeared to counsel resignation rather than resistance." [Jonathan Luxmoore, "Pope John Paul II's Liberation Theology," *The Tablet,* October 11, 1997, p. 1281.]

81. There was one exception to the extensive coverage given the Pope's Mexican pilgrimage. The visit was virtually ignored by Soviet newscasters, as was John Paul's critique of liberation theology. For the Soviet press to ignore such a major international event was usually an indication of the Kremlin's displeasure with something that had happened: embarrassing or ideologically compromising news was best regarded as no news. The fact that Soviet newscasters did not report the Pope's Mexican pilgrimage did not mean that their political masters did not take it seriously—it likely meant precisely the opposite. [See Paul Henze, "Postscript 1985," in *The Plot to Kill the Pope* (New York: Charles Scribner's Sons, 1985), p. 203.]

82. Marek Skwarnicki, "Return from Mexico," in Wierzbianski, *The Shepherd for All People,* p. 85.

83. On the encyclical tradition, see J. Michael Miller, CSB, "Introduction to the Papal Encyclicals," in *The Encyclicals of John Paul II,* edited with introductions by J. Michael Miller, CSP (Huntington, Ind.: Our Sunday Visitor Publishing Division, 1996); hereinafter, Miller, *Encyclicals.*

84. Author's conversation with Pope John Paul II, January 16, 1997.

85. Ibid.; the official date of the encyclical was March 4, 1979, the First Sunday of Lent that year.

86. John Paul II, *Crossing the Threshold of Hope,* pp. 48–49.

87. *Redemptor Hominis* 1.1, 1.2 [the number prior to the period refers to the heading in the original document, the number after the period to the paragraph enumeration added in the Miller volume].

88. *Redemptor Hominis,* 12.2.

89. Ibid., 15.1 – 16.4.

90. Ibid., 17.8.

91. Ibid., 18.1–19.6.

CHAPTER 9

"How Many Divisions Has the Pope?": Confronting an Empire of Lies

1. Davies, *Volume I,* pp. 20–21.

2. John Paul II, *Pilgrim to Poland* (Boston: St. Paul Editions, 1979), pp. 63–72 [emphasis in original].

3. See Timothy Garton Ash, *The Polish Revolution: Solidarity* (Sevenoaks, U.K.: Hodder and Stoughton, 1985), p. 29.

4. On Poland as a communist state, not a communist country, see ibid. It was the writer Julian Stryjkowski who described the papal pilgrimage as "Poland's second baptism"; see Kubik, *The Power of Symbols Against the Symbols of Power,* pp. 138–139.

5. Author's interview with Stefan Swieżawski, April 7, 1997.

6. See John Courtney Murray, SJ, "The Issue of Church and State at Vatican Council II," *Theological Studies* 27:4 (December 1966).

7. Author's interview with Zbigniew Brzeziński, February 7, 1997. On the criminal character of communist regimes, see Stéphane Courtois et al., *Le Livre Noir du Communisme: Crimes, Terreur, Répression* (Paris: Laffont, 1997) and the review essay by Martin Malia, "The Lesser Evil?" in the *Times Literary Supplement*, March 27, 1998, pp. 3–4.

This understanding of the inherently criminal character of communist regimes is missing from a standard reference on the *Ostpolitik* of Paul VI, Hansjakob Stehle's *Eastern Politics of the Vatican 1917–1979* (Athens, Ohio: Ohio University Press, 1981). Stehle's book includes a wealth of interesting detail. But this lacuna on the nature of communist states renders Stehle's judgments less than useful—although the book does opens a window into the way of thinking about the communist world that was prominent in the Vatican's Secretariat of State (where Stehle had many high-placed sources) during the pontificate of Paul VI.

8. Cited in Bogdan Szajkowski, *Next to God . . . Poland: Politics and Religion in Contemporary Poland* (New York: St. Martin's Press, 1983), p. 63.

9. Citations from Jan Hartmann, Bohumil Svoboda, and Václav Vaško, *Kardinal Tomášek: Zeugnisse über einen behutsamen Bischof und einen tapferen Kardinal* (Leipzig: Benno-Verlag, 1994), and from the letter of John Paul II to Cardinal Frantisek Tomášek, *OR* [EWE], June 25, 1979, p. 4.

Tomášek, a native Moravian, had been secretly ordained a bishop in 1949; Pius XII's policy was that each Czechoslovak bishop should secretly ordain a successor to take over in case the bishop in question was arrested. Tomášek was arrested in 1951 and served three years in a labor camp, after which he was permitted to function as a village parish priest in Moravska Huzova; during this period, he was the only Czechoslovak bishop permitted to attend Vatican II, where he met Karol Wojtyła. When Prague's Cardinal Josef Beran agreed to go into exile in Rome in 1965 as part of an attempted Vatican rapprochement with the Czechoslovak government, Tomášek was appointed apostolic administrator of Prague, where he was finally allowed to assume the title of archbishop in 1978. He was named a cardinal *in pectore*, or secretly, by Paul VI in 1976, and was publicly raised to the cardinalate in 1977 when the authorities allowed him to travel to Rome. [Obituary, *The Independent*, August 5, 1992.]

10. Author's interview with Pavel Bratinka, October 23, 1991. For a more detailed analysis of the dramatic transformation of the situation in Czechoslovakia under the impact of John Paul II, see the author's study, *The Final Revolution*, chapter six.

11. "To Cardinal Iosyf Slipyi," *OR* [EWE], July 23, 1979, pp. 3–4.

12. Andrei Gromyko, *Memoirs* (London: Hutchinson, 1989), pp. 212–213.

13. Author's conversation with Pope John Paul II, December 13, 1997. During this conversation I told the Pope an old joke: the reason Gromyko was never seen smiling was that Stalin had told him that smiling was counterrevolutionary, and Gromyko was still waiting for the order to frown to be rescinded. The response was an expressive pontifical grunt. The remark about the Gromyko interview being "tiresome" is from Wilton Wynn, *Keepers of the Keys* (New York: Random House, 1988).

14. Technically, Casaroli was "Pro-Secretary of State" until he was created a cardinal on June 30 and assumed the full, unencumbered title of his office. The *Sostituto* is the functional equivalent of a presidential chief-of-staff and holds a job of wide-ranging influence. For profiles of Silvestrini, Martínez Somalo, and Bačkis, see *OR* [EWE], May 14, 1979, p. 11.

15. On the role of the Final Act's human rights provisions in the collapse of European communism, see the author's study, *The Final Revolution*, pp. 26–30.

16. Author's interviews with Zbigniew Brzeziński, February 7, 1997, and Joaquín Navarro-Valls, January 20, 1997.

17. Author's interview with Joaquín Navarro-Valls, January 20, 1997.

18. Szajkowski, *Next to God . . . Poland*, pp. 61–63.

19. Quotations are from Janusz Rolicki, *Edward Gierek: Przewana dekada* (Warsaw: Polska Oficyna Wydawnicza, 1990), cited in Bernstein and Politi, *His Holiness*, p. 191. Szulc, in *Pope John Paul II*, writes that Gierek recalled saying that the Pope would be received "with dignity" [p. 299].

20. This rodomontade fooled no one. The underground newspaper *Robotnik*, in its April 1, 1979, issue, editorialized that "The authorities of the Polish People's Republic were afraid of the visit and of this date. They were afraid of the date because the cult of St. Stanisław, the perseverant bishop murdered by King Bolesław the Bold, is identified with a dangerous word, *opposition* . . . " [Cited in Kubik, *The Power of Symbols Against the Symbols of Power*, p. 134.]

21. Ewa Czarnecka, "John Paul II Visit to Poland," in Wierzbianski, ed., *The Shepherd for All People*, p. 10 (originally published in the New York–based Polish journal *Nowy Dziennik*).

22. Ibid., pp. 10–11.

23. In Latin, *rutilans agmen*.

24. See John Paul II, *Pilgrim to Poland*, p. 28.

25. John Paul II, "Homily at the Polish Cemetery of Monte Cassino," in *OR* [EWE], May 28, 1979, pp. 6–7.

26. Cited in Kubik, *The Power of Symbols Against the Symbols of Power*, pp. 134–135.

Meanwhile, Moscow was making its views known through one of its most reliable mouthpieces, the hardline Czechoslovak Communist Party weekly *Tribuna*. Who was this Stanisław the Pope was so interested in honoring? With an irony perhaps lost on many of its readers, *Tribuna* described him as a man who had spent his life "implementing the principles of, and demands for, the total domination of the world by the Pope and the Church, as formulated in the Middle Ages by Pope Gregory VII." [Cited in Bernstein and Politi, *His Holiness*, p. 217.]

27. See Kubik, *The Power of Symbols Against the Symbols of Power*, pp. 137–138.

28. Cited in ibid., p. 138.

29. Ibid.

30. Garton Ash, *The Polish Revolution: Solidarity*, p. 28.

31. "Communique of the Polish Episcopate," *OR* [EWE], May 21, 1979, p. 2.

32. John Paul II, *Pilgrim to Poland*, pp. 53–54 [emphasis in original].

33. Ibid., pp. 56–58 [emphasis in original].

34. Ibid., pp. 75, 77.

35. Ibid., p. 82.

36. Ibid., pp. 84–85.

37. Ibid., pp. 89–91, 94 [emphasis in original].

38. Francis X. Murphy, Michael Greene, and Norman Schaifer, *Poland Greets the Pope* (South Hackensack, N.J.: Shepherd Press, 1979), p. 20.

39. John Paul II, *Pilgrim to Poland*, p. 96–97.

40. Murphy *et al.*, *Poland Greets the Pope*, p. 20.

Radek Sikorski was a teenager in the crowd at Gniezno:

[W]e stood and cheered on the square in front of the archbishop's palace . . . waiting for the Pope to come out. A meeting with youth was scheduled; students bands played guitars and sang songs. Suddenly, two men came out onto the balcony: the Pope in white and, in cardinal's crimson, Primate Wyszyński . . . The Pope's face was jolly; one could tell he would have most gladly joined us down below with our guitar playing. Wyszyński was of the prewar school, severe. He stretched out his open palm level with his silk belt and cut through the air in a sideways movement like a Roman emperor. The unruly crowd of teenagers fell silent as if by the touch of a magic wand. I cannot remember what Wyszyński said, but the impression of steely authority emanating from that austere figure is with me to this day. [Sikorski, *Full Circle*, p. 66.]

41. John Paul II, *Pilgrim to Poland*. pp. 99–109 [emphasis in original].

42. David A. Andelman, "Pope Says Mass, Leads Folk Songs and Draw Cheers at Polish Shrine," *New York Times*, June 5, 1979, p. 1.

43. John Paul II, *Pilgrim to Poland*, pp. 121–122.

44. Ibid., pp. 130–151.

45. The *New York Times* editorial of that day had it exactly wrong when the editors wrote that, "As much as the visit of Pope John Paul II to Poland must reinvigorate and reinspire the Roman Catholic Church in Poland, it does not threaten the political order of the nation or of Eastern Europe." ["The Polish Pope in Poland," *New York Times*, June 5, 1979.]

The address to the Polish Bishops' Conference is also a decisive refutation of the claim, advanced by Carl Bernstein and Marco Politi, that John Paul II deliberately toned down his remarks after regime complaints about his statements in Warsaw and Gniezno. Cardinal Franciszek Macharski, who is alleged to have been the conduit between the government and the papal party, has no recollection of any such demarche. [Letter to the author from Cardinal Franciszek Macharski, June 8, 1998.] The authors are also mistaken, as the above citations make clear, in their argument that "religious themes took over from political ones" after Warsaw and Gniezno. John Paul II's evangelism, and his determination to draw out the public consequences of the truths about the human person contained in the Gospel, was consistent throughout the June 1979 pilgrimage. [See Bernstein and Politi, *His Holiness*, pp. 221–222.]

46. Hella Pick, "Party for the People but People for the Pope," *Manchester Guardian Weekly*, June 17, 1979.

47. John Paul II, *Pilgrim to Poland*, p. 185.

48. Murphy et al., *Poland Greets the Pope*, p. 31.

49. John Paul II, *Pilgrim to Poland*, pp. 191–192.

50. Bolesław Wierzbianski, "Cracow and Vicinity," in Wierzbianski, ed., *The Shepherd for All People*, pp. 35–36.

51. Murphy et al., *Poland Greets the Pope*, p. 33.

52. Neal Ascherson, "The Pope's New Europe," *The Spectator*, June 16, 1979, p. 7.

53. Murphy et al., *Poland Greets the Pope*, p. 35.

54. John Paul II, *Pilgrim to Poland*, pp. 198–201.

55. Bolesław Wierzbianski, "A Native Son Comes Home," in Wierzbianski, ed., *The Shepherd for All People*, pp. 38–39; John Paul II, *Pilgrim to Poland*, pp. 202–206.

56. There are two camps in the complex the world has come to know by the double German name Auschwitz-Birkenau. Auschwitz I was in the town of Oświęcim, which lay in a part of Poland that had been absorbed into the Third Reich; it was originally a labor camp for Polish political prisoners, although thousands of executions took place there. Auschwitz II (Birkenau, or in Polish, "Brzezinka") is four kilometers away and was built for the sole purpose of extermination; this is where the gas chambers and crematoria were located.

57. John Paul II, *Pilgrim to Poland*, pp. 207–216.

58. Ibid., pp. 221–222.

59. Bolesław Wierzbianski, "A Native Son Comes Home," in Wierzbianski, ed., *The Shepherd for All People*, p. 44.

60. Murphy et al., *Poland Greets the Pope*, p. 50.

61. Wierzbianskji, "A Native Son Comes Home," pp. 48–50; author's interview with Jerzy Janik, July 17, 1996. Professor Janik is certain that John Paul sensed a political riot brewing amid the unbridled youthful enthusiasm and decided on the spot to "do something else—which was deeper."

62. Henryk Mikołaj Górecki came to international attention in 1993 when his *Third Symphony*, the *Symphony of Sorrowful Songs* for soprano and orchestra, rocketed to the top of both the classical and pop charts. Its Polish premiere in 1976 had made him a national musical hero. Born near Katowice in 1933, Górecki, a deeply committed Catholic, eventually became rector of the Higher School of Music in that Silesian city. His acceptance of Wojtyła's commission and the performance of "Beatus Vir" in Kraków subjected him to endless harassment from communist officials, with his phone calls, correspondence, and meetings under secret or open surveillance. He was prevented from hiring talented young musicians; his image was airbrushed out of photographs of an anniversary celebration at the Higher School in 1979; his home was ransacked by hoodlums. Górecki became, officially, a nonperson, and finally resigned his position as rector. [See Adrian Thomas, *Górecki* (Oxford: Clarendon Press, 1997), pp. xiii, 94–100, and Jane Perlez, "Henryk Górecki," *New York Times Magazine*, February 27, 1994.] This account of Górecki's composition and performance is taken from the author's July 13, 1998, interview with Piotr and Teresa Malecki, old friends with whom Górecki stayed during the papal visit to Kraków in 1979.

63. John Paul II, *Pilgrim to Poland*, pp. 254–270 [emphasis in original].

64. Ibid., p. 278.

65. See Murphy et al., *Poland Greets the Pope*, pp. 59–60; John Paul II, *Pilgrim to Poland*, pp. 277–280.

66. Szajkowski, *Next to God . . . Poland*, p. 72.

67. Garton Ash, *The Polish Revolution: Solidarity*, p. 28.

68. Adam Michnik, "A Lesson in Dignity," in Michnik, *Letters from Prison and Other Essays* (Berkeley: University of California Press, 1987), p. 160.

69. Author's interview with Maciej Zięba, OP, September 10, 1991. After working in the Solidarity movement in the early 1980s, Zięba abandoned his scientific career, entered the Dominican Order, and was ordained a priest. After becoming a prominent columnist in the Polish secular and Catholic press and a friend and adviser to Pope John Paul II, he was elected provincial superior of the Polish Dominicans in January 1998.

70. Author's interview with Father Józef Tischner, June 15, 1991.

71. Quoted in Sławomir Majman, "Road to Damascus," *Warsaw Voice*, June 9, 1991, p. 6.

72. Quoted in Garton Ash, *The Polish Revolution: Solidarity*, p. 29.

73. Author's interview with Sister Emilia Ehrlich, OSU, March 21, 1997. Sister Emilia was told this story by a nun who overheard the miners' conversation.

74. Author's interview with Tadeusz Mazowiecki, April 7, 1997.

75. Adam Michnik was another witness to this phenomenon of personal connection amid mass audiences; see "A Lesson in Dignity," p. 167.

76. Ibid., p. 160.

77. Ibid.

78. Cited in ibid., p. 161.

79. Sikorski, *Full Circle*, pp. 66–67.

80. See Michnik, "A Lesson in Dignity," pp. 161–162.

81. Peter Osnos and Michael Getler, "Poland Indicates Irritation About Pope's Comments," *Washington Post*, June 7, 1979.

82. See Michnik, "A Lesson in Dignity," p. 162.

Other Warsaw Pact countries tried to ignore what was happening, imposing what amounted to a news blackout in their own media. But the news, and the Pope's message, got through on Western radios such as the BBC, the Voice of America, Deutsche Welle, and Radio Free Europe. RFE's Polish service broadcast up to thirteen hours of coverage every day. During the papal visit, the Soviet Union continued jamming U.S.-financed Radio Liberty. [See Michael Dobbs, "Pope's Words Pierce East's Blackout," *Washington Post*, June 7, 1979, p. A34.]

83. Michnik, "A Lesson in Dignity," pp. 162–163.

84. Ibid., p. 164.

85. As the Pope put it to students and faculty of the Catholic University of Lublin when he met with them in Częstochowa on June 6, "Any man who chooses his ideology honestly and through his own conviction deserves respect." The real problem was that communism, by preventing the free pursuit of the truth, had created a society in which a deadening conformity suffocated social life. [Cited in Szajkowski, *Next to God . . . Poland*, p. 69.]

86. Ascherson, "The Pope's New Europe," p. 7.

87. See Garton Ash, *The Polish Revolution: Solidarity*, p. 30.

88. Tad Szulc's comment that "John Paul II's 'Nine Days in June' do not seem—in retrospect—to have fundamentally altered the situation in Poland, except in a general psychological sense" is, to put it gently, unpersuasive. [Szulc, *Pope John Paul II*, p. 309.] It is precisely in retrospect that the Pope's determinative influence on the formation of the Solidarity movement becomes unmistakably clear. Szulc's judgment is shared by virtually no one who participated in the Solidarity movement. It may have been shared by Poland's communist rulers, one of whom, Mieczysław Rakowski, was a principal source for Szulc.

Andrzej Wajda's film, *Man of Iron*, a fictional recreation of the Gdańsk shipyard strike that won the Grand Prize at the 1981 Cannes Film Festival, cinematically captures the change wrought by the Pope. An alcoholic hack journalist for a regime-controlled newspaper is sent to Gdańsk during the heat of the August 1980 strike to smear one of the strike leaders, the "man of iron." But the old communist tactics of lies and violence (which Wajda deftly weaves into the drama through flashbacks using archival footage of the failed strike attempt in 1970) no longer work: not simply because of the regime's ineptness, but because the "man of iron" has learned his own dignity and cannot be intimidated.

89. See Davies, *Heart of Europe*, p. 62.

90. Cited in Garton Ash, *The Polish Revolution: Solidarity*, p. 280.

91. Author's interview with Father Mieczysław Maliński, June 15, 1991.

92. Cited in Garton Ash, *The Polish Revolution: Solidarity*, p. 280.

93. Cited in Timothy Garton Ash, *We the People: The Revolution of '89 Witnessed in Warsaw, Budapest, Berlin and Prague* (Cambridge: Granta Books, 1990), pp. 139–140.

94. Cited in Garton Ash, *The Polish Revolution: Solidarity*, p. 282.

CHAPTER 10

The Ways of Freedom: Truths Personal and Public

1. Author's interview with Cardinal Jan Schotte, CICM, March 14, 1997.

2. Author's interview with Rocco Buttiglione, February 27, 1997.

3. "Ai giovani di Comunione e Liberazione," *Insegnamenti di Giovanni Paolo II, 1979.*

4. John Paul II, "Letter to All the Priests of the Church on the Occasion of Holy Thursday 1979," in John Paul II, *Letters to My Brother Priests*, ed. James P. Socias (Princeton: Scepter Publishers, 1994), p. 35.

5. Ibid., p. 40. The stole is the liturgical vestment that signifies the authority of the priest to consecrate the Eucharist ("the moment of transubstantiation"), which according to Catholic doctrine becomes at the moment of consecration the Body and Blood of Christ. The Latin formula of sacramental absolution in confession begins *Ego te absolvo . . .* [I absolve you from your sins . . .].

6. John Paul II, "To the Italian Episcopal Conference," *OR* [EWE], June 11, 1979, pp. 13–14 [emphasis in original].

7. John Paul II, "To General Assembly of Italian Bishops," *OR* [EWE], pp. 2–3.

8. Paroled in 1985 but refused permission to function publicly as a bishop, Ignatius Gong Pin-Mei came to the United States in 1988 (at age eighty-seven) to live in retirement. Two months short of his ninetieth birthday, his name was publicly revealed and he was formally invested as a cardinal on June 28, 1991.

9. John Paul II, "To the Sant'Egidio Community," *OR* [EWE], July 30, 1979, p. 10.

10. Author's interview with Monsignor Vincenzo Paglia, March 25, 1997. Monsignor Paglia has been chaplain, or "ecclesiastical assistant," to the Sant'Egidio Community throughout the pontificate of John Paul II. When Sant'Egidio did become too big for its small church, its liturgical activities, including a splendid celebration of Vespers every evening, moved to the Basilica of S. Maria in Trastevere, where Monsignor Paglia is rector.

11. See *OR* [EWE], August 20, 1979, p. 3; *OR* [EWE], September 17, 1979, p. 5.

12. Author's interview with Jerzy Janik, July 17, 1996.

13. See *Our Sunday Visitor*, June 3, 1979.

14. Cited in Hebblethwaite and Kaufmann, *Pope John Paul II: A Pictorial Biography*, p. 89.

15. Author's interview with Cardinal Pio Laghi, November 5, 1996.

16. Cited in de Lubac, *At the Service of the Church*, p. 172.

17. John Paul II, *The Theology of the Body* (Boston: Pauline Books and Media, 1997).

18. The confusions attendant on this text had been made obvious, yet again, in the reactions to Jimmy Carter's confession to a *Playboy* magazine interviewer during the 1976 U.S. presidential campaign that he had committed adultery in his heart.

19. This series was interrupted for a year, from February 9, 1983, to May 23, 1984, as the Church observed a special Holy Year of the Redemption and the Pope dedicated his general audience addresses to this theme.

20. Author's conversation with Pope John Paul II, March 20, 1997.

21. Ibid.

22. John Paul II, *Original Unity of Man and Woman* (Boston: St. Paul Books and Media, 1981).

23. Author's conversation with Pope John Paul II, March 20, 1997.

24. John Paul II, *Original Unity of Man and Woman*, p. 73.

25. Ibid., pp. 73–74. On this point, see also Mary Rousseau, "John Paul II's Teaching on Women," in *The Catholic Woman*, Ralph McInerny, ed. (San Francisco: Ignatius Press, 1991), pp. 12–13.

26. John Paul II, *Blessed Are the Pure of Heart* (Boston: St. Paul Books and Media, 1983), p. 19.

27. Ibid., p. 131.

28. Ibid., pp. 142–149.

29. Ibid., p. 150.

30. Ibid., p. 185.

31. Ibid., p. 191.

32. Ibid., pp. 194–195.

33. Ibid., p. 229.

34. Ibid., pp. 241–246.

35. John Paul criticizes pornography in this context. "Privacy" is essential if sexual self-giving is to be genuine mutual self-donation. Pornography violates the "right of privacy" built into the moral structure of human sexuality by turning what is most intensely personal and subjective into public property, an "object." [Ibid., pp. 276–289.] This analysis is particularly interesting in the U.S. context, in which the Supreme Court has declared "privacy" a freestanding liberty right that legally justifies virtually any consensual sexual activity. But this is a "privacy" devoid of moral structure; and as such, it tends to destroy the intensely interpersonal nature of sexual love, by turning the "other" into an anonymous sexual object.

36. Ibid., p. 292.

37. John Paul II, *The Theology of Marriage and Celibacy* (Boston: St. Paul Editions, 1986), pp. 17–38.

38. Ibid., pp. 83–89.

39. Ibid., pp. 96–111; 171–177.

40. Ibid,. pp. 301–307.

41. Ibid., pp. 191–197.

42. Ibid., pp. 215–224.

43. Ibid., pp. 276–282.

44. Ibid., pp. 363–368.

45. John Paul II, *Reflections on* Humanae Vitae (Boston: St. Paul Books and Media, 1984), pp. 13–18.

46. Ibid., pp. 35–40.

47. Ibid., pp. 41–47.

48. Ibid., pp. 61–67.

49. Ibid., p. 93.

50. This brief summary does scant justice to the richness of John Paul's reflections or to their extensive mining of ancient, medieval, modern, and contemporary sources. To take but two examples: The notes to the second address in *Original Unity of Man and Woman* discuss the various positions taken on God's self-definition in *Exodus* 3.14 by Augustine, Anselm, Thomas Aquinas, and Meister Eckhardt—the last as interpreted by the great modern Thomist, Etienne Gilson. The notes to the third address include a lengthy discussion of the different views of "myth" proposed by Rudolf Otto, Carl Gustav Jung, Mircea Eliade, Paul Tillich, Heinrich Schlier, and Paul Ricoeur, with special reference to the latter's analysis of the "Adamic myth" in *Genesis*.

51. Author's interview with Bishop Angelo Scola, February 26, 1997.

52. See Leo G. Walsh, "On the Edge of Europe," in Wierzbianski, ed., *The Shepherd for All People*, pp. 94–95.

53. Cited in ibid., pp. 98–99.

54. Cited in ibid., p. 102.

55. See ibid., p. 110.

56. Cited in *Time*, October 15, 1979, p. 16.

57. John Paul II, *Address to the 34th General Assembly of the United Nations Organization* [hereinafter, John Paul II, *UN-I*], 5.

58. Ibid., 6 [emphasis in original].

59. Ibid., 7 [emphasis in original].

60. Ibid., 9.

61. Ibid., 11.

62. Ibid., 14.

63. See ibid., 17.

64. Ibid., 19 [emphasis in original].

65. Ibid.

66. Ibid., 20.

67. Cited in *Time*, October 15, 1979, p. 24.

68. John Paul II, *The Pope Speaks to the American Church* (San Francisco: HarperSanFrancisco, 1992), pp. 35, 31.

69. Ibid., pp. 38–39.

70. Ibid., p. 46–47.

71. Ibid., p. 56.

72. Ibid., p. 64.

73. Cited in *Time*, October 15, 1979, p. 22.

74. Cited in ibid., p. 23.

75. John Paul II, *The Pope Speaks to the American Church*, pp. 71–80.

76. See James M. Rentschler, "Hooking Up the Vatican Hot Line," *International Herald Tribune*, October 30, 1998, p. 9.

77. "The Pope in America," *Time*, October 15, 1979, p. 28.

78. Author's interview with Zbigniew Brzeziński, February 7, 1997.

79. On the Leadership Conference of Women Religious, see Ann Carey, *Sisters in Crisis* (Huntingdon, Ind.: Our Sunday Visitor Press, 1997).

80. John Paul II, *The Pope Speaks to the American Church*, pp. 102–103.

I was present in the National Shrine of the Immaculate Conception during the papal meeting with American nuns, and remember being struck by two things: first, how John Paul defused the emotional tension within the basilica with his address (not all of the sisters agreed with Sister Teresa Kane by any means); and second, by how many of the nuns who had been standing in silent protest during the papal address stood up on the pews during the Pope's recessional from the basilica to get photographs of him. He was the Pope, after all.

The assertion of former *National Catholic Reporter* editor Thomas Fox that John Paul loathes Sister Teresa Kane, whom he has "never forgiven," is a journalistic speculation based on a sad misreading of John Paul II's character. The Pope who forgave the man who tried to assassinate him and who helped initiate the Polish-German reconciliation statement of 1965 is not given to holding grudges. [See Kwitny, *Man of the Century*, p. 340.]

81. See *OR* [EWE], November 5, 1979, p. 6.

82. John Paul II, *The Pope Speaks to the American Church*, pp. 113–117.

83. "The Pope in America," *Time*, October 15, 1979, p. 28.

84. See John Paul II, "Address to the Sacred College of Cardinals," *OR* [EWE], November 12, 1979, pp. 16–18.

85. "John Paul II at the Commemoration of Albert Einstein," *OR* [EWE], November 26, 1979, p. 9.

86. "John Paul II's Address at the Angelicum University," *OR* [EWE], December 17, 1979, p. 8.

87. Ibid., p. 7.

88. See Hans Küng, *Konzil und Wiedervereinigung*, 3rd edition (Freiburg im Bresgau: Verlag Herder, 1961); English translation, *The Council: Reform and Reunion* (Garden City, N.Y.: Doubleday Image Books, 1965). See also Hans Küng, *Justification: The Doctrine of Karl Barth and a Catholic Reflection* (New York: Thomas Nelson and Sons, 1964).

89. For a critique of Küng's teaching on infallibility from well within the orbit of progressive Catholic theology, see Peter Chirico, *Infallibility: The Crossroads of Doctrine* (Kansas City: Sheed, Andrews and McMeel, 1977).

90. Author's interview with Archbishop Jorge Mejía, November 13, 1996.

91. The official Vatican documentation on the Küng case made by found in *OR* [EWE], January 14, 1980, pp. 17–19; the German bishops' statements may be found in *OR* [EWE], February 25, 1980, pp. 4–5.

92. In 1993, to mark Hans Küng's sixty-fifth birthday, a *Festschrift* of essays was published in his honor. The editors concluded their preface with an appeal for Küng's "rehabilitation" as a Catholic theologian. See *Hans Küng: New Horizons for Faith and Thought*, eds. Karl-Josef Kuscher and Herman Häring (New York: Continuum, 1993), especially the preface, "The Aim of This Book," pp. 7–10. This volume also includes useful documentation on the theologians' response to the CDF declaration.

93. Ignatius's foundation was known as the Roman College. After being generously endowed by Pope Gregory XIII in 1572, it became known as the Gregorian University. "The Greg," as it is universally called, was alma mater to sixteen popes and a vast numbers of cardinals, bishops, and priests; since the Council, nuns and laypeople had also taken advanced degrees there. As of 1979, nineteen of its alumni had been declared saints, twenty-four had been beatified, and many more had been martyred. A bastion of theological conservatism prior to Vatican II (several of its faculty had been among the prominent opponents of John XXIII's plans for the Council), "the Greg," like the Society of Jesus which ran it, had become known for theological adventurousness in the post-conciliar period.

94. John Paul II, "Address to the Pontifical Gregorian University," *OR* [EWE], January 21, 1980, pp. 3–5.

95. Author's interview with Cardinal Edward Cassidy, December 7, 1996.

The Ecumenical Patriarch of Constantinople is first among equals among the leaders of the various self-governing Orthodox Churches. His situation is, politically and theologically, quite different from a pope's. The Turkish government, which requires that he be a native-born Turkish citizen, also claims a role in, and has sometimes interfered with, the selection of the Patriarch of Constantinople, not by vetoing an election but by making known its dissatisfaction with certain potential candidates before voting begins. As for his ecclesiastical role, the governing traditions of Orthodoxy dictate that he can act only with the consensus of his own Synod and at least the tacit agreement of the heads of other self-governing Orthodox Churches. The Ecumenical Patriarch's scope for initiative is thus far more limited than a pope's, because of the peculiar political situation of the Patriarchate of Constantinople and the traditions of authority within Orthodoxy itself.

For an overview of the complex world of Orthodoxy, see Ronald G. Roberson, CSP, *The Eastern Christian Churches: A Brief Survey*, 6th ed. (Rome: Edizioni "Orientalia Christiana," 1999).

96. John Paul II, *Turkey: Ecumenical Pilgrimage* (Boston: St. Paul Editions, 1980), p. 27.

97. Ibid.

98. Ibid., pp. 39–48.

99. Ibid., p. 57.

100. Ibid., p. 62.

101. Ibid., p. 86.

102. The document is cited in Szulc, *Pope John Paul II*, p. 312.

103. These points are detailed in ibid., p. 311.

104. Cited in ibid., p. 359.

CHAPTER 11

Peter Among Us: The Universal Pastor as Apostolic Witness

1. Jerzy Turowicz, "John Paul II in West Germany," in Wierzbianski, ed., *The Shepherd for All People*, pp. 240–259, and Tadeusz Nowakowski, "The Holy Father in Germany," in ibid., pp. 260–268. Turowicz's dispatch was originally written for *Tygodnik Powszechny*, and Nowakowski's for the London-based *Tydzien Polski*.

2. See *Lumen Gentium* [Dogmatic Constitution on the Church], 18–27.

3. Author's interviews with Cardinal Jan Schotte, CICM, March 14, 1997, and Cardinal Jozef Tomko, November 14, 1996.

4. Author's interview with Cardinal Jan Schotte, CICM, March 14, 1997.

5. Ibid.

6. See Bohdan R. Bociurkiw, "The Ukrainian Catholic Church in Gorbachev's USSR," *Problems of Communism* 39, November-December 1990, pp. 6–7.

7. Like Orthodoxy, the Ukrainian Church's canon law permitted the ordination of married men to the

priesthood, but not to the episcopate. There were curial concerns about transferring to the diaspora—and thus to North America and Australia—a practice that had a long tradition in its land of origin but might create difficulties abroad. The Ukrainians, for their part, believed this an essential part of their heritage and resented efforts to limit their historic practice simply because they had been forced into exile.

8. John Paul II, "Address to the Seventeenth General Assembly of the Italian Bishops' Conferences," *OR* [EWE], July 7, 1980, pp. 10–12.

9. See *OR* [EWE], July 14, 1980.

10. *OR* [EWE], December 1, 1980, p. 18.

11. See ibid., p. 17.

12. Broun, *Conscience and Captivity*, pp. 133–136.

13. John Paul II, "Letter to the Church in Hungary," *OR* [EWE], June 23, 1980, pp. 16–17.

14. A variant of this is cited in Broun, *Conscience and Captivity*, p. 145.

15. Author's interview with Cardinal Francis Arinze, November 9, 1996.

16. Christopher Sliwinski, "Prologue to the Holy Father's Visit," in Wierzbianski, *The Shepherd for All People*, p. 158; Sliwiniski wrote originally for Krakow's *Tygodnik Powszechny.*

17. Cited in Greeley, *The Making of the Popes 1978*, p. 210.

18. Christopher Sliwinski, "John Paul II in Africa," in Wierzbianski, ed., *The Shepherd for All People*, p. 166.

19. Ibid., pp. 168–169.

20. Ibid., pp. 169–171.

21. Ibid., pp. 171–172.

22. Ibid., p. 173.

23. Ibid., p. 174. The president, Colonel Denis Sassou Nguesso, told reporters in the papal party that the weather had improved in his country since he had begun employing former medicine men, expert in causing rain, in the state weather service. [Ibid.]

24. Ibid.

25. Ibid., pp. 174–176.

26. Ibid., p. 179.

27. See ibid., p. 182.

28. Cited in Michael Walsh, *John Paul II: A Biography* (London: Fount, 1995), p. 80.

29. Sliwinski, "John Paul II in Africa," p. 183.

30. Author's interview with Cardinal William Baum, November 5, 1996.

31. Sliwinski, "John Paul II in Africa," p. 183.

32. John Paul II, *France: Message of Peace, Trust, Love and Faith* (Boston: St. Paul Editions, 1980), p. 15.

33. Ibid., p. 22.

34. Ibid., pp. 136–137.

35. Ibid., p. 119. John Paul concluded: "Forgive me this question. I asked it as the minister does at the moment of baptism. I asked it out of solicitude for the Church whose first priest and first servant I am, and out of love for man, whose definitive greatness is in God, Father, Son, and Holy Spirit." [Ibid.]

36. The citations above are from ibid., pp. 184–210.

37. Cited in Kwitny, *Man of the Century*, pp. 361–362.

38. A "nuncio" is the Holy See's ambassador to a country with which it enjoys full diplomatic relations. Absent diplomatic relations (as was the case with the United States at this time), the Holy See's representative, who is accredited to the hierarchy of the country rather than to its government, is an "apostolic delegate."

39. Author's interview with Cardinal Pio Laghi, November 5, 1996.

40. A battle of memoranda was one leitmotif of the pilgrimage. A group of Brazilian industrialists had sent the Vatican a memorandum prior to the visit, arguing that São Paulo's Cardinal Paolo Evaristo Arns, a Franciscan sympathetic to liberation theology, should be transferred from his huge archdiocese, to resolve the conflict between the government and the bishops. Another memorandum was waiting for the Pope when he got to São Paolo: it was a petition containing 400,000 signatures, gathered in local parishes, in support of Cardinal Arns.

41. Author's conversation with Pope John Paul II, October 23, 1998.

42. John Paul II left the Brazilian Bishops' Conference the text of an address on "base communities" which he had not had time to deliver. The thrust of the address was to urge that these new forms of local Church community, often formed in the *favelas*, always remain conscious of themselves as *Church* communities, linked to the Church's sacramental system and its hierarchical leadership. This, too was dismissed by some as "conservative," although one has to wonder why a Pope's urging local communities to remain united with the Church and to think with the Church is considered a reproof. If the Office of Peter is an office of fostering unity, this is certainly at least part of what popes are supposed to do. [See Walsh, *John Paul II*, pp. 84–85.]

The details of the Pope's first pastoral pilgrimage to Brazil, and the citations from his addresses, are taken from Maciej Feldhuzen, "John Paul II in Brazil," in Wierzbianski, ed., *The Shepherd for All People*, pp. 212–235; Feldhuzen wrote originally for *Nowy Dziennik* in New York and for the London *Daily Telegraph.*

43. Author's interviews with Archbishop Paul Cordes, March 27, 1997; Cardinal Joseph Ratzinger, September 20, 1997; and Archbishop Christoph Schönborn, OP, December 11, 1997. For an account of the German influence on Vatican II, see Ralph M. Wiltgen, SVD, *The Rhine Flows into the Tiber: The Hidden Council* (New York: Hawthorn Books, 1967).

44. John Paul II, *Germany: Pilgrimage of Unity and Peace* (Boston: St. Paul Editions, 1981), p. 20.

45. Ibid., p. 29.

46. See ibid., pp. 37–52.

47. Ibid., pp. 155–156.

48. Turowicz, "John Paul II in West Germany," in Wierzbianski, ed., *The Shepherd for All People*, p. 259.

49. It was a task magnified by the fact that the USSR had begun a brutal invasion and occupation of Afghanistan in December 1979.

50. See Jan Cardinal Schotte, CICM, "The Synod of Bishops: History, Work, and Recent Synod Experience," a presentation to the Seminar for English-speaking Bishops in Mission Countries, Rome, 16 September–5 October 1996; copy furnished to the author by Cardinal Schotte.

51. Synod of Bishops, *Justice in the World*, "Introduction."

Catholic social doctrine had long taught that Catholic social action was an imperative, not an option, for the Church. The difficulty with this particular Synod statement was twofold: it seemed to suggest that the "liberation from every oppressive situation" could be accomplished by "action on behalf of justice," whereas the Church's constant teaching was that this complete liberation would only happen in the Kingdom of God come in its fullness; and the statement also seemed to suggest that those who did not undertake "action on behalf of justice," either by reason of vocation (like cloistered contemplative nuns) or repression (like the underground Church in situations of persecution), were, somehow, not living the reality of the Church fully.

52. Author's interview with Cardinal Jozef Tomko, November 14, 1996.

53. In addition to general sessions, in which the members of the Synod—bishops chosen by their national conferences, curial officials, heads of men's religious orders, and bishops and priests appointed as members by the Pope—give addresses (or, in Synod jargon, "make interventions") to the entire assembly, the Synod also breaks down into language-based discussion groups (*circules minores*), in which the Pope did not participate.

54. In an intervention that drew considerable media attention, San Francisco Archbishop John Quinn cited survey research showing widespread opposition to the teaching of *Humanae Vitae* on the morally acceptable means of family planning and argued that "unless one is willing to dismiss the attitude of all these people as obduracy, ignorance, or bad will, this widespread opposition must give rise to serious concern." That the situation was cause for serious concern was certainly true. But Archbishop Quinn's intervention did not explore the question of whether the Church's ethic of marital chastity had been adequately proposed to Catholics in the United States by bishops, priests, and theologians. The intervention stressed that too many people did not understand that the Church taught the moral *obligation* of family planning; if ignorance was widespread on this crucial point, might there not be similar ignorance about the rationale for the teaching of *Humanae Vitae* on artificial contraception? The Quinn intervention also seemed to accept at face value the threat of a "population bomb" and the more draconian analyses of certain population-control theorists, while failing to acknowledge the challenges to those analyses that were being mounted by responsible demographers.

But the core of Quinn's proposal was the call for a theological dialogue between the teaching authority of the Church and dissident moral theologians, for the purpose of creating a "new context" for the Church's ethic of marital chastity. This seemed to assume equal status for authoritative teaching and dissent from authoritative teaching, although even that was not entirely clear: the first step in the proposed conversation would be a "listening phase including both theologians who support the Church's teaching and those who do not." How the participation of the latter (whose views were hardly unknown, in any case) squared with one of the ground rules Archbishop Quinn proposed for the dialogue—"recognition that the teaching on contraception is a serious and authentic doctrine of the ordinary magisterium"—was not clarified: unless openness to the "development and amplification of this teaching" that was another Quinn ground rule included openness to a fundamental change in the moral judgment on contraception, which was what the dissidents frankly called for. This second ground rule undercut the first, a further confusion in the proposal. [See *Origins* 10:17 (October 9, 1980), pp. 263–267.]

The Quinn intervention was widely interpreted as a call for a revision of the moral teaching of *Humanae Vitae*. In a later intervention, the archbishop denied that this was his intention.

55. John Paul's sermon on the closing of the Synod is described by one biographer as containing "stinging remarks" about some of the proposals bishops had made during the Synod. [See Walsh, *John Paul II*, p. 87.] The text of the sermon does not sustain the charge. John Paul did address the difficulties spouses experienced in living the ethic of marital chastity contained in *Humanae Vitae*, but distinguished between growth into chastity (which is always difficult, given the high standard set by the Gospel) and a "gradualness of the law" by which the moral bar is set progressively higher as a couple matures. As John Paul noted, a "gradualness of the law" demeans men and women by suggesting that there are different levels of moral law appropriate "for various persons and conditions," a suggestion that dissolves the notion of human equality. [See *Origins* 10:21 (November 6, 1980), pp. 325–329.]

56. Author's conversation with Pope John Paul II, March 20, 1997.

57. John Paul II, *Familiaris Consortio* 6.2, in *The Post-Synodal Apostolic Exhortations of John Paul II*, edited and with introductions by J. Michael Miller, CSB (Huntington, Ind.: Our Sunday Visitor Publishing Division, 1998); hereinafter Miller, *Exhortations*.

58. Ibid., 6.3.

59. Ibid., 11.1, 11.2.

60. Ibid., 21.3.

61. Ibid., 22.3, 23.2.

62. Ibid., 25.5.

63. Ibid., 32.4.

64. Ibid., 36.2, 40.4.

65. Ibid., 46.1–4. The Charter of Rights of the Family was issued in 1983.

66. Ibid., 83–84.

67. Author's interview with Cardinal Joseph Ratzinger, September 12, 1996. Cardinal Ratzinger's impression that *Redemptor Hominis* was not planned at the outset as the first in a three-part series of encyclicals was confirmed by Pope John Paul II in a conversation with the author on January 16, 1997.

68. See *Diary of Blessed Sister M. Faustina Kowalska* (Stockbridge, Mass.: Marians of the Immaculate Conception, 1996).

69. Author's conversation with Pope John Paul II, January 16, 1997. On the theological implications of Sister Faustina's life and work, see Raymond Gawronski, SJ, "'My Name Is Sacrifice': The Mission of Blessed Faustina," *Communio* 24 (Winter 1997), pp. 815–842. Sister Faustina Kowalska was beatified by Pope John Paul II on April 18, 1993.

70. Wojtyła, "Reflections on Fatherhood," in Wojtyła, *The Collected Plays*, p. 368.

71. John Paul II, *Dives in Misericordia*, 4.12, 4.3, in Miller, *Encyclicals*.

72. Ibid., 4.11.

73. Ibid., 8.1.

74. See "Editor's Introduction to *Dives in Misericordia*," in Miller, *The Encyclicals of John Paul II*, p. 100.

75. John Paul II, *Dives in Misericordia*, 5.4, in ibid.

76. Ibid., 6.1–6.5.

77. Ibid., 12.3.

78. See "Editor's Introduction to *Dives in Misericordia*," in Miller, ed., *The Encyclicals of John Paul II*, p. 102.

79. In English, "Aaron." Both spellings are acceptable in French.

80. See *Choosing God—Chosen by God: Conversations with Jean-Marie Cardinal Lustiger* (San Francisco: Ignatius Press, 1991), pp. 17–61, 191–224, 267–282.

81. Lustiger may have been influenced in this analysis by the late Cardinal Pierre Veuillot, who called the young priest to his deathbed in early 1968 and said, "Pure, pure, pure. Everything must be pure. . . . We have to make a true spiritual revolution. The Pope realizes it, few people have; but that is what the Church needs." [See ibid., p. 213.]

82. Author's interview with Cardinal Jean-Marie Lustiger, October 24, 1996.

83. After a French publisher had turned down one of Wojtyła's books in May 1978, a few pages of excerpts were published in the September 1978 *Communio* along with a biographical introduction to the cardinal by Agnes Kalinowski, Jerzy Kalinowski's daughter and Wojtyła's goddaughter. The introduction was "the most accurate and comprehensive biography the French press had in October 1978" when Wojtyła was elected. [Memorandum to the author from Jean Duchesne, special adviser to Cardinal Lustiger, May 27, 1998.]

84. Henri de Lubac, SJ, took this view of the situation in France and undoubtedly had shared it with Wojtyła over the years. [Memorandum to the author from Jean Duchesne, May 11, 1998.]

85. Grammont had reopened the ancient Norman abbey of Le Bec-Hellouin in 1948 and made it into a thriving spiritual and cultural center, combining classical liturgy with ecumenism and an intense interest in Jewish-Christian dialogue: a singular combination of characteristics that gave him a reputation as a master of the spiritual life and a position above the corrosive left/right divide in the French Church. [Memorandum to the author from Jean Duchesne, May 22, 1998.]

86. Author's interview with Cardinal Jean-Marie Lustiger, October 24, 1996; memoranda to the author from Jean Duchesne, May 11, 22, 27, 1998. On Lustiger's early meeting with the Paris clergy, see Kwitny, *Man of the Century*, p. 382.

87. The population of Asia in 1997 was approximately 3.6 billion. Asia's Christian population in 1998 was approximately 286 million. [*International Bulletin of Missionary Research* 22:1 (January 1998), p. 27.]

88. T. Nowakowski, "Destination Far East," in Wierzbianski, ed., *The Shepherd for All People*, p. 269; Nowakowski's report was originally prepared for London's *Tydzien Polski*.

89. Marek Skwarnicki, "John Paul II in the Far East," in Wierzbianski, ed., *The Shepherd for All People*, pp. 285–286.

90. Cited in Nowakowski, "Destination Far East," p. 269.

91. Felix B. Bautista, *Cardinal Sin and the Miracle of Asia* (Manila: Vera-Reyes, 1987), p. 89.

92. Memorandum to the author by Cardinal Jaime L. Sin, December 9, 1997.

93. Bautista, *Cardinal Sin and the Miracle of Asia*, pp. 91–92; Skwarnicki, "John Paul II in the Far East," p. 288.

94. Pope John Paul II, *The Far East Journey of Peace and Brotherhood* (Boston: St. Paul Editions, 1981), p. 43.

95. Marek Skwarnicki, "Light in the Orient," in Wierzbianski, ed., *The Shepherd for All People*, pp. 282–283.

96. John Paul II, *The Far East Journey of Peace and Brotherhood*, pp. 79–86.

97. Nowakowski, "Destination Far East," p. 273.

98. John Paul II, *The Far East Journey of Peace and Brotherhood*, p. 177.

99. Skwarnicki, "John Paul II in the Far East," p. 289.

100. Ibid., p. 289.

101. John Paul II, *The Far East Journey of Peace and Brotherhood*, pp. 280–281.

102. Among those martyred with Lorenzo Ruiz had been a Polish Jesuit from Kraków, Father Wojciech Maczynski. [Nowakowski, "Destination Far East," p. 278.]

103. Marek Skwarnicki, "In Nagasaki and Anchorage," in Wierzbianski, ed., *The Shepherd for All People*, p. 296.

104. "The Pope in Alaska," *Anchorage Daily News*, February 27, 1981, p. B2.
105. Ibid., p. B3.
106. Nowakowski, "Destination Far East," p. 279.

CHAPTER 12
In the Eye of the Storm: Months of Violence and Dissent

1. On the L'viv Sobor, see Bociurkiw, *The Ukrainian Greek Catholic Church and the Soviet State (1939–1950)*, pp. 148–188.

The resolution declaring the L'viv Sobor null and void was adopted by the diaspora bishops in the presence of Cardinal Władysław Rubin, Prefect of the Congregation for Oriental Churches and an old friend of John Paul II. Both the Ukrainians and the Russians assumed that that meant that the Pope knew the details of the resolution and supported its passage. When the resolution was "unofficially" published by the Ukrainians, the Russian Orthodox Patriarchate of Moscow was furious and immediately sent its ecumenical liaison officer, Metropolitan Juvenaly, to Rome. After Juvenaly failed to get the Pope to disown the resolution, Patriarch Pimen himself wrote John Paul on December 22, demanding a papal repudiation of the "direction selected by the Ukrainian Catholic bishops," and threatening a cutoff of ecumenical relations if the Pope did not comply. The Pope's reply, in a private letter of January 24, 1981, defended the Greek Catholics' right to religious freedom while indicating that the resolution had been passed without his having had the opportunity to study it closely. The Patriarchate of Moscow then released the Pimen–John Paul correspondence (presumably to embarrass the Pope, who had not shared Pimen's letter to him, or his to Pimen, with Cardinal Slipyi, the exiled leader of Ukrainian Catholics); the Greek Catholics in the Ukrainian underground were outraged, and discontent rippled through the Ukrainian diaspora. Yet while this incident damaged the Pope's image with Ukrainian Catholics who simply could not understand the ecumenical imperative with Russian Orthodoxy (which they identified not with John Paul's ecumenical commitment, but with the most accommodationist elements of the previous Vatican *Ostpolitik*), the Soviet leadership was further confirmed in its fears that John Paul represented a grave threat, not simply in the Warsaw Pact, but in the Soviet internal empire.

2. Author's interview with Bogdan Bociurkiw, August 10, 1996. See also Bociurkiw, "The Ukrainian Catholic Church in the USSR Under Gorbachev," p. 7.

3. Szajkowski, *Next to God . . . Poland*, pp. 87–90; the poetry is cited in Garton Ash, *The Polish Revolution: Solidarity*, p. 331.

4. Tina Rosenberg, "It Sired a Free Market and It's Paying a Price," *International Herald Tribune*, March 18, 1997, p. 11.

5. Szajkowski, *Next to God . . . Poland*, pp. 90–91.

6. Author's conversation with Pope John Paul II, October 23, 1998.

7. The Pope spoke to the Poles at the August 20 general audience in their common language:

And now, dear countrymen, regarding the news which has come from Poland, I wish to read again before you present here, or rather to recite, two prayers which the Polish Church uses: the first on the Solemnity of Mary, Queen of Poland, on 3 May, and the second on the Solemnity of Our Lady of Częstochowa on 26 August. First that of 3 May:

"O God, who has given to the Polish nation, in the Most Holy Virgin Mary, a wonderful help and shield, grant that through the intercession of our Mother and Queen, the Church may always enjoy freedom, and the country, peace and security."

And now the second, that of 26 August:

"Assist, O Lord, the people which you strengthen with Your Body and Blood, and through the intercession of your Most Holy Mother, deliver them from all evil and every danger, and surround with your protection all their good works."

These prayers by themselves say how much we here in Rome are united with our fellow Poles and with the Church in particular, whose problems are close to the heart, and for which we seek the Lord's aid. [*OR* (EWE), August 25, 1980, p. 1.]

8. Szajkowski, *Next to God . . . Poland*, pp. 91–92.

9. Ibid., pp. 92–93.

10. In the judgment of Jan Nowak, former head of Radio Free Europe's Polish service, Cardinal Wojtyła helped prepare the ground for Solidarity by changing the Polish Church from a Church that defended the rights of believers to a Church that defended everybody, including dissident Marxists and men of the left. [Author's interview with Jan Nowak, May 13, 1998.]

11. Szajkowski, *Next to God . . . Poland*, p. 93.

12. Ibid. pp. 95–97.

13. *OR* [EWE], September 1, 1980, p. 8.

14. Szajkowski, *Next to God . . . Poland*, p. 97.

15. The full text of the communiqué is in *OR* [EWE], September 8, 1980, pp. 6–7. The bishops put the right to unionize and to strike within the framework of the basic human rights that John Paul II had defended at the UN the previous October. Thus the Polish episcopate followed the Pope's—and the workers'—lead in positioning the Gdańsk strike in a broad moral and humanistic context, rather than as an economic squabble.

16. See Garton Ash, *The Polish Revolution: Solidarity*, p. 68.

17. Ibid., p. 74.

18. As Timothy Garton Ash would note later, "It was all faintly reminiscent of a joke current in the late 1970s: 'What is the difference between Gierek and Gomułka?' 'None, only Gierek doesn't know it yet. . . .'" [Ibid., pp. 71–72.]

19. Solidarity was, technically, a national federation of local unions. See ibid., p. 75.

20. Ibid., p. 78.

21. Ibid., pp. 79–80.

22. Author's interview with Tadeusz Mazowiecki, April 7, 1997.

23. Szajkowski, *Next to God . . . Poland*, pp. 102–104.

24. Ibid., pp. 105–106.

25. Ibid., p. 106; Garton Ash, *The Polish Revolution: Solidarity*, pp. 81–82; Kwitny, *Man of the Century*, p. 376.

26. Szajkowski, *Next to God . . . Poland*, p. 107; Garton Ash, *The Polish Revolution: Solidarity*, pp. 84–85.

27. Author's interview with Jan Nowak, May 13, 1998. Kukliński, according to Nowak, knew everything that General Jaruzelski knew about Soviet plans "and more." The Polish colonel provided the United States with the entire operational plan; this was then checked with the Red Army general and by satellite reconnaissance, but cloud cover over east central Europe made photographic confirmation of troop movements difficult.

28. Author's interview with Zbigniew Brzeziński, February 7, 1997; letter to the author from Zbigniew Brzeziński, May 14, 1998.

29. Author's interview with Jan Nowak, May 13, 1998.

30. Author's interview with Zbigniew Brzeziński, February 7, 1997.

31. Ibid.

32. Ibid.; author's interview with Richard V. Allen, November 26, 1996.

33. Jan Nowak is convinced that the two key figures in "saving Poland from Soviet invasion" were Ryszard Kukliński and Zbigniew Brzeziński: "I am sure of it." [Author's interview with Jan Nowak, May 13, 1998.] Colonel Kukliński's recollections may be found in Ryszard Kukliński, "The Suppression of Solidarity," *Kultura*, April 1987. Some of Kukliński's reports may be found in *Cold War International History Project Bulletin 11* (Winter 1998), pp. 53–56.

34. With the authorization of Cardinal Angelo Sodano, the Secretary of State of the Holy See, the text of this letter, which I personally examined, was read to me and translated by Archbishop Jean-Louis Tauran, the Holy See's Secretary for Relations with States, during an interview in the archbishop's office on December 12, 1997.

35. Author's interview with Cardinal Jozef Tomko, November 14, 1996.

36. Lech Wałęsa, *A Way of Hope: An Autobiography* (New York: Henry Holt, 1987), p. 165.

37. Cited in ibid., pp. 164–165 [emphasis in original].

38. John Paul II, "Mass for the Polish Delegation . . . ," *OR* [EWE], February 9, 1981, p. 23.

39. Wałęsa, *A Way of Hope*, p. 166. John Paul's formal address to the Solidarity delegation is in *OR* [EWE], February 9, 1981, pp. 21–22.

40. See Szajkowski, *Next to God . . . Poland*, p. 116.

41. Author's interview with Jan Nowak, May 13, 1998.

By conventional Soviet reckoning, Wojciech Jaruzelski was the classic class enemy: a son of the land-owning gentry, educated in Catholic schools. That a man from this background, alone among the officers of his generation, rose unscathed through the ranks of the Polish military during the purges of the Stalinist and post-Stalinist eras, prospering during every shift of power and every change in personnel, suggests an exceptional degree of confidence in him, which Brezhnev once expressed in the simple phrase, "He is ours." [Ibid.]

42. See Carl Bernstein and Marco Politi (*His Holiness*, pp. 277–278) and Jonathan Kwitny (*Man of the Century*), pp. 386–387.

During our conversation of December 16, 1998, I asked the Pope about the alleged March 28, 1981, meeting. He replied that he remembered no such thing. The Pope's secretary, Bishop Stanisław Dziwisz, then retrieved the detailed diary of John Paul's meetings he had kept for twenty years; the diary includes both the fact of a meeting and the topics discussed. Dziwisz looked through every entry for March 1981, and said, simply, "There was no such meeting." Kwitny cites East German secret police files as a source. The fact that no such meeting ever took place suggests both the unreliability of many such sources and the vulnerability of analysts to disinformation.

43. John Paul II, "Message to Primate of Poland," *OR* [EWE], April 6, 1981, p. 2 (translation revised by the author in light of the original).

44. Szajkowski, *Next to God . . . Poland*, pp. 121–122.

45. Ibid., pp. 122–123.

46. Ibid., p. 123.

47. Both Zbigniew Brzeziński and Jan Nowak believe that "Soyuz 81" was a bluff, intended to keep pressure on the Polish communist leadership, but not a preparation for invasion, as the December 1980 maneuvers surely had been. Author's interviews with Brzeziński, February 7, 1997, and Nowak, May 13, 1998.

48. Cited in Szajkowski, *Next to God . . . Poland*, p. 124.

49. The Brest meeting is described in detail in Bernstein and Politi, *His Holiness*, pp. 280–284, an account based on interviews with Jaruzelski and Kania, on Jaruzelski's memoirs, and on Soviet Politburo minutes of April 9, 1981. The details of the debate are fascinating, but the analysis in which the narrative is lodged seems to accept Jaruzelski's longstanding and self-justifying claim that martial law was the only alternative

to Soviet military intervention—for which Brzeziński and Nowak claim there was no credible evidence at the time, later in the year, or in subsequently released documentation.

50. John Paul II, "Homily at Sotto il Monte," in *OR* [EWE], May 4, 1981, pp. 1–3.

51. See Frossard and John Paul II, *"Be Not Afraid!,"* p. 225. Frossard's account of the assassination attempt and its aftermath is particularly valuable because it is drawn from extended interviews with the Pope's secretary, Monsignor Stanisław Dziwisz, and Dr. Francesco Crucitti, the lead surgeon in the Pope's case.

52. One of these was Cardinal Bernardin Gantin, President of the Pontifical Justice and Peace Commission. The African cardinal gave a photograph of this tableau to every staff member of the Congregation for Bishops when he became its Prefect, as a reminder of what each of them should be prepared to suffer for the Church. Author's interview with Cardinal Bernardin Gantin, December 13, 1997.

53. Author's interviews with Teresa Heydel Życzkowska, April 19, 1997, and Sister Emilia Ehrlich, OSU, March 21, 1997.

54. Frossard and John Paul II, *"Be Not Afraid!,"* p. 251.

55. John Paul had made clear at the beginning of his pontificate that, should he be ill, he should be taken to the hospital like anyone else—another innovation in papal style (Paul VI had had prostate surgery in a specially constructed operating room in the papal apartment). So the Gemelli knew that it was the Pope's hospital of choice. That the suite was constantly on reserve was a precautionary measure that suggests that what had just happened was not entirely unanticipated.

56. Frossard and John Paul II, *"Be Not Afraid!,"* p. 227.

57. Ibid., p. 236.

58. Ibid., pp. 236–237.

59. Ibid., p. 223.

60. Ibid., p. 251.

61. Ibid., p. 225.

62. *OR* [EWE], May 18, 1981, p. 6. The Latin prayer at the end of John Paul's brief message was a reiteration of the motto on his coat-of-arms: "[I am] completely yours." That Jesus Christ was both "priest and victim" was the theme of a litany frequently recited in the Kraków seminary during Karol Wojtyła's student days.

63. Frossard and John Paul II, *"Be Not Afraid!,"* p. 234.

64. *OR* [EWE], May 25, 1981.

65. Author's interview with Gabriel and Bożena Turowski, June 10, 1997.

66. Frossard and John Paul II, *"Be Not Afraid!,"* p. 230.

67. Ibid., p. 246.

68. Ibid., 249.

69. Author's conversation with Pope John Paul II, October 23, 1998; author's interview with Jan Nowak, August 19, 1998.

70. Frossard and John Paul II, *"Be Not Afraid!,"* p. 230.

71. Ibid., p. 231.

72. Ibid., p. 248; author's interview with Gabriel Turowski, June 10, 1997.

73. *OR* [EWE], June 29, 1981, pp. 1, 12; author's interview with Daniella Carozza, May 26, 1998.

74. Author's interview with Jan Nowak, August 19, 1998; Novak said that the Pope had mentioned "reading your book" while he was in the hospital during a subsequent personal conversation.

75. Ibid.

76. See Szajkowski, *Next to God . . . Poland,* p. 132.

77. Frossard and John Paul II, *"Be Not Afraid!,"* p. 240, 249.

78. The feast is also known as the feast of the Dedication of the Basilica of St. Mary Major, built on Rome's Esquiline Hill on the spot where Mary is said to have caused a miraculous snowfall on August 5, 353.

79. Szajkowski, *Next to God . . . Poland,* p. 135.

80. Ibid.

81. Józef Tischner, "Polish Work Is Sick," in Józef Tischner, *The Spirit of Solidarity* (San Francisco: Harper and Row, 1984), pp. 96–100.

82. John Paul II, *Laborem Exercens,* 4.2, in Miller, *Encyclicals.*

83. Ibid., 25.3.

84. Ibid. 6.5.

85. Ibid., 9.3 [emphasis in original].

86. Ibid., 12.1 [emphasis in original].

87. Ibid., 14.2.

88. Ibid., 15.1.

89. Ibid., 15.2.

90. Ibid., 19.3.

91. Ibid., 8.5, 20.3.

92. Ibid., 8.5, 20.3.

93. Ibid., 20.6.

94. Ibid., 25.3–25.4.

95. Ibid., 26.1.

96. Ibid., 27.7 [emphasis in original].

97. On this point see "Editor's Introduction to *Laborem Exercens,*" in Miller, *Encyclicals,* p. 152.

98. Miłosz, *History,* p. 274.

99. *Laborem Exercens,* 1.3, in Miller, *Encyclicals.*

100. Details of the trial and the citation from Judge Santiapichi are taken from Paul B. Henze, *The Plot to Kill the Pope* (New York: Charles Scribner's Sons, 1983).

101. See, among many other examples, Joseph Kraft's column in the *Washington Post* on May 19, 1981, in which he writes that "the root of this terrorist attempt against the Pope is a turbulent Islamic society, pregnant with nasty surprises." [Cited in ibid., p. 6.]

102. Miss Geyer's column was in the *Washington Star* of May 15, 1981; cited in ibid., p. 5.

103. Cited in ibid., pp. 158–159, 172–173.

104. Variants include the prime contractor being the GRU (Soviet military intelligence), operating under Andropov's supervision, and the Stasi, the East German intelligence service, as a possible intermediary between the Soviets and the Bulgarians. In any event, the plot was certainly highly compartmentalized and super-secret. The likelihood is that very few people involved knew all the details of an extremely complex operation.

105. See Henze, *The Plot to Kill the Pope*, pp. 170–172.

106. *OR* [EWE], May 25, 1981, p. 10.

107. See Henze, *The Plot to Kill the Pope*, pp. 15–17.

108. The trial of alleged Bulgarian conspirators that ended in Rome on March 29, 1986, confused matters far more than it clarified them, and may itself have been affected by a Soviet disinformation campaign. But the trial certainly did not, as press coverage at the time suggested, "disprove" the "Bulgarian connection" to Agca. [See Paul Henze, "The Plot to Kill the Pope: A Balance Sheet in the Wake of the Rome Trial," memorandum prepared for the RAND Corporation, June 1986.]

In 1988, a KGB agent posing as a staff member of the Novosti Press Agency asked to see Paul Henze, an American who had published a book in 1983 arguing for a likely Soviet connection to the assassination attempt, and who was then visiting Moscow for the first time. After ten minutes of chatter about international cultural exchange, his ostensible interest, the Soviet visitor asked, "So, do you still hold to your analysis in *The Plot to Kill the Pope*?" [Author's interview with Paul Henze, August 20, 1998.] That the Soviet intelligence service was still so interested in denying its involvement in the late 1980s, two years after many Western analysts and commentators had decided that the "Bulgarian (and thus Soviet) connection" had been disproven, is instructive.

109. On the changes in Jesuit formation, see Joseph M. Becker, SJ, *The Re-Formed Jesuits: A History of Changes in Jesuit Formation During the Decade 1965–1975*, 2 vols. (San Francisco: Ignatius Press, 1992, 1997).

110. Years later, it was made clear that one of the reasons that the Society's highest authorities did not take action against Drinan was that they were never truthfully informed of the situation by Drinan's superiors in the United States. See James Hitchcock, "The Strange Political Career of Father Drinan," *Catholic World Report*, July 1996, pp. 38–45.

When he first ran for Congress in 1970, Father Drinan explained that while he accepted the Church's teaching about abortion as an intrinsically evil act, the Second Vatican Council's *Declaration on Religious Freedom* proscribed his imposing his religious views on others. This was disingenuous at best, as the Church's moral teaching on abortion was based on a natural-law moral analysis accessible to anyone willing to engage the argument. Father Drinan's tacit suggestion that he agreed with those who charged pro-life Catholics with promoting a sectarian position, and his proposal that Catholic religious leaders should withdraw from the legal and political debate over abortion law, ill befit a man positioning himself as a defender of human rights on precisely the same natural-law moral grounds on which the Church based its opposition to abortion. [See Robert F. Drinan, SJ, "The State of the Abortion Question," *Commonweal*, April 17, 1970, pp. 108–109.]

111. The examples are many and various, for example, the public dissent from the Congregation for the Doctrine of the Faith's declaration on the ordination of women signed by virtually the entire faculty of the Jesuit School of Theology at Berkeley (a pontifical faculty chartered by the Holy See) and published in *Commonweal* (April 1, 1977, pp. 204ff.), or Georgetown President Timothy Healy's essay, "The Pope and American Catholic Universities," in *America* (December 8, 1979, pp. 362ff.).

112. Author's interview with Vincent O'Keefe, SJ, September 16, 1997. Father O'Keefe said that John Paul I's talk had been prepared by Father Paolo Dezza, SJ, who had been Pope Paul VI's confessor, and who would figure prominently in the drama to follow.

113. Ibid.

114. Ibid.

115. Prior to the meeting, Arrupe's general assistants had learned that the Holy See had requested that each nunciature or apostolic delegation report on the condition of the Society in its country, but the matter did not come up in the January 17 discussion.

116. Author's interview with Vincent O'Keefe, SJ, September 16, 1997.

117. Ibid.

118. Carl Bernstein and Marco Politi write that O'Keefe's letter "gave advance notice of a general congregation to elect Arrupe's successor." [*His Holiness*, p. 421–422.] O'Keefe said that his letter simply laid out the current situation and the need for a general congregation as he had explained it to the Pope; the former vicar general denied that he had attempted to "convoke a general congregation," stating that "I would have to be crazier than I am to do something like that." [Author's interview with Vincent O'Keefe, SJ, September 16, 1997.]

119. Author's interview with Vincent O'Keefe, SJ, September 16, 1997.

120. Author's interview with Giuseppe Pittau, SJ, December 17, 1997. Father Pittau says that this was precisely what John Paul had told him and Father Dezza at a meeting shortly after the intervention.

121. Ibid.

122. Ibid.
123. Cited in Bernstein and Politi, *His Holiness*, p. 317.
124. John Paul's meeting with Geremek, Tadeusz Mazowiecki, Jerzy Turowicz, and others is described in ibid., p. 316, drawing on Geremek's memories of the meeting.
125. Author's interview with Tadeusz Mazowiecki, April 7, 1997.
126. John Paul II, *The Theology of Marriage and Celibacy*, p. 1.
127. Letter to the author from Monsignor Piero Marini, February 17, 1997.
128. See Bernstein and Politi, *His Holiness*, pp. 329–330.
129. See Szajkowski, *Next to God . . . Poland*, pp. 140–141.
130. Ibid., pp. 155–156.
131. Ibid., pp. 156, 155.
132. See *OR* [EWE], December 21–28, 1981, p. 20.
133. See Garton Ash, *The Polish Revolution: Solidarity*, p. 267–268.
134. Cited in Bernstein and Politi, *His Holiness*, p. 345.
135. See *OR* [EWE], January 4, 1982, p. 3.
136. John Paul II, "Christmas Greetings to Polish People," *OR* [EWE], January 4, 1982, p. 10.
137. See *OR* [EWE], January 11, 1982, p. 1.
138. Author's interview with Zbigniew Brzeziński, February 7, 1997.
139. See *OR* [EWE], January 25, 1982, pp. 1–4, especially section 7.
140. Cardinal Hume, who did not know whether others had previously suggested visiting both Great Britain and Argentina or whether the Pope was already considering the possibility, "thought of it on the spur of the moment when I was with others discussing with the Pope whether he should come to England" under the political circumstances. [Letter to the author from Cardinal Basil Hume, OSB, June 9, 1998.]
141. Citations are from "Papal Times," a supplement to *The Catholic Times* (June 1, 1997) on the fifteenth anniversary of John Paul's visit to the United Kingdom.
142. Memorandum to the author from Cardinal Alfonso López Trujillo, November 24, 1997.

CHAPTER 13

Liberating Liberations: The Limits of Politics and the Promise of Redemption

1. Author's interview with Archbishop Andrea Cordero Lanza di Montezemolo, November 28, 1997.
2. Author's interview with Cardinal Miguel Obando Bravo, SDB, November 24, 1997.
3. See, for example, Szulc, *Pope John Paul II*.
4. See, for example, Bernstein and Politi, *His Holiness*.
5. See, for example, Kwitny, *Man of the Century*.
6. John Paul II, remarks on arrival at Fatima, May 12, 1982, in *Insegnamenti di Giovanni Paolo II, 1982*.
7. Author's interview with Richard V. Allen, November 26, 1996.
8. Ibid.; author's interview with Jan Nowak, May 13, 1998. Reagan had given instructions that the Pope was to be informed of the U.S. government's intelligence sources, as well as of their "product." [Ibid.]
9. Author's conversation with Pope John Paul II, September 10, 1996.
10. The conspiracy theory is most aggressively promoted by Carl Bernstein and Marco Politi in *His Holiness*.
11. See ibid., pp. 319 ff. Bernstein and Politi write that CIA director William Casey and U.S. special ambassador Vernon Walters met with John Paul II "about fifteen times over a six-year period": an average of 2.5 times per year. Fifteen or twenty hours of conversation over six years is not what one usually understands by a conspiracy.
12. Ibid., pp. 270–271. Richard V. Allen characterizes this suggestion, in reference to the intermediate nuclear forces deployment, as "bulls—t." [Author's interview with Richard V. Allen, November 26, 1996.]
13. Sometime after the Bernstein "holy alliance" proposal first appeared in *Time* magazine, John Paul responded to a reporter's question about it on a 1992 flight to Africa. The "holy alliance," he said, was an "a posteriori deduction." Then the philosopher-Pope drew the logical conclusion: "One cannot construct a case from the consequences. Everybody knows the positions of President Reagan as a great policy leader in world politics. My position was that of a pastor, the Bishop of Rome, of one with responsibility for the Gospel, which certainly contains principles of the moral and social order and those regarding human rights. . . . The Holy See's position, even in regard to my homeland, was guided by moral principle. . . ." [*OR* (EWE), February 26, 1992, p. 12.]
14. On Ratzinger's early life and career, see his book-length interview with the German journalist Peter Seewald [Joseph Ratzinger, *Salt of the Earth: The Church at the End of the Millennium* (San Francisco: Ignatius Press, 1997), pp. 41–80], and his autobiography [Joseph Ratzinger, *Milestones: Memoirs 1927–1977* (San Francisco: Ignatius Press, 1998)].
15. Ratzinger's description of why he found Wojtyła attractive is interesting:

The first thing that won my sympathy was his uncomplicated, human frankness and openness, as well as the cordiality that he radiated. There was his humor. You also sensed a piety that had nothing false, nothing external about it. You sensed that here was a man of God. Here was a person who had nothing artificial about him, who was really a man of God and, what is more, a completely original person who had a long intellectual and personal history behind him. You notice that about a person: he has suffered, he has also struggled on his way to this vocation. He lived through the whole drama of the German occupation, of the Russian occupation, and of the communist regime. He blazed his own intellectual trail. He studied German philosophy intensely; he entered deeply into the whole intellectual history of Europe. And he also knew the crucial points in the history of theology that lead far from the usual paths. This intellectual wealth, as well as his enjoyment of dialogue and exchange, these were all things that immediately made him likeable to me. [Ratzinger, *Salt of the Earth*, p. 85.]

16. Author's interview with Cardinal Joseph Ratzinger, September 12, 1996. Ratzinger was concerned that the prefecture would require him to abandon his own theological work and publishing, to which he felt a vocational obligation. John Paul II said he didn't see any problem with the prefect publishing his own work privately, and that settled the matter. [Ratzinger, *Salt of the Earth*, p. 85–86.]

17. See Ratzinger, *Salt of the Earth.*

18. Author's interviews with Cardinal Joseph Ratzinger, September 12, 1996 and December 18, 1997.

19. Author's interview with Cardinal Joseph Ratzinger, September 12, 1996; see also Ratzinger, *Salt of the Earth*, p. 108.

20. Author's interview with Archbishop Zenon Grocholewski, January 13, 1997. Archbishop Grocholewski was a member of the review group, and at the time of our meeting was Secretary of the Apostolic Signatura, the Church's appellate court. On October 5, 1998, John Paul II named Grocholewski the Prefect, or head, of the Signatura.

21. Ibid.

22. Ibid.

23. The citations are from *Sacrae Disciplinae Leges*, in *The Code of Canon Law: A Text and Commentary*, eds. James A. Coriden, Thomas J. Gren, and Donald Heintschel (New York: Paulist Press, 1985), pp. xxiv–xxvi. Interestingly, this edition translates the Latin title of the apostolic constitution as "The Laws of Its Canonical Discipline."

24. Author's interview with Jean Duchesne, August 20, 1997.

25. The phrase "saint of the abyss" is André Frossard's; see *"Forget Not Love": The Passion of Maximilian Kolbe*, (San Francisco: Ignatius Press, 1991), p. 15.

26. See *Insegnamenti di Giovanni Paolo II*, 1982 [emphasis in original].

27. On the controversy over Kolbe's canonization as a martyr, see Kenneth L. Woodward, *Making Saints: How the Catholic Church Determines Who Becomes a Saint, Who Doesn't, and Why* (New York: Simon and Schuster, 1996), pp. 144–147.

28. Hans Urs von Balthasar, "Introduction" to "Thérèse of Lisieux" in *Two Sisters in the Spirit* (San Francisco: Ignatius Press, 1992), p. 24.

29. On this point, see Woodward, *Making Saints*, p. 3.

30. Woodward sums up the changes in ibid., pp. 90–95.

31. See ibid., p. 95.

32. See Joan Estruch, *Saints and Schemers: Opus Dei and its Paradoxes* (New York: Oxford University Press, 1995). Estruch, a scholarly critic of the Work who concedes the movement's key role in Spain's democratic transition, also argues that the transition had effects that Opus Dei did not anticipate, for example, the sharp decline of Catholic practice in a rapidly modernizing Spain.

33. See *Presbyterorum Ordinis* [Decree on the ministry and life of priests], 10.

34. Monsignor del Portillo was ordained a bishop by John Paul II on January 6, 1991. For a study of Opus Dei's quest for a distinctive canonical status in the Church, written from within the movement, see Amadeo de Fuenmayor, Valentin Gómez-Iglesias, and Jose Luis Illanes, *The Canonical Path of Opus Dei: The History and Defense of a Charism* (Princeton/Chicago: Scepter Publishers/Midwest Theological Forum, 1994).

35. This was a point stressed in the author's interview with the Prelate of Opus Dei, Bishop Javier Echevarría Rodríguez, November 14, 1997. Bishop Echevarría succeeded Bishop del Portillo in 1994.

36. See Woodward, see *Making Saints*, pp. 8–12, 384–387.

37. Author's interview with Cardinal Pio Laghi, January 16, 1997; Cardinal Laghi was recounting a conversation he had had with Pope John Paul II in the early 1980s.

When he came to Washington 1981 as apostolic delegate, Laghi used to discuss Central America with President Ronald Reagan. On one occasion, the president asked, "What is this damned theology of liberation?" Laghi, who knew that Reagan had been to an Italian-American function the night before, replied that "The spaghetti is good, but the sauce is poisoned." The "spaghetti" was the Church's work with the poor; the "sauce" was "Marxist analysis" leading to revolutionary violence in the name of the Gospel— "putting a rifle into the hands of the crucified Lord," as Cardinal Laghi once put it.

38. See Teresa Whitfield, *Paying the Price: Ignacio Ellacuría and the Murdered Jesuits of El Salvador* (Philadelphia: Temple University Press, 1994), pp. 102–109. The question of the degree of influence the Jesuits exercised over Archbishop Romero remains controverted almost two decades after Romero's death, and ten years after Father Ellacuría and five other Jesuits were brutally murdered in 1989 by the Salvadoran army. Ms. Whitfield's book, while quite sympathetic to both the archbishop and Father Ellacuría, provides ample evidence that Ellacuría, Sobrino, and their colleagues were influential in shaping Romero's views and actions. Father Ellacuría's theological and political views are outlined in ibid., chapter seven. Piers Paul Read, reviewing *Paying the Price* in the *Times Literary Supplement* [March 24, 1995], praised it as a "scholarly work . . . that manages to remain objective on a theme that still provokes passions of a violent kind"; still, he concluded, "Despite [the author's] sympathies, the information imparted in *Paying the Price* is more than

enough to lead us to question whether Romero, Ellacuría, and the other priests murdered in El Salvador were Catholic martyrs rather than just casualties in a cruel civil war."

The postulator of the cause for Romero's beatification, Monsignor Vincenzo Paglia, disagrees with Read's assessment. Archbishop Romero, he argues, "was not without defects," but Paglia and others who have worked on the cause are "completely agreed" that Romero died a martyr who was not killed simply for political motives. Monsignor Paglia also asserts that Father Sobrino "exploited" his relationship with Romero after the archbishop's murder in order to put pressure on Archbishop Obando in Nicaragua. [Author's interview with Monsignor Vincenzo Paglia, December 9, 1998. See also the "Informatio" submitted to the Congregation for the Causes of Saints on the question of Romero as a martyr, Congregation protocol number 1913.]

39. See *OR* [EWE], March 31, 1980, p. 1.

40. Letter to the author from Ambassador Deane R. Hinton, January 25, 1998.

41. Obando summed up his case against the regime in 1997:

We wanted a revolution that would be good for the people of Nicaragua, but we could see that the revolution was heading another way. Instead of advancing the interests of the people of Nicaragua, progress was reversed . . . [as] they [Sandinistas] continued to violate the human rights of our people. A lot of innocent people were arrested, Catholic radio was closed for a year, homilies were censored; sometimes even the texts of Sacred Scripture were censored. In just one day, ten priests were taken out of Managua. The Sandinistas also militarily occupied our publishing house in Managua. [Author's interview with Cardinal Miguel Obando Bravo, SDB, November 24, 1997.]

The relationship between Archbishop Obando and the Sandinistas had deteriorated quickly after the ouster of Anastasio Somoza in July 1979. By the end of that month, the archbishop had issued a pastoral letter urging the new regime to restore freedom of expression and protesting that the Nicaraguan people were being "compelled to forget their primary respect for life and human values." Two years later, after meeting John Paul II in Rome, Archbishop Obando publicly accused the regime of becoming Marxist; Nicaraguan state television "promptly pulled the archbishop's Sunday Mass off the air." Several days later, the regime shut down the independent newspaper, *La Prensa,* for two days, "for failing to tell the truth" about relations between the Church and the Sandinista government. [Citations from Robert Kagan, *A Twilight Struggle: American Power in Nicaragua, 1977–1990* (New York: Free Press, 1995), pp. 117, 183.]

In light of this pattern of hostility toward the Church, the support for the Sandinista regime by North American Catholics looms as one of the most curious features of the Catholic 1980s. The United States Catholic Conference, the public policy arm of the Catholic bishops of the United States, consistently took a soothing line in its congressional testimony on Nicaragua. But this was mild compared to the support the Nicaraguan regime enjoyed among American Catholic intellectuals and political activists. Readers of *America,* the Jesuit weekly, found praise of the Sandinista neighborhood "defense committees" (which enforced ideological and political orthodoxy through an elaborate spying system and the control of food-ration cards) and were informed that the Sandinista Front was a "flexible" political organization motivated by a "humanistic ethic." Ernesto Cardenal's claim that "there need be no separation between Christianity and communism" was reported without demur. *America* even had room for the argument that Sandinista Nicaragua would eventually evolve into "a far more democratic system than we have in the United States." [See James Brockman, SJ, "Nicaragua in January," *America,* February 24, 1979, p. 138; Chris Gjording, SJ, "Nicaragua's Unfinished Revolution," *America,* October 6, 1979, p. 168; Tennent C. Wright, SJ, "Ernesto Cardenal and the Humane Revolution in Nicaragua," *America,* December 15, 1979, 388; Arthur McGovern, "Nicaragua's Revolution: A Progress Report," *America,* December 21, 1981, p. 378.]

The prominence of Jesuits in what was often uncritical adulation for a Marxist regime should be kept in mind in assessing John Paul II's intervention in the governance of the Society of Jesus in October 1981.

42. Author's interview with Archbishop Andrea Cordero Lanza di Montezemolo, November 28, 1997.

43. Author's interview with Cardinal Miguel Obando Bravo, SDB, November 24, 1997.

44. Author's interview with Archbishop Andrea Cordero Lanza di Montezemolo, November 28, 1997.

45. Author's interview with Roberto Tucci, SJ, September 25, 1997.

46. Author's interview with Archbishop Andrea Cordero Lanza di Montezemolo, November 28, 1997.

47. Ibid.

48. See Humberto Belli, *Nicaragua: Christians Under Fire* (San José, Costa Rica: Instituto Puebla, 1984).

49. See ibid.

50. The Sandinista supporters in front of the altar included the mothers of seventeen Sandinista troops killed by the anti-regime "contras." The Sandinista excuse for the preplanned mob agitation during the Pope's sermon was that the crowd had been righteously indignant when the Pope did not condemn the "contras."

51. Author's interview with Roberto Tucci, SJ, September 25, 1997.

52. Author's interview with Cardinal Miguel Obando Bravo, SDB, November 24, 1997.

53. Author's interview with Cardinal Joseph Ratzinger, January 18, 1997.

54. In *Man of the Century,* Jonathan Kwitny, picking up a speculation widely bruited by others before him, suggests that there was a second instruction on liberation theology because John Paul II was displeased with the *Instruction on Certain Aspects of the Theology of Liberation.* Cardinal Ratzinger flatly denied this in interviews on January 18 and September 20, 1997, noting the essential continuity between the two instructions and the teaching of the Pope at Puebla in 1979 and in Peru in February 1985. At no point in this process, the cardinal said, had the Pope expressed any displeasure that the first instruction had not worked as he had hoped.

Kwitny's suggestion that Cardinal Roger Etchegaray produced the basic draft of a "corrective" second instruction on the Pope's instructions is not persuasive. In the development of texts of this sort, drafts from various quarters are solicited by, or independently sent to, the office finally responsible for writing the document in question.

Kwitny also suggests that the theory which holds that economic factors are dominant in history is "the essence of Marxist analysis" and that John Paul could not have been all that critical of the use of this "Marxist analysis" in liberation theology because he had adopted this view of history in his *Catholic Social Ethics* text in 1953—a text that, as previously discussed, hardly reflects John Paul II's developed social-political views. Moreover, Kwitny seriously misreads both Marxism and John Paul II. The "essence of Marxist analysis" involves far more than economics as a history-shaping force; it includes, for example, class conflict as the chief dynamic of historical change, a view which Karol Wojtyła has always rejected, and could not possibly accept as a Christian. The Pope's 1980 UNESCO speech, with its intense stress on culture as the most powerful force in the human world, was a powerful critique of any "economy first" theory of history. [See *Man of the Century*, pp. 514–518 and the relevant endnotes.]

55. See *Instruction on Certain Aspects of the Theology of Liberation*, X, 5.
56. Ibid., IV, 14–15.
57. Ibid., VIII, 9.
58. Ibid., VIII, 4, 9.
59. Ibid., VIII, 7.
60. Ibid., IX, 10.
61. Ibid, IX, 12.
62. Ibid., X, 12.
63. Ibid., X, 16.
64. Ibid., XI, 17.
65. *Instruction on Christian Freedom and Liberation*, 3.
66. Ibid., 5.
67. Ibid., 14, 44.
68. Ibid., 38.
69. Ibid., 89.
70. Ibid., 68.
71. Ibid., 95,
72. Author's interview with Janusz Onyszkiewicz, June 10, 1991.
73. See Michael Kaufman, *Mad Dreams, Saving Graces—Poland: A Nation in Conspiracy* (New York: Random House, 1989), p. 5.
74. The "Square of the Defense of the Paris Commune" reverted to its pre-communist name after 1989: "Woodrow Wilson Square."
75. See Kaufman, *Mad Dreams, Saving Graces*, pp. 139 ff.
76. The young priest's most quoted sermon summed up his challenge:

Let us put the truth, like a light, on a candlestick, let us make life in truth shine out, if we do not want our consciences to putrefy. . . . Let us not sell our ideals for a mess of pottage. Let us not sell our ideals by selling our brothers. It depends on our concern for our innocently imprisoned brothers, on our life in truth, how soon that time comes when we shall share our daily bread again in solidarity and love. At this time, when we need so much strength to regain and uphold our freedom, let us pray to God to fill us with the power of His Spirit, to awaken the spirit of true solidarity in our hearts. [Cited in Grażyna Sikorska, *A Martyr for the Truth: Jerzy Popiełuszko* (Grand Rapids: Eerdmans, 1985), p. 59.]

77. Antonin Lewek, "New Sanctuary of Poles: The Grave of Martyr-Father Jerzy Popiełuszko" (Warsaw, 1986), pamphlet from St. Stanisław Kostka Church, Warsaw; Father Lewek was a friend and colleague of Father Popiełuszko.
78. Kaufman, *Mad Dreams, Saving Graces*, p. 141.
79. See ibid., p. 138.
80. See "Pope's Mass for the 600th Anniversary of Our Lady of Jasna Góra," *OR* [EWE], September 6, 1982, pp. 1, 2. John Paul celebrated Mass on the anniversary date, August 26, in the chapel as Castel Gandolfo, beneath the reproduction of the Black Madonna given to Pius XI by the Polish episcopate.
81. Author's interview with Roberto Tucci, SJ, September 25, 1997.
In 1982, the regime's internal security apparatus had drafted a memo on "dangers to be anticipated in the event of a visit by the Pope to Poland in August 1982," which spoke of "three hundred fifty terrorist groups" and the "widespread possession of arms munitions, and high explosive"—all part of the continuing smear campaign against Solidarity. The charges of CIA provocations should be understood in the same vein. [See Wałęsa, *A Way of Hope*, p. 275.]
82. See Timothy Garton Ash, "The Pope in Poland," in *The Uses of Adversity: Essays on the Fate of Central Europe* (New York: Vintage Books, 1990), p. 50.
83. Cited in ibid., p. 48.
84. See ibid., p. 48.
85. Cited in ibid., pp. 48–49, 51. As Garton Ash points out, John Paul "effortlessly" expropriated the word odnowa [renewal] from the calcified communist vocabulary, and set it in a true moral context.
86. Author's interview with Cardinal Jean-Marie Lustiger, October 24, 1996.
87. Author's interview with Joaquín Navarro-Valls, March 20, 1997.

88. Garton Ash, "The Pope in Poland," p. 53.

89. See ibid., pp. 57–58.

90. Cited in ibid., p. 58.

91. Ibid.

92. For a more detailed analysis of TCOP and the impact on it of the Vatican consultation, see my *Tranquillitas Ordinis: The Present Failure and Future Promise of American Catholic Thought on War and Peace* (New York: Oxford University Press, 1987), pp. 257–285. Information on the Vatican consultation is from the author's interview with Archbishop Jan Schotte, CICM, May 10, 1991.

93. Letter to the author from Cardinal John J. O'Connor, October 17, 1997.

94. The meeting with Arafat, which caused great controversy in the world Jewish community, had taken place the previous fall, on September 15, 1992.

95. Details on the origins of the IWM and the first Castel Gandolfo seminar are from the author's interview with Father Józef Tischner, April 23, 1997.

96. Ibid.

97. On the Pontifical Council for Culture, see John Paul II's letter to Cardinal Casaroli of May 20, 1982, assigning the Secretary of State the responsibility for its organization. [*OR* (EWE), June 28, 1982, p. 7.]

98. Author's interview with Vincent O'Keefe, SJ, September 16, 1997.

99. "John Paul II's Address to the Jesuit Provincials," *OR* [EWE], March 15, 1982, pp. 10–12, 20.

100. See, for example, Walsh, *John Paul II*, p. 104. Father Vincent O'Keefe confirmed that this was a widespread reaction to the address, and that when news of this got back to the Vatican, it "caused problems" when the time came to get final approval for General Congregation 33. "But we got over it." [Author's interview with Vincent O'Keefe, SJ, September 16, 1997.]

101. "Pope's Address to the Thirty-third General Congregation of the Jesuits," *OR* [EWE], September 12, 1983, pp. 6, 8.

102. Author's interview with Giuseppe Pittau, SJ, December 17, 1997. On July 11, 1998, John Paul II named Father Pittau titular archbishop of Castro di Sardegna and Secretary (the second-ranking position) of the Congregation for Catholic Education. Prior to this appointment, Pittau had been rector of the Pontifical Gregorian University.

103. Author's interview with Roberto Tucci, SJ, September 25, 1997.

104. Ibid.

105. Total membership in the Society was 22,227 in 1996, down from 34,687 in 1960. [See "Public Square," *First Things* 75 (August/September 1997), p. 85.]

106. See John Paul II, *Tertio Millennio Adveniente,* 10.

107. See John Paul II, *Redemptor Hominis,* 1.1.

108. Pilgrims who visit each basilica, pray for the intentions of the Pope, confess their sins, do appropriate penance, and receive Holy Communion are granted a plenary indulgence: a complete pardon from the enduring effects of sin, which, according to Catholic doctrine, require purification in Purgatory in order to make the deceased Christian capable of communion with God and the saints in heaven. [See *Catechism of the Catholic Church,* 1471–1479.]

109. John Paul II, "Homily on the Inauguration of the Holy Year of the Redemption," *OR* [EWE], March 28, 1983, pp. 1, 12.

110. E. M. Jung-Inglessis, *The Holy Year in Rome: Past and Present* (Vatican City: Libreria Editrice Vaticana, 1977), p. 296.

111. At the same time, a Joint Roman Catholic Theological Commission, appointed by the Secretariat for Christian Unity and the Lutheran World Federation, completed ten years of work under the co-chairmanship of Bishop Hans Martensen of Copenhagen and Professor George Lindbeck of the Yale Divinity School. The Joint Commission published a common statement, "Martin Luther—Witness to Jesus Christ," which noted that both communions had achieved "a lessening of outdated, polemically colored images of Luther" who could be "honored in common as a witness to the gospel, a teacher in the faith, and a herald of spiritual renewal."

112. John Paul's letter to Cardinal Willebrands, "Martin Luther—Witness to Jesus Christ," and Cardinal Willebrands's Leipzig address: Secretariat for Christian Unity *Information Service* #52 (1983/II), pp. 83–92.

113. Jung-Inglessis, *The Holy Year in Rome,* pp. 297, 299.

114. See *OR* [EWE], January 16, 1984, p. 1.

115. See *OR* [EWE], February 26, 1984, p. 6.

116. *Reconciliatio et Paenitentia,* which was signed on December 2, 1984, was the first of these Synod-inspired documents to be styled explicitly a "Post-Synodal Apostolic Exhortation." In his introduction, John Paul stressed that "the contents of these pages come from the Synod," including its working papers, its general debates and small group discussions, and the propositions adopted by the Synod Fathers. [*Reconciliatio et Paenitentia,* 4.13, in Miller, *Exhortations.*] At the same time, the Pope wove the Synod-generated material together in a distinctively personal framework.

117. Ibid., 7.7.

118. Ibid., 8.5.

119. See ibid., 13.1, 13.2, 15.4.

120. See ibid., 16.1.

121. See ibid., 17.8–17.17.

122. Ibid., 33.3, 29.3.

123. Ibid., 33.3.

124. Author's interview with Monsignor Andrzej Bardecki, July 11, 1996. Monsignor Bardecki had break-

fast with the Pope the morning after the meeting with Agca, and asked whether the Turk had made a confession. John Paul replied, "No, it wasn't that," and recounted the story of Agca's Fatima obsession. Bardecki later published an account of his breakfast conversation with John Paul in *Tygodnik Powszechny;* the Pope saw it and didn't object to Bardecki's rendering of their discussion.

125. John Paul II, *Salvifici Doloris,* 3, 2.

126. Ibid., 7.

127. Ibid., 12.

128. Ibid., 18.

129. Ibid., 14.

130. Ibid., 14, 15.

131. See ibid., 26.

132. See *OR* [EWE], January 16, 1984, p. 2.

133. See *OR* [EWE], January 30, 1984, pp. 6–8.

134. See Walsh, *John Paul II,* p. 132.

135. See *OR* [EWE], March 20, 1984, p. 1.

136. John Paul II, *Redemptionis Anno, OR* [EWE], April 30, 1984, p. 6.

137. *OR* [EWE], October 10, 1984, p. 16.

138. The Congregation for Bishops presents the Pope with nominees for every episcopal see in the world, except those in mission territories (who are nominated by the Congregation for the Evangelization of Peoples) or Eastern-rite Catholic Churches (which have their own processes for the selection of bishops).

139. The 1975 WCC Assembly in Nairobi had failed to act on a petition from two Russian Orthodox activists, Father Gleb Yakunin and Lev Regelson, asking the WCC's support for religious freedom in the USSR; when Yakunin was subsequently sentenced to five years imprisonment and five years internal exile, the WCC refused to issue a statement on his behalf. [See Ernest W. Lefever, *Nairobi to Vancouver: The World Council of Churches and the World, 1975–1987* (Washington: Ethics and Public Policy Center, 1987, pp. 64–67).]

140. See "Resolution on Afghanistan," in *Gathered for Life: Office Report, VI Assembly of the World Council of Churches,* ed. David Gill (Grand Rapids: Eerdmans, 1983), pp. 161–62.

141. See Ernest W. Lefever, *Nairobi to Vancouver,* pp. 33–45.

142. See ibid., pp. 21–22.

The history of the WCC's politics, based on primary sources, may be found in ibid. and a predecessor volume by the same author, *Amsterdam to Nairobi: The World Council of Churches and the Third World* (Washington, D.C.: Ethics and Public Policy Center, 1979).

143. John Paul II, "Address to the World Council of Churches," *OR* [EWE], June 25, 1984, pp. 6–8.

144. Author's interview with Roberto Tucci, SJ, September 25, 1997.

145. Lewek, "New Sanctuary of Poles."

146. Cited in Garton Ash, *The Polish Revolution: Solidarity,* p. 351.

CHAPTER 14

Reliving the Council: Religion and the Renewal of a World Still Young

1. See "Rome," in *Encyclopedia Judaica,* vol. 14 (Jerusalem: Keter Publishing House, 1972). On the hiding of Jews at Castel Gandolfo, see Emilio Bonomelli, *I Papi in Campagna* (Rome: 1953) and Saverio Petrillo, *I Papi a Castelgandolfo* (Rome: 1995). The major documentary resource on the Holy See and the Pius XII during World War II is *Actes et Documents du Saint-Siège relatifs à la seconde guerre mondiale,* Pierre Blet, Angelo Martini, Robert Graham, and Burkhart Schneider, eds., 11 volumes (Vatican City: Libreria Editrice Vaticana, 1965–1981). One of the editors summarizes the evidence examined in this Vatican-authorized collection of archival materials in Pierre Blet, SJ, *Pie XII et la seconde guerre mondiale d'après les archives du Vatican* (Paris: Perrion, 1997).

2. The addresses of Professor Saban, Rabbi Toaff, and Pope John Paul II at the Synagogue of Rome may be found in John Paul II, *Spiritual Pilgrimage: Texts on Jews and Judaism,* eds. Eugene J. Fisher and Leon Klenicki (New York: Crossroad, 1995), pp. 60–73. The background to the visit is based on the author's interviews with Sister Lucy Thorson, NDS, January 15, 1997, and Bishop Pierre Duprey, M.Afr., January 15, 1997.

3. Author's interview with Paula Butturini, February 18, 1997.

4. See "Homily During the Liturgy of the Word—Cuzco (Peru)," in *Insegnamenti di Giovanni Paolo II, 1985.* Details of the venue are from the author's interview with Paula Butturini, February 18, 1997, and from *Il Mondo di Giovanni Paolo II: Tutti i viaggi internazionale del Papa, 1978–1996* (Milan: Mondadori, 1996).

5. On these points, see Cardinal Joseph Ratzinger and Vittorio Messori, *The Ratzinger Report: An Exclusive Interview on the State of the Church,* translated by Salvator Attanasio and Graham Harrison (San Francisco: Ignatius Press, 1985), pp. 19, 28–29. For Paul VI's remarks on the "Satan's smoke," see *OR* [EWE], July 13, 1972, p. 6.

6. See Neuhaus, *The Catholic Moment,* pp. 112–113.

7. See Berger and Neuhaus, eds., *Against the World for the World.*

8. See Brigitte Berger and Peter L. Berger, "Our Conservatism and Theirs," *Commentary* 82:4 (October 1986), p. 63.

9. See Peter L. Berger, *A Rumor of Angels: Modern Society and the Rediscovery of the Supernatural* (New York: Doubleday Anchor Books, 1970).

10. Author's interview with Joaquín Navarro-Valls, December 18, 1997.

11. Author's interview with Joaquín Navarro-Valls, October 23, 1998.

12. John Paul II, *Spiritual Pilgrimage,* pp. 47–48.

13. "Pope's Address to Colloquium on *Nostra Aetatae,*" *OR* [EWE], April 29, 1985, p. 3.

14. Commission for Religious Relations with the Jews, *Notes on the Correct Way to Present the Jews and Judaism in Preaching and Catechesis in the Roman Catholic Church, OR* [EWE], July 1, 1985, pp. 6–7.

15. See John Paul II, *Spiritual Pilgrimage,* pp. 55–59.

16. Author's conversation with Pope John Paul II, September 30, 1997.

17. Ibid.

18. "History of the World Youth Day," in *Pilgrim Guide Book, JMJ Paris 1997,* p. 12.

19. Citations from *To the Youth of the World,* OR [EWE], April 1, 1985, pp. 1–9.

20. John Paul II, "Address to the Meeting of Delegates of National Ecumenical Commissions," Secretariat for Promoting Christian Unity *Information Service* #58 (1985/II), pp. 71–72 [emphasis in original].

21. See Karl Rahner and Heinrich Fries, *Unity of the Churches: An Actual Possibility* (Philadelphia and New York: Fortress and Paulist, 1985). Karl Rahner's description of the Rahner/Fries proposal may be found in Karl Rahner, "The Unity of the Church to Come," in *Faith in a Wintry Season,* eds. Paul Imhoff and Hubert Biallowons, translations edited by Harvey D. Egan (New York: Crossroad, 1991), pp. 168–174.

22. John Paul II, "The Twenty-Fifth Anniversary of the Secretariat for Promoting Christian Unity: Address to the Roman Curia," Secretariat for Promoting Christian Unity *Information Service* #59 (1985/III), 10 [emphasis in original].

23. See ibid., 2.

24. See ibid.

25. Ibid., 7.

26. See ibid., 6.

27. Ibid., 7.

28. Ibid., 9.

29. The CDF "notification" on Boff may be found in *OR* [EWE], April 9, 1985, pp. 11–12. See also Ratzinger, *Salt of the Earth,* pp. 94–95.

30. Author's interview with Cardinal Edward Cassidy, December 7, 1996 (Cardinal Cassidy was nuncio in the Netherlands during the papal visit); the prime minister's remark is cited in Walsh, *John Paul II,* p. 147.

31. Letter to the author from Frans A. M. Alting von Geusau, January 5, 1997.

32. See Kwitny, *Man of the Century,* p. 533.

33. See Walsh, *John Paul II,* p. 157, note 16.

34. Ibid., see also Walsh, *John Paul II,* p. 147.

35. Letter to the author from Cardinal Edward Cassidy, October 28, 1997.

The new seminary was founded by Bishop Johannes Gerardus ter Schure, SDB, whose appointment was another cause of aggravation to Dutch dissidents; the appointment was denounced by the London Catholic weekly, the *Tablet,* as "a humiliating gesture." [See Kwitny, *Man of the Century,* p. 532.]

36. See Walsh, *Pope John Paul II,* p. 148.

37. See *Insegnamenti di Giovanni Paolo II, 1985.*

38. Author's interview with Cardinal Jozef Tomko, November 14, 1996.

39. On August 15, in Kinshasa, Zaire, John Paul beatified Anwarite Nengapeta, a twenty-five-year-old Zaïroise nun murdered during the Simba rebellion in 1964. Sister Anwarite had told Colonel Olombe, the rebel chieftain who sought to abuse her sexually and who ordered her execution after she resisted his advances, "I forgive you, because you don't know what you're doing." Blessed Anwarite Nengapeta's murderer attended the beatification.

40. See "Historic Meeting in Morocco," *OR* [EWE], September 9, 1985, p. 12.

41. Citations are from "Dialogue Between Christians and Moslem," *Origins* 15:11 (August 29, 1985), pp. 174–176.

42. Author's interview with Cardinal Jozef Tomko, January 19, 1997.

43. Author's conversation with Pope John Paul II, December 13, 1997.

44. The bishops of the United States, heavily influenced by arms control theorists, had expressed serious reservations about the Strategic Defense Initiative in *The Challenge of Peace.* This was not without its ironies, in that the Reagan administration's timing of the announcement of SDI was geared at least in part to taking some of the media play away from TCOP. In any event, the United States Catholic Conference was not speaking for the Holy See in expressing its concerns about SDI.

Gromyko recounts the meeting from his distinctive point of view in his *Memoirs,* pp. 213–214.

45. "Letter of Pope John Paul II to the Clergy of Czechoslovakia on the 1100th Anniversary of the Death of St. Methodius," *OR* [EWE], May 20, 1985, 2.

46. Ibid., 3a.

47. Ibid., 3c, 4.

John Paul also wrote that "the sense of responsibility . . . requires that priests and religious hold in high esteem the doctrinal and disciplinary unity with the Church willed and founded by Christ, that is with the successor of Peter and with the bishops in communion with him." [Ibid., 3c.] This was a response to those parts of the underground Church in Czechoslovakia which were already experimenting with unauthorized ordinations of bishops and the ordination of married men to the priesthood.

48. *Slavorum Apostoli* is John Paul's only encyclical "epistle," a style of encyclical that has less doctrinal content than an encyclical "letter." Unlike other encyclical "epistles," though, *Slavorum Apostoli* is addressed to the whole Church, rather than to an individual bishop or group of bishops—another indication of John Paul's concern to reconnect Slavic Christianity to the Christian West after the artificial Yalta division of Europe, which had resulted in an equally artificial division of Christian consciousness. [See "Editor's Introduction to *Slavorum Apostoli,*" in Miller, *Encyclicals,* pp. 215–216.]

49. John Paul II, *Slavorum Apostoli*, 20, in ibid.

50. Ibid., 14.6.

51. Ibid., 22.2.

52. Ibid., 21.1, 19.2, 11.1, 10.2, 19.1, 18.2, 18.2.

53. See Broun, *Conscience and Captivity*, p. 94.

54. As the Holy See hoped it would. The 1982 instruction had been widely interpreted in the media as aimed at clergy in Latin America. The targets in east central Europe tended to be ignored, but this was where the instruction had its most pronounced immediate effect.

55. Author's interview with Father Václav Maly, October 25, 1991.

The Velehrad event was also the occasion for some typically acerbic Czech humor. After the event, there was the usual argument about the attendance. The cardinal's office said 150,000; the regime said 50,000. The Church resistance said, "We're both right. We're counting ours, and they're counting theirs." [Author's interview with Bishop František Lobkowicz, O.Praem., October 21, 1991.]

56. Author's interview with Cardinal Joseph Ratzinger, January 18, 1997.

57. Cited in Neuhaus, *The Catholic Moment*, p. 110.

Cardinal Danneels was the Synod's relator, responsible for synthesizing the general discussions and the material from the language-based small group discussions into a final report; Danneels was assisted by the Synod's "special secretary," Father Walter Kasper, a distinguished German theologian named bishop of Rottenburg-Stuttgart in 1989. The three Cardinal Presidents of the Extraordinary Synod were John Krol of Philadelphia, Joseph Malula of Kinshasa, and Johannes Willebrands of Utrecht.

58. Ibid.

59. Cited in ibid., p. 122.

60. See, for example, the intervention of Bishop James Malone, "The Value of Collegiality," in *Origins* 15:26 (December 12, 1985), pp. 430–431.

61. Neuhaus, *The Catholic Moment*, p. 121.

62. Cited in ibid., p. 123.

63. As may be inferred from the fact that Etchegaray, then the president of the French Bishops' Conference, did not succeed François Marty as archbishop of Paris in 1981.

64. Memorandum to the author from Cardinal Roger Etchegaray, April 12, 1997.

65. Author's interview with Cardinal Roger Etchegaray, March 19, 1997.

66. Details on the Philippine revolution and the statements of Cardinal Sin and the Philippine Bishops' Conference are taken from Henry Wooster, "Faith at the Ramparts: The Philippine Catholic Church and the 1986 Revolution," in *Religion, the Missing Dimension of Statecraft*, eds. Douglas Johnston and Cynthia Sampson (New York: Oxford University Press, 1994), pp. 153–176. The De Villa family's move to EDSA is from the author's interview with Henrietta T. De Villa, March 25, 1997.

67. Memorandum to the author from Cardinal Jaime L. Sin, December 9, 1997.

68. Ibid.

69. Ibid.

70. Cited in Wooster, "Faith at the Ramparts," p. 162.

71. Cited in ibid., p. 170.

72. Author's interview with Archbishop Jorge M. Mejía, January 20, 1997. At the time of the Assisi initiative, then Bishop Mejía was Secretary, or second in command, at the Justice and Peace Commission.

73. Ibid.

74. Ibid.

75. See *The Pope Speaks to India* (Bandra-Bombay: St. Paul Publications, 1986), pp. 17, 19.

76. Author's interview with Paula Butturini, February 18, 1997.

77. Author's conversation with Pope John Paul II, September 30, 1997.

78. Jorge M. Mejía, "To Be Together to Pray," *OR* [EWE], October 13, 1986, p. 8.

79. Author's interview with Archbishop Jorge Mejía, January 20, 1997.

80. Ibid.

81. Ibid.

82. Cited in John Paul II, *Spiritual Pilgrimage*, p. 4.

83. Cited in ibid., pp. 31–32.

84. Cited in ibid., pp. 52–53.

85. Cited in ibid., pp. 80–81.

86. See *Jewish Perspectives on Christianity*, ed. Fritz A. Rothschild (New York: Crossroad, 1990).

87. See David Novak, *Jewish-Christian Dialogue: A Jewish Justification* (New York: Oxford University Press, 1989).

88. Karol Wojtyła's pre-papal understanding of the Trinity is suggested in his last play, the metaphysical poem *Radiation of Fatherhood*, where, as Józef Tischner suggests, the playwright depicts God, "not [as] an Absolute Solitude but [as] an Absolute Interaction." The Swiss theologian Hans Urs von Balthasar once put a similar idea slightly differently in a sermon for Trinity Sunday. At Christmas, on Good Friday and Easter, at the Ascension, and at the celebration of the coming of the Holy Spirit to the first apostles at Pentecost, Christians celebrate "God with us." But how, Balthasar asks, could God be *with us* if *being with* were not, somehow, part of the essence of God's own life? The doctrine of the Trinity is the expression of the Christian belief, forged from Christian experience in history, that God is an absolute reciprocity of self-giving persons, in which vitality is increased by self-giving and egoism is absolutely excluded. [Balthasar, "Trinity: God Is 'Being With,'" in *You Crown the Year with Your Goodness*, pp. 141–143.]

89. John Paul II, *Dominum et Vivificantem*, in Miller, *Encyclicals*, 33.1.

90. See ibid., 35.2, 36.2, 38.1.

91. See ibid., 42.3, 43.3, 44.3.

92. See ibid., 46.3–4, 47.1.

93. See ibid., 57.2.

94. See ibid., 62.1, 67.1, 67.3.

95. "Reception of Delegation of Patriarch of Constantinople," *OR* [EWE], July 28, 1986, p. 3.

96. "Observations on the Final Report of ARCIC," *OR* [EWE], May 10, 1982, pp. 10–11.

97. See the letter of Cardinal Johannes Willebrands to the co-presidents of ARCIC-II, *OR* [EWE], March 11, 1986, pp. 8–9.

98. See ibid.

99. "Exchange of Letters on the Ordination of Women to the Priesthood," in Secretariat for Promoting Christian Unity *Information Service* #61 (1986/III), p. 106.

100. Ibid., p. 107.

101. See ibid., pp. 109–111.

102. The most recent scholarship on Reformation-era England suggests that the sixteenth-century rupture with Catholicism was far deeper than advocates of the *via media* believed. See Eamon Duffy's magisterial study, *The Stripping of the Altars: Traditional Religion in England c. 1400-c.1580* (New Haven and London: Yale University Press, 1992).

103. On August 6, 1988, Archbishop Runcie wrote a letter to John Paul II, reporting on the discussions at the recently concluded Lambeth Conference; it was the first such report in history. The letter, like the Lambeth Conference itself, confirmed what the 1986 exchange of letters had already made clear: that fundamental differences in understanding the nature of the Church and its relationship to an authoritative and apostolically ordered tradition now lay between Anglicans and Roman Catholics. In his response, dated December 8, John Paul noted that the dialogue he and Runcie had hoped ARCIC-II would conduct on the issues involved in "the mutual recognition of the ministries of our Communions" seemed to have been preempted by "the ordination of women to the priesthood in some provinces of the Anglican Communion, together with the recognition of the right of individual provinces to proceed with the ordination of women to the episcopacy." All of this, John Paul wrote, threatened to set in motion a process of "serious erosion" in "the degree of communion between us."

In his letter, Archbishop Runcie had reminded the Pope that neither he, as Archbishop of Canterbury, nor the Lambeth Conference as a body had "juridical authority over the Anglican Communion." All of the provinces of the Anglican Communion, he wrote, "have the canonical authority to implement the mission of the Church as they deem right in their own cultures." This frank admission touched the nub of the issue, for it amounted to a denial, in effect if not in theory, of an apostolically ordered and authoritative tradition that guided the implementation of the Church's mission in any age or any culture. [See "Exchange of Letters Between Pope John Paul II and the Archbishop of Canterbury, After the Lambeth Conference, 1988," in Pontifical Council for Promoting Christian Unity *Information Service* #70 (1989/II), pp. 59–60.]

On October 2, 1989, Archbishop Runcie and John Paul II signed a Common Declaration during the course of the archbishop's visit to the Holy See. The declaration confirmed that the question of ordaining women to the priesthood engaged "important . . . differences" between Anglicanism and Roman Catholicism about the nature of the Church; emphasized that those working for "visible unity" could neither "minimize these differences" nor "abandon their hope or work for unity"; but frankly conceded that "we ourselves do not see a solution" to the new obstacles that had been placed in the path of ecclesial reunion. [See "The Common Declaration," in Pontifical Council for Promoting Christian Unity *Information Service* #71 (1989/III-IV), pp. 122–123.]

In 1987, when John Paul announced that he would beatify eighty-five martyrs from England, Scotland, and Wales on November 22 of that year, both Cardinal Basil Hume and Archbishop Runcie issued statements calling on both Anglicans and Roman Catholics to see this moment as an occasion for celebrating what Runcie graciously called the "heroic Christian witness" of the Catholic martyrs and to "together deplore the intolerance of the age which flawed Christian conviction." [See "Cardinal George Basil Hume, OSB, "The Significance of the Beatification of Eighty-five Martyrs," and "Statements by Cardinal Hume and Archbishop Runcie on the Beatification," in *OR* [EWE], November 16, 1987, p. 8.]

104. See "Pope's Christmas Address to the Roman Curia," *OR* [EWE], January 5, 1987, pp. 6–7.

105. Author's interview with Monsignor Vincenzo Paglia, December 7, 1997.

106. See "Cardinal's Intervention with UNO Secretary General," *OR* [EWE], February 24, 1986, p. 8; "Expression of Solidarity," *OR* [EWE], April 1, 1986.

107. "Bishops of Nicaragua to All Episcopal Conferences," *OR* [EWE], July 14, 1986, p. 2.

The most recent attack on the Pope, in an editorial in the official daily, *El Nuevo Diario*, was, indeed, vicious:

Between Reagan, who declared yesterday that a smile has broken out on the face of the Statue of Liberty, with the approval of millions for his mercenaries, and this Pope, who dedicates prayers only to the dead Yankees and fills the victims of imperialism with accusations and threats, there exists the most perfidious cohesion and the most serious danger for the peoples, since the period when barbarism and genocide were wrought in the name of the cross and the empire. [Cited in ibid.]

108. "Pope's Message: May the Eucharistic Congress Be an Occasion for Reconciliation," *OR* [EWE], December 15, 1986, pp. 2, 24.

109. According to CDF, Curran publicly denied the Church's teaching on divorce and remarriage, abortion, euthanasia, masturbation, artificial contraception, premarital intercourse, and homosexual acts.

Father Curran did not deny that he denied the Church's teaching on sexual morality, only that that teaching had not been infallibly defined, and was thus not irreversibly normative. [See "Letter of the Congregation for the Doctrine of the Faith to Father Charles Curran," *OR* (EWE), August 25, 1986, p. 3.]

For an overview of Curran's theological method and opinions see the following of his books: *Christian Morality Today: The Renewal of Moral Theology* (Notre Dame: Fides, 1966); *A New Look at Christian Morality: Christian Morality Today II* (Notre Dame: Fides, 1968); *New Perspectives in Moral Theology* (Notre Dame: University of Notre Dame Press, 1976); *Toward an American Catholic Moral Theology* (Notre Dame: University of Notre Dame Press, 1987). Curran's account of his dealings with CDF may be found in his *Faithful Dissent* (Kansas City: Sheed and Ward, 1986).

110. For an overview of the entire Curran case, including a close examination of the legal proceedings, see Larry Witham, *Curran vs. Catholic University: A Study of Authority and Freedom in Conflict* (Riverdale, Md.: Edington-Rand, Inc., 1991).

111. See *Lumen Gentium*, 25.

112. John Paul II, "Address at Taizé," Secretariat for Promoting Christian Unity *Information Service* #62 (1986/IV), pp. 184–185.

113. John Paul II, "To Community of Taizé," in ibid., pp. 185–186.

114. See *Il Mondo di Giovanni Paolo II*, pp. 112–115.

115. See *Insegnamenti di Giovanni Paoli II, 1986*.

CHAPTER 15
Forward to Basics: Freedom Ordered to the Dignity of Duty

1. On Father Popiełuszko saying that "one cannot murder hopes," see Kaufman, *Mad Dreams, Saving Graces*, p. 141. The details of the Kolbe Church's resistance program are taken from the author's interview with Father Kazimierz Jancarz, June 16, 1991. Michnik on post–martial law communism is cited in Kaufman, *Mad Dreams, Saving Graces*, p. 129. Father Maliński's comments are from the author's interview with him of June 15, 1991.

2. Roberto Suro, "Pope, on Latin Trip, Attacks Pinochet Regime," *New York Times*, April 1, 1987, pp. A1, A10.

3. Author's interview with Monsignor Christian Precht, April 25, 1998.

4. Details on the planning and strategy of the papal pilgrimage are from ibid.

5. See Walsh, *John Paul II*, p. 177.

6. Author's interview with Cardinal Angelo Sodano, December 13, 1996.

7. Author's interview with Monsignor Christian Precht, April 25, 1998.

8. See *Insegnamenti di Giovanni Paolo II, 1987*.

9. Teresa "de los Andes" was canonized on March 21, 1993.

10. Author's interview with Monsignor Christian Precht, April 25, 1998.

11. Author's interview with Roberto Tucci, SJ, September 25, 1997. Ever the alert planner, Father Tucci said that he had learned a lesson at the O'Higgins Park riot: always have lemons available, because a cut lemon, held in a handkerchief in front of your face, allows you to breathe through tear gas. [Ibid.]

12. Author's interview with Monsignor Christian Precht, April 25, 1998.

13. Author's interviews with Roberto Tucci, SJ, September 25, 1997, and Monsignor Christian Precht, April 25, 1998. Neither Tucci nor Precht claims that General Pinochet was directly involved in this affair or concocted the idea of a "permitted" riot at the papal Mass. It also remains unclear precisely who "these people" were. What is certain is that they were not the people involved in the National Accord. [Ibid.]

14. Author's interview with Cardinal Angelo Sodano, December 13, 1996. See also *"Alocución a Grupo de Dirigentes Políticos,"* in *El Amor Es Mas Fuerte: Mensajes de Juan Pablo II al Pueblo de Chile* (a booklet of pilgrimage texts given the author by Cardinal Sodano).

15. The text of this address may be found in *Origins* 16:44 (April 16, 1987), pp. 776–777.

16. Author's interview with Monsignor Christian Precht, April 25, 1998.

17. Ibid.

18. Ibid. One bishop who had protested died in an automobile accident, and there were suspicions that his death was not accidental. The bishops' conference protested to the government. [Author's interview with Mario Paredes, December 1, 1998.]

19. Letter from Rabbi Leon Klenicki, director of the Interfaith Affairs Department of the Anti-Defamation League of B'nai B'rith, to Thomas C. Fox, editor of the *National Catholic Reporter*, September 30, 1996; copy to the author from Rabbi Klenicki. Years after his nunciature, while he was Cardinal Prefect of the Congregation for Catholic Education, Laghi was accused of cosseting the military regime of Argentina. One piece of evidence cited was that he had occasionally played tennis with the chief-of-staff of the Argentine navy, a member of the ruling junta. Rabbi Klenicki, who had worked on the Timerman case and many other political prisoner cases with Archbishop Laghi in Buenos Aires, noted this strange charge in his letter and wrote that "I had to take many cups of coffee with the Minister of the Interior, but as a consequence I was able to visit prisoners and get . . . freedom for some of the people imprisoned in the concentration camps."

20. John Paul II, "Discourse to Civil Leaders," *OR* [EWE], May 11, 1987, p. 5.

21. John Paul II, "Homily During Mass in Bahia Blanca," in ibid., p. 7 [emphasis in original].

22. John Paul II, "Homily at Viedma," in ibid., p. 8.

23. See "Liturgy of the Word in Mendoza," in ibid., p. 10.

24. John Paul II, "Homily at Tucuman," in ibid., p. 15; the Pope was citing *Gaudium et Spes*, 75.

25. John Paul II, "Mass at Rosario," in *OR* [EWE], May 18, 1987, p. 11 [emphasis in original].

26. John Paul II, "Address to Young People, Buenos Aires," in ibid., p. 15.

27. John Paul II, "Homily for Palm Sunday, World Day of Youth," in *OR* [EWE], May 25, 1987, p. 12.

28. John Paul II, "Address to the Bishops of Argentina," in ibid., p. 14.

29. She later wrote, "It was my first encounter with the Cross and the divine power that it bestows on those who carry it. For the first time, I was seeing with my very eyes the Church, born of the Redeemer's sufferings, triumphant over the sting of death. That was the moment my unbelief collapsed and Christ shone forth—in the mystery of the Cross."

30. Edith Stein, *Essays on Woman* (Washington, D.C.: ICS Publications, 1987), p. 267.

31. Biographical details on Edith Stein are taken from Waltraud Herbstrith, *Edith Stein: A Biography* (San Francisco: Harper and Row, 1985). See also Edith Stein, *Life in a Jewish Family 1891–1916: An Autobiography* (Washington, D.C.: ICS Publications, 1986) and Edith Stein, *Self-Portrait in Letters 1916–1942* (Washington, D.C.: ICS Publications, 1993).

32. Author's conversation with Pope John Paul II, December 12, 1997.

33. See Woodward, *Making Saints*, pp. 134–144.

34. See ibid., pp. 127–128, 143.

35. See John Paul II, "Homily at the Beatification of Edith Stein," in *Spiritual Pilgrimage*, pp. 91–98.

36. See Woodward, *Making Saints*, p. 216.

37. See James Tunstead Burtchaell, CSC, *Rachel Weeping* (San Francisco: Harper and Row, 1984), pp. 141ff. The phrase *lebensunwertes Leben* was coined by two distinguished German academics, the jurist Karl Binding and the psychiatrist Adolf Hoche, in a 1922 book entitled *The Permit to Destroy Life Not Worth Living*, and was adopted by the Nazis the next decade from this eminently establishmentarian source.

38. On March 10, 1987, the Congregation for the Doctrine of the Faith had released an "Instruction on Respect for Human Life in Its Origin and on the Dignity of Procreation," known by the Latin title *Donum Vitae* [The gift of life]. The instruction sought to clarify the moral issues involved when technology intervened in human reproduction. Its most controversial conclusion was that in vitro fertilization (IVF) using gametes donated by spouses violated the moral integrity of procreation by separating it from marital intimacy. Less controversially, the instruction also rejected IVF with gametes donated by a nonspouse, and "surrogate motherhood." The instruction also taught that so-called spare human embryos created by IVF could never be used for nontherapeutic experimentation, since "the human being must be respected—as a person—from the very first instant of his existence." Moreover, the instruction taught that "it is immoral to produce human embryos destined to be exploited as disposable 'biological material.'"

Donum Vitae was criticized for insensitivity to the plight of childless couples who could, through advances in medical technology, render their marriages fruitful—something the Church had long taught was one purpose of marriage. The Instruction acknowledged the suffering involved in infertility, but disagreed with the claim that a couple had a "right" to have a child, for such a "right" would be "contrary to the child's dignity and nature. The child is not an object to which one has a right, nor can he be considered as an object of ownership: rather, a child is a gift, the supreme gift and the most gratuitous gift of marriage, and is a living testimony of the mutual giving of his parents." For that reason, the "right" involved was the child's: "the right . . . to be the fruit of a specific act of the conjugal love of his parents."

39. For John Paul II's address to the West German bishops, see *Origins* 17:3 (June 4, 1987), pp. 45–47.

40. John Paul II, "Apostolic Letter on the Sixth Centenary of the 'Baptism' of Lithuania," *OR* [EWE], June 29, 1987, pp. 1–3.

41. Lech Wałęsa, *The Struggle and the Triumph* (New York: Arcade Publishing, 1991), p. 115.

42. John Paul II, "Address to Authorities of the Polish People's Republic," *OR* [EWE] July 6, 1987, p. 6 [emphasis in original].

43. John Paul II, "Homily During Inaugural Mass of Eucharistic Congress," *OR* [EWE], July 13, 1987, pp. 3–4 [emphasis in original].

44. See ibid., p. 4.

45. John Paul II, "Homily at Catholic University of Lublin," in ibid., pp. 8–9 [emphasis in original].

46. John Paul II, "Homily During Ordinations at Lublin," in ibid., pp. 10–11 [emphasis in original].

47. John Paul II, "Homily at the Beatification of Karolina Kozka at Tarnów," in ibid., p. 3.

48. See John Paul II, "Homily During Mass at Kraków," in ibid., p. 8.

49. John Paul II, "Address to Seafaring People at Gdynia," in ibid., pp. 7–8 [emphasis in original].

50. The papal visit to the memorial demonstrated yet again the regime's talent for clumsiness. Ordinary Gdańsk citizens were not allowed near the venue; a crowd of sullen party members, dragooned into playing the role of audience, stood by quietly while the Pope, Cardinal Casaroli, and others walked to the monument, prayed, and left. An aside from John Paul to his party indicated that he knew exactly what was happening: "Divine Providence could not do better. In this place, silence is a cry." [See Wałęsa, *The Struggle and the Triumph*, p. 119.]

51. John Paul II, "Homily During Mass for Workers at Gdańsk," in *OR* [EWE], August 3, 1997, pp. 2–3.

52. John Paul II, "Address to Polish Episcopal Conference," *OR* [EWE], August 10, 1997, pp. 6–7 [emphasis in original].

53. "General Jaruzelski's Remarks upon Pope's Departure," *Origins* 17:6 (June 25, 1987), p. 90.

54. Ibid.

55. Ibid.

56. John Paul had discussed this possibility with the Polish bishops, many of whom were enthusiastic

about it. The Pope suggested that caution was in order, given the "credibility" problem involved in reaching an agreement with a regime carrying the historical baggage of the Polish People's Republic. It was another indication of John Paul's intuition that the end of Polish communism was nearer than might be thought. He may also have wanted to avoid a structured relationship between the Holy See and the Polish communist state that might make it even more difficult for other independent social forces, like Solidarity, to gain their rightful position in society. [See John Paul II, "Address to Polish Episcopal Conference," *OR* (EWE), August 10, 1987, p. 7.]

57. Waldheim became Secretary-General when the Soviet Union refused to consider the candidate supported by the United States, Max Jacobsen, a Finnish socialist of Jewish heritage. See Daniel Patrick Moynihan, *A Dangerous Place* (Boston: Little, Brown, 1978), p. 83.

58. The IJCIC is composed of the World Jewish Congress, the Synagogue Council of America, the American Jewish Committee, B'nai B'rith International, and the Israel Jewish Committee on Interreligious Consultations.

59. See, for example, Sergio I. Minerbi, *The Vatican and Zionism* (New York: Oxford University Press, 1990).

60. John Paul II, "Address After Meeting with the President and Mrs. Reagan," in John Paul II, *The Pope Speaks to the American Church*, pp. 142–145 [emphasis in original].

61. John Paul II, "To the Reverend George V. Coyne, SJ, Director of the Vatican Observatory," in *John Paul II on Science and Religion: Reflections on the New View from Rome*, ed. Robert John Russell, William R. Stoeger, SJ, and George V. Coyne, SJ (Rome: Vatican Observatory Publications, 1990), pp. M2–M14.

62. The Synod on the Laity was originally scheduled for 1986, but was moved to 1987 when John Paul decided to summon the Extraordinary Synod for the twentieth anniversary of Vatican II.

63. Questions were raised at the time as to why lay men and women were not members of a Synod that was discussing their vocation and mission in the Church. The answer is that the Synod is a Synod *of Bishops*. To have included lay members would have violated the integrity of the Synod as an institution and would have been redolent of the very clericalism the Synod was trying to overcome: the notion that only members of the clergy (in this case, bishops) "count" in the Church. This understanding of the Synod *of Bishops* is, however, in some tension with the fact that priests have been appointed full members of the Synod.

64. John Paul II, *Christifideles Laici*, 3.2, in Miller, *Exhortations*.

65. See ibid., 1.1–7.6.

66. Ibid., 17.2 [emphasis in original]; on the universality of the call to holiness, see ibid., 16.2.

67. Ibid., 15.8 [emphasis in original], 15.6.

68. See ibid., 23–24.

69. Ibid., 26.1 [emphasis in original].

70. Ibid., 27.6.

71. See ibid., 34.

72. See ibid., 36–44.

73. See *OR* [EWE], December 21–28, 1987, pp. 7–8 [emphasis in original].

74. Secretariat for Promoting Christian Unity *Information Service* #66 (1988/I), pp. 21–22.

75. "The Joint Declaration of Pope John Paul II and Patriarch Dimitrios I," in ibid., pp. 9–10.

76. Thus the so-called hidden encyclical of Pius XI, *Humani Generis Unitas*, a defense of the unity of the human race in the face of racism and anti-Semitism, was never an "encyclical" in any sense of the term; it was a draft—in fact, several drafts—which had never been put into a coherent whole, much less given definitive form by the Pope's agreement and signature. The notion of a "hidden encyclical" is a publisher's trick or a polemicist's device, not a serious appraisal. [See Georges Passelecq and Bernard Suchecky, *The Hidden Encyclical of Pius XI*, transl. Steven Rendall (New York: Harcourt Brace, 1997).]

77. Author's interview with Archbishop Jorge M. Mejía, January 20, 1997.

78. See Roberto Suro, "The Writing of an Encyclical," in *Aspiring to Freedom*, ed. Kenneth A Myers (Grand Rapids: Eerdmans, 1988), pp. 164–166.

79. See ibid., p. 167.

80. John Paul II, *Sollicitudo Rei Socialis*, in Miller, *Encyclicals*, 15.2.

81. Ibid., 15.4.

82. Ibid., 15.5–15.6 [emphasis in original].

83. Ibid., 16.2.

84. Ibid., 44.5 [emphasis in original].

85. Ibid., 21, 22 [emphases in original].

86. Cited in Richard John Neuhaus, "*Sollicitudo* Behind the Headlines," in *Aspiring to Freedom*, p. 135. Neuhaus conceded that there was material in the encyclical to warrant Rosenthal's headline, especially for newspapers obsessed with politics and the superpower rivalry, but he also argued that a better headline would have read, "Pope Says Freedom and Human Rights Essential to Global Development." [Ibid.]

87. William F. Buckley, Jr., "What Is the Pope Saying?" *National Review*, March 18, 1988, pp. 17–18.

88. "Papal Gull," *The New Republic*, March 14, 1988, pp. 5–7.

89. Several progressive celebrations of *Sollicitudo Rei Socialis* are gathered in *The Logic of Solidarity: Commentaries on Pope John Paul II's Encyclical "On Social Concern,"* Gregory Baum and Robert Ellsberg, editors (Maryknoll, N.Y.: Orbis Books, 1989); see also Gregory Baum, "The Anti-Cold War Encyclical," *The Ecumenist*, 26 (1988), pp. 65–74.

For more tempered critical responses to *Sollicitudo Rei Socialis*, see Michael Novak, "The Development of Nations," and Neuhaus, "*Sollicitudo* Behind the Headlines," in *Aspiring to Freedom*. In the same volume, Peter Berger ("Empirical Testings") raises interesting questions about the encyclical's suggestion that democracy is a precondition to economic development.

90. *Sollicitudo Rei Socialis*, 20.3.

91. Author's interview with Joaquín Navarro-Valls, February 18, 1998.

92. See Alejandro Bermudez, "Paraguay's Bishops Strive to Aid Imperiled Democracy," *National Catholic Register*, September 20–26, 1998, p. 1.

93. Cited in Walsh, *John Paul II*, p. 182.

94. Author's interview with Cardinal Joseph Ratzinger, September 20, 1997.

95. Author's conversation with Pope John Paul II, January 16, 1997.

96. The documentation is in an "Informatory Note" published in *OR* [EWE], June 27, 1988, pp. 1–2.

97. Cardinal Ratzinger's telegram is in *OR* [EWE], July 4, 1988, p. 12.

98. The decree of excommunication is in *OR* [EWE], July 11, 1988, p. 1.

99. See John Paul II, *Ecclesia Dei*, in ibid.

100. Author's interview with Cardinal Joseph Ratzinger, September 20, 1997.

101. Author's interviews with Archbishop Zenon Grocholewski, January 13, 1997, and Cardinal Edward Cassidy, January 14, 1997.

On March 25, 1993, the flow chart was rationalized a little further (and in a way that reflected John Paul's understanding of the way the modern world worked) when the Pontifical Council for Dialogue with Non-Believers became part of the Pontifical Council for Culture, which subsequently had two sections: "Faith and Culture" and "Dialogue with Cultures."

102. Author's interview with Archbishop Zenon Grocholewski, January 13, 1997.

103. See Joseph Cardinal Ratzinger, "Homily at the Funeral Liturgy of Hans Urs von Balthasar," in *Hans Urs von Balthasar: His Life and Work*, ed. David L. Schindler (San Francisco: Ignatius Press, 1991).

In his homily, Ratzinger described Balthasar's reluctance to be named cardinal and the Pope's rationale for making the nomination:

> Von Balthasar was hesitant in opening himself to the honor intended for him by being named to the cardinalate. This was not motivated by a coquettish desire to act the great one, but by the Ignatian spirit which characterized his life. In some way, his being called into the next life on the very eve of being so honored seems to show that he was right about it. He was allowed to remain himself, fully. But what the Pope intended to express by this mark of distinction, and of honor, remains valid: No longer only private individuals but the Church itself, in its official responsibility, tells us that he is right in what he teaches of the Faith, that he points the way to the sources of living water—a witness to the word which teaches us Christ and which teaches us how to live. [See ibid., pp. 294–295.]

For an introduction to Balthasar's theology, see Edward T. Oakes, *Pattern of Redemption: The Theology of Hans Urs von Balthasar* (New York: Continuum, 1994).

104. See *Viaggi e visite di Giovanni Paolo II al 18° anno di pontificato e 50° anno di sacerdozio: dati riassuntivi e statistici* (Rome: Radio Vaticana, 1996).

105. See *Santi e Beati Durante il Pontificato di Giovanni Paolo II dal 1978 al 1996* [statistical summary of canonization and beatifications from the Congregation for the Causes of Saints].

106. This pilgrimage includes celebrating Mass at the tombs of Sts. Peter and Paul, in the crypts of St. Peter's Basilica and the Basilica of St. Paul Outside the Walls. Special texts have been prepared for these liturgies by the Congregation for Bishops. [See *Liturgy During the "Ad Limina" Visits* (Vatican City: Typis Polyglottis Vaticanis, 1988)].

107. Author's interview with Cardinal John J. O'Connor, November 8, 1996.

108. Author's interview with Cardinal Francis Arinze, November 9, 1996.

109. Beginning in 1995, the discourse at the group meeting was not delivered personally, but was given to each bishop in an individually addressed envelope after the group Mass in the private chapel.

110. Author's interview with Cardinal Francis Arinze, November 9, 1996.

111. Ibid.

112. The theology and practice of the *ad limina* visit are laid out in the *Directory for the "Ad Limina" Visit*, published by the Congregation for Bishops in 1988. The local preparation of an *ad limina* includes the assembly of a detailed report, often hundreds of pages long, on virtually every facet of life in a particular diocese. This report is forwarded to the Vatican prior to the bishop's arrival.

113. Soloviev had a distinctive view of the Christian failure in modernity: "In earlier times, Christianity was comprehensible to one, incomprehensible to another; but only our age has succeeded in making it repellent and mortally boring." [Cited in Hans Urs von Balthasar, *The Glory of the Lord*, volume three: *Studies in Theological Styles: Lay Styles* (San Francisco: Ignatius Press, 1986), p. 350.]

114. Berdyaev (1874–1948) was a converted skeptic of Marxist sympathies who lived in Paris after 1922. Bulgakov (1871–1944) was a "revert," a one-time candidate for the Orthodox priesthood who became a Marxist activist before returning to Christianity; expelled from the Soviet Union, he was Dean of the Orthodox Theological Academy in Paris from 1925 until he died and died a pioneer ecumenist.

115. Florovsky (1893–1979) taught patristic and dogmatic theology in Paris before becoming Dean of St. Vladimir's Russian Orthodox Seminary in New York and a leading figure in the ecumenical movement.

116. Author's interviews with Irina Alberti, April 13 and 16, 1998.

117. Ibid.

118. Sakharov was born in 1921. His great-grandfather was a Russian Orthodox priest, and his mother was pious, so young Andrei was baptized as a child; but he had never practiced Christianity. After helping create the Soviet hydrogen bomb in 1953, he had taken up the cause of arms control and had become interested in cosmology. Sakharov's security clearance was lifted after the publication of his 1968 dissident essay, "Reflections on Progress, Peaceful Coexistence, and Intellectual Freedom," but his extraordinary

contributions to Soviet science and the self-evident honesty of his dissent gave him a measure of protection for a while. In 1969, his first wife, to whom he had been happily married since 1943, died of a cancer that had been diagnosed too late. The following year, Sakharov met Elena Bonner, a pediatrician and veteran human rights campaigner. They were married in 1972. Sakharov was awarded the 1975 Nobel Peace Prize for his human rights activism and came under immediate and vicious assault in the Soviet media, a process that culminated in his exile to Gorki in 1980. Elena Bonner was similarly exiled to Gorki in 1984.

119. Author's interviews with Irina Alberti, April 13 and 16, 1998.

120. See Edward Kline, "Foreword," in Andrei Sakharov, *Moscow and Beyond: 1986–1989* (New York: Vintage Books, 1992), p. x.

121. Author's interviews with Irina Alberti, April 13 and 16, 1998. For details of Sakharov's evolving views of Gorbachev, see ibid.

122. Author's interviews with Irina Alberti, April 13 and 16, 1998.

123. Cited in Walsh, *John Paul II*, p. 186.

124. Author's interviews with Irina Alberti, April 13 and 16, 1998.

125. "Cardinal Casaroli at the Celebrations for the Millennium of the Baptism of Rus' of Kiev," *OR* [EWE], July 25, 1998, p. 3.

126. Details of the Vatican delegation's experience in Moscow are from the author's interview with Joaquín Navarro-Valls, February 18, 1998.

127. With the authorization of Cardinal Angelo Sodano, the Secretary of State of the Holy See, the Italian original of this letter, which I personally examined, was read to me and translated by Archbishop Jean-Louis Tauran, the Holy See's Secretary of the Section for Relations with States, during an interview in the archbishop's office on December 12, 1997.

The word *animo* is used at the end of the penultimate paragraph, which could also mean an "echo in your mind."

128. With the authorization of Cardinal Angelo Sodano, Secretary of State of the Holy See, Archbishop Jean-Louis Tauran, the Holy See's Secretary for Relations with States, read me an English translation of the Secretariat of State's Italian translation of the Russian original of this letter, which I examined, in an interview in Archbishop Tauran's office on December 19, 1998.

129. Bogdan Bociurkiw, "The Ukrainian Catholic Church in Gorbachev's USSR," p. 9.

130. "John Paul II at 'Moleben' in Honor of the Mother of God in the Millennium of the Baptism of Rus' of Kiev," *OR* [EWE], August 8–15, 1988, p. 4.

131. "Holy Father at Divine Liturgy in St. Peter's for Millennium of the Baptism of Rus' of Kiev," *OR* [EWE], August 8–15, 1998, p. 5 [emphasis in original].

132. That is, from June 7, 1987 until August 15, 1988.

133. John Paul II, "Annual Address to the Roman Curia," *OR* [EWE], January 11, 1988, pp. 6–8 [emphasis in original].

134. See Hans Urs von Balthasar, *The Office of Peter and the Structure of the Church* (San Francisco: Ignatius Press, 1986).

135. John Paul II, *Redemptoris Mater*, 24.3–24.4, in Miller, *Encyclicals*.

136. Ibid., 30.3 [emphasis in original].

137. Ibid., 45.4, citing *John* 19.27.

As *Redemptoris Mater* made clear, John Paul hoped that the Marian Year of 1987–1988 would help foster unity among Rome, Orthodoxy, and the ancient Christian Churches of the East. To further that aim, one of the striking features of the Marian Year was the celebration of a number of Eastern-rite Catholic liturgies in and around Rome at which the Pope presided. In addition, "Eastern-rite usages" were incorporated into the papal celebration of the Latin-rite liturgy. [See *Liturgie dell'Oriente Cristiano a Roma nell'Anno Mariano 1987–1988: Testi e Studi* (Vatican City: Libreria Editrice Vaticana, 1990).]

138. John Paul II, *Redemptoris Mater*, 46.2, in Miller, *Encyclicals*.

139. Ibid.

140. John Paul II, *Mulieris Dignitatem*, 1.

141. Ibid., 2 [emphasis in original].

142. Ibid., 3–5.

143. Ibid., 9–11 [emphasis in original].

144. Ibid., 14.

145. Ibid., 15–16.

146. Ibid., 18–19 [emphasis in original].

147. Author's conversation with Pope John Paul II, October 23, 1998.

148. John Paul II, *Mulieris Dignitatem*, 24 [emphasis in original].

149. Ibid., 30 [emphasis in original].

CHAPTER 16
After the Empire of Lies: Miracles and the Mandates of Justice

1. "The Holy Father's Address to the European Parliament," *OR* [EWE], November 21, 1988, pp. 11–12.

2. See Garton Ash, *We the People*, pp. 26–32.

3. See ibid., from which these highlights are drawn, for a more detailed account of the Roundtable negotiations and the subsequent election campaign.

4. Cited in Broun, *Conscience and Captivity*, p. 97. The entire third Navrátil petition may be found in ibid., pp. 319–320. For a portrait of Augustin Navrátil and the story of his earlier petitions, see Garton Ash, *The Uses of Adversity*, pp. 215–218.

5. Author's interview with Cardinal Edward Cassidy, January 14, 1997.

6. Ibid.

7. Ibid.

8. The communiqué summarizing the joint *plenarium* and the Pope's address to the closing session may be found in Pontifical Council for Promoting Christian Unity *Information Service* #70 (1989/II), pp. 56–58.

9. One source of tension involved the recent history of the Archdiocese of Seattle, where Archbishop Raymond G. Hunthausen had become a controversial figure, beloved by many and heavily criticized by others. After a 1984 apostolic visitation by Washington Archbishop James Hickey had determined that there were serious deficiencies in pastoral practice in Seattle for which Archbishop Hunthausen bore ultimate responsibility, an auxiliary bishop, Donald Wuerl, was appointed and given special authority over certain areas of pastoral life. The arrangement was not well-received by the archdiocesan staff; Bishop Wuerl was poorly treated by many priests; and, after some months, it became apparent to all concerned that the arrangement could not continue. A three-member commission, composed of Chicago's Cardinal Joseph Bernardin, New York's Cardinal John O'Connor, and San Francisco's Archbishop John Quinn, was appointed to mediate the situation. As a result of their work, Donald Wuerl became bishop of Pittsburgh in 1988 and Archbishop Hunthausen, having accepted the appointment of a coadjutor archbishop, Thomas Murphy, took an early retirement on his seventieth birthday, with Archbishop Murphy succeeding him in 1991. It was widely suggested in the press that the Holy See's intervention in Seattle was somehow related to Archbishop Hunthausen's passionate activism against nuclear weapons. In fact, the intervention had nothing to do with that issue, but with liturgical, catechetical, and pastoral practice in the archdiocese.

10. "Archbishop May Describes U.S. Cultural Context," *Origins* 18:41 (March 23, 1989), pp. 679–680.

11. Cardinal Joseph Ratzinger, "The Bishops as Teacher of the Faith," in ibid., pp. 681–682.

12. John Paul II, "Opening Address," in ibid., pp. 677, 679.

13. "Archbishop May Describes U.S. Cultural Context," in ibid., p. 680.

14. The entire exchange between the American bishops and their Roman curial colleagues, which was structured around ten presentations (one by a curial official, one by an American bishop) touching virtually every aspect of the Church's life in the United States, may be found in *Origins* 18:41 (March 23, 1989) and 18:42 (March 30, 1989). The latter includes the "synthesis" of the meeting prepared by Cardinal Joseph Bernardin (with Cardinal Gantin, one of the meeting's two moderators) and remarks by Archbishop May at a teleconference for the press on his return to the United States. Archbishop May's opening statement at the teleconference did not respond to Cardinal Ratzinger's challenge to the cultural analysis May had offered at the opening of the special meeting; indeed, it virtually repeated what the archbishop had said in Rome five days before.

15. Both phenomena were attributable to *Dei Verbum*, the Council's *Dogmatic Constitution on Divine Revelation*.

16. Cited in James Swetnam, SJ, "'A Vision of Wholeness': A Response," in McDermott, ed., *The Thought of Pope John Paul II*, p. 94.

17. See the Pope's 1991 address to the Pontifical Biblical Commission, in *OR* [EWE], April 22, 1991, p. 5. See also Joseph Ratzinger, "Biblical Interpretation in Crisis: On the Question of the Foundations and Approaches of Exegesis Today," in *Biblical Interpretation in Crisis: The Ratzinger Conference on Bible and Church*, ed. Richard John Neuhaus (Grand Rapids: Eerdmans, 1989).

For a more detailed discussion of John Paul II's use of Scripture in his preaching and teaching, see Terence Prendergast, SJ, "'A Vision of Wholeness': A Reflection on the Use of Scripture in a Cross-Section of Papal Writings," in *The Thought of Pope John Paul II*, ed. John M. McDermott, SJ, pp. 69–91. Father Prendergast's conclusion is quite accurate: "John Paul does not preoccupy himself with representing the consensus of scholars on how to interpret [the] Scriptures in our day."

In 1995, the Pope spelled out the ecclesial mission of biblical scholarship to the Pontifical Biblical Commission in even stronger terms than he had in 1989 and 1991:

> Your ecclesial task should be to treat the Sacred Writings inspired by God with the utmost veneration and to distinguish accurately the text of Sacred Scripture from learned conjectures, both yours and others'. It is not unusual today with regard to this matter that a certain confusion can be noted inasmuch as there are some who have more faith in views which are conjectures than in words which are divine. [Cited in Swetnam, "'A Vision of Wholeness': A Response," p. 95.]

18. See *Il Mondo di Giovanni Paolo II*, p. 138, and *Beati Duranti il Pontificato di Giovanni Paolo II dal 1978 al 1996*.

19. See *Il Mondo di Giovanni Paolo II*, p. 138; Walsh, *John Paul II*, p. 208.

20. On the papal message in Malawi and Zambia, see Walsh, *John Paul II*, pp. 207–208.

21. Author's interview with Roberto Tucci, SJ, December 14, 1998; the text of the Pope's address to the Lutheran bishops is in *OR* [EWE], June 19, 1989, pp. 7–8.

22. Pontifical Council for Promoting Christian Unity *Information Service* #80 (1992/II), pp. 17–25.

23. Letter to the author from Cardinal Edward Cassidy, December 28, 1998.

24. See Hans Urs von Balthasar, *In the Fullness of Faith: On the Centrality of the Distinctively Catholic* (San Francisco: Ignatius Press, 1988), p. 77.

25. John Paul II, "Homily at Mass on World Youth Day," *OR* [EWE], September 4, 1989, p. 4 [emphasis in original].

26. See *Insegnamenti di Giovanni Paolo II, 1989*.

27. John Paul II, "General Audience" Address, August 23, 1989, in *OR* [EWE], August 28, 1989, p. 7.

28. See "The Common Declaration," Pontifical Council for Promoting Christian Unity *Information Service* #71 (1989/III-IV), pp. 122–123.

29. See Woodward, *Making Saints*, pp. 132–133.

30. John Paul II, "Reconciling a Divided People," *Origins* 19:20 (October 19, 1989), pp. 321, 323–324.

31. John Paul II, "Prayer for North Korea and China," in ibid., pp. 324–325.

32. With the authorization of Cardinal Angelo Sodano, the Secretary of State of the Holy See, the original of this letter, which I personally examined, was read to me by Archbishop Jean-Louis Tauran, the Holy See's Secretary for Relations with States, during an interview in the archbishop's office on December 19, 1998.

33. Cited in Walsh, *John Paul II*, p. 215. Bishop Belo of East Timor was a co-winner of the Nobel Peace Prize in 1996.

34. John Paul II, "Homily During the Mass for the Faithful of Timor," *OR* [EWE], October 23, 1989, p. 6; John Paul II, "Church and State Relations," *Origins* 19:22 (November 2, 1989), pp. 363–365.

35. *Il Mondo di Giovanni Paolo II*, p. 147.

36. John Paul II, "Message to the Polish Bishops," in *Origins* 19:15 (September 14, 1989), pp. 251–252.

37. Ibid., p. 253.

38. The Pope's analysis here was similar to that of Aleksandr Solzhenitsyn in his 1983 Templeton Prize Lecture, delivered in London on May 10, 1983; see "Men Have Forgotten God," reprinted in *National Review*, July 22, 1983, pp. 872–876.

On learning of Cardinal Wojtyła's election as John Paul II in 1978, the intensely Orthodox Solzhenitsyn threw his arms out and said, "It's a miracle! It's the first positive event since World War I and it's going to change the face of the world!" The Russian author had never met Wojtyła, according to Irina Alberti, but he instinctively knew what Wojtyła's election meant: resistance to communism would now be rooted in religion and culture, which was the strongest force in the world. [Author's interview with Irina Alberti, April 13, 1998.]

39. John Paul II, "Apostolic Letter," in *Origins* 19:15 (September 14, 1989), p. 255.

40. Ibid., p. 254.

41. Ibid., pp. 254–256.

42. Ibid., p. 256.

43. See Serge Schmemann, "East Germany Opens Frontier to the West for Migration or Travel; Thousands Cross," *New York Times*, November 10, 1989, pp. A1, A14.

44. John Paul II, "Homily for the Canonization of Agnes of Bohemia and Albert Chmielowski," *OR* [EWE], December 4, 1989, p. 9 [emphasis in original].

45. The Pope's dinner guests the night of the canonization were two lay Kraków intellectuals, poet Marek Skwarnicki and painter Stanisław Rodziński. [Author's interview with Marek Skwarnicki, July 9, 1998.]

46. John Paul II, "Homily for the Canonization of Agnes of Bohemia and Albert Chmielowski" [emphasis in original].

47. Author's interview with Bishop František Lobkowicz, O.Praem., October 21, 1991.

48. De Lubac, *The Drama of Atheistic Humanism*, pp. 11–12.

49. Cited in ibid., pp. 22–23.

50. Cited in ibid., pp. 24–25.

51. Ibid., p 14.

52. Author's conversation with Father Michael Maslowski, April 22, 1996; author's interviews with Daniela Simpson, March 18, 1997, and Joaquín Navarro-Valls, February 18, 1998.

53. Author's interview with Daniela Simpson, March 18, 1997.

54. Author's interviews with Irina Alberti, April 13 and 16, 1998, and Joaquín Navarro-Valls, February 18, 1998.

55. Author's interviews with Irina Alberti, April 13 and 16, 1998; author's conversation with Pope John Paul II, December 13, 1997.

56. Author's conversation with Pope John Paul II, December 13, 1997; author's conversation with Joaquín Navarro-Valls, February 18, 1998.

57. See Mikhail Gorbachev, *Memoirs* (New York: Doubleday, 1995), pp. 508–509.

58. Author's interview with Joaquín Navarro-Valls, December 17, 1998.

59. Author's interview with Daniela Simpson, March 18, 1997.

60. "John Paul II to President Mikhail Gorbachev of the Soviet Union," *OR* [EWE], December 4, 1989, pp. 1, 12.

61. "Mr. Gorbachev's Greeting to John Paul II," in ibid., p. 1.

62. Author's interviews with Daniela Simpson, March 18, 1997; Victor Simpson, February 17, 1997; and Irina Alberti, April 13 and 16, 1998.

63. Author's interview with Irina Alberti, April 13 and 16, 1998.

64. Author's interview with Joaquín Navarro-Valls, February 18, 1998.

65. See Bernstein and Politi, *His Holiness*, pp. 474–478.

66. Author's interview with Archbishop Jean-Louis Tauran, March 18, 1997.

67. Cardinal Tomášek's statement was drafted by Father Otto Mádr, once condemned to death as a "spy," who had served fifteen years in prisons and labor camps during the worst of Czechoslovak Stalinism. Dur-

ing his time in prison Father Mádr celebrated Mass whenever he could coax ten drops of wine from dried grapes; communion was distributed throughout the camp by the prison barber, who carried bits of consecrated Eucharistic bread to prisoners during his weekly round of shaves and haircuts, using the only ciborium available—a piece of cigarette paper. Father Mádr recited Cardinal Tomásek's message to the November 24 Wenceslaus Square rally by memory at an interview with the author on October 25, 1991, and subsequently sent me the text of the address in a letter of December 13, 1991.

Father Václav Malý declined an invitation to join the new democratic government and became a pastor in Prague. On December 3, 1996, John Paul II named him titular bishop of Marcelliana and auxiliary bishop of Prague.

68. Author's interview with Václav Benda, October 22, 1991.

69. Cited in William H. Luers, "Czechoslovakia: Road to Revolution," *Foreign Affairs* 69:2 (Spring 1990), p. 98.

70. The one exception to the rule of nonviolence was Romania, where the Ceauşescu regime's violent attempt to stem the tide of human rights resistance (triggered by the security forces' attempt to arrest a veteran human rights campaigner, the Baptist minister László Tökes, in Timişoara on December 16) ended with the regime's bloody overthrow on December 22 and the execution of Ceauşescu and his wife on December 25.

71. See Bogdan Bociurkiw, "The Ukrainian Catholic Church in Gorbachev's USSR," pp. 12–13; author's interview with Bogdan Bociurkiw, August 10, 1996.

72. "Communiqué: Archbishop Colasuonno's journey in Romania," *OR* [EWE], January 15, 1990, p. 5.

73. See Bogdan Bociurkiw, "The Ukrainian Catholic Church in Gorbachev's USSR," p. 15; author's interview with Bogdan Bociurkiw, October 10, 1996. See also *OR* [EWE], January 22, 1990, pp. 10, 12, and *OR* [EWE], March 5, 1990, pp. 1, 11.

74. *OR* [EWE], February 19, 1990, p. 8.

75. John Paul II, "Address to the Diplomatic Corps," *OR* [EWE], January 29, 1990, pp. 1–2 [emphasis in original].

76. Ibid., p. 2.

77. "'God Won' in East Europe," *OR* [EWE], February 26, 1990, p. 1.

78. "Truth Has Triumphed," *OR* [EWE], April 2, 1990, p. 12.

79. See John Paul II, "Strength of Solidarity," *OR* [EWE], September 30, 1990, p. 11, and John Paul II, "Poles Need to Learn How to Differ," *OR* [EWE], November 26, 1990, p. 5.

80. John Paul II, "Victory of Fidelity," in *OR* [EWE], April 23, 1990, p. 2 [emphasis in original].

81. "Havel: Sharing in a Miracle," *OR* [EWE], April 30, 1989, p. 4.

82. Cardinal Agostino Casaroli, "Helsinki and the New Europe," *OR* [EWE], April 2, 1990, pp. 6–7.

83. Cardinal Agostino Casaroli, "Ostpolitik: Chipping Away At Marxism's Crumbling House," *OR* [EWE], June 18, 1990, pp. 6–7.

84. Ibid., p. 6.

85. Those attending were Professors Kenneth J. Arrow of Stanford University (the 1972 Nobel laureate in economics); Anthony Atkinson of the London School of Economics and Political Science; Parta Dasgupta of Stanford; Jacques Dreze of the Université Catholique de Louvain; Peter Hammond of Stanford; Hendrik Houthakker of Harvard University; Robert Lucas of the University of Chicago; Edmond Malinvaud, holder of the chair of economic analysis at the Collège de France; Ignazio Musu of the Università degli Studi di Venezia; Jeffrey Sachs and Amartya Sen of Harvard; Horst Siebert of the Institute of World Economics in Kiel; Witold Trzeciakowski of the Polish government; Hirofumi Uzawa, emeritus at Tokyo University; and Stefano Zamagni of the Università degli Studi di Bologna. [Memorandum to the author from the Pontifical Council for Justice and Peace, November 13, 1997.]

86. Letter to the author from Robert E. Lucas, Jr., April 9, 1997.

87. Author's interview with Archbishop Jorge Mejía, January 20, 1997.

88. Author's interview with Rocco Buttiglione, January 21, 1997.

89. John Paul II, *Centesimus Annus*, 5.4, in Miller, *Encyclicals*.

90. Ibid., 6.1–9.1.

91. See ibid., 12.1, 13.1.

92. See ibid., 13–14.

93. Ibid., 23.1–23.3.

94. "Man is understood in a more complete way when he is situated within the sphere of culture through his language, history, and the position he takes toward the fundamental events of life, such as birth, love, work, and death. At the heart of every culture lies the attitude man takes to the greatest mystery: the mystery of God. Different cultures are basically different ways of facing the question of the meaning of personal existence. When this question is eliminated, the cultural and moral life of nations is corrupted." [Ibid., 23.3.]

95. Ibid., 24.2.

96. Ibid., 43.1.

97. See Maciej Zięba, OP, *Kościół wobec Demokratycznego Kapitalizmu w Świetle Encyklik "Centesimus Annus,"* unpublished doctoral dissertation (Kraków: Papal Academy of Theology, 1997), and Maciej Zięba, OP, *Papieze i kapitalizm: od* Rerum Novarum *po* Centesimus Annus (Kraków: Znak, 1998).

98. John Paul II, *Centesimus Annus*, 31.2, in Miller, *Encyclicals*.

99. Ibid., 32.1.

100. Author's interview with Rocco Buttiglione, January 21, 1997.

101. Ibid.

102. John Paul II, *Centesimus Annus*, 42.1–42.2, in Miller, *Encyclicals*.

103. The dean of the Social Science Faculty at the Pontifical Gregorian University in Rome, Sergio Bernal Restrepo, SJ, made this precise argument, in these precise terms, at a seminar sponsored by the Pontifical Council for Justice and Peace to commemorate the centenary of *Rerum Novarum* on May 14, 1991.

104. John Paul II, *Centesimus Annus*, 13.2, in Miller, *Encyclicals.*

105. Ibid., 32.

106. See ibid. [emphasis in original].

107. Ibid., 48.

108. See ibid., 58.

109. See ibid.

110. Ibid., 52.

111. For a more detailed discussion of these points, see Richard John Neuhaus, *Doing Well and Doing Good: The Challenge to the Christian Capitalist* (New York: Doubleday, 1992), especially chapter eight, "The Potential of the Poor."

112. John Paul II, *Centesimus Annus*, 46, in Miller, *Encyclicals* [emphasis in original].

113. Author's interview with Archbishop Jean-Louis Tauran, March 14, 1997.

114. John Paul II, "The International Order Is Severely Threatened," in *John Paul II for Peace in the Middle East/War in the Gulf: Gleaning Through the Pages of* L'Osservatore Romano (Vatican City: Libreria Editrice Vaticana, 1991), pp. 11–12.

115. Author's interview with Archbishop Jean-Louis Tauran, March 14, 1997.

116. John Paul II, "War Is an Adventure with No Return," in *John Paul II for Peace in the Middle East*, p. 36 [emphasis in original].

117. Author's interview with Archbishop Jean-Louis Tauran, March 14, 1997.

118. John Paul II, "Dialogue and Negotiations Must Prevail . . . ," in *John Paul II for Peace in the Middle East*, pp. 40–41.

119. Cited in ibid., p. 42.

120. Author's interview with Archbishop Jean-Louis Tauran, March 18, 1997.

121. Cited in *John Paul II for Peace in the Middle East*, pp. 66–69.

122. Author's interview with Archbishop Jean-Louis Tauran, March 18, 1997.

123. Ibid. Archbishop Tauran was present when the Pope placed his telephone call to the president. President Bush's formal reply to the Pope's January 15 message was delivered to the Vatican on January 16 by U.S. Ambassador Melady. [See Thomas Patrick Melady, *The Ambassador's Story: The United States and the Vatican in World Affairs* (Huntington, Ind.: Our Sunday Visitor Publishing Division, p. 95).

124. "Pontiff Convokes Bishops' Meeting on Middle East," OR [EWE], February 25, 1991, p. 1.

125. The Pope's opening address to the bishops' meeting, his closing address, and the meeting's communiqué all focused primarily on the postwar Middle East. See *John Paul II for Peace in the Middle East*, pp. 113–129.

126. For a history of this latter concern, see David-Maria A. Jaeger, OFM, *The Roman Pontiffs in Defence of Christian Rights in the Holy Land: From* Causa Nobis *to* Redemptionis Anno *(1921–1984)*, unpublished doctoral dissertation (Rome: Pontifical Athenaeum "Antonianum," 1989).

127. This last point is taken from the author's interview with Archbishop Jean-Louis Tauran, March 14, 1997.

128. See James A. Baker, III, *The Politics of Diplomacy: Revolution, War and Peace 1989–1992* (New York: G. P. Putnam's Sons, 1995).

The Bush administration and the Holy See had already experienced a moment of high tension. Just prior to attending the Pope's Christmas midnight Mass on the night of December 24, 1989, Ambassador Melady had been instructed to tell the Holy See that the United States did not want Panamanian dictator Manuel Noriega granted asylum in the Vatican nunciature in Panama City, which he had entered at 9:17 P.M. Rome time (3:17 P.M. in Panama), four days after the December 20 U.S. invasion of the country. Nonetheless, Noriega remained at the nunciature until January 3, 1990, when he surrendered to U.S. forces after days of negotiation. [See Melady, *The Ambassador's Story*, pp. 19–23.]

129. See Melady, *The Ambassador's Story*, pp. 114–115.

130. Author's interview with Archbishop Jean-Louis Tauran, March 14, 1997.

131. Cited in Melady, *The Ambassador's Story*, p. 119. The Catholic population of Iraq was one of the least pressured in the Middle East/Persian Gulf region, and Christians were part of Saddam Hussein's Ba'athist Party and government. In the terror state run by Saddam, of course, public protest against the government was almost always suicidal. But Patriarch Bidawid's defense of the invasion and occupation of Kuwait put him in the position of contradicting the stated position of the Holy See that this had been a clear violation of international law and the UN Charter.

132. Author's interview with Archbishop Jean-Louis Tauran, March 14, 1997.

133. John P. Langan, SJ, "The Just War Theory After the Gulf War," in *Theological Studies* 53:1 (March 1992), pp. 95–112. The original *Civiltà Cattolica* editorial, "Modern War and the Christian Conscience," was reprinted in *But Was It Just? Reflections on the Morality of the Persian Gulf War*, ed. David E. DeCosse (New York: Doubleday, 1992).

134. James Turner Johnson, "Just Cause Revisited," in *Close Calls: Intervention, Terrorism, Missile Defense, and "Just War" Today*, Elliott Abrams, ed. (Washington, D.C.: Ethics and Public Policy Center, 1998, p. 27.

135. Cited in Melady, *The Ambassador's Story*, p. 114.

136. See Efraim Karsh and Inari Rautsi, *Saddam Hussein: A Political Biography* (New York: Free Press, 1991).

137. A more rigorous analysis within the Secretariat of State would have also required confronting those shibboleths about the Arab-Islamic world that dominate Italian political circles and work their way into the Vatican from there. These views were particularly evident in *L'Osservatore Romano* during the crisis.

138. Just prior to this meeting, which he was to have attended, Father Joseph Zvěřina, a survivor of the Czechoslovakian labor camps who lived to become one of the primary advisers to Cardinal Tomášek during the 1980s, drowned while swimming at a beach near Rome.

139. Cited in John Paul II, *Spiritual Journey*, p. 139. The credential ceremony was another occasion to meditate on the meaning of World War II and the *Shoah*:

> It was really the Second World War which came to an end on October 3 [John Paul said] and made many people aware of what fate and guilt mean to all peoples and individuals. We think of the millions of people, most of them totally innocent, who died in that war: soldiers, civilians, women, the elderly and children, people of different nationalities and religions.
>
> In this context we should also mention the tragedy of the Jews. For Christians the heavy burden of guilt for the murder of the Jewish people must be an enduring call to repentance; thereby we can overcome every form of anti-Semitism and establish a new relationship with our kindred nation of the Old Covenant. . . . Guilt should not oppress and lead to self-agonizing thoughts, but must always be the point of departure for conversion. [Ibid.]

140. Author's interview with Cardinal Alfonso López Trujillo, September 22, 1991.

141. Author's interviews with Irina Alberti, April 13 and 16, 1998.

142. The presentation at the press conference was made by Archbishop Pio Laghi, the former nuncio in the United States. Laghi had been appointed Pro-Prefect of the Congregation for Catholic Education the previous April, succeeding Cardinal William Baum, the former archbishop of Washington, D.C.

143. Author's interview with Cardinal William Baum, November 5, 1996.

144. *Ex Corde Ecclesiae*, 4.

145. Ibid., 28.

146. Ibid., Article 1, ¶1.

147. The Profession of Faith may be found in *OR* [EWE], March 13, 1989, p. 3.

148. Author's interview with Monsignor Walter Edyvean, January 16, 1997.

149. See Philip Gleason, *Contending with Modernity: Catholic Higher Education in the Twentieth Century* (New York: Oxford University Press, 1996) and Charles R. Morris, *American Catholic: The Saints and Sinners Who Built America's Most Powerful Church* (New York: Times Books, 1997). For a major study of the patterns by which originally religious institutions of higher education lose their religious identity, see James T. Burtchaell, CSC, *The Dying of the Light: The Disengagement of Colleges and Universities from the Christian Churches* (Grand Rapids: Eerdmans, 1998).

150. Local ordinances applying the general norms of *Ex Corde Ecclesiae* were to have been submitted to the Holy See by March 1992; only one country managed to meet that deadline. By late 1997, seven years after the document was issued, twelve of the forty-eight countries with Catholic institutions of higher education had developed local norms that had been approved by the Holy See. In the United States, the bishops' committee charged with devising the local norms asked for extensions on numerous occasions; the norms finally adopted by the U.S. Bishops' Conference at its November 1996 meeting were not accepted by the Holy See, which sent them back to the U.S. bishops for further revisions.

151. On the relationship between local bishops and Catholic colleges and universities, see Francis Cardinal George, OMI, "Universities That Are Truly Catholic and Truly Academic," *Origins* 28:18 (October 15, 1998).

CHAPTER 17

To the Ends of the Earth: Reconciling an Unreconciled World

1. John Paul II, "Lessons of the Galileo Case," *Origins* 22:22 (November 12, 1992, pp. 369–374. See also Cardinal Paul Poupard, "Galileo: Report on Papal Commission Findings," in ibid., pp. 374–375; and "Galileo, Science and Faith," in *Church & Cultures* (Bulletin of the Pontifical Council for Culture), no. 18 (1992), pp. 3–4.

2. Complicating the situation even further, there was no public reckoning with the records of those scholars, commentators, and politicians who had manifestly and grossly misread the nature of communism. Unlike those who had sympathized with fascism in the 1930s, the anti-anti-communists of the 1960s, 1970s, and 1980s were never called to account for their moral and political blindness. There was a considerable overlap between these men and women and those most fiercely committed to the notion of freedom as radical individual autonomy. The failure to come to grips with the betrayals of the intellectuals during the latter half of the Cold War thus served to strengthen the claim that freedom equaled autonomy, at least indirectly.

3. See Zbigniew Brzeziński, *Out of Control: Global Turmoil on the Eve of the 21st Century* (New York: Scribner's, 1993).

4. The Decree is usually known by its Latin title, *Ad Gentes* [To the nations].

5. See John Paul II, *Redemptoris Missio*, 62.1, in Miller, *Encyclicals*.

6. Author's interview with Cardinal Jozef Tomko, November 14, 1996.

7. *International Bulletin of Missionary Research* 22:1 (January 1998), p. 27.

8. See Paul Griffiths, "One Jesus, Many Christs?" *Pro Ecclesia* 7:2 (Spring 1998), pp. 152–171, for an overview of this debate and a useful bibliography.

9. The Congregation's official post-conciliar name is almost universally ignored in Rome, where every-

one stills refers to it as "the Propaganda," from its old Latin title, *Propaganda Fide*, the Congregation for the Propagation of the Faith.

10. See *Christian Mission and Interreligious Dialogue*, Paul Mojzes and Leonard Swidler, eds. (Lewiston/Queenston/Lampeter: Edwin Mellen Press, 1992), which includes both Tomko's "provocation" lecture and his response to his critics.

11. Author's interview with Cardinal Jozef Tomko, January 19, 1997.

12. John Paul II, *Redemptoris Missio*, 62.1, in Miller, *Encyclicals* [emphasis in original].

13. "Missionary evangelization . . . is the primary service which the Church can render to every individual and to all humanity in the modern world." [Ibid., 2.4.]

14. Ibid., 2.3 [emphasis in original].

15. Ibid., 1.1.

16. Ibid., 5.3.

17. Ibid., 6.1.

18. Ibid.

19. Ibid., 10.1.

20. On this crucial point, see *Redemptoris Missio*, 11: "Mission is an issue of faith, an accurate indicator of our faith in Christ and His love for us." Evangelization is indeed about salvation: the salvation of the members of the Church, no less than those to whom they preach.

21. On these six points, see Richard John Neuhaus, "Reviving the Missionary Mandate," *First Things* 16 (October 1991), pp. 61–64.

22. John Paul II, *Redemptoris Missio*, 37.5, in Miller, *Encyclicals*.

23. See ibid., 37.6–37.10.

24. Ibid., 37.11–37.14.

25. Ibid., 39.2 [emphasis in original].

26. Ibid., 42.1–45.4.

27. Ibid., 45.4. The Pope's reference to martyrdom was no rhetorical flourish; in 1996, for example, forty-six Catholics were killed while working in the missions: three bishops, eighteen priests, eight religious brothers, thirteen religious sisters, and four lay workers. They were martyred in Algeria, Ghana, Zaire, Rwanda, Burundi, Tanzania, Puerto Rico, Colombia, Bosnia, Cambodia, and India.

28. See ibid., 50.1–50.3; 55.1–57.3.

29. See ibid., 52.1–54.2.

30. Ibid., 58.2.

31. Although dated December 7, 1990, *Redemptoris Missio* was not published until January 22, 1991, when it was presented at a press conference by Cardinal Jozef Tomko. Tomko's presentation may be found in *OR* [EWE], January 28, 1991, pp. 1, 21. That the encyclical was presented six days after the Gulf War had started and massive anti-Soviet demonstrations had broken out in Lithuania also made for a problematic reception in the world news media.

One exception to the general neglect of *Redemptoris Missio* in the West was the positive reception the encyclical received in many evangelical Protestant circles. The *International Bulletin of Missionary Research* editorialized that the encyclical was a "refreshingly positive document, breathing confidence, optimism, and encouragement; devoid of condemnations or anathemas, yet pointing to pitfalls to be avoided. . . . It deserves study by all Christians concerned about the Church's missionary mandate." [*International Bulletin of Missionary Research* 15:2 (April 1991), p. 1.]

32. John Paul II, *Redemptoris Missio*, 86.1, in Miller, *Encyclicals*.

33. Richard John Neuhaus, "Christian Mission and the Third Millennium," *First Things* 13 (May 1991), p. 8.

34. On the countercultural character of *Redemptoris Missio*, see Neuhaus, ibid., and "Reviving the Missionary Mandate."

35. The Byelorussian situation was further complicated by the fact that the dioceses in what was now the Byelorussian SSR involved territory that had once been part of czarist Russia and/or interwar Poland.

36. The new Archdiocese of Minsk-Mohilev would serve some 350,000 Latin-rite Catholics, living in some seventy parishes served by thirty priests. The new diocese of Pinsk had approximately 100,000 Catholics with thirty-two parishes and twenty priests. The new diocese of Grodno (established on territory that had belonged to the Archdiocese of Wilno [Vilnius] in interwar Poland) included some 900,000 Catholics served by more than 120 parishes. [See *OR* (EWE), pp. 6–7.]

37. Canon 371§2.

38. The Moscow area had an unknown number of Catholics of Polish, Lithuanian, and Russian origin, as well as Catholic diplomats and students. There were also some 10,000 Catholics in Leningrad, mostly of Polish origin, and Catholic "Volga Germans" were beginning to return to European Russia from their places of deportation in the central Asian steppes. Siberia had been essentially without Catholic priests since the mid-1930s, but Catholic life had begun to revive in the capital, Novosibirsk, and in the cities of Prokopievsk, Irkutsk, Tomsk, and Omsk. In Kazakhstan there were more than 600,000 Catholics of German, Polish, and Ukrainian descent, deportees or the descendants of deportees during the Stalin period. [The remarkably tangled history of the Catholic Church in what then constituted the USSR was summarized in *OR* (EWE), April 22, 1991, pp. 1, 6–7.]

39. The Patriarchate of Moscow's ancient sensitivities were compounded by the fact that the Russian Orthodox leadership had not played a heroic role during the last decades of Soviet communism, in marked contrast to the Catholic leadership in Lithuania, Ukraine, Poland, Czechoslovakia, and elsewhere. The Patriarchate's post–World War II entanglement with the Soviet government, for whom it had frequently served as a mouthpiece in international ecumenical conferences, was a further complication. Russian

Orthodox priests and laity who had resisted the corruption of the Soviet embrace often identified ecumenism with communist manipulations of the Church, and the Orthodox leadership directly involved with world ecumenical activity had not yet persuasively demonstrated its independence from the manipulations of politicians, the state security services, or the new "mafias" of ex-communists that were taking advantage of economic restructuring in the USSR.

40. Author's interviews with Cardinal Edward Cassidy, January 14, 1997, and John Long, SJ, May 5, 1997. Sodano and Cassidy were cardinals-elect at this time, and were created cardinals on June 28, 1991; for the sake of simplicity I refer to them as "Cardinal" here.

41. Bishop Tadeusz Kondrusiewicz, forty-five, the former apostolic administrator of Minsk, was named Apostolic Administrator of European Russia with residence in Moscow, and given the title of archbishop. Father Joseph Werth, SJ, the thirty-eight-year-old son of German parents deported to Kazakhstan, was named Apostolic Administrator of Novosibirsk. Father Jan Lenga, MIC, the forty-one-year-old Ukrainian-born son of Polish parents, was named Apostolic Administrator of Karaganda in Kazakhstan.

42. Author's interview with John Long, SJ, May 5, 1997.

43. The Patriarchate's statement of refusal to participate in the 1991 Eurosynod, and the subsequent Holy See response, may be found in the Pontifical Council for Promoting Christian Unity *Information Service* #81 (1992/III-IV), pp. 84–86. The Patriarchate's statement explicitly cited the establishment of the apostolic administrations as one cause for its refusal to participate. The Holy See responded that it had made a "great effort" to explain the situation to the Patriarchate "in the last six months." Which was a month or two too late.

On May 31, 1991, John Paul wrote a letter to all the Catholic bishops of Europe, explaining what had been done in the past months about regularizing Catholic life in central and eastern Europe, and encouraging the burial of ancient animosities. "Brothers who once shared the same sufferings and trials," the Pope wrote, "ought not to oppose one another today, but should look together at the future opening before them with promising signs of hope." [Pontifical Council for Promoting Christian Unity *Information Service* #77 (1991/II), p. 37.]

44. Author's interview with Henryk Woźniakowski, June 5, 1997.

45. Author's interview with Cardinal Franciszek Macharski, June 12, 1991.

46. Paweł Śpiewak, "Taking Sides," in "Clericalism: Myth or Reality," a pre-visit symposium in *Warsaw Voice*, June 2, 1991, p. 7.

47. Author's interview with Zbigniew Brzeziński, February 7, 1997.

48. "Press Release from the Polish Episcopate," *OR* [EWE], March 18, 1991, p. 12.

49. This anomaly was finally resolved in 1996 when, in what a leading Ukrainian historian described as an "unprecedented act of generosity on the part of the Pope," the Greek Catholic Diocese of Przemyśl was raised to an archdiocese (of Przemyśl-Warszawa) and removed from the jurisdiction of the Primate so as to be subordinate to the Greek Catholic Major-Archbishop of L'viv. [Author's interview with Bogdan Bociurkiw, August 10, 1996.]

50. Author's interview with Jerzy Janik, July 17, 1996.

51. See, inter alia, Bernstein and Politi, *His Holiness*, pp. 489–494.

52. See, again, ibid.

53. Author's interview with Cardinal Jan Schotte, March 14, 1997.

54. Martin Kettle, "John Paul's Grand Design for Europe," *The Guardian*, April 27, 1990, p. 14.

55. John Paul II, "An East-West Exchange for Future of Europe," *OR* [EWE], June 11, 1990, pp. 1, 6–7 [emphasis in original].

56. Author's interview with Cardinal Miloslav Vlk, December 5, 1997. Vlk thought that one exception to this general incomprehension was Cardinal Joachim Meissner of Cologne, who had previously been bishop of divided Berlin. Meissner's appointment to Cologne in December 1988 had caused much controversy, but in light of Vlk's reading of Meissner's knowledgeability, it may have been that John Paul, seeing 1989 coming, wanted a cardinal in Germany's most prestigious See with precisely this kind of understanding.

57. Author's interview with Cardinal Jean-Marie Lustiger, October 24, 1996.

58. Author's interview with Cardinal Jozef Tomko, January 19, 1997.

59. Author's interviews with Cardinal Bernard Law, November 9, 1996; Cardinal Jozef Tomko, January 19, 1997; and Cardinal Jean-Marie Lustiger, October 24, 1996.

60. Author's interview with Cardinal Miloslav Vlk, December 5, 1997.

61. See *OR* [EWE], December 23–30, 1991, pp. 3–4, 13–14.

62. Sodano was, of course, the Secretary of State. Laghi was Prefect of the Congregation for Catholic Education; Sánchez, a Filipino, the Prefect of the Congregation for the Clergy; Cassidy the President of the Pontifical Council for Promoting Christian Unity; Noè, a former papal master of ceremonies; and Angelini, the President of the Pontifical Council for Pastoral Assistance to Health Care Workers.

63. Cardinal Posadas was murdered in still-unexplained circumstances on May 24, 1993.

64. John Paul II, *Spiritual Pilgrimage*, p. 154.

65. See *Insegnamenti di Giovanni Paolo II, 1991*.

66. *OR* [EWE], August 26, 1991, p. 1.

67. The full text of the papal message was as follows:

The announcement of your election as Ecumenical Patriarch has brought me great joy. The bonds of fraternal affection which already unite us will doubtlessly facilitate our collaboration in view of the re-establishment of full communion between our Churches. I ardently hope that the theological dialogue whose opening I had the joy of announcing with your beloved predecessor, Dimitrios I, on the occasion of my memorable visit to the Phanar will continue. May the Lord grant Your Holiness an abundance of his light and strength in your new and difficult pastoral charge. I assure you of my prayer and of all my fraternal charity. IOANNES PAULUS PP. II. [*OR* (EWE), November 4, 1991, p. 12.]

68. Author's interview with Ronald G. Roberson, CSP, March 31, 1997.
For an overview of the difficulties that Bartholomew faced with both the Turkish government and his Orthodox brethren, see Ronald G. Roberson, CSP, *The Eastern Christian Churches: A Brief Survey*, 6th ed. (Rome: Edizioni "Orientalia Christiana," 1995), pp. 43–46.

69. Author's interview with Archbishop Jean-Louis Tauran, March 18, 1997.
70. Ibid.
71. See *OR* [EWE], January 15, 1992, p. 12 for the full list of conditions.
72. Cited in *The Tablet*, January 18, 1992, p. 79.
73. Author's interview with Archbishop Jean-Louis Tauran, March 18, 1997.
74. Author's interview with Monsignor Vincenzo Paglia, December 7, 1997.
75. See *OR* [EWE] April 1, 1992, pp. 6–7 for all the details. John Paul explained the rationale for the changes in an apostolic letter to the entire Church in Poland; the text may be found in ibid., p. 1.
76. The announcement was made in the form of a papal letter to Cardinal Fiorenzo Angelini, President of the Pontifical Council for Pastoral Assistance to Health Care Workers; see *OR* [EWE], May 27, 1992, p. 2.
77. Author's interview with Archbishop Norberto Rivera Carrera, November 21, 1997.
78. In 1979, John Paul II wrote two letters, one to all the Church's bishops and the other to all the Church's priests, on Holy Thursday. In 1980, there was no letter to priests, but rather an apostolic letter to the bishops, *Dominicae Cenae*, "On the Mystery and Worship of the Eucharist," with obvious implications for the priesthood. In 1981, the Pope wrote another letter to bishops on Holy Thursday, marking the 1,600th anniversary of the First Council of Constantinople and the 1,550th anniversary of the Council of Ephesus; once again there was no letter to priests. Beginning in 1982, John Paul wrote an annual "Letter to All the Priests of the Church."
79. See John Paul II, *Letters to My Brother Priests*.
80. See Philip Jenkins, *Pedophiles and Priests: Anatomy of a Contemporary Crisis* (New York: Oxford University Press, 1996).
81. See "Editor's Introduction to *Pastores Dabo Vobis*," in Miller, *Exhortations*, pp. 466–468.
82. *Pastores Dabo Vobis*, 12.4.
83. Ibid.
84. Ibid. 21.2.
85. Ibid. 23.2 [emphasis in original].
Another New Testament image, St. Paul's depiction of Christ as the Bridegroom of the Church (see *Ephesians* 5.21–32), gives further definition to this priestly form of holiness: the priesthood is an office of love, in which the priest is "called to live out Christ's spousal love toward the Church, his Bride." Thus the priest (who, as a man, shares in the human dynamics John Paul analyzed in his *Theology of the Body*) must be a distinctive kind of lover:

> . . . the priest's life ought to radiate this spousal character, which demands that he be a witness to Christ's spousal love and thus be capable of loving people with a heart which is new, generous and pure, with genuine self-detachment, with full, constant and faithful dedication and at the same time with a kind of "divine jealousy" (cf. *2 Corinthians* 11.2), and even with a kind of maternal tenderness, capable of bearing "the pangs of birth" until "Christ be formed" in the faithful (cf. *Galatians* 4.19). [Ibid., 22.3.]

86. Ibid., 36.1 [emphasis in original].
87. See John Paul II, "*Ad Limina* Address to the Bishops of Michigan and Ohio," *OR* [EWE], May 27, 1998, p. 5–6.
88. See John Paul II, *Pastores Dabo Vobis*, 35.2, 34.6, in Miller, *Exhortations*.
89. Ibid., 39.2.
90. Ibid., 41.2 [emphasis in original].
91. Ibid., 51.2.
92. Ibid., 53.1; author's interview with Archbishop Christoph Schönborn, OP, December 11, 1997.
93. See John Paul II, *Pastores Dabo Vobis*, 60.2, 60.3, 60.6, in Miller, *Exhortations*.
94. *Pastores Dabo Vobis* also takes account of the new demographics of seminary life, in which men enter the seminary at a latter stage in life, often after some experience of a professional career, but just as often without a detailed understanding of the Church's doctrine and practice. Thus, following a Synod recommendation, the Pope proposes a "pre-theology" experience of a year or two, in which spiritual formation and charitable service are combined with a broad-based introduction to Catholic thought and culture. [Ibid., 62.1–62.6.] In the wake of *Pastores Dabo Vobis*, "pre-theology" programs of various sorts were launched throughout the world and are now a staple of priestly formation.
The exhortation's stress on rigorous academic formation has raised questions among some responsible Latin American bishops who describe a local situation in which the brief period of formation given evangelical Protestant leaders often results in effective pastors. The bishops' concern is that the academic rigor encouraged by *Pastores Dabo Vobis* risks making the seminary and the priesthood less attractive in these cultural circumstances. It is an issue sure to be debated in world Catholicism well into the twenty-first century.
Pastores Dabo Vobis concludes with the first extended discussion of ongoing education for Catholic priests

in the history of papal teaching. Continuing education programs, focused on theological renewal and pastoral skills, had become a regular feature of Catholic life in the years after the Council. John Paul, convinced that priestly formation is an ongoing task that does not stop at the moment of ordination, reflects on this phenomenon under the biblical rubric of Paul's injunction to Timothy: "I remind you to rekindle the gift of God that is within you" (*2 Timothy* 1.6). That, the Pope suggests, is the deepest reason for ongoing priestly formation: "to release all the extraordinary riches of grace and responsibility" contained in the gift given in ordination. John Paul also discusses continuing education in terms of professional updating and as a matter of justice for the people of the Church, who have the right to hear the word preached effectively. But he characteristically locates a discussion that is usually focused on "professionalization" in an evangelical context. Ongoing clergy education exists to enable each priest "to *safeguard and develop in faith his awareness of the total and marvelous truth of his being*: he is a minister of Christ and steward of the mysteries of God." That, the Pope suggests, is the ground on which the priest can also develop his sense of unity with the people of the Church and his commitment to the Church's saving mission. [Ibid., 70–75.]

95. Author's interview with Cardinal William W. Baum, November 5, 1996.

96. Letter to the author from Archbishop Edwin F. O'Brien, June 10, 1997. Prior to his appointment as coadjutor archbishop of the Archdiocese for the Military Services of the United States, O'Brien had served two terms as rector of St. Joseph's Seminary, Dunwoodie, in the Archdiocese of New York, before and after his rectorship of the Pontifical North American College in Rome.

97. Ibid.

98. The press release from the Gemelli described the procedure in technical terms: ". . . on the morning of July 15, His Holiness, Pope John Paul II, underwent colon resection surgery for a voluminous tubulovillous adenoma of the sigmoid colon accompanied by modest and localized cytological alterations related to a dysplasia of moderate size. The operation was radical and curative because the lesion was of a benign nature. A cholecystectomy for multiple lithiasis of the gall bladder was also performed." [*OR* (EWE), July 15, 1992, p. 1.]

99. John Paul II, "Opening Address to the Fourth General Conference of the Latin American Episcopate," *Origins* 22:19 (October 22, 1992), pp. 321, 323–332.

100. The Special Assembly of the Synod of Bishops for America would meet in November and December 1997, and was completed by the post-synodal apostolic exhortation, *Ecclesia in America*, which John Paul II signed in Mexico City on January 22, 1999 [see *OR* (EWE), January 27, 1999]. For an account of the Synod, see Richard John Neuhaus, *Appointment in Rome: The Church in America Awakening* (New York: Crossroad, 1999).

101. See "Catechism Is Truly a Gift to the Church," *OR* [EWE], December 9, 1992, pp. 1–2. See also Cardinal Joseph Ratzinger's presentation of the book at a press conference on December 9 [*OR* (EWE), December 16, 1992, pp. 4, 6]. The presentation of the *Catechism* was also celebrated at a papal Mass at the Basilica of St. Mary Major on December 8, the solemnity of the Immaculate Conception; John Paul's homily linked the occasion to the solemn closing of Vatican II, twenty-seven years before. [See *OR* (EWE), December 16, 1992, p. 3.]

102. Author's interview with Archbishop Christoph Schönborn, OP, December 11, 1997.

103. Ibid. Christoph Schönborn was ordained bishop in September 1991. He was appointed coadjutor archbishop of Vienna in April 1995 and became archbishop the following September.

104. John Paul II, *Depositum Fidei*, 3.

105. See *Catechism of the Catholic Church*, 173–175.

106. Author's interview with Archbishop Christoph Schönborn, OP, December 11, 1997. See also Joseph Cardinal Ratzinger, *Gospel, Catechesis, Catechism: Sidelights on the "Catechism of the Catholic Church"* (San Francisco: Ignatius Press, 1997), which includes Ratzinger's response to the *Catechism*'s German critics, and Joseph Cardinal Ratzinger and Christoph Schönborn, OP, *Introduction to the "Catechism of the Catholic Church"* (San Francisco: Ignatius Press, 1994).

107. A definitive Latin text of the *Catechism* was published in 1997. Translation of the *Catechism* where the Church lived in poverty became the occasion for exercises in collegial charity; Cardinal John O'Connor of New York, for example, financed the translation of the *Catechism* into Russian, supporting the commission set up by Archbishop Tadeusz Kondrusiewicz. ["Presentation of Catechism of the Catholic Church in Russian," *Vatican Information Service*, January 28, 1997: VIS 970128 (780).]

108. See John Bolton, "Somalia and the Problems of Doing Good: A Perspective for the State Department," and Alberto Coll, "Somalia and the Problems of Doing Good: A Perspective from the Defense Department," in *Close Calls*, ed. Abrams, pp. 145–160 and 161–182.

109. John Paul II, "The World's Hunger and Humanity's Conscience," *Origins* 22:28 (December 24, 1992), p. 475.

110. For a discussion of the moral and policy issues involved in the "humanitarian intervention" debate, see John Langan, SJ, "Humanitarian Intervention: From Concept to Reality," Andrew Natsios, "Complex Humanitarian Emergencies and Moral Choice," and Drew Christiansen, SJ, and Gerard F. Powers, "The Duty to Intervene: Ethics and the Variety of Humanitarian Interventions," in *Close Calls*, ed. Abrams, pp. 109–124, 124–144, and 183–208.

111. John Paul II, "Polish Episcopal Conference—I," *OR* [EWE], February 3, 1993, p. 5.

112. See *Origins* 19:15 (September 14, 1989), p. 250.

113. See ibid., pp. 249–250.

114. For further documentation on the 1987 agreement and the 1989 controversy, see ibid., pp. 249–250.

115. The details above are taken from Władysław T. Bartoszewski, *The Convent at Auschwitz* (New York: George Braziller, 1991).

116. John Paul II, "Letter to the Carmelite Nuns at Auschwitz," in *Spiritual Journey*, pp. 167–168.

117. Bartoszewski, *The Convent at Auschwitz*, p. 137.

118. Author's interview with Monsignor Vincenzo Paglia, December 7, 1997.

119. One of the heroes of the vital Lithuanian Catholic resistance movement that had emerged in the 1970s, the clandestinely ordained Jesuit Sigitas Tamkevičius, had been appointed an auxiliary bishop in 1991. He was named archbishop of Kaunas in 1996.

120. "The Pope in Latvia: Address to the Cultural Leaders," *OR* [EWE], September 15, 1993, pp. 11, 15.

121. On the history of the Union of Brest, see Borys A. Gudziak, *Crisis and Reform: The Kyivan Metropolitanate, the Patriarchate of Constantinople. and the Genesis of the Union of Brest* (Cambridge, Massachusetts: Harvard University Press, 1998).

122. The Balamand Document also cautioned against using recent martyrdoms and sufferings as a weapon against fellow Christians, urged both Orthodox and Eastern Catholics to seek out practical means of cooperation in charitable service to society, and warned against the resort to violence and the civil courts to resolve current grievances (such as the possession or repossession of properties lost during the communist period); these questions should be settled by dialogue. Ecumenism should be part of seminary training; attacks in the mass media should be rigorously avoided; all who had suffered persecution for the sake of Christian faith should be honored by all.

123. Cited in Pontifical Council for Promoting Christian Unity *Information Service* 84 (1993/III-IV), p. 145.

124. Cited in Pontifical Council for Promoting Christian Unity *Information Service* 85 (1994/I), pp. 38–39.

125. On the reception of the Balamand Document by Orthodoxy and the Eastern Catholic churches, see Appendix I in Roberson, *The Eastern Christian Churches*, 5th edition, from which the analysis above is drawn.

Eight months later, in April 1994, Cardinal Lubachivsky sent a pastoral letter, *On Christian Unity*, to all Ukrainian Greek Catholics around the world. In it, the Ukrainian Catholic leader underlined his, and Catholicism's, recognition of Orthodox sacraments and holy orders, and stated that, while Balamand "has its imperfections," it ought to be implemented fully by the Greek Catholics of Ukraine. Lubachivsky's letter was a courageous attempt to bridge an enormous gap, and reflected John Paul II's view that Catholicism should bend every effort to strengthen its dialogue with Orthodoxy, and without expecting immediate reciprocation. [Ibid.]

126. Author's interview with Cardinal Edward Cassidy, September 5, 1996.

127. Author's interview with Cardinal Francis Arinze, November 9, 1996.

128. Ibid.

129. "The Pope in the Sudan: Ceremonies upon Arrival," *OR* [EWE], February 17, 1993, p. 11 [emphasis in original].

130. The government even censored a reference to Blessed Josephine Bakhita, a Sudanese Christian beatified in 1992, in the booklet prepared for the Pope's Mass. Like Sudanese Christians of the 1990s, Blessed Josephine had been kidnaped and sold into slavery.

131. It also gave John Paul the opportunity to publicly honor the memory of his friend Jerzy Ciesielski (who had drowned near Khartoum in 1970) as a "man of authentic faith" who had "made holiness the goal of his life as husband, father, and university teacher." ["Pope's Homily at Mass in Khartoum," in ibid., p. 16.]

132. Turabi, a Sorbonne-trained attorney and former dean of the University of Khartoum Law School, met the Pope briefly at the end of a general audience in the fall of 1993; during the same visit to Rome he also met with the staff of the Pontifical Council for Inter-Religious Dialogue and with Cardinal Arinze. The meetings were criticized, but Arinze argues that his dicastery has an obligation to receive leaders of other religions. The meeting with Arinze and the brief greeting from the Pope after the audience were requested by the Sudanese ambassador to the Holy See (who actually lived in Paris). During their meeting in Rome, Cardinal Arinze told Turabi that if he wanted to have a "dialogue with the Vatican," that conversation had to have roots, which meant "Muslims and Christians in Sudan meeting each other. And then Muslims meeting us in the Vatican would help. But without the first, the second doesn't work." Turabi, Arinze recalled, was "not enthusiastic," and the mild-mannered Arinze was charged by some reporters of speaking "like General Schwartzkopf." "But in this case, some clear talk was necessary," the Nigerian responded. As for John Paul's three-minute encounter with Turabi after the general audience, it may be suggested that the Pope said things about religious freedom that Turabi did not necessarily want to hear. Turabi later said that he had proposed to John Paul a "front against materialism," and that the Pope had received the idea well. It seems unlikely that such a "front" would have been thoroughly discussed in three minutes. [Author's interview with Cardinal Francis Arinze, November 9, 1996.]

133. John Paul II, homily at Agrigento, in *OR* [EWE], May 12, 1993, p. 2 [emphases in original].

134. Ibid.

135. See *OR* [EWE], June 2, 1993, p. 7, and *OR* [EWE], May 19, 1993, pp. 5–6.

136. "Papal Telegram to Florence," *OR* [EWE], June 2, 1993, p. 5.

CHAPTER 18

The Threshold of Hope: Appealing to Our Better Angels

1. Information on the background of the Denver World Youth Day and the opening ceremony: author's interview with Archbishop J. Francis Stafford, February 17, 1997; letter to the author from Dennis M. Gar-

cia, September 25, 1997; memorandum to the author from James Farnan, December 1996; Virginia Culver, "Papal Mass At Park a Bad Precedent?," *Denver Post*, November 21, 1992; Gary Massaro and Bill Scanlon, "Sierra Club Contests Papal Mass," *Rocky Mountain News*, January 27, 1993; *John Paul II Speaks to Youth at World Youth Day*, edited and illustrated by Catholic News Service (San Francisco and Washington, D.C.: Ignatius Press and Catholic News Service, 1993).

2. Addresses in *John Paul II Speaks to Youth at World Youth Day*, pp. 112–115; see p. 78 for John Paul's unscripted dialogue with the crowd at Stapleton International Airport.

3. On the way of the cross at World Youth Day '93, see ibid., pp. 83–89, 116–117.

4. Author's interview with Archbishop J. Francis Stafford, February 17, 1997.

5. On the Cherry Creek Park vigil, see *John Paul II Speaks to Youth at World Youth Day*, pp. 90–101, 120–124.

6. The full text of the homily is in ibid., pp. 124–125.

7. See ibid., p. 127.

8. Memorandum to the author from Archbishop J. Francis Stafford and Monsignor Edward L. Buelt, February 10, 1997.

9. Letter to the author from Dennis M. Garcia, September 25, 1997.

10. Ibid.

11. Author's interview with David Michaud, former Denver chief of police, January 8, 1999.

12. Author's interview with Archbishop J. Francis Stafford, February 17, 1997.

13. Ibid.

14. E. J. Dionne, Jr., "A Church Misrepresented," *Washington Post*, August 17, 1993, p. A21.

15. Peter Steinfels, "Beliefs," *New York Times*, August 21, 1993, p. A7.

16. Author's interview with Archbishop J. Francis Stafford, February 17, 1997.

17. Author's interview with Cardinal John J. O'Connor, November 8, 1996.

18. John Paul II's address to the Roman Curia: *OR* [EWE], January 5, 1994, pp. 6–7 [emphasis in original].

19. *Veritatis Splendor* was dated August 6, 1993, the Feast of the Transfiguration, and publicly released at a press conference led by Cardinal Joseph Ratzinger on October 5. The Latin original of the subtitle just cited is *De Fundamentis Doctrinae Moralis Ecclesiae*.

20. A few sentences in its *Decree on Priestly Formation* [*Optatam Totius*] urged "special attention . . . to the development of moral theology," which was to include deepening the discipline's biblical roots and lifting up the nobility of the lay vocation in the world. [See *Optatam Totius*, 16.]

21. On the situation of pre-conciliar Catholic moral theology, see Pinckaers, *The Sources of Christian Ethics*, pp. 254–279. Pinckaers makes the seminal distinction between a "freedom of indifference" and "freedom for excellence" in ibid., pp. 327–378.

22. See John Paul II, *Veritatis Splendor*, 96, in Miller, *Encyclicals*.

23. See ibid., 97.

24. On this point, see Pinckaers, *The Sources of Christian Ethics*, pp. 278–279.

25. This analysis of the content of *Veritatis Splendor* is indebted to that of Richard John Neuhaus in *First Things* 39 (January 1994), pp. 14–16.

26. John Paul II, *Veritatis Splendor*, 5.3, in Miller, *Encyclicals*.

27. Author's interview with Cardinal Joseph Ratzinger, September 20, 1997. This charge may be found, inter alia, in Morris, *American Catholic*, p. 333.

28. See, for example, Richard K. Ostling, "A Refinement of Evil," *Time*, October 4, 1993, p. 71.

29. Vivian Hewitt, "Encyclical Seen As Declaration of War on Liberals," *Catholic Herald*, August 6, 1993, p. 1.

30. Ann Knowles, "Leaked Draft 'Completely Revised,' " *The Universe*, August 15, 1993, p. 6.

31. Author's interview with Tadeusz Styczeń, SDS, April 14, 1997.

Veritatis Splendor generated a small library of commentaries, among which may be mentioned the following books of essays: *The Splendor of Accuracy: An Examination of the Assertions Made by* "Veritatis Splendor," Joseph A. Selling and Jan Jans, eds. (Grand Rapids: Eerdmans, 1995); "Veritatis Splendor": *American Responses*, Michael E. Allsopp and John J. O'Keefe (Kansas City: Sheed and Ward, 1995); *Understanding* "Veritatis Splendor," ed. John Wilkins (London: SPCK, 1994) and *Moraltheologie im Abseits? Antwort auf die Enzyklika* "Veritatis Splendor," ed. Dietmar Mieth (Freiburg/Basel/Vienna: Herder, 1994). *L'Osservatore Romano* ran an extensive series of commentaries on the encyclical in the winter and spring of 1993–1994; these may be found in the English Weekly Edition of *OR* during that period. Several important commentaries appeared in *The Thomist*: see Martin Rhonheimer, "Intrinsically Evil Acts and the Moral Viewpoint: Clarifying a Central Teaching of *Veritatis Splendor* [*The Thomist*, 58 (1994), pp. 1–39]; Alasdair MacIntyre, "How Can We Learn What *Veritatis Splendor* Has To Teach?" [*The Thomist*, 58 (1994), pp. 171–195]; and Servais Pinckaers, "The Use of Scripture and the Renewal of Moral Theology: The Catechism and *Veritatis Splendor*" [*The Thomist*, 59 (1995), pp. 1–19].

Richard A. McCormick, SJ, comments on the first wave of commentaries and provides a useful international bibliography in "Some Early Reactions in *Veritatis Splendor*," *Theological Studies* 55 (September 1994), pp. 491–506; for a response to McCormick's own criticisms of the encyclical and its defenders, see Richard John Neuhaus, "Moral Theology at its Pique," *First Things* 49 (January 1995), pp. 88–92. For another extensive bibliography of commentaries in *Veritatis Splendor* see Miller, *Encyclicals*, pp. 667–671.

32. On this point, see Josef Fuchs's essay in Wilkins's *Understanding* "Veritatis Splendor," pp. 21–26. The main themes of the German theological criticism of the encyclical are found in Mieth's *Moraltheologie im Abseits?*

33. Cited in McCormick, "Some Early Reactions . . . ," p. 486.

34. Cited in ibid.

35. Cited in ibid., p. 491.

36. This was particularly true of the response of one of post-conciliar Catholicism's most influential moral theologians, Father Bernhard Häring, whose essay may be found in Wilkins's *Understanding "Veritatis Splendor*," pp. 9–13. Father Richard McCormick also thought that the "issue behind the issue" was ecclesiology, and specifically "the attempt to suppress any dissent." [McCormick, "Some Early Reactions . . . ," p. 505.]

37. Gilbert Meilaender, "Grace, Justification Through Faith, and Sin," in *Ecumenical Ventures in Ethics: Protestants Engage Pope John Paul II's Moral Encyclicals*, ed. Reinhard Hütter and Theodore Dieter (Grand Rapids: Eerdmans, 1998), p. 83.

38. Hadley Arkes, in "The Splendor of Truth,: A Symposium," *First Things* 39 (January 1994), pp. 25–26.

39. The problem was acutely described by Ulysses in Shakespeare's *Troilus and Cressida*, some 390 years before *Veritatis Splendor*:

Take but degree away, untune that string,
And, hark, what discord follows. . . .
Force should be right; or rather, right and wrong,
Between whose endless jar justice resides,
Should lose their names, and so should justice too.
Then every thing includes
itself in power,
Power into will, will into appetite;
And appetite, a universal wolf,
So doubly seconded with will and power,
Must make perforce an universal prey
And last eat up himself . . .
[William Shakespeare, *Troilus and Cressida*, I.iii.109ff.]

40. On the nominalist corruption of the idea of freedom see Pinckaers, *The Sources of Christian Ethics*, pp. 327–351.

41. This conviction was translated into detailed pastoral guidelines four years later, on February 12, 1997, when the Pontifical Council for the Family published its *Vademecum for Confessors Concerning Some Aspects of the Morality of Conjugal Life*. These suggestions for how priests should lead penitents to a discernment of the truth of the Church's moral teaching as the framework for making decisions about, inter alia, the morally appropriate methods of family planning was John Paul II's initiative, and reiterates the teaching of *Familiaris Consortio*: "it is part of the Church's pedagogy that husbands and wives would first recognize clearly the teaching of *Humanae Vitae* as indicating the norm for the exercise of their sexuality, and that they should endeavor to establish the conditions necessary for observing that norm." [*Familiaris Consortio*, 34.] In this vision of the moral life and its relationship to the Sacrament of Penance, the confessor is a spiritual and moral guide, not an inquisitor. [See *Vademecum for Confessors*, 1–11.]

42. The *Letter to Families* was another innovation in papal teaching: a more personal reflection, addressed to a specific audience for a specific occasion (in this instance, the 1994 "International Year of the Family"), and not styled an apostolic constitution, encyclical, apostolic letter, or apostolic exhortation.

43. Author's interview with Bishop Stanisław Ryłko, November 12, 1996.

Monsignor Ryłko was ordained a bishop by John Paul II on January 6, 1996 and appointed Secretary of the Pontifical Council on the Laity.

44. John Paul II, address to the diplomatic corps, *OR* [EWE], January 19, 1994, pp. 1–2, 8 [emphasis in original].

45. The account that follows is based on the author's interviews with two of the principal negotiators of the Fundamental Agreement, David-Maria A. Jaeger, OFM (interviews of May 10–11, 1997) and Shlomo Gur (interview of June 17, 1997), and with three other officials of the Holy See: Archbishop Andrea Cordero Lanza di Montezemolo (interview of November 28, 1997), Archbishop Claudio Celli (interviews of January 20 and September 24, 1997), and Monsignor Luigi Gatti (interview of November 25, 1997). At the time of the negotiation leading to the fundamental agreement, Archbishop Montezemolo was apostolic delegate in Jerusalem and Palestine; then-Monsignor Celli was Undersecretary of the Section for Relations with States, or "deputy-foreign minister" of the Holy See); and Monsignor Gatti was the veteran *minutante*, or desk officer, responsible for Middle East affairs in the Secretariat of State.

Additional historical details are taken from Jaeger, *The Roman Pontiffs in Defence of Christian Rights in the Holy Land*. See also George E. Irani, *The Papacy and the Middle East: The Role of the Holy See in the Arab-Israeli Conflict, 1962–1984* (Notre Dame: University of Notre Dame Press, 1986); Andrej Kreutz, *Vatican Policy on the Palestinian-Israeli Conflict: The Struggle for the Holy Land* (New York: Greenwood Press, 1990); and Minerbi, *The Vatican and Zionism*.

Robert L. Wilken's *The Land Called Holy: Palestine in Christian History and Thought* (New Haven, Conn.: Yale University Press, 1992), a richly drawn historical and theological reflection on Christianity and the land of Christ from the first century A.D. to the seventh, provides a perspective essential for grasping crucial aspects of contemporary debates.

46. On Israel, see John Paul II, *Crossing the Threshold of Hope*, p. 100.

47. John Paul II, "Homily in Otranto," *OR* [EWE], pp. 1–2, 8.

48. Author's interview with Monsignor Luigi Gatti, November 25, 1997.

49. John Paul II, "Homily in Otranto," *OR* [EWE], October 13, 1980, p. 8.

50. See O'Brien, *The Hidden Pope*, pp. 284ff.

51. See "Joint Press Communiqué of September 1, 1987," in John Paul II, *Spiritual Pilgrimage*, p. 103.

52. For limited technical purposes (for example, participation in the Internationa! Telecommunications Union), Vatican City State is a subject of international law. But in virtually all other instances. it is the Holy See that participates in international organizations (for example, the International Atomic Energy Agency, where the Church's interest is the moral dimension of nuclear power, not the involvement of Vatican City State in nuclear energy research or production).

53. Montezemolo learned about the back channel and the agreements it had produced in a letter from Cardinal Sodano, who told him that "Father Jaeger will explain it to you." The patrician archbishop didn't flinch (according to Jaeger, who was present when the apostolic delegate opened the letter) and immediately grasped the necessity of doing things this way. Jaeger, he understood, had protected him from being in an impossible position, as the archbishop had no authority to authorize a member of his delegation to engage in such an enterprise without prior clearance through ordinary Vatican channels—which would have tied everything up in knots and jeopardized a process that was producing results.

54. Sabbah, a Palestinian Arab born in Nazareth in 1933, was appointed by John Paul II in 1987 and was the first native Catholic Latin-rite patriarch of Jerusalem in modern times.

55. This language was the subject of lengthy negotiations. The Holy See's position was that it was "upholding" the universal right to religious freedom by, inter alia, urging Israel to "observe" it.

56. Ambassador Shmuel Hadas presented his credentials as the first Ambassador of the State of Israel to the Holy See to Pope John Paul II on September 29, 1994. The Pope's welcoming address and the ambassador's remarks may be found in Pontifical Council for Promoting Christian Unity *Information Service* #88 (1995/I), pp. 38–41.

Archbishop Montezemolo was nominated the first papal nuncio to Israel on June 28, 1994. John Paul took to calling him *il nuncio storico* ["the historic nuncio"], perhaps in part to help take the sting of disappointment out of Monsignor Celli having been the actual signatory of the Fundamental Agreement. In 1998, Montezemolo was named nuncio to Italy.

57. Two years later, at the 1996 Special Assembly for Lebanon of the Synod of Bishops, Latin-rite Patriarch Michel Sabbah made an intervention in which he said that the Middle East, "being in search of stability, needs the resources of all its people and religions, Christianity and Islam." Judaism was noticeably absent. The patriarch went on to describe "the Jewish fact" as a "new reality . . . in the Holy Land," and suggested that the Syrian presence in Lebanon was Israel's fault. [Cited in "One Small Step Backward," *National Catholic Register* February 4, 1996.] See also Michel Sabbah, "The Church of Jerusalem: Living with Conflict, Working for Peace," *Commonweal*, January 14, 1996, pp. 14–17.

58. Father Jaeger summed up the legal implications of the Fundamental Agreement in "The Fundamental Agreement Between the Holy See and the State of Israel: A New Legal Régime of Church-State Relations," *Catholic University Law Review* 47:2 (Winter 1998), pp. 427–440.

59. Arafat's comment was cited in the *New York Times* of December 25, 1995, in a story datelined December 24 and reprinted in the Winter 1995–1996 issue of *Christians in Israel*, a quarterly publication of the Israeli Foreign Ministry.

"Official relations" (the diplomats' technical term) were established between the Holy See and the PLO by a joint communiqué of October 25, 1994. The offices of the PLO representative to the Holy See are in London. There is no counterpart representation of the Holy See to the PLO. Unofficial contacts are maintained with the Palestinian Authority through the apostolic delegate in Palestine/Jerusalem.

60. See "Jerusalem: Considerations of the Secretariat of State," in *Origins* 26:16 (October 3, 1996), pp. 250–253. This text also includes a useful historical overview of the Holy See's position on Jerusalem since 1947–1948.

61. See Melady, *The Ambassador's Story*, pp. 124–136, for an account by the Bush administration's ambassador to the Holy See of his discussions on this issue. Given the impression, widespread in the Vatican, that senior officials of the Bush administration took far less cognizance of the Holy See's concerns than had its predecessor, it seems unlikely that there was a significant causal relationship between the administration's wish for full diplomatic relations between the Holy See and Israel (which Secretary of State James A. Baker, III had written into Ambassador Melady's instructions as a goal to be sought) and the achievement of the Fundamental Agreement.

62. The serious part of the restoration controversy involved questions about the effects of the cleansing agent on some of Michelangelo's late corrections to the ceiling. The less serious part involved complaints from academics and critics whose lengthy speculations about transferences from the dark crevices of Michelangelo's imagination to the ceiling were rendered null and void by the revelation that what had been thought to be artistic shadows were in fact the products of wax, Roman air pollution, and aviary digestive tracts. For technical and scholarly articles on the restoration and its techniques, see *La Capella Sistina: I Primi Restauri—La Scoperta del Colore* (Instituto Geografico de Agostini, 1986), *La Capella Sistina: La Volta Restaurata—Il Trionfo del Colore* (Instituto Geografico de Agostino, 1992), and *La Capella Sistina: Il Giudizio Restaurato* (Instituto Geografico de Agostino, 1997). For the story of the drapings and their removal during the restoration, see Meg Nottingham Walsh, "Out of the Darkness: Michelangelo's 'Last Judgment,'" *National Geographic* 185:5 (May 1994), pp. 102–123.

63. The citations above are from John Paul II, homily at Mass marking the completion of the restoration of the Sistine Chapel, *OR* [EWE], April 13, 1994, pp. 7, 9 [emphasis in original].

64. John Tagliabue, "Cleaned 'Last Judgment' Unveiled," *New York Times*, April 9, 1994, p. 13.

65. The January 24, 1993 editorial was reprinted in *OR* [EWE], January 27, 1993, p. 1.

66. Author's interview with Archbishop Jean-Louis Tauran, March 18, 1997.

67. Reputable demographers believe that there is no such thing as "overpopulation," which has never been scientifically defined. These scholars argue that what we are accustomed to think of as the symptoms of "overpopulation"—disease, hunger overcrowding, high infant mortality—are more accurately described as the results of poverty and material deprivation. On this point, see Amartya Sen, "Population: Delusion and Reality," and Nicholas Eberstadt, "The Premises of Population Policy: A Reexamination," in *The Nine Lives of Population Control*, ed. Michael Cromartie (Grand Rapids: Eerdmans, 1995).

Within three years of the Cairo conference, the UN's own demographic projections were forecasting zero world population growth by 2040 and depopulation thereafter. [See Nicholas Eberstadt, "World Population Implosion?" *The Public Interest* 129 (Fall 1997), pp. 3–22.]

68. See, for example, Peter Singer, *Rethinking Life & Death: The Collapse of Our Traditional Ethics* (New York: St. Martin's Press, 1995).

69. John Paul II, "Letter to Heads of State," in *OR* [EWE], April 20, 1994, p. 1 [emphasis in original].

70. Author's conversation with Pope John Paul II, December 13, 1997.

71. This pattern of misrepresentation—more plainly, lying—had characterized previous interactions between UNFPA representatives and officials of the Holy See. [Author's interview with Monsignor Peter Elliott, September 22, 1997.]

72. In his memorandum to Mrs. Sadik, John Paul emphasized that "what the Church calls responsible parenthood is not a question of unlimited procreation," nor was it based on a "lack of awareness of what is involved in raising children." Rather, what the Church sought was "the empowerment of couples to use their inviolable liberty wisely and responsibly, taking into account social and demographic realities as well as moral criteria." The Pope's memorandum to Mrs. Sadik is in *Origins* 23:31 (March 31, 1994), pp. 716–719.

For Nafis Sadik's reconstruction of this meeting, see Bernstein and Politi, *His Holiness*, pp. 517–524. Their narrative strongly suggests that neither author had read the Cairo draft document thoroughly, much less carefully. Mrs. Sadik's recollections of the meeting may also have been influenced by the fact that her agenda was frustrated at Cairo by, among others, John Paul II.

73. Unclassified memorandum to the U.S. Ambassador to the Holy See, March 21, 1994.

74. See Dennis Proust, "Hostile U.N. Prep Session," *Catholic New York*, April 21, 1994. This reconstruction of Prep-Com III is also based on the author's interviews with two members of the Holy See delegation, Monsignor Diarmuid Martin and Ms. Gail Quinn, shortly after the Cairo conference.

75. The citations above are taken from the "Draft Final Document of the Conference," produced by Prep-Com III as the working text for the final report of the Cairo conference.

The mainstream press seemed uninterested in the strong-arm tactics used at Prep-Com III, which were nevertheless reported extensively in a form of underground journalism: cheaply produced pro-life newspapers and magazines. Attempts to clarify the Orwellian Newspeak of the Cairo draft document were dismissed in one major U.S. news weekly as "Jesuitical obfuscation"—a minor but telling example of the anti-Catholicism that too often tainted coverage of the Cairo conference and the process leading up to it. [Emily MacFarquhar, "Population Wars," *U.S. News and World Report*, September 12, 1994, p. 55.]

76. See Accattoli, *Karol Wojtyła*, p. 272.

77. Author's conversation with Pope John Paul II, January 22, 1997.

78. John Paul II, "Angelus for Trinity Sunday," *OR* [EWE], June 1, 1994, p. 8.

79. Author's interview with Tadeusz Styczeń, SDS, October 23, 1998.

80. The bishops' statement is in *Origins* 24:9 (July 21, 1994), pp. 170–171.

The religious opposition to the Clinton administration's Cairo policy was by no means Catholic alone. On April 22, eleven leading evangelical Protestant leaders faxed a letter of protest to the White House, describing a State Department cable instructing U.S. posts abroad to pressure foreign governments to broaden abortion access in UNFPA programs as "an unprecedented misuse of our diplomatic corps for political ends." The Protestant leaders asked the President how he could reconcile the third part of his campaign promise to make abortion "safe, legal, and rare" with his administration's Cairo policies, which were aimed at promoting precisely the opposite.

81. "Declaration of the Pontifical Academy for Life," *OR* [EWE], June 29, 1994, p. 1 [emphasis in original].

82. "Cairo Population Conference," *OR* [EWE], June 22, 1994, p. 7.

83. See *OR* [EWE], June 15, 1994, pp. 1–2.

84. See *OR* [EWE], June 22, 1994, p. 1.

85. See *OR* [EWE], June 29, 1994, p. 11.

86. See ibid., pp. 1–2.

87. See *OR* [EWE], July 6, 1994, p. 1.

88. See *OR* [EWE], July 13, 1994, p. 1.

89. See *OR* [EWE], July 20, 1994, p. 1.

90. See *OR* [EWE], July 27, 1994, pp. 1–2.

91. See *OR* [EWE], August 3, 1994, p. 1.

92. See *OR* [EWE], August 10–17, 1994, p. 2.

93. See *OR* [EWE], August 24, 1994, p. 2.

94. See *OR* [EWE], August 31, 1994, p. 1.

95. Author's interview with Joaquín Navarro-Valls, December 18, 1997.

96. "Remarks Prepared for Delivery by Vice President Al Gore, National Press Club, Washington, D.C., Thursday, August 25, 1994" (Washington, D.C.: Office of the Vice President), p. 8.

97. Quoted in Christine Gorman, "Clash of Wills in Cairo," *Time*, September 12, 1994, p. 56.

98. Author's interview with Joaquín Navarro-Valls, December 18, 1997.

The Gore/Navarro confrontation came shortly after the U.S. State Department's population coordinator, Faith Mitchell, blamed Vatican disagreement with the Cairo document on sexism and the Church's determination to deny women an education. According to Ms. Mitchell, the Holy See was upset with "the fact that the conference is calling for a new role for women, calling for girls' education and improving the status of women." [Deborah Zabarenko, "U.S. Works to 'Lower Volume' on Population Debate," Reuters World Service, August 19, 1994.]

99. Boyce Rosenberger, "Explosive Abortion Issues Refueled at Forum," *Washington Post*, September 6, 1994, pp. 1, 13.

100. International conferences like the Cairo population conference work on the principle of consensus, with all participants having to agree (or at least having to agree not to formally disagree) with everything in a document before it can be adopted by the conference as a whole. Participants who do not wish to block a final document by "withholding consensus," as the diplomatic vocabulary has it, can add "reservations" to the final document. This was the strategy employed by the Holy See at Cairo after it had achieved its principal objectives at the conference. As the head of the Holy See delegation began his remarks at the closing of the conference on September 13, "the Holy See wishes in some way to associate itself with the consensus, even if in an incomplete or partial manner." The Holy See then affixed an "annexed note" of reservations to the Cairo final report. [See *Origins* 24:15 (September 22, 1994), pp. 257, 259–264 for Archbishop Renato Martino's two interventions at the conference, the "annexed note," and a series of observations by members of the Holy See delegation to the conference.]

101. Barbara Crossette, "Vatican Holds Up Abortion Debate at Talks in Cairo," *New York Times*, September 8, 1994, p. A8.

102. The last major sticking point during the nine-day-long conference involved the "safety" of abortions. It was an important question for the Holy See, which believes that no abortion is "safe," as it results in the death of an innocent human being. The disputed language in the draft final report stated that "in circumstances where abortion is legal, such abortion should be safe." This was unacceptable to the Holy See and the issue was moral principle: to Holy See delegates, the draft language was the equivalent of saying that in circumstances where female circumcision is legal, it should be performed with novocaine. After considerable wrangling, the language was finally changed to read, "in circumstances where abortion is not against the law, such abortion should be safe." On the surface it was a minor change, but from the Holy See's point of view the new language held out the prospect of legal reform and did not concede the moral rectitude of existing permissive abortion laws.

103. The Holy See was criticized by the United States and others for negotiating with Islamic regimes during the conference. Before the Cairo conference, for example, State Department spokesman Mike McCurry publicly warned the Holy See against negotiating with Iran. A week later, in Cairo, U.S. delegates were seen openly negotiating compromise language on abortion and "reproductive rights" with Iranian delegates.

104. The Holy See's last formal statement at Cairo identified those parts of the final report with which it agreed and those parts it still found objectionable. Arguing that the Holy See's views were shared by "many, believers and nonbelievers alike, in every country of the world," Archbishop Renato Martino, the head of the Vatican delegation, welcomed the final report's "affirmations against all forms of coercion in population policies," its recognition of the family as "the basic unit of society," and its stress on "women's advancement and the improvement of women's status through education and better health care services." The archbishop then deplored the fact that the final report "recognizes abortion as a dimension of population policy and indeed of primary health care, even though it does stress that abortion should not be promoted as a means of family planning and urges nations to find alternatives to abortion." The final report's preamble, Martino continued, "implies that the document does not contain the affirmation of a new internationally recognized right to abortion." [The full text of Martino's statement may be found in *Origins* 24:15 (September 22, 1994, pp. 257–260).]

105. See "Accanto a Pietro una preghiera incessante," *L'Osservatore Romano*, May 11, 1994, p. 4.

106. Ibid.

107. The Swiss theologian whom John Paul intended to create a cardinal, Hans Urs von Balthasar, once contrasted the ease with which the early Christian centuries spoke of this "spousal" relationship with the difficulties that contemporary men and women had with it. See Balthasar, "Mother Church," in *In the Fullness of Faith*, pp. 92–93.]

108. See "Declaration on the Admission of Women to the Ministerial Priesthood," in *Vatican Council II: More Post-Conciliar Documents*, Austin Flannery, OP, general editor (Collegeville, Minn.: Liturgical Press, 1982), pp. 331–345.

109. For extensive bibliographies of the debate in the United States and western Europe, see Benedict M. Ashley, OP, *Justice in the Church: Gender and Participation* (Washington, D.C.: Catholic University of America Press, 1996).

110. Details of the development of *Ordinatio Sacerdotalis* and John Paul's comments are taken from the author's interview with Cardinal Joseph Ratzinger, January 18, 1997. The national bishops' conferences represented at the CDF consultation prior to the completion of *Ordination Sacerdotalis* were from England and Wales, the United States, Germany, France, Italy, Australia, and Spain, as well as from the Slavic countries, Africa, and Asia, according to Cardinal Ratzinger.

111. *Ordinatio Sacerdotalis*, 2, in *OR* [EWE], June 1, 1994, p. 1.

112. Ibid., 3, in ibid., p. 1.

113. Ibid., 3, in ibid., p. 2.

114. Ibid., 4, in ibid., p. 2.

115. "Presentation of Letter," in ibid., p. 2.

116. These reactions to *Ordinatio Sacerdotalis* are reported in "Nuances and Defiance Follow Papal Letter," *The Tablet,* June 11, 1994, pp. 749–750.

117. See *OR* [EWE], November 22, 1995.

118. Author's interview with Cardinal Joseph Ratzinger, January 18, 1997.

119. "Reply to the 'Dubium' Concerning the Teaching Contained in the Apostolic Letter '*Ordinatio Sacerdotalis,*'" *OR* [EWE], November 22, 1995, p. 2 [emphasis in original].

120. CDF's official commentary, "Concerning the Reply of the Congregation for the Doctrine of the Faith on the Teaching Contained in the Apostolic Letter '*Ordinatio Sacerdotalis,*'" may be found in *OR* [EWE], November 22, 1995, pp. 2, 9.

121. Cited in Andrew Brown, "Pope Accused of Abusing Power," *The Independent,* December 2, 1995, p. 8. Lash's article was originally published in *The Tablet.*

122. Celestine Bohlen, "Catholics Defying an Infallible Church," *New York Times,* November 26, 1995, p. E3.

123. Peter Steinfels, "Vatican Says the Ban on Women As Priests Is 'Infallible' Doctrine," *New York Times,* November 19, 1995, p. 13.

124. Cited in Tom Roberts, "Dulles Urges Bishops to Enforce Papal 'No,'" *National Catholic Reporter,* July 26, 1996, p. 6. The full text of Dulles's lecture, "Pastoral Response to the Teaching on Women's Ordination," may be found in *Origins* 26:11 (August 29, 1996), pp. 177–180.

125. "Tradition and the Ordination of Women," *Origins* 26:6 (June 27, 1996), pp. 90–94. The final version of the CTSA statement may be found in *Origins* 27:5 (June 19, 1997), pp. 75–79. The response of the staff of the National Conference of Catholic Bishops' Committee on Doctrine to the CTSA statement may be found in *Origins* 27:16 (October 2, 1997), pp. 265, 267–271.

126. On the relationship of the virtue of justice to the debate over women's roles in the Church, see Ashley, *Justice in the Church.*

127. This public perception was, of course, informed not only by the press but by theologians. Even a member of the International Theological Commission, an advisory body to CDF, misstated the nature of the Pope's teaching when he wrote that, "In his apostolic letter *Ordinatio Sacerdotalis* of 13 May 1994, Pope John Paul II declared that he had no authority to change the Church's tradition of ordaining only men to the priesthood." [Hermann Josef Pottmeyer, "The Pope and Women," *The Tablet,* November 2, 1996, p. 1435.] This, of course, framed the question as an issue of personal papal assertiveness. What John Paul had actually written in *Ordinatio Sacerdotalis* was, to repeat with a clarifying emphasis, "I declare that *the Church has no authority whatsoever* to confer priestly ordination on women." [*Ordinatio Sacerdotalis,* 4.] There were, in other words, constitutive elements of the Church that popes—or anyone else—simply could not change; this was a question of the nature of the Church, not of papal *fiat.*

128. Author's interview with Monsignor Vincenzo Paglia, December 7, 1997; "Holy Father May Visit Zagreb and Sarajevo," *OR* [EWE], August 10–17, 1994, p. 12.

129. These texts are reprinted in *OR* [EWE], September 14, 1994, pp. 1–4.

130. Vittorio Messori tells the story of how *Crossing the Threshold of Hope* came to be in his editor's introduction to the book, from which these details are drawn.

131. John Paul II, *Crossing the Threshold of Hope,* p. 222.

132. On this theme in *Threshold,* see Cardinal Joseph Ratzinger, "God in John Paul II's *Crossing the Threshold of Hope,*" *Communio* 22 (Spring 1995), pp. 107–112.

133. The largest hard-cover sales were in the United States (1.2 million) and Italy (957,000). Hard-cover sales were considerably smaller in the United Kingdom (145,000), France (250,000), Germany (200,000), and Spain (300,000). [Sales figures are from a memorandum to the author from Emanuela Canali, November 25, 1998. Royalty information is from the author's interview with Joaquín Navarro-Valls, December 16, 1998.]

134. See Roberson, *The Eastern Christian Churches: A Brief Survey,* 5th ed., pp. 15–19. The implications of this are taken from the author's interview with Father Roberson, March 3, 1997.

135. Author's interview with Ronald G. Roberson, CSP, March 3, 1997.

136. Ibid.

137. John Paul II, *Letter of the Pope to Children in the Year of the Family.* This brief document has no paragraph numbers.

CHAPTER 19

Only One World: Human Solidarity and the Gospel of Life

1. John Paul's address to the extraordinary consistory may be found in *OR* [EWE], June 22, 1994, pp. 6–8 [emphasis in original]. The background to the consistory is drawn from Luigi Accatoli, *When a Pope Asks Forgiveness: The Mea Culpas of John Paul II* (Boston: Pauline Books and Media, 1998), pp. 55–67.

2. John Paul II, "Angelus for Trinity Sunday," *OR* [EWE], June 1, 1994, p. 8.

3. John Paul II, *Redemptor Hominis,* 1, in Miller, *Encyclicals.*

4. John Paul II, *Tertio Millennio Adveniente,* 23.

5. See ibid., 3.

6. See ibid., 4.

7. Ibid., 6 [emphasis in original].

8. Ibid., 7.

9. Ibid., 10–12 [emphasis in original].

10. Ibid., 23.

11. Ibid., 23.

12. Ibid., 25.

13. Ibid., 24 [emphasis in original].

14. Ibid., 33 [emphasis in original].

15. Ibid.

16. See ibid., 34.

17. Ibid., 35 [emphasis in original], citing *Dignitatis Humanae*, 1.

18. Ibid., 36.

19. Ibid., 37 [emphasis in original].

20. Ibid., 40, 42, 44, 46, 49–50, 52.

21. Ibid., 55.

22. Ibid. [emphasis in original].

23. Author's interview with Father Richard John Neuhaus, March 1, 1997.

24. See Thomas J. Reese, SJ, *Inside the Vatican: The Politics and Organization of the Catholic Church* (Cambridge, Mass.: Harvard University Press, 1996), p. 229.

25. For a concise summary of the Calvi/IOR affair, see ibid., pp. 206–207.

26. Author's interview with Cardinal Edmund Szoka, September 4, 1996.

27. See Reese, *Inside the Vatican*, p. 209.

28. Author's interview with Cardinal Edmund Szoka, September 4, 1996.

29. APSA, as it is universally known in Rome, handles the Holy See's investments (including its pension fund) and manages the Holy See's rental properties and payroll.

30. Author's interview with Cardinal Edmund Szoka, September 4, 1996. For documentation on the meeting of the presidents of national bishops' conference, see *OR* [EWE], April 15, 1991, p. 10.

31. "Consolidated Financial Statements of the Holy See: Year 1995" (Rome: Prefecture for the Economic Affairs of the Holy See, 1996).

32. One such point was the 7 billion lire annual subsidy the Holy See was paying to cover the deficits of the Italian newspaper *Avvenire*, which reflected the views of the Secretariat of State, in the late 1970s. The subsidy was in the Holy See budget, which was one of the reasons the budget couldn't be published. John Paul II asked a simple question: "Why are we doing this?" The practice was changed, *Avvenire* now gets no subsidy from the Holy See, and the Vatican's consolidated financial statement could be published. [Author's interview with Joaquín Navarro-Valls, December 18, 1997.]

33. Author's interview with Cardinal Edmund Szoka, September 4, 1996.

34. Various conspiracy theories notwithstanding, these papal donations to support Solidarity never involved the recycling of U.S. government funds through the IOR. American support for Solidarity families during and after martial law was open, with resources coming from the government-funded National Endowment for Democracy, from congressional appropriations to help Solidarity, and from the AFL-CIO. These funds were directed to a Polish priest in Paris who used them to buy food and medicines, and then had the supplies shipped by truck to St. Martin's Church. All of these funds were publicly accounted for by the public, quasi-public, and private organizations involved. [Author's interview with Jan Nowak, August 19, 1998.]

35. Raymond De Souza, "At 77, Pope Still Connects with Youth," *National Catholic Register*, August 31-September 6, 1997, pp. 1, 10.

36. Author's interview with Ambassador Henrietta T. De Villa, March 25, 1997.

37. Ibid.

38. On Ramzi Yousef: Dale Russakoff, "Deliberations Begin in Jet Bomb Plot Case," *Washington Post*, August 30, 1996, p. A3; John Mintz, "Men in Papal Bomb Plot Termed Close to Bin Lade," *Washington Post*, August 22, 1998.

39. John Paul II, homily at the beatification of Peter To Rot, *OR* [EWE], January 25, 1995, pp. 8–9. Details of the life of Peter To Rot may be found in ibid., p. 9.

40. Memorandum to the author from Monsignor Peter J. Elliott, September 18, 1998.

41. See Paul Gardiner, SJ, "Love Was Soul of Mary MacKillop's Virtues," *OR* [EWE], January 25, 1995, pp. 1, 12.

42. John Paul II, homily at the beatification of Mary MacKillop, in ibid., pp. 1–2 [emphasis in original].

43. "Pope's Radio Message to Chinese Catholics," *OR* [EWE], January 18, 1995, p. 1.

44. See Joseph Krahl, SJ, "China," in *New Catholic Encyclopedia*, volume 3, pp. 598–599.

45. Author's interview with Archbishop Oscar V. Cruz, November 22, 1997.

46. Ibid.

47. Author's interview with Cardinal Roger Etchegaray, March 19, 1997.

48. Author's interviews with Archbishop Claudio Celli, January 20, 1997, and Cardinal Jozef Tomko, November 14, 1996. Celli said that, when certain letters to the Pope from PCA bishops can be publicly released, "the world will be astonished at the passionate fidelity to the Holy Father" of many of these men.

49. Jonathan Mirsky, "Pope to Paper over Rift by Meeting Chinese Catholics," *The Times*, January 10, 1995, p. 11. The headline suggests considerable confusion in London.

50. John Paul II, *ad limina* address to the Bishop of Taiwan, *OR* [EWE], August 30, 1995, pp. 3, 6 [emphasis in original].

51. John Paul II, "Message to the Church in China," *OR* [EWE], December 11, 1996, p. 8.

52. "The Pope Asks for Freedom for the Church in China," *Vatican Information Service* VIS 980514 (410), May 14, 1998.

53. "Archbishop Tauran on Holy See's International Relations," *Vatican Information Service* VIS 980515 (890), May 15, 1998.

54. See Cardinal Joseph Ratzinger, "The Problem of Threats to Human Life," *OR* [EWE], April 8, 1991, pp. 2–4.

55. "Pope Asked to Reaffirm Sacredness of Human Life," *OR* [EWE], April 8, 1991, p. 1.

56. There had been internal Vatican discussion about the possibility of a Synod of Bishops on life issues, to conclude with a Synodal statement and an apostolic exhortation. Some argued that such a process would give any papal document on life issues more credibility. The argument was not persuasive to those who thought that John Paul already occupied the world's most authoritative pulpit and who doubted that a Synod's conclusions (which would hardly be surprising, in any case) would add any further authority to what he would say. [Author's interview with Cardinal Jan Schotte, CICM, March 14, 1997.]

57. See John Paul II, *Evangelium Vitae*, 5.2, in Miller, *Encyclicals*.

58. Ibid., 20.2, 18.5, 18.3.

59. On the relationship of *Evangelium Vitae* to the nineteenth-century papal critique of democracy, see Russell Hittinger's contribution to "The Gospel of Life: A Symposium," in *First Things* 56 (October 1995), pp. 33–35. I am also indebted to Professor Hittinger for an earlier, unpublished draft of this article, "A Brief History of Papal Prudence."

60. See John Paul II, *Evangelium Vitae*, 57.4, 62.3, and 65.4, in Miller, *Encyclicals*.

61. See, for example, "Why the Encyclical Was Delayed," *The Tablet*, April 1, 1995, p. 432.

62. Author's interview with Cardinal Joseph Ratzinger, September 20, 1997.

63. *Catechism of the Catholic Church*, 2267. For the *Catechism*'s discussion of the traditional moral rationales for capital punishment, see the two preceding paragraphs, 2265 and 2266.

64. John Paul II, *Evangelium Vitae*, 56.2, in Miller, *Encyclicals*.

65. For an exploration of this and other controverted questions in *Evangelium Vitae*, see *Choosing Life: A Dialogue on* Evangelium Vitae, Kevin Wm. Wildes, SJ, and Alan C. Mitchell, eds. (Washington, D.C.: Georgetown University Press, 1997).

66. John Paul II, *Evangelium Vitae*, 73.1, in Miller, *Encyclicals* [emphasis in original].

67. Ibid., 73.3.

68. For a discussion of the moral ground of the Pope's position on legislative responsibility in unsatisfactory circumstances, see Robert P. George's contribution to "The Gospel of Life: A Symposium," pp. 37–38.

69. Cited in "Bishops Praise Pope's 'Hymn to Life,'" *The Tablet*, April 8, 1995, p. 467.

70. Cited in ibid.

71. See, for example, Richard A. McCormick, SJ, "The Gospel of Life," *America*, 172:15 (April 29, 1995), pp. 10–17. For a bibliography of commentaries on *Evangelium Vitae*, see Miller, *Encyclicals*, pp. 788–789.

72. It certainly spoke to the concerns of the more than 10,000 Dutch men and women who, by 1998, had taken to carrying anti-euthanasia "passports" that read: "I request that no medical treatment be withheld on the grounds that the future quality of my life will be diminished, because I believe that this is not something that human beings can judge. I request that under no circumstances a life-ending treatment be administered because I am of the opinion that people do not have the right to end life." [Steven A. Ertelt, "Dutch Carry Cards That Say: Don't Kill Me, Doctor," *Pro-Life Infonet Digest*, October 20, 1998.]

73. Author's conversation with Pope John Paul II, March 20, 1997.

74. The encyclical could also be read as a critique of the Holy See's own diplomatic practice, although it was surely not intended as such. One American commentator, Russell Hittinger, pointed out that the Holy See had supported a UN-sponsored "Convention on the Rights of the Child" which sometimes abused the language of human rights with the same corrosive effect as did politicians and jurists who defended abortion and euthanasia as rights. Articles 12 and 13 of the Convention had eroded the natural moral authority of parents by defining "the child's right to express an opinion in matters affecting the child and to have that opinion heard," and "the right to seek, receive, and impart information through any media." As one critic put it, the Convention had declared it a human rights violation for a parent to tell an eight-year-old to just turn the television off and go to bed. Yet the Holy See had supported a Convention whose flaccid use of "rights" was conceptually linked to the crisis of "rights-talk" identified in *Evangelium Vitae* and the problems the Holy See had fought so vigorously at Cairo. Hittinger hoped that Vatican policy would eventually catch up with the encyclical. [See Hittinger's essay in "The Gospel of Life: A Symposium," p. 35.]

75. John Paul II, *Evangelium Vitae* 65.2, 65.3, in Miller, *Encyclicals*.

76. "The Only Rock of Our Age," *The Independent*, January 12, 1995, p. 15.

77. The biblical text is *John* 17.21. John Paul II had been struck by the appositeness of John XXIII's last words for years. On October 8, 1983, he quoted John XXIII's on his deathbed: "'I offer my life,' he said, 'for the Church, continuation of the Ecumenical Council, peace in the world, union of Christians . . . My earthly day is ending; but Christ lives and the Church goes on with her task; souls, souls, *ut unum sint, ut unum sint. . . .*' Those were his last words uttered on this earth." [John Paul II, *Prayers and Devotions*, ed. Bishop Peter Canisius Johannes van Lierde, OSA (New York: Viking, 1994), p. 213; the original text is in *L'Osservatore Romano*, October 9, 1983, pp. 1, 5.]

78. According to Cardinal Cassidy, John Paul submitted a draft text for the review of the Pontifical Council. The Pope had written the draft personally, in Polish, through his new dictation-and-editing system, and then had it translated into Italian for review and comment. Speculations and reports to the contrary notwithstanding, *Ut Unum Sint* was not a curial draft to which John Paul II added certain personal reflections. [Author's interview with Cardinal Edward Cassidy, September 5, 1996.]

79. John Paul II, *Ut Unum Sint*, 56.1, 57.1, in Miller, *Encyclicals*.

80. Ibid., 61. Here, John Paul was quoting the apostolic letter issued three weeks before, *Orientale Lumen* [Light from the East], which marked the centenary of Leo XIII's *Orientalium Dignitas* and celebrated the

Eastern Christian heritage as a patrimony common to the entire Church, with which Western Christians must become more familiar. "Every day," the Pope wrote, "I have a growing desire to go over the history of the Churches, in order to write at least a history of our unity and thus return to the time when, after the Death and Resurrection of the Lord Jesus, the Gospel spread to the most varied cultures and a most fruitful exchange began which still today is evident in the liturgies of the Churches." [*Orientale Lumen*, 18, in *OR* (EWE), May 3, 1995.]

81. John Paul II, *Ut Unum Sint*, 88, in Miller, *Encyclicals*.

82. Ibid., 95.2.

83. Ibid., 96.

84. See ibid., 54.2, 57.1.

85. Richard John Neuhaus, "That They May Be One," *First Things* 56 (October 1995), p. 74.

86. Cited in Edward Idris Cassidy, "'That They May All Be One': The Imperatives and Prospects of Christian Unity," *First Things* 69 (January 1997), p. 36. For the full text of Raiser's lecture, see *Centro Pro Unione Semi-Annual Bulletin* #48 (Fall 1995).

87. In 1997, Dr. Raiser also suggested that the Pope's proposal for a common reflection on how a primatial office of unity could be exercised for the benefit of all Christians "begs the question. The issue is not only the different ways of exercising his office, but the rationale behind papal primacy itself. That's still very difficult for me to get hold of." [Gabriel Meyer, "World Council of Churches Chief Counts on Roman Participation," *National Catholic Register*, January 5–11, 1997, p. 5.]

88. John Paul II, homily for the solemnity of Sts. Peter and Paul, *OR* [EWE], July 5, 1995, pp. 6–7 [emphasis in original].

89. "Ecumenical Patriarch's Homily for 29 June," *OR* [EWE], July 12, 1995, p. 4; "Common Declaration," in ibid., p. 5.

90. Ecumenical Patriarch Bartholomew's meditations may be found in Pontifical Council for Promoting Christian Unity *Information Service* #86 (1994/II–III), pp. 112–124. Sister Minke's meditations may be found in ibid., #89 (1995/II-III), pp. 73–82. These invitations were the initiative of the Master of Pontifical Liturgical Ceremonies, Monsignor Piero Marini, who discussed the proposal with the Pontifical Council for Promoting Christian Unity. The invitations were then personally authorized by John Paul II. [Author's interview with Monsignor Piero Marini, December 9, 1996.]

91. "Statements of the Pope in the Czech Republic, May 20–24,1995," Pontifical Council for Promoting Christian Unity *Information Service* #89 (1995/II–III), p. 69 [emphasis in original]. The correspondence between the Czech Protestant leaders, and Cardinal Cassidy and the Pope, is in ibid., pp. 64–69.

92. "Pope Pays Tribute to Calvinists," *The Independent*, July 3, 1995, p. 9.

93. John Paul II, "Forgive One Another's Wrongs," *OR* [EWE], April 30, 1997, p. 3.

94. "Pope to Archbishop," *OR* [EWE], December 11, 1996.

95. John Paul II, "Women: Teachers of Peace," 4, in *OR* [EWE], December 14, 1995, pp. 1–2.

96. John Paul II, *Letter to Women*, 6, in *OR* [EWE], July 12, 1995, pp. 1–3.

97. These addresses began on June 18 and concluded on September 3, 1995. They may be found in *OR* [EWE], June 21, 1995, p. 1 (for the Angelus address of June 18 on equality of personhood); *OR* [EWE], June 28, 1995, p. 1 (for the Angelus address of June 25 on the need to build a "culture of equality"); *OR* [EWE], July 12, 1995, p. 1 (for the Angelus address of July 9 on the complementarity and reciprocity of women and men); *OR* [EWE], July 19, 1995, p. 1 (for the Angelus address of July 16 on women as guardians of life); *OR* [EWE], July 26, 1995, p. 1 (for the Angelus address of July 23 on the "feminine genius" essential for society); *OR* [EWE], August 2, 1995, p. 1 (for the Angelus address of July 30 on women as the primary educators of early childhood); *OR* [EWE], August 9–16, 1995 (for the Angelus address of August 6 on women and the world of culture); *OR* [EWE], August 23, 1995, p. 8 (for the Angelus address of August 13 on women in service to the poor and sick) and p. 1 (for the Angelus address of August 20 on equity for working mothers); *OR* [EWE], August 30, 1995, p. 1 (for the Angelus address of August 27 on women in politics); and *OR* [EWE], September 6, 1995, p. 1 (for the Angelus address of September 3 on women in the Church).

98. John Paul II, "1995 Letter to Priests for Holy Thursday," *OR* [EWE], April 12, 1995, pp. 6–7 [emphasis in original].

99. John Paul II, "Message to Mrs. Gertrude Mongella," *OR* [EWE], May 31, 1995, pp. 2, 7 [emphasis in original]; author's conversation with Pope John Paul II, December 13, 1997.

100. Mrs. Mongella spoke to the Italian Catholic daily, *Avvenire*. See "Worldwatch," *Catholic World Report*, August/September 1995, p. 7.

101. Letter to the author from Janne Haaland Matlary, February 14, 1997. Dr. Matlary was named State Secretary to the Foreign Minister of Norway (deputy secretary or undersecretary in other systems) in October 1997.

102. Annabel Miller, "The Holy See in the Public Square," *The Tablet*, September 23, 1995, p. 1192.

103. Mary Ann Glendon, "What Happened at Beijing," *First Things* 59 (January 1996), p. 30.

104. Author's interview with Joaquín Navarro-Valls, December 18, 1997.

105. Mary Ann Glendon, "What Happened at Beijing," p. 30.

106. See ibid. The full text of Professor Glendon's opening statement is in *OR* [EWE], September 13, 1995, pp. 4–5.

107. Author's interview with Monsignor Peter Elliott, September 22, 1997.

108. The Clinton administration was determined to avoid a direct conflict with the Holy See at Beijing, as there had been before and during the 1994 Cairo world population conference. The new U.S. strategy of working discreetly through other delegations to advance the administration's right-to-abortion agenda

may have been influenced by a set of cables from the U.S. Embassy to the Holy See to the Department of State in Washington in June 1995. The cable described the "skill and tenacity" of Vatican diplomats at Cairo and the "public affairs virtuosity" of Joaquín Navarro-Valls. The Vatican, according to one cable, had "used the media shrewdly to advertise its views" on the impending Beijing conference, and it was likely, the cable concluded, that the Holy See would play as assertive a role in Beijing as it had in Cairo. [Messages 166/95, 167/95, 172/95, 187/95, and 200/95 to the Secretary of State from Embassy Vatican.]

109. Memorandum to the author from Mary Ann Glendon, October 20, 1998.

110. See Mary Ann Glendon, "What Happened at Beijing," for a more detailed analysis of the EU coalition's proposals.

111. Author's interview with Mary Ann Glendon, September 6, 1998.

112. The press release read as follows:

After five days of negotiations at the Fourth World Conference on Women, the Holy See delegation has expressed its concern that a minority coalition is vigorously blocking efforts to bring the Beijing draft Declaration and Program of Action into conformity with the United Nations Universal Declaration of Human Rights and other basic human rights documents. The European Union figures prominently in this group that is impeding consensus.

Pointing out that the conference participants have no authority to undermine the pillars of the human rights tradition, Spokesperson Dr. Joaquín Navarro-Valls cited five respects in which the positions of such delegations are at odds with foundational human rights documents and principles. He [also] criticized the delegations' selective use of human rights language.

1. Where the Universal Declaration provides that "recognition of their inherent dignity" and equal rights of all human beings is the very "foundation of freedom, justice, and peace," a determined coalition of Beijing negotiators is making vigorous efforts to remove all references to human dignity from the Beijing draft.

2. The Universal Declaration makes marriage a fundamental right and provides that "the family is the natural and fundamental group unit of society and is entitled to protection by society and the State." At Beijing, the draft document casts marriage and the family negatively as impediments to women's self-realization (e.g., as associated with violence). Several negotiators, moreover, are pressing to change "family" to the politically correct and ambiguous word "families"—which lends itself to the interpretation that any group of unrelated people may call itself a family.

3. The Universal Declaration provides that "Everyone has the right to freedom of thought, conscience, and religion . . . [including] freedom, either alone or in community with others and in public or private, to manifest his religion or belief in teaching, practice, worship and observance." At Beijing, an active coalition has aggressively sought to remove all references to religion, morals, ethics, and spirituality, except where religion is portrayed negatively (e.g., as associated with intolerance or extremism).

4. The Universal Declaration provides that "Motherhood and childhood are entitled to special care and protection." Beijing negotiators have quashed references to motherhood except where it appears in a negative light.

5. The Universal Declaration and the Convention on the Rights of the Child make special provision for parents' rights and responsibilities concerning the education and upbringing of their children. Beijing negotiators are attempting to eliminate all recognition of parental rights and responsibilities from key sections of the draft—even rejecting direct quotations from the Convention on the Rights of the Child.

The Holy See delegation, in calling attention to these surprising positions, expressed puzzlement about the stances of these negotiators—in view of the fact that most of their own national constitutions mirror the above-cited provisions of the international human rights documents. Surely the provisions of the Universal Declaration of Human Rights should not be so casually brushed aside, he said. [Copy provided to the author by Professor Mary Ann Glendon.]

113. Author's interviews with Joaquín Navarro-Valls, December 13, 1997, and Mary Ann Glendon, September 6, 1998.

114. Mary Ann Glendon, closing statement at the Fourth World Conference on Women, *OR* [EWE], September 20, 1995, p. 4.

A full set of Holy See texts and documents relating to the Fourth World Conference on Women may be found in *Serving the Human Family: The Holy See at the Major United Nations Conferences*, ed. Carl J. Marucci (New York: Path to Peace Foundation, 1997), pp. 415–548.

115. Glendon believed there were some intriguing, unresolved questions about the way the conference had played itself out: "What deals did the affluent nations make with their client states? Why did the EU caucus champion an agenda so far removed from the urgent concerns of most of the world's women? Why did delegates from countries with strong family protection provisions in their constitutions (e.g., Germany, Ireland, Italy) not break ranks with the EU when it attacked the spirit of those provisions? Why were the conference documents so skewed from the beginning? Who paid for the thousands of lobbyists . . . whose main interest was not in women's needs and rights, but in controlling women's fertility?" [Mary Ann Glendon, "What Happened at Beijing," p. 35.] The lack of press interest in such questions post-conference was telling.

116. See Robert D. Kaplan, *The Ends of the Earth: From Togo to Turkmenistan, from Iran to Cambodia, a Journey to the Frontiers of Anarchy* (New York: Vintage Books, 1997), and Paul Johnson, "Wanted: A New Imperialism," *National Review*, December 14, 1992.

117. Author's interview with Cardinal Francis Arinze, November 9, 1996.

The signing of *Ecclesia in Africa* was, Cardinal Arinze believed, another moment in which John Paul was helping new Christians understand that they are as much a part of the Church as Christians who forebears were evangelized in the first millennium. When John Paul came to Nigeria in 1982, Arinze recalled, a local priest had remarked, almost with a sense of wonder, "The Pope is here today, we are the center of the Church today." John Paul's presence had helped this priest and his people to realize in the concrete, Arinze said, that "the Church is not something over there, in the Vatican, the Church is us, including the Africans . . . and when he leaves, he leaves people with the experience that we are the Church, all of us, we belong, we count."

118. John Paul II, *Ecclesia in Africa*, 62, in *OR* [EWE], September 20, 1995.

119. Ibid., 64, with the Pope directly quoting Propositions 35–37 approved by the Synod for Africa.

120. Author's interview with Cardinal Francis Arinze, December 14, 1996.

121. "Two Rwandan Priests Receive Death Penalty," *National Catholic Register*, April 26–May 2, 1998.

122. John Paul II, homily at the beatification of Father Cyprian Michael Iwene Tansi, *OR* [EWE], March 25, 1998, pp. 1–2 [emphases in original].

123. James Rupert, "Nigerians Throng to Papal Mass," *Washington Post*, March 23, 1998, p. A14.

124. Author's interview with Joaquín Navarro-Valls, March 6, 1996.

125. Some things in Nicaragua hadn't changed. Miguel d'Escoto remained a militant Sandinista, and Ernesto Cardenal was still suspended from functioning as a priest. Fernando Cardenal, however, had returned to the Jesuits after disengaging himself from Sandinista politics. There were even opportunities for a bit of banter between old foes. Several months after the Pope's 1996 visit, Cardinal Miguel Obando Bravo, whose anti-Sandinista resistance had been vindicated by the voters, ran into former Commandante Tomas Borgé, once the hardest of Sandinista hard-liners. Obando had founded Redemptoris Mater [Mother of the Redeemer] University, a new Catholic institution, in a building Borgé had once used as the communications center of his internal security network. When Borgé met the cardinal in the headquarters the commandante had once rebuilt, he said a bit ruefully, "You never know who you'll be working for." Obando said that was right, "but I also worked for you: you occupied my offices, our universities, our vehicles, our publishing companies." Borgé had to laugh. [Author's interview with Cardinal Miguel Obando Bravo, SDB, November 24, 1997.]

126. "Holy Father's Inflight Press Interview," *OR* [EWE], February 14, 1996, p. 7; author's interview with Monsignor Vincenzo Paglia, March 25, 1997.

127. John Paul II, "Address to the Fiftieth General Assembly of the United Nations Organization," 1–2 [emphasis in original; hereinafter, John Paul II, *UN-II*].

128. Ibid., 9 [emphasis in original].

129. Ibid., 9–10, 12.

130. Ibid., 16 [emphases in original].

131. Ibid.

132. Ibid., 17.

133. Ibid., 18 [emphasis in original].

134. "The Pope in Newark: Vespers at Sacred Heart Cathedral," *OR* [EWE], October 11, 1995, p. 2.

135. See "The Pope in Brooklyn: Mass at Aqueduct Racecourse," in ibid., pp. 4–5.

136. Robert D. McFadden, "125,000 Join Pope at Mass in Central Park 'Basilica,'" *New York Times*, October 8, 1995.

137. "Holy Father Celebrates Mass in New York," in ibid., pp. 1, 7 [emphasis in original].

138. This was a formulation first coined by England's great historian of liberty, Lord Acton, and frequently cited by the American Jesuit John Courtney Murray, one of the architects, along with Karol Wojtyła, of Vatican II's *Declaration on Religious Freedom*. ["The Pope in Baltimore: Mass at Camden Yards," in ibid., pp. 11, 13.]

139. "The Pope in Baltimore: Visit to the Cathedral," in ibid., p. 13 [emphasis in original].

140. Paul Gigot, "Pope Offers Cure for Those O.J. Blues," *Wall Street Journal*, October 6, 1995.

141. "'The Moral Structure of Freedom,'" *Wall Street Journal*, October 6, 1995 [emphasis in original].

The *New York Times*'s Peter Steinfels dug into one of the mysteries of the Pope's UN address, a reference to the fifteenth-century Cracovian academic, Paweł Włodkowic, whom Steinfels rightly saw as a crucial historic figure in John Paul's understanding of religious freedom because of his rejection of forced conversion at the Council of Constance. The reference, Steinfels suggested, was a subtle reminder to the fifty-year-old UN that the Catholic Church, and particularly the Church in east central Europe, had been wrestling with questions of religious freedom, ethnicity, ethnic cleansing, and so forth for a very long time. The Pope's interest in Paweł Włodkowic, whom he had cited in numerous addresses during the pontificate, also had personal dimensions: Włodkowic's thought was the academic specialty of Dr. Ludwig Ehrlich, a professor of international law, who was the father of Sister Emilia Ehrlich, OSU (John Paul's English tutor and the manager of his personal Vatican library), and an acquaintance of Cardinal Wojtyła's in Kraków. [See Peter Steinfels, "Beliefs," *New York Times*, October 14, 1995; author's interview with Sister Emilia Ehrlich, OSU, March 21, 1997.]

142. "'We Must Not Be Afraid of Man,'" *Baltimore Sun*, October 10, 1995.

For a review of the press coverage of the 1995 papal pilgrimage to the U.S., see James Martin, "The Pope and the Media," *America*, October 28, 1995, pp. 24–25.

143. "TWA Papal Charter Gets Seal of Approval," *USA Today*, October 10, 1995, p. 8B.

144. The texts are in *OR* [EWE], October 18, 1995, October 25, 1995, and November 8, 1995.

145. See *OR* [EWE], November 15, 1995, p. 1.

146. John Paul II, Apostolic Letter for the fourth centenary of the Union of Brest, *OR* [EWE], November 22, 1995, pp. 6–8.

147. "Closing Mass of Synod for Lebanon," *OR* December 20/27, 1995, p. 3.

148. See "Message of the Special Synod for Lebanon," in ibid., p. 11; the Synod was citing John Paul II's January 1991 address to the diplomatic corps accredited to the Holy See.

149. See "Appeals and Announcements," in "General Index for 1995," *OR* [EWE], December 20–27, 1995, p. 15.

150. See "Jean Paul II souffrait de la maladie de Parkinson," *Le Monde*, September 10, 1996, p. 3.

151. Author's interview with Joaquín Navarro-Valls, March 20, 1997.

152. Ibid.; author's interview with Anna Karoń-Ostrowska, April 8, 1997.

153. This reticence was European as well as curial, and paralleled the reticence displayed during the last illness of French President François Mitterand. But the Church, a universal institution, cannot be managed by local standards exclusively, especially when a prior precedent of transparency-through-consultation had been set.

154. Author's interview with Cardinal John J. O'Connor, November 8, 1996.

155. On the pre-Synod process, see "Editor's Introduction to *Vita Consecrata*," in Miller, *Exhortations*, p. 617.

156. John Paul II, *Vita Consecrata*, 3.1, in ibid.

157. See ibid., 19.3.

158. See ibid., 14.3.

159. Ibid., 104.3 [emphasis in original].

160. See ibid., 23.2–3.

161. See ibid., 34.2.

162. See ibid., 91.1–2.

163. Ibid., 87.

164. Ibid., 88.1.

165. Ibid., 87.

166. Author's interviews with John Farren, OP, September 29 and November 17, 1997.

167. "Editor's Introduction to *Vita Consecrata*," in Miller, *Exhortations*, pp. 625–626.

168. For an analysis of the growth of religious communities that take a more classic view of the consecrated life and a refutation of the stereotype of these communities as anti–Vatican II, see Albert DiIanni, SM, "A View of Religious Vocations," *America* 178:6 (February 28, 1998), pp. 8–12.

169. "Sunday Angelus from Gemelli Hospital," *OR* [EWE], October 16, 1996, p. 1.

170. "Vatican Number Two" was Castel Gandolfo.

171. Citations from Josip Stilinovic, "The Witness of Suffering," *Catholic World Report*, June 1998, pp. 30–31.

172. John Paul II, homily at 50th anniversary Mass, *OR* [EWE], November 13, 1996, pp. 1–2.

173. John Paul II, Sunday Angelus address on November 10, 1996, *OR* [EWE], November 13, 1996, p. 2 [emphases in original].

174. John Paul II, *Gift and Mystery*, pp. 89, 100.

CHAPTER 20

A Reasonable Faith: Beyond a Century of Delusions

1. "The Pope in Cuba: Arrival at Jose Martí Airport in Havana," *OR* [EWE], January 28, 1998, p. 2 [first emphasis added; second emphasis in original]. On the alleged parallels between John Paul II and Castro, see Tad Szulc, "When the Pope Visits Castro," *Parade*, December 14, 1997, pp. 6–9.

2. On July 10, 1993, the bishops of the Upper Rhine province, Bishop Karl Lehmann of Mainz, Archbishop Oskar Saier of Freiburg, and Bishop Walter Kasper of Rottenburg-Stuttgart, issued a joint pastoral letter and a set of "principles of pastoral care" that they hoped would advance discussion of the situation of the divorced-and-remarried. The bishops urged Catholics to be "in the forefront of the struggle for successful marriages of lifelong fidelity" and to "work against the trend that would regard divorce-and-remarriage as something normal." The Church, they proposed, has no "right to disregard the teaching of Jesus regarding the indissolubility of marriage," which was rooted, not in arbitrary legalities, but in the original order of creation; moreover, the defense of the indissolubility of marriage "renders an indispensable service to humankind." But neither could the Church, which carried on Christ's ministry of mercy and redemption, "shut its eyes to the failure of many marriages."

Confirming classic Catholic doctrine that was too often ignored or misunderstood, the bishops insisted that divorced-and-remarried people "are and remain members of the Church," who deserve "special care" and must be made to feel "that they are accepted by the congregation," which "understands their difficult situation." But as divorced-and-remarried Catholics returned to active participation in the lives of their congregations, the question inevitably arose: could that participation include the reception of communion at Mass? The bishops affirmed the Church's teaching that "divorced-and-remarried people cannot be admitted to the Eucharistic feast as they find themselves in life situations that are in objective contradiction to the essence of Christian marriage." Anyone who acted otherwise "does so contrary to the order of the Church."

But a distinction should be made, the bishops argued, between "admitting" the divorced-and-remarried to communion (which was a public act that contradicted the Church's teaching) and the divorced-and-remarried "approaching" communion after an intense pastoral dialogue with a priest had led them to the conviction, in conscience, that this was appropriate. That conviction, the bishops proposed, "must be respected by the Church and the congregation." The bishops suggested that this distinction, which they believed guaranteed the integrity of the Church's teaching and responded faithfully to extremely difficult pastoral circumstances, might be particularly appropriate in three particularly hard cases: one in which a remarried person had been abandoned by a first spouse; one in which a prior marriage could not be annulled according to canon law for lack of evidence, despite the remarried person's conscientious conviction that no sacramental marriage had been entered into; and one in which the abandonment of a second, civil marriage would involve a serious injustice to others, including the children of that marriage. [See "Pastoral Ministry: The Divorced and Remarried," *Origins* 23:38 (March 10, 1994), pp. 670–676).]

In late December 1993, the three bishops received a letter from the Congregation for the Doctrine of the Faith [CDF] indicating that they had not "fully upheld" the Church's doctrine in their letter and pastoral guidelines. In February 1994, the bishops met with officials of CDF for a lengthy and frank discussion of the issues, which, they reported, cleared up certain misunderstandings based on distorted media reports and unauthorized, edited translations of their letter and guidelines. But "no full agreement . . . could be reached on the question of the reception of communion." After a further discussion with the Germans in June 1994, CDF issued a letter to all the world's bishops, reiterating that the divorced-and-remarried "cannot receive communion" as long as they "find themselves in "a situation that objectively contravenes God's law."

The theological gravamen of the issue, CDF continued, was the spousal nature of the Church: to be divorced-and-remarried was to be living in a situation that contradicted, objectively, the indissoluble "union of love between Christ and his Church which is signified and effected by the Eucharist." To admit the divorced-and-remarried to communion would be to concede that marriages could be dissolved; that seemed to suggest that the love of Christ for the Church could be dissolved. But the indissolubility of that spousal love was the truth of faith celebrated in the Eucharist and by the reception of communion. The CDF letter acknowledged that the German proposal was not for a "general admission of the divorced-and-remarried to eucharistic communion," and went on to note that canon law "offers new ways to demonstrate the nullity of a previous marriage." Yet CDF's conclusion did not admit the possibility of what the German bishops proposed: that in specific cases divorced-and-remarried Catholics could "approach holy communion when they consider themselves authorized [by] a judgment of conscience to do so," and that a priest could "respect [this] decision in conscience to approach holy communion, without this implying an official authorization." This was impossible, according to CDF, because the reception of communion, like a marriage, was an inherently public reality. [See "Reception of Communion: Divorced-and-Remarried Catholics," *Origins* 24:20 (October 27, 1994), pp. 337, 339–341.]

In a letter to their priests and people dated October 14, 1994, the three German bishops wrote that there was no doctrinal disagreement between them and CDF; nor had they been attempting a unilateral revision of canon law. They further admitted that "we could not and do not wish to claim that we . . . found a solution that is satisfactory in every respect." The CDF letter was not, the bishops had been assured, addressed "to our position in particular," but was a response to a widespread discussion throughout the Church. Yet it was the German distinction between "admitting" to communion and a conscientious decision to "approach" communion which CDF had rejected, and the bishops admitted as much when they wrote that "certain statements in our pastoral letter and in the principles are not accepted by the universal Church and therefore cannot be the binding norm of pastoral practice." They concluded by promising to continue the dialogue, "to come up with answers that are capable of generating a consensus and that are theologically and pastorally responsible."

Reaction to the CDF letter in Germany was harsh: priests were defiant and petitions were organized denouncing John Paul as a shepherd who drove his straying sheep "mercilessly over the cliff." The Central Committee of German Catholics, the country's leading lay organization, was critical. Professor Norbert Greinacher of Tübingen, who had previously condemned the Pope's "declaration of war" on theological liberals, now argued that the Church was entering its *Götterdämmerüng*, the twilight of its spiritual authority. [Patricia Clough, "German Catholics Rebel Against Rome," *The Sunday Times* (London), November 27, 1994.] Although the three German bishops avoided doing so, it was not difficult for others to present the case as one of doctrinal rigidity vs. pastoral sensitivity. The understandable emotions involved were, in this as in other instances, compounded by the image of "authoritarian" many German theologians had successfully pinned on John Paul II and Cardinal Ratzinger.

But perhaps this was a situation where there was no new solution at the legal level. Cardinal Ratzinger suggested as much in a 1996 interview. There, he proposed that, while the principles remained unchangeable, "experienced pastors" could perhaps make "an extrajuridical determination that the first marriage did not exist." [Joseph Cardinal Ratzinger, *Salt of the Earth*, p. 207.] Cardinal Christoph Schönborn of Vienna, the general editor of the *Catechism of the Catholic Church*, also believed that this was an area of the Church's life in which what he termed an "ultimate clarification" was simply impossible at the legal level. [Author's interview with Archbishop Christoph Schönborn, OP, December 11, 1997.] Could the nullity of a marriage become a pastoral rather than juridical determination without jeopardizing the truth about marriage? In a world accustomed to thinking that every problem was susceptible to a legal solution, this was another sign of contradiction; given the degree to which that distinctively modern assumption had entered Catholic consciousness, it also seemed unlikely to meet the criticism of divorced-and-remarried Catholics who felt that they were being treated as second-class members of the Church. But it was the point to which the German bishops' proposal had led the discussion, which was certain to remain one of the most difficult in the Catholic world well into the twenty-first century.

3. John Paul II, homily in Paderborn, Germany, *OR* [EWE], July 3, 1996, pp. 3, 9 [emphasis in original].

4. John Paul II, address to the German Bishops' Conference, in ibid., pp. 6–8.

5. John Paul II, homily in Berlin, *OR* [EWE], June 26, 1996, pp. 1–2.
The Pope's homily also included a defense of Pope Pius XII:

On the basis of his clear principles, Bernhard Lichtenberg spoke and acted independently and fearlessly. Nevertheless, he was almost overcome with joy and happiness when his Bishop, Konrad von Preysing, upon his last prison visit at the end of September 1943, relayed to him a message from my predecessor, Pius XII, in which he expressed his deepest sympathy and paternal appreciation. Whoever is not hampered by cheap polemics knows full well what Pius XII thought about the Nazi regime and how much he did to help the countless people who were persecuted by that regime. [Ibid., p. 2.]

6. John Paul II, Angelus address, in ibid., p. 3.

7. Author's interview with Rocco Buttiglione, February 25, 1997.

8. John Paul II, homily in Reims, *OR* [EWE], September 25, 1996, pp. 1, 4.

9. Those contributions were given official recognition on October 19, 1997, when John Paul proclaimed St. Thérèse of Lisieux a Doctor of the Church, Catholicism's highest accolade for theological accomplishment. The announcement of this, made after the closing Mass at Longchamp on August 24, produced a great burst of applause and much waving of the French *tricolore* on the racecourse infield.

10. The texts of John Paul II's pilgrimage to France during WYD '97 may be found in *OR* [EWE], August 27, 1997, and September 3, 1997.

11. Author's interview with Archbishop Jean-Louis Tauran, November 14, 1997.

12. In addition to roiling domestic Polish politics, Wałęsa, during his presidency, had considered an offer from rogue ex-KGB elements to sell Poland nuclear weapons. It was made clear to him that the Pope would regard any such acquisition as a very bad idea. For numerous reasons the scheme was dropped. [See Sikorski, *Full Circle*, pp. 214–216; author's conversation with Pope John Paul II, December 16, 1998.]

13. One of the country's most knowledgeable interpreters of John Paul's thought, the Dominican Maciej Zięba, did a three-month long series of weekly interviews on Polish public television before the Pope arrived, laying to rest the image of "two Wojtyłas" (the enlightened social progressive and the doctrinal reactionary) by demonstrating how John Paul's teaching was a seamless garment; gathered into book form and published by Znak under the title *Niezwykły Pontyfikat* [*Extraordinary Pontificate*], the book sold briskly throughout the country. Father Zięba's Kraków-based *Tertio Millennio* Institute also sponsored a year-long series of intellectual encounters at which Church leaders, politicians, and journalists—believers and unbelievers alike—met to consider the question, "To what Poland will the Pope return?" Other institutes picked up the idea and conducted similar dialogues.

14. Author's interview with Henryk Woźniakowski, June 5, 1997.

15. Unless otherwise noted, citations of papal addresses during the June 1997 pilgrimage are taken from texts provided by KAI.

16. The texts of John Paul II's 1997 Polish pilgrimage may be found in *OR* [EWE], June 11, 1997, June 18, 1997, June 25, 1997, and July 2, 1997.

17. In the years after communism, Polish Catholicism had not suffered the meltdown many Western observers predicted. In 1993, a survey indicated that eighty-three percent of the population practiced Catholicism "systematically" (fifty-two percent) or "occasionally" (thirty-one percent). Another eleven percent said that they "rarely" practiced. Among eighteen- and nineteen-year-olds, fifty-four percent practiced "systematically" and another twenty-eight percent "occasionally." The percentage of "systematic" practitioners was two points higher among those with advanced academic degrees than among less-educated workers. While recruitment to the priesthood diminished somewhat in the immediate aftermath of the Revolution of 1989, Polish seminaries remained remarkably full by Western standards. Ordinations each year from 1988 to 1992 averaged about 1,100 young men, many of whom were sent to Latin America or Africa as missionaries. The first-year seminary class in 1992 was larger than in 1991, reversing a trend since the peak year of 1987. Poland's religious orders also remained vigorous in the 1990s. [For further data, see George Weigel, "Poland, The Church in, *New Catholic Encyclopedia*, volume 19.]

18. It also had a public effect. In September 1997, John Paul II's politics of culture, combined with exceptional post-communist incompetence in handling a series of catastrophic floods in July, resulted in an election that returned a reconfigured Solidarity coalition to power in the Sejm.

19. See "Holy Father Begins 'Great Prayer for Italy,'" in *OR* [EWE], March 30, 1994, pp. 7–8, and John Paul II, homily at Loreto, in *OR* [EWE], December 21–28, 1994, pp. 3–4.

20. John Paul II, address to the young at a prayer vigil during the National Eucharistic Congress in Bologna, *OR* [EWE], October 8, 1997, p. 7.

21. Author's interviews with Rocco Buttiglione, February 25 and 27, 1997.

22. Author's interview with Leonardo Mondadori, January 16, 1997.

23. Author's interview with Massimo D'Alema, December 10, 1997.

24. The printing press, which would have enabled the Cuban Church to print religious books and catechetical materials, had been purchased by the New York–based Northeast Center for Hispanic Catholic Activities, an agency sponsored by the Catholic bishops of the northeast United States. Under the skillful leadership of its director, Mario Paredes, the Center played a quiet but crucial role in facilitating the "dance" between the Castro regime and the Holy See.

25. Author's interview with Mario Paredes, June 27, 1997; Lorenzo Albacete, "The Poet and the Revolutionary," *The New Yorker*, January 26, 1998.

26. Author's interview with Joaquín Navarro-Valls, December 18, 1997.

27. John Paul II, homily in Santa Clara, *OR* [EWE], January 28, 1998, pp. 3–4 [emphasis in original]. Later that day, four Americans lunching in a restaurant located on the cove from which Ernest Hemingway's "old man" had set off to the sea, were stopped by a guitar-playing gentleman in his seventies. He wanted to tell somebody, he said in broken English, how moved he had been by the Pope's words about the family; for forty years he had been trying to hold his own together under the pressures of an atheistic, totalitarian regime.

28. John Paul II, homily in Camagüey, in ibid., p. 4 [emphases in original].

29. "The Pope in Cuba: 'Meeting at the University of Havana,'" *OR* [EWE], February 4, 1998, p. 4 [emphasis in original].

30. John Paul II, homily in Santiago de Cuba, in ibid., pp. 5, 7.

31. John Paul II, homily in Havana, in *OR* [EWE], January 28, 1998, pp. 1–2 [emphasis in original].

32. John Paul's address to the Cuban bishops is in *OR* [EWE], June 24, 1998, p. 5.

33. On the slow evolution of a civil society in Cuba, see Carl Gershman, "Thanks to the Pope, Civil Society Stirs in Cuba," *Wall Street Journal*, September 18, 1998, p. A11.

34. On this and other points, see Richard John Neuhaus, "The Cuban Revolutions," *First Things* 83 (May 1998), pp. 23–28.

35. *The Catholic Review* [Baltimore], June 25, 1997.

36. "Pope Welcomes Bishops of Vietnam on Ad Limina," Vatican Information Service VIS 961216 (490), December 14, 1996.

37. Author's interview with Archbishop Claudio Celli, October 15, 1998. Celli also visited Laos, Myanmar (Burma), and Cambodia in attempts to "regularize" the Church's position in those countries; the Holy See and Cambodia established diplomatic relations in 1994.

38. "In Brief," *National Catholic Register*, September 28–October 4, 1997, p. 1, citing the news service "Fides," published by the Congregation for the Evangelization of Peoples.

39. *National Catholic Register*, August 23–29, 1998, p. 1.

40. "The Pope in Sarajevo: Arrival at Sarajevo Airport," *OR* [EWE], April 16, 1997, p. 2 [emphasis in original].

41. "The Pope in Sarajevo: Vespers with Priests and Religious," in ibid., p. 3 [emphasis in original].

42. John Paul II, homily in Sarajevo, in ibid., April 16, 1997 [emphasis in original].

43. John Mintz, "Men in Papal Bomb Plot Termed Close to Bin-Laden," *Washington Post*, August 22, 1998.

44. "Visit to Republic of Lebanon: Meeting with Youth," *OR* [EWE], May 21, 1997, pp. 2–3.

45. Author's conversation with Celestine Bohlen, June 7, 1997.

46. Author's conversation with Pope John Paul II, September 30, 1997.

47. Ibid. Eighteen months after Mother Teresa's death, the Pope did agree to dispense with the normal five-year wating period before the formal process of seeking her beatification could be opened by the Archdiocese of Calcutta.

48. In early July, 1997, Patriarch Aleksy tried to revive the idea of a meeting with John Paul with a letter to Rome expressing the hope that such a meeting could still be arranged. No place or date was suggested, but Holy See spokesman Joaquín Navarro-Valls said that some encouragement had been taken from the fact that the letter expressed the hope for a meeting in the indeterminate future. The following year, in his Easter 1998 message, Aleksy continued to complain about "proselytism" and "aggressive triumphalism," and said that "unless serious and clear progress to resolve these problems is under way, the majority of Orthodoxy cannot accept a meeting with the Pope." In 1997, the Russian Orthodox Church was the major institutional supporter of a law "On Freedom of Conscience and Religious Association" that restricted the missionary activities of religious communities unknown in Russia until recent years. Evangelical Protestants were a primary target of the legislation, which the Catholic Church in Russia ineffectually opposed.

49. Details of the plans for the aborted meeting in Vienna and its aftermath are taken from the author's interview with Cardinal Edward Cassidy, September 19, 1997; from the Secretariat for Ecumenical and Interreligious Affairs *Newsletter on the Eastern Churches and Ecumenism* 21 (June 5, 1997), p. 1; from Arthur DuNunzio, "Far from Unity, *Catholic World Report* (August/September 1997), pp. 34–35; from "World Watch," *Catholic World Report*, June 1998, pp. 12–13; and from "World Watch," *Catholic World Report*, August/September 1998, p. 6.

50. Bartholomew I, "Dialogue, from an Orthodox Perspective," *Origins*, 27:20 (October 30, 1997), pp. 333, 335–337.

51. Author's interview with Ronald G. Roberson, CSP, October 31, 1997. Ecumenical Patriarch Bartholomew would later insist that his remarks about an "ontologically different" way in which Catholicism and Orthodoxy existed had been misinterpreted, suggesting that he had been referring to different ways of life rather than essential differences. (Author's interview with Ronald G. Roberson, CSP, March 1, 1999.)

52. "The Church in the World," *The Tablet*, February 14, 1998, p. 223.

53. John Paul II, *Spiritual Pilgrimage*, pp. 98–99.

54. See Daniel T. Wackerman, "The Pope's Maestro," *America* 171:17 (November 26, 1994), pp. 5–8, 26.

55. John Paul II, "The Roots of Anti-Judaism," *Origins* 27:22 (November 13, 1997), pp. 365, 367.

56. "Joint Press Communique: Meeting in Rome and Castel Gandolfo," in John Paul II, *Spiritual Pilgrimage*, p. 103.

57. Reactions to *We Remember*: Celestine Bohlen, "Vatican Repents Failure to Save Jews From Nazis," *New York Times*, March 17, 1998, pp. A1, A11; William Drozdiak, "Vatican Apologizes to Jews," *Washington Post*, March 17, 1998, pp. A1, 15; Paul Elie, "John Paul's Jewish Dilemma," *New York Times Magazine*, April 26, 1998, pp. 34–39.

58. Information on the *Joint Declaration* and *Response* is taken from the author's interviews with Cardinal

Edward Cassidy, October 10, 1998, and June 7, 1999, and Cardinal Joseph Ratzinger, December 16, 1998. See also Richard John Neuhaus, "Setback in Rome," *First Things* 86 (October 1998), pp. 80–82. A copy of Cardinal Cassidy's July 30, 1998, letter to Dr. Noko was provided to the author by Cardinal Cassidy. The texts of the *Joint Declaration* and *Response,* and Cardinal Cassidy's press conference statement on June 25, 1998, may be found in *Origins* 28:8 (July 16, 1998), pp. 120–132. Dr. Noko's letter to the LWF executive committee may be found in *Origins* 28:17 (October 8, 1998), pp. 288–290.

59. John Paul II, *Universi Dominici Gregis,* prologue.

60. Ibid., 44, 55, 61.

61. Ibid., prologue.

62. Ibid., 62.

63. Ibid., 74.

64. See Reese, *Inside the Vatican,* p. 87.

65. Author's conversation with Pope John Paul II, October 23, 1998.

66. Pope Pius XII was photographed by a physician during his death agonies and the pictures peddled to the tabloid press. The managers of popes also managed to botch Pius XII's embalming; the decomposing body could be heard bursting inside the casket during the pre-funeral ceremonies.

67. *Universi Dominici Gregis,* 30.

68. Ibid., 17.

69. Ibid., 77.

70. Ibid., prologue.

71. "World Watch," *Catholic World Report,* June 1998, pp. 10–11.

72. Dziwisz took as his episcopal motto *Sursum Corda* ["Lift up your hearts"], the phrase from the Mass that Henryk Siekiewicz used as the epigram for his great trilogy of novels.

73. Shortly after the consistory, two of the new cardinals died: Alberto Bovone, the Prefect of the Congregation for Saints, and Jean Balland, the archbishop of Lyons.

74. Author's interview with Irina Alberti, April 16, 1998; Vatican Information Service 980212 (February 10, 1998).

75. Author's interview with Tadeusz Styczeń, SDS, October 23, 1998. The texts of John Paul II's 1998 Austrian pilgrimage may be found in *OR* [EWE] June 24, 1998, July 1, 1998, and July 8, 1998.

76. "Austrian Catholics Vote for Sweeping Reforms to Church," *The Tablet,* October 31, 1998.

77. See *Catholic World Report,* June 1998, pp. 6–7.

78. "Portugal's Voters Reject Attempt to Liberalize Abortion Law," *National Catholic Register,* July 12–18, 1998, pp. 15–16.

79. Author's interview with Cardinal Edward Cassidy, October 10, 1998.

80. The *New York Times* headlined the story, "Attend Mass on Sundays, Pope Reminds the Wayward" [*New York Times,* July 8, 1998, p. A5]; "Catholics Told to Improve Mass Attendance: Pope Says Weekend Leisure Pursuits Must Leave Time for Obligatory Worship," readers of the *Washington Post* were informed [*Washington Post,* July 8, 1998, p. A20].

81. John Paul II, *Dies Domini,* 1, 2.

82. Ibid., 4.

83. Ibid., 11.

84. ". . . the Sabbath's position as the seventh day of the week suggests for the Lord's Day a complementary symbolism, much loved by the Fathers. Sunday is not only the first day, it is also the "eighth day," set within the sevenfold succession of days in a unique and transcendent position which evokes not only the beginning of time but also its end in the 'age to come.' Saint Basil explains that Sunday symbolizes the truly singular day which will follow the present time, the day without end which will know neither evening nor morning, the imperishable age which will never grow old; Sunday is the ceaseless foretelling of life without end which renews the hope of Christians and encourages them on their way." [Ibid., 26.]

85. Ibid., 30.

86. *New York Times,* July 24, 1998, p. A1.

87. On this point, see "Episcopal Conferences: Theological Bases," unpublished lecture delivered by Cardinal Francis George, OMI, September 8, 1998.

88. See *Lumen Gentium,* 12.

89. The diverse expressions of the Catholic charismatic renewal were likely the most numerous expression of this phenomenon after Vatican II. One of its manifestations, the "El Shaddai" movement in the Philippines, regularly drew between 800,000 and a million people to revival-type meetings every Saturday of the year. By the late 1990s, renewal movements and new communities with global reach and a significant numbers of members included the Focolare, the Neocatechumenal Way, Communion and Liberation, and the "Regnum Christi" movement associated with the Legionaries of Christ, a new religious community of priests. Opus Dei, which was fitted into the hierarchical structure of the Church through being created a "personal prelature," functions as a renewal movement but is not the quite the same, structurally. [Author's interviews with Archbishop Paul Cordes, March 22, 1997, and Cardinal J. Francis Stafford, December 18, 1998. See also Paul J. Cordes, *In the Midst of Our World: Forces of Spiritual Renewal* (San Francisco: Ignatius Press, 1988).]

90. The celebration in St. Peter's Square was preceded by a four-day-long international congress of "renewal movements and new ecclesial communities," as the curial terminology had it.

91. The testimonies may be found in *Il Papa e i Movimenti* (Milan: Edizioni San Paolo, 1998), pp. 17–39.

Chiara Lubich's spirituality, like John Paul II's, is deeply Carmelite, stressing Christ's abandonment on the Cross as the model of, and warrant for, abandoning one's own life to God's providential plan. The abandoned Christ, Chiara Lubich once said, "married atheism and God-forsakenness," which is the modern condition. [Author's interview with Chiara Lubich, February 25, 1997. See also Chiara Lubich, *Unity and Jesus Forsaken* (New York: New City Press, 1985).] John Paul II personally encouraged the stipulation in the Focolare's statutes specifying that a woman will always be the movement's president. [See *Chiara Lubich: A Life for Unity—An Interview with Franca Zambonini* (New York: New City Press, 1992), pp. 142–143.]

Luigi Giussani's most influential book is *The Religious Sense* (Montreal and Kingston: McGill-Queen's University Press, 1997).

92. The Pope's address is in *OR* [EWE], June 3, 1998, pp. 1–2.

93. See Paul J. Cordes, *Born of the Spirit: Renewal Movements in the Life of the Church* (South Bend, Ind.: Greenlawn Press, 1994), pp. 64–66.

94. John Paul II, homily for the canonization of Edith Stein, 2, in *OR* [EWE], October 14, 1998, p. 1; author's conversation with Pope John Paul II, October 23, 1998.

95. John Paul II, homily for the canonization of Edith Stein, 6.

96. Ibid., 4.

97. The canonization of St. Edith Stein was severely criticized by the Anti-Defamation League of B'nai B'rith [ADL], which charged that it was part of an attempt to "Christianize" the Holocaust and deflect attention from what ADL suggested was the considerable Christian responsibility for the Nazi genocide of the European Jews. Rabbi David Novak of the University of Toronto said of the ADL statement, "What it says in effect is that the Catholic Church killed Edith Stein and is now trying to cover up its guilt by making her a saint. It is an obscene statement." [See Abraham H. Foxman and Rabbi Leon Klenicki, "The Canonization of Edith Stein: An Unnecessary Problem," a statement issued by the Anti-Defamation League of B'nai B'rith; Rabbi Novak's comment is cited in *First Things* 90 (February 1999), p. 71.]

98. John Paul II, homily at twentieth anniversary Mass, 2, in *OR* [EWE], October 21, 1998, p. 2.

99. Author's conversation with Pope John Paul II, October 23, 1998.

100. John Paul II, *Fides et Ratio*, 1.

101. See ibid., 45–48.

102. See ibid., 48.

103. Cited in ibid., 79.

104. Ibid., 1.

105. Ibid., 107.

EPILOGUE

The Third Millennium: To See the Sun Rise

1. Author's interviews with Anna Karoń-Ostrowska, April 8, 1997, and Danuta Michałowska, April 22, 1997. *I Without Name* was subsequently produced on stage in London, and published in Poland as Volume 87 in the "*Więź* Library" series.

2. Statistics on the first twenty years of the pontificate of John Paul II are taken from the Vatican Information Service: "The 20 Years of John Paul II: 11th Longest Papacy in History" (# VIS 981013 [1500], "Some Statistical Data on the Pontificate of John Paul II" (# VIS 981013 [1930]), and "14 Million Attend General Audiences in 20 Years of Papacy," (# VIS 9810103 [60]).

3. In the 1998 encyclical *Fides et Ratio,* John Paul wrote that *Gaudium et Spes* 22 had been, throughout the pontificate, "one of the constant reference-points of my teaching." [*Fides et Ratio*, 60.]

4. On this point, see Ratzinger, *Principles of Catholic Theology*, p. 378.

5. John Paul II, *UN-II*, 2.

6. Balthasar, *In the Fullness of Faith*, p. 105.

7. One who was excommunicated, the Sri Lankan Tissa Balasuriya, OMI, was reconciled to the Church in short order.

8. Author's interview with Teresa Malecka, November 9, 1998.

9. On these points, see Balthasar, *In the Fullness of Faith*, pp. 55–57.

10. On "tradition" beginning inside the Trinity, see Hans Urs von Balthsar, *Theo-Drama IV: The Action* (San Francisco: Ignatius Press, 1994), pp. 52–53.

11. Historian of doctrine Jaroslav Pelikan claims that the pedigree of this famous distinction is impossible to determine; see Pelikan, *The Melody of Theology: A Philosophical Dictionary* (Cambridge, Mass.: Harvard University Press, 1988), pp. 252ff.

12. Author's conversation with Pope John Paul II, December 13, 1997.

13. For a critical yet affirming view of the Synod from inside, see Neuhaus, *Appointment in Rome*.

14. Author's conversation with Pope John Paul II, October 23, 1998.

15. Restorationist critics must also recognize that John Paul has, in fact, addressed key theological and practical themes in liturgy in the 1980 apostolic letter *Dominicae Cenae*, in the 1998 apostolic letter *Dies Domini*, and in several *ad limina* addresses to various groups of bishops; for examples of the latter, see the Pope's *ad limina* address to the bishops of Provence on March 8, 1997 (*OR* [EWE], March 19, 1997, pp. 5–6) and his October 1998 *ad limina* address to the bishops of the Northwest United States (*OR* [EWE], October 14, 1998, pp. 3, 10).

16. Author's interview with Cardinal Jozef Tomko, November 14, 1996.

17. See Reese, *Inside the Vatican*, pp. 192–201.

18. Letter of Pope John Paul II to Maciej Zięba, OP, June 21, 1994.

19. Author's interview with Rocco Buttiglione, January 21, 1997.

20. Author's interview with Bishop Pierre Duprey, M.Afr., January 15, 1997.

21. See "Evangelicals and Catholics Together: The Christian Mission in the Third Millennium," *First Things* 43 (May 1994), pp. 15–22, and "The Gift of Salvation," *First Things* 79 (January 1998), pp. 20–23. The intricacies of "translating" these kinds of initiatives into a Latin American context are explored in Neuhaus, *Appointment in Rome*, pp. 117–149.

22. Author's interview with Archbishop Oscar Cruz, November 22, 1997.

23. That hope was exemplified in a memorial address delivered by Cardinal Agostino Casaroli in Rome on November 22, 1997, at a commemoration of the centenary of the birth of Pope Paul VI. In a lengthy encomium to the late pontiff, delivered before John Paul II, the Roman Curia, and thousands of invited guests, the former Secretary of State suggested, in so many words, that while the past two decades had been an interesting and stimulating period, they should be understood in the manner of an interregnum, after which it would be time to return to the kind of papacy modeled by Paul VI, the man perfectly prepared to be Pope. It was, in more ways than one, an extraordinary statement. A close reading of it, set against the record of the previous nineteen years, suggested that this most accomplished of curial officials had not begun to grapple with the sea change that John Paul II, whom he had served for twelve years, had effected in the papacy.

The dramatic difference in preparation for the papacy between Giovanni Battista Montini and Karol Wojtyła was captured by Casaroli in a single sentence, which readers outside the curial milieu could only regard as ironic in its implications: "It is an old and beatiful tradition of the ecclesiastics in the Roman Curia to reserve part of their free time for some form of direct exercise of the priestly ministry." However unintended, and with no attempt to demean the pastoral passion of Paul VI, the contrast here between Wojtyła's formation as a priest and bishop and that of veteran Curialists could not have been more pronounced. [See "Il Discorso del Cardinale Agostino Casaroli," in *L'Osservatore Romano*, November 24–25, 1997, pp. 6, 8.]

24. As of October 8, 1998, Italian cardinals constituted less than twenty percent of the electoral college that will choose John Paul II's successor. The electoral college created in part by John XXIII was, by contrast, thirty-six percent Italian; and in his first consistory, in December 1958, John XXIII actually increased the percentage of Italian and curial cardinals in the college.

25. Letter to the author from Pope John Paul II, January 2, 1995.

26. Author's interview with Father Józef Tischner, April 23, 1997.

27. John Paul II, *Crossing the Threshold of Hope*, p. 22 [emphasis in original].

28. See ibid., pp. 20, 22.

29. Alasdair MacIntyre, *After Virtue: A Study in Moral Theory* (Notre Dame: University of Notre Dame Press, 1981).

30. See Balthasar, *Theo-Drama IV: The Action*, p. 73.

31. Author's interview with Halina Bortnowska, April 7, 1997; Chesterton on More is cited in James Monti, *The King's Good Servant but God's First* (San Francisco: Ignatius Press, 1997), p. 15.

32. On this point, see Balthasar, *In the Fullness of Faith*, pp. 20–21.

33. Author's interview with Piotr and Teresa Malecki, July 13, 1998; author's conversation with Pope John Paul II, December 16, 1998.

Bibliography

I. Works by Karol Wojtyła/Pope John Paul II

Works by Karol Wojtyła

The Acting Person. Dordrecht: D. Reidel Publishing Company, 1979.

The Collected Plays and Writings on Theater, with introductions by Bolesław Taborski. Berkeley: University of California Press, 1987.

Człowiek w polu odpowiedzialności. Rome-Lublin: John Paul II Institute, 1991.

En Esprit et En Vérité. Paris: Le Centurion, 1980.

Faith According to St. John of the Cross. San Francisco: Ignatius Press, 1981.

I miei amici. Rome: CSEO Biblioteca, 1979.

Love and Responsibility. San Francisco: Ignatius Press, 1993.

Miłość i odpowiedzialność, edited by Tadeusz Styczeń, Jerzy W. Gałkowski, Adam Rodziński, and Andrzej Szostek. Lublin: KUL Press, 1986.

Osoba y czyn: oraz inne studia antropologiczne, edited by Tadeusz Styczeń, Wojciech Chudy, Jerzy W. Gałkowski, Adam Rodziński, and Andrzej Szostek. Lublin: KUL Press, 1994.

Person and Community: Selected Essays. New York: Peter Lang, 1993.

The Place Within: The Poetry of Pope John Paul II. New York: Random House, 1994.

Poesie: L'opera poetica completa. Rome: TEI Newton, 1994.

Poezje i dramaty. Kraków: Znak, 1979; rev. edition, 1998.

Rozważa nia o istocie człowieka [mimeographed texts of November 1951 lectures on the nature of the human person, provided to the author by Danuta Rybicka].

Sign of Contradiction. New York: Seabury, 1979.

Sources of Renewal: The Implementation of Vatican II. San Francisco: Harper and Row, 1980.

The Way to Christ: Spiritual Exercises. New York: HarperCollins, 1994.

The Word Made Flesh: The Meaning of the Christmas Season. New York: HarperCollins, 1994.

Wykłady lubelskie, edited by Tadeusz Styczeń, Jerzy W. Gałkowski, Adam Rodziński, and Andrzej Szostek. Lublin: KUL Press, 1986.

Zagadnienie podmiotu moralności, edited by Tadeusz Styczeń, Jerzy W. Gałkowski, Adam Rodziński, and Andrzej Szostek. Lublin: KUL Press, 1991.

Works by Pope John Paul II

Ad Limina Addresses: The Addresses of His Holiness Pope John Paul II to the Bishops of the United States During Their Ad Limina *Visits, March 5–December 9, 1988*. Washington, D.C.: United States Catholic Conference, 1989.

Assisi: World Day of Prayer for Peace. Vatican City: Pontifical Commission "Iustitia et Pax," 1987.

Blessed Are the Pure of Heart. Boston: St. Paul Books and Media, 1983.

Crossing the Threshold of Hope. New York: Alfred A. Knopf, 1994.

Curriculum Philosophicum [unpublished autobiographical memorandum provided to the author].

The Encyclicals of John Paul II, edited with introductions by J. Michael Miller, CSB. Huntington, Ind.: Our Sunday Visitor Publishing Division, 1996.

The Far East Journey of Peace and Brotherhood. Boston: St. Paul Editions, 1981.

France: Message of Peace, Trust, Love and Faith. Boston: St. Paul Editions, 1980.

Germany: Pilgrimage of Unity and Peace. Boston: St. Paul Editions, 1981.

Gift and Mystery: On the Fiftieth Anniversary of My Priestly Ordination. New York: Doubleday, 1996.

Giornata Mondiale di Preghiera per la Pace nei Balcani: La pace e possibile!. Vatican City: Tipografia Vaticana, January 23, 1994.

God, Father and Creator: A Catechesis on the Creed. Vol. 1. Boston: Pauline Books and Media, 1996.

The Holy See at the Service of Peace: Pope John Paul II Addresses to the Diplomatic Corps (1978–1988). Vatican City: Pontifical Council for Justice and Peace, 1988.

Insegnamenti di Giovanni Paolo II. 18 vols. Vatican City: Libreria Editrice Vaticana.

Jesus, Son and Savior: A Catechesis on the Creed. Vol. 2. Boston: Pauline Books and Media, 1996.

John Paul II at the Gregorian University and the Biblical Institute. Rome: Tipografia P.U.G., 1980.

John Paul II for Peace in the Middle East. Vatican City: Libreria Editrice Vaticana, 1991.

John Paul II Speaks to Youth at World Youth Day. San Francisco/Washington, D.C.: Ignatius Press/Catholic New Service, 1993.

Letters to My Brother Priests: Holy Thursday (1979–1994), edited by James P. Socias. Princeton/Chicago: Scepter Publishers/Midwest Theological Forum, 1994.

Original Unity of Man and Woman. Boston: St. Paul Books and Media, 1981.

Papal Allocutions to the Roman Rota, 1939–1994, edited by William H. Woestman, OMI. Ottawa: Saint Paul University, 1994.

Pilgrim to Poland. Boston: St. Paul Editions, 1979.

The Pope Speaks to the American Church: John Paul II's Homilies, Speeches, and Letters to Catholics in the United States. San Francisco: HarperSanFrancisco, 1992.

The Pope Speaks to India. Bandra-Bombay: St. Paul Publications, 1986.

The Post-Synodal Apostolic Exhortations of John Paul II, edited with introductions by J. Michael Miller, CSB. Huntington, Ind.: Our Sunday Visitor Publishing Division, 1998.

Prayers and Devotions, edited by Peter Canisius Johannes Van Lierde. New York: Viking, 1994.

Le Mie Preghiere. Rome: Grandi Tascabili Economici Newton, 1995.

Priesthood in the Third Millennium: Addresses of Pope John Paul II, 1993. Princeton/Chicago: Scepter Publishers/Midwest Theological Forum, 1994.

Puebla: A Pilgrimage of Faith. Boston: St. Paul Editions, 1979.

Reflections on Humanae Vitae. Boston: St. Paul Books and Media, 1984.

The Social Teaching of John Paul II: The True Dimensions of Development Today, Texts of John Paul II (August 1979–February 1982). Vatican City: Tipografia Poliglotta Vaticana, 1982.

The Spirit, Giver of Life and Love: A Catechesis on the Creed. Vol. 3. Boston: Pauline Books and Media, 1996.

Spiritual Pilgrimage: Texts on Jews and Judaism 1979–1995, edited by Eugene J. Fisher and Leon Klenicki. New York: Crossroad, 1995.

The Theology of the Body. Boston: Pauline Books and Media, 1997.

The Theology of Marriage and Celibacy. Boston: St. Paul Editions, 1986.

Turkey: Ecumenical Pilgrimage. Boston: St. Paul Editions, 1980.

PAPAL DOCUMENTS CITED IN THE TEXT

ENCYCLICALS

Redemptor Hominis. 1979.
Dives in Misericordia. 1980.
Laborem Exercens. 1981.
Slavorum Apostoli. 1985.
Dominum et Vivificantem. 1986.
Redemptoris Mater. 1987.
Sollicitudo Rei Socialis. 1987.
Redemptoris Missio. 1990.
Centesimus Annus. 1991.
Veritatis Splendor. 1993.
Evangelium Vitae. 1995.
Ut Unum Sint. 1995.
Fides et Ratio. 1998.

POST-SYNODAL APOSTOLIC EXHORTATIONS

Catechesi Tradendae. 1979.
Familiaris Consortio. 1981.
Reconciliatio et Paenitentia. 1984.
Christifideles Laici. 1988.
Pastores Dabo Vobis. 1992.
Ecclesia in Africa. 1995.
Vita Consecrata. 1996.

APOSTOLIC CONSTITUTIONS

Sapientia Christiana. 1979.
Sacrae Disciplinae Leges. 1983.
Divinus Perfectionis Magister. 1983.
Pastor Bonus. 1988.
Ex Corde Ecclesiae. 1990.
Fidei Depositum. 1992.
Universi Dominici Gregis. 1996.

APOSTOLIC LETTERS

Dominicae Cenae. 1980.
Egregiae Virtutis. 1980.
Redemptionis Anno. 1984.
To the Youth of the World. 1985.
Euntes in Mundum. 1988.
Ecclesia Dei. 1988.
Mulieris Dignitatem. 1988.
On the Fiftieth Anniversary of the Beginning of the Second World War. 1989.
Ordinatio Sacerdotalis. 1994.
Tertio Millennio Adveniente. 1994.
Orientale Lumen. 1995.
For the Fourth Centenary of the Union of Brest. 1995.
Ad Tuendam Fidem. 1998.
Dies Domini. 1998.
Apostolos Suos. 1998.

LETTERS AND MESSAGES

For the Sixth Centenary of the Death of St. Catherine of Siena. 1980.
To Leonid Brezhnev. 1980.
For the Fifth Centenary of the Birth of Martin Luther. 1983.
Salvifici Doloris. 1984.
To Mikhail Gorbachev. 1988.
To George Bush and Saddam Hussein. 1991.
Letter to Families. 1994.
Letter to Children. 1994.
Letter to Women. 1995.

II. STUDIES OF KAROL WOJTYŁA/POPE JOHN PAUL II

Accatoli, Luigi. *Quando Il Papa Chiede Perdono: Tutti i Mea Culpa di Giovanni Paolo II.* Milan: Arnoldo Mondadori Editore, 1997. English edition: *When a Pope Asks Forgiveness: The Mea Culpa's of John Paul II.* Boston: Pauline Books and Media, 1998.

———. *Karol Wojtyła: L'uomo di fine millennio.* Milan: San Paolo, 1998.

Baum, Gregory, and Robert Ellsberg, eds. *The Logic of Solidarity: Commentaries on Pope John Paul II's Encyclical "On Social Concern."* Maryknoll, N.Y.: Orbis Books, 1989.

Beigel, Gerard. *Faith and Social Justice in the Teaching of Pope John Paul II.* New York: Peter Lang, 1997.

Bernstein, Carl, and Marco Politi. *His Holiness: John Paul II and the Hidden History of Our Time.* New York: Doubleday, 1996.

Biffi, Franco. *The "Social Gospel" of Pope John Paul II: A Guide to the Encyclicals on Human Work and the Authentic Development of Peoples.* Rome: Pontifical Lateran University, 1989.

Blazynski, George. *Pope John Paul II: A Man from Kraków.* London: Sphere, 1979.

Boniecki, Adam, MIC. *Kalendarium życia Karola Wojtyły.* Kraków: Znak, 1979. English translation by Irena and Thaddeus Mirecki et al.

Bujak, Adam, and Michał Rożek. *Wojtyła.* Wrocław: Wydawnictwo Dolnośląskie, 1997.

Buttiglione, Rocco. *Karol Wojtyła: The Thought of the Man Who Became Pope John Paul II.* Grand Rapids: Eerdmans, 1997.

Cielecki, Jarosław. *Wikary z Niegowici: Ksiądz Karol Wojtyła.* Częstochowa: Tygodnik Katolicki *Niedziela,* 1996.

Coyne, George V., SJ, Robert John Russell, and William R. Stoeger, SJ, eds. *John Paul II on Science and Religion: Reflections on the New View from Rome.* Rome: Vatican Observatory Publications, 1990.

Craig, Mary. *Man from a Far Country: A Portrait of Pope John Paul II*. London: Hodder and Stoughton, 1979.

Dulles, Avery, SJ. *The Splendor of Faith: The Theological Vision of Pope John Paul II*. New York: Crossroad, 1999.

Filipiak, Maria, and Andrzej Szostek, MIC, eds. *Obecność: Karol Wojtyła w Katolickim Uniwersytecie Lubelskim*. Lublin: Redakcja Wydawnictw KUL, 1989.

Frossard, André. *Portrait of John Paul II*. San Francisco: Ignatius Press, 1990.

Frossard, André, and Pope John Paul II. *Be Not Afraid!* New York: St. Martin's Press, 1984.

Gasidło, Władsysław. *Duszpasterska troska Kardynała Karola Wojtyły o rodzin*. Kraków: Archdiocese of Kraków, 1996.

Hebblethwaite, Peter, and Ludwig Kauffman, *John Paul II: A Pictorial Biography*. New York: McGraw-Hill, 1979.

Henze, Paul B. *The Plot to Kill the Pope*. New York: Charles Scribner's Sons, 1983; rev. paperback edition with a new postscript, 1985.

Hitchcock, James. *The Pope and the Jesuits: John Paul II and the New Order in the Society of Jesus*. New York: National Committee of Catholic Laymen, 1984.

Hütter, Reinhard, and Theodor Dieter, eds. *Ecumenical Ventures in Ethics: Protestants Engage Pope John Paul II's Moral Encyclicals*. Grand Rapids: Eerdmans, 1998.

Janik, Jerzy, ed. *Nauka Religia Dzieje: Co to znaczy realnie być . . . ? VII Seminarium w Castel Gandolfo, 8–10 sierpnia 1995*. Kraków: Wydawnictwo Uniwersytetu Jagiellońskiego, 1996.

Karolak, Tadeusz. *John Paul II: The Pope from Poland*. Warsaw: Interpress Publishers, 1979.

Kijowski, A., and J. J. Szczepański, with the collaboration of Krzysztof Zanussi. *From a Far Country: The Story of Karol Wojtyła of Poland*. Santa Monica, Calif.: ERI/NEFF, 1981.

Kupczak, Jarosław, OP. *The Human Person as an Efficient Cause in the Christian Anthropology of Karol Wojtyła*. Unpublished S.T.D. dissertation. Washington, D.C.: John Paul II Institute for Studies on Marriage and Family, 1996.

Kwitny, Jonathan. *Man of the Century: The Life and Times of Pope John Paul II*. New York: Henry Holt, 1997.

Leuzzi, Lorenzo, ed. *Etica e Poetica in Karol Wojtyła*. Torino: Societa Editrice Internazionale, 1997.

Maliński, Mieczysław. *Pope John Paul II: The Life of Karol Wojtyła*. New York: Seabury, 1979.

————. *Przewodnik po życiu Karola Wojtyły*. Kraków: Znak, 1997.

Mary: God's Yes to Man, John Paul's Encyclical Redemptoris Mater, introduction by Joseph Cardinal Ratzinger, commentary by Hans Urs von Balthasar. San Francisco: Ignatius Press, 1988.

McDermott, John M., SJ, ed. *The Thought of Pope John Paul II*. Rome: Editrice Pontificia Università Gregoriana, 1993.

Michener, James. *Pilgrimage*. Emmaus, Pa.: Rodale Press, 1990.

Il mondo di Giovanni Paolo II: tutti i viaggi internazionale del Papa, 1978–1996. Milan: Mondadori, 1996.

Moody, John. *Pope John Paul II*. New York: Park Lane Press, 1997.

Murphy, Francis X., CSSR, and Norman Shaifer. *John Paul II: A Son from Poland*. South Hackensack, N.J.: Shepherd Press, 1978.

Myers, Kenneth A., ed. *Aspiring to Freedom: Commentaries on Sollicitudo Rei Socialis*. Grand Rapids: Eerdmans, 1988.

O'Brien, Darcy. *The Hidden Pope: The Personal Journey of John Paul II and Jerzy Kluger*. New York: Daybreak Books, 1998.

O'Carroll, Michael. *Poland and John Paul II*. Dublin: Veritas Publications, 1979.

Oram, James. *The People's Pope: The Story of Karol Wojtyła of Poland*. San Francisco: Chronicle Books, 1979.

Parker, Michael. *Priest of the World's Destiny: John Paul II*. Milford, Ohio: Faith Publishing Company, 1995.

Piedra, Alberto M. *A View of Pope John Paul II's Trip to Cuba: His Messages, Addresses, and Homilies*. Washington, D.C.: Institute for U.S.-Cuba Relations, 1998.

Pontifical Council for the Laity. *Il Papa e i Movimenti*. Milan: Edizioni San Paolo, 1998.

Schmitz, Kenneth L. *At the Center of the Human Drama: The Philosophical Anthropology of Karol Wojtyła/Pope John Paul II*. Washington, D.C.: CUA Press, 1993.

Schall, James V., SJ. *The Church, the State and Society in the Thought of John Paul II*. Chicago: Franciscan Herald Press, 1982.

Sterling, Claire. *The Time of the Assassins: Anatomy of an Investigation*. New York: Holt, Rinehart, and Winston, 1983.

Svidercoschi, Gian Franco. *Letter to a Jewish Friend*. New York: Crossroad, 1994.

Szulc, Tad. *Pope John Paul II: The Biography*. New York: Scribner, 1995.

Tamaro, Susanna. *"Caro Papa": Lettere del Popolo di Dio*. Milan: Mondadori, 1998.

Valente, Leonardo, Krzysztof Zanussi, and Giorgio Cajati, *Giovanni Paolo II: Il Profeta del Terzo Millennio*. Rome: RAI, 1997.

Viaggi e visite di Giovanni Paolo II al 18° anno di pontificato e 50° anno di sacerdozio: dati riassuntivi e statistici. Rome: Radio Vaticana, 1996.

Walsh, Michael. *John Paul II: A Biography*. London: Fount, 1995.

Wierzbianski, Bolesław, ed. *The Shepherd for All People*. New York: Bicentennial Publishing Corporation, 1993.

Wildes, Kevin, SJ, and Alan C. Mitchell, eds. *Choosing Life: A Dialogue on* Evangelium Vitae. Washington, D.C.: Georgetown University Press, 1997.

Willey, David. *God's Politician: Pope John Paul II, the Catholic Church, and the New World Order*. New York: St. Martin's Press, 1992.

Williams, George Huntston. *The Mind of John Paul II: Origins of His Thought and Action*. New York: Seabury, 1981.

———. *The Contours of Church and State in the Thought of John Paul II*. Waco, Texas: Baylor University, 1983.

Zięba, Maciej, OP. *Niezwykły Pontyfikat*. Kraków: Znak, 1997.

III. OTHER CHURCH DOCUMENTS

THE SECOND VATICAN COUNCIL

Lumen Gentium [Dogmatic Constitution on the Church]. 1964.

Nostra Aetate [Declaration on the Relation of the Church to Non-Christian Religions]. 1965.

Dignitatis Humanae [Declaration on Religious Freedom]. 1965.

Gaudium et Spes [Pastoral Constitution on the Church in the Modern World]. 1965.

SYNODAL AND CONGREGATIONAL DOCUMENTS

Justice in the World. Synod of Bishops, 1971.

Inter Insigniores. Congregation for the Doctrine of the Faith, 1975.

Instruction on Certain Aspects of the "Theology of Liberation." Congregation for the Doctrine of the Faith, 1984.

Notes on the Correct Way to Present the Jews and Judaism in Preaching and Catechesis in the Roman Catholic Church. Commission for Religious Relations with the Jews, 1985.

Instruction on Christian Freedom and Liberation. Congregation for the Doctrine of the Faith, 1986.

Donum Vitae. Congregation for the Doctrine of the Faith, 1987.

Vademecum for Confessors Concerning Some Aspects of the Morality of Conjugal Life. Pontifical Council for the Family, 1997.

We Remember: A Reflection on the Shoah. Commission for Religious Relations with the Jews, 1998.

IV. THE PAPACY: GENERAL BACKGROUND

Bunson, Matthew. *The Pope Encyclopedia: An A to Z of the Holy See*. New York: Crown Trade Paperbacks, 1995.

Chirico, Peter. *Infallibility: The Crossroads of Doctrine*. Kansas City: Sheed, Andrews and McMeel, 1977.

Duffy, Eamon. *Saints and Sinners: A History of the Popes*. New Haven: Yale University Press, 1997

Granfield, Patrick. *The Limitations of the Papacy: Authority and Autonomy in the Church*. New York: Crossroad, 1987.

Hughes, John Jay. *Pontiffs: Popes Who Shaped History*. Huntington, Ind.: Our Sunday Visitor Publishing Division, 1994.

Jedin, Hubert, ed. *History of the Church*. 10 vols. New York: Crossroad, 1986–1989.

Jung-Inglessis, E. M. *The Holy Year in Rome: Past and Present*. Vatican City: Libreria Editrice Vaticana, 1997.

Kelly, J. N. D. *The Oxford Dictionary of Popes*. New York: Oxford University Press, 1986.

Martin, Jacques. *Heraldry in the Vatican*. Gerrards Cross, Buckinghamshire: Van Duren, 1987.

McBrien, Richard P. *Lives of the Popes: The Pontiffs from St. Peter to John Paul II*. San Francisco: HarperSanFrancisco, 1997.

Miller, J. Michael, CSB. *The Shepherd and the Rock: Origins, Development, and Mission of the Papacy*. Huntington, Ind.: Our Sunday Visitor Publishing Division, 1995.

V. THE CATHOLIC CHURCH AND THE PAPACY IN THE TWENTIETH CENTURY

Abeln, Reinhard, and Adelbert Ludwig Balling. *Martyr of Brotherly Love: Father Engelmar Unzeitig and the Priests' Barracks at Dachau.* New York: Crossroads, 1992.

Alberigo, Giuseppe, and Joseph A. Komonchak, eds. *History of Vatican II, Volume I: Announcing and Preparing Vatican Council II, Toward a New Era in Catholicism.* Maryknoll, N.Y.: Orbis Books, 1995.

Brown, Robert McAfee. *Observer in Rome: A Protestant Report on the Vatican Council.* Garden City, N.Y.: Doubleday, 1964.

Cornwell, John, *A Thief in the Night: The Mysterious Death of John Paul I.* New York: Simon and Schuster, 1989.

Fappani, Antonio, and Franco Molinari. *Giovanni Battista Montini Giovane: Documenti inediti a testimonianze.* Turin: Marietti, 1979.

Fesquet, Henri. *The Drama of Vatican II.* New York: Random House, 1967.

Frossard, André. *"Forget Not Love": The Passion of Maximilian Kolbe.* San Francisco: Ignatius Press, 1991.

Gałązka, Grzegorz. *Cardinali del terzo millennio.* Vatican City: Libreria Editrice Vaticana, 1996.

Graham, Robert A., SJ. *The Vatican and Communism During World War II: What Really Happened?* San Francisco: Ignatius Press, 1996.

Granfield, Patrick. *The Papacy in Transition.* New York: Doubleday and Company, 1980.

Greeley, Andrew M. *The Making of the Popes 1978: The Politics of Intrigue in the Vatican.* Kansas City: Andrews and McMeel, 1979.

Hebblethwaite, Peter. *The Year of Three Popes.* New York: William Collins, 1978.

————. *Pope John XXIII: Shepherd of the Modern World.* Garden City, N.Y.: Doubleday, 1985.

————. *In the Vatican.* Oxford: Oxford University Press, 1986.

————. *Paul VI: The First Modern Pope.* New York: Paulist Press, 1993.

————. *The Next Pope: An Enquiry.* London: HarperCollins Publishers, 1995.

Herbstrith, Waltraud. *Edith Stein: A Biography.* San Francisco: Harper and Row, 1985.

Irani, George E. *The Papacy and the Middle East: The Role of the Holy See in the Arab-Israeli Conflict, 1962–1984.* Notre Dame: University of Notre Dame Press, 1986.

Jaeger, David-Maria A., OFM. *The Roman Pontiffs in Defense of Christian Rights in the Holy Land: From Causa Nobis to Redemptionis Anno (1921–1984).* Unpublished doctoral dissertation. Rome: Pontifical Athenaeum "Antonianum," 1989.

Kaiser, Robert Blair. *The Politics of Sex and Religion.* Kansas City: Leaven Press, 1985.

Küng, Hans. *Konzil und Wiedervereinigung.* 3d ed. Freiburg im Bresgau: Verlag Herder, 1961. English translation, *The Council: Reform and Reunion.* Garden City, N.Y.: Doubleday Image Books, 1965.

Liturgie dell'Oriente Cristiano a Roma nell'Anno Mariano 1987–1988: Testi e Studi. Vatican City: Libreria Editrice Vaticana, 1990.

Luciani, Albino. *Illustrissimi: Letters from Pope John Paul I.* Boston: Little, Brown, 1978.

McDowell, Bart. *Inside the Vatican.* Washington, D.C.: National Geographic Society, 1991.

McGarry, Cecil, SJ, ed. *What Happened at the Africa Synod?* Nairobi, Kenya: Pauline Publications Africa, 1995.

Melady, Thomas Patrick. *The Ambassador's Story: The United States and the Vatican in World Affairs.* Huntington, Ind.: Our Sunday Visitor Publishing Division, 1994.

Minerbi, Sergio I. *The Vatican and Zionism.* New York: Oxford University Press, 1990.

Nichols, Peter. *The Pope's Divisions: The Roman Catholic Church Today.* New York: Penguin Books, 1982.

Nights of Sorrow, Days of Joy. Washington, D.C.: National Catholic News Service, 1978.

Reese, Thomas J., SJ. *Inside the Vatican.* Cambridge: Harvard University Press, 1996.

Rhodes, Anthony. *The Vatican in the Age of the Dictators 1922–1945.* New York: Holt, Rinehart and Winston, 1973.

Roberson, Ronald G., CSP. *The Eastern Christian Churches: A Brief Survey.* 6th ed. Rome: Edizioni "Orientalia Christiana," 1999.

Santini, Alceste. *Agostino Casaroli: Uomo del dialogo.* Milan: Edizioni San Paolo, 1993.

Stehle, Hansjakob. *Eastern Politics of the Vatican 1917–1979.* Athens, Ohio: Ohio University Press, 1981.

Stein, Edith. *Life in a Jewish Family 1891–1916: An Autobiography.* Washington, D.C.: ICS Publications, 1986.

————. *Essays on Woman.* Washington, D.C.: ICS Publications, 1987.

————. *Self-Portrait in Letters 1916–1942.* Washington, D.C.: ICS Publications, 1993.

Whitfield, Teresa. *Paying the Price: Ignacio Ellacuría and the Murdered Jesuits of El Salvador.* Philadelphia: Temple University Press, 1994.

Wiltgen, Ralph M., SVD. *The Rhine Flows into the Tiber: The Hidden Council.* New York: Hawthorn Books, 1967.

Wynn, Wilton. *Keepers of the Keys.* New York: Random House, 1988.

Zizola, Giancarlo. *I papi del XX secolo.* Roma: Tascabili Economici Newton, 1995.

————. *Il successore.* Rome-Bari, Laterza, 1997.

VI. ISSUES IN CONTEMPORARY CATHOLICISM

Balthasar, Hans Urs von. *The Office of Peter and the Structure of the Church.* San Francisco: Ignatius Press, 1986.

————. *Dare We Hope "That All Men Be Saved"?—With a Short Discourse on Hell.* San Francisco: Ignatius Press, 1988.

————. *In the Fullness of Faith: On the Centrality of the Distinctively Catholic.* San Francisco: Ignatius, 1988.

————. *You Crown the Year with Your Goodness.* San Francisco: Ignatius Press, 1989.

————. *Theo-Drama: Theological Dramatic Theory—Volume IV: The Action.* San Francisco: Ignatius Press, 1994.

————. *Tragedy Under Grace: Reinhold Schneider on the Experience of the West.* San Francisco: Ignatius Press, 1997.

Bartoszewski, Władysław T. *The Convent at Auschwitz.* New York: George Braziller, 1991.

Bautista, Felix B. *Cardinal Sin and the Miracle of Asia.* Manila: Vera-Reyes, 1987.

Becker, Joseph M., SJ. *The Re-Formed Jesuits: A History of Changes in Jesuit Formation During the Decade 1965–1975.* 2 vols. San Francisco: Ignatius Press, 1992, 1997.

Belli, Humberto. *Nicaragua: Christians Under Fire.* San José, Costa Rica: Instituto Puebla, 1984.

Berger, Peter L., and Richard John Neuhaus, eds. *Against the World for the World: The Hartford Appeal and the Future of American Religion.* New York: Seabury Press, 1976.

Carey, Ann. *Sisters in Crisis.* Huntington, Ind.: Our Sunday Visitor Publishing Division, 1997.

Cromartie, Michael, ed. *The Nine Lives of Population Control.* Washington, D.C.: Ethics and Public Policy Center, 1995.

Curran, Charles. *Christian Morality Today: The Renewal of Moral Theology.* Notre Dame: Fides, 1966.

————. *A New Look at Christian Morality: Christian Morality Today II.* Notre Dame: Fides, 1968.

————. *New Perspectives in Moral Theology.* Notre Dame: University of Notre Dame Press, 1976.

————. *Faithful Dissent.* Kansas City: Sheed and Ward, 1986.

————. *Toward an American Catholic Moral Theology.* Notre Dame: University of Notre Dame Press, 1987.

DeCosse, David, ed. *But Was It Just? Reflections on the Morality of the Persian Gulf War.* New York: Doubleday, 1992.

De Fuenmayor, Amadeo, Valentin Gómez-Iglesias, and Jose Luis Illanes. *The Canonical Path of Opus Dei: The History and Defense of a Charism.* Princeton/Chicago: Scepter Press/Midwest Theological Forum, 1994.

De Lubac, Henri, SJ. *At the Service of the Church.* San Francisco: Ignatius Press, 1993.

————. *The Drama of Atheistic Humanism.* San Francisco: Ignatius Press, 1995.

————. *Theology in History.* San Francisco: Ignatius Press, 1996.

Duffy, Eamon. *The Stripping of the Altars: Traditional Religion in England c. 1400-c.1580.* New Haven and London: Yale University Press, 1992.

Fries, Heinrich, and Karl Rahner, SJ. *Unity of the Churches: An Actual Possibility.* Philadelphia and New York: Fortress and Paulist, 1985.

Gleason, Philip. *Contending with Modernity: Catholic Higher Education in the Twentieth Century.* New York: Oxford University Press, 1996.

Hick, John, and Paul Knitter, eds. *The Myth of Christian Uniqueness: Towards a Pluralistic Theology of Religions.* Maryknoll, N.Y.: Orbis Books, 1987.

Imhoff, Paul, and Hubert Biallowons, eds. *Faith in a Wintry Season: Interviews with Karl Rahner.* New York: Crossroad, 1991.

Johnston, Douglas, and Cynthia Sampson, eds. *Religion, the Missing Dimension of Statecraft.* New York: Oxford University Press, 1994.

Joaquin, Nick. *The Book of Sin: From Golden Salakot to Red Hat.* Manila: Weekly Graphic Publishing Company, 1992.

Lefever, Ernest W. *Amsterdam to Nairobi: The World Council of Churches and the Third World.* Washington, D.C.: Ethics and Public Policy Center, 1979.

————. *Nairobi to Vancouver: The World Council of Churches and the World, 1975–1987.* Washington, D.C.: Ethics and Public Policy Center, 1987.

Little, Joyce. *The Church and the Culture War: Secular Anarchy or Sacred Order.* San Francisco: Ignatius Press, 1995.

Lubich, Chiara. *Unity and Jesus Forsaken.* New York: New City Press, 1985.

————. *A Life for Unity: An Interview by Franca Zambonini.* London: New City, 1992.

Lustiger, Jean-Marie. *Choosing God—Chosen by God.* San Francisco: Ignatius Press, 1991.

McInerny, Ralph, ed. *The Catholic Woman.* San Francisco: Ignatius Press, 1991.

Morris, Charles R. *American Catholic: The Saints and Sinners Who Built America's Most Powerful Church.* New York: Times Books, 1997.

Neuhaus, Richard John. *The Catholic Moment: The Paradox of the Church in the Postmodern World.* San Francisco: Harper and Row, 1987; rev. paperback ed., 1990.

————. *Doing Well and Doing Good: The Challenge to the Christian Capitalist.* New York: Doubleday, 1992.

————. *Appointment in Rome: The Church in America Awakening.* New York: Crossroad, 1999.

Novak, David. *Jewish-Christian Dialogue: A Jewish Justification.* New York: Oxford University Press, 1989.

Novak, Michael. *Freedom with Justice: Catholic Social Thought and Liberal Institutions.* San Francisco: Harper and Row, 1984.

————. *Will It Liberate? Questions About Liberation Theology.* New York: Paulist Press, 1986.

————. *The Catholic Ethic and the Spirit of Capitalism.* New York: Free Press, 1993.

Oakes, Edward T., SJ. *Pattern of Redemption: The Theology of Hans Urs von Balthasar.* New York: Continuum, 1994.

O'Brien, Conor Cruise. *On the Eve of the Millennium: The Future of Democracy Through an Age of Unreason.* New York: Free Press, 1994.

Ogden, Schubert. *Is There Only One True Religion or Are There Many?* Dallas: Southern Methodist University Press, 1992.

Oliver, Robert W. *The Vocation of the Laity to Evangelization: An Ecclesiological Inquiry into the Synod on the Laity (1987), Christifideles Laici (1989), and Documents of the NCCB (1987–1996).* Rome: Editrice Pontificia Università Gregoriana, 1997.

Pasotti, Ezekiel. *The Neocatechumenal Way According to Paul VI and John Paul II.* Middleborough, U.K.: St. Pauls, 1996.

Pinckaers, Servais, OP. *The Sources of Christian Ethics.* Washington, D.C.: Catholic University of America Press, 1995.

Ratzinger, Joseph. *Principles of Catholic Theology: Building Stones for a Fundamental Theology.* San Francisco: Ignatius Press, 1987.

————. *Church, Ecumenism, and Politics: New Essays in Ecclesiology.* New York: Crossroad, 1988.

————. *A Turning Point for Europe? The Church in the Modern World—Assessment and Forecast.* San Francisco: Ignatius Press, 1994.

————. *Milestones: Memoirs 1927–1977.* San Francisco: Ignatius Press, 1998.

Ratzinger, Joseph, and Vittorio Messori. *The Ratzinger Report: An Exclusive Interview on the State of the Church.* San Francisco: Ignatius Press, 1995.

Ratzinger, Joseph, and Peter Seewald. *Salt of the Earth: The Church at the End of the Millennium.* San Francisco: Ignatius Press, 1997.

Riccardi, Andrea. *Sant'Egidio: Rome et le Monde.* Paris: Beauchesne Editeur, 1996.

Rothschild, Fritz A., ed. *Jewish Perspectives on Christianity.* New York: Crossroad, 1990.

Scola, Angelo. *Hans Urs von Balthasar: A Theological Style.* Grand Rapids: Eerdmans, 1995.

Skwarnicki, Marek. *Podróże po Kościela.* 2d ed. Paris: Editions du Dialogie, 1990.

Smith, Janet E. "Humanae Vitae": *A Generation Later.* Washington, D.C.: Catholic University of America Press, 1991.

Stark, Rodney. *The Rise of Christianity.* New York: HarperCollins, 1997.

Weigel, George. *Tranquillitas Ordinis: The Present Failure and Future Promise of American Catholic Thought on War and Peace.* New York: Oxford University Press, 1987.

————. *Soul of the World: Notes on the Future of Public Catholicism.* Grand Rapids: Eerdmans, 1996.

Weigel, George, and Robert Royal, eds. *Building the Free Society: Democracy, Capitalism, and Catholic Social Thought.* Grand Rapids: Eerdmans, 1993.

Witham, Larry. *Curran vs. Catholic University: A Study of Authority and Freedom in Conflict.* Riverdale, Md.: Edington-Rand, 1991.

Woodward, Kenneth L. *Making Saints: How the Catholic Church Determines Who Becomes a Saint, Who Doesn't, and Why.* New York: Simon and Schuster, 1996.

VII. The Catholic Church in Central and Eastern Europe/The Revolution of 1989

Baran, Zbigniew, and William Brand. *Cracow: Dialogue of Traditions.* Kraków: Znak, 1991.

Bardecki, Andrzej. *Zawsze jest inaczej.* Kraków: Znak, 1995.

Bilinski, Piotr. *Żywoty sławnych biskupow krakowskich.* Kraków: Archdiocese of Kraków, 1998.

Bociurkiw, Bohdan R. *The Ukrainian Greek Catholic Church and the Soviet State 1939–1950.* Edmonton: Canadian Institute of Ukrainian Studies Press, 1996.

Bourdeaux, Michael. *The Gospel's Triumph over Communism.* Minneapolis: Bethany House Publishers, 1991.

Bourdeaux, Michael, ed. *The Politics of Religion in Russia and the New States of Eurasia.* New York: M. E. Sharpe, 1995.

Braun, Kazimierz, *A History of Polish Theater, 1939–1989: Spheres of Captivity and Freedom.* Westport, Conn.: Greenwood Press, 1996.

Broun, Janice, ed. *Conscience and Captivity: Religion in Eastern Europe.* Washington, D.C.: Ethics and Public Policy Center, 1988.

Bujak, Adam, *Cracow from the Air.* Kraków: Parol, n.d.

———. *Mystical Cracow.* Kraków: Parol, 1996.

Bukovsky, Vladimir. *Jugement à Moscou: Un dissident dans les archives du Kremlin.* Paris: Laffont, 1995.

Chronicle of the Catholic Church in Lithuania. Multiple issues, 1979–1988.

Courtois, Stéphane, et al. *Le Livre Noir du Communisme: Crimes, Terreur, Répression.* Paris: Laffont, 1997.

Davies, Norman. *God's Playground: A History of Poland.* 2 vols. New York: Columbia University Press, 1982.

———. *Heart of Europe: A Short History of Poland.* Oxford: Oxford University Press, 1984.

Deak, Istvan. *Beyond Nationalism: A Social and Political History of the Habsburg Officer Corps 1848–1918.* New York: Oxford University Press, 1990.

Garton Ash, Timothy. *The Polish Revolution: Solidarity.* Sevenoaks, U.K.: Hodder and Stoughton, 1985.

———. *The Uses of Adversity: Essays on the Fate of Central Europe.* New York: Vintage Books, 1990.

———. *We the People: The Revolution of '89 Witnessed in Warsaw, Budapest, Berlin and Prague.* Cambridge, England: Granta Books, 1990.

Gorbachev, Mikhail. *Memoirs.* New York: Doubleday, 1995.

Gromyko, Andrei. *Memoirs.* London: Hutchinson, 1989.

Groch, Juraj. *Riport o Nežnej Revolúcii/Report of the Soft Revolution.* Bratislava: Vydavatel'stvo Obzor, 1990.

Gudziak, Borys A. *Crisis and Reform: The Kyivan Metropolitanate, The Patriarchate of Constantinople, and the Genesis of the Union of Brest.* Cambridge, Mass.: Harvard University Press, 1998.

Hartmann, Jan, Bohumil Svoboda, and Václav Vaško. *Kardinal Tomášek: Zeugnisse über einen behutsamen Bischof und einen tapferen Kardinal.* Leipzig: Benno-Verlag, 1994.

Havel, Václav. *Disturbing the Peace: A Conversation with Karel Hvizdala.* New York: Vintage Books, 1991.

———. *Open Letters: Selected Writings, 1965–1990.* New York: Alfred A. Knopf, 1991.

———. *Summer Meditations.* New York: Alfred A. Knopf, 1992.

Havel, Václav, et al. *The Power of the Powerless: Citizens Against the State in Central-Eastern Europe.* Armonk, N.Y.: M. E. Sharpe, 1985.

Kaufman, Michael. *Mad Dreams, Saving Graces—Poland: A Nation in Conspiracy.* New York: Random House, 1989.

Kostrzewa, Robert, ed. *Between East and West: Writings from Kultura.* New York: Hill and Wang, 1990.

Kowalska, Faustina. *Diary of Blessed Sister M. Faustina Kowalska.* Stockbridge, Mass.: Marians of the Immaculate Conception, 1996.

Krčmery, Silvester. *In Prisons and Labour Camps.* Bratislava: Milada Cechova, 1995.

Kubik, Jan. *The Power of Symbols Against the Symbols of Power: The Rise of Solidarity and the Fall of State Socialism in Poland.* University Park, Pa.: Pennsylvania State University Press, 1994.

Lewek, Antonin. "New Sanctuary of Poles: The Grave of Martyr-Father Jerzy Popiełuszko." Warsaw: St. Stanisław Kostka Church, 1986.

Luxmoore, Jonathan, and Jolanta Babiuch. *The Vatican and the Red Flag: The Struggle for the Soul of Eastern Europe.* London: Geoffrey Chapman, 1999.

Markowski, Stanisław. *The Cathedral at Wawel.* Kraków: Postscriptum, 1993.

Micewski, Andrzej. *Cardinal Wyszyński: A Biography.* San Francisco: Harcourt Brace Jovanovich, 1984.

Michałowska, Danuta, ed. *". . . trzeb da wiadectwo": 50-lecie powstania Teatru Rapsodycznego w Krakowie.* Kraków: ArsNova, 1991.

Michnik, Adam. *Letters from Prison and Other Essays.* Berkeley: University of California Press, 1987.

———. *The Church and the Left.* Chicago: University of Chicago Press, 1993.

Mikloško, Frantisek. *You Can't Destroy Them: Catholic Church in Slovakia, 1943–89.* Unpublished manuscript, 1992.

Miłosz, Czesław. *The History of Polish Literature.* 2d ed. Berkeley: University of California Press, 1983.

Mindszenty, Joseph. *Memoirs.* New York: Macmillan, 1974.

Murphy, Francis X., CSSR, Michael Greene, and Norman Schaifer. *Poland Greets the Pope.* South Hackensack, N.J.: Shepherd Press, 1979.

Nagorski, Andrew. *The Birth of Freedom: Shaping Lives and Societies in the New Eastern Europe.* New York: Simon and Schuster, 1993.

Pelikan, Jaroslav. *Confessor Between East and West: A Portrait of Ukrainian Cardinal Josyf Slipyj.* Grand Rapids: Eerdmans, 1990.

Pierwszy Synod Prowincji Krakowskiej. Kraków: Archdiocese of Kraków, 1994.

Pipes, Richard. *Russia Under the Bolshevik Regime.* New York: Alfred A. Knopf, 1993.

Pipes, Richard, ed. *The Unknown Lenin: From the Secret Archive.* New Haven, Conn.: Yale University Press, 1996.

Połtawska, Wanda. *And I Am Afraid of My Dreams.* London: Hodder and Stoughton, 1987.

Remnick, David. *Lenin's Tomb: The Last Days of the Soviet Empire.* New York: Random House, 1993.

Rolicki, Janusz. *Edward Gierek: Przewana dekada.* Warsaw: Polska Oficyna Wydawnicza, 1990.

Sakharov, Andrei. *Moscow and Beyond: 1986–1989.* New York: Vintage Books, 1992.

Sikorska, Grażyna. *A Martyr for the Truth: Jerzy Popiełuszko.* Grand Rapids: Eerdmans, 1985.

———. *Light and Life: Renewal in Poland.* Grand Rapids: Eerdmans, 1989.

Sikorski, Radek. *Full Circle: A Homecoming to Free Poland,.* New York: Simon and Schuster, 1997.

Il Sinodo Pastorale dell'Archidiocesi di Cracovia 1972–1979. Vatican City: Libreria Editrice Vaticana, 1985.

Szajkowski, Bogdan. *Next to God . . . Poland: Politics and Religion in Contemporary Poland.* New York: St. Martin's Press, 1983.

Tischner, Józef. *The Spirit of Solidarity.* San Francisco: Harper and Row, 1984.

Under One Heaven: Poles and Jews. Special edition of *Więz,* 1998.

Volkogonov, Dmitri. *Autopsy for an Empire: The Seven Leaders Who Built the Soviet Regime.* New York: Free Press, 1998.

Wałęsa, Lech. *A Way of Hope: An Autobiography.* New York: Henry Holt, 1987.

———. *The Struggle and the Triumph.* New York: Arcade Publishing, 1991.

Watt, Richard M. *Bitter Glory: Poland and its Fate 1918–1939.* New York: Simon and Schuster, 1979.

Webster, Alexander, F. C. *The Price of Prophecy: Orthodox Churches on Peace, Freedom, and Security.* Grand Rapids: Eerdmans, 1995.

Weigel, George. *The Final Revolution: The Resistance Church and the Collapse of Communism.* New York: Oxford University Press, 1992.

Wyszyński, Stefan. *All You Who Labor: Work and the Sanctification of Daily Life.* Manchester, N.H.: Sophia Institute Press, 1995.

Zamoyski, Adam. *The Polish Way: A Thousand-Year History of the Poles and Their Culture.* New York: Hippocrene Books, 1994.

Acknowledgments

While the narrative, analysis, and judgments in *Witness to Hope* are entirely my responsibility, it is a pleasure to acknowledge the great debt of gratitude I owe to those whose cooperation, assistance, and counsel made the work possible.

In Rome: Here, the first word of thanks must go to His Holiness, Pope John Paul II. When we met to discuss the procedures we would follow in the project, I told him that, while I understood and respected his sense of privacy, I would have to try to violate it over the next several years. He understood. During ten interviews and more than twenty hours of conversation over meals in the papal apartment and at Castel Gandolfo, he opened his mind, his memory, and his heart so that I might understand his life, his thinking, and his work better. On no occasion did the Holy Father suggest that I avoid some topic, nor did he ever propose how an issue might be handled. He believed, from the beginning and throughout, that the responsibility for this book was mine.

John Paul II's secretary, Bishop Stanisław Dziwisz, was unfailingly helpful in arranging what needed to be arranged, in the Vatican and elsewhere. My work would have been quite impossible without his assistance and support.

Dr. Joaquín Navarro-Valls, director of the Holy See Press Office, will, I hope, write his own study of John Paul II someday. For the present, I wish to thank him for his insight, enthusiasm, and advocacy, all of which were indispensable.

I owe a considerable debt of gratitude and friendship to Bishop James M. Harvey, Prefect of the Papal Household, for his counsel and his company.

The Pontifical North American College was my Roman home during the preparation of the book, and a finer home cannot be imagined. I am deeply grateful to the rector, Monsignor Timothy M. Dolan, and to the college faculty, students, and staff, for their welcome, their friendship, their interest, and their support. A special word of gratitude goes to Michael Woods, and to the 1996–1997 students from the Archdiocese of Washington, who acted as impromptu research assistants. To NACers one and all: *ad multos annos*.

I should like to thank the following officials of the Holy See for their cooperation in providing interviews, suggestions, and/or materials: Cardinal Francis Arinze; Cardinal William Baum; the late Cardinal Alberto Bovone; Monsignor Timothy Broglio; Archbishop Agostino Cacciavillan; the late Cardinal Agostino Casaroli; Cardinal Edward Cassidy; Archbishop Claudio Celli;

Archbishop Andrea Cordero Lanza di Montezemolo; Archbishop Paul Cordes; Bishop Pierre Duprey, M.Afr.; Monsignor Robert J. Dempsey; Monsignor Walter Edyvean; Cardinal Roger Etchegaray; Father Brian Farrell, LC; Father John Farren, OP; Archbishop John Foley; Father Reginald Foster, OCD; Cardinal Bernardin Gantin; Archbishop Luigi Gatti; Archbishop Zenon Grocholewski; Cardinal Pio Laghi; Cardinal Alfonso López Trujillo; Cardinal Jorge Medina Estévez; Bishop Piero Marini; Bishop Diarmuid Martin; Archbishop Jorge Mejía; Archbishop Giuseppe Pittau, SJ; Cardinal Luigi Poggi; Monsignor Joseph Punderson; Monsignor John Radano; Cardinal Joseph Ratzinger; Archbishop Giovanni Battista Re; Bishop Stanisław Ryłko; Cardinal Jan Schotte, CICM; Cardinal Angelo Sodano; Cardinal J. Francis Stafford; Cardinal Edmund Szoka; Archbishop Jean-Louis Tauran; Monsignor Daniel Thomas; Cardinal Jozef Tomko; and Father Roberto Tucci, SJ.

My thanks go as well to Mrs. Irina Alberti; Ambassador Corinne Claiborne Boggs; Father Alvaro Corcuera Martínez del Río, LC, and the faculty and students of the Pontifical Athenaeum "Regina Apostolorum"; James Crowley; Ambassador Henrietta T. De Villa; Father Frederick Dolan; Bishop Javier Echevarría Rodríguez; Sister Emilia Ehrlich, OSU; Ambassador Raymond Flynn; Stanisław Grygiel; Jerzy Kluger; Chiara Lubich; Father Marcial Maciel, LC; Marta and Filippo Manzi; Krzysztof Mięsożerny and his colleagues; Father John Navone, SJ; Brother Robert Oliver, BH; Monsignor Vincenzo Paglia; Lisa Palmieri-Billig; Bishop Angelo Scola; Sister Lucy Thorson, NDS; and Father Thomas Williams, LC. Rocco Buttiglione was, as always, a steady source of insight. My thanks, too, to Prime Minister Massimo D'Alema and former President Francesco Cossiga for discussing John Paul II's impact on Italian public life. As in the past, Leonardo Mondadori was both publisher and friend.

Among present and former members of the Roman press corps, I should like to thank Celestine Bohlen, Richard Boudreaux, Greg Burke, Paula Butturini, Candice Hughes, Joan Lewis, Victor and Daniela Simpson, Alessandra Stanley, John Tagliabue, John Thavis, and Cindy Wooden. Father Paul Mankowski, SJ, and two students at the Pontifical North American College, Daniel Gallagher and Roger Landry, helped with Latin translations. John Vargas helped with Spanish translations.

In Poland: Father Maciej Zięba, OP; Father Jarosław Kupczak, OP; and Father Jarosław Głodek, OP, were invaluable in arranging my research periods in Poland. My best thanks, too, to Father Mirosław Pilśniak, OP, and the Dominican community in Kraków, and to Father Jacek Buda, OP, and the Dominican community in Warsaw's Old Town, for their hospitality.

I owe a very special debt of gratitude to several men and women of Karol Wojtyła's *Środowisko* for their assistance and their trust: Danuta Ciesielska, Teresa Malecka, Piotr Malecki, Danuta Rybicka, Stanisław Rybicki, Karol Tarnowski, Bożena Turowska, Gabriel Turowski, and Teresa Życzkowska. For my understanding of Karol Wojtyła's forty years in Kraków, I am also indebted to Monsignor Andrzej Bardecki; Monsignor Władysław Gasidło; Father Wojciech Giertych, OP; Jerzy Janik; Archbishop Marian Jaworski; Halina Kwiatkowska; Cardinal Franciszek Macharski; Father Mieczysław Maliński; Monsignor Stanisław Małysiak; Marek Michałewski; Danuta Michałowska; Andrzej Połtawski; Stanisław Rodziński; Bishop Stanisław Smoleński; Maria Swieżawska; Father Michal Szafarski, SDB; Father Józef Tischner; the late Jerzy Turowicz; Henryk Woźniakowski; and Jacek Woźniakowski. Marek Skwarnicki gave me invaluable help in translating Karol Wojtyła's poetry and exploring his poetic imagination. Anna Orla-Bukowska and Paweł Malecki helped with other translations.

For introducing me to the Catholic University of Lublin and discussing Karol Wojtyła's work there with me, I am grateful to Jerzy Gałkowski; Cezary Ritter; Stefan Sawicki; Father Tadeusz Styczeń, SDS; Stefan Swieżawski; Father Andrzej Szostek, MIC; and Sister Zofia Zdybicka, OSU.

Elsewhere in Poland, I am happy to acknowledge the help of Halina Bortnowska; Maria Kotlarczyk Ćwikla; Piotr Dardziński; Bohdan Cywiński; Anna Karoń-Ostrowska; Piotr Kimla; Tadeusz Mazowiecki; Wojciech Ostrowski; Bishop Tadeusz Pieronek; Radek Sikorski; Monsignor Kazimierz Suder; Brother Viktor Tokarski, OFM; Adam Zamoyski; Krzysztof Zanussi; and Archbishop Józef Życyński.

In the United States: My agent, Loretta Barrett, has been a great support throughout the project. Diane Reverand did a superb job of editing, assisted by Carolyn Fireside; they have my thanks, and should have the readers'. I am also grateful to Susan Llewellyn and Eleanor Mikucki for their meticulous production editing and copyediting, respectively. Ann Derstine and Ever Horan, my assistants during the project, were unfailingly gracious, organized an immense amount of material, did translations from the German, French, and Italian, juggled phone calls, faxes, and e-mails over six time zones, and kept my office in order during my frequent absences. Patrick Prisco also provided important research assistance, as did Kristina Fox. Thanks, too, to my colleagues at the Ethics and Public Policy Center, and particularly to my successor as the Center's president, Elliott Abrams.

Father Richard John Neuhaus helped me think through the project from the beginning; his reading and critique of the manuscript were extremely helpful.

I am also in debt to Richard V. Allen; Robert Andrews; Susan Bailey; Monsignor Thomas Benestad; Zbigniew Brzeziński; Anna Carozza; Daniela Carozza; Father Romanus Cessario, OP; Thomas Crooks; Father Joseph Augustine DiNoia, OP; Father Avery Dulles, SJ; Fritz Ermarth; Mary Ann Glendon; Paul Henze; Cardinal James Hickey; Father David-Maria A. Jaeger, OFM; Cardinal William Keeler; M. Jean Kitchel; Father Joseph A. Komonchak; Cardinal Bernard Law; Joyce Little; Father John F. Long, SJ; Francis X. Maier; Father Michael Maslowsky; Brother Charles McBride, CSC; Father Vincent McMurry, SSJ; Father Seraphim Michalenko, MIC; Father J. Michael Miller, CSB; Irina and Thaddeus Mirecki; Victor Nakas; Father Jay Scott Newman;

Louis J. Nigro, Jr.; Michael Novak; Jan Nowak; Cardinal John O'Connor; Father Vincent O'Keefe, SJ; Ethan Reedy; Mario Paredes; Magdalena Potocka; Rodger Potocki; the board of the Institute on Religion and Public Life; Father Ronald G. Roberson, CSP; Father Robert Sirico; Mary Catherine Sommers; John H. Weigel; and Herman Wouk.

Elsewhere: I must also thank Bohdan Bociurkiw; Rémi Brague; Yigal Carmon; Archbishop Oscar Cruz; Jean Duchesne and his gracious family; Bishop Dominik Duka, OP; Monsignor Peter Elliott; Father Borys Gudziak; Shlomo Gur; Canon Gustaaf Joos; Archbishop Emery Kabongo; Cardinal Franz König; Cardinal Jean-Marie Lustiger; Jean-Luc Marion; Krzysztof Michalski; Cardinal Lucas Moreira Neves, OP; Cardinal Miguel Obando Bravo, SDB; Archbishop Karil Otčenašek; Father Hugo Pitel, O.Praem.; Monsignor Christian Precht; Cardinal Norberto Rivera Carrera; Ernesto Rivas-Gallont; Cardinal Christoph Schönborn, OP; Cardinal Jaime Sin; Anthony Sivers; Lawrence Uzzell and his colleagues at Keston News Service; Cardinal Miloslav Vlk; and the priests and parishioners of St. Jane Frances de Chantal Church in Bethesda, Maryland, for various forms of assistance and support.

Finally: My profound thanks to my wife, Joan, and to our children, Gwyneth, Monica, and Stephen, for their love, and for their patience, perseverance, and support during this project. This book is dedicated to them.

G.W.
14 February 1999
Feast of Sts. Cyril and Methodius

Index